S0-ATR-828

GENEALOGICAL GLEANINGS
IN ENGLAND

Henry F. Waters

Genr.
929.1
WAT v.1

GENEALOGICAL GLEANINGS

IN ENGLAND

REFERENCE

ABSTRACTS OF WILLS RELATING TO EARLY AMERICAN FAMILIES, WITH GENEALOGICAL NOTES AND PEDIGREES CONSTRUCTED FROM THE WILLS AND FROM OTHER RECORDS

By

HENRY F. WATERS, A.M.

With the Addition of

GENEALOGICAL GLEANINGS IN ENGLAND

(New Series) A-Anyon

(1907)

VOLUME I

Baltimore

GENEALOGICAL PUBLISHING CO., INC.

1981

AMADOR COUNTY LIBRARY
530 SUTTER STREET
JACKSON, CA 95642

Originally published in serial form in *The New England
Historical and Genealogical Register*, July 1883-January 1899.
First published complete in book form by the New England
Historic Genealogical Society, Boston, 1901.

Reprinted, with permission, with the addition of
Genealogical Gleanings in England (New Series, Salem, 1907),
by the Genealogical Publishing Co., Inc.
Baltimore, 1969. Reissued 1981.
Library of Congress Catalogue Card Number 78-88096
International Standard Book Number: Volume I: 0-8063-0925-3
Set Number: 0-8063-0371-9
Made in the United States of America

PUBLISHER'S NOTICE

The indexes of persons and places mentioned in these two volumes will be found on pages 1449-1643 in Volume II, just as they were originally published in 1901. The publisher has added the New Series, which was originally published in 1907, on pages 1645-1760 following the indexes; since the entries in the New Series were in alphabetical order, it was deemed unnecessary to add an index to the New Series.

—GENEALOGICAL PUBLISHING COMPANY

CONTENTS

ILLUSTRATIONS AND PEDIGREES.

VOL. I.

INTRODUCTION.

The efforts made by the New England Historic Genealogical Society, through its Committee on English Research, to procure funds sufficient to enable it to make an exhaustive search of
the English Records, on a plan never before attempted, for everything which concerns the family history of the early settlers of
this country ; its great good fortune in securing the services of
the eminent antiquary, Henry FitzGilbert Waters; his peculiar qualifications for the task, and the superiority of the method
adopted by him, are all set forth in the New England Historical and Genealogical Register for July, 1883 (xxxvii., 305) ;
July, 1884 (xxxviii., 339) ; and January, 1888 (xlii., 40).

Mr. Waters sailed for England May 5, 1883, and at once entered upon his great work. The step thus taken was a most important one, and marked a new departure in genealogical research.
The notes printed in the Register for July, 1883 (xxxvii., 233),
were the results of Mr. Waters's first few days' work among the
records of the Prerogative Court of Canterbury, Somerset House,
London. They arrived here barely in time for publication in that
number of the Register, and were a foretaste of what was to
come. Before a twelvemonth had passed he had accumulated a
vast amount of historical and genealogical material, including
abstracts of more than six hundred wills relating to American
families, and he has since then industriously added to his invaluable collections, until they are now unequalled both in extent and
in importance.

Some of the results of his researches, under the title of "Genealogical Gleanings in England," have been given to the public in
the New England Historical and Genealogical Register,
the organ of the Society. It has now been deemed advisable to
reprint some of these "Gleanings" in a form more convenient for
reference. The present volumes include the various instalments
published in the Register from July, 1883, to January, 1899,
inclusive.

In addition to these genealogical researches, Mr. Waters has
made historical discoveries of the highest value. We owe to him
the finding of the Winthrop map and the Maverick MS., two of

the most important contributions made in our day to our early colonial history. For an account of the former, the reader is referred to the "Proceedings of the Massachusetts Historical Society" for June, 1884 (xxi., 211), and the REGISTER for July, 1884 (xxxviii., 342). The Maverick MS. was printed in the "Proceedings of the Massachusetts Historical Society" for October, 1884 (xxi., 231), and in the REGISTER for January, 1885 (xxxix., 33). These discoveries excited great attention among historical students, not only in this country, but also in England.

Mr. Waters also contributed "Papers in Egerton MS. 2395," to the REGISTER for April, 1886 (xl., 175) ; the will of Alexander Selkirk — the real Robinson Crusoe — to the REGISTER for October, 1896 (l., 539), and the will of Thomas Hobson, carrier ("Hobson's choice, that or none"), to the REGISTER for October, 1898 (lii., 487). A facsimile of the will of Alexander Selkirk may be found in the REGISTER for April, 1897 (li., 150).

Mr. Waters also made a most valuable collection of "Extracts from Marriage Licenses granted by the Bishop of London, 1598 to 1639," which he intended should be printed in the REGISTER as an instalment of these Gleanings, but being unable, much to his regret, "to get it before the genealogical world through that channel," and as it seemed to him "too valuable not to be published," he contributed it to the Historical Collections of the Essex Institute (xxviii., 57–150).

To some of the various instalments of Gleanings published in the REGISTER I added certain explanatory remarks by way of introduction, and these remarks it has been thought advisable to reprint here in this preface, in order not to break the continuity of Mr. Waters's notes.

The article in the REGISTER for July, 1883 (xxxvii., 233–240) (pp. 1–8 this book), was introduced by a note from which the following extract is made:

It has been found almost impossible heretofore, in most cases, to establish satisfactorily the relationship between English and American families of the same name, and this failure to connect has been to the American genealogist the source of his greatest trouble. The searches now undertaken promise for the first time to meet and overcome this difficulty. The method adopted by Mr. Waters, so different from that of his predecessors, cannot fail to bring to light information which must necessarily have escaped the attention of all other investigators.

The article on "John Harvard and his Ancestry," Part I., in the REGISTER for July, 1885 (xxxix., 265) (pp. 117–134 this book), was preceded by the following introductory note:

The Committee on English Research of the New England Historic Genealogical Society, under whose direction Mr. Waters is now pursuing his investigations in England, have on more than one occasion asserted that the method of search adopted by him — so different from that of his predecessors — would without fail enable him to bring to light what had escaped the notice of all other antiquaries. Striking proofs of the correctness of this statement have been already afforded by the remarkable discoveries Mr. Waters has hitherto made, and the following paper, in which the parentage and ancestry of John Harvard are for the first time conclusively shown, will add still another.

In 1842 the late James Savage, President of the Massachusetts Historical Society and author of the "Genealogical Dictionary of New England," went to England for the express purpose of ascertaining what could be learned of the early history of John Harvard; but although Mr. Everett, then our minister to the court of St. James, rendered every assistance in his power, no trace of Harvard could be found, except his signature on taking his degrees at the University of Cambridge. Mr. Savage tells us that he would gladly have given five hundred dollars to get five lines about him in any capacity, public or private. Since that date others have made efforts equally unavailing.

The late Col. Joseph L. Chester, in a letter written the year before his death to the editor of the Register (Register, xxxvi., 319), says that he had carried about with him daily for many years a bit of pedigree of Harvard in the hope of being able to perfect it; that he thought he had found the will of the father of John Harvard, but could not yet prove it; that he disliked to put forward a mere theory, but hoped to come upon further evidence some day.

At a meeting of the New England Historic Genealogical Society held in Boston, June 3, 1885, a paper by Miss Frances B. James, of Cambridge, Mass., was read, on "John Harvard's English Home, a Caveat in Behalf of Devonshire." It contained the results of some researches made by her in the summer of 1883, in Plymtree, co. Devon, England, where there formerly lived a family of Harward or Harvard, but no claim was made by her that any relationship could be shown to exist between this family and that of John Harvard.

Mr. William Rendle, in an article in the "Genealogist" for April, 1884, on "Harvard University, U. S., and the Harvards of Southwark," gives a list of certain Harvards of the Parish of St. Saviour's noted by him, but he failed to find the baptism of John Harvard, and was unable to connect him with this family of Harvards. In the South London "Press" for April 11, 1885, and in the "Athenæum" for April 18, 1885, Mr. Rendle has something further to say about the Harvards. He gives the date of baptism of a John Harvye, whom he says he believes to be the founder of Harvard College, but is unable to prove the fact, and offers no evidence to support it. These articles, however, contain nothing new. Everything of importance in them had been previously made known to us by Mr. Waters. The record of this very baptism had been already found by him, and a copy of it sent to the committee. Mr. Rendle's knowledge of it seems to have been obtained from a person to whom Mr. Waters had mentioned it as a discovery of his own, and its appropriation by Mr. Rendle without acknowledgment, and its publication in this manner, was certainly a most extraordinary proceeding.

It had long been known that there was a family of Harvards in St. Saviour's Parish, Southwark; that John, son of Richard, was baptized there 11 Dec., 1606; another John, son of Robert, baptized 29 Nov., 1607; another John, son of John, baptized 2 Feb., 1611; and still another John, son of John, baptized 10 April, 1614; but whether the benefactor of the College was one of these, or whether he was of Southwark at all, has not been known, until now at last the proof is presented to us by Mr. Waters. Colonel Chester, as we have seen, years ago surmised that he was the son of Robert Harvard, but, like a true genealogist, waited for evidence before making a positive statement. Probably nearly every one in America who was interested in Harvard, and had given the subject much thought, suspected, at least, if not believed, that he was the son of Robert Harvard, of Southwark. So that Mr. Rendle offers nothing new and merely adds his belief to theirs, for which he fails to offer evidence. That Southwark was a field for persecution, and therefore its people must have been ready to emigrate to New England, carries no weight, for there was persecution in other parts of England; and it would be difficult for Mr. Rendle or any other investigator to show that more people came to New England for religion's sake from the county of Surrey than from the counties of Somerset, Dorset, or Wilts, in all of which Harvards were to be found. Could he say that John Harvard was not from either of these counties, or from St. Katherine's near the Tower in co. Middlesex where a family of Harvards lived, or that he was not the son of Robert Harvey, alias Harverde, of Rugby in Warwickshire?

Mr. Waters, however, is the first to show conclusively that John Harvard, from whom the College takes its name, was one of the sons of Robert Harvard of the parish of St. Saviour's, Southwark, London, and Katherine (Rogers) Harvard his wife, and that he was baptized in that parish Nov. 29, 1607. Ample proof of this is afforded by the documentary evidence now for the first time published, to which the attention of the reader is directed. The parentage of John Harvard is no longer a mystery. Mr. Waters gives us here, among others, the wills of his father and mother, his brother Thomas Harvard, his uncle Thomas Harvard, his aunt by marriage Margaret Harvard, his stepfathers John Elletson and Richard Yearwood, and his father-in-law John Sadler.

But although so much has been accomplished that a few months ago would have been thought impossible, much remains to be done. There are other fields of research as yet unexplored, which will richly repay all the expenditure of time and labor which a thorough investigation of them will require.

The expense of the search thus far has been met by voluntary contributions of the Alumni, particularly the Harvard Club of New York.

The article in the REGISTER for October, 1885 (xxxix., 325) (pp. 134–145 this book), was introduced by the following note:

The following is the tenth in the remarkable series of papers contributed to the REGISTER by Mr. Waters, and modestly styled by him "Genealogical Gleanings in England." The article on "John Harvard and his Ancestry," published in the REGISTER for July last, although it appears under a separate title, was the ninth in that series. There is no need to enlarge upon the importance of Mr. Waters's dis-

coveries in relation to John Harvard; but it will not be out of place
to make the announcement here that Harvard College, in grateful recognition of his patient labors in these investigations, conferred upon him
on Commencement Day, June 24, 1885, the honorary degree of Master
of Arts. The words of President Eliot on that occasion were :

Henricum Fitz-Gilbert Waters investigatorem antiquitatis curiosum, de Uni-
versitate ob genus Johannis Harvard feliciter exquisitum bene meritum, artium
magistrum causa honoris.

At the Commencement Dinner President Eliot said :

The class of 1855, this day thirty years out of college, the class which boasts
Agassiz the naturalist, Francis C. Barlow the general, Theodore Lyman the
independent, and Phillips Brooks the great preacher and large minded man,
has won a new distinction this year. One of its members, Henry Fitzgilbert
Waters, genealogist and antiquarian, has discovered, by most patient and
ingenious research, the family of John Harvard. We have only known about
our first benefactor that he was a master of arts of Emmanuel College, and a
non-conforming minister, that he had a well chosen library of three hundred
volumes and some property, and that he was admitted a freeman in this colony
in November, 1637, and died at Charlestown within a year, leaving his library
and half of his estate to the infant college at Cambridge, which was thereafter
called by his name. Nothing has been known about his family or the sources
of his property, until now, when Mr. Waters has brought to light the wills of
his father, two step-fathers, mother, brother, uncle, aunt, and father-in-law,
besides other documents of importance in connection with these wills.

John Harvard, whose faith and piety planted this institution, was baptized
in the parish of St. Saviour's, Southwark, London, Nov. 29, 1607, being
the son of Robert Harvard, a well-to-do butcher, and Katherine Rogers. The
mother's maiden name was discovered through the will of William Ward, a
goldsmith, who, in 1624, bequeathed a ring of gold to the value of 20s. to his
brother Robert Harvard. Rose Rogers, the wife of William Ward, was the
sister of Katherine Rogers, John Harvard's mother, so that William Ward
could speak of Robert Harvard as his brother. The father, youngest brother,
and older brother of our benefactor died in 1625, perhaps of the plague which
raged that year in London, and the father disposed by will of a property considerable for those days, the widow and her two surviving sons receiving
most of it. Katherine Harvard married John Elletson, a cooper, in January,
1626 ; but he died in the following June, leaving another considerable property
to his widow Katherine. In December, 1627, John Harvard was entered at
Emmanuel College, Cambridge, at the age of twenty, presumably by the
advice of the Rev. Mr. Morton or the Rev. Mr. Archer, ministers of the parish
of St. Saviour's, both of whom are remembered in the will of John Harvard's
mother and in that of his brother Thomas. Five years later this mother
appears as the widow and principal heir of Richard Yearwood, a grocer, who
was mentioned in the will of her first husband, Robert Harvard, as " my good
neighbor and friend Richard Yearwood." In July, 1635, Katherine (Harvard)
(Elletson) Yearwood made her will and died, leaving her property, which had
been derived from her three husbands, the butcher, the cooper, and the grocer, chiefly to her two sons, John and Thomas Harvard, with a preference,
however, for the elder son, " John Harvard, clarke." In this year John took
his master's degree at Cambridge. In February, 1637, he appears married to
Ann Sadler, seven years younger than himself, and the daughter of a clergyman settled at Ringmer in Sussex. In July, 1636, John's younger brother
Thomas, a cloth worker, being " sick and weak in body," made his will, in
which he disposed of a fair property, a good portion of which he gave to his
well beloved brother John. The executors named in this will were his brother
John and Nicholas Morton, preacher ; but when the will was proved on the
5th of May, 1637, only Mr. Morton appeared, John Harvard having sailed

with his young wife for New England. In 1638 the young minister at Charles-town, dying at thirty years of age, became the first private benefactor of this college, started in the New World a stream of-beneficence which has never ceased to flow in ever widening channels, and won for himself, and now at last for his family, an enduring remembrance.

In the twelve years from 1625 to 1637 John Harvard had lost his father, two step-fathers, his mother, and his two brothers, and almost the whole family property had fallen to him. He appears to have been the only scholar in the family, although his brother Thomas seems to have signed his name to his will. His father and mother both made their marks. The whole family con-nection were trades-people; but his mother, by her marriages, came into pos-session of property enough to give a college education to her oldest son. The education of that one delicate youth has had far-reaching consequences indeed. No prince or potentate, civil or ecclesiastical, founded this college; it sprang from the loins of the common people. It was founded by the General Court of the Colony of Massachusetts Bay, and first endowed by an educated son of pious London trades-people. When I had read these Harvard wills, I asked myself how closely the college is bound — after two hundred and fifty years — to the sort of people who established it. I went to the admission books in which the occupations of parents of the students are recorded, and found to my great satisfaction that more than a quarter part of its students are to-day sons of tradesmen, shopkeepers, mechanics, salesmen, foremen, laborers, and farmers. I found sons of butchers, coopers, grocers, and cloth-workers — the Harvard trades — on the roll of its students to-day. May no exclusive policy or spirit ever separate the university which bears John Harvard's name from that laborious, frugal, self-respecting part of the community to which he and his belonged.

Since the article on John Harvard in the REGISTER for July was printed, Mr. Dean, the editor, has received from Mr. E. S. Shuckburgh, the librarian of Emmanuel College, a facsimile, which is reproduced here, of Harvard's signature in 1635, when he took the degree of A. M. It is from the original University register in the custody of the Rev. H. Luard, D. D., registrar of the University. "There is," Mr. Shuck-burgh writes, "no doubt whatever about its genuineness. All persons admitted to a degree had to sign these books, which have been preserved since 1544— unhappily not earlier."

It is to be hoped that funds sufficient to prosecute still further these interesting investigations may be speedily obtained.

To the article in the REGISTER for January, 1886 (xl., 34) (pp. 145–158 this book), was prefixed the following note, which was also printed in part in the London "Athenæum" for Jan. 2, 1886 :

MR. WILLIAM RENDLE has published in the "Athenæum" of April 18, July 11, and Oct. 24, 1885, some communications as to the genealogy of John Harvard, and in certain quarters allusions have been made to a "controversy" on the subject. There is, properly speaking, no con-troversy at all. There is and can be no question whatever in the minds of those conversant with the facts in the case as to who discovered the parentage and ancestry of John Harvard. The credit of this remark-able discovery belongs undeniably to Mr. Henry F. Waters, and to him alone.

The facts in the case are briefly these: Mr. Rendle seems to be a local antiquary who has, I believe, lived many years in Southwark, and who has spent much time among the records there, and has undoubtedly there done good work. But unfortunately for Mr. Rendle, there is not in this case so far a single scrap of evidence to show that there is anything whatever in the Southwark records to establish the slightest possible connection between the Harvards of that Borough and John Harvard of Emmanuel College and of New England. There were Harvards in Southwark, it is true, and perhaps in other parts of Surrey, just as there were Harvards in Devonshire, Somerset, Dorset, Wilts, Middlesex, Warwickshire, and doubtless in other parts of England. The problem was to identify, among them all, the father of John Harvard. So far as Mr. Rendle was concerned, this problem might have remained unsolved to the end of time, for there was nothing in the Southwark records which would have enabled him to solve it.

The proof of this relationship Mr. Waters discovered after much research in the records of the Prerogative Court of Canterbury. There he found, among others, the wills of John Harvard's father, mother, brother, uncle, aunt, two step-fathers, and father-in-law. This proved the whole family connection. If Mr. Waters had stopped there and gone not a step farther, it would have been enough to completely dispel the mystery which had so long enveloped the birth and early life of the benefactor of the noble University. After thus finally solving the problem, he went to Southwark merely for supplemental evidence, not at all necessary, however, to substantiate his case, and there in the parish registers he found the record of the baptism of John Harvard and other collateral matter.

Information of this visit of Mr. Waters to Southwark and its successful result was communicated to several persons. That Mr. Rendle was apprised of it by one of them can be shown by evidence both direct and circumstantial.

In articles published by Mr. Rendle in the "Genealogist" for April and July, 1884 (N. S., i., 107 and 182), he gives the names of the Harvards found by him in the records of St. Saviour's, Southwark. But there nowhere appears in his list the name of our John Harvard. He even quotes the late Chaplain Samuel Benson as saying that "he cannot find the name of John Harvard, the founder, but that he had no doubt he was born of this family of Harvard of St. Saviour's." Mr. Rendle then adds: "After careful, I will not say exhaustive, examination of the original books and papers, I am quite of the same opinion." On page 182 he quotes the entry in the books of Emmanuel College, where Harvard is said to be of Middlesex, and in a foot-note talks of drawing the "attention of officials of Middlesex churches to the name of John Harvard, and the dates *circa* 1605 and after." Mr. Rendle, although fully apprised of the fact that Harvard, Harverde, and Harvye were merely different forms of the same family name, had evidently overlooked the entry of Harvard's baptism, or had failed to recognize it, or to appreciate the importance of the entry, even if his eye had ever rested upon it, and was as late as July, 1884, turning to Middlesex for the record of it, having apparently given up all hope of finding it in Southwark. The "extremely diverse spelling" of the name, being already well known to him, will by no means account for this failure.

On the 11th of April, 1885, a date, be it remembered, subsequent to

Mr. Waters's visit to Southwark and his discovery of the record of this baptism, Mr. Rendle published in the South London "Press" a letter, which, with some additions, he again published in the "Athenæum" of April 18th.

In this letter he printed conspicuously in italics the record of this baptism, and added, "I believe" him "to be the founder" of Harvard College, but he neither then nor has he since offered any proof of his own to substantiate his belief or to show any reasonable grounds for it. Sometime, therefore, between July, 1884, and April, 1885, Mr. Rendle saw a great light. He evidently does not mean to tell us how or when this flashed upon him. But he unwittingly, in the very letter above referred to, shows us the source of his information in these significant words: "The clue, or rather the result of the clue, is before me. I believe that some American friends, anxious to do honor to their benefactor and his birth-place, are now among us. It would have been pleasant to me to have known them; probably now I may." Of course he did not know "them." But when we consider that at the very time he penned these lines Mr. Rendle knew that the long search for John Harvard was over, that even the record of his baptism had been found and that Mr. Waters was the successful discoverer, the extremely disingenuous and misleading nature of this allusion to American friends can be readily seen. What is the "clue" the result of which Mr. Rendle had before him? Does he mean to say that somebody else had the clue and that he had only the result? The general denial made by W. D. in the "Athenæum" of July 11, 1885, is altogether too vague. It should be more specific if it is expected that much weight should be attached to it.

There seems indeed to be a confusion or haziness in Mr. Rendle's mind as to what constitutes not merely legal but even genealogical proof. Mr. Waters, on the other hand, like a true genealogist, has made a scientific treatment of the subject, and shows us step by step how he reached the successful result of his search, and on what his conclusions are based. He gives us the pedigree of Harvard and the proof by which it can be substantiated. That the search was an independent one is shown by Mr. Rendle's chief and only witness W. D., who, in the letter above referred to, kindly proves Mr. Waters's case for him by admitting that Mr. Rendle's offer of assistance was "neither acted on nor acknowledged" by Mr. Waters.

In an article in the NEW ENGLAND HISTORICAL AND GENEALOGICAL REGISTER for July, 1885, I expressed my astonishment at what I called this "extraordinary proceeding" on the part of Mr. Rendle. That such a proceeding is happily considered as extraordinary in England as it is here, and that the standard of literary morality is at least as high there as here, is shown by the fact that I have before me, as I write, letters from several English antiquaries whose names are known on both sides of the Atlantic, and who are fully cognizant of the facts in the case, who express surprise at what they call the "strange conduct" of Mr. Rendle. As these are private letters, not intended for publication, I have no right to quote them in this matter, but the evidence thus afforded is overwhelming.

Mr. Rendle's pamphlet, a copy of which I have only lately seen, will, I understand, be reviewed elsewhere and by abler hands than mine. I will therefore not take up space to point out certain inaccuracies in it, which are patent to every one who has given much thought to the subject. I will content myself with calling attention to the fact that it furnishes not an iota of proof of the connection of John Harvard of Southwark with John Harvard of New England, except what is taken from Mr. Waters's pamphlet on the subject. This indebtedness Mr. Rendle is, however, careful to acknowledge, and he has conspicuously marked with a W. the source of information thus obtained. It is instructive to notice how plentifully sprinkled Mr. Rendle's pages are with this initial letter.

I freely admit — now that Mr. Waters has conclusively shown that John Harvard was a Southwark man, and has put this statement in print so that all may read — that Mr. Rendle's local knowledge as a Southwark antiquary may enable him to carry on still further the investigations in that Borough, and I certainly trust that he may supplement and add to the already accumulating data concerning the early life of the benefactor of America's oldest and most famous University. Any such supplemental and corroborative material will command the attention of antiquaries on both sides of the ocean, and will deserve and receive due recognition on their part.

The article on "John Harvard and his Ancestry," Part II., in the REGISTER for October, 1886 (xl., 362) (pp. 180–197 this book), was preceded by the following introduction:

In the article in the REGISTER for July, 1885 (xxxix., 265), entitled "John Harvard and his Ancestry," which formed the ninth instalment of his "Genealogical Gleanings in England," Mr. Waters conclusively established the fact that John Harvard was one of the sons of Robert Harvard of the parish of St. Saviour's, Southwark, London, and Katherine (Rogers) Harvard, his wife, and that he was baptized in that parish Nov. 29, 1607. In support of this statement he published, among others, the wills of Harvard's father, mother, brother, uncle, aunt, two step-fathers, and father-in-law.

In the present paper he continues still further the investigations so successfully begun. He here gives us, with other new and important matter now for the first time published, the probate of the will of Thomas Rogers of Stratford-on-Avon, Harvard's maternal grandfather, the wills of Rose Reason, his aunt, and Thomas Rogers, Jr., his uncle, both on his mother's side, with extracts from the Parish Registers of Stratford, setting forth the baptisms, marriages, and burials of the Rogers family. Harvard's grandfather, Thomas Rogers, was, at the time of his death, an alderman of Stratford, and the house which he built there in 1596 is still standing. From it John Harvard's father and mother were married in 1605. It is one of the oldest and certainly the best remaining example of ancient domestic architecture in Stratford. The illustration in this number is a heliotype copy, slightly reduced, of an excellent photograph just taken.

When it is remembered that the late Hon. James Savage, LL.D., the author of the "Genealogical Dictionary of New England," made a voyage to England for the express purpose of ascertaining what could be learned of the early history of John Harvard, and that he would gladly have given, as he himself tells us, five hundred dollars to get five lines about him in any capacity, public or private, but that all his efforts were without avail, the accumulation of material now brought to light by the perseverance of Mr. Waters is certainly most surprising. From being almost a semi-mythical figure in our early colonial history, John Harvard bids fair to become one of the best known of the first generation of settlers on these shores. The mystery which surrounded him is now dispelled. No better illustration could be given of the importance of the work Mr. Waters is doing in England, no more striking instance could be found of the extraordinary success which is attending his labors there.

The Committee earnestly hope that funds sufficient to carry on still further these valuable investigations may be speedily raised.

That the interest excited by Mr. Waters's discovery of the parentage and ancestry of John Harvard is not confined to those who speak the English language, is shown by an editorial article in the Paris journal, "La Renaissance," which was reprinted in the REGISTER for April, 1886 (xl., 180).

The article on the "Family of John Rogers of Dedham," in the REGISTER for April, 1887 (xli., 160) (pp. 209–236 this book), was introduced as follows:

The article in the REGISTER for October, 1886 (xl., 362), on "John Harvard and his Ancestry, Part Second," which, although published under a separate title, formed the fourteenth instalment of Mr. Waters's "Genealogical Gleanings in England," related especially to the family of John Harvard's maternal grandfather, Thomas Rogers of Stratford on Avon, co. Warwick. Mr. Waters's investigations in this direction resulted in the accumulation of a mass of material in regard not only to this but to other families of the name of Rogers, but a part of which is as yet ready for publication.

The article in the present number of the REGISTER, the sixteenth in the series of "Genealogical Gleanings," concerns more particularly the Rogers family of Essex Co., England, and of Essex Co., Massachusetts. It is by no means complete, nor is it intended to be a final report of the results of Mr. Waters's signally successful researches. Mr. Waters has evidently thought it advisable simply to "report progress" in this line of search rather than to wait until he could perfect his work so as to present a finished pedigree of this family. The latter course would necessitate a long delay, while the course he has adopted, although open to the objection of being perhaps a fragmentary and unsatisfactory mode of dealing with the subject, has the positive merit of enabling him to make at once available for the use of antiquaries some of the new and important discoveries he has made in relation to this family.

As is well known to the readers of the REGISTER, the Committee on English Research have repeatedly asserted that the method of search adopted by Mr. Waters would without fail enable him to bring to light what had escaped the notice of all previous investigators, and they have from time to time called attention to the most striking points in the evidence relied upon to support this assertion. The Harvard discoveries undoubtedly made the most impression on the minds of the general public, but Mr. Waters's whole work, in every part, is proof enough to the mind of the trained antiquary that here at last is a new departure in genealogical investigation which cannot fail to produce results not otherwise to be attained. And this present paper on the Essex Rogers is by no means inferior to the Harvard papers as evidence of the truth of the statements above referred to.

It has long been a tradition in New England that the Rev. Nathaniel Rogers of Ipswich, Mass., son of the Rev. John Rogers of Dedham, co. Essex, England, was a descendant of John Rogers the Martyr. This tradition was disproved by the late Col. Joseph L. Chester, himself a descendant of the Ipswich minister. Indeed, it was through the researches that he then made into the history of this branch of the Rogers family that Colonel Chester was first led to turn his attention to the genealogical pursuits in which he subsequently became preëminent. His "Life of John Rogers the Martyr," published in London in 1861, was his earliest antiquarian work, and was the means of first bringing him to the notice of genealogists in this country and England. Although the result of these investigations was personally unsatisfactory to him, as he himself tells us, and his disappointment was great in finding that the Martyr could not have been the ancestor of the Ipswich minister, he never lost his interest in the subject, and continued almost to the day of his death to accumulate material in relation to the Rogers family in all its branches.

Through the kindness of Augustus D. Rogers, Esq., of Salem, Mass., I am permitted to make the following extracts from three letters written to him by Colonel Chester.

In the first, dated Jan. 13, 1877, after referring to his "Life of John Rogers the Martyr," he says :

I may say generally that I have since discovered nothing to vary the conclusions I then arrived at, but much to confirm them. We shall never, I fear, carry the Rogers pedigree back beyond Richard Rogers of Wethersfield. I have sought earnestly in vain to ascertain who his father was, but I quite accept Candler's statement that he was of the North of England. . . . I have often been at Dedham, where the bust of John Rogers is still in the chancel of the church. I have spared no pains to ascertain his parentage, but in vain. My Rogers collections alone would make a small library.

In the second, bearing date Feb. 17, 1877, he says :

For eighteen years I have been collecting everything I could lay my hands on, from every possible source, concerning the Rogers families, all over England. All this material I have kept carefully worked up in pedigree form, and, with all my personal interest in the descent, I have never been able to get back a step beyond Richard Rogers of Wethersfield, nor even ascertain who was the father of John Rogers of Dedham. If any further progress is ever made it will be by accident. But my impression is that the earlier ancestors of the family were of a rank in life so humble that they never got into the public records. If I could think of anything more to do, you may be sure that I would do it. . . . My Rogers collections are enormous, and I know of nothing that has escaped me.

The third is dated March 9, 1878, and he there says :

You must recollect that I take as deep an interest in the Rogers pedigree as you or anybody else can, as there is no doubt about my descent from Rev. John Rogers of Dedham, and if I had been able to add anything to what I have heretofore published, I should have done so. I have been pursuing these inquiries here for now nearly twenty years, and you may be sure I have left no stone unturned.

It will be seen that these letters were written but a few years before the death of the writer.

It is with no wish to detract from the fame of Colonel Chester — for that is now secure, and he is admitted by all to have been preëminent among the genealogists of our day, without a superior indeed either in this country or in England — that attention is called to the fact that in the history of the very family in which Colonel Chester had the greatest interest, for it was his mother's mother's family, to which he had devoted so much exhaustive labor with the tireless energy and perseverance for which he was so remarkable, discoveries have now been made by Mr. Waters which but a short time ago would have been pronounced impossible.

Mr. Waters now shows us that the Rev. John Rogers of Dedham was the son of John Rogers, a Chelmsford shoemaker, and that this shoemaker and the Rev. Richard Rogers were probably brothers, the sons of another John Rogers, when John Rogers the Martyr was living elsewhere. Nor has this discovery been made by accident, as Colonel Chester prophesied, but by a laborious, systematic, and exhaustive search on a plan never before attempted. It is another proof that the baffled investigator hereafter need never despair of his case, that genealogical problems apparently impossible of solution are by no means to be abandoned as hopeless. It is a reminder also of the necessity of establishing a permanent fund, by means of which we can carry on these investigations on a grander scale than ever before, and with proportionately greater results.

Of surpassing interest as were these discoveries of the parentage of John Harvard and John Rogers, they were followed by the equally remarkable establishment of the ancestry of Roger Williams and George Washington. All of these problems had long baffled the efforts of the most eminent antiquaries, and their solution by Mr. Waters forms a series of perhaps the most brilliant achievements in the whole history of genealogy.

But the story of the final determination of the Washington ancestry — ending as it did the long search first begun by Sir Isaac Heard in 1791, in the lifetime of Washington, and since then continued by other genealogists without success, until at last brought to a close by Mr. Waters nearly a century afterward — is best told in Mr. Waters's own words, and to his account the reader is referred.

It has been thought advisable to reprint here for the sake of convenience (pp. 523–539) the article on the " Wills of the American Ancestors of General George Washington," communicated by the late Joseph M. Toner, M.D., of Washington, D.C., to the REGISTER for July, 1891 (xlv., 199–215).

But Mr. Waters has by no means limited himself to the work of preparing complete and finished pedigrees of noted families, nor has he confined his attention to determining the parentage of historic personages, however famous. His aim has been to make accessible in print everything which can serve to connect American families, distinguished or obscure, with the parent stock in England. Nowhere else can there be found in print genealogical data bearing on this connection which concern so large a number of the families of our early settlers. These pages contain wills relating not only to New England families, but to those of Virginia, Maryland, South Carolina, New York, Pennsylvania, and the West Indies. These researches, in short, have been conducted in no narrow spirit, and they should interest every one of English descent in every part of our country.

The valuable table prepared by J. Challenor Covington Smith, Esq., late Superintendent of the Department for Literary Inquiry, Principal Registry of the Court of Probate, Somerset House, London, giving the numbers of the Calendars, the names and dates of the several registers — as well as his paper explaining the method of identifying the Will Registers of the Prerogative Court of Canterbury, which was contributed by him to the REGISTER for July, 1892 (xlvi., 299–303) — may be found reprinted here (pp. 569–573). The genealogical investigator cannot fail to appreciate its great usefulness.

Page 845 has been divided. The probate of the will of William Dyre and the Editor's note at the top of that page are to be found in Vol. I. The will of Nicholas Pynchon which fills the rest of the page begins Vol. II.

The index to these volumes of "Genealogical Gleanings" is the work of Miss Edna F. Calder.

In the Index of Persons, the names of those whose wills were probated, or whose estates were administered upon, are printed in full-face type, the number of the page on which such will or administration is to be found being printed in italics.

JOHN T. HASSAM.

BOSTON, Jan. 1, 1901.

GENEALOGICAL GLEANINGS IN ENGLAND.

GREGORY COFFIN, of Stepney, co. Middlesex, mariner, shipped on board the William & Jane of London, Mr. John Baker commander, on a voyage to New England and Bilboe, by will dated 15 February, 1660, proved 20 August, 1662, appointed John Earle of Shadwell, mariner, his attorney, and left all his estate to the said John Earle and his wife. Joane Earle, whom he appointed joint executors. Laud, fol. 105.

JOHN COCKERELL, of Great Cogshall, co. Essex, clothier, made his will 14 July, 1662, proved 12 August, 1662. He bequeathed to his wife Mary all the lands and tenements in Bradwell, in the county aforesaid, which were her jointure; and also lands, &c., in Cressing, which he had lately purchased of one Mr. Jermyn and one Joseph Raven, during her natural life, and after her decease then to his son John Cockerell and his heirs forever. He devised to her also that part of the messuage which he had lately purchased of John Sparhauke, then in the tenure and occupation of Mistress Crane, for life, with remainder to son John, &c. The residue of his estate to son John at age of twenty-one years. He made bequests to two daughters, Mary and Elizabeth, and to the child his wife was then going withall. He appointed said wife executrix, and directed her to redeem the mortgage which he had made to Mrs. Hester Sparhauk of the messuage he then lived in, and which was in the occupation of the said Mrs. Crane.

Laud, 106.

BENJAMIN KAINE furnished an account of his goods and chattels, 16 October, 1654. Among the items was a tenement in Shoe Lane, and property in the hands of Mr. Coddington, his attorney, in Bow Lane, and in keeping of other persons (among whom a Mr. Walter Gibbons, cutler in Holborn). Thomas Blumfield spoken of, and called a brother of Mr. Withers. By his will, of same date, he gave his whole estate to his daughter Anna Kaine, except some particular legacies, viz., to his father Mr. R^t Kaine of Boston in New England, to whom he left (*inter alia*) a Japan cane with a silver head, which was in the trunk at Mr. Blumfield's, to his dear mother, to his cousin Dr. Edmond Wilson, to his Colonel, Stephen Winthrop, to Cornet Wackfield, to Mr. Mastin, to Mr. Richard Pery and his wife, to Mr. William Gray, late of Burchin lane; the said Gray and Pery to be trustees for his estate in England; to his servants John Earle and Thomas Lamb. The will was signed in Glasgow, in presence of Nicholas Wackfield and Richard Pery. On the sixteenth of May, 1662, emanavit comissio Simoni Bradstreet prox. consanguineo in hoc regno angliæ remanenti dicti defuncti, etc. Laud, 67.

[This was Benjamin, only son of Capt. Robert Keayne. of Boston, founder of the Ancient and Honorable Artillery Company. He married Sarah, daughter of Gov. Thomas Dudley. Gov. Simon Bradstreet, named in the probate, married another daughter, Anne (see REG. viii. 313 ; ix. 113; x. 130). Bradstreet sailed, November, 1657, for England, as the agent of the colony, and remained there three years, returning July 17, 1661. Probably the application for probate on Keayne's will was made before Bradstreet left England. For notices of the Keayne family, see REG. vol. vi. pp. 89-92, 152-8 ; xxxv. 277.—EDITOR.

See Savage Gen. Dict. iii. 1, where the date of Benjamin Keayne's death is incorrectly given. See also Suffolk Deeds, Lib. i. fol. 83 and 84.

John Morse, of Boston, in New England, salt-boiler, by deed of mortgage dated Nov. 9, 1654, recorded with Suffolk Deeds, Lib. 2, f. 180, conveyed to his uncle, Mr. Robert Keaine of said Boston, " my third part of that tennement or howse in shoe lane in London which comes to me by the right of my wife mary Jupe now mary morse which was left and given to hir by m^{rs} Grace Jupe hir mother by will before hir decease with all the right title or Interest that myself and wife or either of vs haue therein," and also their interest in one half part of five certain tenements in Gravel Lane, in the Parish of St. Buttolph without Aldgate, London, to secure the payment of £32. See also fol. 86 and 182. See fol. 183 and 184 for a bond and an order from said John Morse to Mr. Simeon or Symon Smith of Southwark to pay " my Couzen majo^r Benjamin Keajne " of London, £15 advanced by " my vnckell m^r Robert Keajne " to pay for the passage of said Morse, his wife, and his wife's brother Benjamin Jupe from New England back to Old England. This sum was to be paid at the Golden Crown in Birchin Lane, London, on or before April 26, 1655, out of the rents belonging to his said wife, or brother Benjamin Jupe, remaining in the hands of said Smith as executor.—J. T. H.]

CAPTAIN HUMPHREY ATHERTON, 25 December, 1661, proved 3 July, 1662, by John Atherton, his brother and one of the executors. He named his brother Francis and his two sisters, Elizabeth Osborne, widow, late wife of Robert Osborne, and Anne Parker, wife of Richard Parker, of the city of Bristol. There was due to him by bond from Lieut. Col. Maurice Kingswell the sum of one hundred pounds, of which he ordered twenty pounds to be given to his worthy friend Mr. Richard Smith, one of the life guard to his Grace the Duke of Albemarle, to buy him a mourning suit and a cloak, thirty pounds apiece to his two sisters and ten pounds apiece to his two brothers, John and Francis Atherton, and also ten pounds apiece more which was owing unto him by Mr. William Walker at the Green Dragon in Cornhill, London. To the said Richard Smith he devised fourteen pounds owing to him by bill from Capt. Nathaniel Disborough. The residue of his estate, with arrears due from his Majesty for his service at Dunkirk, he left to his brothers, whom he named executors.

Laud, 94.

[It is singular that this Capt. Humphrey Atherton died about the same time as our Maj. Gen. Humphrey Atherton of Dorchester. The latter died Sept. 16, 1661, less than a year before his English namesake. For facts concerning the Atherton family, see REGISTER, ii. 382 ; x. 361 ; xxxii. 197 ; xxxv. 67.—ED.]

JOHN BURGES, the elder, of Westly, lying sick in Richman's Island, in New England, 11 April, 1627, proved 24 May, 1628, by Joanna Burges. alias Bray, relict and executrix. Besides his wife, he mentioned his three sons, Robert, John and William ; and he enumerated, among other things, his bark, called the Annes, with her boat, tackling and provisions, and what she had gained that summer, his whistle and chain, and all his instruments that belonged to the sea.   Barrington, 45.

[Richmond's or Richman's island is situated near Cape Elizabeth, Maine. Walter Bagnall had a trading post there from 1628 till October 3, 1631, when he was killed by the Indians. The same year, Robert Trelawney and Moses Goodyeare of Plymouth obtained from the Council of Plymouth a grant which included this island. John Winter was their agent there. The papers relating to this plantation, fortunately preserved to this day and discovered by the late J. Wingate Thornton, A.M., are in press, edited by James P. Baxter, A.M., and will soon be issued as a volume of the Collections of the Maine Historical Society.—Ed.]

CAPT. JOHN WILCOCKS, late of Plymouth, now of Accomac, intending to go on service against the Indians, made his will, dated in Elizabeth City, Virginia, 10 September, 1622, proved the last of June, 1628. He named wife Temperance, his daughter in law, Grace Burges, legitimate daughter of his said wife, and his sisters Katherine and'Susanna Wilcocks.

Barrington, 55.

EDWARD GREEN, late of Bristol, grocer, and now at present at Capt. Robert Dudley's in the county of Middlesex, in Virginia, 22 August, 1697, proved 9 August, 1698, by Robert Green, his brother and executor. He desired his body to be buried in a decent and christian manner at the discretion of John Barnard, then residing at John Walker's in King and Queen County in Virginia. The residue of his estate he left to his brother Robert Green of Bristol, haberdasher of hats. The witnesses to his signature were Robert Dudley, Senior, William Reynolds and Robert Dudley.

Lort, 186.

BENJAMIN WILLIAMS, of Stoake, near Guldeford, co. Surrey, schoolmaster, 2 July, 1695, proved 22 September, 1698, by Nathaniel Williams his brother and executor. To cousin Susanna Hall, John, Samuel and Daniel Hall, now or late of Whetenhurst in co. Gloucester, twenty shillings apiece, within six months after decease of the testator. To cousins Anna Cliffold (Clifford?), of Bisley, and her two brothers, Richard and Nathaniel Tindall of Nibley, and to my cousin Joseph Tindall, of Nibley, sometime of Trotton Hinton, ministers, ten shillings apiece, within six months, &c. To my cousins Samuel, Thomas and Benjamin Williams, of New England, and to my cousin Elizabeth Bird, of Dorchester in New England, and to the eldest child of my cousin Williams, of New England, deceased, in case there (are) any of them living, and also to the eldest child of my cousin Joseph Williams, deceased, in case he have left any living and who shall be living at the time of my decease, to every and each of the said last mentioned persons the sum of twenty shillings, within one year, &c. To the poor of the parish of Eastington fifty shillings, and to the poor of the parish of Whetenhurst fifty shillings, any poor people of my father's kindred principally recommended. To my brother in law Nathaniel Williams, of Brandley, in co. Worcester, and his heirs forever, all those my freehold, tenements, lands tenements and hereditaments, &c., in Eastington and Frampton, and elsewhere in Gloucestershire, and all the residue ; he to be executor.

Note that the name Nathaniel is by my mistake omitted, and also the eldest child of my cousin Hannah Parmater is to be comprehended. B. W.

Lort, 208.

[The children of Richard Williams, one of the first settlers of Taunton, N. E., were 1. John, 2. Samuel, 3. Joseph, 4. Nathaniel, 5. Thomas, 6. Benjamin, 7. Elizabeth, wife of John Bird, 8. Hannah, wife of John Parmenter. See Reg. v. 414[4]. All these children, except John, who may have died young, are named in the above will.

Emery, in his " Ministry of Taunton," i. 43–5, quotes " a manuscript of considerable antiquity," but evidently not written before 1718, which states that " Richard Williams was descended from a family of that name in Glamorganshire, in Wales, and found a wife in Gloucestershire, England." The same manuscript

states that his wife was Frances Dighton, sister of Katharine, second wife of Gov. Thomas Dudley. Baylies, in his "Historical Memoir of New Plymouth," part i. p. 284, says there was a tradition that Williams was a relative of Oliver Cromwell. He also prints (i. 272) a letter from the Rev. Roger Williams, in which reference is made to "my brother." Baylies thinks this may be Richard Williams, of Taunton.
    John Bird, the husband of Elizabeth Williams, was a son of Thomas Bird of Dorchester. See Bird Genealogy, REG. xxv. 21–30.—ED.]

THOMAS BEAVAY, waterman, of the city of Bristol, 21 Jan. 1656, proved by Mary Beavay, widow and executrix, 24 April, 1657. To be buried in the churchyard of St. Phillipps. To son Thomas Beavay, now a planter in Virginia, my best suit of clothes and all belonging to it. To my godson, Samuel Gosner, a small boat or twenty shillings in money. To godson Edward Martin the younger, twenty shillings. To godson Thomas Webb, twenty shillings. To wife Mary, the passage boat, with all the term of years that is yet to come.   Ruthen, 145.

EZEKIEL SHERMAN, of Dedham, clothier, the last of December, 1656, proved 12 May, 1657, by Martha Sherman, widow and sole executrix. To son Ezekiel one hundred pounds at age of twenty-one years. To daughters Grace and Hannah one hundred pounds each, at the age of twenty-one. To daughter now born eighty pounds at the age of twenty-one. To my brother John Sherman ten pounds within a year and a day after my decease. To Mary Sherman five pounds at the same time. After decease of wife Martha, son Ezekiel to enter on lands, &c. If he die without lawful issue, then the property to go equally among the daughters then living. Wife Martha to be executrix. The overseers to be Robert Stevens, of Dedham, my father-in-law, and Robert Stevens of Ardleigh, brother-in-law.
    William Grindell one of the witnesses.   Ruthen, 147.

[Ezekiel Sherman probably was of the same family with the Rev. John Sherman, of Watertown, whose ancestors came from Dedham, co. Essex, England. See "Sherman Family," REG. xxiv. 66.—W. B. TRASK.]

WILLIAM SUMPNER, of Waltham Holy Cross, co. Essex, 12 February, 1656, proved 7 May, 1657, by Roger Sumpner, one of the executors. To daughter Susan Williams, daughter Mary Sumpner, son William; wife Jane and youngest son Roger executors. The overseers to be brother Roger Sumpner and brother-in-law William Sawdrie.   Ruthen, 148.

[There seems to be a similarity in early names between this family and that of the Sumner or Somner family of Bicester, co. Oxford, who settled in Dorchester, Mass., before 1637. See REG. viii. 128e; ix. 300.—W. B. T.]

JOHN MASON, of Mashburie, co. Essex, husbandman, 2 December, 1656, proved 7 May, 1657, by Sarah Mason, his widow and executrix. Real estate in Much Waltham to wife for twelve years and then to John Mason, the eldest son, he to pay certain legacies to daughters Mary, Lydia and Sarah Mason. Stileman's Croft, in Good Easter, Essex, to wife for six years, and then to son David Mason, he to pay to two (sic) other children, Abraham Arthur Mason and Samuel Mason, five pounds at age of twenty-one years.   Ruthen, 150.

ROGER BAKER, of Wapping, co. Middlesex, 15 August, 1676, proved 24 January, 1687, by Mary Johnson, alias Baker, wife of Thomas Johnson and daughter and residuary legatee of the testator named in the will. He mentions some land in Maryland, in Virginia, which he directs to be sold.

He leaves to his brother-in-law Abraham Hughs, of Ockingham, co. Berks, yeoman, ten pounds. The residue to two daughters, Honner Baker and Mary Baker, both under twenty years of age. Failing them, then to the four youngest children of his sister Mary Cleves, widow, ten pounds apiece, and the rest to such child or children as brother John Baker shall have then living. Exton, 1.

JOHN HILL, of London, merchant, 14 December, 1665, proved 8 February, 1687. To wife Sarah one thousand pounds. To daughter Sarah one thousand pounds and a silver bason. To daughter Elizabeth eight hundred pounds and a silver "sully bub pott." To daughter Hannah eight hundred pounds and a silver sugar box. Wife now great with child. If it prove a son then he is to have land and tenements in Winthorpe and Croft and elsewhere in Lincolnshire, of the yearly value of twenty-four pounds, and six hundred pounds in money. Whereas my brother Valentine Hill, late of New England, deceased, did owe me at the time of my (*sic*) decease, above three hundred pounds, not yet satisfied, I give and bequeath the said debt unto the children of my said brother Hill and to the children of my brother-in-law Mr. Thomas Cobbett, to be equally divided amongst them, share and share alike. To my niece Bridget Cobbett five pounds. To cousin Garrett's children ten pounds, to be equally divided among them. To cousin Thomas Browne and his wife forty shillings, for rings. To cousin John Browne forty shillings. To brother Hutchinson and sister each forty shillings, and cousin Elizabeth Meredith twenty shillings, to buy rings. To my brother Nathaniel Hunt and brother Richard Hunt, each five pounds. To brother-in-law John Miles and to his wife, each five pounds, and to their son John Miles, five pounds. To my maid-servant Prudence, forty shillings if dwelling with me at time of my death. To my cousins Charles, Margaret and Katherine Watkins, each twenty shillings, for rings. To the poor saints in London ten pounds, to be distributed at the discretion of my overseers. To the poor of the parish where I now dwell, forty shillings. The residue to wife Sarah, who is appointed executrix. Friends Mr. William Allen, Mr. William Sawyer, and Mr. Robert Wakeling, overseers. Witnesses, Nathaniel Hunt and Charles Watkin. Exton, 16.

[Valentine Hill was extensively engaged in real estate and other transactions in Boston, Lynn, Rumney Marsh, Dover, Oyster River and Pascataqua River, between the years 1637, when he was of Boston, and 1660. In 1651 he conveyed to Mr. Thomas Cobbett, of Lynn, styled " Clarke," afterwards minister of Ipswich, and others, all grants of land made to him, the said Hill, by the town of Dover, at Oyster River, and the saw-mills erected thereon. *Suffolk Deeds*, Lib. i. 182. See REGISTER, vii. 49, and Wentworth Genealogy, i. 138.—W. B. T.]

JOHN PARGITER, of St. Martins in the Fields, co. Middlesex, 8 February, 1687, proved 24 February, 1687, by John and Samuel Pargiter, sons and executors. To the four sons of my brother William Pargiter, deceased, viz., Robert, Edward, Samuel and William, and to his daughter Knight's children. To my cousin Frances Meade, wife to Mr. Francis Meade, of Battersea. To Mr. Thomas Pargiter, son to my brother Thomas Pargiter, deceased, to his son, my godson. To my sister Pargiter, his mother-in-law. To George Pargiter, his brother. To my cousin Sarah Louell at Virginia, by Yorke River, ten pounds. To Elizabeth, widow of cousin Robert Pargiter, deceased. To cousin Austin, of Hampton, and his wife. To cousin Benjamin Billingsby, bookseller, and his wife. To cousin Cal-

lendrine and his wife Mary. To my cousin Brewer. To my sister Blagrave. To Daniel and Deborah Blagrave. To Mr. Soffier, draper. To
my grandson John Fleetwood and my grand-daughter Mary Fleetwood.
My worthy friend Sir William Cowper, the elder. Sir Gerald Fleetwood
(father of John and Mary). To my son John Pargiter, lands, &c.,
at Nordley wood, Ashley and Abbots Ashley, or any part of Shropshire,
Pamber and Bramley in Hampshire, large house next the Northumberland
House in the Strand, the Standard Tavern in the Strand, &c. &c. Son Samuel Pargiter.   Exton, 21.

JOHN ANTHONY, of Rhode Island, in America, mariner, 16 June, 1701,
proved 10 December, 1703. To son John Anthony all the estate. Richard and Elinor Potts executors. Proved by Eleanor Potts.
                                                    Degg, 205.

[Query.—Which John Anthony was this? See Anthony Genealogy, REGISTER,
xxxi. 417.—ED.]

THOMAS READE, aboard the ship "Kingsoloman," now riding in the
hope, being bound a voyage to Virginia. All my estate to loving brother
William Reade, of the parish of St. Sepulchres, London, corn chandler,
who is made executor. Signed 2 October, 1662, in presence of John Budd,
scr. and Robert Bray. Proved by William Reade, 22 June, 1663.
                                                    Juxon, 84.

ROBERT RAND, of Barham, co. Suffolk, 27 February, 1651, proved the
last of March, 1651, and a commission issued to Jane Rand, the widow, no
executor having been named in the will. To William Brooke, my grandchild, all my hooks and one hatchet and one pair of cobirons and one hale.
To William Brooke, my son-in-law, all my wearing apparel and the "dobbe"
house, and my cart and my biggest Danske chest and two brass pans and
four pieces of pewter; and all the rest pewter that is mine to be divided
among his children. To my son Robert, after my wife's decease, if he do
come over, my best feather bed and my best bedstead. To wife Jane all
the moveable goods, &c., "not disposed before of," and excepting three
cows which are letten to Lionel Cooke until next Michaelmas, which,
after decease of wife, are to go to son-in-law William Brooke.
                                                    Bowyer, 64.

DENNIS GEERE, of "Sagust," in New England, 10 December, 1635,
approved 6 August, 1637, before us, Tho. (sic) Winthrop Gov', Tho. Dudley dep Gov', Jo. Endecott. To wife Elizabeth three hundred pounds. To
Elizabeth and Sarah Geere, my two daughters, three hundred pounds
apiece. To cousin Ann Pankhurst so much as shall make her portion fifty
pounds. To Elizabeth Tuesley twelve pounds to make up that eight pounds
I owe her twenty. Roger Carver, of Bridhemson,* and John Russell, of
Lewis, in Sussex, appointed overseers for estate in old England. My children to be paid at day of marriage, or at age of eighteen years. And whereas the Lord our God of his great goodness, since my coming into New
England, hath discovered to me all usury to be unlawful, I do hereby
charge my executor to restore all such moneys as any in England can
make appear I have received from them by way of usury, whether it were
6 or 8 per cent, not thinking hereby to merit anything at the hands of God

* This, or Brighthelmston, is the old name for Brighton, as I am assured by J. C. C.
Smith, Esq., who kindly called this and the succeeding will to my notice.   H. F. W.

but laboring hereby to attend my duty and manifest my distaste against every evil way. Of the estate in New England, to Thomas Topper five pounds, Thomas Braines three pounds, Thomas Launder three pounds, Benjamin Nye thirty shillings, Thomas Grenuill ten shillings, all which deducted and paid together with the sending my two servants with my child into England, the residue shall be employed to the advancement of such works as in the wisdom of my executors for that purpose shall seem good for the plantations settled within the Patent of the Massachusetts; and for the discharging of these legacies and sums, and the right ordering of my estate for the public good I appoint for my executors John Winthrop, the elder, and John Humphry, esquires, John Wilson and Hugh Peter, Preachers. Witnesses, Edmond Freeman and John Greene.

28 June, 1642. Emanavit comissio Edwardo Moonke avunculo Elizabethe Geere et Sare Geere filiarum dicti defuncti durante minori etate, &c. It appeared that the widow Elizabeth had departed this life.

Campbell, 79.

[Dennis Geere with his family embarked June 15, 1635, in the Abigail of London, Hackwell master, "having brought Certificate from the minister of Thiselworth," probably Isleworth in Middlesex. Those who embarked that day were Dennis Geere, 30; Elizabeth Geere, uxor, 22; Elizabeth Geere, 3; Sara Geere, 2, children; Anne Pancrust, 16; Eliz: Tusolie, 55; Constant Wood, 12." (Reg. xiv. 315.) His fellow passengers, Anne Pancrust and Eliz: Tusolie, are no doubt the "cousin Ann Pankhurst" and "Elizabeth Tuesley" mentioned in the will. "Thomas Brane, husbandm. 40," and "Tho: Launder, 22," were also fellow passengers, having embarked in the Abigail, July 1, 1635. (Reg. xiv. 318.) In the "Addenda" to Winthrop's Journal, under date of "1635, Dec. 10," among the "gifts bestowed upon the colony," is this entry: "Denis Geere of Sagus gave by his will (at the motion of Mr. Hugh Peter) £300."—Ed.]

Thomas Geere, of the parish of Falmer, near Lewes, co. Sussex, 6 March, 1649, proved 25 April, 1650, by Dennis Geere, son and executor. To wife Mary. To eldest son Thomas Geere and his wife Mercy, and their children, Mercy and Mary. To grand-children Dennis and Richard Geere and grand child Thomas Geere. To the poor of Falmer and the poor of Stamer. Youngest son, Dionice Geere, executor. Friend John Russell, of Southover, near Lewes, and Stephen Towner, of Kingston, to be overseers. Witnesses, Richard Banckes and Tho. Russell.

Pembroke, 51.

Dorothy Parker, of Mildenhall, co. Wilts, widow, 10 October, 1649, proved 11 April, 1650, by Benjamin Woodbridge, one of the executors. To son Mr. Thomas Parker, of New England, two hundred pounds now in hands of my brother, Mr. Richard Stevens, of Stanton Bernard, co. Wilts, not doubting that if he die unmarried he will bestow what remains at his death, thereof, upon the children of my daughters Sarah Baylie and Elizabeth Avery. Of the other one hundred pounds in my brother Stevens' his hand I give five pounds to my son Mr. Thomas Bayly and the remainder to my daughter Sarah Bayly and her four children, John Woodbridge, Benjamin Woodbridge, Sarah Kerridge and Luce Sparhawke, equally. For the one hundred pounds due to me from my son Avery, for which his house was mortgaged, I bestow it upon my daughter Avery and her children. To my son-in-law Mr. Timothy Avery, &c. My loving daughter Sarah Bayly to be executrix in trust with her son, my grandson, Mr. Benjamin Woodbridge, executor, with his mother. Son Mr. Thomas Baylie and Cousin Mr. John Taylor to be overseers. Witnesses, John Barges and Anthony Appleford.

Pembroke, 54.

[An abstract of this will, made by the late Horatio G. Somerby for the Hon. Francis E. Parker of Boston, was published in the REGISTER, xxxii. 337. Mr. Waters has thought that a fuller abstract would be of service to the readers of the REGISTER. —J. T. H.

Mrs. Dorothy Parker was the widow of the Rev. Robert Parker, the famous Puritan author. Benjamin Woodbridge, the executor who proved the will, was the first graduate of Harvard College. See Woodbridge Genealogy, REG. xxxii. 292–6. See also the " Woodbridge Record," New Haven, 1883, large 4to., compiled from the papers of Louis Mitchell, Esq., by his brother Donald G. Mitchell, Esq. The will of the Rev. John Woodbridge, of Stanton, Wilts, the father of Rev. John and Benjamin Woodbridge, is printed in this work from a copy lately obtained in England.—ED.]

EDWARD BELL, of St. Brevells, co. Gloucester, 16 August, 1649, proved 21 January, 1649. He mentions nephew John Gorges, Esq. In a codicil. 20 August, 1649, he mentions lady Elizabeth Gorges of Ashton Phillips, Mrs. Mary Cutts, "my" godson Mr. Edward Perkins, Mr. Thomas Pole, &c. &c. He discharges sundry persons (among whom Mr. Wymond Bradbury, deceased) " of all debts owing by them to me or my brother William which became due unto me by his gift." Pembroke, 3.

[I suppose that this Edward Bell was a brother of Ann, daughter of Edward Bell of Writtle, Essex. Ann Bell was the first wife of Sir Ferdinando Gorges, and her eldest son, John Gorges, probably the " nephew John Gorges, Esq." named in this will, was the father of Ferdinando Gorges, author of " America Painted to the Life." See Johnson's Wonder Working Providence, edited by William F. Poole, LL.D., and the notice of it by the Rev. Edmund F. Slafter in the REGISTER, xxii. 213–19. " Lady Elizabeth Gorges of Ashton Phillips " was no doubt the fourth wife and widow of Sir Ferdinando. See REGISTER, xxix. 42–7. Wymond Bradbury may be Wymond Bradbury of Wicken Bonant, co. Essex, whom the late John M. Bradbury, Esq., supposed to be the father of Thomas Bradbury, of Salisbury, Mass. (see REGISTER, xxiii. 262–6), but if so he died before 1650.—EDITOR.]

NATHANIEL PARKER, of East Berghoult, co. Suffolk, Esq., 5 August, 1684, proved 19 August, 1684. To be buried at the East end of the churchyard near the church of Great Wenham, co. Suffolk. He mentions his farm of Great Wilsey in Wrating, co. Suffolk. To nephew Philip Parker, Esq., son and heir apparent of Sir Philip Parker, Baronet, all my farm called the Priory in Great Wenham and East Berghoult, and the advowson of the church of Great Wenham, for life, and then to his son Philip. Nephew Calthorp Parker, son of Sir Philip Parker. Nephew Sir Philip Parker. Niece Mercy Parker, nieces Dorothy and Mary Parker, daughters of my late brother Sir Philip Parker, Knight. Niece Mary Parker, daughter of Henry Parker, Esq., my late brother. Nephew Henry Parker, son of said brother. My nephew Philip Gurdon, Esq. To John Gurdon, son of my nephew Mr. Nathaniel Gurdon. To Sir John Barker, Baronet. To my godson Winiff Sergeant. My god-daughter Elizabeth Walker. My god-daughter the daughter of my nephew Bernard Saltingstall. My nephew in law Anthony Gaudy, Esq., and my god-son Anthony Gaudie, son of the aforesaid, and his sister Winifred Gaudie. My cousin Elizabeth Garnish, widow.   Hare, 104.

JANE WILLIAMS, of Whetenhurst, co. Gloucester, spinster, 31 May, 1650, proved 30 June, 1655. To brother Samuel Williams my Scottish print bible. To my brother Richard Williams and my sister Elizabeth Williams that are in New England, each of them twenty shillings apiece. To Benjamin Williams and Nathaniel Williams, the two sons of my brother Samuel Williams, ten pounds apiece when they reach the age of twenty-one years. To John Hall, the younger, my sister's eldest son, ten pounds and a standing bedstead that is in his father's parlour chamber, my brother-in-law John Hall's. To Samuel, Daniel and Susanna Hall, the other three children of my brother-in-law, John Hall, twenty pounds apiece at 21. Brother-in-law John Hall to be executor. Aylett, 292.

[It is evident that the Richard Williams, named above, as in New England, was Richard Williams of Taunton, Mass. (*ante*, p. 3).

See also REGISTER, li. 209. — ED.]

WILLIAM GOODRICK, of Walton Head, co. York, 21 September, 1662, proved 25 January, 1664. My two daughters, Sarah and Elizabeth. My daughter Mary and her husband Matthew Elwald. My nephews Sir John Goodricke and Sir Francis Goodrick. My wife Sarah. My son William Goodrick. Hyde, 4.

[See REGISTER, xxxvi. 384.—H. F. W.]

JOSEPH HOLLAND, citizen and clothworker of London, 25 December, 1658, with codicil dated 29 December, 1658, proved 17 January, 1658. To be buried on the south side of the christening pew in the parish church of St. Sepulchre, London, between my two former wives. To Elizabeth, my now wife, late the wife and administratrix of Jeffery Cumber, deceased. To son Joseph Holland the lease of my house in Green Arbour in said parish. To son-in-law John Perry and Johanna, his wife, my daughter, and their sons John Perry and Josias Perry and daughter Elizabeth Perry. To my said daughter Johanna, certain needle work "wrought by my first wife, her mother." To daughter Elizabeth, wife of Richard Bessy, in Virginia. To my son Nathaniel Holland, of Waterton in New England twenty pounds in goods; to son Samuel Holland, in Virginia, thirty pounds in goods or money; and to each a bible. To son-in-law Miles Rich and daughter Prudence, his wife. To good friend Mr. John White, grocer, of above-named parish, and his wife. To Mr. John Andrewes in Fleet Lane. To my servant John Arnott. To the poor of said parish, in bread, twenty shillings, to such as Master Gouge will distribute unto. The executor to be Master John White; the overseer to be Master Andrews. The witnesses to the body of the will were Hen: Travers Scr: Ellen Booth (her mark). The witnesses to the codicil were Hen: Travers, John Arnatt and Thomas Bargett. Pell, 9.

[The family of Nathaniel Holland of Watertown, named in this will, is found in Bond's Watertown, p. 302. Dr. Bond erroneously conjectures that he was a son of John and Judith Holland of Dorchester, Mass., and he has been followed by other writers.—ED.]

[I find a grant of land on record in the Virginia Land Registry Office, of 189 acres, to Edward Besse, on the south side of Chickahominy River, April 7, 1651, Book No. 2, p. 321. The names Arnott, Gouge, Booth, Perry and Travers appear in the early annals of Virginia. Francis Willis, the ancestor of the worthy Virginia family of that name, married, about the middle of the 17th century, Ann Rich.—R. A. BROCK, of Richmond, Va.]

MARGARET LANE, of London, widow, 16 January, 1661, with addition made 3 September, 1662. To be buried in the grave of my late husband, Edmond Lane, in the parish church of St. Dunstan's in the East, London. To my sister Martha, wife of William Eaton, now, I think, in New England, one hundred pounds within one year next after my decease. To her five children twenty pounds, to be equally divided amongst them, and also within the like time, to their said father or mother for their use, and whose acquittance shall be a sufficient discharge to my executor for the same. To my cousin Sarah Barett, daughter of my late brother Daniel Jenkin, deceased, and now wife of John Barett, twenty pounds. To her eldest daughter, Sarah Barett, thirty pounds, and to her son John Barett and her other daughter, Mary Barett, twenty pounds apiece. To the three children of my late sister Priscilla Haṁond, deceased, late wife of William Hammond, ten pounds apiece within one year after my decease. To Thomas Jenkins, eldest son of said deceased brother Daniel Jenkins. To my other cousin Daniel Jenkins, son of said deceased brother, &c. &c.

The addition, or codicil, mentions cousin Thomas Jenkins, of Minster, co. Kent, who is appointed overseer, the said 3 August (*sic*) 1662.

The witnesses to the will were Henry Travers, Scr. in Smithfield, Jo. Newland, Micah Machell and Samuel Fox, his servants.

Elizabeth Jenkin, relict and administratrix, with the will annexed, of Daniel Jenkins, deceased, executor of above will, received commission to administer on the estate of the above, 5 August, 1667.   Carr, 107.

["William Eaton of Staple, husbandman, Martha, his wife, three children and one servant," embarked for New England in 1637 (REG. xv. 29). They settled at Watertown (Bond's Watertown, p. 202). They had two children born in this country, making in all five children, the number named by Mrs. Lane.—ED.]

EDMUND MUNINGES, of Denge, co. Essex, the unprofitable servant of God, 2 October, 1666, proved 18 July, 1667, by Hopestill Muninges, executor. To wife Markiet ten pounds within one month after my decease, and the household goods which her father gave her, and that is to say, one bed, one table, cubbord, one guite (*sic*) chest, one brass pot, one dripping pan and four little platters. To second son, Return, twenty pounds within one year after demand be made for it. To third son, Takeheed, forty pounds within six months after my decease. To eldest daughter, Harry (*sic*) ten pounds within one year after demand be made for it. To second daughter, Rebecca, ten pounds. Eldest son, Hopestill, to be executor. If wife Markit prove with child, then to such child ten pounds at age of twenty-one years, &c. Testator made his mark in presence of William Cooch, John Spencer and Takeheed Muninge.   Carr, 95.

[Edmund Munnings, aged 40, came to New England in 1635, in the Abigail, Robert Hackwell, master, bringing with him his wife Mary, aged 30 years, daughters Mary and Anna, and son Mahalaleel, respectively nine, six and three years of age. He settled in Dorchester, where he had grants of land, among them that of Moon Island, "layd to Dorchester" by the General Court, June 2, 1641. This Island contained about twenty acres of land, and was used for pasturage, it may have been, for two and a half centuries. On the northerly side was a high bluff; southerly it was connected at very low water, by the bars or flats of the island, with the promontory of Squantum. This island is named on the Dorchester Records, in 1637 and 1638, "Mannings Moone." It is, however, no longer an island, having recently been joined to Squantum by an artificial isthmus in connection with the great Boston sewer, the reservoir of which is being built here.

Mr. Munnings had three sons, born and baptized in Dorchester, bearing the singular names of Hopestill, born April 5, 1637, Return, Sept. 7, 1640, and Take Heed, Oct. 20, 1642. The Dorchester Church Records say that Hopestill went to England. We have also evidence that the father returned and died in his native clime. Return removed to Boston. Goody Munnings, the mother, was admitted to the Dorchester church, 16. 2. 1641. On the "9 (8) 59, Mahallaeell Munings" was dismissed from this church "vnto ye new," or second "church at Boston, & dyed ye 27 (12) 59, being drowned in ye Millcreek at Boston in ye night."—Dorchester Church Records. He married Hannah, daughter of John Wiswall. The widow subsequently married Thomas Overman. By the inventory of the estate of Mahalaleel Munnings, made in 1659, and proved Jan. 30, 1660, occupying three large folio pages in volume three of Suffolk wills and inventories, pages 229 to 231, the last inventory in the book, it would appear that he invested largely in English goods, and was a prominent merchant of his day. In 1667 widow Munnings was taxed three pence, among those rated for lands at the neck in Dorchester, at a half penny per acre for the plow land. Mahalaleel went to England, it may have been with his father, and is doubtless the person who returned to New England in the Speedwell in 1656, Capt. Locke, master, notwithstanding the slight discrepancy in age, as given at the two arrivals.

The name of Edmund Munnings, on the 7th of 12 mo. 1641, is affixed to the list, consisting of seventy-one, of the inhabitants of Dorchester, who agreed that a rate of twenty pounds per annum should be paid out of the rents of Thompson's island towards the maintenance of a school in Dorchester. We are not certain that Mr. Munnings was there subsequent to 1641. On the 8th of March, 1663-4, his name stands the fifteenth on the list of rights in the New Grant of undivided land, which did belong to William Stoughton. Mr. Munnings had an interest in 10 acres, 3 quarters, 12 pole. Mr. Savage says Mr. Munnings " had probably gone home, I think, to Malden, co. Essex, there at least, was somehow connected with Joseph Hills, who before coming over had given M. £11 in a bill for bringing one bullock for the use of H." Maldon is a few miles only from Dengie, and is "locally in the hundred of Dengie." See REGISTER, i. 132 ; vii. 273; viii. 75 ; x. 176 ; xiv. 316 ; Fourth Report of the Record Commissioners, Boston, pages 29, 32, 106, 120 ; Savage's Genealogical Dictionary, iii. 255 ; Lewis's Topographical Dictionary of England, ii. 20 ; iii. 206 ; History of Dorchester, p. 68 ; King's Handbook of Boston Harbor, pp. 100, 106.—W. B. TRASK.]

JOHN NORRIS the elder, of Westminster, co. Middlesex, yeoman, 8 June, 1667, proved 4 (or 5) July, 1667. To son William Norris seventy-five pounds to make up the twenty-five pounds formerly given him to one hundred pounds, &c., and also house, &c., at Mooret-clack,* co. Surrey, which I bought of him, and a tenement at Tame in co. Oxford, held by lease. To son John Norris ninety pounds, to make up the ten pounds formerly given him to one hundred pounds, and a tenement at Mooretclack, bought of son William, &c. To grand child Annanias Andrews thirty pounds at age of twenty-one or day of marriage. To grand child John Andrews thirty pounds at twenty-one. To daughter Elizabeth Bell, now beyond the seas, forty pounds, if she be living and come to England to receive the same herself, and that Samuel Bell, her husband, shall not meddle or have to do therewith. To grand-child Edward Norris, son of Christopher Norris, thirty pounds, five pounds whereof to put him forth an apprentice, and the remaining twenty-five pounds, with the benefit and increase, at age of twenty-one years. Remainder to two sons, William and John Norris, equally. Carr, 95.

Sir ROBERT PEAKE, Knight, citizen and goldsmith of London, 15 May, 1666, with codicil made 27 September, 1666, proved 26 July, 1667, by Gregory and Benjamin Peake. To my cousin and sometime servant, George Lyddall, in Virginia, gentleman, three hundred pounds in three years (one hundred pounds per year payable on Michaelmas day). To my sometime servant, Michael Tucker, in Virginia, husbandman, ten pounds. To servant Elizabeth Essington, of London, widow, twenty pounds. To my cousin James Waters, the son of Joseph Waters, fifty pounds. To my cousin —— Waters, relict of Samuel Waters, skinner, deceased, twenty pounds. To friend Doctor James Hide of Oxford, and his wife Margaret Hide, fifty pounds, and to their son Robert, my godson, fifty pounds. To my good friend and valentine Mary St. Loe, of the Parish of Dunstans in the East, London, widow, one thousand pounds in ten years (one hundred pounds a year, payable on Michaelmas day). To Mrs. Mary Burton, wife

* Mortlake.

of Mr. Thomas Burton of London, gentleman, and their son Robert, my godson, &c. To my godson Tristram Huddlestone, son of Nicholas Huddlestone of London, skinner, &c. To good friend Thomas Pulteney, of London, salter, and his wife, &c. To Edward Hunt, of London, vintner, and Elizabeth his wife. To my friend Edward Jerman. To good friend Richard Loans, of London. To John Peake, Esq., eldest son of Sir William Peake, Knight, of London, Alderman, and his brother Benjamin, second son of Sir William, &c. To Mrs. Elizabeth Vanbrugh, wife of Mr. Giles Vanbrugh, merchant, both my singular good friends—and to others.

Carr, 96.

[Much about the English family of Waters will be found in Emmerton and Waters's Gleaning from English Records, pp. 121–30.—ED.]

[In the Virginia Land Registry Office the following grants are recorded: George Lyddal, "Gentleman," 1750 acres in York County, Nov. 25, 1654; "Captain" George Lyddal, 2390 acres in New Kent County (formed from York County in 1654) Jan. 20, 1657. Book No. 4, p. 214. The name Lyddall is a favored Christian name in a number of Virginian families, notably in the Bowles and Bacon. I find on record in Henrico County court, in June, 1754, the will of Langston Bacon. Wife Sarah is named, and also as Executors, Nathaniel Bacon, Lyddal Bacon and John Williamson. John Lyddall Bacon, Esq. is at this date President of the State Bank of Richmond.—R. A. BROCK, of Richmond, Va.]

WILLIAM BURGES, of South River, County of Ann Arundell, Province of Maryland, 11 July, 1685. To son Edward Burges five thousand pounds of tobacco in casque within one year, provided he deliver to my executors one half of certain live stock that belonged to the estate of George Puddington, deceased. To William and Elizabeth, the children of said son Edward. To son George Burges five thousand pounds of tobacco in casque, within one year. To sons William, John, Joseph, Benjamin and Charles, and daughters Elizabeth, Ann and Susanna Burges. To daughter Susannah, the wife of Major Nicholas Sewall, five pounds in money and my seal ring. To my grandson Charles Sewall and my granddaughter Jane Sewall. To son William my messuage, &c., near South River, Ann Arundell county, which I purchased of one George Westall, and on a part whereof is a town called London. Wife Ursula to have the use of it till son William accomplish the age of twenty-one years. (It is again referred to as the town or port of London.) Also to son William a tract in Baltimore County, near land of Col. George Wells, containing four hundred and eighty acres. To son John a tract near Herring Creek, in Ann Arundell County, containing eight hundred acres. To son Joseph a tract lately bought of Richard Beard, gentleman, near the South River, &c., containing thirteen hundred and forty acres. To son Benjamin a tract near the Ridge, in Ann Arundell County, which I bought of Thomas Besson, containing three hundred acres, and another near the head of South River, containing four hundred acres. To son Charles my interest in land bought of Vincent Low, near the head of Sasafras River, in Cecil County, formerly granted to Nicholas Painter, since deceased, and containing sixteen hundred acres, also a tract lately purchased by me from said Vincent Lowe, on the south side of the Susquehanock River in said county of Baltimore, containing five hundred acres. (These sons appear to have been all under twenty-one years of age.) Wife Ursula to be executrix, and Major Nicholas Sewall, Major Nicholas Cassaway and Captain Henry Hanslapp, supervisors. The witnesses were Thomas Francies, Michael Cusack, John Harrison, William Elridge (his mark) and John Edwards.

5 July, 1689. Emanavit Comissio Micajæ Perry attornato unice depu-

tato per Ursulam Moore als Burges (uxorem Mordecai Moore) jam in com. de Ann Arundell in Provincia de Maryland comorand. relictam et executricem, &c. &c. Ent. 91.

THOMAS BRINLEY, of Datchett, co. Bucks, Esq., 13 September, 1661, with codicil of 16 October, 1661, proved 11 December, 1661. My third of tenements in the town of Newcastle upon Tyne, and two thirds of the manor of Burton in Yorkshire, to eldest son, Francis Brinley and his heirs. My half of the township or manor of Wakerfield, heretofore parcell of the Lordship of Raby, and my lands and tenements in Wakerfield, county and Bishoprick of Durham, purchased in the names of William Wase of Durham and of Robert Worrall, lately deceased, and of Michael Lambcroft, lately deceased, and of John Maddocke, of Cuddington, co. Chester, in trust for the use of me, the said Thomas Brinley, and the said Robert Worrall and our heirs and assigns forever, to my wife, Anne Brinley, during her natural life; at her death to eldest son, Francis Brinley. My lands in Horton and Stanwell, in the several counties of Middlesex and Bucks, &c., by me purchased of Henry Bulstrode of Horton, to wife Anne for life; then to my second son, Thomas Brinley, a lease of ninety-nine years. Certain other lands, &c., lately bought of James Styles, the elder, of Langley, to wife Anne; at her death to my third son, William Brinley. A legacy to daughter Mary Silvester, widow, and her daughter, my granddaughter, Mary Silvester the younger, who are both left destitute of subsistence by the decease of my said daughter's late husband, Peter Silvester, &c. To the children of my daughter Grissell, the now wife of Nathaniel Silvester, gentleman, dwelling in New England, in the Parts of America, in an island called Shelter Island, one hundred pounds within one year after my decease. The witnesses to the will were Robert Style and Rose Baker. In the codicil he bequeaths legacies to his brother Lawrence Brinley and Richard Brinley his son, both of London, merchants, to the intent that they shall with all convenient speed sell that half of said lands, &c. (in Wakerfield), for the best rate and value that they can get for the same, &c. The witnesses to this codicil were William Wase, Budd Wase, William Carter and William Brinley. The will was proved by the widow, Anne Brinley. May, 193.

[Thomas Brinley, who made this will, was the father of Francis Brinley, who emigrated to Barbadoes, but, the climate not being " suited to his habits and constitution," came to New England and settled at Newport, R. I., as early as 1652. Francis Brinley wrote an "Account of the Settlements and Governments in and about the Lands of Narraganset Bay," which is printed in the Massachusetts Historical Collections, 1st S., vol. v. pp. 217-20. A catalogue of his library is printed in the REGISTER, xii. 75-8.
Brief genealogies of the Brinley family will be found in Bridgman's King's Chapel Epitaphs, 219-228, and in the Heraldic Journal, vol. ii. pp. 31-2. The former is by the Hon. Francis Brinley, now of Newport, R. I. From it we learn that Thomas Brinley, " one of the auditors of the Revenue of King Charles the First and of King Charles the Second," besides the children named above in his will— Francis, Thomas, William, Mary, widow of Peter Sylvester, and Grizzell, wife of Nathaniel Sylvester—had three other daughters who lived to be married, namely : Rose, who married Giles Baker, lord of the manor of Riple in Kent ; one, christian name unknown, who married William Coddington, governor of Rhode Island ; and the other, whose christian name is also unknown, who married Richard Hackle, Esq. Grizzell was baptized at St. James's Church, Clerkenwell, Jan. 6, 1635-6. Abstracts of the wills of Peter and Nathaniel Sylvester will be found later in this article.—ED.]

LAURENCE BRINLEY, citizen and haberdasher of London, 10 August, 1662, proved 11 December, 1662, by the oaths of Samuel and Richard

Brinley, sons and executors named in the will. The following bequests appear : to Mary Limbrey twenty pounds ; to Philip Limbrey, of Virginia, twenty pounds ; to my sister Susan Gregory, of Exon (Exeter), widow, ten pounds ; to my cousin Elizabeth Brinley, of London, widow, and her two daughters, twenty pounds apiece to buy them a ring ; to Master Calamy, my dearly beloved pastor and faithful minister of Jesus Christ, five pounds ; to poor Presbyterian ministers out of their places for conscience sake, thirty pounds, to be disposed of according to the discretion of my executors with Mr. Calamy ; to my daughter Jenne Jackson, the wife of ——, the sum of twenty pounds, and, in case Weaver's Hall money cometh in, eighty pounds ; to my daughter-in-law Elizabeth Earnly, widow, the sum of twenty pounds ; to my son Nathaniel Brinley fifty pounds when he cometh out of his time. I do constitute and appoint my two sons Samuel and Richard Brinley to be my executors, and give ten pounds apiece to them. The residue, &c., to my five children, viz., Nathaniel, Susannah, Hester, Philip and Isaac Brinley, according to equal proportions. My real estate of land in Ireland and England, after my decease, to be sold according to the uttermost value, for the payment of my wife's and the children's portions.

The witnesses -to this will were William Webb, Richard Brinley and John Jackson.   Laud, 151.

NATHANIEL, son of Laurence Brinley, of London, merchant, was a legatee to the amount of five pounds, under the will of Henry Hazlewood, citizen and currier of London, proved in the same year as the foregoing will.   Laud, 108.

[From Lipscombe's History of Buckinghamshire, published in 1847.] In an account of the church at Datchett are found the following copies of inscriptions on a slab in the floor of the nave :

Here lieth the body of Thomas Brinley, Esq., who was one of the auditors of the Revenue of King Charles the First and of King Charles y[e] Second. Born in the City of Exeter. He married Anne, youngest daughter of W[m] Ware* of Petworth, in Sussex, gent., who had issue by her five sons and seven daughters. He dyed the 15th day of October in the year of our Lord 1661.

Here also lieth buried y[e] body of the above said William Ware,* who died the 19th of Sept. 1642, aged 62 years and 5 months.

Vol. iv. page 441.

[From Visitation of London, 1634, vol. i., printed by the Harleian Soc.]

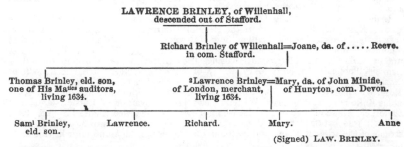

LAWRENCE BRINLEY, of Willenhall,
descended out of Stafford.

Richard Brinley of Willenhall=Joane, da. of ..... Reeve.
in com. Stafford.

Thomas Brinley, eld. son,   2Lawrence Brinley=Mary, da. of John Minifie,
one of His Ma[ties] auditors,   of London, merchant, of Hunyton, com. Devon.
living 1634.   living 1634.

Sam[l] Brinley,   Lawrence.   Richard.   Mary.   Anne.
eld. son.

(Signed) LAW. BRINLEY.

* This is undoubtedly a mistake for Wase ; for a pedigree of which family see Berry's Sussex Genealogies, p. 125, and Dallaway's History of the Western Division of Sussex, Vol. 2, Part ii. p. 123. It will be noticed that William Wase and Budd Wase were witnesses of Thomas Brinley's will.—H. F. W.

[From Randall Holmes's Heraldic Collections for Cheshire, Harleian MS., No. 2119 British Museum.]

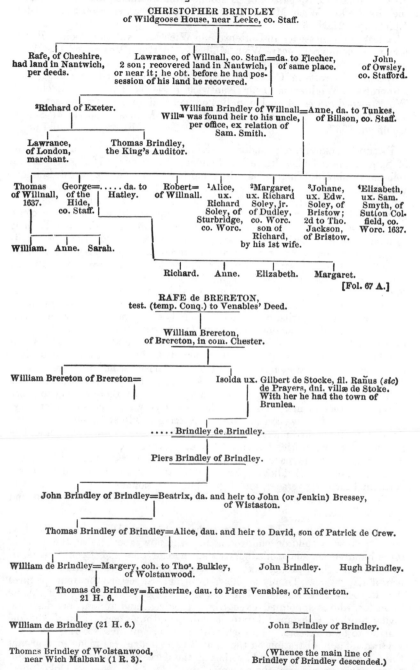

CHRISTOPHER BRINDLEY
of Wildgoose House, near Leeke, co. Staff.

Rafe, of Cheshire, had land in Nantwich, per deeds.

Lawrance, of Willnall, co. Staff.=da. to Flecher, 2 son; recovered land in Nantwich, of same place. or near it; he obt. before he had possession of his land he recovered.

John, of Owsley, co. Stafford.

²Richard of Exeter.

William Brindley of Willnall=Anne, da. to Tunkes, Willᵐ was found heir to his uncle, of Billson, co. Staff. per office, ex relation of Sam. Smith.

Lawrance, of London, marchant.

Thomas Brindley, the King's Auditor.

Thomas of Willnall, 1637.

George=.... da. to of the Hatley. Hide, co. Staff.

Robert= of Willnall.

¹Alice, ux. Richard Soley, of Sturbridge, co. Worc.

²Margaret, ux. Richard Soley, jr. of Dudley, co. Worc. son of Richard, by his 1st wife.

³Johane, ux. Edw. Soley, of Bristow; 2d to Tho. Jackson, of Bristow.

⁴Elizabeth, ux. Sam. Smyth, of Sutton Colfield, co. Worc. 1637.

William. Anne. Sarah.

Richard. Anne. Elizabeth. Margaret.

[Fol. 67 A.]

RAFE de BRERETON, test. (temp. Conq.) to Venables' Deed.

William Brereton, of Brereton, in com. Chester.

William Brereton of Brereton=

Isolda ux. Gilbert de Stocke, fil. Rañus (sic) de Prayers, dni. villæ de Stoke. With her he had the town of Brunlea.

..... Brindley de Brindley.

Piers Brindley of Brindley.

John Brindley of Brindley=Beatrix, da. and heir to John (or Jenkin) Bressey, of Wistaston.

Thomas Brindley of Brindley=Alice, dau. and heir to David, son of Patrick de Crew.

William de Brindley=Margery, coh. to Thoˢ. Bulkley, of Wolstanwood.

John Brindley. Hugh Brindley.

Thomas de Brindley=Katherine, dau. to Piers Venables, of Kinderton. 21 H. 6.

William de Brindley (21 H. 6.)

John Brindley of Brindley.

Thomas Brindley of Wolstanwood, near Wich Malbank (1 R. 3).

(Whence the main line of Brindley of Brindley descended.)

[Abstracts of deeds in evidence.]   William, son of Thomas de Brindley, gives to Rich⁴ Reffs, parson of Bastomley, all his lands, tenements, &c., in the Hundred of Wich Malbank.   Dated at Wolstanwood on the Feast of Epiphany—21 H. 6.

A lease of a messuage in Rottenrow in Wich Malbank, by Thomas Brindley of Wolstanwood, near Wich Malbank, to Hugh Boston of the Wich, gentleman, dated 6 February, 1 R. 3.

A lease of Crofts in Copenhall and Wolstanwood, and a messuage and two crofts in Wighterson, near Nantwich, made by Thomas Brindeley of Wolstanwood aforesaid, to Hugh Boston, gent. aforesaid, of same date.

Mr. Garside to pay me for this pedigree for Mr. Sam. Smyth of Sutton Coldfield, 1637.   Ff. 40, 67 A. and 68.

PETER SILVESTER of London, merchant, now inhabitant in the parish of Saint James, Dukes Place, in London, 26 January, 1657, proved 11 February, 1657.   Whereas my dear mother, Mary Silvester, of London, widow, did oblige herself by promise to give unto me the sum of one thousand pounds of lawful money of England, for which said sum of one thousand pounds, &c., my said mother, at my request, hath this day become bound by obligation of the penalty of two thousand pounds unto Thomas Middleton of Stratford Bow, in the County of Middlesex, Esquire, conditioned for the payment of the said one thousand pounds within six years after the date of the said bond unto me or to Mary my now wife, &c. &c. I do give and bequeath the said sum to wife Mary.   To only daughter Mary six hundred pounds at the age of one and twenty years or day of marriage.   If she die in the mean time, then two hundred pounds of it to my dear and loving wife, one hundred pounds to my brother Nathaniel Silvester, one hundred pounds to brother Joshua Silvester, one hundred and fifty pounds to brother Giles Silvester, and fifty pounds to my sister Cartwright.   The said sum of six hundred pounds to be sent to my loving brother Constant Silvester, now resident in the Barbados, he to become bound for the payment, as above.   To each and every of my own brothers and brothers-in-law forty shillings apiece to make each of them a ring to wear in remembrance of me.   To my uncle Jeofrie Silvester the sum of twenty-five pounds.   To my cousin Joseph Gascoigne fifteen pounds.   To my Aunt Gascoigne five pounds, and to her daughter Anne Gascoigne five pounds.   To loving friend Richard Duke, scrivener, forty shillings to make him a ring.   To the poor of the parish of St. James, Duke's Place, five pounds.   Thomas Middleton, Esq., to be sole executor, and loving uncle Nathaniel Arnold overseer, and I give him fifty pounds.

The witnesses to the above were Edw: Warren, Hum: Richardson and Richard Duke, scr.   Wootton, 95.

GILES SILVESTER, of London, merchant, 2 March, 1670, proved 26 May, 1671.   To such child or children as my wife now goeth with, the sum of three hundred pounds at his, her or their age of one and twenty years, if sons, and at age of twenty-one, or on day of marriage, which shall first happen, if daughters.   To my nephew, Constant Silvester, the four pictures that were my late fathers.   The residue of the estate to loving wife, Anne Silvester, who is appointed executrix.   I entreat and appoint my dear and loving brother, Constant Silvester Esquire, and my good friend Redmaine Burrell to be overseers.   To each of them forty shillings, for rings.

Grant of administration on the estate of the above was made to Constant Silvester, natural and lawful brother of the deceased, the widow Anne Silvester having renounced the executorship.   Duke, 68.

CONSTANT SILVESTER made his will 7 April, 1671, proved 7 October, 1671, by Grace Silvester, relict and executrix. All my lands, plantations, houses and tenements in the island of Barbados, &c., to wife Grace and to Henry Walrond, Senr Esq., brother of the said Grace, Col. Richard Hawkins, Samuel Farmer, Esq., and Mr. Francis Raynes (being all of the said island of Barbados) for one thousand years from the day of my decease, in trust, &c.; wife Grace to enjoy one moiety during her natural life, and my eldest son, Constant, to enjoy two thirds of the other moiety during his mother's life, and my second son, Humphrey Silvester, to have and hold the remaining third of said other moiety during his mother's life. After her death Constant to have two thirds of the whole, and Humphrey the remaining third. If there should be more sons, the eldest son (in that case) to have a double share, and each other son a single share. If wife Grace should marry again, then she to have one third, instead of one half, of the above described property. To daughters Grace and Mary two thousand pounds sterling each at day of marriage, or at age of twenty-one years, and, over and above that, the sum of one hundred pounds sterling each, to buy them a jewel at the age of sixteen years.

Item, I give and bequeath to my brother Nathaniel Silvester, his heirs and assigns forever, one sixth part of all the lands which I and my said brother hold in partnership in Shelter Island, upon the coast of New England; so that, whereas he had a third part of the said lands before, now he shall have a moiety. And the remaining moiety of the said lands I give and bequeath to my two sons before named, equally, and to the heirs of their bodies lawfully begotten, forever; and, for want of such issue, to my brother Joshua Silvester and the heirs of his body, forever; and, for want of such issue, to my brother Nathaniel, his heirs and assigns, forever. To brother Joshua Silvester eight hundred pounds sterling. To my sister Mary Cartwright a mortgage on the estate made over to me by her deceased husband, Isaac Cartwright, during her natural life, and after her decease to my nephew, Constant Cartwright, he paying out of the same to each of his sisters, Mary and Anne, two hundred pounds sterling at their day of marriage or arrival at age of twenty-one years, whichever shall first happen. To my nephew Richard Kett, six hundred pounds sterling, and sixty pounds sterling per annum so long as he shall remain upon my Plantation after my decease, to keep the accompts thereof and taking care no injury or prejudice be done to the estate by any without giving notice thereof to my trustees beforenamed.

Wife Grace to be executrix so long as she remain unmarried, then the other trustees, &c. To each of these fifty pounds sterling apiece to buy them what they shall think fit to remember me by after my decease.

The witnesses were Henry Walrond, Grace Walrond, Peter Blackler, Anne Guillett, Dorothy Marshall, Samuel Ainseworth, jun^r and Will. Swepson.

17 June 1702 emanavit commissio Dominæ Gratiæ Pickering, uxori Domini Henrici Pickering, Baronetti, filiæ naturali et legitimæ dicti Constantii Silvester defuncti, etc. etc.   Duke, 124.

In the Chancel Aisle of the church in Brampton (co. Huntington), is a stone with this inscription: " Here lieth the body of Constant Silvester Esqre who departed this life the 2nd September, 1671." The church Register contains the following : " Mr Humphrey Silvester, son of Mr Constant

3

Silvester & Mrs Grace his wife, was buried April ye sixteenth 1673." " Mr Constant Silvester was buried the 4th day of September a: d: 1671." Add. MS. 24493, Fol. 341, Brit. Mus. (Joseph Hunter's Colls.).

The following is an abstract of the last will and testament of NATHAN-IEL SYLVESTER of Shelter Island, proved 2 October, 1680. He calls him-self the right, true and lawful owner and proprietor of one moiety or half part, in fee simple, of all that Island whereon he was then dwelling, for-merly called Manhansack-Ahaqua-Shuwamock, now Shelter Island, &c. &c. also of one moiety or half part, in possession and reversion, of one other Island, formerly called Robert's Island. He gives and bequeaths to his en-deared wife Grizzell Sylvester, Francis Brinley, James Lloyd, Isaac Arnold, Lewis Morris and Daniel Gould, all the above described property, and also the other moiety or half part of Shelter Island which is claimed in partner-ship by my brother Constant Sylvester and Thomas Middleton, or any part or parts thereof which may happen to fall due unto me from the said Con-stant Sylvester and Thomas Middleton by reason of the great disburse-ments made by me for the said moiety, &c., in their behalf since the year 1652 until this present year, and likewise by reason of the great sums of money which my brother Constant doth in particular stand indebted unto me, as per accounts doth appear, and furthermore by reason of the confis-cation of the said moiety, &c. &c., by the Dutch men of war at their taking of New York with their fleet of nineteen men of war, they also taking and surprising the said moiety, &c. &c., as by the chief commanders of the said Dutch men of war their instrument of confiscation and Bill of Sale given unto me for the same, as doth at large appear, the said commanders also sending one of their men of war to Shelter Island where the Captain land-ed with about fifty soldiers, taking possession of the said moiety, &c., and to strike the greater dread in my family they beset my house, the better to obtain the money which they forced from me and myself constrained to pay to prevent their suing of said moiety, &c. &c. The above described prop-erty is to be held in trust for certain purposes. Reference is made to his wife's jointure, as by a deed left in hands of brother William Coddington of Rhode Island may at large appear. My children to be brought up in the fear of God, and to have such education bestowed upon them as may be conveniently gotten in these parts of the world, and as shall seem meet to my endeared wife, their mother, &c. My brother Joshua to be convenient-ly maintained both with diet, lodging, clothing and necessaries, decent and becoming him, as hitherto he hath enjoyed, that he may in no manner of way want, and in no wise put off from the Island, unless he shall think good to live elsewhere, &c. To son Giles (certain property) ; to son Nathaniel ; to son Peter ; to daughter Patience at age of twenty-one or marriage ; to daughter Elizabeth at twenty-one or marriage ; to daughter Mary at twen-ty-one or marriage; to daughter Ann at twenty-one or marriage ; to daugh-ter Mercy at twenty-one or marriage. To sons Constant and Benjamin at twenty-one. Son Nathaniel (a minor) to have certain bricks lying at Tho-mas Moore Senior's farm and at the Oyster Pond. Son Peter (also a minor) to have part of the said bricks. Property at Southold spoken of. The executors of the above will to be wife Grizzell Sylvester, brother-in-law Francis Brinley, son-in-law James Lloyd, cousin Isaac Arnold, Lewis Morris and Daniel Gould.

The witnesses were John Colling, Ann Colling (by mark), Peter Al-dritch and Jaques Guillott. These made deposition 2 October, 1680, under authority given by the Governor 2 September, 1680.

Additional MS. 24493, Fol. 344, British Museum (Joseph Hunter's Collections).

[On the 9 of June, 1651, Thomas Middleton, Thomas Rouse, Constant Sylvester and Nathaniel Sylvester, purchased Shelter Island, on the east end of Long Island, for sixteen hundred pounds of good merchantable Muscovado sugar, from Stephen Goodyeare, of New Haven, who had purchased it May 18, 1641, from the agent of the Earl of Sterling. Full particulars of the transactions of Nathaniel Sylvester in relation to Shelter Island will be found in Thompson's Long Island, vol. i. pp. 364-9. Nathaniel Sylvester died in March, 1680, according to Thompson, who gives an account of his descendants. Savage, in his Genealogical Dictionary (iv. 99), says : " There is no slight reason to believe this Nathaniel to be the son of the celebrated poet Joshua Sylvester, translator of the divine rhapsodies of Du Bartas." I do not know what reason Mr. Savage, who was a cautious genealogist, had for thinking so. It is possible that he was a son, or more likely a grandson.—ED.]

SAMUEL WARD, the elder, of Ipswich, clerk, 19 October, 1639, proved 24 April, 1640, by Nathaniel and Joseph Ward, sons of the deceased and executors of his will; to whom he left all his books, all his loadstones, shells, papers, pictures and maps. Item—I will and bequeath all that money which doth belong to me upon the house where I now dwell, situate in Ipswich aforesaid (which money was given by many gentlemen and townsmen my friends), to be equally divided between them and their heirs forever ; also all my lands and houses in Brickelsea, both free and copy, equally, &c. &c., on condition that every year during the natural life of Deborah, my loving wife, and Samuel Ward, my eldest son, they pay to the said Deborah and Samuel twenty pounds a year apiece,—to either of them at four times or terms in the year,—upon the feast-day of the Nativity of our Lord God, upon the feast day of the Annunciation of our Blessed Lady St. Mary the Virgin, upon the feast day of St. John the Baptist, and upon the feast day of St. Michael the Archangel, by even and equal portions, &c., at the now dwelling house of Mr. Robert Knapp in Ipswich; or, in lieu of said twenty pounds a year to son Samuel, to keep and maintain him in a comely and decent manner for and during his natural life, at the election and choice of the said Nathaniel and Joseph. To my mother forty shillings yearly, to be paid her at her now dwelling house in Weathersfield, quarterly. My watch to my daughter Deborah, and my fair English Bible, printed anno domini 1633, to my said daughter Deborah, only my wife to have the use of said bible during her life. Sundry chattels to daughter Abigail, after decease of wife. All the plate and wearing clothes to son Nathaniel. My Greek Testament, of Robert Stephens print, to my brother John Ward. My best gloves to my son Robert Bolton. A Greek Testament to son John Bolton. To Margaret my maid, twenty shillings. To John Boggas, my servant, ten shillings. To the poor of the parish of St. Mary Tower and of St. Mary Key in Ipswich, either of them twenty shillings apiece. To Mr. Robert Knapp, my ancient friend, a pair of gloves of five shillings price, or a book of the same value.

The witnesses to the signature were Thomasin Willis and Daniel Ray.

Coventry, 47.

[The Rev. Samuel Ward, B.D., the maker of the above will, was the town preacher at Ipswich, and a celebrated Puritan author. He was the eldest son of the Rev. John Ward of Haverhill, in Suffolk, and brother of the Rev. Nathaniel Ward, author of the Massachusetts Body of Liberties, or code of laws adopted in 1641. Samuel Ward married, January 2, 1604-5, Deborah Bolton, widow, of Isleham, Cambridgeshire. It seems from this will that she had two sons, Robert and John Bolton, by her first husband. For further details of his life, see a brief memoir of Rev. Samuel Ward, appended to the editor's memoir of the Rev. Nathaniel Ward (Albany, 1868).   An abstract of his will, furnished by the late Col. Chester, will be found on pages 154-5 of that work.—Ed.]

MARGARET SIMONDS, late widow of John Simonds, late of Kunckles Alley in London, deceased, her nuncupative will, August, 1665 ; To daughter Margaret Burton, who is now beyond the seas.   Proved 6 March, 1667, by Margaret Burton.   Hene 36.

TIMOTHY SNAPE, London, yeoman, one of the sons of Edmond Snape, late of the parish of St. Saviors, in Southwark, co. Surrey, clerk, deceased, being bound forth on a voyage to Virginia in the parts beyond the seas, executed his will 10 September, 1624, proved 9 July, 1629.   He names brothers and sisters, Samuel, Nathaniel and John Snape, Hannah, now wife of John Barker, citizen and haberdasher of London, and Sarah Snape, spinster.   Ridley, 67.

SAMUEL IVE, of Portsmouth, 13 July, 1667, proved 17 August, 1667, by John Ive, brother and executor.   To sister Sarah Putland, of Strood, wife of Elias Putland, four score pounds.   To brother John Ive.   To Mary Alderidge or any other of our kindred.   To my brother Thomas Ive twenty pounds.   To Mary Alderidge, my sister's daughter, twelve pence.   To Robert Reynolds, carver, all my working tools and the time of my servant John Rauly which he has yet to serve, only six months of the time I do give to the said John Rauly.   To M^{ris} Reynolds what goods I have in the house, except my desk and trunk of linen and wearing clothes, which I do give to my brother Thomas Ive if he live to come home ; or, else, to my brother John Ive, to whom all the residue.   Carr, 107.

[Much about the Ive family will be found in Emmerton and Waters's Gleanings from English Records, pp. 60-1.—Ed.]

WILLIAM QUICKE, citizen and grocer of London, 26 October, 1614, proved 21 January, 1614.   He mentions daughter Apphia, wife Elizabeth, daughter Elizabeth, daughter Debora, brother Nicholas Quicke and his children, the rest of brothers' and sisters' children, kinswoman Mary Marshall the younger, brother-in-law Thomas Hodges, merchant taylor, &c.

" I give and bequeath to and amongst my three daughters aforesaid, all my pte of all such landes, tenements and hereditaments as shall from time to time be recovered, planted and inhabited eyther in Virginia or in the somer Ilandes heretofore called the Bermoodas togither wth all such mynes and mineralls of gold, silver and other mettalls or treasure, perles, precious stones or any kinde of wares and merchandices, comodities or profitts whatsoever which shalbe obtayned or gotten in or by the said voyages and plantations accordinge to the adventure and portion of money that I have employed to that use."   Rudd, 1.

[John Smith, in his " Generall Historie," Ed. 1626, page 126, gives the name of William Quicke in the List of the Adventurers for Virginia.—R. A. BROCK, of Richmond, Va.]

NATHANIEL WARDE, of Old Winsor, co. Berks, Doctor in Divinity, 3 December, nineteenth of K. Charles, proved 11 February, 1667.   He mentions wife Susanna and marriage contract, a bond of one thousand pounds unto Mr Thomas Hanchett and Mr Solomon Smith, in trust for said wife. Son Nathaniel to be executor.   The witnesses were Robert Aldridge, Elizabeth Reynolds and (the mark of) Edward Stokes.   Hene, 26.

SMALEHOPE BIGG, of Cranbrooke in the County of Kent, clothier, 3 May, 1638, proved 3 October, 1638, by John Bigg. Brother John Bigg, of Maidstone, to be executor. To the poor of Cranbrooke ten pounds. To my Aunt Mary Bridger of West Peckham and her two sons, Robert and Thomas Betts; to my kinswomen, the wife of William Hunt of Brenchley, Anne Bottinge of Brenchley, widow, and the wife of John Saxby of Leeds; to Judith, wife of Thomas Tadnall, late of Dover; to Godfrey Martin of Old Romney and his sisters; to the children of Robert Pell of New Romney, jurat, deceased.

To my kinsfolk Thomas Bate, of Lydd, James Bate, Clement Bate, the wife of William Batchelor, John Compton, Edward White and Martha his wife, all which are now resident in New England, twenty shillings each. I give ten pounds to be distributed to them or to others in New England by my mother and my brother John Stow. To Peter Master of Cranbrook who married my sister. To my mother Rachell Bigg one hundred pounds. Lands &c. at Rye in County Sussex to my wife Ellin. To my sisters Patience Foster and Elizabeth Stow in New England. To Hopestill Foster, son of my sister three hundred pounds. To Thomas and John Stow, sons of my sister Stow two hundred pounds each. To Elizabeth Stow and the other three children (under age) of my said sister Stow. Lands in Horsmonden to my brother John Bigg. Lands at Wittersham, Lidd and Cranbrook to Samuel Bigg, my brother's son, at the age of twenty-three years. My friends John Nowell of Rye, gentleman, James Holden and Thomas Bigg the elder, of Cranbrook, clothiers, to be overseers. To my cousin Hunt's children and John Saxbey's children; to the two sons of my Aunt Betts; to my cousin Bottenn's children; to my cousin Pell's children, viz., Joan Pell, Elizabeth Pell, Richard Pell and Thomas Baytope's wife.

After a hearing of the case between John Bigg, brother and executor of the one part, and Hellen alias Ellen Bigg (the relict), Patience Bigg alias Foster, wife of Richard Foster, and Elizabeth Bigg alias Stow, wife of Richard (*sic*) Stow, testator's sisters, of the other part, sentence was pronounced to confirm the will 4 April, 1639 (the widow having previously died, as shown by date of probate of her own will which follows).

Consistory Court, Canterbury, Vol. 51, Leaf 115.

ELLEN BIGGE, of Cranbrooke, widow of Smalehope Bigge, of Cranbrook, clothier, 24 November, proved 12 February, 1638. To be buried in Cranbrooke Cemetery, near my husband. To Samuel Bigge, son of my brother John Bigge, of Maidstone. Lands and tenements at Rye in the County of Sussex to my only sister Mary, wife of Edward Benbrigg, jurat, of Rye, for her life, remainder to her son John Benbridge; to Anne Benbridge, alias Burrish, and Elizabeth and Mary Benbrig, daughters of my aforesaid sister Mary. To John Benbrigg, clerk, Thomas Benbrigg and Samuel Benbrigg, sons of my deceased sister Elizabeth; also her daughters Anne Benbrigge, alias Puttland, and Elizabeth Benbrigg (the last named under age). My said sister Mary Benbrigg and her son John Benbrigg to be executors. To Peter Master, son of my brother Peter Master, of Cranbrooke; to my sister-in-law Katherine Master. To William Dallett (son of my dec'd sister Bridgett) and his son (under age). To William Edwards, son of my sister Mercy. To Thomas Pilcher, Elizabeth Pilcher alias Beinson, Judith Pilcher alias Burges, and Anne Pilcher, son and daughters of my uncle John Pilcher of Rye, deceased. To Mary, wife of Robert Cushman and their son Thomas (under age). James Holden of

Cranbrooke, clothier, and my brother-in-law Peter Master of Cranbrooke, mercer, to be overseers.

Archdeaconry, Canterbury, Vol. 70, Leaf 482.

Will of JOHN BIGG, of Maidstone, co. Kent., jurat. begun Aug. 17, 1640, finished March 27, 1641, probated Feb. 7, 1642.

Mr. Andrew Broughton, Ex[r], friends James Bolden of Cranbrook and Thomas Lamb of Staplehurst, overseers. Legacies to Roger Ball, John Bowden, William Whetston, Samuel Browne, Samuel Skelton, widow Clarke, widow Peirce, Susan the wife of Daniel Clarke my ancient servant, William Lawraman, William Ayerst, Richard Weller Sen[r], of Cranbrook, —Cheeseman, my porter and fetcher in of my water, old goodman Greensmith of Loose, widow Darby of Staplehurst, old goodman Humphry or his wife of Harresham, widow Warren late of Sandwich, Mr. Harber Minister of Raish beside Mallinge, Mr. Elmeston schoolmaster of Maidstone, Mr. Goodacker and Mr. Bramston, brother to widow Charleton of Loose, " two poore godlie ministers, I think of Sussex," Damarys Wilson now living with me and her father and mother, Mary Tatnell daughter of Thomas T. now living with me and her sister Judah Tatnell.

Also to Packnam Johnson, now living with me, my sister Johnson his mother, my cousin Milles widow, living at Raysh, my cousin Botten, widow, living at Brenchley, my aunt Bredger of Peckham, my cousin Hunt's wife of Brenchley, my cousin Saxbey's wife of Leeds, my cousin Gaskyne and my cousin Betes living about Lengly. My mother Bigg, my sister Foster, my brother Stowe, all these living in New England. Hopestill Foster, Thomas Stowe, John Stowe, Nathaniel Stowe, Samuel Stowe, my brother Stowe's two daughters, Elizabeth Stowe, Thankful Stowe. My wife Sibella Bigg. Elizabeth Pell dwelling with me. My cousin Beatupes wife of Tenterden. Marie Terrie in New England. My cousin Godfrey Martyne, my cousin Smith's wife of Ladomi, late Saltman. My cousin William Boysse. John Crumpe, son of Thomas Crumpe. My brother Beaccons. Cousin Yonge of Canterbury. My brother Peter Masters of Cranbrooke and his four children. My cousin James Bate of New England. My cousin Lyne of New England. Clement Bate and William Bachelor. Edward Whitt, John Compton, John Moore, Thomas Bridgden, Goodman Beale that went from Cranbrook and my cousin Betts there. My brother Robert Swinocke and his wife. Mr. John London. My mother Mrs. Dorothie Maplisden, my brother Mr. Jervis Maplisden and his wife, my brother Mr. Nynion Butcher and his wife, Mr. Thomas Swynocke, my brother in law, Mr. Wilson and his wife, my brother Wildinge, Mrs. Marie Duke. Mr. Elmeston of Cranbrook. James Holden of Cranbrook. My brother Smallhope Bigg, late of Cranbrook. My brother Beaccon's will. Mr. William Randolph. Mr. Robert Drayner.

Crane, 11.

A copy of this will was printed in the REGISTER, xxix. 256.—H. F. W.

[See will of Christopher Gibson, Suffolk Probate Records, vi. 64. He and Hopestill Foster, Jr., married sisters, daughters of James Bate.

For the foregoing abstracts of the wills of Smalehope Bigg and his widow, Mrs. Ellen Bigge, the readers of the REGISTER are indebted to the kindness of Joseph Eedes, Esq., who has, moreover, given me numerous clews and references to other

American names, to be followed up hereafter. Indeed all my fellow workers here are constantly exhibiting proof of that good will and kindly fellowship which my experience, in America as well as England, has shown me to be characteristic of the brotherhood of antiquaries. HENRY F. WATERS.

By an instrument dated Sept. 10, 1653, recorded with Suffolk Deeds, lib. i. fol. 318, Hopestill Foster of the one part and Thomas, Nathaniel and Samuel Stowe of the other part, all of New England, for the purpose of ending the " many & vncomfortable differences " which have arisen concerning the wills of their deceased uncles Mr. Smallhope Bigg and Mr. John Bigg both of the County of Kent in old England, and which " haue occasioned much trouble each to other p'tie & likewise vncomfortable suits att Lawe," agree that each party shall " enioy what they now enioy namely Hopestill ffoster or his assignes the one half of all those lands In Crambrooke Withersham & Lidd wch m^r Smallhop [ ] Bigg gaue vnto Samuell Bigg his Brothers Sonne & Thomas Stowe and his sonne John as heires to John Stowe his Uncle deceased And Nathanicll & Samuell Stowe the other half of the said land and likewise quietly & peacably to enioy the lands of m^r John Bigg of 60^li a yeare or thereabou^ts wch hee deuided as by his will is exp^rsed Unto Hopstill ffoster 15^li a yeare, John Stowe 15^li a year, Thomas Nathaniell & Samuell ye remainder."—JOHN T. HASSAM.

Smallhope Bigg, in his will, mentions sisters Patience Foster and Elizabeth Stow They were the wives of Hopestill Foster of Dorchester (see Dorchester Antiq. Society's Hist. Dorch., p. 118) and John Stow of Roxbury (see the Apostle Eliot's Ch. Records, REGISTER, xxxv. 244). Of the kinsmen whom he names, Edward White, Dorchester, Mass., had married in 1616, at St. Dunstan's Church, Cranbrook, Kent, Martha King, according to a pamphlet printed in 1863, entitled, In Memoriam Lieut. W. Greenough White ; John Compton was probably the person of the name who settled at Roxbury (REG. xxxv. 244), and William Batchelor may have been the Charlestown settler who had wives Jane and Rachel (Wyman's Charlestown, i. 42). Clement Bate settled at Hingham (Barry's Hanover, p. 245) and James Bate at Dorchester (Hist. Dorch. p. 106). For the parentage of the latter, see REGISTER, xxxi. 142.

John Bigg in his will (REG. xxix. 259), mentions as persons " that went from Cranbrook," " Edward Whitt [White], John Compton, John Moore, Thomas Brigden and Goodman Beale."—EDITOR.]

THOMAS BELL, senior, of London, merchant, 29 January, 1671, proved 3 May, 1672, by Susanna Bell, his relict and sole executrix.

I give unto Mr. John Elliott, minister of the church and people of God at Roxbury in New England and Captaine Isaac Johnson, whom I take to be an officer or overseer of and in the said church, and to one such other like godly person now bearing office in the said church and their successors, the minister and other two such Head Officers of the church at Roxbury, as the whole church there, from time to time, shall best approve of successively, from time to time forever, all those my messuages or tenements, lands and hereditaments, with their and every of their appurtenances, scituate, lying and being at Roxbury in New England aforesaid, in the parts beyond the seas—To Have and To Hold to the said Minister and Officers of the said church of Roxbury for the time being and their successors, from time to time forever,—In Trust only notwithstanding to and for the maintenance of a Scoole-master and free schoole for the teaching and instruction of Poore mens children at Roxbury aforesaid forever, And to and for no other use, intent or purpose whatsoever.

Whereas my son Thomas Bell did pay unto me the sum of three hundred pounds which he received in marriage with his wife, I therefore give, &c., over and besides two hundred pounds formerly given him, the sum of twelve hundred pounds within twelve months after my decease. If he be dead then to his wife Jane the sum of five hundred pounds. To grand child Clement Bell three hundred pounds at the age of one and twenty. To grand child Thomas Bell three hundred and fifty pounds ; to grand child

Simon Bell one hundred and fifty pounds at one and twenty. Whereas I gave in marriage with my daughter Susan to John Wall deceased the sum of three hundred pounds and afterwards the sum of four hundred pounds to Mr John Bell her now husband, I do give to Mr John Bell and to said Susan his wife the sum of eighty pounds between them. To grand child John Wall the sum of one hundred and twenty pounds at the age of one and twenty. To Simon Baxter, my son-in-law, and Sarah his wife eighty pounds, and for Edward and Simon their sons, and to Sarah and Susan Baxter, my grand children, one hundred pounds apiece at age of one and twenty or on day of marriage, &c. To my daughter Mary Turpin, wife of John Turpin; to Edward Bell, son of my brother Edward, at age of twenty one years; to Elizabeth and Sarah Bell, at age of twenty one; to Susanna ――, late wife of Edward Bell, and to her two children which she had by the said Edward; to the poor of the parish of Allhallows Barking, London, where I now dwell, &c.

I do hereby give and bequeath unto Thomas Makins, my sister's son, in New England, the sum of twenty pounds and to the other child of my said sister, whose name I remember not, twenty pounds. And to all the children of my sister Christian, on her body begotten, who married one Chappell* or Chapman, I give and bequeath twenty pounds apiece, &c. To my cousin Ann Bugg, widow, an annuity of three pounds for life. To cousin Thomas Wildboare (my cousin Sarah's son) ten pounds at age of twenty one, and to Susan, her daughter, ten pounds. To said cousin Sarah Wildboare the sum of twenty pounds, and her husband to have no power over it. A legacy to Mr Isaac Daffron. The sum of one hundred pounds to be distributed among poor necessitous men late ministers of the Gospel, of which number I will that that Mr Knoles and Mr John Colling, both late of New England be accounted. Legacies to the said Mr Knoles and Mr Samuel Knolls his son, Mr John Colling and one Mr Ball. To my cousin Mr John Bayley of little Warmfield, in co. Suffolk and his wife and daughter Martha and his other four children; to my cousin William Whood and his wife; to my uncle's daughter of St Edmundsbury whose husband's name is John Cason; to Mary Bell, daughter of brother Bell. Houses in Grace church St., London, to wife Susan for life, then to son Thomas. I omit to give anything to his daughter.   Eure, 56.

[Thomas Bell of Roxbury and his wife " had letters of Dismission granted & sent to England an^o 1654 7mo," according to the Apostle Eliot's records (REG. xxxv. 245). Thomas Meakins and his wife Catherine were admitted to the church in Boston, Feb. 2, 1633-4. His son Thomas settled in Braintree, and thence removed to Roxbury and Hadley (Savage). " Mr Knoles and Mr John Colling," mentioned as " ministers of the Gospel," were the Rev. Hanserd Knollys and the Rev. John Collins. Knollys preached at Dover, N. H., awhile, and returned in 1641 to England. He died in London, September 19, 1691, aged 93. See his Life and Times, London, 1692, and articles by A. H. Quint, D.D., in the Congregational Quarterly, xiii. 38-53; and by J. N. Brown, D.D., in Sprague's Annals of the American Pulpit, vi. 1-7. A society in England for publishing Baptist historical works was named for him. The Rev. John Collins, graduated H. C. 1649, returned to England, was chaplain to Gen. Monk, and afterwards pastor of an Independent Church in London, where he died, Dec. 3, 1687. (See Sibley's Harvard Graduates, i. 186-91.) He was a son of Edward Collins, of Cambridge, N. E., who with sons Daniel, John and Samuel and daughter Sible, are mentioned in 1639, in the will of his brother Daniel Collins, of London. (Emmerton and Waters's Gleanings, p. 20.) Mr. Waters sends us, as confirmatory of his queries four years ago, in Emmerton and Waters's Gleanings, p. 21, about the Collins family, the two following short pedigrees:

* Perhaps William Chappell of New London. (See Savage's Gen. Dict. i. 363.)—H. F. W.

Sam¹ Bedle of Wolverston, Suff.=Abigail, dau. of .... Collins in com. Essex.

| John. | Samuel. | Nathan'l. | Dorothy. | Abigail. |

Have we not here, Mr. Waters adds, Abigail widow of Samuel Bedle, wife of William Thompson, sister of Daniel Collins, Dorothy daughter of above and first wife of John Bowles, and Abigail her sister wife of Michael Powell?

John Collyns of London, Salter=Abigail, dau. of Thos. Rose of Exmouth, co. Devon, 3d wife.

Daniel Collyns of London, merch¹. 1633, s. p.=Sibil, dau. of Thos. Francklyn of London, goldsmith.

—Editor.]

NATHANIEL EELES, of Harpenden in the County of Hartford, 28 March, 1678, with codicil of 9 April, 1678, proved 12 February, 1678. To wife Sarah one third of household goods and the lease of Denhames house and land, and the money made of her lands at Boringdon, now in the hands of Mʳ Combes of Hemsted, for her natural life, and my watch and largest English bible in folio, with annotations thereon, in two volumes, and Deodate's Annotations, and all the books I have of Mʳ Carill upon Job, &c. Certain property to three daughters at day of marriage or age of twenty four years. To son Nathaniel ten pounds and my sealing ring, he having formerly received his portion, for which I have a writing under his hand. To son John ten pounds, he having received his portion and part formerly, the said ten pounds to be paid to him within one year after my decease, or be then or as soon as may well be after sent over to him into Virginia, if he be then living; and if he die before the time limited for the payment thereof to him, I give the said ten pounds unto my son Nathaniel. To son Isaac my lease of Denhames, with the rents and profits thereof, after the decease of my wife, and all my books, he to pay ten pounds unto my son Daniel within one year after the decease of my wife. To sons Jacob, Joseph and Jeremiah, to each one hundred and fifty pounds for to educate, maintain, and put them forth to callings and for the setting them up in their trades after they shall have served up their apprenticeships or times with them to whom my wife shall put them; and the like sum of one hundred and fifty pounds to son Daniel for the same ends and purposes.

The portions to my four sons last named shall be paid unto them at their ages of twenty four years or when they shall have served out their apprenticeships and need the same to set up with, at the discretion of my wife. To daughter Sarah two hundred pounds; to daughters Rebecca and Mary one hundred and fifty pounds each; and to every of my sons and daughters I give a practice of Piety (a book so called) and Mʳ Alley his Treatise of Conversion and Mʳ Baxter his call to the unconverted, and a new bible to such as need the same. To my very loving brother Mʳ William Eeles and my dear and loving sister Mʳˢ Foster, both which I appoint to be overseers of this my will, I give twenty pounds to each of them and desire them, by all the love they ever bare to me, to give my destitute and afflicted wife the best assistance, counsel and advice they can in all cases, from time to time, as need shall require. To loving sisters Mʳˢ Eeles and Mʳˢ Pearse, to each of them ten pounds, to buy them rings. My dear and loving wife Sarah to be sole executrix. The one hundred pounds in Mʳ Coombe's hand is of right my wife's during her life.

The witnesses to the will were William Eele, John Eeles, Will: Eeles jun[r] and Jos: Marlow. All but the first named were witnesses to the codicil.   King, 16.

[In Calamy and Palmer's Nonconformist's Memorial (1802), Vol. II., page 306, under the head of Harden, in Hertfordshire, we learn that Mr. Nathaniel Eeles (of Emmanuel College, Cambridge) was born at Aldenham in that county, of good parentage. Having prosecuted his studies till he was senior bachelor and then studied two years at Utrecht, he was ordained a Presbyter, returned to England and preached at Caddington in Bedfordshire. In 1643 he was called by the people of Harding to be their preacher. There he continued till the year 1661, when he was ejected. He preached in private in sundry places till 1672, when he took out a license for his own house at Harding, where he preached, gratis, to all who would come. He died 18 December, 1678, aged 61, leaving, we are told, a wife and ten children.—H. F. W.
I do not know of any present representative of the name Eeles in Virginia. I find that Samuel Eale and John Stith received a grant of 500 acres in Charles City Co., Va., in 1652. Va. Land Registry, Book 5, p. 268.—R. A. B.]

MARMADUKE GOODE, of Ufton, in Berkshire, clerk, 5 September, 1678, proved 20 February, 1678, by Samuel and Mary Goode, executors. To brother Samuel Goode all that messuage or tenement, with the appurtenances, lying in Sulhamsteed Abbots and South Bannister which I hold by lease from Francis Perkins Esquire, to said Samuel to enjoy the same during his natural life; and, after his death, I give the said messuage &c. to my niece Mary Goode, the daughter of my brother John Goode, to enjoy for the remaining term of the said lease. To my brother John Goode, citizen of London, & to Susanna his now wife all my house, tenement, lands and hereditaments &c. in Sylchester in the County of Southhampton, which I purchased of John Carter of Sylchester, and after their decease, to my nephew Marmaduke Goode, son of the said John Goode, he to pay to his sisters, Elizabeth, Susanna and Anne, forty pounds apiece within twelve months after he shall be possessed of the said lands and premisses at Silchester. To my brother William Goode my messuages or tenements, &c. called or known by the name of the Heath lands or heath grounds, situated, lying & being in the several parishes of Ufton and Sulhamsteed, in the county of Berks, and which I lately purchased of Richard Wilder of Theale in the parish of Tylehurst, in the said County of Berks, innholder, during his natural life and afterwards to my nephew Robert Goode, son of the said William Goode and his heirs forever, he to pay to his two sisters, Elianor and Mary, forty pounds within twelve months, &c. To my sister Mary Haines and her two maiden daughters fifty pounds apiece within one year after my decease; to my brother John Goode in Virginia ten pounds within twelve months after my decease, according to the appointment of my brother John Goode, citizen of London; to my brother Thomas Goode, in Ireland, ten pounds (in the same way); to my sister Ann Wickens of Upton ten pounds; to my servant Alice Payce ten pounds; to my servant Hugh Larkum five pounds. All the rest of the property to brother Samuel Goode and niece Mary Goode, daughter of my brother John Goode, who are appointed joint executors.
The witnesses were Samuel Brightwell and Robert King.
                                                                          King, 17.

[By family tradition John Goode came to Virginia from Whitby, England, about 1660, with his wife, and purchased the plantation of one Gough (situated on the south side of James River, about four miles from the city of Manchester) which he named "Whitby." His descendants have intermarried with many prominent families of Virginia, including the Harrisons, Blands, Turpins, Gordons, Scotts, Cookes and others. Col. Thomas F. Goode and Hon. John Goode of Virginia, and Prof. G. Brown Goode of the Smithsonian Institution, are descendants of John Goode. "Whitby" is now the property of A. D. Williams, Esq., Richmond, Virginia.—R. A. B.]

Mary Hoskins, of Richmond in the County of Surrey, widow, 30 July, 1678, proved 28 February, 1678. To my dear mother Anne Githins, widow, all my plate and linen and diamond locket and five hundred pounds within three months after my decease. To Mrs Mariana Carleton, the wife of Matthew Carleton, gentleman, my best diamond ring and twenty pounds. Ten pounds apiece to be paid to the three children of my late deceased brother John Githins in Meriland, Philip, John and Mary Githins. To Mary Evererd, daughter of Robert Evererd of Godstone, five pounds and five pounds to Richard Nye, whom I placed with Mr Taw. Twenty pounds to be laid out in placing two boys to trades, whereof one to be of Oxted and the other of Godstone. All my houses in the Maze in Southwark, held of St Thomas Hospital and all other personal estate, &c. to my loving brother William Githins, Gentleman, whom I appoint executor.

The witnesses were Thomas Jenner, Richard Smith (by mark), Winefrut King of Petersham and Jeoffrey Glyd. King, 19.

The pedigree of the Hoskins Family of Oxted is given in various MSS. in the British Museum. The marriage of any Hoskins with the testatrix named above has not been found.

[The name Everard has had most prominent representatives in Maryland, Virginia and North Carolina, and is a favored Christian name in the distinguished Meade family of Virginia.—R. A. B.]

Anne Jones, of St Clement Danes in the County of Middlesex, widow, 20 February, 1676, proved 6 February, 1678. To Bridget Waite, wife of William Waite (certain household effects) and the lease of my house wherein I now dwell, she paying the rent, &c. All the rest to my son Thomas Daniell who is in Virginia, beyond the seas. And I do hereby make my said son Thomas Daniell full and sole executor, and my friends Charles Stepkin Esq. and Mr Richard Southey overseers, they to keep the estate in trust for my said son Thomas Daniell. In case he die before he comes from beyond the seas, then I bequeath to Edward Jones and Patience Jones, son & daughter of John Jones, of the parish of St Clement Danes, taylor, five pounds apiece; and all the rest of my estate to Mark Workman and Elizabeth Workman, son and daughter of Mark Workman, late of the parish of St Mary Magdalen, old Fish Street London, deceased, equally.

The witnesses were Richard Southey, Junr. John Searle and Ro: Stone. King, 19.

[I find of record in the Virginia Land Registry, Book No. 8, p. 428, a grant of 130 acres in the Counties of Isle of Wight and "Nanzimond," Va., to Owen Daniell, in 1695.—R. A. B.]

Robert Lucas, of Hitchin, in the County of Hertford, in his will of 13 January, 1678, proved 14 February, 1678, speaks of land purchased of William Papworth of New England, lying close to land which was heretofore that of the testator's father, Simon Lucas, deceased, and lands heretofore the lands of William Willis. King, 21.

[*Query*. Where did William Papworth reside?—Ed.]

ANTHONY ROBY, of the Province of Carolina, 6 December, 1686, proved 11 July, 1688. To mother Early Roby, in England, all my estate in Carolina or elsewhere ; if she be dead then to her next heirs then living. My friend Andrew Percivall Esquire, of the said Province, to be sole executor. The witnesses were David Harty, James Wyatt and John Shelton.

Exton, 99.

JOHN REED, mariner, 4 April, 1688, proved 6 July, 1688. I bequeath all my concerns aboard the ship Richard, of London, John Reade Master, riding at anchor in the York River, to my loving wife Mary Reade of Bristol. I desire my loving friend Capt. Trim, commander of the ship Judy, riding at anchor in York River, to take accompt. The witnesses were Benjamin Eyre, George Lodge and Charles Perkes.

Exton, 99.

[John Read was granted 145 acres in Gloucester Co., March 18, 1652. Va. Land Registry Office, Book 5, p. 280. There are grants within a short period thereafter to Alexander Argubell and James Read or Reade.

The Eyres have been continuously seated in Northampton Co., Va., from the 17th century. They early intermarried with the Severns, Southeys and Lyttletons, and these latter names are now favored Christian names in the family.—R. A. B.]

HENRY WOODHOUSE, of the parish of Linhaven, of lower Norfolk in Virginia, 29 January, 1686, owned to be his will 31 January, 1686-7, and proved 24 July, 1688. To eldest son Henry Woodhouse my plantation where I live (containing five hundred acres, and described) ; to second son, Horatio, property called Moyes land (adjoining the above) ; to son John (other real estate) ; to son Henry two negroes Roger and Sarah ; to daughters Elizabeth and Lucy, daughter Mary, wife of William More, and daughter Sarah, wife of Cason More.   Exton, 102.

[I find the following grants of land to the name Woodhouse, of record in the Va. Land Registry Office : Thomas Woodhouse, 200 acres in James City Co., March 24, 1644, Book No. 2, p. 1 ; Henry Woodhouse, 200 acres in Lynhaven parish, Lower Norfolk Co., April 5, 1649, p. 167 ; the same, 275 acres in same, May 11, 1652, Bk. No. 3, p. 254 ; the same, 749 acres in the same, April 3, 1670, Book No. 6, p. 357, Hamond Woodhouse. 340 acres in Charles City Co., April 20, 1669, Book No. 6, p. 216.—R. A. B.]

MICHAEL GRIGGS, of County Lancaster, Colony of Virginia, gentleman, 17 April, 1687, proved 10 September, 1688. To my father-in-law Robert Schofield. To wife Anne Griggs the residue. The witnesses were William Lee, Richard Farrington and William Carter.

The above will was proved at London "juramento Annæ Bray, als Griggs (modo uxoris Richardi Bray) relictæ dicti defuncti et executricis," &c.

Exton, 117.

[William Lee was doubtless the son of Col. Richard Lee, the founder of the distinguished family of the name in Virginia.

The name Bray is of early seating in Virginia. John Bray received a grant of 200 acres in " Worrosquinack " Co., June 4, 1636. Va. Land Records, Book No. 1, p. 362. His descendants intermarried with the Harrison and other prominent families. The Brays intermarried early also with the Plomer, Plommer, Plummer or Plumer family.—R. A. B.]

JOHN CURTIS, of Boston, Co. Middlesex, New England, mariner, belonging to Majesty's ship the English Tyger, appoints Robert Chipchace in County Middlesex, Old England, his attorney and sole executor, 31 January, 1689-90, in presence of Thos. Coall and Tho' Browne. Proved 3 December, 1690, by Robert Chipchace.   Dyke, 200.

ELIZABETH BRETLAND, late the wife of William Bretland, deceased, Barbados, 6 October, 1687. Legacies to daughters Elizabeth Taylor and Millecent Acklam; to grandson Peter Jones; to grandsons John and Jacob Legay. I give and bequeath to my brother Adam Coulson's children, of Reading near Boston, in New England, the sum of one hundred pounds, to be equally divided among them or the survivor of them.

Cousin Edward Munday and Mr John Mortimer of London, merchants, to be executors of the will.

Item I give unto my brother Adam Coulson's children, of Reading, near Boston, in New England, one negro woman, by name Sarah, being my own proper purchase, or to the survivor of them, to be sent to them the first opportunity after my decease. I leave, according to the desire of my dear husband, Mr. Edward Munday, to my three daughters, Elizabeth, Millecent and Mary, thirty five pounds of silver, at twelve ounces to the pound.

Friends, Capt. Elisha Mellowes and Mr. John Hooker, to be executors for that portion of the estate in the Barbados.

The witnesses made deposition as to this will 3 April, 1689. It was entered and recorded in the Secretary's Office, 17 February, 1689. Proved in London 5 December, 1690.   Dyke, 199.

[Adam Colson, of Reading, Mass., married Sept. 8, 1668, Mary, daughter of Josiah Dustin. He was schoolmaster there from 1679 to 1681. He died March 1, 1687. See Eaton's Reading, p. 58, and Savage.—ED.]

ROBERT HATHORNE, the elder, of the parish of Bray in the county of Berks, yeoman, 15 February, 1689, proved 16 February, 1691. He left all his estate to his son Robert Hathorne, the younger, of the parish of Bray in the county of Berks.   Fane, 49.

[The testator of the above will was doubtless a brother of Major William Hathorne of Salem, Massachusetts, ancestor of the distinguished writer Nathaniel Hawthorne. (See Emmerton & Waters's Gleanings from English Records.)—H. F. W.]

EDWARD GADSBY, of Stepney, in the county of Middlesex, mariner, bound out to sea "with Mr Penn to Virginy" in the Charity of London, appointed John Duffield, citizen and barber-surgeon of London, his attorney, &c. 30 January, 1692, proved 28 April, 1696. He wished all his estate to be given to his brother Samuel Gadsby, of Woodborough, in the County of Nottingham, basket-maker.   Bond, 47.

DANIEL JOHNSON, of Lynn in New England, trumpeter, 22 June, 1695, appointed Patrick Hayes of Bermondsey in the County of Surrey, victualler, to receive and collect his bounty or prizemoney, pursuant to their Majesties' Gracious Declaration of 23 May, 1689, and all such money, &c. as should be due to him for service in any of their Majesties' ships, frigates or vessels or any merchant ships, &c. He gave and bequeathed all unto his beloved children (without naming them) equally to be divided among them. Proved 6 April, 1696.   Bond, 51.

[There was a Daniel Johnson at Lynn, Mass., who married March 2, 1674, Martha Parker, and had Abigail, born April 21, 1675, Stephen and Nathaniel, twins, born Feb. 14, 1678, Sarah, born July 5, 1680, Elizabeth, born March 7, 1682, and Simon, born Jan. 25, 1684 (Savage).—ED.]

JOHN ROLFE, of James City in Virginia, Esquire, 10 March, 1621, proved 21 May, 1630, by William Pyers. Father-in-law Lieut. William

Pyers, gentleman, to have charge of the two small children of very tender age. A parcell of land in the country of Toppahannah between the two creeks over against James City in the continent or country of Virginia to son Thomas Rolfe & his heirs; failing issue, to my daughter Elizabeth; next to my right heirs. Land near Mulberry Island, Virginia, to Jane my wife during her natural life, then to daughter Elizabeth. To my servant Robert Davies twenty pounds.

The witnesses were Temperance Yeardley, Richard Buck, John Cartwright, Robert Davys and John Milwarde.   Scroope, 49.

[It would appear that John Rolfe was three times married, his first wife bearing him in 1609 one male child, which died on the Island of Bermuda. His second wife was Pocahontas, and his third Jane Pyers, or Poyers, of the text, the mother of the daughter Elizabeth. The son Thomas appears to have married in England, having issue Anthony, whose daughter Hannah married Sir Thomas Leigh of co. Kent, the descendants of that name and of the additional highly respectable names of Bennet and Spencer being now quite numerous. Died prior to 8 Nov. 1682. See *Richmond Standard*, Jan. 21, 1882.

The witness Richard Buck (sometimes rendered Bucke) was doubtless the minister of the name at Jamestown, who died sometime prior to 1624, leaving a widow, and children—Mara, Gershom, Benoni and Peleg.—R. A. B.]

Sir GEORGE YARDLEY, 12 October, 1627, proved 14 February, 1628. To wife Temperance all and every part and parcell of all such household stuff, plate, linen, woollen or any other goods, moveable or immoveable, of what nature or quality soever, as to me are belonging, and which now at the time of the date hereof are being and remaining within this house in James City wherein I now dwell. Item, as touching and concerning all the rest of my whole estate consisting of goods, debts, servants, "negars," cattle, or any other thing or things, commodities or profits whatsover to me belonging or appertaining either here in this country of Virginia, in England or elsewhere, together with my plantation of one thousand acres of land at Stanly in Warwicke River, my will and desire is that the same be all and every part and parcell thereof sold to the best advantage for tobacco and the same to be transported as soon as may be, either this year or the next, as my said wife shall find occasion, into England, and there to be sold or turned into money, &c. &c. The money resulting from this (with sundry additions) to be divided into three parts, of which one part to go to said wife, one part to eldest son Argoll Yeardley, and the other part to son Francis & to Elizabeth Yeardley equally.

The witnesses were Abraham Peirsey, Susanna Hall and William Clayborne, Scr.

A codicil, dated 29 Oct. 1627, was witnessed by the same scrivener.
                                                                    Ridley, 9.

Commission to administer on the estate of Sir George Yeardley, late in Virginia, deceased, was issued 14 March, 1627-8, to his brother Ralph Yeardley during the absence of the widow, relict, Temperance Yeardley, in the parts beyond the seas, &c.   Admon Act Book for 1628.

[From the Calendar of State Papers, Colonial Series (London, 1860), we learn that Governor Francis West and the Council of Virginia certified to the Privy Council, 20 December, 1627, the death of Governor Sir George Yeardley and the election of Captain Francis West to succeed him in the government. In July, 1629, Edmund Rossingham sent in a petition to the Privy Council stating that he was agent to his uncle Sir George Yeardley, late Governor of Virginia, who dying before any satisfaction was made to the petitioner for being a chief means of raising his estate to the value of six thousand pounds, Ralph Yeardley, the brother, took administration of the same. He prayed for relief and that his wrongs might be examined into. This was referred, July 11, 1629, to Sir Dudley Diggs, Sir Maurice Abbott, Thomas Gibbs and Samuel Wrote, late commissioners for that plantation, to examine into the true state of the case. Annexed is the report of Gibbs and Wrote, made 25 Sept. 1629, describing in detail the petitioner's employments from 1618, and awarding three hundred and sixty pounds as due to him in equity ; also an answer by Ralph Yeardley, administrator, &c., to Rossingham's petition. In January or February, 1630, Rossingham sent in another petition praying for a final determination. In it he styles Ralph Yeardley an apothecary of London. On the nineteenth of February the Privy Council ordered Ralph Yeardley to pay two hundred pounds to the petitioner out of his brother's estate, twelve hundred pounds having already come into the administrator's hand.

Captain Yeardley was chosen Governor of Virginia in 1618, in place of Lord De la Warr, who is said to have died in Canada, and he departed immediately thither with two ships and about three hundred men and boys. On the twenty-eighth of November Chamberlain writes that Captain Yeardley, " a mean fellow," goes Governor to Virginia, two or three ships being ready. To grace him the more the King knighted him this week at Newmarket, " which hath set him up so high, that he flaunts it up and down the streets in extraordinary bravery, with fourteen or fifteen fair liveries after him." He arrived in Virginia in April, 1619, and is said to have brought the colony from a very low state to an extremely flourishing condition. He was governor again 1626–27.—H. F. W.

Colonel Argoll Yeardley married Sarah, daughter of John Custis, of Northampton Co., Va., a native of Rotterdam and the founder of the socially distinguished family of the name in Virginia.

" Colonel " Francis Yeardley (died August, 1657) married Sarah the widow of Adam Thorowgood and of John Gooking, the latter being her first husband.

The name Yeardley, or properly Yardly, is still represented in the United States, but I know of none of the name in Virginia.

One Abraham Piersey, or Percy, was treasurer of the colony of Virginia in 1619. He may have been the father of the first witness. The other witness was doubtless Col. William Clayborne, or Claiborne, as it is now rendered, the son of " the rebel " of the same name, who had the command of a fort in New Kent county in 1676 (Major Lyddal serving with him), and who distinguished himself in the Indian wars of Bacon's Rebellion. There was of record in King William County, Va., a certificate of his valorous service, signed by Gov. William Berkeley and attested by Nathaniel Bacon (senior, of the Council) and Philip Ludwill.—R. A. B]

EDWARD COLE, of East Bergholt, in the county of Suffolk, clothier, 18 August, 1649, proved the last of May, 1652. To wife Abigail; to youngest son Peter Cole ; to my two daughters Sarah and Mary Cole ; to the children of my son Edward Cole; to my grandchildren in New England twenty pounds.

The witnesses were John Layman and Richard Royse.

Bowyer, 103.

ROBERT FEVERYEARE, the elder, of Kelshall in the county of Suffolk, yeoman, 24 June, 1656, proved 5 September, 1656. To wife Elizabeth. Frances Brothers of Kelshall owes me on bond. To Edmund Feveryeare, my brother, the sum of forty shillings within six months after my decease. To William Feveryeare, my brother, three pounds. To Margaret Feveryeare, my sister, forty shillings within six months, &c. To Margery, my sister, wife of Robert Goodwin, forty shillings within twelve months, &c. ; also eight pounds within twelve months, &c. To Anne, my sister, wife of John Miles, five pounds within six months, &c. To Richard Eade, mine uncle, twenty shillings ; to Mary Minstrell, my former servant, twenty shillings within six months, &c. To Robert Goodwin, the elder, my new suit of apparel. To Henry Minstrel, the elder, a legacy. Brother William and wife Elizabeth to be executors and residuary legatees. Berkeley, 333.

CLEMENT CHAPLIN, of Thetford, in the county of Norfolk, Clerk, 16 August, 1656, proved 23 September, 1656, by Sarah Chaplin his relict and sole executrix. To wife, Sarah, all my houses and lands in Hartford and Weathersfield in New England, to her and her heirs forever. Loving brother Thomas Chaplin of Bury St Edmunds in old England, and my kinsman Mr. William Clarke, of Rocksbury in New England to be supervisors. Witnessed by Elizabeth Gurnham (her mark) and John Spincke.

Berkeley, 332.

[The testator of the above will, son of William Chaplin " of Semer " (see the Candler MS. No. 6071 of Harleian Collection, British Museum), we are told was a chandler in Bury, went over into New England, and was one of the elders in the congregation whereof Mr. Hooker was minister. His wife Sarah was one of five daughters and co-heiresses of —— Hinds, a goldsmith in Bury. Her sister Elizabeth was wife of Thomas Chaplin (mentioned above), linen draper in Bury, alderman and justice of the peace for the County of Suffolk, her sister Margaret Hinds was married to George Groome of Rattlesden, Justice of the Peace, Abigail Hinds was married to Richard Scott of Braintree (who married secondly Alice Snelling), and Anne Hinds was married to —— Alliston. Mr. Chaplin had, besides the brother Thomas whom he names, a brother William of Blockeshall, who had issue, a brother Richard, of Semer (sine prole), a brother Edmund of Semer, who had many children, and a brother Capt. Robert Chaplin of Bury, who had issue. A sister Martha is said to have been married to Robert Parker of Wollpit, who went into New England, another sister, whose name is not given, was wife of —— Barret of Stratford, and mother of a Thomas Barret, and a third sister (also unnamed) was married to —— Smith of Semer. Alderman Thomas Chaplin had a daughter Anne who was married to Jasper Shepheard, an alderman of Bury, and a daughter Abigail married to Robert Whiting of —— in Norfolk.—H. F. W.]

JOHN SMITH, citizen and merchant tailor of London, by reason of age weak in body, 17 December, 1655, proved 20 October, 1656, by Sarah Whiting, daughter and executrix. To wife the sum of five pounds in money, as a token and remembrance of my love, and I will and appoint that it shall & may be lawful for her to dwell and abide in my dining-room and wainscot chamber belonging to my dwelling house in the old Bailey, London, by the space of three months next after my decease ; and I confirm the indenture bearing date 30 August, 1654, between me and Thomas Fitz Williams, of the one part, and my said wife, known by the name of Sarah Neale, and Vincent Limborowe, of the other part, &c. &c. To the children of my loving daughter, Sarah Whiting, ten pounds apiece towards putting them out to be Apprentices, &c., and also forty pounds apiece to the sons at twenty four years of age and to the daughters at twenty one.

Likewise I give to the children of my cousin William Smith, in New England, and Mary, his now or late wife, the sum of three pounds apiece, to be paid to them, the said children, at the ages as above is limited to my grandchildren, &c. &c.

Legacies to brother Thomas Smith and to the daughter of James Smith, son of brother Thomas. To grandchild John Whiting, son of daughter Sarah Whiting, the half part of certain lands, tenements, &c. in Hogsden, alias Hoxden, in the County of Middlesex, and to the male and female issue of the said John ; failing such issue, then to grandchild Nathaniel Whiting, &c. &c. ; with remainder to grandchildren Robert and Stephen Whiting ; then to Samuel Whiting, another son of my said daughter, &c. The other moiety to grandchild Nathaniel Whiting ; then to John ; then to Robert and Joseph ; then to Stephen Whiting. Legacy to son-in-law Timothy Whiting.

Berkeley, 337.

[There was a Nathaniel Whiting in Dedham who had sons John, Samuel and Timothy.—H. F. W.]

JOSIAS FIRMIN, the elder, of Nayland, Co. Suffolk, tanner, 27 August, 1638, proved the last of November, 1638. To the poor of Nayland. To wife Anne, houses and lands in Nayland and also in Stoke next Nayland (called Noke meadow in Stoke), then to Gyles Firmin my youngest son and his heirs, but if he die before he arrives at twenty four years of age, then to the rest of my children. Lands in Stoke called Edmondes Field, after death of wife, to eldest son Josias Firmin and his son Josias, my grand child. To John Firmin, my son, ten pounds within one year after my decease. To my daughter Mary, now wife of Robert Smith, forty five pounds. To daughter Martha Firmin one hundred pounds at age of twenty one. To daughter Sara Firmin tenement, &c. at Foxyearth, co. Essex, which I purchased of one Thomas Partridge, &c., to said Sara at age of twenty years. To grand child, John Firmin, son of Josias Firmin. Sons Josias and Gyles and my three daughters. Executors to be wife Anne and son in law Robert Smith of Nayland, mercer.   Lee, 146.

[See abstracts of wills and extracts from parish registers relating to the name of Firmin in Emmerton and Waters's Gleanings, pp. 34–9.—ED.]

JOSE GLOVER, of London, being by the providence of God forthwith to embark myself for some parts beyond the seas, 16 May, 1638, proved 22 December, 1638, by Richard Daveys, one of the executors, power being reserved for John Harris, another executor. To my dear and loving wife all my estate, &c. both in New England and old England for life, she to maintain and liberally educate all my children. After her decease the property to go to two eldest sons, Roger and John, equally. To my three daughters, Elizabeth, Sara and Priscilla, four hundred pounds apiece (then follows a reference to a decree and order of the court of chancery), my three daughters to release to Edmond Davyes Esq. and Thomas Younge, merchant of London, at day of marriage or arrival at full age, all their interests, &c. in tenements, &c. in Dorenth* and Stone in co. Kent, &c. To my ancient, faithful servant John Stidman fifty pounds. To all my brothers & sisters that shall be living (except my sister Collins) five pounds. To friend Mr Joseph Davies and his wife five pounds apiece. The executors to be John Harris, my loving uncle, warden of the College of Winchester, and Richard Davies, my ancient loving friend. The witnesses were E. Davies, Joseph Davyes, Thomas Yonge, Samuel Davyes & John Davyes.   Lee, 176.

[See the article by J. Hammond Trumbull, LL.D., on the christian name of Mr. Glover, in the REGISTER, xxx. 26–8. His will, from a copy preserved on the Middlesex Court Files, is printed in full in the REGISTER, xxiii. 136–7.—ED.]

Sir ROBT CARR, of Ithall, co. Northumberland, knight. All estate in America, &c. to eldest son William Carr, the other estate in England being formerly settled. To James Deane, my now servant and his heirs, for and in consideration of his service, a plantation within any of the six islands granted unto me, except in Carr's Island. This having been read to him, 29 May, 1667, he did declare, &c. Proved 16 July, 1667, when commission was issued to William Carr, natural son and lawful heir and principal legatee named in the will of Sir Robt Carr, knight, lately of Carr's Island, in New England, in the parts beyond the seas.   Carr, 90.

[See notice of Sir Robert Carr, with remarks on his will, in the REGISTER, xxiv. 187.—ED.]

* Darent.

NOWELL HILTON of Charlestown, co. Middlesex in New England, mariner, appoints his trusty and loving kinsman Nathaniel Cutler, of the parish of Stepney in co. Middlesex, sawyer, his attorney, &c. The amount due for my service done or to be done on board of any of his Maties ships, vessels or frigates, &c. Signed 6 October, 1687, in presence of Mary Story (her mark), Cuthbert Stoy (*sic*) and Samuel Sapp, at the two Anchors and three Stars on Wapping Wall. 17 September 1689 emanavit comissio Nath^{li} Cutler, &c.   Ent, 123.

[Nowell Hilton, the testator, was born in Charlestown, May 4, 1663. He was a son of William Hilton of Charlestown by his second wife Mehitable, a daughter of Increase Nowell. After the death of his father his mother married (2) 29: 8th, 1684, Deacon John Cutler. Timothy Cutler, a son of Deacon John Cutler, married, Dec. 22, 1673, Elizabeth Hilton, a sister of the testator. See the articles entitled "Some of the Descendants of William Hilton," REGISTER, xxxi. 179. See also Wyman's Genealogies and Estates of Charlestown, 255, 257, 504, 710. This will was printed in full in the REGISTER, xxxii. 50.—JOHN T. HASSAM.]

THOMAS GOLLEDGE, his will in form of a letter written from Charde in Somerset, 10 May, 1645, and addressed to his wife Mrs. Mary Golledge at Chichester ; proved by Mary Colledge, 1 June, 1648.

" My Deere Wyffe   I am now goinge in the service of my Lord and Master Jesus Christ.   I knowe not howe hee will dispose of my fraile lyfe in breife I shall desire thow wilt take all fitt opportunity yf the Lord soe dispose to leave thee wth out an husband as to transport my sweete poore innocent children into New England or some such place voyd of Trouble because the Lord ys ready to shoote his fiery darts of wrath against this sinfull land and yo^u wthout an husband and they wthowt a ffather may suffer the black darknesse of Egiptian Popery or Athisme pray sell what of mine is to bee sould for though I cannot wthowt helpe of a lawyer make a fformall will yet my desire in breife ys that thow bee my sole executor & have full power."   Essex, 98.

Notes on Abstracts previously printed.

JOSEPH HOLLAND.   Will Dec. 25, 1658.   [Page 9.]

[We have received the following note from Prof. Arthur L. Perry, LL.D., of Williams College :

If Mr. Waters's abstract of the will of Joseph Holland of London, citizen and clothworker, discredits one conjecture of Dr. Bond in his history of Watertown, it strikingly confirms another conjecture of that author in the same volume. A John Perry died in Watertown in 1674, aged 61. Another John Perry of Watertown married Sarah Clary, of Cambridge, Dec. 1667. Bond says the first John was " probably father " of the second John. Joseph Holland's will makes that guess a certainty. He leaves bequests " *to son-in-law John Perry and Johanna his wife, my daughter, and their sons John Perry and Josias Perry and daughter Elizabeth Perry.*" In another clause : " To my said daughter Johanna certain needle work wrought by my first wife, her mother." In another clause he leaves twenty pounds in goods " *to my son Nathaniel Holland of Waterton in New England.*" The first John Perry was therefore brother-in-law of Nathaniel Holland, and the second his nephew. The Perrys came to Watertown eight years (1666) after this will was drawn (1658). They were clothworkers, i. e. weavers and tailors, like the Hollands in London. The London names, John and Johanna and Josiah and Joseph, were kept up constantly among the Perrys in Watertown and after their removal to Worcester in 1751, and some of them are not even yet disused as christian names in the family. It is a matter of record in the family Bibles that the two Perrys came to Watertown from *London.* Inferentially, therefore, but certainly, they were among the heirs mentioned in Joseph Holland's will.

That will was drawn before the great fire of London in 1666. The mother of Mrs. John Perry the elder was already buried in St. Sepulchre Church in 1658 ; and the good Joseph Holland, citizen and clothworker, directed that his own body should be buried " on the south side of the christening pew " of that parish church.

A grandson of the second John Perry, Nathan, became deacon of the old South Church in Worcester in 1783, and continued in that office till his death in 1806 ; his son Moses succeeded in the office immediately, and continued in it till his death in 1842 ; and his son Samuel succeeded his father and sustained the office thirty-five years longer, making ninety-four years of continuous service in one family.

ARTHUR L. PERRY,
Seventh generation from first John.]

NATHANIEL DOWNEINGE of London, gentleman, 7 May, 1616, proved 14 May, 1616, by his wife Margaret Downeinge. To be buried in the parish Church of St. Dionis Backchurch, London, or elsewhere it shall please my executrix. To the poor of St. Dionis and of St. Gabriel Fanchurch, London. To my brother Joseph Downeinge, now dwellings in Ipswich, in the County of Suffolk, twenty pounds. To my sister Abigail Goade, wife of John Goade, skinner, twenty pounds, and to their son, John Goad, forty shillings to make him a cup. To my sister Susanna Kirby, wife of John Kirby, skinner, twenty pounds. To my mother in law Mary Cellyn, widow, ten pounds and the " Hope [hoop] Ringe " which was my mother's. To my brother Joshua Downinge the seal ring of gold that I do wear on my hand. And to my brother Emanuel Downeinge I give the like ring of gold of the same value & fashion. The residue to my wife Margaret Downeinge, whom I make sole executrix. Whereas I am now seized in fee of and in the late dissolved monastery of the " Fryers Carmelites, or the White-ffryers," in Ipswich in the County of Suffolk, with the appurtenances, &c. —this to wife Margaret and her heirs forever. Cope, 48.

Sir GEORGE DOWNING of East Hatley, in the County of Cambridge, Knight and Baronet; 24 August, 1683, with codicil added 7 July, 1684 ; proved 19 July, 1684. My body to be interred in the vault which I have made under the chancel at Crawden, alias Croyden, in the county of Cambridge, by the body of my wife Frances. Son George Downing, Esq., and son William named. Houses in or near King Street, in the city of Westminster, lately called Hampden House, which I hold by long lease from the Crown, and Peacock Court there, which I hold by lease from the Collegiate Church of St. Peter, Westminster ; all which are now demolished and rebuilt, or rebuilding, and called Downing Street. To Edward Lord Viscount Morpeth and Sir Henry Pickering,* Baronet, my son-in-law, in trust, &c. Bequests to sons Charles and William Downing, and to three daughters, Lucy, Mary and Anne, at age of twenty-one years or day of marriage. The guardianship and custody of the persons of these three daughters entrusted to my dear daughter Frances Cotton. Bequests to daughter Cotton's children, Francis, John and Thomas, and to Elizabeth and Frances, the two daughters of my late daughter Pickering deceased; also to nephew John Peters, niece Lucy Spicer, nephew Joshua Downing and Mʳ Edmond Woodroffe, one of my clerks in my office in the Exchequer. Hare, 139.

* This Sir Henry Pickering was son and heir of Sir Henry Pickering of Whaddon, who was created a Baronet 2 January, 1660. He was of Barbados in 1695, and had two wives, Philadelphia, daughter of Sir George Downing, by whom he had two daughters, Mary and Anne (who both died without issue), and secondly, Grace, daughter of Constant Silvester, Esq. (See REG. xxxvii. 385.) At his death, in 1705, the title became extinct. (See Add. MS. 24493, British Museum.)—H. F. W.

This Indenture made the Thirteenth day of Sept. Anno Doᵐ. one thousand seuen hundred and in the twelfth yeare of the Reigne of our Soueraign Lord William the third, by the grace of God of England, Scotland, ffrance and Ireland King, defender of the Faith &cᵃ. —— Between Charles Downing of London in the Kingdome of England Esqʳ of the one part and Thorndike Procter of Salem in the Countey of Essex within his Majᵗⁱᵉˢ Province of the Massachusetts Bay in New England in America, yeoman, on the other part [then follows the ordinary phraseology of conveyance of a tract of three hundred acres in Salem which was] formerly the farme of Emanuel Downing of Salem aforesaid Gent: Deceased, Grandfather of the said Charles Downing, purchased by the said Emanuel Downing of one Robert Cole unto whome the same was granted by the said town of Salem one thousand six hundred thirty and five* [together with other parcels of land which had belonged to Emanuel Downing. And the grantor warrants the purchaser that he may hold these premisses] free and clear or well and sufficiently Indemnified saued and kept harmless of and from all and all manner of former and other gifts, grants, bargaines, sales, leases, releases, mortgages, Joyntures, Dower, Judgments, Executions, Extents, wills, Entails, ffines, fforfeitures, titles, troubles, charges and Incumbrances whatsoever had, made, done, committed, knowledged or suffered by the said Charles Downing, Sʳ George Downing, Baronᵗ, late father of the said Charles, and the abouesaid Emanuel Downing or any of them.

This Indenture was signed by the grantor, Charles Downing, Esqʳᵉ, and his wife, Sarah Downing, and their seals affixed on the day and year first abovewritten.   Deeds of Essex Co., Mass., Book 7, Lvs. 7 to 10.

The will of Sir George Downing, Knight of the Bath & Baronet, providing (in default of male issue to his cousin) for the foundation of a new college in the University of Cambridge, "which college shall be called by the name of Downing College," was dated 20 December, 1717, and proved 13 June, 1749.   Lisle, 179.

[The foregoing extracts show clearly enough the connection of this family with New England, a family whose name, associated as it is with a street in which has been, for so many years, the official residence of the Prime Minister of England, the centre of the greatest and most wide-spread empire of modern times, and with a college in one of the most famous universities of the world, is known wherever the English language is spoken, and bids fair to last so long as English history shall be read.

From some MS. notes furnished me by my very obliging friend Mr. T. C. Noble, whose authority on matters connected with the history of the great metropolis of the world and its surrounding parishes is unquestioned, I find that Sir George Downing was rated for a house in "New Pallace" (New Palace Yard, Westminster) for twenty years previous to 1683, that in 1728 the rentals of the whole of Downing Street (for assessment) amounted to less than £1000, and in 1828 the total was £3000. At the present time (1883) the whole street is occupied by the offices of the government and the residences of the First Lord of the Treasury, Chancellor of the Exchequer, &c. From the "Memorials of Westminster," by the Rev. Mackenzie E. C. Walcott, we learn that "The official residence of the First Lord of the Treasury formerly belonged to the Crown : King George I. gave it to Baron Bothmar, the Hanoverian Minister, for life. After his death King George II. offered the house to Sir Robert Walpole, who only accepted it upon the condition that it should be attached to the Premiership forever. Since that time, therefore, Downing Street is inseparably connected with the name of every successive Prime Minister of England." Chapter III. of the Appendix to these Memorials gives us additional information, including a list of the successive occupants of the official residence down

* This must be a mistake for 1638. (See Book of Grants, Salem, edited by William P. Upham, Esq.)—H. F. W.

to July 6, 1846. " Sir Robert Walpole accepted it in 1732, and came to reside here 22 Sept. 1735." " In the small waiting-room of No. 14, for the first and only time in their lives met Sir Arthur Wellesley and Lord Nelson ; the latter was well known to Sir Arthur from the prints in the shop windows ; they conversed together for some minutes ; on parting Lord Nelson went out of the room and asked the name of the stranger whose conversation and appearance had made a deep impression upon him."

I am informed by William H. Richardson, Esq., F.S.A., who is now annotating " The Annals of Ipswiche, by N. Bacon,"* that George Downing, who was undoubtedly the father of Emanuel and Nathaniel Downing, was master of the Grammar School, Ipswich, about the years 1607 to 1610. His son Emanuel, baptized in the parish church of St. Lawrence, Ipswich, 12 August, 1585, married at Groton, Suffolk, 10 April, 1622, Lucy (baptized 27 January, 1601), daughter of Adam Winthrop, Esq., and sister of Governor John Winthrop. Mr. Downing was a lawyer of the Inner Temple, London, Attorney in the Court of Wards, and seems to have lived in the parishes of St. Bridget and of St. Michael, Cornhill. He came over to New England in 1638, took up his abode in Salem, was admitted into the church 4 November of the same year, and frequently represented the town in the General Court of the colony. The date of his death is not known, nor has any record yet been found of any will made by him. We have seen what became of his farm in Salem. His town residence was conveyed, 8 August, 1656, by Lucie Downing of Salem, with consent of Emanuel Downing her husband (as is recited in the deed) to their son Lieut. Joseph Gardner, as the dower of their daughter Ann on her marriage with Lieut. Gardner. It was described as a messuage or tenement in Salem situated upon four acres of ground entire, having the Common on the east, the street or highway that runs from the meeting-house to the harbor on the south, and the lane that goes to the North River on the West. This property comprises the various estates now included between St. Peter, Essex, Newbury and Browne Streets. Lieut. Gardner and his wife sold various lots at either end to sundry members of the Gardner family, and to Deacon Richard Prince and Mr. William Browne, Jr. The house, which stood where the residence of the late Col. Francis Peabody stands, remained as the homestead of Mrs. Gardner. After the untimely loss of her first husband, who was killed in the great Swamp Fight, 19 December, 1675, she took for a second husband Simon Bradstreet, Esq. ; but by the terms of the marriage contract of 2 May, 1676, the ownership of the homestead remained with her. It was afterwards commonly known as the Bradstreet house, and was torn down in 1750, having previously been used as a tavern. On page 75 of the first volume of the REGISTER, and on page 185 of the fourth volume of Historical Collections of the Essex Institute, may be seen an engraving representing this house, in which Sir George Downing probably passed his boyhood while under the tuition of the Rev. John Fisk, preparing for entrance into Harvard College, from which he was graduated in that famous first class of 1642. For a long account of him and his family, and a list of his published works, see Sibley's Harvard Graduates, vol. i. pp. 28–51.

Nathaniel Downing, brother of Emanuel and uncle of Sir George, was baptized in the church of St. Mary at the Tower, Ipswich, 8 October, 1587. He married, 6 May, 1613, Margaret, daughter of Doctor Daniel Selyne (or Selin), a French physician, who died 19 March, 1614–15, and in his will (Rudd, 23) mentions his son-in-law Nathaniel Downing. Mr. Downing seems to have had one son, Daniel, baptized at St. Dionis Backchurch, 5 April, 1614, and buried five days afterwards.

In the Whitehall Evening Post of Febr. 11, 1764, is this letter :

" To the Printer &c.   Sir

By the death of Sir Jacob Garrard Downing Bar* an estate of about 5 or 6000 pr annum falls to the University of Cambridge, to build a college, to be called Downing College. The late Sir George Downing, of Gamlingay, in Cambridgeshire, Bar*, having left it to the late Sir Jacob Garrard, and his Heirs male ; & for want of such Issue, to the rev. M* Peters, late Lecturer of S* Clement-Danes & his Heirs male : both of whom having died without such Issue, the Estate descends as above. The Original of the Family was D* Calibut Downing, one of the Preachers in the Rebel Army, & a great man with Rump : and his son, afterwards Sir Geo: Downing & the first Baronet of the Family, was made Envoy from Cromwell to the States-General, and got a great Estate, owing to this Incident. When King Charles

* The valuable MS. referred to in note, pp. 197–8, vol. xxxvii. REG.

the 2ᵈ was travelling in Disguise in Holland, to visit the Queen Mother, attended only by Lord Falkland, & putting up at an Inn, after he had been there some Time, the Landlord came to these strangers and said, there was a Beggar-man at the Door, very shabbily dressed, who was very importunate to be admitted to them ; on which the King seemed surprised, & after speaking to Lord Falkland, bid the Landlord admit him. As soon as this Beggar-man entered, he pulled off his Beard (which he had put on for a Disguise) & fell on his knees, & said he was Mʳ Downing, the Resident from Oliver Cromwell ; & that he had received Advice of this intended visit from his Majesty to the Queen ; and that, if he ventured any farther, he would be assassinated ; & begged secrecy of the King, for that his Life depended upon it, & departed. The King was amazed at this, & said to Lord Falkland, How could this be known ? there were but you & the Queen knew of it. Therefore the Queen must have mentioned this to somebody who gave Advice of it to his Enemies. However, the King returned back, whereby this Design was prevented. Upon this, after the Restoration, Sir George Downing was rewarded, made a Baronet & Farmer of the Customs, &c. &c., whereby this large Estate was raised.

Besides the above Estate of Sir Jacob Garret Downing Barᵗ. which devolves on the University of Cambridge, another fine Estate, with a handsome house at Putney, falls to his Lady."

In the London Chronicle of Jan. 9, 1772, is this Article :

" We are assured that the Heirs at Law [B. P. Ewer of Bangor who married a Barnardiston] of Sir Jacob Downing Barᵗ have applied for a Royal Charter to found & incorporate the College at Cambridge. A spot is fixed upon for erecting this edifice, which is a spacious Piece of ground, fit for the Purpose, on the South Side of the Town, opposite the Physic Garden, & between Pembroke & Emanuel Colleges. A Design is preparing & Application making to the Owners of the Ground which belongs to several Bodies Corporate ; & as soon as an Act of Parliament can be obtained to impower them to sell, this noble Benefaction will be carried into immediate Execution."—H. F. W.

The English genealogical works which attempt to give the ancestry of Sir George Downing, baronet, give it erroneously. The error seems first to have been promulgated by Anthony a Wood in his Athenæ Oxoniensis, published 1691-2, where, in an account of Dr. Calybute Downing, the Puritan writer, son of Calybute Downing of Shennington, Gloucestershire, Sir George is called his son. The error has been copied into several Baronetages. Dr. Downing's ancestry has been carried back through his grandfather, Arthur, of Lexham in Norfolk, to his great-grandfather Geoffrey Downing of Norwich, who married Elizabeth, daughter of Thomas Wingfield. There are no indications of a relationship between this family and that of George Downing of Ipswich, Suffolk, who, as Mr. Waters shows, was father of Emanuel, the father of Sir George. Savage names Mary, wife of Anthony Stoddard ; James ; Anne, wife of Capt. Joseph Gardner and afterwards of Gov. Simon Bradstreet ; John ; and Dorcas, as other children of Emanuel Downing ; and there was probably also a son Joshua (Mass. Hist. Coll. 4th S. vi. 79). Emanuel Downing announces his intention to leave New England in the fall of 1654 with Gen. Sedgwick (Ibid. p. 84). He was living as late as Sept. 6, 1658, in Edinburgh (Ibid. p. 86). His wife was living in England, June 27, 1662 (Ibid. p. 544). The place and date of death of neither are known. Interesting letters from Emanuel Downing and other members of his family, are printed in the volume of the Mass. Hist. Coll. cited.

Henry Downing, father of Col. Adam Downing, distinguished as an officer in William III.'s army in Ireland, may have been, as represented by Burke (Ext. and Dorm. Baronetage, ed. 1844, p. 163 ; Landed Gentry, ed. 1853, i. 453), a son of Dr. Calybute. We find no evidence that Sir George had a brother Henry.

It is not probable that Wood obtained his information from the family, for the deed of which Mr. Waters gives an abstract proves that Charles Downing, son of Sir George, knew that his grandfather's name was Emanuel so late as 1700, eight years after the publication of Wood's Athenæ. The following letter, copied for us by G. D. Scull, Esq., of Oxford, England, from the original, shows that Wood, while engaged on his work, applied to the Rev. Increase Mather for information about the Downings, but with little success :

" Sir

I have yours of 20ᵗʰ Instant. There never was any Dr Downing in New England. It is true yᵗ Sir George Downing (who was knighted by Charles 2ⁿᵈ) had his education in yᵉ Colledge there ; but had no other degree there besides yᵗ of

Bachelor of Art. Nor do any in that colledge proceed further than Master of arts after seven years standing, as 'tis in Oxford and Cambridge. We never (which is pity) had any Doctors. I am ashamed to tell you that I cannot procure any further account concerning non conformist writers. I have really laboured to gratify you to my power. I heartily wish there were more publick spirits in the world.

Sir   Your servant,   I. MATHER.

London July 23—1691.

To Mr Anthony Wood near Merton College in Oxford."

An equally inexplicable error will be pointed out in this article when we come to the will of Sir William Phips, who is represented in English books to be ancestor of the present Marquis of Normanby. Both errors have years ago been pointed out by our countrymen. The second volume of Hutchinson's Massachusetts, which was reprinted in England in 1768, gives the true christian name of the father of Sir George Downing.—EDITOR.]

THOMAS WARNETT, now of James City in Virginia, merchant, 13 February, 1629, proved 8 November, 1630, by Thomazine Warnet, relict and executrix. To M^{ris} Elizabeth Pott one Corfe and crosse cloth of wrought gold and to Dr John Pott (1) five thousand of several sorts of nayles. To Francis Pott four score pounds of tobacco which he oweth me. To Mr Francis Boulton, minister, one firkin of butter, one bushel of white salt, six pounds of candles, one pound of pepper, one pound of ginger, two bushels of meal, one rundlett of ink, six quires of writing paper and one pair of silk stockings. To John Johnson's wife six pounds of soap, six pounds of white starch and one pound of blue starch. To John Browning's wife one thousand of pins, one pair of knives carved with two images upon them, twelve pounds of white starch and two pounds of blue starch. To the wife of Mr John Uptone one sea green scarf edged with gould lace, twelve pounds of white starch and two pounds of blue starch. To my friend Mr Thomas Burges my second best sword and my best felt hat. To John Grevett's wife one pair of sheets, six table napkins, three towels and one table cloth marked with T. W., six pounds of soap, six pounds of white starch and one pound of blue starch. To Thomas Key's wife one gilded looking glass. To Sarg^t John Wane's (2) wife four bushels of meal and one rundlett of four gallons of vinegar, one half pound of "threed" of several colours, twenty needles, six dozen of silk and thred buttons, one pewter candlestick & one pewter chamberpot. To Roger Thompson's wife one half bushel of white salt, one pound of pepper and one jar of oil. To Benjamin Symes (3) one weeding hoe. To George Muleston one " howing" hoe & one axe. To John Goundry one bar of lead of twenty pound weight and three pound. To John Hattone one black felt hat, one suit of grey kersie, one shirt marked T. W., four pairs of Irish stockings, two pairs of my own wearing shoes, one bar of lead and six pounds of powder. To John Southerne (4) six pounds of candles, one Poland cap furred and one pair of red slippers. To Michael Batt (5) his wife two bushels of meal.

The rest of my temporal estate in Virginia, my debts being paid and legacies paid & discharged, to wife Thomazine, whom I appoint executrix. Friends John Southerne and James Stome overseers. To the former one black beaver hat and gold band, one doublet of black chamlet and one pair of black hose; and to James Stome my best sword and a gold belt.

The witnesses were Francis Boltone (6) & John Southerne.

Scroope, 105.

[The following, from Harl. MS. (Brit. Mus.), 1561, f. 142, undoubtedly gives the pedigree of the testator of the above will, and indicates his place of residence before his migration.

John Warnet of = Susan, d. of .... Ridley
Hempsted, Sussex. | of Whellebeech, Sussex.

Francis Warnet=Anne, d. of	Thomas Warnet=Thomazin, d.	Catharine.	Susan,
of Hempsted,	Edw. Boys,	of Southwark	and heir of	uxʳ Edmond
ob. v. p.	of co. Kent.	in co. Surrey,	Wm. Hall of	Jordan of Gat-
		1623.	Woodalling,	wick, co. Surrey.
			co. Norfolk.	

Edmond Warnett.   Thomas, 3 y. old 1623.   Judith.

H. F. W.

1. Dr. John Pott, the legatee mentioned, was doubtless the John Pott, A.M., M.D., physician for the colony of Virginia, who arrived with his wife Elizabeth in October, 1621, in the ship George. He was appointed on the recommendation of Dr. Theodore Gulston, the founder of the Gulstonian lectureship of Anatomy, still maintained by the London College of Physicians. In the Virginia Land Records, Book No. 1, p. 8, he appears as a grantee, on August 11th, 1624, of three acres of land in "James Cittie," and is mentioned as a "Doctor of Physicke" and a member of the "Councill." Francis West, the governor of the colony and a younger brother of Lord Delaware, departing for England March 5th, 1628, Dr. Pott succeeded him as governor, and so served until some time in March, 1630, when he was superseded by Sir John Harvey. Pott was then arraigned for pardoning Edward Wallis, condemned for murder and cattle stealing. This was the first trial by jury in the colony. Pott was found guilty and confined to his plantation at Harrope, now Williamsburg, until the King's pleasure could be ascertained. Governor Harvey forwarded the recommendation of the Council for his pardon, and Mrs. Pott crossed the ocean and pleaded her husband's cause. The commissioners to whom the petition was referred reported to the King that "condemning him for felony was very rigorous, if not erroneous," and recommended that he should be restored to liberty and his estate, and the practice of his profession.

2. I find in the State Land Registry a grant of 300 acres to John Wayne (rendered in the Index, Waine) in Charles River County (as the County of York was first called), May 10th, 1638. Book No. 1, p. 569.

3. It may be recalled that Benjamin Symmes is reported in 1648 as having founded in the colony a free school, which he endowed with two hundred acres of land, a good house, forty milch cows and other appurtenances.

4. There is a grant also of record to John Southerne, "Gent." (in all probability him of the will), of twenty-four acres in "James Cittie," September 1st, 1627. Book No. 1, p. 55.

5. Michaell Batt appears as a grantee of one acre of land in "James Cittie Island," September 20th, 1643, Book No. 1, p. 890. Grants also appear contemporaneously to John, William and Henry Batt, Batte or Batts, as the name is variously rendered. The descendants of William and Henry Batte (as the name now obtains), brothers, are quite numerous in Virginia, and of high respectability.

6. The Rev. Francis Boulton, Boltone or Bolton, as the name is variously rendered, who had been recommended by the Earl of Southampton for some vacant parish in Virginia, arrived in the colony in the ship George, as above, and was assigned to Elizabeth City, to reside with Captain Thomas Newce.—R. A. Brock, *of Richmond, Virginia.*]

WILLIAM PEPPERELL of St. Stephens by Launceston, in the County of Cornwall, 5 June, 1655, proved 15 October 1655, by Jane Pepperell, his widow, and William Pepperell, his son. Daughter Alice (under 12) and Jane Pepperell, second son Robert, wife Jane, son Thomas (under 12) and eldest son William. Richard Call my brother-in-law, John Roe of Launceston, Thomas Facy of St. Thomas, and Robert Pepperell my brother (of whose unfained affection and fidelity I have had long and frequent experiments), to be overseers. The witnesses were Nevill Blighett, Will Blagdon and Nicholas Dodge.   Aylett, 387.

[The testator could not have been the grandfather of Sir William Pepperrell, bart., the captor of Louisburg. Possibly he may have been his great-grandfather. William Pepperrell, the father of the baronet, was born about 1646, having died Feb. 13, 1733-4, in his 87th year. Usher Parsons, M.D., in the biography of the son (Boston, 1856), states that the father was born in Tavistock, Devonshire: but ten years later (REGISTER, xx. 1) he calls him a native of Wales. The Wentworth Genealogy (ed. 1878, p. 307) calls him a native of Cornwall. "Tradition," according to Dr. Parsons, "says that he spoke broad Welsh, as Boll and Woll for Bill and Will." He had three sisters. One married a Phillips, another a Gilbert, and the third, Grace, died unmarried. His children were Andrew, Mary, Margery, Joanna, Miriam, William the baronet, Dorothy and Jane. For an account of the descendants of the baronet, among whom is Edward Walford, M.A., of London, Eng., editor of the *Antiquarian Magazine*, see REGISTER, xx. 1-6.—EDITOR.]

GEORGE FENWICK, of Worminghurst, co. Sussex, Esquire, 2 February, 1656, with codicil of 9 March, 1656, proved 27 April, 1657, by Elizabeth Fenwick, daughter and executrix. To wife Katherine, &c. &c.; to my most natural and dear mother, Mrs Dorothy Clavering; to brother Claudius and his heirs male my lands in Brenckborn and Nether Framlington in the county of Northumberland; to my nephew Thomas Ledgard and his heirs male land in Thirston and Tillington in Northumberland; to my sister Ledgard and my sister Cullick each fifty pounds; to my brother Ledgard and my brother Cullick, each ten pounds; to my sister Cullick's children one hundred pounds apiece; to my niece Clifton fifty pounds, and to niece Bootflower's boy fifty pounds; to my daughter Elizabeth and daughter Dorothy; to Ralph Fenwick, a scholar of Christ Church, Oxford, ten pounds a year; to my daughters land in Sussex that descends to them from their uncle Edward Apsley, Esquire, deceased.

The above he declared to be his will 10 March, 1656. In the codicil he bequeaths to his sister Cullick and her children all his estate in New England; and also five hundred pounds to the public use of that country of New England if " my " loving friend Edward Hopkins think fit. He makes bequests to his friend Robert Leeves and to his servant Moses Fryer. To Dame Elinor Selby of Barwick he leaves ten pounds and desires her to undertake the education of Dorothy. His father-in-law Sir Arthur Hesslerigg to accept the mean remembrance of forty shillings to buy a ring. He also mentions his cousin Lawrence and his wife, his cousin Strickland and his lady, his ancient acquaintance and dearly beloved friend Sir Thomas Widdrington, his dear and good friend Mr Edward Hopkins, late warden of the fleet, his friend Aaron Gourdon, Dr. of Physic, his friend Mr Tempest Milner, alderman of London, and the latter's kinsman Robert Key, his father-in-law, Mr Claveringe, and Thomas Burrell of Brinckborn, Northumberland. He gives six pounds per annum to Tristram Fenwick for life, forty shillings to Mr Ogle of Leith in Scotland, and twenty shillings to the widow Clarke of Weldon. Ruthen, 138.

[The family of Forster, of Newham, from which Col. George Fenwick and his sister Mrs. Elizabeth Cullick derived their descent, are said by Mundy to be descended out of the house of Forster of Etherston. In this latter family the baptismal name of Reignold often occurs, suggesting the possible origin of Reginald Forster of Ipswich. They bore *Argent, a chevron vert between three bugle-horns stringed sable.* " these verses were sett about the Armes," says Mundy :

" let us derly them hold
to mind ther worthynes
that wch our parent's old
hath left us to posses."

Col. Fenwick's first wife and the mother of his children, was Alice, relict of Sir John Botteler, knight, and daughter of Sir Edward Apsley of Thackham in county Sussex, knight. One of her sisters, Elizabeth, was the wife of Sir Albert Morton, Secretary of State to King James. His second wife, Catherine, was eldest daughter of the famous Sir Arthur Hazelrigg of Noseley Hall, in Leicestershire. The monument erected to the memory of Col. Fenwick in the church at Berwick, which he is said to have been principally instrumental in building, shows that he died 15 March, 1656. It will be noticed that his sister Elizabeth, wife of Capt. John Cullick, does not appear on the following pedigree, probably not having been born until after 1615, when the visitation was made. The " sister Ledgard " was Mary, wife of Thomas Ledgard.

The following pedigree is extracted from Richard Mundy's copy of Visitations of Northumberland, 1575 and 1615, Harl. MS. 1554, ff. 20, 54 :

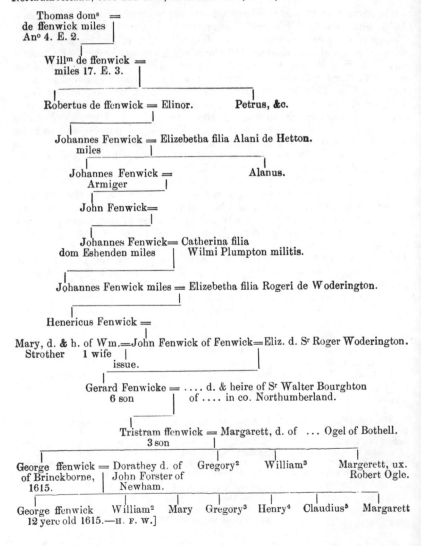

Thomas dom^s =
de ffenwick miles
An° 4. E. 2.

Willm de ffenwick =
miles 17. E. 3.

Robertus de ffenwick = Elinor.   Petrus, &c.

Johannes Fenwick = Elizebetha filia Alani de Hetton.
miles

Johannes Fenwick =   Alanus.
Armiger

John Fenwick=

Johannes Fenwick= Catherina filia
dom Eshenden miles   Wilmi Plumpton militis.

Johannes Fenwick miles = Elizebetha filia Rogeri de Woderington.

Henericus Fenwick =

Mary, d. & h. of Wm.=John Fenwick of Fenwick=Eliz. d. Sr Roger Woderington.
Strother   1 wife
            issue.

Gerard Fenwicke = ... d. & heire of Sr Walter Bourghton
6 son   of .... in co. Northumberland.

Tristram ffenwick = Margarett, d. of ... Ogel of Bothell.
3 son

George ffenwick = Dorathey d. of   Gregory²   William³   Margerett, ux.
of Brinckborne, John Forster of   Robert Ogle.
1615.   Newham.

George ffenwick   William²   Mary   Gregory³   Henry⁴   Claudius⁵   Margarett
12 yere old 1615.—H. F. W.]

WILLIAM HATHORNE, of Binfield in the County of Berks, yeoman, 18 May, 1650, proved 2 May, 1651, by Sara Hathorne, the widow and executrix. To the poor of the parish of Binfield twenty shillings, to be distributed on the day of my burial. To Robert Hathorne, my son, all that my messuage or tenement now in the tenure of my brother-in-law John Lawrence, situate and being in Bray, in the County of Berks, together with all barns, stables, outhouses, orchards, gardens, backsides, easments, profits and hereditaments thereto belonging; and also that my cottage closes and parcels of land, pasture and meadow, lying and being in Bray aforesaid, and hereafter particularly mentioned. That is to say, one barn with two orchards and five closes of pasture and meadow called Neatherhouse barn, neathouse mead, the two Butts, Bishopps cloase and the backside, containing in all eighteen acres, more or less, lying together near unto the said messuage and abutting upon Oakely Greene towards the North,—(other lots, of four acres and of eighteen acres respectively, abutting upon Oakely Green towards the South), one cottage, with a hay house and backside, late in the tenure of Richard Braiser, containing one acre, more or less, abutting upon Okely Greene aforesaid towards the North; also one close and one pidle of pasture ground called Godlers, containing seven acres, adjoining to a lane leading out of Okeley Greene into Didworth Green towards the South, to have unto the said Robert Hathorne my son & his heirs forever, upon trust, &c.—that they shall give and pay unto William Hathorne, my eldest son, his executors or assigns, the sum of one hundred pounds of lawful money of England within two years next after my decease, and unto John Hathorne, my son, &c., twenty pounds within three years, &c. Item, I give unto Nathaniel Hathorne, my son, twenty shillings in money. Further unto John Hathorne twenty pounds, if living, otherwise to his wife and children, within one year next after my decease. To Edmond Hathorne, my youngest son (thirty acres and more in Bray) upon the trust and confidence and to the end, intent and purpose that the said Edmond Hathorne, my son, his heirs or assigns, shall give and pay unto Elizabeth, my daughter, the wife of Mr Richard Davenporte, her executors or assigns, the sum of forty pounds of lawful money of England within two years next after my decease. To Anne, my daughter, wife of Hugh Smith, twenty shillings, and to Elizabeth, her daughter, five shillings. To Robert, Sara, Anne and Katherine, the children of my son-in-law Philip Lee, five shillings apiece.

The residue, my debts being paid, my funeral expenses discharged and this my last will and testament in all things duly performed, to Sara Hathorne, my wife, whom I ordain and make sole executrix.

The witnesses were John Sowthey als Hayle, Thomas Dyer and Robert Southey als Hayle. Grey, 87.

SARA HATHORNE (by mark) of Binfield in the County of Berks, widow, 5 September, 1655, proved 14 March, 1655, by Nathaniel Hathorne, son and sole executor. To the poor of Binfield twenty shillings, to be bestowed on such as have most need, at the discretion of my executors, on the day of burial. To Robert Hathorne, my son, a round table in the chamber over the Hall, with a drawer to him, a great joyned chair in the parlor, my elm chest in the chamber over the parlor, a great pair of andirons standing in the parlor, two pillow beares, one of them Holland pillow beare and the other of them a flaxen pillow beare, two silver spoons, one of my best joined stools in the hall, a cupboard cloth wrought with blue at the ends and a great brazen candlestick.   To Anne, my daughter, the wife of Hugh Smith, my best feather bed and bolster belonging to him, a feather pillow, two blankets, my green rug, my green sea curtains and valians to them, two pair of my better sheets, the fourth part of all my pewter, my lesser brass pot and pothooks, my little skillett, all my wearing apparell, three of my bigger milk bowls, a low leather chair, my best green matted chair, the biggest chest that was her fathers and ten pounds of lawful money of England.   To my two grandchildren Anne Lee and Katherine Lee, twenty shillings apiece.   To all the residue of my grandchildren, that is to say, Sara Hathorne, Elizabeth Hathorne and Elizabeth Hathorne, Susanna Hathorne, Nathaniel Hathorne, William Smith and Elizabeth Smith, the several sums of ten shillings apiece.   To Anne Middleton, my late servant, ten shillings.

The residue to son Nathaniel Hathorne, who is to be sole executor.   The witnesses were John Yonges and Henrie Otwaie (by mark).

Berkley, 34.

[The foregoing will of William Hathorne of Binfield confirms the guess made in 1879, as to the English home of the American family of Hathorne, and the intermarriage of Lieut. Richard Davenport, of New England, with that family. (See Gleanings from English Records, &c., by Emmerton and Waters, Essex Institute, Salem, Mass., where sundry abstracts of English wills may be found, and paternal and maternal pedigrees of the distinguished author Nathaniel Hawthorne.)   Binfield, Bray and Oakley Green are all in the North Eastern part of Berkshire, a little West and South West of Windsor. From a History and Antiquities of the Hundred of Bray, by Charles Kerry, London, 1861, I learn that there was a manor of Cruchfields and Hawthorne, that a William Hawthorne was one of the tenants of " Queen Lease " in the parish of Bray and Manor of Bray, 1650 ; in the " Rentall of the Manor of Bray, 1650," William Hawthorne is charged one pound per annum for all lands holden of the manor, Thomas Hawthorne is charged three shillings, the heirs of Robert Hawthorne five shillings, and William Hawthorne, Jr., five pence.   In " The Assert Rent of Bray, 1658," under the title " Oakley," I find "Robert Hauthorne for house and lands," six shillings four pence, " Thomas Hauthorne ditto," three shillings three pence half penny, and " Henery Hauthorne for lands," seven shillings.   William Hawthorne was one of the church wardens in Bray, A.D. 1600.   By Indenture dated 10 January, 6 James (1609), Sir John Norris confirmed unto William Goddard, William Hathorne, Thomas Westcott and five others, and their heirs, all those piddles or parcels of ground severally lying in certain hamlets and tithings of the parish of Bray in the county of Berks, whereupon small cottages and other edifices were erected and built, containing in the whole, by estimation, five acres," &c., in trust for the " relief of such poor, impotent and aged persons as from time to time thereafter should be dwelling within the said parish, and to the intent that the poorest and most aged and impotent persons of the said parish should be provided for ever of houses and habitation."   By an Indenture dated 14 January, 1621, it appears that William Hawthorn and Thomas Westcott, who were the surviving trustees, associated with themselves eight other substantial inhabitants of the parish as feoffees in trust, &c. By Indenture of feoffment bearing date 1 September, 1657, it appears that Thomas Wilcox was the surviving trustee.   On page 110 of the History may be found " The Legend of Hawthorn," which narrates the finding of two pots of gold on Hawthorn Hill, near Cruchfield (but a little way from Binfield), and on page 111 sundry notices of the name of Hawthorne, gathered from court rolls, registers and other authentic sources ; from which it appears that John Hothorn died 1520, leaving Henry Hothorn his son and heir.   Henry died 1531, leaving Roger his son and heir.   In 1535 a field of Thomas Hothorne adjoined one held by John Bysshop in " Crychefeld."   In 1533 Thomas Hothorne was appointed collector for the lands he (Bysshop) held called " Chaunters " by the yearly rent of twenty shillings nine pence. William Hothorn died 1538, leaving William his son and heir.   William Hawthorne was a copyhold tenant 1601 and church warden 1600–02.   Thomas Hawthorn jun. purchased " Brownings " in Holyport, 1602.   John Hawthorne held a coppice at Binfield called " Picking's Points," 1605.   One of this family married Anne, daughter of Gilbert Loggins, circa 1605.   And Robert Hawthorne's name occurs 1656 to 1664.—H. F. W.]

NATHANIEL HATHORNE, of Cookham in County Berks, gentleman, 27 September, 1652, proved 29 July, 1654, by Martha Hathorne, the relict and executrix. To wife Martha eight hundred pounds in lieu of her jointure and thirds, &c. My manor of South Braham* in the county of Somerset. Estates in the counties of Devon, Somerset and Berks. My four brothers-in-law, Thomas Loggins, John Whistler, Ralphe Whistler and Thomas Whistler, gentleman. My three own sisters, Elizabeth, Mary and Anne, and John Laurence, the husband of Anne. My son-in-law William Mattingly and Jone his wife. My kinsman William Eldridge and Judith his wife. Anne Winche, the wife to my nephew John Winch. My nephew William Winche. The poor of Cookham and South Braham. Wife Martha to be executrix, and two loving kinsmen, Dr. Daniel Whistler of Gresham College, and John Winche, of London, haberdasher, to be overseers. One of the witnesses was John Hathorne. Alchin, 251.

[This testator was, of course, brother to the foregoing William Hathorne and uncle to the American immigrant.

It is with a peculiar satisfaction, it must be confessed, that the compiler of these Gleanings, himself a native of Salem, has at last been able to prove beyond a doubt whereabouts in "Our Old Home," that elder England beyond the seas, we must look for the ancestry of the most widely known among the distinguished sons of old Salem, the most original of the prose writers of our New England, and the one whose writings are most native to her soil ; a satisfaction tinged with the regret, however, that the discovery was not made in the great writer's life-time. We can easily imagine with what delight he would have made a pilgrimage into Berkshire, how gladly he would have loitered about Binfield and Bray, Cruchfield and Oakley Green, making new sketches to illustrate his English Note Book, and how eagerly his quaint and vivid fancy would have seized even upon the scanty materials offered to it in the Legend of Hawthorn Hill and its pots of gold, to weave therefrom a story that should rival in weirdness any of his "Legends of New England."

The eldest son and namesake of William Hathorne of Binfield, and first American ancestor of the distinguished writer, was, next to Governor Endicott, by far the most important personage in the civil history of Salem during the first generation. By sheer force of natural talent and commanding character, this son of a plain English yeoman easily came to the front rank among the many wise and active New England men who were then engaged in the tremendous and to them solemn task of founding a state, opening up the wilderness, treating with "the barbarious Heathen," justly and peaceably if possible, but with fire and sword if need be, allotting lands to the new comers in proportion to their means and ability and to the numbers of their families, establishing offices of record, settling disputes, levying taxes, making provision for meeting-house and school-house, regarding justice and morality, a careful religious training and the free education of all, as the only sure basis of good order and sound government, the only firm and stable foundation whereon to erect the superstructure of a mighty new state. In all this work Major William Hathorne bore a prominent part, whether as an enterprising and prosperous merchant, a trusted citizen and deputy, an honored speaker of the House, a wise and influential magistrate in the highest court, or an active and successful commander in the wars ; and his career illustrates most happily the wonderful capacity of the Anglo-Saxon race, that imperial race of modern times, its adaptability and readiness to cope with new conditions of life, to adjust itself to strange and heretofore untried surroundings, its plain and homely common sense, its union of native practical sagacity and sound judgment with a love of law and order, and at the same time a spirit of adventure, which has made Great Britain not only the most prosperous of nations, but the greatest colonizing people in the world, the mother of Nations, and which is so conspicuously manifested in the marvellous career of her daughters, the "Greater Britain" in America and Australia and elsewhere throughout the world wherever a love of enterprise or any other cause has led its people to settle and plant new homes.—H. F. W.]

---

* Probably South Bruham (or Brewham) in the Hundred of Bruton.—H. F. W.

Sir WILLIAM PHIPS, Knight, of Boston in the county of Suffolk, Province of Massachusetts Bay, in New England, 18 December, 1693, sworn to by Dame Mary Phips 10 September, 1696; proved 29 January, 1696. To brother James Phips or his heirs, the sum of five shillings. To my dear and entirely beloved consort Mary Phips, and to her heirs forever, all my estate, real and personal, &c. &c., with power to alienate by deed of gift, will or codicil. If she should die without having, by will, disposed of my estate, &c., it shall all descend and fall to my adopted son, Spencer Phips als Bennett and the heirs of his body. If he should die without issue surviving, what is left shall be equally divided and shared, one half thereof by my sisters Mary, Margaret and the heirs of my sister Anne deceased, or their heirs forever, and the other half in like manner, to the relations of my beloved consort, reserving only out of the whole estate one hundred pounds current money of New England, which my said relations and the relations of my said wife shall cause to be paid unto John Phipps, son to my brother John Phipps deceased, or to his heirs, if this clause be not repealed by my wife aforesaid. If my dear consort should die before my said son is come to age or is married, then I do nominate and appoint my friends Capt. John Foster, Esq., and Capt. Andrew Belcher of Boston, merchants, to be trustees of my estate and guardians to my said son, until he shall be of full age or married.

The witnesses were John Phillips, John White, John Hiskett, Josiah Stone and John Greenough.   Pyne, 15.

FRANCIS PHIPPS, the elder, of Reading, in the county of Berks, mentions (inter alios) son Constantine Phipps, in his will proved 1668.
                                                              Hene, 69.

[A flattering sketch of the mathematical and inventive ability of Sir William Phips—our governor during the time of the witchcraft delusion; with a copy of the epitaph from his monument in St. Mary Woolnoth's Church in London, are given in "The Peerage of Ireland," by John Lodge, vol. vii. p. 84, of the edition of 1789, edited by Mervyn Archdall, as a prelude to the history of the ancestry of Lord Mulgrave; which is followed by the statement that Sir William Phips was father of Sir Constantine Phipps, Lord Chancellor of Ireland from 1710 to 1714, who was grandfather of the first Baron Mulgrave.

Sir William (whose will is given above) was son of James Phips, a gunsmith, who came from Bristol, England, and settled near the Kennebec River. Cotton Mather states that James had twenty-one sons and five daughters. Sir William mentions in his will but one brother and three sisters, and having *no* child adopts his wife's nephew, afterward known as Spencer Phips, who lived and died in New England. Sir Egerton Brydges copied the statement from Archdall and incorporated it in his celebrated edition of Collins's Peerage (1812), but having noticed later the Life of Sir William Phips by Cotton Mather, corrects the statement in an appendix, so far as Sir *Constantine* was concerned, by suggesting that Spencer Phips, the adopted son of Sir William, was the true ancestor of Lord Mulgrave. Debrett, in his annual Peerage, carried the original story for years, but finally left it out entirely. Burke substituted "cousin" for "father," still keeping Sir William Phips for the "figure-head" of the family by saying he was cousin of Sir Constantine. Savage (1861) Vol. iii. p. 422, calls attention to the "preposterous fable," and quotes "Smiles's Self-Help, p. 169," as a present example of its continuance. The Heraldic Journal (1865), Vol. i. pp. 154-5, contains a full and interesting account of this "popular error." The latest promulgation of the old story which has come to my sight is in an elegant volume purchased by the Boston Athenæum during 1881, "Picturesque Views of Seats of Noblemen, &c.," by Rev. F. O. Morris, no date, but evidently a *very* recent publication, Vol. ii. pp. 11 to 12, with a view of Mulgrave Castle, the seat of the Marquis of Normanby.

This magnificent place was inherited by Constantine Phipps (a grandson of Sir Constantine previously mentioned) from his maternal grandmother, whose paternity was a question of historic doubt.

Catherine Sedley, created Countess of Dorchester *for life*, was the acknowledged mistress of James II.; the keeper of his privy purse, Col. James Graham, also had intimate relations with her. It happened that her daughter—Lady Catherine Darnly—bore an exact resemblance to his daughter, the Countess of Berkshire. Col. Graham was not inclined to deny the paternity, while the mother asserted that her daughter "need not be so proud, as she was *not* the King's child, but Col. Graham's." (Jesse's Lives of the Stuarts, Vol. iii. p. 508.)

Lady Catherine Darnley was married first to the Earl of Anglesey, from whom she was divorced; she then married the Duke of Buckingham. From him she received Mulgrave Castle, and she gave it to Constantine Phipps, the son of her daughter by her first husband.

This Constantine Phipps was created Baron Mulgrave *of the peerage of Ireland* in 1768, but the titles have accumulated upon his descending line until the present head of the family is "Marquis of Normanby, Earl of Mulgrave, Viscount Normanby and Baron Mulgrave of Mulgrave, co. York, *in the Peerage of the United Kingdom;* Baron Mulgrave of New Ross, co. Wexford, *in the Peerage of Ireland.*" The armorial bearings are quarterings of those of James II.! and of Sir William Phips!

Mr. Waters has found a father for *a* Constantine Phipps, and we hope the whole question of relationship to Sir William (if any existed) will be fully settled soon. Dr. Marshall in "The Genealogist," Vol. vi., gave new material as to the marriages and children of the first Constantine.—J. C. J. BROWN.

From Hist. and Antiquities of Reading, by the Rev. Charles Coates, LL.B., London, 1802, p. 445, we learn that there was a tradition that Sir Constantine Phipps, the ancestor of the Mulgrave family, was born at Reading.—H. F. W.]

SYMON BRADSTREETE, citizen and grocer of London, 22 February, 1627, proved 28 February, 1627, by Samuel Bradstreete. Daughter Margaret, now wife of Edmond Slater, citizen and mercer of London, married without my love, leave or consent. My nephew, Samuel Bradstreete, to be residuary legatee and sole and absolute executor. Barrington, 14.

[Simon Bradstreet, the "Nestor of New England," who was governor of Massachusetts, 1679–86 and 1689–92, was probably related to the testator. Gov. Bradstreet used on his will a seal with these arms: On a fesse three crescents, in base a greyhound passant (REGISTER, viii. 313). The tinctures are not indicated. The arms of Sir John Valentine Bradstreet, baronet, descended from Simon B. of Kilmainham, co. Dublin, Ireland, created a baronet in 1759, are, Arg. a greyhound passant gules; on a chief sable three crescents or.

The father of Gov. Bradstreet was named Simon, according to the statement of the Rev. Simon B. of New London (REG. ix. 113). Cotton Mather, who does not give the christian name, says that he was "a minister in Lincolnshire who was always a nonconformist at home as well as when preacher at Middleburgh abroad" (Magnalia, ed. 1702, Bk. ii. p. 19; ed. 1853, vol. i. p. 138). Gov. Bradstreet, according to Mather, was "born at Horbling, March, 1603." He died at Salem, March 27, 1697, "æt. 94," according to the inscription on his monument (REG. i. 76). He was bred at Emmanuel College, Cambridge, A.B. 1620, A.M. 1624, came to New England in 1630, being then secretary of the Massachusetts Company. He married first, Anne, daughter of Gov. Thomas Dudley, by whom he had eight children—Samuel, Dorothy married Rev. Seaborn Cotton; Sarah wife of Richard Hubbard; Rev. Simon, Hannah or Ann, wife of Andrew Wiggin; Dudley, John, and Mercy wife of Nathaniel Wade. He married secondly Mrs. Anne (Downing) Gardiner. See memoirs, REGISTER, i. 75–7; viii. 312–13. Lists of descendants of him and his gifted wife, the first female poet in New England, including some eminent American writers, are printed in the REGISTER, viii. 312–25; ix. 113–21.—EDITOR.]

JOHN SEDGWICKE, of the parish of St Savior's, Southwark, in county Surrey, brewer, 27 November, 1638, proved 5 December, 1638, by Martha Sedgwicke, widow and executrix. To be buried in the parish church of St Savior's. To wife Martha two thousand pounds of money and certain personal property at my house at Barnes in county Surrey, late in the occupation of Mr Hubland deceased. To my mother Elizabeth Sedgwicke, of Woburn in the county of Bedford, widow, the sum of five hundred pounds in money within one year after my decease. But if she die before the expiration of said year, then two hundred and fifty pounds of that money to be given to my wife and the other two hundred and fifty pounds to be at the disposal and ordering of my said mother to such of her children as she shall think most meet, at her own will and pleasure. To my sister Mary Houghton, now wife of Robert Houghton, and their daughter Martha, my god-daughter, the sum of one hundred and fifty pounds within one year, &c. To my brother William Sedgwicke, minister of Farnam, near Bishops Starford, fifty pounds within one year, &c. " Item I give and remitt to my loving brother Robert Sedgwicke, of Charlestowne in new England Thirtie and eight pounds which hee oweth mee by bill and fourty shillings to buy him a ring." To my father and mother in law, Edward and Joan Wicke, of Leighton in the county of Bedford, the sum of five pounds each; to sister Joan Wicke ten pounds ; to brothers Matthew, Mark and Thomas Wicke ten pounds apiece; and to brother Luke Wicke thirty pounds ; all within one year after my decease. To my friend and brother Nicholas Crisp, citizen and girdler of London, ten pounds, and to his wife Sarah Crisp, ten pounds within one year, &c. To the poor of the parish of Woburn in the County of Bedford, the sum of twenty pounds, &c., it being the parish in which I was born. To the poor of the town of Leighton twenty pounds. To the poor of the Liberty of the upper ground, on the Bankeside, in the parish of St. Saviors, ten pounds. To ten poor godly ministers of God's word the sum of forty pounds, to be distributed at the discretion of my overseers. To Mr Nicholas Morton, minister of the parish of St. Saviors, forty shillings to preach my funeral sermon. To Mr James Archer, minister also of the said parish, forty shillings. To my uncle, Mr Stephen Sedgwicke, brewer, five pounds to buy him a ring. To servant Nathaniel Barrow five pounds. Wife Martha to. be executrix, and kinsmen and friends Edward Wicke, Stephen Sedgwicke, Nicholas Crisp and Robert Houghton to be overseers. Lee, 181.

[Robert Sedgwick, named in this will as brother of the testator, was a prominent man in early New England history. It is noteworthy that Sarah Sedgwick, second wife of Gov. John Leverett (REG. xxxv. 348), who has been supposed to be a sister of Robert, is not mentioned here. Robert Sedgwick settled in Charlestown as early as 1636, was one of the founders of the Artillery Company in 1638, was chosen Major-General, the highest military office in the colony, May 26. 1652 ; went to England and was appointed by Cromwell commander of the expedition which captured in 1654 the French posts in Acadia. He was sent as a commissioner to Jamaica after the capture of that island (REG. ante, p. 24), where he died May 24 (Drake), or June 24 (Palfrey), 1656. His children were Samuel, Hannah, William and Robert (Wyman's Charlestown). His widow Joanna became the second wife of Rev. Thomas Allen of Charlestown, whose first wife was Anna, widow of John Harvard, founder of Harvard College. Descendants have been distinguished in literature and in civil and military life.—EDITOR.]

Notes on Abstracts previously printed.

CONSTANT SYLVESTER. (*Ante*, p. 17.)

GRACE SYLVESTER.—In the REGISTER for October last, page 385, Mr. Waters gives an abstract of the will of Constant Silvester, made in Barbadoes in 1671. In this will the testator gives his two daughters, Grace and Mary, " two thousand pounds each on the day of their marriage, besides One hundred pounds each to buy them a jewel at the age of 16 years." The following deposition, made by the mother of these two young ladies, has been transcribed from the "Proceedings in the Spiritual Court of the Diocese of London," and brings to light an interesting episode in the annals of the family of Sylvester :

"12 Die Menses Decembris Anno Dom̄ 1685 which day appeared p'sonally Grace Sylvester, widdow and Relict of Constant Sylvester, Esquire, dec^d and by vertue of her oath deposed that about Ten years since her husband being dead, her affaires called her into Barbadoes ; she left her children, vizt one Sonn and two daughters under the care and tuition and government to Anne Walrond her sister, who dyed in ffebruary last, as she was informed and she was likewise informed y^t one Mr John Staples being an acquaintance of this deponents sonn Constant Sylvester, thereby became acquainted with Grace Sylvester this deponents daughter and pretended to make his addresses to her in the way of marriage and the same (as this deponent was informed) Came to the Knowledge of the said Anne Walrond & she forbad the said John Staples to come to the said House and he thereupon did desist and she doth farther depose that she this deponent arrived at London on the 28th of September last and after such her arrival Sir Henry Pickering Bar^t made courtshipp in the way of marriage to her this Deponents daughter Grace Sylvester and he made also his addresses to this deponent therein to whom she gave her consent, upon Information of his Quality, State and Condition and after some tyme the said Mr John Staples came to her this deponents lodgings in St James S^t vizt. on or about the 3^d day of Novr last and in the p'sence of this Depon^t, Henry Walrond Senr Esqre and severall other p'sons the said m^r John Staples told this deponent that he understanding that her daughter Grace was speedily to be married to Sir Henry Pickering and he thought good to acquaint this deponent that her daughter could not justly p'ceed in the s^d match, for she was by promise engaged to him or to that effect and he being asked, when, where, and in whose p'sence, he answered, in the Mall in St James and that her sister Mary and Mrs Mary Seaman were with them, but were either soe much before or behind them that they could not heare theire discourse and the s^d Grace Sylvester being then p'sent absolutely denyed that she made any such p'mise, but declared that she told him that she would never marry any p'son wth out her mothers consent and approbation, or to that very effect, whereupon the s^d John Staples replyed that the p'mise made to him had that condiĉon and the s^d Grace denying any p'mise, the s^d John Staples said that this was noe more than he expected and in a little tyme after departed, but im̄ediately before his departure had some private discourse with Henry Walrond Senr Esqr and this depon^t findeing that her s^d daughter Grace Sylvester was noe wayes engaged to the s^d John Staples nor had any kindness for him, This dep^t did consent that the said Sir Henry Pickering should pursue his addresses to the s^d Grace her daughter which he did accordingly and hath obteyned the affections of her s^d daughter and there was and is an agreement made between them by and with the Consent of this dep^t and that order was and is given for drawing up writings and settling of a Joynture and preparation for the marriage between him the s^d Sir Henry Pickering and the s^d Grace to be solemnized before any ——— or Inhibition was served on the said Grace which was not served as she believeth untill the fourth of this Instant—December and upon designe (as this dep^t doth verily believe) by the s^d John Staples to gett some money or other sinister end. In witness whereof she hath hereunto sett her hand.

Grace Sylvester.

12 Decemb. 1685.   p' fata Gratia Sylvester ⎱
vidua jurat coram me,   Th° Exton. ⎰

Henry Walrond, Sen[r] also made a deposition similar to the above, and also adds that Staples in a private discourse with him said " he knew the Consent or promise made to him, was no such promise, as thereby to oblige her, meaning the s[d] Grace, to marry him, or to make null or void her marriage to any other person, but he could thereby putt a stopp, or hindrance if he pleased to her marriage with any other person and desired this deponent (Henry Walrond) to consider thereof."

Sir Henry Pickering was the only son of Sir Henry, the first Baronet, of Whaddon, co. Cambridge, by Elizabeth, daughter of Sir Thomas Vinor, 1st Baronet, Lord Mayor in 1653. He succeeded his father in 1667-8, and married first the daughter of Sir George Downing, Bart., of East Hatley, co. Cambridge; second, Grace Sylvester, by whom he had no children. He resided in Barbadoes, where he died in 1704-5. With him the Baronetcy became extinct.—G. D. SCULL, *of Oxford, England.*

ABSTRACT of the last Will and Testament of the most reverend Father in God Edmund Grindall, Archbishop of Canterbury, made 8 May, 1583, and proved 15 July, 1583.. All other wills revoked (except one bearing date 12 April, 1583). My body to be buried in the choir of the parish church of Croydon, without any solemn hearse or funeral pomp. To her Majesty the Queen the New Testament in Greek of Stephanas his impression. To my next successor the pictures of Archbishop Warham and of Erasmus and all such instruments of music and other implements as were bequeathed and left unto me by my predecessor that last was. To Lord Burghley, the Lord High Treasurer of England that my standing cup which her Majesty gave unto me at New Years Tide last before the date hereof. And I make him supervisor, &c. (Gifts to sundry other legatees.) To my faithful friend M[r] Nowell, Dean of Paul's, my ambling gelding called Gray Olyphant. To the poor of the town and the lower part of the parish of S[t] Beghes ; to the use of the parish church of S[t] Beghes. To M[r] Doctor Gybson. To William Woodhall, my nephew (*inter alia*), " my blacke straye nagg called Nixe." To Mr. Wilson my chaplain (certain books) and the advowson of the parsonage of Wonston in the diocese of Winchester if it shall fall void in his life time; if not, then to M[r] Robinson, now provost of Queen's College, Oxford. To my nieces Mabell, Anne, Barbara and Frances, the daughters of Robert Grindall, my brother. To my nieces Dorothy, Katherine, Elizabeth and Isabell, the daughters of Elizabeth Woodhall, my sister, late deceased (fifty pounds to each). To the children of Mabel, daughter of my sister, fifty pounds, to be divided amongst them at the discretion of William Woodhall, their uncle. To my niece Woodhall a bowl. To my niece Isabell Wilson, one other bowl, double gilt, without a cover. To Edmond Woodhall, my godson. To my niece Frances Younge, widow. To John Scott, Esq., steward of my household. To my servant William Grindall, my servant William Hales (and other servants named). To John Sharpe. To my loving friend master Thomas Eaton and his wife. To M[r] William Strycland, M[r] Atherton, John Browne, fellow of Pembroke Hall, Cambridge, M[r] Redman, Archdeacon of Canterbury.

I ordain & constitute William Redman, Archdeacon of Canterbury, John Scott, Esq., Steward of my Household, and William Woodhall, my nephew, executors.

Clause, referring to a Free Grammar School, to be founded in St. Beghes in the county of Cumberland, blotted, and " stroken" out 3 July, 1583. about 11 A. M.

A codicil bequeathing to Mr Redman, Archdeacon, &c., all his antique coins of the Roman Emperors. To Mr Wilson, his chaplain, his watch. He did forgive his niece Ann Dacres, widow, &c. &c. Rowe, 39.

Sñia pro allocacõe cõmpi bonorum Reuřendissimi prīs Edī Grindall nup Caut Archipi defti—in judicio inter Alexandru Willson Mariam Willson et Aliciam Willson nepotes ex sorore dc̃i defuncti partem hmõi negotiũ promoveñ ex una et Johannem Scott Armigerum executorem superstitem testamenti siue ultime voluntatis dc̃i defuncti partem contra quam hm̃oi negotium promovetur necnon Mabillam Windor ffranciscum Dacres Elenam Dacres Dorotheam Dacres aĩs —— Barbaram Raper ffranciscam Latus-Johēm Wilkenson Robertum Wilkenson Dorotheam Bowman Dorotheam Willson Johannem Gibson Thomam Gibson Edmundum Willson Willum Willson Johannem Willson Thomam Willson Mariam Willson Mariam Sheafe et Isabellam Willson proximos consanguineos dc̃i defuncti in specie ac omnes et singulos alios jus titulum aut Interesse in bonis dicti defuncti habeñ aut pretendeñ in genere ad videndum compūm dc̃i defuncti exhiberi et in debita Juris forma iustificari ltm̃e citāt etc. etc.

Lecta lata et promulgata fuit hec sñia diffinitiua etc Tertia sessione Termini Pasche die Jovis decimo octauo vizt die menss Maii Anno Domini millesimo sexcentesimo nono. Dorset, 60.

[This celebrated puritan Archbishop, the son of William Grindall, was born at St. Bees, in the County of Cumberland, in 1519. He was fellow, president and master of Pembroke Hall, Cambridge, and filled successively the Sees of London, York and Canterbury. He died July 6, 1583, and was buried in the chancel of Croyden church, where are his monument and epitaph. The free school of St. Bees was incorporated by Queen Elizabeth in the name of Edmund Grindall, Archbishop of Canterbury, and the school and master's house were built by his executors. The founder's donation was fifty pounds a year, twenty pounds whereof he appointed to be paid to the master of Pembroke Hall, Cambridge. By the foundation the master of the school is to be a native of Cumberland, Westmoreland, Yorkshire, or Lancashire, and is to be nominated by the Provost of Queen's College, Oxford. King James I. augmented this foundation. Lord Bacon says he was the gravest and greatest prelate of the land. (Hutchinson's His. of Cumberland.)—THOMAS MINNS.]

JAMES WOODHALL of Walden in the county of Essex, yeoman, 21 February "in ye thirtith yere of the raigne of oure Soueraigne Ladie Elizabeth," &c., proved 30 June, 1601. My body to be buried at the discretion of my executor. To William Woodhall, my son-in-law and Mary his wife, my daughter, all my lands and tenements, both free and copy hold lying within the parish church of Littlebury in the county of Essex, and to their heirs forever, "in consideration of ye great kindness which I have found in him towards me and for a Remuneration of his fatherly goodnes and charges and benevolence bestowed upon the children of William Bird deceased, his said wyves late husband." To the same all that my messuage wherein I now dwell, situate in Walden aforesaid, in a street there commonly called Threshwell hundred, &c., two acres I bought of William Pumfrett, two parcels I bought of Thomas Crofte, one and a half acre of land lying between the land I bought of Thomas Crofte and the lands of George Nicholls Esq., two acres of land in Windmill lane which I lately bought of John Crofte, two and a half acres of land I bought of Richard Chapman, lying on Windmill Hill, &c., and my two houses in Duck Street, in the parish of Walden, (one) now in the tenure of Richard Austen, the other late in the tenure of Davy Hodson. James Woodhall, eldest son of the said William Woodhall, my godson, Edmond Woodhall (second son) and William Woodhall (third son). Certain land at the Sandpits, next the land lately Richard Plommers. Land near William Shelford, land near Thomas Howard, bought of William Bowling. To William Bird and George Bird, sons of my daughter Mary. To Mary Bird, one of the daughters of my said daughter and now the wife of John Kyng, clerk and canon of Windsor. To Debora Woodhall, a daughter of William and Mary Woodhall and every of the other sons and daughters of the said William and Mary, viz. Elizabeth, Mary, Edmond, Dorothy, Jane, Katherine and Johane Woodhall. Whereas Johane my wife, after my marriage had with her, did faithfully promise that she would not claim any title of dower, &c. To Robert Nicholls, her son, and to James, her son, and Henry, her son. William Bird, my daughter's eldest son, to be the overseer of this my will.

The testator's signature was Jamys Woodhall. The witnesses were William Willson, clerk, John Kyng, clerk, and James Crofte Not. Publique.

In a codicil, made 29 August, 1596, referring to his wife's dowry and the bequests to Robert, James and Henry Nicholls, her sons, and to the children of William Woodhall of Walden Esq., his son-in-law and daughter Mary his wife, we learn that " synce that tyme it hath pleased god to blesse hym with one sonne more named Grindall Woodhall," &c. The witnesses to this codicil were William Bird, George Bird, John Sharpe, Robert Longe No. Pub., William Lawe and Josaphat Webbe.

In another codicil, bearing date 22 March, 1598, he makes bequests to his wife and to the poor of Walden. The witnesses to this were George Bird, Thomas Bird, William Burroughs, John Sharpe and John Rice.

Woodhall, 1.

WILLIAM WOODHALL, of Walden in the County of Essex Esq., 30 May First of James, proved 29 November, 1604. To be buried in the parish church of Walden, either on the North side of the church in a place where I appointed or else by my father-in-law and my son James, at the discretion of my executor.

" Nowe whereas my wife and I haue bin mareyed this foure and thirtie yeres and I haue had nott onely by her many children but alsoe haue founde her a moste kinde and loving wief I should farr forget myself if I should nott soe prouide for her as she may haue sufficient," &c. &c. I leave unto my said wife, according to her father's will all such lands as he hath bequeathed unto her, lying either in the parish of Walden or Lytlebury. To John, Archbishop of Canterbury (certain bequests) humbly beseeching his Grace to be good and favorable to my son Edmund whom I leave behind me to succeed in my office. To loving cousin Doctor Duñ, Mr of the Requests and Dean of the Arches. To my dear and faithful brother Mr William Wilson. To Doctor Birde and Michael Woodcock (spoken of in another place as "son Woodcock"). " I had a purpose to bestow my sonne William Woodhall either at the study of the common lawe or at the Universitie of Oxforde; but pceiving his tabackicall humor I see he hath nott anie minde either to the one or to the other, And therefore for anythinge I see he must be a souldyer or servingman both places commendable for a younge man especially if he may haue a pipe of tobacco. And to that ende least a farther inconvenience mighte followe for his better maintenaunce I giue unto the said William the place wherein Thomas Lynne was," &c. &c. " Nephew John Wilkinson now in London," referred to.—" Son Grindall Woodhall to be an apprentice either with a mercht Venturer or some other good trade." My three eldest daughters, Debora Calton, William Burroe and Michael Woodcock. My four other daughters, Mary, Jane, Katharine and Jone Woodhall.

" Memorandum that on Thursday being Ascenĉôn day and the second daie of June 1603 betweene the howers of seauen and eight in the fore-noone the testator within named lieing in his bed in his chamber within Mr Chayre's house in Pawles church-yarde London did with his owne hande subscribe his name to every leafe of this Will being fiue in nomber," &c.

The witnesses were Jo: Lawe not. pub., William Birde, Antho: Calton, George Birde, Rich. Theker, Christopher Yowle, Robert Longe, William Cooke and Timothy Paget. Harte, 86.

[The following pedigree from Harleian MS., 1541, fol. 55, in the British Museum, shows the connection between Archbishop Grindall and the Woodhalls, whose wills follow his :

John Woodhall of Ullock= in Com. Cumberland.

John Woodhall=Jennett, d. of Thomas Woodhall=Joane, d. of .... Longdale. .... Crakeplace.

John* Woodhall = Elizabeth, da. of Wm. Grindall and sister of Edmond of Walden in Essex. Grindall, Archbishop of Canterbury

William Woodhall=Mary, da. of James Woodhall=William Byrd of Walden in Essex. son of Jas. Woodhall of Cockes- 1 Husband more in Com. Cumberland. vide London.

Debora ux^r Elizabeth Mary ux. Dorothy† Katherine Joanne Anthony ux. William Tho. Harrison Jane ux. .... Barley ob. s.p. Calton Burrows of Wickhambroke in Com. Suff.

Edmond Woodhall=Margaret dau. of William James Grindall of Walden in Essex .... Law. ob. s.p. ob. s.p. ob. s.p.

Edmond John Mary ux. Penelope ux. Thos. Goade John Gibson of Crake D^r of Civil Law. Welborne in Com. York.

—H. F. W.

In Lipscomb's County of Buckingham is an interesting account, tracing one branch of the Woodhall family from Walter De Flanders, Lord of Wahal, alias Woodhal, 20 William the Conqueror, and giving the coat of arms.

In the Chapel of Eton College is a Latin inscription in memory of " Jane Goad dau. of Edmund Woodhall aged 34 1657 the mother of 3 sons & 2 daughters." (v. iv. p. 312,486.)

In the church of Walden in Essex, are epitaphs of the following persons : James Woodhall, Assistant and Treasurer, died 1529 ; William Woodhall, Esq., Register of the Prerogative Court of Canterbury, died 1603 ; Mary, daughter of James Wood-hall, first wife to William Byrd, afterwards married to William Woodhall. She died 1613. William Byrde, Gent., d. 1568. (Salmon, His. of Essex, p. 142.)—T. M.

I have a conviction that the Birds mentioned in the abstracts of the wills of the Woodhalls *et al.*, were of the same lineage of William Byrd, of " Westover,"

* Willm Woodhall had evidently been written first, in the same ink as the rest of the pedigree, and John Woodhall written over this in blacker ink.—H. F. W.
† Dorothy became the wife of Michael Woodcock. (See Cussans' Herts, vol. ii. p. 149.' H. F. W.

James River, Va., whose parents were John and Grace (Stagg, or Stegge) Byrd, (or Bird, or Birde), of London. The christian names John, Thomas and William, appear to be favored ones in his pedigree. William Byrd, the first of the name in Virginia, came thither a youth as the heir of large landed estates of his maternal uncle Colonel Thomas Stegge (as he wrote it), whose will is dated 31st March, 1690, and it is presumed that Byrd arrived in the latter part of the year. If the arms are given of the Bird legatees under the Woodhall wills, the family identification would be of easy solution.—R. A. BROCK.]

EDMUND WOODHALL, Esq. Registrar of the Prerogative Court of Canterbury, 25 January, 1638, proved 3 February, 1638. My body to be decently interred, near the bodies of my two wives, in the "Ile" belonging to me in the church of Little Munden in the county of Hartford, "there to sleep free from further molestaĉon till it be awaked at the last day by the Angels trumpe with a Surge—Arise thou that sleepest & come to Judgment." I will that the like monument be there erected for me as I did set up for my father in the church of Walden, but my desire is that my funeral may be without any great cost, my will & meaning being that only my children and two sons in law have mourning provided for them; the charges of my funeral not to exceed fifty pounds. My two eldest daughters, Mary Goad, now wife of Thomas Goad, Doctor of Laws, and Dame Penelope Gibson, the now wife of Sir John Gibson the younger, Knight. To Bridget Woodhall, my third daughter, one thousand pounds and to Jane Woodhall, my youngest daughter, the like sum, at four & twenty years of age or day of marriage. Son Edmond and son John (who appears to be at King's College, Cambridge). Brother-in-law Alexander Southwood, gentleman. Brother mr. Michael Woodcock. Cousins and friends Nicholas Hawes Esq. and John Wilkinson gentleman.

" And soe Lord Jesu come quickly."   Harvey, 20.

WILLIAM WILSON, Canon of St. George's Chapel, Windsor Castle, 23 August, 1613, proved 27 May, 1615. To be buried in the chapel near the place where the body of my dear father lies. If I die at Rochester or Cliff, in the County of Kent, then to be buried in the cathedral church of Rochester, near the bodies of wives Isabel and Anne. To my cousin Collins, prebendary at Rochester. To the Fellows and Scholars of Martin College, Oxford. My three sons Edmond, John and Thomas Wilson, daughter Isabel Guibs and daughter Margaret Rawson. My goddaughter Margaret Somers which my son Somers had by my daughter Elizabeth, his late wife. To my god-son William Sheafe, at the age of twenty one years. Son Edmond, a fellow of King's College, Cambridge, eldest son of me, the said William. To son John the lease of the Rectory and Parsonage of Caxton in the County of Cambridge, which I have taken in his name. To Thomas Wilson, my third son. Son Edmond to be executor and Mr Erasmus Webb, my brother-in-law, being one of the Canons of St. George's Chapel, and my brother, Mr Thomas Woodward, being steward of the town of New Windsor, to be overseers.

The witnesses were Thomas Woodwarde, Joh. Woodwarde, Robert Lowe & Thomas Holl.

In a codicil, dated 9 May, 1615, wherein he is styled William Wilson Doctor of Divinity, he directs his son Edmond to give to his son John forty pounds and to his wife forty marks, he gives to Lincoln College Oxford ten pounds towards a Library, and mentions son-in-law Mr Doctor Sheafe and daughter Gibbes. To this Thomas Sheafe was a witness, amongst others.

In another codicil, of 12 May, 1615, he says, I have provided for the husband of my daughter Isabel Gibbes a place in Windsor, in reversion, of some worth. His signature to this codicil was witnessed by David Rawson and William Newman.

Rudd, 36.

[Rev. William Wilson, D.D., of Merton College, Oxford, was also a prebendary of St. Paul's and Rochester cathedrals, and held the rectory of Cliffe, in the county of Kent. In 1584 he became canon of Windsor in place of Dr. Will. Wickham promoted to the see of Lincoln, being about that time chaplain to Edmund (Grindall), Archbishop of Canterbury. He married Isabel Woodhall, daughter of John and Elizabeth Woodhall of Walden in Essex, and niece of Archbishop Grindall. He was buried in St. George's Chapel, Windsor Castle, near the body of his father, William Wilson, late of Wellsbourne, in Lincolnshire, Gent.

His eldest son, Edmund Wilson, M.D., of London, gave the infant colony of Massachusetts one thousand pounds sterling about 1633, which was invested in arms and ammunition. See Mass. Colonial Records, v. 1, p. 128, and 2d Mass. Hist. Soc. Collections, v. 8, p. 228.

His second son, Rev. John Wilson, of Christ's College, Cambridge, married Elizabeth, daughter of Sir John Mansfield and sister of the wife of Mr. Robert Keayne, the first commander of the Artillery Company of Massachusetts, and in 1630 accompanied Winthrop's company to New England, and became the first minister of the First Church in Boston, dying in office in 1667. For a fuller account of him, see Mather's Magnalia, vol. ii. p. 275. For his will, see REGISTER, vol. xvii. p. 343–4.

His daughter Margaret married for her first husband David Rawson, of London, and was the mother of Edward Rawson, secretary of the Massachusetts Colony from 1650 to 1686. For her second husband she married William Taylor. For a further account of them, see the Taylor Family, prepared by the late Col. Chester for Mr. P. A. Taylor.—T. M.

Since these abstracts were in type, the editor has received from Mr. Waters abstracts of the wills of Edmund Wilson, M.D., of William Taylor his brother-in-law, and of William Taylor, son of the latter. They will appear in another number.—EDITOR.

The following notes, taken from the History and Antiquities of Berkshire, by Elias Ashmole, Esq. (Reading, 1736), give the inscriptions found by that famous antiquary in the Chapel of St. George, Windsor Castle, relating to this family.

On the North Side lies a Grave-stone, on which, in Brass Plates, is the Figure of a Man, and this Inscription.

To me to live is Christ, and to dye is Gain.
Philip. I. 21.

Here underneath lies interr'd the Body of William Wilson, *Doctour of Divinitie, and Prebendarie of this Church by the space of* 32 *yeares. He had Issue by* Isabell *his Wife six sons and six daughters. He dy'd the* 15th *of May, in the Year of our Lord* 1615, *of his Age the* 73. *beloved of all in his Life, much lamented in his Death.*

> *Who thinke of Deathe in Lyfe, can never dye,*
> *But mount through Faith, from Earth to heavenly Pleasure,*
> *Weep then no more, though here his Body lye,*
> *His Soul's possest of never ending Treasure.*

On another small Brass Plate, on the same Grave-stone, is the following Inscription.

Neere unto this Place lyes buried William Willson, *the third Son, Who, after a long Trial of grievous Sickness, did comfortably yield up his Spirit in the Yeare of our Lord* 1610. *of his Age* 23.

Pp. 305–306.

On a Brass Plate, on a Grave-Stone Northward of the last,* is this Inscription.

William Wilson, *late of* Wellsbourne, *in the County of* Lincolne, *Gent. departed this Lyfe, within the Castle of* Windsor, *in the Yeare of our Lord* 1587. *the* 27th *Day of August, and lyeth buried in this Place.*

P. 309.

---

* The "last" monument referred to is a white marble monument erected to the memory of Henry Somerset, Duke of Beaufort, at the east end of a small chapel, dedicated to the Virgin Mary, in the south-west corner of the church.

Arms of " Will'm Wilsonn, of Welborne, per Norroy flower, 1586."

Per pale argent and azure three lions' gambs barways, erased and counterchanged.
Crest :—*A lion's head erased argent guttée de sang.*

Harleian Coll., No. 1550, Fol. 192, British Museum ; Richard Mundy's
copy of the Visitations of Lincolnshire, 1564 and 1592.

—H. F. W.]

JOHN WILKINSON, of London, gentleman, 3 May, 1614, acknowledged
27 May, 1628; acknowledged again 18 June, 1634; with three codicils,
dated respectively 18 June, 1634, 11 October, 1638, and 21 March, 1638 ;
proved 12 September, 1639. To my brother Robert Wilkinson the land
whereon he now dwelleth, at Preston Howes, pish of St. Bees, in the county of Cumberland. Sister Jeane Pyper, wife of William Pyper, mariner.
Sister Mary Wilkinson and brothers Henry and James Wilkinson.
" I do give and bequeath unto the Right Worshipfull my loving uncle
William Wilson, Doctor of ˙ Divinity, five pounds, and to every one of my
loving cosens, his children, twenty shillings apiece." To my loving uncle
Henry Bowman and every one of his children by my aunt, the right Worshipful, the lady Margaret Gibson, my good Aunt, &c. The right Worshipful Sir John Gibson, Knight, my loving cousin, and his now wife and
virtuous lady, the lady Anne Gibson. My cousin Thomas Gibson and his
brother Edward Gibson. The right Worshipful my loving kinsman William Byrd, Doctor of the civil laws. My loving kinsman Mr Thomas Byrd,
his brother. My loving kinsman Mr George Byrd. My loving cousin Mrs
Elizabeth Burroes and every one of her children. My loving cousin Mrs
Dorothy Woodcocke, wife of Mr Michael Woodcocke, and every one of her
children. My loving cousin Mrs Jane Warren, wife of Francis Warren.
My loving cousin Katherine Barley. My loving cousin Mr William Woodhall. My loving cousin Grindall Woodhall. My dear and loving cousin
Edmund Woodhall Esq. & my loving cousin his wife, and his two daughters, Mary & Penelope Woodhall. Mr John Law, Actuary, and Mrs Ann
Law, his wife. My loving friend John Sharpe of Walden. My cousin
Robert Wilkinson, of Everdale, in the county of Cumberland. The poor
of Preston Howes, where I was born. My loving cousins Mary Wilson
and Aylce Wilson. Michael, Anthony and George Calton, sons of my
cousin Debora Calton deceased. Edmond Calton, another son, when master
of arts.
    In the first codicil he mentions his friend & kinsman Mr William Wil-
kinson, mercer in Pater Noster Row, cousin Mrs Grace Pyne, Jane Warren, deceased, and the children of brother Edward Bowens. Friend William Sharpe and his three sisters. To Ralph Brownerigg, Doctor in Divinity, a seal ring of gold. Nephew John Wilkinson goldsmith of London,
son of brother James. The children of my sister Mary Bowen. My cousin Alice Swallowe and her husband Mr Thomas Swallowe, my cousin.
Others mentioned.   Harvey, 151.

    Dame MARY ROWE, widow of Sir Thomas Row, Knight, late citizen
and alderman of London (and evidently a sister of William Gresham deceased and of Edmond Gresham), by her will of 21 March, 1579, proved
in the year 1582–3, bequeathed to William Wilsonn, parson of Cliff, als
Clyve, in Kent, a ring of gold, of three pounds or three pounds in money,
and to his wife a ring of gold or its equivalent in money.   Rowe, 1.

EDWARD RAWSON, of Colbrooke, in the parish of Langley Marris, in the County of Buckingham, mercer, 16 February, 1603, proved 4 May. 1604. To my wife Bridget Rawson for and during her natural life, my house and tenement and the appurtenances, &c. lying in Colbrooke, now in the occupation of Edward Whitlock, and, after her decease, unto David Rawson my son and to the heirs male of his body lawfully begotten; and, for want of such issue, unto Henrie Rawson, my eldest son, & to the heirs male of his body lawfully begotten; and, failing such issue, to the right heirs of me, the said Edward, for ever. To son Henry all that house called the "Draggon" and the two shops thereunto adjoining, lying and being in Colbrooke aforesaid, and to his heirs male, &c., with remainder to son David & his lawful issue, &c.; and failing such issue, unto Raphe Warde, my brother-in-law and his heirs for ever. To the said David Rawson, my son, the sum of two hundred pounds at his full age of one and twenty years. Henry Rawson, also a minor. My executors, at their costs and charge, shall bring up my said son David in some reasonable learning until he may be fitt to be putt to apprentice unto some good trade or mystery. My brother Henry Rawson doth owe me fifty pounds.

Wife Bridgett and son Henry to be executors, and friends John Bowser, gentleman, Raph Warde, Philip Bowreman and George Charley to be overseers. Harte, 40.

DAVID RAWSON, citizen and merchant tailor of London, a most unworthy servant of Jesus Christ, 15 June, 1616, proved by his widow Margaret Rawson 25 February, 1617. My goods, &c. shall be divided into three equal & just parts and portions according to the laudable custom of this honorable city of London. One of the three parts to Margaret Rawson, my loving & well-beloved wife. One other part to William and Edward Rawson and such other child or children as I shall hereafter have or as my wife shall be with child withall at the time of my decease, to be equally divided amongst them all, part and part alike. The other third part I reserve towards the payment of legacies, gifts and bequests, &c. To William Rawson, my eldest son, a double gilt salt and a standing cup with a cover, double gilt, and half a dozen of Postle spoons and two double gilt spoons, and a silver porringer, a silver spoon and a silver bowl. To Edward Rawson, my son, a great standing bowl, double gilt, and six silver spoons, and two double gilt spoons, "which was given him by those which were his witnesses at his christening," and a silver bowl. All the rest of the plate to my wife. To the relief of the poor of the Town of Colbrooke, in the County of Buckingham, where I was born, the sum of five pounds of lawful money of England, to be paid within one year next after my decease. To John Emery, son of John Emerie of Colbrooke, clark, deceased, five pounds, to be paid him on the day when he shall be made a freeman of the city of London. To William Fenner, a poor scholar in Pembroke Hall in Cambridge, five pounds within three years after my decease. To David Anngell, my godson, five pounds at the age of twenty one years. To John Nayle, the son of Nicholas Nayle, of Iver in the County of Buckingham, five pounds on the day he shall be made a freeman of the city of London, if he take good courses. To the poor people at my funeral the sum of forty shillings. To John Anngell, clothworker, forty pounds, & to Alexander Dubber, clothworker, forty shillings, which I will shall be deducted out of such money as they shall owe unto me at the time of my decease (if any be). Item, I give unto my godson Edward Rawson, the son of my brother Henry Rawson, the sum of ten pounds to be paid unto him at his age of twenty one years.

I give and bequeath to my dear mother, Bridget Woodward, the sum of ten pounds, which I desire her to give to Mr Winge and Mr Foxe, forty shillings apiece, if she so please. To my sister-in-law, Jone Rawson, the sum of forty shillings to make her a ring, and to my sister-in-law Isabel Gibbs the like sum of forty shillings to make her a ring, and to my sister-in-law, Elizabeth Wilson, the like sum of forty shillings to make her a ring; which said four legacies so given to my mother and three sisters I will shall be paid within one year next after my decease. Item, I do give & bequeath to my brother-in-law, Thomas Wilson, the sum of five pounds, to be paid within one year, &c.; and to Andrew Warde, son of my uncle Raphe Warde, the sum of five pounds, to be paid him at his age of twenty-one; and to my uncle John Warde the sum of forty shillings, if he be living at my decease. To my master, Mr Nathaniel Weston, the sum of forty shillings to make him a ring, and I desire him to be assisting to my executrix to help get in my debts. To Isabel Sheafe, daughter of Doctor Sheafe, three pounds, to be bestowed in a piece of plate and given her at her age of twenty one years or at the day of her marriage, which ever shall first happen. To my son Edward Rawson, over and above his said part, the sum of one hundred pounds; and to my apprentice Matthew Hunte, the sum of six pounds, thirteen shillings and four pence, to be paid unto him on the day he shall be made a freeman of the City of London; and to William Beard and John Samford, my apprentices (the like sums & on the like conditions).

If all my children die the portions shall remain & come to Alexander Rawson, the eldest son of my said brother Henry Rawson (if he be then living); but if he die then to John Rawson and Edward Rawson, two other of the children of my said brother, &c. equally. The Residue to wife Margaret and son William. I constitute my loving friends, Mr Thomas Woodward, of Lincoln's Inn, in the County of Middlesex, Esq., my father-in-law, my brother Henry Rawson and Edmond Wilson, Doctor of Physic, and John Wilson, master of Arts, my brothers-in-law, overseers and give them five pounds apiece. If wife should die then the above to be executors during the minority of my said sons William and Edward. The witnesses to this will were John Wilkinson & Arthur Viger scr.

In a codicil made 27 November, 1617, he bequeaths to daughter Dorothy Rawson, besides her (child's) portion, the sum of one hundred pounds at her age of twenty one or day of marriage; to sister Anne Wilson, the wife of brother Thomas Wilson, the sum of forty shillings; to uncle John Warde the sum of seven pounds, thirteen shillings and four pence and some of my cast apparell; to my cousin Elizabeth Glover the sum of twenty shillings; to cousin Jane Lawrence twenty shillings; to Isabel Cave twenty shillings; to Aunt Fenner ten shillings; to Mr Frogmorton forty shillings; to Mr. Houlte twenty shillings; to Mrs Jane Bartlett ten shillings; to Mrs Martin of Windsor ten shillings; to cousin Dorothy Sheafe a piece of plate of fifty three shillings price; all these legacies to be paid within one year and a half next after my decease by my executrix.

The witnesses to the codicil were John Wilkinson & John Hill.

Meade, 15.

[These wills carry the pedigree of Edward Rawson, secretary of the Massachusetts Colony from 1650 to 1686, back two generations. They give his father David

Rawson of London, and his grandfather Edward Rawson of Colebrook. For a memoir of Secretary Rawson, with a portrait, and a genealogy of his descendants, see REGISTER, vol. iii. pp. 201–8 and 297–330 ; also The Rawson Family, editions of 1849 and 1875.—EDITOR.

In Lipscomb's Buckingham is the following mention of the Rawson family. In 1540 Sir John Rawson is Grand Prior in Ireland of the Knights Hospitallers. Sir Michael Stanhope, Knt., knighted at Hampton Court, 37 Henry VIII., governor of Hull, &c., married Anne, daughter of Nic. Rawson, Esq., of Aveley, Essex. Ob. 20 Feb. 1587. The ancestress of the noble families of Earls Stanhope, Chesterfield and Harrington. Richard Rawson, LL.B., was presented rector of Beaconsfield, 26 July, 1525, by John Scudamore, Esq. He was Canon of Windsor and Archdeacon of Essex ; and rebuilt the parsonage here where his arms remained in 1728. He died 1543. James Rawson, inst. vicar of Wingrave, 8 August, 1508. Edward Rawson, inst. Rector of Hedsor, 13 May, 1664 ; also vicar of Wooburn. Edward Rawson, presented vicar of Wooburn, 5 Feb. 1662. John Rawson, presented vicar of Turville, 5 Dec. 1532. V. i. p. 265, 479 ; v. iii. p. 195, 536, 580, 637, 631. (See also Maskell's History of Allhallows Barking, in London, p. 47.)

The wife of Edward Rawson of Colebrooke, mother of David Rawson of London, and grandmother of Edward Rawson of Boston, Mass., married for her second husband Thomas Woodward of Lincoln's Inn.—T. M.]

WILLIAM RAWSON of the town of Northampton, Notary Publique, 4 May, 1603, proved 27 February, 1604. To be buried in S‎ᵗ Gyles church, Northampton, near to the door of the pew where I use to sit. To Joane Glover my sister ten shillings and to every one of her children ten shillings apiece which I will shall be paid to her husband to their uses ; and he shall have the use thereof until the said children accomplish the age of one and twenty years. To my brother Richard his children ten shillings apiece in same manner and form as is above rehearsed concerning my sister Glover's children. To Mary my eldest daughter, one "gymold Ringe " of gold, with a sharp diamond in it. To Elizabeth my daughter a little gold ring enamelled that the lady Cromwell gave her mother, with the poesie (*Decreui in aeternum*) in it, which rings are in the keeping of Martha now my wife. I will and charge these my said children to keep the said rings so long as they shall live in remembrance of their good mother, my late wife Francys. My children William, Mary, Thomas, Elizabeth and Timothy. To son James my greatest silver bowl; to William my second silver bowl ; to Thomas my best silver salt parcel gilt; to Timothy a stone pot garnished with silver double gilt and six silver spoons which I bought of Mᵣˢ Warde. My eldest daughter Mary. My three youngest children, Mary, Frances and Melior. My wife Martha, her father Christopher and mother Alice and brother Robert. My cousin William Ive. My brother-in-law Mʳ Francis Morgan of Kingsthorp. Son James to be executor. Hayes, 11.

[Although in the above will there is no direct reference to the family of Secretary Rawson, yet the mention of the names Glover and Warde has led me to save it foi printing. (See will of Secretary Rawson's father, who speaks of a cousin Glovei and of the Warde family.)—H. F. W.]

RICHARD PERNE, of Gillingham in the County of Dorset, Gentleman one or two days before his death. All to wife ; only my eldest son to have an eldest son's part. Wife to be executrix, and Mr. Edward Rawson and my uncle Foyle to be overseers. Sworn to 10 April, 1636, by Edward Rawson, Mary Perne and Jane Clark (by mark). Proved 17 May 1636, by Rachael Perne, widow, relict of the deceased. Pile, 59.

RACHEL PERNE of Gillingham in the County of Dorset, widow, 31 March, 1656, proved 13 November, 1656, by John Perne, son and executor. My body to be buried in the parish church of Gillingham. I am possessed of a living called Easthaimes in Gillingham, as by a lease bearing date 12 October, 12th of late King Charles, under the hand & seal of William, Lord Stowerton, for and during the term of four score and nineteen years, if I, the said Rachel, and Richard Perne and John Perne, my sons, or either of us, shall live so long; and am also possessed of the lawful right of a certain ground called Wagger and one other ground called Ramsleare, allowed and assigned unto me for & in lieu of the fee fostership; and of & in certain lands called Linches, by virtue of a lease and assignment to me made by John Tyse, clerk, for a long term of years, if William Bull, Thomas Bull and Joane Bull, sons & daughter of Edward Bull, shall so long live; and of two acres of mead in Combermeade, by virtue of a lease and other assurances to me made for divers years to come, which said two acres were heretofore the lands of one Augustine Matthew; and of one acre of allotment heretofore allowed and assigned to the said two acres, &c. in lieu of common upon the dissaforestation of the late forest of Gillingham; and of five acres of meadow or pasture upon the top of Bowridge Hill, now in the possession of Richard Gornish, baker, &c. All the above to John Tyse of Orcheston St. George in the County of Wilts, clerk, Simon Crocker, of Winterborne Stoake in said County of Wilts, clerk, and John Greene, of the parish of St. James in the said county of Dorset, gentleman, &c., upon the trust and to the intents following, that they shall permit and suffer my eldest son, Richard Perne, to take & receive the rents, &c. for so long time as he shall live; and after his death, &c. such woman as shall be his wife at the time of his death, so long as she shall live; then the child or children or grandchild or grandchildren of the said Richard Perne; In default of such then John Perne (in the same way). I give to the said Richard Perne half my plate and half my household stuff and half my bacon and half my cheese in my house at Easthaimes and half my stock of bees there in my beefold or garden at Easthaimes and all my timber and wood at Easthaimes, except the two woodpiles abutting against the great meade there at Easthaimes and one of my cheese steanes and all my doors with their locks and keys, loose boards, "gice" planks, about or belonging to my said house of Easthaimes, ———— my biggest white mare and great colt and all the panes of glass about or upon my windows of my house at Easthaimes. To John Perne (certain property similar to a portion of the above) and also my lease which my husband took of Mr William Whittaker the elder deceased, with all my right and title in the same. To my son-in-law John Tyse one shilling.

"Also I give and bequeath unto my sonne in Lawe Edward Rawson one shilling." To daughter Marie Tyse thirty pounds and the goods that I formerly delivered to my said daughter which are now in her house at Orcheston St. Georges aforesaid. "Also I give and bequeath unto my daughter Rachell Rawson the summe of ffortie pounds of lawfull monie of England to be paid at Mr Webb's house in London unto such friend as my daughter Rachell Rawson shall nominate or appoint to receive it for her." To grandchildren John Tyse and Mary Tyse, ten shillings each, to daughter Rachell Rawson's children the sum of ten pounds to be divided among them according to the discretion of my said daughter,—& likewise to be paid at Mr Webb's house aforesaid. To my brother Peter Greene twenty shillings to buy him a ring, to sister Anne Stagg, six pounds, to be paid by forty shillings yearly, to Marie Tyse my great bible, to maid servants Alice Clemont, Anne Frippe and Margerie Bateman, to the minister or the curate of the parish & to the poor of the parish. Son John Perne to be sole executor.

The witnesses were Richard Perne, Mary Tyse, John Hiscock (by mark), Alice Clement (by mark) and Anne Fripp (by mark).

Berkley, 405.

[It seems probable from the following pedigree of Stagg of Little Hinton, printed in Hutchins's Hist. of Dorset, vol. i. p. 55, from the visitation book 1623, that the maiden name of Rachel Perne was Green.

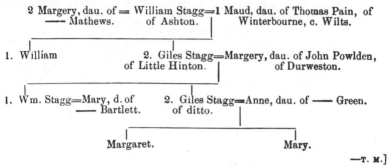

2 Margery, dau. of = William Stagg=1 Maud, dau. of Thomas Pain, of
—— Mathews.   of Ashton.   Winterbourne, c. Wilts.

1. William   2. Giles Stagg=Margery, dau. of John Powlden,
                              of Little Hinton.   of Durweston.

1. Wm. Stagg=Mary, d. of   2. Giles Stagg=Anne, dau. of —— Green.
    —— Bartlett.   of ditto.

Margaret.   Mary.

—T. M.]

Sir HENRY LELLO of Ashdon in the County of Essex, Knight, 7 January, 1629, proved 18 January, 1629. To be buried in the church of St. Brides als Bridgett, London, in the " Isle " of the said church where my predecessors, Wardens of the Fleet, have been buried, if I depart this life in London. If in Ashdon, then in the parish church there. I do give and bequeath to my most Honble and loving friends the gifts, sums and bequests hereafter named. To the Right Honorable Thomas, Lord Coventrie, Lord Keeper of the Great Seal of England, my great Beaserstone. To my loving friend, Dr William Paske, twenty nobles. To Mr John Eldred the elder twenty pounds. To Mr Binge five pounds. To Mr James Ingram twenty pounds and also, as a token of my love to him, my " cristall cabonite," lying now in a chest in the fleet, for his great respect and good service done unto me and in hope of his future care of the place for my executor. To Mr Robert Bailey twenty pounds. To my brother in law Edmund (sic) Hopkins twenty pounds. To my kinsman Cuthbert Macklyn twenty pounds, to his wife five pounds and to his son Henry five pounds. To the said Cuthbert Macklyn the office of Chamberlain of the Fleet during his life, with this direction that who shall execute the clerk's place shall be in the nomination of my very loving friend Mr James Ingram and my executor, because it shall be well executed. To John Lello, my godson and kinsman, twenty pounds at his setting up of shop to begin his trade. To the servants at Ashdon. To the poor of Clenton, where I was born, ten pounds. To the poor of Ashdon, if I die there, five pounds. To Abigail and Margaret, my sister Hopkins' daughters, two hundred pounds apiece, and to Patience and Judith, other two of her daughters, which are already preferred by me in marriage, to Patience one hundred pounds and to Judith fifty pounds. To Edward Hopkins, my nephew, all my adventure in the East India Company. And whereas I have already given him four hundred pounds for which I am indebted and stand bound for the payment thereof unto Benjamin Eldred, if before my decease I shall not have paid and discharged the same then I do ordain my executor to pay it or so much as shall be unpaid at my decease.

I give unto my sister Katherine Hopkins, the wife of Edward (*sic*) Hopkins, all my lands, tenements and hereditaments in Clenton and Clun in the County of Salop, during her natural life, and, after her decease, to Matthew Hopkins her son, to him and his heirs forever. Further, whereas I and John Eldred aforenamed purchased the Fleet and keeping the Palace of Westminster jointly, to us and our heirs forever, since which said purchase the said John Eldred, for and in consideration of the sum of eight thousand pounds, &c. &c. hath released all his right, title and interest of the said office and keeping of the Palace of Westminster to me and my heirs forever, and for non-payment of the said eight thousand pounds at the several times aforementioned I have made to him a lease for three score and ten years, as by the said lease doth likewise appear, whereof the " counterpaine " is amongst my writings, now for the payment of the said sum of eight thousand pounds, as all my debts and legacies, I do ordain and appoint Henry Hopkins, my nephew, whom I do make my sole executor, to see paid and discharged. In consideration whereof and for the due accomplishment of the same I do give and bequeath unto the said Henry all that my manor or capital messuage called the Fleet, otherwise " the King's Gaole of the Fleete," situate in the parish of St. Brides London, with the office of " Boarden of the Fleete," &c. &c., and also the keeping of the Palace of Westminster, called the old and new Palace, with the benefits and rents of the shops and stalls in Westminster Hall and without &c. &c., in as large and ample manner as I and M[r] Eldred had and purchased the same from Sir Robert Tirrell, Knight. Also I give unto the said Henry Hopkins my farm or messuage of Thickho, in the County of Essex, and all my lands, tenements and hereditaments belonging to the same, &c. ; provided that if the said Henry Hopkins do sell the office of the Warden of the Fleet, for the performance of this my last will and follow not the course I have by the same set down then I do, by this my will, appoint him to pay out of the said purchase money to his brother Edward Hopkins two hundred pounds, to his brother Matthew Hopkins two hundred pounds and to every one of his four sisters before named one hundred and fifty pounds apiece. I advise him to continue the execution of the office in M[r] James Ingram, &c. &c., because he is a sufficient and able man for the place, well acquainted therewith and one that I have always found very honest and most ready to do me any service for the good of the office.

Bequests are made to the poor of St. Brides, to my servant Robert Freeman, my loving friend James Weston Esq., my loving friend Sir Paul Pindor, Knight, to M[r] John Eldred's son Nathaniel, my godson, to my servant John Lightborne, and his son, my godson, to the children of Josias Piggott, to my kinsman Willowe Eve and to his wife Judith, my niece.

The witnesses were Robert Holmes, Edward Hopkins and Virgill Reynolds.   Scroope, 6.

HENRY HOPKINS, Esq[r]. Warden of the Fleet, 30 December, 1654, proved 24 January, 1654, by Edward Hopkins, brother and sole executor.

I desire to lie in my own ground in S[t] Bride's church, near my uncle and predecessor Sir Henry Lello, if I expire in London or near thereunto ; to which parish I give & bequeath five pounds if I be buried there. Of my temporal estate,——first, because there is the greatest need, I give and bequeath to my sister Judith Eve thirty pounds per annum, with that stock I have at Ashdon and household, provided that none of it may come into her husband's hands but be disposed of for her own subsistence. I will that my executor defray the charges of the commencement of our nephew Henry Dalley at Cambridge and allow him some competent means for his subsistence until he obtain some preferment there or abroad. I will that my executor take special care of our dear sister Margaret Tompson and her two children, with two more of sister Dally's, according as the estate will arise to and according to their several deserts, which are very different, and so are their necessities. And this I reserve the rather to him because he is equally related with me unto them all. To master James Jackson, fellow of Clare, that ten pounds which his brother, master Richard Jackson, oweth me and all that household stuff he possesseth of mine in Clare Hall. I give unto Henry Hopkins, now at Barbadoes, ten pounds ; unto my godson William Hall, the son of William Hall at Lackford, one silver tankard which is now in my possession at the Fleet. To my loving friends Doctor Thomas Paske, master James Ingram, Doctor John Exton, Doctor William Turner, Dr Robert King, Doctor John Leonard, Doctor Cornelius Laurence, Master William Hall of Lackford, Master John Sicklemore, Master Charles Jones, Master John Fifield, Master Charles Bushie, Master Jackson, Master Peele, Master Moungague (*sic*) Newse and Master Wilson, fellows of Clare Hall, Master Thomas Hall of the Exchequer, Master Thomas Rivett, Master Thomas Newcomen, Master Cutbert Macklin, Master Henry Walthew, to each of them a ring of thirty shillings price, with this motto inscribed—*Præ eo non pereo.* The like I give to my loving cousins, Mr John Harris of Elton, Master Edward Mathewes of Burraton and my brother, Master William Lowe of Hereford. To the poor of the parish of Elton, where I was born, ten pounds, to be disposed of at the discretion of my executor and my cousin John Harris. To my servant Richard Walker five pounds and I will that my executor continue him in the place of Tipstaff of the Exchequer as long as he behaves himself well. To my servant Matthew Pitt the place he now holds of Tipstaff in the Common Please, during his good behavior, and ten pounds in money, with all my wearing clothes & do commend him to the care of my executor as judging him very fit his employment here as long as he continue it. I give unto Thomas Lell the son of Thomas Lello, draper, ten pounds ; unto Mistress Bridget Exton, the daughter of my most loving friend, my crimson damask canopy and my best crimson quilt.

I do make and constitute my dear and loving brother Edward Hopkins, merchant, sole executor, &c.; and to my said executor all that office of Warden of the Fleet and Keeper of the Palace of Westminster in as ample a manner as I had it from my uncle Sir Henry Lello, Knight. To my said brother and executor all that my farm of Thickho, in the parish of Ashdon, to him and his heirs forever——and all else, &c. &c.

Henry Hopkins.

" There haue bin many interlinings but all of my owne hand."

H. Hopkins.

The witnesses were William Ball, Henry Nevill and John Milett.

Aylett, 41.

EDWARD HOPKINS, esquire, at his house in London, 7 March, 1657, proved 30 April, 1657, by Henry Dalley, nephew and sole executor. If any debts shall appear to be due in New England that they be paid out of my estate there. As for the estate I have in New England (the full accompt of which I left clear in my books there, and the care and inspection whereof was committed to my loving friend Capt. John Culleck) I do in this manner dispose. To eldest child of Mrs Mary Newton, wife of Mr Roger Newton of Farmington and daughter of Mr Thomas Hooker deceased, thirty pounds; and also thirty pounds to eldest child of Mr John Culleck by Elizabeth, his present wife. To Mrs. Sarah Wilson, the wife of Mr John Wilson, preacher of the gospel, and daughter of my dear pastor, Mr Hooker, my farm at Farmington, &c. To Mrs Susan Hooker, the relict of Mr Thomas Hooker, all such debts as are due to me from her upon the Account I left in New England. The residue of my estate to my father, Theophilus Eaton, Esq., Mr John Davenport, Mr John Culleck and Mr Goodwyn, in trust, &c.—to give some encouragement in those foreign plantations for the breeding up of hopeful youths in a way of learning, both at the Grammar School and College, for the public service of the country in future times.

Of the estate in England one hundred & fifty pounds per annum to be paid to Mr David Yale, brother to my dear distressed wife, for her comfortable maintenance and to be disposed of by him for her good, she not being in a condition fit to manage it for herself; this income to be paid in quarterly payments. The thirty pounds per annum given me by the will and testament of my brother Henry Hopkins, lately deceased, to be given to our sister Mrs Judith Eve, during her natural life, and to be made up to fifty pounds per annum. To my sister Mrs Margaret Thomson fifty pounds within one year after my decease. To my nephew Henry Thomson, eight hundred pounds, whereof four hundred pounds to be paid him within sixteen months after my decease, and the other four hundred pounds within six months after the decease of my wife. To my niece Katherine Thomson, but now Katherine James (over and above her portion of five hundred pounds formerly given her), the sum of one hundred pounds. To my nieces, Elizabeth and Patience Dallye, two hundred pounds each, provided they attend the directions of their brother or aunts, &c., in disposing of themselves in marriage. To brother Mr David Yale two hundred pounds; to brother Mr Thomas Yale two hundred pounds; to my sister Mrs Hannah Eaton two hundred pounds. Within six months after the decease of my wife the sum of five hundred pounds to be made over into New England according to the advice of my loving friends Major Robert Thomson and Mr Francis Willoughby (for public ends, &c.). Twenty pounds apiece to Mr John Davenport, Mr Theophilus Eaton and Mr Culleck; a piece of plate of the value of twenty pounds to my honored friend Mr Wright; (a bequest) to my servant James Porter; to my friends Major Robert Thomson and Mr Francis Willoughby twenty pounds each in a piece of plate; to my servant Thomas Hayter; to my sister Yale wife of David Yale twenty pounds; to John Lello, a youth with sister Eve, twenty pounds; to my nephew Henry Dally, M.A. in Cambridge, my land and manor in Thickoe in the County of Essex and I appoint him executor, and Major Robert Thomson and Mr Francis Willoughby overseers, of my will.

Ruthen, 141.

Edward Hopkins, governor of Connecticut, one of the early settlers of Hartford, an abstract of whose will is given above, was born in Shrewsbury, England, in 1600, and died in London, March, 1657. For action of the General Court of Connecticut in relation to his legacy to Theophilus Eaton and others, trustees, see Colonial Records of Connecticut, edited by J. H. Trumbull, vol. i. p. 374; and for correspondence in relation to it, see the same volume, page 578. The £500 for "public ends" was paid to Harvard College under a decree in chancery in 1710. With it a township of land was purchased, which was named Hopkinton in honor of the donor. See Savage's notes on Winthrop's New England, vol. i. 1st ed. pp. 228-30; 2d ed. pp. 273-5, where large extracts from the will of Gov. Hopkins are made. It seems from the wills here abstracted that he was the son of Edward or Edmund Hopkins, that his mother was Katherine, sister of Sir Henry Lello, and that he had two brothers, Henry and Matthew; and four sisters, Abigail, Margaret, Patience and Judith. For an account of the insanity of his wife, see Winthrop's New England, vol. ii. 1st ed. p. 217; 2d ed. p. 266. Another early settler of Hartford was John Hopkins, who could not have been a brother of Gov. Edward, though he may have been related. He was the ancestor of President Mark Hopkins of Williams College, and of the late Mark Hopkins, Esq., an enterprising citizen of San Francisco, Cal.—EDITOR.]

THOMAS YALE of London, merchant, the poorest of what is stamp'd with my Creator's image and most unworthy his mercy; 29 September, 1697 ; proved 17 January, 1697. As to my temporal estate here, in India, and elsewhere, &c. To my dear mother Mrs Ursula Yale and my beloved brother M[r] Elihu Yale. The hereditary estate in the county of Denbigh to my brother Elihu Yale's male issue, if he have any. Failing such, then to the heirs male of my uncle Thomas Yale, in New England and to his right heirs forever.

The Revd Doctor John Evans of London and M[r] Robert Harbin of London to be trustees and overseers.

Then follows an account of his estate. Lort, 26.

July, 1721. Undecimo die em[t] com° Catharinæ Yale viduæ Relc̃æ Elihu Yale nup p̃oae S̃ci Andrew Holborn in Com̃ Middxiæ ar̃i defti hẽntis etc. ad adm̃strandum bona jura et credita d̃ci defti de bene etc. jurat.

Adm̃co de bo: non etc. em[t] mense Febr̃ii 1727.

Admon. Act. Book 1721 P. C. C.

[The name Ursula here given as that of the testator's mother, shows that he and his brother Elihu, the founder of Yale College, were sons of David Yale and not of Thomas, as has been asserted (REG. iv. 245; Savage's Gen. Dict. iv. 666). This agrees with the entry on the register of the private school of William Du Gard, where Elihu (there written *Eliah*) is called the son of David (REG. xiv. 201). Du Gard had previously been head master of Merchant Taylors' School, London.— EDITOR.]

ROBERT THOMSON (residence not stated in will), 14 April, 1691. To my wife, in addition to her jointure, my household stuff, plate, coach and horses and five hundred pounds; and, during her natural life, the profits of my houses, lands and stock at Gelford in New England, the rents of my farm at Culpho and Felsham, in the county of Suffolk, and of that bought of M[r] Denham in Kent. I give unto my wife and son Joseph five hundred pounds to dispose as they know is my mind without being accountable to any. I will that there be not above three hundred pounds expended on my funeral in mourning and all other expenses. I will that what is expended on those one thousand apiece (which I have by deed settled on my daughters Ashhurst, Clark, Miller and Duckinfield) of land at Nipmugg in New England be made up a one hundred pounds to each for their further settlement, as Mr Staughton shall direct. To my grandson William Thompson, son of my deceased son William, during his natural life, after he shall attain the age of twenty five years, Esham in Lincolnshire, with its appurtenances, bought of my cousin Oldfield, and the farm in Kent bought of Mr Denham, and that, in the mean time, my executors receive the profits and lay them out in land for his use as aforesaid; and this in discharge of the twelve hundred pounds which my executor is to pay : after his decease to his first son, then to the second son (and so on); failing male issue, to my grandson Joseph, son of my son Joseph (in the same order, &c.) ; then to my daughters that shall be living, during their natural lives, and after their deaths to such of their sons as are or shall be baptized Robert. Whereas upon my son William's marriage I did settle several lands in Yorkshire and Kent upon my brother Glover and son Clarke in trust, &c. &c.

On examining Mr Richard Bradly's account of Kintledg, I found an overweight which, for the reasons writ in my waste book, may be my just right, yet, least there should be an error, I will that his heirs or executors be paid the sixty four pounds. I give unto each of my grandchildren (except Joseph Ashurst) that shall be living at my death, when they marry or come of age, fifty pounds. My dear wife & son Joseph to be executors.

The witnesses were Ann Cunliffe, Henry Scoupholme, John Rooke and William Watson.

The testator declared it to be his will 12 March, 1693. Signed and delivered in presence of Henry Scoupholme, Mary Watson and A. Hatway. Proved by Joseph Thomson, 6 December, 1694. Confirmed by decree 3^d Session Trinity, 1695. The receipt of the original will acknowledged by Joseph Thomson 13 July, 1695.   Box, 42.

Sententia pro valore Testamenti Roberti Thompson, nuper de Stoke Newington in comitatu Middlesexiæ armigeri defuncti etc. etc. in judicio inter Franciscam Thompson, relictam, et Josephum Thompson, filium, dicti defuncti, executores hujusmodi negotium promoventes, ex una, et Dominam Elizabetham Ashurst (uxorem domini Willielmi Ashurst, militis) Mariam Clerke (uxorem Samuelis Clerke armigeri) Annam Miller, viduam, et Dominam Susan Duckingfeild (uxorem Domini Roberti Duckingfeild Baronetti), filias naturales et legitimas dicti defuncti, ac Guilielmum Thompson nepotem ex filio ejusdem defuncti, partes contra quas idem negotium promovetur, &c. &c. 1695.   Irby, 201.

In connection with the foregoing it may be well to note that Thomas Sprigg of London, merchant, in his will of 19 May, 1675, proved 14 January, 1678, appointed Mr Maurice Thomson, Col. George Thomson, Sir William Thomson and Major Robert Thomson his executors and trustees, &c.   King, 10.

[Major Robert Thompson of London purchased of the Rev. Henry Whitefield of Guilford, Ct., who returned to England in 1651, his property in that town including the famous "stone house" built in 1639—one of the oldest buildings in New England now standing. The property remained in Thompson's family "to the great detriment of the town till October 22, 1772, when Andrew Oliver, Esq., of Boston, as attorney for Thompson's heirs, sold it all to Mr. Wyllys Elliott for £3000 of the current money of Massachusetts." (Smith's Guilford, p. 92.) Savage (Gen. Dict. iij. 288) conjectures that Thompson married a sister of Gov. Hopkins. We see by the Hopkins wills that the governor had a sister Margaret who married a Thompson ; but the names of her children, Henry and Katherine, are not found as the children of Robert Thompson in the probate of his will. It is possible, however, that they and their mother died after 1657 and before 1691. Several letters from Major Robert Thompson are printed in Hutchinson's Collection of Papers. Winthrop, in his History of New England, under 1639 (vol. i. p. 307 of 1st ed., p.

370 of 2d ed.), states that "a fishing trade was begun at Cape Ann by one Mr. Maurice Tomson, a merchant of London." (See also Mass. Colony Records, i. 256.) This was probably Maurice, eldest brother of Maj. Thompson, son of Robert of Watton, and grandson of Maurice of Cheshunt. "He was Governor of the East India Company in the reign of King Charles the First, as was also his brother Sir William in the reign of King Charles the Second." His son, Sir John Thompson, bart., was created Baron Haversham, May 4, 1696. (Collins's Peerage, ed. 1741, pp. 230–233.) For other facts concerning Major Thompson and his brothers and their families, see Collins's Peerage, as cited. See also Wotton's Baronetage, iv. 488.—EDITOR.

[From Hartfordshire Pedigrees.]

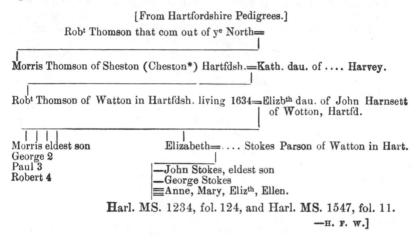

Robt Thomson that com out of y^e North=

Morris Thomson of Sheston (Cheston*) Hartfdsh.=Kath. dau. of .... Harvey.

Robt Thomson of Watton in Hartfdsh. living 1634=Elizbth dau. of John Harnsett of Wotton, Hartfd.

Morris eldest son
George 2
Paul 3
Robert 4

Elizabeth= .... Stokes Parson of Watton in Hart.

—John Stokes, eldest son
—George Stokes
≡Anne, Mary, Elizth, Ellen.

Harl. MS. 1234, fol. 124, and Harl. MS. 1547, fol. 11.

—H. F. W.]

HANNAH WALLIN, alias Poulter, of St Andrews Undershaft, London, spinster, 15 March, 1661, proved 7 August, 1663, by Joseph Alston. To be buried in the parish church of St. Mary Hill, London, as nigh to the place where my dear brother John Wallin als Poulter was buried as conveniently may be with such charge of my funeral as is answerable to my degree and estate, with the remainder of my estate which is hereby undisposed of, which I have purposely left sufficient to perform the same in a handsome and plentiful manner. To Mr Joseph Alstone of London, Norwich merchant, and Mary his wife ten pounds apiece. To Joseph, Edward, Isaac and Clare Alstone, children of said Joseph and Mary, five pounds apiece, the sons at the age of twenty one years and the daughter at the age of twenty one or day of marriage. To Mr Edward Ashtone, kinsman of the said Joseph Ashtone (sic) the father, and unto Thomas Spring servant unto the said Joseph Ashton, the father, five pounds apiece within six months after my decease. To John Baldridge, son of Mr Baldridge, now dwelling with the said Joseph Alstone the father, five pounds at the age of twenty one. To my kinsman Thomas Hunt, the elder, thirty pounds within six months after my decease. To his son Thomas Hunt five pounds at the age of twenty one. To my god-daughter Hannah Hunt, daughter of the same, twenty pounds at the age of twenty one years or day of her marriage. To my kinsmen Edward and John Hunt, brothers of the said Thomas Hunt the elder, ten pounds within six months. To Elizabeth ——,

---

* My friend Mr. Eades suggests that Cheshunt may be intended, he having seen the name in this form before.—H. F. W.

Collins gives Cheshunt as the residence of this person.—EDITOR.

sister of the said Thomas Hunt the elder, ten pounds within six months. To my cousin John Poulter of Hitchin, in the county of Herts, forty pounds within three months after my decease ; and to Mary Poulter his daughter twenty pounds at the age of twenty one or the day of her marriage.

Item I give and bequeathe unto Thomas Poulter (being now at Virginia or some parts beyond the seas), brother of the said Mary Poulter, the sum of ten pounds of like lawful money, to be paid unto him within six months next after my decease. To the son and daughter of my cousin Isaac Poulter, late of Hitchen aforesaid deceased, whose names I know not, five pounds within six months. If they die, then amongst the children of my cousin John Poulter equally. To the poor of the parish of St. Andrew Undershaft three pounds ; to the poor of the parish of Hitchen, where I was born, five pounds. To my cousin Katherine, wife of my cousin Thomas Hunt the elder, to Mary Poulter, daughter of my said cousin John Poulter, and to my cousin Elizabeth ——, sister of my said cousin Thomas Hunt the elder, all my wearing apparel.

The executors to be M[r] Joseph Alstone the father and Mary his wife. When the will was proved by the former, power was reserved for the latter.   Juxon, 112.

This family of Poulter, or Pulter, were long settled in Hitchin in Hertfordshire. They bore—*argent, two bendlets Sable, in the sinister chief a Cornish chough of the Last.* Crest—*Out of a ducal coronet Azure a demi bear rampant Ermine.*

SAMUEL PURCHAS, rector of S[t] Martins near Ludgate, 31 May, 1625, proved 21 October, 1626. Five pounds to the poor of Thaxted where first I received light. To my son Samuel all that messuage and tenement in the parish of Thaxted which I lately bought of Absolon Onion, &c. A portion lately bought of my brother William Purchas and by him purchased of one —— Kent als Reynolds, who formerly had bought of Absolon Onion, unto Martha my daughter and her heirs, also lands near a hamlet called Beyton End, which were lately belonging to my father George Purchas, of pious memory, in the parish of Thaxted, now in the tenure of my brother William. My wife Jane to have the use of the said lands so long as she shall continue a widow. If my son & daughter die without issue these premises shall descend to Daniel Purchas, son of my brother William, with remainder to Samuel, son of the said William. If my brother William's posterity should fail then to the heirs of my brother George Purchas, i. e. to his eldest son John. In defect of issue of brother George then to Samuel, son of my brother Thomas Purchas of Eastwood and to his heirs forever.

My library and all my books, globes, maps and charts unto Samuel my son, except all those books or works or any part of them whereof I have been the author, namely my Pilgrimage, Pilgrim and Pilgrims, of which he hath already had one printed copy of each of them. The other printed books thereof now in my custody or now due or hereafter to be due upon reckonings from M[r] Fetherstone I reserve & bequeath to the performance of my will. One of each to my daughter Martha, my brethren George and William and to my brother in law William Perkins, to each of them one entire work of my Pilgrims in four books. Wife Jane to be executrix. Brethren George & William and William Perkins to be overseers. My seal ring to my son Samuel.   Hele, 137.

[Samuel Purchas, rector of St. Martins, Ludgate, London, and author of Purchas his Pilgrimage and Purchas his Pilgrimes, was born in Thaxted, Essex, about 1577, and died in London probably in 1626. For an account of him and his writings, see Allibone's Dictionary of Authors, vol. ii. p. 1706. See also Drake's Dictionary of American Biography, p. 745; and Notes and Queries, London, 1867, 3d S. xi. 57. For notices of his son Samuel, rector of Sutton, Essex, also an author, see Allibone's Dictionary, and Notes and Queries, 1868, 4th S. ii. 541.

It seems, from the following note by Dr. Perkins, of Salem, that the christian name of the father of the author of the "Pilgrimes" was George.—EDITOR.

"William Perkins, merchant taylor, who is mentioned in the will of Samuel Purchas, was the son of George Perkins of Abbots Salford in the county of Warwick, yeoman, by his wife Katherine; he was baptized January 1, 1579. He married first, Katherine ——, May 22, 1603. She died Sept. 18, 1618. He married second, Mary, daughter of George Purchas of Thaxted, in the county of Essex, March 30, 1619. She died Oct. 29, 1629 (REGISTER, x. 369). This Mary must have been a sister of the testator, Samuel Purchas, and of 'Brethren William and George.' William Perkins had, by his first wife Katherine, a son (inter al.) William, born Aug. 25, 1607, who immigrated to N. England about 1630–1, and whose name appears in various places in our early history as Rev. William Perkins. He was first in Boston and afterwards in Weymouth, Roxbury, Ipswich, Gloucester, and last in Topsfield, where he died, May 21, 1682. He was a man of education and very varied accomplishments. He has descendants now living in Topsfield and elsewhere. His daughter Mary was the second wife of Oliver Purchase, of Lynn.—
G. A. PERKINS.]

MARGARET STONE, wife of Simon Stone of St. Andrews Holborn, gentleman, and relict and executrix of John Fawne, late of St. Buttolph without Aldergate, London, gentleman, deceased, did, about the beginning of May, 1605, and about "sevenights" before her death and at divers other times, &c. make her test. nuncupativ. Her husband the said Simon Stone to have the keeping and bringing up of her daughter Judith Fawne.

The above will was proved 23 May, 1605, by Simon Stone.

Hayes, 35.

THOMAS FOULKS, planter, lying in Princess Ann's county in Virginia, 1 August, 1692, proved 19 Sept. 1692. I do leave my plantation in Princess Ann's County in Virginia & all my servants & my stock & all other things belonging to it, also in cash 250^{li} sterling which is now in the hands of John Vicary mariner living in the city of Bristol, to the said John Vicary, my sole executor.

Wit: John Barwick, Edward Cocks, John Vicary.

Confirmed per sententiam 31 October, 1692.   Fane, 141.

[William Fookes, an ancestor probably of the testator Thomas Foulkes, received a patent of 450 acres of land lying on "Nanzamond" river, November 24th, 1636. Va. Land Records, Book No. 1, p. 399. The name, variously rendered: Foulkes, Fowlkes, Folkes, and Foulks, is quite numerously and respectably represented in the states of Virginia and North Carolina.—R. A. BROCK.

JOSEPH WADE (called also Ward) of Boston in New England, on board the ship Mary, 21 October, 1691, proved 17 October, 1692. He speaks of clothes lent to John Trinby, 4^s to Mr Collins the waterman at Barbadoes, 6^s lent to William Jewry, messmates Thomas Linch, Valentine Baker, William Barten & George Golden. All money goods & chattells in New England left to Frances Gibbs of Boston aforesaid spinster.

Wit: John Marshall, Edward Mobryd, Richard Hazard.   Fane, 193.

JONE COLE, of the city & County of Exon, spinster, 12 September, 1687, proved 16 February, 1693. Referring to will of husband John

Cole, left with her when he took a voyage to America, intended for the city Philadelphia; to Alice Stoker's children, to William Home, to Fortuna Martin's brothers and sisters. Residue to Fortuna Martin, kinswoman. James Kearle executor of husband's will & mine.   Box, 28.

JOHN LARABEE of New England (evidently a mariner) appoints Elizabeth Crawford of London his attorney, &c. 30 April, 1694. Proved 19 June, 1694.   Box, 130.

RICHARD CHARLETT in the Province of Maryland in the County of Calvert, in Pawtuxen River, in Swanson's Creek, 28 August, 1686, proved 4 April, 1694. To cousin Hannah Kings forty pounds, to cousin Richard Kings ten pounds. All the rest to my brothers & sisters. Brother Richard Kings to be executor.   (Signed) Richard Charlet.

Wits : Philip Rogerson, Thomas Vuett, Ann Rogerson, William Goode.
                                                                    Box, 72.

MARY GODWYN of Lyme Regis in the County of Dorset, widow, the last of March, 1665, proved 6 June, 1665. To the poor of Lyme Regis five pounds upon condition that my body is permitted to be buried in the church of Lyme Regis aforesaid without a sermon or the Service Book in such order as is therein appointed. To my three cousins William, James, Ynatius, the sons of my brother William Hill, in New England, one hundred & fifty pounds, to be equally divided amongst them. To John Tyderleigh, & Susan & Mary Tytherleigh, children of Nathaniel Tytherleigh of Lyme Regis & to Grace, wife of the said Nathaniel & to Nathaniel their son, ten pounds each. To my sister Elizabeth Kerridge five pounds (& some land) to cousin William Hill of Lyme, son of my late brother Benjamin Hill & to Mary his now wife & Benjamin their son & their four daughters, at ages of one & twenty years. To cousin Joane Berry, wife of John Berry. To sister Martyn. To Mr Wyatt, clerk. To Mrs Thomazine West, wife of Mr Walter West. To Henry Fry of Weyford, my sister's son & to his daughter Elizabeth. To my cousin John Shute, to my cousin Anne Whitfield, to Elizabeth Sprake, daughter of my cousin William Kerridge, to Mary Hoare, my now servant, to James Gollopp of Taunton, to Mr Bartholomew Westley, to Mrs Sara Kerridge, late wife of Mr John Kerridge of Wooten, to my sister Paveatt, to my cousin Mr John Kerridge who lives in Lyme churchyard, to Grace, daughter of mr. Nathaniel Tyderleigh, to William & Samuel Courtney, sons of William Courtney, one of my executors, to Elizabeth daughter of my cousin John Whetombe (sic), to my cousin Elizabeth Hart, to the widow Isaacke, the widow Hockett, the widow Pike & John Palmer's wife, to my cousin Judith, sister of my cousin Ann Whitfield, to my cousin Mary Fry of Woathill, to Mrs Elizabeth West, wife of Mr Gabriel West, to Mr Richard Farrant's two children. To Mr John Farrant, Mr Robert Burridge & Mr William Courtney all my right, title & interest in the dwelling house & garden, with the appurtenances wherein I do now live in Combestreete, the issues & profits thereof to be to the use of such and to be given & disposed to such poor outed and ejected ministers from time to time as they shall think fit & in their judgments have most need & best deserve the same. All the residue to the said three whom I make executors.

                                                            Hyde, 61.

[The above will answers the query printed in the REGISTER (vol. xxxv. p. 184). The widow of William Hill and mother of William, James and Ignatius, became the wife of Mr. Edmund Greenleaf (ancestor of the New England families of that name) who, in a paper appended to his will and recorded in the Suffolk Registry at Boston (B. 7, L. 112), says: " When I married my wife I kept her grandchild, as I best remember, three years to schooling, diet & apparel ; and William Hill, her son, had a bond of six pounds a year, whereof I received no more than a barrel of pork of 3^{li} 0. 0. of that 6^{li} 0. 0. a year he was to pay me, and sent to her son Ignatius Hill to the Barbadoes, in mackerel, cider & bread & pease, as much as come to twenty pounds, and never received one penny of it. His aunt gave to the three brothers 50^{li} apiece—I know not whether they received it or no; but I have not received any part of it. Witness my hand Edmund Greenleaf."

" Besides when I married my wife she brought me a silver bowl, a silver porringer and a silver spoon. She lent or gave them to her son James Hill, without my consent."—H. F. WATERS.

See Mr. Appleton's article on the Greenleaf family in the REGISTER for July, 1884 (xxxviii. page 299).

Mrs. Sara Kerridge, named by Mrs. Godwyn, was perhaps Sarah, sister of the Rev. John Woodbridge of Andover, Mass., and of the Rev. Benjamin Woodbridge, whose name heads the list of the graduates of Harvard College. (REG. xxii. 337, 342; xxxvii. 240.) Sarah Woodbridge married, Dec. 27, 1632, John Kerridge (Mitchell's Woodbridge Record, p. 9), probably the Rev. Mr. Kerridge of Wooton Fitz-Paine, Dorset, who was ejected in 1662 and died soon after (Palmer's Nonc. Mem., ed. 1778, p. 487). His son John Kerridge, M.A , of Corpus Christi College, Oxford, was for a time schoolmaster at Abingdon, Berks ; thence went to Lyme Regis, where he was ejected as a schoolmaster ; was afterwards pastor of a dissenting church in Culleton, Devonshire, and died April 15, 1705 (Ibid. p. 460).—ED.]

JOSEPH TILDEN citizen & girdler of London, 1 February, 1642. To my brother Freegift Tilden five pounds, to my niece Sara Smyth ten pounds, to my sister Lydia Tilden, late wife of my brother Nathaniel Tilden, ten pounds, and to her two daughters who are married in New England twenty nobles apiece. The livery of the company of Girdlers whereof I am a member to attend my corps to burial. To the said company for poor members and widows ten pounds. To the poor of Smallhead Street in the parish of Tenterden, Kent, three pounds for the poor at the discretion of Mr Thomas Huckstropp. To the widow Hamond three pounds. To the widow Prestwich of Lambheth in the County of Surrey thirty shillings, to Jane Ranndall a diaper table cloth with the napkins belonging to it, to my maid servant Margaret Smart ten shillings, to my nurse five shillings, to the poor of the parish of St John Baptist, London, the several legacies following i. e. the widow Armefield thirty shillings and to the rest of the said parish fifty shillings, to be distributed among them at the discretion of my brother Thatcher. To Hudnall the hairdresser of our parish twenty shillings. My nephew Joseph Tilden, son of my brother Nathaniel Tilden, to be sole executor. My brother Hopestill Tilden to be administrator in trust for the use of the said Joseph until he shall take upon him the executorship and I give to the said Hopestill ten pounds for his pains. To my brother George Thatcher the half year's rent due next Lady day for my lands in Sussex. George Thatcher to be overseer.

(Signed) Jos Tillden.

Wit : Henry Randall Francis Helmes Val: Crome.

By a codicil he bequeaths the residue to nephew Joseph Tilden.

Letters of administration were issued 18 March, 1642, to Hopestill Tillden, brother of the deceased, during the absence of Joseph Tillden, executor named in the will & now dwelling in the parts beyond the seas.

Crane, 28.

[Elder Nathaniel Tilden, brother of the testator, settled in Scituate, Mass. For an account of him and his descendants, see Deane's History of Scituate, pp. 353–5. One of his descendants is the Hon. Samuel J. Tilden, formerly governor of the state of New York, and the democratic candidate for president of the United States in 1876 (see REGISTER, vol. xxxviii. p. 6).—EDITOR.]

THOMAS SPELMAN of Virginia, gentleman, declared his will that his daughter Mary Spelman in Virginia should have all that he had here in England & what he had in Virginia his wife should have, in presence of Jane Bridges (her mark) Mary Rowe (her mark) & Fran: Spelman. Letter of administration was granted 24 April, 1627, to Francis Spelman natural and lawful brother of the said Thomas Spelman lately of Truro in the county of Cornwall deceased, &c. &c. during the absence of Hannah Spelman the relict of the said deceased in the parts of Virginia then dwelling, &c.   Skinner, 40.

[Thomas Spilman, of " Kicoughton in the corporacion of Elizabeth Citty," received a grant of fifty acres, his " first personall divident " as an " ancient planter, * * * to be augmented and doubled by the Company," December 1st, 1624. *Va. Land Records*, Book No. 1, p. 35.—R. A. BROCK.

Query. Was this Thomas Spelman a relative of Henry Spelman, whose " Relation of Virginia," 1609 (see REGISTER, xxvii. 332), was edited by J. F. Hunnewell and printed for him in 1872? The author of the Relation was a son of Sir Henry Spelman, the antiquary, whose pedigree will be found in Blomefield's Norfolk, 2d ed. vol. vi. pp. 150–5.—EDITOR.]

RALPH HOOKER, of Barbadoes, 14 March, 1663, proved 27 May, 1665. To my good friend and neighbor M[rs] Judith Pinney eight hundred and twenty one pounds eight shillings and three pence which she oweth me, and also one hundred thousand pounds of Muscovado Sugar. And for the remainder of her debt to me my executors to forbear to call on her for it until February next, excepting only the debt which she owes me as executrix of M[r] Robert Challoner deceased, which I desire may be paid this year. To my friends Capt. Jeremy Egginton, M[r] John Knight, M[r] Stephen Spicer, M[r] John Bawdon and M[r] John Sparks each a ring with a death's head, value three pounds sterling. To my friend D[r] Peter la Rous fifty pounds sterling to buy himself a ring. To M[r] Jeoffrie Body two thousand pounds of Muscovado Sugar. To Thomas Peake one thousand pounds of Muscovado Sugar. To Edward Russell my servant one half piece dowlas. To my cousin M[r] James Woods of London merchant, ten pounds sterling and to his wife ten pounds sterling. To my cousin M[rs] Woods, relict of my cousin John Woods deceased ten pounds sterling and to her son John Woods five pounds sterling. To my cousin Edward Hooker his children that are alive in England five pounds sterling each. To my cousins Robert & Edward Boys, my cousin Soane & her sister & my cousin Anne Boys, to each of them five pounds sterling.

Item I give and bequeath unto my young cousin Peter Bennett the son of Richard Bennett of New England (the which Peter was my own sister's son) the sum of one hundred pounds sterling, to be paid him when he shall accomplish the age of eighteen years of age. To my poor kindred in England one hundred & fifty pounds sterling, to be distributed by my cousin James Woods, something of it to be given to my aunt Webbe her children of Ottebourne, if any alive, my cousin Edward Hooker of Chilcombe can inform. For goods consigned to Capt. Samuel Davis & myself he to make returns to the principals in London, but not to meddle or intermedle with any of my other consignations. A reference to goods sold in this island on account of Sir Andrew Riccard & Co. To Capt. Davis five pounds sterling and a horse. To my friend Capt. William Porter ten pounds & a gold hat band & my best beaver if he please to wear it for my sake. To Hugh Lewis three pounds sterling to buy him a ring. My executor to confer with Mr Stephen Spicer who is administrator with me about Mr John Williams' estate. Reference to shipments home to Mr Mico on ac't of John Williams deceased,—much more sugar than I have received on ac't. My executor may employ Mr Jeoffery Body on my books and accounts. He knows the accounts between Mr John Knights & myself and also about Mr John Williams' estate, Mr John Lewis' estate and all the accounts in my books. My loving cousin John Hooker, now residing in the Island of Barbadoes, to be sole executor and my cousin James Woods of London, merchant, to be overseer in trust.

Wit: John Hawkesworth, Josias Cox, John Watkins.

Barbadoes —— By the Deputy Governor.

This Fifteenth day of April, 1664, personally appeared before me Major John Hawkesworth & Mr Josias Cox & made oath that they saw Major Ralph Hooker sign, seal & publish the foregoing Writing, &c. &c.

Henry Willoughby.

A true copy of the Original recorded in the Secretary's Office of Barbadoes attested 17 August, 1664. Edward Bowden Dep: Secretary.

Hyde, 50.

[The Richard Bennett, referred to in the above will, said by Savage to have been of Salem in 1636, afterwards of Boston, had a wife Sybil, the mother of his children, whose maiden name is here shown to be Hooker, and a second wife Margaret. His will of 21 June, 1677, with a codicil of 6 July, 1677, was proved at Boston 8 September, 1677. In it he mentions grandchild Susanna Bennett, daughter of son Peter, wife Margaret Bennett, son Jonas Clarke and Susanna his wife, and cousin Anthony Bennet of Bass River, New England. (Suffolk Probate Registry, B. 6, p. 195.)—H. F. W.]

ELIZABETH VANSOLDT of Whitegate Alley in the parish of Buttolph Bishopsgate London, widow, 7 September, 1665. Five pounds to be spent about my funeral. To my son Abraham Vansoldt in Virginia or elsewhere twenty pounds within three months after my decease (and certain moveables). Legacies to daughter Mary Wills, cousin Mrs Judith Bonnell of the Old Jury, daughter Anne White (inter alia two pictures made & drawn for my brother Stripe & his wife), grand child James White, & loving friend Thomas Parker of Walbrook London & his wife. My loving son James White to be full and sole executor.

James White having died, letters of administration were granted 12 October, 1665, to Anna White. Hyde, 126.

Notes on Abstracts previously printed.

Sir WILLIAM PHIPS, Knight (*ante*, pp. 46).

The following inscription on a monument in St. Mary Woolnoth Church, between Lombard and King William Street, London, is contributed to the REGISTER by A. M. Haines, Esq., of Galena, Ill.

" Near this place is interred the body of Sir William Phipps, Knight; who in the year 1687 by his great industry, discovered among the rocks near the banks of Bahama on the north side of Hispaniola a Spanish plate-ship which had been under water forty four years, out of which he took in gold and silver to the value of £300,000 Sterling; and with a fidelity equal to his conduct, brought it all to London, where it was divided between himself and the rest of the adventurers. For which great service he was knighted by his then Majesty King James II. ; and afterwards, by the command of his present Majesty, and at the request of the principal inhabitants of New England, he accepted of the government of the Massachusetts, in which he continued to the time of his death; and discharged his trust with that zeal for the interest of his country, and with so little regard to his own private advantage, that he justly gained the good esteem and affections of the greatest and best part of the inhabitants of that Colony.

" He died the 18th of February, 1694, and his Lady, to perpetuate his memory, hath caused this monument to be erected."

ROBERT THOMPSON.—The following notes, appended by Mr. Waters to the will of Major Thomson (*ante*, pp. 65–6), were accidentally omitted in the last number :

[Information of Hugh Squier. Heard three men of quality, one seemingly a Dutchman, rejoice that the Dutch had done so well, and attribute it chiefly to the care and diligence of Maurice Thompson and his brother Major, in supplying them with information of the motions of the English fleet; they said these men served much better than Scott for his thousand guilders a year. Finds that Maurice Thompson was always violent against kingly government, was intimate with the Protector, sat on some of the high courts of justice, and sentenced some beheaded lords to death, so that he is incapable of bearing any office. He was a poor man in Virginia, but got a great estate, chiefly from the king's party. He, Hugh Peters and Nich. Corsellis, a Dutchman, went over in the beginning of the war to collect money in Holland for the distressed Protestants in Ireland, and was always in great favour with the Dutch. As to Major, can hear of no one of that name but a rich Mr. Major, who married his daughter to the Protector's son Richard, but he is no brother of Maurice Thompson, so thinks they must mean his brother Major Rob. Thompson, who was so great with Cromwell that he had nearly married his daughter : he began with nothing, rose high enough to purchase 2,200¹ a year in bishops' lands, and lost it on the Restoration, so that he brags that he hates not the persons but the office of bishops ; he is bold, full of malice, and embittered against government ; he was six or seven years a navy commissioner for the Protector, so that he knows all the ways of the navy, and is thus able to commit this treason. Thinks their houses should be searched, and Council should consider whether to seize them. Asks directions in case he should again meet the three men whose discourse he heard. [2 pages with postscript in cypher undecyphered.] Westminster, 24 June, 1666.

Account of two other brothers of these Thompsons : George, who lost his leg fighting against the King, but got a great estate. When the army had fallen into the posture of a brand-iron, with the Rump in the middle, threatening a battle royal, Haselrigg and Morley to support the Rump, and Lambert and his party to pull them down, this Col. George Thompson was with some thousands in St. George's-in-the-Fields, Southwark, and with Bibles in their hands, and good swords also, they declared for King Jesus, which signified what they pleased, except King Charles. " Endorsed Col. G. Thompson, of Southwark, a Millenary, &c." 24 June, 1666.

Calendar of State Papers, Domestic Series, 1665–1666.

The great interest taken by this family in the affairs of the British Colonies of North America, and the important parts played by them (directly or indirectly) in the management of those affairs, as shown by the State Papers, would seem to warrant the giving of so much space to this account of them. From this family were derived the baronial house of Thomson Lords Haversham, created 4 May, 1696, and extinct on the death of Maurice, the last Baron Haversham in 1744, a family closely allied, by intermarriages, to the house of Annesley, Earls of Anglesey. Of the children of Major Robert Thomson, the testator of the foregoing will, Elizabeth became the wife of William Ashhurst, son of Henry Ashhurst,* an eminent merchant of London, descended from an old Lancashire family. This William was himself Lord

---

* Of this Henry Ashhurst, Morant (vide History of Essex, ii. 296) says: " He had the chief hand in settling the corporation for the Propagation of the Gospel in America, of which he was treasurer; and also zealously promoted the translation of the Bible into the Indian language. He dyed in 1680."—H. F. W.

Mayor of London in 1693, one of the representatives of the city in several parliaments, received the honor of knighthood from King William III., and died 12 January, 1719 ; his lady survived till 22 March, 1723. His brother Henry was created a Baronet in 1688. Her sister Mary was the wife of Samuel Clarke, Esq., of Snailwell in the county of Cambridge (of Kentish stock), who was created a Baronet 25 July, 1698, and died 8 March, 1719. Another sister, Susan Thomson, was the second wife of Sir Robert Duckenfield, of Duckenfield Hall, Cheshire, created a Baronet 16 June, 1665, who died Nov. 1729.—H. F. W.]

JOHN SCOTCHFORD of Brenchlie in the county of Kent, clothier, 26 December, 1600, proved 16 January, 1600. To be buried in the parish church of Brenchley. To the poor of the parish. To Jasp Saxbie, Henry Alchin and Lawrence Bycie, to every of them ten shillings. To my servants. To every one of my godchildren twelve pence apiece. To John Scotchford my uncle ten shillings. To Laurence Briggenden ten shillings. To Jone, my sister, wife of Richard Browne, forty shillings, and to her son, Noe Stone, three pounds. To every one of the children of the said Jone, my sister, ten shillings. To my sister Martha, wife of Richard Glydd, twenty shillings. To her son John my godson, twenty shillings, and to the rest of her children ten shillings apiece. To every one of my daughters, Elizabeth, Anne, Margaret, Mary and Martha, one hundred pounds at one and twenty years of age or day of marriage. To my daughter Elizabeth, at the age of one and twenty years, the sum of ten pounds, which ten pounds was given her by her grandmother, my mother. To my wife Elizabeth one hundred and fifty pounds within one year after my decease (and other bequests made to her).

To every one of the daughters of John Bigge two shillings, and to his son Hope Bigg ten shillings ; to Mary wife of John Bett ten shillings ; to Mary wife of George Stacie ten shillings ; all within twelve months after my decease. To my mother nine pounds ten shillings yearly (in quarterly payments) &c. To George Saxbie, my uncle, twenty shillings, and to William Saxbie, my uncle, ten shillings ; both within three months after my decease. To Edward Henshall, vicar of Brenchley, twenty shillings. The residue to my son Thomas Scotchford and his heirs forever. John Saxbie and Robert his son, both of Brenchley, clothiers, to be my executors. Richard Glidd, of the parish of Brightling, in the County of Sussex, yeoman, and John Maynard of Brenchley, yeoman, to be the overseers.

The witnesses were Edward Henshall, Script. and John Maynard.

Woodhall, 40.

[The testator of the above will was probably the ancestor of John Scotchford, town clerk of Concord, who married Susanna (perhaps) daughter of George Meriam, and died 10 June, 1696. The will is at any rate of interest as relating to the Bigg family.—H. F. W.]

NINION BUTCHER, of Mary Aldermanbury, London, 25 February, 1658, proved 13 October, 1660. To the poor of the parish of Staplehurst. To eight poor people of the parish of Marden five shillings apiece, and to ten poor people of the same parish two shillings apiece. To Mᵗⁱˢ Lawrence, widow, twenty shillings, to Mᵗˢ Southen forty shillings, and to Henry Parsons ten shillings. To eight poor people of the parish of Aldermanbury five shillings apiece, and to eight more poor people two shillings and sixpence. To my loving daughter Elizabeth Houlden five hundred and fifty pounds if my said daughter is living in twelve months, &c. if not then to her children at their respective ages of eighteen years. To my sister Re becca Glover five hundred pounds within one year, if my sister is living, if not then to her children at eighteen. To my daughter Mary Pointell five hundred pounds in one year, &c. if alive, if dead then to her children at their several ages of eighteen. To my grand children, Elizabeth Butcher, fifty pounds at eighteen, William Butcher, twenty pounds at one and twenty, and Hannah Butcher twenty pounds at eighteen. To my grandchildren, James Houlden, fifty pounds at one and twenty, and Mary Houlden, fifty pounds at eighteen. To my grandchildren, Rebecca Glover, fifty pounds at eighteen, and Thomas Glover, twenty pounds at one and twenty; and twenty pounds to every other child of my daughter Glover's that shall be born before my death, and to be paid at eighteen if daughters and at one and twenty if sons. To my grandchildren, Judith Pointell, forty pounds at eighteen, Daniel Pointell, twenty pounds at one and twenty, and Edward Pointell, twenty pounds at one and twenty. To my reverend Pastor Mr Edmund Calamy four pounds within 6 months. To every one of my brother William's children that shall be alive six months next after my decease twenty shillings. To my kinswomen Mary and Elizabeth Sheefe twenty shillings apiece at eighteen. To my kinsman Thomas Butcher of Staplehurst twenty shillings in twelve months. To my kinsman Richard Butcher twenty shillings in twelve months. To my cousin Tunnell twenty shillings a year during natural life. To my cousin Elizabeth Busnell twenty shillings in twelve months. To my cousins Joseph, Samuel and Caleb Swinoke twenty shillings apiece in twelve months. To my cousin Elizabeth Crosse, in Southwark, twenty shillings in twelve months. To my cousin Mary Hasleden twenty shillings in twelve months. To my loving sister Johnson forty shillings in twelve months. To Mr Bland and his wife ten shillings apiece in twelve months. All my lands to my son John Butcher and his heirs forever, and the residue to him. My three daughters, Elizabeth Houlden, Rebecca Glover and Mary Poyntell. Grandchildren Elizabeth and Hannah Butcher, daughters of son John. Son John Butcher to be executor and sons Daniel Poyntell, Francis Willoughby and Thomas Glover to be overseers.   Nabbs, 176.

[I suspect Thomas Glover (husband of Rebecca) was son of John Glover of Dorchester.—H. F. W.]

JOHN IVE of Naylonde, in the county of Suffolk, clothier, 4 Dec. 1618, proved 17 June, 1619. To wife Anne the house wherein I dwell, for and during her natural life. Friends William Forth, gentleman, and Thomas Blythe to be executors. To my eldest son John Ive twenty pounds within one year after the decease of my wife. My son Thomas Ive of London oweth unto me forty pounds by a bond bearing date 9 January, 1617. To my son Myles Ive the sum of five pounds to be paid unto him within one year after the decease of my wife. To my son Ambrose fifteen pounds, within one year, &c. To my two daughters Anne and Mary five pounds apiece, &c. To my grandchild John Ive, son of my son Thomas, three pounds at the age of one and twenty years. To every one of my grandchildren, the children of my son John, Miles and Anne, now living, twenty shillings apiece, the sons at twenty-one and daughters at eighteen. The younger children of my son Thomas. The children of my son Miles. The children of my daughter Anne Frost.

The witnesses were Edmund Wells, John Smyth and Richard Robinson.
                                                    Parker, 57.

EDMUND CHAPLIN of Little Waldingfield in the County of Suffolk and the Diocese of Norwich, gentleman, 6 October, 1618, proved 8 February, 1618, by John Wincoll and Thomas Brian, with power reserved for the widow Martha Chaplin to act. To my grandchild Edmunde Chaplin, eldest son of my late son Edmunde, my messuage called Lyons, in Whatfield, Suffolk, at the age of five and twenty years. To grandchild William Chaplin, another son of said Edmund and to Ursula and Elizabeth Chaplin, his daughters (minors). To John Wincoll, my grand child, at the age of fourteen, Anne Wincoll, my grand child, at sixteen, John Wincoll, my son in Law, Awdry Wincoll, my daughter, his wife. Thos. Brian my son in law and Martha Brian, my daughter, his wife. John Howe of Melford, my nephew, and Judith his wife. To my friend Mʳ Thomas Iles of Hammersmith, Middlesex, gentleman, a ring of gold (value forty shillings) desiring him, of all kindness, to stand good grand father and friend unto the young poor fatherless children of my late son and his son-in-law Edmund Chaplin and his wife Anne the daughter of Mʳ Iles. If interred at Little Waldingfield, then, &c. If interred at Lindsey, &c. To Pernell Wilkinson, wife of Wilkinson the elder, and to the widow Mallard, both of Little Waldingfield, five shillings apiece. A bequest to four household servants of John Wincoll. All the residue to wife Martha, appointed executrix, with sons John Wincoll and Thomas Brian.

The witnesses were George Wincoll, Francis Wincoll and Joseph Briante. Parker, 40.

Sententia pro confirmaĉone testi Edmundi Chaplin dēf in judicio inter Johannem Wincoll et Thomam Bryant partes hm̄oi negotium promoventes ex una et Martham Chaplin aĭs Bryant filiam n'raĭem dicti defuncti Edmundum et Wĩm Chaplin nepotes, Ursulam et Eliz. Chaplin neptes ex filio eiusdem defuncti, etc. 21 June 1619. Parker, 56.

Testamentum nuncupativum THOME AYRES, of the parish of Froome in the County of Somerset, broadweaver, 14 January, 1638. To the church there three shillings and fourpence; to the poor six shillings and eight pence. Having a debt of five pounds, eight shillings due him by bond from one Nathan Doale, of Brooke in com. Wilts, his will was that Symon Ayers, his brother, should have that debt to his own use ; also his wearing apparel and a piece of new green cloth which lay in the chest, of five yards; also his broad loom unto Simon Ayers and William Ayers, his brother Simon Ayers his children, to each the moiety. A cupboard at his father's to Anne Ayers, daughter of Simon Ayers. His wife consents to these legacies. Witnesses John Lacie and Richard Eyers.

A commission issued forth 20 March, 1638, to Mary Ayers, the relict.
Harvey, 54.

SYMON EYRE of Osmington in the County of Dorset, yeoman, 29 April, 1659, proved 4 October, 1660, by William Eyre. To wife Joan and son William Eyres, &c. To my daughter-in-law Mary Eyres the sum of three score pounds which was promised her at the marriage of her unto my son Symon Eyres, provided the portion promised by her friends in marriage be truely and duely paid and for those children she had by my son Symon. To my four grand children twenty shillings to be divided equally amongst them. Son William to be executor and my good friends Robert and Henry Godshall to be overseers. One of the witnesses was a John Eyre.
Nabbs, 182.

NATHANAELL SMITH, 19 February, 1650. "I dispose of my money and goods that is now in new England and elsewhere in wise and manner following." The sixty three pounds in Mʳ George Corwin's hands due by bond, twenty pounds of it to my kinsman Thomas Edwards, eighteen pounds to my sister Ruth Halford, ten pounds to Mʳ John Nicolls, flaxman, five pounds to my cousin Nathaniel Edwards and ten pounds to my uncle John Smith. The money in James Brown's hand and that which is in Master Makepeace his hand, Brown's being eight or ten pounds and Mʳ Makepeace's four pounds ten shillings, my will is that my sister Hanna Mellowes shall have, &c. The linen that I have I do give the napkins, towells and tablecloths and one half the sheets to my kinsman Thomas Edwards and the other half of the sheets to my sister Hanna Mellowes in New England. Linen of mine in my brother Mr. Samuel Wandley's hands I do freely bestow it upon him. Also if there should be any allowance for the plundered estate, one half whereof is due to me, I do give one half to my brother Mʳ Samuel Fisher and the other half to be distributed between my sister Walford and my sister Wandley. My kinsman Thomas Edwards and cousin Nathaniel Edwards to be administrators.

The witnesses were Samuel Brinsmeades and Samuel Oliver.

20 March 1650 emanavit cõmissio Thomae Edwards et Nathanaeli Edwards, consanguineis dicti defuncti, ad administrand͠ bona jura et credita dict. defuncti iuxta tenorem et effectum testamenti ipiũs defuncti, eo quod dictus defunctus nullum omnino in hujusmodi testamento nominaũit Executorem etc.   Grey, 53.

[In the Massachusetts Archives, at the State House in Boston (B. 15, No. 70), may be found a copy of this will. Another copy is in the Court House at Salem, among the records of Ipswich Court, 1651, in the present office of the Clerk of Courts for the County of Essex. I have (scanty) minutes of what seems to be an earlier will, made 1 January, 1648 (Mass. Archives, B. 15, No. 72), in which the testator mentions William Halford, " my brother Andrew Halford's sonne," cousin Nathaniel Wandley, cousin Hannah Mellowes to have the linen and Abraham Mellowes my books, my brother Edward Mellowes and my brother Samuel Wandley to be executors.—H. F. W.]

EDWARD APSLEY of Apsley in the County of Sussex. The yearly profits of all my real and personal estate, in Sussex, Middlesex and Kent, to my brother George Fenwick, till my nephew Edward Fenwick attain the age of twenty one years. Then my will is that he should change his name to mine ; and so I give to him the said Edward Fenwick als Apsley all mine estate, both real and personal, he paying to his father one hundred pounds per annum during his life, to Jo: Apsley, son to my cousin Jo: Apsley of Pulberrow fifty pounds per annum during his life, to my servant Margaret Moyse twenty pounds per annum, to Thomas Stringer, my servant, ten pounds per annum, to Moses Fryer ten pounds per annum, to be paid to him at the house his father-in-law, Mʳ Evernden, now lives in, to Jo: Adams als Humphrey ten pounds per annum and a lease for twenty one years of all the lands he holdeth of me, at the rents he now payeth, to the town of Steyning five pounds per annum, to Sir Thomas Middleton one hundred pounds. To Sir Arthur Heislerige two either of my stone horses or mares. To Duncombe Colchester such of my geldings as he shall choose and twenty pounds, ten pounds by the year. To my cousin Richard Coldicott one hundred pounds. I would have one hundred and fifty pounds paid to Mʳ Bartholomew; Mʳ Pierce knoweth where he liveth. Other bequests. There issued forth letters of administration, 13 August, 1652, to Sir Arthur Haslerigg, one of the members of the right honorable the Parliament of the Common Wealth of England, and a "legatary" named in this will, for that the said deceased named no executor, the pretended will or "scrowle" of the said deceased, bearing date 11 October, 1651, being declared and decreed null and void.   Bowyer, 215.

[See will of Col. George Fenwick, *ante*, p. 41.—H. F. W.]

NATHANIEL ELES late of Harden in the County of Hartford, husbandman (nuncupative) 26 July, 1653, proved 18 February, 1653. To every one of the children of Mr William Eles twenty shillings apiece. To John Eles, son of the said William, a two and twenty shilling piece of gold over and above, &c. To every one of the children of Mr Nathaniel Eles twenty shillings apiece. It was his will that Richard White who liveth with Mr Nathaniel Eles should have all the money due unto him from goodman Salmon. To the two sisters of the said Richard White the rents of his house and lands till his brother John's son shall come to age. To the poor of Harnden and Essenden twenty shillings apiece to each parish if his money would hold out. To Mrs Wilton and Mary Smith twenty shillings apiece. To goodwife Lewis one shilling. To his brother's daughter all the remainder of the money in his chest. To his brother's son his house and lands when he cometh of age. To his sister in-law a bond which is in his chest. Master William Eles to be sole executor.   Alchin, 179.

[See will of Nathaniel Eeles, *ante*, p. 25.—H. F. W.]

RICHARD CROUCH (by mark) of the parish of St. Gyles without Cripplegate, London, Brewer's Servant, 27 October, 1660, proved 29 November, 1660. My body to be buried at the discretion of my executrix.

Imprimis I give and bequeath unto my brother William Crouch in New England beyond the seas one shilling of English money, to be paid unto him within one twelvemonth next after my decease if the same be demanded. To my sister Elizabeth Ayres, wife of Richard Ayres, the sum of twelve pence of like money if the same be demanded in twelve months. The residue to my loving wife Anne Crouch, who is to be executrix.

The witnesses were William Howe, Daniel How and Thomas Gill, Scr.
                    Nabbs, 206.

[William Crouch, of Charlestown, married Sarah, daughter of Barnabas Lamson, of Cambridge. See Wyman's Charlestown, pp. 251, 597; Paige's Cambridge, p. 597.—EDITOR.

In connection with the above it may be well to notice the will of Peter Lidget of Boston, merchant, made 10 February, 1670-71, with a codicil dated 21 April, 1676, proved 5 May, 1676. (Suff. Reg. Prob., B. 6, pp. 160-162.) The following persons are named : My wife Elizabeth, my daughter Elizabeth, wife of John Usher, my only son Charles, my daughter Jane, my three children, the three children of my sister Elizabeth Cornel, lately deceased, viz: Peter, Mary and Robert, my sister Mary Smith's two children, John and Peter, they living in Essex, to be paid in London, my three kinswomen, cousin Crouch of Charlestown, cousin Cooke of Cambridge and cousin Rice of Sudbury, the three children of my aunt Lampson, my grandchild Elizabeth Usher, jr. My son Charles to marry Mrs Bethiah Shrimpton.—H. F. W.]

THOMAS BURNELL, citizen and clothworker of London, 5 July, 1661, with a codicil bearing date 19 August, 1661, proved 2 October, 1661, by the oath of Hester Burnell his widow.

Remembering the saying of St. Jerome which soundeth daily in mine ears, *Surgite mortui et venite ad judicium.*

If I die in London, to be buried within the chancel door of the parish

church of Allhallows Barking, near Tower Hill, under the gravestone there
lying where my dear brother John Burnell and his virtuous wife Mary (of
worthy memory) lie buried.   But if it shall please the almighty God that I
shall die at Stanmore Magna then my desire is that I may be buried there in
the vault within that chancel door of the said parish church where the bones
of my dear deceased father and mother lie buried, at the discretion of my loving and dear wife Hester Burnell.   To my she cousin Hasell, my nephew
John Burnell Senr, and his three sisters, An, Katherine and Elizabeth, and
to the three sons of my deceased brother William Burnell, viz: Thomas,
John and Henry Burnell ; also unto my sister Rewse, my two nephews
John and Richard Ball and their five sisters, An, Barbara, Jane, Margaret
and Elizabeth, my cousin Sarah Edlin and also my cousin William Pindar,
jun^r, for his help for the getting in of mine estate,—to all of them the sum
of thirty pounds apiece.   Also I give unto my nephew John Morley, resident in New England, and to his sister-in-law, the wife of his brother Thomas Morley deceased, the sum of ten pounds apiece, and unto her son Thomas Morley, both resident in or about Hamburgh, together with all the
children of my nephews John Burnell, Senr, and Thomas and Henry Burnell, lawfully begotten in wedlock, that shall be living at my death, the sum
of five pounds apiece.   To my loving and dear wife fifty pounds.   Also
unto her loving brother, Henry Wollastone, Esq. and his son Henry, my
brother-in-law Robert Smyth, my nephew Doctor Richard Ball, my cousin
Doctor William Pindar, my cousin Thomas Reeve, my cousin James
Gough, my nephew John Burnell, sen^r, my cousin Doctor Coe, Bourcheirs
and Rudyere, my cousins Thomas and Henry Burnell, and all their wives,
also my sister Rewse, my cousin Anne Young and her sister Allett, and my
cousin Sarah Edlin, widow, also unto my cousin John Ball, Esq. and my
cousin William Robinson and my cousin John Cooke ; also unto my cousins
Doctor Trench and Doctor Deake and Doctor Winter and their wives, and
old Mrs Churchman, the sometime bedle's wife of Marchant Taylor's Hall ;
to all the sum of six pounds apiece towards their mourning.
    My copyhold land and houses in Stanmore Magna, in the County of Mid-
dlesex unto my wife for and during her natural life.   Whereas I have lately purchased another house and land lying in or near upon Weald Green in
the parish of Harrow upon the Hill, called or known by the name of
Brookes, another field, wood ground and springs called Sander's Hill, and
now both in the tenure and occupation of John Dancer ; and also my present house and garden wherein I now dwell here in London, &c. &c., with
five other tenements, all lying in the court or alley called Nunn's Court or
Alley, in the street or parish of St. Stephens, Coleman Street, London,
(and other leases, &c.) ;—all these to my wife for life ; and then to my
nephew John Burnell, Senr, my chief house and lands lying in Stanmore
Magna, called and known by the name of Fiddles (and a lot of other lands
there-to my said nephew for life, then to his wife, if he do marry again, and
his children equally, during the natural life or second marriage of his said
second wife, if he marry again, then equally among his children and their
heirs forever ; failing such issue, equally among the children of the three
daughters of my eldest brother John Burnell long since deceased.   Also,
after my wife's decease, I give, &c. to my nephew Thomas Burnell, eldest
son of my brother William Burnell deceased, my two thirds of the house
and land he now lives in, called, &c. Buggs, for life, then to his wife and
children during her life or second marriage, then to the children.   To my
nephew John Burnell, jun^r now resident in the East Indies (estate in Har-

row, &c). To my nephews John and Richard Ball (the house, &c. in London). Legacies to godson Burnell Ball, son of said nephew Richard Ball, to my brother Robert Smyth, my brother Thomas Wollaston and my brother-in-law Justice Henry Wollaston.

The witnesses to the will were Robert Fenn, Peter Whitinge and William Pindar, Jun[r]. It was published by the said Thomas Burnell for his will 19 August, 1661.

In the codicil he names his nephew Thomas Burnell, citizen and haberdasher of London, nephew Henry Burnell, citizen and leatherseller of London and his three daughters, Elizabeth, Mary and Barbara, nephew John Burnell, citizen and clothworker of London, now in the East Indies, nephew William Pindar, citizen and clothworker of London and niece Elizabeth Gough, wife of James Gough.

The witnesses to the codicil were John Mosse, Notary Public, and Edward Bullocke. May, 150.

[Stanmore Magna lies at the extremity of the County of Middlesex, towards Hertfordshire, from which county John Morley probably came, as shown by his will, wherein he disposes of real estate in Cheshunt, Hertfordshire. John Burnell, Esq., was lord of the manor of Stanmore, and died in 1605. After her death it was for some time the property of her son Thomas Burnell, Esq., as we learn from Lyson's Environs of London (vol. 3), in which also are given the arms of this family :—*Sable on a bend Or three escallops of the field.—*H. F. W.]

JOHN ASTWOOD, of Milford in the Colony of Newhaven in New England, 27 June, 1654, proved 31 August, 1654, by his son Samuel Astwood.

To my loving wife Sarah Astwood all my estate in New England whatsoever it be in household stuff or cattle or debts, to be disposed by her as she shall see meet for her own proper use. Of my estate here in England, in Abutley, I do give my brother William Astwood ten pounds sterling within one year after my decease. To my loving mother five pounds sterling and the use of two rooms of my house so long as she please. To my brother Robert Astwood do I give five pounds sterling within two years after my decease. To John Rute do I give ten shillings after my decease. The rest of my property to my executor. My son Samuel to be sole executor. The witnesses were Nicholas Hudley and Robert Swan (by mark).

Alchin, 505.

[See REGISTER, xiv. 304 ; xxxv. 245.—EDITOR.]

PETER CUSHING, citizen and turner of London, 2 February, 1663, proved 12 January, 1664. To wife Godly Cushing (referring to contract with John Greenhill of London and William Newbold of London, gent.). The messuage or tenement wherein I now dwell, in or near Broad Street, London, and other tenements. To my brother Thomas Cushing. To ten ministers (who are named). To the " M[r], Warden and Cominalty of the Mistery or Arte de lez Turnors," London, whereof I am a member. To Abigail Phillips, Margaret Bull and Sarah Norris, my god-daughter. To my loving friend Francis Gillow of Stratford Bow, in the county of Middlesex, gent. To Martha Gamlin, now wife of Henry Gamlyn and daughter of the said Francis Gillow. To my sister Katherine. To William and Robert Cushing, sons of my brother William Cushing. My loving friend M[r] William Devonshire. My God daughter Sarah Norris, the daughter of David Norris, in St. Clement's Lane. To my wife's kinsman, Richard Hill, twenty pounds. My loving brother Theophilus Cushing. My brother William Cushing's youngest daughter. To Anne Cushing, daughter of my said brother William.

"I give and bequeath unto each one of the children of my nephew Daniell Cushing, son of my late brother Matthew Cushing, which shalbe living at my death fiftie pounds a peece." To Deborah Briggs, wife of Matthew Briggs, one hundred pounds.—all within twelve months next after the decease of my wife Godly. The residue to my brother Thomas Cushing. The tenement in Bread Street which I purchased of William Swayne, Esq. Loving friends Arthur Remington, Thomas Hartley and William Greenwood to hold property in trust. After payment of debts, legacies, annuities, &c. the residue to my said nephew Daniel Cushing and to Jeremy Cushing, Matthew Cushing and John Cushing, sons of the said Matthew "Cushion." my brother deceased.

The witnesses were Francis Gillow, Henry Woods, John Dawson and Thomas Stevens.   Hyde, 3.

[See REGISTER, x. 79, 173.—H. F. W.]

ELIZABETH HAILES of Lower Shadwell in the parish of Stebunheath als Stepney, in the County of Middlesex, widow, 28 September, 1664, proved 22 March, 1664, by Thomas Parker and William Bugby, the executors. My executors to invite such a number of my christian friends as they shall think fit to accompany my corps to my funeral, and to disburse and lay out for the accommodation of those friends the full sum of thirty pounds. To my cousin Thomas Parker twenty pounds, and to my cousin Ann Parker, his wife, twenty shillings. To my cousin John Parker, son of my said cousin Thomas Parker, thirty pounds. To my cousin Thomas Little ten pounds; to Elizabeth Little, his wife, thirty pounds; and to Mary Little, his daughter, ten pounds. To my grandchild William Bugby, five pounds. To my cousin John Foster, of Tower Hill, and to ——, his wife, five pounds apiece. To my cousin William Foster, at New England, the full sum of ten pounds of like lawful money. To my cousin —— Graves, of Tower Hill, widow, twenty shillings. To my cousin Elizabeth Harris ten pounds, and to her daughter ——, my husband's goddaughter, four pounds. To my cousin —— Appleby, of London, Beavermaker, and to ——, his wife, five pounds apiece. To my cousin Isaac Foster's daughter, four pounds; to my cousin Elizabeth Parsons twenty pounds; to my cousin Martha Goodwin twenty pounds; to my cousin John Hutchinson twenty pounds. To my said cousin John Hutchinson's five sons (that is to say) John, Henry, Edmond, Thomas and George Hutchinson, ten pounds apiece. To my cousin Ann Barber, widow, twenty pounds, to her daughter Susan, now the wife of Robert Aldons, ten pounds, and to the children of the said Susan ten pounds. These legacies to be paid within one month next after my decease to the several respective legatees, or to so many of them as shall demand the same; they to give absolute discharges of any further claim to mine or my deceased husband's estate.

To my cousin Thomas Parker the full sixteenth part of the good ship William and Elizabeth, of London, &c. &c., of which ship he the said Thomas Parker, under God, at the date hereof, is master. To Jane Bugby, the wife of my aforesaid grandchild William Bugby, my full two and thirtieth part of the good ship called the Owners Adventure, of London, &c. &c., of which ship, under God, the said William Bugby, at the date hereof, is master. To my aforesaid cousin John Parker my other two and thirtieth part of the aforesaid ship. Twenty pounds amongst the poor of Shadwell, to be "distributed to and amongst the Auntient poore and such as are not Idle, drunken or of badd conversation," within one month next after my decease. Twenty pounds to another division of Stepney, respect being first had to aged poor seamen and their families in want.

My loving cousin Thomas Parker and my loving grandchild William Bugby to be my executors, and my loving friends Mr John Hall and Mr Day to be the overseers. Two twenty shilling pieces of gold to be given to Doctor William Clarke, minister of Stepney, for his pains to preach my funeral sermon, if he shall please to undertake the same. To my nurse Margaret Wybrow forty shillings.

The witnesses were John Hulme, Elizabeth Hill, Raph Matthews and William Bissaker.   Hyde, 25.

ROGER GLOVER of London, merchant, being now at the Island of Meavis, 14 November, 1636, proved 5 Sept. 1637. William Hawkins, citizen and waxchandler of London, to be overseer. Goods, &c. in the Increase of London to be disposed of for the advantage of Richard Rowe of London, merchant, my loving brother Richard Glover of London, merchant, and my loving sisters Elizabeth and Sara Glover, whom I appoint, &c. executors. Debts due in the Indyes and debts formerly due in any part of the West Indyes. To my niece Elizabeth Glover, daughter of my loving brother Joss: Glover fifty pounds. To William Rowe, son of the said Richard Rowe, thirty pounds. To my niece Elizabeth Pemmerton forty pounds. To John Worcester ten pounds. To my friend Capt. Thomas Sparrowe, Governor of the Island of Meavis two thousand weight of tobacco. To Mr George Upcote of the same Island five hundred weight of tobacco. To Nicholas Godsalve, Secretary, three hundred pounds of tobacco. Debts due from Thomas Littleton late Governor of the abovesaid Island. To James Littleton, his son, one hundred pounds.

The witnesses were Thomas Sparrow, John Worcester, Thomas Hinde and Nicholas Godsalue, Secr.   Goare, 126.

THOMAS NELSON of Rowlay in the County of Essex in New England, being by Providence called now to make a voyage into Old England " this sixt of Sextilis, here called August, 1648." To wife Joane for her natural life my mill, millhouse, &c. in Rowlay and all that ground near unto the said mill, lately in the occupation of Joseph Wormehill, and all my upland and meadow or other ground between Rowley Oxe Pasture on one part, the common on another part and the Mill River and the Brook that goeth from the town on the other part,—all containing fifty acres more or less, provided she make no claim to any other part of my houses, lands, &c.,—also two acres of ground in the Pond field next Mrs Rogers, during her natural life (leaving out the pond), to build her an house. The reversion of said mills, &c. I give amongst my children and their heirs, as well that child which my wife is withall as the rest. To my eldest son Philip Nelson a double portion, and to son Thomas Nelson and daughter Marie Nelson and the child or children she is withall their equal parts. Richard Bullingtam (sic) Esq. and my honored uncle Richard Dumer gen^t shall have the education of my son Philip Nelson and Thomas Nelson and the proportions of both their estates, &c. for their education and maintenance, till they come to the age of twenty-one years, &c. My uncle Richard Dummer to have the education of my daughter Marie Nelson and the other children. To my son Philip Nelson the sum of ten pounds which was given him by my aunt Katharine Witham and is in my hands, &c. Mr Richard Bellingham and my uncle Richard Dumer to be executors. I would intreat Mr Ezekiell Rogers of Rowly and Mr John Norton of Ipswich to be overseers. Signed Dec. 24th, 1645, in presence of Jeremy Howchin and Ezechiell Northens.

I Thomas Nelson being about to return to Rowland in New England do by these present test-my confirming of my last will and testament which I made and left in New England with my wife's uncle Mr Richard Dumer.

—— My youngest child Samuel Nelson being born since that will was made, &c. &c.

The witnesses were Henry Jacike a͟ls Jesse, Daniel Elly (by mark), Sara Appleyard (by mark).

The above will was proved 21 February, 1650, by Richard Dummer one of the executors, power being reserved for Richard Bellingham, the other executor, &c.   Grey, 30.

[See Essex Co. Court Papers, vol. iii. Nos. 65 and 70.—H. F. WATERS. This will was also proved and recorded in the Suffolk County Probate Court. An abstract is printed in the REGISTER, iii. 267-9. An account of Thomas Nelson is printed in the REGISTER, xxxv. 271 ; see also pp. 261, 267, 269.—EDITOR.]

BENJAMIN WOODBRIDGE of Englefield, in the county of Berks, 25 October, 1684 (nuncupative) in presence and hearing of Dame Elizabeth Alleyn, Mrs Mary Alleyn and Mrs Mariabella Charles. He bequeathed all to his wife Mary. As no executor was named, Letters of Administration were issued to his widow 3 April, 1685.   Cann. 51.

[His name stands first on the list of graduates of Harvard College. See REGISTER, xxxii. 293.—EDITOR.]

PARGITER.

London ye 2^d of August 1654

Brother Francis —— I beinge now intended by divine providence for Ireland desireinge in my absence that you would be pleased to receive and open whatsoever letters shall come to mee from beyound Seas, or from freinds here ; And for what goods of mine or others that shalbe consigned to mee from the Barbadoes or elcewhere I request you to enter them in the custome house and take them up and to dispose of them at price Currant (except you see anie probability to advance by keepinge of them which I leave to yor discretion And withall you may please to take notice that I stand indebted to the Account of John Washington (as per Account sent him thirty eight pound tenn shillings and tenn pence, which monies is to pay the fraught of Servants to the Barbadoes in case his freinds have or shall provide anie to send him   And for the dischargeinge of part of this debt I herewith leave you a bond of Thomas Pargiter's for twenty and three pounds payable to mee the Sixth day of September next, but since hee made this bond to mee I have had of him to the value of aboute Seaventeene shillings   Soe rests due but twenty two pounds and three shillings.   The rest (or this if his occation require it sooner) I desire you wilbe pleased to disburse for mee And to pay yo^rselfe out of the proceeds of such goods of mine as shall come to your hands   There is likewise due from mee to my cosen Robert Wards account five pounds which monies as soone as you shall have soe much monies of mine in your hands I then desire it may be paid to James Yeates for my Cosen Robert Wards Account   I likewise leave one bill of Ladinge for my cosen John Washington's goods shipt in the Advice Mr Robert May which I desire may be sent him the verie next shipp after Mr Mays that shall goe for the Barbadoes And if Mr Lapsey will doe mee the favour (as hee hath promised mee) which is to lett mee have aboute halfe a dozen hoggs heads of his Virginia Tobacco at price Currant to Satisfie the debt of thirty two pound Seaventeene shillings and eleaven pence which hee owes mee I shall then desire my Cosen Thomas Pargiter the groser, or some others of Judgment whom you shall thincke fitt to looke it over that it be found marchantable and good and worth the monie And then desire you to receave it and shipp it out in his name for Waterford or Dublin in Ireland And this is all the materiall at present: only (in case of mortallity) I then bequeath to you the hundred and fifty pounds now restinge in my brother Robert Pargiters hands for which a yeares interest was due to mee in may last And there is three pounds tenn shillings and nine pence due to mee from my nephew William Pargiter And I doe stand indebted unto Thomas Pargiter's brother who lives at Wardington five pounds And five pounds more to my ffather which hee lett him have long since And for what other estate of mine shalbe cominge to mee from beyound Seas together with the ffifty pounds my brother ffrancis Smith hath of mine upon a mortgage I doe as before (only in case of mortallity) bequeath it to my brother William Pargiter and my brother Ezechiell Pargiter to bee equally devided betweene them. Soe wishinge you health and prosperity in all your affaires I take leave and rest Your Loveinge brother to Comand Theodor Pargiter.

Commission or Letters of Administration issued 20 May, 1656, to William Pargiter and Ezekiel Pargiter, natural and lawful brothers of the deceased. Berkeley, 164.

[What is known of this John Washington who was in Barbadoes just before the emigrant ancestor of George Washington settled in Virginia?—EDITOR.]

Letters of Administration on the estate of JOHN LLOYDE, late in Virginia, deceased, granted 27 August, 1653, to his daughter Mary Lloyde.
Admon Act Book P. C. C., 1653, fol. 24.

[Though I have not met with the name of John Lloyde in early record or print of Virginia, the following data of others of the same name may prove of interest. The State Land Registry Office presents of record, grants to Cornelius Lloyd, 800 acres in Elizabeth City county, June 2, 1635; 400 acres on the west branch of Elizabeth River, March 13, 1636; 100 acres on the east side of Elizabeth River, Dec. 22, 1636—Book No. 1, pp. 394, 359 and 406 severally. Cornelius Lloyd of London, merchant, Wm. Tucker, Maurice Tompson, George Tompson, William Harris, Thomas Dobson, James Stone and Jeremiah Blackman, mariner, 8000 acres in Charles City county, February 9, 1636, Book No. 1, p. 410. Edmund Lloyd, 400 acres in James City county, May 20, 1636, Book No. 1, p. 359. Humphrey Lloyd, 250 acres in Charles River county, November 6, 1637, Book No. 1, p. 523. Cornelius Lloyd was a member of the House of Burgesses from Lower Norfolk county, March 2, 1642-3, Oct. 1, 1644, and Nov. 3, 1647. "Leftenant Colonel" Cornelius Lloyd as a burgess from Lower Norfolk county, May 6, 1652, and July 5, 1653.—Hening's Statutes, i. pp. 239, 283, 340, 373 and 379. Edward Lloyd as burgess from Lower Norfolk county, Feb. 17, 1644-5.—Hening, i. p. 289.—R. A. BROCK, Richmond, Va.]

Letters of Administration on the estate of ROBERT BOUGHTON the younger, late in New England, bachelor, deceased, issued to his father Robert Boughton, 31 January, 1655.
Admon Act Book P. C. C., 1656, fol. 6.

Letters of Administration on the estate of SAMUEL FRYE, late in Virginia, bachelor, deceased, issued 12 March, 1655, to his mother Ann Frye, widow. Admon Act Book P. C. C., 1656.

[The following grants of record in the Virginia Land Registry Office may have some connection with the testator Samuel Frye :—To William Frye, 250 and 500 acres in James City county, May 20, 1637, and Aug. 29, 1643, Book No. 1, pp. 421 and 906 ; to Joseph Farye, 250 acres in Charles City county, May 27, 1638, Book No. 1, p. 561.—R. A. BROCK, Richmond, Va.]

Letters of Administration on the estate of ANDREW GILLIARD, in ship King of Poland, late in Virginia, deceased, issued 2 April, 1656, to John Pulling, cousin German.   Admon Act Book P. C. C., 1656.

Letters of Administration on the estate of MARGARET GIBBONS, late of New England, but at her death of Plymouth in County Devon, issued 28 February, 1656, to Jerusha Rea, now the wife of Capt. Thomas Rea, natural and lawful daughter of the deceased.

Admon Act Book P. C. C., 1657.

[This was Margaret, widow of Maj. Gen. Edward Gibbons. See REGISTER, viii. 276; ix. 346; Savage's Gen. Dict. ii. 245; Wyman's Charlestown, i. 406.—ED.]

Letters of Administration on the estate of RICHARD PATE, late in Virginia, deceased, issued 30 October, 1657, to John Pate, his brother's son.

Admon Act Book P. C. C., 1657.

[The following grants are of record in the Virginia Land Registry Office :—Richard Pate, 1141 acres, of land on the north side of York River, Dec. 12, 1650, Book No. 2, p. 271.   John Pate, 1000 acres in Rappahannock county, Dec. 31, 1662, Book No. 5, p. 201.   The name Pate is numerously represented in Virginia at the present day.—R. A. BROCK, Richmond, Va.]

FRANCIS ANTHONY, Doctor of Physick, 25 May, 1623, proved 19 June, 1623.   To be buried in the parish church of St. Bartholmewes.   My lease at Barnes I bequeath to my beloved wife, consisting of mansion house, garden, orchard, &c., late in the occupation of Thomas Erskins, and ten pounds a year to be paid out of my dwelling house in St. Bartholmewes, during her natural life, and all moneys in the hands of Sir Stephen le Sure, Knight, and Mr Richards.   To my daughter Martha, as her dowry money, three hundred pounds.   The inheritance of this my dwelling house in St. Bartholmewes to Francis my son, my copyhold lands, &c. in Barnes to my youngest son Charles.   Other estates to eldest son Francis.

To my sons Francis, John and Charles all that state of mine in Virginia, together with all disbursements of all and singular such moneys as the Company have received from me for thirty shares, and all the appurtenances in Southampton Hundred there, to be divided amongst them by equal portions as long as they shall be living, "and so to the longest liver of them three."   To my wife the basin and ewer of silver and all such other plate as was in her possession at the time of my marriage with her.   To my daughter Vickars twenty pounds a year.   To my son Charles twenty pounds a year during the term of the lease at Barnes.   To my daughter Smith and my daughter Martha each twenty pounds, in the same manner. To John and Charles, my sons, all my books equally except my written books, which I bequeath to Charles.   To them I give and bequeath all my medicines equally.

I appoint my wife and Sir Stephen le Sure, Knight, my executors, and Mr Humfrey Selwood overseer.

The testator made his mark 26 May.   Probate was granted to Elizabeth Anthony the relict and one of the executors, power being reserved for the other.   On the 17th of March, 1629, commission issued to Sir Stephen le Sieur, Knt, the other executor.   Swann, 60.

FRANCIS ANTHONY of London, gentleman, 11 Aug. 1623, proved 18 Aug. 1623.   To be buried in the parish of St. Gyles without Crepelgate, London.   To wife Judith Anthony all those two leases of the mansion house, &c.

&c. situate, lying and being in Barnes in the County of Surrey, sometime in the tenure of one Thomas Erskins, and my right, title, interest, &c. in the same by virtue of the last will and testament of Francis Anthony, my father deceased, on condition she do suffer my mother in law Elizabeth Anthony to enjoy such part of the same mansion house and premisses as by the last will and testament of my said father she is appointed to enjoy, and that she pay such legacies as are or shall be due to be paid to my said mother for her dower, my brother Charles Anthony, my sister—Robinson, my sister—Smith and my sister Martha, out of the same two leases, &c. or out of my messuage or tenement in the tenure of John Anthony my brother, situate, lying and being in the parish of Great St. Bartholmewe near West Smithfield. To my son Edmond Anthony all my said messuage or tenement in Great St. Bartholmewe, &c. to hold forever ; but if my said son Edmond shall depart this present life before he shall accomplish his full age of twenty and one years then to Elizabeth Anthony my daughter. If both die before accomplishing the age of twenty one then to my said wife Judith for and during the term of her natural life, my wife to receive the rents, &c. until they attain their several ages, as aforesaid. To my said daughter Elizabeth one hundred and fifty pounds at her age of twenty one or day of marriage. To Sara Russha my daughter in law fifteen pounds due me by bond from my brother Charles Anthony within four years next after the date hereof. To my said wife all the arras hangings, the best taffata bed, &c. To the poor of St. Gyles without Crepelgate ten shillings. The residue to my wife Judith whom I appoint executrix. My brother John Anthony, Doctor of Physicks, and Edmund Bollyvant to be overseers. Wit: John Wandley Scr., Edward Leche, John Duesh.

Swann, 87.

[Frauncis Anthoyne obijt one Wensdaye the 13 of August buryed in St Giles Criplegatt before the Pulpett the 15 of ye same 1623 wt 7 escochens.—*Harleian MSS.* 1754, f. 63.—H. F W.]

EZEKIELL CULVERWELL, of London, clerk, 5 July, 1630, proved 9 May, 1631. To Nicholas Piccard my kinsman ten pounds. To Katherine my kinswoman ten pounds. To Mrs Johnson, wife to Frederick Johnson, five pounds. Item to Margaret Chevers, for herself and her son Ezekiell, ten pounds. To John Hudson, student at the University in Dublin, forty shillings. To Josiah, son to Martha Wilson, five pounds. To old Alice Grinder twenty shillings. To old Ellyn Smith, a maid, forty shillings. To Ezekiell Washbourne, son of Robert Washbourne, five pounds. To my daughter Sarah one hundred pounds to her own use. To Benedict, son of my daughter Sarah Barfoot, two hundred pounds. To poor faithful preachers and godly poor students in either University one hundred pounds. For all my English books (my bible in quarto excepted, which I give to Martha Wilson) I leave to my executrix for her own use. All my Latin books I will to be divided in three parts, equally as may be, and then, by lot, to give to Nicholas Piccard one lot, to Josias Wilson another lot, a third lot to Ezekiell Cheuers. The residue to my daughter Sara, whom I appoint sole executrix. Wit: Arthur Harbur.

Reg. of Commissary Court of London (1629–34), fol. 147.

[Ezekiel Culverwell, a Puritan divine and author, was curate of Felsted in Essex, but in 1583 was suspended for not wearing the surplice ; was afterwards rector of Stambridge magna in the same county, of which living he was deprived about 1609, his successor having been instituted March 27 of that year. He was afterwards curate of St. Antholin's, London. The register of that church, contains this entry

under the year 1631 : " April 14, Mᵣ Ezekiel Culverwell, minister, bur." Biographical sketches are printed in Brook's Puritans, iii. 512, and Davids's Nonconformity in Essex, p. 125. See also Newcourt's Repertorium, ii. 542 ; Register of
St. Antholin (Harl. Soc.), p. 65. Brook and Davids give the titles and dates of his
works ; as does also Allibone in his Dictionary of Authors, i. 458.—EDITOR.

Ezekiel Cheever, one of the legatees named in the foregoing will, was doubtless
the famous master of the Boston Latin School. He was born in London, Jan. 25,
1614, came to Boston in New England in 1637, and died there Aug. 21, 1708, in the
ninety-fourth year of his age. For a biographical notice of him and an account of
his family, see the articles entitled " Ezekiel Cheever and Some of his Descendants,"
in the REGISTER for April, 1879 (xxxiii. 164), and April, 1884 (xxxviii. 170).—JOHN
T. HASSAM.

In vol. i. p. 395 London Visitations (edited by Dr. Howard and Col. Chester),
appears the marriage of Thomas Horton, of London, merchant, aº 1634, 3d son to
Margaret, dau. of Lawrence Culverwell.—J. C. J. BROWN.]

JAMES HOLT of Virginia, planter, 8 December, 1629, proved 12 May,
1631. To my son James Hoult all and singular my goods, catells, chat-
ells, household stuff and all my houses and ground and all other things
which I have or may have in Virginia or elsewhere ; and also all the servants which are or shall be mine in Virginia, and all the time that they
have yet to serve with me ; only to my servant William Bond one year of
his time. To my servant Richard Bawinton four years of his time. My
executors to be Nathaniel Flood, planter, Henry King, planter, Theophilus Berrestone, planter.

Wit : Theophilus Berrestone and Peter Perkins.

Emanavit commissio Wᵐᵒ Donne, curatori ad lites Jacobi Houlte, &c.
(for the reason, it appears, that those named executors in the will were beyond the seas).

Reg. of Commissary Court of London (1629–34), fol. 150.

[The following grants from the Virginia Land Registry Office may be informatory
in connection with the above.

Randall Holt, 400 acres in James City county, Sept. 18, 1636 ; Thomas Holt, 500
acres in New Norfolk county, May 22, 1637 ; Robert Holt, 700 acres in James City
county, July 23, 1640.—Book No. 1, pp. 386, 423 and 727.

John Fludd, 2100 acres in James City county, May 12, 1638, Book No. 1, p. 548.
John Flood, " Gentleman," " an antient planter," 1100 acres in James City county,
June 7, 1650—" Mary Flood, John Flood, John Lawrence and John Connaway,"
being among the " head-rights."—Book No. 2, p. 227. Francis Flood, 300 acres
on York river, April 1, 1651, Book No. 2, p. 318. John King, 300 acres in Charles
River county, Dec. 10, 1642 ; " Anne his wife, Katharine Kallaway, Thomas Clary,
Phillip Neale, Alice Smith and Alice Cocke," " transports " or " head-rights " ;
John King, 500 acres in York county, Nov. 9, 1649.—Book No. 2, p. 192. John
King; 200 acres in " Gloster " county, October 10, 1651, Book No. 2, p. 345.—R.
A. BROCK, Richmond, Va.]

Notes on Abstracts previously printed.

THOMAS SPELMAN (*ante,* p. 72).

[The Thomas Spelman (Spilman) of Virginia, an abstract of whose will is found
in the Genealogical Gleanings of Henry F. Waters, in the REGISTER of July, 1884, p.
323, came to Virginia in A.D. 1616, when he was about sixteen years of age. His
wife Hannah, when about eighteen years old, arrived in A.D. 1620. In the Muster
of Inhabitants, taken in January, 1624–5, and published in *Hotten's Lists,* Thomas
was then listed as twenty-four years old and his wife as twenty-three. The daugh
ter Mary, in England, in 1627 could not have been more than six years old. Spilman in 1625 had four white servants in his employ, and lived at Kecoughton in

Elizabeth City Corporation, now Hampton. At the same time there was another Thomas Spilman living at James City, twenty-eight years of age, who came in A.D. 1623, and was a servant of Richard Stephens, who arrived in the ship George with him. Stephens was for several years a prominent colonist.—From Rev. EDWARD D. NEILL, of St. Paul, Min.]

RACHEL PERNE (*ante*, pp. 60–61).

[I may add from my own family papers, that " John Tyse, clerk," son-in-law of Richard and Rachel Perne, mentioned on p. 60, had two children, John and Mary. The former, I think, died unmarried ; but Mary married, first, John (or Nicholas) Goddard, of Gillingham, and, secondly, in 1681, ᷇William Weston, of Weston in Stalbridge, both in Dorsetshire. She died about the year 1725, having had an only son, John Goddard of Gillingham, who died in 1702, leaving, by his wife Martha Cox, who predeceased him, Mary Goddard, sole heiress. She became in 1717 the wife of William Helyar of Coker, co. Somerset, eldest son of William Helyar of Coker, M.P. for Somersetshire in 1714, and from this marriage is descended the present Horace Augustus Helyar of Coker Court, Secretary of the British Embassy at the Hague.—*Letter of the Rev. Charles J. Robinson, M.A., of West Hackney, London, England.*]

THOMAS BROWNE, 17 April, 1663, proved 17 July, 1663. List of Property &c. viz :—on board the Samuel, Jemaico, one half of fifty thousand pounds of Sugar, the other half belonging to George Thompson. Goods coming per George Ladd. I left behind, in hands of George Thompson, &c. I have in Abraham Brown's hands, in New England, one hundred and fifty pounds. I have in brother William's hands about one hundred pounds. I have in Virginia employment fifty pounds, &c.

For the hundred pounds to brother William, I freely forgive him. To my sister Joane Browne twenty pounds, besides ten pounds I owe her. To my cousin Joane Browne ten pounds. Which sums I desire may be paid out of the sugars I have in Barbados. The balance ; to my son Thomas, God sending him to age, one third, and two thirds to my wife Priscilla Browne.

Wit: Argent Tuttle, William Browne.   Juxon, 89.

[Abraham Browne, an early settler of Watertown, is supposed by Bond, in his history of that town, to be a son of Thomas Browne of Swan Hall, in the parish of Hawkedon, co. Suffolk, by his wife Joan. A tabular pedigree of this family from John Browne, alderman of Stamford, co. Lincoln, in 1376 and 1377, is found in that book, pp. 116–17.—EDITOR.]

JOHN PEMERTON (by mark) of Lawford in the County of Essex, weaver, 9 September, 1653, proved 25 March, 1654, by John Beeston, sole executor. For my worldly goods being in New England, in the custody of Hercules Woodman, living in Newbery in the County of Essex, or his assigns, I give and bequeath unto my daughter-in-law Deborah Gofe, there born, and to her heirs forever, and all my moveable goods which I now possess in this England, both within doors and without, whatsoever. I make and ordain my loving kinsman and faithful friend, John Beeston of Dedham, my executor. My debts to be paid within six months next after my decease. My desire is likewise that if my said daughter-in-law should happen to die without heirs that then all the forementioned estate should be equally divided, that is, for my means in New England, to my brother James Pemerton and to my sister Robinson, to be equally divided between them. And for such my other goods my desire is that they may be divided equally between my three brothers, William, Richard and Thomas.

The witnesses were William Winge, John Stud and Thomas Boston.

Alchin, 191.

[The above will throws light upon the family of the Reverend Ebenezer Pemberton, minister of the old South Church in Boston, 700–1717, the testator evidently being his uncle John, who was of Boston 1632, and afterwards of Newbury. Savage suggests that he may have been living in Winnesemit in 1662 ; but that suggestion is disproved, not only by this discovery but also by a document among the Massachusetts Archives (B. 15, No. 43), wherein John Pamerton of Winnesimmet distinctly calls himself (14 April, 1662) son of James, of Malden.   H. F. W.

The name of " Hercules Woodman, of Malford [probably Christian-Malford, Wiltshire], mercer," appears in the list of passengers who embarked " aboute the vᵗ of Aprill 1635 " in the James of London, William Cooper, master. (See REGISTER, xiv. 333.) He settled at Newbury. His true name was Archelaus, at least that is the name he went by in this country.

Another person by this surname, namely, Edward Woodman, settled at Newbury, Mass., about the same time as Archelaus. He was deputy from Newbury and held other important offices. A genealogy of the Woodman family by a descendant, Cyrus Waterman, A.M., was published in 1874. The author supposes that Edward Woodman came from Corsham in Wiltshire, about eleven miles from Christian-Malford. No connection has been traced between Edward and Archelaus Woodman. Who was the Deborah Goffe named as born in New England?—EDITOR.]

RICHARD LARDNER of Portsea, in the County of Southampton, merchant, nominated Mʳ Urian Oakes of Southweeke, Southampton, gentleman, and Mʳ Thomas Mills and Mʳ John Mills, of Portsmouth, overseers to the carrying out of his will, proved 1670–71.   Duke, 64.

ALICIA LISLE of Moyles Court in the County of Southampton, widow, 9 June, 1682, with codicil of same date, proved 11 November, 1689. To the poor of the parish of Ellingham two pounds within one year after my decease. I have settled upon Thomas Tipping of Wheatfield in the County of Oxford, Esq., and Christopher Warman of Milborne Weekes in the County of Somerset, gentleman, their heirs and assigns, the reversion and inheritance of the moiety of the manor of Moyles Court, alias Rockford Moyles and over-Burgatt and several other manors, lands, tenements and hereditaments in the said County of Southampton and in the County of Dorset and elsewhere, mentioned in an indenture tripartite, dated 19 Feb. 1678, to be conveyed to William Tipping, Esq., for five hundred years, who hath since conveyed and assigned over his interest, &c. to the said Thomas Tipping and Christopher Warman ; which said conveyance is in trust for the payment of certain debts in a schedule thereunto annexed, &c. &c. The overplus (after payment of such debts) to my worthy friends, the said William Tipping and Mrs. Frances Tipping his sister, Richard Lloyd, citizen and linen-draper of London, and Triphena his wife, to hold forever upon this especial trust, &c. to discharge my funeral expenses and pay debts, &c. and to pay unto my daughter Anne twelve hundred pounds at the age of one and twenty years or day of marriage, to pay unto my grandaughter —— Hore, daughter of my daughter Bridgett, now in New England, the sum of one hundred pounds at age of one and twenty or day of marriage, to pay unto my daughter Mary one annuity or yearly rent of six pounds during her natural life, but if said daughter Mary marry against their consent said annuity shall cease, to pay to daughter Mabella Lisle an annuity of forty pounds (under same conditions). The residue to be distributed among my daughters or daughters' children as they (the trustees) shall think fit. To cousin Judah Rie ten pounds within two years after my decease. To William Carpentar, my servant, thirty pounds (in two years). In the codicil she bequeaths to daughter Margaret, now the wife of Mʳ Whitaker, seventy pounds (in two years). Witnesses Anne Tipping, William Withrington, John Swan and Abiah Browne.   Ent, 159.

[I am indebted to Henry Marillier, Esq., for the reference to the above will.

The following pedigree is from Berry's County Genealogies, County of Hants, pages 173–175.

ARMS.—*Or, on a chief az.*
    three lions rampant,
    of the field.
CREST.—*A stag statant ar.*
    attired or.

Jordan de Insula = Hawise.
lived in time of
King Henry I. and
K. Stephen.

Geffrey de Insula = ...
gave lands in franc almoine
for the soul of Earl Baldwin
of Devonshire.

Walter de Insula, in time of King John = Margaret

Baldwin de Insula = ...
Lord of Wodeton & Plomp-
ton in the Isle of Wight,
lived in time of Henry III.

John de Insula = ...
a baron in the time
of Edward I., and Governor
of Carisbrooke Castle,
ob. 32 Edw. I.

Walter de Insula, Lord of Wodeton = Margaret.

Walter de Insula, Lord of Wodeton = Florence.

William de Insula, Lord of Wodeton = ...

William de Insula = ...
Lord of Wodeton, 44th Edward III.

Sir John de Insula or Lisle, Knt. = Margaret dau. of John
Lord of Wodeton. | Bremshot of Bremshot
in co Southampton.

George Lisle = Anna, dau. of ......
| Montgomery, of Calais.

Lancelot Lisle = Anne, dau. of
| Sir Thos. Wroughton, Knt.

Thomas Lisle = ..., dau. of ..... Moore
of Moore Court, Esq.

Anthony Lisle of Wodeton, Esq. = Elizabeth, dau. of John Dormer
temp. 30th Elizabeth. | of Steeple-Barton in co. Oxon, Esq.

Sir William Lisle = Bridget, dau of Sir John Hungerford
Knighted in 1606: living 1622. | of Down-Ampney in co. Gloucester, Knt.

John Lisle of Moyles Court = Alice, dau. & co-heir of Sir White Beconsawe Knt.,
co. Southampton; he was one of the | beheaded at Winchester, 1685,
judges who condemned King Charles | by the order of Judge Jeffries.
the First, for which he was obliged to
fly the kingdom, and ob. abroad.
2d son. | H. F. W.

Mrs. Bridget Hoar (daughter of John and Alicia Lisle and widow of Leonard Hoar, president of Harvard College) married 1686, Hezekiah Usher, Jr., who died *s. p.* July 11, 1697. She died May 25, 1723. See Usher Genealogy, REG. xxiii. 410–13.—EDITOR.]

THOMAS COTTON, of Pond Street, Hampstead, in the County of Middlesex, gentleman, 9 May, 1730, proved 11 August, 1730, by Bridget Cotton, his widow, and Thomas Cotton, his son. To dear wife Mʳˢ Bridgett Cotton, who for many years has been a dear and tender wife to me and a faithful partner with me in all my joys and sorrows of life and a tender mother to all my dear children, &c.   I appoint her executrix, in conjunction with my son Thomas Cotton, as soon as he shall become of age, which will be, God willing, on the 20 July next ensuing.   To wife I give and bequeath whatever money, bonds, leases or estates that yet belong unto me in any wise upon the death of our dear Honoured mother, Mrs Bridgett Usher, late of Boston in New England, left in trust with the Honoured Judge Sewal or others.   At her decease all my effects, &c. to be equally divided between our two dear children Thomas Cotton and Alicia Cotton.   For, as our eldest son Mr Leonard Cotton wherever he at present is has long ago received from me far above the property of worldly goods I had to bestow upon my children, I only give him ten pounds.

The witnesses were Edward Morton, Anne Tanton and Eleanor Brearecliff.   Auber, 152.

[The following pedigree is from Add. MS. 24458 (Brit. Museum), p. 54.

Thomas Cotton of...... ▬ ....   Wm. Fownes of Kendley = Eliz'th, dau. of ......
    Auditor to Sir Thos.   near Wenlock in co. Salop. | Bought the upper Haigh
    Weston; supposed to be   &c. of Anthony Urton,
    son or gr. son of Richard   30 Sept. 1656. Will dated
    Cotton of Combermere.   7 April, 1655, pro. 22
                                                                                                    January 1658.
                                                                                                    Bur. at Wortley, Feb.
                                                                                                    1657, æt. 62.

....   William Cotton of Nether Denby = Eleanor Fownes,   John.
wife of Leeke   parish of Peniston, gen., an iron | bur. at Peniston,   Gilbert.
of Criggau.   master, living at Wortley 1656, at | 30 Nov. 1699.   George.
                        Hawkhurst, parish of Silkston 1667.
                        Will dated 24 Feb. 1674. Died 13
                        March following and was bur. at
                        Peniston church on 17th.   He
                        bought the Haigh of Wm. Fownes,
                        24 Sept. 1660.

William,   Daniel,   Joanna,   Joshua,   Eleanor,   John,   Susanna.
mar. 1st Barbara,   married   ux. Thos.   drowned   ux. James   d. young.   Elizabeth.
dau. of Thos.   & had issue.   Hall (issue).   at sea, or   Wright, a   Ann.
Curwen; 2d Anna,   died in   silenced   Mary.
dau. of Geo. Westby.   Holland.   minister.
Issue by both.

Thomas Cotton, V.D.M. = Bridget, dau. of Leonard Hoare, Pres'dt of Cambridge
born at or near Wortley 1657. | University in N. E., by Bridget his wife, dau. of the
A minister in London many | Lord Lisle; who remarried ...... Usher.   Portraits
years.   Died 1730 & was buried | of some of this family are in poss'n of Mr. Bayes Cotton.
in Bunhill Fields.

Thomas Cotton = Rebecca, dau. of   Leonard Cotton = ...   Alicia,
of Hackney,   Joshua Bayes,   eldest son,   d. unmarried.
Atty. at Law,   V.D.M., minister   settled in America.
second son,   in London,
d. 23 March, 1797, | d. 7 Feb. 1799, æt. 82.   Colonel Cotton,
æt. 87. Buried at | Bur. in Bunhill Fields.   an American Loyalist.
Bunhill Fields.

Bayes Cotton,   Joshua.
living.

Mrs. Bridget Cotton is mentioned by her step-father, Hezekiah Usher, of Boston, in his will, recorded in Suffolk Co. Probate Registry (B. 11, p. 318), in which, after speaking in very strong terms of his wife, he goes on to say : " But as for her daughter Bridget, if her mother had not been so undermining and over-reaching for her I should a been willing to have done what I could for her and I do give her the tumbler with the armes of a spread eagle with two heads but I think one head for a body is enough." This doubtless refers to the arms of the Hoare family. If so, is it not the earliest sign of their use in New England?

In Massachusetts Archives at the State-House in Boston (Book 8, No. 22), in the case of Samuel Sewall, surviving trustee to Mrs. Bridget Usher, vs. Winthrop, may be found a certificate from the Rev. Joshua Richardson, Rector of the parish church of Allhallows on the Wall, London, 1692, showing that Mr. Thomas Cotton of Peniston in the County of York, and Mrs. Bridgett Hoar of the Parish of St. Buttolph, Bishopsgate in the city of London, were married 21 June, 1689. And, in the same volume (No. 67) is a deposition made by Henry Newman that Mrs. Bridgett Hoar, daughter of Madame Usher, is the wife of Mr. Thomas Cotton, &c.   H. F. W.

I do not find the name Cotton among the patentees of land in the Virginia Land Registry Office. The following extracts from the Parish Register of Sussex County, Va., 1737–1775, in which the entries are made alphabetically by Christian not surname, may however be of some interest to the Cotton family of New England.

Amelia dau.	of John	and Lucy	Cotton	b. Dec. 1, 1739.	
Sarah "	"	"	"	"	b. Sept. 24, 1741.
Ephraim son	"	"	"	"	b. Dec. 13, 1747.
Drury, son	Thos.	"	Jane	"	b. Aug. 10, 1741.
Mary dau.	Thos.	"	Jean	"	b. Apr'l 3, 1743.
Frederick son	Joshua and	Susanna	"	b. June 11, 1760.	

Sponsors: Drury, Henry & Eliz[h] Cotton.

Jesse son	"	"	"	"	b. Dec. 28, 1758.
Drusilla dau.	"	"	"	"	b. Dec. 9, 1763.
Howell son	"	"	"	"	b. Mch 3, 1765.
Edmund son	"	"	"	"	b. Mch. 30, 1769.

Sponsors: Thos. Whitfield, W[m] Sela & Eliz[h] Hight.

Susanna dau.	"	"	"	Cotton b. Oct. 3, 1775.
Becky dau.	Richard &	Betty	Cotton	b. Mch. 29, 1756.
Cary son	"	"	"	"	b. Mch. 12, 1765.
Jane dau.	"	"	"	"	b. Apl. 14, 1762.
Sally dau.	"	"	"	"	b. June 2, 1748-9.
Seth son	"	"	"	"	b. Nov. 1, 1750.
Weaver son	"	"	"	"	b. July 2, 1768.
Betty dau.	Henry "	Sarah	Cotton	b. Jan. 3, 1762.
Thomas son	"	"	"	"	b. May 2, 1766.
John son	Seth "	Rebecca	"	b. Oct. 22, 1772.
William son	"	"	"	"	b. Nov. 6, 1769.
Hardy son	William "	Eliz[h]	"	b. Feb. 1, 1766.
Selah dau.	"	"	"	"	b. Dec. 14, 1759.
Alsobrook son	"	"	"	"	b. Aug. 20, 1768.
Lucretia dau.	William "	Lucy	"	b. Nov. 14, 1762.
Littlebury son	Drury "	Phebe	"	b. Mch. 10, 1764.

R. A. BROCK, of Richmond, Va.]

ROBERT PECKE, minister of the word of God at Hingham in the County of Norfolk, 24 July, 1651, proved 10 April, 1658, by Samuel Pecke, one of the executors. To Thomas, my son, and Samuel, my son, and their heirs forever the messuage wherein I now dwell, situate and lying in Hingham, and an enclosure called the Lady Close (of eight acres). To Robert Pecke, son of my son Robert deceased, twenty pounds at the age of twenty three years. To John Pecke, son of said Robert, ten pounds at the age of twenty two years. To Benjamin Pecke, the youngest son of said Robert Pecke deceased, twenty pounds at the age of twenty two years. To the children of Anne Mason, my daughter, wife of Capt. John Mason, of Seabrooke, on the river Connecticot in newe England, forty pounds to be divided equally and to be sent to my son John Mason to dispose of it for their use. To my son Joseph during his natural life fourteen pounds yearly to be in hands of sons Thomas and Samuel, and I commit said son Joseph to the care of my two sons Thomas & Samuel. To the children of Thomas & Samuel, my sons, five pounds apiece at age of twenty one years. To my now wife Martha Pecke forty pounds within two months after my decease. If I depart this life in Hingham my body may be interred in the churchyard near unto Anne, my wife deceased.

When the will was proved power was reserved to Thomas Pecke, the other executor, to act.   Wootton, 153.

[" The Lord and patron of Burgate is Sᵣ Edmund Bacon, Baronet. James Bacon, sonne of Sᵣ James Bacon of Friston, Kⁿᵗ, was Rector of Burgate in the time of K. Charles, an excellent preacher, but he had a very weake body, he married .... daughter of .... Honeywood Esq. She was grandchild of that famous Mʳˢ Mary Honeywood, so often made mention by devines in regard of her long distresse of conscience, and brought up by her. The husband of yt Mʳˢ Mary Honeywood was a man of 3000£ pr annum, in those times. She was after the death of Mʳ Bacon married to Mʳ Robert Pecke Rector of Hingham in Norff. a woman of singular parts."—Add. MS. 15520, British Museum.

This MS. is entitled on the cover, Church Notes for the County of Suffolk, 1655-1665, and, on fly leaf, inside, " Ryece's Collections of the Antiquities of Suffolk :" but this is undoubtedly a mistake. Robert Rice or Ryece, the antiquary, died in 1637-8, as will be seen from his will (which follows). The handwriting shows these Notes to be the work of one of the Candler family.

" John Hale, Mʳ in Arts, was preacher there [in Mildenhall] in the time of the Long Parliament and there lived in very good esteeme, his father was a citizen of London—hee married Mary daughter of Thomas Sothebie Rector of Combes. She was since his death married againe to Thomas Peck of Prittlewell in Essex—whose first wife was —— daughter of John Rogers the famous preacher of Dedham his 2ᵈ was daughter of —— Caley, this was his 3ᵈ."—Add. MS. 15520 British Museum.—H. F. W.

More about the Rev. Robert Peck and his connection with the Bacon family will be found in the Register, xxxvii. 193. Rev. Robert Peck and his brother Joseph came to New England in 1638 (Reg. xv. 26) and settled at Hingham. The former returned to England. The latter remained here and has numerous descendants, one of whom, Ira B. Peck, Esq., of Woonsocket, R. I., published in 1868 a large volume on the family (Reg. xxiv. 96, 187). The will of Rev. Robert Peck, and that of his father, Robert Peck of Beccles in Suffolk, England, are printed in full by Mr. l. B. Peck, who also gives a tabular pedigree of the ancestors of the two New England emigrants for twenty generations.

The descendants of Anne, daughter of the Rev. Robert Peck and wife of Capt. John Mason, the conqueror of the Pequots, are the subject of an article by the late Chancellor Walworth in the Register, vol. xv. pp. 117–22, 217–24, 318 ; xvii. 39–42, 214–19.—Editor.]

Robert Rice of Preston in the County of Suffolk gentleman ; " This Seaventh daie of ffebruary In the latter dayes of this miserable world from Christs birth 1637 " ; proved 16 February 1638 by Sara Allen executrix. My body to be buried in the South side of the Chancell in the church yard of Preston as near unto my wife as conveniently may be. To Mʳ Thomas Willis, now minister and Vicar of Preston. .... To my reverend and good friend, late minister and Curate in Great Waldingfield, Mʳ Peachie, now resident in Clare or thereabouts. To my reverend good friend Mʳ Stanesbie, sometime minister of Little Waldingfield, and to Mʳ William Lambert now present minister of Little Waldingfield. To my cousin Robert Hobert of Lynsey in the County of Suffolk, gentleman. To my cousin Mʳ William Munnings, late resident at Sir Henry Myldmayes in the County of Essex. More, I give unto him and his heirs forever, my copyhold meadow in Monkes Illigh in the County of Suffolk: between the common river there and the King's highway leading from Monkes Illigh church to Brent-Elligh, containing four acres, commonly called Skipps meadows, and now in the occupation of Katherine Munninge, widow ; he to sell it and divide the proceeds between three of his sisters, Ann, Katherine and Ellen Munninge, so as one half shall go to Anne Munninge, aged, lame and impotent, and the other half to Katherine and Ellen. To Thomas Munning, sometime my servant. To my cousin Robert Doe, of Bardwell.

To my nephew John Appleton, the second son of my loving brother in the law John Appleton of Chilton, in the county of Suffolk deceased, my Latin bossed Bible, of Trimelius, in folio. To William Mills, of Lanham, in the County of Suffolk, painter and glazier, forty shillings, with all my boxes of Painting Colours, with the desire that, so long as he shall live and be able to work, that he do from time to time keep, renew and amend, as need shall require, the decays of colours, words, letters, compartments and forms of those tables, writings and inscriptions which he hath at any time made for me, as they are fixed in the Parish church or chancell of Preston aforesaid. To Zouch Allen the son of my niece Sarah Allen, widow, my customary tenement called Perkins-Bronds, in Preston. To the aforesaid John Appleton my copyhold lands and tenements holden of the manor of Brettenham Hall in the said County of Suffolk. To my loving cousin Richard Kymbould of Braintree in the county of Essex. To my cousins Rice Munning and his sister the wife of Francis Lucas. To Robert Johnson, my godson, and William Johnson, his brother, sometime my servant. To my loving brother-in-law Samuel Appleton, gentleman, now dwelling at Ipswich in New England. To Sarah Allen, sister of Zouch Allen, at the age of twenty one years. To Edmond Betts, of this town, my tenant. My niece Mrs Sarah Allen, widow, to be the sole executrix. Harvey, 36.

[" Riece was yeoman of the Guard to K. Hen. 7 note y^t all the kings Guard were gentlemen borne at ye first hee was Capt of Riece banke (?) and came to inhabit in Suff. with little John Vere E. of Oxford. His sone was justice of Peace and setled himselfe at Preston his name Roger he liued in Preston in the dayes of Edw. Mary & Eliza : (thus far Tilletson). Robert Riece his sonne had his education in Geneua in the house of Theodore Beza he liued in Preston in ye dayes of Q. Eliza: k. James and K. Charles and died lamented leauing a good name behind him but sine prole. He was a man very skilfull in Heraldy and set up the Royall armes of England in a faire Table in ye church of Preston in Suff. and in the glasse windowes the coats of very many of the cheife gentry of Suff. in his time where they remaine this 25 of March 1655." Harleian MS. 6071 (Candler's), p. 343, British Museum.

H. F. W.

Samuel Appleton, named in this will, a son of Samuel Appleton of Little Waldingfield, Suffolk, England, was born in that parish in 1586, and was baptized there Aug. 13 of that year. He died in Rowley, Mass., 1670. Messrs. I. A. Jewett (1850), John Appleton (1867) and W. S. Appleton (1873 and 1874) have published books on this family. Mr. Jewett prints the will of Robert Ryece in full.—ED.]

AGNES DARBY, relict of Augustine Darby of Bisley in the County of Surrey (nuncupative), 21 May, 1650, proved 18 June, 1650. To Henry Collier of Horsell, yeoman. He to pay unto Edward Darby in New England ten pounds when he shall come and demand the same. To Richard Darby five shillings. To John Darby twelve pence. To Margaret Lee, wife of John Lee, five shillings. Youngest son Austen Darby. Son John Ellis. Joane Bowbrick, wife of Thomas Bowbrick. Henry Lee a witness.

Pembroke, 90.

[Edward Darby or Derby was of Braintree, Mass. He married Jan. 25, 1659–60, Susanna Hook. Several others of the surname settled in New England. Roger Derby, from Topsham, Devonshire, settled in Ipswich, Mass., about 1671, and among other sons had Richard, born Oct. 1679, who settled in Salem, Mass., and was the ancestor of a distinguished family.—EDITOR.]

RICHARD HOUGHTON, citizen and Merchant Taylor of London, 30 July, 1652, proved 4 August, 1652. To my sister Alice White forty shillings and to her son twelve pence. To my sister-in-law Anne Houghton twenty shillings and to her sons who are now in the Common Wealth of England forty shillings apiece, and to her other son who is now beyond the seas, if he be now living and come home safe and alive within one year after the date hereof, forty shillings. Furthermore unto one of my said sister in laws sons who is now married (a bequest) and to the other son here residing, &c. To my uncle Hanmer twenty shillings and to his children twelve pence apiece. To my cousin Thomas Cooke, living in Fow lane, Southwark, thirty shillings and to his children twelve pence apiece. To Daniel Cooke, where I now lodge, five pounds, whom I desire to be sole executor. George Horne, cordwainer, and Mr Whittle, merchant taylor, to be overseers. A bequest to cousin Anne Cord, widow, and her children. To fifty poor taylors ten shillings apiece; to fifty poor bodiesmakers ten shillings apiece; to fifty poor glovers ten shillings apiece; to fifty poor widows ten shillings apiece. To the two eldest daughters of my executors wife twenty shillings apiece; to his own daughter Mary forty shillings and to Mrs Cooke herself thirty shillings to buy her a ring; and to Daniel Man, to buy him a coat, ten shillings. Sundry other bequests made.   Bowyer, 227.

GEORGE MOODY of Moulton in the County of Suffolk, yeoman, 20 February, 1651. To wife Lydia my mansion house commonly called Fryatts &c. &c. To my cousin Mary Smith thirty pounds in the second year after my death. To my cousin Jonas Alston's wife thirty pounds four years after my decease. To my cousin Alstone's daughter, Ann Alstone ten pounds in the sixth year after my decease. To my cousin Samuel Warren, son of my sister, Margaret Warren, forty pounds in the third year after my decease. To my cousin Clement Warren, son of my sister Margaret Warren, ten pounds in the fifth year after my decease. House to sister Margaret Warren and her son George Warren after her decease. To George Warren's wife ten pounds in the fifth year after my decease. To her daughter Sara five pounds in the sixth year, &c. and five pounds among the rest of her children in the seventh year, &c. To my brother John Salmon's eldest son thirty pounds in the eighth year, &c. Ten pounds to the rest of his children in the ninth year. To Francis Hovell's children five pounds in the tenth year, &c. To Richard Hovell of Ashfield Magna, to Mr Croxen, to Mr Archer, to Mr Chatchpole, to Mr Deaken at Newmarket, to Mr Westwood of Dallam, to the poor in Newmarket, of Gaseley, of Dallum, of Barrow, of Denham and of Moulton. Mr Jonas Alston and John Salmon the younger to be executors. Certain lands to go to brother Samuel Moody in Berry (*sic*) and to his heirs forever. Mr. Eyres to preach my funeral sermon. The witnesses were Thomas Warren and Nathaniel Eyre.

Administration with the will annexed was granted 3 May, 1654, to Samuel Moody, brother of the deceased, &c. the executors having renounced the trust.   Bowyer, 61.

SAMUEL MOODY, of Mowlton, in the County of Suffolk, Esquire, 18 February, 1657, proved by his son John Moody, executor, 28 June, 1658. To eldest son George Moody, houses, lands, &c. in Mowlton. My late mansion in Bury, where my son George now dwells, the lease renewed in my son's name. A son Henry named. To son John all my lands in Ireland. To Henry lands in Gaywood near Lynn, in Norfolk (forty acres). To daughter Anne in three years after my death or at her day of marriage, and to daughter Elizabeth (with the same condition). To daughter Mar-

garet Westropp, daughter Sarah Cooke and grandchild Mary Browne. To
the poor of James Parish in Bury. To Mr Slater, minister in Bury. To
the children of my sister Greenwood one hundred pounds in full for the
debt which she or her husband claims from my brother George Moodye or
his executors or administrators.

The witnesses were Thomas Stanton and Edward Oxborough.

Wootton, 492.

[The following pedigree is from Harl. MS. 6071 (British Museum), p. 512 (or
fol. 254).

MOODY.

George Moody of Moulton = ...
famous for his house keeping
and wast and plaine dealing.

George = ...	John	Samuell Moody = Mary, daughter	Daughter.
Moodye	daughter	a wollen Draper	of John Boldro,
of Moulton	of Houill,	in Bury.	Gent. (of St.
s. p.	**als. Smith.**	Alderman, of	Edmunds Bury).
	went over to	great power in	
	New England.	committees. Justice	
		of the peace since	
		the death of K.	
		Charles, chosen by	
		the Bourugh in Bury	
		into seuerall parlia-	
		ments in that time.	
		After the death of	
		his Brother he had	
		his father's estate	
		in reuertion.	

George=Anne, dau.	John Moody=Anne, one	Samuel Moody,	Mary=John Browne,
Moodey	of Ambrose	Capt. of foote	of the daus.	a Capt.—	Moody,	Alderman of
a wollen	Bigge of	& afterward	& co-heirs of	Thomas.	eldest	Bury this
Draper	Glemsford,	sergeant-major	..... of Flowton.	Henry.	daughter.	yeare 1658.
in Bury.	Gent.	of horse in the		all of		
		service of the		them		
		Parliament.		**s. p.**		
		Since a merchant				
		in Ipswich.				

Samuel.
Ambrose.
George.

Margaret Moody,	Sarah Moody,	Anne Moody.	Elizabeth Moody.
married to	m. to Wm. Cooke		
Major Westhorp	of Bury,		
of Hundon.	a Linen Draper.		**H. F. W.**

John Moody, according to the Apostle Eliot's records, came to New England in
1633 and settled at Roxbury. His wife was named Sarah. He removed to Hartford, Ct. His widow died in 1671 at Hadley. (See REG. iv. 179 ; xxxv. 242 ; Winthrop's New England, ed. 1853, i. 126 ; Savage's Dict. iii. 225).—EDITOR.]

THOMAS COBBET of Moorton, parish of Thame, in the County of Oxford,
12 November, 1617, proved 11 February, 1617. My body to be buried in
the church of Thame. To Thomas Cobbet, eldest son of my son John, five
pounds within one year after my decease. To each of the rest of my son
John's children forty shillings apiece within one year, &c. To son Raphe
Cobbet forty pounds within one year & six months, &c. To Thomas, eldest
son of Raphe five pounds within one year and six months, &c., and to each
of the rest of son Raphe's children forty shillings (within the same period).
To my son Christopher Pytts ten shillings, as a token of my love, and to
my daughter Johane Pytts twenty pounds within one year, &c. To each
of my god children twelve pence apiece.

Item, I give to my cousin Thomas Cobbett of Newbury forty shillings of good & lawful money of England, to be paid him within one year after my decease. My son John Cobbett to be sole Executor ; and my brother John Cobbett and my son in law Christopher Pitts to be overseers and to have five shillings apiece for their pains.   Meade, 10.

[Rev. Thomas Cobbet, of Lynn and Ipswich, Mass., is said by Mather to have been born in Newbury, England, in 1608. (See *Magnalia*, ed. 1853, vol. i. p. 518.) He was probably related to this family.—EDITOR.]

FRANCIS FAWCONER, of Kingscleare in the County of Southampton, Gentleman, 1 September, 1662, proved 21 May, 1663. To the poor of the parish of Kingscleare three pounds, to be distributed within six days next after my decease. To my cousin Peter Fawconer, son of Richard Fawconer deceased, all my freeland containing thirty acres, more or less, and the barn and timber and wood thereupon growing, in Kingscleare Woolands, which I purchased and bought of James Waite, and all the rents issuing out of the said lands, to the said Peter Fawconer and his heirs forever, and twenty pounds and all my wearing apparel. To his sister Elizabeth Fawconer one hundred pounds.

Item I give and bequeath to my brother Edmond Fawconor that is living in New England two hundred pounds of lawfull money of England. To John Fawkner of Kingscleare twenty pounds. To Alice Person, widow, one hundred pounds. To Elizabeth Fawconer, their sister, forty pounds. More, to the abovenamed Peter Fawconor a joyned bedstead, a bedmatt, a bedcord, a feather bed, a feather bolster, two feather pillowes, a pair of pillowbeares, a pair of sheets of the best, a pair of blankets, a coverlet and curtains and my great chest, &c. To Alice Person, widow, a brass pot, &c., and all the brewing vessell that I have standing at her brother John Fawconer's house except the brewing tub. To Nicholas Knite of Kingscleare, miller, ten shillings ; to Elizabeth, his wife, forty shillings ; to her five children that she had by her first husband, that is, to Richard, Francis, John, Daniel and Anthony Fawkoner, twenty-five pounds to be equally divided amongst them, five pounds apiece, at the age of twenty one years. To Elizabeth Fawconer, sister of Peter (some pewter). To my brother in law, John Carter, and to Elizabeth, his wife, each a twenty shilling piece of gold. To John Carter the younger (some furniture standing at Coldhenly House). To Agnes Fawkener, widow, twenty shillings. To Winifrit Waite, wife of James Waite of Kingscleare ten shillings in gold ; and to their son James and daughter Katherine Waite ten shillings each. To Francis Friser, of Kingscleare, the elder, ten shillings. To Alice Alle ten shillings. To Christopher Dugdale of Husborne* ten shillings. To his five children that he had, by Master Webber's daughter, one hundred pounds, equally to be divided amongst them, twenty pounds apiece, at age of twenty years. I appoint John Atfield of Kingscleare, gentleman, overseer, and give him two twenty shilling pieces of gold, and to his wife one twenty shilling piece of gold.

The residue to my sister's son, Matthew Webber, whom I make executor ; and it is my will that he should agree with my Lord's officers for the Heriotts that were due to the Lord at my decease and to pay them in money or in goods, as they can agree.

Wit : John Atfiell, Nicholas Bartholomew (his mark).
                                                                      Juxon, 60.

* This is probably meant for Hurstborne.—H. F. W.

[The following pedigree of the Fawknor family of King's Clear, to which the testator of the preceding will and his brother Edmund (who settled in Andover, Massachusetts) must have belonged, is from the Visitation of Hampshire, 1634.

Arms.—Sa. three falcons ar., beaked, legged and belled or.
Crest.—A garb or, banded ar.

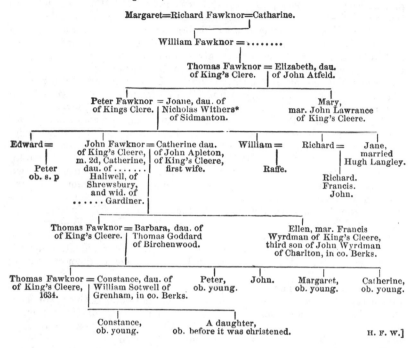

Margaret=Richard Fawknor=Catharine.

William Fawknor = ...

Thomas Fawknor = Elizabeth, dau.
of King's Clere. | of John Atfeld.

Peter Fawknor = Joane, dau. of   Mary,
of Kings Clere. | Nicholas Withers*   mar. John Lawrance
                   of Sidmanton.   of King's Cleere.

Edward=   John Fawknor=Catherine dau.   William =   Richard =   Jane,
       | of King's Cleere, of John Apleton, | | married
Peter   m. 2d, Catherine, of King's Cleere, Raffe. | Hugh Langley.
ob. s. p dau. of .... | first wife.   Richard.
          Haliwell, of   Francis.
          Shrewsbury,   John.
          and wid. of
          ..... Gardiner. |

Thomas Fawknor = Barbara, dau. of   Ellen, mar. Francis
of King's Cleere. | Thomas Goddard   Wyrdman of King's Cleere,
                    of Birchenwood.   third son of John Wyrdman
                                         of Charlton, in co. Berks.

Thomas Fawknor = Constance, dau. of   Peter,   John.   Margaret,   Catherine,
of King's Cleere, | William Sotwell of ob. young.   ob. young. ob. young.
1634.   Grenham, in co. Berks.

Constance,   A daughter,
ob. young.   ob. before it was christened.   H. F. W.]

THOMAS FAWNE, 25 December, 1651, proved 17 August, 1652. To Robert Williams, the chirurgeon of the ship called the Peter, one watch and a cornelian ring. To my servant, William Martin, his passage to Virginia and his freedom there and one suit of clothes with black ribbons. To the poor of Skendley† parish in Lincolnshire forty shillings. To Mr Hatch, woollen draper, nine pounds; to Mr Crayford seven pounds ; to Thos. Dagger one chest with whatsoever is in it. To my father one pair of silver fringed gloves and one pair of white gloves ; to my mother two rings with stones in them. To Mr Murrell, Mr John Richards, Mr Corbin, Matt. Johnson (sundry bequests). To my brother Robert my rapier and belt. To John Younge and John Stone, whom I make executors .... all my debts due to me in Virginia, and likewise the disposing of all my estate now shipped in the ship called the Peter, and the return whereof is to be divided among my brothers and sisters, whereof Mrs Francis White is to have one part. To the seamen two cases of drams.

The witnesses were John Richards and James Frisby.

Bowyer, 220.

* Harleian MS. 1139 (fol. 22), in British Museum, gives the surname Whitacres, instead of Withers, as above.
† This is so written. Probably Skendleby is meant.—H. F. W.

ROBERT NICKOLSON, of London, Merchant, and son of Francis Nickolson, Esq. 10 November, 1651. Ten pounds sterling towards the relief of
the English captives in Turkey. Forty shillings to Mr Pickett, sometime
minister of Chappell alias Pontibridge, Essex, and twenty shillings to the
poor of the said parish. To Capt. Sam: Matthewes of Virginia, Esq. one
pair of Buckskin gloves, cost five shillings, and to Mrs Matthewes his wife
two pairs of kid skin gloves. To Sam: Matthewes, the son of said Capt.,
one pair of Buckskin gloves and to his brother one pair of corderont (*sic*)
gloves. To Mrs. Mary Bernard of Warwick River six pairs of kid gloves
and to her daughters three pairs of gloves apiece. Item fourteen shillings
more of gloves or other ware which Stephen Wooderife oweth me. I give
unto John Younge, M^r of the ship Peter of London twenty shillings sterling to buy his wife a ring and to himself a buckskin pair of gloves of five
shillings. To Mr John Richards two pairs of cordevant gloves and M^r
Lockers Sermons. To Mr Thomas Fawne two pairs of cordevant gloves
and Leo Afer, a History book. To John Stone twenty shillings, two pairs
of Cordevant gloves, all the rest of the syrups and all the books in the cab-
in. Gloves to Mr Driver, Mr Freizby and Matthew Johnson. To John
Corbin my coasting coat, my stuff coat and one turkey waistcoat and two
pairs of cordevant gloves. To the seamen one case of Drams. To the
steward, boatman, carpenter and gunner all my clothes and bedding, whereof the steward is to have one half. To the poors box five shillings. To
Robert and Peter, each of them, one pair of gloves. To Mrs Veheath Land
Vernald one diamond ring, one gold ring, the motto *Idem qui pridem*, which
said Mrs Veheath Land is daughter to Mrs Mary Vernail of Warwick
River, widow. To Mr Murrell and the Doctor, to each of them one pair of
gloves.

All the which gifts are to be given and satisfied unto every and several
said party or parties by the said John Younge and John Corbin at or near
the Barbadoes or at or near Virginia upon demand, if the said John Younge
and John Corbin shall think fit. And the said John Younge and John Corbin are to lay out four or five pounds upon my burial at the Barbadoes or
at Virginia, &c. All my goods or all goods consigned to me, Robert Nickolson, now shipped in the ship called the Peter, to be sold for the best advantage and the returns to be paid to my father Mr Francis Nickolson,
Esq. in Ipswich.

All the rest of my estate to be distributed equally between my brothers
and sisters. Eldest·brother Francis Nicholson mentioned.

The witnesses were John Richards, Thomas Fawne and John Stone.

The executors named in the will renounced the executorship and letters
of administration issued 26 August, 1652, to Francis Nicholson the father,
the testator being referred to as late in the parts beyond the seas deceased.

Bowyer, 228.

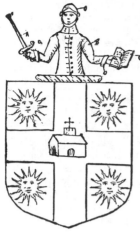

Nicholson, Virginia mercht
(ms ware. 1085 fo. 57)

[I am indebted to Mr. Eedes for the sketch of the Nicholson coat of arms, of which an engraving will be found in the margin. It will be noticed that no colors are indicated on the shield.—H. F. W.

Robert Nicholson was granted 500 acres of land in Charles City County, Virginia, Jan. 3, 1655, Book No. 4, p. 11, *Va. Land Reg. Office.*

The Samuel Matthews mentioned in the will, is presumably " an ancient planter " who was a member of the Council of the Colony of Virginia as early as 1629. In March, 1630, he built the fort at Point Comfort, James river. He served continuously in the Colonial Council or House of Burgesses, and latterly as County-Lieutenant of Warwick County, deriving thence his title of Lieutenant-Colonel. In 1656 he was sent as one of the agents of the Colony to England, and on March 13, 1658, was elected by the assembly Governor of the Colony to succeed Edward Digges. He was an honest, energetic and faithful servant of the Colony, and his death, which occurred in January, 1660, was universally lamented.

The following grants to the name Matthews are on record in the Virginia Land Registry :
Thomas Matthews " chirurgeon " 1100 acres in Henrico County, May 11, 1639, Book No. 1, p. 646.
Thomas Matthews " chirurgeon " 470 acres in Henrico County, Oct. 10, 1641, Book No. 1, p. 777.

" Captain Samuel Matthews Esq." 3000 acres upon Warwick river, Aug. 20, 1642, Book No. 1, p. 814.
" Captain Samuel Matthews Esq. " 200 acres upon Warwick river, Aug. 20, 1642, Book No. 1, p. 815.
" Captain Samuel Matthews Esq." 4000 acres on the North-side of Rappahannock river, Jan'y 6th, 1639, Book No. 1, p. 882.

In regard to the name Barnard, mentioned in the will, it may be said that to Mrs. Anna Barnard was granted 1000 acres in Northumberland County, Apl. 3, 1652, and among the " transports " or " head-rights " was " Mr. Richard Bernard," Book No. 2, p. 306. *Va. Land Reg. Office.* R. A. BROCK, of Richmond, Va.]

THOMAS STEGGE, now bound forth in a voyage to Vergenia, 6 October, 1651, proved 14 July, 1652, by Elizabeth Stegg, relict and sole executrix. To sister Alice ten pounds per annum during her natural life, to be paid her every half year. To my brother Christophers two daughters twenty pounds apiece, to be paid them within two years after my decease. To my wife's sister Emelion Reade one full sixteenth part of the good ship now called the Seven Sisters, with the profits, &c. I give to my son Thomas Stegg in Virginia all my whole estate in Virginia, as also one quarter part of the Seven Sisters, now bound to Virginia, and all goods and apparel I have in that ship or any other servants and ought else belonging to me ; as also one quarter part of the ship Increase and all that shall accrew unto her for her voyage now at sea ; and for more I leave it to the consideration of his mother. To my daughter Grace Byrd and her children the houses I bought of Mr Neale in Bedlam, as also, after the decease of my wife or at the next marriage of my wife, I give her and her children my houses in the cloisters at St. Katherines that I bought of Mr. Tokely ; also, in like kind and case, I give her and her children my annuity at Elinge, if it so long continue, until the death of my said wife or her second marriage. To Elizabeth Byrd, my daughter's eldest daughter, one hundred pounds if she live until the age of fourteen years. To wife Elizabeth Stegg, during her natural life or widowhood, my whole estate, after debts and legacies are paid, excepting what is directly given away before to my son and houses at Bedlam to my daughter. But in case my said wife should marry again I give her out of my estate eight hundred pounds; and the rest to be equally divided between my two children. Wife Elizabeth to be executrix and loving friend M^r . . . . Loton, Mr. Roger Draiton and Mr Robert Earle to be overseers, and ten pounds apiece to buy them each a cloak.   Bowyer, 202.

[Thomas Stegge, "merchant," was granted 1000 acres of land between "Old man's and Queen's Creeke," January 6th, 1639, Book No. 1, p. 694.— *Virginia Land Records.*—R. A. BROCK, Richmond, Va.]

THOMAS STEGGE of the county of Henrico in Virginia Esq. 31 March, 1669–70, proved 15 May, 1671. To beloved wife Sarah Stegge, for ornaments for her person and as a token of my loving remembrance of her affectionate and tender care for me in sickness and in health (sundry personals) and more one Indian girl named . . . . . And if she resolve to go for England my will is that she have free power to accommodate herself with bedding, provisions and other necessaries for her voyage without the contradiction of any person whatsoever. And further she is hereby given free power to bestow upon her friends at her departure the value of twenty pounds sterling. I desire Mr Thomas Grindon of London to pay unto my said wife or her order as soon as conveniently he may after her advice received all such sums of money as are due, belonging or appertaining to me in his hands or custody. To my dearest mother Elizabeth Grindon, wife of Mr Thomas Grindon, citizen of London, twenty pounds sterling yearly &c. during her natural life. To my loving sister Mrs Grace Byrd wife of Mr John Byrd,[1] citizen and goldsmith of London, two hundred & forty pounds due to me in the hands of her said husband, as by his account sent me last year doth appear, and to my said sister one diamond ring given me by my mother when I was last in London, which I promised to give my sister if I died before her. To every child of my said sister and brother Bird of London now living one hundred pounds sterling to each of the sons at the age of twenty one years respectively and to the daughters at the age of twenty one or day of marriage. I give and bequeath all the right, title and interest I at present have or hereafter shall have to part of a house bought by the Honorable Thomas Ludwell Esq.[2] and myself of Henry Randolph and now in the possession of us together with all my interest in the furniture in the house and all lands &c. thereto belonging, to him the said Thomas Ludwell and his heirs forever, requesting him to pay out of the same to the Right Honb^{le} Sir William Berkley K^{nt}, Governor, fifty pounds sterling within six months after my decease, as a token of that unfeigned respect I am and ever shall be obliged to pay his Honor for his many graces and favors.

All other lands, messuages, tenements &c. in Virginia or England to William Bird,[3] eldest son of the aforementioned John and Grace Bird in London, to him and his heirs forever. But because my cousin is yet young and not so well experienced in the transactions of the world I desire my loving wife, for a year or two that she continues in the country, to continue the managing of the estate &c., charging my cousin not to be led away by the evil instructions he shall receive from others but to be governed by the prudent and provident advice of his aunt; further desiring and charging my cousin, in all matters of moment and bargains of consequence, to make his address to the Honb^{le} the Secretary[4] for his assistance, whom I earnestly entreat, for the dear friendship we have so long mutually enjoyed, that he will please to continue his kindness to my Remains and accept the trouble of being overseer to this my last Will and Testament.

The witnesses were Henry Randolph,[5] Edward Hill[6] and John Knowles. The above will was proved by the oath of Sara Stegge, relict and executrix.

Duke, 69.

["Captain Thomas Stegge, Gentleman," received the following grants of land: 800 acres in Henrico county Dec. 29th, 1662, Book No. 4, page 583; 1280 acs. in Henrico county, on the north side of James river [including the present site of the city of Richmond], January 5th, 1663, and 1850 acres in the same county, December 29th, 1663, Book No. 5, pp. 200 and 528. *Va. Land Rec.* It is recorded in the family Bible of the Byrds of "Westover," that "he was an Officer in King Charles's Army." He was for several years a member of the county court of Charles City, and was a man of prominence and influence.

[1] Of the family of Byrd, Brexton, Cheshire.

[2] The ancestor of the prominent Virginia family of Ludwell [REGISTER, xxxiii. 220]. He was appointed a member of the Colonial Council in 1674. He appears to have been previously Clerk of the House of Burgesses. The following grants of land are of Record: Thomas Ludwell, 961 acres in Henrico county, June 16th, 1663, Book No. 4, p. 599. Thomas Ludwell and Thomas Stegge [they were probably merchants and partners in business], one-half acre in "James Cittie," January 1st, 1667, Book No. 6, p. 223. Thomas Ludwell, 1432 acres in Westmoreland County, October 15th, 1670, Book No. 6, p. 327. His son Philip Ludwell, who was successively governor of North Carolina and secretary of the colony of Virginia, who married Lady Frances (she was thrice married, her first husband being Samuel Stephens; no issue by the first or second marriage), the widow of Sir William Berkeley, and was the ancestor, maternally, of the distinguished patriots of the Revolution, Richard Henry, Francis Lightfoot, Thomas Ludwell, William and Arthur Lee, was a beneficiary in the following grants of land: Philip Ludwell, 200 acres in Rappahannock county, April 17, 1667, Book No. 6, p. 121; "Collonel" Philip Ludwell, 400 acres in New Kent county, October 22d, 1673, Book No. 6, p. 474. Philip Ludwell, Robert Handfort and Richard Whitehead, 20,000 acres in New Kent county, Oct. 24th, 1673, Book No. 6, p. 467.

There appears to have been a John Ludwell, "planterin," Charles City county in 1662.

[3] According to the family Registry, "The Honorable William Byrd Esquire the first of the name who settled in this Colony was born in 1652 and died in 1704 at 'Westover,' Virg. He came from Brexton in Cheshire to inherit the effects of his uncle Captain Stagg." October 27th, 1673, "Captain William Bird" was granted 1280 acres of land on the north side of James river, "formerly granted Collo. Thomas Stegg, by patent dated January 5th, 1663." *Va. Land Records.* He subsequently received other extensive grants, was a member of the Council, and for a number of years Receiver General of the Colony. He married Mary, daughter of Colonel Warham Horsmonden of "Purley in Essex, England," a member of the Virginia Council.

William Byrd, son of the preceding, was born at "Westover" March 10, 1674; died there August 26th, 1744. He was educated in England; "called to the bar in the Middle Temple, studied for some time in the Low Countries, visited the Court of France and was chosen Fellow of the Royal Society." He succeeded his father as Receiver General of the Colony, "was thrice appointed public agent to the court and ministry of England, and, being thirty-seven years a member, at last became President of the Council." His genius is embalmed in our national literature as the author of the *Westover Manuscripts*, which contain, with other papers, the " History of the Dividing Line between Virginia and North Carolina as run in 1728-29," Colonel Byrd being one of the Commissioners on the part of Virginia. He was the founder of Richmond, Va., which was laid off by Major William Mayo in April, 1737. He married twice. First, Lucy, daughter of Colonel Daniel Parke, Governor of the Leeward Islands ; secondly, May 9th, 1724, " Mrs. Maria Taylor, eldest daughter and co-heiress of Thomas Taylor of Kensington, England," born November 10th, 1698, died August 25th, 1771.

William, the eldest son by the second marriage, born September 6th, 1728, died January 1st, 1777, was a member of the Virginia Council ; and in 1756 served as Colonel of the 2nd Virginia regiment in the French and Indian war. He was married twice—first, April 10, 1748, to Elizabeth (born October 13th, 1731 ; died July 14th, 1760), daughter of John Carter of " Shirley," James river ; secondly, January 29th, 1761, to Mary, daughter of Charles and Ann (daughter of Joseph Shippen) Willing of Philadelphia, Pa., who survived him. Charles Willing was son of Thomas and Ann Willing of Bristol, Eng.

⁴ Major Robert Beverley, the father of the historian of Virginia.

⁵ Henry Randolph, long the clerk of Henrico county. Joseph W. Randolph, the veteran bookseller of Richmond, is a descendant.

⁶ Colonel Edward Hill, Senior, a member of the Council.—R. A. BROCK.]

REBECCA SAINTBURY of St. Olave Southwark, in County of Surrey, widow, 30 November, 1677, proved 2 January, 1678. To grandson John Leeson my houses in Shoreditch for term of my lease. To Sarah Leechfield twenty shillings, to Susanna Leechfield twenty shillings, to Anne Leechfield, their mother, twenty shillings to buy her a ring. To niece Rebecca Tapley forty shillings. The remainder of my ready money, legacies & funeral expenses being thereout first paid, born and discharged, I give to my grandsons Thomas & James Spicer, equally. All the residue of my estate (excepting twenty pounds which I give unto my niece Elizabeth Griffin⁷ now inhabiting in Virginia, and excepting my iron and brass goods which I give to my grandson John Leeson and granddaughter Anne Spicer, to be divided betwixt them &c., and excepting two silver spoons which I give to the children of my grandson John Tomlinson) I give unto Anne, Elizabeth, Sarah and Mary Spicer, daughters of John Spicer, gentleman, to be divided amongst them, share and share alike. John Spicer, gentleman, to be the sole executor.

The witnesses were Mary Bowder, Ruth Halsey (by mark) and George Miniett. King, 11.

[⁷ The following early grants of land to the name of Griffin are of record :

Thomas Griffin, 1064 acres in Lancaster county, July 4th, 1653, Book No. 3, p. 79.

Samuel Griffin, 1155 and 1046 acres in Rappahannock county, April 16 and Jan. 1, 1660, Book No. 4, pp. 472 and 473.

William Griffin, 400 acres in Northampton county, December 9, 1662, Book No. 4, p. 570.

Humphrey Griffin, 200 acres " in the south branch of Nancimond river on Matthews Creek," March 11th, 1664, Book No. 5, p. 67.

Richard Griffin, 57 acres in Westmoreland county, September 30th, 1664, Book No. 5, p. 129. Judge Cyrus Griffin, last president of the Continental Congress, was the son of Leroy Griffin and his wife Mary Ann, daughter of John Bertrand and his wife Charlotte Jolly, Huguenot refugees—all of Rappahannock county. The family tradition is that the paternal ancestor of Judge Cyrus Griffin was from Wales. From the christian names of the first two grantees cited above, Thomas and Samuel, which were borne by two brothers of Judge Griffin, and have been perpetuated in succeeding generations, I am inclined to think that they were brothers, and that one or the other of them was the ancestor of Judge Griffin.—R. A. B.]

BATT of Virginia.

[From Pedigrees of Yorkshire Families, West Riding, collected about 1666–67, with additions made 1702.]

Batt of Okewell, near Birstall in the Wapentake of Agbrigg and Morley, bears *Arg. a chev. betw. 3 reremice displayed sable.*

Henry Batt of Okewell in Birstall, lived in the reign of K. Henry VIII., Edw VI., and until second year of Q. Mary ; was witness to the last Will and Testament of Sir Henry Savile of Thornhill, K^nt^ of the Hon. Order of the Bath, and had forty shillings yearly annuity for life given him out of his lands, by the said will, and the keeping of his courts. He purchased the manors of Birstall, Heckmondwyke and Heaton, in Bradford dale, with other lands. He married ...., dau. of .... and had issue—Henry, ——, John.

Henry Batt (son & heir of Henry) married ..., dau. & co.-h. of Mr Richard Wilkinson of Bradford, and had issue—Henry (s. p.), Robert, Richard who lived at Spenn in Gomershall, ... married to Mr Geo. Parry, ... married to Mr Thos Crowle, and Margaret married to Mr Anthony Hopkinson of Birstall.

Robert Batt (son & heir of Henry) was fellow and vice master of University College, Oxford, married Mary, daughter of Mr. John Parry, of the Golden Valley in Herefordshire and had issue—John, William and Henry^s^ (both lived in Virginia), Robert, Mary married 1st to Mr Reresby Eyre, afterward to Mr Henry Hirst, Elizabeth married to Richard Marshe D^r^ of Divinity, Dean of York, Rebecca unmarried, Catherine married to Mr Philip Mallory. The said Mary survived her husband and was afterwards married to Mr Richard Rawlinson of Rotheram.

John Batt Esq. (son and heir of Robert) was captain of a foot company in the Reg^t^ of Agbrigg and Morley, & Justice of Peace in the West Riding ; married Martha, daughter of Mr Thomas Mallory, Dean of Chester, and had issue—John, drowned in the Irish Seas coming from Virginia with his father, William, Thomas and Henry in Virginia 1667, and Martha.

William Batt Esq. (son & heir of John) is captain of a foot company in the same Reg^t^, Justice of the Peace 1667 ; married Elizabeth daughter of Mr William Horton & hath issue—William, Gladdhill, John, Thomas died young, Elizabeth, Martha and Judith.

John Batt Esq. (third son and h. of William) is now living 1702; married .... daughter of .... Metcalfe.

Harl. MS. 4630, page 26.

[A partial genealogy of Batte of Virginia was published in the Richmond *Standard*, June 4th, 1881, a copy of which is in the library of the New England Historic Genealogical Society.

The following grants of land are of record to the name :

John Batte and John Davis, 750 acres in Charles river county (now York), April 2nd, 1667, Book No. 1, p. 638.

William Batt, 220 acres on Mobjack bay, September 5th, 1643, Book No. 1, page 901 ; 182 acres on "Chipoke Creek, called by the natives in the Indian, Paco lacke, in James Cittie county," April 11th, 1649, Book No. 2, p. 161.

Thomas and Henry Batte, 5878 acres "on the south side of James river in Appamattock in Charles Cittie county," August 29th, 1668, Book No. 6, p. 126.

William Batt, 700 acres in Charles City county, April 22d, 1670, Book No. 6, p. 285.

Henry Batte and John Sturdivant, 3528 acres in Charles City, October 28th, 1673, Book No. 6, p. 480.

Thomas Batt and John Bevill, 400 acres in Henrico county, October 25th, 1690, Book No. 8, p. 122.

Henry Batt, 700 acres in Charles City county, and 200 acres in Bristol parish, do., Book No. 8, p. 44.
William Batte, 250 acres in Prince George county, March 22d, 1715, Book No. 10, p. 280.— *Va. Land Records.*
  ⁸ Henry gave his estate in England and Virginia to his brother William. The descendants of the last in Virginia include the names of Cox, Poythress, Eppes, Colley, Gilliam, Russell, Maddox, Hinton, Ritchie, Poindexter, French and Friend.— R. A. B.]

HENRY BENSKIN, lately arrived in England from the Plantation of Virginia, 26 September 1692, proved 19 October 1692. Touching the estate which I have in England (having already settled that which I have in Virginia before I left that place) I give & bequeath to my mother Benskin, Mʳ Alexander Roberts of Shadwell, shipwright and Mʳ Thomas Whitfield twenty shillings for rings. All the rest to my two daughters, Mary Harman, wife of William Harman of New Kent County, on York River, Virginia, and Frances Marston, wife of William Marston, living upon Shipperhominy River, in James City County, Virginia, equally between them. The said Mʳ Alexander Roberts and Mʳ Thomas Whitfield to be executors, &c.
  Wit : Benj. Jones, Thomazine Harris, Robert Sandford, serᵛᵗ to Mʳ Whitfield, Scr.   Fane, 181.

[I fail to find of record any grants of land in Virginia to the testator Henry Bunskin, or to any of his surname. The following grants may however be of interest in connection with the names of two of the legatees named :
Henry Harman and John Bishop, 168 acres, 3 perches and 23 poles in Charles City county, Sept. 20, 1683, Book No. 7, p. 305.
  Robert Harmon, 1200 acres in New Kent county, April 20, 1687, Book No. 7, p. 552.
  Thomas Marston, 1300 acres on the north-east side of Chickahominy river, in James City county, Sept. 20, 1691, Book No. 8, p. 211.
  Eliza Marston, 349 acres in St. John's parish, New Kent county, April 21st, 1696, Book No. 8, p. 249.— *Va. Land Records.*
  The name Marston is quite a common one at the present day in eastern Virginia, while that of Harman is prominently represented in the Valley District.—R. A. B.]

GEORGE WHITTACRE, passenger aboard the good ship called the William, of London, bound from Virginia to London, 13 May 1654, proved 26 June 1654. Seven hogsheads of tobacco to my brother Edward Duckworth, living in the backside of Sᵗ Clements Deanes hard by the new Inn, London, if the said Edward or his wife be then living. If not to be found, then to William Scott, who is made executor. Some sugar aboard Mr. Webber's ship.
  Wit : Solomon Williams, Owen James.   Alchin, 252.

[The Rev. Alexander Whittaker, " the apostle," who accompanied Sir Thomas Dale to Virginia in 1611 ; married and baptized Pocahontas in 1614, and was drowned in James river in 1616, may be mentioned in this connection. The following grants of land to the name in its various renderings are of record :
Edward Whittaker, 100 acres " adjoining the pallisadoes of middle plantacon," February 8, 1638, Book No. 1, p. 365.
  Captain William Whitacre, 90 acres in James Cittie county, June 5th, 1656, Book No. 3, p. 381.
  William Whitacer, 90 acres in James Cittie county, March 18th, 1662, Book No. 5, p. 157.
  Richard Whittaker, 135 acres in " James Cittie " county, October 22d, 1666, Book No. 5, p. 153 ; 158 acres in Middlesex county, February 17th, 1667, Book No. 6, p. 275.
  William Whitacar, 400 acres in James City county, April 20th, 1680, Book No. 7, p. 25.

Richard Whicker, 300 acres on Knoll's Island, Currituck, Lower Norfolk county, April 20th, 1682, Book No. 7, p. 141.—*Va. Land Records.*

The descendants of one Richard Whitaker, a settler in Warwick county, Virginia, in the 17th century, are now quite numerous in and around Enfield, N. C.—R. A. B.]

JOSEPH WALKER of St. Margarets in the City of Westminster, gentleman, 13 February 1666, proved 27 February 1666. To my kinsman John Walker, now living or being in Virginia in the parts beyond the seas, ten shillings, provided he release & discharge my executors of & from all other claims &c. To my kinsman Andrew Walker, citizen & draper of London, ten shillings (with the same proviso) and to my kinsman Samuel Walker, seaman (under the same condition) ten shillings. All other property to my kinswoman Mary Snow, now the wife of Nicholas Snow, citizen and armorer of London, whom I nominate executrix.   Carr, 33.

[Peter Walker was granted 150 acres in Northampton county, September 20th, 1645, Book No. 2, p. 44.

John Walker (probably him of the text), 1000 acres, and 150 acres " on Ware river, Mobjack Bay," January 29th, 1651, Book No. 2, pp. 356 and 357. There are numerous subsequent grants to " Lieut. Collo." John, Henry, Richard and William Walker.—*Va. Land Records.* John Walker was a member of the Virginia Council, 1658–1660.—R. A. B.]

Charta Donationis Georgii Chauncey.

GEORGE CHAUNCEY Sen' of Barking in the county of Essex Esq. 28 November 1621, proved 25 August 1624. I grant, bargain & sell unto George Chauncey, my son, all my goods &c. on condition &c. He to pay, after my decease, to Edward Chauncey my son two hundred pounds, to be paid out of that one thousand pounds which Alexander Williams of Gilston in the county of Hartfordshire doth now owe unto me, to Charles Chauncey my son one hundred marks and Judith Chauncey my daughter three hundred pounds. To Frances Porter my daughter nine & twenty pounds yearly, to her hands and not to any other, for her sole use &c., and not to the hands of Ambrose Porter or to any other for his use. This annuity to be paid immediately after my decease, at Cranbrooke House in Barkinge in the said County of Essex, or at some other place that the said George, my son, and Frances Porter shall appoint the same to be paid. To William Chauncey my nephew five pounds within one year after my decease. To Alice Clarke twenty pounds yearly during such years as are to come in an annuity granted by me to one John Clarke deceased late husband to the said Alice.

If I the said George shall tender at any time during my life the sum of twenty shillings at my now dwelling house in Barking to the use of George Chauncey my son, that then and at all times after this present deed of gift to be frustrate and of none effect.

The witnesses were William Chauncy, Matthew Chauncey & Nathaniel Rowdon (by mark). There issued commission to George Chauncey, natural & lawful son of George Chauncey late of Barking in the County of Essex deceased.   Byrde, 62.

JUDITH CHAUNCY of Yardley, in the County of Hertford, spinster, 2 December, 1657, proved 1 March, 1657, by Henry Chauncy and Mountague Lane.

" To my deare and lovinge brother M' Charles Chauncy minister of gods word and nowe liveinge in newe England Twentie pounds of currant English money which I desire to haue paid and conveyed unto him as soone as

it may be safely done after my decease. And I doe likewise will and bequeath unto my loveinge Cousens Isaac Chauncy and Ichabod Chauncy,
twoe of the sons of my said loveinge brother ffive poundes apeece. And I
doe giue and bequeath unto the rest of my said brothers children which are
nowe in newe England with him (and are sixe in number as I am informed) fforty shillings apeece to be paid to them as soone after my decease as
it may conveniently and safely be done."

Bequests are made to loving cousin Mr Mountague Lane, cousine M^r
Henry Chauncye the elder of Yardley and M^ris Anne Chauncy his wife,
cousin George Chauncy the third son of the aforesaid Henry and godson of
the testatrix, said godson's mother, his brother Peter Chauncy and his sisters Anne, Elizabeth and Mary Chauncy, cousins Henry, John and Peter
Chauncy, three of the sons of cousin Henry Chauncy, cousin Alexander
Chauncy the elder now living in the County of Kent, nephew Mr John
Humberston and his daughter Judith Humberston, Mr. John Sykes, clerk,
and his son John Sikes, godson of testatrix, John Starr, son of Edmond
Starr, late of London, dyer, and to Thomas Burges whom she had put an
apprentice to a tailor. The residue she left to her cousins George Chauncy, Henry Chauncy the elder of Yardley and Mountague Lane.

The witnesses were John Sykes, Hannah North (by mark) and Grace
Couch.   Wootton, 109.

Ichabod Chauncey of the City of Bristoll, Doctor in Physick, 19
March 1688, with codicil made 26 September 1690, proved 17 February
1691. My body to be laid near my children in St. Philip's church yard
in the said city. To Nathaniel Wade Esq. Daniel Gwillim, merchant,
and William Burgesse, grocer, property in trust. Wife Mary, sons Staunton, Charles & Nathaniel. To brother Nathaniel Chauncy's children. To
brother Isaac and to cousin Oziell Chauncy, my cousins Charles, Elizabeth
and Isaac Chauncy.   Fane, 138.

Sñia pro Valore Test^i et Codicilli Ichabod Chauncey nuper civitatis
Bristoll, in medicinis Doctor defuncti, Quod coram nobis in judicio inter
Mariam Chauncey viduam relictam et executricem in Testamento sive ultima voluntate dicti defuncti nominatam, partem humoi negotium promoventem ex una et Stanton Chauncey minorem filium naturalem et legitimum
dicti defuncti per Josephum Wetham ejus curatorem agentem partem contra quam dictum negotium promovetur etc.

Die Jovis decimo die mensis Decembris Anno Dñi milliñio sexceñmo
nonagmo primo.   Vere, 233.

Isaac Chauncy, having by the tender mercy of the most High been
preserved in life unto an old age, 26 February 1712, proved 15 March
1711. To son & daughter Nisbet each five pounds. The House I live in,
in Little Moorfields &c. Wife Jane Chauncy. To daughter Elizabeth Nisbet my gold non striking watch. To my daughter in law, the relict of my
late son Uzziel Chauncy, five pounds. To my grand daughters by her two
pounds apiece. To the widow & relict of my late son Charles Chauncy
the sum of money due me from the African Company. Reference to the
children of said son as infants. Brother Wally, Son Isaac. Wife Jane executrix. Son Nisbet & friend Richard Tailor to aid her.   Barnes, 46.

[We have here abstracts of the wills of George Chauncy, the father, Judith, a sister, and Ichabod and Isaac, sons of the Rev. Charles Chauncy, president of Harvard College. Isaac and Ichabod Chauncy both graduated at Harvard College in 1651, and sketches of their lives, with lists of their publications, are to be found in Sibley's Harvard Graduates, i. 302–9. For a genealogy of the family, see REGISTER, x. 106–120, 251–62, 323–36 ; xi. 148–53. Tabular pedigrees will be found at x. 257 and xi. 148.—EDITOR.

Henry Chauncy, the half brother of Judith and of Charles the president of Harvard College, had a son Henry, who with his wife and children are all mentioned in the will of Judith. His wife was Anna, daughter of Peter Parke of Tottenham, co. Middlesex ; their children were Henry, John, George, Peter, Anne, Elizabeth and Mary. Henry, the eldest of the sons, was the author of the History of Hertfordshire ; he was admitted to Caius College, Cambridge, Eng., 1647 ; to the Middle Temple, 1649 ; Degree of the Bar, 1656 ; Justice of the Peace, 1661 ; called to the bench of the Temple, 1675, and the same year made Steward of the Borough Court in Hertford ; Charter Recorder, 1680 ; Reader of the Middle Temple, 1681 ; the same year he was Knighted ; in 1685, Treasurer of the Middle Temple ; 1688, called by Writ to the State and Degree of a Serjeant at Law.

The details of the Chauncy family history have been gathered by a descendant, William Chauncy Fowler, and published as the " Chauncy Memorials." On p. 312 is given an account of the marriages and children of George ; on p. 313, extracts from the will of Judith ; on pp. 46, 337, pedigree of Isaac's descendants and his will in full ; his grandson, Rev. Charles Chauncy, was the minister of the 1st Church of this city, and his name is perpetuated here by Chauncy Street, where the church was then located ; on p. 78 is a pedigree of the descendants of Isaac. President Chauncy, like other early presidents of Harvard College, sacrificed his own and his family's pecuniary prospects by his devotion to the college interests ; he had an estate of £60 income given him by a Mr. Lane—probably a relative, of Bristol, England. President Quincy wrote of the early presidents, that " they experienced the fate of literary men of that day,—thankless labor, unrequited service, arrearages unpaid, posthumous applause, a doggerel dirge and a Latin epitaph."

The Chauncy family of England is referred to in the Histories of Hertfordshire by Sir Henry Chauncy, vol. ii. 400 ; Clutterbuck, pp. 60, 189 ; Harl. Soc. Pub. viii. 353 ; Norfolk Arch. So. i. 113 ; Histories of Northamptonshire, by Bridges, i. 119 ; Baker, i. 494.—See p. 312 of Chauncy Memorials.—JOHN COFFIN JONES BROWN.]

FRANCES HANHAM (or Hannam) of Boston in the County of Lincoln, widow, 4 April 7th of Charles (1631) proved by William Hastinges, brother & executor 13 June 1631. To be buried in the parish church of Boston. To the poor of Boston thirty shillings. To Mr. John Cotton and M[r] Anthony Tuckney, the ministers, at Boston, to each of them as a token of my hearty affection and true respect unto them, to either of them the sum of twenty shillings, to be paid them presently after my decease. To my brother M[r] Ambrose Hayes twenty shillings, within three months &c., to make him a ring. To my brother Thornell ten shillings and to his wife twenty shillings, within three months &c. To my brother M[r] William Hastinges of Asterby ten shillings to buy him a ring. To the wife of M[r] Thomas Askham & to the wife of M[r] Richard Westland ten shillings each within three months &c. To my daughter Pollixena all my rings & jewells & my taffety petticoat. To John Howseman my man servant my sorrel mare &c. To my sister the wife of the said M[r] William Hastinges all my wearing apparell not before given. To the widow Yates six shillings eight pence presently.

Item I give to Jonas Horrax, nephew to M[rs] Cotton, ten shillings to be presently paid after my decease. Item I give to M[r] Thomas Leveritt & to his wife to be paid them within three months next after my decease either of them ten shillings. To Philip Hannam my son, in full of all legacies & bequests given him by the last will of his late deceased father, the sum of two hundred & fifty pounds (at full age of one and twenty). To

Rudyard Hannam my son &c. two hundred pounds & to daughter Pollixena two hundred pounds (at one & twenty). If all my said children depart this life before said ages of one & twenty then to Anne, Frances Pollixena and Pascha Hastinges daughters of my said brother William. M^r
Thomas Askham of Boston to be guardian of Pollixena Mr Richard Westland of Boston guardian of Philip and brother William Hastinges guardian
of Rudyard.   St. John, 73.

[The first wife of the Rev. John Cotton, according to Mather (Magnalia, ed. 1853,
i. 58), " was Elizabeth Horrocks, sister of Mr. James Horrocks, a famous minister of
Lincolnshire." Perhaps Jonas was his son. It is stated in Palmer's Nonconformists' Memorial (ed. 1778, i. 510), that Christopher Horrocks of Bolton in the Moors,
and his family, came to New England with Mr. Cotton. Has any one met with
other evidence of their residence here? They left their son Thomas at Cambridge
University. After taking his degrees he became a clergyman, and after the restoration was ejected from the living of Malden, in Essex.—EDITOR.]

MARY USHER, late of the parish of St. Anne, Westminster, in the County of Middlesex, widow, deceased. Administration on the goods, chattells
and credits pertaining to her estate was granted, 3 April 1739, to Patient
Usher, the Wife and lawful Attorney of James Usher, the natural and lawful son and only issue of the said deceased, for the use and benefit and during the absence of the said James Usher, now at Philadelphia in America.
                                           Admon. Act Book, 1740.

PATIENT USHER, late of Philadelphia in Pennsylvania, in North America, widow, deceased. Administration on her estate was granted 29 April
1749, to Elias Bland, the lawful Attorney of Margaret Kearsley, formerly
Brand, wife of John Kearsley, the niece and next of kin of the said deceased, for the use and benefit of the said Margaret Kearsley, formerly
Brand, now residing at Pennsylvania aforesaid, having first made a sincere
and solemn affirmation or declaration, according to Act of Parliament &c.
                                           Admon. Act Book, 1750.

THOMAS SCOTTOW of Boston in New England, chirurgeon, now bound
forth on a voyage to sea in the ship Gerrard of London, Captain William
Dennis commander, 14 November 1698, proved 4 September 1699. To
my loving sister Elizabeth Savage of New England aforesaid all my real &
personal estate in New England of what kind soever. To my loving friend
Margaret Softley of the parish of St Paul, Shadwell, in the county of Middlesex, widow, all & singular such moneys, salaries and wages whatsoever as is and shall become due to me for my service in the said ship and
all other my goods and chattels and estate whatsoever in said ship to her
own use in satisfaction of what I shall owe and be indebted unto her at
my death ; and I appoint her executrix.
The witnesses were James Richmond, Richard Baddeley & Theo:
Pomeroy.   Pett, 150.

[Thomas Scottow was a son of Joshua Scottow, and was graduated at Harvard
College in 1677. His sister Elizabeth married Thomas, second son of Maj. Thomas
Savage. See Hist. Catalogue of Old South Church, ed. by Hill and Bigelow, page
220.—EDITOR.]

PHILIP GIBBS of the City of Bristol, ironmonger, now bound to Virginia, 26 August, 1658, proved 23 October 1674. To brother Jacob Gibbs.
To brother in law Philip Marshall of Evisham, in the County of Worcester, shoemaker, and his sons Anthony, Philip and Francis Marshall. The
said Philip Marshall to be executor.   Bunce, 113.

JOHN WAYTE of the city of Worcester, glover, 13 August 1691, proved 14 November 1691. My body to be decently interred according to the discretion of my dear and loving wife; and my worldly goods and estate I bequeath in such manner as herein after is expressed, vizt. As for and concerning my land in Pennsylvania which I have impowered Milicent Hoskins to sell and dispose of I give the money to be raised by the sale thereof to my son Benjamin, and five pounds more, for the raising him a stock to be paid him, with the improvement thereof, when he shall accomplish the age of one & twenty years, or have served out an apprenticeship, which shall first come or be. And I give to my daughter Elizabeth the sum of five pounds, to be paid her, with the improvement of the same, when she shall attain the age of one & twenty years or be married, which shall first come or be. And in case either of my said children shall depart this mortal life before the said legacy shall become due & payable, as aforesaid, then I give the whole to the survivor of them. And I give Francis Willis, my servant, ten shillings as a token of my love and to the intent he may be assisting to my wife in all things she desires of him, And my will is my children may be bred up & well educated by my dear wife ; and I appoint her guardian to my said children. And all the residue of my goods & chattells, after the payment of my just debts, legacies and educate (*sic*) and breeding up of my said children, I give to my dear and loving wife Elizabeth Wayte, and I do appoint and ordain her executrix and the said Francis Willis executor. Wit : John Lacy, Stephen Cosens, Tho: Taylor.

Vere, 200.

WILLIAM WHITTINGHAM, of Sutterton in the County of Lincoln, yeoman, 22 December 1591, proved 1 October 1599 by Richard Whittingham, son and executor. To the poor of Sutterton ten shillings. Towards the reparation of the church twenty shillings. I give unto Baruke Whittingham, mine eldest son, twenty pounds within one year after my decease. To Anne Pell, my daughter, the wife of Stephen Pell, twenty pounds within one year &c. To Agnes Whittingham, the daughter of my son Richard, twenty pounds at the age of eighteen years or day of marriage. To every of the four children of Robert Harvie of Kirton, yeoman, which he had by my daughter, five pounds at their several ages of eighteen or days of their several marriages, which shall first happen. To the said Richard Whittingham, my son, my "swane marke," called the "Romaine A," marked as it appeareth in the "margent" of this my will.

All the residue to the said Richard, my son, whom I make executor; my body in decent manner to be brought to the earth and buried in the church of Sutterton; and I appoint Anthony Irbie, of Whapload, Esq. supervisor &c., to whom I give forty shillings for his pains in that behalf, advising and charging my sons Barucke and Richard that if any trouble or difference arise between them concerning this my last will and testament, &c. that they be directed therein by my supervisor.

Concerning my lands, I give to William Whittingham, my nephew, one of the sons of Barucke Whittingham, my son, two acres and a half acre of arable land, lying in Bicker in the said County of Lincoln, in the tenure of the widow Rowte, to him and his heirs forever. To Richard Whittingham, my nephew, one other of the sons of the said Barucke, my son, two and a halfe acres in the tenure of Kenelm Philips, in Bicker aforesaid. To Barucke Whittingham, my nephew, one other of the sons of Barucke &c. one acre & a half acre. To Agnes Roote, widow, late wife of William

Roote, deceased, one cottage with the appurtenances in Donnington, for term of her life, the remainder thereof, after her decease, to the uses mentioned in the last will of John Whittingham, my cousin. I give and devise to Richard Whittingham, my son, and to his heirs forever all that my mansion house wherein I now dwell, together with that house at the end of my yard which I had by the gift of my son Thomas Whittingham, and my house called my mother's house &c. (and a lot of other lands and tenements).

Wit: Anthony Irbye, Thomas Landsdaile (his mark), William Bennett.
Kidd, 80.

RICHARD WHITTINGHAM of Sutterton in the parts of Holland, in the County of Lincoln, gentleman, 6 March 1615, proved 18 April 1618. My body to be buried in the Church of Sutterton. To Elizabeth my wife one messuage and twenty acres and one rood in Algorkirke, in Lincoln, lying in seven parcels, which were late my brother William Whittingham's, to wife for term of life, then to the heirs of my body by the said Elizabeth lawfully begotten; and, for fault of such issue, to remain unto William Field, son of George Field of Algarkirke, and the heirs of his body &c.; and, for want of such heirs, then to remain to Elizabeth Stowe, wife of Thomas Stowe of Algarkirke &c. husbandman, and sister of the said William Field, and to the heirs of her body &c.; next to Jane, now the wife of Christopher Passmore, one other of the sisters of the said William Feyld, and to the heirs of her body &c.; then to the right heirs of me the said Richard Whittingham forever. If my wife be with child then to such child nine acres of pasture, in Algarkirke, called Oxholme, late my brother William Whittingham's, subject to the payment of forty pounds, by will of my said brother William, unto the children of Nicholas Thompson of Wigtoft. If wife be not with child then the above to the children of the said Nicholas and to their heirs forever.

All the lands &c. in Sutterton late my uncle Richard Whittingham's (subject and chargeable with my Aunt Whittingham her annuity of forty pounds by the year) unto Hannah Foster, now wife of Christopher Foster, and daughter of Stephen Pell deceased, and to her heirs forever. Sundry lands &c. (after decease of my wife without heirs of her body by me, as aforesaid) to remain to Kellam Harvie, son of Robert Harvie, and to his heirs forever. Other lands to remain to Thomas Harvie of Kirton, son of Robert Harvie, and to his heirs. After the decease of my wife without issue &c. my messuage and twelve acres of pasture in Kirton, in a place called Willington there, unto William Taylor, my cousin of Northkyrne, and to his heirs forever. Other land to Anne Richards, wife of Walter Richards and daughter of Robert Harvie of Kirton, and to her heirs forever. I give and bequeath unto the aforesaid Thomas Harvie, my cousin, and his heirs, one acre of land arable in Sutterton, in a place called Shettlefield, between the lands of William Hewitson, on the North, and my lands, South, &c., in trust &c. I give my revertion, after my Aunt Whittingham's decease, of all my messuages & lands & tenements in Boston, in the said County of Lincoln, to Elizabeth my wife, for term of life; then to the heirs of her body by me &c.; then to Kellam Harvie. To the poor of Sutterton five pounds over and above the ten pounds given by my father. To my servants William Barker and Thomas Handley and John Roote. To Alice Parkynson, Percy Brandon, Fraunces Christian. To the daughter of William Hewitson, my god daughter. To Ellen Diggle, daughter of

Edmond Diggle, clerk, my god daughter &c. I give unto my brother Mellowes his children ten shillings apiece. To William Ingoldsbie, one of the sons of my brother Ingoldsbie, clerk, to be paid at his first commencement, when he shall bachelor of Art, or within three years after my decease, which shall first happen. To all the rest of my sister Ingoldsbie's children. To Olive Welbie and to all the rest of her brothers and sisters. To my Aunt Whittingham, my Aunt Massingberd, my father-in-law, Mr Doctor Buckley, my brother-in-law. Mr Peter Buckley and to Edward, his son. To Mr. Cotten. To Michael Harbert. To James Wilkinson. To Robert Johnson of Kirton.

My wife to be executrix and residuary legatee, and my friends Mr Thomas Middlecott, of Boston, Esq., Mr Anthony Ingoldsbie, of Fishtoft, clerk, and Mr Edmond Diggle of Sutterton, clerk, to be supervisors.

Wit: Anthony Ingoldsbie, Edmond Diggle & Thomas Knott.

Meade, 28.

[Articles on the Whittingham family, by Mrs. Caroline H. Dall, now of Georgetown, D. C., will be found in the REGISTER, xxvii. 135–9; xxxiv. 34–7. Compare the above abstracts with the extracts from the parish registers of Sutterton, near Boston, Lincolnshire, in REG. xxxiv. 35–6.

An account of the ancestry of the New England Whittinghams is given in the obituary of Mrs. Mary (Whittingham) Saltonstall, widow of Gov. Gurdon Saltonstall of Connecticut, in the *New England Weekly Journal*, Boston, January 26, 1730. There are important errors in it. The obituary is copied into the REGISTER, xi. 26–7.

It would seem from the will of Richard Whittingham, that he married a daughter of the Rev. Edward Bulkley, D.D., of Odell (REG. xxiii. 303), whose son, the Rev. Peter Bulkley, named in the will, was the first minister of Concord, Mass. Perhaps the Mr. Mellowes also mentioned, was related to Abraham Mellows of Charlestown, Mass. There was a subsequent connection between the Bulkley and Mellows families, Hannah Smith, a niece of the Rev. Peter Bulkley, having married Edward, son of Abraham Mellows (Wyman's Charlestown, ii. 665).—EDITOR.

With one exception the Whittingham family material published before 1880, stands unrivalled for blunders. In the REGISTER (xxxiv. pp. 34–37) Mrs. Dall began the work of correction by printing extracts from the Registers of the parish of Sutterton in Lincolnshire, which had been furnished to her by the curate, Rev. W. W. Morrison. The two wills which Mr. Waters has sent may be most valuable aids towards the discovery of the ancestry of the John Whittingham who married Martha Hubbard. The names correspond exactly with those given from the parish records. So far we stand on secure ground. The evidence is wanting which *proves* John of New England to be son of Baruch, who was born in Sutterton A.D. 1588, and is said to have died there in 1610; possibly Mrs. Dall has this evidence, at any rate she refers to a list of deaths of the Whittinghams of Sutterton, which it is hoped she will contribute to the next number of the REGISTER. I have the strongest doubts of the quotation "From Mad. de Salis, copied from *Alie's Norfolk*"—(vol. 34, p. 36). *A lie* I am afraid it is—as I never heard of the book, and know of no reason to suppose that the record of a marriage on this side of the ocean should have been recorded and printed in a County History of England. The grossest frauds have been discovered in pretended copies from abroad, especially when the American correspondent informed the searcher what he wanted.

Mrs. Dall mentions "William[1] Whittingham with wife Joanna, who was buried at Sutterton Feb. 3, 1540." William,[2] in his will of 1591, mentions "my house called my mother's house," and I should judge that it was so called because William[1] had married an heiress or resident of Sutterton, he having been the first of the name in that locality. The parish records contain baptisms between 1540 and 1570 of the children of Roger[2] and William[2] only. Supposing them to be brothers and sons of William[1] I have made this pedigree, marked with * if mentioned in the will of William,[2] and with † if mentioned in the will of Richard.[4]

William[1] Whittingham m. Joanna ———. They were probably parents of:
Roger,[2] who married and had Margaret,[3] b. 1544; Dorothea,[3] b. 1548; Jane,[3] b. 1549; Anna,[3] b. 1555, and an only son John[3]* (styled cousin in the will of William[2]).

William,[2] will given above, who married and had Thomas,[3*] b. 1540 [who married and had daughters *Agneta*,[4] b. 1570, and Susanna,[4] b. 1572] ; Joan,[3] b. 1546, m. 1569, Thomas Percye; Baruch,[3*] b. 1547, m. 1577, Eliz. Taylor [they had *Baruch*,[4*] b. 1588, *Eliz.*,[4] b. 1593, *William*,[4*] *Richard*,[4*] will given above, m. Elizabeth Bulkley, daughter of Mr. Doctor Bulkley] ; Richard,[3†] b. 1563, m. Mabell, daughter of Francis Quarles (see Harl. Soc. Pub. Vis. of Essex, 1612, p. 271) [they had Agnes,[4*] b. 1590, and perhaps Richard,[4] b. 1610]; Ann,[3*] b. 1568, m. Stephen Pell*† [they had Hannah Pell†] ; Dorothea,[3] b. 1552, and Almira,[3] b. 1554; one of these was the wife of Robert Harvie,*† of Kirton, who had four children,* of whom Kellam,† Anne† and Thomas† are mentioned by their cousin Richard.

John Whittingham, who married Martha Hubbard, had a son William, who married Mary Lawrence ; she died in childbirth, November, 1671. Their son William (5th child) was born November 9, 1671. William, the husband, was probably sick at the time, and hastened over to England to arrange for the legal acquirement of his hereditary property in Lincolnshire; making a home in Cambridge, co. Middlesex, England, at " Marie le Savoy." His will is dated 25th March, 1672: " Wm Whittingham late of Boston in Massachusetts &c. Gentleman, being sick, gives to his eldest son Richard,—House, Barn, Mill-house, &c. together with 20 acres arable land, and 84¼ acres of pasture, now in possession of Wm Pakey in the town of Sutterboro', in the parts of Holland (low-lands) in the County of Lincoln—gives to son William, one dwelling house and barn, &c. with 42¼ acres of land in tenure of John Trigg ; also One Cottage and barn with 5 acres of land in tenure of Thomas Baily in Sutterboro'. To daughter Mary one messuage, &c. with 18 acres land in tenure of John Wilson and Mr. Baker ;—to daughter Elizabeth one messuage, &c. with 15½ acres of land, also one cottage and 1 acre of land—John Gidny, George Ledman and John Baker tenants;—to daughter Martha two cottages and 12½ acres of land in the possession of John Pakey, Wm Walker and Richard Gunn,—daughters to have possession at the age of 20 years or days of marriage, &c. &c. Mentions Uncle Nathaniel Hubbard of London, Gentleman ; brother Richard Whittingham ; brother in law John Clark of Boston in New England and his mother Mrs. Martha Eire (annuity to her). Gifts to James Whitcomb of Boston; cousins Mary Hubbart and Anne Hubbert. Father in law John Lawrence of New York in America, William Hubbert of Ipswich, of America, and said Uncle Nathaniel Hubbard of London, Gentleman, and John Lewine of London Esq. Executors. Proved " Arch. Canterbury " same month and year as dated.—In the certificate he is styled as " formerly of Boston in New England, now of Marie le Savoy of Middlesex." Proved in Boston, New England, 23d July, 1672; recorded Suffolk Deeds, vol. 7, p. 224.

I suppose the " town of Sutterboro' " is the same as Sutterton. With proof as to the missing link, consanguinity would be easily established.—JOHN COFFIN JONES BROWN.]

RICHARD BIFIELD minister of the word of God, of Isleworth in the County of Middlesex, 23 August 1633, proved 24 October 1633. To Richard, my eldest son twenty shillings. To the children of the said Richard viz. to Mary twenty shillings, to Timothy twenty shillings, to Sarah Bifield ten shillings and to his other three children Samuel, Anne, & Richard ten shillings apiece. To my son Nathaniel Bifield six pounds and a mark‡ within two years after my decease (and other property). To my grandchild Bathshua Clifford, wife of Mr William Clifford, clerk, twenty shillings, the which twenty shillings the said Mr William Clifford oweth me. To my grandchild Richard Weston four pounds in one year &c. To grandchild Mary Weston three pounds in two years &c. To my loving wife Margaret Bifield twenty five pounds which was owing to me from Edward Browne my son in law deceased and now is due to me from the executors

---

‡ This amount, commonly written vi£ xiiiˢ iiiiᵈ, seems to have been a favorite amount to bequeath previous to the 17th century. It is just ten marks or twenty nobles, and very likely (as my friend J. C. C. Smith, Esq. suggests) would be so read and spoken of, rather than six pounds thirteen shillings and four pence. The noble was one half of a mark, or six shillings and eight pence.—H. F. W.

of his last will and testament. To said Margaret twenty pounds which my eldest son Richard doth owe me. If my son Richard shall depart this life before my wife Margaret his mother aforesaid then the said twenty pounds shall be paid within one month after his decease unto the said Margaret, my wife & his mother. All the rest of my estate, saving my three cloakes and all my study of books which I give and bequeath unto Nathaniel Bifield clerk, my son aforesaid, I leave unto my loving wife Margaret and appoint her sole executrix. Russell, 85.

RICHARD BYFEILD minister of the Gospel, pastor of the church in Long Ditton in the County of Surrey, 15 August 1662, proved 11 June 1665. (The will begins with an interesting confession of Faith.) A reference to a statute or Recognizance of the nature of statute staple ordained & provided for the recovery of debts, bearing date 17 June 1662, taken & acknowledged before Sir Orlando Bridgeman, Knight, Lord chief Justice of His Majestie's Court of Common Pleas at Westminster and a bond of six hundred pounds to Maurice Gethin & John Kay, citizens and merchant taylors of London, for the payment of a debt of five hundred pounds, the security being a messuage or tenement in Ilield in the County of Sussex, now in occupation of John Richardson my tenant.

Bequests are made to "my five daughters" Rebecca, Dorcas, Priscilla, Mary & Debora, to eldest son Mr Samuel Byfeild (inter alia the works of Thomas Aquinas in fourteen volumes and one gold ring which hath engraven on it Thomas Lancashire) and to second son Mr Richard Byfeild. Whereas God hath blessed me with ten children more born to me by my dear & loving wife Mrs Sarah Byfeild which ten children are all now living (praised be the name of our God) —— To my daughter Sarah (at one & twenty or day of marriage), to son Tymothy that fifty pounds given unto me as a legacy by my godly, loving friend Mr Herring, citizen of London deceased. Mention is made of land & tenement in the West end of Little Heath in East Sheene in the parish of Mortlake in the County of Surrey, house &c. in the tenure & occupation of Abraham Baker, a little tenement leased out to Robert Hartwell deceased & now in the occupation of Benjamin Feilder of East Sheene, a tenement in the occupation of John Cooke of East Sheene, a tenement leased to Lucy Northall widow deceased and now in the occupation of Margaret Parker her daughter, in East Sheene, lands lately in the occupation of John Poole of East Sheene, carpenter and other lands. Sons John, Nathaniel & Thomas. To son Nathaniel the three tenements now in the tenure & occupation of William Lytter of Thomas Greaves & of John Best. To son William Wagstaffe forty shillings to buy him books, to daughter Mrs Elizabeth Bowers three pounds, to my three grandchildren the daughters of Mr Robert Goddin, the husband of my daughter Mary deceased, to my grandchild Ann Wickins, my daughter Mrs Ann Wickins, my daughter Mrs Elizabeth Berrow, my two grand children John & Sarah Wright. In the codicil (dated in one place 21st, in another 31st, May, 1664) the testator says, " God hath taken to himself my youngest son Thomas "—" the Lord hath also made a great breach upon us in taking to himself by death our son William Wagstaffe."

The above will was proved by Sarah Byfeild, relict & executrix.

Hyde, 58.

[" Richard Bifield, minister, was buried the 30th of Decr 1664." He was rector of Long-Ditton, had been one of the assembly of divines, and published several sermons and religious tracts.—Extract from Parish Register of Mortlake, with remarks thereon. Lysons's Environs of London, vol. i. p. 371.
Richard Byfield, M.A., who was ejected from the Rectory of Long Ditton in Surrey, retired to Mortlake and continued to preach to the last sabbath of his life. He died December 26, 1664, aged 67, and was buried in the parish church."—Surrey Congregational History, by John Waddington, D.D. Printed in London, 1866. P. 250.—H. F. W.
Nathaniel Byfield, son of Rev. Richard of Long Ditton, came to New England about 1674, and settled first in Boston and afterwards in Bristol, but returned to Boston, where he died June 6, 1733, in his 80th year (see Lane's Manual of the First Church in Bristol, R. I , p. 74). It is said that he was one of twenty-one children (Savage's Dict. i. 325). Rev. Nicholas Byfield of Chester and Isleworth (Bliss's Wood's Ath. Ox. ii. 323, and Brook's Puritans, ii. 298), whom Brook calls a half brother of Richard of Long Ditton, is more likely to have been an uncle. Nicholas was father of the celebrated Rev. Adoniram Byfield.—EDITOR.]

Notes on Abstracts previously printed.

THOMAS COTTON (*ante*, p. 91) :

[Benj. Woodbridge, of Boston, deposes 30 Dec. 1697, that, when I was in London 2 years ago and since, I was often to see Mrs. Bridget Usher the wife of Mr. Hezekiah Usher (lately deceased) who dwelt with her son in law Mr. Thomas Cotton a minister of the Gospel who married her daughter and who had one son living about 5 years old. They dwelt in Hodsdon's Square near Shoreditch. He complained how he was unjustly kept from his wife's portion for about 7 years it being here in New England, and that he would be glad to have relief in that case. (*Mass. Archives*, viii. 66.)—WILLIAM M. SARGENT, of Portland, Me.]

STEPHEN WHEATLAND of the city of Winchester in the County of Southampton, 6 January, 1737, proved 18 June, 1739. To my son Stephen Wheatland, clerk, one shilling. To my daughter Elizabeth Barlow, wife of Henry Barlow, one shilling. To my granddaughter Elizabeth Barlow one shilling. To Henry Barlow one shilling. To my grandchildren Susanna Whitehead, Anna Whitehead, Stephen Wheatland Whitehead and Elizabeth Whitehead and their heirs, and, for want of such heirs, to William Whitehead, my grandson, and his heirs forever, all my freehold messuages and tenements, lands and hereditaments situate, lying & being in the city of Winchester. My loving son and daughter Edward Whitehead & Susanna his wife to be executor & executrix.
Wit: Tho: Cropp, Richard Rimes, James Pledger.

Henchman, 142.

[Possibly there may be some connection between Stephen Wheatland, the testator, and the family from which Henry Wheatland, M.D., of Salem, Mass., president of the Essex Institute, is descended. The name Stephen is found in both. Dr. Wheatland writes to us : " My father, Richard Wheatland, was born in Wareham, England, in 1762. His parents were Peter and Bridget (Foxcroft) Wheatland, who were married about 1752. Their eldest child was born in 1753. We have in Salem the family bible given to my father by his mother, during a visit to England in 1799. It contains the records of the births of the children, 7 sons and 3 daughters, viz. : John, Stephen, Peter, George, Richard, Robert, 2d John, Bridget, Margaret and Anne. My impression is that my father's father was born about midway between London and Wareham, probably in the vicinity of Winchester."
See Gleanings by Emmerton and Waters, p. 130, in relation to William Wheatland, who died 19 Feb. 1575.—EDITOR.]

MEMORANDUM   That the tenth daye of July i6ii John Harvard of the
pishe of St Sauior in Southwarke wthin the County of Surrey Butcher beinge then sicke and very weake in body but of good memory, beinge moved
to dispose of his temporall estate uttered theise or the like wordes in effect
(in the presence of us whose names be subscribed) vizt, I give unto Francis
Rodgers tenn poundes —— And all the rest of my goodes and estate I giue
unto my broth^r Thomas Harvard, and I make my said brother Tho: Harvard my sole Executor, And to witnes the same we haue hereunto sett our
handes   Tho: Harvard his m^{r}ke Ric^d Yearwood Robert Harvard his m^{r}ke.
   The above will was proved 21 July 1611 by Thomas Harvard brother
and executor &c.   158, Berry
                                                   (Archdeaconry of Surrey).

Marche the 27. Anno i622.

IN THE NAME OF GOD, AMEN.   I Thomas Harvard of the precinct of
St Katherins neere the tower of London beinge sicke in bodie but of perfect memory thankes be to God doe ordaine this my last will and testament
in manner and forme followinge.   ffirst I doe bequeath my Soule into the
handes of almightie god that gave it me, and to his sonne Jesus Christ that
Redeemed me by whose death and merritts I doe trust onelie to be saved
and my Sole receyved into eternall ioye. for my bodie to be committed to
the Earthe from whence it came and to be buryed at the discretion of my
Executrix hereundernamed   And for the rest of the porcion of goodes
which the lorde hath lent me duringe my life my will is my welbeloved
wife shall fullie and whollie enioy it whatsoeuer and to give unto my children that the lorde hath sent me whatsoever it pleaseth her into whose
handes after my decease I comitt all that my estate and porcion ether in
England or elsewhere beyonde the Seas and this I ordaine as my last will
and testament and disanull all former whatsoeuer making my deerly beloved wife Margarett Harvarde my sole executrix.   In witnes whereof I
have hereunto put my hande.   The marke of Thomas Harvard.
   Subscribed and deliuered by Thomas Harvard in the presentes of us
hereunder named   Edmond Swettenham   the marke of Ann Blaton.

   PROBATUM FUIT TESTAMENTUM suprascriptum apud London coram venerabili viro mag^{r}o Richardo Clarke legum doctore Surrogato venerabilis viri
domini Willimi Bird militis legum etiam doctoris Curie Prerogatiue Cantuar-
ens^s mag^{r}i Custodis siue Commissarii ltime constituti. Vicesimo tertio die
mens^s Augusti Anno Dñi Millesimo sexcentesimo vicesimo secundo.   Juramento Margarete Harvard relicte et executricis dicti defuncti in eodem testamento nominat. Cui Commissa fuit Administracio bonorum iurium et creditorum dicti defunct de bene et fideliter administrañd &c.   Ad sancta Dei
Evangelia Jurat.   78, Saville.

July the xxvith: 1625

THE LAST WILL AND TESTAMENT of Margaret Harwar* of St Katherines widdowe sicke and weake in bodie but in perfecte memorie thanks be
gee geven to god in this manner and forme followeinge; ffirst I bequeathe
my soule into the hands of Allmighty god that gave it me, and to Jesus
Christ my saviour that redeemed me hopinge and trustinge only to be saved
by his merritts death and passion and my bodie I committ to the earth

---

* This name in the original will appears invariably as Harvard.—H. F. W.

from whence it came and to be buried att the discretion of my executors hereunder named And my worldly goodes I bequeathe in this manner and forme followeinge ; ffirst my will and desire is that the howse I now dwell in, commonly called by the name of the Christopher scittuate and beinge in St Katherins neere the Tower of London be sould to the best advantage, And to him or her that will give most money for it, And beinge sould the money to be devided in this manner followeinge, The money to be devided between my three daughters Margarett Harward Alse Harward, and Jone Harward, And if any of my said daughters doe chance to dye before their legacies come to their hands or growe due, my will is that their parte or parts shall come to the survivors of those three; Item my will is and I bequeathe unto John Walbank my sonne the some of Twenty Pounds of Currant English money if he be livinge And if it please god that he be dead then my will is that this Sonne Thomas Walbancke my Grandchilde shall have it paid him when he comes to lawfull Age. It. my will is and bequeath unto my daughter Susan Walbanck the some of ffive Pounds to be paid unto her when my said howse is sould It. my will and desire is that those worldly goodes that god hath blessed me withall shall be equally devided betwixt my said three daughters Jone, Margarett Harward and Alse Harward parte and parte alike; every one there share; And if any of them happen to dye before their part come to their hands my will is it shall come to the survivor or survivoᵗˢ. It. my will is and I doe give unto Thomas Wallbanck my grandchild the some of Tenn Pounds to be paid unto him out of my two daughters porc͞o͞ns Jane and Alse. It. I give and bequeathe unto Thomas Harward the sonne of Thomas Harward my late husband the some of Tenn Shillins. It. my will is and I bequeathe unto my frend Edmond Swettenham of East Smithfeild the some of ffourty shillinges to make him one gould ringe withall to weare for my sake; And I doe ordaine my daughter Margarett Harward my sole executrix of this my last will and testamente ; And I doe appointe and desire my two lovinge frends Robert Evebancke and Edmond Swettenham my two overseers of this my will and I doe give unto Robert Evebanck for his paines twenty shillings ;   *The marke of Margarett Harward.*

Witnes Edmond Swettenham Rob't Ewbancke The marke of Marie psons.

PROBATUM fuit Testamentum suprascriptum apud London corā Magistro Thoma Langley Clic͞o Surrogato venerabilis viri domini Henrici Marten Millitis legum doctoris Curie Prerogative Cantuariensis Magistri Custodis sive Commissarii legitime constituti Nono die mensis Septembris Anno D͠ñi Millesimo sexcentesimo vicesimo quinto, Juramento Thome Gouldan Notarii Publici Procur̃is Margarete Harward filie et executricis in hum͠oi Test͞o nominat Cui Commissa fuit Administrac͞o bonorum iurium et creditorum dc̃i defunct de bene et fidelit Administrañd eadem Ad sancta Dei Evangelia Jurat.   91, Clarke.

IN THE NAME OF GOD AMEN. The eight and Twentyth daie of July Anno D͠ñi one Thousand sixe hundred Twentie five, & in the ffirst yere of the Raigne of our Soveraigne lord Charles by the grace of God Kinge of England Scotland ffraunce and Ireland defender of the faith &c. I Robert Harvard of yᵉ pish of St Saviours in Southwarke in the Countie of Surrey Butcher, being not well in body but sound in minde in memory (laud and praise bee to allmightie god therefore) doe make and ordayne this my present last will and Testament in manner and forme following that is to saie, ffirst and principally I bequeath and commend my soule into the hands of allmighty God trusting through his mercie and for the meritts of his deere Sonne my lord and Saviour Jesus Christ to haue forgivnes of all my Sinnes, and after this life ended to bee made ptaker of life eu^rlastinge in the kingdome of heaven And I will that my body bee decently and Christianly buried in the pish Church of St Saviours aforesaid, after the discretion of my executrix hereundernamed, And as touching that Temporall estate of goods and Chattles wherew^th it hath pleased god of his goodnes to blesse, my minde and will is as followeth vizt, Inprimis I give and bequeath unto the poore of the pish of St Saviour aforesaid forty shillings and to bee payd and distributed according to the discrecon of my said Executrix & Overseers hereunder mencõned Item I give and bequeath unto John Harvard my Sonne Two hundred pounds To bee payd unto him when he shalbee accomplish his age of one and Twentie yeres Item I give & bequeath unto Thomas Harvard my Sonne the like somie of two hundred pounds to be payd likewise unto him when he shall accomplish his age of one and Twenty yeres Item I give and bequeath unto Peter Harvard my Sonne the like somie of Two hundred pounds to bee payd likewise unto him when he shall accomplish his age of one and Twenty yeres And if any of them my said three sonnes depart this life before his said pte and porcõn shall growe due to bee payd by this my will, Then I give ye pte or porcõon of him deceaseinge to the residue of them Surviving equallie to bee devided betwixt them, or wholly to the Survivor yf two of them decease And if it shall happen all my said three Children to decease before they shall accomplish theire severall ages of twenty and one yeres as aforesaid Then and in such case I give and bequeath unto my Cosin Thomas Harvard and his Children ffifty pound to bee payd within three moneths next after the decease of the last Child Item I give and bequeath unto Robert Harvard my godson sone of my said cosin Thomas Harvard Ten pounds to be payd unto him when he shall accomplish his age of one and Twenty yeres All the rest and residue of my goods and Chattles whatsoever my debts (if any be) beinge first payd and my funerall expences discharged I give and bequeath unto Katherin Harvard my welbeloved wife whom I constitute ordayne and make full and sole Executrix of this my last will and Testament And it is my will that shee shall haue the use of my said Childrens porcõns for theire educacon and bringing up untill the same shall growe due to them as aforesaid And I make and ordayne my good neighbour and friend Mr Richard Yearwood Citizen & Grocer of London and the said Thomas Harvard my Cosin Overseers of this my last will and Testament desireing them as much as in them shall consist and lie to see the same pformed according to my true intent and meaneing herein declared And I give unto them for theire paynes to bee taken in seeing this my will performed Twenty shillings a peece to make them rings for a remembrance Provided alwaies & I will and oidayne hereby that my saide wife shall wth sufficient Suerties w^thin three moneths next after my decease or at least before shee shalbe espoused or married agayne to any other, enter and become bound in the somie of one Thousand pounds unto my said Two Overseers, if they shalbe both liveing or to the Survivo^r of them if either of them shallbee deceased, wth condicon to pay the pts and porcõons of my said Children wch I haue before bequeathed unto them, accordinge to my true intent and meaning herein declared, and at such tyme or times as before is limyted and set downe for the payment thereof, In witnes whereof I the said Robert Har

vard haue to this my p^rsent last will and Testament put my hand and Seale
the daie and yere first aboue written, The marke of the said Robert Harverd Sealed acknowledged and delivered by the said Robert Harverd
for and as his last will and Testament the daie and yere first aboue written
in the presence of Ric: Saudon Scr The m^rke of Richard Rayner.

PROBATUM FUIT Testamentum suprascriptum apud London coram magistro Thoma Langley Cliĉo Surrogato venerabilis viri Domini Henrici Marten militis legum doctoris Curie Prerogative Cantuariensis magistri Custodis sive Comissarii ltim̄e constituti Sexto die mensis Octobris Anno Dñi
millesimo sexcentesimo vicesimo quinto Juramento Katherinæ Harvard
Relicte dicti defuncti et executricis in huiusmodi Testamento nomināt Cui
Comissa fuit administrat &c. de bene et fideliter administrando eadem, ad
sancta dei Evangelia Jurat.   111, Clarke.

JOHN ELLETSON citizen and cooper of London 15 June, 1626, proved
the last day of June, 1626. To Mr William Quelch, clerk, sometimes minister of St Olaves in Southwarke, forty shillings, & to Mr Archer, minister
of St Saviours in Southwarke, twenty shillings, within six months after my
decease if they be then living. To my sister's son Stephen Hall, Bachilor of
Divinity at Cambridge twenty pounds, to be paid him within six months
next after my decease. To my sister Elizabeth Rigate full power and
authority to dispose of the house wherein she now dwelleth for the term of
two years next after her decease conditionally that a pepper corn be paid
yearly therefore to my executrix. The residue of the term of years unexpired of the said house I will and bequeath unto my nephew Robert Elletson, son of my late deceased brother Robert Elletson, his executors and
assigns. To my aforesaid nephew Robert all those my two messuages or
dwelling houses, &c. situate & being in the liberties of East Smithfield in
the parish of St Buttolph's Algate, to him and to the heirs of his body lawfully to be begotten, and, for want of such issue, to his brother William
Elletson & to the heirs of his body, &c., and, for lack of such issue, to
George Elletson his brother and to his heirs forever, which houses I bought
and purchased of Mr Norton, gentleman. And my will and mind is that
my loving wife Katherine Elletsonne shall have her thirds out of the same
during the term of her natural life. Item I give and bequeath unto my
said loving wife Catherine Elletson and her assigns during her natural life
the yearly sum of twelve pounds of lawful money of England to be paid
unto her quarterly and to be issuing and going out of all and singular my
lands tenements and hereditaments whatsoever lying and being in the several parishes of Alverstoke and Rowner in the County of Southampton.
To my sister in law, Mary Elletson, and her two daughters, Elizabeth
Elletson and Margaret Elletson, and their assigns, during the natural life
of my said loving wife Catherine Elletson, the like yearly sum of twelve
pounds, &c. To my nephew George Elletson, son of my said brother
Robert, all that my messuage, barns, lands & commons, &c. called or known
by the name of Hemeleys, situate in the parish of Alverstoke (with remainder first to William, then to Robert, brothers of the said George),
which aforesaid premises I bought and purchased of Thomas Rabenett,
mariner. To nephew Robert my messuage, &c. situate in Brockhurst in
the parish of Alverstocke and Rowner, &c. (with remainder to his brothers
William and George, &c.) which premises I bought of Robert Nokes of
Brockhurst, yeoman. To nephew William my messuage, &c. in Newton

in the parish of Alverstocke, &c. (with remainder to Robert and George), which premises I bought of my brother Robert Elletson. To Thomas Elletson, son of Anthony Elletson, born at Lymehouse in the parish of Stepney, the sum of ten pounds, to be paid him at the age of one and twenty years if he shall be then living. To Robert Wilson in Southwark all such sum or sums of money which he oweth me upon one certain obligation conditionally that he give unto Mr Thomas Foster Bailiff of the Borough of Southwark, as a legacy and bequest from me the sum of three pounds, &c. within three months next after my decease, and three pounds more to the poor of the parish of St Olaves, where he is a parishioner, &c. &c. To my kinswoman Jane Merricke one quarter or fourth part of the good Bark called the Jane of Gosport, with the fourth part of the tackle, munition and apparell, which said Bark is in partnership between her husband Walter Merricke and myself. And I give and bequeath to my sister Mary Elletson and her two daughters the other quarter or fourth part of the same Bark. To my sister Elizabeth Bygate, widow, twenty pounds yearly & every year during her natural life, to be paid her by five pounds the quarter, or within one and twenty days after the quarter day, out of the tenements which I lately purchased by lease of the wife of James Turner, holden by the masters, brethren and sisters of St Catherine's and which is situate and being in the parish of All Saints Barkin near unto Tower Hill. To my eldest brother George Elletson, dwelling in the County of Lancaster, five shillings, conditionally that he shall give to my executrix a general acquittance of all demands whatsoever from the beginning of the world until the day of the receipt of the same legacy. To my brother William Elletson, dwelling in the said County of Lancaster, ten shillings (on the same condition). To my sister Agnes Stables, the sum of twenty shillings, to be paid her upon lawful demand. To my sister Ellen Towers, dwelling in the County of Lancaster, the sum of twenty shillings (upon lawful demand). I absolutely release and discharge Richard Edwards, dwelling at White Waltham in the County of Berks, of all sum or sums of money which he oweth me, and particularly of one specialty of thirty pounds which I freely forgive him.

Item I give unto my son in law Joseph Knapp and unto Agnes his wife, my kinswoman, all that my house, together with my buildings, yards and appurtenances thereunto belonging, and to his son John Knap after his decease, during the term of a lease which I took of Mr John James, gentleman, paying the rents, &c.; also the goods, household stuff &c in and about the said house, which is in their possession and which I left freely to them at my coming away from Mill Lane. To my said son Joseph Knapp all that my third part and bargains of boards whatsoever remaining in the County of Sussex which is in partnership between Mr Anthony Keeme, Mr Richard Waker and myself, citizens and coopers of London. To the said Joseph my best livery gown and my second cloak. Item I give and bequeath two silver cups, gilded, with my name to be ingraven upon them, to the value of twenty pounds, which shall be bought by my executrix and given to the company of coopers of the city of London within six months next after my decease. To twenty poor people which is in the Almshouse at Ratcliffe twenty shillings to be equally divided amongst them. To Mrs Suttey, my mistress, dwelling at Ratcliffe, over and above the part of the said gift of twenty shillings, the sum of ten shillings.

Item whereas Hugh Horsell of Southwarke, Innkeeper deceased, by his last will and testament did give and bequeath unto his children the sum of six hundred pounds as by his said will appeareth, of the which I have already paid the sum of one hundred pounds to Mary one of the children of the said Hugh Horsell for her legacy, as also the sum of twenty pounds which I gave with Nicholas Horsell, one of the said children, to bind him an apprentice, so that there is remaining now of the said six hundred pounds the sum of four hundred and eighty pounds to be paid unto them as in their said father's will more at large and plainly appeareth. Therefore my desire and meaning is and it is expressly my will that my executrix hereafter named shall truly pay and satisfy unto the children of the said Hugh Horsell or to the survivors of them the said sum of four hundred and eighty pounds in every point according to their father's will and to see them well educated and brought up in all things necessary in the fear of God and in learning. And I do further will that my executrix shall within one month next after my decease enter into obligation of one thousand pounds to my overseers hereafter named in every kind to see these legacies performed and the said children well brought up and educated. To the poor of the parish of Alverstocke and Gosport the sum of twenty shillings. To the poor of the parish of All Saints Barking in Tower Street, twenty shillings. To George Browne my kinsman twenty shillings to be paid upon lawful demand. I absolutely acquit and discharge Richard Graye, waterman, a bill of debt of three pounds which he oweth me. I absolutely acquit and discharge Nicholas Parsons, ostler at the Queen's Head in Southwark, of a debt of twenty and eight shillings which he oweth me. To my kinsman William Hughs and Agnes his wife one hundred pounds &c.

Item I give and bequeath unto my said loving wife Catherine Elletson the lease of all and singular the premises which I hold of the Master, brethren and sisters of St Katherines, together with all the rents and profits that shall arise by reason of the same ; to have and to hold the same lease and the rents and profits thereof unto my said loving wife, Katherine Elletson, for and during the term of her natural life, she paying the rents and performing the covenants contained in the same lease on my part to be performed, the remainder of the years that shall be to come from and after the death and decease of my said wife and the rents and profits that shall arise by reason of the same I give and bequeath unto my said kinsman Robert Elletson, son of my said brother Robert Elletson, and the issue of his body lawfully begotten. And if it shall fortune my said kinsman to die and depart this life before the expiration of the term of years in the said lease granted having no issue of his body lawfully begotten then living that then I give and bequeath the said lease and the benefit and profits thereof arising unto his brother William Elletson, his executors and assigns. The rest and residue of all and singular my goods and chattels whatsoever moveable and immoveable not before by me given and bequeathed, my debts and legacies being paid and my funeral expenses discharged I wholly and absolutely give and bequeath unto my said loving wife Catherine Elletson whom I make and ordain the sole and only executrix of this my present last will and testament, desiring her to see the same in all things performed according to my mind and meaning herein plainly declared, and I do hereby nominate and appoint my loving friends Mr Anthony Kemme, Mr George Preston and Mr Richard Waker, citizens and coopers of London, overseers thereof, desiring them according to my trust in them reposed to be aiding and assisting to my said executrix in the due " exequition " of this my present last will and testament; and I give unto each of them for their pains taking therein the sum of three pounds apiece &c. Provided always that if my said wife shall not be contented to accept of the said legacies before given unto her and to pay and perform the legacies herein by me bequeathed according to the true intent and meaning of this my present last will and testament then my will is that she shall have only so much of my estate and no more as shall justly belong unto her by the custom of the city of London and then I make and ordain my said kinsmen William Hewes & Robert Elletsonne, son of my said brother Robert Elletson, executors &c. Wit: William Manbey Scr. Edward Thomas William Hedges.

91, Hele.

RICHARD YEARWOOD of Southwarke in the County of Surrey and citizen and grocer of London, 8 September 1632, proved 6 October 1632, and confirmed by Decree of the Court in the last session of Trinity Term 1633, After my funerals done and discharged I will that an Inventory shall be taken of all my estate in goods, chattells, wares, merchandizes plate and other things whatsoever and be indifferently valued and appraised, and that therewithall the debts which I do owe shall be first duly satisfied and paid. But because the debts which my wasteful son hath brought me unto are so great that I fear much that my personal estate will not be sufficient to satisfy the same or at the least will not be collected and got in convenient time to give that satisfaction which is fit and just much less to pay and satisfy such other legacies as by this my will I have appointed and given I do therefore will, ordain and appoint that my executors hereafter named or the survivor of them with as much convenient speed as they can after my decease for the speedier payment of my debts and discharging of my legacies shall sell and dispose all those my tenements and hereditaments situate lying & being in the parish of St Mary Magdalen of Bermondsey within the County of Surrey, near the church there, which I purchased of Walter Oliver, being three tenements or houses &c in the several occupations of Thomas Miller Robert Fisher and John Bould their or some of their assignee or assignees. And my will is as well the leases which I bought of the same and which are in being in friends' names as also the inheritance of the said houses be sold for the uses aforesaid by mine executors or the survivor of them and by such other persons and friends who have any interest or estates in the same for my use or benefit. They shall sell &c. all that my tenement &c. in the tenure or occupation of John Blacke, in the parish of Lingfield within the County of Surrey which I bought of Edmond Rofey, and my tenement &c. in the parish of Frinsbury within the County of Kent, now or late in the tenure & occupation of —— Jones, which I bought of Henry Price. I give and bequeath unto Richard Yearwood my son all that my manor or farm with the appurtenances &c. in the parish of Burstow within the County of Surrey, now or late in the tenure &c. of Edmond Rofey &c. to have & to hold during the term of his natural life (then follow conditions of entailment on the issue of the body of the said Richard Yearwood the son). And for default of such issue to Hannah Payne my daughter during her natural life; and after her decease to Richard Payne her second son and the heirs of his body lawfully to be begotten; and for default of such issue to my right heirs forever. Item I give unto the poor of the parish of St Saviours in Southwark inhabiting within the liberty of the Borough of Southwark whereof I am a parishioner the sum of ten pounds &c. I give unto Mr Morton and Mr Archer ministers of the said parish forty shillings apiece. I give to William Brayne apprentice with Nicholas King grocer twenty pounds &c. to be paid unto him at the expiration of his time of apprenticeship. I give unto Margaret Dallin wife of Christopher Dallin cooper the sum of ten pounds &c. to be paid unto her in five years by forty shillings a year. To Hannah Groue daughter of Richard Groue of Middle Wiche in the County of Chester ten pounds at day of marriage or age of twenty and one years.

Item I give to Katherine my well beloved wife her dwelling in all that part of my dwelling house wherein I do now live during so long time as she shall continue a widow and dwell in the same herself if my lease thereof shall so long continue, my said wife paying therefore yearly to my executors hereafter named the sum of five pounds per annum by half yearly payments &c. And I do further give unto her all such household stuff and so much value in plate as she brought with her when I married her. And I give and bequeath unto my cousin Nicholas King grocer and Margaret his wife and the longer liver of them the lease of my now dwelling house, onely I will that my said wife do dwell and continue in such part thereof as I have before appointed during such time as aforesaid. To my loving friend and cousin Mr Stephen Street grocer ten pounds. The said Nicholas King and Stephen Street to be executors.

The residue and remainder of all my personal estate and which shall remain of my lands and tenements by me appointed to be sold as aforesaid, my debts being paid and my funeral expenses and legacies discharged, I will the same shall be distributed and divided by my executors in manner following vizt two third parts thereof unto Richard Yearwood my son if he shall be then living and that my said executors shall discern him to be reformed and become a frugal man, and the other third part thereof I will shall be divided to and amongst my daughter Payne's eight children now living vizt Edward, Richard, John, George, Anne, Timothy, Susan and Katherine, and the survivors of them; the same to be paid to their father for their uses. And I appoint my loving friends Mr Drew Stapley grocer and my son in law Edward Payne to be overseers of this my will. And I do give to either of them for a remembrance of my love and their pains to be taken therein the sum of five pounds apiece.

Wit: Thomas Haruard, William Frith William Sheappard John Fincher.

13 march 1661 administration de bonis non was granted to his daughter Hannah Payne, the executors being dead.   98, Audley.

IN THE NAME OF GOD AMEN. I Katherine Yarwood of the parrish of St Saviours in the Burroughe of Southwarke in the Countie of Surrey widdowe being at this tyme weake in bodie but of perfect memory praised be God therefore doe ordayne this my last will and Testament revoakeing all former wills and Testamentes whatsoever ffirst I bequeath my soule into the mercifull hands of my Deare Redeemer Jesus Christ the eternall sonne of God whoe by his holy Spirit as my trust and hope is will p^rserve me to his heavenly kingdome; And my bodie to be interred at the discretion of my executors And for my worldly goods I thus dispose of them. Inprimis I give to my eldest sonne John Harvard Clarke all that my messuage Tenement or Inne comonly called or knowne by the name of the Queenes head in the Borroughe of Southwarke aforesaid with the appurtenances and all my deedes and writings touching and concerning the same and all my estate right title interest terme of yeares and demand whatsoever which I have of and unto the same and of and unto everie part and parcell thereof. Item I give unto the said John Hervard and unto Thomas Hervard my sonne equally to be devided betweene them all my messuages Tenements and hereditaments whatsoever wth their and every of their appurtenances scituate and being in the parrish of All Saintes Barkeing nere unto the Tower of London whereof I am possessed under two severall leases made by the Master brethren and Sisters of the Hospitall of St Katherine's nere the Tower of London unto John Elletson deceased ; and all my deedes and writeings touching and concerning the same. And all my severall and respectiue estates right title interest terme of yeares and demaund which I have of and unto the same, and of and unto every part and parcell thereof. Nevertheless my will and meaneing is and soe I doe hereby appoint and declare that the said John Harvard and Thomas Harvard their executors Administrators and Assignes shall yearly and every yeare dureing the continuance of the severall tymes in the said severall leases graunted, paye or cause to be payed out of the rentes issues and proffits of the said last menc̃oed premises at the feast of the nativity of our Lord God twentie shillings to fower poor people that are reputed of honest conversation dwelling in the parrishe of St Saviours aforesaid by five shillings apeece And that the said John Hervard and Thomas Hervard their executors Administrators and Assignes shall paye or cause to be payed the residue and remainder of the rentes issues and proffites of the said last menc̃oned premises unto such of the Children of Hugh Harsall late of the Burrough of Southwarke aforesaid Innkeeper deceased as have not their porc̃ons paied and was given and bequeathed unto them by the last wills & testam^{tes} of the said John Elletson and Hugh Harsall or either of them untill such tyme as the said Children shall have all their said porc̃ons paied unto them and afterwards that the said John Hervard and Thomas Hervarde their executors adm'strat^{ors} and assignes shall enioye the residue of the said rentes issues and proffits of the said last menc̃oned premises to their owne proper uses and behoofes equally to be devided betweene them Item I give to my said sonne John Hervard two hundred and fiftie poundes in money And I doe appoint two hundred pounds parcell thereof to be payed wth the moneys due upon one obligac̃on of the penall som̃e of fower hundred poundes beareing date the first daye of this instant moneth of Julie made by my sonne Thomas Hervard unto my Overseer Mr Mooreton for my use condic̃oned for the payment of two hundred pounds at or upon the first daye of January now next ensueing Item I give to my sonne Thomas aforesaid one hundred poundes in money Item to the Children of my Brother Thomas Rogers I give fortie shillings a peece. Item to the poore of this parrish of St Saviours I give fortie shillinges Item to Mr Archer one of our Ministers I give twentie shillings. Item to M^{ris} Moreton our other Ministers wife I give my best gould wrought Coyfe which of my two best shee please to make choice of Item my Sister Rose Reason and my sister Joane Willmore to each of them I give a ring at the discretion of my executors Item to old M^{ris} Blanchard I give my best paire of Gloves Item to my Cosen Joseph Brocket the younger I give twentie shillings; and to my Cosen Mary Brocket I give my best scarlet Petticoate or the value thereof in money at the discretion of my executors Item I make and ordayne my two sonnes John and Thomas Hervard aforesaid ioinct executors of this my last will and Testament. Item for the overseers of this my last will and Testament I appoint my loveing frend Mr Moreton our minister of St Saviours aforesaid for one, and to him in token of my love I give three pounds and my paire of silver hafted knyves ; And for my other Overseer I appoint my Cosen Mr Thomas Hervard Butcher of St Saviours aforesaid and to him like-

wise in token of my love I give three pounds   Item I give to my said executo^{rs} and Overseers eight pounds by them to be bestowed on such Christian poore as they thinke fitt   And I will that all my legacies formerly given and bequeathed except the two hundred pounds payable by the obligačon as aforesaid shalbe paied and deliuered by my executors wthin one moneth after my decease   The residue of all and singular my goods Chattells and psonall estate after my debts payed and funeralls discharged I give and bequeath unto my said sonnes John Hervard and Thomas Hervard equally to be devided betweene them   In wittnes whereof I have unto every sheete being seaven in number put to my hand and have sealed the same this second daye of Julie in the eleaventh yeare of the reigne of our Soūaigne Lord Charles by the grace of God of England Scotland ffrance and Ireland Kinge Defender of the faith &c.   Annoꝗ Dñi 1635.   The marke of
Catherine Yarwood.

Memorandum that theis wordes vizt porčons in the seaventh lyne and John in the fourteenth lyne of the fourth sheete were interlyned and afterwards this will was read sealed and published to be the last will and Testament of the said Catherine Yarwood in the p^rsence of us ; Sealed and published by Katherine Yarwood aforesaid in the presence of us William Brayne Robert Greaton William Sheap.

PROBATUM fuit Testamentum suprascriptum apud London coram mr͞o Johanne Hansley Clič͞o Surrogato veñabilis viri Dñi Henrici Marten militis legum etiam Dc͞oris Curie Prerogative Cantuar mag͞ri Custodis siue Com^{rii} ltim͞e constituti vicesimo septimo die mensis Julii Anno Dñi millesimo sexcentesimo tricesimo quinto Juramentis Johi͞s Hervard et Thome Hervard filiorum dc͞e defunctæ et executorum in huiusmodi Testamento nominatorum Quibus comissa fuit administrač͞o omn͞i et singulor͞u bonor͞u iuri͞u et creditor͞u dc͞æ def de bene et fideliter administrando ead^m &c   Ad sancta dei Evangelia Jurat.   77, Sadler.

IN THE NAME OF GOD AMEN the fiefteenth daie of July Anno Domini one thousand six hundred thirtie and six And in the twelueth yeare of the raigne of our Soveraigne Lord Charles by the grace of god kinge of England Scotland ffraunce and Ireland Defender of the faith &c   I Thomas Harvard of the pishe of Saint Olave in Southwarke in the County of Surry and Cittizen and Clothworker of London beinge att this presente sicke and weake in bodie but of good and pfecte mynde and memorie all laude and praise be given to Allmightie god therefore and consideringe with my selfe the frailtie and mutabilitie of this present life and the certaintie of death, And to the end that I may bee the better prepared and settled in my mynde whensoever it shall please god to call me out of this transitorie life I doe by the pmission of god make and declare this my last will and Testament in manner and forme followinge, That is to saie, ffirst and principally I comend my Soule into the hands of Allmightie god hopeinge aud assuredly beleevinge through the death and passion of Jesus Christe his only sonne and alone Saviour to obtaine Remission and forgivenes of all my Synns and to be made ptaker of everlastinge life My bodie I comitt to the earth from whence it came to be decently buried att the discrečon of my executors here under named, And as concerninge all such worldly goods Chattelles and psonall estate as it hath pleased god to endue me wth in this life I give and bequeath the same in manner and forme followinge, That is to saie Inprimis I give and bequeath unto my deere and welbeloved wife Elizabeth Harvard the some of fower hundred poundes of lawful English money to be paied unto her within six monethes next after my decease More I giue and bequeath to my said lovinge all my plate and howsehold stuffe exceptinge only my best standinge bowle of silver guilte and my great Cheste with two lockes Item I give and bequeath unto my said lovinge wife Elizabeth Harvard one Annuitie or yearely payment of thirty poundes of good and lawfull Englishe mony to be yearely due goeinge out issuinge and payable unto my said wife out of all those messuages and Tenementes with thappurtenñces And the rentes issues and proffites of them scituate lyinge and beinge att or neere Towerhill in the parishe of All Saintes Barkinge in London which I hould ioyntly togeather with my brother John Harvard by vertue of a lease to us thereof made by the M^r. brothers and sisters of the Hospitall of Saint Katherines neere the Tower of London, To have and to hould the said Annuitie or Rente charge of Thirtie poundes p Anñ unto my said loveinge wife for and duringe the tearme of her naturall life to be paied unto her att fower feastes or tearmes in the yeare, That is to saie att the feastes of Saint Michaell Tharchangell, the birth of our lord god, Thannuntiacõn of the blessed virgin Marie and the Nativitie of Saint John Baptist or within one and twentie daies nexte ensuinge everie of the same feaste daies by equall and even porcõons, The first paimente thereof to beginn and to be made att the feaste of the feastes aforesaid which shall first and next happen and coñe after my decease, or within one and twentie daies then nexte ensuinge with power to distreyne for the same Annuitie in and upon the said tenementes or anie of them, if the same añuitie shall happen to be behinde and unpaied contrary to this my will, Provided that my ffather in lawe M^r. Nicholas Kinge or his heires att any time duringe the tearme of my naturall life doe assure and conveie unto me and my heires or within six moneths after my decease to my executors hereunder named or to such pson or psons as I the said Thomas Harvard shall by anie writinge under my hand name and appointe, And theire heires and assignes, And to such use and uses as I shall thereby lymitt and declare and in such good sure and sufficiente mannor and forme as by learned Councell shall be advised and required All that messuage or Tenement with thappurtenñces and the rente and Re, vercõn thereof scituate and beinge in or neere Shippyard in the pishe of Saint Saviours in Southwarke now or late in the tenure or occupacõn of Owen Jones or his assignes Item I give and bequeath unto such childe or Children as my wife nowe goeth with or is with childe of the some of three hundred poundes of lawfull Englishe money to be paied and deliuered into the Chamber of the Cittie of London for the use of such Child and children within one yeare nexte after my decease to be imployed for the use and benefitt of such childe and children untill they shall accomplishe the age of Twentie and one yeares Item I give and bequeath unto such childe and children as my wife goeth with or is with childe of all that my moitie or halfe parte of the lease of the said Tenem^{tes}. with thappurtenñces att or neere Tower hill in the said pishe of All Saintes Barkinge holden of and from the Hospitall of Saint Katherines and the moitie of my rentes and revercõns thereof, And all my estate tearmes of yeares and demaund therein charged with the said Annuity of Thirtie poundes p Anñ by me herein before given unto my said wife, Prouided allwaies and my mynde and will is that if my said wife shall not be with childe att the time of my decease, or that such childe and children shall happen to miscarry or dye or departe this life before he she or theie shall accomplishe the age or

ages of twentie and one yeares then in such case or cases and not otherwise
I doe giue and bequeath unto the severall persons hereunder named the
seu'all legacies and somes of money hereunder menčoned, That is to saie,
To my said lovinge wife one hundred poundes. to my said brother John
Harvard one hundred poundes. To and amongst the children of my unckle
Rogers fforty poundes To my godsonn William Harvard ffiefteene poundes,
To the eldest sonne of my Cossen Thomas Willmore ffower poundes to my
Cossen Robert Harvard five poundes to John Brockett the sonne of Joseph
Brockett ffortie shillinges, And then alsoe and in such case, I doe give and
bequeath unto my said brother John Harvard my said moitie or half parte
of the lease of the said Tenementes with the appu'tenñces att or neere
Towerhill aforesaid and the rentes and the Reverčons thereof, And all my
estate tearme of yeares and demaunde therein charged with the said
Annuity of Thirtie poundes. p anñ by me given to my said wife, Item
I doe alsoe by this my will give and bequeath unto my said brother John
Harvard the sume of one hundred poundes lawfull English mony, and my
standinge bowle of silver guilt and my Chest with twoe lockes before ex-
cepted, Together with my best whole suite of appell and my best cloake,
And all things belonginge thereunto, Item I give and bequeath unto Mr
Nichollas Morton Minister and Preacher in the pishe of Saint Saviors in
Southwarke the some of fforty shillinges in recompence of a Sermon which
I desire he should preach at my funerall, for the better Comforte edifyinge
and instrucčon of such my freinds and neighboures and other people as
there shalbe assembled, Item I giue and bequeath unto James Archer Minister twentie shillinges. Item I giue and bequeath unto Mr Osney Minister
the some of twenty shillinges, Item I give and bequeath unto Mr Clarke
Minister the some of twenty shillinges, Item I give and bequeath unto my
said ffather in lawe Mr. Nicholas Kinge the some of three poundes to make
him a ringe, Item I giue and bequeath unto my Cossen William Harvard the
some of Tenne poundes, Item I give and bequeath unto my said Cossen
Robert Harvard the some of six poundes, Item I give unto the said Joseph
Brockett my seale Ringe of gould, I will that there shalbe distributed
by my executors on the day of my buriall the some of ffortie shillinges, that
is to saie to and amongst the poore people of Saint Saviours in Southwarke
the some of twenty shillinges and to And amongst the poore people of the
pishe of Saint Olave in Southwarke the like some of twenty shillinges Att
the discrečon of my Executors where moste neede shall appeare.

Item I give and bequeath unto my Mother in lawe Margarett King ffortie
shillinges and unto her twoe daughters Margaret and Hanah the like some
of ffortie shillinges a,peece to make them Ringes. The rest residue and Remainder of all and singuler my goodes chattelles and worldly substance whatsoever not herein before given or bequeathed, I give and bequeath in forme
followinge, that is to saie, Twoe full third pts thereof unto such.childe and
children as my said wife nowe goeth withall or is with childe of And thother
twoe third ptes thereof I fully and wholly give unto my said lovinge wife
Elizabeth, and my said lovinge brother John Harvard equally betweene
them to be devided pte and porčon alike. And in case my said wife shall
not be with childe att the time of my decease or that such child and children shall dye before theie shall accomplishe theire age or ages of twentie
and one yeares Then in such case I give and bequeath the residue and remainder of my estate my debtes funerall expences, and my legacies beinge
paied and pformed unto my said lovinge wife and my said brother equally
betweene them to be devided pte and porčon alike, And my will and mean

iñge is that the legacies by me in and by this my last will given and bequeathed unto my said wife and such childe and children as she nowe goeth
with or is with childe of is and are in full Recompence and satisfacčon of
such parte of my estate shee they or anie of them shall or may claime or challenge by the custome of the Citty of London, And to the end they shall
make noe clayme or challege thereby, And if they shall make such Claime
or challenge by the said custome Then I will that the said legacies by me
to them given shall cease and bee voide and not be paied, And I doe ordaine and make my said welbeloved brother John Harvard And the said
Nichollas Morton preacher executors of this my said last will and Testament in trust for the due pformance of this my said laste will and the payment of the legacies herein included and given and especially and before
all of such debtes as in right and conscience I shall owe to anie pson or
psons att the time of my decease as my trust is in them, And in recompence of theire paines therein to be taken, I give and bequeath unto either
of them the sume of fiue poundes lawfull englishe mony apeece, And I doe
nominate and appoint my said lovinge ffather in lawe Mr Nicholas Kinge
and my lovinge Cossen Thomas Harvard and my lovinge freind Mr. John
Spencer Merchante to be overseers of this my will desiring them to se the
same pformed accordinge to my true meaning and to be aidinge and assist-
inge to my said Executors with theire best advice And for theire paines
therein to be taken I give and bequeath unto every one of them three
poundes apeece of like mony, And I doe hereby revoke and disalowe of
all former willes and bequestes by me in any wise heretofore made And this
to stand and continewe for and as my last will and testament, In witnes
whereof to this my said last will and testament conteyninge with this sheete,
Nyne sheetes of paper, I the said Thomas Harvard have sett my hand and
seale the daie and yeare first aboue written Thomas Harvard Sealed and
published by the said Thomas Harvard for and as his last will and testament the daie and yeare abovesaid in the prsence of me Richard Greene
Scr: Richard Barlowe.

PROBATUM fuit Testamentum suprascriptum apud London coram magro
Willmo Sames legum dcōre Surrogato venerabilis viri domini Henrici
Marten militis legum etiam dcōris Curie Prerogatiue Cant magri Custodis
sive Comissarii ltime constitut, Quinto die mensis Maij Anno domini millimo sexcentesimo tricesimo septimo Jurament Nicholai Morton Cleric
executorū in humōi testament nominat; cui comissa fuit administracio
omñi et singulorū bonorū iuriū et creditorū dict def de, bene et fidle adº
eadm ad scta dei evang: iurat, Reservata ptate similem comissiōem faciend
Johanni Harvard alteri execut etiam in dicto testament nominat cum vene-
rit eam petitur.   69, Goare.

[At last, thanks to the mother that bore him, and who by her careful mention of
him in her will as "my eldest son, John Harvard, clarke," has again, as it were,
brought him to light, we are enabled to lift the veil that for nearly two hundred
and fifty years has hidden our modest and obscure, but generous benefactor, the
godfather of America's oldest University, the patron Saint of New England's scholars; to learn his parentage and birthplace, and to form some idea of his youthful
surroundings. The will of his brother Thomas, to be sure (discovered by me on
Washington's birth-day, 1884), furnished the first important evidence in regard to
him. It will be noticed in that will, made 15 July, 1636, that he appoints his brother,
John Harvard, and the Rev. Nicholas Morton, parson of St. Saviour's, joint executors; that this will was presented for probate 5 May, 1637, by Mr. Morton alone, and
power granted only to him, a similar power being reserved for John Harvard, the

other executor, *when he should come to seek it.* This seemed to show plainly enough the absence of John Harvard, the brother of Thomas, on that fifth of May, 1637 Well, that was the year of the first appearance of *our* John Harvard on the soil of New England, as shown by the records of Charlestown ; so that probably on that very day in May he was on his way across the Atlantic. The inference then was a reasonable one that the John Harvard named in the will of Thomas Harvard of Southwark and the wise benefactor after whom our ancient University was named were one and the same person. But it needed just the mention of him in his mother's will as " clarke," taken in connection with this fact of his absence at the proving of his brother's will, to put the matter beyond question. Here too it seems as if envious chance had sought to hide him, for in the Calendar of 1637 the name of the testator, which in the record is plainly enough " Harvard," was entered " Haward," a name which might be passed over by any one hunting for the name of Harvard. It was only by *gleaning* that I came upon it.

Again—the Register Books of St. Saviour's, Southwark, the parish in which our benefactor first saw the light, seem to have lent themselves to increase the mystery that has enveloped the English surroundings of John Harvard, as will appear from the following list of baptisms :*

    1601 May 31 Marye Harverde d. of Robert, a Butcher.
    1602 July 15 Robert Harverde s. of Robert, a Butcher.
    1606 September 30 Robert Harvye s. of Robert, a Butcher.
    1607 November 29 John Harvye s. of Robt. a Butcher.
    1609 December 3 Thomas Harvye s. of Robt. a Butcher.
    1610 November 1 William Harverd s. of Robert, a Butcher.
    1612 September 27 Katherin Harverd d. of Robert, a Butcher.
    1613 December 12 Ann Harverd d. of Robt. a Butcher.
    1615 April 2 Peter Harvye d. of Robt. a Butcher.

Why, if his name was Harvard, should we accept the baptism of John Harvye as the baptism of our John Harvard? Here again the mother comes to our assistance. It can readily be seen that Katherine Yearwood must have been the widow of Robert Harvard and mother of the John, Thomas and Peter named in his will. It may not appear so evident that John Elletson, whose will I have given in its order of time, had married the widow Harvard before she became the wife of Richard Yearwood. The will of John Elletson makes no mention of any of the Harvard family ; yet no one can read attentively that will and the will of Mrs. Katherine Yearwood in connection with each other, without being forced to the conclusion that Katherine Yearwood must have been the widow of John Elletson and the executrix of his will, and, as such, the successor of his trust in regard to the children of Hugh Horsall, or Harsall, deceased. So convinced was I of this that almost the first object of my quest in the register of St. Saviour's, was the record of the marriage of John Elletson with the widow Harvard. And I soon found it entered thus :

    1625 Januarie 19 John Ellison & Katherine Harvie.

Here we find mother and son both appearing under another and the same name, viz., Harvie or Harvye. I found too in the will of Thomas Cox, citizen and vintner of London, made 12 September and proved 21 September, 1613 (79 Capell) bequests made to sundry members of this family (John Harvard's uncles?) as follows':
" I give Mrs Herverd als Harvey wife of Mr Thomas Harverd als Harvey of St Katherines Butcher six payre of best sheets," &c.—" I doe give and bequeath unto Richard Harverd als Harvey of St Saviour's parish aforesaid butcher, my now tenant, the sum of ten pounds," &c. A Robert Harvy als Harverde the elder of Rookeby (Rugby) was mentioned by Thomas Atkins of Dunchurch, Warwickshire, in his will, 41st Elizabeth. (48, Kidd.)

The burial of the father of John Harvard is thus entered :

    1625 August 24 Mr Robert Harvey, a man, in the church.

The youngest son, Peter, mentioned in his father's will (of 28 July, 1625) but not in the widow's, was buried four days before the father, also in the church, where also Richard Yearwood (a vestryman) was buried 18 October, 1632, and Katherine Yearwood 9 July, 1635. John Harvard's elder brother Robert was buried the very day before his father made his will. Evidently the family were suffering

---

* The first two children in the list, viz. Mary (bapt. 1601) and Robert (bapt. 1602), were probably the children of Mr. Harvard by his first wife, Barbara Descyn, whom he married 26 June, 1600.

from the visitation of the plague in the summer of 1625. I saw other burials entered, but did not have time to note them. All, however, I think, were buried in the church. As I passed through this venerable edifice, once the place of worship of our modest benefactor, I noticed that the great window in the South Transept was of plain glass, as if Providence had designed that some day the sons of Harvard should place there a worthy memorial of one who is so well entitled to their veneration.—HENRY F. WATERS.]

WILLIAM WARD of the parish of St Savior in Southwarke in the County of Surrey citizen and goldsmith of London 2 April 1624.

My body to be buried within the parish church of St Saviors in Southwark aforesaid. My estate shall be divided into three equal parts or portions according to the laudable custom of the city of London. One of which said third parts of my estate I do give, devise and bequeath unto my now wellbeloved wife Roase Ward. One other third part of my said estate I do give and bequeath unto my loving son Edward Ward and unto my well beloved daughter Roase Warde equally between them to be divided part and part alike (both minors). The other third part I reserve towards the payment of debts, funeral expenses and legacies &c.

To loving aunt Margaret Wood widow forty shillings per annum, in quarterly payments. To the poor of the parish of St Savior's four pounds sterling. To Mr James Archar our minister twenty shillings sterling. To the churchwardens and vestry men of the parish of St Saviors aforesaid of which society I am now a member the sum of six pounds sterling to make a dinner for them. To my good friend Mr Richard Yarwood one silver bowl of the weight of twelve ounces. Item I do give and bequeath unto my brother Mr Robert Harverd and to my friend George Garrett and my cousin William Shawarden to every of them a ring of gold to the value of twenty shillings or twenty shillings apiece in money. The remainder shall be divided into three equal parts or portions, two of which I do give and bequeath unto my said son Edward Ward to be likewise paid unto him at his age of one and twenty years, and the other third part of the said remainder I do give and bequeath unto my said daughter Roase Ward to be paid unto her on the day of her marriage or at her age of one and twenty years, which shall first happen. If both my said children shall happen to die before the legacies by this my last will bequeathed unto them and either of them shall grow due then I do will and bequeath all and every the legacies, herein by me before bequeathed unto my said children, unto my said loving wife Roase Ward and unto my cousin Elizabeth now wife of the forenamed William Shawarden equally between them to be divided &c. And I do make and ordain my said son Edward Warde and my said good friend Mr Richard Woodward executors of this my last will. And I do nominate and appoint the foresaid Robert Harvard, George Garrett and William Shawarden to be overseers of this my will.

This will containing four sheets of paper was read signed sealed and delivered in the presence of us Josua Whitfeild and me William Page Scri. Memorandum that this word Woodward was mistaken in the fifteenth line of this sheet and that according to the true intent of the said William Ward the same was meant and should have been written Yearwood who is the man mentioned to be nominated in the eighth line of the — sheet to be Richard Yearwood and mistaken by me the writer, witness William Page Scri.

Administration was granted to Roase Ward, the widow, during the minority of Edward Warde the son. 5 October 1624.   80, Byrde.

[The foregoing abstract was found in the course of my gleanings nearly a year ago, and preserved on account of its mention of Robert Harvard and Richard Yearwood. It now turns out to be very important as evidence that Robert Harvard's wife Katherine, the mother of our John Harvard, was a Rogers; for in my reading of the registers of St. Saviour's I came upon the following marriage :

1621 Oct 17 William Warde and Rose Rogers.

This I made note of at the time, not remembering this long preserved abstract of William Ward's will, but solely because I recalled that Katherine Yarwood had mentioned a sister Rose Reason, and as I fully believed the testatrix would turn out to be a Rogers, the name Rose Rogers struck me as worth noting. Rose Ward and Rose Reason were probably one and the same person.

Another most important evidence of John Harvard's identity remains to be shown. Knowing that he must have been the owner of landed property, and believing that before leaving for America (in the spring of 1637) he would be selling some of this property, I surmised that some record of such sale would appear in some of the documents preserved in the Public Record Office, although I had been informed that the Record Office had been searched for trace of John Harvard, and that it was hardly worth the while for me to make a search there. However, I laid the matter before my young friend Francis Grigson, Esq. (a son of the late Rev. William Grigson, our former corresponding member), and sought his advice. He said that my surmise was quite reasonable, and that the best field of investigation would be the Feet of Fines. No one could be kinder than he in showing me how to look for the evidence I wanted. After almost a whole day's labor, in which I found many suggestive items bearing on American names, I, at last, found an entry which led me to send for the Feet of Fines of the Hillary Term, 12th Charles I., County Surrey. The following is a copy of the first (and important) part of this document:

Hēc est finalis concordia fca) in cur) Dni Regis apud Westm) in Octavis Purificac)ois Be) Marie Anno regnorum caroli Dei gra) Angli Scotie ffranc et Hibn)ie Regis fidei Defens etc a conqu) duodecimo coram Johe) ffinch Rico) Hutton Georgio Vernon et ffrancisco Crawley justic' et aliis dni Regis fidelibus tunc ib) p'sentibus Int' Johe)m Man et Johannam uxo)m eius quer) et Johe)m Harvard et Annam uxo)m eius deforc) de uno mesuagio et tribus Cotagijs cum p'tin) in Parochia Sci) Olavi in Southwarke.

The next day, after a long search, I was able to examine the Concord of Fines, relating to the same transaction, where I hoped to find the signatures of the parties to this agreement, as was the custom. This case, to my great regret, proved an exception to the rule, and I was unable therefore to get a tracing of John Harvard's autograph. However, I was enabled to fix the precise date of the transfer, vizt. 16 February, 12th Charles I. The consideration given by John and Johan Man was one hundred and twenty pounds sterling.

Here we find John Harvard appearing in February, 1636–7, as a grantor of real estate in St. Olave (where his brother Thomas was living) and with wife *Ann;* surely most important evidence that he was the John Harvard who six months afterwards was in New England with a wife Ann; and the above date of transfer and the date of probate of his brother Thomas Harvard's will undoubtedly furnish the limits of the period of time within which John Harvard left old England to take up his abode in our New England. He must have set sail some time between 16 February and 5 May, 1637. The four tenements thus conveyed were, without doubt, the same as those described in the following extract:

John Man of the parish of St. Olave in Southwarke in the County of Surrey, sea captain, 6 August 1660, proved 25 November 1661.

" I giue and bequeath all those my foure houses or Tenements with thappurtenances thereunto belonging scituate in Bermondsey streete in the parish of S⁺ Olave in Southwarke and County aforesaid which I purchased of one —— Harbert, being in the occupation and possession of one —— Greenball or his assignes at yearely Rent of eight and twenty pounds unto Mary my Loveing wife dureing her naturall life and from and after her decease to the heires of our bodyes lawfully to bee begotten forever and for want of such issue to the heires of the said Mary my wife Lawfully to bee begotten of her body forever."—H. F. W.]   180, May.

IN DEI NOMINE AMEN. The Sixt Daye of the moneth of ffebruary Anno dñi 1637 I John Sadler of Ringmer in the County of Sussex Clerke Compos mentis et Corpore sanus thankes be to God therefore doe make & ordayne this my last will & Testament vizt ffirst I will & bequeath my poore sinfull Soule to God the father Beseechinge him of his mercy to save it for his sonne Jesus Christ his satisfacc͂ons sake And my Body I will to be buryed where & by whome & in what manner God hath appointed. ffor my worldly goodes I will & bequeath them in maner followinge ffirst I will and bequeath to my daughter Anne the wife of John Haruard Clarke Twentie shillinges to be payd her after my deĉease when shee shall demand it. Item I will and bequeath to my sonne John Sadler Twenty Shillinges to be payd him within a moneth after my death if it be demaunded Alsoe I will and bequeath to the poore of the parish of Worsfield in the County of Salop Twenty shillinges to be distributed amongst them after my death And I will to the poore of ye p͂ish of Ringmer abouenamed the summe of Tenn shillinges to be distributed amongst them after my departure And for the rest of my worldly goodes whatsoever legally bequeatheable I will and bequeath them to Mary my deare and loveinge wife not doubtinge of her good and godly diposeinge of them whome I make the sole and onely Executrix of this my will In wittnes whereof I say In wittnes whereof I haue hereunto sett my hand & seale   JOHN SADLER.

Witnesses hereunto John Shepherd John Legener.

PROBATUM fuit Testamentum suprascriptum apud London coram venerabili viro dño Henrico Marten milite legũ dc͂ore Curiæ Prerogative Cant Mag͂ro Custode sive Com͂issario ltim͂e Constituto vicesimo primo die mensis Octobris Anno dūi Millm͂o sexcentm͂o quadragesimo Juramento Marie Sadler Relictæ dicti defuncti et Execntricis in hm͂oi Testamento noiāt Cui Com͂issa fuit Administrac͂o omniũ et singlor͂um bonorum iurium et Creditorum eiusdem defuncti de bene et fideliter Administrando eadem Ad sancta dei Evangelia coram Mag͂ro Esdra Coxall Clic͂o vigore Com͂issionis in ea parte aĺs emanat Jurat.   Coventry, 128.

[John Sadler, M.A., whose will is given above, was instituted Vicar of Patcham in the county of Sussex, 3 November, 1608, as I have been informed by E. H. W. Dunkin, Esq., who has for years been making careful researches among the records relating to this county. In Patcham Mr. Sadler's children were baptized as follows :

          Ann d. of Jn. Sadler, Mary, August 24, 1614.

          John s. of Do. .... April 6, 1617.

Afterwards he was settled at Ringmer, where I find he was inducted 12 October, 1626, and was buried there 3 October, 1640.* His son John was a graduate of Emanuel College, Cambridge, M.A. 1638, Fellow of the College, Master in Chancery, Town Clarke of London and Master of Magdalen College, Cambridge, we learn from Cole's Collection (Add. MS. 5851, British Museum). From Le Neve's Fast. Eccl. Angl. we get this confirmed and with further information, under the title St. Mary Magdalene Coll. Masters. John Sadler, M.A., was admitted 1650, and deprived at the restoration.

* The Burrell Collection (Add. MSS. 5697, &c. British Museum), from which I took the above item, gives the date 1642, a manifest error as shown by date of probate of will ; besides, Burrell convicts himself in the next line, showing the date of induction of Mr. Sadler's successor, 1640. My friend Mr. Dunkin gives me the entry from the Ringmer Register as follows : "1640 Oct. 3 buryed Mr John Sadler minister of Ringmer." H. F. W.

In the same MS. Cole gives the admission of John Harvard, P 1631, and the same year Tho. Allen P. June 22, Suff. Mr. Harvard's graduation is shown to be 1635. His pastor, Nicholas Morton, M.A. 1619, born in Leicestershire, was Dixy Fellow and afterwards chaplain of St. Mary Overies, London (i. e. St. Savior's, Southwark).

In the Sussex Archæological Society's Collection (vol. 11, p. 225) is given " A Rolle of the several Armors and furniture with theire names of the clergie within the Arch Deaconry of Lewes and Deanery of South Malling with the Deanry of Battell in the County of Sussex. Rated and appoynted the 11th day of March A° D'ni 1612 by the Right Reverend father in God Samuell (Harsnet) Lo. Bishoppe of Chichester." I extract the following item : " Petcham, Mr Jo. Sadler, vicar —— a musquet furnished."

As the widow Ann Harvard became the wife of the Rev. Thomas Allen, the following abstract may be worth noting here :

Mense Octobris 1673, Vicesimo Septimo die. Emt. Como. Thomæ Allen filio nrāli et ltimo Thomæ Allen nup Civtis Norwicen vid def hentis etc. Ad Admistrand bona jura et cred d'ci def de bene etc jurat.   Admon. Act Book 1673, fol. 128.

I cannot refrain from expressing the gratitude I feel towards my brother antiquaries in England for the kindly sympathy and generous assistance I have received from them ; and I desire to name especially Messrs. E. H. W. Dunkin, Francis Grigson, David Jones, Robert Garraway Rice and J. C. C. Smith, who have shown kindness without stint in this matter, as in all other matters connected with my genealogical work in England.—HENRY F. WATERS.]

Testamentatum Georgii ffox.

I do give to Thomas Lower my sadle and bridle they are at John Nelson's and spurrs and Bootts inward leathers and the New England Indian Bible and my great book of the signifying of names and my book of the New Testament of Eight languages and all my physical things that came from beyond the sea with the outlandish cupp and that thing that people do give glisters with and my two dials the one is an Equinoctiall Diall And all my overplus Books to be divided among my four sons in law and also all my other books And my Hamock I do give to Thomas Lower that is at Benjamin Antrobus his closett and Rachell may take that which is at Swarthmore. And Thomas Lower may have my Wallnutt Equinoctiall Diall and if he can he may gett one cut by it which will be hard to do, and he shall have one of my prospect glasses in my Trunck at London and a pair of my gloves and my seale. G: ff: And the flameing sword to Nath: Meade and my other two seals I: Rouse and the other Dan: Abraham And Tho: Lower shall have my Spanish Leatherhood and S: Meade shall have my magnifying glass and the tortoise shell comb and cace. G. ff.

And let Tho: Docra that knoweth many of my Epistles and written Books which he did write come up to London to assist ffriends in sorting of my Epistles and other writings and give him a Guinea. G. ff.

And all that I have written concerning what I do give to my Relations either money or otherwise John Loft may putt it up in my Trunck at John Elsons and write all things down in a paper and make a paper out of all my papers how I have ordered things for them and John Loft may send all things down by Poulesworth Carryer in the Trunck to John ffox at Poulesworth in Warwickshire And lett John ffox send John Loft a full Receipt and a discharge and in this matter none of you may be concerned but John Loft only. And my other Little Trunck that standeth in Benjamin Antrobus his closett with the outlandish things Thomas Lower shall have and if it be ordered in any other papers to any other, that must not stand so, but as now ordered. G. ff. And Sarah thou may give Sarah Freckelton halfe a guinea for she hath been serviceable to me an honest carefull young woman G. ff. Make no noise of these things but do them in the life as I have ordered them And when all is done and cleared what remains to the printing of my Books Benjamin Antrobus and Mary hath one 100 pounds of mine. take no use of them for it when you do receive it And in my chest in Benjamin Antrobbus his Chamber there is a little Guilt Box with some gold in it Sarah Meade to take it and let it do it service among the rest so far as it will goe the Box is sealed up.

G. ff.

I do order William and Sarah Meade and T. Lower to take care of all my Books and Epistles and papers that be at Benjamin Antrobuses and att R. R. Chamber and those that come from Swarthmore and my Journall of my life and the passadges and travells of ffriends and to take them all into their hands And all the overplus of them they may have and keep together as a Library when they have gathered them together which are to be printed ; And for them to take charge of all my money and defray all as I have ordered in my other papers and anything of mine they may the my (sic) take, and God will and shall be their reward The 8ᵗʰ moᵗʰ 1688.

G. ff.

Thomas Lower and John Rouse may assist you And all the passages and Travels and sufferings of ffriends in the beginning of the spreading of the truth which I have kept together will make a fine History and they may be had at Swarthmore with my other Books and if they come to London with my papers then they may be had either at W: M: Ben: Antrobus his closett, soe it is a fine thing to know the beginning of the spreading of the Gospel, after so long night of Apostacy since the Apostles' days that now Christ reigns as he did in the hearts of the people. Glory to the Lord for ever Amen. The 8ᵗʰ moᵗʰ 1688 G: ff:

30 December 1697: Appeared personally Sarah Meade, wife of William Meade of the parish of Sᵗ Dyonis Back church, London, citizen and merchant Taylor of London, and did declare that she is of the number of dissenters commonly called Quakers; and she did declare in the presence of Almighty God, the witness of the truth of what she said, that she has known George Fox, late of Swarthmore in the County of Lancaster Gentleman, deceased, he marrying with her, the declarant's mother ; and she has often seen him write and is well acquainted with his handwriting and she, having now seen and perused three papers hereunto annexed and marked No 1, 2 & 3, containing the last Will & Testament of the said George Fox deceased, the first beginning thus (I do give to Thomas Lower, &c) and ending thus (" Torkel shel com & case. G. ff."), the second beginning thus (and all that I have written, &c.) and ending thus (the Box is sealed up. G. ff.) and in the margin (give him a guinea), the third beginning thus (I do order William & Sarah Meade, &c.) and ending thus. (glory to the Lord forever Amen. G.ff. the 8ᵗʰ mon 1688) she did declare that she did & does verily believe that the same three papers were and are all wrote by & with the proper handwriting of the said George Fox deceased And she farther declared that above a year before the death of the said George Fox (who died on or about the thirteenth day of January in the year of our Lord

one thousand six hundred & ninety) the said George Fox did deliver to her a parcel of papers sealed up & thus superscribed with his own hand, viz (Papers of George Fox which are to be laid up in the Trunk of his at William Meade's and not to be opened before the time) and on the next day after the deceased's death the said bundle was opened in the presence of the declarant and of several other persons and they the three papers hereunto annexed and marked No 1, 2 & 3 were found amongst other papers relating to his concerns.   Sarah Meade.

30 Decembris 1697 dicta Sara Meade fecit declarationem suprascriptam coram me   George Bramston Surr.

30 December, 1697   Appeared personally William Ingram of the parish of Sᵗ Margaret's, New Fish Street London, citizen & Tallow Chandler of London, aged about fifty seven years, and declared that he is of the number of Dissenters commonly called Quakers; and he did declare in the presence of Almighty God, the witness of the truth of what he said (then follows a declaration similar to the foregoing as to handwriting of deceased testator, &c.).

A similar declaration was made, the same day, by George Whitehead of the parish of Sᵗ Botolph without Bishopsgate, London, gentleman, aged about sixty years and also of the number of Quakers, &c.

Tricesimo die mensis Decembris Anno Dñi Milliม̃o Sexcenм̃o nonageм̃o septima emanavit coм̃co Margaretæ ffox relictæ et Legāriæ nominatæ in Testamento Georgii ffox nuᵖ de Swarthmore in coм̃ Lancastriæ sed in Þoâ omniū Sanctorū Lombard Street London dēfti hēntis &c ad administrañd bona Jura et credita dicti dēfti juxta tenorem et effectū Testamenti ipsius dēfti (eo quod nullū omnino nōiaverit extorem) declaraĉone in presentia dei Omnipoteñ juxta Statutum parliamenti in hac parte editum et provisū de bene et fideliter administrañd eadem ᵖ dictam Margaretam ffox prius facta.   Pyne, 280.

[George Fox, born in July, 1624, married 27 8mo. 1669, in Bristol, Margaret, widow of Thomas Fell of Swarthmore Hall, Lancashire. She is said to have died at Swarthmore in 1702, near the eighty-eighth year of her age. Of her children by her first husband, Margaret is said to have been the wife of John Rous, Bridget of John Draper, Sarah of William Meade, Mary of Thomas Lower, Susanna of (William?) Ingram, and Rachel of Daniel Abraham.—H. F. W.]

Letters of administration on the estate of the Rev. GEORGE PIGGOTT clerk, late chaplain in the regiment of marines under the command of the Hon. Col. John Wynyard, at Jamaica in the West Indies, granted, 30 June, 1743, to the Rev. George Piggott, clerk, son and lawful attorney of Sarah Piggott, widow, the relict of the said deceased, for the use and benefit of the said Sarah Piggott, now residing at the Massachusetts Bay in New England.   Admon. Act. Book, 1743.

[For this abstract the readers of the REGISTER are indebted to Robert Garraway Rice, Esq., of Acar Lodge, Bramley Hill, Croydon, Surrey.—H. F. W.
The Rev. George Pigot was settled as Rector of St. Michael's Church, Marblehead, 1728; he came to Marblehead from Providence, and in addition to his parochial duties officiated every month in Salem, where in a short time he gathered a congregation of between two and three hundred persons.
In 1730 Mr. Pigot made what proved to be an unsuccessful attempt to regain a right to the Baronies of Morley and Monteagle, to which he was an heir, and requested permission to return to England to attend to the matter, which was evidently not granted. His rectorship ended in 1736. During his rectorship there are recorded 454 baptisms, among them four of his own slaves, 95 marriages, 145 burials. In going from the house of a poor and sick parishioner whom he had been visiting in the winter of 1736, Mr. Pigot fell on the ice and broke his left arm, which

he fractured again the following summer ; his health consequently became broken, and he obtained leave to visit England, and is supposed to have died there or on the passage. His wife was buried in the churchyard fifteen years after.

Samuel Curwen, Esq., in his Diary, writing of Cardiff, 1st August, 1777, says: " After my departure I learnt that a daughter of the late Parson Pigot of Marblehead was an inhabitant of this place."—GEORGE R. CURWEN.

The baronies of Morley and Monteagle in 1686, on the death of Thomas Parker, the third inheritor of the two baronies, fell into abeyance between the issue of his two aunts, Katharine who married John Savage, earl of Rivers, and Elizabeth who married Edward Cranfield, Esq. (Burke's Extinct Peerage, ed. 1846, p. 409). Rev. George Pigot, of Marblehead, wrote to the secretary of the London Society for Propagating the Gospel, August 1, 1730 : " I think it proper at this juncture to notify the Hon'ble Society of one affair which might otherwise deserve their blame : It is that I have made a claim by Mr. Speaker of the House of Commons to be restored to my right to the Baronies of Morley and Monteagle, and that I do not know how soon I may have a call to make out the same. Therefore I request the Hon'ble Society to give me leave to come home upon a proper invitation." (Bp. Perry's Massachusetts Historical Papers, p. 262.) Mr. Pigot, in a letter Dec. 27, 1734, speaks of having a large family (Ibid. p. 304).

May 1, 1718, " Mr. George Piggott " of Newport was admitted to the freedom of the colony of Rhode Island (R. I. Records, iv. 227). May 5, 1724, " George Pigot " of Warwick was admitted freeman to that colony (Ibid. p. 340). Was either of these the minister?—EDITOR.

A year or two ago I met at the rooms of the New England Historic Genealogical Society, Rev. Mr. Pigot, an English clergyman, who said he was a descendant of Rev. George Pigot, of Marblehead. He visited the rooms to obtain genealogical information concerning his ancestor. He had an elder brother in Australia who had sufficient property to maintain the dignity of a baron. He wished to obtain documentary evidence to substantiate the claim to the barony which he said was in abeyance in their line of the Pigot family.—JOHN COFFIN JONES BROWN.]

WILLIAM HORSFORDE of Dorchester in the County of Dorset, gentleman, 30 June, 1621, proved 25 January, 1622. To be buried in the church of St Peters. To the poor of the Hospital of Dorchester five pounds. I give & bequeath my house and lands, with the appurtenances, in the parish of St Peter's, in the lane there going towards the Fryery, wherein George Hooper, needle maker, lately dwelt, and which I purchased of Mr Joseph Longe and Thomas Bullocke, unto Joane my wife for the term of her life ; then to Joane my daughter and the heirs of her body, &c. ; then to my own right heirs forever. My daughter Sarah and her husband, my son in law, John Hardey. To their children, John, Jane and Sarah Hardey and the child wherewith my daughter Sarah is now great, one hundred pounds, which was meant to be given unto them by my brother Hugh Horsforde deceased, and one hundred pounds besides. To my daughter Joane Horsforde four hundred & fifty pounds. My daughter Grace, the wife of Thomas Frye, and her children. My friends John Strode of Chantmarrell, Richard Bingham of Melcombe, Richard Kesier and William Clapcott, of Frampton, to be executors. Swann, 27.

[There was a William Horsford, spelled, in other places on the record, Horseford, Hosford, Hosseford, who was an early inhabitant of Dorchester, Mass. He is first mentioned October 8, 1633, when he is styled " Goodman Hosseford "; freeman 1634 ; went to Windsor, Conn. ; was a Commissioner to the General Court in 1637. With his old Dorchester companions and friends, Mr. John Witchfield, and Mr. John Branker " the schoolmaster," he became associated as ruling elders of the church in Windsor. They frequently delivered the weekly lecture before the church. Mr. Savage says, he probably removed to Springfield, and there preached from October, 1652, to October, 1656, " when Moxon gave up in disgust." It seems that he returned to England with his second wife Jane, widow of Henry Fowkes. In 1656, being then in England, he gave land at Windsor to his two children. His wife also gave some of her land to Windsor church and to her husband's children, &c. " In

1671," says Mr. Savage, "she was at Tiverton, co. Devon." William had a son John, whose nine children were living at their father's decease, August 7, 1683. (See Savage, Hinman, Stiles's Windsor.)—WILLIAM B. TRASK.]

MORGAN HOLMAN of Barwicke within the parish of Swyre, in the County of Dorset, gentleman, in his will, dated 19 June, 1614, proved 19 April, 1623, mentions (among others) cousin Humphrey Jolyff, and speaks of land which he lately purchased of Nicholas Darbye, Lawrence and Roger Darbye.   Swann, 33.

BOLD BOUGHEY, Esq., Warden of the Fleete, 17 October, 1669, published and acknowledged by testator the next day. Whereas since my marriage with Jane the widow & relict of William Celey, Esq., by whom I have had no children, and who either hath or pretended to have a reasonable good estate, which I have not wasted or intermedled with; since which marriage I have lived but an uncomfortable life; I do therefore give and bequeath unto my said wife, for her better support and as an addition to her own estate, the sum of twenty pounds per annum, to be paid to her yearly and every year during the life of M^{ris} Challener alias Bamfield, her mother in law, now living, to be paid unto her by my executors by ten pounds at the end of every six months after my decease. To my daughter Martha Boughey the sum of one thousand pounds,.to be paid unto her at the day of her marriage, or within such short time after as my executors can raise the same; and in the mean time I give unto her thirty pounds per annum for her maintenance; and if she happen to die before she be married, then I give and bequeath the said sum of one thousand pounds between my two sons John & Bold Boughey. Reference is made to an engagement of John Boughey, son and heir of the testator, to come into partnership with Edmond Peirce, Esq., in the business and office of Wardenship of the Fleete. To my son Bold Boughey three hundred pounds at his age of one and twenty, or when he shall be a Freeman of London and set up his trade of a Linendraper. Unto the poor prisoners of the Fleete five pounds per annum, to be paid on Christmas Eve during all the time that any of my name or family shall be Wardens of the Fleete. To my brother Thomas Boughey one hundred pounds to be paid him within twelve months after my decease. To my two nieces Priscilla and Margaret Roe ten pounds apiece, to put them out to some trades such as my executor shall think fit. To my good friends Mr Robert Leighton, Capt. William Oakes, Sir John Carter, Mr Griffith Boderdo, Mr James Johnsen, Charles Cornwallis, Esq., Mr Samuel Fisher, Mr Richard Beale and Mr Robert Wigmore, forty shillings apiece, to buy them rings. The same to my old servant Christopher Story. To my servant Thomas Corbett the like sum; and it is my desire that he be continued in his place of Tipstaff in the exchecquer so long as he shall "abare" himself honestly. My friends Edmond Peirce, Esq., and William Church, gentleman, to be executors, and to each ten pounds for their pains therein. My loving brother in law Robert Wiggmore, Esq., and Charles Cornwallis, Esq., to be overseers.

The above will was proved by Edmond Peirce, who took out letters 15 November, 1669, and by William Church, 25 June, 1672.   Coke, 133.

[The testator of the above will, although he makes no mention therein of New England or New England people, is clearly enough the writer of the letter bearing date "London, 4th may 1662," and superscribed "For my Deare Sist^{er} Mrs Elizabeth Harris att Wroxbury These in New England," which was printed in the July number of the N. E. HIST. AND GEN. REGISTER, 1851 (vol. v. pp. 307–8). In it he

speaks of his family thus : " our youngest Bro^{er} Timothy is Chaplaine to the Kings Rigimt of Guards in Dunkirke, Thomas Imployed by me in business, our sister Katherine .... is married to one Mr Thorpe in London, ... our Sist^{er} Hannah is married to one Mr Wilding and lives in Shrewsbury. Mary is married to Mr Roe, who hath an Imployment under me in London, and lives well, Priscilla is married to an honest minister one Mr Bruce and at present Lives in London, is Chaplaine to mee, at the ffleete. Our Sisters, except Katherine, are all mothers of children." ....
" I was married but it pleased god to remove my wife by death about foure yeares since : I have only two sonnes and a daughter (viz) John, Bold and Martha living ; my wife was with child of the tenth when she died."
We are told that " Robert Harris & Elizabeth Boffee were married Jan. 24, 1642," in Roxbury.—H. F. W.]

PETER HODGES late of East West Guersey in America, planter, and now in the parish of St Mary Magdalen, Bermondsey, in the County ot Surrey, the one & twentieth of July, 1697, proved 21 December, 1697. To my dearly and well beloved friend Elizabeth Willis, of the said parish, spinster, whom I intended for my lawful wife, as well for the natural love and affection I have and bear to her as for divers other good causes and considerations me hereunto especially moving, all those two hundred acres of woodland in East West Guersey in America by me held and granted from the Governour of the said Island, together with the deed or writing by which the same premisses are granted, which is now left in the hands of Thomas Revell of Burrington in East West Guersey aforesaid ; also all my horses, hogs and other cattle whatsoever in the said Island, marked with a half Gad; and also all and singular my estate, both real and personal, as well within the said Island of East West Guersey as any other place or places whatsoever, &c. To all or any of my Relations that shall lawfully claim any estate or interest in the said premisses, &c., I give and bequeath one shilling if demanded and no more. The said Elizabeth Willis to be executrix.
Wit : Joann Pryor Senior, Mary Pryor, Joann Pryor Junior, Hannah Richeson and John Parry Scr.   Pyne, 284.
[Burrington should be Burlington. Thomas Revell was at this time a member of the West Jersey Council. See New Jersey Archives, ii. 146 et seq.—EDITOR.]

JAMES MONTGOMERY, of James River in Nantzimum in the Island of Virginia, and late chirurgeon of His Majesty's ship St Albans, being sick and weak of body in Richmond in the County of Surrey, 25 August, 1697, proved 24 December, 1697. My body to be buried in such parish as it shall please God to call my soul from thence. To my two loving brothers Robert and Benjamin, all such writings, obligatory bills and accounts which are my property in Virginia aforesaid. To my brother Benjamin one bed. To my brother Robert all the residue of my estate (lands excepted). To Sarah, wife of William Cranbury, of the place above named in Virginia aforesaid, I give and bequeath one warming pan now in the custody of the said Sarah ; and touching all such wages or pay as shall appear due to me for my service performed on board His Majesty's Ship St Albans above named I dispose thereof as follows (vizt) to my sister Jane and to her youngest son now living, and to her daughters Jane and Elizabeth three pounds apiece, to be paid unto them or either of them on his or her respective marriage day. This money is to be raised out of such pay as shall appear due to me from the Right Honorable the Treasurer or Paymaster to His Majesty's Navy. To my godson James Buxton two pounds, and to his brother Richard one pound ten shillings. To Martha, daughter of my brother Benjamin, five pounds. To my nephews James and Benjamin five pounds apiece. To my nephew Robert Montgomery five pounds. To Joseph Halford of Richmond in the County of Surrey, chandler, I devise and bequeath one hogshead of tobacco, freight and custom of the same being hereby appointed to be paid by him for the same when arrived from Virginia. Papers relating to my said ship's affairs, &c. now in the custody of .... Bird of Wapping in the County of Middlesex, Instrument Maker. My will is that if my executors shall think fit to authorize him their Attorney to receive the money due thereupon or shall recall them out of his said custody that there shall be an allowance of twelve pence per each pound to such person as shall take care in the management and receipt of the same. My brother Robert and William Wilson of London, merchant, to be joint executors.

Wit: Thomas Ryley, Nathaniel Clark Not. Pub^e in Richmond in the County of Surrey.   Pyne, 290.

[Benjamin Montgomery appears as the patentee of 450 acres of land in Nansemond County, October 26th, 1699, Book No. 9, p. 241. The following grants, also of record, may be of interest: Robert Montgomery, Edmund Belson and other inhabitants of Coward Creek, Nansemond County, 850 acres in Nansemond County, April 30th, 1671, Book No. 6, p. 678; Hugh Montgomery, 280 acres in Lower Norfolk County, October 21st, 1687, Book No. 7, p. 615, Virginia Land Records.

R. A. BROCK.]

EDWARD FRAUNCES of Vere in Jamaica but now in London in Great Britain Esq. 24 Dec. 1740. All my property to my loving brother James Fraunces of Cheapside, London, apothecary. If he die without issue, lawfully begotten, then all to my cousins Elizabeth Jacquelin now the wife of Richard Ambler of York Town in Virginia Esq., Mary Jacquelin the now wife of John Smith of Gloucester County in Virginia, merchant, and Martha Jacquelin of York Town aforesaid, spinster, equally, share & share alike. To my negro servant maids Madge & Maria to each an annuity of twenty shillings Jamaica money for & during their respective lives. To Henry Smallwood, Esq., John Verdon, Esq., Varney Phelp, Esq., and Moses Kerrett, Esq., each a gold ring of twenty shillings value. My brother James Fraunces, the said Varney Phelp & Moses Kerrett to be joint executors.

Wit: John Hyde, Jn° Harwood, Jn° Hawkesworth.

Proved 3 April, 1741, by James Fraunces, with power reserved for the other executors.   Spurway, 89.

[Edward Jaquelin, son of John and Elizabeth (Craddock) Jaquelin, of county Kent, England, and a descendant of a Protestant refugee from La Vendee, France, during the reign of Charles IX., of the same lineage as the noble family of La Roche Jaqueline, came to Virginia in 1697 ; settled at Jamestown ; married Miss Cary, of Warwick county, and died in 1730, leaving issue three sons (Edward the eldest) —neither of whom married—and three daughters : Elizabeth, of the text, who married Richard Ambler ; Mary, of the text, who married John Smith, who is believed to have been a member of the House of Burgesses, of the Council, and of the Board of Visitors of William and Mary College ; Martha, who died unmarried in 1804, aged 93 years. Edward Jaquelin " died as he had lived, one of the most wealthy men in the colony."

Richard Ambler, son of John Ambler, sheriff of county York, England, in 1721, migrated to Virginia early in the 18th century ; settled at Yorktown ; married Elizabeth Jaquelin and had issue nine children, all of whom died at an early age, except three sons : Edward, Collector of the Port of York ; married and left issue. He was a man of consideration in the colony, and when Lord Botetourt came over as Governor he brought a letter of introduction to him from Samuel Athawes, merchant, London (see Virginia Hist. Reg. iii. 1850, pp. 25, 26) ; John, born 31st December, 1735, Burgess from Jamestown, and Collector of District of York river, died 27th May, 1766, in Barbadoes; Jaquelin, born 9th August, 1742, married Rebecca, daughter of Lewis Burwell, of " White Marsh," Gloucester County member of the Virginia Council during the Revolution, and long State Treasurer. He left issue : Eliza, married first, William Brent of Stafford County, and secondly, Col. Edward Carrington of the Revolution and member of Congress (no issue) ; Mary Willis, married Chief-Justice John Marshall ; Anne, married George Fisher, of Richmond ; Lucy, married Daniel Call, lawyer and legal reporter, Richmond. Upon the tomb of John Ambler, of Jamestown, Virginia (born 25th September, 1762, died 8th September, 1836), in Shockoe Hill Cemetery, Richmond, Virginia, the Ambler and Jaquelin arms are quartered : Ambler—*Sa. on a fesse or, bet.* 3 *pheons ar. a lion passant guard. gu.* Jaquelin—*On a bird* 3 *roses* (no tinctures discernible).

Much information regarding the Amblers and Jaquelins of Virginia is given in Meade's Old Churches and Families of Virginia, i. p. 97, *et seq.* The descendants of Edward Jaquelin and Richard Ambler have intermarried with the families of Baylor, Byrd, Carter, Nicholas, Norton, Randolph and others of prominence.

R. A. Brock, of Richmond, Va.]

Anna Coltman of London, widow, 10 February, 1622, proved 25 August, 1623. To my grand daughter Anne Coltman, daughter of my son William, one hundred pounds at her day of marriage or age of twenty-one years. If she die before that time then this sum to her father and his younger daughter Alice and his son Richard, to be equally divided between them. To my son Francis Coltman twenty pounds, to be paid him within three months after my decease.

Item, I give and bequeath unto my son Henry, if he be living, the sum of ten pounds of the lawful money of England, to be paid unto him within three months next after his return from Virginia. Francis my eldest son, William my youngest son. Other legacies to children. To my daughter Margaret, the wife of my son William, a ruby ring of gold. To Ralphe Canning, citizen and ironmonger of London, forty shillings ; and I appoint him sole executor. To his wife a ruby ring of gold. To my friend Mrs. Anne Hebb of London, widow, whom I appoint overseer, forty shillings and a saphire ring of gold. Swann, 78.

Solomon Stedman of Boston in New England, mariner, 20 October, 1696, proved 1 December, 1697. Henry Cole of St Pauls, Shadwell, Baker, to be my attorney to demand and receive of and from the Right Honorable the Treasurer of His Majesty's Navy and Commissioner for Prize money, &c. &c. I bequeath all my estate to my brother John Stedman.

Wit: Abraham Card, Sam¹ Forrest, John Smith. Pyne, 298.

Augustine Fish of Bowden Magna in the County of Leicester, yeoman, 7 April, 1646, proved 23 September, 1647, by Christian Fish the relict and executrix. To Thomas Fishe my second son, and to my wife, during her life, and after her life ended to Thomas and his heirs males forever one farm, whereon my eldest son liveth, called by the name of Royses Farm, with all that John Fish had there during my life, both in town and field ;—moreover seven "pastors" in Acharhads which sometimes did belong to Palmer's House in the neather end, I give unto Thomas Fish and his heirs males as aforesaid, with this caution and proviso that he shall pay unto his youngest sister, Elizabeth Fish, one hundred marks at her age of twenty three years or on her marriage day, which shall first happen, if her marriage be with the liking of the overseers and her mother and brother. If Thomas Fish die without issue male his land to return unto Bartholomew Fish. In like manner if Bartholomew die without issue male it is to return to William Fish which is in New England, if he be then living. I give unto Christian my daughter the cottage house wherein " Jhon "

Warde and his sister liveth, with that spot of ground adjoining, bought of Richard Watts, to enter at the death of Jhon Warde, with one cow and five sheep. I give unto Jhon Halliake the eldest son of William Halliake, after his father and mother's decease, the three acres which did belong to Palmer's farm, unto him forever; and all the rest of his other children which will be ruled by parents and grandmother I give five pounds apiece, to be paid at their marriage or at twenty years old. I give unto Bartholomew Fish my youngest son five pounds. I give unto William Fish in New England, if he return, five pounds. Further to my son Thomas Fish, after the lease is expired which now my son John Fish holdeth, called by the name of Waters his close, to my son Thomas and his heirs forever. To my grandchildren at Brigstock, to help to buy every one a sepp,* —— nobles apiece. I also give unto my grand children at Thorpe, in Rutland, three ewes, to be given at the discretion of my executrix. I also give unto my servants half a crown apiece more over than their wages. I make my wife full and sole executrix, praying Thomas Fish my second son, to assist her with his power. I also wish, if be thought good unto my executrix, to give unto my eldest son's children two nobles.

The Test. of Augustine Fishe " Ritten " with his own hand. Intreating these two my sons, Edward Marriat and Robert Sly to be overseers. Wit : Maurice Dix and William Whittwell.   Fines, 186.

[The William Fish mentioned is probably William of Windsor, Ct. See Savage's Gen. Dict. ii. 161 ; Connecticut Col. Records, i. 144, 148; ii. 519.—Editor.]

JAMES CARTER of Hinderclay in the County of Suffolk, yeoman, Saturday, 8 Sept. 1655. " I give unto the children of my brother Thomas Carter who now is in the new England, to every of them Tenn pounds apeece as Conveyniently as the same may bee raysed out of my parsonall Estate." To the two sons of my brother William Stubbs of Harleston, by his late wife who was my sister, and his two daughters by her, &c.   To Frances Edwards, my wife's kinswoman.

Commission was issued 24 October, 1655, to Mary Carter widow of the said James Carter.   Aylett, 391.

[The Thomas Carter mentioned was probably Thomas of Sudbury, who died Aug. 14, 1659. There were at least two others who may have been the man, viz., Rev. Thomas, of Woburn, who died Sept. 5, 1684 (REGISTER, xvii. 51) ; and Thomas, of Charlestown, who died about 1652. (Wyman's Charlestown, i. 186.)—EDITOR. Mr. Samuel R. Carter, Paris, Oxford County, Maine, in letter of July 21, 1884, surmises that the Rev. Thomas Carter may have first landed in Virginia (emigrating thence to New England), and that he may have been a relation of John Carter, the ancestor of the well-known Virginia family of the name. There is, however, nothing of tradition or record to substantiate the theory.—R. A. BROCK.]

JOHN COOPER, of Weston Hall (in the County of Warwicke), 21 November, 1654, proved 1 October, 1655, by Elizabeth Cooper, his widow and executrix.   To brother Timothy Cooper, now in New England, the sum of thirty pounds, but if it happen that he shall die before this shall be due then to his children that shall be living.   To sister Dorcas ten pounds, but if she die, &c. then to brother Timothy if living, if not then to his children.   My wife to have the benefit of the said sums of thirty pounds and ten pounds during her widowhood.   " Yet notwithstandinge if it shall please god to afflict my wife in anie of his providences towards her that shee hath neede of all that I have as it shall evidently appeare to supply her-

---

* Interesting as a survival of the Anglo Saxon term for sheep.—H. F. W.

selfe in her want Then my will is that that I have bequeathed to my brother and sister shalbe voyde and shall not be exported from her." Wife
Elizabeth to be executrix. Friends Humphrey Hale and John Buttery
" to be helpefull to my wife as her occation shall require."
The witnesses were John Sutton & John Buttery.   Aylett, 392.

[The Timothy Cooper mentioned was probably the person of that name at Lynn,
who died March, 1659, and had sons John and Timothy, and several daughters.—
EDITOR.]

JOSEPH TOWNSEND, now of London, gentleman, but late of South Carolina in America, 4 February, 1732, proved 16 August, 1736. Money to
be raised to satisfy my brothers in law Mr John Glasse of Cary Street,
gentleman, all such sum & sums that I am or shall be indebted unto him
together with interest thereon. If any thing remain I give & bequeath the
same unto my loving sister Hannah Glass, wife of the said John Glass, in
trust, to divide and give the same unto my dear son William Sinclar Townsend and Hannah Townsend, equally to be divided between them, to be
paid at their several ages of one & twenty years ; and I desire her to take
care of them, &c. My dear sister to be sole executrix, without the control
of her said husband.
Wit : Do Strangways G. Thornton, Robt: Thornton.   Derby, 185.

JOHN ENDICOTT of Salem in New England, chirurgeon, now resident
in London, being bound on a voyage to New England, 12 August, 1689,
proved 30 March 1695 by Anne Endicott, his widow. He mentions wife
Anne and the child she goes with, brother Samuel, and refers to the will
of his father Zerubbabel Endicott.   Irby, 208.

[This John Endicott was a grandson of Gov. John Endicott. See REGISTER, i. 336.
—EDITOR.]

WILLIAM MARCH of Charlestown in New England, but now residing in
the parish of Stepney in the County of Middlesex, mariner, being very
sick, &c. makes his friend Mr Richard Robison of Shadwell, shipwright,
executor and gives him two guineas. " I can hold my pen no longer." 29
October, 1694, proved 13 September, 1695. The witnesses were Anne
Pearce & Jane Willoughby.   Irby, 220.

[This William March was the son of Nicholas and Martha March of Charlestown.
His mother married for a second husband William Dadey. Administration on this
estate in this county was granted to Mrs. Dadey. Inventory, Sept. 12, 1695, £24.
See Wyman's Charlestown, ii. 655.—EDITOR.]

Letters of administration granted 11 November, 1633, to John Conant,
clerk, uncle on the father's side (patruo) of CALEB CONANT, lately in the
parts beyond the seas, bachelor, deceased.
        Admon. Act Book for 1633, Leaf 204.

JOHN PARRIS of the Island of Barbadoes, Esq., 15 May, 1660, proved
23 October, 1661. To wife Susanna Parris one hundred pounds a year, in
quarterly payments; and I do bind my third part of three plantations in the
said Island for performance of the same. To Thomas Parris, son of my
brother Thomas, one hundred pounds out of the revenue of said plantations. To Samuel Parris, another son of brother Thomas, one hundred
pounds (as before), and to Martyn Parris, another son (a similar bequest).
If any of my said three nephews die before they attain the age of twenty
one years, the legacies shall remain equally to the survivors. To Sarah

Parris, daughter of my brother Richard Parris, deceased, one hundred pounds to be paid within one year after my decease. To my sister Margaret Bully ten pounds. To my sister-in-law Susanna Parris, forty shillings to buy her a ring. To my sister Rebecca Parris forty shillings to buy her a ring. To Thomas Martaine, son of my cousin Thomas Martaine of this Island, one thousand pounds of Musko sugar within twelve months after my decease. To Hugh Leman, one half piece of fine dowlas, &c. Bequest to James Minge. To Thomas Newman, son of George Newman deceased, fifty pounds at age. To my brother Thomas Parris all my third part of three plantations (as above) as also all my part of the stone house at Reades Bay and land at the Bridge, &c., provided he pay annuity & legacies, &c. To John Parris, eldest son of my said brother Thomas, after the death of his father (all the above real estate), with remainder to Thomas, next to Samuel, then to Marrine (*sic*) Parris, sons of my said brother. And my said cousin John Parris shall have my gold ring with the signet. The residue to brother Thomas Parris. Richard Evens, Capt. James Klinkett, Left. Anthony Woodward and my cousin Thomas Martine to be my executors, in trust, until other orders shall be given by my brother Thomas Parris who is at London.

The above will was proved by Thomas Parris, brother of the deceased.

May, 161.

ANNE PARRIS of St Mary Islington, in the County of Middlesex, wife to Thomas Parris now or late resident at the Island of Barbadoes beyond the seas merchant, 9 June, 1665, proved 10 June, 1665. Reference to bond of husband, before marriage, to one Mr William Freeman, in trust for the use of me, for the payment of five hundred pounds, &c. To Samuel Halsey, now an apprentice in —— three hundred pounds. To my loving cousin Thomas Bent, citizen & merchant taylor of London, cousin Frances Ascue & cousin Elizabeth Smith fifty pounds apiece. Their mother, my sister, Elizabeth Smith, my sister Tanser. Others mentioned. Mr Thomas Doelittle & Mr Peter Royle to be executors.   Hyde, 65.

[The Rev. Samuel Deane, in his History of Scituate, Mass. (page 320-1), speaking of Thomas Parris, of Scituate, who was born at Pembroke, May 8, 1701, says : " From undoubted documents, now [1831] in the possession of Rev. Martin Parris, of Marshfield, we learn that this gentleman was son of Thomas Parris, who came to Long Island, 1683, from London, from whence he removed to Newbury, 1685, and to Pembroke, Mass., 1697 ; which latter was son of John Parris, a dissenting minister of Ugborough, near Plymouth, England,—whose father was Thomas, a merchant of London. The last named Thomas had a brother John, a merchant and planter of great wealth, who deceased in Barbadoes, 1660. His original will is in the possession of Rev. Martin Parris."

The testator is undoubtedly the wealthy merchant and planter of Barbadoes referred to by the Rev. Mr. Deane, and the Rev. John Parris of Ugborough must be his nephew John, whom he calls " the eldest son of my said brother Thomas." The late Hon. Albion Keith Parris, the second governor of Maine, was the sixth in descent from Rev. John. (See Historical Magazine, vol. i. (1857) pp. 130-1.)

Mr. Thomas Parris was Assistant Justice in Barbadoes, April 11, 1631 (REGISTER, xxxix. p. 138).

The Rev. Samuel Parris, of Danvers, of witchcraft notoriety, appears to have been the son of Thomas Parris, of Barbadoes, who died in 1673, and who was probably Thomas, a younger brother of Rev. John Parris, also named by the testator. (See REGISTER, x. 34.)—EDITOR.]

JOSEPH WILKINSON of Calvert County in the Province of Maryland merchant, 25 April, 1734. To my brother in law Mr John Skinner an handsome suit of mourning and a mourning ring of twenty shillings sterling price. To my dear and loving wife one full third part of my personal estate. To my daughter Elizabeth one other full third part. To my son Joseph the remaining third part. If my wife be with child then my estate is to be equally divided among all my children. My wife to be executrix. In case of her death my brother in law Mr John Skinner to be executor. Wit: John Smith, Pos^{ths}: Thornton, Roger Boyce, Alex^r Lawson.

22 July, 1736, there issued a commission to William Torver the lawful attorney of Mary Wilkinson the widow and executrix of the deceased, &c., to administer according to the tenor & effect of the said will, for the use & benefit of the said executrix, now residing in Maryland.

Derby, 168.

EDWARD PARKS citizen & merchant tailor of London, 23 January 1650 To wife Mary Parks, in lieu of her thirds, fifteen hundred pounds (in various payments) and one third of the plate and household stuff, and all that my freehold messuage or tenement with its appurtenances, &c. which I lately purchased of William Pennoyer of London, merchant, wherein I now dwell, in the parish of Stepney, being the North western part of that great messuage formerly the possession of the Right Hon. Henry Earl of Worcester. My wife to have the education of my children.

If my son Henry Parks shall within three months, &c. and after notice given, release and quitclaim, &c. all his part of all my goods, &c. (according to the custom of the city of London) and release to George Jackson of Sandhurst in the county of Kent all his part of lands, &c. in Maidstone in the County of Kent which I lately have sold to George Jackson, then I give & bequeath unto him three hundred pounds (in various payments). And further I give & bequeath unto my said son Henry Parks and his heirs forever, in consideration as well of the release by him to be made to my brother George Jackson of the lands in Maidstone, &c. all my messuages, houses, lands, tenements & hereditaments situate, lying and being in New England in the parts of America beyond the seas.

If my son Edward Parks, within three months next after notice given him of my death and after he shall attain the age of twenty & one years, release his part of personal estate according to purport of an indenture, dated 26 June 1640, between me the said Edward Parks, of the one part, and Thomas Westby of Fresby in the county of York, gentleman, and Edward Gell of Brimington in the county of Derby Esq., of the other part, then I give and bequeath unto the said Edward three score pounds for his preferment & placing him to apprentice. To my son John five hundred pounds within three months after he attains the age of twenty-one years, and to sons William & Stephen (the same amount with the same limitation). To daughter Elizabeth Parks five hundred pounds at twenty-one or day of marriage. To sons Thomas, Dannett, Francis & Samuel (legacies similar to their brother John's above). To Mark, Francis & Susan Wilcox, three of the children of my sister Alice Wilcox, ten pounds apiece, & to Anne Wilcox another daughter twenty pounds, to be paid, the sons at twenty-one and the daughters at that age or day of marriage. Bequeaths to the widow Brewer, to Martha Wilson now wife of Thomas Wilson, being both my late servants, to my daughter Mary, now wife of Thomas Plampin and my two grand children Thomas and Edward Plampin. Reference to lands in Hadleigh in the county of Suffolk lately bought.

My son in law Thomas Plampin and cousin John Bagnall, both of London, merchant tailors, to be my executors and my brothers Dr William Forth and Dannett Forth of London, woollen draper, to be overseers. A Thomas Forth a witness.

The above will was proved 29 January 1650; but the executors having died before fulfilling their trust a commission was issued 29 March 1673 to John Parkes, a son & legatee. He also died before completing his administration, and commission was issued 3 November, 1681, to Mary Cawley als Parkes, the widow relict of said defunct, &c.   Grey, 10.

[A full abstract of this will was printed in a note in Mass. Hist. Soc. Collections, 4th S., vol. vii. p. 385, from a copy obtained for me by Col. Chester. The note was appended to several letters from Edward Parks to John Winthrop, Jr. These show that Parks terms Henry Bright of Watertown his uncle. In the genealogy of the Brights of Suffolk, Eng. (Boston, 1858), we find on pp. 270–71, an abstract of the will of Mrs. Elizabeth Dell, sister of Henry Bright, in which she mentions her nephew William Parks. She also mentions her brother Henry Bright, William Forth and —— Blowers, her sister Martha Blowers, her cousin —— Cawby, Esq., and her nephew Dr. William Forth.

Henry Parks, son of Edward, sold in 1655, his land in Cambridge to John Stedman, and very probably came here for the purpose. This particular branch, however, then ceased to have any connection with New England. But at Cambridge one of the early settlers was Dea. Richard Parke, 1638–1655, whose son Thomas had a son Edward. At Roxbury was William Parke, whose will of 20 July, 1684, mentions only three daughters and their children, brother Thomas Parks of Stonington, deceased, and brother Samuel with his sons Robert and William. Savage says that these three were sons of Robert of Wethersfield and New London, who died in 1665. Very probably this Robert was the man who wrote to John Winthrop in 1629 from Easterkale in Lincolnshire (see Mass. Hist. Soc. Coll., 5th S. vol. i. p. 194), proposing to go to New England.

These *may* have been relatives of Edward Parke, who was clearly allied to Winthrop through the Forths. The family name of Dannett ought also to lead to some trace of this family.

The Alice Wilcox, sister of Edward Parks, recalls the William Wilcockes of our Cambridge, who died in 1653, leaving a widow Mary (Powell) but no children, and a sister Christian Boiden in Old England. A John Wilcox was of Dorchester, 1661, and went to Middletown. The names Wilcox, Hastings, Fox and Hall are in the Leicestershire Visitations, and Wilcox also in Rutland.—W. H. WHITMORE.]

WILLIAM GOORE of Nether Wallop in the county of Southampton gentleman, 9 November 1587. To wife Joane, eldest son William, all my land called Garlacks. To my four youngest sons Richard, John, Nicholas and William Goore the younger all my land in Newington, in the county of Wilts, and in Basingstoke, in the county of Southampton, and two hundred pounds apiece. To my four daughters Agnes, Elizabeth, Barbara and Margery Goore two hundred pounds apiece. The executors to be my eldest son William Gore and Margaret Reade, the supervisors to be John Pittman of Quarley, Thomas Elie, Clerk vicar of Nether Wallop and Leonard Elie of Wonston.

10 May 1588. Emanavit cõmissio Will^mo St John armigero marito sororis naturalis et ltiñie dict def et Leonardo Elie generoso uni supervisorum &c. cum consensu W^ml Gore filii &c. durante minori etate eiusdem Willmi et Margarete Reade als Gore alterius executorum &c.

                                                       Rutland, 37.

WILLIAM GORE of Nether Wallop in the county of Southampton, gentleman, 22 January 1655, proved 29 March 1656. Wife Elizabeth to be sole executrix. To the poor of Nether Wallop three pounds to be distributed in one month after my decease. To my wife a portion of my now dwelling house at Garleggs in the parish of Nether Wallop and part of the orchard. To my cousin Richard Hamon. To Amy Singer, daughter of my late sister Margaret, and Jane Singer, another daughter, and Roger Singer, a son. To my cousin Mary Poore the now wife of John Power thirty pounds. To Nicholas & Margaret, son and daughter of my late sister Wallingford, twenty pounds apiece in one year after my decease. To my cousin Nicholas Gore, son of Nicholas Gore late of Farley deceased, ten pounds in one year. To Nicholas Hatchet of Nether Wallop five pounds in one year. My brother in law Mr Robert Sadler, my cousin John Poore and my cousin Richard Miller of Broughton. To the now five children of Richard Hamon forty pounds apiece and to William Poore and Elizabeth Poore, son & daughter of my late cousin William Poore deceased, forty pounds, and to the now children of my late cousin Thomas Singer deceased, forty pounds. To my godson Richard Sherfield, son of my late brother Roger Sherfield, gentleman, deceased. If my cousin Nicholas Wallingford shall have issue of his body or Margaret Wallingford have issue of her body then, &c. To John Gore, son of my late uncle Richard Gore. To my uncle Hugh Mundy. Berkeley, 110.

[In these Goore wills Mr. Waters is evidently probing the connections of the ancestors of our Merrimac Valley settlers. The villages of Wallop, like those of Choulderton, lie upon the edges of the Counties of Wilts and Southampton, and when Dummer, Saltonstall and Rawson, with their English associates, had arranged for developing a stock-raising town in New England, they arranged also to secure from co. Wilts and its vicinity the transfer of a colony of practical men not only accustomed to the care of live stock, but to the trades which interlaced in the products of a stock-raising community. The matter of first importance was to secure ministers with whom the community would feel at home. Rev. Thomas Parker and his relatives the Noyes family, natives of Choulderton, were secured, and with them the Wiltshire men were glad to join.

In the will, proved 28 March, 1657, the names of many of the Poore family are mentioned as cousins of the testator, and so is Nicholas Wallingford, who came in the Confidence from Southampton in 1638, with others—Stephen Kent, John Rolfe, John Saunders, John and William Ilsley, and more recruits to join their relatives who established the town of Newbury. Joseph Poore, of Newbury, married, 6 August, 1680, Mary Wallingford, daughter of Nicholas, born 20 August, 1663. Anthony Sadler was a passenger in the same vessel. In the Visitation of co. Wilts in 1623 are pedigrees of the Sadler family on p. 63. The son and heir of the family given there is Robert Sadler, born in 1608, who may have been the person mentioned as " brother-in-law " in the will given above.

The will proved in 1588 contains an instance, not uncommon at that period, but a terrible annoyance to genealogists, of two sons having the same baptismal name— *eldest* son William, and four youngest sons, among whom is William the *younger*. The name of Margaret Read recalls the fact that the Read and Noyes family intermarried in the locality of these testators.—JOHN COFFIN JONES BROWN.]

JOSEPH BLAKE of Berkley County in the Province of South Carolina, 18 December, 1750. My whole estate to be kept together until it raises the sum of two thousand pounds sterling money of Great Britain and one thousand pounds Proclamation money, or the value thereof, in the currency of this province, exclusive of the maintenance of my sons Daniel and William and my daughter Ann Blake. After said sums are cleared—to be kept at interest and the interest applied towards educating & maintaining my sons Daniel & William and daughter Ann until they arrive at full age. Then one thousand pounds sterling to my son Daniel, the same to son William and the remaining thousand pounds Proclamation money to daughter Ann. To son Daniel the plantation I now live on called Newington and a tract of land on the Cypress Swamp lying between the lands of Mr James Postell and Barnaby Brandford, part of which I purchased of Mr James Postell deceased, the remainder I took up of the King; and that part of my land on Charles Town Neck which lies between the High Road and Cooper River; and fifteen hundred acres to be taken out of my lands on Cumbee River between Mrs Hudson's land and the land I bought of Colonel William Bull, the line to run towards Calf Pen Savanah as far back as will take in the quantity of fifteen hundred acres; and a plantation containing five hundred & ninety-seven acres in·two tracts bounding on Mrs Donings and Mrs Drake to the North East and to the North West on Mrs Donings, Mrs Sacheveralls and Doctor Brisbanes, to the South West on a tract of land which was formerly Mr Dowses but now mine and on Mr Ways, to the South East on Mr Richard Warings. To son William & his heirs forever my plantation containing more or less on Wadmelaw River and new cut, commonly called Plainsfield, lying between lands of Mr John Atchinson and Mr Fuller; and that part of my land on Charles Town Neck that lies between the High Road and Ashly River, bounding on Mr Gadsdens, Mr Hunts & Mr John Humes; and two tracts of land lying between Mr Atchinsons and Mr Stoboes, one tract containing two hundred & thirty acres, the other seventy-six acres; and two tracts of land containing four hundred & forty acres purchased of Stephen Dowse by Mrs Jennis, bounding on Mr William Elliott, Mr John Draytcn & Mr Graves.

I give and bequeath unto my loving daughter Rebecca Izard, to her and her heirs forever a tract of land containing eighteen hundred & seventy three acres in Granville County on the Lead of Coosaw, Hatchers and Chili Phina Swamp, bounding on James Therrs to the North West; and an Island on Port Royal River in Granville County commonly called Cat Island, containing four hundred acres. I give and bequeath to my loving daughter Ann Blake one thousand acres of land to be laid out by my executors and executrix on the Calf Pen Savanah to be taken out of my lands on Cumbee on the head of the said tracts and an island containing two hundred and eighty-six acres of land in Granville County on the North East side of Port Royal River and on all other sides on marshes and creeks out of the said River. I give all my Real estate, not already given, devised or bequeathed, unto my two sons Daniel & William Blake, all my household goods & plate to be divided between my two sons Daniel & William & my daughter Ann Blake, to each a third. To son Daniel my coach & harness and Prime Thorn, his wife Betty Molly & all their children which they have or shall have. To son William Wally Johnny Molatto Peter Mol Juda & all their children, &c. To daughter Ann Blake Lampset Nanny Patty & Molly child of Hannah & all their children, &c. All the residue of my personal estate (not already given, devised or bequeathed) unto my four children Rebeccah Izard, Daniel Blake, William Blake & Ann Blake, to be equally divided.

I nominate, &c. daughter Rebecca Izard, son Daniel Blake and son Ralph Izard executrix & executors & guardians to my children until they attain the ages of twenty-one years, &c. & to improve the estate of my said children either by putting money at Interest, buying slaves or any other way they shall judge most advantageous.

Wit: Jacob Molte, William Roper, Alexander Rigg.

Charles Town So: Carolina   Secretarys Office.

The foregoing Writing of two sheets of paper is a true copy from the Original will of the Honble Joseph Blake Esquire deceased. Examined & certified p William Pinckney Dep^{ty} Sec^{ty}.

11 **February** 1752 Depositions of John Ouldfield, of South Carolina, planter, & William George, freeman of South Carolina, at present residing in
the city of London, gentleman.

The will was proved 20 February 1752 by Daniel Blake Esq. son, &c.
&c. Power reserved for the other executors.   Bettesworth, 30.

GEORGE JONES, of the City of Philadelphia in the Province of Pennsylvania, yeoman, having a design by the Permission of the Almighty to
pass over the seas, 22 September 1743. To Sarah Toms daughter of Robert Toms twenty pounds current money of Pennsylvania, to be paid her at
her age of eighteen years. To Thomas Howard of the city of Philadelphia, joyner, all my right & title of & to my seat in Christ church in Philadelphia. To Mary Howard, daughter of Thomas Howard, ten pounds at
age of eighteen. To Andrew Robertson, miller at Wesschicken, my horse,
saddle & bridle, my watch & seal thereto affixed. To Kattrine Hinton
one hundred pounds immediately after my decease, &c. provided that the
said Katrine do not marry till after my decease. To Abraham Pratt, of
the city of Philadelphia joyner, twenty pounds, &c. To the children of
my brother James Jones deceased, of the parish of St John at Brogmore
Green in the County of Worcester in Great Britain, & to my sister Elizabeth Clay, of the city of Worcester, & to her children, all the rest & remainder of my estate, Real & Personal, to be equally divided.

I do nominate & appoint Jonathan Robeson of Philadelphia Esq., Lawrence Anderson, of Philadelphia merchant, and Jacob Duchee, shopkeeper
in Market Street, executors.

Wit: William Cunningham, Warwick Coats John Chapman.

14 February 1752 Admon. with the will annexed of the goods & chattells, &c. of George Jones late of the city of Philadelphia, in the Province
of Pennsylvania, but at the city of Worcester deceased, lying and being in
that part of Great Britain called England only but no further or otherwise,
was granted to Elizabeth Clay, widow, the natural & lawful sister of the
said deceased & one of the Residuary Legatees named in said will, for that
Jonathan Robeson Esq., Lawrence Anderson & Jacob Duchee, the executors appointed in said will, have taken upon them the execution thereof so
far as concerns that part of the estate of the said deceased within the Province of Pennsylvania, but have respectively renounced the execution of the
said will and their right of administration of the said deceased's estate in
that part of Great Britain called England.   Bettesworth, 39.

[Probated in Philadelphia, 1751, Book i. p. 404.—C. R. HILDEBURN, of Philadelphia.]

WILLIAM STOCKTON, Clerk, parson of Barkeswell in the County of
Warwick, 2 March 1593, proved 17 June 1594 by Elizabeth his relict & executrix, through her attorney Thomas Lovell Not. Pub. The will mentions brother Randulph Stockton, brother Raphe Stockton, the children of
cousin John Stockton, parson of Alcester, the children of cousin Thomas
Gervise, son Jonas Stockton, eldest daughter Debora Stockton, wife Elizabeth & daughters Judith & Abigail, cousins John Stockton & Thomas Ger-
vis and Thomas Benyon of Barkeswell yeoman, & John Massame of the
city of Coventry, clothworker, to be overseers.   Dixey, 49.

[I suppose the " cousin John Stockton, parson of Alcester," mentioned in the above
will, was the father of Patience, wife of Edward Holyoke of New England, whose
father, John Holliock, of Alcester in the county of Warwick, mercer, made his will
21 November 30th Elizabeth (proved 31 January, 1587) in presence of John Stock-

ton. If this be so, then Mr. Stockton must have removed before 1607 to Kinkolt in Leicestershire, where he was living (probably as Rector of that parish), as shown by a letter from young Edward Holyoke to his betrothed, dated 21 Nov. 1607. (See Emmerton & Waters's Gleanings from English Records, pp. 57–59.)—H. F. W.]

ROBERT WILCOX, the younger, of Alcester in the county of Warwick, mercer, xiiii October 1626, proved 14 February 1626. To my father M[r] Robert Wilcox, over and above the two hundred pounds due to him by bond, one hundred pounds within one year after my decease (and some chattell goods). To my son Robert fifty pounds to be put out for his best use at his age of xiiii years. My will is that Ann & Elizabeth Heath shall have x[li] between them for the money I received by their brother Richard's will. To each of my sisters xl[s]. To Humfry Bedowe x[s]. To Joane my maid servant xv[s], to Elenor my maid servant x[s]. I give x[li] to be from time to time lent gratis to honest tradesmen at the discretion of M[r] Bay-liffe for the time being, with the assent of my father Wilcox, brother Bridges, brother Holioke and M[r] Jeliffe, or of three, two or one of them so long as any of them shall live, and, after the death of the survivor of them, at the discretion of M[r] Bayliffe for the time being. To mine apprentice xx[s] at thend of his term. The rest of my goods chattells, &c. to Martha, my beloved wife, whom I make sole executrix. The overseers to be my well beloved father in law John Halford and George Jelliffe and my brother Florisell Bovey and I give them ii[s] vi[d] apiece for their pains.

Wit: Samuel Hulford, Edward Holioke.   Skinner, 12.

[An article on the Wilcoxes of New England is printed in the REGISTER, xxix. 25–9, but no connection with Robert of Alcester is found. There is probably some relationship between his " brother Holioke " and Edward Holyoke, the immigrant ancestor of the Holyokes of New England, who seems to have come from Alcester (see will of Edward Holliock, 1587, in Emmerton and Waters's Gleanings, p. 57). Two other New England immigrants, William and Richard Waldern (written by descendants, Waldron), were natives of Alcester (see REG. viii. 78).—EDITOR.]

Mr. THOMAS ROPER's will. John West my servant to be set free. Alexander Gill, servant to Capt. Peirce, to be set free or else if Capt. Peirce shall refuse to release him, then that the said Alexander receive two hundred pounds of Tobacco from Capt. Peirce. I give and bequeath all tobaccoes due unto me in Virginia to my brother John Roper in England and that M[r] George Fitz Jefferyes receive it to the use of my said brother. Item a pair of Linen breeches to William Smith of James City. To the said William Smith a waistcoat. To my brother John · Roper three· hundred and odd pounds of good & lawful money of England, in the hands of my father in law M[r] Thomas Sheaperd of Moine in Bedfordshire. The residue to my brother John Roper. Fifty shillings in money to M[r] Haute Wyatt, minister of James City.

Wit: Haut Wyatt, William Smith, George Fitz Jefferey.

In the letter of administration (5 February 1626) to John Roper Thomas Shepard is spoken of as the natural & lawful father of John, Elizabeth and Constance Shepard, brother and sisters of the deceased on the mother's side (*ex materno latere*), the letters of administration granted in the month of May 1624 having been brought back and renounced.

Skinner, 11.

[According to a pedigree of the Wyatt family furnished me some years ago by Reginald Stewart Boddington, Esq., London, England, the Rev. Hawte Wyatt (a younger brother of Sir Francis Wyatt, twice governor of Virginia, married 1618, buried 24 August, 1644, at Boxley) was the second son of George and Jane (daughter of Sir Thomas Finch of Eastwell, Knight, by his wife Katherine, elder daughter and co-heiress of Sir Thomas Moyle of Eastwell) Wyat (of Allington Castle, Boxley, and in right of his wife, Lord of the Manor of Wavering, son of Sir Thomas Wyat by his wife Elizabeth, daughter of Thomas Brooke, Lord Cobham, beheaded 11 April, 1554) and Jane (married 1537), younger daughter and co-heiress of Sir William Hawte of Bishopbourne, co. Kent, Knight, and to whom Queen Mary granted the Manor of Wavering) ; inducted after his return to England to the living of Boxley, 3 October, 1632, and Rector of Merston, co. Kent; died 31 July, 1638 ; buried at Boxley.

He was married twice, " *and his issue said to have gone to Virginia.*"

The following document in my possession may be of interest in connection with the immediately preceding paragraph :

" Oct. 29, 1655. This day Pindabake the Protector of the young King of Chiskoyack was at my house [punctuation mine], intending to have spoken with the Governor, then expected to be heer'd, but he came not, & therefore hee desyned to leave his mind with mee, Maior Will Wiat & divers others, as followith, viz : that Wassahickon the —— [illegible] had freely given unto Mr. Edward Wyatt and his heyres, executors, administrators or assigns, all the land from Mr. Hugh Guinn's old marked trees to Vttamarke Creeke, including all Pagan —— [illegible] high Land, being freely given, and with the consent of all the rest of the Indians, it was also agreed among them all that neither the King nor any other of his Indians should sell, alienate or dispose of any land belonging unto them without the consent of Mr. Ed. Wyatt, which was the only business that he had to acquaint the Gov'r therewith in the behalfe of Mr. Ed. Wyat, as we heere doe testify under our hands, this present 29th of October, 1655."

John West

The marke of

[mark]

Pindabake, Protector of
the young King of
Chiskoyake

Will'm Benett
John West Junior
Toby West

The marke *[mark]* of Wm Godfrey

The marke of   John Talbutt
John King   *[mark]*

Signed and sealed in the presence of
all whose names are here subscribed:

I find the following grants of land to the name Wyatt and Wyat of record in the Virginia Land Registry Office : Ralph Wyatt, " Gent." Book No. 1, p. 590, lease to Richard Johnson, Roger Davis and Abraham Wood, " planters," " one parcell of Islands," 1636 ; Henry Wyat, Esq., eldest son of Sir Francis Wyat, p. 757, lease for 21 years, of 50 acres in Pasbylaiers James City county for the raising of corn for the better protection of the plantation, Dec. 16, 1641 ; Thomas Wyat, p. 916, 2000 ac. on the south side of the Rappahannock river, " twenty miles up," Sept. 24, 1643 ; George Wyatt, No. 2, p. 54, 250 acres in James City county, April 12, 1642 ; Richard Wyatt, p. 154, 500 acres in Mobjack bay, Aug. 20, 1645 ; William Wyatt, No. 3, p. 4, 400 acres in Gloucester county, April 27. 1653 ; p. 354, 300 acres in New Kent county, June 6, 1665 ; Edward Wyatt and Robert Grig, 4, p. 439, 370 acres in Kingston parish, Gloucester county, April 19, 1662 ; William Wyatt, 5, p. 286, 400 acres in Gloucester county, March 16, 1663 ; Major William Wyatt, p. 439, 1940 acres in New Kent county, May 20, 1664 ; William Wyatt, p. 453, 300 acres in New Kent county, May 20, 1664 ; Anthony Wyatt, p. 510, 282 acres in New Kent county, June 28, 1664 ; Thomas Wyatt, p. 608, 500 acres in Mobjack bay, May 9, 1666 ; William Wyatt, 6, p. 322, 500 acres in New Kent county, June 20, 1670 ; Anthony Wyatt, p. 247, 398 acres in Charles City county, July 24, 1669 ;

William Wyatt, p. 296, 2240 acres in New Kent county, April 17, 1669; p. 364, 1900 acres in New Kent county, Oct. 21, 1670; 7, p. 32, 850 acres in New Kent county, April 25, 1680; Henry Wyatt, p. 123, 649 acres in New Kent county, April 20, 1682; John and Richard Wyatt, p. 321, 650 acres in New Kent county, Sept. 20, 1683; Nicholas Wyatt, p. 510, 115 acres in Brandon parish [Charles City county?], April 27, 1686; John Wyatt, 9, p. 654, 700 acres in King and Queen county, May 2, 1705; James Wyatt, No. 10, p. 85, 139 in upper parish of Nansemond county, May 2, 1713; Richard Wyatt, p. 247, 285 acres in Charles City county, Aug. 15, 1715; Francis Wyatt, 23, p. 635, 377 acres in Prince George county, Nov. 25, 1743; Francis Wyatt and Mary Hawkins, No. 28, p. 208, 100 acres in Prince George county, Aug. 20, 1747, and in same, p. 211, 200 acres in Amelia county, Aug. 20, 1747.

Anthony Wyatt was a prominent citizen of Charles City County, Virginia, 1660–70.—R. A. Brock, of Richmond, Va.]

Nicholas Jupe, citizen & merchant Taylor of London, 10 March 1650, proved 13 October 1651. To cousin Benjamin Jupe, his executers & assigns, all my moiety or half part of two houses, &c. in the parish of St Buttolph Aldgate, London, in the occupation of Richard English and Edward Mott, and the house where a stone-cutter did dwell and my own dwelling house and so much of the dwelling house as is now in Mr Finch's occupation,—which I and Richard English bought of Matthew Beanes. To the said Benjamin fifteen pounds and to his brother John & his sister Margaret five pounds apiece. To Anthony and Mary Jupe, equally between them, my half of five houses which were bought by me and the said Richard English, standing in Gravel Lane in the Parish of Saint Buttolph without Aldgate, London, being in one row or rank, they to pay, out of the profits, to Christopher Jupe & Thomas Evans ten pounds apiece within two years after my decease. I give to Simeon Smith my half of four tenements granted by lease from the Hospital of Christ Church London. To Rebecca Smith, daughter of my brother Joseph Smith, my lease of tenements in the occupation of Mr Mason & Mr Harman. To the poor of Bishopsgate, to the minister, Mr Fuller, to the poor of Aldgate. To Richard English & John Euerett & to each of their wives twenty shillings apiece, to Sarah Martin & Mrs Katherine Jackson twenty shillings apiece, to Mr Dye and his wife twenty shillings apiece, to Simeon Smith forty shillings, to Sarah Wilmott ten pounds, to Rebecca Unckles three pounds & to her mother four pounds, to my brother Christopher's daughter Mary five shillings, to my cousin Evans forty shillings, to my cousin Christopher Jupe forty shillings, to cousin John Jupe twenty shillings, to cousin Margaret Jupe twelve pounds, to Anne Foster twenty shillings, to my wife's sister Denton three pounds & to her daughter twenty shillings, to Mr Hedges & his wife twenty shillings apiece, to Edward Smith the elder and Edward Smith the younger and to Elizabeth Smith (certain legacies), to William Harper forty shillings, to Thomas Jackson twenty shillings, more to Benjamin Jupe ten pounds, more to Joseph Smith & his daughter Rebecca Smith, &c. Loving friends Mr Grimes, Richard English & John Everett to be overseers. Simeon Smith to be executor.   Grey, 189.

[At the time of the decease of the testator, the five houses in Gravel Lane above devised were in the occupation of "John Trigg senior mrs oakeman; widdow Izard widdow Bocken and mr Chambers" and the interest of the testator's niece Mary Jupe, afterward Mary Morse, therein, was conveyed with other property by her husband John Morse of Boston in New England, salt boiler, by deed of mortgage dated Nov. 9th, 1654, recorded with Suffolk Deeds, Lib. 2, fol. 180, to Capt. Robert Keaine of said Boston, uncle of said mortgagor, to secure the payment of £32. Capt. Keaine had advanced £15 to pay for the passage of Morse, his wife and his wife's brother, Benjamin Jupe, from New England back to Old England, and the latter sum was to be paid at the Golden Crown in Birchin Lane, London, on or before April 26, 1655, out of the rents belonging to the said wife or brother Benjamin Jupe remaining in the hands of Simeon Smith of Southwark. the executor of the foregoing will, as appears by a bond and order recorded fol. 183 and 184. See also fol. 86 and 182. See note to the will of Benjamin Kaine (*ante*, page 2). See also the abstract made by Stanley Waters of an indenture, found by him in the Suffolk Court Files, dated March 10, 1652, " between Benjamin Kayen of London Esquire, sonne and heire apparent of Robert Kayen of Boston in N. E., Esquire, on the one part, and Simeon Smith, Cittizen and Haberdasher, of London, the executor of the last will &c. of Nicholas Jupe, Cittizen & Marchant Tayler of London, deceased, of the other part." This abstract was published in the REGISTER for July, 1881 (xxxv. 277).—JOHN T. HASSAM.]

FRANCIS NEWTON of London, grocer, 24 August 1660, proved 11 January 1661, now bound out on a voyage to Virginia. To wife Mary Newton six hundred pounds within six months after my decease. The residue to my loving sisters Elizabeth and Susan Newton and loving brother Joseph Newton, equally, &c. Friends John Berry, Anthony Stanford & Joseph Wilson to be executors.   Laud, 8.

[See note " Newton of Kingston upon Hull, England," REG. April, 1885, p. 194.—R. A. BROCK.]

RICHARD SMITH, of St Dunstan's West, London, Cook, 13 January 1660, proved 17 January 1661. To be buried in the parish church of St Dunstans in the West. Wife Joane, brother John Smith. To my sister Ann Hawthorne five acres in the possession of John Alley, butcher, of the yearly value of five pounds for her natural life, &c. and then to her two sons John & Nathaniel Hawthorne and their heirs equally. To my brother John Smith the reversion I purchased (after the decease of Anne Henman, widow) of William Backhouse Esq., with remainder to his eldest son Samuel Smith & his heirs male, next to Richard Smith, second son of said brother John, then to the right heirs of the body of the said John Smith.

I give and bequeath to William Hawthorne, son of Anne Hawthorne, my sister, the reversion of one pightle called Leachrye or Tan-house Pightle, containing by estimation three acres, in the possession of John Vincent. One third part of land called Welshman's (after my wife's decease) to my loving sister Mary Holloway and the heirs of her body, one third to my loving sister Rachel Horton & the heirs of her body, the remaining third to the children of John Topping begot upon the body of my sister Prudence and their heirs. To my wife the lease or leases of the two houses in Chancery Lane, &c. To my loving friend Mr Robert Hawe of Wokeingham twenty shillings to buy him a ring. To Mr —— Sedgwick, without Temple Bar, ten shillings to buy him a ring. To the poor of the town of Wokeingham twenty shillings. To the poor of the parish of Wokeingham and dwelling in the said town twenty shillings. Lands, &c. in Wokeingham in the County of Berks. Brother John Smith to be executor & Richard Palmer of Wokeingham Esq. to be overseer.

Wit: L. Astry, George Chapman.   Laud, 9.

[The Salem Hathornes, as well as the Hawthornes named above, were allied with a Smith family, the immigrants, William and John Hathorne (REG. xii. 295 ; Emmerton and Waters's Gleanings, pp. 52-5) having had a sister Anne who was the wife of Hugh Smith (*ante*, pp. 43-5).—EDITOR.]

HENRY SEWALL of the parish of St Michael in the city of Coventry, alderman, aged fourscore years or thereabouts, 1 Sept. 1624, proved the last of June 1628 by Margaret Sewall his relict and executrix. To my wife Margaret an annuity or yearly rent charge of eleven pounds, eight shillings, issuing out of certain lands in Ansley in the county of **Warwick**, granted to me & my heirs forever, and now in the tenure of Elizabeth Throckmorton widow, and all my lands, tenements and hereditaments, with the appurtenances, &c. in the city of Coventry & in Corley and Coundon in the County of Warwick and in Radford Coundon in Urchenfield & Stoke in the county of the city of Coventry. To Henry Sewall, my eldest son, all my lands, tenements and hereditaments, &c. &c. in the hamlet of Radford in the county of the city of Coventry and in Coundon in Urchenfield in the county of the city of Coventry and in Coudon in the County of Warwick, and all my lands, tenements & hereditaments, &c. in Dog Lane in the said city, in the occupation of Richard Baldwyn, a messuage or tenement & one garden, with the appurtenances, in Much Park Street, in Coventry, in the tenure of Henry Critchlowe, draper, and all those messuages or tenements, &c. &c. in the said city in the several occupations of John Harbert, William Heyward, Richard Heyes or Walter Wiggens, and all those three tenements in Little Park Street, in the occupation of Mr Henry Davenport, —— Thorton, Katherine West, or their assigns, after the decease of my wife Margaret, and during his natural life ; then to the heirs of his body lawfully begotten, &c. ; also to the said Henry, my son, a tenement & garden, &c. &c. in Heylane in the said city, in the tenure of Bryan Conigrave.

To Richard Sewall, my younger son, after the decease of my wife Margaret, lands & tenements, &c. in Corley, in the county of Warwick, which I lately purchased of Stephen Hales Esq. with the wyndell thereupon now standing, and other lands, &c. purchased of Richard Patchett, of Martin Whadocke & of Thomas Nicklyn and of Thomas Barre; also to the same Richard one messuage, &c. in Smithford Street, Coventry, in the tenure of Jefford, barber, and a tenement & certain stables called the Sextree in Coventry.

To my daughter Anne, now the wife of Anthonie Power, my messuage & tenement, &c. &c. in Corley, now in the occupation of me the said Henry, which I lately purchased of Daniel Oxenbridge, and other lands, &c. purchased of Thomas Patchet & of George & Walter Holbech, and two tenements in Bailie Lane in Coventry, one in the tenure of Theophilus Washington, and a messuage in High Street, Coventry, in the tenure of Mr William Hancock, and a messuage in the suburbs of Coventry in the tenure of John Lindon, and a messuage in the tenure of Roger Bird and a tenement in the tenure of Joyce Hobson, a widow and late in the occupation of Lawrence Armeson.

To Margaret, my youngest daughter, now the wife of Abraham Randell, tenements without Newgate in the several tenures of Francis Robinson & Edward Coles, lands, &c. purchased of John Horne of Stoke, gentleman, lands in the tenure of John Wilkinson, & of William, or Thomas, Pywall, that my messuage or tenement & garden in Bailie Lane, in the city of Coventry wherein I now dwell, tenements, &c. in Bailie Lane in the occupation of Roger Dudley, James Knib, William Miller, Edward Malpas, Johane Newland, widow, William Cumberledge & Edward Bissaker, a tenement in Earl Street in the occupation of John Wright, a garden in the occupation of Mr Richard Clarke, a tenement I purchased of John Hammond, Doctor in Physick and tenements in Darbie lane in the occupation of the widow Wothon & the widow Kinsman. Reference also made to tenements in the occupation of Richard Faulkner, Raphe Mellowes, Peter

Baxter, Henry Wetton, Randall Cleaver, Clerk, Thomas Hobson and John Hill. To my loving friend Humphry Burton forty shillings, &c. &c. Wife Margaret to be executrix and friends Mr William Hancock, of Coventry, alderman, and my loving kinsman Reginald Horne, gentleman, to be overseers. To my cousin John Horne a cloke cloth.

Wit: John Brownell, James Brownell.   Barrington, 63.

[The eldest son of the testator of the above will, Mr. Henry Sewall, came over to New England and was the ancestor of the distinguished family of that name in Massachusetts. In Essex County Court Papers (Book xxvi. No. 59) may be found a deposition made 10 April, 1679, by Robert Walker, of Boston, Linen webster, aged about seventy-two years, in which he testified that about fifty-six years before, living with his father in the town of Manchester, in Lancashire, within the realm of England, he did then know one Mr. Henry Sewall who lived at the same town and in the same street with the deponent's father, being his overthwart neighbor, and that afterwards the said Mr. Henry Sewall removed with his family to New England, and there dwelt in the town of Newbury, &c. &c.   H. F. WATERS.

This will furnishes another example of the wisdom of the course pursued by the associated collection and publication of material of this kind. In the introduction to the Sewall Papers, now in course of publication by the Mass. Historical Society, after stating the investigations made by Col. Chester, the main results of whose search was placed in their hands, the editors state that the Sewall family cannot be traced beyond the two brothers (Henry, whose will is here given, and his brother William, both of whom had been mayors of Coventry in England). It is to be supposed that neither the editors nor Col. Chester had the detail which Mr. Waters furnishes your readers, for in the closing paragraphs of the will here given, the mention of his "loving kinsman Reginald Horne, gentleman," who was made an overseer of the will, and the bequest to his "cousin John Horne," furnish direct guides to obtain the name of the father of Henry and William Sewall. It appears from the pedigree of the Horne family, which is given below from the Visitation of Warwickshire, 1619 (see Harleian Soc. Pub., vol. xii. p. 343),* that William Shewell married Matilda Horne, and that her brother John was the father of both Reginald and John, who are mentioned in this will of Henry Sewall respectively as his "kinsman" and "cousin."

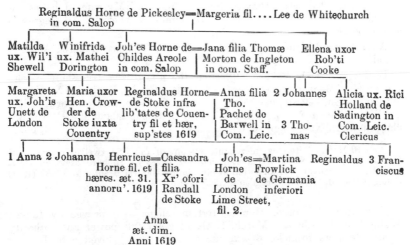

Reginaldus Horne de Pickesley=Margeria fil....Lee de Whitechurch
  in com. Salop

Matilda ux. Wil'i Shewell	Winifrida ux. Mathei Dorington	Joh'es Horne de Childes Areole in com. Salop	=Jana filia Thomæ Morton de Ingleton in com. Staff.	Ellena uxor Rob'ti Cooke
Margareta ux. Joh'is Unett de London	Maria uxor Hen. Crowder de Stoke iuxta Couentry	Reginaldus Horne de Stoke infra lib'tates de Couentry fil et hær, sup'stes 1619	=Anna filia Tho. Pachet de Barwell in Com. Leic.	2 Johannes —— 3 Thomas	Alicia ux. Rici Holland de Sadington in Com. Leic. Clericus

| 1 Anna | 2 Johanna | Henricus=Cassandra Horne fil. et filia hæres. æt. 31. Xr' ofori annoru'. 1619 Randall de Stoke | Joh'es=Martina Horne Frowlick de de Germania London inferiori Lime Street, fil. 2. | Reginaldus Franciscus 3 |

Anna
æt. dim.
Anni 1619

Judge Samuel Sewall was always sharp in money matters, from the time when he received the dowry upon his marriage with the mint-master's daughter until his

* Was John Horne (otherwise Orne), of Salem, descended from this Warwickshire family?

death, and whether his visit to his relatives was one of affection or for mercenary motives, it is plain that if he could get an honest penny, he went for it. He evidently had a full copy of this will, and displayed this paragraph from it in his Diary, under date of April 9, 1689 :

" To the said Margaret during her natural Life and after her decease to the Heirs of her Body issuing, and for want of such issue of her body, to remain to the right heirs of me, the said Henry the Testator, for ever."

This extract is followed by a memorandum of the date of Margaret Randall's will, May 4, 1646. If this will could be found it might throw some light upon other relations.

The Judge saw some of the real estate which had been left to his grandfather's sister Margaret, *with the above proviso*, and she had given it to the descendants of her sister Anne, ignoring the rights of the descendants of Henry, her brother, the grandfather of the judge. He told them who he was, and offered to confirm the right (for a consideration ?), and he received the emphatic answer that his relatives would not give him 3d. for it.   JOHN COFFIN JONES BROWN.]

NOELL MEW being intended by God's permission to go to old England, 3 August, 1691, proved 4 April, 1700. To my wife Mary Mew, during her widowhood, all my estate, real and personal. But if she sees cause to marry, then she is to have out of my estate in England one hundred and ten pounds sterling in lieu of her dowry, in one year after her marriage, and all the household stuff. To my son Richard Mew all my farm Rockey Farm, &c., with the mulatta boy called George and fifty pounds sterling, he paying each of his sisters five pounds per annum to help bring them up till of age or married, and then to be acquitted of the said payment. To him also my great bible and silver tankard. To my daughter Mary Mew one hundred pounds sterling, &c., an Indian girl called Jenny, one Spanish silver cup, one round silver cup, one silver dram cup with a funnel. To my daughter Patience one hundred pounds sterling, the negro woman Bess, six silver spoons. All my land in West Jarsey to be sold and the proceeds to be equally divided betwixt my said three children. My wife to be executrix and my friends William Allen, Benjamin Newberry and Peleg Sanford to be overseers.

Wit : Richard Jones, Joseph Blydenburgh, Thomas Roberts, William Cload.

Testimony, 22 December, 1692, that the above is a true copy. John Easton Gov[r], John Greene Dep. Gov[r], Walter Clarke, Benjamin Newberry, William Allen, Christopher Almy. In the Probate the testator is called Noell Mew late of Newport in the Colony of Rhode Island and Providence plantations, in New England, deceased.   Noel, 59.

[Richard Mew, of Stepney, merchant, was one of the first twelve proprietors of East Jersey, 1681 (N. J. Archives, i. 366, 383 *et seq*.). Richard Mew, of New-port, R. I., merchant, had an action at law against Jahleel Brenton in 1708. (R. I. Colonial Records, iv. 39. See also iii. 555.)—EDITOR.]

NATHANIEL WEBB of Mountserrett, merchant ——, proved by Robert Webb, Esq., his son, 26 March, 1741. I grant full power and authority to my executors to make & execute a lease to my beloved wife Jane of all my negroes on and belonging to a certain plantation in the parish of St Anthony in the said Island, commonly called Carrolls Plantation, with the house & lands in town (and sundry movables) for her natural life, she paying to my executors in trust for my children the yearly sum of two hundred and fifty pounds sterling. This in full satisfaction of her dower, also the use of half my house in the town of Taunton one half of the furniture, &c. To my eldest son Robert my estate in the County of Somerset formerly under lease to John & Richard Barber of Taunton, and all my houses and lands in said Taunton or elsewhere in England, and five thousand pounds sterling, &c. To my son Nathaniel my plantations in Mountserratt now under lease to John Dyer of the said island, and all my houses & lands in the said island, and my house and land in the town of Bassterre in the island of St Christophers. Item I give & bequeath to my son John all my lands in the County of Connecticut in New England near the town of Seabrook, they containing about five hundred acres. To my brother John Webb of Abington one hundred pounds sterling, at the same time forgiving him what he owes me. To my brother Harry Webb fifty guineas to buy him a mourning ring. To my executors ten guineas each to buy them mourning rings. To my sisters Anne Stone & Sarah Smith twenty pounds sterling each to buy them mourning & mourning rings. The rest & residue to my five children, Robert, Ann, Ruth, Nathaniel & John.

I appoint William Gerrish, Esq., in London, Isaac Hobhouse of Bristol, merchant, John Paine of Taunton, mercer, Dominick Trant, Thomas Meade, George French and Peter Lee of this Island, Harry Webb of Antigua and my son Robert Webb executors & the guardians of my children.

Spurway, 78.

BENJAMIN PLUMMER of Portsmouth in the Province of New Hampshire in New England Esq. 7 May, 1740, proved 12 March, 1740. To my esteemed friend Mrs Mary Macphederis my gold watch, my negro boy named Juba and a ring of five guineas price. To Theodore Atkinson Esq. my saddle Horse and to him & his wife each of them a gold ring. To Mr John Loggin one suit of mourning apparel. The whole of my apparel to be sold for the most they will fetch in the town of Boston. To my honored mother one hundred pounds sterling. The residue to be equally divided amongst my brothers. My brother Mr Thomas Plummer of London, merchant & Theodore Atkinson of Portsmouth Esq. to be the executors.

Wit: Arthur Browne, James Jeffrey, Josh Peirce.

Proved at London by Thomas Plummer, power reserved for Theodore Atkinson the other executor. Spurway, 73.

[I extract the following from a letter to me from Miss Plumer, of Epping, N. H., dated Nov. 1, 1885, in reply to an inquiry about Benjamin Plumer: " In a note at the end of my father's manuscript genealogy of the Plumer family, my father writes, ' Benjamin Plumer was appointed collector of Piscataway in New England. His commission, of which I have a copy in the handwriting of R. Waldron, Secry, is dated Feb. 11, 1736. It was sworn to before Gov. Belcher, June 8th, 1736. He was perhaps the progenitor of the Portsmouth Plumers. There is a silver vase in the Atkinson family on which is inscribed the deaths of various persons, among the rest that of Benjamin Plumer, Esquire, who died May 8th, 1740, aged 24 years. If this was the collector he was but twenty when appointed.' "—*Com. by George Plumer Smith, Esq., of Philadelphia, Pa.*

In the New Hampshire Provincial Papers, vol. iv. p. 864, is a letter from John Thomlinson to Theodore Atkinson, dated " London, 5 April, 1737." Mr. Thomlinson writes : " Altho the Bearer Mr. Plummer his coming over Collector in your place may be some Disadvantage or Disappointment to you, yet when I tell you I dare say he will prove the most agreeable Gentleman that you could have had, in every respect, you will excuse my here recommending him to your friendship. ....
He is a gentleman of good sense and of a very good family and good circumstances." I presume that Plumer was an Englishman.—EDITOR.]

Notes on Abstracts previously printed.

NATHANIEL PARKER (*ante*, p. 8).

[" My god-daughter the daughter of my nephew Bernard Saltingstall."
The pedigree of the Saltonstall family, given in Bond's Watertown, shows that
Bernard Saltonstall was a great-grandson of Gilbert Saltonstall, from whom the
New England family descended, through Sir Richard of Huntwicke. The Bernard
Saltonstall referred to in the will was son of Sir Richard Saltonstall of North Ock-
enden, co. Essex. Susanna, sister of Bernard, married William Pawlett of Cottles
in co. Wilts, who was a grandson of William Pawlett, first Marquis of Winchester.
(See Dr. Marshall's Visitation of co. Wilts, 1623, p. 92.)
                                            JOHN COFFIN JONES BROWN.]

RICHARD PERNE ; RACHEL PERNE (*ante*, pp. 59–61 and 89).

[It was noticed in Rachel Perne's will that she cut off Edward Rawson, our faithful Colonial Secretary, with the proverbial shilling, although she bequeathed to
Rachel, his wife and her daughter, £40.
By a deed of his recorded in Suffolk Deeds, vol. iii. pp. 413 and 414, he acknow-
ledges receipt of a marriage " portion of £300, which he long since Received with
his wife." This accounts for the omission to bequeath any more of the Perne estate to him on its final distribution by will.   JOHN COFFIN JONES BROWN.]

DOROTHY LANE of London, widow, 17 January, 1605. My body to be
buried in the parish church or churchyard of St Dunstans in the East, London, where I am a parishioner. To Susan Harrys, daughter of my late son
in law William Harrys, late of Wapping in the County of Middlesex, mariner deceased, and of Dorothie my daughter, late his wife, ten pounds. To
George Stake, son of my late sister Elizabeth, thirty shillings. To my cousin
Jeffery Thorowgood twenty shillings. To my cousin Bennet Burton twenty
shillings. To my cousins Elizabeth and Sara Quaitmore, daughters of
Rowland Quaytmore and of my said daughter Dorothie, his now wife, five
pounds apiece. To the said Rowland Quaytmore, my son in law, thirty
shillings to make him a ring. To Helen Averell, late wife of William Averell, Schoolmaster, deceased, my small joyned chair with a back. To the
said Dorothie Quaytmore,* my daughter, and William Harrys, her son, and
to the heirs of the said William Harrys, the son, lawfully begotten, all those
my two tenements and two acres in Saffron Walden in the County of Essex,
which late were Symon Burton's, my late brother's deceased, the said
Dorothie Quaytmore & William Harrys her son to pay out to Samuel
Harrys, son of my said daughter Dorothie Quaytmore, ten pounds upon
reasonable request, within two months next after such day or time as the
said Samuel Harrys shall attain and come to the lawful age of twenty-one
years, and unto Jane and Joane Burton, daughters of my said late brother
Symon Burton of Saffron Walden aforesaid, five pounds apiece within four
years next after such day or time as my said daughter Dorothie & William
her son or her heirs or assigns shall first enter and enjoy the said two tenements, &c. To Susan & Dorothie Harrys, daughters of my said daughter Dorothie Quaytmore (certain bequests). To Mary Quaitmore five
pounds. To my cousin Elizabeth Quaytmore (certain table linen) and to
Sara Quaytmore her sister (a similar bequest). To Mary & Sara Thorowgood, daughters of my cousin Jeffery Thorowgood, twenty shillings. To
Richard Weech of London, merchant, twenty shillings. The residue to my
daughter Dorothie and she and the above named William Harrys the son
appointed full & sole executors. The said Jeffery Thorowgood & Richard

---

* Rowland Coitmore and Dorothy Harris (widow) married at Whitechapel, co. Mid. 28
March, 1594–5. Elizabeth, their daughter, bapt. 25 Feb. 1595–6.—I. J. GREENWOOD.

Weech appointed overseers. To my cousin Walter Gray five shillings, and to his wife my stuff gown lined with furr.

The witnesses were William Jones, Scr., Jeffery Thorowgood, signum Roberti Powell, shoemaker, and me Richard Perne.

Commission was issued 4 March 1608 to Dorothie Quaytmore, with power reserved for William Harrys, the other executor, &c.

Dorsett, 23.

THOMAS RAINBOROWE of East Greenwich in the County of Kent, mariner, 4 December 1622, proved 23 February 1623. My body to be buried in the church yard of East Greenwich with such solemnity as my executors in their discretion shall think fit. My wife Martha and eldest son William Rainborowe to be executors. Ten pounds to be given for the putting forth of poor children of the parish of Greenwich aforesaid, &c. To said Martha my wife all my plate and household stuff and the furniture of my house and also my one sixteenth part of the good ship called the Barbara Constance of London and my one sixteenth of the tackle, apparel, munition, furniture, freight, &c. of the said ship. To my said son William two hundred pounds within one year next after my decease, and one sixteenth of the good ship Rainbowe of London & one sixteenth of her tackle, &c., one sixteenth of the ship Lilley of London (and of her tackle, &c.), one forty eighth part of the ship Royal Exchange of London (and of her tackle, &c.). To my son Thomas Rainborowe two hundred pounds within one year, &c. To my daughter Barbara Lee two hundred pounds within one year, &c. To my daughter Martha Wood two hundred pounds within one year, &c. To my daughter Sara Porte two hundred pounds within one year, &c.

Whereas I have taken of the Right Honorable Edward Lord Dennie, Baron of Waltham Holy Cross in the County of Essex, by Indenture of Lease bearing date the eight and twentieth day of September Anno Domini 1619, a capital messuage called by the name of Claver Hambury and certain lands, with their appurtenances, situate, lying & being in the said County of Essex, for the term of two and twenty years, and for and under the yearly rent of a peppercorn, &c.; for which said lease I have paid to the said Lord Denny the sum of two thousand three hundred pounds of currant English money; and the said messuage and lands, &c. are worth yearly in rent (de olaro) two hundred and twenty pounds or thereabouts, &c. &c. it is my will that there shall be paid out of the rents, profits, &c. to Martha my wife one annuity or annual rent of one hundred pounds, to my son William an annuity, &c. of twenty pounds, to my son Thomas an annuity, &c. of twenty pounds, to my daughter Barbara Lee an annuity, &c. of twenty pounds, to my daughter Martha Wood an annuity, &c. of twenty pounds, to my daughter Sara Port an annuity, &c. of twenty pounds.

The residue of my personal property to my two executors to be divided equally, part and part alike. My dwelling house and lands in East Greenwich shall be sold by my executors for the most profit they can & within as short time after my death as conveniently may be, and of the money arising therefrom one third shall go to my wife Martha, one third to my son William and the other third to my said four other children, Thomas, Barbara, Martha & Sara.

The witnesses were J. W. the mark of John Wotton, of the precinct of St Katherine's, mariner, John Woodward, Not. Pub., and John Brooke his servant.

Byrde, 8

ANTHONY WOOD of Redrith in the county of Surrey, mariner, 13 August 1625, proved at London 3 January 1625 by the oath of Martha Wood his relict and executrix. To wife Martha all my lease &c. in my now dwelling house in Redrith & my part of the good ship Exchange of London & of the Charity of London. To son Richard all my portion of the good ship Rainbow of London & my adventure in her &c. To my sons Richard, Thomas & Anthony five hundred pounds apiece, & to my daughter Sara five hundred pounds, at one & twenty. To my brother John Wood five pounds a year for eighteen years. To my mother Raynborrowe three pounds for a ring. To my brother William Raynborowe five pounds for a cloak. To my brother Francis Port three pounds for a ring. To my brother Thomas Lee three pounds. To my brother Thomas Raynborowe three pounds. To my uncle William Wood & his wife four pounds, for & in remembrance of tokens of my love unto them. I give to my said wife all my lease of certain lands at Waltham which I have & hold from the Lord Denny, &c. My said wife & my said son Richard to be full & sole executors &c., and I name & appoint overseers of this my will my loving friends the wor¹¹ Henry Garway & William Garwaye of London merchants.

A codicil made Tuesday the 23ᵈ of August A.D. 1625 revokes the bequest of his portion of the ship Rainbow to son Richard & bequeaths it to Martha Wood his wife.   Hele, 4.

ROWLAND COYTEMORE of Wapping in the County of Middlesex, mariner, 5 June, 1626, proved 24 November 1626 by Katherine Coytemore, relict and executrix. To son Thomas Coytemore and his heirs, &c. the messuage or tenement, lands, hereditaments and appurtenances in the manor of Milton in the parish of Prittlewell als. Pricklewell, in the County of Essex, now in the tenure and occupation of John Greene, &c. and my farm and copyhold land of forty four acres or thereabouts, in the parish of Great Bursted in the County of Essex; wife Katherine to have the use and rents until my son Thomas shall accomplish his age of one and twenty years. To my daughter Elizabeth Coytemore three score pounds at her age of one and twenty years or day of marriage, also the tenement or messuage known by the sign of the Blewboare in the town or parish of Retchford, in the County of Essex, now in the tenure of William Ashwell als. Hare. To my son in law Thomas Gray* and his heirs my two copyhold tenements, &c. in Rederith als. Rederiff, in the County of Surrey, now in the several occupations of Francis Welby and John Moore. If my children and children's children die before they accomplish their several ages of one and twenty or be married, then my aforesaid lands shall remain, come and be unto my kinsman Hugh Hughs als. Gwyn, my sister Elizabeth's son. To my grandson William Ball, son of William Ball, forty shillings. To my daughter in law daughter Dorothy Lamberton forty shillings. To the poor of Wapping three pounds and to the poor of the Upper Hamlet of Whitechapel forty shillings. To the masters of Trinity House, for their poor, ten pounds within one year, &c.

My wife Katherine to be executrix and sons in law Thomas Gray and William Rainsborough of Wapping aforesaid, mariners, to be overseers. The witnesses were Raphe Bower pub. scr. and John Wheatley servᵗ to the said scr.   Hele, 125.

---

* See Gray and Coytmore Families, REG. xxxiv. 253.—ED.

MARTHA RAINBOROWE of the parish of St Bridget als. Brides, near Fleet St. London, widow, late wife of Thomas Rainborowe, late of East Greenwich in the county of Kent, mariner, deceased, made her will 29 November 1626, proved 23 September 1631. In it she referred to her husband's will & the lease of the messuage called Claverhambury and the disposition of its rents, bequeathed her own annuity among her five children, devised to her daughter Barbara Lee her sixteenth part of the good ship called Barbara Constance and gave the residue of her goods, chattels, &c. to her said daughter Barbara, wife of Thomas Lee, citizen & armorer of London, whom also she appointed sole executrix.

The witnesses were Robert Woodford, Thomas Turner and Tho: Eastwood. St John, 102.

WILLIAM RAINBOROW of London Esq. 16 July 1638, with codicil of 1 February 1642, proved 8 April 1642. To the Hamlet of Wapping as a stock for their poor fifty pounds ; to the Hamlet of Whitechapel ten pounds, &c. To the Trinity House fifty pounds, with the condition that they give to poor seamen or their widows of the Hamlet of Wapping, every St. Thomas Day, forty shillings. To my eldest son Thomas Rainborowe all those my houses in Southwark purchased of Mr William Gambell and some of them lately built. To my son William Rainborowe those my houses in Gun Alley in Wapping purchased of my father in law Renold Hoxton and also one thousand pounds. To my son Edward twelve hundred pounds. Item I give and bequeath to my daughter Martha Coytmore, the wife of Thomas Coytmore now in New England, the sum of seven hundred pounds, if she be alive at the time of my death. To my daughter Judith Rainborowe one thousand pounds & to my daughter Joane Rainborowe one thousand pounds. All this to be paid to them, by my executors, at their several days of marriage or at their age of one and twenty years, and those that be of age at six months after my decease. To the four sons and one daughter of my deceased sister Sara Port, namely Robert, John, Thomas, William and Martha Porte, two hundred and fifty pounds, that is to each fifty pounds, at twenty one. To my brother Mr Thomas Rainborowe fifty pounds. To my sister Buckridge fifty pounds. To my sister Wood fifty pounds. To my father in law Renold Hoxton and to my mother in law Joane Hoxton ten pounds apiece to buy them each a ring. My executors to be my loving sons Thomas and William Rainborowe and I appoint them to bring up my younger children to their age of twenty one years or day of marriage and to have the tuition of them and be at the charges of meat & drink & clothes & learning. For overseers I desire my loving brothers in law Mr Robert Wood and Mr John Hoxton to have a care that this my will be fulfilled and do give them twenty pounds apiece for their pains. Witnesses Robert Wood and William Ashley.

To my mother in law Jone Hoxton my house at Wapping now in the occupation of Mr Sander Bence, during her natural life, toward her maintenance. To my grand child William Rainborowe one hundred pounds.

Codicil. Whereas the said William Rainborowe hath by his will given to Martha Port fifty pounds the said William Rainborow did about a year since and at other times afterwards declare his mind and will to be that the said Martha should not have or expect the said legacy because he had given her the sum of ten pounds and all her wedding clothes in marriage with William Ashley. Subscribed by witnesses 1 February 1641.

Witnesses to the codicil, John Hoxton, Thomas Hoxton & Mary Bennfes. Campbell, 51.

STEVEN WINTHROP of James Street, Westminster, Esq., 3 May 1658, proved 19 August, 1658. To wife Judith the house wherein I now dwell, with the house adjoining, lately erected, for her life, and then to all my children. All the rest to my daughters Margaret, Joanna and Judith and such child or children as my said wife shall now be great withall. To my nephew Adam Winthrop, son of my brother Adam Winthrop deceased; to the children of my brother Deane Winthrop; to my brother Samuel Winthrop's children; to my half brother John Winthrop's children; to my cousin Mary Rainborowe daughter of my brother in law William Rainborowe Esq.; to my cousin Judith Chamberlaine, daughter of my brother in law John Chamberlaine Esq.—sundry bequests. "To the poor of Boston in New England one hundred pounds of lawfull money of England upon Condition that the Inhabitants of Boston aforesaid doe build and erect a Tombe or Monument, Tombes or Monuments, for my deceased ffather and Mother upon their graue or graues of ffifftie pounds value att the least, whoe now lyeth buried att Boston aforesaid, according to the Loue and honour they bore to him and her in theire life time." The executors to be my wife Judith Winthropp, my brother in law John Chamberlaine Esq. and Thomas Plampyon, gentleman.

The witnesses were Leo: Chamberlaine, Elizabeth Baldrey and Clement Ragg (by mark).   Wootton, 418.

[In Suffolk Registry of Deeds (Book 8, p. 193) may be found record of conveyance made by Judith Winthrop and John Chamberlain, executors of Stephen Winthrop, 20 April, 1671, to Edward Rainborow of London, of all the said Winthrop's land in New England, consisting of one half of Prudence Island and fifteen hundred acres in Lynn or Salem, &c. This latter property included the well known Pond Farm (Lynnfield), originally granted to Colonel John Humfrey.—H. F. W.

In addition to the ten letters of Stephen W., printed in Part IV. of the Winthrop Papers (5 Mass. Hist. Coll., viii. pp. 199-218) we have found several others, but they are of no importance. Before his final return to England he was Recorder of Boston and a Representative; and, but for the failure of his health caused by sleeping on the damp ground, there is reason to believe Cromwell would have made him one of his generals, as Roger Williams, writing to John Winthrop, Jr., in 1656, says, "Your brother Stephen succeeds Major-General Harrison." By his own desire he was buried with his ancestors at Groton in Suffolk, where were also interred a number of his children, most of whom died young. Only two daughters are known with certainty to have survived him: Margaret, who married 1st, Henry Ward, and 2d, Edmund Willey, R. N., and had issue; and Joanna, who married Richard Hancock, of London, and died s. p. During his military service his wife resided partly at Groton and afterwards at Marylebone Park near London, a portion of which estate he had purchased. This gave rise to an absurd tradition, perpetuated in some pedigrees of the last century, that the Winthrops were "of Marylebone Park before they settled in Suffolk." Besides his house in James Street, Westminster, he owned, at the time of his death, his father's house in Boston, on the southerly portion of which estate the Old South Church now stands; this was subsequently sold by his widow, but whether she ever returned to New England I do not know. My kinsman Robert Winthrop, of New York, has a portrait (of which I have a copy) of a young officer of the Stuart period, which has been in our family for generations, and is called "Colonel Stephen Winthrop, M.P." If authentic, it must have either been sent by him as a present to his father before his death, or subsequently procured by his brother John, or his nephew Fitz-John, during their residence in England.—R. C. WINTHROP, JR.]

THOMAS RAINBOROWE of East Greenwich in the County of Kent, gentleman, 24 November, 1668, proved 2 January 1671 by Mary Rainborowe, his widow & executrix. To wife Mary, for life, an annuity bought of Ralph Buskin of Oltham in the County of Kent Esq. one bought of Edward Turner of East Greenwich, gentleman, and all my other goods, moneys, &c.

She to be executrix and to pay two hundred pounds (on a bond which testator made to his mother*). I give to my brother's son Edward Rainborowe twenty pounds, to my brother's daughter Judith Winthrop twenty pounds and to my said brother's daughter Joane Chamberlaine fifty pounds. To the poor of East Greenwich ten pounds. The witnesses were William Richardson & John Fuller. Eure, 7.

[The following notes on the Rainsborough family, collected some years ago, will throw light on Mr. Waters's abstracts :

1537.—Reynold Ravynsbye, freeman of the Co. of Cloth Workers, London.
1598.—Roger Rainseburye of Stawley, co. Somerset. Will dated July 24, proved Aug. 23, 1598. Bequeaths to the poor of Kettleford 3-4. To the poor of Ashbrittle 3-4. To his goddaughter Agnes Gover 20s. To each of his other godchildren, not named, 4d. To Edward Blackaller his wife's godson 20s. Residue to wife Honor, whom he appoints executrix, and her friends John Gover and William Golde overseers.—*Book Lewyn*, fo. 68.
1603.—Nicholas Rainbury of Stawley. Will dated April 19, 1603; proved May 4, 1611. To the poor of Stawley the interest of £10,—to be used in keeping them at work. To each of his godchildren, not named, 6s. To Mary, dau. of Richard Wyne 20s. To each of the children of John Grover 12d. To the poor of Ashbrittle 10s. To the poor of Kettleford 5s. To each of the ringers 12d. To Parson John Blackeallor 10s. Residue to his sister-in-law Honour Rainsbury, whom he appoints executrix, and William Golde and John Gover, overseers.—*Book Wood*, fo. 46.
Stanleigh or Stowley, Kittesford and Ashbuttel, all in Milverton Hundred.
1615.—Henry Raygnesburye of Culmstock, co. Devon, husbandman. Will dated Feb. 8, 1615; proved March 9, 1615. To his son Henry £60. To daughter Alice R. £80, to be paid to her uncle Christopher Baker, clothier, for her use. To George, son of Andrew Bowreman 10s. To each of his godchildren, not named, 12d. To the poor 20s. Residue to wife Susan whom he appoints executrix.—*Book Cope*, fo. 29.
During the Protectorate the Baker family held the Manor of Columbstock, Hemyoke Hundred, co. Devon.
1636.—Henry Raynsbury, of the parish of St. Austin (Augustine) in London, factor. Will dated March 15, 1636, proved May 8, 1637. To Mr. Stephen Denison, Doctor and Lecturer, of Great All Hallows, 10s, to preach a sermon at his burial, and to the minister of the parish, where he shall be buried, for giving him way to preach the sermon £5. To each poor man and woman of the parish as the church wardens may select 10s. To the parish of Cullumstock, co. Devon, where he was born £100—for the use of the poor forever, the interest to be divided once a year among eight poor men and women. To the poor of Samford Arundel (Milverton Hund.) co. Somerset, £10—for the use of the poor forever. To his sister Alice Wood, widow, of Henryoke, co. Devon, all his inheritage lands in the county of Lincoln, during her life, then to be divided among her five children. To Mrs. Susan Fleming, wife of Mr. John Fleming of St. Austin's, London £100. To their three children, Roland, Mary and Susan, each £10. To each of his godchildren, not named, 20s. To ten poor laboring porters of Blackwall Hall (market for selling woolen cloths), each 10s. To cousin Edward, son of cousin Edward Baker of Henryoke £20. To ten poor servant-maids of Cullumstock, each 20s. Residue to his godson Henry Baker, son of cousin John Baker the elder, of Cullumstock, clothier, when 21 years of age. Appoints the said John Baker executor, and his uncle Christopher Baker, cousin Henry Holwaye, and gossip John Rew, overseers, and gives each of them £5.—*Book Goare*, fo. 59.
The Hundreds of Milverton, co. Somers and Henryoke, co. Devon adjoin.
The parish registers of Whitechapel, co. Mid., which begin in 1558, record the marriage of
Thomas[1] Raineborow and Martha Moole, Nov. 11, 1582.
In Chancery Proceedings, temp. Elizabeth, P.p. No. 23, occurs a bill, filed 1641 ; Thomas Raynsbury and others, to vacate an annuity charged by George Peirce *plaintiff* on a freehold messuage in Gate Lane, parish of St. Mary Staynings, London, for use of plaintiff's daughter Eliz. Peirce.
Thomas Rainborowe of East Greenwich, mariner, had a lease of certain lands, 28 Sept. 1619, at Claverhambury, co. Essex, from Lord Edward Denny, which manor,

---

* His mother had been dead many years.

with Hallyfield Hall, &c., had been granted by Henry VIII., 1542, to his lordship's grandfather Sir Anthony Dennye.

His children, baptized at Whitechapel, were :

1. 1583, April 28. Barbara,[2] m. Thomas Lee, armorer, of London, and after Mr. —— Burbridge, or Buckridge.
2. 1584–5, Feb. 21. Elizabeth,[2] d. unm. before 1619.
3. 1587, June 11. William.[2]
4. 1589, Sept. 23. Martha,[2] m. Anthony Wood.
5. 1591–2, Feb. 20. Thomas,[2]·d. young.
6. 1594, Oct. 15. Thomas.[2]
7. 1597, June 19. Sarah,[2] m. Francis Porte.

The name is spelled variously on the registers, as Rain(e)borow(e), Rain(e)sborow(e), Raynsborow, Raineburrow(e), Rainsberry, and, though possibly it is synonymous with Ramesbury or Remmesbury [of co. Wilts, &c.), the armorial bearings of the two families do not coincide, the Rainsborowe arms being similar to those of the Raynes, Reynes, or Reymes.

The will of Thomas[1] Rainborowe, mariner of East Greenwich, co. Kent, dated 4 Dec. 1622, and proved 23 Feb. 1623, is given in this article by Mr. Waters, as also that of the widow, Martha Rainborowe, who afterwards resided in the parish of St. Bridget's, London, where she died in 1631.

Before considering the elder son William,[2] it may be briefly stated that the second son—

THOMAS[2] RAINBOROW, bapt. at Whitechapel 15 Oct. 1594, in his will of 24 Nov. 1668, proved 2 Jan. 1671 (as given by Mr. Waters), is styled " of East Greenwich, gent." He evidently died without issue surviving him, though he had a son Thomas,[3] bapt. at Whitechapel, 18 Sept. 1614. The will of his widow is as follows : Mary Rainborow of Greenwich, co. Kent, widow ; dated 11 Feb. 1677, proved 9 Apr. 1678. Whereas she has heretofore expressed her kindness to her brother and sister, not named, to the utmost of her ability, she now gives them but twelve pence. Appoints her niece Sarah Trott, who now lives with her, executrix, and makes her residuary legatee.—Book Reeve, fol. 37.

WILLIAM[2] RAINBOROW (eldest son of Thomas[1]), bapt. at Whitechapel, 11 June, 1587. In Nov. 1625, we find him a part owner and in command of the Sampson of London, 500 tons, built at Limehouse, and now granted the privilege of carrying great guns. His name occurs frequently in the Cal. Dom. State Papers. Secretary Lord Edward Conway writes him, 20 March, 1626, relative to taking aboard the trunks, &c. of Sir Thomas Phillips, Ambassador for Constantinople. Letters of Marque were granted 24 Oct. 1627, and finally, when the reconstruction of the navy was paramount with King Charles, the merchantman Sampson, well fortified with iron ordnance, was one of the vessels presented, in Dec. 1634, by the City of London, for his Majesty's service. William Raynisborowe, as one of the inhabitants in the vicinity of the Tower, complained, in the summer of 1627, of the nuisance of an alum-factory erected at the west end of Wapping. Five years later we find his knowledge and experience of maritime matters duly recognized by the Lords of the Admiralty, who in their order of 21 April, 1632, appoint Capt. Rainsborough one of the gentlemen to attend a meeting of the Board on the 26th, to give their opinion concerning the complements and numbers of men to be allowed for manning each of his Majesty's ships.

Jan. 2, 1634–5, the King in Council had expressed his desire that the Merhonour, the Swiftsure, the City of London and other vessels should be presently put forth to sea. The order was confirmed March 10, and the first named vessel was ordered to be fitted out and victualled by April 24· for six months' service, the charge to be defrayed with moneys paid by the several ports and maritime places. To the Merhonour, at Chatham, the Lords of the Admiralty appoint Capt. William Rainborough, March 30, with Capt. William Cooke as Master. This 44 gun vessel (800 tons), sometimes called the May Honora, had been rebuilt and launched, 25 April, 1614, at Woolwich, by Phineas Pett. Other vessels commissioned at the time were the Constant Reformation, Capt. Thomas Ketelby ; the Swallow, Capt. Henry Stradling ; the Mary Rose, Capt. George Carteret ; the Sampson, Capt. Thomas Kirke, &c. &c. ; and these were under the command of Sir William Monson, Vice Adm. in the James, and Sir John Pennington, Rear Adm. in the Swiftsure. Since the death of the Duke of Buckingham in 1628, the office of Lord Admiral had remained in commission, but on May 14, 1635, one of the Navy Commissioners, Robert Bertie, Lord Willoughby de Eresby and Earl of Lindsey, was appointed Admiral, Custos Maris, General and Governor of His Majesty's Fleet, for the guard of the Narrow Seas. He was to defend the King and the Kingdom's honor, which had been lately called in question by a fleet of French and Dutch off Portland, and to exact " the due homage of the sea " from passing ships, and so restore to England her ancient sovereignty of the Narrow Seas ; he was also to clear the neighboring waters of pirates and Turks ; to convoy merchants and others desiring it ; to guard against any infringement of the custom on the part of returning vessels, &c. About the middle of April the Merhonour repaired to Tilbury Hope to receive the remainder of her stores ; and on May 16 the Admiral came on board, the ships meeting twelve days later in the Downs. Rainsborough's vessel, though a good sailer, proved somewhat leaky, and the Admiral was desirous at first of changing to the Triumph ; however, the leaks having been found and her foremast repaired, he concluded she would do well for her present employment, and continued cruizing in her until he brought the fleet into the Downs once more on Oct. 4. Most of the ships were now ordered to Chatham and Deptford, though a few continued out under Sir John Pennington. The Earl despatched his journal of the expedition to the King, and hoped he might, with his Majesty's favor, return home. The Hollanders, who in pursuit of the Dunkirk frigates, had been accustomed to land on the English coast, committing depredations upon the inhabitants, had been checked ; one of their armed bands had been arrested at Whitby, and a vessel of 21 guns had been taken and sent into Hull ; moreover, Capt. Stradling, in the Swallow of 30 guns, being off the Lizard alone, had met the French Admiral Manti with two vessels, who after receiving an admonitory shot apiece, had each struck their flags and topsails, and saluted with three pieces of ordnance.

Writs were now sent to the sheriffs of the various counties of England, to levy money to defray the charge of a fleet for next year of double the strength of that which had just been employed, and attention was paid to the improvement of the vessels in the removal of the cumbersome galleries, as suggested by Capt. Rainsborough. This gentleman, together with one of the commissioners, Sir John Wostenholm and others, was appointed Dec. 9 to inquire into the institution, state, order and government of the Chest at Chatham, as established in 1588 by Queen Elizabeth, with Adms. Drake and Hawkins, for the relief of wounded and decayed seamen, and to certify their doings to the Co. of Chancery.

Towards the close of Feb. 1635–6, a list of Naval Captains, twenty-five in number, was handed in for the year, with Algernon, Earl of Northumberland, as Adm., Sir John Pennington as V. Adm., and Sir Henry Mervyn as Rear Adm. The Earl, in the Triumph, had chose Rainborow as his Captain, with William Cooke as Master, and during the next month he desired the Lords of the Admiralty that his Captain's pay might be made equal to theirs, and that he might have a Lieut., as he had more business to do than any other captain of the fleet. April 9, the ships at Portsmouth were awaiting the arrival of Capt. R. to take them out to sea, the Admiral having promised to send him down for that purpose.

At this time, and for a long series of years previous, England was and had been suffering from a grievous scourge, viz. : the pirates from the north of Africa. So bold and venturesome had they become during the summer of 1636, as to land within twelve miles of Bristol and successfully carry off men, women and children. Their chief place of refuge was the port of Cardiff and its vicinity, whence they carried on their depredations along either coast of the St. George's Channel. No relief, save an occasional collection for the redemption of captives, had heretofore been devised, and numerous were the petitions and statements now being presented to the King and the H. of Lords. The Court was moved to proclaim a general fast, and a sermon was preached in October by the Rev. Charles Fitz-Geffry, of St. Dominick, in Plymouth, from Heb. 13, 3 ; this was printed at Oxford, and entitled, " Compassion towards Captives, chiefly towards our Brethren & Countrymen who are in such miserable bondage in Barberie." A cotemporaneous document reads : " It is certainly known that there are five Turks in the Severne, wher they weekly take either English or Irish ; and that there are a great number of their ships in the Channell, upon the coast of France and Biscay. Whereby it is come to passe that our mareners will noe longer goe to sea, nor from port to port ; yea, the fishermen dare not putt to sea, to take fish for the country. If timely prevention be not used, the Newfoundland fleet must of necessity suffer by them in an extraordinary manner." The greater part of the captives, reported to be some 2000 in number, had been taken within the last two years, and the sea-rovers, most to be dreaded, were the pirates of New Sallee, who had revolted from the Emperor of Morocco, headed by a rebel who was called the Saint. The matter coming to be more seriously discussed, three plans were suggested—peace, war, or suppression of trade. Finally it was proposed that Capt. Rainsborough should be employed in an expedition against Sallee, and he and Mr. Giles Penn (father of the future Adm. William Penn) were called upon by the King, Dec. 28, to give their opinion concerning the particulars. In a letter, some three weeks earlier, Capt. R., then an invalid at Southwold, on the Suffolk coast, states his great willingness to attend the Lords and further their project, as soon as he can set out for London. The plan, which he subsequently submitted, states that to redeem the captives would require over 100,000*l.*, the payment of which would but encourage the pirates to continue their present course. Whereas to besiege them by sea would not only effect the purpose, but give security for the future, or a fleet might be kept on their coast for two or three years, until their ships were worm-eaten. That " the maintenance of the suggested fleet would be very much to the King's honor in all the maritime ports in Christendom, &c." He recommends himself to go as Admiral in the Leopard, Capt. George Carteret as V. Adm. in the Antelope, Capt. Brian Harrison in the Hercules, Capt. George Hatch in the Gt. Neptune, Capt. Th. White in the largest pinnace, and Capt. Edmund Seamon in the lesser. The plan was adopted, and, Feb. 20, 1636-7, Sec. Coke writes from Whitehall to the Lord Dep. Strafford : " This day Capt. Rainsborough, an experienced & worthy seaman, took his leave of his Majesty, and goeth instantly to sea with four good ships and two pinnaces to the coast of Barbary, with instructions & resolution to take all Turkish frygates he can meet, & to block up the port of Sally, & to free the sea from these rovers, which he is confident to perform."

March 4 the little squadron was in the Downs and on the eve of departure. The port of Sallee was reached in good season, and the enemy's cruisers, about to start for England and Ireland, were hemmed in and twenty-eight of their number destroyed. A close siege was now maintained, assisted on the land side by the old Governor of the town, and the place was delivered up to the English, July 28th.

The Emperor now agreed to join in a league with King Charles, promising never again to infest the English coasts, and forthwith delivered up some 300 captives, with whom Capt. Carteret immediately returned homeward. Rainsborough, however, on Aug. 21, proceeded to Saffee to treat for about 1000 English captives who had been sold to Tunis and Algiers. Here he remained till Sept. 19, when the Emperor's Ambassador came aboard, accompanied by Mr. Robert Blake, a merchant trading to Morocco, for whom the Emperor had formed a friendship, and who had obtained the position of Farmer of all his Ports and Customs. On the 21st they left the coast, and arriving fifteen days later in the Downs, landed, Oct. 8, at Deal Castle. Detained at Gravesend through sickness, it was not until the 19th that the Ambassador was conducted to London by the Master of Ceremonies, and, landing at the Tower, was taken to his lodgings " with much display & trumpeting." In the procession were the principal citizens and Barbary merchants mounted, all richly apparelled, and every man having a chain of gold about him, with the Sheriffs and Aldermen in their scarlet gowns, and a large body of the delivered captives, some of whom had been over thirty years in servitude, arrayed in white, and though it was night, yet the streets " were almost as light as day." Sunday, Nov. 5, the Ambassador was received by the King, to whom he brought, as a present from his imperial master, some hunting hawks and four steeds, " the choicest & best in all Barbary, & valued at a great rate, for one Horse was prized at 1500 pound." These, led by four black Moors in red liveries, were caparisoned with rich saddles embroidered with gold, and the stirrups of two of them were of massive gold, and the bosses of their bridles of the same metal. An account of the proceedings was printed towards the close of the month, entitled, " The Arrival & Entertainment of the Morocco Ambassador Alkaid (or Lord) Jaurar Ben Abdella, from the High & Mighty Prince Mully Mahamed Sheque, Emperor of Morocco, King of Fesse & Susse, &c."

Great was the enthusiasm created by the successful issue of the expedition, and even Waller was prompted to eulogize the event in the following rather ponderous lines :

> " Salle that scorn'd all pow'r and laws of men,
>   Goods with their owners hurrying to their den ;
> *   *   *   *   *   *
>   This pest of mankind gives our Hero fame,
>   And thus th' obliged world dilates his name.
> *   *   *   *   *   *

With ships they made the spoiled merchant moan;
With ships, their city and themselves are torn.
One squadron of our winged castles sent
O'erthrew their Fort, and all their Navy rent:
*   *   *   *   *   *
Safely they might on other nations prey;
Fools to provoke the Sov'reign of the Sea!
*   *   *   *   *   *
Morocco's Monarch, wondering at this fact,
Save that his presence his affairs, exact,
Had come in person, to have seen and known
The injur'd world's revenger, and his own.
Hither he sends the chief among his Peers,
Who in his bark proportion'd presents bears,
To the renown'd for piety and force,
Poor captives manumis'd and matchless horse."

Even grumbling Master Andrew Burrell, who, in a pamphlet of 1646 condemns the entire Navy, its officers, &c., though he had himself built for them the Marie Rose, "the most sluggish ship" they had afloat, confesseth that Rainsborough's Fleet "performed better service than England's Navie did in 44 years before." The King was very willing and forward to have knighted the gallant Admiral, but he declined the honor, and order was given that he should have a gold chain and medal of the value of 300*l.*; a memorial of loyal service perhaps still extant, "should not very opposite family feelings have melted it down in the days of the Rump," observes Disraeli in his Life of Charles I. An augmentation to the family arms was undoubtedly conferred at the time in the shape of "a Saracen's head couped ppr. in the fesse point."

Meanwhile the raising of funds and supplies for the equipment of the fleet for the following year had again become necessary, and Strafford, writing to the Abp. of Canterbury from Dublin, 27 Nov., says in connection, "this action of Sallee, I assure you, is so full of honor, that it will bring great content to the subject, and should, methinks, help much towards the ready, cheerful payment of the shipping monies." Early in Feb. 1637-8, the list of ships, which were to keep the seas during the following summer, was published, headed by the Sovereign of the Seas. This vessel, launched at Woolwich the preceding year, had been in progress since May, 1635, and surpassed in size, tonnage and force anything heretofore constructed for the English Navy. Thomas Heywood published an account of it, with a view of this "his Majesty's royal Ship, the Great Glory of the English Nation, and not to be paralleled in the whole Christian World," while Marmaduke Rawdon, of York, mentions in his Life,* a visit, in 1638, to the Royal Sovereign, Capt. Rainsberry, then newly finished and riding at Erith, below Woolwich.

Burrell, in his pamphlet before alluded to, condemns the vessel as "an admirable ship for costly Buildings, & cost in keeping; and, which adds to the miracle, the Royall Ship is never to be used for the Kingdom's good," &c. The Commissioners of the Navy answered in reply: "Capt. Rainsborough, whom Master Burrell confesseth, in his time, was the most eminent Commander in this Kingdom, had the trial of her in the Channel of England, and at his return reported to his Majestie that he never set his foot in a better conditioned Ship in all his life. And as for her Forces, she is not inferior to the greatest Ship in Christendom."†

On Sunday, March 18th, Algernon, Earl of Northumberland, obtained the position of General at Sea, or Lord High Admiral, during his Majesty's pleasure, the King designing to eventually bestow that office upon his younger son, the Duke of York.

That Capt. Rainsborough was ever in active naval service after his cruise in the Sovereign does not appear. He and others, owners of the 200 ton ship Confidence of London, were allowed Feb. 19, by the Lords of the Admiralty, to mount her with 20 pieces of cast-iron ordnance, and, during the fall of the year, together with some 155 other sea-faring men, he signed his consent to a proposition made by the Lord High Admiral and the Att. General, that an amount be deducted from their wages for the establishment of the Poor Seamen's Fund, to be administered by the officers of the Trinity House. The following year, as appears by a paper among the Duke

* Camden Soc. Pub.
† She subsequently did such good service that the Dutch nicknamed her "the Golden Devil."

of Northumberland's MSS., he submitted a proposition, in the form of articles, suggesting that 10,000 pieces of ordnance, with carriages, &c., be kept in readiness to arm 100 collier-ships, which may fight with a great army; stating their superiority for such service. Commission was given, Oct. 20, 1639, to Sir Edward Littleton, Solic. General, Sir Paul Pindar and Capt. William Rainsborough, to inquire into the truth of the statements made in the petition to the Privy Council, by Edward Deacon, who with his goods had been seized and detained in Sallee for debts there contracted by Mr. Robert Blake, as factor for some London merchants; petitioner having come to England, after leaving his son in Barbary as a pledge, in pursuit of said Blake, who, at the time, or immediately subsequent, was one of the gentlemen of the Council.

As William Rainsborough, Esq., he, with Squire Bence, merchant, were members from Aldborough, a seaport of co. Suffolk, in the Fourth Parl. of Charles I., held at Westminster from 13 April to 5 May, 1640 ; as also in the Parliament which convened 3 Nov. following ; that most notable of English Parliaments, before which, a week later, Thomas, Earl of Strafford, was accused of high treason.   May 27, 1641, he with others took the oath of Protestation, for the defence of the religion established, of the King's person, and the liberty of the subject; the same having been assented to by both houses on the 3d and 4th of the same month.   Aug. 25th Capt. R. was at the head of the committee for taking the whole state of the navy into consideration, and providing ships for transporting the ordnance and ammunition from Hull and other parts of the north.   Five days later the merchants' petition for erecting a Company for America and Africa, &c., was referred to Sir John Colpeper and Mr. Pymm especially, assisted by twenty-three other members, among whom was Capt. Rainsborough.   The same day he was included in a committee to whom had been referred the Act for making Wapping Chapel parochial.   He was also appointed, Sept. 9, a member of the Recess Committee, during the adjournment of Parliament till Oct. 20th ; and on Nov. 19, was on a committee for naval affairs, with some other members, including Sir Henry Vane.   Three days later it was ordered " that citizens that serve for the City of London and Capt. Rainsborough do inform themselves what shipping are now in the River that are fit to transport the Magazine at Hull to the Tower, and to give an account of it to-morrow morning " ; this was in pursuance of a resolution of the 3d.

And so ends his life and public services, for no more is heard of him till Feb. 14, 1641-2, when the Speaker of the House was ordered to issue a warrant to the Clerk of the Crown in Chancery for a new writ to be issued forth for the election of a new Burgess to serve for the town of Alborough in co. Suffolk, in the room and stead of Capt. Rainsborough deceased, and Alex. Bence, Esq., was accordingly elected.   On the 17th his body was interred in St. Catherine's (Tower), London.   At the time of his decease the Captain was a widower, his wife Judith, a daughter of Renold and Joane Hoxton, having been buried at Wapping, 3 March, 1637-8.   The will of William Rainsborow of London Esq., dated 16 July, 1638, with codicil of 1 Feb. 1641 proved 8 April, 1642, has been already given.

1.   THOMAS[3] RAINSBOROWE, Esq., of Whitechapel, co. Midd. (William,[2] Thomas[1]), commonly known in history as Col. Rainsborough.   A naval captain at first under the L. H. Adm. Warwick ; then a colonel of infantry under the Parliament, and finally V. Adm. of their Fleet.   A member of the Long Parliament.   A more detailed account of this prominent and distinguished individual may be given hereafter.   Suffice it to say that the Rev. Hugh Peters, alluding to the services of this officer at the taking of Worcester, that last stronghold for the King (in July, 1646), observes, " and truely I wish Colonell Rainborow a suitable employment by Sea or Land, for both which God hath especially fitted him ; foraine States would be proud of such a Servant "[*]   Resisting a seizure of his person on the part of the royalists, he was killed at Doncaster, 29 Oct. 1648, and buried at Wapping, 14 Nov.   Administration on his estate was granted, 24 Nov., to his widow Margaret, maiden name probably Jenney.

   1.   *William,*[4] eldest son ; mentioned in wills of his grandfather 1638, and his uncle Edward 1677.   He was a Captain in the army, it would appear, during the Protectorate, and judging from the Winthrop Letters (Mass. Hist. Soc. Col. 5, viii.) was in Boston, N. E., 1673 ; living 1687.

2.   WILLIAM[3] RAINSBOROW (William,[2] Thomas[1]) ; mentioned in Savage's Geneal. Dic. as being of Charlestown, Mass. Col. 1639 ; Artillery Co. same year ; purchas-

* King's Pamphlets, Brit. Mus., E. 351.

ed 17 Dec. 1640, of Th. Bright, house and land in Watertown, which had been the homestall of Lt. Robt. Feake. Budington mentions his purchase of the old meeting-house. He was evidently a trader or sea-captain. March 7, 1643-4, the treasurer of the Colony was ordered to attend to the discharge of Mr. Rainsborow's debt, with allowance of £20 forbearance for the time past, and the loan of two sachars for two great pieces for one voyage. He had been in England in 1642, when in April his name, and that of his brother Thomas, are found on the list of the proposed Adventurers by Sea, against Ireland. This was the expedition against Galway, &c., whereof, under Lord Forbes, his brother Thomas was commander, and the Rev. Hugh Peters chaplain.

Judging from the discharge of his debt and the loan of cannon, Capt. R. again returned to the old country in 1643-4, and though there are subsequent entries as to the debt, the moneys are always to be paid to parties abroad on R.'s account. He immediately espoused the people's cause and joined that division of the army which was in the west under Lord Essex. Finding himself in a critical position, the Lord General despatched Stapleton, his General of Horse, to Parliament, calling for aid, and on the night of Aug. 30th, Sir William Balfour, his Lieut. General, passed safely through the King's Quarters with 2300 horse, and reached London. Two nights thereafter Essex himself and Lord Roberts fled in a cock-boat to Plymouth, and the following day, Sept. 2, 1644, the commanding officer, Serj. Major General Skippon, surrendered with all the infantry and a few horse. According to a return* found in the quarters of Sir Edward Dodsworth, Com. Gen. of the Horse, we find that the cavalry had previously mustered at Tiverton, co. Devon, 39 troops, 420 officers and 2785 men. The first division of 8 troops, 639 men, under Sir Philip Stapleton, Major Gen. Philip Skippon and Maj. Hamilton; the six troops of the second division (62 officers, 432 men), being commanded by Sir William Balfour, 14 officers, 100 men; Major Balfour, 9 officers, 77 men; Sir Samuel Luke (Gov. of Newport Paganel, co. Bucks), 10 officers, 72 men; Capt. Rainsborow, 9 officers, 57 men; Capt. Sample, 10 officers, 61 men; Capt. Boswell, 10 officers, 65 men.

Prestwich's " Respublica " describes the cornet of Capt. Rainsborough's troop as follows: " Azure; from the sinister base point all over the base, and up to the middle of the dexter side, clouds Argent, shaded with black and crimson; near the middle or base, a book in pale closed and clasped and covered Or, on the front or side thus: $\begin{smallmatrix} \text{VERBUM} \\ \text{DEI} \end{smallmatrix}$; between this book and the dexter side, and a little above the base, an armed arm and hand uplifted, as issuant from the clouds, and as in pale, holding in his hand a Hussar's sword as barrways, and waved on both sides, and the point burning and inflamed with fire proper, hilted Or; in chief a scroll, its end turned or doubled in, and then bent out and split, and fashioned double like two hooks, endorsed Argent, lined Or, and ends shaded with crimson and Argent, and in Roman capital letters Sable, VINCIT VERITAS. Arms.—Chequered Or and Azure, and in fess a Moor's head in profile, bearded and proper, his head banded with a wreath Argent."

In the list of officers for the New Model of the army, which was sent up from the House of Commons to the House of Lords, 3 March, 1644-5, and approved on the 18th, Col. Sheffield's squadron of horse consisted of his own troop and those of Major Sheffield and Captains Eveling, Rainsborow, Martin and Robotham. He subsequently obtained the rank of Major, and Whitelock informs us of letters received, July 2, 1647, from the Commissioners in the Army, certifying "that the General had appointed Lt. Gen. Cromwell, Cols. Ireton, Fleetwood, Rainsborough, Harrison, Sir Har. Waller, Richard Lambert and Hammond, and Major Rainsborough, or any five of them, to treat with the Parliament's Commissioners upon the papers sent from the Army to the Parliament, and their Votes."

From the Journals of the House of Commons, under date of 27 Sept. 1650, we read that " Mr. Weaver reports from the committee for suppressing lycentious and impious practices, under pretence of religious liberty, &c., the confession of Lawrence Clackson (or Claxton), touching the making and publishing of the impious and blasphemous booke called the ' Single Eye,' and also Major Rainsborrow's carriage " in countenancing the same. Claxton, departing from the established church, appears to have joined all the prominent sectaries of the day, and from a tract of his published in 1660, entitled " the Lost Sheep Found," we gather that much of his trouble and imprisonment resulted from his own licentious behavior, he maintaining that " to the pure all things are pure." He was sent to the house

* Symond's Diary of Marches, Camden Soc. Pub.

of correction for one month and then banished, and his book was burned by the common hangman. Major Rainsborough, residing at the time at Fulham, was one of his disciples, " and seems to have been an apt scholar in improving his relations with the female part of the flock."* It was resolved by the House that he be discharged and disabled of and from being and executing the office of Justice of Peace in cc. Middlesex, or any other county within England or Wales.

For almost nine years we hear nothing of him, but on Tuesday, 19 July, 1659, he presented a petition to the House on behalf of the Sheriffs, Justices of the Peace and Gentry of the co. of Northampton, and on the same day was made a Commissioner for the Militia for the same county. In accordance with a report from said commissioners, he was appointed by Parliament, Aug. 9, Colonel of a Regiment of Horse in co. Northants.† After the Restoration, a warrant was issued, 17 Dec. 1660, to Lieut. Ward for the apprehension of Col. William Rainsborough at his residence, Mile End Green, Stepney (near London), or elsewhere, for treasonable designs, and to bring him before Secretary Sir Edward Nichols. He was accordingly arrested and confined in the Gatehouse. On his examination next day he declared he was a Major of horse, but dismissed by Cromwell in 1649; that the Rump Parliament made him a Colonel of Militia-horse, 1659, but nothing was done; that he had bought 40 cases of pistols for militia, and had since tried to dispose of them. He gave bond for 500l., Feb. 7, 1661, with Dr. Richard Barker of the Barbican as security for his good behavior.

His wife's name was Margery, and, as we have seen before, the will of Capt. Rowland Coytmore of Wapping, in 1626, mentions a son-in-law William Rainsborough, mariner, of Wapping; while the will of Stephen Winthrop, 1658, leaves a legacy to "cousin Mary Rainsborowe, daughter of my brother-in-law William Rainsborowe, Esq." From the Winthrop Letters (Mass. Hist. Soc. Coll. 5, viii.) he appears to have been in Boston, N. E., in 1673, with his nephew William.

3. MARTHA,³ bapt. at Whitechapel, 20 April, 1617; married at Wapping, 14 June, 1635, Thomas Coytmore,‡ son of Capt. Rowland Coytmore, an East India trader. He came to N. England next year and was wrecked, 27 Dec. 1644, on the coast of Spain, leaving issue. Her second husband, whom she married 4 Dec. 1647, was Gov. John Winthrop, to whom she was fourth wife; he died 26 March, 1649, aged 61. She married thirdly, 10 March, 1652, John Coggan of Boston, as his third wife; he died 27 April, 1658, leaving issue. Disappointed of a fourth marriage, we are given to understand that she committed suicide in 1660.

4. JUDITH,³ bapt. at Wapping, 14 Sept. 1624; married about 1644, Stephen Winthrop, son of Gov. John W., born 24 March, 1619. He returned to England 1645, became a Colonel of Horse under Parliament, receiving 474l. 10s. per annum, and in 1656 was M.P. for Banff and Aberdeen. Resided at time of decease in James Street, Westminster. His will of 3 May, proved 19 Aug. 1658, mentions three daughters, Margaret, Joanna and Judith, as before given. She is mentioned 1668, in her uncle Thomas's will.

5. SAMUEL,³ b.   ob. infs.; buried at Wapping, 24 Nov. 1628.

6. JOANE,³ b. ; m. John Chamberlain, a captain under Parliament; living in May, 1687, a brewer at Deptford, co. Kent. She is mentioned 1668 in her uncle Thomas's will. The will of S. Winthrop, 1658, mentions their daughter Judith.

7. REYNOLD,³ bapt. at Whitechapel, 1 June, 1632.

8. EDWARD,³ bapt. at Whitechapel, 8 Oct. 1633. Richard Wharton, writing from Boston, N. E., Sept. 24, 1673, to a kinsman of rank and influence in England, suggests that his Majesty should send out two or three frigates, by the ensuing February or March, with some 300 soldiers, for the recapture of New York from the Dutch. That the expedition should be assisted by a colonial force, the whole to be under the command of some native leader, such as Maj. Gen. Daniel Dennison. He continues: " for a more certain knowledge of the constitutions of oᵣ government & complexions of the people I refer you to Mʳ Edwᵈ Rainsborough an intelligᵗ

---

* Notes and Queries, 4th Series, xi. 487.
† In the limits of Charleton, parish of Newbottle, co. Northants, is a camp and hill commonly called "Rainsborough Hill," supposed to be of Danish origin.
‡ Katherine, daughter of Thomas and Martha Quoitmore, bapt. at Wapping, 13 April, and buried 19 April, 1636.

Gentleman who went home three months since. I have requested him to wait on you & communicate w^t I have advised him. .... Mr Rainsborough dwells at Knights bridge & is to be heard of at Mr Whiting's shop upon the old Exchange."* He appears to be the same party whose will runs as follows: Edward Rainborow of Cranford, co. Middlesex, gentleman; Sept. 14, 1677 (proved May 4, 1682), being in good health, but going beyond the seas, do make this my last will, &c. Bequeaths to his wife Christian one fourth of all his real and personal estate during her life. To his dear friend Mary Alcock, widow, for and in consideration of a very considerable sum of money for which he stands indebted to her, one fourth part of his real and personal estate either in England or N. England, during her life; one eighth part to be at her absolute disposal. To son Mytton Rainborow one fourth of all his real and personal estate when twenty-one years of age. To daughter Judith Rainborow one fourth of his real and personal estate until her brother Mytton shall enjoy that part which is given to his mother and also the eighth part given to Mary Alcock. To his nephew William Rainsborow five pounds to buy him a ring. Appoints his wife's sister, Mrs. Sarah Mackworth of Shrewsbury, and Mrs. Mary Alcock of Cranford, executors.—*Book Cottle*, folio 62.

Concerning the New England estate referred to by Edward Rainsborowe in his will of 1677, as above, we have evidence on file in the Registry of Deeds, Salem, of which the following is a summary: Whereas Judith Winthrop and John Chamberlain, two of the Executors of Stephen Winthrop deceased, had by certain deeds of Indenture, Bargain & Sale conveyed to Edward Rainsburrowe of London, merchant, all those parcells of lands lying & being in N. England in America, viz: one moiety of Prudence Island, lying in or near ye bay of Narragansett, in Rhode Island Colony, and all that Farm at Lynn or Salem, containing by estimation 1500 acres more or less, now, considering the great hazard of transmitting ye conveyances beyond sea, the said Executors do acknowledge before a notary public the said deeds of bargain and sale, 21 April, 1671. The document was signed in presence of Nich. Hayward, Not. Pub., Symon Amory, Tim^o Prout sen^r, and his son Wm Prout. Timothy Prout, shipwright of Boston, testified to the same before Dep. Gov. John Leverett, 5 Mar. 1672-3, and the instrument was recorded and compared 5 July following. As late as 21 March, 1695-6, the above was compared with the original and found an exactly true copy of ye record in ye booke of Deeds Lib: 8° Page 195.

Meanwhile John Chamberlain, the sole surviving executor of Stephen Winthrop deceased, having been shown a copy of the instrument above referred to, as being on file in some court in N. England, made oath 31 May, 1687, that he had never signed nor executed any such writing or instrument, nor did he believe that Judith Winthrop, widow & executrix, had made any such conveyance to the late Edward Rainsburrow. This testimony of Mr. Chamberlain appears to have been given at the request of his nephew William[4] Rainsburrowe, son of Vice Adm. Thomas[9] Rainsburrowe, being, we may infer, at the time the only, or at least the eldest, male representative of the family, and acting in the interest of his cousins the children of Stephen Winthrop deceased. Robert Wildey, of the parish of St. Paules Peters, co. Middlesex, cook, and "Thomasine Jenney, of the same place spinster, aunt of ye said William Rainsburrowe," swore to their knowledge of and acquaintance with John Chamberlayn for thirty years and upwards last past; that he and Stephen Winthrop, Esq., whom they had also known, had married two sisters, "this deponent William Rainsburrow's Aunts, and sisters of Edward Rainsburrow in ye above written affidavit named, &c. &c." Nicholas Hayward, the Notary Public, mentioned in the first instrument, swore that he had never drawn up such a paper, and the whole denial was witnessed by four parties on the point of departure from London for New England, and was also compared with the original about nine years later, viz: 21 March, 1695-6. I. J. GREENWOOD.]

EDMUND SPINCKES of Warmington in the County of Northampton, clerk, 2 October 1669, proved 11 August 1671. I give out of that seven hundred & fifty pounds which will be due to me or mine from the heirs or executors or administrators of Thomas Elmes of Lilford Esq. (after the decease of himself the said Thomas Elmes and the Lady Jane Compton),

* Hist. Mag., 1867, p. 299.

to my eldest son Nathaniel Spinckes one hundred pounds, to Seth, my second son, one hundred and fifty pounds, to William, my third son, one hundred & fifty pounds, to Elmes, my fourth son, one hundred & fifty pounds, and to Martha, my only daughter, two hundred pounds. To Nathaniel Spinckes, my eldest son & heir, all that land in Ireland, in King's County, which is now in the possession of the heirs or assigns of Thomas Vincent sometimes alderman of London, which is due to me according to a writing signed by him to that purpose 6 March 1642. Item I give to the said Nathaniel Spinckes all that fifty pounds, more or less, with the profit of it, that is now in the Iron works in New England, acknowledged received by John Pocock then Steward of the Company and living then in London, his Acquittance bearing date March 19th 1645. Item, I give to the said my son Nathaniel all that estate whatsoever it be that falleth to me or shall fall in New England, as joint heir with John Nayler of Boston in Lincolnshire, clerk, to Boniface Burton, now or late of Boston in New England, my uncle and mother's brother and only brother; also my library of books, only such excepted as his mother shall choose out for her own use. To Seth Spinckes, my second son, five pounds at the age of twenty-four years, to William five pounds at twenty-four, to Elmes five pounds at twenty-four and to Martha, my only daughter, five pounds at twenty-four. All the rest to my wife Martha, whom I appoint sole executrix. My loving friend Mr. Sam¹ Morton, clerk & rector of the parish church of Haddon, in the County of Huntingdon, and my much respected cousin Mr Richard Conyer, clerk and rector of Long Orton and Butolph-Bridge in the County of Huntingdon, to be overseers. A schedule to be annexed to the said will &c. that Seth shall have paid him out of the estate that my father Elmes left my wife &c. &c. (So of all the other children.)

18 May 1693 Emanavit commissio Nathanieli Spinckes, clerico, filio et administratori Marthæ Spinckes defunctæ &c. &c. Duke, 107.

[I presume that this is the " Edmond Spinckes " whose name immediately precedes that of John Harvard in the *Recepta ab ingredientibus* of Emmanuel College (REGISTER, xxxix. 103).

Boniface Burton, whom Mr. Spinckes calls his mother's only brother, died June 13, 1669, " aged 113 years," according to Judge Sewall, who calls him " Old Father Boniface Burton " (REG. vii. 206). Hull in his Diary (Trans. Am. Antiq. Society, iii. 279) gives his age as " a hundred and fifteen years." Both ages are probably too high. Burton's will was dated Feb. 21, 1666-7, and proved June 24, 1669. An abstract of the will is printed in the REGISTER, xx. 241, and on page 242 are some facts in his history. He left nothing to the family of Mr. Spinckes nor to John Nayler. After bequests to Increase Mather, to his niece Mrs. Bennet, her husband Samuel Bennet and their children, Burton leaves the rest of his property to his wife Frances Burton.

For an account of the Iron Works in which Mr. Spinckes had an interest, see " Vinton Memorial," pp. 463-74. John Pococke is named among the undertakers. —EDITOR.]

GEORGE LUDLOWE¹ of the County and Parish of Yorke in Virginia Esq. 8 September 1655. To my nephew Thomas Ludlow, eldest son to my brother Gabriel Ludlowe Esq. deceased, all my whole estate of lands and servants, &c. that I have now in possession in Virginia, to him and his lawful heirs forever; also my sixteenth part of the ship Mayflower, whereof Capt. William White is commander, which part I bought of Mr Samuel Harwar of London, merchant, only this year's "fraught" excepted, which I have reserved for my tobacco &c. My executor, yearly and every year during the natural life of my now wife Elizabeth Ludlowe, to pay unto her fifty pounds sterling in London. My crop wholly this year to be consigned to M[r] William Allen of London, merchant, and one M[r] John Cray that lives at the Green man on Ludgate Hill, whom I make my overseers of my estate in England. Moneys due from M[r] Samuel Harwar at the Sun and Harp, in Milk Street, London. To my brother Gabriel all his children, now in England, one hundred pounds apiece, and the remainder of the money (in England) to my brother Roger Ludlowe's[2] children equally; and M[r] Thomas Bushrode[3] to be paid seventy five pounds.

Whereas my brother Roger Ludlowe hath consigned divers goods to me as per my book appears, as debts in New England and in Virginia as by his letters and other writings appear &c. To my said brother the hundred pounds I lent him. To my cousin Samuel Langrish three thousand pounds of tobacco &c. To George Bernard,[4] son to Col. William Bernard, my great silver tankard with my arms on it &c. To George Webster,[5] son to Capt. Richard Webster of Jamestown the silver tankard that M[r] Bowler brought in the year 1655. To Col. William Bernard, Major William Gooch[6] and Capt. Augustine Warner[7] ten pounds apiece, and I desire and nominate them to be overseers here in Virginia. To Doctor Henry Waldron all the debt he owes me on book, and the physic I have sent for for him. To M[r] Bushrode five pounds. To my man Archyball a cloth suit &c. To Jane Greeham my servant one year of her time. To M[rs] Rebecca Hurst all the clothes that I have sent for her in full of her time being with me in my house.

Wit: Nicholas Trott, Augustine Hodges.

Codicil:—I Colonel George Ludlowe &c. My nephew Thomas Ludlowe intends to intermarry with one Rebecca Hurst that is at this present living in my house. In that case my will is and my desire that my overseers here in Virginia take into their custody all my whole estate and dispose of the same until they can send into Ireland to my nephew Jonathan Ludlowe, eldest son to my brother Roger, who lives in Ireland at Dublin. Now in case my aforesaid nephew Thomas shall marry with the said Rebecca then it is my will that I give and bequeath unto my said nephew Jonathan all the estate that I did formerly give unto my nephew Thomas Ludlowe and make and constitute the said Jonathan my full and sole executor. Otherwise my former bequest to stand valid and the said Thomas shall enjoy what I have formerly given him to his use and heirs as my executor and heir. 23 October 1655. Witness:—James Biddlecombe.

On the first day of August, in the year of Our Lord God 1656, there issued forth Letters of administration to Roger Ludlow Esq., the father of and curator lawfully assigned to Jonathan, Joseph, Roger, Anne, Mary and Sarah Ludlowe, minors, the nephews and nieces and residuary legataries in this will, during the minority of the said minors; —— —— for that no executor is therein named as touching the said deceased's estate in England.

Berkeley, 256.

Administration on the goods &c. of John Ludlow, late of Virginia bachelor, deceased, granted to his brother Francis Ludlow 15 September 1664.

Admon Act Book p. c. c.

[1 George Ludlow (or Ludlowe), of the text, was a prominent and influential colonist. Grants of land to him, aggregating some 17,000 acres, are of record in the Virginia Land Registry; the first, of 500 acres, " in the upper county of New Norfolk," being dated August 21, 1638. He was long County Lieutenant of York county, and thus by title " Collonell "; Member of the Council 1642-55. There is a tradition that his brother Roger Ludlow was a fugitive in Virginia from Connecticut near the close of the 17th century.—R. A. BROCK, of Richmond, Va.

The testator was probably the Mr. George Ludlow whose name appears on the list of those who desired Oct. 19, 1630, to be made Freemen of Massachusetts. He must have returned soon after to the old world, as a petition received from him in England was acted upon by the General Court of Massachusetts, March 1, 1630-31. —EDITOR.

[2] Roger Ludlow was an assistant of the Massachusetts colony, 1630-4, and was deputy governor in 1634. In 1635 he removed to Windsor, Ct., and was the first deputy governor of Connecticut colony. In 1639 he removed to Fairfield. He was a commissioner of the United Colonies in 1651, 2 and 3. He removed to Virginia subsequent to April 13, 1654, but probably about that time. A full memoir of him by Hon. Thomas Day, LL.D., is printed in Stiles's History of Ancient Windsor, pp. 687-8. Mr. Day styles him the "Father of Connecticut Jurisprudence." We have in this will, for the first time, the names of his children. His daughter Sarah, who is said to have been "distinguished for her literary acquirements and domestic virtues," married Rev. Nathaniel Brewster, of Brookhaven, Long Island, whose memoir will be found in Sibley's Harvard Graduates, i. 73.—EDITOR.

[3] Thomas Bushrod was a Burgess from York county, March, 1658-9. Richard Bushrod was granted 2000 acres in Westmoreland county, Oct. 15, 1660 (Land Registry, Book No. 4, p. 450). There were probably marriages of members of the Washington family with that of Bushrod, and hence the transmission of Bushrod as a Christian name, instanced in Bushrod Washington, nephew of George Washington, and Justice of the United States Supreme Court.—R. A. BROCK.

[4] The name Bernard is of early mention in the records of Virginia. Thomas Bernard was granted 189 acres of land in James City county, January 20, 1641, No. 1, p. 762 ; William Bernard, 1050 acres in Warwick county, December 16, 1641, No. 1, p. 761; "Collonell" William Bernard, 800 acres in Lancaster county, October 8, 1659, No. 4, p. 372. William Bernard, with title of Captain, was a Member of the Council in 1647, and with that of "Collonell," 1655-58. Captain Thomas Bernard, Burgess from Warwick county in 1644.—R. A. BROCK.

[5] Major Richard Webster was a Burgess from James City county, March, 1657-8. Thomas Webster was granted 251 acres in Henrico county, October 20, 1665 (No. 5, p. 519, Land Registry). Lucy, daughter and heir of Roger Webster, dec'd, was granted 250 acres in Hampton parish, Nov. 19, 1642. Head rights : Edward Spark, Stephen ———, Thomas Webster, Susan Webster, Book No. p. 857. Lucy, Judith and Jane Webster were granted 500 acres in James City county, July 20, 1646, No. 2, p. 52.—R. A. BROCK.

[6] William Gooch, "Gent.," was granted 1050 acres on the south side of the Potomac river, Oct. 18, 1650 (No. 2, p. 251, Land Registry). Captain William Gooch was a Burgess from York county in 1654. Major William Gooch died October 29, 1655, aged 29 years. His tomb in the burying ground at "Temple Farm," York county (where Gov. Alexander Spotswood was also buried), bears the arms of Gooch of Norfolk county, England (of which family was Sir William Gooch, Lieutenant Governor of Virginia, 1727-40), as follows: Paly of eight, ar. and sa. a chevron of the first, between three dogs of the second, spotted of the field. *Crest*.—A greyhound passant ar. spotted sa. and collared of the last.

Jeffery Gooch was granted 500 acres in Northumberland county, January 30, 1650 (No. 2, p. 279, Land Registry). The Gooch family, descended probably from Major William Gooch or Jeffery Gooch, as above, has been most estimably represented in Virginia.—R. A. BROCK.

[7] Colonel Augustine Warner (son, it is presumed of Augustine Warner) granted 250 acres "called Pine Neck, on New Pocoson," October 12th, 1635 (No. 1, p. 298, Land Registry), born June 3, 1642; died June 19, 1681; Burgess from Gloucester county, 1658, and Member of the Council during the administration of Governor Sir William Berkeley, is buried at "Warner Hall," Gloucester county. The Lewis, Washington and other prominent families have intermarried with that of Warner, which is a favored Christian name in Virginia.

John Lewis, second son of Robert Lewis, from Brecon, Wales, of Abington, Ware parish, Gloucester county, Virginia, married Isabella Warner, "daughter of a wealthy and retired India merchant;" called his seat "Warner Hall," a spacious mansion of 26 rooms, in which was long illustrated the refined hospitality typical of the Old Dominion. This Isabella Warner was probably a daughter of the Augustine Warner, the first grantee as above. — See article, "Descendants of Robert Lewis from Wales," *Richmond Standard*, Feb. 5, 1881.—R. A. BROCK.]

JOHN CUTLER of Ipswich in the County of Suffolk, merchant, 10 November 1645, with codicil dated 6 January 1645, proved 29 January 1645. To Robert Cutler, my cousin, youngest son of my deceased uncle Samuel Cutler, one half of my manor of Blofields als Burnivalls and of all lands, tenements, hereditaments, rights, members and appurtenances thereunto belonging &c. in Trimly St Mary and Walton in the said County of Suffolk. If the said Robert die without heirs of his body lawfully begotten or, having such heirs, if the same shall die before they come to the age of one & twenty, then the said half to my cousin Martha Noore, the wife of Raphe Noore of Ipswich, merchant, sister of the said Robert (on certain conditions). The other half to the said Martha Noore. John Smithier of Ipswich, to be assistant to my executor in & about the getting in of my estate beyond the seas and elsewhere. To Elizabeth Smithier his daughter and all the rest of his daughters and to his three sons John, William and Henry and to Nicholas Kerrington, the said Mr John Smithier's wife's brother's son. The said Mr John Smithier and his wife and the longer liver of them shall dwell in my messuage or tenement wherein they now dwell in St Nicholas' Parish, Ipswich, rent free for three years. To Mr Samuel Snelling, son in law to my cousin Mr Ralph Noore, and to my cousin Martha Snelling his wife, and Mary Noore and Alice Noore her sisters and Richard Noore her brother. To my cousin Thomas Cutler Secretary to the Company of Eastland merchants, resident at Ipswich. To Elizabeth Hubbard and Mary Ward, maidservants to my cousin Mr Raphe Noore. To Mrs Ward, widow, late the wife of Mr Samuel Ward, late town Preacher of Ipswich, and to Samuel & to Mr Joseph Ward her sons. To the poor of St Nicholas, Ipswich, to the poor of the parish of Whatfield, near Hadley in Suffolk. To Mr Lawrence, common preacher or lecturer of the said town of Ipswich. Mr John Revett, merchant, to assist my executor in getting in of my estate beyond the seas. To John Cressall, to Johan Nowell. To my cousin Margaret Skinner, wife of Jonathan Skinner, clerk, and all her children now alive. Others named. George Raymond one of the witnesses. Twisse, 3.

[There were several early emigrants to New England by the name of Cutler :—1. John Cutler, who came from Sprowston in Norfolk, with his wife, seven children and one servant, and settled in Hingham, Mass., in 1637 (REG. XV. 27) ; 2. James Cutler, who settled at Watertown as early as 1634; 3. Dea. Robert Cutler, who was here as early as 1636. See Genealogical Record of the Cutler Families, by Rev. Abner Morse, Boston, 1867.

Mr. Samuel Ward named in the will was the author of The Life of Faith. He was a brother of Nathaniel Ward, the compiler of the Massachusetts Body of Liberties. A sketch of his life is appended to the Memoir of Rev. Nathaniel Ward by the editor of the REGISTER. His son Joseph, also named in the will, was rector of Badingham in Suffolk.—EDITOR.]

MARIANE SEVIER of Yenstone, in the parish & peculiar of Henstridge in the County of Somerset, widow, 9 May 1607, proved 26 June 1607. To be buried in the churchyard of Henstridge. To the parish church of Henstridge ten shillings. To the poor folk of Henstridge parish ten shillings. To Deane Haskett, the daughter of Ellis Haskitt forty shillings. To Ellis Haskett's three other daughters and William Haskett his son four pounds, provided if any of them die before they come to the age of one & twenty years or be married then the money to remain to the survivors. To Margaret Sevier, daughter of Richard Sevier, a gown cloth and ten pounds ; to Alce Sevier, another daughter, a gown and ten pounds. To Marie Royall

of Henstridge, widow, one featherbed and three pounds. To Annis Harte
twenty shillings. To Cicely Royall, daughter of Marie Royall, three
pounds ; to Richard & to Dorothie Royall, son & daughter of Marie Royall, twenty shillings apiece. To brother in law Reynold Sevier three
pounds & to John Sevier, his son, forty shillings. To Dorothie Pennie a
gown. To Marrian Harris, wife to Richard Harris, five sheep. To John
Moores nine sheep. To the children of John Wollfres nine sheep. To
Thomas Seavier the younger nine sheep. To the children of Gregorie
Royall four pounds eight shillings and four pence, which money is in the
hands of the said Gregorie, the father of the said children. To John &
Dorothy Penny, my servants, ten shillings apiece. To Rose Collis, wife of
John Collis, three pounds. To Marie Haskett, wife of Ellis Haskett, twenty shillings. To every of my godchildren twelve pence apiece. All the
rest of my goods to Gregory Royall, whom I ordain & constitute sole executor &c. The overseers to be Ellis Haskett & Richard Chippman and I
bequeath to them three shillings four pence apiece.

The witnesses were John Bryne, William Pittman, Richard Chippman,
Ellis Haskett & John Royall.   Huddleston, 62.

KATHERINE SAMPSON, of the parish and peculiar jurisdiction of Hengstridge, in the Diocese of Bath & Wells, maiden, 30 April 1627, proved 14
June, 1627. To be buried in the parish church of Hengstridge. To the
said church, in money, twenty shillings. To the poor of the said parish ten
shillings. For the love I bear to my cousin Nicholas Locke I do forgive
him all the debts that he to me doth owe &c. To my mother my best
band of linen and my best apron. I forgive my cousin John Sampson, out
of the bond of forty shillings which he oweth unto me, twenty shillings
thereof, and the other twenty shillings of the said Bond I do give unto my
cousin Susan Sampson. To my sister Joane Sampson one silver spoon.
To cousin Mary Sampson, my brother William's daughter, my best gown,
my best petticoat, my best hat and sixteen pounds ten shillings which is
due to me upon bond from Ellis Hasket and William Haskett, his son &c.
To my two sisters Jane & Edith Sampson the residue, and they to be executrices. The overseers to be Richard Sampson the younger & Thomas
Morris the younger. Brother Henry Sampson oweth me twenty six
pounds. Richard Eburne, vicar, was one of the witnesses. Skinner, 63.

JOHN CARTER of the parish of St Mary Matfellon, alias Whitechapel, in
the county of Middlesex, gentleman, 14 February 1691, proved 16 June
1692. To my two attorneys in Barbadoes, Mr Peter Fluellin and Capt.
George Paine, twenty pounds each to buy them mourning. To my executors Mr Samuel Shepheard and Mr Samuel Perry twenty pounds each (for
mourning). " Item I doe give, devise & bequeath unto my brother RoBert
Skelton of New Yorke in America the full summe of five hundred pounds
soe soone as Assetts shall come into my Executors hands to that value" &c.
on condition that he pay to Samuel Shepheard seventy pounds that he owes
to the said Shepheard. To Mr William Shawe, Mr Edwarde Shawe and
Mr Francis Shawe, to each six pounds to buy mourning and to each of
their wives twenty shillings to buy rings to wear for my sake. The residue
to my sister Sarah Slaymaker, wife of Thomas Slaymaker, of the city of
Oxford, cook. (By a codicil made the same day bequests to Mr Mark Bedford Whiteing, and his wife and two daughters, Angellick & Annett, to

Alexander Staples Esq and his wife, and son Alexander and *his* wife, and son John and daughter Dorothy. To John Hickman, Elizabeth Hickman, Hannah Hickman and Mary Staples (gold rings). To cousin Elizabeth Carter of Barbadoes, widow and her children Thomazine Gibbs, James Carter, and her other children James, Anne, William, Richard, Jane, Damaris, John & Agnes (gold rings). To cousin John How, of Barbadoes, his wife Elizabeth and daughter Mary, to every of them a gold ring of the value of ten shillings.   Fane, 103.

Mem. that on or about the first day of March 1691 John Lee, heretofore of Charlestown in New England, carpenter, lying sick on board the ship Swallow &c. I desire the captain, meaning and speaking of and to Gyles Fifield, Captain of the said ship, to take care of all my concerns and get in what is due me in England or elsewhere. I give two parts of my whole estate to my two children. The other part I give to the captain and desire he would bestow something of the ship's company. Witness Geo. Robeson, Samuel Boyes. 2 June 1692, the witnesses were sworn.

11 June 1692 Emanavit Commissio Egidio Fifield fidei commissario et legatario nominat in Test Nuncupativo Johannis Lee aliquandiu de Charlestowne in Nova Anglia sed in nave Le Swallow super alto mari deceden &c.
                                                        Fane, 112.

I, William Read of New England in the parts beyond the seas, mariner, have constituted John Harlock of Ratcliff, Stepney, in the county of Middlesex, gentleman, and Elizabeth his wife my attorneys &c. On board the good ship Granado, Capt. Loader commander, on a voyage for Jamaica. 2 October 1691.

Witness Fred. Johnson, Jaˢ Travers. Proved 12 September 1692.
                                                        Fane, 173.

JOHN SYMONDS of Yeldham Magna in the County of Essex, Esq. 20 March, 1691, with codicil dated 16 February 1692, proved the last of May 1693. I do confirm the jointure made to my wife (Jane) and give her my mansion house called the Poole, &c. Manors of Panfield Hall & Nichols in Panfield & Shalford, in the County of Essex, to my kinsman Mʳ Martin Carter and his heirs (& other lands). To my niece Elizabeth Pepys all moneys due to her by bond or otherwise by Martin Carter decᵈ, father of the said Martin Carter. To my nephew Mʳ John Pepys, of Cambridge ; to my sister Thomasin Pepys; to my nephew Thomas Pepys; to my nieces Anne Whaples and Elizabeth Pepys, to my niece Ellen Bacon. To each of the children of Martin Carter decd. (except the two eldest sons) fifty pounds. To my sister Mrs Judith Burgoyne, to my nephew and godson Mark Guyon, to my niece Jane Guyon, to my nephews Roger and Lucy Burgoyne, sons of Sir John Burgoyne, Baronet. To Mʳ John Brooke our worthy minister. To the Society of Lincoln's Inn of which I am a member. My wife and sister Thomasine Pepys and nephew John Pepys to be executors.

(In the codicil) to my cousin Mʳ William Simonds of Ipswich in New England one hundred pounds. To Mʳ Fisk forty shillings. To my cousin John Carter and his heirs (certain lands). My nephew Thomas Pepys of Felsted. Mr Fisk my chaplain.

Sworn to &c. die Lunæ vizᵗ Decimo die mensis Aprilis A.D. 1693.
                                                        Coker, 86.

The testimony of the witnesses shows that Mr. Symonds had been cursitor for Lincolnshire and Somersetshire.

[John Symonds was the 2d son of John and Ann (Elyott) Symonds, and was born in Yeldham Magna, Sept. 4, 1618. He was a nephew of Samuel Symonds of Ipswich, deputy governor of Massachusetts. See Appleton's Ancestry of Priscilla Baker, pp. 19-102.—EDITOR.]

JANE COAKER of Kingsbridge in the County of Devon, widow, 6 June 1651, proved 1 August 1651. To the poor of Kingsbridge twenty shillings at the day of the funeral. To son Robert Coaker forty pounds within one month after my decease, and I release him of all debts owing unto me, and ten shillings a year to be paid him by my executor so long as they shall live together. To grandson James Coaker, son of William Coaker, my son, all my right &c. in the messuage wherein I live. To grandchild Jane Ball ten pounds within two years after my decease. To son Richard Coaker five shillings, to be paid him at his return into England. To daughter-in-law Agnis Coaker thirty shillings. To daughter Agnis Bound, wife of Thomas Bound, ten pounds within a quarter of a year, and to Jane Kingston five shillings. To daughter Johane Borton (wife of Henry Borton) twenty pounds within one month after my decease and ten bushels of barley malt. To Agnes Risdon, wife of Thomas Risdon, to godchild Thomas Phillipps, to Francis Hingston & to Johane Heyman, my godchildren. To grandchild Jane Coaker forty shillings. To grandchildren Anne Davie and Elizabeth Coaker ten shillings apiece. To grand children Leonard & Francis Kent fifty shillings apiece. To grand children Richard, Henry, Robert, William, Flower and John Coaker ten shillings apiece. To grand child Henry Borton six silver spoons. To grand child Jane Coaker three pounds besides the forty shillings before bequeathed. Residue to son-in-law John Hardie, who is made sole executor. The will was proved by John Hardye.   Grey, 157.

[The foregoing will may refer to Richard Coaker who was of New England in 1640.—H. F. W.
It may not be relevant, but I offer that the following grants are of record in the Virginia Land Registry:—John Corker, 6 acres in James Island, Feb. 10, 1637, Book No. 1, p. 521 ; John Cocker, 1150 acres in Surry county, March 20, 1677, Book No. 4, p. 301.—R. A. BROCK.]

SARAH ELMES, of the parish of St. Saviour's, Southwark, in the County of Surrey, widow 25 August 1653, proved 20 April 1654. To son Anthony Elmes five pounds. To son Radolphus Elmes (now in parts beyond the seas) the sum of ten pounds if he shall be living at the time of my decease. To son Jonathan Elmes ten pounds within one month after my decease. To grand child Jonathan Elmes, son of the said Jonathan, ten pounds, and to such child as Mary, the wife of the said son Jonathan, now goeth withall ten pounds. To son Henry Elmes ten pounds within one month. To my two grand children Curtis and Henry Elmes (minors) sons of my said son Henry, ten pounds apiece. To my two grand children John and Sarah Maries, children of my daughter Margaret Maries, of the parish of St. Saviour's, Southwark, widow, twenty pounds apiece at the age of one & twenty years or day of marriage. To my loving cousin Sarah Best twenty shillings (for a ring) and to sister Elizabeth Sturmey, twenty shillings and good friend Mrs Hamond of Pudding Lane twenty shillings (for rings). Daughter Margaret Maries to be sole executrix and Mr John Chelsham and loving cousin Mr Ralph Collins overseers.
                                                    Alchin, 83.

[The testatrix of the above will was undoubtedly the mother of Rhodolphus Ellmes (see Savage), of Scituate, who came in the Planter, 1635, aged 15, and married, 1644, Catharine, daughter of John Whitcomb.

See deed of Rodolphus Emes of Scituate to John Floyd, Oct. 2, 1656, for money lent and paid for passage, in Suffolk Deeds, vol. ii. p. 204.—H. F. W.]

EDWARD WINSLOW, of London, Esq., being now bound in a " Viage " to sea in the service of the Common Wealth, 18 December 1654, proved 16 October 1655 by Josias Winslow, son and executor. All my lands and stock in New England and all my possibilities and portions in future allotments and divisions I give & bequeath to Josia, my only son, and his heirs, he allowing to my wife a full third part thereof for her life. To the poor of the church of "Plimouth" in New England ten pounds. To the poor of Marshfield, where the chiefest of my estate lies, ten pounds. I give my linen which I carry with me to sea to my daughter Elizabeth; and the rest of my goods which I carry with me to sea to my son Josias, he giving to each of my brothers a suit of apparell. Son Josias to be executor and Col. Venables my overseer of my goods in the voyage and my four friends, Doctor Edmond Wilson, Master John Arthur, Master James Shirley and Master Richard Floyd, to be overseers for the rest of my personal estate in England.

The witnesses were Jon Hooper, Gerard Usher servant to Hen: Colbron.

Aylett, 377.

[Edward Winslow, the third governor of Plymouth Colony, was the son of Edward and Magdalen Winslow, of Droitwich in Gloucester, England, and was born Oct. 18, 1595. (See REGISTER, xxi. 209–10, where his pedigree is given.) He was one of the Mayflower passengers. He was appointed by Cromwell one of three commissioners to superintend the expedition against the Spaniards in the West Indies, and died May 8, 1655, on the passage between Hispaniola and Jamaica. An article on his life, by G. D. Scull, Esq., was printed in the REGISTER, xxxviii. 21–6. See also REGISTER, iv. 297; xvii. 159; and xxxvii. 392.—EDITOR.]

JOHN STOUGHTON Doctor "in devinitie" & curate of the parish of St Mary Aldermanbury, London, beginning " Laus Deo the fowerth daie of May 1639 " [on which day he died], proved 20 May 1639. To my poor kindred twenty pounds to be disposed of according to the discretion of my wife Jane Stoughton, one of my executors. To the parishioners of the parish of St Mary, Aldermanbury aforesaid five pounds, to be bestowed unto the poor of the said parish.

To my two daughters Jane & Marie five "hundreth" pounds, to say, to my eldest daughter Jane "fower hundreth marks which twoe hundred three score and six poundes thirteene shillings and fower pence, and the remainder beinge twoe C. hundreth thirtie three poundes six shillings and eight pence to my youngest daughter Marie Stoughton, to be paied them att theire age of one & twenty yeares or the day of theire marriage, which shall first happen " &c. If both depart this life before they attain the age specified or day of marriage that then " two hundreth and fieftie poundes thereof shall come unto my wife and two hundred poundes thereof to my nexte of kynn, and twentie fiue poundes thereof to Emanuell Colledge in Cambridge and the other five and twentie poundes to Master Hartlipp a Dutchman."

To four or five persons such as my loving wife & one of my executors shall think fit twenty shillings apiece for a ring, provided Mr Janeway be one of them. The executors to be my dear and loving wife Jane Stoughton and my loving father in law and her father John Browne of Frampton in Dorsetshire Esq. and for overseers Robert Edwards and Edmond Foord of London merchants.

The remainder to my wife Jane Stoughton.

Wit: Robert Edwards   Thomas Davies.   Harvey, 69.

[May 4, 1639, " Dr. Stoughton of Aldermanbury died." See Smyth's Obituary. —H. F. W.

The Rev. John Stoughton was a brother of Israel and Thomas Stoughton, early settlers of Dorchester, Mass. Israel was the father of Lieut.-Gov. William Stoughton. Thomas removed from Dorchester to Windsor, Conn. Rev. John Stoughton, the testator, was also the stepfather of Gen. James Cudworth, of Scituate, New England, and of the Rev. Ralph Cudworth, author of The Intellectual System of the Universe. See articles on Stoughton and Cudworth in the REGISTER, xiv. 101 ; xxi. 249.—EDITOR.]

MENSE APRILIS 1611.

Thomas Rogers   Vicesimo Septimo die probatum fuit testim̄ Thome
Sen.   Rogers señ nup de Stratford sup Avon in Cõm̄ Warwici def heñts etc. Juramento Thome Rogers filii dicti def et exr̄is etc. cui etc de bene etc iurat.   Probate Act Book.

[The will of which the above is the Probate Act, does not seem to have been copied into the Register, which I examined leaf by leaf, with hopes to find it. My friend J. C. C. Smith, Esq., then hunted through the bundle of original wills for that year, but in vain. That the testator was the father of Mrs. Harvard, and grandfather of our John Harvard, there can be no doubt. The extracts from the Parish Register of Stratford upon Avon, together with the wills of his daughters, &c., prove that. Among the Feet of Fines of the Easter Term, 23d Elizabeth (1581), I find a conveyance made to him by one Henry Mace, of two messuages and two gardens with their appurtenances in Stratford upon Avon. He seems to have been a prominent citizen of that borough, as will appear from the extracts I shall give from the records, and, in 1596, while he was holding the office of Bailiff, built the house still standing in High Street, now known as " Ye Ancient House," the best specimen now left in that street, or perhaps in the borough. On the front, under the broad window of the second story, appear these characters :

T R   1596   A R

In this house, therefore, Katharine Rogers lived from 1596 until her marriage to Robert Harvard, and to it she may have come with her little son John to attend the obsequies of her father. A heliotype of this house illustrates this volume.

—H. F. W.]

The Parish Registers of Stratford upon Avon commence Anno 1558. By the kind permission of the Vicar, the Rev. George Arbuthnot, M.A., I was enabled to devote the whole of one day, from the close of the morning service to the beginning of the afternoon service, to an examination of them. I took notes of the following marriages :

```
1562   January 31, Thomas Rogers and Margaret Pace.
1563   November 27, Henry Rogers and Elizabeth Burback.
1566   July 6, Edward Huntington and Matilda Rogers.
1570   October 15, John Rogers and Anne Salsbury.
1579   July 20, William Rogers and Elizabeth Walker.
1581   October 30, Richard Rogers and Susanna Castell.
  "    November 5, Richard Rogers and Ales Calle.
1592 (?3)  December 30, Antherin Russell and Joyce Rogers.
1596   November 21, William Rogers and Jone Tante.
1600   October 28, John Nelson to Elizabeth Rogers.
1602   April 13, Lewes Rogers to Joane Rodes.
  "    October 12, Francis Rogers to Elizabeth Sperpoint.
1603 (4)  January 1, William Smith to Ales Rogers.
1605   " Apriell 8, Robertus Harwod to Katherina Rogers."
1608 (9)  February 6, Henry Stanton to Phillip Rogers.
1609   July 18, Thomas Chestley to Margaret Rogers.
```

The early home of JOHN HARVARD's mother.

I looked through the record of the marriages down to 1637 inclusive, and found a few other Rogers marriages, which it hardly seems worth the while to print. Thomas, Henry, John, William and Richard Rogers had numerous children baptized and buried. Of these I pick out the children of Thomas.

Baptized.	Buried.
Margaret, September 26, 1562.	Margaret, December 1, 1562.
Elizabeth. October 28, 1563.	Johanna, February 21, 1566 (7).
Charles, March 28, 1565.	Alice, October 3, 1568.
Johanna, January 24, 1566 (7).	Anne, July 24, 1581.
Alice, September 2, 1568.	Thomas, August 13, 1584.
Joanna, October 14, 1571.	" Infant," January 15, 1591.
Joyce, February 9, 1572 (3).	Charles Rogers, " homo " March 30,
Ales, September 11, 1574.	1609 (10).
Richard, November 10, 1575.	Thomas Rogers, August 31, 1639.
William, June 8, 1578.	
Edward, February 18, 1579.	
Thomas, July 22, 1582.	
Katherin, November 25, 1584.	
Thomas, June 11, 1587.	
Rose, March 29, 1590.	
Frances, March 10, 1593.	

The burial of Margaret, the wife of Mr. Rogers, I did not find. He evidently married again; for I found the burial of " Alice wyf to Mr Thomas Rogers," August 17, 1608. His own burial is thus given :

1610 (11) February 20, Thomas Rogers, one of the Aldermen.

THOMAS ROGERS of Stratford upon Avon in the County of Warwick yeoman 27 Aug. 1639, proved at Worcester 21 May 1640. To Anne my beloved wife all that my messuage or tenement wherein I now dwell, with the appurtenances, and all other my lands and tenements whatsoever situate & being in the said town of Stratford &c. to have and to hold for life or until marriage, and, after her decease or day of marriage, to my four daughters Lydia, Alice, Ruth & Hannah & their assigns until Edward Rogers my son shall well & truly pay unto my said four daughters the sum of twenty pounds apiece, and after such payment, then to the said Edward & to the heirs of his body Lawfully to be begotten ; failing such to my right heirs forever. To the poor of Stratford twenty shillings. Towards the repair of Stratford church twenty shillings. John Whinge of Blackwell in the county of Worcester, yeoman to be the executor and my loving kinsman John Woolmer the younger and Henry Smyth of Old Stratford, yeoman, to be the overseers of this my will.

The Inventory of his goods, &c. was taken · 1 October 1639 by John Wolmer the younger, gentleman, John Wynge and Henry Smith. The sum total was 86^{li} 13^s 0^d.

The widow Anna Rogers was appointed administratrix with the will annexed and gave her bond 23 May 1640, with Francis Baggott of Witley Parva in the parish of Holt in the County of Worcester, as her surety.

WILLIAM SMYTHE of Stratford upon Avon in the County of Warwick mercer, 30 March 1626, proved at Worcester 10 May 1626. To Thomas, my eldest son my shop & the cellars lying in the Middle Row & now in the tenure of William Ayng, butcher, and also my three tenements in the Henley Street, now in the tenures of Thomas Alenn & Thomas Woodwarde and that I late did dwell in, &c. & for want of lawful issue then to

Francis my son & to his lawful issue & for want of such issue to my two daughters Mary & Alice (equally). To daughter Mary twenty pounds to be paid to her within two years after my decease by my son Francis, and in consideration thereof I give to my son Francis the lease of the house wherein I now dwell, &c. To my daughter Alice Smythe all my household stuff, &c. &c. and I make Alice Smyth my said daughter executrix of this my last will & testament, and I make my brother Henry Smythe and John Wolmer overseers, &c.

The Inventory of his goods & chattels was taken 28 April 1626.

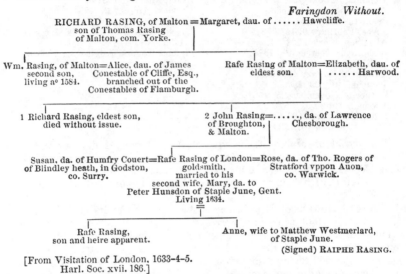

Faringdon Without.

RICHARD RASING, of Malton = Margaret, dau. of ...... Hawcliffe.
son of Thomas Rasing
of Malton, com. Yorke.

Wm. Rasing, of Malton = Alice, dau. of James   Rafe Rasing of Malton = Elizabeth, dau. of
second son,   Conestable of Cliffe, Esq.,   eldest son.   ...... Harwood.
living a° 1584.   branched out of the
                     Conestables of Flamburgh.

1 Richard Rasing, eldest son,   2 John Rasing = ..., da. of Lawrence
died without issue.   of Broughton,   Chesborough.
                             & Malton.

Susan, da. of Humfry Couert = Rafe Rasing of London = Rose, da. of Tho. Rogers of
of Blindley heath, in Godston,   goldsmith,   Stratford vppon Auon,
co. Surry.   married to his   co. Warwick.
                    second wife, Mary, da. to
                    Peter Hunsdon of Staple June, Gent.
                    Living 1634.

Rafe Rasing,   Anne, wife to Matthew Westmerlard,
son and heire apparent.   of Staple June.
                        (Signed) RAIPHE RASING.

[From Visitation of London, 1633-4-5.
Harl. Soc. xvii. 186.]

Mense Junii 1647. Undecimo die em᷑ Com° Rose Reason Relce Radulphi Reason nup poe Ste Bridgitte als Brides prope Fleetstreete Civitat London deft haben & ad adstrand bona iura et credita dict deft de bene &c. iurat.   Admon. Act. Book. Fol. 76.

[The two forms of spelling this surname are interesting for two reasons; first, as showing the loss of the guttural final *g* sound in Rasing (in connection with which it may be well to note that the crest of this family was a hand grasping a bunch of *grapes*), and, secondly, as illustrating the sound of the diphthong *ea* in *Reason*. I have seen many similar instances showing that in Shakspeare's time the word was pronounced like *raisin*. Recall Fallstaff's play on the word in Henry IV. Part I. Act ii. Sc. 4: " Give you a reason on compulsion ! If reasons were as plenty as blackberries I would give no man a reason upon compulsion."—H. F. W.]

IN THE NAME OF GOD AMEN. I Rose Raysings of the Parish of Saint Bride London Widdowe being weake in bodie but of sound and perfect memorie thankes be to God doe make this my last Will and Testament in manner and forme following (videlicet) ffirst I bequeath my soule to Almighty God who gaue it me and my bodie to the Earth from whence it Came to be buried in Saint Brides Church London in Christian decentlike manner as my Executor hereafter named shall thinke fitting. Item I giue to my daughter Rose Haberly the Wife of Anthony Haberly the summe of Tenne poundes and alsoe my best Gowne and petticoate and a payre of Hollande sheetes and one douzen and to her husband twentie shillinge.   Item I giue to the Children of my daughter Rose Haberley (that is to say) to Anthonie John Mary and Rose I giue fiue poundes apeece   But to my Grandchild Elizabeth Haberley who is my God daughter I giue Tenne poundes.   Item I giue to Katherine Wilmour my Executors Wife here after named fiue poundes.   Item I giue to Joane Wilmour her Kinswoeman fiue poundes.   Item I giue to John Wilmour the younger my sisters Grand-Child fiue poundes.   Item I giue to my Cousin Brockett's sonne Joseph Brockett in Southwarke fiue poundes and to his Mother twenty shillings to buy her a Ring.   Item I giue to Marie Right That Tends me in my sick-nes fiue pounds.   Item I giue John Corker my Godsonne Twenty shillings and to his Mother and his brother Tenne shillings a peece.   Item I giue to William Suthes the sonne of James Suthes twenty pounds to be paid att his age of one and twentic ycarcs.   Item I giue to Master James Palmer formerly the Viccar of Saint Brides London fiue poundes.   Item I giue to Master Alexander Baker of Cliffords Inne London Gentleman that Bond wherein Master Morgan and Master Powell stands bound unto my late husband Ralph Raysing which is now in suite in the upper Bench and in the Chancerie and I doe hereby giue power to the said Master Baker to sue in my Executors name for the same provided alwaies That if the said James Suches shall att anie time hereafter trouble my Executor hereafter named for any concerning mee or my late husband Ralph Raysing That then my Legacie to the said Willià Suthes his sonne shall be absolutely voyd. Item I giue to Thomas Smith the sonne of my sister Alice Smith in War-wickshire the summe of fiue pounds.   And last of all I make my loueing Kinseman Master John Wilmour of Stratford upon Avon in the Countie of Warwick my full and sole Executor of this my last Will and Testament de-sireing him to doe all things accordingly as I haue by this my last Will re-quired him.   And the remainder of all my goods and Chattells not formerlie bequeath I doe hereby give and bequeath to my said Executor and I doe hereby renounce all former Wills and Testam[ts] whatsoever and doe hereby revoake the same and publish this to be my last Will and Testament and desire that none may stand for my last Will but this and I doe alsoe giue and bequeath to Mistris Susan Annyon Widdowe the summe of Thirtie shillings to buy her a Ring.   In Witnes whereof I haue to this my last Will and Testament sett my hand and seale dated This first Day of December in the yeare of our Lord One Thousand six hundred fifty and fower.   Rose Raysings Signed sealed published and delivered as her last Will and testam[t] Theise words (videlicct) and alsoe my best gowne and petticoate and a payre of Holland sheetes and one douzen of Napkins and my Bible Kinsewoeman to be paid att his age of one and twenty yeares   Avon in the Countie of Warwicke being first interlined in the presence of us Susan Annyon Alex Barker.

This Will was proved in London the twentith Day of June in the yeare of our Lord God One Thousand six hundred fiftie and fiue before the Judges for probate of Wills and granting Administrations lawfully authorized by the oath of John Willmour The Sole Executor named in the aboue written Will To whome Administration of all and singular the goods Chattells and debts of the said deceased was Committed he being first legally sworne truly and faithfully to administer the same.   291, Aylett.

Joh. Sadler clerk M.A. adm., on the resignation of Simon Aldriche, to the Vicarage of Ringmer, 6 October, 1626.

Archbishop Abbot's Reg. p. 2, f. 349[b].

JOHN SADLER was inducted into the possession of ye vicaridge of Ringmer Octob^r xijth 1626.

1640 Oct. 3 buryed Mr John Sadler minister of Ringmer.
Ringmer Parish Register.

Sussex, Ringmer Vic. John Sadler 14 Nov. 1626 (to Nov. 1628), William Thomas of Lewes and William Michelborne of Westmiston (his sureties).   Compositions for First Fruits.

EDWARD FENNER of Auburne in the County of Sussex (13 July 1603 proved 9 October 1605) wishes his body to be buried in the parish church of Auburne and leaves all to his wife Mary whom he appoints executrix & entrusts the children to her care.   69, Hayes.

License granted 12 May 1613 to the Rector, Vicar or Curate of Stepney in the county of Middlesex to solemnize the marriage between John Sadler, clerk, and Mary Fenner, widow, late the relict of Edward Fenner, while he lived of Auburne in the County of Sussex, gen. dec'd.
Vicar General's Book.

[Albourne is a parish in Sussex near Cuckfield.—H. F. W.]

MARY SADLER of Mayfield in the County of Sussex, widow, 16 January 1645, proved 13 November 1647. " My Corpes to bee interred where ever ytt shall please God by my surviving freindes to dispose of ytt." I do nominate & appoint my daughter Elizabeth James to be my sole Executrix. And I bequeath and give unto her one hundred pounds of money which is in her husband's hands, and such bedding and chests and wearing clothes as I have (saving one chest which is full of linnen and pewter, and other small things). My will is that she shall buy & give to my grandchild Mary Russell two silver spoons of ten shillings apiece price and to Thomas Russell my grandson ten shillings of money. I will & bequeath unto my son John Sadler the money which I have in Mr William Michilborne's hands. Item I give unto my grandchild Mary James one chest of linen and pewter except two pair of the sheets and one pair of pillowcoats therein, which I give unto Anne James, and one other pair of sheets which are also in the said chest, which I give unto Elizabeth James my grandchildren. Item I give to each of my son Russell's children not before named in this my will one shilling apiece for the buying them gloves. Item I give unto my daughter Mary Sadler and to each of her children which I suppose to live in " newe " England one shilling apiece. Item I give unto my daughter Anne Allin and to her daughter Mary one shilling apiece, and this I do appoint and intend my last will and testament.   231 Fines.

ALLEN.—THOMAS, son of John Allen, dyer, of Norwich. At school under Mr Briggs eight years. Age 15. Admitted sizar litt. grat. July 6, 1624. Surety Mr Moore.   Admissions Caius Coll. Cambridge.

THOMAS HERVY, citizen & " Bocher " of London, 16 June 1505, proved at Lambeth 3 October 1505. " I bequeth my soule to god to our blissed lady Virgyñ Mary his moder and to all the holy company of heveñ And my body to be buried in the churchyerd of Seynt Clementes in Candilwykstrete of London on the Northside of the same Churchyerd where the body of William more late Citezein and bocher of London my groundfader lyeth buried. And if it fortune that I dye or decesse owte of Londoñ thañ I will that my body be buried where as it shall please god for it to dispose. Item I bequeth to the high aulter of the said churche of Seynt Clementes for myñ offerynges forgoteñ or negligently w'draweñ in dischargyng of my soule iij⁸ iiijᵈ. It I bequeth unto Margarete my wife for hir parte purparte and porcioñ of all my goodes moevable and unmoevable in redy money xlˡⁱ sterl and all my stuff of household and plate hole as it shalbe the day of my decesse. It I bequeth unto my sonnes Thomas Hervy and Nicholas Hervy and to the Infaunte beyng in my wiffs wombe if she now be wᵗ childe in redy money xlˡⁱ evenly to be devided and departed amonges theym and to be deliūed to theym and eūry of theym whañ they or eny of theym shall cõme to their laufull ages or mariages the which money I will my moder mawde Hoppy haue the keping to the use of my said childerñ till they shall cõme to their laufull ages or mariages. And if it fortune any of my said sonncs or the Infañt in my wiffes wombe for to dye or decesse afore they or any of theym shal cõme to their laufull ages or mariages, thañ I will that the parte of hym or theym so decessyng remayne to hym or theym beyng on lyve. And if it fortune all my said childerñ to dye afore they cõme to their laufull ages or be maried thañ I will that my said moder dispose the same xlˡⁱ to my said childerñ before bequethed for my soule my faderes soule my childerñ soules and for all my goode frendes soules in deedes of almes and of charitie as she shall thinke best for the helth and saluacioñ of my soule. It I will that my saide moder haue the keping of my said childreñ duryng their noonage It I will that the saide Mawde my moder take haue & receyve the proffittes and revenues cõmyng and growying of my fermes called Gubbons and Waltoñs in the Countie of Essex and of my ferme in Madebrokes long mede and Wottons croftes lying in the pisshe of Retherhith in the Countie of Surrey towardes the sustentacioñ and fynding of my said childerñ duryng their noonage and the surplusage of the same revenues and proffittes cõming & growyng of the same fermes I will it be evenly devided and depted amonges my said childerñ and Infaunt by the said Mawde my moder. It I bequeth to my suster Elyñ fflynte the wif of John fflynte all my state and Tñie of years which I haue to cõme of and in my ferme called preestes ñshe sett and lying in the pisshe of Retherhed aforesaid. And I will that thendentur of the same ferme be deliūed unto my said suster incontinent aftʳ my decesse. Itñ I bequeth unto my cosyñ Thomas Hervy myñ state and termes of yeres which that I haue to cõme of and into the tenementes called the Dogge and the Shippe in Estchepe in the pisshe of Seynt Clementes aforesaid and in seynt Leonardes. And I will that thendentures of the same houses be deliūed unto my said cosyñ Thomas assone aftʳ my decesse as is possible. It I bequeth unto my sūnt William Anderby xx⁸ in money. It I bequeth unto Johñ ffelix xx⁸. It I bequeth unto Richard ffelix xx⁸. It I will that my moder or hir Executo'rs fynde the said Johñ ffelix to gramʳ scoole and to writting scole by the space of a yere aftʳ my decesse. The Residue of all my goods moevable and unmoevable aftʳ my dettes paid my burying done and this my pʳsent testament in all thinges fulfilled I geve and bequeth unto the forsaid Mawde my moder she therewᵗ to doo ordeyne and dispose hir owne freewill for eūmore. Which Mawde my moder I make and ordeyne executrice of this my pʳsent testament. In witnesse wherof to this my pʳsent testament I haue setto my seale. Youeñ the day and yeʳ aforesaid." 36 Holgrave.

In the name of God amen The xxixᵗʰ day of the moneth of July In the yere of oʳ lord god mᵗ vᶜ and viij. I Thomas Hervy bocher of the pisshe of seynt Oluff in Suthwerk in the diocise of Winchester beyng hole of mynde and memory thanked be almighty god sett make and ordeyne this my p^{r}sent testament and last will in man^r and fo^{r}me folowing ffirst I bequeth and recom̄end my soule unto almighty god my creato^r and savio^r, my body to be buryed in the church of seynt Oluff aforesaid And I bequeth unto the high aulter of the same churche for my tithes & oblacioп̄s here before necligently paid or forgoteп̄ ij^s. Also I bequith to my moder church of Wynchestre iiij^d And I geve and bequeth to the aulter of our lady in the said pisshe church of seynt Orluff iiij^d. Also I bequeth to the ault^r of seynt Anne there iiij^d. Also to the aulter of seynt Clement iiij^d. The Residue of all my goodes and catalles not bequethed nor geven after my fuп̄all expences dooп̄ and my dettes paied I will and geve unto Guynor my wif she to dispose theym after hir discrecioп̄ as she shall thinke moost convenyent. And of this my present testament and last will I make and ordeyne myп̄ executrice my said wif Thiese witnesses Sr William Priour Curat of seynt Oluff aforeseid William Bulleyп̄ grocer William Symsoп̄ and other.

Probatum fuit suprascript testm̄ corã Dп̄o apud Lamehith xv° die mens Augusti Anno Dп̄i Millim̄o quingētesimo octauo Jur Guynoris Relicte et executricis in huioi testō noiãte Ac approbat & insinuat Et cōmissa fuit adm̄istra° om̄ bonorum & debit dicti defuncti prefate executrici de bene & fidelit adm̄istrand Ac de pleno & fideli Inuētario citra p^{r}imū diem Septembr̃ p̃x futur exhibend necnō de plano et vero com̄pto reddend ad sca dei euп̄g in debita iuris forma iurat.   4 Bennett (P. C. C.)

William Herford citizen & tallowchandler of London, 31 August 1518, proved 10 Nov. 1518. My body to be buried in the parish church of St. Olave in the old " Jure " of London in the same place where my late wife Johan resteth buried. " And I haue bought & payed for the stone that lyeth on her. And therefor I woll haue the same stone layed on my body & I woll have a scripture graveп̄ & fyxed yn the same stone makyng mension off the tyme off my deceasse requiryng the people to pray for me." To the high altar of the same church for tythes & oblations forgotten or negligently withholden iij^s iiij^d. Towards the gilding of the tabernacle of St John the Baptist at the south end of the high Altar of the same church xx.^{s} Towards the maintenance of Olave's Brotherhood within the same church xij^d. To the company & brotherhood of Our Lady & St John Baptist Tallowchandlers of London my silver pot. To John Hone my best dagger the sheath garnished with silver as it is. To Richard Chopyn my purse garnished with silver. " It I beqweth to Nicholas Pynchyn my best Jaket." Touching the disposition of my lands & tenements in the parish of St. Stephen in Colemanstreet I will that my wife Agnes Herford shall have them during her life and after her decease they shall remain to my children and to the heirs of their bodies lawfully begotten & for lack of such issue they shall remain to the company of Butchers of London forever, they finding forever in the same church of St. Olaves the day of my decease dirige " on nyght and masse of Requiem on the morne by note dispendyng at eūry such obyte amongyst prestes and clerkes wex Ryngyng off belles & poū people 20^s foreu^r. And if the same Company of Bouchers make defaute of and yn kypyng of the same obyte yn man^r & forme a bouesayd then I woll that the same landes and tenūtes shall full & hole remayne to the cōpany & felyshippe of Talow chauudelers of London foreū they doyng and dyspendyng yerely therfore at an obytt yerly yn man^r and forme as the forsayd cōpany off Bouchers ar bounde to doo yn kepyng of the forsayd Obyte as they wyll answere before God." ———— To my cousin Richard Baynbery my tawney gown furred with black, to John Kyttelwell & Rob[t] Kyttelwell either of them my single Ray gowns, to John Ryve my best dublett to William Knott my second Dublet, to William Pyper, George Chelsey & James Quick mine apprentices, so that they continue & serve out their terms well & truly to my wife their mistress, to either of them vi[s] viij[d]. when their terms of prenticehood shall be finished. To my god children that at time of my decease shall be living xii[d]. The residue shall be divided amongst my wife & children accordinge to the laws & custōms of the city of London. And Executors of this will &c. I make & ordaine my said wife Agnes & the said Nicholas. To Robert Whetecroft my riding coat.

102 Bennet (Commissary Court of London).

CRISTIANA HARVYE of Shenley in the County of Hertford widow, and John Harvye, son and heir apparent of the said Cristiana, give a bond 30 June 10 Elizabeth, of one hundred pounds, to Lawrence Greene, citizen and cutler of London, that they will carry out an agreement specified in a pair of Indentures bearing date 30 June 10 Elizabeth.

Claus Roll 10 Elizabeth, Part 13.

THOMAS HARVARD of the precinct of S[t] Katherine's near the Tower of London, butcher, conveys to Henry Rawlins of Lee in the county of Essex, mariner 29 January 1621, for the sum of one hundred and fifty pounds already received, all those three several messuages and tenements, with all shops, cellars, rollers, warehouses, backsides, entries, lights, easements, commodities and appurtenances whatsoever to the said three several messuages or tenements, or any of them, belonging, situate, &c. at the North end of Bermondsey Street, near Battle Bridge, in the parish of S[t] Olaves, *als.* tooles in Southwark, &c. now or late in the several tenures or occupations of William Pilkington, William Hatcham and William Fells or their assigns, &c. to be delivered up the 2[d] day of July next. His wife Margaret unites. (What follows seems to indicate that this conveyance is a mortgage.)

Claus Roll 20 Jac. I. Part 37.

HILL. 6 H. viij (1514) Apud Westm̄ a die Sci Martini in quindecim dies. Int[r] Johēm Kyrton Nichū Tycheborñ Henr̄ Tyngylden & Johem Fowler quer. et Ricū Harvy & Cristinam uxeм̄ eius deforc de uno mesuagio & uno gardino cum ptin in Southwerk Et preterea iidem Ricus & Cristina concesserunt pro se & hered ipius Cristine qd ipi warant pdcis Johi Nicho Henr & Johi & hered ipius Johis Kyrton pdca ten cum ptin contr̄ Johem Abbem monastri Sc Petri Westm̄ & successores suos &c. &c.

The consideration was twenty marks of silver.

Feet of Fines, Surrey.

Trin. 10 Elizabeth (1568). Hec est finalis· concordia fc̄a in cur Dn̄e Regine apud Westm̄ in crastino Sc̄e Trinitatis anno regni Elizabeth dei gra Anglie ffranc & hibñie Regine fidei defensoris etc a conqu decimo, coram (&c.), Int Laurenciū Grene quer et Cristianam Harvye viduam & Johem Harvye geñosum deforc de septem messuagiis septem gardinis & una acra trē cum ptin in pochia Sc̄i Georgii in Southwarke etc. Consideration eighty pounds sterling.

Feet of Fines, Surrey.

Trinity Term 37 Elizabeth, Essex. Oliver Skinner quer. and Thomas Harvard and Johann his wife, Hugh Gullifer and Anne his wife, William Smarte, Henry West and Margaret his wife and William Spalding and Elizabeth his wife deforc,—for one acre of pasture with the appurtenances in Westham. Consideration 40[li] sterling.

Feet of Fines.

Hillary Term 37 Elizabeth, Surrey. Thomas Harvard & Johan his wife quer. and John Leveson mil. deforc,—for three messuages with the appurtenances in the parish of St Olave alias St Toolyes in Southwark. Consideration 160^{li} st.   Feet of Fines.

Easter Term 38 Elizabeth, Essex. Christopher Poyner gen. quer. and Thomas Harvey & Johan his wife deforc, for one messuage with the appurtenances in Foxyearth & Pentrowe.   Consideration 80^{li} st.
                                                         Feet of Fines.

Easter Term 38 Elizabeth, Essex. John Jefferson and Thomas Smyth quer. and Thomas Harvard & Johan his wife & Henry West & Margaret his wife deforc, for three parts of one messuage, one barn, one garden, one orchard and twelve acres of arable land with the appurtenances, into four parts to be divided, in Westham & Stratford Langthorne.   Feet of Fines.

Mich. Term 39–40 Elizth (1597) Surrey. Thomas Harvard quer. and John Anwyke and Alice his wife and William Crowcher (Crowther?) and Agnes his wife deforc; for two messuages, two gardens with the appurtenances in the parish of St Olave, Southwark.   Consideration 80^{li} st.
                                                         Feet of Fines.

Easter Term 40 Elizabeth, Essex, David George quer. and Thomas Herverd and Johan his wife and William Spaldinge and Elizabeth his wife deforc,—for one messuage, one barn, one garden, one orchard, twenty acres of land (arable), four acres of meadow and six acres of pasture with the appurtenances in Westham. Consideration 100^{li} sterling. Feet of Fines.

Mich. Term 22 James I. Surrey. Robert Harverd quer. and Thomas Harverd deforc,—for three messuages, with the appurtenances in the parish of St Olaves in Southwark. Consideration 240^{li} sterling.
                                                         Feet of Fines.

THOMAS ROWELL of the Parish of Westham in the County of Essex yeoman, 12 August 1583, proved 23 August 1583. My body to be buried in the churchyard of Westham.
  "Also I doe giue unto my sonne in Lawe Thomas Harford butcher dwellinge in London one redd cowe and he havinge the said Cowe to giue unto his mother in Lawe the some of xl^s." To John Bestone my wife's son all my wearing apparell. To Joane my wife all the rest of my goods & I make her Executrix.
  Wit. John Hall curate, John Rowell yeoman Richard Cannon yeoman Isabell Spike widow.   306 Bullocke, Consistory Court of London.

Married, 1582, Nov. 19, Thomas Harvarde & Jane Rowell.
                    Register of St Saviour's Parish, Southwark.

JONE HARVARD wife of Thomas Harvard buried June 10, 1599.
                    Register of St Savior's Parish, Southwark.

RICHARD YEARWOOD and Katherine Ellettsone were mar^d xxviiith of May 1627.   Parish Register of Wandsworth, Surrey.

[This is the third marriage of John Harvard's mother. I am indebted to J. T. Squire, Esq., for his kind permission to extract the above from his MS copy of this Register, and to my friend J. C. C. Smith, Esq., who discovered this important entry.—H. F. W.]

PETER MEDCALFE of the parish of St Olave's in Southwark in the County of Surrey clothworker 24 August 1592, proved 6 September 1592. To Mr Richard Hutton Deputy of the Borough of Southwark my best gown faced with Foynes. To my very friend Mr Thomas Lynne in Pater Noster Rowe my best gown faced with satin. To Richard Barker my gown faced with Budge or Damask at his choice. To Peter Keseler one of my gowns faced with budge. To the poor of St Olave's in Southwark forty shillings To the poor of Redderiffe in the County of Surrey twenty shillings. To my very good friend Mr John Nokes a ring of gold with an agate cut. "Item I giue and bequeathe unto Robert Harvey a boye which I keepe the somme of ffyue poundes lawfull money of Englande to be paied unto hym at his age of one and twentie yeres. So that-he be ordered and ruled by my executrix and that he do liue to accomplishe the age of one and twentie yeres aforesaied." To Symon Harvye my servant my great anvil & two of my best vices with the bellows thereunto belonging. To my other servants viz Francis, Thomas & Peter being my household servants each of them 20 shillings. Others mentioned. Wife Margaret Medcalfe to be executrix.

71 Harrington (P. C. C.).

Admon de bonis non was granted 26 (September) to Christopher Medcalf, the next of kin.

JOHN GUY of the parish of St Saviour in Southwark, in the County of Surrey, brewer (17 June 1625, proved 28 June 1625) bequeaths to Richard Harford citizen & brewer of London the sum of thirty shillings to make him a ring for a remembrance.

64, Clarke.

ROBERT GREENE of the parish of St. Savior in Southwark in the county of Surrey, yeoman (8 November 1645, proved 19 January 1645) appoints as one of the overseers of his will Mr Thomas Harvard of the said parish Butcher, calling him friend & neighbor, and gives him five pounds. In a codicil, made 11 January 1645, he bequeathes unto Robert Harvard son of Thomas Harvard (above) the sum of ten shillings. The testator had a sister Jane Marshall of Billorica, Essex.

3, Twisse.

RAPH YARDLEY citizen & merchant tailor of London 25 August 1603, proved 27 February 1603. After my debts paid and my funerals discharged I will that all and singular my goods chattels & debts shall be parted & divided into three equal parts & portions according to the laudable use and custom of the city of London. One full third part thereof I give and bequeath to Rhoda my wellbeloved wife, to her own use, in full satisfaction of such part and portion of my goods, chattells & debts as she may claim to have by the custom of the same city. One other full third part thereof I give & bequeath unto and amongst my children, Raphe, George, John, Thomas and Anne Yardley and to such other child or children as yet unborn as I shall happen to have at the time of my decease, to be equally parted, shared & divided between them, and to be satisfied and paid to my said sons at the accomplishment of their several ages of one and twenty years, and to my said daughter at the accomplishment of her age of one & twenty years or marriage, which shall first happen, &c. &c. And the other third part thereof I reserve to myself therewith to perform & pay these my legacies hereafter mentioned, that is to say, Item I give & bequeath to the poor of the parish of St Saviours in Southwark where I now dwell twenty shillings, to be divided amongst them by the discretion of the overseers of the poor there for the time being, and to such of the bachelors and sixteen men of the company of merchant tailors London as shall accompany my body to burial twenty shillings for a recreation to be made unto them, and to the Ves-trymen of the same parish twenty shillings more for a recreation to be made unto them. Item I give and bequeath to my sister Palmer a ring of gold to the value of six shillings eight pence, and to my cousin John Palmer her husband a like ring to the like value, and to my daughter Earby my first wife's wedding ring, and to my son Erbye her husband my best cloak, and to my cousin Richard Yearwood my black cloth gown of Turkey fashion. The rest & residue of all & singular my goods &c. I wholly give unto my said children &c. &c. Item I give & bequeath to my brother Thomas Yardley a ring of gold to the value of six shillings eight pence. And I ordain & make the said Raph Yardley my son to be the Executor &c. and the said Richard Yerwoode and my son Edward Earbye overseers.

As to my freehold lands tenements & hereditaments I will demise give & bequeath my messuages, lands &c in Southwark or elsewhere unto my said children &c.   24, Harte.

John Hall, Not. Pub., one of the witnesses.

AGNES PARKER of London, spinster, 27 November 1617, proved 9 January 1617.   Brother in law Edward Smyth and sister Julian, his wife, Sister Margery, the wife of Thomas Flinte of Litterworth in the County of Leicester, glazier. To M^ris Elizabeth Bygate, sometime my M^ris the sum of twenty pounds &c. To Anne the wife of William Hughes, Elizabeth Turner, the daughter, and Elizabeth Turner, the wife, of James Turner citizen & haberdasher of London. To the poor of all Hallows Barking London where I am now inhabiting. Item I do bequeath to Mr John Ellatson & his wife for a remembrance a piece of gold of five shillings & six pence. And likewise to Mr William Bygate & his now wife a like piece of gold. And to Mr William Turner & wife another piece of gold. To Sarah the wife of Thomas Skinner ten shillings. The residue to James Turner whom I hereby make ordain & constitute my full & sole executor.

122, Vol. 23, Commissary Court of London.

ANN PALMER of London widow, 30 January 1621 proved 31 December 1624. My body to be buried in the parish church of St. Olaves in South-wark in the county of Surrey, where now I am a parishioner, as near the place where my late deceased husband was buried as conveniently may be. I give & bequeath to my son Michael Palmer all such debts duties sum & sums of moneys as are and shall be due & owing unto me at the time of my decease by Jacob Manninge Percival Manninge or either of them or by any other persons by or for them or either of them, all which debts do amount unto the sum of three score and five pounds and twelve shillings or thereabouts principal debt besides all the interest long due, the which money he caused me to lend. Item I give to John Palmer son of my son Michael Palmer three hundred pounds of lawful English money besides I have given to his master the sum of thirty pounds of like money, and unto Andrew Palmer one other son of my said son Michael Palmer twenty pounds &c. and unto Mary Palmer daughter of my said son Michael Palmer one hundred & fifty pounds of like money, and unto Thomas Palmer one other son of my said son Michael twenty pounds &c. & unto Elizabeth Palmer one other daugh-ter of my said son Michael Palmer twenty pounds of like money. To my son William fifty pounds besides I have heretofore given him two hundred pounds and one hundred & fifty pounds before hand, which sums were intended to have been given him for a legacy ; of both which sums I do discharge him, the which may appear partly by his bond of three hundred pounds, dated 19 July 14 James &c. and partly by other writings, and I give him his plate remaining in my hands as a pledge for twenty pounds more, which twenty pounds I forgive unto him also. To John Palmer, son of my said son Michael (*sic*) two hundred pounds, besides I have given with him to his master the sum of forty pounds. To the said John Palmer, son of my said son William, the lease of my now dwelling house situate upon London Bridge, &c. &c., provided that the said William Palmer, his father, shall, from and after the end of two months next after my decease, until the said John Palmer his son shall accomplish his full age of four & twenty years, have hold & enjoy my said dwelling house, given unto his said son, paying & discharging the rent to be due for the whole to the Bridgehouse and one pepper corn yearly at the Feast of the Birth of our Lord God unto his said son if he lawfully demand the same. Reference made to the will of John Palmer, the late husband of the testatrix, and legacies to John and Mary Palmer, children of Michael, and John Palmer, son of William.

Item I give and bequeath unto my daughter Anne Faldo, late wife of Robert Faldo Esquire, deceased, two hundred and three pounds of lawful money of England and my chain of gold, and unto Thomes Faldo, her son, forty pounds, and unto Francis Faldo, her son, forty pounds, to be paid to my said daughter their mother, and by her to be paid to the said Thomas &-Francis when they shall accomplish their ages of two & twenty years. To Anne Faldo, her daughter, forty pounds, and to Jane Faldo, one other of her daughters, twenty pounds, and to Elizabeth Faldo, one other of her daughters, forty pounds, at their several ages of one and twenty years or at the days of their several marriages &c.

To my daughter Elizabeth Fawcett, wife of William Fawcett, gentleman, two hundred pounds, besides four hundred pounds to them formerly given &c. and my bracelets and all my rings of gold &c.

Reference to an Obligation wherein the said John Palmer deceased (former husband of the testatrix) stood bound with the said Michael Palmer (the son) to Mr Jacob Vercelin in the sum of twelve hundred pounds, with condition thereupon endorsed to leave Mary, then wife of the said Michael Palmer & daughter of the said Jacob, if she survive the said Michael, worth in goods & chattels the sum of one thousand pounds &c.

Item I give and bequeathe unto my cousin Anne Streate and to my cousin Ellen Yarwoode twenty shillings apiece to buy them rings to wear in remembrance of me. As touching blacks to be worn at my funeral I dispose them as hereafter followeth, that is to say, I give and bequeathe unto my son Michael Palmer & William Palmer and unto my son-in-law William Fawcett and unto John Fawcett, husband of Jane Faldoe, and to my loving friends & cousins Stephen Streate and Richard Yarwoode and John Grene and Ralphe Yardley, to every of them a cloak of brown blue cloth containing three yards and half quarter in every cloak at twenty shillings every yard or thereabouts. I give and bequeathe unto my cousin Robert Poole a cloak cloth of forty shillings price, to my cousin Richard Hinde a cloak cloth, about forty shillings price and unto his wife a piece of stuff about fifty shillings price to make her a gown. Similar bequests to " my " cousin Nicholas Cowper and his wife, and cousins Anne Streate and Ellen Yarwood, and to Elizabeth Blinkensopp and Margaret Kinge and to Christopher Blinkensopp and Nicholas Kinge their husbands. Other bequests.

And I do ordain and make the aforesaid Richard Yarwoode & Stephen Streete grocers, "my cosens," full executors &c. and I appoint my loving friends John Grene Esq. and "Richard (*sic*) Yardlye Pottecary my cosen" overseers of this my will and testament, and I give and bequeath unto the said John Grene and Ralphe Yardeley for their pains therein to be taken twenty nobles apiece &c.

In a codicil dated 17 June 1624 the testatrix refers to her daughter Anne Faldoe as since married to Robert Bromfield. 111, Byrde.

Inquisition taken at St Margaret's Hill, St Savior's Southwark in the County of Surrey, 11 March 22 James I. *post mortem* Ralph Yardley, lately citizen and merchant taylor of London Deceased, who was seized, before death, in fee of one capital messuage with the appurtenances called the Horn, lately divided into two several messuages, and situate lying and being in the parish of St Savior in the Borough of Southwark, in the County of Surrey, now or late in the several tenures or occupation of George Fletcher, fisherman, and Lawrence Lunde, or their assigns; and the said Ralph Yardley, being so seized, did on the 25th day of August 1603, 1 James, by his last will in writing, give and bequeath all and singular these premisses, in English words, as follows (then follows an extract from the will). And he died, so seized, on the 1st day of July 1618, and Ralph Yardley, named in the will, is son and next heir, and was aged at the time of the death of the said Ralph Yardley the father, twenty one years and more ; and the said capital messuage, into two separate messuages divided (as above) with the appurtenances, is held and, at the time of the death of the said Ralph Yardley, was held, of the Mayor, Commonalty and Citizens of the City of London in free soccage, as of their manor of Southwark, in Southwark aforesaid, by the annual rent of two shillings per annum, and is worth clear per annum, during a certain lease made by the said Ralph Yardley to a certain Richard Yerwood, citizen and grocer of London, bearing date 10 July 1603, and during the term of one hundred years, one peppercorn, and after the determination of the said lease will be worth clear and in all events and beyond reprise, three pounds per year.

Chancery Inq. p. m., Miscel., Part 4, No. 130.

[These Yardley items are interesting as showing the connection of Sir George Yardley, the governor of Virginia, to Richard Yerwood, one of John Harvard's step-fathers. I believe a little research would show that these Yardleys were of the Warwickshire family of that name. Richard Yerwood and his kinsman Stephen Street were of Cheshire, I have no doubt.—H. F. W.] .

RICHARD BOWMER of the parish of St Saviours in Southwark in the county of Surrey Innholder, 7 January 1593 proved 20 March 1593. My body to be buried in the parish church of St Saviours. To the poor people of the said parish forty shillings and to the poor of the parish of St George in Southwark twenty shillings. For a sermon made at the time of my burial for me (by Mr Ratliffe if it please him) ten shillings. To the three daughters of Agnes Lackenden widow, vizt Joane, Alice and Mary, twenty shillings apiece. To Stephen Lackendon ten shillings, and to my godson, his son, five shillings. To my godson Richard Smyth of Plumpstede in the county of Kent five shillings & to my godson William Cleere of Walworthe five shillings. To my goddaughter Ellyn Beech five shillings. To Thomas Vaugham five pounds and to Henry Vaugham, brother to the said Thomas, three pounds six shillings & eight pence. To Cisly Vaugham, their sister, four pounds. To Richard Emmerson, son of William Emmerson, five shillings.

To Richard Emmerson son of Humfrey Emmerson, five shillings. To Robert Rodes, youngest son now living of Roger Rodes of said parish of S[t] Saviours, goldsmith, three pounds six shillings and eight pence, and to Elizabeth Rodes mother to the said Robert five pounds. To my kinsman Peter Bowmer of Sevenocke in Kent, sadler, ten pounds. To Elizabeth Mitchell wife of Abraham Mitchell feltmaker dwelling at Horseydowne near Southwark, thirty shillings, and to my godson, her son, ten shillings. To Lambert Bowmer of the parish of S[t] Ollifes twenty pounds, and to Robert Bowmer, his son, twenty pounds, also to the two daughters of the said Lambert now living five pounds apiece. To Henry Yonge twenty shillings, to John Yonge twenty shillings, to Gregory Francklyn twenty shillings, to Abraham Allyn twenty shillings, and to every one of their wives twenty shillings apiece to make every of them a ring of gold withall. To Richard Cuckowe ten shillings and to Peter Holmes scrivener ten shillings (for rings) and to Isaac Allen twenty shillings.

"Allso my full intente will and mynde ys : and I doe herebye giue and graunte the lease of my nowe dwellinge house called the queens heade scituate in the sayd parrishe of St. Saviors wythall my Intereste and tytle therein after my decease unto Rose my wife duringe all the yeares therein to come. Provided allwayes and my will and mynde is that the sayd Rose my wife shall haue one years respitte after my decease to pay and dischardge my legacyes herein bequeathed, and therefore I doe appoynte hereby that shee the sayd Rose shall wythin one month nexte after my decease become bounde in good and sufficyente bonde in lawe unto my ouerseers here after nominated in the some of two hundred poundes of lawfull money of Inglande that shee the sayd Rose or her assignes shall well and truly performe fulfill and keepe the tenor of this my will : and pay and discharge : all legacyes and other duetyes by me hereby given and appoynted accordinge to the tennor and true meaninge of this my last will and Testamente."

To the Society of the Vestry of St. Saviors thirteen shillings & four pence. The residue to Rose my well beloved wife whom I make & ordain my full & sole executrix. Thomas Jackson, merchant Tailor, & Miles Wilkinson, Baker, to be overseers. 23, Dixey.

ROSE BOOMER of the parish of Saint " Savyoure " in Southwark in the County of Surrey, widow, 29 March 1595, proved 9 August 1595. My body to be buried in the parish church of S[t] Saviour's where I am a parishioner. To the preacher that shall make a sermon at my funeral ten shillings. To the poor people of the said parish forty shillings, to be distributed amongst them at the discretion of my Executor & the Collectors for the poor there for the time being. To the poor people of the parish of Bossham in the County of Sussex, where I was born, the sum of forty shillings, whereof I will that ten shillings shall be paid to Alice Reade, the widow of Richard Reede (if she be then living) And if she be then deceased then the same ten shillings to be paid to Richard Chapman. To the poor people of S[t] John's house in the city of Winchester forty shillings. To Richard Braxton, son of Cornelius Braxton, the sum of six pounds thirteen shillings and four pence, which I will shall remain in the hands of such person as shall keep him towards his education until he shall be bound apprentice and then delivered over to use for the best profit of the same Richard and the same, with the interest, to be paid him at the expiration of his apprenticeship. And if he happen to decease before the said sum shall come unto his hands then I will to his half brother Edmond Braxton

ten shillings & to his sister ten shillings, and the residue to his other two
whole brethren both by father and mother, equally. To Richard Mapcrofte
six pounds thirteen shillings & four pence, or if he dies to his children (in
hands of his wife). To Matthew Barnard the younger, dwelling in Yorkshire three pounds. To Matthew Barnard the elder ten shillings. To
William Hildrop a piece of gold of ten shillings, for a remembrance. And
a similar bequest to his brother Barnabie & his brother Richard and to
John Hildrop and their sister ——, also to Johane Hoskyns, widow, and
to her sister the daughter of Edward Hildroppe, and to William Braxton
and —— Hardam of Chichester, son of Margery Braxton, and to Richard
Wallys of Winchester, to Margaret Bathe, to John Homeade's wife of Winchester and to Richard Homeade her son, to Mrs Bird, to Mistress Denham,
to Mr Thomas Thorney, of Portsmouth, to John Androwes, to Robert
Boomer, to Thomas Vaughan, to his sister Cicely, to Robert Roades, & his
brother Henry Clarke, and to my servant that shall attend upon me at the
time of my decease, ten shillings. To Johane Allen, my daughter, fifty
pounds (and certain household stuff). To Isaacke Allen, her son, & to
Rosanna Allen the sum of twentie five pounds each. To my daughter
Alice Francklin (certain household stuff).

"Item I will and bequeathe unto Gregorye ffrancklyn my sonne in lawe
and the sayed Alice his wife (yf she the same Alice shalbe living at the
tyme of my decease) all my Righte title and interest of and in so muche
and suche partes and parcells of the mesuage or Inne called the Quenes
hed in the parishe of Sainct Savyoure in Sowthwarke aforesayed as I lately
demised by Indenture of Lease unto one Oliuer Bowker and of in and to the
gatehouse of the sayed Jnne nowe in the occupaĉon of Bryan Pattenson:
The Interest of which premisses I haue and hould by vertue of a Lease
heretofore made and graunted by one John Bland unto Richard Boomer my
late husband deceased and me the said Rose for diuers yeres yet to haue con-
tynewance. Except allwayes and my meaning ys that the sayed Devise by
me as aforesayed made shall not extend to certeyne garden plottes lying on
the East syde of the Dytche or Common Sewer extending and passing by the
Tenter yard and the garden behinde the sayed mesuage. Prouided allwayes
that yf the sayed Gregory and Alice shall not permitt and suffer Abraham
Allen and Jone his wife Isaacke Allen and Rosanna Allen and theire
assignes peaceablye and quietly to hould and enioye the sayed excepted garden plottes according to the tenure of suche graunte and assuraunce as I
haue lately made unto them That then and from thencefourthe the Devise
made to the sayed Gregorye and Alice as aforesayed shall cease and be
utterlie frustrate and voyde (any thinge before expressed to ye Contrary
notwithstandinge)."

To my daughter Anne Younge the lease of my now dwelling house and of
certain grounds at Wallworth and one hundred pounds (and certain household stuff). To my son in law John Younge and Anne his wife towards
the buying of their blacks for my funeral four pounds. The same to
Gregory Franckling & Alice his wife & to Abraham Allen & Johane
his wife. Bequests to others. John Younge to be executor and Thomas
Jackson & Myles Wilkenson supervisors.   53, Scott.

GREGORY FRANCKLIN of the parish of St Savior in Southwark in the
County of Surrey, citizen & sadler of London, 11 September 1624, proved
22 September 1624. My body to be buried within the church of the
parish of St Savior, at the discretion of Katherine my wife & sole executrix.

To the poor of the said parish forty shillings. To the Wardens of the Company of Sadlers in London four pounds to make them a supper withall.
" Itm̃ whereas I the said Gregory ffrancklin by my deede indented bearing date the Second day of ffebruary in the Thirteenth yeare of the Kings Ma^{ts} Raigne aforesaid of England ffraunce and Ireland, And of Scotland the Nyne and ffortieth (ffor the Consideracõns in the said deede expressed) did graunte enfeoff and confirme unto Gilbert Kinder Cittizen and Mercer of London All that Capitall Messuage or Inne called or knowne by the name of the Queenes head Scituat and being in the p̃ish of St Savio^r in the Borrough of Southwark in the County of Surr. and one garden to the same belonging To certen severall uses in the said deede expressed As by the same more plainly may appeare, I the said Gregory ffrancklin doe hereby publish and declare that the only cause and consideracõn wch moved me to Seale unto the said deede was for that at the tyme of the making and sealing thereof I was a widdower and a sole p̃son, not having any yssue of my body then living nor then intending to marrye. Nevertheles wth a Res^{r}uacõn unto myselfe in case I did marrye and had yssue, That not wthstanding the saide deede, or any estate thereupon executed, the power should remaine in me to giue and dispose of the said Inne and p^{r}imsses at my owne will and pleasure, In such manner as I should thinck fitting. And therefore for significacõn of my will intent and meaning concerning the same, And forasmuch as it hath pleased God that I have marryed the said Katherine my nowe wiffe by whome I have yssue Gregory ffrancklin my sonne and heir who is very young and of tender yeares, unto whome I have but small meanes to conferre and settle upon him both for his educacõn and bringing upp and otherwise wch wth care I would willingly provide for after my decease, And not minding or inteṅding that my said sonne should be disinherited or deprived of his lawfull right of and to the said Messuage or Inne doe hereby renounce and frustrate the said deede and all thestate thereupon had Togeather wth the severall uses and limitacõns therein expressed, And doe declare the same to be of noe force or vallidity at all. And doe hereby giue deuise and bequeath the said Messuage or Inne and garden wth thapp^{r}tenñces to the said Gregory ffrancklin my sonne and the heires of his body lawfully to be begotten, And for default of such yssue unto Gilbert Kinder and Margarett his wife and unto theire heires for ever."
Reference made to a deed indented dated the last day of August 1616 for the jointure of the said Katherine (if she should happen to survive), conveying certain tenements in the parish of St Savior in Southwark & in the parish of St Sepulchre without Newgate London and confirmation of that deed. Also to the said Katherine the moyty or one half part of the Rents Issues and Profits, when and at such time as the same shall grow due and payable of all and singular those gardens or garden plots with the Alley way or passage to the same leading and used with all the appurtenances thereunto belonging lying and being on the backside of the Messuage or Inne commonly called &c. the Queen's Head &c. now in the tenure or occupation of Isaac Allen Gen^t or his assigns. And the other moiety or half part of the Rents &c. of the same gardens and premisses I give, will and bequeath to the said Gregory Francklin, my son, at such time as he shall accomplish his full age of one & twenty years. And after the decease of the said Katherine, my wife, I give will & bequeath all the said premisses unto the said Gregory my son & the heirs of his body lawfully begotten. If my son shall happen to depart this transitory life before his said age &c. (having no issue of his body living) then the said Katherine, my wife, shall

freely have, hold, possess & enjoy all & singular the same gardens & premisses &c. for & during her natural life, and from & after her decease then to the Wardens or keepers & Commonalty of the mystery or Art of Sadlers of the City of London & to their Successors forever the moiety or half part of the said gardens &c., And the other moiety &c. to the Governors of the Free School of the Parish of St Saviour in Southwark, aforesaid, and to their successors forever, to this use, intent and purpose only (that is to say) for & towards the maintaining & bringing up of some one child or youth which shall from time to time forever hereafter be born within the said parish. And I hereby will that such one always may be first taught learned and instructed sufficiently in the said free school and afterwards by them the said Governors and their successors for the time being put forth and brought up in learning, during the term of eight years, so that from time to time such one scholar may attain to the degree of M^r in Arts in one of the Universities of Oxon or Cambridge if such one scholar shall so long continue both scholar and student in either of the same, as by their discretions shall be thought most meet and convenient, whereunto I refer myself.

To the said Katherine, my wife, the lease which I hold of & from the Wardens &c. of the said mystery or Art of Sadlers &c. of all that Messuage or Tenement with the appurtenances &c. called or known by the sign of the Three Kings set, lying and being upon Snowe Hill near the Conduit there, within the parish of St Sepulchre without Newgate London, now in the Tenure or occupation of Josias Curtis, tailor &c. If she die before the expiration of the term granted by the same lease, then to the said Gregory Francklin, my son, for the time &c. unexpired. To my said son Gregory my gold seal ring (and other personal property).

Item my special will & meaning is that the said Katherine my wife shall within the space of six months next after my decease well & truly satisfy & pay or cause to be paid unto Ann Parkhurst & Katherine Parkhurst, daughters of Edward Parkhurst, late citizen & merchant tailor of London deceased & of the said Katherine my wife, the sum of one hundred pounds of lawful money of England for the redeeming of the said Gardens or garden plots, and two tenements with the appurtenances thereupon erected, which I mortgaged and stand engaged to pay the said sum by my deed as thereby appeareth.

A bequest is made to John Parvish, "my old servant," and the residue is bequeathed to wife Katherine who is made sole Executrix, and friends Richard Yerwood grocer and Robert Bucke glover are appointed supervisors, and to either of them, for their pains, a ring of gold of twenty shillings apiece is bequeathed.

Witnesses Richard Harrison, Richard Haukins, Antho: Rogers Scr., John Dodsworth, servant to Edr̃d Jackson Scr.

Probate granted to the widow 22 September 1624.

Decimo quinto die mensis Junii An° Dñi 1637° Emanavit Comissio Henrico Creswell p̄oe St Bothi extra Aldersgate London aurifabr̃ ad administrand boua iura et crēd dc̄i Gregorii ffrancklyn def iuxta tenorem et effc̄um testī prēd p̄ Catherīnam Creswell als̃ ffrancklyn als̃ Blackleech nup̄ relcam et execūt testī dc̄i Gregorii (iam etiam demort.) non plene adm̃istrat de bene etc iurat.   73, Byrde.

ANNE WHITMORE of Lambehith in the county of Surrey, widow, 9 August 1624, proved 12 October 1624. I give all my worldly goods, money, jewells, plate and household stuff whatsoever unto my grandchild

Martha Smith and to the heirs of her body, lawfully begotten, provided always that if the said Martha shall happen to die and depart this life without such issue of her body lawfully begotten then my will is and I bequeath unto my grandchildren Gregory Francklin, Anne Parkhurst & Katherine Parkhurst, the son and daughters of Katherine Francklin, wife of Gregory Francklin, to every of them the sum of ten pounds; also I give and bequeath unto Richard Smith and Thomas Bradbridge, the sons of Anne Bradbridge. my daughter, of Lambehith aforesaid, widow, the like sum of ten pounds and also to the said Anne Bradbridge the sum of forty pounds. And I nominate appoint and ordain the said Martha Smith to be sole executrix &c. And my will is that she shall within six months after my decease give unto her Aunt Katherin Francklin the sum of three pounds sterling to buy her a cup or bowl, in token of my love unto her, and I do appoint my loving friend Mr William Childe to be overseer &c.   118, Byrde.

GREGORY FRANCKLYN 19 February 1635. I do bestow all the estate that is or shall be mine upon my sister Ann, conditionally that she shall help, succor & relieve my mother in all her wants and necessities so far as she is able. And to my sister Kate I give a pair of sheets, a dozen of napkins and a towel, and to my cousin Mrs Martha Marshall a pair andirons, and to Thomas Day a piece of gold of five shillings.

Administration was granted 1 March 1635 to Anne Parkhurst natural & lawful sister of the said Gregory Francklyn of the Parish of St Buttolph without Aldersgate London deceased.   32, Pile.

RICHARD QUINEY, citizen & grocer of London, 16 August 1655, proved 3 January 1656. To be buried at Stratford upon Avon in the county of Warwick, where my father & other my ancestors are interred. One half of my personal estate (having no wife) I bequeath among my five children Richard, Adrian, Thomas, William and Sarah Quiney. To my cousin Dr. Richard Bayley and Master William Wheate forty shillings apiece. To my cousin master George Naoh forty shillings, to buy rings. To my brother master John Sadler and my sons in law Edward Pilkington and Thomas Booth and my cousin Richard Chaundler five pounds apiece. To my brother in law William Smith five pounds. To my cousin William Watts and his wife forty shillings apiece. To cousin William Smith & his wife forty shillings apiece to buy rings. To cousins John & Robert Smith ten pounds apiece. To my daughter Ellen Pilkington fifty pounds and to her husband the said Edward Pilkington, ten pounds to buy mourning, to my daughter Elizabeth Cooper ten pounds, to my brother in law master John Sadler and my sister Elizabeth his wife ten pounds, to my son in law Thomas Booth & daughter Ann his wife ten pounds, to son John Lilburne & my daughter Isabell his wife ten pounds, for mourning. To my cousin Charles Watts twenty five pounds when he shall have faithfully served out the term of eight years of his apprenticeship. Ten pounds to be distributed among the children of my cousin Ellen Parker equally. To my cousins John Sadler & William Baker forty shillings apiece, to cousin Margaret Jones forty shillings to buy rings. To my grand child Elizabeth Pilkington ten pounds at one & twenty years of age or marriage, to Gr. children William & Richard Cooper ten pounds apiece at their several ages of one & twenty years. To grand child Richard Booth ten pounds at one & twenty. To such child as my daughter Lilburne now goeth withall ten pounds at one & twenty. To the worshipful

Company of Grocers of London whereof I am a member a piece of plate of the value of ten pounds sterling. To master Watson minister of the Word of God in St Stephen's in Walbrooke, London, five pounds, to master Beane, minister, &c. at Stratford upon Avon forty shillings. To the poor of Stratford upon Avon ten pounds. To my son Thomas my part, share & interest in the Ship called the Seven Sisters, Abraham Reade commander, to be managed for his use until he shall have served out the remainder of his apprenticeship; also several leases estates & interests which I have in the Tyth of Drayton & a certain house at Stratford upon Avon which I hold by lease of the chamber of Stratford upon Avon.

The residue of all & singular my goods chattells, &c. I give & bequeath to John Sadler, Edward Pilkington, Thomas Booth, William Smith & Richard Chaundler, in trust, &c. for my four younger children, Adrian, Thomas, William & Sarah Quiney. To my brother Thomas Quiney, for natural life, an annuity of twelve pounds out of my messuages & lands at Shottery, with the appurtenances, in the County of Warwick; and at the decease of the said Thomas my executors to take out of the said lands the sum of five pounds to bear & defray the charges of my said brother's funeral. (Other lands, &c. bequeathed and devised to his sons.)

Also I give & devise all my land in Virginia in the parts beyond the seas together with all the stock of cattle, servants & other things thereunto belonging unto my said son Thomas Quiney & to his heirs & assigns forever. All my land in Ireland to son Richard. To the town of Stratford upon Avon my two small tenements near the meer side in Stratford towards the maintenance of the Bridge, &c. & for the poor alms men. Son Richard to be executor. If he shall not at the time of my decease be resident in England then my sons in law Edward Pilkington & Thomas Booth to be executors in trust for him in his absence.   Ruthen, 6.

[The testator, it seems, was a brother-in-law of Rev. John Sadler, but whether this Rev. John Sadler was related to the father-in-law of Rev. John Harvard we have no means of ascertaining. Shakspeare's daughter Judith married, Feb. 10, 1615-16, Thomas Quiney, a wine merchant residing in the High Street of Stratford-upon-Avon (See Outlines of the Life of Shakspeare by J. O. Halliwell Phillips, F.R.S., F.S.A., 2d ed. 1882, p. 182). There was a Richard Quiney, son of Adrian Quiney, who about 1598 resided at the Bell in Carter Lane, London (Ibid. p. 579. See also pp. 575-82).—EDITOR.

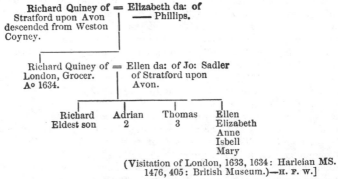

(Visitation of London, 1633, 1634: Harleian MS. 1476, 405: British Museum.)—H. F. W.]

BENJAMIN KEYSAR the elder of Westham in the County of Essex, tanner, 10 April 1650, proved 3 May 1650, by William Salter executor. Whereas George Keysar my grandfather, late of Layton Buzzard in the

County of Bedford, tanner, deceased, did by his last will & testament give me twenty two pounds four shillings & five pence at my age of one and twenty years as my third part of one hundred marks which my grandfather gave unto the three sons of Benjamin Keysar, &c. and it now remains in the hands of Edmond Keysar my uncle, of London, ironmonger, being the executor of my said grandfather, I give and bequeath ten pounds thereof to my loving brother Gabriel Keysar and ten pounds to my sister Mary Keysar at their several ages of one and twenty years. A bequest to friend William Salter yeoman in the County of Essex, who is to be executor.

Pembroke, 74.

[George Keysar was the name of the tanner who first settled in Lynn, Massachusetts, and carried on his business alongside of Strawberry brook, to the westward of the Water Mill, which itself stood just west of the road now known as Federal Street. He bought the land 19th 1mo. 1649, of Mr. Samuel Bennett who then held the mill property. In October, 1654, he seems to have settled in Salem, buying of Major William Hathorne a lot of land near the South River, as it was often called, or the Harbor, as now termed, at the foot of Burying Point Lane, now Liberty Street. He still retained his estate in Lynn, which passed to Benjamin Keysar.—H. F. W.]

MARGERY COX of Debtford in the County of Kent, widow, 30 May 1656 proved 11 June 1656. To my well beloved brother Giles Webb[1] living now in Virginia, twenty pounds. To my brother William Lews of Titbury in the County of Gloucester ten pounds. To my sister Elizabeth Waight wife of Giles Waight, of Titbury aforesaid, twenty pounds. To William Stone and John Rooper, both of Debtford, five pounds apiece, they being overseers. To the poor of the parish of Debtford twenty shillings. Mary and Elizabeth Waight, daughters of the abovesaid Giles Waight, to be executrixes.

The witnesses were William Huttun, Joane Phillips (by mark) & George Martin.

Berkley, 224.

[1 Captain Giles Webb commanded a company of rangers in Henrico County, Va., in 1692. A Captain Giles Webb died in Henrico County in June, 1713. The last married the widow of Henry Randolph, Jr., Clerk of Henrico County. In his will he mentions a brother Thomas, and his step-son Henry Randolph. The name Webb has been prominent in Virginia. John Webb, "Mariner," was granted 50 acres of land in Accomac County, Dec. 13, 1627. Va. Land Records, No. 1, p. 81. Stephen Webb was a Burgess from James City in October, 1644. George Webb was elected, Dec. 17, 1776, by the Virginia Assembly, treasurer of Virginia, to succeed Robert Carter Nicholas, resigned.—R. A. BROCK, Richmond, Va.]

MARK PIERCE, of London, in his will & enumeration of assets dated 10 February 1654 (proved in 1656) mentions forty pounds in the hands of Master Robert Newman,[1] citizen & vintner of London, and ten pounds in money in the hands of Elizabeth Higginson, widow, which I lent to her deceased husband, Theophilus Higginson[2] in New England and ought to have been paid presently at our arrival in England.

Berkley, 233.

[Mark Pierce was a resident of New Haven as early as 1639 and as late as 1646 (See New Haven Colony Records, vol. i. pp. 18 and 302). Savage, in his Geneal. Dict., vol. iii. p. 430, says he was of Cambridge 1642, but he is not mentioned in Paige's History of Cambridge.

1 Probably the Robert Newman who was one of the settlers of New Haven, Ct., and one of the seven pillars of the church there. He resided there as late as 1649 (See New Haven Colony Records, vol. i. pp. 9, 20, 492). Savage, in his Gen. Dict. vol. iii. p. 275, says he returned to England. He thinks he was the Robert Newman whose name is among the passengers in the Mary and John, 1634, printed in the REGISTER, vol. ix. pp. 265-8.—EDITOR.]

2 Theophilus Higginson, son of Rev. Francis Higginson. See Hist. Coll. Essex Institute, vol. v. p. 34.—HENRY WHEATLAND.
Savage (Gen. Dict. ii. 414) says that Theophilus Higginson, of New Haven, died about 1657, aged 37. This will shows that he was dead three years earlier.—ED.]

THOMAS DUMER of Chicknell within the parish of North Stonham in the County of Southampton, gentleman, 12 April 1650, proved 9 November 1650 by Thomas, John, Robert and Stephen Dummer, his executors. To be buried at discretion of the executors. To the poor in North Stonham and South Stonham and Bishopstoake twenty six shillings and eightpence to every of said parishes. To my wife ten pounds within one month after my decease. To four of my daughters, viz. Susan, Hester, Jane and Mary Dumer, two hundred pounds to either of them at their several days of marriage. &c. To my eldest daughter Joane Nelson, widow, twenty shillings within one year, &c. To my two grand children namely Samuel and Mercie Nelson, son and daughter of my daughter Joane Nelson, fifty pounds apiece at ages of twenty one years. To my daughter Margaret Clements, being my second daughter and now in New England, twenty five pounds, and to her child she now hath twenty five pounds within six months, &c. To my only son Thomas Dumer and his heirs forever all my freehold land of inheritance in North Stonham or elsewhere within the kingdom of England, to have and enjoy at the age of twenty one years. If he die without lawful issue then to my said four first named daughters, being now virgins and unmarried, &c. My beloved kinsmen John Dumer of Townhill, Stephen Penton of Winton, Robert Dumer of Durley, Thomas Dumer of Fairethorne and Stephen Dumer of Bishopstoake to be executors in trust, &c.

The witnesses were Stephen Dumer, Thomas Baylie and Ann Baldry (by mark).   Pembroke, 174.

[For an account of Thomas Dummer, the testator, and his children, see Col. Chester's Dummer genealogy in the REGISTER, vol. xxxv. pp. 269-71. His eldest daughter Joane married Thomas Nelson of Rowley, whose will is printed in the REGISTER, vol. iii. pp. 267-8. His second daughter Margaret married Dec. 25, 1644, Job Clement, of Haverhill, Mass., afterwards of Dover, N. H.

If the testator was the Mr. Thomas Dummer, who was one of the first settlers of Salisbury, Mass. (REGISTER, vol. iii. p. 55; Coffin's Newbury, p. 301), he must have returned early to England.—EDITOR.

In an account against the estate of Mr. Thomas Nelson, deceased, presented to the court held at Salem by Mr. Richard Dummer, the last Tuesday in June, 1656, is a claim for " charges in England, from South-hampton to Yorke & Hull which is 400 miles (18 dayes) [wit]h the hire of three horses & 2 men & Expences yᵘpon : to Endeauour to gaine the [mon]ey yʳ due :"

Among the papers also in this case is a copy of a release made the first of July, 1654, by the widow Jone Nelson, who calls herself " of Wecom or Duphy or Dulye neare Southampton in old England." In 1650 she calls herself of North-stoneham.

Another of these papers is a copy of a bond of Thomas Nelson, dated 15th 12th month, 1641, in which reference is made to the " Contract of marriage betwixt Thomas Nelson of Rowley in New-England gent: & Joane Dumer Spinst: the dafter of Thomas Dummer of Badgely in ould England gent:."

Another is interesting as containing the word " nayther," thus perhaps showing what the sound of this word was as then pronounced.—County Court, Ipswich, March, 1657. Mr. Richard Dummer v. Mʳ Phillip Nelson. Review.—H. F. W.]

JEREMY DUMMER late agent of His Majesty's Provinces of Massachusetts and Connecticut, in New England, and now resident at Plaistow in Essex, in the Kingdom of Great Britain, 7 June 1738, proved 1 June 1739. In the chief place & before all things I do on this solemn occasion commend my soul to Almighty God and render him Infinite thanks for the many Blessings with which he has been pleased to fill up the short scene of my life, firmly confiding in the Benignity of his Nature that he wont afflict me in another World for some follys I have committed in this, in common with the rest of mankind, but rather that he will graciously consider the frail & weak frame which he gave me and remember that I was but Dust.

As to the Interment of my body I should think it a trifle not worth mentioning but only to desire my executors kindly to invite to my funeral all such New England gentlemen as shall be in London at the time of my decease and to give each of them a twenty shilling ring without any name upon it but only this motto which I think affords a good deal of reflection —*Nulla retro via.*

As to the small fortune I have acquired I bequeath, &c. as follows—To Mrs Kent where I now live and to Mrs Mary Stephenson lodging in the same house one hundred pounds each and a ring. To my worthy countryman Henry Newman Esq. twenty pounds. To Miss Hook Jacob twenty pounds. To my good kinswoman Mrs Lloyd of New England, formerly Pemberton and Campbell, one hundred pounds. To Dudley Woodbridge[1] of Barbadoes fifty pounds for the pleasure I had in his company when in England. To Commissioner Pearse of the Navy his eldest son by his former wife twenty pounds. Item, I give a fifty pound New England bill to Mrs Burr[2] of New England, and, in case of her death, to her children, as an acknowledgment of a civility I received from her husband at the college, I mean that Burr who was schoolmaster at Charlestown. To Col^o & Capt. Mandell, Swedes in London, ten guineas each. To Stephen Whateley of Gray's Inn, gentleman, my little Library, and to my brother Dummer of Newbury twenty pounds New England money to distribute among the poor Indian Squaws that may come a begging at his door in the country. I leave to my sister Dummer her husband's picture set in gold which will be found in my Scrutore. The Bulk of my estate I make no disposition of, being content it should go according to the Act of Assembly in New-England for distributing the estates of Intestates. And lastly I desire that Francis Wilks Esq. and Mr Samuel Storke will be my executors and accept of me a small specific legacy, vizt Mr Wilks the Diamond ring which I usually wear and Mr. Storke my gold watch with the appurtenances. —Made & published in presence of Benj^a Rutland, Ann Silver.

A Codicil, dated 8 April 1739, refers to a deed bearing date 20 March last between the testator of the first part, Dorothy Keant of the second part and Francis Wilks of the third part for the conveying of a house in Clarges street to the said Mrs Kent "and which I have ordered to be registered" according to Act of Parliament in consideration of the trouble I have given her during a long fit of sickness. I do hereby revoke the legacy I have given her of one hundred pounds in the foregoing will.

Witnesses F. Hutton, James Howgill.

Plaistow 15 November 1738. I desire my executors will give my scrutore to Mrs Kent, all my wearing apparell to Mrs Mary and to my coachman a guinea, and the same to each of the maids. JER. DUMMER.

30 May 1739 appeared Francis Hutton of Gray's Inn in the County of Middlesex, gentleman, and James Howgill of the Middle Temple, London, gentleman, and deposed, &c. Henchman, 126.

[Jeremy Dummer, the testator, was a brother of Lieut. Governor William Dummer of the Province of Massachusetts. He was the author of " Defence of the New England Charters " (1721). He died in England May 19, 1739, and was buried at West Ham in Essex. See Col. Chester's account of him and his ancestry in the REGISTER, vol. xxxv. pp. 268-9. See also Massachusetts Historical Collections, 5th S. vol. v. pp. xxi.-ii.

¹ Rev. Dudley Woodbridge, probably the eldest son of the Hon. Dudley Wood-bridge, of Barbadoes, was rector of St. Philip's, Barbadoes. He died in 1747. See "Woodbridge Record," compiled by Donald G. Mitchell, from the papers of his brother Louis Mitchell, p. 37 ; REGISTER, vol. xxxii. p. 294.

² Mrs. Elizabeth Burr, widow of Samuel Burr, master of the Grammar School at Charlestown, Mass., a preparatory school for Harvard College, which is said to have had a reputation in the New England colonies similar to that of Eton in England. He was born at Fairfield, Ct., April 2, 1679, and died there while on a visit, Aug. 7, 1719. See Todd's "Burr Family" (1878), pp. 148 and 431.—EDITOR.]

NATHANIEL HULTON citizen and Salter of London, 20 July 1692, proved 13 March 1693, with three codicils, the last of which was dated 1 January 1693. To son in law James Greene and his sons James, Richard and John, daughters Margery & Elizabeth Greene ; to Joseph Scriven ; to John Greene, brother of James Greene the elder ; to the poor of Newington Green where I live. Wife Elizabeth Hulton ; William Hulton, son of my late kinsman William Hulton deceased; Joseph Hulton son of my late kinsman Adam Hulton deceased ; the widow and daughter of the said Adam Hulton ; kinsman Samuel Haward ; Thomas Crompton, son of my late kinsman Adam Crompton deceased & also his second & third sons & two daughters ; sister Hulton, widow ; the daughter of kinsman George Cromp-ton ; kinsman John Hill ; Nathaniel Hill son of Edmund Hill deceased ; kinswoman Elizabeth Hill ; my sister Elizabeth Dickins, widow of John Dickins deceased ; kinswoman Ann Prinlott and her two sons now living and her daughter ; Mrs Mary Pickford & her eldest son & her other six children now living ; kinsman Nathaniel Hulton's wife & daughter; my son in law Thomas Horrocks ; my daughter in law Jane Perry, &c. &c. My body to be interred at Bolton in Lancashire near my father & mother.

In the last codicil he makes a bequest of one hundred pounds to Mr Encrease Mather, minister of the Gospel in New England for the use of the College there of which he is President.   Box 54.

MARY BUTCHER, daughter of Francis Butcher, late of Staplehurst in the County of Kent, Clothier, proved 6 June 1651. Mention made of uncle John Hide, of Sounteine in the County of Sussex, and his daughters Jude & Margaret Hide, brother Thomas Butcher, mother Ann Lambe, father Thomas Lambe, brothers Thomas, James, Christopher & John Lambe (all under 21), uncle Thomas Watersfield & Dorothy his wife, uncle Ninian Butcher & Francis his wife and his two daughters, Mary and Re-becca, Aunt Elizabeth Batherst, widow, cousin Mildred Stace, wife of Cap-tain Stace, Hanna Butcher, wife of Capt. Butcher, and her daughters Eliz-abeth and Hanna Butcher, Elizabeth Holden, wife of James Holden of Crambroke, Cousin Elizabeth Holden daughter of Richard Holden of Fe-vershame in Bedfordshire (sic), Mary & Dorothy Lambe daughters of Christopher Lambe late of Westrum and the widow Dupper. Father Tho-mas Lambe to be executor.   Grey, 109.

[See the will of Ninian Butcher, uncle of the testator, in the REGISTER, vol. xxxviii. p. 415 ; ante, p. 75.—EDITOR.]

ARTHUR SOMNER of Chittlehampton in the County of Devon, fuller, 25 May 1637, proved 10 October 1637. Son John, son Roger (under twenty one), daughter Ales Somner, godson John Somner, my brother John's three other children, my brother William Somner's two children, uncle John Tanner's children. Wife Mary to be executrix and brothers John Somner, William Somner & Lewes Smale to be overseers.

Goare, 129.

[Whether Arthur Somner was related or not to the New England family of Sumner I have no means of determining. William Sumner, of Dorchester, the stirps of that family, came from Bicester in Gloucestershire. See REGISTER, vol. ix. p. 300, vol. xxxvii. p. 237. The name Roger occurs in the Bicester family of Sumner.—ED.]

THOMAS WATERS of Herstmounseux, in the County of Sussex, yeoman, 13 May 1614, proved 11 December 1617. To be buried in the church yard of Herstmonseux aforesaid. To eldest son Andrew Waters fifty pounds within one year after my decease, and, after the decease of Winifrede my wife, six acres of marsh land in the Levell of Horsey & in the parish of Pevensey in the aforesaid county. To son Thomas Waters one parcel of land in the parish of Ashborneham in said county, called Blackland fields, containing five acres, more or less, and forty pounds in one year, &c I give unto my son Sampson Waters a lease of half an acre known by the name of Lusted's Croft, joining unto Bawley Lane, in the parish Herstmonseux aforesaid, and ten pounds in three years, &c. To Nicholas Waters my brother six pounds that he oweth unto me. To John Waters, my godson, twenty shillings and to the other of my brother's children ten shillings apiece in one year, &c. To Thomas Waters, my godson, son of Andrew Waters, ten pounds & to James, the son of Andrew Waters ten pounds, to be employed to their best advantage within two years after my decease. The residue to my wife Winifred whom I ordain and make sole executrix. Loving friends William Parker, gentleman, and Jerimy Grint, yeoman, of the said parish, to be overseers.

Wit: William Parker, Samuel Parker & Mathy Pinson.

Weldon, 124.

[See Savage. Sampson Waters of Boston.—H. F. W.

Lieut. Edward Waters was granted 100 acres of land in Elizabeth City, Va., "in tho precincts of Buck Roe," Oct. 28, 1628. *Va. Land Records*, No. 1, p. 93. William Waters, probably a son, was Burgess from Northampton County, 1654-60. His will is dated 1685 ; died soon after, leaving issue—1. William, Naval Officer for Accomac, 1713; Burgess for Northampton County, 1718 ; had son William, whose only child Mary married David Meade of Nannemond County, 2. Obedience ; 3. Thomas.—R. A. BROCK.]

JOHN KIRTLAND of Tickford in the parish of Newport Pagnell, county Bucks, gentleman, 12 December 1616, proved 1 August 1617. To son Nathaniel all that part of my dwelling house in Tickford wherein I now inhabit sometime called by the name of Emberton's,[1] adjoining to the tenement in tenure of William Coningham and to the house and ground of me the said John Kirtland, sometime Thomas Horton's. Legacies to Mary Kirtland my now wife, sons Francis and Joseph Kirtland, and daughters Abigail, Susanna & Mary Kirtland. To my eldest son John Kirtland the house or tenement sometime Thomas Horton's (next the above) and adjoining a tenement of heirs of William Barton deceased. Wife Mary and her five children (as above). To godson John Kirtland, son of my brother Philip Kirtland, xiiii^s iiii^d and to the rest of the children of the said Philip ii^s vi^d each, to be paid unto the said Philip for their use. To the children of my brother Francis Kirtland ii^s vi^d apiece. To Francis Foster, clerk, ten shillings. Wife Mary to be executrix, friends George Hull and John Horley, inhabitants of Newport Pagnell, to be overseers. Phylipp Kyrtland one of the witnesses. Weldon, 82.

[Probably the family of President Kirkland of Harvard College. A number of settlers of Lynn came from about Olney in Bucks. Sherrington, from which Philip Kirtland of Lynn is said to have come, is only about two miles from Newport Pagnell on the road to Olney.—H. F. W.

President Kirkland was a great-grandson of John Kirtland of Saybrook, Conn., said to be a son of Nathaniel Kirtland, an early settler of Lynn. Philip and John Kirtland were also early settlers of Lynn. (See Chapman's Kirtland Genealogy in the REGISTER, vol. xiv. pp. 241–5, and Lewis and Newhall's History of Lynn (1865), pp. 154–5.—EDITOR.

¹ Paganus de Emberton, of Tykford Priory, Bucks, 1187. Dugdale's Monastikon.—JAMES A. EMMERTON.]

JOHN DOWNING of S[t] Clement Danes in the County of Middlesex, skinner, 15 May 1623, proved 7 July 1623. To the poor of the said parish twenty shillings. To my daughter Katherine a ring with a flower de luce which I wear upon my finger. To my daughter Abigail twenty shillings. And moreover my will and meaning is that if my said daughter Abigail shall determine to go to Virginia that upon her going away my executors shall pay to and for use unto the Virginia Company the sum of six pounds towards her charges. To my grand child Sara Smith ten pounds, to be put out to the best advantage by my executors until the day and time of her marriage. To my grand child Katherine Smith and her sister Dorothy Smith twenty shillings apiece, to be paid them at their several marriages, or sooner, at the discretion of my executors. To my grand child Francis Smith forty shillings, at his accomplishment of the age of twenty and one years. To my grand child Sibell Smith twenty shillings, at her day of marriage, or sooner, &c. To my grand child John Smith five pounds towards the placing and putting him forth an apprentice; and my will is that until he shall be fit and capable for service my executors shall maintain him & keep him to school, to write and read. To my son Smith's daughter Mary ten shillings within three months after my decease. To the two sons of my son Drake, vid[lt] to John and Richard, twenty shillings between them, in three months, &c. To my sister Joyce Wilson a seal ring with a faucon in it, which I had of her, and twenty shillings in money, to be paid unto her within three months, &c. To my grand child Abraham Downing ten shillings. To my well beloved son Richard Downing the lease which I hold from and under the countess Dowager of Arundell by the houses now in the occupation of me the said John Downing, together with the shop, &c. of Jane Barkested widow, &c. &c. To my well beloved son Francis Downing twenty pounds over and besides his part of the remainder of my goods, which my will is he shall have within three months after my death. The residue shall be equally shared & divided between my said two sons Richard and Francis Downing ·and they two to be co-executors.

Wit: Elias Allin, George Courthopp, Thomas Dannett & John Browne, Scr.   Swann, 67.

JAMES RAND, citizen & apothecary of London, 20 June 1685. Legacies to son James and to son Ralph. I have advanced my daughter Mary in marriage. There is a debt owing to me from one William Baucks now or late resident at Virginia, in the parts beyond the seas. My daughter Grace Rand to be executrix. M[r] John Fisher and my son in law Christopher Gould to be overseers.

Wit: Leonard Bates, scr., Robert Burges and George Gittens his servant. In a codicil, dated 26 March 1686, he refers to his daughter Grace as very sick and appoints his daughter Mary Gould executrix in her stead, if she shall happen to die.

The will was proved 3 May 1686 by Mary Gould, wife of Christopher Gould.   Lloyd, 63.

THOMAS DOBSON, citizen and skinner of London, 13 September 1626, proved 30 May 1627, directs his body to be buried in the parish church of St. Michael Bassishawe, makes bequests to sundry people dwelling in Colman Street and to sundry ministers, among whom Mr. Davenport, minister at St Stevens in Colman Street. In a codicil of 11 November 1626 he revokes a bequest of ten pounds made in his Will to his sister Dobson, and bequeaths that sum to Thomas Davenport, son of his neighbor Mrs. Mary Davenport, widow, to be paid to the mother for the use of the said Thomas Davenport. In another codicil, of 13 March'1626, he changes this bequest to one of ten pounds to the widow Davenport and ten pounds to her son Thomas. Skinner, 46.

Inducco m̃ri Joh̃is Davenport cliĉi in artibus probati ad vicariam ecc̃liæ pochiæ S̃ci Steph̃ in Colman strete cits et archiñ p̃r vacañ per mortem nal̃em m̃ri Samuelis Jerman cliĉi ulti vicarii et incumbents ib̃m̃ etc em̃t sub sigillo etc quarto die novembris A° Dñ̃ 1624°.

Prob. & Admon. Act Book, Archdeac.
of London, 1611—1626, fol. 190.

Inducc̃o Johis Goodwyn cliĉi in Artibus mag̃ri ad vicariam p̃petuam ecc̃liæ p̃och s̃ci Stephañi Coleman streete cits et Archiñat London def p̃ liberam et spontaneam Resignac̃oem Joh̃is Davenport cliĉi ultimi vicarii et Incumbeñ pred̃ ad quam p̃ discretos viros Simonem Laurence Willm̃um Spurtlowe Augustinũ Garland Johēm Stone Henricum Wood Henricum Austin Ludovicu Roberts et Michaelem Warner pochianos dĉe p̃oe veros et indubitatos patronos p̃rntatus extitit.

Prob. & Admon. Act Book, Archdeac.
of London, 1626—1637, fol. 139.

[Rev. John Davenport was the fifth son of Henry and Winnifred (Barnabit) Davenport, of Coventry, co. Warwick, where he was born in 1597. On the 9th of April in that year he was baptized in the Church of the Holy Trinity, of which the Rev. Richard Eaton, father of Theophilus Eaton of New Haven, Ct., was rector. He was admitted to Merton College, Oxford University, in 1613, and after passing two years in that college he removed to Magdalen Hall, but the same year, Nov. 15, 1615, left the University and commenced preaching. On the 5th of October, 1624, he was almost unanimously elected vicar of St. Stephen's, Colman Street, London, to which living he was inducted Nov. 4, as the above record shows. On the death of Archbishop Abbot he left London, Aug. 5, 1633, for a hidden retreat in the country, and after waiting three months, finding the messengers of Laud, the new archbishop, were on his track, he crossed over to Holland, landing at Haarlem in November. He resigned the vicarage of St. Stephen's, and John Goodwin was admitted as his successor Dec. 18, 1633. In 1637 he came to New England, arriving at Boston June 26, 1637, with another minister and Mr. Eaton and Mr. Hopkins, merchants, as Winthrop informs us (Hist. of New England, vol. ii. p. 226, 2d ed. p. 272). It is possible that the other minister may have been John Harvard, who probably arrived about this time. It is true that Trumbull (Hist. of Connecticut, vol. i. p. 89) says that Rev. Samuel Eaton accompanied his brother, but it is hardly probable that Winthrop, who gives his brother's name, would omit his. Davenport was the first minister at New Haven, Ct., 1638–67, and was pastor of the First Church of Boston, Mass., 1667, to his death 1670. For further details in the life of Rev. John Davenport, see History and Genealogy of Davenport Family, by A. B. Davenport, 1851, and Supplement to do. 1876; Life and Writings of John Davenport, by F. B. Dexter, in New Haven Historical Society Papers, vol. ii. pp. 205–38; and REGISTER, vol. ix. p. 147. Mr. Waters has much other matter relative to the Davenports, including a will of an uncle of the Rev. John Davenport, who mentions him as at the University. This matter will appear in a future number.— EDITOR.]

JOHN GREENE, late of the parish of Petsoe in the County of Gloucester, Virginia, and now at present of the parish of St Butolph's without

Aldgate, mariner, now bound out to sea for a voyage unto Virginia in the good ship Thomas & Francis, Capt. Simmons Commander, 15 April 1685, proved 8 January 1693, by Anne Greene, relict and executrix. He appoints his wife Anne his attorney & the executrix of his will, and mentions six hundred acres in the parish of Petsoe, with certain dwelling houses, &c. given and bequeathed to him by his late father John Greene deceased, now in the tenure and possession of one Wm. Grimes, his undertenants or assigns. He gives and bequeaths unto every one of his relations or near kindred nominated or usually called by any name or names whatsoever, unto each one of them particularly twelve pence apiece, to be paid unto each one of them upon their several demands.

The witnesses were Edward Gibson, Thomas Forne and Thomas Eccleston.   Box (1694).

[Ralph Greene received grants of 50 and 300 acres of land on the north side of York River, July 18, 1650. *Va. Land Records*, No. 2, p. 265. He received subsequently grants aggregating 3500 acres. Oliver Greene was granted 120 acres in Gloucester County, July 24, 1633, No. 3, p. 16, and 450 acres March 30, 1657, No. 4, p. 122. Thomas Greene was granted 270 acres on Elizabeth River, June 11, 1652, No. 3, p. 145. John Green was granted 200 acres on the West Branch of Elizabeth River, June 1, 1655, No. 3, p. 349 (among the "transports" or "head rights" were Richard and Katherine Greene); 350 acres in Gloucester County, Jan. 13, 1661, No. 4, p. 407. There are numerous other grants of record in the 17th century to William, Peter, James and Robert Greene.—R. A. BROCK.]

MILES PRICKETT (by mark) of the parish of Holy Cross near & without the walls of the City of Canterbury, baker, 30 November, 2^d Charles (1626), proved 30 June 1627.

Whereas there is or will be certain money due to me in consideration of my adventuring into Virginia under the Worshipful Captain Pryn his charge, which goods, if they shall prosper well in the said voyage, I freely dispose of the benefit that shall be due to me unto my brother John Prickett, by him equally to be divided and shifted between my brethren as the same shall come into his hands. To brother William Prickett's two children ten pounds, equally to be divided, &c. as they come to age, which sum of money is now remaining in the hands of my brother Thomas. To brother John nine pounds now remaining in the hands of Jane Prickett my sister & by her due to me. To the son of my said brother John my cloak. To Edward Hollett (certain wearing apparel). Brother John to be sole executor. I give to him and his heirs two hundred acres of land lying in Elizabeth City in Virginia, near Salford's Cricke.

The witnesses were William Brooke, John Slade, Thomas Boudler (by mark) & Edward Turfett.   Skinner, 65.

WILLIAM WHITE of London, linen-draper, 20 August 1622, proved 26 June 1627. I give and bequeath all my lands in Virginia, with all my servants, goods, debts, chattells and whatsoever else I have unto my beloved brother John White of London Esq., whom I constitute and ordain to be the sole heir and executor of this my last Will & Testament. The witnesses were Erasmus Ferior & John Wade.   Skinner, 65.

[George White, "Minister," was granted 200 acres of land on Nansemond River, June 3, 1635. Head Rights: Geo. White, William Moore, John Joyce, Thomas Catchman. *Va. Land Records*, No. 1, p. 240; 100 acres in County of New Norfolk, Aug. 19, 1637. Head Rights: Wife Blanche White, Peter White, Zach. Taylor, No. 1, p. 458; 150 acres do. do. Head Rights: George White, William Moore, John Joyce, Thomas Catchman, No. 1, p. 459; 300 acres in upper county of New

Norfolk, March 6, 1638, No. 1, p. 589 ; John White was granted 50 acres in upper county of New Norfolk, June 10, 1639, No. 1, p. 659. James White and John Richeson 200 acres in Mobjack bay, Aug. 15, 1642, No. 1, p. 810.—R. A. BROCK.]

WILLIAM SAKER of Surrey gentleman, 1 December, 1627, proved 7 December 1627. House & lands in Lambeth to nephew Christopher Saker if he live to be of the age of one & twenty years. If he die before then my cousin John Rayner and his heirs shall have the same. To niece Dorothy Saker one hundred & fifty pounds.

Item, I give my servant Thomas Gregory, if he return alive out of Virginia into England, fifty pounds. To Mrs Machett a piece of plate, which she hath in her custody, of the fashion of a cock, and to Mr Machett two hundred weight of my Virginia Tobacco, to the end he may be assisting to my executors. To Mr Thomas Clarke ten pounds & to Mr John Upton the elder fifteen pounds which he owes me and five pounds to buy him a ring. My executors to be Sir Thomas Jay of the Precinct of Blackfriars, London, Knight, and Nathaniel Finch of Gray's Inn. Wit : G. Hastings & Benjamin Jeay. Skinner, 117.

PAUL DE REUOIRE, gentleman, born in Savoye, at present in London, sick in bed, 30 November 1627, proved 18 December 1627. Small legacy to a servant. All the rest to good friend Alexander Toriano, minister of the Italian church, who is appointed executor. Skinner, 118.

[This surname was borne by the ancestors of Paul Revere of Boston, of Revolutionary fame, whose grandfather, Gilbert de Rivoire, a Huguenot, emigrated from St. Foy, in France, and settled in the island of Guernsey. Apollos de Rivoire, son of Gilbert, at the age of thirteen was sent to Boston to learn the trade of a goldsmith. Here he changed his name to Paul Revere, married and settled. His oldest son Paul, above named, was born Dec. 21, 1734, O. S., Jan. 1, 1735, N. S., and died May 10, 1818.—E. H. Goss, *of Melrose, Mass.*]

MARY SYMES, now of Beamister, late of Poorstock, in county Dorset, widow, 7 June 1736, proved 17 November 1738. To be buried in the Church Yard of Poorstock at the end of the chancell there, near my late son in law Mr Bendle deceased, and to the Parson or Vicar of the same parish two guineas for the breaking the ground for my grave and burying me. I give unto my grand son Richard Chichester,[1] now in Virginia (son of my late daughter Elizabeth Chichester deceased) one Bond for one hundred & thirty pounds lately given or entered into by son Chilcott Symes to me and all the moneys, principal & interest now due or to grow due on the same. To John Chichester (son of the said Richard Chichester) eighty pounds sterling within one year next after my decease, and in case he shall not then have attained his age of one & twenty years it shall be paid to his said father in trust for him. To Elizabeth Beer widow and relict of Francis Beer late of Long Bredy, in said County of Dorset, deceased, thirty pounds sterling, in one year, &c. To Mrs Elizabeth Foster, wife of Mr. John Foster of West Milton in the said county, maltster, ten pounds sterling in one year, &c. To my old servant Grace Moores the sum of five pounds sterling. It is my will that in case any right or thing shall happen or accrue to me from or out of the personal estate or effects of my late uncle George Richards Esq., deceased, that the same shall go and be equally divided between my said son Chilcott Symes, my daughter Mary Symes (wife of Mr Arthur Symes of Beamister aforesaid) and my said grandson Richard Chichester. The residue to said son Chilcott & daughter Mary, equally to be divided between them ; and I appoint them jointly to be executor & executrix. Wit : Merfield Cox & Richard Hussey.

In a codicil, of same day, she directs that her silver tankard be exchanged or converted into a flagon or other necessary piece of plate for the communion service of the parishioners of the said parish of Poorstock. To Dinah, wife of John Darby of Loscombe, Dorothy, wife of John Bailey of Poorstock, taylor, Mary Courtenay, wife of John Courtenay of Poorstock, blacksmith, and Anne wife of ————, formerly Anne Wench, one guinea apiece.   Brodrepp, 272.

[¹William Chichester was granted 220 acres of land in Lower Norfolk County, Va., Sept. 14, 1667. *Va. Land Records*, No. 6, p. 220. The name is extensively represented in Virginia.—R. A. BROCK.]

ANNE NOYES, of Cholderton, in the County of Wilts, widow, 18 March, 1655, proved 20 April, 1658, by Robert Rede, sole executor named in the will. To James Noyes and Nicholas Noyes, my two sons, now in New England, twelve pence apiece and to such children as they have living twelve pence apiece. To son-in-law Thomas Kent of upper Wallop twelve pence, to his wife five shillings and to their children twelve pence apiece. To Robert Read of East Cholderton, in County of Southampton, gentleman, all the rest & residue, and I ordain that the said Robert Rede shall be sole executor.

The witnesses were John Tesdale and T. Tesdale.   Wootton, 130.

[Mrs. Anne Noyes, the testator, was, as her grandson the Rev. Nicholas Noyes of Salem states, a "sister of the learned Mr. Robert Parker" (Mather's Magnalia, Bk. iii. ch. 25, Appendix; ed. of 1853, vol. i. p. 484). She was therefore an aunt of Rev. Thomas Parker of Newbury. Her husband was Rev. William Noyes, rector of Choulderton, Wilts, instituted in 1602, and resigned in 1621 (Savage, iii. 296). Of her sons, Rev. James the eldest, born in 1608, died Oct. 26, 1656, was the colleague of his cousin Rev. Thomas Parker of Newbury; and Nicholas, who also settled at Newbury, was the father of Rev. Nicholas Noyes of Salem.—EDITOR.]

Notes on Abstracts previously printed.

GEORGE LUDLOWE (*ante*, p. 174.)

[In a note on Roger Ludlow, in the July number of the REGISTER, it is stated that he went to Virginia about 1654. This assertion was doubtless made on the authority of Dr. Trumbull (*Hist. of Conn.* i. 218), and he based it on what he found in the New Haven records. Ludlow had hired a vessel to transport himself and family to Virginia, probably intending to take shipping there for England; for a MS. Roger Wolcott expressly says that Ludlow returned to England, and a deposition of John Webster, dated Dec. 18, 1660, in the Conn. Archives, speaks of "the time that Mr. Ludlow went for old England." If one will examine the printed N. Haven Colonial Records, ii. 69–74, he will find nothing to show that Ludlow went to Virginia, but rather the contrary; for Manning, the captain of the vessel Ludlow had hired, was arrested for illicit trading with the Dutch, and upon trial, being found guilty, his vessel, in spite of Ludlow's protests was declared by the court to be a lawful prize, and ordered to be sold "by an inch of candell, he that offers most to have her."—CHARLES J. HOADLY, of Hartford, Conn.]

John Rogers the Younger.

OF CHELMSFORD, ESSEX.

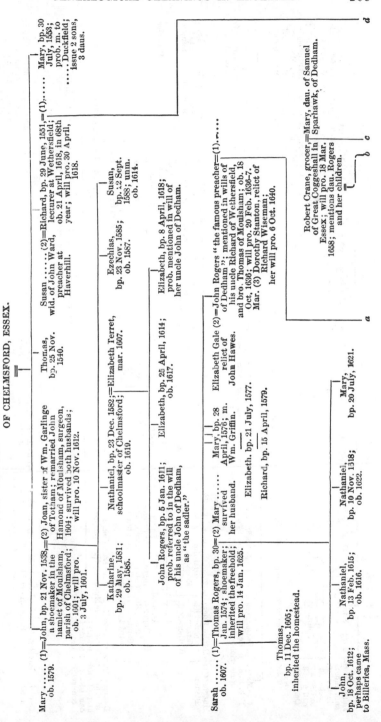

Mary...... (1). ob. 1579.

John, bp. 21 Nov. 1538,=(2) Joan, sister of Wm. Garlinge
a shoemaker in the   of Totham; remarried John
hamlet of Moulsham,   Hamond of Moulsham, surgeon,
parish of Chelmsford;   1604; survived both husbands;
ob. 1601; will pro.   will pro. 10 Nov. 1612.
3 July, 1601.

Thomas, bp. 25 Nov. 1540.

Susan.....(2)=Richard, bp. 29 June, 1551,=(1).....
wid. of John Ward,   lecturer at Wethersfield;
preacher at   ob. 21 April, 1618, in 68th
Haverhill.   year; will pro. 30 April,
                         1618.

Mary, bp. 30
July, 1553;
prob. m. to
....Duckfield;
issue 2 sons,
3 daus.

Katharine,
bp. 29 May, 1581;
ob. 1585.

Nathaniel, bp. 23 Dec. 1582,=Elizabeth Terret,
schoolmaster of Chelmsford;   mar. 1607.
ob. 1619.

Ezechias,
bp. 23 Nov. 1585;
ob. 1587.

Susan,
bp. 2 Sept.
1588; unm.
ob. 1614.

John Rogers, bp. 5 Jan. 1611;
prob. referred to in the will
of his uncle John of Dedham,
as "the sadler."

Elizabeth, bp. 25 April, 1614;
ob. 1617.

Elizabeth, bp. 8 April, 1618;
prob. mentioned in will of
her uncle John of Dedham.

Sarah ......(1)=Thomas Rogers, bp. 30=(2) Mary......
ob. 1607.   Jan. 1574; shoemaker;   survived
                inherited the freehold;   her husband.
                will pro. 14 Jan. 1625.

Mary, bp. 28
April, 1576; m.
Wm. Griffin.

Elizabeth Gale (2)=John Rogers "the famous preacher=(1).....
relict of   of Dedham"; mentioned in wills of
John Hawes.   his uncle Richard of Wethersfield,
                      and bro. Thomas of Moulsham; ob. 18
                      Oct. 1636; will pro. 20 Feb. 1636–7.
                      Mar. (3) Dorothy Stanton, relict of
                      Richard Wiseman;
                      her will pro. 6 Oct. 1640.

Elizabeth, bp. 21 July, 1577.

Richard, bp. 15 April, 1579.

Robert Crane, grocer,=Mary, dau. of Samuel
of Great Coggeshall in   Sparhawk, of Dedham.
Essex; will pro. 18 Mar.
1658; mentions dau. Rogers
and her children.

Thomas,
bp. 11 Dec. 1605;
inherited the homestead.

Nathaniel,
bp. 10 Nov. 1618;
ob. 1622.

Mary,
bp. 20 July, 1621.

John,
bp. 18 Oct. 1612;
perhaps came
to Billerica, Mass.

Nathaniel,
bp. 13 Feb. 1615;
ob. 1616.

a   b   c   d

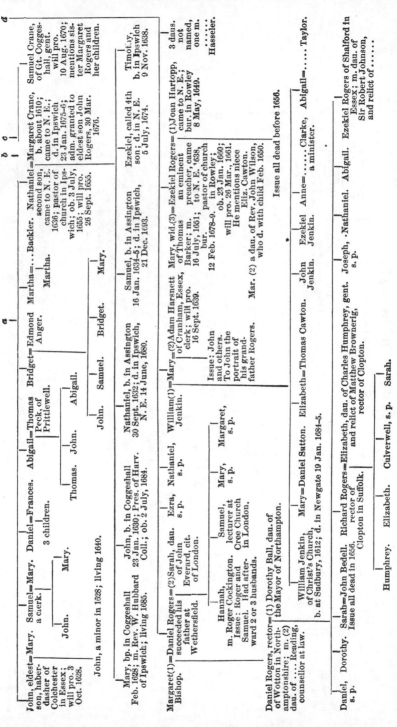

John, eldest=Mary.   Samuel=Mary,   Daniel=Frances.   Abigail=Thomas   Bridget=Edmond   Martha=...Backler.   Nathaniel=Margaret Crane,   Samuel Crane,
son, haber-   a clerk.   3 children.   Peck, of   Anger.   Martha.   second son,   b. about 1610;   of Gt. Cogges-
dasher of   Prittlewell.   came to N. E. came to N. E.;   hall, gent.
Colchester   Mary.   1636; pastor of d. in Ipswich   will pro.
in Essex;   church in Ips- 23 Jan. 1675-6; 10 Aug. 1670;
will pro. 3   Abigail.   wich; ob. 3 July, adm. granted to mentions sis-
Oct. 1628.   1655; will pro. eldest son John ter Margaret
                                                                                                    26 Sept. 1655.   Rogers, 30 Mar. Rogers and
        John.   Thomas.   John.   Samuel.   Mary.   1676.   her children.

John, a minor in 1628; living 1640.

Mary, bp. in Coggeshall   John, b. in Coggeshall   Nathaniel, b. in Assington   Samuel, b. in Assington   Ezekiel, called 4th   Timothy,
Feb. 1628; m. Rev. W. Hubbard   23 Jan. 1630; Pres. of Harv.   30 Sept. 1632; d. in   16 Jan. 1634-5; d. in Ipswich,   son; d. in N. E.   b. in Ipswich
of Ipswich; living 1685.   Coll.; ob. 2 July, 1684.   N. E. 14 June, 1680.   21 Dec. 1693.   5 July, 1674.   9 Nov. 1638.

Margaret(1)=Daniel Rogers=(2)Sarah, dau.   Ezra,   Nathaniel,   William(1)=Mary,=(2)Adam Harsnett   Mary, wid.(3)=Ezekiel Rogers=(1)Joan Hartopp,   3 daus.
Bishop.   succeeded his   of John   s. p.   s. p.   Jenkin.   of Cranham, Essex,   of Thomas   an eminent   came to N. E.;   not
        father at   Everard, cit.   clerk; will pro.   Barker; m.   preacher, came   bur. in Rowley   named,
        Wethersfield.   of London.   16 Sept. 1639.   16 July, 1651;   to N. E. 1638,   8 May, 1649.   one m.
                                                                              bur.   pastor of church   ......
        Hannah,   Samuel,   Mary,   Issue: John   12 Feb. 1678-9.   in Rowley;   Hasseler.
        m. Roger Cockington.   lecturer at   s. p.   Margaret,   and others.   ob. 23 Jan. 1660;
        Issue: Roger and   Cree Church   s. p.   To John the   Mar. (2) a dau.   will pro. 26 Mar., 1661.
        Samuel. Had after-   in London.   portrait of   of Rev. John Wilson,   He mentions niece
        ward 2 or 3 husbands.   his grand-   who d. with child Feb. 1660.   Eliz. Cawton.
                                                   father Rogers.

                                                                                                      Issue all dead before 1656.

                                                                          John   Ezekiel   Anne=....Clarke,   Abigail=.....Taylor.
                                                                          Jenkin.   Jenkin.   a minister.
                                                                                            Ezekiel   Joseph,   Nathaniel.   Abigail.   Ezekiel Rogers of Shalford in
                                                                                            Jenkin.   s. p.   Essex; m. dau. of
                                                                                                                                       Sir Robert Johnson,
                                                                                                                                       and relict of......

Daniel Rogers, rector=(1) Dorothy Ball, dau.
of Wotton in North-   of the Mayor of Northampton.
amptonshire; m. (2)
dau. of .... Reading,   William Jenkin,   Mary=Daniel Sutton.   Elizabeth=Thomas Cawton.   Richard Rogers=Elizabeth, dau. of Charles Humphrey, gent.
counsellor at law.   of Christ's Church,   rector of   and relict of Matthew Brownerig,
                     b. at Sudbury, 1612; d. in Newgate 19 Jan. 1684-5.   Clopton in Suffolk.   rector of Clopton.

Daniel,   Dorothy,   Sarah=John Bedell.   Richard Rogers=Elizabeth, dau. of Charles Humphrey, gent.
s. p.   Issue all dead in 1656.

        Humphrey.   Elizabeth.   Culverwell, s. p.   Sarah.

FAMILY OF JOHN ROGERS OF DEDHAM.

IT is with intense gratification that, at last, I am able to answer the long vexed question who was the father of John Rogers, "the famous preacher of Dedham," and to show pretty clearly what was the name of his grandfather, father of the no less famous Richard Rogers of Wethersfield. For more than a score of years has this question been discussed in the New England Historical and Genealogical Register and other publications, without eliciting a particle of positive evidence bearing on this subject. The late Col. Chester, in his memoir of John Rogers the martyr, produced a mass of negative evidence which seemed to refute the wide-spread belief in a descent from that heroic sufferer in the cause of the English Reformation. But all that we actually knew of the family in which so many of our New England people are interested, was what we could gather from the will of Richard, who speaks of his cousin (i. e. nephew) Rogers of Dedham, the inscription on his tombstone, the will of John Rogers himself, his epitaph on the north wall of the chancel in Dedham church, and the Candler pedigrees in the Harleian MSS., British Museum, and in the Bodleian Library, Oxford. Add to these Giles Firmin's Journal and the very significant statement in Nichols's Literary Anecdotes (1812), vol. ii. p. 556 (see Memoir of John Rogers the Martyr, by Col. J. L. Chester (London, 1861), p. 243), in reference to Daniel Rogers, the father of the Rev. Dr. Jortin's mother, that he was "descended from Mr. Rogers, Steward to one of the Earls of Warwick, whose residence was at Lees, near Chelmsford, in Essex, *temp.* Henry VIII.," and we have, I believe, the sum total of our knowledge of this family in England, so far as the genealogical aspect is concerned. In order that we may get our exact bearings at this point of departure, I venture to reproduce the most important of these facts.

The inscription on the tombstone of Richard Rogers of Wethersfield (see Col. Chester's Life of John Rogers, pp. 239, 240) shows that he died 21 April, 1618, in the sixty-eighth year of his age, and was born therefore about A.D. 1551. The following is a very concise abstract of his will, which was published in full in the October number of the REGISTER for 1863 (vol. xvii. p. 326).

RICHARD ROGERS of Wethersfield, Essex, preacher, 16 April 1618, proved 30 April 1618. He mentions John Clarke, a neighbor at the brook, Samuell Waight, a son in law,[*] Walter Wiltsheir and Jeremy Boozy. To wife Susan all such goods and household stuff as were hers before I married her. I give to my son Danyell my best cloak &c. I give to my son Ezekiell all my Latin and Hebrew and Greek books, but if his brother have not St Austin's Works, I give them him; other books written by myself

---

[*] Samuel Waite, of Wethersfield, married Mary Ward, either a sister or daughter of Rev. John Ward, of Haverhill (see my Memoir of Rev. Nathaniel Ward, p. 129 ; REGISTER, xxxii. p. 188; also xxxi. p. 160). If this reference is to the same person, as is probable, it is evident that his wife was a *daughter* of Rev. John Ward.—EDITOR.

and all my written lectures and papers I give to sons Danyell and Ezekiell "and to my Cosen Rogers of Dedham" &c. Twenty pounds, out of
remainder of my annuities, to wife, and whatsoever shall remain I give it
among all my six children. Of the ninescore pounds and twenty marks
which Allen Mountjoy gen^t owes me I give the said ninescore pounds to
sons Daniell and Ezekiell and the twenty marks to my daughter Hassel-
der's children which she had by her husband now living. Daughter Has-
seler again mentioned. To my wife's children forty shillings apiece. To
my sister Mary Duckfield's three daughters and her son John forty shillings apiece. To my kinswoman Mary Smallwood twenty shillings &c.
To Cousin Daniel Duckfield* twenty shillings. My meadow in Wethersfield lying between the Lords meadow and John Clarke's. Goodman Parker's daughter, the widow Barnard.

My executors to be Cousin Mr John Wright esq. of Romford, in Essex,
Susan, my wife, and Francis Longe, my son in law. My brother Cooke
and my son Makin to be overseers.

Wit: John Clarke Samuell Wayte.

B. Hamer 314, Consistory Court of London.

The inscription in Dedham church gives us the following dates :

Johannes Rogersius hic, quam prædicavit expectat Resurrectionem

Oct 18   *Año* $\begin{cases} D\bar{n}i & 1636 \\ ætatis & 65 \\ ministerii & 42 \\ Huic\ Ecclesiæ & 31 \end{cases}$

Obijt &c

An abstract of his will (also given in full, vol. xvii. of REGISTER,
p. 329) is as follows :

JOHN ROGERS, minister of God's word in Dedham, 14 October 1636,
proved 20 February 1636. The house I dwell in &c to Dorathie my wife,
during her life, and then to John Rogers my grandchild, son of my eldest
son John Rogers of Colchester, deceased, and to his heirs, and for default
of such heirs to his mother, my daughter in law, for term of her natural
life, then to my son Nathaniel and to his heirs male, failing such then to
my son Samuel and his heirs male, with remainder to my son Daniel and his
heirs forever. To my sister Garood and her children twenty pounds.
Item to Sara, Hanna and Marke twenty pounds. To my cousin Webb of
Colchester ten pounds, and to John her son ten pounds. To my son Anger's children fifty pounds. To my son Nathaniel's children forty pounds.
To son Samuel's son thirty pounds. To son Daniel's child five pounds.
To son Peck's children ten pounds. To my daughter Martha's child five
pounds. To these poor men, Abraham Ham, Robert Ham, John Ham,
John Cannon, Simon Cowper, widow French, John Shinglewood, John
Weed, Edmund Spinke, William Wood five shillings each. To my servants, Martin Garood ten shillings, George Havill twenty shillings, Tame-
son Princett ten shillings, goodman Allen of Santoosey (St Osithe?) twenty shillings, and to Elizabeth, now my maid two pounds. To my cousin

---

* Daniel Duckfield vicar of Childerditch, signs a petition in favor of Mr. Thomas Hooker, preacher at Chelmsford, November, 1629. He died in January, 1653. (See Annals of
Evangelical Nonconformity in Essex, by Davids, pp. 156, 360.)—H. F. W.

Elizabeth Rogers ten pounds, and to her brother, the sadler, five pounds. Remainder to all my children in old England. My wife to be sole executrix.

Wit : Richard Backler, Samuel Sherman.

B. Goare 22 (P. C. C.).

The Candler pedigree is in substance as follows :

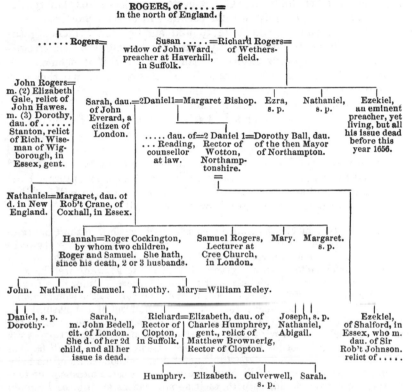

Candler shows the parentage of Margaret, the wife of our Nathaniel Rogers, as follows :

Robert Crane = Mary, dau. of Samuel Sparhawke of Dedham in Essex.
of Coxhall in Essex |

Margaret, m. to Nathaniel Rogers, rector of Assington, whence he went into New England.

Besides the pedigree are the following entries by Candler, " closely huddled together," as Col. Chester says :

" Her 2ᵈ Husband was Harsnet clarke."
" William Jenkin, of Christ's Church in London."
" Mary, ma. to Daniel Sutton."
" Elizabeth, m. to Tho. Cawton."
" John, Ezekiel, Anne, to Clarke, a minister."
" Abigail."

All these entries, but the first, Col. Chester was able very clearly to explain. The Rev. William Jenkin, of Sudbury, clerk, married a daughter of Richard Rogers of Wethersfield, and had a son, William Jenkin the younger, of Christ's Church, and daughters Mary, wife of Daniel Sutton, Elizabeth, wife of Thomas Cawton, Anne Clarke and Abigail (Taylor). Probably, therefore, John and Ezekiel were also his children. Col. Chester's suggested explanation of the first entry is probably not correct, as will be seen shortly.

To the foregoing I was able to add sundry new evidence gathered, from time to time, in my gleaning among the wills registered in the Prerogative Court of Canterbury. But it seemed evident that the field of labor should be the Essex wills, whether registered or preserved in the Commissary Court of London, the Consistory Court of London, the Commissary Court of London for Essex and Herts, the Archdeaconaries of Essex and of Colchester, or any of the other various peculiar courts in that county. So, when my researches into the maternal ancestry of John Harvard called for an investigation into the Rogers family and one or two Roses* gathered by me proved to belong to Essex, I eagerly embraced the opportunity and settled down to an examination of the wills of that county, with what result the following notes will show.

JOHN ROGERS of Mulsham in the parish of Chelmsford in the County of Essex, shoemaker, 10 June, 43 Elizabeth, proved 3 July 1601. My body to be buried in the churchyard of Chelmsford by the good discretion of my executrix undernamed. Item I give and bequeath to Joan my well beloved wife all that my freehold messuage or tenement wherein I now dwell, with all the houses, buildings, yards, garden and hop-yard to the same belonging, with their appurtenances, for and during the term of her natural life, and after her decease I give and bequeath the same messuage or tenement and other the premises, with their appurtenances, unto Thomas Rogers my son and to the heirs of his body lawfully begotten. And if it shall happen the said Thomas my son to depart this natural life without heirs of his body lawfully begotten then my will and mind is that the same messuage or tenement or other the premises with their appurtenances shall be and remain to and amongst all my other children and their heirs, part and part alike. Item I give unto the aforesaid Joan my wife and her assigns all those my three tenements, with their appurtenances, that I bought of one John Sames and his wife until my daughter Susan shall come to her full age of twenty and one years, for and towards the payment of the legacies hereafter given to Nathaniel Rogers, my son. And at the full age of the said Susan I give and bequeath unto the said Susan and to the heirs of her body lawfully begotten all those my three tenements, with their appurtenances, before given to my said wife till the said Susan should come of full age. And if it shall happen the said Susan my daughter to depart this natural life without heirs of her body lawfully begotten then my mind and will is that the same three tenements with their appurtenances shall be and remain to and amongst all my other children and their heirs, part and part alike. Item I

* I was on the look out especially for any mention of a Rose Rogers, that being the name of John Harvard's aunt.—H. F. W.

give unto my daughter the wife of William Gryffyn the sum of five pounds of lawful English money. Item I give and bequeath to Nathaniel my son the sum of ten pounds of like lawful money, to be paid unto him within two months next after he shall have served the time of his Indenture of apprenticeship by which he now standeth bound for certain years yet to come. Item I give and bequeath unto the aforesaid Thomas my son my standing bed over the hall wherein I usually do lie, with the settle to the same, one feather bed whereon he usually doth lie, with a covering and a blanket belonging to the same, and two pair of sheets, one table, a form and a little cupboard standing in the chamber over the shop, two beds with their furniture, that my servants do usually lie on, one great old table and form, one brass pot and little kettle, one posnet, three pewter platters, two pewter dishes, one pewter bason, two fruit dishes, a copper, an old currying pan and the currying board, all the lasts and other working tools in the shop belonging to my occupation, and my stall and tilt which I use in the market. Item I give and bequeath unto my said son Thomas all my shoes and boots already made and all my leather of all sorts now being bought, upon condition that he pay unto my son John his brother the sum of ten pounds of lawful money of England within two months next after my decease; provided nevertheless that if such shoes, boots and leather as shall remain unsold at the time of my decease shall not amount to the full value of twenty pounds, being valued and prized by four honest and indifferent men, two to be chosen by my said son Thomas and other two by my executrix, that then my executrix shall make up the said shoes, boots and leather to the full sum and value of twenty pounds in ready money at such time as my said son is to pay to his brother John the aforesaid sum of ten pounds by force of this my will. Item I give and bequeath to the aforesaid John my son the sum of five pounds of lawful money of England to be paid to him by my executrix within two months next after my decease. Item I give and bequeath unto the aforesaid Thomas my son the sum of three pounds of like lawfull money to be paid to him by my executrix within two years next after my decease. Item I give and bequeath to the aforesaid Nathaniel Rogers my son all that my copyhold orchard with the appurtenances which I late bought of John Ashbye, to have and to hold unto the said Nathaniel his heirs and assigns for ever according to the custom of the manor of Mulsham Hall, whereof the same is holden.

The residue of all my goods, chattles, movables, household stuff, debts, ready money and implements of household whatsoever not before in and by this my last will and testament given, devised and bequeathed, my debts, legacies being paid and my funeral expences discharged, I fully and wholly give and bequeath unto the aforesaid Joan my wife, whom I make and ordain sole executrix of this my last will and testament.

Wit: John Cooke, Thomas Parker, Michael Newman, Richard Brodway, Urias Spilman.

Commissary of London, Essex and Herts, 1601–2, No. 157.

License granted, 27 September, 1604, to the Rector or Curate of Chelmsford to solemnize the marriage between John Hamond of Moulsham, chirurgeon, and Joan Rogers, late relict of John Rogers, late of Moulsham, shoemaker, deceased. Vicar General's Book, London.

JOHN HAMOND of Moulsham, in the parish of Chelmsford, surgeon, 24 September 1612, proved 10 November 1612. To wife Joane all the household stuff and other goods which were her own before I married her and twenty pounds to be paid her by her brother William Garlinge. To my son Abraham a house and land called Pypers in Much Baddow, and other land there, with remainder to William, son of said Abraham, and to Thomas, another son. To my son John a house in Moulsham called Cowles. To my daughter Elizabeth forty shillings. To my daughter Margery three pounds. To Mary Barnes, my daughter's child, three pounds. To Richard Edlinge, my daughter Joan's son, forty shillings. To my wife Joane five pounds. To my son Richard five pounds.

Wit : Thomas Rogers, Thomas Jones and Hugh Barker.

Commissary Court of Essex and Herts, 1612.

JOANE HAMOND of Moulsham, in the parish of Chelmsford, widow, 3 November 1612, proved 10 November 1612 (the same day as the foregoing). To my son Nathaniel and to my daughter Susan the twenty pounds in the hands of my brother William Garlinge of Tottham, to be equally divided between them, and also four pounds due by legacy from my late husband John Hamond deceased, also to be divided equally between them. The residue of goods and chattels &c. to my daughter Susan, except an old bedstead, the frue, a pan, a chair and some shelves and boards in the buttery which I give to my son in law (step son) Thomas Rogers. Daughter Susan to be executrix.   Commissary Court of Essex and Herts, 1612.

THOMAS ROGERS of the hamlet of Mulsham in the County of Essex shoemaker, 23 May, 1st Charles (I.), proved at Chelmsford 14 January 1625. To Mary, my loving wife, my three tenements with all and singular their appurtenances, the which I lately bought of my brother John Rogers of Dedham, clerk, for and during the time or term that my daughter Mary shall attain to one and twenty years or day of marriage ; the which my wife shall be contented with. And upon one of those times I will the said Tenements, &c. to my said daughter and to her heirs. But if it shall please God to call her out of this mortal life before she shall come to her several age or day of marriage then I will the same to my son John and to his heirs. And if both of them die before their several ages of one and twenty years then I will the said tenements to the next heirs of me the said Thomas the testator ; provided always that if both my said children do die before they come to their several ages my mind and will is that my wife shall have the said tenements for and during her natural life, and after her decease to the next heirs of me the said testator. I further give and bequeath to my said wife twenty pounds of lawful money of England to be paid unto her within three months next after my decease, conditionally that she shall make, seal and deliver to my son Thomas a sufficient release of all her thirds of the house and backsides I now dwell in, at the time of the payment of the said twenty pounds, or else she shall lose the said sum. I give her further all the household stuff in the chamber over the cistern (except the bed and bedsted and furniture therewith), the stuff in the chamber over the Buttery (except one old flock bed). I further give her the bedsted and flockbed in the chamber over the Hall and all the hutches that be mine. I further give her two feather beds and one standing bedsted in the chamber over the buttery and all the moveable stuff in the said chamber. My said wife shall have three chambers in my house until the Michaelmas next after my son Thomas shall be married, viz. the chamber over the Hall, the chamber next the street over the shop, the chamber used for an apple chamber, and the shop, paying therefore to my said son Thomas forty shillings yearly at Michaelmas and our Lady by even portions.

Item I give unto my said son Thomas all that my messuage or tenement I now dwell in situate in Mulsham aforesaid, with all and singular their appurtenances, to him and his heirs for ever, except those the rooms formerly willed to my said wife, upon condition that he pay or cause to be paid unto his brother John thirty pounds of lawful money of England, so soon as he shall come to the age of twenty and two years. The residue to my son Thomas. The executors to be my loving brother John Rogers of Dedham, clerk, and my said son Thomas, to which said brother, for his pains herein, I will and devise by this my last will that my son shall bear his charges in proving of my will and other charges of his expences herein, and give unto him for a remembrance of me one piece of gold of ten shillings towards the making of him a gold ring.

Wit: Petter de Court, Tho. Sherlock Scr.

Commissary Court, Essex and Herts, 1624–5.

Here at last we strike a broad trail, and it becomes evident that this family were at the end of the sixteenth century settled in Chelmsford.

This town, as we learn from Morant, gives name both to the Deanery and Hundred, and is a pretty large and populous place, twenty-nine miles from London. It is seated at the confluence of two rivers, the Can, which flows from the south-south-west, and the Chelmer from the north. From the latter it probably derived its name, which in Domesday-book is written Celmeresfort and Celmeresforda, and in other records Chelmeresford, Chelmerford and Chelmesford; there having been undoubtedly a ford here across the river on the great road from London to Colchester, Harwich and Suffolk County. Close adjoining, on the north-east, is the little village of Springfield, which was the English home of another of our New England families, the Pynchons. A stone bridge over the Can leads directly into Moulsham or Mulsham, a manor and hamlet which before the Conquest was holden by the Abbot and convent of St. Peters, Westminister, and remained in their possession until the suppression of monasteries, when, falling to the Crown, it was granted 23 July, 1540, to Thomas Myldmay, Esq., who built a magnificent manor house, commonly called Mulsham Hall. This hamlet is really a part of the town of Chelmsford, and is but a continuation of its main street. The oldest and most noticeable house on the right, but a short distance from the Bridge, was, I learned, a freehold that had belonged from time immemorial to the Rogers family, and was still owned and occupied by one of that name. I could not but think that this might be the homestead passed down in the preceding wills from father to son, *the birth place of John Rogers of Dedham.*

The Church Registers of Chelmsford go back to A.D. 1538 (when parish registers were first ordered to be kept in England). I spent the latter half of a long summer day in the examination of their contents, while day light lasted, or until nearly nine, P. M. Too late I discovered from internal evidence that the volume which had been handed me was a copy of the original record and made by some rector or curate, who was evidently something of an antiquary, about two hundred years ago. So I offer my notes of baptism with a great deal of diffidence. I found at last the missing volume, but had no time to examine it thoroughly. The parish clerk had fancied it lost.

I found that this family were evidently settled here in Chelmsford as early as the first year noted in the Register, so that it seems needless to visit the Lees or Leighs, with the hope of carrying our history of the family further back by the aid of Church Registers.

There was a John Rogers the elder, carpenter, whose wife Jone was buried in 1540, and a John Rogers the younger, who had a son Richard baptized 29 June, 1551. This I have no doubt was Richard Rogers of Wethersfield (see the inscription on his tomb-stone). Taking this for granted, the problem was to find the baptism of John, the father of John of Dedham and brother of this Richard.

The following were all the baptisms I gathered from 1538 to 1558 inclusive :—

> John, of John Rogers the younger, 21 Nov. 1538.
> Thomas, of John Rogers the younger and Ann, 25 Nov. 1540.
> Mary, of John Rogers joiner (?) and Agnes, 11 Feb. 1542.
> John, of John Rogers and Jone, 19 Oct. 1545.
> John, of John Rogers and Agnes, 10 Sept. 1548.
> *Richard, of John Rogers the younger*, 29 June, 1551.
> Mary, of John Rogers the younger, 30 July, 1553.
> Thomas, of John Rogers, 29 Oct. 1557.
> Ellyn, of John Rogers, 1 Nov. 1558.

Whether John Rogers the younger was the father of all these children it is impossible, without further evidence, to say. Assuming that he had two wives, Ann and Agnes, then all but one are accounted for ; and in that case John the father of John of Dedham and of Thomas the shoemaker was born in 1548. A John Rogers married Agnes Carter in 1541. Coming down to the next generation I found the baptisms of the following children of a John Rogers :—

> Thomas, 30 January, 1574.
> Mary, 28 April, 1576.
> Elizabeth, 21 July, 1577.
> Richard, 15 April, 1579.
> Katherine, 29 May, 1581.
> Nathaniel, 14 December, 1582.
> Ezechias, 23 November, 1585.
> Susan, 22 September, 1588.

The baptism of John, who must have been born about 1569 to 1571, I did not get, though I have note of the baptism of a Johan, son of John Rogers, 9 August, 1579 (the very same year as the baptism of Richard, son of John). If this be our man, then his baptism was postponed nearly ten years after his birth. In New England 1 have noticed several instances of the postponement of this rite until the individual had even reached the age of manhood. Very likely such cases may be found in English records. At any rate the names of Thomas, Nathaniel and Susan show that we have here the family of John, the shoemak&r, while it must have been their sister Mary who was married in 1596 to William Griffyn (mentioned in will of John, the father, in 1601). This John Rogers's first wife was probably Mary, buried in 1579: and the children born after that year (viz. Katherine, Nathaniel, Ezechias and Susan) were his children by his second wife Joan, who in her will, made 1612, left the bulk of her property to two of them, Nathaniel and Susan. The others both died young, Katherine in 1585 and Ezechias in 1587.

Later on I found the baptisms of the children of Thomas, Nathaniel and Richard, all of Moulsham. Thomas was called a shoemaker, and was, without question, the one who was buried in 1625, and by his mention of his brother John as " of Dedham, clerk," has enabled us to place this family. He seems to have had two wives, Sarah, buried 1607, by whom a son Thomas baptized 11 December, 1605, and Mary who outlived him, by whom he had the following children :—

John, bapt. 18 October, 1612; perhaps died in Billerica, Mass., 25 Jan. 1685–86, æt. 74.
Nathaniel, bapt. 13 February, 1615; d. in Moulsham, 1616.
Nathaniel, bapt. 10 November, 1618; d. in Moulsham, 1622.
Mary, bapt. 20 July, 1621 ; mentioned in her father's will.

Nathaniel Rogers, of Moulsham, brother of the preceding and of John of Dedham, was called schoolmaster, and, very likely, was master of the Free School in Moulsham, founded by King Edward VI. A.D. 1552. He probably died in 1619, having had by his wife Elizabeth Terret (m. 1607) the following children :

John, bapt. 5 January, 1611 ; probably referred to in his uncle John's will as " the sadler."
Elizabeth, bapt. 25 April, 1614; d. in Moulsham 1617.
Elizabeth, bapt. 6 April, 1618 ; adopted, I think, by her uncle John who mentioned her in his will, and mentioned also by the latter's widow, who speaks of her as " my maid Elizabeth Rogers."

Richard Rogers, of Moulsham, called a "Poulter," married Anne Cooke 1613, and had the following children :—

  Jeane, bapt. 27 February, 1613.
  Mary, bapt. 21 January, 1615.
  John, bapt. 28 January, 1618.

Besides all these there was a Thomas Rogers (buried, probably,

1598) who was having children from 1575 to 1580 inclusive. There is no reason to doubt that he belonged to this Chelmsford family.

And there was a William Rogers, who was buried in Chelmsford, 1587, having buried his wife Margaret the year before, who must have belonged to a family of Rogers seated at Stanford le Hope and the neighboring parishes of Fobbinge and Curringham, near the Thames. I have a few abstracts of wills relating to them. One of these, John Roger of Fobbinge, refers to the above, in 1584, as cousin William Roger of Chelmsford, and his wife, and in a nuncupative codicil, made 21 October, 1584, he willed that John Roger his (own) son should remain at Chelmsford, where he then was, until our Lady day next.

There are other references to the name of Rogers on the calendars of Wills and Admons. in Essex County, not yet examined. When they are, we may get more light on the relationship of all these parties. Some of these are as follows :—

John Rogers, 1592.   [bury).
Rose Rogers (widow), 1599–1600 (prob. wid. of Robt. R., of Buttis-
Richard Rogers, 1601–2.
William Rogers, of Colchester, 1618.
Mary Rogers (wid.), of Moulsham, 1626–8.
Richard Rogers, of Moulsham, 1628–31.
Thomas Rogers, of Moulsham, 1639–41.
Jeremiah Rogers, of Chelmsford (test.), 1676–77.
Daniel Rogers, of St. Nicholas, Colchester, 1679–80.
Nehemiah Rogers, Hatfield Brodocke (test.), 1686–7.
Jeremiah Rogers, Chelmsford (adm.), 1686–7.

And in calendars of the Archd. of Colchester,

Barnaby Rogers, of Boxted, 1626–7.
William Rogers, of Bentley Magna, 1638–9.
Elizabeth Rogers, of Witham, 1646–7.
Timothy Rogers, of Tey Magna, 1662–3.
Rachel Rogers, of Tey Magna (Book Symons 46).
James Rogers, of St. Buttolph (Book Symons 43).

Whether this family can be traced farther remains to be proved. I find in Burke's General Armory the following :—

Rogers (Chelmsford, co. Essex ; Purton, co. Gloucester ; Kent ; and Evesham, co. Worcester). *Ar. a chev. betw. three bucks, sa. Crest A buck's head sa. attired or, in the mouth an acorn of the second, stalked and leaved vert.*

In the Visitation of Gloucestershire, published by the Harleian Society, Vol. XXI. p. 141, may be found a pedigree of the family undoubtedly referred to. If of this stock, then, our New England family may surely claim kinship with the protomartyr, by virtue of a descent from a common ancestor. I confess that I am somewhat inclined to think that further research may not only establish this connection, but also trace the ancestry of John Harvard's mother back to the same source.

On the other hand, it will be remembered, Candler says that this family came from the North of England, while the Jortins believed that one of their ancestors was a steward of the Earl of Warwick, without, however, stating which Earl.

Before giving extracts from any other wills, I ought to call attention to a clause in the will of John Rogers the shoemaker (1601), which, taken in connection with a similar one in the will of Thomas Rogers the shoemaker (1625), furnishes a significant bit of evidence to prove that these two stood to each other in the relation of father and son.

John, the father, gave the three tenements bought of John Sames* to his wife for life, then to daughter Susan and the heirs of her body; failing such, then to the testator's other children. Now Susan died young and unmarried, her brother Nathaniel died; whether Mary Griffyn was alive or not I cannot say, but in 1625 Thomas Rogers is found disposing by will of "three tenements lately bought of my brother John Rogers, of Dedham, clerk."

I was fortunate enough to discover the wills of John Hawes, whose widow Elizabeth became the second wife of John Rogers of Dedham, of Richard Wiseman, whose widow Dorothy became his third wife, of Dorothy Rogers herself, who by her conscientious mention of her step-children and their children, adds much to our knowledge of the family; of John Rogers of Colchester, eldest son of the famous preacher of Dedham, and of John Ray† of Stradishall, Suffolk, who calls him brother in law.

Short abstracts of these wills here follow :

JOHN HAWES the elder of St. Lawrence in the County of Essex, yeoman, 7 August 1613, proved 12 October 1613. Mentions son John and Elizabeth his daughter; kinsman John Anthony ; Charles Anthony the younger, a sister's son; Martha Anthony, youngest daughter of said sister; Frances, the eldest daughter of sister Alice Anthony ; John Olmsted, son of Richard Olmsted and of daughter Elizabeth, Israel their second son, Jedidiah their third son and Elizabeth their daughter ; daughter Elizabeth wife of Richard Olmstead, clerk; Julian Veale of Malden, widow ; wife Elizabeth. Commissary Court, Essex, Herts, 1613.

RICHARD WISEMAN, of Much Wigborowe, in the County of Essex, yeoman, 12 October 1616, proved 24 May 1617. To my son Marke Wiseman, at his age of one and twenty years, my copyhold lands and tenements called Sheereinges and Cuckoes &c in Much Wigborowe. My brother Henry Wiseman, of Elsingham, Essex, gentleman, to take charge of said estates &c until then, to collect rents, &c. after the death of Anne Lawrence, widow. My said brother to pay unto my daughter Sara one hun-

---

* There was a John Sames in New England among the early settlers.—H. F. W.

† I have found two or three other wills of this family of Ray, which do not throw any light on the Rogers alliance.

dred pounds, and to my daughter Anne one hundred pounds, at their several ages of twenty years. To my daughter Sara three hundred pounds and to my daughter Anne three hundred pounds, at their several ages of twenty years. To my son Marke one hundred pounds at his age of four and twenty years. To my wife Dorothie my freehold lands, tenements &c in West Mersey, Essex, for and during her natural life, and then to my said son Marke Wiseman forever. To Sir Edward Bullock Kn^t five pounds and to the Lady Elizabeth, his wife, five pounds within one year after my decease. To John Whitacres, gentleman, three pounds six shillings and eight pence within one year after my decease. To Mr Harrison, of Layer-delahay, clerk, one piece of gold of twenty two shillings. To Mr Nichol-son of Little Wigborowe twenty shillings. To Christian Bridge, my wife's mother, ten shillings to make her a ring. To Jo: Makyn now servant with William Bond of Colchester, baker, five pounds, at age of four and twenty years. To Matthew London of Colchester, yeoman, five pounds and to Mary his wife, my sister, ten pounds, upon condition that they shall not claim &c anything by force or virtue of the last Will and Testament of Margaret Wise-man, my late mother deceased. To Rachell, Bridgett and Anne London, daughters of the said Matthew London, to every one of them three pounds. To Henry Bridge, my man servant thirty shillings. To my son Marke Wiseman one silver salt parcel gilt, one dozen silver spoons and one silver bowl or cup.

All the rest of my goods and chattels &c to my wife Dorothy, except my gray ambling gelding which I give and bequeath to my said brother Henry Wiseman. Said wife Dorothy to be executrix.

Weldon, 39 (P. C. C.).

DOROTHY ROGERS of Dedham in the County of Essex, widow, 16 April 1640, proved 6 October 1640. She mentions son Mark Wiseman; daughter Sarah Cole, and her children Mary, Samuel, Sarah and Mark; daughter Hannah Hudson and her children John, Samuel, Hannah and Sarah; Sister Garrod and Jeremy Garrod her son; the house where Edmond Spinke lives; Nathaniel Rogers, eldest son of late deceased husband, and Margaret his wife, and their four children, John, Mary, Nathaniel and Samuel; Mary, wife of Samuel Rogers, clerk, another son of deceased husband, and his two children, John and Mary; Frances, wife of Daniel Rogers, another son of deceased husband, and his three children; Abigail, Bridget and Martha, daughters of late husband; the three children of daughter Pecke, Thomas, John and Abigail; the four children of daughter Anger, John, Samuel, Bridget and Mary; Martha, the daughter of daughter Backler; the widow Howchen and widow Reinolds; the wife of John Ham, the wife of Abraham Ham, Michael Ham and the wife of Bezaliel Ravens; her maid Elizabeth Rogers; her god children Robert Webb, Susan Gutteridge and William Thorne; the widow Downes and the widow French; her sister Marshall; John Rogers, her late husband's eldest son's son; cousin Page of Haverhill; and John Garrod of Colchester, her sister's son.

Commissary Court, Essex & Herts, 31, 1641–2.

JOHN ROGERS of Colchester in the County of Essex, haberdasher, 7 July 1628, proved 3 October 1628. To son John one hundred pounds at his full age of one and twenty years. My executrix shall, within three months after my decease, put in good security to Nathaniel Rogers of Bockinge, Essex, my brother, clerk, and Edmond Anger, my brother in law, of Dedham, in said County, clothier, to their liking and content, for the true payment of the said one hundred pounds. My wife Mary shall have the use and consideration of the said one hundred pounds yearly towards the bringing up of my said son John until his said age of one and twenty years. My said wife Mary to be executrix and the said Nathaniel Rogers and Edmond Anger to be supervisors, and to either of them twenty shillings apiece. To every of my brothers and sisters ten shillings apiece for a remembrance. To the poor of Colchester twenty shillings. Wit: John Rogers,* John Marshall and Tho: Cockerell.

Arch. of Colchester, 11, 1628-9.

JOHN RAY of Stradishall in the County of Suffolk, yeoman, 31 January 1630, one of the sons of Richard Ray, late of Stradishall, deceased. Mentions brother Robert Ray; lands &c in Wichambroke and Stradishall; brother Richard Ray; cousin John Ray of Denston; brother Thomas Ray; John Ray, son of brother Henry deceased; brother Abraham Ray; *brother in law John Rogers, clerk;* brother in law John Benton, clerk; John Ray, son of brother Ambrose deceased; *Elizabeth Page of Haverhill, widow of Michael Page;* Susan Ray, wife of Richard Ray.

Admo[n] granted, 30 June 1631, to Ellene Ray relict &c of Robert Ray, brother and executor. S[t] John, 72 (P. C. C.).

EXTRACTS FROM FEET OF FINES.

Between Thomas Cotton gen. *quer.* and William Turner gen., Mary Twidow, John Rogers clerk and Dorothy his wife, *deforc.*, for one messuage, one garden, one orchard, thirty acres of arable land, six acres of meadow, twenty six acres of pasture and four acres of wood, and common pasture for all animals in Goldhanger, Tolshunt Major *als.* Tolshunt Beckingham and Totham Parva. Consideration 100[li] st.

Mich. 4 Car. I. Essex.

Between Henry Towstall, esq *quer.* and John Rogers, clerk and Dorothy his wife, *deforc.*, for one cottage, one garden, two acres of arable land, thirteen acres of freshmarsh, and two acres of saltmarsh, with the appurtenances in Fingringhoe. Consideration 60[li] sterling.

Trin. 11 Car. I. Essex.

The following is an abstract of the will of the Rev. John Ward, whose widow became the second wife of Richard Rogers of Wethersfield.

JOHN WARD, preacher of God's word in Bury S[t] Edmunds, Suffolk, 9 October 1589,† proved 31 October 1598. To youngest son John one hun-

---

* I would suggest that this may be the signature of his father, John Rogers of Dedham.
H. F. W.

† Col. Joseph L. Chester furnished me with a copy of this will which I printed in full in 1868 in my "Memoir of Rev. Nathaniel Ward." In the will as recorded the date is in words, "The nythe daie of October One Thowsand Fyue Hundredth eightie nyne Elizabethe Quadragesimo." Soon after receiving the copy I called Col. Chester's attention to the discrepancy between the regnal and the common year, and suggested that if the year of our Lord had been in arabic numerals instead of words, I should have supposed that the last two figures had been transposed, and that the true date was 1598 instead of 1589. Col. Chester found the original will, and it was as I supposed in arabic numerals, as was also the regnal year. "The year," he wrote, "should unquestionably be 1598, for it is simply impossible that a man writing in the 31st Elizabeth could have written 40th." Besides, Samuel is mentioned in a way that conveys the idea that he was of age, whereas in 1589 he was only twelve years old. *See Memoir of N. Ward,* p. 132.—EDITOR.

dred pounds at twenty one ; daughter Abigail one hundred pounds at eighteen, and daughter Mary one hundred pounds at eighteen. To son Samuel all my books and apparell, and to son Nathaniel six score pounds at two and twenty. Wife Susan to be sole executrix. If she refuse then my brother Edward Ward to be executor.

Wit : Lawrence Neweman, John Woodd.   Lewyn, 85 (P. C. C.).

ADAM HARSNETT of Cranham in the County of Essex, clerk, 30 November 1638, proved 16 September, 1639. Mentions wife Mary, widow of John Dawson, daughter Elizabeth Dawson; brothers John Pope of London, salter, and Samuel Harsenett, grocer, executors. To son John the picture of his grandfather Rogers, to son Ezekiell two beer bowls marked with E. R. and E. H., a silver wine goblet marked S. H. and spoons marked M. H. To daughter Anne (certain things which Mr Cotton gave unto her). Daughter Abigail, 'son Nathaniel annuities to be received out of lands of Grace Reinolds and Elizabeth Boreham of Bubbingworth, Essex. Mother Mercie Harsenett. Brothers William Harsenett, William White and John Pope. To daughters Torshell and Stanyon five pounds each.   Harvey, 148 (P. C. C.).

The above is evidently the "Harsnet clarke" of the Candler pedigree. I would suggest that he married the daughter of Richard Rogers, widow of William Jenkin, and survived her. He was born, I found, in Colchester, son of Adam Halsnoth (as the name was often spelled), a joiner, by his wife Mercy or Marcey, and was a near kinsman of the well-known bishop, Samuel Harsnett, whose baptism I also found in Colchester under the name of Halsnoth. The will of Adam Halsnoth the elder, joiner, I found among the wills of the Archd. of Colchester (1612–13). He mentions wife Marcey, sons Adam, William, Samuel and Joseph, and daughters Marcey, Tamazin and Elizabeth.

The connection of the Crane family with the Rogers family is shown in the following extracts.

ROBERT CRANE of Great Coggeshall in the County of Essex, grocer (without date) proved 18 March 1658. Mentions wife ; refers to marriage contract entered into with brother in law Mr Nathaniel Bacon ; lands &c in West Mersey, Essex ; son Samuel Crane and his lawfull issue and son Thomas Crane ; they to pay my son Robert Crane and his issue ; lands &c in Stocke Street, lands in Gr^t Coggeshall in occupation of myself and William Cottyes, lands in Church Street, sometime Spooners and other estates ; refers to a surrender made unto the William Turners (father and son) of Markes Tey &c.

To my daughter Rogers, wife of Nathaniel Rogers, now of New England, clerk, four hundred pounds ; to my grand children Samuel, Nathaniel, Ezekiel, Timothy and John Rogers fifty pounds apiece ; they to accept of a bond of four hundred pounds made to me from Mr Joshua Foote, now or late of New England, on which there is now due for principal one hundred and fifty pounds, besides use ; to daughter Mary Whiting wife of Henry Whiting of Ipswich, two hundred pounds, the remainder of her portion ; to my grand children Henry and Mary Whiting one hundred pounds apiece at their ages of one and twenty years or days of marriage respectively ; to my daughter Elizabeth, wife of William Chaplyn two hundred pounds; to my grand children Robert and Mary Crane, children of my son Thomas Crane, one hundred pounds apiece; to Diana, Elizabeth, Margaret, Frances and Bridget, daughters of my brother Thomas Crane deceased, five pounds apiece; to my kinswoman Frances Stafford,,widow, five pounds; to Susan Voyse wife of John Voyse of Great Coggeshall, five pounds; to my three kinswomen, the residue of the daughters of my sister Johan Foulsham, forty shillings apiece; to Robert Crane, son of my cousin Robert Crane of Braintree, twenty pounds at his age of one and twenty years; to William Fowleger, my servant, for his faithful service &c. thirty pounds; to my son Samuel all my goods and wares in the shop and warehouses, my debts &c., and the lands and tenements in Lowhard &c had of John Edes, clerk, &c.; sons Samuel and Thomas to be executors.

Proved by the oath of Samuel Crane, the surviving executor.

Pell, 179 (P. C. C.).

SAMUEL CRANE of Great Coggeshall, in the County of Essex, gentleman, —— November, 1669, proved 10 August 1670. To my sister Mrs Margaret Rogers, now of Ipswich, in New England (lands and tenements in various places) for life, and then to her children; my sister Mary Whiting, wife of Mr Henry Whiting of Ipswich, Suffolk, and her children; my sister in law —— wife of —— Daynes, late the wife of my brother Robert Crane; my sister Mrs Elizabeth Chaplin, late the wife of Mr William Chaplin, of Bury St Edmunds; my brother Mr William Clopton and his children; my cousin Mr Lawrence Stisted of Ipswich, grocer, and my niece Mary, his now wife; my uncle Mr. Edward Sparhawke and his son Samuel and daughter Sarah Sparhawke; my kinswoman Mrs. Bridget Andrews, wife of Mr William Andrews, citizen and cheesemonger of London; John Garwood; my father in law Mr. Robert Feltham; my uncle Mr. John Crane, living about Horram in Suffolk, and his son John; my cousin Cooper, widow, and cousin Burgis, widow; children of my cousin Robert Foulsam, deceased; my cousin Robert Crane of Braintree and his son Robert; my cousin John Sparhawke; my cousin John Sherman; my cousin Mr John Blomfield; my cousin Mr John Rogers and Mr William Hubbard, both in New England; Christian Whiting, daughter of Henry; Isaac Hubbard; others mentioned. Penn, 97 (P. C. C.).

ROBERT CRANE of Hadleigh in the County of Suffolk, gentleman, 14 May, 18 Charles II. 1666, proved 22 May 1669. My sister Mary Crane to be executrix, to whom all my tenements &c in Kelvedon, in the County of Essex, the reversion of the jointure of my mother in law, the wife of Mr Robert Andrewes; if my sister die the premises to be sold by Thomas Goulding and the product to be equally divided betwixt the children of my uncle Whiting and aunt Rogers in New England and the children of my cousin Thomas Goulding; to the aforesaid Thomas Goulding and his heirs forever my house in Brantray; my two messuages in Coggeshall to William Fowler and his heirs forever; to William Hawkins my two messuages on Fering Hill; to Mr Whiting of Sermer, for preaching my funeral sermon, five pounds; to the poor of Kelvedon five pounds.

Proved by Mary Stisted *als* Crane, wife of Lawrence Stisted, sister of the deceased and his executrix. Coke, 51 (P. C. C.).

The following rough table will serve to show the relationship of most of these parties :

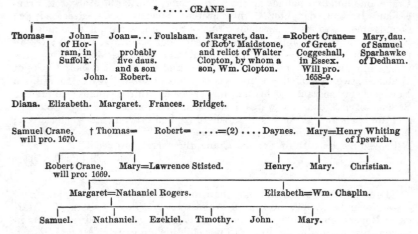

```
                                    *......CRANE=

  Thomas=   John=   Joan=... Foulsham.   Margaret, dau.   =Robert Crane=   Mary, dau.
           of Hor-                       of Rob't Maidstone,  of Great      of Samuel
           ram, in    probably           and relict of Walter Coggeshall,   Sparhawke
           Suffolk.   five daus.          Clopton, by whom a   in Essex.     of Dedham.
                      and a son           son, Wm. Clopton.    Will pro.
           John.      Robert.                                  1658-9.

  Diana.  Elizabeth.  Margaret.  Frances.  Bridget.

  Samuel Crane,   † Thomas=   Robert=  ....=(2)....Daynes.   Mary=Henry Whiting
  will pro. 1670.                                               of Ipswich.

     Robert Crane,   Mary=Lawrence Stisted.       Henry.   Mary.   Christian.
     will pro: 1669.

        Margaret=Nathaniel Rogers.           Elizabeth=Wm. Chaplin.

  Samuel.   Nathaniel.   Ezekiel.   Timothy.   John.   Mary.
```

The following extracts from the Registry of Deeds of Suffolk County, Mass., refer evidently to the legacy of Robert Crane to his grandchildren, the sons of his daughter Margaret Rogers.

By an Indenture made 24 October 1653 between Joshua Foote, late citizen and Ironmonger of London, then of Roxbury in the County Suffolk in New England, on the one part, and Robert Crane of Coggeshall in the County of Essex within the Commonwealth of England, on the other part, the former made conveyance to the latter of his dwelling house, lately purchased of Joshua Hues, situate in Roxbury, with four acres of land &c belonging, as security on his bond to pay 184£ 7ˢ 2ᵈ, due to the said Crane &c.

Suffolk Deeds I. 335.

Testimony of Samuel Danforth, Thomas Weld William Park and David Richard 1–9–1655 that Nathaniel Rogers of Ipswich and William Barthelmew did enter upon the dwelling house, formerly possessed by Joshua Hewes in Roxbury and since belonging to Joshua Foote deceased and did legally take possession of the said dwelling house &c. and order to give warning that the said house and land in the deed of sale made by the said Joshua Foote unto and for the use of Mr Robert Crane &c. 20 October 1653, do legally and properly belong unto Nathaniel Rogers of Ipswich and to his brethren Samuel, Ezekiel and Timothy Rogers of Ipswich.

Suffolk Deeds II. 210.

It seems to me worth the while to add abstracts of the wills of Ezekiel, the son of Richard of Wethersfield, and of Nathaniel, the son of John of Dedham, and certain other notes gleaned in Salem Court House and elsewhere.

EZEKIEL ROGERS " Borne at Wethersfeild in Essex in old England Now of Rowley in Essex in new England " 17 April 1660, sworn to 26 March 1661 Renders praise to God for three special blessings : " flirst for my Nurture and Education under such a father Mr Richard Rogers, in Catechisme and knowledge of the holy scriptures the want whereof I see to be the main cause of the Errors of the times. Secondly that (whereas till I was aboue twenty yeares of age I made but ill use of my knowledge but liued in a formal profession of Relligion) the lord pleased by occation of a sore sicknes which was like to be death to make me to see the worth and Neede of Christ and to take such houlde of him as that I coolde never let him goe to this houre whereby I am now encouraged to bequeath and committe my soulle into his hands who hath Redeemed it, and my Body to the Earth since he will giue me with these very eyes to see my Redeemer. Thirdly for my Calling even to be a minester of the Gospell the most glorious Calling in the worlde which the lord brought into noth without difficulty for my .... ing in the time of the hottest Persicution of that Bloody Hirarchy and being inlightened concerning the euell and snare of Subscrip...n and Cerimonies I was advised to give over the thought of the minestry and to betake my selfe to the study and practise of Phis..ke But the lord mercyfully prevented that ; for though it be a good and Nessecary Calling, I haue observed that the most through these o..e Coruption haue made it to them selues the very Temptation to couetousnes or lust or both, I therefore chose rather to lye hide abo.. a dozen yeares in an honerable famelly exerciseing my selfe in minesteriall dutyes for a bout a dozen yeares after my leaving the uneversity. Then the lord Gaue me a Call to a Publique charge att Rowley in Yorke shire whereby The Gentlenesse of —oby Mathewe I was fauoured both for subscription and Cerimonies and injoyed my liberty in the minestry about seaventeene ..ars in Comforthable sort Till for refuseing to reade that accursed Booke that allowed sports on God's holy Sabbath or lords day I was suspended and by it and other sad signes of the times driven with many of my hearers into New ...land where I haue liued in my Pastor all Offlce about ———— years with much Rest and Comforth beleeueing the way .. the Churches here to be according to the present light that God hath giuen the purest in the wholle world.

Now Age and Infir...es calling upon me to looke daly for my change I profese my selfe to haue liued and to dye an unfeigned Hater of all the Base Opinnions of the Anabaptists and Antinomians and all other Phrenticke dotages of the times that springe from them which God will ere longe cause to be as doung on the earth. I doe also protest against all the evell ffashions and guises of this age both in Apparr.. and that Generall Disguisement of longe Ruffianlike haire A Custome most generally taken up at that time when the Graue and modest weareing of haire was a part of the Reproch of Christ: as appeared by the tearme of Roundheads and was carryed on with a high hand not with standing the knowne offence of soe many Godly persons, and without publique expression of these reasons for any such libertie taken."

Then follows his disposal of his estate : to wife Mary the dwelling house &c. during her natural life ; to nephew Mr Samuel Stone of Connecticut thirty pounds ; to " my cousen his son John ten pounds ;" to dear brother and fellow officer Mr Phillips five pounds and Aquinas his Sum. in folio ; to my sometimes servant Elizabeth Tenney ells Parratt ten pounds ; to loving neice Mrs Mary Matosius of Malden in Essex in old England ten pounds ; to loving niece Mrs Elizabeth C..ton wife of the Preacher of Roterdam in

Holland ten pounds ; to the wife of cousin Rogers of Billerica five pounds ; sundry gifts to servants ; all his Latin books to Harvard College and some English books, as appears in the Catalogue.

The rest of the estate in lands not given to wife during her natural life, he gives to the Church and town of Rowley upon condition that they pay or cause to be paid &c. unto Ezekiel Rogers the son of Mr Nathaniel Rogers late pastor of the Church of Ipswich deceased the sum of eight score pounds.

The real estate given to wife, for term of her life, after her decease to go to the church and town of Rowley to enable them the better to maintain two teaching elders in the church for ever, on condition that they settle an elder within four years and so from time to time when changes occur by death or removal any other way. On failure of this condition the said houses and lands to be to the use of Harvard College. Wife Mary to be sole executrix.*

The amount of his estate as rendered in the Inventory was over 1535£, of which 400£ was in lands that were Thomas Barker's (his wife's former husband).

This will is on file among the probate papers of Essex County ; but I do not find any copy of it in the Registry or any record of probate or administration granted. In the March term of the Ipswich Court, 1665, Ezekiel Rogers, the son of Mr. Nathaniel Rogers of Ipswich, deceased, brought suit against Mrs. Mary Rogers, the executrix of the above will, for not performing a promise and engagement made to the said Nathaniel in the behalf of his son, wherein the said Mr. Ezekiel Rogers, of Rowley, had obliged himself to provide for Ezekiel the son of Nathaniel, and to make his portion as good as the rest of the sons of the said Nathaniel. The plaintiff in his declaration says that his father for that reason gave him no portion in his estate, except a small pledge of his love, and discharged himself from any care concerning him, and, indeed, looked upon him as the elder brother, though but his fourth son.

This case is valuable and important, since it furnishes evidence that the wife of the Rev. William Hubbard was Mary,† and not Margaret, as all our New England authorities have had it, and thus confirms Candler's statement, made in his account of the Knapp family. I fail to find the least bit of evidence, either that Nathaniel Rogers had a daughter Margaret or that William Hubbard had a

---

* Rev. Ezekiel Rogers's will is printed in full in the REGISTER, vol. v. pp. 125-8.—ED.
† Candler in his Knapp pedigree gives the name of the husband of Mary Rogers as " Wm. Hobert," and in his Rogers pedigree as " Wm. Heley " (*vide* REGISTER, xvii. 47). Mr. Waters makes it evident that the surname in the Knapp pedigree (Hobert, *i. e.* Hubbard) is correct.

William Hubart or Hubbard of the County of Essex, England, who afterwards settled at Ipswich, Mass., married Judith, daughter of John and Martha (Blosse) Knapp, of Ipswich, England (see The Visitation of Suffolk, ed. by Metcalf, 1882, p. 149 ; REG. xvii. 47). He was father of Rev. William Hubbard, who married Mary Rogers.

The first book in which I find the christian name of the wife of Rev. William Hubbard given is John Farmer's Genealogical Register, published in 1829, where on page 152 she is called " Margaret daughter of Rev. Nathaniel Rogers." Subsequent writers have repeated Farmer's error.—EDITOR.

wife bearing that name. This Mary Hubbard seems to be living as late as 26 March, 1685, whĕn she joins her husband in a conveyance of certain land in Ipswich. The following are some of the depositions filed in this case.

The testimony of MARY HUBBERT.

I can affirme that aft^r my Father Rogers' death my Brother Ezekiell Rogers was very desirous to have lived wth his Cousen Mr Ezekiell Rogers of Rowley & he rendred this as ye reason, w^n sundry complaints were made to his mother against him, that he knew he could please him, if he lived with him, wch he knew he should never doe, unlesse he lived there, in reg^d that sundry informations would be carried to his Cousen agst him, wch he should be able no otherwise to prevent. And farth^r I know that our friends did endeavour to insinuate so much into my Couzen, but were discouraged therefrom by a report they heard from presseing it over farr, wch report was, that one nere to my Cozen should say, nameing of him by some opprobrious terme, that he should not come there. Also when my Brother lived with him before, he wore his haire longer, by my Cosins sufferance, contrarie to my Fathers desire, then the rest of his Brethren; Farther my Bro: rendred this as the reason why he was not willing to live constantly at the Colledge, because he had not convenient maintenance allowed, my Cosin not allowing above five pound a year at ye most. To the truth of w^t is above written I can attest upon oath if called thereunto.

March 31. 1665.   MARY HUBBERT.

The Deposition of Mrs MARGARET ROGERS aged about 55 yeares.

This Deponent sayth that soon after her husbands death, goeing to visit her cousin M^r Ez. Rogers of Rowly, he told her that he would doe for her son Ezekiel according no hore followeth viz. That he would give him his house where he then lived wth severall parcells of land, wch he then mentioned, & shewed ye place of them, altho she had now forgotten the particulars: She thinks also he promised her then to allow 10£ a year towards his education, yet (being long since she cannot speak so punctially thereunto). Further at another time since this Deponent went to the sayd M^r Ez. Rogers to speake wth him about her son Ezekiels hayre, y^t was complayned of, to be too long: but when M^r Ez. Rogers would have had her son bound to let his hayre be no longer then to ye lower tip of his eares, she told him she would never yeild to such a snare for her child, tho he never had peny of him while he lived. Also this Deponent sayd y^t James Baily told her that M^r Ez. Rogers had appoynted him to pay fourty pound to her upon the account of her son Ezekiel, but she never knew but of ten pound thereof paid: Also that she would have been glad if her son Ezekiel might have lived wth her Cousin M^r Ez. Rogers at Rowly, and was troubled that there was no way appearing to have it so, altho her son Ezekiel alwayes about those times seemed very desirous so to doe. The Deponent also saith that Mr Ez. Rogers told her he had appointed James Baily to pay her fourty pound in four years towards the education of her son Ezekiel, And further saith not

March 3065.   Sworne before me   DANIEL DENISON.

"MATHEW BOYES* of Leeds in the County of Yorke Clothworker aged fifty yeares or thereaboutes" sworn at York 16 Jan'y 1661, makes a deposition concerning the matter.

The testimony of JOHN PICKARD, aged forty three years, made 28 March 1665, is to the effect that he understood from Mr Ezekiel Rogers of Rowly that there were three reasons why he would not give his kinsman more. "'1 Because he refused to dwell wth him. 2 Because he would not keep at Colledge though there he would have maynteyned him. 3 Because he spake to his mother to have his haire cutt, but could not gett it done, And seuerall other things were the mention not here materiall."

Essex Co. Court Papers, Vol. X. Nos. 90–98.

A notable error has been made by all who have written about Ezekiel Rogers, of Rowley. They have all, one after another, stated that he brought over "the wife of his youth," Sarah Everard, who lived here about ten years, and died in Rowley, etc. That he brought over the wife of his youth I do not deny; but that her name was Sarah Everard I can deny with confidence, for I find her provided with another husband, in the person of Ezekiel's eldest brother Daniel, who had by her, as his second wife, four children. Who then was the first wife of Ezekiel Rogers? That he had a wife buried in Rowley about ten years after his coming over is true. Her name, however, was *Joan*, buried 8 May, 1649. This is a strong confirmation of a pedigree which I had constructed in England before I had the opportunity to discover this important fact. I had already been led to give Mr. Ezekiel Rogers a wife Joan by the following evidence which I had discovered in my researches among Wills and Feet of Fines :—

Between Richard Raynton, gen. *quer.* and Ezekiel Rogers, clerk and Johanna his wife, *deforc.*, for one messuage, one garden, nine acres of meadow and six acres of pasture, with the appurtenances &c in Bermondsey. Consideration 100^{li} sterling.   Trin. 11 Car. I. Surrey.
(Feet of Fines.)

THOMAS DAMPIER *als* DAMPORT of Stratford at Bow, gentleman, 26 March 1617, proved 15 February 1627. Mentions son James, daughter Katherine, wife Joane, sister Joane, now wife of John Creed of Shepton Mallett in the County of Somerset, and her sons Matthew, Stephen and John Webb, cousin Marmaduke Moore and daughter Katherine now wife of Hugh Cressie, of London, merchant.

To my daughter in law Joane Hartopp, now wife of Ezekiel Rogers of Hatfield, Essex, gentleman, twenty pounds within six months after my decease.   Barrington, 18 (P. C. C.).

He must have married his second wife (Sarah?), daughter of Mr. John Wilson, very soon after; for Emanuel Downing writes from

---

* Matthew Boyes was an early settler of Roxbury (REGISTER, xxxv. 24). He was freeman of Massachusetts May 22, 1639 ; removed to Rowley, which he represented in the General Court in 1641, 3, 5 and 50; returned to England as early as 1657. He was father of Rev. Joseph Boyse, of Dublin, Ireland, a famous Puritan author. (See REGISTER, xii. 65.)—EDITOR.

Salem, 24. 12. 1650, to John Winthrop, Jr., "Mr. Rogers of Rowly hath last weeke buryed his wife and childe within a few dayes after shee was brought to bed."

21 Feb. 1621. Ezekiel Rogers, Clerk, instituted to the Rectory of Rowley, void by the death of Henry Pickard, Clerk, on the nomination of Sir Francis Barrington, Baronet. Institution Books, York.

Extract from a Letter of Robert Ryece to John Winthrop, 1 March, 1636.

" One accidente which I credibly hard, I can not omytte;—While the Bishop his chancelor, Dr. Corbett, was vpon his seate of justice at Bury, newes was broughte hym that Mr. Rogers of Dedham dyed the last nighte. Is he so? sayd the chancelor, let him goe in reste, for he hath troobled all the contry these 30 yeeres, & dyd poyson all those partes for x myle rounde abowte that place,—the manner of whose death is thus reported; whiles the Bishop was at Ipswiche, one daye, havinge occasion to ryde forthe, comanded his servantes to hyer poste horses; who browght hym worde that all the horses were taken vp, by suche as wente to the sermon at Dedham. Is the wynde at that doore? sayde the Bishop, I wyll soone ease that; & so not long after, as the Commissary synce confessed, he had commande from Canterbury vpon the complaynte of Norwich to stay the lecture at Dedham : wherevpon the Commissary wrote a friendely letter to Mr. Rogers, shewenge hym he had commandemente from Canterbury to require hym to stay his lecture now for a whiles the plague continewed, which by suche concourses was daylie encreased. Mr. Rogers, beleevinge, as was pretended, stayed his lecture, & after harvest ended, the Doctor & Comissary was moved for renewene of the lecture ; the Comissary gave fayer woordes, promysynge uery shortely thay shoolde haue liberty, which after sondry promyses, withowte all in all intention, Mr. Rogers seinge there was a secrett determination wholly to suppresse that leeture, this strooke hym to the harte, hastened all his natural malladies to his vttermost periode." Winthrop Papers, Mass. Hist. Coll.
Fourth Series, Vol. VI. p. 412.

Extract from a Letter of Emanuel Downing to John Winthrop, 6 March, 1636.

" I was at Mr. Rogers of Dedham his funerall, where there were more people than 3 such Churches could hold : the gallery was soe over loaden with people that it sunck and crackt and in the midle where yt was Joynted the tymbers gaped and parted on from an other soe that there was a great cry in the Church: they vnder the gallery fearing to be smothered, those that were vpon yt hasted of, some on way some an other, and some leaped downe among the people into the Church: those in the body of the Church seing the tymbers gape were sore afrighted, but yt pleased God to honour that good man departed with a miracle at his death, for the gallerie stood and the people went on againe, though not so manie as before; had yᵗ faln as blackfryars did vnder the popishe assembly, yt would haue ben a great wound to our religion." Winthrop Papers, Mass. Hist. Coll.
Fourth Series, Vol. VI. p. 47.

Mr. Nathaniel Rogers arrived in New England 17 Nov. 1636.*

* Winthrop's New England, vol. i. p. 205 (2d ed. p. 244).

Concerning his voyage, the following extract from a Letter of
Brampton Gurdon to John Winthrop, dated Assington, this 30 of
August (1636), seems worth inserting. here.

"It hathe faulne out verry hard with the shipe whear in Mr.
Nathaniel Rogers imbarked himselff, his wiff who locke for* at the
end of 7^{bur}, 4 children, & 3 other pore fameles out of this towen;
won is Robinson that lived in Litle Waldenfeld, with his wiff & 6
children; they went abord at Grauesend the furst of Jeuen, & have euer
scins ben houareng to the Ile of Wite, & this day Mris Crane, their
scister, & Mris Rogers mother in law tould me her husband had a letter
from them from Plimworth, writ on Saturday scenight. This will fall
exceding heui to dyuers in the ship who had mad som prouicyon for their
liuelyhod in New England. Thay will be inforsed to spe[nd] it before
they goe, & all for want of a constant Est wind. Thay haue had the
wind for a day or 2, & then brought backe agayen. Thay haue had dyuers
feruent prayers to geue them a good wind, but the tyem is not yet coum
for God to haue the prayes of it."

Winthrop Papers, Mass. Hist. Coll.

Fourth Series, Vol. VI. p. 560.

The will of the Rev. NATHANIEL ROGERS, Pastor of the Church at
Ipswich, taken from his own mouth, July 3, *Anno Domini* 1655,
was proved in court at Ipswich, 25–7–1655. He reckons his estate
in Old and New England at about twelve hundred pounds, four
hundred pounds of which "is expected from my father M^r. Robert
Crane in England." He makes the portion of John, though his
eldest son, equal only with the others, viz. Nathaniel, Samuel and
Timothy, and gives to each one hundred pounds out of his estate in
Old England and one hundred pounds out of his estate in New England. To his son Ezekiel he gives twenty pounds, which he may
take in books if he pleases. To his daughter he had already given
two hundred pounds. To his three grandchildren, John, Nathaniel
and Margaret Hubbard, he gives forty shillings each. To his cousin,
John Rogers, five pounds, in the hands of Ensign Howlett. To
Elizabeth, Nathaniel, John and Mary, children of his cousin John
Harris,† of Rowley, he gives twenty shillings each. To Harvard
College, five pounds. The remainder he leaves to his wife Margaret,
whom he appoints executrix.

The original will is on file in the Probate Registry of Essex
County, and a copy of it is preserved among the papers of the case
of Rogers *vs* Rogers already referred to.

Mrs. Margaret Rogers died in Ipswich, 23 January, 1675, and
admon. was granted to her eldest son, John Rogers, 30 March
following (1676.)

Administration of the estate of Margaret Rogers, of Ipswich in

---

* I am inclined to think that this must refer to her expected confinement. Ezekiel must
have been born just about this time.—H. F. W.

† The wife of John Harris of Rowley was named Bridget. I would suggest that she may
have been Bridget Anger, one of the children of Edmond and Bridget Anger (see the wills
of Dorothy Rogers of Dedham and of John Rogers of Colchester).—H. F. W.

New England, widow, was also granted in England, 21 March, 1677, to William Hubbard, principal creditor.

From her age, as given in her deposition, it would appear that she was born about 1610. Her mother, therefore, could not have been the Mary Sparhawke, daughter of Samuel, baptized 1 February, 1600. (See New Eng. Hist. Gen. Reg., Vol. XIX. p. 125.)

There remains John Rogers, of Billerica, who undoubtedly belonged to this family, as we may learn from the will of Ezekiel of Rowley. The recent history of Billerica, by our associate, Rev. Mr. Hazen, furnishes a good account of him and his descendants. His will can be found on record in the Suffolk Registry (X.—23). It was "declared" 22 January, 1685, and letters were granted 8 June, 1687, to Thomas and Nathaniel, the executors. He gives to Nathaniel one half the house, etc., and to Thomas the other half after the death of the widow, who is to have the use of it. Other bequests to sons John and Daniel, daughter Priscilla, grandchild Mary French (at 21), son George Browne and wife's daughter Mary Browne. He is said to have died 25 January, 1685(6), æt. 74, and was born therefore about 1611 or 1612. On the Tabular Pedigree which accompanies these notes will be found two Johns, either of whom might be this individual, so far as date of birth would indicate. I cannot help thinking that John, the son of Nathaniel, the schoolmaster, was the one referred to in will of his uncle John, of Dedham, as "the sadler," brother to Elizabeth Rogers. This sister, I doubt not, was adopted by her uncle, and was the one mentioned by the widow Dorothy Rogers in her will, as "my maid Elizabeth Rogers." The John Rogers who lived in Billerica was evidently a baker (as I am informed by Mr. Hazen). Whether a man would change an occupation requiring an apprenticehood for another is a question. We have still left John, the second son of Thomas Rogers, who probably was placed by his father to learn some other trade than the ancestral one of shoemaking, in which the eldest son, Thomas, was to succeed him. I am therefore inclined to think that we are to look here for our Billerica Rogers.

It was my good fortune to find in the British Museum two Elegies which seem to have escaped notice hitherto; one in manuscript, which I found in the well known Harleian collection; the other a printed broadside, in a collection known as the Luttrell collection. I found in this latter collection divers other elegies and eulogies which deserve to be known; among them one on the Rev. William Jenkin the younger, I remember, and another on Col. Rainborough.

The two elegies referred to here follow :—

Upon the death of old Mr Rogers of wethersfield minister of god his word,
late deceased.

In Rama once a voyce was heard   W^{ch} now in weathersfield doth sound
  Of bytter lamentation,   An heavy visitation.

He is not now who lately was
  As Rachells children were not
Soe we shall hardly fynd the lyke
  Crye loud therefore & spare not.
The cloudie piller now is gone
  That guyded in the day
And eke ye fire wch in the night
  Did poynt us out the way.
Alas therfore what shall we doe
  Our Moses cannot crie,
Nor stand up in the gapp to stay
  Gods iudgements when they flie.
How shall we passe to Canaan now
  The wildernesse is wide
Soe full of Tygers, Beares & wolues
  And many a beast besyde.
Who shall stand up to plead wth God
  ffor to supply our neede.
Our waters stand, our Manna feast
  Whereon our soules did feede.
Oh happie it was wth weathersfielde
  And neighboure townes about
When they enioyed y^t worthy light
  Which now is cleane worne out.
Noe greater proofe of loue to god
  Doth Christ himself require
Then was p'formed of this man
  Wthall his hartes desire
Wth wisedome and discretion both
  He fedd Christs lambs indeede
Devydeinge out them portions all
  According to their neede.
To stronge ones he gave stronger meat
  Who better could apply y^t
And to the weaker sort also
  As best might fitt their dyett.
The sicke and feeble ones alsoe
  He nourished paynefully
And evermore his hart did yerne
  To heare ye poore mans crie.
He bound up broken hearted ones
  He did ye hungrie feed
He brought the wandringe home againe
  And did supplie their neede
He sought their peace continually
  He ended all their striefe
Reioyceing neuer more then when
  They ledd a Christian lyfe.
He spared noe labour of the mynde
  Noe bodilie griefe nor payne

That tended to his peoples good
  And to his masters gayne. [fayle
When strength of leggs and feete did
  On horseback he did ryde
And wheresoeuer he became
  His tallent well emploid.
Soe deerely did he loue gods house
  When Arons bell did call
Noe winde or weather might him lett
  He ventred lyfe and all.
Thus did he leade them forth wth ioy
  To pastures fresh and greene
And to the lyuely water pooles
  As cleere as hath beene seene.
Rare was his order to catechise
  His doctrine sound & playne
And by this holy ordynance
  He many soules did gayne.
Thus hath he spent his vitall breath
  In honour and renowne
His hower is past, his glasse is runne
  And he hath gott the crowne.
And now behold ye shepehards all
  Whom god hath given this station
See here a patterne to behoulde
  fit for your imitation.
The better sort neede yet to learne
  This patterne to behould
As for the rest, learne you were best
  Looke better to your soulde.
And now Oh woefull weathersfield
  Whose fame soe farr hath sounded
Looke how thou hast received & heard
  And how thy faith is grounded.
And to thy faith and godly life
  As thou before hast learned
Wthout the wch thy faith is deade
  And cannot be discerned.
ffor now the Lord doth call for fruite
  To answere all his payne
And wher he hath bestowed much
  He lookes for much agayne.
Loue thou therefore gods ordynance
  Sell all, that to obteyne
And buy the fielde wher treasure is
  That euer shall remayne
Then thou wth him thats gone before
  Shall 𝔥allelujah singe
And Reigne in heaven for euermore
  Wth Christ our lord and kinge.
         finis.
         [Harleian MS. 1598.]

A mournefull Epitaph upon the death of that reverend vvorthy Pastor Mr JOHN
ROGERS, late preacher of Gods vvord at Dedham in Essex, vvho departed this
life the 18 of October in the yeere 1636.

        1.
Come helpe us mourn good Shepherds all,
  who love Christs flock indeed
Helpe us to beg, pleade, cry & call,
  in this our time of need.

        2.   [old,
Come weep and mourne, both yong and
  your harts to sorrow move
Both Sheepe and Lambs all of his fould
  shew forth your deerest love.

3.
Our joy is gone, our soules delight,
  our blessed sonne of thunder,
Our valiant champion in Gods sight,
  to breake sinnes boults in sunder.

4.
Our famous light which lately stood
  on hill within our towne :   [abroad,
Whose beames were spread   so   farre
  is now by death tooke downe.

5.
Those lively christall streames so pure,
  with pastures fresh and greene ;
From us alas are lock't full sure,
  and can no more be seene.

6.
Oh mournefull flocke who art deprived
  of such a faithfull guide ;
Whose drooping soules he hath reviv'd
  Full many a time and tide.

7.
Our faithfull Moses now is gone,
  Which stood up in the breach ;
To stay Gods wrath with many a groane,
  his hands to heaven did stretch.

8.
His life Gods glory did advance,
  his doctrine good and plaine :
And by Gods holy ordinaace
  he many a soule did gaine.

9.
No paine nor labour he did spare,
  the hungry soules to feed,
Dividing out each one his share,
  according to their need,

10.
A person grave, a patron rare,
  most humble, godly, wise,
Whose presence made the wicked feare,
  when they beheld his eyes.

11.
His ears were open and attent,
  To heare the poore mans cry :
And speedily his heart was bent,
  to find a remedy.

12.
To rich and poore, to old and yung,
  most courteous, mild and meeke,
The mourning soules he brought along,
  and comforted the weake.

13.
Much comfort heere his soule possest,
  his life fame, and renowne,
And now with Saints and Angels blest,
  he weares a glorious crowne.

14.
Where many a soule is gone before,
  Which he through Christ hath gain'd,
His glory shines as Sunne therefore,
  And never shall be stained.

15.
You pastors all of Christ his fould,
  of soules who have the charge,
See here a patterne to behold
  Your duties to your charge.

16.
His faith, his love, his godly care,
  his zeale sinne to suppresse :
His pitty showes to such as were,
  in griefe and heavinesse.

17.
His humble heart did soon make peace,
  by arbitration wise,
All jars and strifes he made to cease,
  twixt neighbours that did rise.

18.
But now those ioyfull dayes are gone,
  which made our hearts so glad,
And comfort brought to many one,
  when sorrow made them sad.

19.
Our Zion temple songs doe cease,
  our burning shining light
Is gone to everlasting peace,
  and bids us all good night.

20.
Our constant Lector twelve dayes fame,
  and ioy of Saints all round,
To which Gods armies flocking came,
  To heare his doctrine sound.

21.
Gods holy Law and Gospel pure,
  he preach't with courage bould,
Whereby he many did allure,
  and brought to Christ his fould.

22.
The poore and hungry soules alway,
  with good things he did fill,
The rich, nor any went away,
  Without Gods mind and will.

23.
Most faithfully he preach't Gods will,
  with wisedome from above,
And left for to direct us still,
  his booke of faith and love.

24.
Gods counsell and the narrow way,
  he clearely did unfold
Without excuse to leave all they,
  That would not be controld.

25.
His proudest foes on every side,
  who sought his deprivation,
He still did overcome their pride,
  by humble conversation.

26.
Against hels force and Satans rage,
  God kept him in his station,
And still preserved him in his old age,
  In *Dedhams* congregation.

27.

From weeke to weeke, from day to day,
he cryed in our eares :
And this he did without delay,
the space of thirty yeeres.

28.

In zeale he was a flaming fire,
yet humble and discreet,
Which made his chiefest foes admire,
and swadged their malice great.

29.

They often sought for to prevaile,
to take away our joy,
To quench our light they did assaile
our glory to destroy.

30.

But God did guard his choice elect,
who worthy was through Christ,
From dangers all did him protect,
and tooke home at last.

31.

The time of life that God him lent,
was three score yeeres and seven,
The greatest part of which he spent,
to bring soules into heaven.

32.

Oh happy change and blessed gaine,
good time for him to die :
Vnhappy we that still remaine
more sinfull dayes to see.

33.

Yet happy now likewise are they,
which are in state of grace,
And were so wise that in their dayes,
with God they made their peace.

34.

Now magnifie the providence,
of Gods election strong,
That he such dayes by sure defence,
In mercy did prolong.

35.

And now hold fast with diligence,
the trueths which you have learn'd
And bring forth fruit with patience,
that grace may be discern'd.

36.

Those graces learne to imitate,
in him which shine so bright,
So shalt thou live in happy state,
and pleasing in Gods sight.

37.

A wife hath lost a heavenly head,
children a father deare,
A losse to all on every side,
and to his flocke most neere.

38.

His house a blessed *Bethel* was,
as plainely did appeare :
He lived to see his fruits in grace,
on all his children deare.

39.

But now alas what shall we doe
Gods anger to revoke,
Our sinfulnesse have brought us to
This sad and heavy stroake.

40.

Our sleepy formall carelessnesse,
in hearing of Gods word :
Vnfruitfull barren heartednesse,
though we with meanes were stored.

41.

All those that have worne out this light,
and yet remain all darke,
How shall it now their soules affright,
to weare this cursed marke.

42.

Now let us all repent and pray,
with zeale and fervency,
That of the Lord obtaine we may,
some comfort and supply.

43.

Our King and Counsell Lord preserve,
and all of each degree,
That from his trueth we may not swerve,
but therein live and die.

44.

That with him that's gone before,
a kingdome may obtaine,
And then with Saints for evermore,
in glory may remaine.

AN EPIGRAM.

In morning wake with God, and beg his
    grace,
Offend not his good spirit in any case,
Hang fast on Christ, cleave closse unto
    his word,
No time forget to weare the christian
    sword,

Run cheerefully your generall is before,
Our blessed captain Christ hath opened
    the doore
Got victory against sin, death and hell,
Eternall life for aye with him shall
    dwell,
Returne my soule, goe foorth unto thy
    rest,
Strange joyes are gone which cannot be
    exprest.

                    I. L.

FINIS

Printed for the yeere, 1642.
Eulogies and Elegies
            Luttrell Coll. Vol. I.
               British Museum.

A FINAL CONCORD was made between Richard Grene, *quer.*, and William Convers, *deforc.*, about three acres of arable land with the appurtenances in Navestock, the consideration being forty pounds sterling.
Feet of Fines, Co. of Essex, Easter Term, 36th Eliz[th].

Will of THOMAS CONVERS, of Westmersey, Co. Essex, yeoman, 9 May 1599, proved 11 January 1599. To my sons Thomas and Edward Convers all my lands and tenements, whatsoever they be in this realm of England, towards the education and bringing up of my children &c. To my son John Convers ten score pounds out of the lands &c. in two years after he shall accomplish the full age of twenty one years, provided if my said son shall happen to enjoy by inheritance one cottage and orchard (copyhold) in Chessen (Cheshunt?) in Co. Herts, then he to have but nine score pounds. To my daughters Lettes, Katren and Frances Convers fifty pounds each in one year after marriage or at the age of twenty four years. My son Thomas Convers to be executor and son Edward to be supervisor.   Commissary Court, Essex and Herts.

WILLIAM CONVERS of Layndon, Essex, husbandman, 15 June 1607, proved 17 July 1607. To my son William ten pounds at the age of twenty one years. To my daughters Agnes and Joane Convers thirty pounds each at the age of eighteen years. To my mother Joane Convers three pounds if she will depart from my wife and not be at her keeping. To the poor of Layndon ten shillings, and to the poor of Ramsden Bellhouse three shillings and four pence. To my wife Agnes Convers all my goods and chattels &c. and she to be executrix. My brother John Convers to be overseer and I give to him ten shillings.   Com. Court, Essex and Herts.

JOHN CONVERS of Basildon, Essex, yeoman, 5 May 1614, proved 6 June, 1614. He mentions wife Elizabeth, three daughters Joane, Elizabeth and Lydia Convers, son in law William Pullen (and his brother Thomas Pullen), sister Ruth, and cousin Robert Vyncet.
                       Com. Court, Essex and Herts.

ALLEN CONVERS of Southweald in the County of Essex, yeoman, 3 January 1636, proved at Brentwood 28 June 1639. To the poor of the upland of Southweald the sum of twenty shillings, to be paid to the overseers of the said parish &c. within one month next after my decease. To Elizabeth my wife all my house and land in Navestock and Stanford Ryvers, for the term of her natural life, and after her decease to my son Gabriel Convers and to his heirs forever. To Elizabeth, my wife, all my house & land in Fyfield alias Fyfed for term of her natural life, and after her decease to my son Daniel and to his heirs forever according to a deed of feoffment. To my son Andrew the sum of four pounds a year for the term of five years, to be paid unto him by my son Daniel, the first payment to begin at the second feast of S[t] Michael the Archangel next after my decease, and so from year to year until the said term of five years be expired. I give and bequeath to Richard Convers, my son, other four pounds a year, &c., to be paid unto him by my son Daniel in manner & form as aforesaid. To Anne Shelton, my daughter, the sum of forty shillings a year &c. &c. To Hester Skynner my daughter other forty shillings a year &c. Item I give & bequeath to Edward my son the sum of five shillings to be paid unto him by my executrix. To my son Gabriel the sum of five shillings &c. To my son Daniel five shillings. To my son Andrew five pounds, to be paid him within two years after my decease. To Richard my son the sum of ten pounds, to be paid within one year after my decease. To Anne Shelton my daughter five pounds within two years &c. To Richard & Gabriel my sons one great brass pot and one caldron between them and to take them after the decease of Elizabeth my wife. Other personal property to daughter Hester Skynner. All the rest of my said goods, not bequeathed nor given away, to Elizabeth my wife whom I make executrix &c., to pay such legacies as I have bequeathed and given away and to see my body buried in a decent and comely manner. Wit: Samuel Luckin, Thomas Osborne.

Whitehead, 56. [Registry of Archdeaconry of Essex.]

ELIZABETH ADAMS of the parish of Rederith [Rotherhithe] in the County of Surrey, widow, late the wife of John Adams, late of Branston in the County of Northampton, yeoman, deceased, being weak and aged, 10 December, 1660, proved the last of December 1660. I give and bequeath unto my son Thomas Adams (who about twelve years ago went into Virginia) five pounds to be paid him or his assigns within six months after my decease. To my son George Adams (who about three years since went into France) twenty pounds within six months &c. To Hugh Thompson twelve pence, and no more, within six months &c. To my daughter Rebecca Brownlow, wife of Peter Brownlow, forty pounds within six months. To my daughter Sarah Adams fifty pounds within six months. My daughter Mary Adams to be sole executrix and residuary legatee. Wit: Joane Vahun (by mark), Jane Hilles, William Barrett (by mark) and John Fuller, Scrivener.   Nabbs, 260.

At Sea Latitude 24 degrees 7ber ye 9th 1662. Aboard ye Restauraĉon.

Loveinge Brother These certifie yow that wee sett sayle from New England upon the ffifth day of August since which time wee have had two exceedinge great stormes of winde insomuch that wee have lost all our mast and throwne overboard a great deale of ffish and mickrell and pipe staves as alsoe three horses drowned one of which was betwixt yourselfe and my brother Thomas soe that you have lost all as well as my brother Thomas and myselfe and Peter. I knowe not whether I have saved anything or noe till I come to some port soe much as some of my wearinge Cloathes were thrown over board it was the Lord's Grt mercy that hee did spare our lives and was more then we did expect (twice) the Lord give us hearts to bee truely thankfull for his mercies wee lye like the wracke in the Sea and know not what harbour wee shall gett to and are scarce of provisions and water, but three pints of water a man a day (the Lord deliver us) I hope yow have paid the three pounds three shillings I charged to yow from Deale if yow have not pray doe. But I doe not question but it is paid long ere this I have abt fifty pounds or sixty pounds or seventy pounds of Tobacco in Captaine Thomas Carter's hande at Nancemund in Jeames River if I come not home this twelve monethes then pray looke after itt for then yow may conclude the Lord hath taken mee out of this world. But I hope ere that he will fitt mee for a better world I had a servant run away in Virginia that makes mee not knowe what Quantitie of Tobacco is in Captaine Carter's hands I pray if it should please God to deale otherwise then yow expect with mee that yow would see after that and lett my brother Peter my sister Mary and William have it Captaine Jno Whitty who uses Virginia knowes the man and if yow can speake to him hee will bring it home hee knowes the man is a very honest man and lett them three have their shares of what is due to mee which wilbee seventy or eighty pounds apeece and seventy or eighty pounds amongst all of yow for mourninge. I am in hast the shipp being under saile—soe leavinge yow to the protection of Almighty God with my kinde Love to yourselfe and all freinds rest

Yo^r Loveing brother   STEPHEN FOX.

20 October, 1663 emanavit commissio Johanni Fox fratri nrãli etc.

Juxon, 119.

FRANCIS WILLIS of the parish of Ware River, in the County of Gloucester, in Virginia, but now resident in the parish of East Greenwich in the County of Kent, Gentleman, 6 July 1689, proved 25 April 1691. My body to be decently buried, my executor not exceeding one hundred pounds sterling at my funeral, in costs & charges. To my loving sister Grace Feilder one hundred & twenty pounds sterling to be paid in manner & form following (that is to say) fifteen pounds per annum during her life, or until the sum of one hundred & twenty pounds be fully paid, which first shall happen. To Charles Feilder, the son of my sister Grace aforesaid, one hundred pounds sterling (in payments of twenty pounds per annum until the sum of one hundred pounds be fully paid). To my cousin Elizabeth Butler and her daughter Sarah Butts ten pounds sterling apiece. To my cousins Frances and Elizabeth Willis, sisters to Hugh Willis, clerk, deceased, the sum of ten pounds sterling apiece. To Francis & Christopher Willis, the sons of the said Hugh Willis, the sum of twenty pounds sterling apiece. To the widow of Hugh Willis ten pounds sterling. To Susanna Willis, the daughter of my brother Henry Willis, ten pounds sterling. To my cousins John & Joane Lipton one hundred pounds sterling and to her two children, Henry & Mary, one hundred and thirty pounds sterling apiece. To my cousin Mary Herren, the daughter of my brother Henry Willis deceased, the sum of three hundred and fifty pounds sterling. To Alice Willis, daughter of said brother Henry, three hundred & fifty pounds sterling. To my loving cousin Elizabeth Ironmonger one hundred pounds sterling and to her two sons Charles & Matthew Ironmonger one hundred pounds sterling apiece. To William Willis, the son of my brother William Willis deceased one hundred & fifty pounds sterling. To the poor of the parish of St Fowles als St Algate in the city of Oxford, the place of my birth, one hundred pounds sterling. And all my legacies I desire may be paid within eighteen months after my decease.

To my dear & loving wife Jane Willis, the sum of one thousand pounds sterling, to be paid her in the first place, within one year after my decease, and all the household vessels of plate, linen & bedding which she brought over with her from Virginia to England (& other personal estate).

I give unto the said William Willis, the son of my brother William Willis deceased, all that land & plantation which his father formerly lived upon & held of me, with the appurtenances, situate on the South side of Crany Creek, containing one hundred acres or thereabouts, to him & the heirs of his body lawfully begotten or to be begotten, and for want of such heirs then to the right heirs of me the said Francis Willis.

I give & devise unto the said Francis Willis, the son of my brother Henry Willis, all the rest & residue of all my other estate & estates whatsoever in lands, goods, moneye, cattle & chattells that I now at this time stand seized or possessed in Virginia and not herein already devised, also one thousand pounds, to be paid him within eighteen mouths after my decease.

I ordain & make William Willis, the son of brother Henry Willis deceased, sole executor of this my will & testament. I give unto Mr Edward Polter, of the Parish of St Peters in the East in Oxford city, milliner, and Mr George Richards of London, merchant, whom I desire & appoint to be overseers &c., the sum of ten pounds sterling apiece.

Wit: Richard Jones, Margaret Nicholson, Joseph Busfield.

Vere, 201.

[Francis Willis, the progenitor of the worthy and prominent Virginia family of the name Willis, was granted, July 3, 1642, 450 acres of land in that portion of York County from which Gloucester County was formed by act of Assembly in the same year. (*Va. Land Registry*, Book No. 2, p. 199.)

He represented Gloucester County in the House of Burgesses in 1652, and later. Francis (born 1685–90), son of Hugh Willis, the last presumably his brother, is said to have married " Lady " Ann Rich in England about the year 1716. She was interred near the chancel of Ware Church, Gloucester County. The fragments of the broken slab above her grave present the following inscription :

" Here lyeth the body of Mrs. Ann Willis the wife of Col. Francis Willis, who departed this life the 10th of June, 1727, in the 32nd year of her age; Also the body of A** daughter of the above aged 7 days."

There are a number of extensive land grants of subsequent record, to Thomas, Coll^o Francis, William, John, Richard, Robert, Major Henry, David, Francis, Augustine and Herod Willis, to the year 1772, inclusive, located in the counties of York, Lancaster, Gloucester, Westmoreland, Middlesex, Henrico, Spotsylvania, Orange, Goochland, Albermarle, Brunswick and Pittsylvania counties. Major, subsequently Colonel Henry Willis, was one of the Trustees of the town of Fredericksburgh, Va., laid off in 1727. Col. William Byrd, visiting the town in 1732, says: " Col. Willis, who is the top sunn of the place .... walked me about his town of Fredericksburg." A Henry Willis was member of the House of Burgesses from Gloucester County in 1726, and Francis Willis in 1736. Lewis Burwell married between Oct. 22–29, 1736, Mary, presumably a daughter of the last; and Rebecca, daughter of this Lewis and Mary (Willis) Burwell, of " White Marsh," Gloucester County, married Jaquelin, seventh child of Richard and Elizabeth (Jaquelin) Ambler (see *Genealogical Gleanings*, p. 140).

Lewis Willis was one of the signers of the articles of " Association," dated Feb. 27, 1766, composed chiefly of residents of Westmoreland County, and known as the " Westmoreland Association, " protesting against the stamp act, and binding themselves not to use any articles imported from Great Britain subject to such tax.

Representatives of the Willis family have been allied with nearly every family of prominence in Virginia.—R. A. BROCK, *Richmond, Va.*]

JOHN WEST, late of New York but now of Boston in New England, Esquire, 29 January 1689, proved 25 November 1691. My just debts to be paid and all the rest & residue of my estate, both real & personal, and all my land & tenements, of what nature or kind soever or wheresoever they be, I give, devise & bequeath to my dear & well-beloved wife Anne West; and I make her my executrix.

Which day appeared personally Charles Lydgett of the parish of St Midreds Poultry, London, merchant, aged about thirty four years, and John Palmer of the parish of St Clement Danes in the County of Middlesex, gentleman, aged about forty two years, and, being sworn upon the Holy Evangelists to depose the truth, did generally say & depose that they did very well know John West late of Boston in New England, Esquire, deceased (who as they have been informed and do verily believe departed this life in or about the month of July last past) and so had done for the space of about seven years together before his death and these deponents do severally depose that they were and are very well acquainted with the manner and character of writing of the said John West deceased and have often seen him write, and that they were and are well assured & do believe in their consciences that the schedule of paper hereunto annexed purporting the Will of the said John West is totally wrote by and with the proper hand-writing of the said John West deceased. And further these deponents do depose that they have severally heard the said John West deceased, in his life time, say that he had made his will and that he had left the same in New England when he came away and that they really believe the schedule aforesaid to be a true copy thereof.

CHARLES LIDGET, J. PALMER.

14° Novembris 1691 Jurati fuere dicti Carolus Lydgett et Johannes Palmer super veritate præmissorum coram me Ri: Raines.

Which day appeard personally Elizabeth Hughes of the parish of St Martins Ludgate London, widow, aged about forty three years, and being sworn upon the Holy Evangelists made oath that John West Esqr lately deceased had lodged at her house in the parish aforesaid about six months before his death, which happened in or about the month of August last, and that after his death search was made for a will of the said deceased and that the copy hereunto annexed purporting the Will of the said deceased was among other writings of the said deceased in a trunk of his found by this deponent, Elizabeth Hughes.

25° Novembris 1691 Jurata fuit dicta Elizabetha Hughes super veritate præmissorum coram me. Ri: Raines. Vere, 201.

Capt. SAMUEL STYLE, at Eastra Moss in Portugal, 21 May 1663, proved 26 April 1665 by Henry Boade, power being reserved for Symon Smith and John Midleton. To my father James Style fifteen pounds sterling, to my brother William Style fifteen pounds sterling and to brother John Style fifteen pounds sterling. To my brother Joseph Style all that money which he hath in his hands of mine. I give unto my sister Elizabeth Style, in New England, fifteen pounds sterling. To my brother William's eldest daughter ten pounds. To my brother James his eldest child ten pounds. To my brother John his eldest child ten pounds. These several legacies, amounting to the sum of ninety pounds, I desire may be paid by my brother James Style to each. And what he hath remaining in his hands after I give to himself. There is in the Consul's hands, Mr Tho: Maynyard at Lisbon, seventy two pounds in English money and six dollars and gold nine pieces, great and little ; all is seventy two pounds now in the Consul's hands, of Portuguese crusadoes one hundred and fourteen, at Eastra Moss four pieces of gold thirty eight crusadoes &c. &c. &c. These several sums of money that is left in Portugal I desire that they be exactly divided betwixt my father and my brothers and my sister Elizabeth Style.

The executors to be Symon Smith, Capt. Leift. Henry Boad and Leift. John Midlton. My brother James Style he did live in Lusam* Kent &c. my brother Joseph Style did live at the sign of the Ball in Bedlam, London. Hyde, 34.

THOMAS DEANE of London, merchant, 19 February 1683. My body to be decently buried, the charge thereof not to exceed one hundred pounds. To wife Anne the rents, issues, and profits of all my messuages &c. in the County of Sussex, and of my houses in old Fish Street Hill, London, during her natural life (and certain furniture described), one fifth of the plate, all her own rings and jewells and three hundred pounds, in case

---

* The town of Lewisham, Kent.

her father do not require the same sum of me for which I have given him my notes.   To my daughter Sarah Deane twelve hundred pounds; and also eight hundred pounds which I lately received from her grandfather M[r] William Browne of Salem in New England, which was due to me from him as a part of her mother's portion; which will make my daughter's portion two thousand pounds.   This two thousand pounds to be paid at her age of eighteen or day of marriage first happening.   To my said daughter all the plate which was her mother's and one fifth of all my plate.   To my sons Thomas and James Deane and my daughter Rebecca Deane the rents, issues and profits of all my messuages, &c. in the County of Southampton, towards their education and maintenance, to hold the same unto my said three children until such time as my said son Thomas shall attain his full age of one and twenty.   (Then follow special legacies to these three children.)

If all my children die before they come to full age or day of marriage, all their estate, both real and personal, to my two cousins Henry Deane and Thomas Deane,[1] sons of my brother M[r] John Deane, and to their heirs forever.   To my brother M[r] John Deane and to my brother-in-law M[r] William Browne[2] fifty pounds apiece, and they to be joint executors.   To my friend John Midgley of London, scrivener, ten pounds.   The witnesses were John Midgley, scrivener, and Thomas Cason and William Halford, his servants.

In a codicil added 13 August 1685, he says, it hath pleased Almighty God to bless me with another son to whom I have given the Christian name of Samuel, &c.   Witnesses J. Packer, Tho: Farr and Ro: Smyth.

The above will was proved 12 May, 1686, and commission issued forth to John Deane, with power reserved for William Browne, the other executor.   A commission issued forth 20 April, 1695, to Thomas Deane, son of the deceased, John Deane, the former executor, having also deceased, and William Browne, the other executor named in the will, having renounced the executorship.   Lloyd, 56.

[Thomas Deane, the testator, was a merchant of Boston, Massachusetts, from 1664 to about 1678, when he returned to England and settled in London. He was a son of James Deane of Deanelands and Oxenwood, and was born about 1640. He married first, Sarah, daughter of William Browne of Salem, Mass., by whom he had, 1, *Sarah*, born at Boston, Oct. 27, 1666, m. Rev. Dr. Robert Woodward, Dean of Salisbury, whom she survived. Their daughter Henrietta m. Nathaniel Hyde, and had three children. 2. *Elizabeth*, born at B. Dec. 29, 1667, died young. He m. second, Anne, daughter of William Farr of London, and had, 3. *Thomas*, born at B. March 18, 1673-4, a portrait of whom is found in the British Museum ; m. Jane Gray of Nether Stowey, Somerset, by whom he had a daughter Jane, born about 1700, m. Sir John Cullum, bart. (see *Betham's Baronetage*, vol. ii. p. 55). 4. *Rebecca*, born at B. Dec. 7, 1677, m. Mr. Pearse. 5. *James*. 6. Dau. died young. 7. *Samuel*, born about 1685. For other facts, see REGISTER, vol. iii. p. 380; vol. xxvii. p. 420. A letter from him to Joseph Dudley, March 4, 1683-4, is printed in the REGISTER, vol. xiii. pp. 237-8. A mural tablet to his memory in Freefolk Chapel bears this inscription: " Here lyeth the body of Thomas Deane Esq. who died the 27th day of April 1686, Aged 46. And Anne, his wife, daughter of William Farr, Grocer and Citizen of London. She departed this life the 31st day of January 1706-7 aged 52 years."

Mr. William Dean, 53 Rowan Road, West Kensington, London, England, has sent me an extract from the MS. Pedigree of Deane of Deanelands, by the Rev. John Bathurst Deane, M.A., F.S.A., of Bath, England, from which and other documents sent me by Mr. Dean, and MSS. of the late Mr. William Reed Deane, of Boston, Mass., the following pedigree of Thomas Deane of Freefolk is derived :

RICHARD[1] DE DENE, or DENEFIELD, temp. Edw. III., had Walter de Dene of Iwood (Hackwood) in the parish of Basing; *Richard de Dene.*

RICHARD[2] DE DENE, ob. 2d Henry IV., by wife Isabella, daughter and heir of William Holowell, had William at Dene, d. s. p. ; *Richard de Dene.*

RICHARD[3] DE DENE of Odiham, by wife Isabel, daughter of Ralph Yonge, had *William at Dene.*

WILLIAM[4] AT DENE had *Matthew at Dene*, or, according to pedigree Harl. MS. 1544, p. 784, *Walter Dene.*

MATTHEW[5] AT DENE, or WALTER DENE, by wife Agnes, daughter and heir of John Leeche, had John at Dene of Odiham, d. s. p. ; *James at Dene:* Richard at Dene, whose son John[7] was father of Sir James[8] Deane, knt. of London, who d. in 1608, aged 63.

JAMES[6] AT DENE, by wife Amy, had Christopher; James, Richard, *John*, Elizabeth, Amy and Margery.

JOHN[7] AT DENE, m. Margery Dunhurst of Sussex, and had *Henry;* Richard, m. Bridget, daughter of Thomas Berington of Streightly, Berks, and had Francis,[9] John.[9]

HENRY[8] DEANE of Deanelands, Hants,* m. 1st, Ann Hall, m. 2d, Alice Berington, sister of his brother Richard's wife, and had John, m. Alice Turner, d. s. p ; *James ;* William of Havant, m. Frances Vachell, sister of John Hampden's second wife; Elizabeth ; Alice; Mary.

JAMES[9] DEANE of Deanelands, Hants, and Oxenwood, Wilts; m. first, Elizabeth Pigott, who d. s. p. ; m. second, Frances, daughter of Thomas Baynard of Wanstrow, Somerset (see Visitation of Wiltshire, 1623, ed. by Marshall, p. 34), and had Henry, Chancellor of Bath and Wells, æ. 37 in 1672, m. Anne, daughter of William Pearce, D.D., and had daughter Elizabeth ; John, buried Jan. 4, 1694–5, at Tidcombe ; Thomas of Freefolk, the testator, whose family is given above; Frances ; Susannah.

[1] Mr. William Dean, of London, suggests that the testator's nephew, Thomas Deane here named, of whom he finds no later trace in England, may have emigrated to New England, and that the Thomas Deane of Boston, Mass., 1692 (see REGISTER, xxxvii. p. 288), who owned pasture and wood lots in Wrentham, Mass., where Thomas Deane of Freefolk was an early proprietor, may be identical with him. It is possible that this conjecture is true, and facts to disprove or confirm it are solicited. It is worthy of note that Thomas Deane of Boston, 1692, married a niece of Peter Lidget of Boston, the intimate friend of Thomas Deane of Freefolk. Still it should be borne in mind that this can only be called a conjecture.—EDITOR.

[2] See *Slaughter's History of Bristol Parish*, 2d ed. p. 168.—R. A. BROCK.]

Notes on Abstracts previously printed.

STEPHEN WINTHROP (*ante*, p. 162).

[In my note to the will of Colonel Stephen Winthrop, in the REGISTER, I stated that his daughter *Joanna* married Richard Hancock. My friend Mr. Henry Saltonstall has since shown me papers in his possession which conclusively establish that the Christian name of Mrs Hancock was *Judith*. The mistake undoubtedly arose from the fact that Stephen W. had an elder daughter Judith who died in childhood, and the compiler of the old Winthrop pedigree (from which I quoted) evidently confused the second Judith with her sister Joanna, who died unmarried.

Mr. H. Saltonstall's papers also establish that the said Judith Hancock and her sister Margaret Ward, afterwards Willey, were joint owners of the well-known Humphrey farm, embracing Suntaug Lake, in Salem and Saugus (now Lynnfield and Peabody), the said farm having been acquired by Stephen Winthrop from Robert Saltonstall in 1645. It is now the property of Mr. Henry Saltonstall.

R. C. W., JR.

The record of the laying out of " the bounds of the Pondes Farme," belonging to Major Stephen Winthrop," may be found in the printed Records of the Colony of the Massachusetts Bay in New England, vol. iv. Part I. p. 95.—H. F. W.]

* Deanelands was located between Basing and Newnham, on the left hand side of the road to Newnham, and is marked on the Ordnance map. In the act of Parliament, 4th and 5th Anne, cap. 57, for the sale of lands of Thomas Deane, Esq., mention is made of the disposition of *Deanelands*, alias *Leeches* near Basing. A small house stood on it in 1874. The arms confirmed in 1598 by Dethicke, Garter King of Arms, to Henry[8] Deane and his cousin Sir James[8] Deane, are Gu. a lion sejant guardant or, on a chief ar. three crescents of the first. *Crest*—A demi-lion rampant or, holding in the dexter paw a crescent gu. An engraving of these arms is printed in the REGISTER, vol. iii. p. 375.—EDITOR.

JEFFERY DISBEROWE of Borowghe in the County of Cambridge, yeoman, 19 July, 1588, pro: 18 April 1589, mentions John Disberowe of Elsely, Cambridge, yeoman, and his heirs, sister Agnes Disberowe and George Knock *alias* Ansell of Binckley, blacksmith.   Leicester, 37.

WILLIAM DISBEROWE of Walden in the County of Essex, joiner, 30 March 1610, pro: at Dunmowe 4 Oct. 1610. Wishes to be buried in the churchyard at Walden, mentions wife Katherine and appoints son Nicholas Disberowe executor.

Consistory Court of London, Vol. for 1609–21, L. 21.

ISAAC DISBROWE, of Elseworth in the County of Cambridge gentleman (by mark) 6 December 1660, proved 21 December 1660. I give my farm house or messuage situate and being in Eltisley, in the County of Cambridge, and all my freehold land there and in the fields of Gronsdon Magna in the County of Huntingdon, unto John and Isaac Disbrowe, my grandsons, children of Isaac Disbrowe, deceased. John the elder to have the homestall and twenty acres of free land in Eltisley, at twenty one years of age. Isaac to have the remainder of my free lands, being twenty four acres, more or less, in Eltisley, at twenty one. To my son John Disbrowe, twenty acres of copyhold in the fields of Eltisley and one close or pasture between the grounds of James Disbrowe on the West and the ground of Mr Charles Baron on the East, worth four pounds per annum, and one pasture lying behind a barn lately William Michell's, worth seven nobles per annum, to him & his heirs forever. To my grandchild Elizabeth Disbrowe two acres of copyhold land and my close called Great Bottles at the age of twenty one years. To my grandchild Anna Disbrowe eight acres at the age of twenty one years, and the same amount of land to Susan and Mary Disbrowe, two other granddaughters, each, at the same age. To my son Nathaniel Disbrowe my close called Rodins, lying in Eltisley. Elizabeth, Ann, Susan and Mary referred to as the four sisters of John and Isaac. To my son Samuel ten pounds. To my daughter Elizabeth Johnson ten pounds. To my daughter Hannah Stocker five pounds and five pounds among her ,children. To my daughter Sarah Croxon ten pounds and another ten pounds to my granddaughter Sarah Croxon. To Richard Kempton ten shillings. To Alice Toll five shillings. The residue to my son in law Thomas Croxton whom I make executor.

Wit: John Deane and Richard Croxton.   Nabbs, 264.

JAMES DISBROWE of Stepney in the county of Middlesex, Doctor in Physick 26 November 1690. I give & devise the lease of my house at Stepney Causey unto my dear & loving wife Abigail if she survive me, but, if not, unto Mrs Whitfield, spinster, for & during so many years of the said lease as the said Mary Whitfield shall live; and, after her decease, I give the said house & lease, during the residue of the years therein then to come, equally between Mrs Elizabeth Hayter & Mrs Rebecca Hayter. My silver watch to Mr Charles Polhill when he shall attain the age of eighteen years; also Dr. Goodin's book on the Ephesians. All the rest & residue of my goods and chattels &c. to my said wife Abigail. I give & devise all that my " manner " of Elsworth, with the rights, members and appurtenances thereof, and all my lands & hereditaments in Elsworth in the County of Cambridge, from and after the decease of my father & mother Disbrowe, unto my said wife Abigail until my daughter Elizabeth shall attain her age of eighteen years or die, which shall first happen, if my said wife shall so long live & continue a widow, upon trust that my said wife, during such time as she shall enjoy the said man' & hereditaments at Elsworth, shall pay the yearly sum of sixty pounds by equal quarterly payments unto my daughter Elizabeth for her maintenance ; and from & after my said daughter Elizabeth shall attain her said age of eighteen years, or from & after my said wife's second marriage, which shall first happen, I give & devise the yearly rent of sixty pounds unto my said wife Abigail during her life, to be issued & had out of my said manor & lands in Elsworth, by equal quarterly payments.

If it shall happen that my said daughter Elizabeth shall die without issue of her body in the life of my said dear & honored father Samuel Desbrowe then I give my said manor of Elsworth & my manor of ffandrayton in the said County of Cambridge & all other my manors & lands & hereditaments unto my said father Samuel Desbrowe & his heirs forever.

My wife to be sole executrix during her life ; and, after her death, my said honored father to be sole executor. 14 January 1690, A Commission was issued to Joseph Marsh during the minority of Elizabeth Disbrowe minor daughter, Abigail Disbrowe, widow, the relict and one of the executors having died before the Testator and Samuel Disbrowe, the father and the other executor having died before he had accepted the burden of the execution. Vere, 4.

Sa: Disbrowe of Elsworth in the County of Cambridge, gentleman, 20 September 1680. My Deare wife Rose being provided of a jointure out of my estate in Elsworth which according to the law she ought to enjoy during the term of her natural life,—my son to take care that my said wife do and may enjoy without interruption or molestation from him. My will is that my wife do enjoy all that household stuff, plate, jewells or other goods whatsoever which was her own at the time of our marriage, and that she be not put to the trouble to prove what was her own but what she shall say and affirm to be hers before our marriage, as aforesaid. I give to my said dear wife during the term of her natural life all that my farm in Elsworth, now in the possession of James Rooke, with all the appurtenances belonging, and that necklace of pearls which I gave her at our marriage, and any other jewells or plate I have or shall give her before my death ; also an ebony cabinet & the best coach and horses, with the furniture &c. ; and forty pounds in money, to be paid her within one month after my decease. And because I have not yet been able to purchase so much land as might make my dear wife's jointure two hundred pounds a year, as I intended, therefore my will is & I expressly request my executor, my son & heir, that he give sufficient satisfying security to my said dear wife to pay unto her the sum of twelve pounds per annum by half-yearly payments during the time of her natural life. I give her also (for the further bettering of her jointure) all that messuage or tenement with the close of pasture thereto belonging which I lately purchased of Thomas Allin and is now in the possession of Thomas Cole & William Pamplin, to be enjoyed by her during the time of her natural life, provided that if my said wife or any other person claiming by, from or under her shall cut down or destroy any trees or grovage or young spirrs now growing or that hereafter may grow upon any part of those grounds which are her jointure that then and from that time those three legacies aforementioned shall cease and be wholly void &c. I give to my three grand children, Christopher, Samuel & James Mills, twenty pounds apiece to be paid unto them and each of them when they shall attain to their respective age of one and twenty years.

All the rest of my lands, tenements and hereditaments, goods, chattels &c. to my son & heir James Disbrowe, and I appoint him Executor. To the poor of the parish of Elsworth five pounds to be distributed amongst the most necessitous of them at the discretion of my executor : Thomas Cole, my old, diligent servant to have twenty shillings thereof ; and if the said Thomas Cole shall happen to be in want I desire and charge my said son to give him some competent relief. All such men and women servants as shall be my actual household servants at my death ten shillings apiece; and to all my other servants I would have my son give them gloves or two six pences apiece. And as to my sister Greene I earnestly require and charge my son and executor that (if God makes him able) he continue the annuity of four pounds a year unto her during her life which I have formerly bestowed on her. Also to my said son James all my right, title & interest to a lease of fifteen hundred acres of land, Irish measure, be it more or less, in the Barony of Nanan in the County of Meath or in any other place or County it shall happen to be or lie in the Kingdom of Ireland, now or late in the possession of John Preston Esq. Alderman of Dublin or his assigns, which lease is granted to me from the Company of Drapers, London, for one and thirty years after the decease of my dear wife.

I would have my son give my son Mills and my grand children mourning.

Wit: John Woodbridge, John Allin, John Cole (by mark), Sarah Berriff.

Decimo sexto mensis Aprilis Anno Doñi millimo sexcenno nonageȓo primo Emᵗ Comᵒ Josepho Marsh ar. avunculo et curatori ltīme assignat Elizæ Disbrowe minori Nepti ex filio Samuelis Disbrowe nuper de Ellsworth in Coȓ Cantabrigeiæ arm dȇft heñtis etc Ad admȋstrandum bona jura et credita dc̄i dȇft durante minori ætate et in usum et beneficium dc̄æ Elizabethæ Disbrowe minoris juxta tenorem et effectum Testamenti ipsius defuncti eo quod Jacobus Disbrowe filius dc̄i dȇft et executor in Eodem Testaȓto nōiatus in Vita Testatoris mortem obiit etc.

Vicesimo quarto die mensis Oct. Anno Dōni 1728 Emᵗ Comᵒ Elizæ Holworthy viduæ Nept ex filio et prox consanguiñ Saȓlis Disbro nuper de Ellsworth in Coȓ Cantabrigeiæ Armʳⁱ etc.   Vere, 66.

Honʳᵈ & Deare Sʳ
          In my last I certifyed you of the receipt of yoʳˢ dated March 5ᵗ (53) in wᶜʰ lr̄e: I receiued a Coppy of one you pleased to write to the Protectoʳ at my request in behalfe of yoʳ ffreinds in these pts of New England, entreating his wise & gratious contriuemᵗ & help in their afflicted & straitned Conditiō. I haue made knowne yoʳ writeing to many so yᵗ it is spread (I suppose) thorough the Cuntry & I ρceiue is marvailous well resented & you laid up in the breasts of many people as one of the Cordiall ffreinds of New England there. Captaine Astwood writes that he had admittance to speake wᵗʰ his highnes who expʳssed his tender respect of New England & thoughtfullnes wᶜʰ way to doe yᵐ good, but said wᵗʰall, that the landes in Ireland were disposed to yᵉ souldyers & Adventurers &c so yᵗ nothing there could be done, nor can the dutch be remoued (unless by Compositiō), since the peace wᵗʰ holland (being pʳvented as by speciall providence to be done before,) as in my last I touched. But Capt: writes yᵗ my Lord asked him whether it would not be better that New England were remoued to some place where they might haue Cittyes ready builded & land ready tilled & where staple Comodityes might be raised, than either to remoue the dutch or plant in Delawar, the place he hinted it seemes was Hispaniola, But Captaine Astwood answered at pʳsent that he thought we would rather

chuse the nearer & probably more peaceable though the poorer, Than be remoued farther wth more hazard to loose peace, & gaine riches. The answer
was true for the maine so farr as it went, But we app^rhend some   should
haue beene added, as we haue inserted in a l<del>r</del>e frō our Generall Court to y^e
Protecto^r this yeare, viz: That w^teuer we might upō selfe respect chuse, yet
wee are free in adherence & complyance wth his highnes & our godly na-
tiue Cuntrymen to be remoued to any place whether the lord our god shall
call where we may but carry on C<del>h</del>s worke under our handes & provide
necessary Comforts for us and ours. The Captaine saith my lord wished
him to Consider further of the matter & come to him againe, when (I hope)
he will bethink himselfe of an answer that may shut up no doore of provi-
dence towards us, wthout first acquainting us y^t so the positiue answer may
imediatly proceed frō our selues, ffor the p^rsent I pceiue the cuntry doe
most desire to keep themselues in ye most apt waiting posture wch may
suit any further discouery of gods minde & will concerning them, whatsoeuer, or whersoeuer, onely attending the p^rsent duty of the day or yeare,
wch frame cannot chuse but be somew^t detrimenting to settlem^t here, if so
should proue to be our way after all, yet for my pt I think if many
had knockt in lesser stakes into the Rocky sandy pts of this wildernes, it
might better haue suited a wildernes state, in its infancy esp^{ly}. I heare
that Mr Evance his house & ffarme, wch you well know, will not reach to
make 20^{li} & many more are so lowly esteemed at Newhauen, for matters
here I referre you to conferrence wth yor Cousen, Jordan & yor brother Nathaniell; who fully understand the state of thinges here & can make some
apology or excuse for me in regard of the remainder of yor estate here not
being returned as yet, haueing had some tast of the difficulty of makeing
returnes themselues. If New England Tobacco would vend at some rate
considerable, both I & my Boyes would leaue off some other improuem^t, to
procure a quantity to pay you wthall. That seeing our stock will not be
converted that way, we might see to pay you wth worke, wch you haue accepted in New England for Currant pay   Our neighbours at Seabrook
haue raised about 20000 weight this yeare they say it is good Tobacco; it
may be if it were p^rveledged in England it might turne to Account they doe
send some to try w^t will come of it, & I purpose to send a hogshead upō
Mr Stapeleys Acc^t: who wrote to me this yeare to order his estate here, &
meeting wth a debt of Corne upō the Acco^t: frō yor brother Nath: wch I knew
not els w^t to doe wthall, it haveing lyen upō losse & charge a good space, I adventured to turne into Tobacco, by wch experiment you may pceiue w^t it will
make in England & see w^t it is if you please, But if this way liketh you not,
then haue I propounded somewhat to yor Consideration in my last l<del>r</del>e wch I
much entreat may be by yor fauor & Contriuem^t brought about, wch if you
please to cause to take effect, (as I see not ought to ye contrary) but you may
in a faire way unlesse my brother be unwilling either to doe it or resign to
another who may, wch I (suppose) he will not, Then may three lawfull
ends be attained, viz 1 yor estate returned, 2 I here settled 3 The people
here more satisfyed wth me & their iealousy remoued of yor being an instru-
m^t of my remoueall frō them, Concerneing w^{ch}, Truely I was much afflicted
& troubled at some passages the other day y^t fell frō some, seemeing to be
affected & to affect others euilly against you in refference to ye goodwill
you shewed towards me. Nowthstanding I told them ouer & ouer That you
had wrote nothing to me to invite or giue a call, but onely exp^rssions of
loue showing reall freindship in a willingnes & gladnes of heart to doe good
wth the Talent of opportunity that god had lent you, to me or any other of

yo[r] New England freinds in case god called them where they might use you, & I haue said that I wished some mens eyes were not euill because yo[rs] was good & doe professe they take the wrong course to settle me, if they take up euill surmises or cast any aspersions upō you; since w[ch] my showing my selfe greiued w[th] such thinges I hear no more, I wished them if they thought anything of duty were to be done, in order to p[r]vent or to exhort anything w[ch] frō yo[r] selfe might have euill Consequence I desired they would be silent here & write their mindes, I told them I was Confident you would take it well & attend y[m] in anything y[t] was right & for their good. I pray mention nothing as haueing a hint frō mee, you may know any of y[e] matters w[th] us Viua Voce, by our brethren in England, And if you doe anything in order to my settlem[t] here, be pleased to Exp[r]sse yo[r] selfe as doeing it much respecting them therein, It may be that such convicting testimony of yo[r] non alienation but still continued tender affectiō toward the Church of Christ here may cast inward shame upō some spirits, & my desire is not to raise any thing in yo[r] spirit but to bring Convictiō upō some others y[t] seeing their ffolly, (in an aptnes to haue harsh thoughts on almost all men y[t] goe for England, as if they regard not Cħs poore people here, haueing [soug]ht & obtained great thinges for themselves there,) might learne to be more wise or more charitable for the future, w[n] they see yo[r] enlarged loue not onely putting forth itselfe to help such as come to you into old England, But also to seeke the upholdm[t] & encouragem[t] of them whome god requires to stay in New England, I might well haue left out these latter passages of advise concerneing hints of directiō how you should carry it & exp[r]sse yo[r] selfe to us, not knowing whether you will please to doe the things I request or no, and also haueing so good knowledge of yo[r] better wisedome than mine in euery matter, but onely that I saw somethings here w[ch] you at a distance could not so well understand, & I desire euery thing you doe may turne to the best acco[t]: The thing w[ch] I haue propounded in my last l̃re y[t] here I referre unto, is That you would please to consult or contriue wth my brother how to produce out of y[t] place w[ch] my brother writes he holdes as for me so much as may bring me out of yo[r] debt, w[ch] you may see how much by this enclosed Acco[t]: if it can be but in some annuall way raised (I suppose) it may answer to w[t] is like to be done here unlesse the times turne, The experience whereof makes Willm Dudley y[t] he will take no Compositiō for his other 25[li]: I haue tendered him mares Cowes or Corne &c he saith he had rather it should lye dead in yor handes there, then to haue much more here as thinges stand. I pray carry it wth great & tender regard to my brother that he may be very free to w[t] is done, for I would not loose an inch either of naturall or christian loue & affectiō for an Elle of profit or worldly Accomõdatiō; pray S[r] forget [not?] to show loue & helpfulnes to poore brother Hodley whose wife & Children are come ouer according to his order this yeare he was my Constant Nocturnall Associate, whome I dearely misse, But least I should be tedious wth Cheife respectes & dearest affectiō from my selfe & wife to both yo[r] selfe & deare M[rs] Disbrow recomending you & all yo[rs] to the blessed protectiō & guidance of god our father, The lord Jesus Christ & the holy spirit of grace to lead you through all the troubles and difficult turneings & tergiversations of thinges in this age to enter into rest & finde eternall satisfactiō so prayeth:

S[r] he who euer desires to be

Guilford Octob[r] 10th (54)

Yo[r] most Cordiall loueing freind
to his power to serue you:

WILLM LEETE.

Pray S^r remember my respects to Mr Jones & Mr John Whitfeild I desire you may fall in Actes & Consult wth yor owne brother, Mr Hopkins & Maior Haynes &c our New England freinds in this iuncture of time to pro [   ] w^t may be for releife of these pts & for o^r Comfortable encouragm^t here or elsewhere as god shall dispose: One thing I must entreat that in case you should exp^{r}sse y^t you haue done in order to my stay here, that you do carry it as not to giue y^m advantage to wthdraw w^t they doe for me but rather as expecting they should continue their encouragm^t in some certaine way seeing y^t I put by what in reason might more advantage me & mine in our low estate

To his much honrd & worthy freind
Mr Samuell Disborow
one of the Comission^{rs}
for Customs at
Leith these
p^{r}sent
Scotland

S^r

His Highness the Lord Protector haveing sent into this Nation the publicque seales to be affixed to the evidences and rights of the people according to the rules in that case formerly given & observed and the Great Seale being comitted to yor custody The Councill have thought fit to acquaint you that as by Comission to you from the Councill you were directed only untill the comeing of the said seale to subscribe yor name to dispatches duely comeing to the Great Seale. Soe the subscribeing yor name to such dispatches is not longer to bee used but the said seale is to bee affixed or áppended to them by you, according to the rules in that case formerly given & observed. Signed in the name and by the order

Edinburgh 25 Juny 1656   of the Councill

BROGHILL, Presid^t.

To Samuell Disbrowe Esqr
One of his Highness Councill in
Scotland appointed Keeper of
the Great Seale of Scotland
these

A Commission from Oliver, By the Grace of God Lord Protector of the Commonwealth of England Scotland and Ireland and dominions and Territories thereunto belonging, giving and granting unto Samuel Disbrow Esquire, one of his Highnesse Privy Councill of Scotland, The Office of Keeper of the Great Seall of Scotland &c.

Given at Edinburgh the Sixteenth day of September (1657)

Whereas by his Maiestyes declaration from Breda the $\frac{4}{14}$ day of Aprill (1660) His Maiesty is gratiously pleased to graunt a free & generall Pardon unto all his Subiects of what degree or quality soeuer, who within forty dayes after the publication thereof shall lay hold upon his grace and fauour, and shall by any publique act declare theyr doing so. And that the returne to the loyalty and obedience of good subiects

I Samuell Disbrowe of Elsworth in the County of Cambridge gent. his Maiestyes most loyall & faythfull subiect with all humblen[.] & unfayghned thankfulnes doe hereby declare that I doe lay hold of & accept of his Maiestyes grace fauour & pardon in the sayd declaration held forth, And that I am and shall continew by the Asistanc of god a loyall and obedient subiect to his Maiesty Charles the second by the grace of god king of England Scotland ffrance & Ireland Defender of the fayth &c: Witness my hand this 21th day of May (1660)   SA: DISBROWE.

This declaration by Samuell Disbrowe was sighned owned & acknowledged before mee   GEORGE MONCK.

Charles R.

Our Will & Pleasure is That yoᵘ forthwᵗʰ prepare a Bill fitt for oʳ Royall signature conteyning a Graunt of our gracious Pardon unto Samuell Disbrowe of Elsworth in yᵉ County of Cambridge Esqʳ. of all such offences & with such restitucõn of Lands & Goods & such Excepc̃ons & Clauses in all things as are expressed in the forme of a Pardon prepared for that purpose & remayning wᵗʰ yoᵘ under Our signnett & signe manuall. And for soe doeing this shalbe yoʳ Warrᵗ: Given att our Court att Whitehall the 24th day of October 1660 in the Twelfe yeare of our Reigne.   S.

By his Maᵗˢ Comand

To oʳ Attorney or   EDW: NICHOLAS.
    Sollicitor Generall
Vera copia   Papers of General Desborough
                                   1651–1660. Egerton, 2519.

The following is a mem: of Pedigree in Coll. of Arms, Signed by Samˡ Desbro 1684.

James Disbrowe == . . . . Daughter of
of Eltisley—Co. Cam- | . . . . Hatley of
bridge. Died about 1630 | Over, Cambridgesh:

¹James, died young   ²John, Major Genˡ = Jane, daughter   ³Nathaniel, died young
                      Admiral, member   of Robert Cromwell
                      of the Upper House. & sister of Protector
                      Died about 1680

Rose Hobson of London = Samuel of Elsworth,   1 = Dorothy Whitfield
2d wife. No child.   Co. Camb. living in 1684   of Surrey
       2   aged 65. One of the Com-
                        m̄rs for Scotland May 4,
                        1655. In 1656 M. P. for Mid
                        Lothian. In 1657, Sept. 16,
                        Keeper of Great Seal of
                        Scotland.

James Desbro = Abigail, dau.
Dʳ of Physic, Step- | of John Marsh of
ney, Middˣ | Sᵗ Albans.

Elizabeth, aged 3 years in 1684.

The following account is taken from Cole's (MS.) Collections for Cambridgeshire, in his description of the church & monuments at Elsworth :—

— " A very handsome large black marble slab with these arms at top : viz : 3 *Bears heads eras'd & muzzled on a Fess for* Disbrow impaling *on a Cheuron int : 3 Bezants 3 Quaterfoils, & a Cheif vairé* for . . . . On yᵉ Wall is an Atchievemᵗ with yᵉ same Arms in Colours viz : *O. on a Fess S. 3 Bears Heads er : A. muzzled G.* for Disbrow, impaling *A. on a Cheu. B. 3 Cinquefoils O. int : 3 Torteuxes a Cheif vairé O. & B.* with a Crest viz: *a Bears Head er: A. muzzled G.* & Motto *Mors Iter ad vitam.* Under them is this inscription:

Here lyeth the body of
Samuell Disbrow Esquire late
Lord of this Manour, aged 75
He dyed the 10 of *December* in
the *year* of our *Lord* 1690.

Close to this on yᵉ N. lies another black marble of yᵉ same sort with yᵉ aforesaid Arms in a Lozenge, except that yᵉ Cheif is Checquy & yᵉ Quaterfoils are Cinquefoils. I suppose a mistake, but where it lies I know not; for I put them down as I find them: on yᵉ wall is an Atchievemᵗ with the said arms blazoned, where yᵉ mistake is continued & yᵉ Cheife Checquy O. & B. for .... Under these Arms on yᵉ marble is this Inscription:

Here lieth yᵉ Body of yᵉ virtuous
& pious *Mʳⁱˢ Rose Disbrow
Relict* of *Samuel Disbrow Esqʳ*
who Soul returned to *God*
who gave it yᵉ 4 Day of *March*
1698 in yᵉ 83 *year* of her age.

[The genealogical contents of Isaac Disbrowe's will may be shown by the following table:

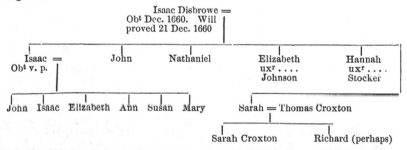

Isaac Disbrowe =
Obᵗ Dec. 1660. Will
proved 21 Dec. 1660

| Isaac = Obᵗ v. p. | John | Nathaniel | Elizabeth uxʳ .... Johnson | Hannah uxʳ .... Stocker |

John Isaac Elizabeth Ann Susan Mary   Sarah = Thomas Croxton

Sarah Croxton   Richard (perhaps)

Isacke Desbrough, husbandman, of Ell-Tisley in Com. Cambridge (æt.) 18 embarked early in April, 1635, on the Hopewell of London, for New England, having, as fellow passengers, the families of Cooper, Farrington, Purryer, Griggs and Kyrtland, from Olney, Laundon and Sherrington, Bucks, most of whom settled in Lynn, and a lot of Christians from the neighborhood of Nazing in Essex and Stansted Abbey in Herts, many of whom formed a part of the flock of John Eliot at Roxbury. Mr. Disbrowe (as the name seems to have been more commonly spelled) probably lived in Lynn, although I find no record of the transfer of real estate either to or from him. His name appears in the Court records of Essex County, Mass., as a party to sundry suits in the years 1638 and 1639, and then disappears altogether from the records here.

The following is the record of the cases referred to, taken from the earliest Court Record at Salem.

25: 10ᵗʰ mo.: 1638.

Isaack Disberoe pl. agᵗ Ann Burt def. who being absent hir husband Hugh Burt Answered to acō of case. Jury finds for pl. viijˢ damages & iiij costes.

Isaack Disberoe pl. agᵗ Hugh Burt def. in acō of defamacōn Jury finds for pl. ffiftie shillinges damag & iiij costes

Isaack Disberoe pl. agᵗ Nath: Kertland def. in acō of case Jury finds for pl. xvijˢ dama. & iiij costes

25 : 4th mo : 1639

John Goit pl. ag[t] Isaack Disberoe def. in acō of Debt To grant out attachm[t] ag[t] him fo[r] x[s] costes and to app[r] next Court

24 : 7th mo : 1639

Hugh Burt of Lynn pl. ag[t] Isaack Disberoe def. in an acō of case Referred to next Court ag[t] wh tyme Hugh Burt is to p'cure y[e] iudgm[ts] granted ag[t] him att Boston last Court

31 : 10th mo : 1639

Hugh Burt commensing an acō Last Court ag[t] Isaacke Disberoe def. now tryed viz The Jury bring in for pl. 4[li] 10[s] damages & 10[s] costes　John ffarrington was surety

From the Record of the Court of Assistants held at Boston the 3th day of the first month, 1639–1640, we learn that Isaack Deesbro and John Farrington forfeited their recognizance.

Whether he was the Isaac Disbrowe, above named, who died A.D. 1660, or Isaac the son, who died in his father's life-time, remains to be proved. I am inclined to think, however, it was the son.

That Isaac Disbrowe, Senior, was nearly related to Samuel Disbrowe of New Haven and Guilford, Connecticut (brother of the Major-General), there can be no shadow of a doubt. As to the names of his daughters' husbands, I would suggest that Stocker was and is a Lynn name, and it was John Johnson of Guilford, Conn., who married the daughter Elizabeth, 1 Oct. 1651, after her divorce from her first husband, Thomas Relfe or Rolfe.

One of the fellow passengers of Isaac Disbrowe the immigrant, was a John Astwood, who was undoubtedly the Captain Astwood to whom Governor Leete refers in his letter to Samuel Disbrowe. His will may be found in the "Gleanings," Page 81.

From Lyson's Magna Britannia (London, 1808) we learn that Burgh or Burrough Green (called Borowghe in Jeffery Disberowe's will) is in the Hundred of Radfield and deanery of Camps, about four miles south of Newmarket, and about eight miles north of Linton. Close to it is the parish of Brinkley, called Binckley in the will.

Elsworth, in the hundred of Papworth and deanery of Bourne, lies about eight miles nearly west of Cambridge, and about the same distance south-east of Huntingdon. The manor of Elsworth and the manor of the rectory were purchased in 1656 by Samuel Disbrowe, Esq., who died in 1690; his granddaughter brought it in marriage to Matthew Holworthy, Esq. (called the only son of Sir Matthew Holworthy, knt., of Great Palsgrave in Norfolk). After Mr. Holworthy's death it was possessed by his daughter, Mrs. Heathcote, who, having no children, devised it to Matthew Heathcote, who took the name of Holworthy, and was grandfather of the Rev. Matthew Holworthy, Lord of the manor, patron of the rectory and incumbent. In the parish church, besides the monument of Samuel Disbrowe, are several memorials of the Holworthy family.

Eltisley, in the hundred of Stow and deanery of Bourne, lies about 12 miles nearly west of Cambridge. The manor of Stow, or Goldinghams, afterwards called the manor of Eltisley, belonged successively to the families of Stow, Ward and Goldingham. In 1656 it was sold to Major General Disbrowe, whose descendant, Mr. John Disbrowe, devised it in 1741 to the two sons of his nephew, William Walford of Bocking. The rectory, with the advowson (we are further told) was purchased, about the year 1600, by the Disbrowe family. John Disbrowe, who was buried there in 1610, is called the grandfather of Major General Disbrowe and of Samuel Disbrowe, Keeper of the Great Seal in Scotland, both of whom were born at Eltisley, the former in 1608, the latter in 1619. The Major General was married at Eltisley to Jane Cromwell, Oliver's youngest sister, in 1636; James Disbrowe, elder brother of the Major General, inherited the estate at Eltisley, where he resided. His descendants possessed this estate until the year 1713. The parsonage house, which had been the seat of the Disbrowes, has been pulled down.

This adds one generation to the pedigree found in the College of Arms, and supplies, perhaps, a father for Isaac Disbrowe, who died in December, 1660.

Of Samuel Disbrowe, an abstract of whose will is given above, our friends in Connecticut can give a better account. I would only suggest that the pedigree gives us important information by disclosing the maiden names of his two wives. The first (Dorothy Whitfield) must have been one of the daughters of his minister and next neighbor in Guilford, the Rev. Henry Whitfield, a reference to whose will I have, but of which unfortunately I have no abstract at hand. His second wife we had known as the widow of Samuel Pennoyer. May not the John Marsh, whose daughter Abigail became the wife of Samuel Disbrowe's son, and the Joseph Marsh, her brother, to whom administration was granted, have been related to John Marsh, of Hartford, Conn.?

The ancestry of the Rev. Henry Whitfield and his wife Dorothy, I expect to show in a future instalment of the Gleanings, having gathered a very large collection of material relating to their families.

It is my intention, also, at some future day, to give some account of the Holworthy family, which became connected by marriage with this Disbrowe family.

Mr. Evance, who is mentioned in Gov. Leete's letter, was doubtless Mr. John Evance, of New Haven, Conn., a son of Hugh and Audrey Evance, of London (see Hist. Coll. Essex Inst., vol. xvii. pp. 27–33). Hugh Evance was a citizen and clothworker of London, according to his will proved in London 28 March, 1636—(Pile 32). Mrs. Audrey Evance, whose will was proved in London, 25 Oct. 1651 (Grey, 184), was a daughter of William Jefferay of Chiddingly, or Chittingleigh, in the County of Sussex, and sister of William Jefferay, who came to New England, it is said, before Endicott's colony was planted. It is well to note that her sister Ann was married to a William Goffe. John Evance went back to England and lived in Aldermanbury, London. In his will, made 13 Dec. 1660, proved 2 May, 1661 (May, 71), he mentions wife Susanna and sons Daniel, John, Stephen and Thomas. His wife, I suspect, was a sister of Capt. Francis Norton, of Charlestown, Mass., for in 1640 Mr. Evance (then of New Haven) called Capt. Norton's wife Mrs. Mary Norton, sister, and again spoke of his brother Norton. Mrs. Mary Norton, I have found, was a daughter of Mr. Nicholas Houghton, of London, and sister of Robert Houghton, who married Mary, sister of Major-General Sedgwick. She does not appear to have had any sister Susanna; so the connection would seem to have been through the Nortons.

John Evance's son Stephen, born in New Haven, Conn., 21 April, 1652, was probably the Stephen Evance, citizen and goldsmith of London, who was knighted at Kensington, 14 Oct. 1690, as we learn from Le Neve (Harl. So. Pub. 8, p. 435).

HENRY F. WATERS.

Mr. Samuel Disbrowe was an early settler of Guilford, Ct., which was founded in 1639. The late Hon. Ralph D. Smith, in his *History of Guilford*, states that he was " one of the first settlers of the town, and one of the seven pillars of the Church at its formation here." He was also a magistrate there, and is mentioned as " holding courts in the town with three or four deputies appointed by the freemen for that purpose. He was associated with Gov. Eaton, Gov. Leete and other distinguished men in forming and establishing the combination and government of the New Haven Colony in 1643, and, while in this country as one of its magistrates and the civil father of one of its towns, shared some of its highest honors. Upon his return to England with Mr. Whitfield, says President Stiles in his History of the Judges (p. 35), quoting from Noble, he became one of the commissioners of the revenues, and in the same year represented the city of Edinburgh in Parliament, at a council held at Whitehall, May 4, 1655. He was appointed one of the nine counsellors of the Kingdom of Scotland, and the same year Keeper of the Great Seal of that nation, and allowed £2000 annually. The year following he was returned a member of the British Parliament for the sheriffdom of Midlothian, and was continued in all his employments under the Protector Richard. Burton, who kept a diary of the doings of Cromwell's Parliament, of which he was a member, makes frequent and honorable mention of Samuel Disborough as one of the most active and talented members of that body. 'This shows him,' says President Stiles, 'a man of political abilities to sustain so many and such high betrustments with the reputation and acceptance with which he discharged them.' "

The Hon. Lewis H. Steiner, M.D., the editor of the History of Guilford, which was printed after the author's death, adds this foot-note :

"Samuel Disborow was born on the manor of Ettisley in Cambridgeshire, on the 30th of November, 1619, and was the third surviving son of James Disborow, Esquire, and a younger brother of the famous Major General John Disborrow, who married Jane Cromwell, a sister of the Lord Protector Oliver Cromwell, and was a member of several Parliaments, and one of the Judges appointed to try Charles I.

" Mr. Samuel Disborrow studied law with his brother John Disborrow, who in early life was a barrister." See *History of Guilford*, pp. 120–1.   EDITOR.

The Disbrow gleanings, and particularly Leete's letter, are quite interesting. As the records of New Haven jurisdiction from 1644 to 1653 are lost, and the Guilford records as we have them now only begin with 1645, I can add very little to the notice of Disbrow given in R. D. Smith's History of Guilford, p. 120-1. There are, however, in Part II. of Vol. VI. of the Acts of the Parliaments of Scotland, published by the government, some letters, &c., by and relating to him, which Mr. Smith never saw.

I suppose the brother Nathaniel, mentioned in Leete's letter, was Nathaniel Whitfield, D.'s brother-in-law.

Brother Hodley, named in Gov. Leete's letter, was John Hoadly, born Jan. 1616-17, who came to New England in the same ship with Leete, 1639, and was one of the "seven pillars" of the first church gathered in Guilford June 19, 1643, as were also Leete and Desborough. John Hoadly married in G. in 1642, Sarah Bushnell, by whom he had twelve children, seven of them born in Guilford, where three died infants. Of two sons born in G. the younger became rector of Halsted, Kent,—the elder also took orders in the Church of England, and died master of the free school in Norwich, in the cathedral of which city he is buried. He (Samuel, born Guilford, Sept. 23, 1643) was father of Benjamin Hoadly, successively Bishop of Bangor, Hereford, Salisbury and Winchester (born 1676, died 1761), and of John Hoadly, successively Bishop of Leighlin and Fernes, Archbishop of Dublin, Archbishop of Armagh (born 1678, died 1746).

John Hoadly the emigrant returned to England in the autumn of 1653; the next year was appointed (presumably through Desborough's influence) chaplain of the garrison of Edinburgh Castle. His family went over (as the letter states) in 1654. He continued at Edinb. until 1662, when he settled at Rolvenden, Kent, where he died June 28, 1668. His widow survived him more than twenty years.

Charles J. Hoadly.

William Leete, whose letter is here printed, was also an early settler of Guilford. From the Visitations of Huntingdonshire, 1613 and 1684, we learn that he was a son of John Leete of Diddington, co. Huntingdon, and a grandson of Thomas Leete of Oakington, co. Cambridge. His mother was Anna, daughter of Robert Shute, and his wife Anne was daughter of John Payne, a clergyman of Southoe, co. Hunt. (See *The Family of Leete with special Reference to the Genealogy of Joseph Leete, Esq., F.S.S.* London, 1881, pp. 11, 12 and 64.) He was born about 1612, and died April 16, 1683. He was governor of New Haven Colony, 1661-3, and of Connecticut from 1676 till his death. A biographical sketch of him will be found in Smith's *History of Guilford*, pp. 121-2.

For Cromwell's plans for the removal of the people of New England to what he supposed would be a more favorable location, which is mentioned in Gov. Leete's letter, see Palfrey's *History of New England*, vol. ii. pp. 389-93.—Editor.]

2: April 1621.

In the name of God Amen: I comit my soule to God that gave it and my bodie to the earth from whence it came. Alsoe I give my goodes as followeth That fforty poundes wch is in the hand of goodman Woodes I give my wife tenn poundes, my sonne Joseph tenn poundes, my daughter Priscilla tenn poundes, and my eldest sonne tenn poundes. Alsoe I give to my eldest sonne all my debtes, bonds, bills (onelye yt forty poundes excepted in the handes of goodman Wood) given as aforesaid wth all the stock in his owne handes. To my eldest daughter I give ten shillings to be paied out of my sonnes stock Furthermore that goodes I have in Virginia as followeth To my wife Alice halfe my goodes . 2 . to Joseph and Priscilla the other halfe equallie to be devided betweene them. Alsoe I have xxj dozen of shoes, and thirteene paire of bootes wch I giue into the Companies handes for forty poundes at seaven years end if thy like them at that rate. If it be thought to deare as my Overseers shall thinck good And if they like them at that rate at the devident I shall have nyne shares whereof I give as followeth twoe to my wife, twoe to my sonne William, twoe to my sonne Joseph, twoe to my daughter Priscilla, and one to the Companie. Allsoe if my sonne

William will come to Virginia I give him my share of land furdermore I give to my twoe Overseers Mr John Carver and Mr Williamson, twentye shillinges apeece to see this my will performed desiringe them that he would have an eye over my wife and children to be as fathers and freindes to them, Allsoe to have a speciall eye to my man Robert wch hathe not so approved himselfe as I would he should have done.

This is a Coppye of Mr Mullens his Will of all particulars he hathe given. In witnes whereof I have sett my hande   John Carver, Giles Heale, Christopher Joanes.

Vicesimo tertio: die mensis Julii Anno Domini Millesimo sexcentesimo vicesimo primo Emanavit Commissio Sare Blunden als Mullins filiè naturali et legitime dicti defuncti ad administrand bona iura et credita eiusdem defunct iuxta tenorem et effectum testamenti suprascripti eo quod nullum in eodem testamento nominavit executorem de bene etc Jurat.

                                                                68, Dale.

Mense Julij An^o Dñi 162j.

Vicesimo tertio die emanavit coñissio Sare Blunden als Mullens filie nŕali et ltiñe Willñi Mullens nup de Dorking in Coñ Surŕ sed in partibus ultra marinis def heñtis etc ad administrand bona iura et credita ejusdem def iuxta tenorem et effcūm testamenti ipsius defuncti eo quod nullum in eodem nominavit exŕem de bene etc iurat.

                                        Probate Act Book, 1621 and 1622.

[William Mullins, the testator, was one of the passengers in the Mayflower, and the father of Priscilla Mullins, the heroine of Longfellow's poem, " The Courtship of Miles Standish." The will was evidently drawn up at Plymouth, New England, which was then considered a part of Virginia. The date of the will is not given, but it must have been on or before Feb. 21, 1620-1, for on that day Mr. Mullins died, according to Gov. Bradford's Register, as quoted by Prince in his Chronology, part ii, p. 98. The date April 2, 1621, is probably that on which the certified copy was signed.

Gov. Bradford, in his list of passengers in the Mayflower, has this entry : " Mr William Mullines and his wife, and 2. children, Joseph & Priscila ; and a servant, Robert Carter." In the margin he gives the number of persons in Mr. Mullins's family, " 5." *

In Bradford's memoranda of the changes that had occurred in these families in the course of thirty years, we find this entry : " Mr Molines, and his wife, his son and his servant, died the first winter. Only his daughter Priscila survied, and married with John Alden, who are both living, and have 11. children. And their eldest daughter is married & hath five children."†

This will gives the names of Mr. Mullins's two children who were left in England, William the eldest son, and Sarah, who married a Mr. Blunden. The Probate Act Book supplies the English residence, Dorking in the county of Surrey.

Mr. Williamson, who is named as an overseer of the will, I take to be the " Master Williamson," who, according to Mourt's Relation, p. 36 (Dexter's edition, p. 92), was present, March 22, 1620-1, when the first treaty was made with Massasoit. Rev. Alexander Young, D.D., finding no person by the name of Williamson among the signers to the compact, concludes that the name Williamson was probably an error of the press, and suggests that of Allerton instead. (See Chronicles of the Pilgrims, Boston, 1841, p. 192.) Dr. Young's conjecture has generally been adopted by later writers.

Christopher Joanes may have been the Captain of the Mayflower, whose surname we know was Jones. Rev. Edward D. Neill, however, in the REGISTER, xxviii. 314, gives reasons for believing that his christian name was Thomas.—EDITOR.]

* Bradford's New Plymouth, Boston, 1856, p. 446.
† Ibid. p. 452.

JOHN HARWOOD of London, merchant, 13 November 1684, proved 22 June 1685. To wife Elizabeth all my household goods and plate during her life and after to dispose of them as she shall judge meet, and all my five tenements &c. in St. George's Lane and Pudding Lane London, which I hold by lease from the company of fishmongers and two messuages in Pudding Lane which I hold by lease from Christ Church Hospital. To son Jacob Harwood the messuage near the Monument in London late in the occupation of Mr. Selby, to hold after the decease of my said wife. To son Joseph Harwood the messuage now in the occupation of Mr. Strood, after the decease of my wife.

"Item I give to my daughter Elizabeth Sedgwick now in New England and to her sonne Samuell those three houses in St George's Lane aforesaid which I hold by lease from the said company of ffishmongers now in the occupation of Mr. Bodkin, Jerome Hall and —— Norrice, to hold to them the said Elizabeth Sedgwick and her sonne Samuell their Executors, Administrators and assignes imediately from and after the decease of my said wife for and dureing all the rest and residue which shall bee then to come and unexpired of the terme in the said Lease by which I hold the same, they paying to the ffishmongers company aforesaid the remainder of the yearly ground rent which is Eleaven pounds thirteene shillings and four pence neverthelesse my will is that my said daughter Sedgwick and her said sonne Samuell or one of them shall pay and allow to my sonne John now in New England fifteene pounds a yeare out of the rents and profitts of the said three messuages or tenements dureing all the time they or either of them shall hold the same and if it shall happen that the said Elizabeth Sedgwick and her said sonne Samuell shall dye then I give the said three Messuages or tenements (after the death of my said wife and after the deceases of the said Elizabeth Sedgwick and her said sonne) to my said sonne John his Executors Administrators and assignes."

To my daughter Hannah Manwaring the two messuages in Pudding Lane now in the occupation of Mr. Bird and Thomas Smith &c. and after her decease to Elizabeth, her daughter. To my son Jacob one thousand pounds if he shall faithfully and honestly serve out his time of apprenticeship &c. To son Joseph the like sum at his age of two and twenty years &c. To wife Elizabeth six hundred pounds to be at her own disposing. To said daughter Manwaring five hundred pounds out of such money her husband owes me &c. To her daughter Elizabeth. Manwaring two hundred pounds at her age of seventeen years.

"Item I give to my brother Thomas Harwood in New England fifty pounds to bee paid him there. Item I give to Nathaniel Harwood of New England fifty pounds to bee paid him there. Item I give to Hannah Wheeler of Concord in New England fifty pounds to bee paid her there. Item I give to Sarah Tucker formerly Scotto of New England fifty pounds which fower last mençoned summes I will shall bee paid out of My Stock in New England. Item I give to Mr. John Collins forty pounds to Mr. Samuel Belchamber five pounds to poor Suffering Christians such as the said Mr. John Collins and my said wife shall nominate appoint and agree one hundred pounds and I doe hereby nominate appoint and desire Mr Isaac Dafforne to bee my trustee for my said two sonnes Jacob and Joseph," &c. My said wife Elizabeth to be sole executrix, desiring her to take the assistance and advice of the said Isaac Dafforne, "and as for the remainder or overplus of my estate which I value to bee above two thousand pounds as by note inclosed of what is beyond Sea which when it is returned home to

London I doe give the one halfe thereof to my sonne John and the other halfe to my said wife and my two other sonnes Jacob and Joseph which is over and besides what is in the hands of Mr Hezechia Usher and John Usher and which by account is above five thousand pounds and is Stock in their hands the one halfe whereof belongs to mee and if they have not complyed with my proposalls made by Peter Buckley Esqr then my power that I gave to the said Peter Buckley is to bee null and void and then I doe give the proceed thereof to my said sonne John and my sonne in law Ralph Manwaring equally to bee divided betweene them."

To Mr. Matthew Meade ten pounds, to Mr Lawrence ten pounds, to Ann Gillman five pounds, to my sister Harwood five pounds, to Mary Scatergood five pounds and to such poor Christians as Mr. Meade Mr. Lawrence and my said wife shall think fit ten pounds.

Wit. Hen: Bosworth, Humph Hackshaw, Jacob Bosworth.

Cann, 72.

[John Harwood, the testator, was no doubt the John Harwood of Boston 1645, freeman of Mass. May 2, 1649, who by wife Elizabeth had Elizabeth, bp. 17 March, 1650; Hezekiah, b. 17 April, 1653, d. young; Hannah, b. March 6, 1655. He was admitted to First Church, Dec. 25, 1647, when he was called taylor. He sold his estate in 1657, and went home, and in 1677 was of London (See Savage's Gen. Dict.). Savage suggests that he may have been a son of George Harwood, the first treasurer of the Massachusetts Company.

Thomas Harwood, of Boston, presumably the brother Thomas named by John, m. July 7, 1654, Rachel, wid. of Robert Woodward and dau. of John Smith, and had Rachel, b. June 20, 1655, d. young; Jeremiah, b. June 4, 1656; Ann, b. Aug. 1657, d. young; Rachel, b. Feb. 28, 1661; and Benjamin, b. Feb. 4, 1663.

Nathaniel Harwood, of Boston, by wife Elizabeth, had William, b. March 28, 1665.

Elizabeth Sedgwick, daughter of the testator, must have been the widow of Samuel Sedgwick, who was a son of Major Robert. Her husband was b. in Charlestown, N. E., where he was bap. March 31, 1639. He went to England as early as 1657. "It is curious that his signature was proved in England by his widow [Elizabeth], 1 Dec. 1683, then aged only 33 years, and she says he was her husband six years. 'Citizen and clothworker of London,' he calls himself in a deed of 20 May, 1667, whereby he sold his house and land in Charlestown to Francis Willoughby." (Savage.) See Sedgwick wills, post.—EDITOR.]

Memorandum that NICHOLAS HOUGHTON late of the parish of St Margaret New Fish Street, London, deceased, did on the one and twentieth day of January one thousand six hundred forty eight, stilo Angliæ, or thereabouts, utter and speak these words &c. I give to my son Robert Houghton the sum of ten pounds and my ring, to my daughter Mary Norton forty shillings to buy her a ring, and to my daughter Van Court forty shillings, and for the rest of my goods I give unto Ellinor my wife, and do make her my full executor .... in the presence of Arthur Wind and Susanna Houghton.

Admon. was granted 2 March 1648 to the son Robert Houghton, the widow having renounced. Fairfax, 33.

ROBERT HOUGHTON of the parish of St Olave's, Southworth, in the County of Surrey, brewer, 25 December 1653, proved at Westminster 7 January 1653. To wife Mary Houghton six hundred pounds in money and all my plate and household stuff whatsoever; also my house and land at Lewsham which I purchased of Thomas Hill, gentleman, deceased (and other real estate). To our daughter Martha four hundred pounds, to be paid her at her day of marriage or age of twenty-one years, and to daugh-

ters Sarah and Hannah (the same sum on similar conditions). To John
Planner the younger, son of John Planner, citizen and girdler of London,
and of my daughter Mary Planner the sum of fifty pounds within seven
years after my decease.

"Item I will and bequeath unto my dearely loveinge and pious sister
Mary Norton wife of ffrancis Norton of Charles towne in New England
the some of twenty poundes to be paied to her within two yeares after my
decease." I will and appoint that the five hundred pounds due unto my
son in law John Willcox who lately married my daughter Elizabeth Houghton be paid unto him within the compass of two years as the remainder of
the portion which I agreed to give him with my said daughter. To my
son in law John Planner five pounds to buy him a ring and to my daughter
Mary Planner ten pounds (similar sums to son and daughter Willcox).

"Item I allsoe give and bequeath unto my very loueinge brother Mr
William Sedgwicke five pounds to buy him a ringe. Allsoe to my loueinge brother ffrancis Sedgwicke five pounds to buy him a ringe." To *three*
clerks, William Piggott, John Nobes and Robert Maisters and Lawrence
West fifty shilling apiece and also to widow West the sum of twenty shillings. All the residue to wife Mary Houghton whom I appoint sole executrix. And I desire my brothers Mr William and Mr Francis Sedgwicke to
be overseers.   Alchin, 372.

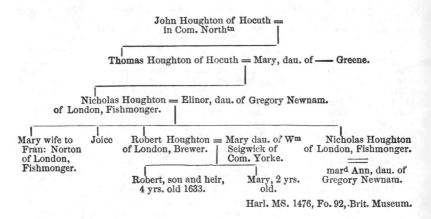

John Houghton of Hocuth =
in Com. North^{tn}

Thomas Houghton of Hocuth = Mary, dau. of —— Greene.

Nicholas Houghton = Elinor, dau. of Gregory Newnam.
of London, Fishmonger.

Mary wife to   Joice   Robert Houghton = Mary dau. of Wm   Nicholas Houghton
Fran: Norton   of London, Brewer. | Seigwick of   of London, Fishmonger.
of London,   Com. Yorke.
Fishmonger.
                             Robert, son and heir,   Mary, 2 yrs.   mard Ann, dau. of
                             4 yrs. old 1633.   old.   Gregory Newnam.

Harl. MS. 1476, Fo. 92, Brit. Museum.

[A pedigree of the same family may be found in the Visitation of London, published by the Harleian Society (vol. xv. p. 369). In the latter Francis Norton is
called a haberdasher, which is more probably correct, if we may judge from the
character of his inventory as shown in the Middlesex Records, he being the well-
known Capt. Francis Norton, who was admitted into the church of Charlestown,
Mass., 10-2-1642, and died in Charlestown, 27 July, 1667. He left no male issue,
but has probably many descendants in New England through his daughters, of
whom Abigail was the wife of John Long, Mary of Joseph Noyes, Deborah of Zech-
ary Hill, and Elizabeth of Timothy Symmes and Ephraim Savage. In social, political and military relations Capt. Norton seems to have stood high.

The Houghton pedigree is interesting and valuable for the light it incidentally
casts on the origin of the family of Sedgwick of Charlestown. The will of John
Sedgwick, already printed in these Gleanings (*ante*, p. 47), by its reference to his
brother Major-Gen. Robert Sedgwick, of New England, and his sister Mary, wife
of Robert Houghton, establishes this connection clearly.—HENRY F. WATERS.]

STEPHEN SEDGWICK of London Brewer 19 July 1638. One third to wife Catherine and one third to children now living viz. Job, Sara, Susanna, Rebecca, Abigail and Joshua Sedgwick at their several ages of twenty and one years or days of marriage. The other third in special legacies. To the poor of the parish of Engleton where I was born and had my first breath, the poor of Horton, the poor of St Bride's &c. To my uncle Thomas Checheley of St Ives. To Arthur Browne of the same town. To my cousin Jane Prichard in Moore Lane. To my brother William Sedgwick's children living at my decease. To my brother Thomas Browne's children and his wife. To my brother Norton and his wife. To my cousin William Sedgwick and John Sedgwick and cousin Robert Houghton. To my aunt Anne Rundall. To my cousin Elizabeth Browne the daughter of my sister Elizabeth Norton. And I do forgive all such debts and sums of money as are due and owing unto me by any of my cousins Sedgwickes in Yorkshire. The rest and residue to loving wife Catherine Sedgwick, whom I make and ordain to be my full and sole executrix &c. My loving brother Mr Thomas Browne, my loving brother Mr Henry Norton and my said loving cousin Mr Robert Houghton to be my overseers &c.

On the 15th day of December, A.D. 1649, issued forth a commission to Job Sedgeswick, natural and lawful son and principal legatee of Stephen Sedgeswick, late of the parish of St Bridget *alias* Bride's, Fleet Street, London, deceased, to administer the goods, &c., according to the tenor of the will, for the reason that Catherine Sedgeswick, wife and executrix of the testator, before his death, hath also departed this life.   Fairfax, 192.

January 1655.   English Stile.

The fifth day Letters of Administracōn issued out unto Martha Sedgewicke the Relict of ffrancis Sedgwicke, late of the parish of Mary Somersett in London deced   To adtēr the goods chēlls & debt's of ye said decēd She being first sworne (by Com̃ission) truly to Administer &c.   Fo. 12.

September 1656

On ye Thirtieth day issued forth Letters of Adc̃on To Johanna Sedgwick widdow ye relict of Maior Robert Sedgwick late in the parts beyond the Seas Esqr decd To Administer all and singuler ye goods chēlls and Debts of ye sayd decd   Shee being first sworne truely to Administer &c.
Fo. 221.

WILLIAM SEDGWICKE, the elder (of Lewisham, Kent, says the Probate Act) 28 November 1663, proved 26 February 1663. To son in law Nicholas Ashton and his wife, my daughter, two parcels of land in Great Sampford and Little Sampford, Essex. To daughters Susan and Mary Sedgwicke. To son in law Timotheus Van Vleteren three hundred pounds, which with three hundred pounds already paid makes in all six hundred pounds his full share and more of that money which fell to me by the death of Mr James Harewin. To son in law Nath: James. To my nephew Zach. Sedgwicke one hundred pounds, to be paid him within one month after my brother Sedgwicke, his father, shall have paid the hundred and fifty pounds that I stand bound for him, with the interest. To my nephew William Barrett one hundred pounds to be paid to his father for his use &c. To my sister Mary Houghton. To my son Francis Commins. To my friend Robert Bacon. To my faithful servant Robert Boult. To my loving friend Joshua Sprigge one hundred pounds to be disposed to charitable uses &c. William Sedgwicke my only son and heir and sole executor. He to consult with his loving brothers Nath: James, Nich: Ashton and Timotheus Van Vleteren.   Bruce, 22.

WILL. SEDGWICK, Son of William Sedgwick of London, Gen. became a
Commoner in Pembroke Coll. Oxon. in Michaelmas Term A. 1624, aged
15 years. Having taken his Degrees and H. Orders he was admitted into
this Church [Farnham] at the Presentation of two of his Relations* in 1634,
where he behav'd himself conformable to the Ch. of England; but upon the
turn of the times in 1641 he clos'd with the Presbyterians; after the Loyal
Clergy had been ejected from their Livings he became the chief preacher in
Ely and was called the Apostle of that Isle. What he enjoy'd there and
elsewhere, for several Years, he lost after the King's Restauration, by Non-
Conformity. He was a conceited whimsical Person and one very unsettled
in his Opinions; sometimes he was a Presbyterian, sometimes an Independent, and at other times an Anabaptist, sometimes he was a Prophet, and at
other times pretended to Revelations; and upon pretence of a Vision that
Doomsday was at hand he retired to Sir Francis Russells in Cambridgeshire, where he call'd upon certain Gentlemen as they were at Bowes to
prepare themselves; for that he had lately received a Revelation that
Doomsday would be some Day the next Week; whence he was afterwards
call'd Doomsday Sedgwick; after the Restauration he lived mostly at Lewes-
ham in Kent. In 1668 he retired to London, where he soon after dy'd.
Ath. Ox. Vol. II. p. 335.   Newcourt's Repertorium, &c. II. 256.

REBECCAH THORNE of Hornsey in the County of Middlesex, 17 September 1660, proved 20 November 1660. To my sister Blackwell my
diamond ring that was my mother's. To my sister Clarke the little cabinet of mother of pearl that was my mother's. To my son John Thorne
my silver watch. To my daughter Sarah Thorne my diamond ring with
one stone. To my brother Job Sedgwicke and wife and brother Joshua
Sedgewicke twenty shillings apiece to buy each of them a ring. To Mary
Noble the forty shillings that she oweth me, and a small ring that I had at
my Aunt Randall's funeral. To my cousin Moore the satin petticoat that
was my mother's. To my cousin Elizabeth Ash the ring that I had at
cousin William Sedgwicke's wife funeral. My sister Blackwell to be sole
executrix, desiring her to take upon her the care and charge of my son
Robert Thorne.

The will was proved by Susanna Blackwell.   Nabbs, 301.

Letters issued 21 July 1670 to Stephen Sedgewicke son of Job Sedgewicke lately of Sᵗ Peter's Paul's Wharf London but dying in the City of
Bristol, to administer on his goods, &c.

Admon. Act Book (1670) 113.

Inrollment of Letters Patent and other Instruments of State during the
Protectorate of Oliver Cromwell, of his son Richard, and of the Government of the persons styling themselves Keepers of the Liberties of England, from 24 June, 1654, to 23 January, 1659.

Fol. 31. 6 June 1655. That the sum of 1793ˡⁱ 7ˢ 8ᵈ remaining due and
owing unto Major Robᵗ Sedgwick upon his Accompts (examᵈ by the Comˢˢ
of our Navy) as he was employed in the publique service in New England and elsewhere against the ffrench, be paid him.

Stowe MSS. (Brit. Mus.) 215.

* He was presented to the living, Feb. 5, 1634-5, by Stephen and John Sedgwick (See
Newcourt, II. 256, and Bliss's ed. of Wood's Athenæ Oxonienses, III. 894). The latter
work contains a good sketch of William Segdwick's life, with a list of his publications.
Wood and Newcourt (ubi supra) and Palmer (Nonconformist's Memorial, London, 1778,
I. 248) are in error in placing his death after 1668.—EDITOR.

[By the preceding documents and the will of John Sedgwick above referred to, we learn that Major Robert Sedgwick of Charlestown, N. E., was son of William[2] Sedgwick of London, gent., who had a brother Stephen[2] a brewer.

WILLIAM[2] SEDGWICK, of London, had a wife Elizabeth who survived him and was living a widow in Woburn, Beds. in 1638. He had at least five children, namely: Maj. *Robert*,[3] *John*,[3] of St. Savior, Southwark, will 27 Nov. 1638, pr. 5 Dec. 1638, wife Martha. *William*,[3] a clergyman, rector of Farnham in Essex 1634 to 1644, afterwards held a living in the city of Ely, but was ejected under the Bartholomew act, retired to Lewisham, Kent, and died between Nov. 28, 1663, and Feb. 26, 1663-4. He had William,[4] and several daughters. *Francis*,[3] who was living in 1653, and was probably the Francis of the parish of St. Mary, Somerset, London, whose widow Martha was granted administration on his estate, January, 1655-6. *Mary*,[3] wife of Robert Houghton, who had Robert, Mary married John Planner, and Martha.

———[2] SEDGWICK, brother of William, perhaps Stephen above named, had: *Stephen*,[3] will July 19, 1638, proved Dec. 15, 1649, had wife Catherine, who died before him. He had Job,[4] Sarah,[4] Susanna[4] and Rebecca;[4] of whom Rebecca married —— Thorne and died in 1660, leaving a daughter Sarah Thorne. *William*,[3] probably dead in 1638, leaving children. *Elizabeth*[3] married Henry Norton, both living in 1638. She had a daughter Elizabeth Browne.

William[2] Sedgwick, above, of London, is said in the Houghton pedigree (*ante*, p. 66) to have been of the county of York. He resided afterwards, it is presumed, in Bedfordshire, as his son Rev. William[3] is stated in Wood's *Athenæ* to have been born in that county, and another son John[3] in his will (REG. XXXVIII. 207) calls Woburn, Beds, the parish in which he himself was born. Elizabeth Sedgwick, wife of William[2] and the mother of these children, resided in Woburn after her husband's death. Probably Major Robert[3] Sedgwick and the other children were born in Woburn.

There is a Sedgwick pedigree traced to "Edward Sedgwik of Dent in com. York" in the Essex Pedigrees in the Publications of the Harleian Society, vol. XIV. page 600. In 1642, Edward Sedgwick, a great-great-grandson of the above Edward, resided at Chipping Ongar in Essex. I can find no evidence that the two families were related, though both were from the same county.—EDITOR.]

JOHN JOLLIFE of Fyfhed Magdalen in the County of Dorset, 29 October 1583, proved 30 January 1583. To the poor people of Stower Preaux, Stower Estower and Fyfhed Magdalen. To eldest daughter Rebecca Jollife and daughter Susan Jollife at ages of fourteen years. Son John Joliffe. Mother in law Helen Newman, widow, late wife of Robert Newman deceased. Reference to a lease granted by father Richard Jollife, 20 December 22[d] of Elizabeth. Father still living. To brother Edmond Jollife. To kinswoman Christian Galler. To sister Mary Jollife. To brother John Jollife. Wife Elizabeth Jollife to be sole executrix. Uncle Henry Newman, brother in law Richard Estemond, brother Edmond Jollife, Nicholas Joyce and Nicholas Clarke, vicar of Fifehed, to be overseers.

Butts, 23.

Letters issued forth 9 December 1639, to Catherine Joliffe relict of John Joliffe lately of East Stower in the county of Dorset deceased, to administer on his goods, &c.   Admon. Act Book (1639) fo. 89.

"Memorandum that GEORGE JOYLIFFE, Doctor in Physicke, ye Sixteenth Day of November one thousand sixe hundred fftie Eight made his last Will." Proved 24 November, 1658. My body to be buried with as little funeral pomp as may be. To my cousin Francis (my servant) the sum of fifty pounds to be paid when all my debts are satisfied. To my maid-servant Elizabeth five pounds and to Susan four pounds. To my brother Richard Joyliffe my black mare. To my cousin Francis (as above) all my Latin Books. To my daughter Katherine five hundred pounds, with the interest thereof, to be paid her at the age of sixteen or the day of her mar-

riage, and the same to be put out for her use by my brother William Bigg
and my cousin Richard Newman. All the residue of my estate to my loving wife Ann Joyliffe and she to be executrix. Brother William to be
overseer. None of these legacies to be paid or disposed of until Mrs
Mymms's account be satisfied and paid. Wit: Thomas ffrewen and Sara
Mills.   Wootton, 631.

ANNE JOYLIFFE relict and executrix of George Joyliffe late Doctor of
Phisick, 25 May 1660, proved 29 November 1660. My body to be buried in Trinity church near Garlick Hill, London, near the body of my late
husband. To my daughter Katherine Joyliffe one thousand pounds, to be
paid her at the age of sixteen years. A reference to a legacy of five hundred pounds left to her by the husband of the testatrix and to be paid her
at the same age. The amount of this legacy to be recovered out of a debt
due the said George by one Francis Drake of Walton, in the County of
Surrey. If that debt should not be recovered then five hundred pounds
more to make the thousand pounds fifteen hundred. To my mother Mary
Bigge two hundred pounds. To my brother William Bigge* one hundred
and fifty pounds. To my brother John Bigge one hundred pounds. To
Francis Cave, nephew to my said husband, forty pounds, and to Alice
Cave, his sister, ten pounds. To my said daughter Katherine my diamond
ring set with one stone only, my diamond locket, my plate, linen and other
household stuff. My brother William Bigge to be executor.

Wit: St. Frewen, Thomas Frewen, Miles Beales.

A codicil refers to fifteen hundred pounds secured in the names of Sir
Charles Harford, my cousin Newman and my cousin Frewen, in trust for
my use, and refers also to a deed from my brother Joyliffe.

Nabbs, 285.

THANKFUL FREWEN, of St Andrew, Holborn, in the County of Middlesex, esq., in his will of 25 September, 1656, proved 18 March, 1656, mentions, among others, his brother Accepted Frewen, cousin George Joyliffe,
Doctor in Physick, niece Ann Joyliffe, wife of the said Dr. Joyliffe, and
sister Mary Bigg.   Ruthen, 110.

PEDIGREE OF JOLLIFFE.

Ricardus Joleiff de Canning Court in = ... relict .... Rogers
p'ochia de Pulhā in Com. Dorset. | de Com. Som.

Johannes Joleiff de Caning Court in = Elizab. filia et coh Robtt Newman
Com. Dorset fil. et heres. | de Fifeild Magdalen in Com.
| Dorset.

¹Rebecca vxor | Johannes Jolliffe de Estouer | Katherin da. of | ²Susanna vx. Will:
Wili. Starre de | in Com. Dors. fil. et hæres | Johēs Henninge | Holman de
Bradford in Com. | Patris et matris sup'stes | de Paxwell in | Estouer in
Dors. | 1623. | Com. Dorset. | Com. Dorset.

Ricardus Joleiff fil. | ²Johannes æt. 8. | ⁴Georgius æt. 3. | Catherine æt. [14].
et hacr ætat, 12 | ³Robtus æt. 4. | | Dorothea æt. [13].
annorū 1623. | | |

                                                    (Signed) Jo. JOYLIFFE.

Harl. MS. 1166, fo. 32b.

* Much about the Bigg family will be found in the REGISTER, xxix. 253–60; and *ante,*
pp. 21–3.—EDITOR.

JOHN FREWEN the elder, of Northiham, in the County of Sussex, clerk, aged, &c., in his will, dated 1 June 1627, mentions son Accepted Frewen (President of Magdalen College, Oxford), son Thankfull Frewen and daughter Mary wife of John Bigg, lands &c. in Sussex and in Newenden and Sandherst, Kent. Barrington, 38.

[From the Roll of the Royal College of Physicians of London, compiled from the Annals of the College and from other authentic sources, by William Munk, M.D., Fellow of the College, etc. etc., previously referred to, we learn that "George Joyliffe, M.D., was born at East Stower, in Dorsetshire. In the early part of 1637 he was entered a commoner of Wadham College, Oxford, where he remained about two years, and then removed to Pembroke College, as a member of which he took the two degrees in arts, A.B. 4th June, 1640 ; A.M. 20th April, 1643. He then entered on the study of physic, pursued anatomy with the utmost diligence, and 'with the help' (as Wood says) 'of Dr. Clayton, master of his College, and the king's professor of Physick, made some discovery of that fourth set of vessels plainly differing from veins, arteries and nerves, now called the lymphatics.' He finally removed to Clare Hall, Cambridge, and, having there proceeded doctor of medicine, settled in London ; was admitted a candidate of the College of Physicians, 4th April, 1653 ; and a Fellow, 25th June, 1658. Dr. Joyliffe lived in Garlick Hill; and, as I learn from Hamey, died 11th November, 1658, being then barely forty years of age."

There is nothing, to be sure, in the foregoing wills of Dr. Joyliffe and his widow, to show any connection with English families in America. Fortunately we may learn, from another source, that he was a brother of John Joyliffe, Esq., an eminent merchant of Boston, Mass., who, as we are told by Savage, was of "Boston 1656, m. 28 Jan. 1657, Ann wid. and extrix. of. Robert Knight, who had also been wid. and extrix. of Thomas Cromwell, the wealthy privateersman, had only ch. Hannah, b. 9 May, 1690. He was freem. 1673, many yrs. a selectman, one of the patriots of 1689 who put Andros in prison, town recorder in 1691 ; and was made by Increase Mather one of the Counc. in the Chart. of William & Mary, but drop. at the first popular choice ; died 23 November, 1702." Savage is in error as to the year of his death, as is shown by the probate of Joyliffe's will (see below), and by Sewall's Diary.* It should be 1701. The daughter of his wife, by her first husband, viz., Elizabeth Cromwell, was married first to Richard Price of Boston, and secoudly to Isaac Vickars of Hull, and by the first husband had, among other issue, a daughter, Elizabeth Price, who became the second wife of James Townsend of Boston, ancestor of a distinguished Boston family, and whose granddaughter Rebecca, daughter of James and Elizabeth (Phillips) Townsend, was the wife of John Winthrop, LL.D. and F.R.S., Fellow of Harvard College and Hollis Professor of Mathematics and Natural Philosophy.

The will of John Joyliffe of Boston, merchant (Suffolk Registry, B. 14, L. 432), made 7 February, 1699 (1700), proved 27 December, 1701, devises his mansion house to Martha, daughter of his late wife and wife of Jarvis Ballard, allowing the heirs of Richard Price power of redemption. He also makes numerous bequests to friends and relatives in England, viz. : Katherine Bowles, daughter of his brother Dr. George Joyliffe, Katherine Coope and Alice Morley, daughters of his sister Dorothy Cave, John Cooke of London, merchant, son of his sister Martha Cooke, Rebecca Spicer, daughter of his sister Rebecca Woolcot, John Drake, son of his sister Margaret Drake, and Margaret and Katharine Drake, daughters of his sister Margaret and Esther, daughter of his sister Mary Biss, sometime wife of James Biss of Shepton Mallett, in the County of Somerset. He also bequeaths sums of money to the Rev. Samuel Willard (of Boston), and to Mr. Simon Willard, his son, and to the poor of Boston. For a further account of his wife and her relatives, see "Family of William Townsend of Boston," Essex Institute Historical Collections, Vol. 19, pp. 274-5 (1882).—H. F. W.]

* "Novr 23. 1701. John Joyliffe Esqr. dies. He had been blind, and laboured under many Infirmities for a long time."—Diary of Chief Justice Samuel Sewall in Coll. of Mass. Hist. Society, 5th Series, vol. vi. p. 48.

WILLIAM GREY citizen and merchant tailor of London 1 September 1657 ; proved at London 18 November 1663. To son Abraham the copyhold house and orchard in Hamerton, in parish of Hackney. To son Josia part of another copyhold house in Hamerton with two barns, stable and cowhouse &c. To daughter Rebecca Grey another part. To youngest daughter Susanna Grey another part. Other lands in Hackney to these four children. To son Abraham the fee farm rent of the watermills at Barking, Essex, of fifteen pounds per annum or thereabouts. To son Josiah all other rents or tenths payable to me in the manors or parishes of Barking, East Ham or West Ham in said county of Essex, which amount in the whole about nine pounds three shillings and two pence. To daughter Rebecca (other rents) and all that Last of red herrings due unto me yearly from the bayliffs of Great Yarmouth in the County of Norfolk. To daughter Susanna (other rents). If wife be with child then such child to have an equal portion with the other four children.

Item I give and bequeath unto my loving brother John Grey of New England the sum of five pounds of lawful money of England as an expression of my love to him. To brother Henry Grey the like sum of five pounds &c. And these two five pounds not to be paid until two years after my decease. To brother Isaac Grey my buff coat and five pounds to buy a piece of plate. To wife Susanna leases at Hamerton and lease of tenement in Birchin Lane, London, known by the sign of the Cross Keys. To brother in law M\r John Price twenty shillings to buy him a ring. And the like sum to cousin John Smith, potter. To the poor of the church at Stepney of which M\r Will\m Greenhill is pastor the full profit of that Last of red herrings &c. for one year only next after my decease and no longer. And that year's profit I appoint to be paid unto the assissors and deacons of the said church whereof one M\r Robert Williams my dear brother in Christ is one.

Wife Susanna to be executrix and guardian to all the children and brother in law John Price and brother Isaac Grey to be overseers.

Juxon, 130.

[Savage has several John Grays who were in New England.—EDITOR.]

ROBERT GREENE, Bodie maker, dwelling in the parish of Stepney, in the County of Middlesex, 5 August 1658, proved 22 September 1658. To be buried near my wife Dorothy in the church of S\t Leonard, Shoreditch. To Thomas Reynolds at Martin Branden in Virginia I bequeath forty pounds, but if he die before he receive it I bequeath it to Joanna Canon, widow, in Trinity Lane, London, or her heirs. To John Greene, a barber in Norwich, my brother, five shillings and to his son Francis Greene twenty shillings. To Alexander and Richard Greene, students in Cambridge, and to Christopher Greene, cook or Katherine Hall there, sons of my brother Christopher, five shillings apiece. To my kinswoman Elizabeth Gray, at Chelmsford, in Essex, four pairs of flaxen sheets, and to her brother Christopher Gray four pairs of sheets, and to Ann Gray, their sister, dwelling with me, ten pounds. To John Wright, bodie maker, once my servant, now dwelling in the parish of St. Leonard, Shoreditch, five pounds. To Richard Thorington, of the same parish, my mourning cloak. To Robert Marshall, bodie maker, of the same parish, ten shillings. To Nicholas Myriall, of the same parish, clothworker, a cloth suit. To Thomas White, virginall maker in the old Jury, a mourning hat and hatband. To

Mary Jenkes, of Grub Street, forty shillings.   To my servant Jone Beercroft twenty shillings.   To Christopher Greene, my brother Nicholas Greene's eldest son, a carrier of Cambridge, five shillings, and to my loving friend Thomas Snow, gardener, forty shillings, whom I appoint executor, dwelling in the parish of St Leonard, Shoreditch.   And the residue I leave to him.   Wit: Roger Ley, Thomas White.   Wootton, 417.

JOHN DINGLEY of the parish of St Olaves in the old Jewry, London, grocer, 21 August, 1626, proved 9 October, 1626.   Begins with reference to an assignment made of property consisting of five leases three years and a half ago to brother-in-law, Sampson Cotton of London, draper, in trust, with consent of chiefest and greater part of his creditors.

To my sister in law Mrs Anne Fuller, widow, twenty five pounds yearly.   To Alice Longe, my sister's daughter, now remaining in my service, ten pounds a year.   To Robert Johnson the younger, of London, grocer, two thirds part of the benefit & profit which shall be made and raised of my said five leases, after the expiration of the term &c. of the trust deed.

I give and bequeath to my said brother in law Sampson Cotton, in respect of the pains and trouble which he hath taken and sustained for me, the sum of one hundred pounds &c.   To Elizabeth Cotton, his daughter and my god daughter, fifty pounds; and to the rest of his children twenty pounds apiece.   To my loving friend Mr John Eldred the younger, five pounds.   To my kinswoman Anne Jarvis, now the wife of George Jarvis, gentleman, fifty pounds within eight years after my decease.   If she die before that time, then to her son —— Jarvis, now living.   To John Warton, of Winchester, my kinsman, twenty pounds within seven years after my decease.   To William Allen the younger, my godson, twenty pounds, at the age of twenty one years.   To my godson Thomas Strange five pounds within eight years.   To my servant William Hudson, twenty pounds in seven years.   To John Rosewarden, my servant, an augmentation of his wages if he shall continue workmaster in the "Coperous works" at Gil lingham in the County of Kent &c.   Other names.

Robert Johnson the younger to be sole executor, and loving & good friends Mr Alderman Johnson, the said Sampson Cotton and the said John Eldred to be overseers.   Hele, 141.

HARVARD AND SADLER (*ante*, p. 133).

The following is only another, though a very marked, evidence of the friendly interest taken in my work by my fellow workers at Somerset House.   Hardly a day passes, in fact, that I do not have occasion to express my gratitude for some new genealogical fact brought to my notice by my friends here.

It was to Mr. Dunkin that I was indebted for the extract from the Archbishop's Register, showing the date of institution of Mr. Sadler at Ringmer, and the extract from the parish register giving the date of his induction, confirming, in the latter respect, the notes of Burrell which I had copied in the British Museum.   HENRY F. WATERS.

Kenwyn House, Kidbrooke Park, Blackheath,
17 Feb. 1888.
DEAR MR. WATERS:
   Knowing the interest that is felt in the Harvard pedigree by yourself and others, I feel sure you will be glad to know that I have recently had the good fortune

to find, in contemporary records, the exact date and place of marriage of John Harvard to Anne Sadler, daughter of John Sadler, vicar of Ringmer—facts which have hitherto baffled the patient and diligent inquiries of genealogists.

The following extracts will speak for themselves. The first is a marriage license among the archives of the see of Chichester, while the second is the entry of marriage in the parish register of South Malling near Lewes, a parish adjacent to Ringmer, where John Sadler was beneficed.

[i.] "xviij°: Apri: pređ (*i. e.* 1636) Quo die magi' Anthonius Huggett Cĺicus in artibus magi' Surr': &c. Concessit ĺiam m̄ro Esdræ Coxall Cĺico Curato de Southmalling sive eius locū tenenti Cuicunque ad solem̄ m̄rioniū in eadem Eccĺia inter Joh̄em Harvard Cĺicum p̄oe Sᵗⁱ. Olavi iuxta London et Annam Sadler de Ringmer pueł pʳstito prius Jurament' ad sancta &c. p dcum̄ Harvard nil impedimenti rac̄oe consanguiñ affiñ pʳcont' vel alterius Cause Cuiuscunque de Jure ᵱhibito de eius scientia obsistere seu intervenire posse quominus m̄rioniū inter eos ĺtime solem̄ Obligantur Idem Johannes Cĺicus et Samuel Jeames de Glinde yeoman in C łj:"

[ii.] "Maryed the 19 day of Aprill 1636. Mʳ. John Harvard of the p̄ish of Sᵗ. Olives, neere London, and Anne Sadler of Ringmer."

I am desirous that this discovery should be made known to your American genealogical friends, and I think there is no better medium than your own "Gleanings," in which perhaps you will not mind inserting this letter.

I am, dear Mr. Waters,

Yours very truly,

E. H. W. DUNKIN.

[Thomas Harvard, brother of Rev. John, in his will (*ante,* page 126) calls himself of the parish of "Saint Olave in Southwarke in the county of Surrey." It will be noted that John Harvard is described as of that parish in the above records found by Mr. Dunkin. Thomas Harvard describes himself also as "Citizen and Clothworker of London." A little over two years ago the records of the Clothworkers' Company of London were searched for entries relating to him, and those of his being bound an apprentice and his admission to the freedom of the company were found. An English correspondent of the New York *Nation,* April 8, 1886, writing from Cambridge, Eng., March 22 of that year, says : "The records of Clothworkers' Company show that Thomas Harvarde bound himself an apprentice to William Coxe for eight years from June 24, 1627. I give the entry, extending the abbreviated Latin of the original :

"'Thomas Harvarde filius Roberti nuper de Southwarke in comitatu Surrey lanii defuncti posuit scipsum Apprenticium Willielmo Coxe Civi & Clothworker London par [pro] Octo Annos A festo Nativitatis Sancti Johannis Baptistæ preterito Datum undecimo Septembris 1627.' (Apprentice Book, 1606–1641.)'

Thomas Harvard was admitted a freeman of the Company December 3, 1634, as is shown by an entry found in the accounts of Henry Browne, Quarter Warden, 1634–1635. Printed fac-similes of these entries were sent to me by a friend in England, April 16, 1886, and they are reproduced in the margin on the preceding page.

The writer just quoted, noting the fact that Harvard was admitted to the freedom of the Company before eight years had expired, says : "The explanation is that he had fulfilled the term of seven years, which was all that the use and custom of the city of London,required."

Dr. Oliver Wendell Holmes presented to the Massachusetts Historical Society, February 10, 1887, similar printed facsimiles of both of these entries. See Proceedings Mass. Hist. Soc., 2d series, vol. iii. p. 221. The record of Thomas Harvard being bound an apprentice is found in the Register of Apprentices Bound, 1606–1641.

An autograph of Thomas Harvard and another autograph of his brother John, have recently been discovered attached to a document dated July 25, 1635, found among the muniments of the Hospital of St. Katherine near the Tower of London. See REGISTER, XLII. pp. 109–110.—EDITOR.]

KATHERINE WILSON, wife of Alexander Wilson of St. Martin le Grand of London, taylor, 25 November 1583, proved at London 9 January 1583. I give and bequeath unto Alexander Wilson my only husband that part, parcell and portion that I, Katherine Wilson, had given and bequeathed unto me by my own uncle Edmond Grindall, late Archbishop of Canterbury deceased, with all my right and interest that I, the said Katherine Wilson, had or by any ways might have had hereafter to whatsoever part or parcell and portion of the residue of my said uncle's will and goods by any ways or means howsoever, in as large and ample manner as it doth appear in his will more plainly, and make executor of my said will my said husband Alexander Wilson.   Butts, 20.

GUY BRISCOWE of the parish of Sundriche in the County of Kent, clerk, 26 May 1594, proved 1 March 1594. To my godchild Lawrence Gascony three shillings four pence. To all the rest of my godchildren twelve pence apiece. To my father, Edward Briscowe, of Crostananby in the Co. of Cumberland, if he be living, ten shillings. To my sister Margaret in the said county ten shillings. To my sister-in-law Mistress Isabel Wilson ten shillings. To my daughter Mary Briscowe three score pounds &c; to my daughter Anne Briscowe fifty pounds, to my daughter Isabel Briscowe fifty pounds, to every of my said daughters at their several ages of twenty years or at their several days of marriage. To my eldest son Thomas, forty pounds, and if all my lands are sold, other forty pounds. To my second son Edward fifty pounds. To my third son William fifty pounds. To my fourth son John fifty pounds. To the child my wife now goeth withal fifty pounds. Provision made in case of death of any of them.

Item I give and bequeath unto my loving wife Mary Briscowe daughter of William Willson, late of New Windsor in the County of Berks, deceased, &c all my lands and tenements with their appurtenances whatsoever within this realm of England to the only intent and purpose that she my said wife shall sell the same by the advice of my overseer or overseers of this my last will and testament hereafter named for the payment of the said legacies and of my said childrens' portions. If my wife die before my said lands be sold &c. then they shall be sold by my loving brother-in-law William Wilson, clerk, for the same purpose &c. And if he die &c. then these lands shall be sold by my loving cousin Alexander Briscowe of Wattford, besides Aldenham, in the County of Hartford &c. And if the said Alexander die &c. then my loving cousins Edward and Robert Briscowe, of the parish of Aldnam (Aldenham) aforesaid &c. The residue to wife Mary, whom I make sole executrix &c. I nominate constitute and appoint my said brother-in-law William Willson, clerk, governor and gardiner of my said daughter Mary Briscowe.   Scott, 20.

EDMUND WILSON of the parish of St Mary Bowe, in London, Doctor in Phisick, 28 September, 1633, with a codicil dated 30 Sept. 1633, proved 11 Oct. 1633 by William Taylor one of the executors, power reserved for John Wilson, the other. I bequeath my soul unto the lord my Creator, Redeemer & Comforter, my body to the earth to the great day. And concerning my burial my will is that my funeral shall be by night and decently accompanied by such kindred, physicians, friends and patients as may be thought fit to be nominated and will come to my burial and my will is that there shall be no manner of mourning at my burial either by my executors nor kindred nor any other.

To Mr Payne all debts he oweth unto me and five pounds. To Anthony Medcalfe five pounds and to Martha his wife forty shillings. To Bartholomew Edwards of Aldermanbury twenty pounds. I do remit to Mr Edward Alman of Cambridge the eight pounds he oweth me and give him twenty pounds as a testimony of my love & requital of his presents in my life time. I remit to my cousin William Briscoe the ten pounds he owes me, and give him ten pounds which my brother William Taylor owes to me by bond made in his name and also I give him the said bond. I remit to my cousin Blissenden the five pounds he oweth unto me and I give unto her five pounds more. I give unto my cousin Haies for his son twenty pounds. To Mr. Leech five pounds for his pains at my burial. To Mr Vocher five pounds. To my servant Robert twenty nobles. To my servant Geoffrey twenty pounds. To my maid servant Grace (money, bedding &c.). To my man Robert my old coloured rideing cloak lined with baize & my coloured cloth suit I wore at St Albans. To cousin Daniel Taylor fifty shillings. I remit to my neighbor Mr Ball the debt which he owes me. All the legacies before mentioned shall be discharged within six months after my death, or sooner if money come into my executor's hands.

And whereas there is none of my kindred to whom I would enlarge myself more than to my sister Taylor's children, if they had need, but because they have a loving & careful father & of good ability therefore I know what I should give them would not much augment their portions. Nevertheless in remembrance of my love unto them I give them these legacies following, viz. To Margaret Taylor ten pounds, to Hanna Taylor ten pounds, to Edmund Taylor twenty pounds. Item I give and bequeath to William Rawson one hundred & fifty pounds which legacy my executors shall retain in their hands and keep until the said William shall be recovered of his sickness and they, in the mean time, to allow unto him the profits of the said legacy towards his maintenance. To Edward Rawson, my sister's son, one hundred pounds. To my brother Gibbs five pounds, and to my sister Gibbs twenty pounds. To my cousin William Gibbs one hundred & fifty pounds &c. To Elizabeth Gibbs one hundred pounds, to be paid her on her day of marriage or age of one & twenty years. To my cousin Edmond Gibbs one hundred pounds, at the end of his apprenticeship, and thirty pounds more to bind him apprentice when such a master shall be provided as my executors shall approve of &c. And my will is that none of the legacies of my sister Gibbs' children shall lie dead but shall be bestowed & adventured in some lease or annual rent or in some other respectable way with the advice and consent of my sister Isabel Gibbs and of William Gibbs &c. And because my sister Summer's children have (by) many expressions of their love & respect to me " interested " themselves in my favor I must not neglect them : therefore I give to my cousin Hart one hundred & fifty pounds &c., to my cousin Page one hundred pounds, to cousin Thomas Summers one hundred pounds. To my cousin Whitfield ten pounds, to Thomas Sheafe ten pounds, to cousin Edmond Sheafe ten pounds, to cousin Grindall Sheafe ten pounds, to cousin Norwood ten pounds, to cousin Wesley ten pounds, to cousin Rebecca Haselrig ten pounds. To my sister Anne Wilson five pounds. To my brother Thomas Wilson forty pounds. I give to Elizabeth Wilson, wife to my brother John, in regard of her much pains & love towards me, the sum of thirty pounds and to cousin Edmond Wilson, son to my brother John, one hundred pounds. To Mr Stevens the apothecary thirty pounds.

Whereas by my father's will I should have given ten pounds to Lincoln College in Oxon and had a desire to present it with my own hand, but have not had opportunity so to do, my will is it shall be forthwith paid and moreover I give to the said college ten pounds. The rest and residue to be divided into three equal parts, two parts whereof to brother John Wilson's children, and the other third to brother Thomas Wilson's children.

My brother John Wilson and brother in law Mr William Taylor to be executors, and to each fifty pounds. The overseers to be my brothers in law Thomas Sheafe Doctor of Divinity, and Mr John Summers and Mr Bartholmew Edwards of Aldermanbury and to each of them twenty pounds. Reference is made to leases of house in Woodstreet, house at Charing Cross, house in Friday Street, lease of lands near Durham. To my cousin Edmond Wilson, my brother Thomas Wilson's son, my house and all my lands, tenements & hereditaments situate in Parshur in the county of Worcester and all my lands in the Isle of Bermudas, and to his heirs forever. To my sister Elizabeth (*sic*) Gibbs for and during the joint lives of the said Isabell and of my brother John Wilson one yearly annuity of ten pounds to be issuing, perceived and taken out of all my lands, tenements and hereditaments in the counties of Hartford & Kent &c. And whereas I have given to my sister Isabel Gibbs ten pounds yearly ever since my father's death my will is the same shall continue.

All my said messuages &c. in St Albans in the county of Hertford and all my lands &c. in the county of Kent, with their appurtenances, chargeable with the said annuities, to my brother John Wilson during his natural life and after his decease to my brother Thomas Wilson and to my sister Isabel Gibbs (for their lives) then to my cousin Edmund Wilson, son of my brother John & his heirs. All the lands, hereditaments &c in Charing in the County of Kent (let at fifty pounds per annum) to cousin John Wilson, my brother John's son, after decease of brothers & sister John, Thomas & Isabel as aforesaid. A provision insisting that brother Gibbs is not to intermeddle. To Mr Nye, the minister, five pounds. To my executors further, to each sixteen pounds six shilling eight pence, to make their legacies one hundred marks. To my sister Margaret Taylor five pounds.

The witnesses were Tho⁸ Andrew, Nicholas Viner, Jeffrey Wilson and Henry Colbron Scr.

The codicil provides for Mʳ Rolles, the minister, forty shillings, Mʳ Davis, the minister, forty shillings, Mʳ Smith, in or near Coleman St., twenty shillings, Dʳ Clarke my horse, saddle & bridle, so that he use him himself & not suffer any other to ride him nor sell him to any other. I also give him my best beaver hat. To brother John Wilson and his eldest son all my physic, books with my notes of physick added to the same. The legacy to my cousin Edmond Sheafe to be made up fifty pounds. Mʳ Votior's legacy to be made up ten pounds. To Mʳ Foxley, minister, forty shillings. To my brother John my three beaver hats. To Dʳ Fox three and a half yards of black satin for a doublet, and to Dʳ Meverel the same.

Wit: Bartholl: Edwards, Edmund Payne, William Gibbes, Robᵗ Steppinge his mark.

To Mʳ Daves, the minister, twenty shilling more in regard of his pains taken with him before his death.

Wit: Mare Hart.   Russell, 89.

EDMUND WILSON, M.D., was the second son of the Rev. William Wilson, D.D., canon of Windsor and rector of Cliffe, in Kent, who died 14ᵗʰ March, 1615, and was buried in Sᵗ George's chapel, Windsor. Dr. Edmund Wilson was educated at Eton and at King's College, Cambridge, and in that university proceeded Doctor of Medicine. He was incorporated at Oxford, 12ᵗʰ July 1614; was admitted a Candidate of the College of Physicians 22ⁿᵈ December 1615, and a Fellow the same day. On the 18ᵗʰ December, 1616, Dr. Wilson was installed canon of Windsor, but, because he was not ordained priest within a year following, he was deprived, and Dr. Godfrey Goodman succeeded, being installed 20ᵗʰ December 1617. Dr. Wilson practised his faculty for a few years at Windsor, but subsequently removed to London, was Censor in 1623 and Anatomy Reader in 1630. He died in the parish of Sᵗ Mary-le-Bow in September 1633. Dr. Hamey says of him: "Syphar hominis, nec facie minus quàm arte Hippocraticus, nec facultate magis quàm religionis titulo celebris."

> The Roll of the Royal College of Physicians of London, by William Munk, M.D., London, 1861, pp. 157–8.

[The "brother Gibbs" mentioned in Dr. Wilson's will, was Thomas Gibbs, of Windsor, second son of John and Mary Gibbs. By Isabella, daughter of the Rev. William Wilson, D.D., he had William, Edmund, Elizabeth and two other children (a son and daughter) not named, according to Additional MS. 5507, in British Museum. In the same MS. (which is a copy of Philipot's Visitation of Kent, 1619–1621, with additions by Hasted) is a pedigree of the Somer Family, of whom John, son of John Somer of St. Margaret's, is shown to have taken, for a first wife, Elizabeth, daughter of William Wilson, S.T.P., and to have had issue by her. His second wife was Elizabeth, daughter of Anthony Dering of Charing. The Rebecca Haselrig, who was called cousin, was one of the daughters of Thomas Sheafe, of Windsor, and wife of Thomas Haselrig, of London, mercer, who was a brother of the famous Sir Arthur Haselrig (or Heselrigge) of Noseley, and third son of Thomas Heselrigge of Noseley. (See Harleian MS. 1476, British Museum.)—H. F. W.

An abstract of the will of William Wilson, D.D., father of the above Dr. Edmund Wilson of London, and of Rev. John Wilson of Boston, Mass., will be found in the REGISTER, vol. XXXVIII. p. 306 (ante, p. 54), with an account of the family appended. Abstracts and annotations of the wills of other relatives will be found in that volume, pp. 301–12 (ante, pp. 50–61).—EDITOR.

Munk's Roll of the Royal College of Physicians of London, from which is quoted above an account of Dr. Edmund Wilson, the testator, contains also (page 227) an account of Dr. Edmund Wilson, the eldest son of the Rev. John Wilson, of Boston, Mass. He is named in his uncle's will as "cousin Edmund Wilson son of my brother John."—THOMAS MINNS.]

WILLIAM TAYLOR citizen & haberdasher of London 29 March 1650 proved 19 July 1651. To be buried in the parish church of Hacknay whereof I am a parishioner. Money to be expended in mourning apparel for my well beloved wife and my son Samuel Taylor & my daughter Rebecca Taylor &c. To my son and heir Daniel Taylor ten pounds for a piece of plate and to Rebecca Taylor his wife forty shillings for a ring. To my second son Edmond Taylor five pounds to buy him a piece of plate, and to my two daughters Margaret Webb, wife of William Webb, grocer, & Hanna Claxton, wife of Robert Claxton, mercer, forty shillings each for rings. These children have already received &c. My house in Paternoster Row, London, called the Three Nuns. Houses &c. at or near Charing Cross in the county of Middlesex. Reference to agreement made with the friends of Margaret my dearly beloved wife. Her lease of messuages or tenements at or near Paul's Chain, lately purchased of Stephen Goodyeare & other estates. To wife Margaret all the firing which shall be remaining in my house at Hackney at my decease. To my daughter in law Rebecca Howard & to Mrs Malpas forty shillings each as a remembrance of my love. To my brother Robert Taylor, at the Summer Islands, forty shillings for a ring and forty shillings yearly during his natural life, and to his son Samuel Taylor, of New England, eight pounds &c. To my sister Elizabeth Owen forty shillings yearly during her natural life and to live without paying rent in the house where she now liveth in the town & county of Bucks: her husband Robert Owen to keep it in good repair. To Robert Owen the apprentice of my cousin Graunt ten pounds at his age of twenty two years. To my sister Martha Vocher, widow, five pounds and sixteen pounds yearly for maintenance of herself & children. To Elizabeth Vocher, the blind daughter of my said sister and to Mary and Martha Vocher two other daughters (certain bequests). Sundry other bequests. Residue of personal estate to youngest son Samuel Taylor and he to be executor. Wife Margaret and sons in law Mr William Burroughes & Mr Samuel Howard to be overseers & to each ten pounds. Shop in Paternoster Row in parish of St Faith's, London, called the Brood Hen, and a parcel of ground behind it whereupon part of the messuage called the Bishop of London's palace was situate. Another tenement in Paternoster Row, in parish of St Gregory's, formerly called the Golden Lyon and since the Three Cocks &c. all to son Samuel and his heirs. Failing heirs then the Brood Hen to son Daniel and the Three Cocks to daughter Rebecca Taylor. To Samuel also, after death of my wife, the Three Nuns, and after decease of Elizabeth Owen the messuage in Buckingham in County Bucks, now in occupation of Robert Owen, &c. House & land in Hackney, bought of Mr Francis Coventry & wife, to son Samuel. Grey, 155.

[William Taylor was the step-father and Daniel Taylor was a step-brother of Edward Rawson, secretary of the Colony of Massachusetts. See REGISTER, vol. XXXVIII. p. 310 (ante, p. 58). The Samuel Taylor of New England, son of Robert Taylor of the Summer Islands, is supposed by Col. Joseph L. Chester to have been the person of that name who resided at Ipswich, Mass., and whose will was proved June 29, 1695, aged 81. See Some Account of the Taylor Family by P. A. Taylor, London, 1875, p. 76.—EDITOR.

William Taylor, the testator, had three wives. His second wife Margaret was sister of Rev. John Wilson, the first minister of Boston, and the mother, by a former husband, of Secretary Rawson.

Her children by this marriage were a son Edmund Taylor, and daughters Margaret Webb and Hanna Claxton mentioned above.

Sister Martha Vocher was the second wife of Rev. Daniel Votier, Rector of St. Peter's Cheap. and was buried in that church, 4th May, 1651.—THOMAS MINNS.]

DANIEL TAYLOR of London, Esq., 22 February 1654, with codicil of 28 March, 1655. Son William (under twenty one) and my three daughters Katherine, Rebecca and Margaret. Brother master William Webb and Master Samuel Howard. Messuage in or near Paternoster Row, London, in occupation of Israel Knowles &c. Brother Howard. Brother Edmond Taylor and his heirs. Brother Samuel Taylor and his heirs.

In codicil he names wife Margaret, mother Taylor, sister Margaret Webb (to be guardian of my children), sister Clarkson, brother Clarkson, sister Juxon and brother Juxon, brother and sister Howard, cousin Sarah Howard, cousin Matthew Howard, brother Burroughs, cousin Votier, cousin Martha Knolls, cousin Mary Singer, cousin William Taylor at Newcastle, Aunt Owen at Buckingham, cousin Timothy Owen, cousin Anne Graunte, cousin Katherine Busby the elder and her daughter Katherine Busby (under twenty one & unmarried). To my brother Edward Rawson in New England ten pounds. To father and mother Locke, cousin Tucker (to buy her a ring). My two partners & brothers Robert Clarkson & Samuel Howard. To cousin Timothy Owen to be laid out for wife & children of his brother Robert Owen. To cousin Temperance Pratt, to aunt Gibbs forty shillings for a ring, to cousin Nicholas Juxon & to others. Mark Hildesley Esq. late alderman of London, sole executor.

The above will was proved 28 April, 1655.   Aylett, 348.

[Daniel Taylor was the son of William Taylor by his first wife.—THOMAS MINNS.]

Sir EDMOND ANDROS, of Guernsey, and now residing in the parish of St Anne, in the Liberty of Westminster, in the County of Middlesex, 19 July 1712, proved 8 March 1713, by John Andros Esq., executor. My body to be decently buried without ostentation. I give one hundred pounds for the placing of ten poor children to be apprentices to some Trader &c., i. e. ten pounds for each child. I am entituled to two several annuities of fifty pounds per annum, payable out of the Exchequer, by virtue of an Act of Parliament; these I leave to Dame Elizabeth my wife, during the term of her natural life; and one hundred pounds to her immediately after my death: these bequests in lieu of a jointure and in full recompence of her dower. After her death these two annuities shall go to my executor. I give the sum of two hundred pounds which is due me by bond from Thomas Cooper, near Maidstone, in Kent, taken in the name of my late sister in law Mrs Hannah Crispe, and all the interest that shall be due thereupon, unto Christopher Clapham Esqr., son of my late dear deceased wife, if I do not, in some other manner, give or secure to the said Christopher Clapham the said debt of two hundred pounds and interest. I give to Edwin Wiat Esqr. Sergeant at Law, if he shall survive me, and, in case of his death before me, to his executors, administrators or assigns, the sum of three hundred pounds which is due and owing to me by mortgage made from Mrs Mary Hurt unto my said late wife, by the name of Elizabeth Clapham, widow, &c., upon condition that the said Serg^t Wiat shall pay

&c. unto the said Christopher Clapham Esq. the sum of two hundred pounds. To my niece Elizabeth, the daughter of my late brother John Andros, deceased, the sum of two hundred pounds, and to Ann, another daughter, one hundred pounds. To my nephew, Cæsar, a son of my said brother John, one hundred pounds; to Edmund, another son, the yearly sum of twenty pounds for his maintenance, and to William, another son, the sum of one hundred pounds. To my nephew George, son of my late brother George, deceased, all my estate and interest in the Island of Alderney, &c., and also five hundred pounds (with other property). To my niece Anne Lemesurier, daughter of my said late brother George Andros, the sum of one hundred pounds. To Cæsar Knapton, gentleman (certain sums due from him). To William Le Merchant, son of my late niece, Elizabeth Le Merchant, deceased, the sum of one hundred pounds, and to his sister Elizabeth, the now wife of Mr Elizea Le Merchant, the like sum of one hundred pounds. I release and discharge my cousin Magdalen Andros, widow, the relict of my cousin Amos Andros, deceased, &c., of and from all sums due from the said Amos Andros, &c. To my cousin Mary Andros, daughter of the said Amos, the sum of one hundred pounds (and other legacies). A legacy to John Andros, eldest son of my brother John Andros, deceased. To Mrs Margaret Baxter, widow, ten pounds per year, out of the interest and profits of a mortgage due from the estate of my late cousin Margaret Lowdon, deceased (her estate in Harrow Alley, without Aldgate, London).

All my other estate in Great Britain, Guernsey, or elsewhere, to my said nephew John Andros, he to build, within two years, a good, suitable house on or at the manor of Sacuares, in Guernsey. E. ANDROS.

Wit: James Spencely, Rob Hodson, Jn° Hodson. Aston, 44.

[One of the Articles on Official Seals, published in the Heraldic Journal, Boston (Vol. I. (1865), pp. 140-2), conveys so much information about the testator of the foregoing will and his family, that no apology seems necessary for inserting the greater portion of it here.

"The seal of Sir Edmond Andros" . . . "is of frequent occurrence, and the following reply to an interrogation made in Notes and Queries last year [1864], gives us some valuable information about a peculiarity in the arms."

" 'Sir Edmund Andros, of Guernsey, bore for arms : Gules, a saltire gold, surmounted of another vert ; on a chief azure, three mullets sable. *Crest,* a blackamoor's head in profile, couped at the shoulders and wreathed about the temples, all proper. *Motto,* ' Crux et præsidium et duces.' "

"In 1686 he made application to the Earl Marshal to have his arms 'registered in the College of Arms in such a manner as he may lawfully have them with respect to his descent from the ancient family of Sausmarez in the said Isle ' (Guernsey). In this petition it is set out that—' His Great Grandfather's Father, John Andros als Andrewes, an English Gentleman, born in Northamptonshire, coming into the Island of Guernsey as Lieutenant to Sir Peter Mewtis, Kⁿᵗ, the Governor, did there marry A° 1543 with Judith de Sausmarez, onely Daughter of Thomas Sausmarez, son and heir of Thomas Sausmarez, Lords of the Seignorie of Sausmarez in the said Isle,' &c."

" ' The warrant, granting the petition, is dated September 23, 1686 ; and from this time Sir Edmund Andros and his descendants "(?) "as Seigneurs de Sausmarez, quartered the arms of De Sausmarez with their own, and used the crest and supporters belonging thereto, as depicted in the margin of the warrant. These arms are thus blazoned :—Argent, on a chevron gules between three leopards' faces sable, as many castles triple-towered, gold. *Crest,* a falcon affrontant, wings expanded, proper, belted, gold. Supporters : Dexter, a unicorn argent, tail cowarded; Sinister, a greyhound argent, collared gules, garnished gold.' This reply, by Edgar MacCulloch, Esq., of Guernsey, is in Notes and Queries, 3d series, v. 425."—H. F. W.

Sir Edmund Andros was born in London, Dec. 6, 1637, where he died Feb. 24, 1713-4, and three days later was buried at St. Anne's, Soho, Westminster. A memoir of him by William H. Whitmore, A.M., with portrait, is prefixed to the first volume of " The Andros Tracts " (Prince Society, 1868). The pedigree placed by Sir Edmund on record at the Herald's College, in September, 1686, and his will, are printed in full in that volume.—EDITOR.

In the Sir Edmund Andros abstract I note the name of his step-son Christopher Clapham. We had one William Clapham, a planter in Warrosquaike County (subsequently Isle of Wight) as early as 1620 ; and I have the additional notes as to grants of land : William Clapham, 1100 acres on the south side of the Rappahannock river, in consideration of the transportation of 22 persons, Aug. 22, 1650, Book No. 2, p. 238, and George Clapham 670 acres on the south side of York river, Dec. 24, 1652, Book No. 3, p. 162, *Virginia Land Registry.*—R. A. BROCK.]

FRANCES LUDLOW.—Sententia pro confirmatione testamenti Franciscæ Ludlowe, ——nuper dum vixit parochiæ Sancti Egidii in Campis in Comitatu Midd. etc. —— in judicio inter Danielem Ketteridge etc. executorem etc., ex una et Henricum Ludlowe, armigerum, Elizabetham Penny *als* Ludlowe, Luciam Ludlowe, Margaretam Vernon *als* Ludlowe necnon Bridgittam Keene *als* Ludlowe, fratrem et sorores naturales et legitimos ex utroque latere dictæ defunctæ, ac Henricum Ludlowe militem, Edmundum Ludlowe, Humfridum Ludlowe, Benjaminum Ludlowe, Ellenoram Ludlowe et Catherinam Hall *als* Ludlowe, fratres et sorores naturales et legitimos ex paterno latere ejusdem defunctæ, necnon Rogerum Ludlowe consanguineum, etc.   Hele, 28 (1626).

[These Sententiæ are often very valuable as evidence, and should be more studied.
                                                                                                             H. F. W.

An abstract of the will of George Ludlow, who came to Massachusetts in its early days, but returned to England, will be found in these Gleanings (*ante*, p. 172), and much information about the Ludlows is printed there and in *ante*, p. 208.

In 1884 a " Pedigree of Ludlow of Hill Deverill, co. Wilts," in tabular form, was printed. The arms of this family are given as—" Argent, a chevron between three martins' heads erased, sable. Crest, a demi martin rampant sable. Motto : *Omne solum forti patria.*" This pedigree was compiled by Henry Hungerford Ludlow-Bruges, Esq., M.A., and G. D. Scull, Esq., the latter a contributor of valuable articles to the REGISTER, and now residing in London, England. A copy of the pedigree printed on vellum, presented by Mr. Scull, is in the library of the New England Historic Genealogical Society. It shows exhaustive research, giving fourteen generations of the family.

I give below the early generations reduced to REGISTER FORM. It will be seen that Frances Ludlow was an aunt of Edmund Ludlow, the English patriot, who was a member of the High Court of Justice which condemned Charles I. to execution, and that Edmund was a cousin-nephew of George Ludlow, whose will may be found in abstract at the above reference, and of his brother Roger Ludlow, deputy governor of Massachusetts.—EDITOR.]

1. WILLIAM[1] LUDLOW, of Hill Deverill, co. Wilts, Butler to Henry IV., V. and VI. M. P. for Ludgershall, Wilts. Buried in St. Thomas' Church, Salisbury. Married Margaret, daughter and heiress of William Rymer. (*Vide* will of John Ludlow, son and heir, proved 26 April, 1488.) Children :

2. i.   JOHN[2] LUDLOW, married Lora Ringwood.
    ii. MARGARET[2] LUDLOW, married William Sandes.
    iii. MARGERY[2] LUDLOW, married William Earle.
    iv. JOAN[2] LUDLOW, married 1st, John Norwood ; m. 2d, Thomas Ringwood of Southampton.
    v.   MARGARET[2] LUDLOW, the Younger. Buried at Corsham Church. Married Thomas Trapnell or Tropenell of Great Chalfield, near Trowbridge, Wilts, Esq. Buried at Corsham Church ; tomb existing.

2. JOHN² LUDLOW. Will proved 26 April, 1488. Married Lora, daughter of Thomas Ringwood of Ringwood, Hants. Child:
   3. i. JOHN² LUDLOW, married Philippa Bulstrode.

3. JOHN³ LUDLOW, buried in chancel of Hill Deverill Church. *Vide* will proved 14 Nov. 1519. Married Philippa, daughter and heiress of William Bulstrode of London. Children:
   4. i. WILLIAM⁴ LUDLOW, married Jane Moore.
     ii. EDWARD⁴ LUDLOW, unmarried.
     iii. DOROTHY⁴ LUDLOW, married William Horsey of Martin, Wilts.

4. WILLIAM⁴ LUDLOW. *Vide* will proved 6 May, 1533. Married Jane, daughter and co-heiress of Nicholas Moore of Withford, co. Southampton. Children:
   5. i. GEORGE⁵ LUDLOW, married Edith, daughter of Lord Windsor.
     ii. MARY⁵ LUDLOW, married Richard Scrope of Castle Combe, Wilts. (*Vide* Pedigree of Lord Scrope.)

5. GEORGE⁵ LUDLOW. High Sheriff of Wilts, 1567. Will proved 4 Feb. 1580. Married Edith, third daughter of Lord Windsor of Stanwell, Middlesex. Children:
   6. i. EDMUND⁶ LUDLOW, married 1st, Bridget Coker; m. 2d, Margaret Manning.
   7. ii. THOMAS⁶ LUDLOW, married Jane Pyle.
     iii. ANNE⁶ LUDLOW, married Thomas Hall of London, gent.
     iv. MARGARET⁶ LUDLOW, married Robert Vaux of Odiham, Hants.
     v. JANE⁶ LUDLOW, married —— Bassett.
     vi. MARY⁶ LUDLOW, married Hugh Ryley of New Sarum, gent.
     vii. URSULA⁶ LUDLOW, married Rev. William Earth, rector of Mildenhall, Wilts.
     viii. PHILIPPA⁶ LUDLOW, married Thomas, son of Sir John Zouch, Knt., Dorset.

6. Sir EDMUND⁶ LUDLOW. M. P. for Hindon 1603. Administration 1621. Married 1st, Bridget, daughter and sole heiress of Henry Coker of Maypowder, co. Dorset. She was buried at Hill Deverill, Sept. 1587. Children:
     i. HENRY⁷ of Hill Deverill and afterwards of Tadley, co. Hants, b. 1577. Matriculated at "Aula Cervina," Oxford, 22 Oct. 1591, aged 14. Graduated B.A. 17 Dec. 1594. Administration 28 Oct. 1639. Married Lettice, daughter of Thomas West, Lord De La Warre. *Vide* Monument in Hill Deverill church. Descendants given in the tabular pedigree.
     ii. GEORGE,⁷ died young.
     iii. JOHN.⁷
     iv. ANNE,⁷ died young.
     v. ELIZABETH.⁷
     vi. LUCY.⁷
     vii. MARGARET.⁷
     viii. BRIDGET.⁷
     ix. JANE.⁷
     x. FRANCES,⁷ bapt. at Hill Deverill, 15 Sept. 1787. Will proved 8 Feb. 1624-5. Describes herself as a daughter of Sir Edmund Ludlow, and twice refers to her cousin Roger Ludlow.

He married 2d, Margaret, daughter of Henry Manning of Down, co. Kent, Marshall of the Household, relict of Thomas Howard, viscount Bindon, third son of Thomas, Duke of Norfolk. She was bapt. at Down, 30 Nov. 1559, and buried at Maiden Bradley, Wilts, 14 Dec. 1643. Children:

8. xi. HENRY,[7] married Elizabeth Phelips.
   xii. EDMUND,[7] of Kingston Deverill, bapt. at Hill Deverill, 25 June, 1595.
     Matriculated at Brasenose College, Oxford, 19 June, 1610, age 14.
     M.P. for Hindon. Will proved 23 Nov. 1666. Married Katherine.
     Died without issue.
   xiii. HUMPHREY,[7] matriculated at B. N. C. Oxon, 1611. Living at Allington,
     1633.
   xiv. BENJAMIN,[7] killed at the siege of Corfe Castle. Administration 1659-60.
     His second son,
        Edmund,[8] of Ealing, co. Middlesex, was executor to the will of his
        uncle, Edmund Ludlow the Elder, of Kingston Deverill. Will
        dated 13 June, 1586, proved in London, 4 Feb. 1689-90. Married
        Douglas, daughter of Sir Francis D'Aungier, Knt. Ch.: 1. Tho-
        mas.[9] 2. Emilia.[9]
  [xv. ELEANOR.   xvi. CATHERINE.]*

7. THOMAS[5] LUDLOW, of Dinton and Baycliffe. Buried at Dinton, 25
Nov. 1607. Will proved June, 1608. Married Jane, daughter of Thomas and sister of Sir Gabriel Pyle, Knt., of Bapton, in the parish of Fisher-
ton de la Mere. Her will proved 6 July, 1650. Children:

   i. GEORGE,[7] born at Dinton, 7 Sept. 1583, died young.
   ii. GABRIEL,[7] bapt. at Dinton, 10 Feb. 1587. Called to the Bar 15 Oct. 1620.
     Elected a Bencher 3 Nov. 1637. Particular Receiver of the Duchy of
     Lancaster possessions in Norfolk, Suffolk and Cambridge. His patent
     dated 5th of Charles 1. Resigned the office 28 June, 1639. Deputy
     Ranger of Sellwood Forest, 1638. Married Phillis, who sold Baycliffe
     to Sir James Thynne, 1653. Children:
       1. Gabriel,[6] bapt. at Warminster, 13 Aug. 1622. Admitted to the
         Inner Temple 13 June, 1638. Killed at the Battle of Newbury,
         1644. Vide Ludlow's Memoirs, in which he describes the death
         of his cousin Gabriel at Newbury.
       2. Thomas,[8] bapt. at Warminster, 1 November, 1624.
       3. Francis,[8] bapt. at Warminster, 10 Sept. 1626. Living at Maiden
         Bradley, 1666. Married. Issue.
       4. Anne,[8] bapt. at Warminster, 4 Dec. 1628.
       5. Elizabeth,[8] bapt. at Maiden Bradley, 18 Oct. 1632.
       6. John.[8] Vide Jane Ludlow's will, proved 6 July, 1650.
       7. Sarah.[8] Vide Jane Ludlow's will, proved 6 July, 1650.
   iii. ROGER,[7] bapt. at Dinton, 7 March, 1590. Matriculated at Balliol Coll.,
     Oxford, 16 June, 1610. Gained distinction in New England. Mar-
     ried; issue. Vide Ludlow's Memoirs; also George Ludlow's will,
     proved 1 Aug. 1656.
   iv. ANNE,[7] bapt. at Dinton, 5 July, 1591. Buried at Dinton, 8 July, 1613.
   v. THOMAS,[7] bapt. at Baverstock, 3 March, 1593. Inventory taken 16 June,
     1646. Married at Warminster, 15 Feb. 1624, Jane Bennett, daugh-
     ter of John Bennett of Steeple Ashton and Smallbrook, who was
     bapt. at Warminster, 15 April, 1604, and died 19 Dec. 1683. Children:
       1. Thomas,[8] bapt. at Warminster, 3 March, 1631. Buried 13 Nov.
         1668. Administration granted to Sarah Ludlow, 18 Aug. 1669.
         He married 18 Aug. 1658, Sarah Sutton, born (according to John
         Ludlow, her son) 1639. She survived her husband, remarried,
         and died as Mrs. Langley, 16 April, 1700, at Warminster. Their
         son Thomas[9] Ludlow was father of Christopher,[10] whose son Ben-
         jamin[11] was father of Benjamin Pennell,[12] whose son William
         Heald[13] Ludlow, Esq., assumed the name and arms of Bruges by
         royal license in 1835, on succeeding to the landed estates of Tho-
         mas Bruges of Seend, Esq. Mr. W. H. Ludlow-Bruges was
         father of Henry Hungerford[14] Ludlow-Bruges (one of the compil-
         ers of the tabular pedigree from which this is extracted), born at
         Seend, 10 June, 1847; graduated at St. John's College, Oxford,
         M.A. 1872.

  * These two names in brackets are entered by Mr. Waters on the authority of the preceding Sententia.—EDITOR.

2. *Gabriel*,[8] of Frome, bapt. at Warminster, 27 Aug. 1634.*
3. *William*,[8] of Sarum, bapt. at Warminster, 11 April, 1637.
4. *John*,[8] bapt. at Warminster, 9 Jan. 1640.
vi. GEORGE,[7] bapt. at Dinton, 15 Sept. 1596. Will proved 1 Aug. 1656. Member of the Virginian Council. *Vide* Ludlow's Memoirs.

8. Sir HENRY[7] LUDLOW, Knt., born at Maiden Bradley, 1592. Matriculated at Brasenose College, Oxford, 16 Oct. 1607, aged 15. Graduated as B.A. 6 Feb. 1609. High Sheriff for Wilts 1633. M. P. 1640. Died intestate; buried at St. Andrews, Holborn, 1 Nov. 1643. Administration of effects granted to his eldest son, General Edmund Ludlow, 20 March, 1646–7, which grant being subsequently revoked, a new grant was made to Nathaniel Ludlow, 8 Feb. 1660–1. He married Elizabeth, daughter of Richard Phelips of Montacute, Somerset. Her will, dated 18 May, 1660, was proved at London, 19 Jan. 1660–1. She was buried at St. Andrews, Holburn, 6 Nov. 1660. Children:

i. EDMUND[8] LUDLOW, the celebrated Republican, born at Maiden Bradley, 1616–17. Matriculated at Trinity College, Oxford, 10 Sept. 1634, aged 17. Graduated as B.A. 14 Nov. 1636. Admitted to the Inner Temple 13 June, 1638. M. P. for Wilts. High Sheriff 1645. Was one of the King's Judges. Commander of the forces in Ireland. Died an exile at Vevay, 1693. Married Elizabeth Thomas of Wenvoe Castle, co. Monmouth. Left no issue. *Vide* monument at Vevay.
ii. ROBERT,[8] second son, born 1621. Matriculated at Magdalen College, Oxford, 12 July, 1636, aged 15. Died a prisoner of war 1643. *Vide* Ludlow's Memoirs.
iii. THOMAS.[8] *Vide* Ludlow's Memoirs.
iv. NATHANIEL,[8] bapt. at Maiden Bradley, 13 April, 1624. Administrator of his father Sir Henry Ludlow's effects. Executor to his mother, his uncle Edmund, and his brother Philip. Will proved 12 May, 1701.
v. FRANCES,[8] bapt. at Maiden Bradley, 0 Oct. 1626. Buried at Maiden Bradley, April, 1632.
vi. PHILIP,[8] bapt. at Maiden Bradley, 15 April, 1628. Died at sea, 13 Aug. 1650. Administration 1 Oct. 1650.
vii. HENRY,[8] bapt. at Maiden Bradley, 19 Feb. 1629–30. Ancestor of Earls Ludlow. The peerage became extinct in 1042.
viii. ELIZABETH,[8] married Col. Kempstone. *Vide* Ludlow's Memoirs.
ix. MARGARET.[8] married Giles Strangeways, Esq., of East Charlton, Somerset. *Vide* Ludlow's Memoirs.

STEPHEN SEDGWICK (*ante*, pages 259 and 261).

[I think the EDITOR is wrong, on page 261, in supposing that this Stephen Sedgwick, brewer, was a nephew of William[2] Sedgwick, of London, and a cousin of Major General Robert Sedgwick, of New England. I had looked on this Stephen as a brother of the first William and an uncle of Robert. Stephen Sedgwick calls Robert Houghton cousin. I almost always understand, by this word what we now express by the words nephew or niece, and not a cousin german. He is referred to by John Sedgwick (*ante*, page 47) as my uncle "Stephen Sedgwick, brewer." Why suppose another Stephen Sedgwick, brewer?—H. F. WATERS.

With regard to the references to the Sedgwick family in the Gleanings in the January REGISTER, the Major Robert Sedgwick mentioned was *Major General* Robert Sedgwick, the first of the name to emigrate to this country. He was the son of William Sedgwick and Elizabeth Howe, who were married, according to the registers of St. Mary's Church at Woburn, Bedfordshire, England, on April 10th, 1604. His father, William, was a warden of that church, and was buried there on July 25th, 1632. General Sedgwick was baptized May 6th, 1613. The earliest date on the St. Mary's registers is 1558, and the earliest Sedgwick record there is of the baptism of Richard, son of James Sedgwickes, Sept. 18th, 1580. With the General's

* He is said to have been the ancestor of the New York Ludlows.—G. D. SCULL.

father, born about 1585, the record is lost, and researches at Woburn, York, London and elsewhere, have so far failed to reveal any *authentic* trace of his grandfather, though the numerous appearances of the name in Yorkshire, Lancashire and Bedfordshire, and in the lists of members of the great guilds in London and elsewhere, prove that the family was one of distinction, and that further search will discover the missing link in the chain.

General Robert Sedgwick married in England, Johanna ———. After his death she married the Rev. Thomas Allen, pastor of the Congregational Church in Norwich, England, formerly teacher of the church in Charlestown, Mass., from about 1639 to 1651, when he returned to England, by whom she had no children. General Robert Sedgwick emigrated to this country in 1635, and was one of the most distinguished men of his time. He was one of the earliest settlers of Charlestown, Mass. In 1641, 1645 and 1648 he commanded the Ancient and Honorable Artillery Company, of which he was a founder, and in 1641, the Castle. He was an officer under, and friend of, Cromwell, with whom he corresponded, and by whom he was sent in July, 1654, from Boston to Jamaica, after the capture of that Island by the British, with a fleet under his orders with reinforcements for the army under Gen. Venables. He was one of the Commissioners for the Government of Jamaica, and died there on May 24th, 1656, leaving several children. Professor Adam Sedgwick, of Trinity College, Cambridge, England, in a letter written some years before his death, in 1873, says that the clan was settled from very early times among the mountains which form the borders of Lancashire, Yorkshire and Westmoreland; and he believed that every family of the name could trace its descent from ancestors who were settled among these mountains. The name among the country people in the north of England is sometimes pronounced Sigswick, and the oldest spelling of it is Siggeswick,—at least so it is written in many of the parish records going back to the reign of Henry VIII. It is good German, and means the *Village of Victory*, probably designating some place of successful broil where our rude Saxon or Danish ancestors first settled in the country, and drove the old Celtic tribes out of it, or into the remote recesses of the Cambrian Mountains, where many Celtic names are met with to this day. But in the valley where the Sedgwicks are chiefly found, the names are almost exclusively Saxon or Danish. Ours, therefore, was a true Border Clan.

The name Sedgwick was probably a correction given, like many others, through a wish to explain the meaning of a name (Siggeswick), the real import of which was quite forgotten. The word *Sedge* is not known in the northern dialects of England, and the plant itself does not exist among the Yorkshire valleys. But a branch of the clan settled in the low regions of Lincolnshire, and seem to have first adopted the more modern spelling, and at the same time began to use a bundle of sedge as the family crest. This branch was never numerous, and is now believed to be entirely extinct. Indeed, the Sedgwicks never seem, at least in England, to flourish away from their native mountains. If removed to the low country, they droop and die away in a few generations. A still older crest, and one suited to the history of the race, is an eagle with out-spread wings. Within a comparatively few years, eagles existed among the higher mountains on the border. The arms most commonly borne by the Sedgwicks, and accorded to them by Burke in his Encyclopædia of Armorial Bearings, are composed of a field or, a cross gules, with five bells of the field, and a lion passant through sedge on a cap of maintenance.—ROBERT SEDGWICK, *of New York City.*]

WILLIAM AMES of Wrentham, in the County of Suffolk, Preacher of the Gospel, 27 September 1683, proved 8 August 1689. To Robert Smith, my son-in-law, my houses and lands in Needham, in the County of Norfolk, for life; then to my grandchild Ames Smith: for want of lawful issue to the said Ames Smith, then to my cousin Samuel Angier, pastor of the Church of Christ at Rehoboth in New England, and to his heirs. To Mary Rix, my niece, twenty pounds. To my sister, the wife of Mʳ Thomas Wales the elder, my brother in law, of Needham aforesaid; he to be my executor. The rest of my goods to said grandchild, Ames Smith, when twenty one years of age. If he die without issue, then fifty pounds to my cousin Mʳ Thomas Wales the younger, fifty pounds to my cousin Mʳ John

Wales, (money) to my brother in law Mr Symon Rix and to the children of my late brother John Rix. Remainder then to my cousin Samuel Angier, pastor of the church of Rehoboth in New England, and to Ruth the wife of Mr Samuell Cheevers of Marblehead in New England.

Consistory Court, Norwich, 1689–90.

[For the above abstract we are indebted to the kind thoughtfulness of our corresponding member, Joseph J. Muskett, Esq., now of Knysna, Cape of Good Hope.

The following pedigree of this Ames family has been compiled chiefly from the History of Congregationalism in Norfolk and Suffolk, by John Browne, B.A., London, 1877, pp. 66–71 and 422–9.

William Ames = Joan, dau. of . . . . Snelling.
merchant adventurer. | Died during minority of son William.
Died during minority of son William.

Elizabeth, wife of John Phillip, Rector of Wrentham, m. there 6 Jan. 1611-12. He d. 2 Sept. 1660, aged about 78 yrs.

Joan Fletcher = Wm. Ames, b. at Norwich, 1576. = First w. a dau.
Second wife, embarked for America 1637, then aged 50. Buried at Cam. Ms. Dec. 1644.
Fellow of Christ Coll. Camb. minist. of Engl. Ch. at the Hague. Prof. of Divinity at Franeker 1622. Attended Synod of Dort. Minister of Engl. Cong. Ch. at Rotterdam. Died there 14 Nov. 1633, aged 57 years, and there buried.
of his predecessor at the Hague.

Ruth Ames, a. 18 in 1637, m. to Edm. Angier of Cambridge.

Susan or Susanna, first wife. Bur. at Wrentham 6 Jan. 1651-2.

=William Ames, A.M. H. C. 1645, ret. to England 1646, d. 21 July, 1689, a. 65 yrs. Bur. at Wrentham.

=Elizabeth Wales, m. 26 Jan. 1652 -3, d. 19 Feb. 1682-3. Bur. at Wrentham

John Ames, bur. at Wrentham.

Elizabeth, = Robert Smith, m. 6 Nov. 1672. Buried at Wrentham 2? July, 1679.
ejected from Blithborough. Bur. at Wrentham 24 August, 1705.

Ruth and Philip. Died young.

Mr. John Phillip, who married the sister of Dr. Ames, obtained the living of Wrentham in 1609, was of Dedham, New England, in 1638, and went home in the autumn of 1641, and was one of the Assembly of Divines at Westminster. He received his degree of A.B. at Catharine Hall, Cambridge, 1596, of A.M. in 1600, and of B.D. at Clare Hall, 1608. His wife Elizabeth was buried 22 January, 1659.

The widow Joane Ames came to New England, bringing her three children, Ruth, William and John, from Great Yarmouth, in the ship Mary Ann, William Goose, master, in company with a great many, chiefly from Norfolk and the borders of Suffolk, many of whom, including the master of the vessel, took up their abode in Salem and its neighborhood, or at least applied for admission as dwellers in that town. Mrs. Ames evidently first intended to make Salem her home in the New World, but finally took up her abode in Cambridge, where she was buried 23 December, 1644. The General Court granted her forty pounds, 15 November, 1637, referring to her as "the widow of Dr. Ames of famous memory." Her son William was a graduate of Harvard College in the class of 1645, and for an account of his life and works the reader is referred to the first volume of Sibley's Harvard Graduates, Savage's Gen. Dict. and the History of Congregationalism in Norfolk and Suffolk, above referred to. The following inscription from his gravestone in Wrentham churchyard, is copied from the last named book :

HERE . LYETH . INTERRED . THE . BODY . OF . WILLIAM . AMES . (ELDEST . SON . TO . THE . LEARNED . DOCTOR . AMES .) . TEACHER . OF . A . CONGREGATIONAL . CHURCH . IN . WRENTHAM . WHO . DEPARTED . THIS . LIFE . ON . JULY . 21, . 89, . AND . IN . THE . 66 . YEARE . OF . HIS . AGE.

The following entries from the Town Records of Salem seem to refer to this family :

"The xxxith day of the 10th moneth 1638. —— At a generall towne meetinge. —— Agreed and voted that there should be a Village graunted to Mr Phillips & his company uppon such conditions as the 7 men appointed for the towne affaires should agree on."

"At a meeting the 21th of the 11th moneth (1639) —— *Granted to Hugh Stacy, John Thurston, Tho. West & w[idow] Payne 20 acres of land apeece. Granted to Austen Kilham, Nicholas Pacy, Philemon D[ickerson], and Joseph Yongs 30 Acres of land apeece. Granted to Henry Chickering & John Yongs 50 acres of [land] apeece. Granted to M^{ris} Ames 40 acres of land. Granted to William Browne, Shopkeeper, 80 acres of l[and]. Granted to Mr Phillips to be an Inhabitant & to have 80 acres of land. Provided y^t these 6 last grants from this m^rke * is wth the condicion that they continew in the Plantation to use the same."

In that most valuable List (in the handwriting of Roger Conant) showing the allotment of marsh and meadow land, made in accordance with a vote passed at town meeting 25th of the 10th month, 1637, which gives us the number of persons in each family, M^{ris} Amies is credited with 6 persons.—H. F. WATERS.

The Rev. Samuel Cheever, the first settled minister of Marblehead, Mass., and eldest son of Ezekiel Cheever, the master of the Boston Latin School, was graduated at Harvard College in 1659. He m. June 28, 1671, Ruth Angier, daughter of Edmund and Ruth (Ames) Angier, of Cambridge, Mass. His son, the Rev. Ames Cheever (Harv. Coll. 1707), was the first settled minister of Manchester, Mass.

For a further account of the Rev. Samuel Cheever, the Rev. Ames Cheever, and the Rev. William Ames, D.D., see the REGISTER for April, 1879 (xxxiii. pp. 193–198.—JOHN T. HASSAM.]

ROBERT SMITH of Wrentham in the county of Suff: gent: 27 December, 2d Anne, 1703, proved at Beccles 15 September 1705. To wife Sarah the sum of fifteen pounds of lawful English money to buy her a piece of plate. To John Lincolne and Sarah Badeley my son and daughter in law twenty shillings apiece, to buy each of them a ring. To my sister Smith now or late of Yoxford & to Margaret Fynn my niece, her daughter, twenty shillings apiece to buy each of them a ring. To Tabitha Aldred, my late servant, forty shillings. To Margaret Dennington, the wife of Edmund Dennington, three pounds.

Item I give and bequeath unto Ames Smith my son and his heirs all my messuages, lands, tenements and hereditaments whatsoever, both freehold and copyhold, situate, lying and being in Yoxford &c., and all that my messuage or tenement &c. in Beccles which I late had and purchased of Mary Blomfield, widow, and Augustine Blomfield; also all my copyhold messauge or tenement, shop, stalls &c. in the new Market Place in Beccles. All the residue &c. to the said Ames Smith, whom I constitute executor.

Ipswich Wills, Archd. of Suff. B. Yallop (1705–9) L. 41.

SARAH SMITH of Wrentham, widow, 30 October 1705, proved 1 November 1706. To John Lincolne, my son, and his heirs all my lands lying in Walingham, he to pay unto Sarah Badeley my daughter, within one year after my decease, the full and entire sum of one hundred pounds at the south porch of the parish church of Wrentham. If she depart this life before the said sum shall become due and payable I give and bequeath it unto my grandchildren John Badeley, Sarah Badeley and Lydia Badeley &c. Son John Lincolne to be executor.

Ipswich Wills, Archd. of Suff. B. Yallop (1705–9) L. 82.

[Robert Smith, the testator, was the incumbent of the living of Blithborough in Suffolk, from which he was ejected under the Act of Uniformity. Blithborough is about six miles distant from Wrentham. Mr. Smith, as will be seen in the preceding pedigree of Ames, married in 1672, Elizabeth, daug r of William Ames,

H. C. 1645. She died in July, 1679. His last wife Sarah seems to have been a widow Lincoln. An abstract of her will is found above. In 1672 Mr. Smith was a " minister of the gospel in Wrentham." Rev. Mr. Browne says : " His ministrations were not confined to Wrentham, for in the License Book 1672, we find that Robert Smith, M.A., was a ' Congregational Teacher at the house of Joseph Gilder, yeoman, of Westleton.' "—*Congregationalism in Norfolk and Suffolk*, p. 428.

Mr. Smith had by his first wife two children who survived her, Elizabeth and Ames. Elizabeth seems to have been dead when her father made his will. Ames Smith resided at Denton. He had a son Ames whose daughter Sarah (the sixth in descent from Dr. William Ames) married Rev. Thomas Bocking, who was minister at Denton from July 27, 1757, till his death, April 21, 1805, in his 73d year.—*Ibid.* pp. 340 and 428.—EDITOR]

EVERARD FAUKNER citizen and grocer of London 10 December 1705. To my dear and loving wife Elizabeth Faukener all my goods, household stuff, debts due to me, moneys, plate, jewells, chattells and personal estate whatsoever to her own sole use and disposing. Also all my real estate, free and copy hold, messuages, lands, tenements and hereditaments whatsoever and wheresoever the same are or is or shall hereafter be, to have and to hold the same and every part thereof to her the said Elizabeth Faukner her heirs and assigns forever to her and their own use.

All the rest, residue and remainder of my estate &c. I give, devise and bequeath the same to my said dear wife Elizabeth Fawkner and to her heirs, executors and assigns forever. And I do hereby declare, constitute nominate and appoint my said dear and loving wife Elizabeth Faukner sole Executrix &c.

Then follow instructions for the widow, at her death to give certain sums to Everard Faukner, the son of " my brother " John Faukner and to all the other children of the said John, born or to be born, and provisions against any suit that may be brought against the widow in relation to the will.

Proved in the P. C. C. 30 July, 1707, by the widow.

Poley, 164.

ELIZABETH FAWKNER of Epsom als Ebisham in the County of Surry Widow, 4 June, 6th George, 1720. My body to be decently interred, at the discretion of my executors herein after named, with and by my late indeared husband Mr Everard ffawkner deceased. And inasmuch as he now lies crowded or liable so to be in the church of Epsom aforesaid my Will and mind is and I so hereby direct my executors to prepare and provide with all convenient expedition after my decease a fit and proper vault in the church yard of Epsom aforesaid or some other fitting and convenient place and thereunto to remove and lodge the "corps" of my said Husband together with my own. The management of which (together with my funeral) I leave unto my executors so as they lay out therein a sum not exceeding six hundred pounds &c. &c.

I give, devise and bequeath all those my lands, tenements and hereditaments, situate and lying in the town & parish of Epsom aforesaid, held by copy of Court Roll of the Manor of Epsom aforesaid and which I have surrendered to the use of my Will (except a small piece of Land or ground-parcel of the premises) by me allotted and set out or agreed or intended to be allotted and appropriated for the erecting thereon a Meeting Place for Religious Worship) and also all other my Copyhold and Customary Estate in England unto my nephew Thomas Bulkley now or late Factor at Fort St George in the East Indies and the heirs of his body lawfully begotten or to be begotten, and for want of such issue I give and devise the same premises (except before excepted) unto Stanley West of London Gent. and the Reverend William Harris of London aforesaid Minister of the Gospel (my executors &c.) and their heirs upon Trust to make absolute sale thereof for such price as can be reasonably obtained for the same and to bring in and add all such money as shall arise thereby unto my personal estate to the end and intent the same may go with and be applied in like manner as the Surplus and Residuum of my Personal Estate is herein by me willed and appointed.

Then follows a clause bequeathing the parcel of land before excepted for building a house for religious worship, &c.

I give and bequeath all my share and interest (being One thousand pounds nominal stock) in the Capital Stock or Fund of the Bank of England and the growing dividends and profits thereof &c. unto my Executors &c. in trust to permit & suffer my cousin Edward Bulkley & his assigns to take and receive to his and their own use the Interest &c. of my said Stock for & during the term of his natural life, and from & after his decease to permit and suffer my cousin Sarah Bulkley, now wife of the said Edward Bulkley, & assigns, to take & receive to her & their use one moiety or equal half part of the Dividends &c. for & during the term of her natural life.   And as to the same moiety from & after the decease of the said Sarah Bulkley, & the other moiety of my said Stock from & immediately after the decease of the said Edward Bulkley &c. &c. in trust for Elizabeth Bulkley daughter of the said Edward & Sarah Bulkley; but if she happen to die &c. before she shall attain her age of one & twenty years or day of marriage &c. then in trust &c. &c. for such person or persons who at the time of the decease of the said Elizabeth Bulkley shall be the heir at law of me the said Elizabeth Fawkner &c. &c.   Provision made for allowing the said stock to be sold and the proceeds invested otherwise.

I give unto the said Elizabeth Bulkley if and when she shall attain her age of one and twenty years or day of marriage the sum of five hundred pounds &c. &c.   To my nephew Everard Fawkner four hundred pounds & to my three neices, his sisters, Sarah, Jane & Susanna three hundred pounds apiece, which said last mentioned sums make together the sum of one thousand & three hundred pounds and is the sum directed, intended or appointed them in and by the last will and testament of my said late husband &c. (with deductions for advances made in my life time).   To each of them my said nephew & neices the Fawkners the further sum of three hundred pounds.   To my cousin Mary Rotheram one hundred pounds.   To my brother in law William Brudenall fifty pounds and to him and his wife forty pounds more for mourning.   To the Lady Catherine Taylor one hundred pounds.   To the Reverend Mr Thomas Valentine of Epsom one hundred pounds and ten pounds more for mourning.   To Mrs Reddall of Northtonshire twenty pounds.   To Mrs Martha Barrow one hundred pounds.   To my cousin Ann Barrow daughter of my cousin Thomas Barrow fifty pounds.   To my said cousin Edward Bulkley and his wife and daughter and my said nephew & neices the Fawkners ten pounds apiece for mourning.   To M^r —— Barrow & Mrs Elizabeth Barrow ten pounds apiece for mourning and to the Bishop of Peterborough and his Lady ten pounds apiece for mourning.   To the Reverend Mr Woodford minister of Epsom ten pounds.   To Mr Anderson of the same place twenty pounds.   To Mrs Drury five pounds, to whom I also remit four pounds of the debt she oweth me.   To Jane Furness ten pounds.   To my god daughter Eliz-

abeth Heskins twenty pounds and so will & appoint my Executors to pay
unto or for the benefit of Mrs Elizabeth Heskins (wife of John Heskins)
the sum of ten pounds for her separate & peculiar use &c. To Izan Patrick ten pounds. To my maid Susanna Fletcher twenty pounds &c. &c.
To John Stonestreet five pounds. For the Dissenting Congregation at
Epsom one hundred pounds. One hundred pounds sterling to be distributed among twenty dissenting preachers or teachers in the Country.

Item I give and bequeath unto such the children or grandchildren of my
uncles Edward Bulkley, Peter Bulkley and Gersham Bulkley late of New
England as shall be living at the time of my decease the sum of five hundred pounds sterling &c. To his grace the Arch Bishop of Canterbury &
his Lady twenty shillings apiece for rings. To Mrs Hester Vicaridge fifty
pounds. To Rachel Dent of Coleman Street ten pounds. To the Reverend Mr Joshua Bayes five pounds. To the Lady Ward & her four daughters each a ring of twenty shillings value. To Mrs Royston & her two
eldest daughters & Mr Thomas Wooley & his wife & their two daughters
each a ring of twenty shillings value and to Mrs Elizabeth Diston M^{rs} Ce-
ney Mrs Bridges and her nephew John Bridges & his sister twenty shillings
apiece for rings. To my coachman George (certain bequests). My will
is that my cousin Edward Bulkley & his said wife & daughter &c. do inhabit in my present dwelling house in Epsom until my said nephew Thomas
Bulkley shall arrive in England or my executors have certain advices of
his death.

The rest and residue of goods, chattels & personal estate to my executors in trust for my said nephew, if living at the time of my decease; if he
be then dead then in trust for his child or children lawfully begotten &c.;
failing such, then in trust to pay to my said nephew and neices the Fawkners
(then living) the sum of sixteen hundred pounds sterling in equal parts and
shares; and upon further trust to pay unto such of the children of the said
Hester Vicaridge (except that he is the chyrurgeon) as shall be then living
the sum of fifty pounds apiece; and upon further trust to pay unto such
the child or children, grandchild or grandchildren of my said late uncles
Edward, Peter and Gersham Bulkley as shall be then living one half part of
the then remaining surplus of my said personal estate in such parts and proportions at such times and in such manner as my executors or the survivor
of them or the executors or administrators of such survivor shall think fit.
Other provisions for the rest of the legatees. Mr Stanley West and M^{r}
William Harris to be the executors, and to each of them two hundred
pounds sterling.

A codicil, of 4 June, 1720, provides for giving to Philip Papillon Esq.
a ring of twenty shillings value, to Mrs Elizabeth Papillon a five pounds
broad piece of gold and to Mrs Susanna Papillon my broad piece of gold in
nature of a medal, to the Lady Wostenholme and her two daughters Elizabeth and Ann Allstone each a ring of twenty shillings value, to Mrs Stephens, Mrs Catherine Devinck, Mr Christopher Todd and Mrs Cole and her
daughter Hiller each a ring of twenty shillings value.

Mrs Elizabeth Fawkner's Directions and Orders to Mr Stanley West
June 21th 1720. Imprimis I order my household goods to remain unsold until my Nephew
Bulkley comes home from India, or until my executors have News of his
death. Item I appoint Mr Page and Mr Reynolds to be the undertakers of
my funeral which I would have performed in a solemn and decent manner.
I doubt not but my executors will wisely and carefully discharge that affair

which I leave to their prudence and conduct. I appoint and desire Sr Wm Stewart, Mr Ruth, Mr Diston, Mr Betts, Mr Cresnor and Mr Devinck to hold up my Pall. —— I give one hundred pounds to my cousin Edward Bulkley. I give ten pounds to poor families in Epsom in such proportions as my executors shall think fit to each family. I give to Mr Sheldon Vicaridge twenty pounds. I give to the Lady Ward, Mrs Bridges and to Mrs Stephens a mourning ring to each of them set in " christall " and diamonds of each side of it about five or six pounds value. I give all the daughters of the Lady Ward, Lady Napper, Lady Harrison, Mrs Sabet Bridges, Mrs Anne Rotheram, Mrs Curgaven, Mrs Cresnor, Mr Churchill, Mr Loeffs, Dr Criston and his Lady, Mrs Crittenden rings of twenty shillings value each.

I order that all the rings I have given away both in my will and in this paper to the ladies and gentlewomen shall be with a " christall " glass, although the charges should exceed twenty shillings a ring. I give five pounds to Mr Tongue the minister. I order that the six gentlemen who shall hold up my Pall may have rings of twenty shillings each, and also Belts, Hatbands and gloves of the best sort. I give the daughter of my cousin Edward Bulkley my pearl necklace my diamond ring, my set of lockets my chintz gown and petticoat with small flowers, my laced headcloaths, six my new Holland shifts and also my Holland and Dimity which lies in Boxes unmade up and my " Marselles " and white damask petticoats. I give to my cousin Edward Bulkleys wife my imbroidered gown and petticoat my new silk wrapping gown, my ten new callico shifts, my purple chintz, my dark coloured Norwich crape gown with a luitstring lineing, my best alamode hood and laced net. I give to my cousin Martha Barrow my best chints gown and petticoat lined with green. I give to my servant Susan my white Dimity gown and petticoat, my callico gown, my black silk gown and petticoat my six new callico shifts my under petticoats and all my headclothes except my best edgings and broad laced ones. I give my niece Sarah Fawkner my gold watch. I give my niece Jenny Fawkner one of my large silver salvers. I give my nephew Everard Fawkner one of my large silver salvers. I give my niece Susan Fawkner my middle size silver tankard. I give my two nieces Sarah and Jenny Fawkner my three pieces of chintz. I order that my blue satin petticoat with gold and silver flowers and my buff coloured petticoat shall be kept and not disposed of. I order that the rest of my wearing apparel shall be distributed according to the will of my executors. I give to the Lady Ward my fine chintz counterpane unlined and not made up. I give to Mr Stanley West my large china Punch bowl with a cover, my china sallet dish, my china mug and my fork and spoon with coral handles. I give to Mr Valentine my silver Presenter and my great Bible and my silver mug. I order that my nephew Bulkley shall have what books he pleases for his own use out of my study and the remainder to be disposed of by my executors for some public place or library either in New England or where else they shall think most proper. But I give liberty to my executors and Mr Valentine to choose out any particular books for their own use. I give my said cousin Edward Bulkley my set of castors my pair of salvers and my silver cup with a cover and six silver spoons. June the 21st these are my dircctions to Executors.   ELIZ: FAWKNER.

Then follow depositions made 2 July, 1720, by Sarah Fawkner and Jane Fawkner, spinsters, of the parish of St Magnus the Martyr, London, concerning the foregoing Directions and Orders. The will and these two codicils were proved at London, 1 July, 1720.   Shaller, 153.

[In the will of John Bulkeley (Bulkeley Family, p. 64) he mentions wife Avis ; daughter Elizabeth, wife of Everard Fawkner ; sons Thomas and Edward ; sister Mrs. Eleanor Frye [Trye ?] ; brother and sister Vicaridge and their children ; late nephew Trye Vicaridge, his eldest son ; three brothers in New England, Edward, Gershom and Peter, if then living; sons of deceased brother Thomas if to be heard of and living; nephew Edward Bulkeley* here in England; nephew Thomas Trye, son of brother-in-law William Trye. Dated 1689. Executors, son Edward, wife Avis, daughter Elizabeth Fawkner.

This will of Elizabeth Fawkner throws some light upon a document which has been hitherto unexplained (REG. xxv. 89), and of which the following is an abstract : " Whereas Mrs Elizabeth Fawkner of Epsom Surry did by her Last Will bequeath the sum of five hundred pounds Sterling to her Relations the familyes of the Buckleys in New England know ye that I John Hancock of Lexington in yᵉ county of Middlesex Clerk one of yᵉ persons Interested in yᵉ sᵈ Legacy having received my proportion of yᵉ aforesᵈ Legacy Do fully discharge," &c. &c. Dated 1723.

The following is of course the clause referred to : " Item I give and bequeath unto such the children or grandchildren of my uncles Edward Bulkley Peter Bulkley and Gershom Bulkley late of New England as shall be living at the time of my decease the sum of five hundred pounds sterling."

Now Rev. John Hancock of Lexington, born 1671, died 1752, was the son of Nathaniel (Nathaniel and Joan) Hancock, and Mary (Henry and Joan) Prentice. As he was therefore neither the child nor the grandchild of a Bulkley, he must have received the legacy in right of his wife. He married about 1700 (eldest son John born June 1, 1702) Elizabeth Clarke (died 1760), daughter of Rev. Thomas (Jonas and Elizabeth) Clarke of Chelmsford ; and his wife Mary —— (died Dec. 2, 1700). As Elizabeth (Clarke) Hancock was not the daughter, she must have been the granddaughter and her mother the daughter of one of " my uncles " Edward, Peter or Gershom Bulkley. Before inquiring which of these could have been the father of Mary (——) Clarke, it is necessary to fix approximately the date of her birth. She had several children, but the only dates of birth known are those of her sons in 1684 and 1694. As her daughter Lucy was married in 1700 and Elizabeth probably the same year, their mother could scarcely have been born later than 1660, and the probability is that the date was earlier ; perhaps not far from 1655. Her husband, Rev. Thomas Clarke, born March 2, 1652-3, H. C. 1670, served with the Narraganset army seven weeks before Oct. 17, 1676 (Sibley, II. 330) : and made a return voyage from England in the summer of 1677.† Articles of Agreement with the church at Chelmsford were signed by " Thomas Clarke " on the " 5th of the 12 month, i. e. Feb. 5, 1677 " (1677-8). He was ordained and probably married soon after, which again would give 1655 as a probable approximate date for the birth of his wife Mary. We have now to consider whose daughter she could have

---

* Mentioned also in Elizabeth Fawkner's will as being in England in 1720 with wife Sarah and daughter Elizabeth. John Bulkley's nephew Edward, son of Gershom Bulkley (born 1672, died 1748 in Weathersfield, Conn.), married in 1702 Dorothy Prescott, and had eleven children from 1703 to 1713; an Elizabeth in 1705. In Gershom's will, 1712, he mentions son Edward's " present wife Dorothee " and a clock " standing in his house." The only other " nephew Edward " that John Bulkley seems to have had, was his great-nephew Edward,⁴ eldest son of Hon. Peter³ (Rev. Edward,² Rev. Peter¹), who was born March 18, 1668-9, and of whom nothing further is recorded. His father, Hon. Peter Bulkley (Bulkeley Family, p. 40 ; Savage, I. 291-2; Sibley's Harv. Graduates, II. 68), was born in Concord, Jan. 3, 1640-1; H. C. 1660 ; was Assistant, Major, etc. ; and Oct. 30, 1676, sailed on a special mission to England, from which he returned Dec. 23, 1679. It is not impossible that he may have taken his son Edward to England with him and left him there. Hon. Peter Bulkley died March 25, 1688. Mr. Sibley made one of his rare mistakes in crediting his history to Peter,² the youngest son of Rev. Peter of Concord.—E. F. WARE. [A portrait of Hon. Peter Bulkeley, said to have been painted by Sir Godfrey Kneller, and another painting, the Bulkeley arms, were deposited with the New England Historic Genealogical Society in its early days, by its president Mr. Charles Ewer, in behalf of the owner of the paintings, Mr. Richard B. Hewes of Boston. In 1877 they were returned to the owner's widow, Mrs. Mary Hewes. Subsequently they were, for a year or two, deposited again with the society by Mrs. George D. Sargent of Boston, a granddaughter of Mrs. Hewes, who probably has them now.—EDITOR.]

† Savage (IV. 578) gives for the death of Francis Willoughby, Jr., which took place on this voyage, the date June 15, 1678 ; but this must be a mistake, since Mr. Clarke was in Chelmsford in February, 1677-8. In March, 1694-5, he says the voyage was " about seventeen years ago." May he not have gone to England with Hon. Peter Bulkley, Oct. 30, 1676 ? (REG. XXXI. 309.)—E. F. W.

been ; and a process of elimination will bring us as nearly to a certain conclusion as we can come in the absence of actual records.

Peter, the youngest son of Rev. Peter Bulkley of Concord (born in Concord 1643, died 1691, removed to Fairfield, Conn., with his mother about 1663), married and had children Gershom, Peter, Grace, Margaret and Dorothy. (Bulkeley Family, pp. 40, 83, 190. Mr. Sibley credits to this Peter[2] the history that undoubtedly belongs to Hon. Peter,[3] son of Rev. Edward.) He could scarcely have been the father of Mary Clarke. *Gershom*, the next older son of Rev. Peter (born in Concord 1636, H. C. 1655, removed to Connecticut about 1661, died 1713), married October, 1659, Sarah Chauncey (born in Ware, England, 1631, died 1669), and had a son Peter, born in Concord 1660, Dorothy 1662 or 3, Charles 1663 or 4, etc. ; and Edward. Neither could he have been the father of Mary Clarke. There remains then only the eldest son, Rev. *Edward* Bulkley, who was born in England 1614, was in Concord until 1642 or 1643, and in Marshfield from that date to 1657,* when he returned to Concord, succeeded his father and finally died in Chelmsford, Jan. 2, 1695-6, but was buried in Concord.† The only children whose names have been given hitherto are *Peter*, born in Concord Jan. 3, 1640-1 ; *John*, buried in Marshfield Feb. 26, 1655 (1655-6) ; *Elizabeth*, who married 1665 Rev. Joseph Emerson, and after his death in 1680 John Moody of Reading ; and *Jane*, who married 1684 (?) Ephraim Flint. A daughter *Mary* may well have been named after two daughters of Rev. Peter of Concord, born in 1615 and 1621, both of whom died young. The following tables show the relationship of the parties.

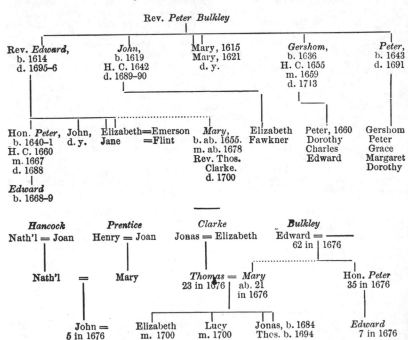

The church records of Marshfield, previous to 1696, are no longer in existence ; and the town records give no dates of birth of any children of Rev. Edward Bulkley, only the burial of John. Now, however, that this clue has been discovered, it

* The town records of Marshfield, under date Aug. 13, 1657, speak of " the house and land that Mr. Bulkley late lived in." Jan. 7, 1657-8, a committee is appointed " to go to Mr. Bulkley at Concord," &c.

† Shattuck in his history of Concord says he died " probably " at the house of his grandson Edward Emerson; but it may have been at that of his daughter Mrs. Thomas Clarke.—E. F. W.

is greatly to be hoped that some old record in deed, letter or family bible will be found, which, explained in the light of the foregoing documents, may place beyond question the fact that the first wife of Rev. Thomas Clarke of Chelmsford was a daughter of Rev. Edward Bulkley of Marshfield and Concord. That this fact should have remained until now undiscovered, which is perhaps the chief argument against its being a fact, is no more strange than that the name of Rev. Edward Bulkley's wife should still be unknown.—EMMA F. WARE.

These wills of Everard Faukner and his widow Elizabeth are printed in Chapman's Bulkley Family, Hartford, 1875, pp. 68–77. The will of John Bulkley, " of the Precincts of St. Katherines, near the tower of London, Gent.," father of Mrs. Fawkner, dated Oct. 10, 1689, proved Jan. 28, 1689-90, is printed in that volume, pp. 64-67.—EDITOR.]

ROGERS (*ante*, p. 180).

Some References to Thomas Rogers in the Stratford Records.

Among the expired Leases, High Street Ward :—

One to Roger Smith, mercer, of a messuage or tenement in High Street,* between the dwelling-house of Thomas Rogers on the north part and the dwelling-house of Mr John Wolmer on the south part; and also a messuage in Elie Street alias Swyne Street, between the barn and backside of Thomas Rogers on the west part and the backside of Mr John Wolmer on the east part, 26 November, 19 James I. The High Street frontage was 19 ft. 2 inch. Lease and counterpart.

Lease to Francis Smyth of London, haberdasher, of a messuage in High Street between the dwelling-house of Thomas Rogers (on the North) and John Woolmer (on the South), and also a tenement in Ely Street (see above). 25 February, 6 Charles I.

Expired Leases. Henley Street Ward.

Thomas Rogers, draper, —— two tenements in Windsor Street or Henley Lane alias Hell Lane, 10 June, 20 James I.

Expired Leases. Chapel Street Ward.

Charles, the son of Thomas Rogers, —— a messuage and garden in Church Street. January, 1 James I.

Early Sessions Papers.

The presentmente of Thomas Rogers and his felowes of all such thinges geven them in charge at the Quarter Sesson holden the xiiijth dai of Januarii, 1602, as much as came to their knowledg or remembrance.

Court of Record Manuscripts.

Charles Baynton and George Bardoll v. Thomas Rogers for a debt of 37£ 6d. (relates to a lease of lands at Bridgetown) 16 Eliz.

John Smythe (pinsor) summoned to answer Thomas Rogers touching a parole agreement about the upper part or end of a certain close in Bridgetowne called Wythibed Lees, 34 Eliz. (I find that John Shaksper was a juror in this case.)

Thomas Rogers attached to answer John Rogers (clerk) for ten *fasces radiorum sinuosorum*, at 6^d the bundle, 10 Jac. I.

Thomas Rogers, executor of the will of Thomas Rogers gentleman, summoned to answer John Rogers, clerk, in a bill of obligation (dated 6 Jac. I.).

---

* The High Street tenement conveyed in this lease was, I believe, a building which must have stood on the site of the present Garrick Inn, which is still corporation property, and still bounded, as then, north and south, by private property.　　　　H. F. W.

Miscellaneous Documents.

The accompte of Thomas Rogers, chamberlayne to the Borrowghe of Stretforde-uppon-Avon, made the thyrde of October, 1589, which he then yelded upp in respecte he was elected to be Bayleef for the yeare followeinge, 31 Elizabeth.

The noate of corne and malte taken the iiij[th] of ffebruarii, 1597, in the xl[th] yeare of the raigne of our moste gracious soveraigne ladie Queen Elizabethe, &c.

High Street Warde.   Townsmens Corne.

M[r] Thomas Rogers vij. quarters, rye iiij. quarters, myle corne ij. quarters.

Straingers.

M[r] Rogers hath of M[r] Hubands v. quarters iiij. str.

Hamnet Sadler summoned to answer Thomas Rogers, on money matters, 39 Eliz.

Thomas Rogers, gentleman, summoned to answer Thomas Bridges since by request of the said Thomas Rogers he sold to one William Rogers all his part of the collection of the County of Surrey for the sustenance of the poor inhabitants of Stratford by letters patent granted, &c., 38 Eliz.

Richard Dixon alias Waterman summoned to answer Thomas Rogers senior respecting the purchase of some barley straw, 26 Eliz.

Richard Dixon v. Thomas Rogers, the jurors' names and verdict in a suit respecting the rent of a house inhabited by Rogers.

Thomas Rogers summoned to answer to the suit of Richard Dixon about the lease of a tenement, 37 Eliz.

Richard Quiney summoned to answer Thomas Rogers concerning a loan of money, 38 Eliz.

Thomas Rogers v. William Rogers, concerning a bill of obligation, 40 Eliz.

Richard Dixon v. Thomas Rogers concerning the lease of a tenement to Charles Rogers son of defendant, 36 Eliz.

Charles Rogers summoned to answer Richard Dixon alias Waterman for an assault, 43 Eliz.

A bond of obligation by Abraham Sturley of Stratford, yeoman, and Richard Quyney of the same, mercer, to Thomas Rogers of the same, woollen-draper, and Henry Wilson of the same, fishmonger, in 40[li], 38 Eliz.

A Court of Record was held 7 January, 38 Elizabeth, before Thomas Rogers bailiff.

I found numerous references to other individuals of the name of Rogers. The earliest, I think, was a deed of John Clopton etc. to John Rogers and others, of one shop and a chamber built over it, in Middle Row. This was dated 13 Edward IV. There was a William Rogers on the Subsidy Roll 34–5 Henry VIII. The church registers contain baptisms, burials, &c., of the families of Henry, William, Richard and John Rogers, all contemporary with Thomas Rogers the bailiff. John Rogers was a clergyman, and seems to have succeeded (in 1610) Mr. Richard Bifield (grandfather of Nathaniel Bifield, of Boston) as vicar of Stratford. In 1619 a Mr. Thomas Wilson became vicar. The following are a few of the notes relating to this John Rogers, taken from the Stratford records.

M[r] John Rogers, vicar, to have towards the building of a stable and woodhouse on his own backside thirty shillings. 3 November 1610.

Mr Rogers to deliver up possession of his house 15 October, 17 James I. A fit gown cloth given to Mr John Rogers our Vicar in the hope that he will deserve the same hereafter and amend his former faults and failings, 30 January 1614.

In 1615 he was complained of for creating a nuisance by building a pigstye just opposite the back court of New Place (Shakespeare's residence). He besought the corporation that they " would consent to the finishinge of that small plecke which I have begunne in the lane, the use whereof was noe other but to keepe a swine or two in, for about my howse there is noe place of convenience without so much annoyance to the Chappell, and how farre the breeding of such creatures is needefull to poore howsekeepers I referre myselfe to those that can equall my charge; moreover the highway will be wider and fayrer, as it may now appeare."

[From Hist. of New Place, by J. O. Halliwell (now Halliwell-Phillipps), Esq., London, 1864.]

It is thought probable that he performed the service at the funeral of Shakespeare.

As to the occupation of Mr. Thomas Rogers, there may be found, in Mr. Halliwell Phillipps's " Outlines of the Life of Shakespeare " (2d ed. 1882), page 207, " Illustrative Notes—*The concentration of several trades*," the following :

" Thus it is recorded that ' Thomas Rogers, now baieliefe of this towne ' (1595) ' besydes his butchers trade, which until now of late hee allwaies used, hee ys a buyer and seller of corne for great somes, and withall useth grazinge and buyinge and selinge of catell, and hathe in howsehold xiiij persons.' "

Notes from Feet of Fines.

Int^r Thomam Rogers quer et Henricū Mace deforc de duobs messuagiis & duobus gardinis cum p̄tin in Stretford sup̄ Avon &c.

Pasch. 23 Elizabeth (1581).

Int Thomam Rogers geñosum quer et Willm̄ Rogers & Johannam uxēm eius & Elizabeth Rogers viduam deforc de uno mesuagio uno curtilagio & uno gardino cum p̄tin in Stretford sup̄ Avon &c.

Mich. 44–5 Elizabeth.

Int Johem Wolmar quer et Thomam Rogers geñosum & Aliciam uxēm eius deforc de uno mesuagio uno curtilagio & uno gardino cum p̄tin in Stratford sup̄ Avon &c. Mich. 2 James I. (1604).

THOMAS JADWYN citizen and cutler of London, 4 November 1626, proved 5 March 1627. To the poor of the parish wherein I am a parishioner forty shillings. I forgive to Daniel Colwall my apprentice the last year of his term. To my son Robert Jadwyn, "who" I pray to bless and reform, the sum of five pounds and a feather bed and such other household stuff as my executrix shall think good to give him. To my daughters Hanna Dunscombe and Susanna Sharrowe, to either of them three pounds to dispose of as they please, and to be paid into their own hands within one year next after my decease. To Jadwin Dunscombe, my daughter Hannah her son, twenty marks at his age of twenty one years. To Philip and Thomas Dunscombe, his brothers, five pounds each at twenty one. I am seized and possessed of and in three several messuages or tenements called or known by the names of the Unicorn, the Saracen's

Head and in the Crown, in the parish of St. George in Southwark in the county of Surry (the messuage called Saracen's Head divided into several tenements). These to my wife Elizabeth during her natural life; then to my son Robert and his lawful heirs; next to my daughters Hanna and Susanna and their heirs; failing such then to the Master, Wardens and Commonalty of the cutlers of London forever. To my son Robert all my lands in Virginia except such lands there as is or shall be allotted to go with my two shares in the Sommer Islands. These two shares and the land going with them to ·ᵒy son in law Thomas Dunscombe, Hanna his wife, Philip and Thomas their sons, to have and to hold for one hundred years if they or any of them or any issue from them or any of them shall so long live and dwell and abide in the said Sommer Islands, yielding and paying therefor yearly only ten pounds weight of Tobacco at the Feast of St. Michael the Archangel, and paying and discharging all other charges and impositions which from time to time during the said term shall be lawfully taxed and imposed upon the said land. My wife Elizabeth to be executrix. The overseers to be the Master and Wardens of the said Mystery and Commonalty of Cutlers of London.

Wit: Thomas Coffyn, Daniel Colwell.   Barrington, 30.

[Thomas Jadwyn or Jadwine was an " adventurer for Virginia " and was present at several meetings of the Virginia Company in 1619.—R. A. BROCK, *of Richmond, Va.*]

ANTHONY BARHAM of Mulberry Island in Virginia, gentleman, and at this present resident in England, 6 September 1641, proved 13 September, 1641. Reference to a will made before my departure out of Virginia. My wife Elizabeth to be sole executrix. Reference made to goods and chattels, money &c. due to me in England. Goods and commodities to be sent over to Virginia to my wife. Money owing me by Mʳ Thomas Lyne. One hundred pounds to be sent over to my wife for the use and behoof of my daughter Elizabeth. To my mother Bennet five pounds. To my brother in law Richard Bennet[1] five pounds. To my sister Mrs Mary Duke five pounds. To my sister Graves her son forty shillings. To my friend Edward Maior[2] ten pounds. To my friend and gossip William Butler ten pounds. To Mʳˢ Joane Perce, wife of Mʳ William Perce,[3] fifty shillings to make her a ring. To Martha Maior, wife of my loving friend Edward Maior, fifty shillings to make her a ring. To my god daughter Sara Butler, daughter of my said gossip William Butler,[4] thirty shillings for a wine cup. To my loving friend Mʳ Edward Aldey, minister of Sᵗ Andrews in Canterbury, forty shillings to make him a ring. To Thomasine Doves forty shillings for a ring. Mr. Edward Aldey to deliver unto my executors the Deed of covenant touching the two hundred & twenty six pounds ten shillings due to me from the said Mʳ Thomas Lyne. · Edward Maior and William Butler to be the executors of my said will in Virginia and for payment and satisfaction of the legacies herein given &c. Three pounds apiece to them to make them rings to wear in remembrance of me.

Wit: Thomas Collyns, Katherine Myns (per signum) Richard Barlowe Scr.   Evelyn, 115.

[Anthony Barham was Burgess for Mulberry Island, 1629–30.

¹ This was Richard Bennett, Acting Governor of Virginia under the Commonwealth of Cromwell, from April 30, 1652, to March, 1655. There are grants of land to him of record in the Virginia Land Registry of 6,700 acres in the counties

of James City, Lower Norfolk and Rappahannock, between 1637 and 1642. There appear also the following grants to the name Bennett. Joane Bennett, "widdow," Book No. 1, p. 346, 400 acres in Charles River (York) county, May 6, 1636; Ambrose Bennett, Book No. 1, p. 529, 300 acres in Isle of Wight county, May 8, 1638; Morris Bennet, one of the "Head Rights" mentioned, No. 1, p. 746, 1150 acres, do. June 23, 1641; Thomas Bennett, No. 1, p. 761, 1050 acres in York county, Dec. 16, 1641; William Bennett, No. 1, p. 798, 1200 acres in Isle of Wight county, Aug. 10, 1642; W^m. Bennett, a "Head Right;" Philip Bennett, No. 1, p. 932, 515 acres in Upper Norfolk county, Dec. 20, 1643.

2 Edward Major was Burgess for Upper Norfolk county, in 1645; for Nansamond 1646, and April, 1652, and speaker of the House; Lieut. Col. in Nansamond in 1653. The following grants of land to him and others of the name are of record in the Virginia Land Registry: Edward Major, Book No. 1, p. 416, 450 acres in Upper county of New Norfolk, May 18, 1637. Edward Major, among the "Head Rights;" Edward Major, "Gent.," No. 2, p. 17, 450 acres in Upper Norfolk county, Oct. 4, 1644, p. 45; 300 acres in Warwick county, April 24, 1645, p. 89; 500 acres in Nansamond county, Feb. 20, 1645. Richard Major, No. 1, p. 566, 300 acres in Charles River, York county, May 12, 1638, p. 687; 500 acres, do. Nov. 5, 1639, No. 2, p. 200; 300 acres at the mouth of Mattapony River, June 17, 1640, No. 3, p. 382; 1350 acres in New Kent county, June 30, 1656, No. 4, p. 367; 350 acres on the North side of York, on Pierce's *alias* Major's Creek, April 27, 1659. John Major, son of Richard Major, No. 1, p. 572, a deed or gift of cattle from " John Brocke in Virginia, Chirurgeon," his god-father, June 12, 1638, p. 947; 200 acres in Northampton county, Nov. 10, 1643, p. 948; 400 acres do. Sept. 4, 1643, No. 2, p. 269; 400 acres in Northampton county, Oct. 24, 1650. John Major, among the "Head Rights"; No. 3, p. 8, 1000 acres in Gloucester county, March 20, 1653; No. 4, p. 203, 300 acres on the North side of York river, Feb. 28, 1657.

3 Captain William Pierce and Joane his wife, were living at Jamestown in 1623-4. He was a member of the Council, 1631-44. His daughter Jane married, in or before 1620, John Rolfe, one of whose previous wives was Pocahontas. The following grants are of record to the name Pierce in the Virginia Land Registry: Captain William Pierce, Book No. 1, p. 255, 2000 acres, June 20, 1635; "Captain William Pierce, Esq.," p. 879, 360 acres near Baber's Neck on James river and near the lands of Thomas Harwood, called Queen's land, and bounded by Pierce's Creek, July 24, 1653; do. p. 927, 2100 acres near the dwelling house of Captain Pierce, Dec. 16, 1643; Thomas Pierce (George Lobb and Otho Warne) No. 1, p. 605, 1550 acres in James City county, Sept. 12, 1636; Richard Pierce, No. 1, p. 379, 600 acres in James City county, Sept. 12, 1636.

4 The following grants are of record to the name Butler in the Virginia Land Registry: William Butler, "Gentleman," Book No. 1, p. 900, 700 acres on the south side of James river at the head of Lawne's Creek (mouth in Surry county), near the lands of Captain William Pierce, Aug. 29, 1643, Head Rights; William, Jon, Elizabeth and Mary Butler, Amory Butler, No. 6, p. 230, 280 acres in New Kent county, April 17, 1669; John Butler "of Westmoreland county," p. 296, 597 acres in Rappahannock county, April 18, 1670; Christopher Butler, p. 297, 339 acres in Rappahannock county, June 18, 1670; William Butler (probably son of Wm. Butler, "Gentleman," above), p. 449, 590 acres in Surry county, adjoining land where "Major William Butler" (as above) "formerly lived," in Lawnes Creek parish, March 1, 1672-3.

William Butler was a Burgess, April, 1642; "Captain" William Butler, Burgess from Surry county, 1653; "Major" William Butler, Burgess, 1657-8. The Butler family continued long in Surry county. Robert Butler was Adjutant General of Virginia troops in the war of 1812; Robert Butler, M.D. was State Treasurer about 1840. He married a daughter of Rev. John Bracken, president of William and Mary College, and mayor of Williamsburg, 1810. William Mahone, late Major General C. S. A. and U. S. Senator from Virginia, married Oteia Butler, a cousin of Dr. Robert Butler, above.—R. A. BROCK.]

NICHOLAS BACON of Shrubland Hall, Bargham, in the county of Suffolk, Esq.; 30 March 1658, proved 25 February 1658. My body to be buried in the parish church of Bargham, in the tomb where my father and mother and wife were interred. Whereas my two sons Philip and Nathaniel have undutifully left me in my old age and are gone beyond the

seas without my leave, privity or consent I do therefore give and devise
unto my eldest son Nicholas Bacon and his heirs &c. To Charles George
Cocke, Esq., my son-in-law. My grand-child Anne Vaghan. My son-in-
law Sir Edward Vaghan, Knight.

The witnesses were Philip Bacon, Phillip Gillett als Candler, Edmund
Purpett Senr, Nicholas Candler, George Burton.

To my brothers to buy rings. Brother Lionell, Mr. George Burton the
attorney that lives at Wickham.   Pell, 93.

[John Bacon, of New Kent county, was granted Oct. 13, 1727, 1600 acres of
land in Henrico county, Book No. 13, p. 282. Captain Edmund Bacon was granted
243 acres in the upper part of New Kent county, Oct. 21, 1687, No. 7, p. 614.
He may have been the father of John above, who has numerous descendants in the
names of Bacon, Crenshaw, Rice, Pryor and others. It is a family tradition that
John Bacon was a descendant of Nathaniel Bacon "the rebel," but it is not known
that he left other issue than a daughter Elizabeth, who married Dr. Chamberlain.
Could it have been that Nathaniel Bacon of the text was the ancestor—transmitted as "the rebel"?—R. A. BROCK.
See article on the Bacon family in the REGISTER, vol. XXXVII. pp. 189–98.—EDITOR.]

FRANCIS HANNSWORTH (of the parish of St Sepulchre's, London), 11
April 1656, proved 28 February 1656. To John Hamond a hogshead
of tobacco. Bequests to Thomas Wilkinson[1] of Rosewell, Virginia, Elizabeth Ramsey, daughter of Thomas Ramsey, of Virginia, Francis Wheeler
& his wife, master John White & his wife. My nearest of kindred in
Tatel Thrope, Lincolnshire; if they do not appear then to John Creed of
Virginia, planter. To Michael Tillard—my things in a bag I have in the
ship Phillip. Master John White[2] to take up my fourteen hogsheads of
tobacco in the Ship Phillipp and sell them for my best advantage.

Wit: Michaell Tyllyard, Edw: Symons.

In an account of the debts which Master Hannsworth oweth appears one to
Robert Williams of Virginia.   Ruthen, 59.

[1 The following grants to the name Wilkinson are of record in the Virginia Land
Registry:
Wm. Wilkinson, Book No. 1, p. 315, 700 acres opposite to Captain Thorowgood's
land on Lynn Haven alias Chisopeên Bay, Nov. 20, 1635. Mr. William Wilkinson
and Mrs. Naomy Wilkinson, assumedly his wife, among the Head Rights, p. 400,
700 acres, by assignment from Robert Newburke, Nov. 10, 1635; p. 431, 700 acres
in Lower county of New Norfolk, May 25, 1637. Thomas Wilkinson, No. 2, p. 257,
500 acres on the south side of Potomac river, Oct. 18, 1650; No. 3, p. 25, 320 acres
on both sides of a creek on the south side of Rappahannock river, June 8, 1653.
William Wilkinson, "Minister," No. 2, p. 9, 100 acres in Elizabeth city county,
June 21, 1644. Richard Wilkinson, No. 2, p. 107, 237 acres opposite Pagan's Point
in Isle of Wight county, Aug. 13, 1646.
2 John White received the following grants of land, Book No. 2, Virginia Land
Registry, p. 10: 1 acre "East upon the land adjoining the State House" in "James
Cittie," and North towards the lands of Thomas Hampton, Aug. 28, 1644; No. 6,
p. 1, 100 acres in Mobjack Bay, near lands of William Armistead, Nov. 25, 1653.
The counties of Gloucester, Matthews and Middlesex bordered on Mobjack Bay.—
R. A. BROCK.]

ELIAS ROBERTS, citizen and merchant tailor of London, the elder, January 1624, proved 20 February 1626. To wife Sarah Roberts, my loving
and lawful yokefellow, the third part of my goods, two shares of lands in
Martins Hundreth. To my son Elias Roberts in Virginia, and one share
and fifteen acres in the Somer Islands and my house that I dwell in, allowing my wife Sarah her dwelling with the rest of my daughters until it
please God that they be bestowed in marriage, paying to each of my three
daughters the third part of my goods and to each of them one share of land

apiece in the Somer Islands and for my son to make it over to the husbands in the Somer Islands Court, if they be married; but if they have no children then to my son Elias; but if it please God he wanting issue with my three daughters, then my will is that the increase of my lands in Virginia and in the Somer Islands or in Ireland, which is amongst the merchant tailors, towards the maintaining a "lector" in the parish church of Queen Hoope, called the Eastin Church, in Flintshire, upon the Lord Day in the Welsh language.

I William Wight do testify that the handwriting above is in the hand of Elias Roberts.

[The above, not wholly intelligible, will seems to be followed by a more formal testament, to make his intentions clear, viz.: To wife Sara one third of the goods. To son Elias the two shares of lands in Martin Hundreth in Virginia, and the land in Ireland amongst the merchant tailors and one share of lands in the Somer Islands and fifteen acres in St. Davids Island, and my house that I dwell in, he allowing to my wife Sarah and all the children, &c. &c. The children's names are Elias, Sarah, Mary and Prudence Roberts.—H. F. W.]

Reg. of Commissary Court of London (1626–29), Fol. 143.

JOHN SHAWE the elder, citizen and draper of London, being of the age of three score and fourteen years or thereabouts, 20 September 1625, proved 6 March 1627. To be buried in the parish church of Kingston upon Thames in the county of Surrey. My sole heir to be John Heydon, my nephew and godson. To him my messuages, lands, tenements & hereditaments in Surton als Surbyton, in the parish of Kingston upon "Themise" &c. and also the thirty pounds and five pounds of lawful money of England which I have already disbursed and adventured to and with the company of Drapers of the City of London for and towards a plantation as well in Ireland as in Virginia, and the profits &c. and all and singular the lands, tenements and hereditaments whatsoever which I have or ought to have or which shall or may happen to fall, come or descend to me or my heirs of or by the said plantation either in Ireland or Virginia &c. &c. Bequests to William Williams, my servant, and John Hodgson my other servant, and Alce the wife of the said William Williams and Grace the now wife of the said John Hodson and to Edward Hodson. To my godson John Shawe my seal ring of gold which hath my name engraven therein, being worth three pounds or thereabouts. To my wife Susan. To Arthur Panther, my cousin Harris and his wife and son John Harris, my godson. To Thomas Copley, to Mr Willett my loving friend and his wife. To Robert Shawe, barber, to little Thomas Shaw of Richmond. To William Davys my servant. To Robert Harris my late scholar in St John's College, Oxford. To Robert Shawe my now scholar in St John's College, Oxford. To the poor of Great St Bartholomew parish by West Smithfield and of St. Michael's Woodstreet, London, and to the poor of St. Martins in the Fields where I was born. To James Davys. To George Symcott, citizen and clothworker (my loving friend). The said John Heydon, my nephew and my only kinsman and sister's son to be my sole and absolute executor.

Wit: John Hall, Oliver Man, Thomas Bishop, Nathaniel Nicholles and Joseph Fairebancke Scr. Barrington, 28.

RICHARD EVE of Willingaldoe in the county of Essex, gentleman, one of the yeomen of His Majesty's Chamber, 14 December 1629, proved 12

February 1629. To the poor of the parish twenty shillings. To son Richard Eve fifty pounds, to.be paid him within twelve mouths next after my decease if he shall be then returned into England from the parts beyond the seas. To son Seath Eve four score pounds at the age of one & twenty years and to daughters Sarah and Anne Eve four score pounds apiece at age of one & twenty or marriage. To my son Adam Eve all my freehold lands, messuages &c. in the county of Essex or elsewhere. The Residue to my wife Anne & son Adam whom I constitute joint executors. Brother in law Thomas Gathings, gentleman, overseer.

The witnesses were Richard Merrydale, Isabell Sykes (by mark) and Dudley Meares.   Scroope, 10.

[Adam Eve married July 5, 1694, Elizabeth, daughter of William Barsham of Watertown, and had a daughter Annabella, who married Jonathan Benjamin of W., Dec. 23, 1714. See Bond's Watertown, p. 18; Savage's Dictionary, II. 129.— H. F. W.]

JAMES OLIVER, merchant of Bristol, now servant to the Honorable Company of the English now trading to the East Indies and now chief of the English in the factory of Mocho, 25 March 1620, proved 22 August 1629. He leaves his property to his four children and his wife. His widow Frances received grant of admon.   Ridley, 75.

RICHARD ADDERLY of Romsy in the county of Southampton, mercer, in his will of 21 October 1629, proved 5 January 1629, appoints Bartholomew Gilbert, gentleman, and Peter Osgood overseers.   Scroope, 6.

JOHN CARNABYE of Ipswich, in the county of Suffolk, merchant, 22 May 1631, proved 2 July 1631. To son Samuel (inter alia) one halfe quarter or eight pte of & in the good shipp called the Mayflower of Ipswich. To daughter Mary Carnaby a two & thirtieth part of the same ship ; & to son in law John Brandlinge, a sixteenth part with the stock, tackle, furniture & apparell unto the same. belonging &c. Other children. St John, 90.

CHRISTOPHER BEALE of Eastfurleigh in the county of Kent, tailor (by mark) 31 May 1651, proved 20 June 1651. To my daughter Ann, now wife of George Climpson, twenty shillings within one year after my decease. To my daughter Margaret, now living in New England, ten shillings within one year &c. To my daughter Elizabeth ten pounds in lieu of eight pounds which her uncle Robert Beale gave her, to be paid within one year &c. To my youngest daughter Katherine four pounds which she oweth me and one shilling more in one month &c. To my two sons Christopher and Thomas Beale all my messuages, lands and tenements in the parish of Eastfurleigh, or elsewhere, in Kent. My youngest son Christopher to be executor.

Wit : Richard Fletcher, Nicholas Amhurst, John Ward (by mark) and Henry Burden.   Grey, 108.

Col. EDWARD HOOKER, citizen and Tallow Chandler of London, of the parish of St Mary at Hill, 8 May 1650, proved 16 July 1651. My body to be interred in the vault where my late wife was, Mrs Ellen Hooker, in Mary Hill Church, near Sir Christopher Buckell's tomb. To the poor of Mary at Hill parish six pence a week for ever in money to be distributed to three poor inhabitants that live orderly by two pence a person every Sabbath day in the morning. To ten poor ministers and ministers' wid ows (whereof Mrs Hill to one if she be then living) forty shillings a person. To fifty eight poor men ten shillings a person to accompany my corpse with a decent black mourning gown, sixteen of these persons to be taken out of the division of East Smithfield, in the parish of St Buttolphs Algate, eight out of Mary at Hill, four out of St Buttolphs, three out of Andrews Hubberd, two out of St Georges, two out of Margarets, Pudding Lane, and two out of Margaret Pattons. To Christ Hospital fifty pounds. To the repair of Chilcombe church & chancel twenty marks. To the public use of that part of the parish out of Barton Farm five pounds. To the parish of Chilcombe twenty five pounds, to pay four nobles a year quarterly, viz six shillings eight pence quarterly, to the minister of the said parish, to preach one sermon yearly the Fifth of November and to catechize the inhabitants once a month at least in the grounds of Religion.

To my brother Peter the house he liveth in, or three pounds per annum for life, and ten pounds per annum during his life (in consideration of his pains for looking to the business there and gathering up the rents for my executors). I forgive him what he properly owed me at my decease and all his errors of accompts, praying God to forgive him. To Ralph Hooker, my brother's son ten pounds. I forgive Henry Hooker, another of his sons, all he oweth me, at death. To Sibbell Hooker, my brother Peter's daughter, five pounds. To Anne Hooker, the eldest daughter of my late brother Richard, forty pounds. To Mary Hooker, her sister, that is now in New England, ten pounds. To my brother and sister Boyse ten pounds to buy mourning, viz five pounds each. I forgive my sister Eger all she oweth me at death and give her four pounds per annum during life, out of my rents at Nightingale Lane (and other bequests). To my cousin Edward Hooker of Chilcombe forty shillings, for a ring, and to my cousin John Hooker, his brother (the same). To my god son Edward Boyse five pounds. To Edward Eager ten pounds. To Rose Eager twenty pounds. To John Boyse, son of Henry Boyse deceased, five pounds. To goodwife Millner forty shillings and twenty shillings to goodwife Forrest. To Mrs May, in Philpott Lane, twenty shillings. To goodwife Freeman, in Tower St. twenty shillings. To my cousin John Woodes forty shillings, to buy a ring, and ten pounds for mourning for him and his wife.

To my wife, if she renounce her thirds, one hundred pounds per annum for life ; and she is to have the rent of that of Chilcombe copyhold and that of Compton, during her widow's estate, which will be about twenty seven pounds per annum; and ten shillings; five hundred pounds also in ready money, besides what I owe her by bill of one hundred & fifty pounds; and my lease of house in Love Lane, for life, to dwell in or to let. My library of books to my son Cornelius, except the bible that was my last wife's. That I bestow upon my wife. To Mrs Underhill at Brumley in Kent, my wife's sister, five pounds ; and five pounds to her sister Almond. To my daughter in law twenty pounds as a token of my love, to buy a ring. To my Company of Tallow Chandlers thirty pounds, to lend unto two young brothers. Legacies to brother Peter & his wife, to cousin John Hooker, to cousin Edward Hooker of Chilcombe, to Anne Hooker, to Henry Hooker my brother Peter's son, to cousin Ralph Hooker (mention made of Chilcombe & Compton in the county of South'ton), to my godson Edward Hooker, son of my cousin Edward Hooker of Chilcombe & to Jane my sister Eger's daughter. Wife Elizabeth and son Cornelius to be joint executors. Cousin Woods to be assisting.   Grey, 144.

Isaac Birkenhead, Adjutant General of the forces raised and to be raised in America. A case of Barbers' instruments to my lady. A pair of silk stockings &c. to Mr Richard Scott, Secretary to his Excellency General Robert Venables. My best bedstead to Mr Scott, his father. Forty shillings to be paid to Quarter Master General John Rudyard, and he to pay twenty shillings of it to Mr. Thomas Venables, son to his Excellency General Venables. All my " cocoe " nuts and such like I give to the Quarter Master General. " To my nephew Tom a parcell of money depending betwixt Coll. Buller and I," about three pounds six shillings. All the rest to my nephew Randolph Birkenhead. I do likewise desire that half crown apiece may be given to the people that throw me overboard.

Wit: John Rudyard, Richard Scott.

29 September 1655 there issued forth letters to Randolph Birkenhead the nephew and residuary legatary of the deceased.   Aylett, 196.

Margaret Beard of the Charterhouse yard, in the parish of St. Sepulchres, London, widow, 23 November 1664, proved by Francis Flexmer 17 April 1665. To my two grandchildren Charles and Elizabeth Beard my lease and all my messuages &c. at Castle Bitham and Bitham Parke, in the county of Lincoln, which I hold by lease from the Earl of Worcester for the remaining term of four score and nineteen years (if my brothers Francis Flaxmer and George Flaxmer, or either of them, shall so long live) to be divided share and share alike, they paying (certain annuities) to George Flaxmer, Francis Flaxmer jun^r and Jeane Beard widow. To my said grand daughter Elizabeth Beard my freehold messuage in Beckenham Kent, and to the heirs of her body; remainder to my grandson Charles Beard and the heirs of his body; remainder to my niece Anne Flaxmer and her heirs forever. My brother Francis Flaxmer to be the executor. Grand daughter Elizabeth Beard under eighteen years of age, and grandson Charles Beard under twenty one. Nephews Stafford Leaventhorpe and William Flaxmer. To my godson William Rainsford five pounds. To my god daughter Mary Flaxmer fifty shillings.

The witnesses were John Elye of Charter House Lane, victualler (by mark) & Bartho: Pickering, scr. in Foster Lane.

In a codicil, bearing date 26 November 1664, she mentions daughter Jane Beard (not to be troubled) sister Susan Flaxmer, niece Elizabeth Flaxmer and Mr. Heather. The witnesses were J. Ravenscroft and John Ealy (by mark).

In another codicil, dated 9 March 1664, she says : Whereas at the time of the making of my said last will I did presume and verily believe that my son Thomas Beard was dead in some parts beyond the seas. And since having been credibly informed that my said son Thomas Beard is yet living beyond the seas and if it shall please god that my said son Thomas shall live and return home into England, then I do hereby give and bequeath unto my said son Thomas Beard five pounds. My brother Francis Flaxmer shall receive and take the rents and profits &c. of all my copyhold messuage &c. of Frimley in the county of Surrey (which after my decease will lawfully descend and come to my said son Thomas, if he be living, or, if he be dead, to my said grandson Charles Beard, as right and next heir) until such time as my said son Thomas Beard shall return home into England again, or that my said brother Francis Flaxmer or my other executors " shall bee ascertained of my said son Thomas his death " &c. Other changes in the disposition of her estate set forth.   Hyde, 38.

[Savage, in his Genealogical Dictionary, names three persons in New England named Thomas Beard,—1st, a shoemaker, Salem, 1629; 2d, a resident of Scarborough, perhaps of Dover, who died 1679; 3d, a resident of Ipswich, freeman, perhaps of Boston 1675, a mariner.—EDITOR.]

MARGARET KEMB, of the parish of St. Saviour's, Southwarke, in the County of Surrey, widow and administratrix of Andrew Kembe, late deceased, citizen & stationer of London, made her will 4 November 1665, proved 16 November 1665, by Sarah Feake, daughter & executrix. To my son Thomas Kembe, now in Virginia, all my books, copies of books, stock in the Hall, all my dwelling house as I now use, occupy and enjoy; also that part which is now in the occupation of Jane Curtis,—some furniture and plate,—and one hundred pounds in money and all the money that is due me from Mr Gibbens upon a mortgage. To my daughter Sarah Feake, widow, my two leases of my houses in Old Street and Grub Street, or lying near thereabouts, in the parish of St Giles without Cripplegate in the County of Middlesex and city of London &c. To my sister Mary Meredith ten pounds,—and ten pounds apiece to every child she hath living at my decease. To my brother David Meredith his children that shall be living at my decease ten pounds apiece. To my cousin Sarah Huffin thirty pounds at her day of marriage or age of twenty one years. To Anne Holt five pounds. To Mary Marshall five pounds. To my sister Kembe five pounds. To my cousin Wells his wife twenty shillings to buy her a ring. My loving daughter Sarah Feake aforesaid to be full and sole executrix. To Margaret Allington, widow, twenty shillings a year, by five shillings a quarter, during her natural life. To Henry Waller five pounds. To Mr George Ewer ten pounds. To Elizabeth Martimore ten pounds at her day of marriage or age of one & twenty years. To Jane Curtis and the widow Alley twenty shillings apiece. To Sarah Chandler and Mr Scott and his wife twenty shillings each.

If my daughter Sarah Feake die before she marrieth, I nominate and appoint Mr Ewer and Henry Waller joint executors in trust for my son Thomas Kembe, now in Virginia as aforesaid. Then, in case he die without issue or unmarried, that is, leaving neither wife nor child behind him, in such case I give my sister Mary Meredith and her children and my brother David's children, as aforesaid, my whole estate, to be divided amongst them equally, share and share alike, after my debts and legacies are paid. My cousin Wells, Henry Waller, of the parish of St. Giles, Cripplegate, scrivener, and my loving friend Mr Ewer to be overseers.

Wit: William Bodd, Hum. Willoughby, Joane Church (by mark).

Hyde, 130.

JOHN PAYSON, of Nasing in the County of Essex, yeoman, 7 October 1666, proved 13 January 1667. To son William Payson tenements in the parish of Raydon hamlett in the County of Essex, with barn and stable yard, garden and orchard and two closes thereunto belonging and containing by estimation four and one half acres, being freehold. To son Thomas Payson and his two children Julian and Mary. To daughter Lydia Borham. To daughter Mary. To wife Lydia Payson. To John Borham's four children. To son Wm Payson's two children. Son James Payson to be executor, and cousin Ambros Chanler and John Foord overseers. The witnesses were John Sheelley and John Foord. Hene, 8.

[Giles Payson, from Nazing in Essex, aged 26, embarked for New England. April 3, 1635, in the Hopewell, William Bundick, master (See REGISTER, XIV. 304),

He settled at Roxbury, Mass., and became deacon of the church there. He was admitted freeman of Massachusetts, April 18, 1637, and the same month was married to Elizabeth Dowell. He had several children. (*See* Savage's Gen. Dict.) For other Nazing families, see REGISTER, XXVIII. 140–5 ; XXXIX. 365–71 ; and Memorials of the Pilgrim Fathers, John Eliot and his friends of Nazing and Waltham Abbey, by W. Winters, 8vo. 1882.

Edward Payson, perhaps a brother of Giles, of Roxbury as early as 1637, admitted freeman of Massachusetts, May 13, 1640 ; married August 20, 1640, Ann Park, daughter of William and Martha (Holgrove) Park. She died September 10, 1641, and he married 2d, January 1, 1641-2, Mary Eliot, daughter of Philip and a niece of the Apostle Eliot. She died his widow March 26, 1697, aged 76. Edward Payson was the ancestor of Rev. Seth Payson, D.D., of Rindge, N. H., whose son Rev. Edward Payson, D.D., was the celebrated divine of Portland, Me. (*See* Stearns's History of Rindge, N. H., p. 623 ; Eliot's Roxbury Records in REGISTER, XXXV. 245-7, and Savage's Gen. Dict.) A manuscript genealogy of the Payson Family by the late Rev. Abner Morse, A.M., is in the library of the New England Historic Genealogical Society.—EDITOR.]

NATHANIEL SNELL, of Hillingdon in the County of Middlesex, gentleman, 20 September 1684, with codicil of 27 August 1688, proved 16 April 1692. Lands in the manors of Colham and Colkennington alias Kempton in the County of Middlesex, to my wife Sarah and her heirs. The blood or kindred of the Snells or the Atlees, the name or kindred of my wife. Fifty pounds to George Maybanke and to David Maybanke (now in Carolina) fifty pounds and to Sarah Loughton fifty pounds, being sons and daughter of my eldest sister Sarah ; and fifty pounds to Thomas Cock and fifty pounds to Nathaniel Cock, sons of my second sister, Mary Cock. To wife Sarah. To Sarah Cock, daughter of sister Mary. Lands and tenements in Amersham als. Agmondesham and Chalfont St Giles in the county of Bucks. My third sister Bethia Shrimpton and her eldest son Nathaniel Shrimpton and three daughters, Susanna, Bethia and Martha. To Mary & Bethia Cock, daughters of sister Mary.

The witnesses to the will were William Crosier, James Atlee & Richard Perkins, and to the codicil Richard Perkins, Henry Bishop and Sarah Lidyard.   Fane, 74.

ROBERT HACKSHAW, of London, merchant, in a codicil to his will (in form of a letter to his executors) bearing date 15 May 1738 desires all lumber to be sold excepting what his daughter shall desire & excepting a trunk in the Ware-house (to which I have no keys) belonging to Mrs Hutchinson of New England and to be reserved there till she sends for it. Proved 7 December 1738.   Brodrepp, 285.

ANNE NOYES (*ante*, page 208.)

[Your note on Mrs. Anne Noyes in the January, 1887, REGISTER (*ante*, p. 208), says, Rev. William Noyes, Rector of Cholderton, Wilts, resigned in 1621.

I have received a letter from the present Rector of Cholderton, the Rev. Edwin P. Barrow, in which is the following extract from the Registry Book :

" Mr. William Noyes Rector of Choldington about 30 years departed this life anno 1616. Mr. Nathan Noyes succeeded his father in the Rectorie of Choldrington and departed this life in ye year 1651."

I notice your authority is Savage's Gen. Dictionary, but as there seems to be a difference in the date I thought you might like to know it.

Among the burials extracted from the register, is " Mrs. Ann Noyes widow & Relict of Mr. William Noyes sometime Rector of Choldrington, March 7 1657, æt. 82."—EDWARD DEERING NOYES, *of Portland, Me.*]

LAWRENCE WASHINGTON, of Washington Parish in the County of West-moreland in Virginia, gentleman, 11 March 1697–8.   To be buried, if please God I depart in this County of Westmoreland, by the side of my father and mother and near my brothers and sisters and my children.   To friends Mr William Thomson, Clerk, and Mr Samuel Thompson, each a mourning ring of thirty shillings price each ring.   To my godson Lawrence Butler one young mare and two cows.   To my sister Anne Writts children one manservant apiece of four or five years to serve, or three thousand pounds of tobacco, to be delivered or paid to them at age of twenty years. To my sister Lewis a mourning ring of forty shillings.   To my cousin John Washington Senr., of Stafford County, all my wearing apparel.   To cousin John Washington's eldest son Lawrence Washington, my godson, one man-servant of four or five years to serve, or three thousand pounds of tobacco, the same to be delivered at his age of twenty years.   To my godson Lawrence Butler and Lewis Nicholds that tract of land joining upon Meridah Edwards and Daniel White, being two hundred and seventy five acres, to be equally divided between them.   To the upper and lower churches of Washington parish, each of them, a pulpit cloath and cushion.   It is my will to have a funeral sermon at the church and to have no other funeral to exceed three thousand pounds of tobacco.   After debts and legacies paid and discharged, my personal estate to be equally divided in four parts, my wife Mildred Washington to have one part, my son John another part, my son Augustine another part and my daughter Mildred the other part, at their ages of twenty years.   To my son John this seat of land where I now live and that whole tract of land where I now live and that whole tract lying from the mouth of Mathodack extending to a place called the round Hills, with the addition I have thereunto made of William Webbs and William Rush, to him and his heirs forever.   To my son Augustine Washington all the dividend of land that I bought of Mr Robert Lessons children in England, in Mattax between my brother and Mr Baldridges land where Mr Daniel Lessons formerly lived, by estimation four hundred acres; likewise that land that was Mr Richard Hills, and all that land where Mr Lewis Markham now lives, after the said Markham and his now wife's decease, by estimation seven hundred acres more or less.   To my daughter Mildred Washington all my land in Stafford County lying upon Hunting Creek where Mrs Elizabeth Minton and Mr William now lives, by estimation twenty five hundred acres. I give my water-mill to my son John Washington.

If my children should die before they come of age or marriage my broth-ers children shall enjoy all their estates real, excepting that land that I bought of Mr Robert Lissons children, which I give to my loving wife and her heirs forever.   I give that land which I bought of my brother Francis Wright, being two hundred acres, lying near Stocks quarter, to my son John Washington.   My cousin John Washington, of Stafford County, and my friend Mr Samuel Thompson, to be my executors and my loving wife Mildred my executrix.

The witnesses were Robert Readman, George Wadon, Thomas Howes and John Rosier.

The will was proved 10 December 1700 by the oath of Mildred Gale als Washington (wife of George Gale), one of the executors, power being reserved for John Washington and Samuel Thompson, the other executors, to act.   Noel, 186.

[The will of Lawrence Washington here printed was sent to us by Mr. Waters several years ago, not long after he commenced his researches, at Somerset

House. We learn from him that he has since collected much important genealogical information concerning the Washingtons, which we hope before long to receive from him and print.—EDITOR.

This is the will of the grandfather of President George Washington, and was proved in England by Mildred Gale the widow of the testator and grandmother of the President. Mr. J. C. C. Smith, an intimate friend of the late Col. Chester, published in the seventh volume of *The Genealogist*, Jan. 1883, some extracts from the will of Mildred Gale, which was proved March 18, 1700-1, dated Jan. 24, 1700-1, in which she is described as the wife of George Gale, of Whitehaven, Cumberland, "being doubtfull of the recovery of my present sickness," and mentions that "by an Indenture of Marriage made and executed by and between John Washington one of the executors of my late husband's will of the one part, and my present husband George Gale with my own consent and approbation thereof of the other part, bearing date 16 May in the present year 1700, I am empowered to demise by will or other instrument the estate and legacys of my late husband to the uses and purposes therein mentioned," and she proceeded to bequeath £1000 to her said husband and the residue of her property equally between her said husband and children. When George Gale took probate of her will, he had to give bond for the tuition of the children, and their names appear as John, Augustine (father of the President) and Mildred Washington. In the Parish Register of St. Nicholas Church, Whitehaven, appears the baptism, Jan. 25, 1700-1, of Mildred, daughter of George Gale, and her mother was buried five days afterwards, while the infant was buried March 26, 1701. In a pedigree which Mr. Smith furnished with his article it appeared that George Gale had removed to Maryland, where he had four sons living in 1712.

In 1866, Col. Chester contributed an article to the London *Herald and Genealogist*, which was reprinted in the REGISTER, vol. 21, pp. 25-35, proving that the brothers John and Lawrence Washington, who emigrated to Virginia in 1657, could not have been identical with those of the same names in Sir Isaac Heard's *supposititious* pedigree, which Baker incorporated into his History of Northamptonshire as historic truth, for the John of Baker's Northamptonshire was a Knight and would not have relinquished his title; besides, he was living in England in 1662, while *his* brother Lawrence was a clergyman in England after the restoration (1660).

The point of interest, in the proof of the will above given, is that it leads towards the support of the tradition of the older members of the Virginia family "that their English ancestor came from some one of the Northern counties of England."

John Washington (the father of the testator), and Lawrence brother of John, came to Virginia in 1657; both died in 1677, leaving real and personal property in England. Lawrence left his English possessions to a daughter Mary, who was in England, and her half brother John Washington (of Stafford Co., Va., in the above will) may have gone there with some self-interest to see his sister, if he was in England when the marriage settlements were made for Mildred, the widow, to marry George Gale. In the *Whitehaven Guardian*, of Nov. 11, 1875, it was shown that there lived in that town, from 1692 to 1766, a family of Washingtons, and that the christian name of one of them who was married there in 1731 was Lawrence.

This town is not many miles from WARTON in Lancashire, which was for centuries the home of the Washington family from which the Northamptonshire branch descended. The Church Registers begin in 1568, and by reference to them the generally unreliable Albert Welles could be tested as to the statement that James Phillippe, of London, his authority for the English Pedigree of the Washington family, found the dates of baptisms which are given thus:—
Leonard Washington (grandfather to the testator above), born at Warton about 1595; his children,

Robert,	baptized at Warton, co. Lancaster, A.D. 1616.
Jane,	"	"	"	"	"	"	1619.
Francis,	"	"	"	"	"	"	1622.
Laurence,	"	"	"	"	"	"	1625.
John (father of testator),	"	"	"	"	1627.

Is there any truth in Welles's work? The Vicar of Warton will undoubtedly give the information if a copy is sent him of this imprint, and a desire for him to do so.—JOHN COFFIN JONES BROWN.]

WILLIAM PALMER of London Esquire, 23 March 1635 (sealed and published 6 April 1636), with a codicil dated 12 September 1636, proved 27 September 1636. My body to be buried in the parish church of St. Mary Aldermanbury,[1] in London, where I now dwell. All my personal estate shall be (in respect I am a citizen and freeman of the City of London) divided into three equal parts, according to the ancient custom of the same city, whereof one part I give unto Barbara Palmer, my wellbeloved wife, as due unto her by the said custom. Another third I give unto my three sons, Archdale, William and John, to be divided equally amongst them, according to the said laudable custom. And the other third part thereof, commonly called the Testator's third part, being devisable by me according to the custom of the same city, I do dispose of as followeth. (Then follow sundry bequests, among which) To my sister Mrs Mary Palmer the late wife of my brother Mr Robert Palmer, to my brother John Palmer, to my cousin Thomas Palmer of Marston and his brother Robert Palmer, to my cousin Mr George Clarke, to my Kinsman Thomas Cooke of Salte in the co. of Stafford and his sister Katherine Holte and his sister Frances Backhouse, to my cousin Walter Sedgley, for a divinity lecture or sermon in the Chapel of Marston where I was born, to my son John, at the age of twenty one. My cousin Mr George Clerke and my son Archdale Palmer to be executors.

In the codicil he mentions "our minister Mr Doctor Stanton," cousin Bydolphe and his wife, cousin William Palmer and his wife, cousin Williams and his wife, cousin Mr Richard Archdale and his wife, cousin Gardner, the company of Haberdashers, the poor in St. Bartholomew's Hospital, "whereof I am a Governor," and others.   Pile, 100.

[1 The parish Church of St. Mary Aldermanbury, in which Wm. Palmer was buried in 1636, was totally destroyed by the great fire in London in 1666. His cousin George Clarke, one of the executors of the will, was a merchant of London, of which he was elected Sheriff in 1641; he was created Knight at Hampton Court on 3d Dec. 1641. His wife was Barbara Palmer of Hill in Bedfordshire, whose brother William was also knighted in 1641 or 1642. It is uncertain whether he or his cousin William (son of the testator), and the brother of Archdale, was first knighted, one of them being made Knight at Whitehall 18 April, 1641, the other at Oxford 2 November, 1642. William Palmer, the brother of Sir George Clarke's wife, married a sister of Sir Thomas Gardiner, the Recorder of London, who was knighted at Kingsland 25 November, 1641, and is styled "Cousin Gardner" in the codicil.—JOHN COFFIN JONES BROWN.]

BARBARA PALMER of Onelepe in the co. of Leicester, widow, 13 September 1650, proved 10 June 1651. It is my earnest desire that the younger children of my sons Archdale Palmer Esq. and Sir William Palmer, Knight, shall have those moneys paid them which I have given them by their said fathers. To my son John Palmer a messuage in or near Page Green in the parish of Tottenham, Middlesex (and other tenements). To my cousin Sarah Willett, wife of James Willett clerk, to John Sare, son of Archdale Sare, at twenty one, to my cousin John Combe's wife, to my cousin Mary Ditchfield, to my cousin Susanna Dutten. Other bequests and legacies.
                    Grey, 126.

ARCHDALE PALMER, of Oneleppe in the co. of Leicester, Esq., 3 April 1672, proved 20 September 1673. My body to be buried in the parish church of Oneleppe by my dear mother, Mrs Barbara Palmer, widow, deceased. To my son William Palmer and Martha his wife, to my son Archdale Palmer and his wife Anna and son Thomas, to my son Thomas Pal-

mer and Mary his wife, to my son Samuel Sleigh and Barbara his wife (my
daughter), to my daughter Martha Palmer, to my son Samuel Palmer, at
one and twenty, to my son Joshua Palmer, at one and twenty. My houses
&c in Stepney to my four sons, Archdale, Thomas, Samuel and Joshua.
To my brother Mr John Palmer and Mary his wife. To my brothers in
law Mr John Smith, Mr Henry Smith and Mr Thomas Smith. To my
sisters in law Mrs Jane Gore and Mrs Elizabeth Danvers. My brother in
law Mr John Pegg and his wife. My cousin Thomas Palmer of Stafford.
My cousin Robert Palmer of Bassie-shaw, London. My wife Martha to be
the guardian of sons Samuel and Joshua, and also to be executrix of this
my will &c.   Pye, 115.

WILLIAM PALMER of Wanlippe ałs Oneleape, in the co. of Leicester
Esq. 13 April 1692, proved 14 July 1693. To my wife Martha and my
daughter Martha, at her age of one and twenty. My eldest son and heir
Archdale Palmer. Three of my children, Thomas, William and Henry.
Reference to adventures in Barbadoes. To my son John Palmer & his heirs
the reversion and inheritance, after the death and decease of my sister in law
Mrs Anne Appleton, of and in all my lands &c in Astbury ałs Newbold
Astbury, in the co. Palatine of Chester, with remainder to my youngest son
Samuel, then to my right heirs. My late mother Mrs Martha Palmer de-
ceased. My loving uncle John Palmer Esq. My two brothers, Samuel
Palmer and Joshua Palmer, and their two wives. My wife's three brethren,
Rowland Hunt Esq., Thomas Hunt merchant and John Hunt Esq., and
her sister Mrs Elizabeth Beale. My brother in law, John Moorewood Esq.,
and his wife.   Coker, 115.

WILLIAM PALMER of London, Doctor in Physic, 21 April 1708. Wife
Mary. Brother Archdale Palmer of Wanlip Esq. and his children, whether
of first or second marriage. My nephew John Palmer, the eldest son of
his first marriage, and my nephew Charlton Palmer, the eldest son of his
second marriage, already provided for. My wife to be executrix.
Commission issued, 15 December 1716, to Henry Palmer, the paternal
Uncle and lawfully appointed guardian of Mary Palmer, minor daughter,
and only issue of William Palmer lately of the parish of St. Mary Aldermary, London, Doctor in Medicine deceased &c., for the reason that Mary
Palmer, wife of the deceased and executrix named in the will, hath departed
this life.   Fox, 234.

JOHN PALMER of the Middle Temple, London, Esq., 7 July, 1738, proved 22 December 1738. To be buried in St Laurence church by my dearly
beloved spouse. To my loving brother Mr Thomas Palmer, of New
England,[2] fifty pounds, and in case of his death to his eldest son Eliakim
Palmer. To my dear brother Mr Henry Palmer one hundred pounds.
To my dear brother Mr Samuel Palmer five hundred pounds. To
my beloved sister Mrs Martha Palmer five hundred pounds. To my
nephew William Palmer five hundred pounds, and my two sets of chambers in Essex Court in Middle Temple. To my niece Barbara Palmer and
her sister Mrs Mary Palmer, daughters of the said Samuel Palmer, five hundred pounds apiece. To my daughter in law Mrs Graves one hundred
pounds. To my grandson Mr Joseph Andrews one hundred pounds. To
my brother in law Mr Thomas Palmer & his sister Mrs Mary Palmer twenty pounds apiece. To my niece Bakewell ten pounds. To all my brother
Archdale Palmer's children by his last wife ten pounds apiece. To my

niece Molesworth ten pounds. To Mr Andrews & Mr Graves, my sons in law ten pounds apiece. To my nephew Eliakim Palmer ten pounds. To the Fund for supporting dissenting ministers fifty pounds. To Dr Earl ten pounds, Mr Newman, Dr Wright's assistant five pounds, the poor of Dr Earl's church five pounds & to Mrs Gascoign five pounds. I give plain gold rings of sixteen shillings value to all my brothers & sisters, nephews & nieces, Mr Andrews & his lady, Mr Graves & his lady, Dr Earl, Dr Allen & my dear friend Thomas Hunt Esq. The rest & residue to my nephew William Palmer aforesaid whom I nominate and appoint executor. Wit: John Launder, John Launder, jun^r & William Thirkill.

Mention of bonds & other property in Mr Hoare's hands &c. I give rings to cousin Joshua Palmer, cousin More his sister, cousin Lloyd, cousin Birch, cousin Tom Beal, my diamond ring to said niece Barbara & all my other rings to my niece Molly, her sister.

The above was sworn to, 22 December 1738, by Henry Palmer of St Mary Aldermanbury, merchant, and Eliakim Palmer of the same parish, merchant. Brodrepp, 293.

[^2 His "loving brother Mr. Thomas Palmer of New England," married Abigail Hutchinson the daughter of Eliakim, of Boston, who gave Thomas a piece of land at the foot of Fort Hill, upon which the beneficiary erected a large house which he subsequently altered into two tenements as mentioned in his son Eliakim's will. He was one of the most useful public men in Boston, and during a long contest between the town and himself in relation to some of his father-in-law's property, he was still selected for the most important positions. He held advancing positions throughout life.

By the will of Thomas he gave to his son Eliakim all of his "houses and lands wharves and real-estate wherever to be found," except one of the tenements above referred to; he gave him also "one moiety of all my personal estate in what part of the world soever it may be found." Son Thomas was to have the other moiety of the personal property and the tenement which was left after Eliakim had taken his choice; but the "Tappestry hangings in the end of the House Mr. Job Lewis now possesses shall not be taken down, but belong to that tenement whoever chooses it. To granddaughters Hannah and Abby Lewis £500 each; all my plate to be divided between my children Eliakim Palmer and Sarah Lewis. To son Thomas wearing apparel, household goods, negro woman Fanny, with my horse and furniture and chaise. To brother Samuel, with my sister Martha Palmer and sister Arch. Palmer, each a Ring of suitable value, as also a Ring to my brother's wife. To my partner Nathl Balston, Esq., £100 as a token of my love. £30 to the poor of Brattle St. Church and £10 each to Rev. Ben^n. Colman and Rev. Thos. Cooper." Mourning clothes provided, &c. &c. Nathaniel Balston was Executor, and evidently the intended way of managing the property was a family secret as he never rendered any account until forced to do something at the death of the son Thomas in 1752, brother of Eliakim, when he reported *personal* property in his hands belonging to the brothers, undivided, amounting to nearly £10,000. It will be noticed in Eliakim's will that he gave all the real estate inherited from his father, in trust to Nathaniel Balston, for the ultimate use of Abigail and Hannah Lewis his nieces.

Thomas Palmer, the brother of Eliakim, left Boston for England in January, 1750, and beside his will he gave written orders that his sister Mrs. Lewis should remain in his house rent free, in case of his death, not returning from England, or not giving contrary orders. Whether he died abroad or at home the writer does not know; his son Thomas under 14 years of age was put under the guardianship of James Boutineau and Nathaniel Bethune with bonds of £4000, increased in 1760 to £10,000.—JOHN COFFIN JONES BROWN.]

HENRY PALMER the elder of St Mary Aldermanbury, London, Merchant, 19 April 1739, proved 22 May 1740. To my brother Thomas Palmer of Boston in New England Esq. five hundred pounds and to his son Thomas Palmer and his daughter Sarah Lewis five hundred pounds

each. To Job Lewis, the husband of the said Sarah Lewis, and to Hannah
and Abigail Lewis, children of the said Job and Sarah, one hundred pounds
each, and to Mary Palmer, wife of my said nephew Thomas Palmer, twenty
pounds. To Anne Palmer, widow of my brother Archdale Palmer Esq.
deceased, fifty pounds. To Anne Palmer, widow of my nephew John
Palmer Esq. deceased, twenty pounds, and to Anne Palmer, her daughter,
thirty pounds. To my nephew William, son of my brother Archdale Palmer Esq. deceased, twenty pounds and to Elizabeth Palmer, his wife, one
hundred pounds, and to Henry Palmer, son of the said William and Elizabeth, three hundred pounds. To my niece Elizabeth Bakewell one hundred
pounds and to Mr John Bakewell, her husband, twenty pounds. To my
nephew Henry, son of my brother Archdale Palmer Esq. deceased, three
hundred pounds. Reference to a bond of his to William Fauquire Esq.
and other debts. Nephew Thomas, son of my brother Archdale Palmer
Esq. deceased. Nephew Archdale Palmer, son of my brother Archdale
Palmer Esq. deceased. Nephew Henry Palmer of London, Merchant.
Niece Mary Faris, wife of William Faris, and John Faris her son. Anne
Ewer, Katherine Handley,[3] Martha Lewis, Barbara Palmer, Charlton Pal-
mer and Betty Palmer, children of my late brother Archdale Palmer Esq.
deceased, and Walter Ewer, Samuel Handley, Benjamin Lewis and William
Faris, my nephews in law, and Rebecca Palmer, my niece in law. To the
Hon. Doctor Coote Molesworth and his wife Mary Molesworth. My brother Samuel Palmer and his wife Elizabeth and William, Barbara and Mary
Palmer, children of the said Samuel. My sister Martha Palmer. My
cousin Mary Palmer, spinster, and Sarah Blundell, widow of Benjamin
Blundell. My much esteemed friend Lieut. Gen. Peers Esq. of the Barbadoes. Item I give to the incorporated Society for propagating the Gospel
in New England, whereof Sir Robert Clark is the present Governor, the
sum of one hundred pounds. To my nephew Eliakim Palmer, eldest son
of my brother Thomas Palmer, and his heirs and assigns my freehold
house of inheritance situate on Ludgate in London, known by the name of
the Swan and Star, and now in the occupation of Bernard Townsend, which
house I purchased from Nicholas Charlton Esq., and to the said Eliakim
the residue of my estate, as well in foreign parts as in England. The said
Eliakim Palmer to be executor.   Browne, 153.

[³ There is a full pedigree of the family of Sir Samuel Handley in the College
of Arms, London.—J. C. C. SMITH.]

MARTHA PALMER of Newgate Street, London, spinster, 19 April 1744,
proved 14 January 1745. To my sister Anne Palmer, widow of my brother
Archdale Palmer, thirty pounds. To my nephews, Harry Palmer and
Charlton Palmer, and my nieces, Elizabeth Bakewell, Anne Ewer, Katherine Handley and Martha Lewis, all children of my said brother Archdale
Palmer, twenty five pounds each. To my nephew Archdale Palmer, in
whose house I now dwell, and my nieces Barbara and Betty Palmer, likewise children of my said brother and yet unmarried, one hundred pounds
each. To my nephew Eliakim Palmer and my niece Mary Molesworth
twenty five pounds each. To my grand-nephew Harry Palmer, now in the
East Indies, sixty pounds. To my nephew Thomas Palmer, son of my
said brother Archdale, one hundred and fifty pounds. To my sister Elizabeth Palmer, widow of my brother Samuel, fifty pounds. To my nephew
William Palmer, only son of my said brother Samuel, five hundred pounds,
and to his sisters Barbara and Mary Palmer seven hundred pounds each.

My said nephew William to be executor, and to him three hundred pounds
new South Sea Annuity stock, on trust to pay the interest and dividend
arising therefrom to my niece Mary Faris, to her sole and separate use
exclusive of her present husband &c. To her son John Faris one hundred
pounds at his age of twenty five years, or at the decease of his said mother, the
which shall first happen. The Rev. M^r. Samuel Chandler and others.

Edmunds, 25.

ELIAKIM PALMER of London, merchant, 14 May 1749, proved 24 May
1749, as to the deceased's estate in England or in any other parts except
in New England. Reference to contract on marriage with wife Elizabeth.
To said wife fifteen thousand pounds. My father Thomas Palmer, of Boston
in New England Esq. deceased, being seized in fee &c of a mansion house,
by him built, at the foot of Fort Hill in Boston aforesaid and divided into
two tenements, by his last Will and Testament gave and devised to me such
one of the said two tenements as I should choose and the other tenement to
my brother Thomas. I hereby make choice of that one now or late in the
occupation of Charles Paxton Esq. and release &c to my said brother Thomas
all my right and claim in and to the other tenement in which he now lives
or lately lived. To Nathaniel Balston of Boston Esq. and my said brother
Thomas Palmer, all my houses, buildings, wharves, lands and Real Estate
whatsoever at Boston, during the life of my sister Sarah Lewis, wife of Job
Lewis of the said town of Boston, in trust to pay the rent &c into the hands
of my said sister for her sole and separate use. And after her decease I
give the said houses &c to my nieces Abigail and Hannah Lewis, her daughters, as tenants in common &c. To the said Nathaniel Balston Esq. and my
brother Thomas Palmer one hundred pounds each, to Mrs Mary Barker,
widow of Dr. John Barker deceased, one hundred pounds, To John Faris,
son of my cousin Mary Faris, one hundred pounds. To George Walker
and the Hon. John Lyte of the Island of Barbadoes, esquires, fifty pounds
each, making it my humble request to them that they will assist my executors
in getting in that part of my effects which I shall (—) possessed of in the
said Island. To Beeston Long Esq.[4] and Mr Henry Norris Junior of London,
merchants, my executors hereafter named, and to my cousin William Palmer of London, Attorney at Law, also one of my executors, the several sums
of one hundred pounds each. Certain servants and others. My house in
London. My house at Ealing. Ann Palmer widow of my late uncle
Archdale Palmer. My late uncle Henry Palmer. The poor of the congregation of Protestant Dissenters in the Old Jewry, London.

The residue to my son William Finch Palmer and the child or children wherewith my wife is now "Ensient." The said Nathaniel Balston
Esq. and my said brother Thomas Palmer to be executors as to my estate
in New England and the said Beeston Long, Henry Norris and William
Palmer, as to the estate in England or any other parts except New England.

Lisle, 157.

[4 Beeston Long was a West India merchant (see memoir of him in Gentleman's
Magazine, 1785). One of his sons was created Baron Farnborough, and from one
of his daughters descend the Prescotts baronets.—J. C. C. SMITH.]

THOMAS SMYTH the elder of Aldermanbury, London, Esq. 24 February
1665, proved 13 June 1666. My two younger sons, Henry and Thomas
Smith. My eldest son John Smith, with my consent, did marry Mary,
one of the daughters of Sir Edmond Wright, knight, late Alderman of the

PALMER OF MARSTON, CO. STAFFORD.

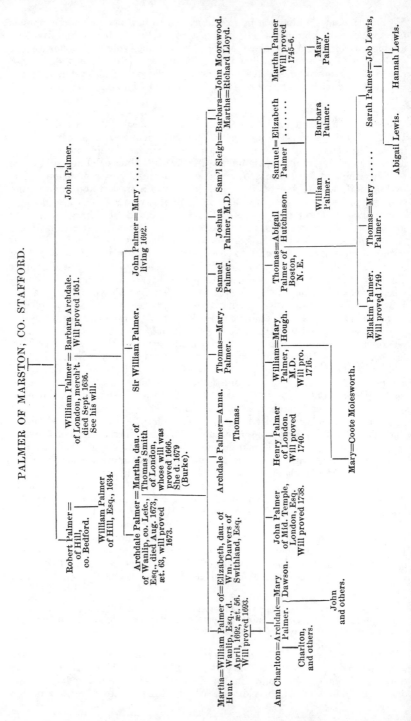

City of London deceased. My daughter Jane was married unto William Gore Esq; My daughter Martha was married unto Archdale Palmer Esq.; Elizabeth, Margaret and Anne Smyth, three of the daughters of my said son John Smith, not yet married. My grandchild Jane Bennett and her father, Sir Humphry Bennett, knight. My brother in Law John Robinson Esq. and my brother William Robinson. The poor of St. Margaret Moyses parish in Friday Street, where I was born and christened. To Mr Edmond Callamy, late minister of Aldermanbury Church, and to Dr. Walker, now minister &c. My three sons to be executors. Mico, 104.

[The Arms of this family of Palmer may be thus described: Ar. two bars Sa., charged with three trefoils slipped, of the field. In Chief a greyhound courant, of the second, collared Or.

Crest: On a mount Vert a greyhound sejant Sa., gorged with a Collar Or, rimmed Gu., and charged on the shoulder with a trefoil slipped Az.

The pedigree on the opposite page is based on those in Burke's Landed Gentry and the Visitation of London 1633-34 (Harl. So. Pub.), which, by the way, differ as to the name of the father of William Palmer of London.

I have many notes relating to the Archdale Family, which I shall send for publication later on.—H. F. Waters.]

I, Thomas Palmer of the Parish of St James, in the Island of Barbadoes, Gentleman, being bound on a voyage to Barbadoes &c. &c., whereas my brothers and sisters are already well provided for, in and by, my Father's will and I am engaged to marry Mrs. Mary Wethread of Boston, Spinster, daughter of Mrs. Dorothy Wethread, widow &c. &c., 18 Sept. 1733— Proved Oct. 27, 1740.—No. 7508, Suffolk Probate Papers.

[The above abstract is furnished by John C. J. Brown, Esq., who adds this note. Luke Vardy who kept the Royal Exchange Tavern on King St., was a witness to the will, and the name of Wethered will be recognized as belonging to another inn-keeper of the time. In Vardy's house Benj. Woodbridge began the war of words which led to his death by the hands of Henry Phillips; it was noted as a place of assemblage for gaming and drinking, and possibly this will of Thomas Palmer was obtained by a black-mail game of the olden time, which undoubtedly resulted in nothing. It will be noticed that seven years had elapsed before it was offered for probate, and there seems to have been nothing more done about it.]

John Chamberlaine of London, gentleman, 18 June 1627, proved 13 March 1627. To be buried in the parish of St. Olaves in the Old Jury, where I was born and christened and where my father, my mother, my brother Robert and other friends are interred. "My funerall I would haue performed wth as little trouble and charge as maibee answearable to the still and quiett course I haue allwaies sought to followe in my life time." To the poor of that parish five pounds and to the poor of St. Mary Aldermanbury ten pounds. To poor prisoners at Ludgate ten pounds, in the Counter in the Poultry five pounds, in the Counter in Woodstreet five pouds, the poor distracted people in Bedlam five pounds. To the Right Honorable the Lord Carleton, Baron of Imbercourt, a basin and ewer of silver of one hundred ounces or thereabouts, to the value of thirty pounds. To Lady Winwood, late the wife of Sr Ralph Winwood, knight,[1] principal Secretary to King James, and to the Lady Fanshawe, late wife to Sir Henry Fanshawe, knight, to each of them a basin and ewer of silver to the same value of thirty pounds. To Sir William Borles, knight (the elder), a ring of gold of forty shillings. To my sister Poole a ring of gold of forty shillings. To Mr Alexander Williams, of the Pipe Office, and to his wife, to each of them a ring of gold of forty shillings. To Mr Dudley Carleton, son of George

Carleton Esq., a ring &c.   To Mrs Anne Smith, sister to Dr. Gilbert and wife to ———— Smith, gentleman, a ring &c.   To my nephew S^{ir} Thomas Stewkeley, knight, two hundred pounds and to his eldest son Sir Hugh Stewkeley, knight and Baronet, and to his second son Thomas, to each of them twenty pounds.   To my niece Lady Drewrie, late wife of S^{ir} Henry Drewry, twenty pounds.   To my nephews Edmond, John, Zachary, Francis, George, sons of my sister Windham deceased, and to my niece the Lady Stroode, their sister, to each of them twenty pounds.   To my cousin Edmund Windham (eldest son of my nephew Thomas Windham) twenty pounds.   To my god-daughter Rebecca Tothill, daughter of my cousin Tothill, widow, dwelling in the parish of St. Giles without Cripplegate, twenty pounds.   To Anne,[2] late wife to my brother George Chamberlain deceased, and now wife to John Poole Esq., alderman of the City of London, an annuity or yearly rent of fifty pounds for the term of her natural life, to be issuing out of all that my manor or lordship of Suttonn Gannocke in the County of Lincoln and out of all my lands, tenements and hereditaments in Suttonn Gannocke, in said County of Lincoln, during her natural life.   I do give and bequeath unto her, the said Anne Poole, in lieu and recompence of one annuity &c., of fifty pounds pr annum heretofore usually paid unto her the said Anne by my late brother Richard Chamberlain deceased, in consideration of accounts cleared between my said brothers George and Richard, as being joint executors of the last Will & Testament of my late brother Robert Chamberlain Esq. deceased, one annuity &c of forty pounds &c.   I give also to the said Mrs Alice Carleton five hundred pounds and my inlaid cabinet that usually standeth upon the low chest near my bedside, with all that shall be in it at the time of my decease, and whatsoever she hath else of mine in her custody; and this I do in regard of the sincere good will and honest affection I bear her and of the true and long continued friendship between us.   To my nephew Thomas Windham of Hensforde in the County of Somerset Esq., all that manor of Minsterworth in the County of Gloucester and the manor of Etloe in the same County and two hundred pounds.   To John Cuffe, sometime servant to my brother Richard Chamberlain, twenty pounds and one of my parts or shares in Bermudas or Summer Islands.   Another part or share in the same Islands I give & bequeath to my servant Richard Reeve, also forty pounds and all my wearing apparel if he be in my service at the time of my decease.   To all the servants that shall be in my nephew Hugh Windham's house, at the time of my decease, to each forty shillings.   To my nephew Hugh Windham and his heirs forever my manor or lordship of Suttonn Gannocke &c (charged with the several annuities) as likewise all other lands that I shall leave undisposed or quillets or houses in Greenwich, Sollihill, Studlie, or elsewhere, and likewise all my parts and shares, title and interest that I shall have at the time of my decease in the Bermudaes or Sommer Islands or in Virginia, to him and his heirs forever.   He to be executor.

Wit: Antho: Ouldfield, Law. Chambers, John Burton, Richard Reeue.

Barrington, 25.

Sententia pro confirmatione etc. etc., in judicio inter Hugonem Wyndham, etc., et Dnm̃ Thomam Stewklie militem Dnãm Susanam Drewrie Thom. Wyndham armigerum Johan. Wyndham Franciscum Wyndham et Georg^{m} Wyndham generosos necnon Dominam Margaretam Strowde nepotes et neptes ex sorore ac proximos consanguineos etc. ———— 26 June 1628.

Barrington, 61.

[John Chamberlain, the testator, seems to have been a son of Richard Chamberlain, " alderman and sherif of London & of Anne his wife da. & heire of Robert Downes of Yalding in Kent, gent." Elizabeth, sister of the testator, married Hugh Stewkley or Stukeley. Their son, Sir Thomas, knt., and their grandson, Sir Hugh, bart., are named in the will. Their daughter Susan married Sir Hugh Drewry, knt., and she is named in the will. Margery Chamberlain, another sister of the testator, married Edmund Windham of Kenesford, co. Somerset, whose pedigree is given in the Visitation of London, Publications of the Harleian Society, vol. 17, page 357. The arms and crest of Robert Chamberlain, brother of the testator, are given in the above volume on the same page. See also Burke's Extinct Baronetage, ed. 1844, page 311.

The names of Richard and John Chamberlain are found early in New England. At a later date, 1681 to 1686, Richard Chamberlain was secretary of the Province of New Hampshire. He was the author of "Lithobolia," London, 1698.—EDITOR.

¹ Sir Ralph Winwood, buried at St. Bartholomew the Less, London, Sept. 30, 1617; his widow buried there Sept. 28, 1659.—J. C. C. SMITH.

² Mrs. Anne Poole was the daughter and heiress of Lawrence Overton of London. She married, first, George Chamberlain; second, alderman Poole of London; and third, Sir John Ramsden of Byrom and Longley, Yorkshire, knt., ancest⌐r of the Ramsdens baronets. (See Betham's Baronetage, vol. 3, page 93, a⌐d Foster's London Marriage Licences, pp. 259 and 1110.)—EDITOR.]

Wᴵᴸᴸᴹ TARBOXE of par. Lowton, Bucks, husbandman, dat. Mch. 20, 1562, p. Mch. 21, 1563 (Arch. Bucks.) Son-in-law Wm. Line (living), Luce Line (unmarᵈ). Isabell Line, Brygett Line, "their father's legacis Wiᴵᴸᵐ Line lette of Lowton." Wife Agnes.

THOS. TARBOX of Mentmore, yeoman, dat. Oct. 10, 1636, p. Mch. 16, 1648 (? 7-8, or 8-9) (Arch. Bucks). Brother Wm. T. & his 3 sons 1ˢ. each, brother Richᵈ. T. & his 4 childⁿ, Henry, Mary, Elizᵗʰ & Joane, 1ˢ. each. Sister Agnes Emerton, £6; her son Richᵈ. E. £5. Sister Sarah Carter, her childⁿ. Robᵗ. Wm. & Sara, also her dau. Elizᵗʰ C. & her son John C., Thos. Curtis, eldᵗ. son of said Sara C.

ALICE TARBOX of Mentmore, widow, dat. Feb. 1, 1628, p. Feb. 11, 1631-2 (Arch. Bucks). Dau. Agnes Emerton, her son Ric. E., dau. Sara Carter, Thos. Curtise, Elizᵗʰ. Carter, Robᵗ. Carter & his father, Wᵐ. Carter, John Carter, my cosen Sarah Carter, my son Wm. his three sons, son Richᵈ. & his 3 childⁿ., son John T.

THOMAS TARBOX of Mentmore, yeoman, dat. Sep. 30, 1613, p. Sep. 28, 1614 (Arch. Bucks). Thos. Curtice, 20ˢ, each of Wm. Tarbox childⁿ, Annis my daur's childⁿ., my dau. Saraes childⁿ., son John, Wife ——.

GEORGE TARBOX of St. Peter's, Herts, milner, dat. Dec. 27, 1641, p. Feb. 18, 1641-2 (12 Cambell). Eldᵗ. dau. Mary, dau. Sarah, dau. Ellen, dau. Sarah Newton, dau. Hannah Newton, son Thos. Newton, dau-in-law Sarah Newton, brother Joseph T.

RICHᵈ. TARBOX of Dunton, Bucks, yeoman, dat. Sep. 8, 1655, p. Oct. 14, 1658 (551 Wootton). To wife Elizᵗʰ, Summerleyes Close, etc. at Mentmore for life, Remʳ. to my grandchild Richard T., grandchⁿ Richᵈ. Miller, Richᵈ. Wigg & Richᵈ. Simpson, Richᵈ. Carter, Mary Chandler, grandchild Elizᵗʰ. Tarbox sister of said Richᵈ.

THOMAS TARBOXE of Brockhampton, Hereford, 1653 (237 Brent). Wife Ann, daurs. Margᵗ. T. Ellenor & Alice, son Thos. T.

WILLIAM TARBOX the elder of Mentmore, Bucks, yeoman, being aged, dat. Mch. 6, 1658, p. May 14, 1662 (Arch. Bucks). Grandchild Thomas T., grandchild William T., Rebecca T., grandchild Susana T., grandchild

Rebecca T., my sister Sarah's daughters, sons Thomas T. & Edward T. Executors.

THOMAS TARBOX of Mentmore, yeoman, dat. Sep. 8, 1673, p. Oct. 30, 1673 (Arch. Bucks). Grandson Tho⁸. Glenister, son of Wᵐ. & Susanna G. of Piddlestone, Bucks, grandson Wᵐ. Glenister, granddau. Mary Tarbox, the 2 eldᵗ. sons of Tho⁸. Stevens of Cheddington, Bucks, godson Tho⁸. Tayler of Soulbury, Bucks. Son Wᵐ. T. my house etc. at Mentmore, also lands in Cheddington field, son Thos. T., son-in-law Wᵐ. Glenister, Kinsman Mʳ. Richᵈ. T. of Cubblington, Bucks.

WILLIAM TARBOX of Mentmore, husbandman, dat. Dec. 20, 1658, p. Feb. 12, 1658–9 (112 Pell). Wife Anne, £420, brother Edward, brother Thomas, Thomas son of said Thomas, under 21. Rebecca T. dau. of said Thomas, £5 at 21, Susanna T. dau. of said Thos., Wᵐ. T. son of said Tho⁸. Residue of houses, etc., to brother Edward and he Executor.

THOMAS TARBOX of Mentmore, Bucks, yeoman, dat. Sep. 6, 1564, p. May 7, 1565 (Arch. Bucks). Wife Elizabeth, son Thomas T.

EDWARD TARBOX of . . . . . . Admoñ Arch. Bucks, ... 1665 to (Thomas?) Tarbox, brother (perished).

[The preceding abstracts of Tarbox wills were contributed by a London friend of Mr. Waters, who had read in the REGISTER for January last (vol. 42, pp. 27–8), the remarks of the late Rev. Increase N. Tarbox, D.D., on the origin of his surname. These abstracts show that the name in its present form was found in England, three quarters of a century before John Tarbox settled in Massachusetts. Dr. Tarbox was in North Carolina when these abstracts arrived, but copies of the earliest ones were sent to him. He died a few days after his return, but expressed to me his gratification at receiving them, stating that he was more inclined to the opinion that Tarbox was of English origin, and not unlikely a corruption of the Lancashire name, Tarbock or Torback.—EDITOR.]

GEORGE WAY of Dorchester in the County of Dorset, merchant, 30 September 1641 and signed 1 October 1641, proved 3 December 1641. I give unto Sarah, my loving wife, the house, burgage and tenement wherein I now dwell situate in East side of the North Street in Dorchester aforesaid, with all outhouses and appurtenances thereunto belonging, and all my houses, burgages and tenements, garden and ground in Bridport in the said County of Dorset, to hold the same unto my said wife during her life. And from and after my wife's decease and from and after Eliezer Way, my son, shall attain the age of six and twenty years I do devise and bequeath my said lease, burgage and tenement with the appurtenances in Dorchester aforesaid unto my said son and the heirs of his body. But in case my said son shall die without heirs of his body, or for want of such heirs, then I give the same unto all my daughters and their heirs. And in case my said wife shall die before my said son shall attain his age of six and twenty years then I do give and bequeath my said house, burgage and tenement in Dorchester unto my loving and dear friends, Mʳ. William Derbie, Mʳ. Richard Savage and Mʳ. Thomas Clench of Dorchester aforesaid and Mʳ. Walter Baily of Bridport until my son shall attain that age. And from and after my said wife's decease I give and devise my said houses, burgage, garden and ground in Bridport aforesaid unto my said friends, in trust for and towards the raising the legacies hereby given to my younger two daughters &c. &c. Then the remainder of my term unto my said son, if he live to attain the age of six and twenty years or be married, or if he die before then I give the same amongst all my said daughters. To my daughter Sarah one hundred pounds, to my daughter Mary fourscore pounds, to my daughter Elizabeth threescore and ten pounds, and to my daughter Martha threescore pounds, all payable at their several ages of four and twenty years, except my said daughter Martha's legacy which I appoint to be paid as the same may be raised out of my said houses &c. in Bridport.

And, whereas there is of my estate four and thirty pounds in money in Thomas Ford's[1] hands in New England and in the hands of Roger Clap and Stephen Tayler in New England, "the provenew" of fifty pounds worth of goods and divers moneys and goods of mine in the hands of Henry Cogan there, and other cattle and corn that I have in New England aforesaid, I do appoint that all the said moneys and goods or the provenue thereof, shall go and be employed towards the raising of my said daughters' legacies, and also such money and provenue of the benefit of my plantation at Beshipscot in New England, which is due to me from my brother in law Thomas Purchase. And I do give and devise all my moiety of that plantation, houses, land and grounds in New Beshipscot aforesaid and my lot in Dorchester in New England aforesaid and all other my lands and grounds in New England unto my said son Eleazer and the heirs of his body; and for want of such heirs then I give the same to all my daughters and their heirs. All the residue &c. I give to Sara my wife whom I ordain sole executrix.

Will: Derbie a witness.

Proved at London by Sarah Way, widow and executrix, in the presence of John White, clerk, by virtue of a commission &c.

Evelyn, 155.

[George Way, the testator, was one of the forty-one persons who subscribed* in May, 1628, to the stock of the company which obtained a grant from the Council of Plymouth under which the Massachusetts Colony was settled. On the 16th of June, 1632, he and Thomas Purchase obtained from the Council of Plymouth a grant of certain lands in New England called the River "Bishopscotte, and all that bounds and limits the main land adjoining the river to the extent of two miles."† Thomas Purchase is called by Way in the above will his brother-in-law. It is probable that Way either married Purchase's sister or his wife's sister. Purchase had settled on the lands about 1628, a few years before the grant was obtained, somewhere within the limits of the present town of Brunswick, Maine.‡ The tract of land is sometimes known as the Way and Purchase Grant, but more often as the Pejepscot Purchase.

George[1] Way's son Eleazer settled in New England and died at Hartford, Ct., July 12, 1687. It seems from the will that Eleazer had four sisters, Sarah,[2] Elizabeth,[2] Mary[2] and Martha,[2] but I find no evidence that any of them came to this country. Eleazer Way, the heir and only son of George Way, brought suit Oct. 10, 1657, against Thomas Purchase his father's partner. A long litigation ensued. Way's suit was settled in 1683 by the sale of the tract by him and the heirs of Purchase to Richard Wharton. During the litigation with Purchase, Eleazer Way was in Boston, when he married Mary ———. His name is found on the Boston records as early as 1659. He was admitted freeman at Hartford, May 13, 1669. He left five children: 1, *Mary;*[3] 2, *Sarah,*[3] m. Ichabod Wells; 3, *Lydia,*[3] m. Jabez Whittlesey; 4, *Elizabeth,*[3] m. Joseph Wells; 5, *Ebenezer.*[3]

Ebenezer[3] Way was a physician and settled at Southold, L. I. He had: 1, *Mary,*[4] m. William Hops or Hobson; 2, *Althea,*[4] or *Esther,*[4] m. Nathaniel Overton; 3, *Josiah;*[4] 4, *Daniel;*[4] 5, *Eleazer.*[4] The last named Eleazer[4] had an only daughter *Ann,*[5] who died unmarried at Southold in 1821. She was the only living descendant of George[1] Way who then bore his surname. For further genealogical details and other particulars relative to the litigation above referred to, see my pamphlet, "George Way and his Descendants," Boston, 1887.—CHARLES GRANVILLE WAY.

---

* See the agreement, with the names of the subscribers, in Felt's Salem, Vol. 1. pp. 508-9.
† Sainsbury's Calendar of Colonial State Papers, Vol. I. p. 152.
‡ Wheeler's History of Brunswick, Topsham and Harpswell, p. 7.

Eleazer Way, son of George, calls Purchase his uncle in a release, dated June 1, 1669, by which he makes over to his "honoured vnkle, Mr. Thomas Purchas, of Pudgipscott," and his heirs forever, all right said Eleazer had in the one half of the Plantation, "in Pudgipscott," by the above said Will of his father, George Way, of Dorchester, "or any other wayes;" giving full power to his said uncle to sell or dispose of it, provided, that after said sale, one half of the effects of it shall be delivered in specie to said Eleazer, or his heirs or assigns. See extracts from Howard's Notarial Records, REG. xliii. 149.—W. B. TRASK.]

[1] Thomas Ford and family came from England to Dorchester, in the year 1630; and he was made freeman the same year. He had four daughters. Abigail married John Strong, the ancestor of Gov. Caleb Strong, Joanna became the wife of Roger Clap whom she married Nov. 6, 1633, when in the 17th year of her age; they lived together in the conjugal relation 57 years, and had 14 children, the youngest of whom, named Supply, Judge Sewall, in his Journal, styles "a very desirable man." Another daughter of Thomas Ford wedded Aaron Cooke; Hepzibah married Richard Lyman.

Thomas Ford, Ensign Stoughton, William Phelps and William Gaylord, were appointed by the General Court, March 4, 1633–4, "to set the bounds between Boston and Roxbury." Thomas Ford had a grant of land in Dorchester, June 27, 1636, and not far from that time, it may be, went to Windsor. On the 16th of January, 1636, old style, two acres of land in Dorchester, on M^r. Ludlow's neck, were "ordered" to John Holland, it being land formerly granted to Thomas Ford; also "a little plott of marsh," without inclosure, Holland paying said Ford "the charges he hath been at in ditching." Mr. Ford was an active and useful man, both in Dorchester and Windsor, and his name appears a number of times on the records of those towns. In 1633, the Town of Dorchester ordered that a fort be built "upon the Rocke, above Mr. Johnson's," and a double rate, to that end, be paid to Thomas Ford and Roger Clap "at the house of the said Thommas Ford." While in Dorchester he was one of the twelve men selected by the plantation for ordering their affairs. He was chosen to that office June 27, 1636; constable in Windsor in 1654; approved to be made freeman at the latter place, Oct. 4, 1669 (REGISTER, v. 247); was on the Grand Jury in 1662. He had a grant of 50 acres of land at Massacoe, now Simsbury, Conn., "whereof forty-four acres had been improved by plowing and mowing, as it was measured by Matthew Graunt," ancestor of the late President Grant.

Mr. Ford married for his second wife, Ann Scott, widow of Thomas Scott, of Hartford, Conn., Nov. 7, 1644. REGISTER, xiii. 53. He subsequently removed to Northampton, Mass., where he died Nov. 9, 1676.—W. B. TRASK.]

JOHN BOYS, bound for Virginia, 7 August 1649, proved last of May 1650. To my sister two hundred pounds. To my uncle & aunt Boys. To my Aunt Jaggar and her daughter. To Uncle Sea. To my cousin Harrison. To the rest of my uncle Boys's children. To my cousin Gasen and his wife. To my three cousins, Maior Boys's sons, that live in London. To Mrs. Ann Berisford of Chidgwell, Essex, Mr Thomas Allen, Em Paine, John Beaumont, Allen Arundell and Robert Bowrne. My executors to be my uncle Boys and brother Thomas Maior. Wit: John Beaumont and Em Paine (by mark).   Pembroke, 59.

[In the first Legislative Assembly of Virginia, in 1619, was a John Boys. Chene or Cheney Boys or Boise, born 1586, was living in Virginia in 1624; was Burgess for Shirley Hundred Island, Oct. 1629, March 1629–30 and Sept. 1632. Neill (*Virginia Carolorum*, Appendix, p. 408) says that he was probably of the family of John Boys above, and also a relative of Captain Isaac Bargrave, the first person with Captain Ward in 1618, to establish a private plantation in Virginia. Doctor Bargrave, Dean of Canterbury, was the brother of Isaac, and the successor of John Boys (who had married his sister) in the Deanery. The following grants of land are on record in the *Virginia Land Registry:* Hannah, daughter and heir of Luke Boyse of Henrico county, 300 acres in the same county Nov. 11, 1635; Cheney Boyse, 1550 acres in Charles City county, May 31, 1636, Book No. 1, pp. 351, 352. Luke Boyse was a Burgess, 1623–4. Christopher Boyse was a land owner in Harwood's Creek, Warwick county, 1635, and was alive in 1652.—ROBERT A. BROCK, of Richmond, Va.]

JOSEPH THOROWGOOD of London, merchant, 11 October 1683, proved 19 January 1684. To my brother William Thorowgood, of London, merchant, the use, benefit and profit of all my plantation and lands in Carolina beyond the seas and of such servants, utensils, cattle, stock and things that I shall have thereon at the time of my decease, and all my other lands, tenements &c. &c. for and during the term of his natural life; then to such son of my said brother William, lawfully begotten, as my said brother shall think most fit to enjoy the same; for default of such son, then to such son of my loving brother Benjamin Thorowgood Esq, as my said brother Benjamin shall think most fit &c.; failing such, then to such son of my sister Elizabeth Ashby as my said sister, or my brother-in-law John Ashby shall think most fit &c.; next to such son of my sister Mary Dod as my said sister or my brother in law John Dod shall think most fit. My brother William Thorowgood and the said John Ashby to be the executors.

Wit: John Bookey, Tho: Sandford, Sam: Thorowgood.   Cann, 12.

[Adam Thoroughgood "Gent." was granted 200 acres on Back river in Virginia in 1634 (*Virginia Land Registry*, Book No. 1). He was a brother of Sir John Thoroughgood, Kn't, of Kensington, was born 1602 and came to Virginia in 1621, settling at Kicotan. In a subsequent patent to Captain Adam Thoroughgood it is stated that the grant is made "at the espetiall recommendation of him from their Lordships and others of his Majesty's Most honble Privie Councill." He was commissioner and Burgess for Elizabeth City county 1629, and Burgess in 1630. About 1634 he moved to Lynhaven Bay in the present county of Princess Anne; was a member of the Virginia Council 1637, and in the same year President of the County Court of Lower Norfolk; died in the spring of 1640; married Sarah ——, and had issue: i. Lt. Col. Adam, Burgess for Lower Norfolk Co., Oct 1666, and High Sheriff 1669. ii. Elizabeth, married Jacob Chandler of Maryland, a member of the Council. iii. Sarah. The representatives of these include among others the names of Lawson, Moseley, Smith, Keeling, Nimmo, Haynes, Sayer, Harper, Jamieson, Singleton and McPheeters.—R. A. BROCK.]

HENRY HARTWELL late of Virginia Esq., now of the parish of Stepney als Stebonheath, 3 July 1699, with codicil dated 4 July 1699, proved 2 August 1699. To Nicholas Merryweather,[2] nephew of my late wife, two hundred pounds. To Francis Merryweather, another nephew, one hundred pounds. To Thomas Merryweather, another, one hundred pounds. To Jane Browne, wife of William Browne and niece to my late wife, one hundred pounds. To Elizabeth Browne, daughter to Coll. William Browne and niece to my late wife, one hundred pounds. To my kinsman John Spratly one hundred pounds. To my kinswoman Mary Sanders one hundred pounds (and other personal property). To Elianor Say daughter of Capt. Edward Say one hundred pounds, to be put into the Bank of England until she shall arrive to the age of eighteen or day of marriage; but in case the Bank shall be redeemed before such time that then it shall be put out at the discretion of my executors till the time aforesaid. In case of the death of the said Elianor Say, before she arrive to the age of eighteen or day of marriage then to Anne Say daughter to the above Capt. Edward Say. To Mrs. Susan Say his wife twenty pounds. To the poor of Maidenhead in the County of Berks twenty pounds.

I give and bequeath unto the use of the College of William and Mary in Virginia the sum of fifty pounds. To my niece Mary Hartwell daughter of my late brother William Hartwell[1] three hundred pounds at age of eighteen or day of marriage. To my nephew William Hartwell eldest son of my late brother William four hundred pounds at the age of twenty one. To John Hartwell the youngest son four hundred pounds at age of twenty one.

If the said Mary, William or John or either of them die before they arrive at their respective ages &c. the portion of such shall be equally divided to the survivors of them and their brother Henry Hartwell. To my coachman William Anderson five pounds. To my maid servant Isabella Leigh ten pounds. To my nephew Henry Hartwell, the second son of my late brother William, all my land in Surrey County, over against James City in Virginia, and to his heirs forever. To Thomas Lane and Mary his wife, each five pounds to buy them rings. To Mrs. Sarah Perry wife of M[r]. Richard Perry five pounds to buy her a ring. To Micajah Perry and Richard Perry in consideration of their trouble in the management of the Trusts fifty pounds each. And it is my express will that my executors do send for my said nephew Henry Hartwell out of Virginia to England and that they give him the best education they can till he shall so arrive to the age of one and twenty years. If my said nephew Henry Hartwell shall not live to attain the age of one and twenty years my will then is that my land in Surrey County &c. shall be to my nephew William Hartwell and his heirs forever. And all other my personal estate, in case of my nephew Henry Hartwell's death if he die before he attain the age of one and twenty years, I give as follows. I then give unto the College of William and Mary in Virginia, more, one hundred pounds for and towards the founding Scholarships in the said College, and I do hereby desire the Governors of the said College to see it faithfully laid out to that end.

The residue of the personal estate, in case of the death of my nephew Henry Hartwell, I give to my nephews William and John Hartwell and my niece Mary Hartwell and to Nicholas, Francis and Thomas Merryweather and Jane the wife of William Browne and Elizabeth the daughter of Colonel William Browne, and John Spratly and Mary Sanders and Elianor Say, equally to be divided among them.

I appoint my trusty and well beloved friends Micajah Perry and Richard Perry of London, merchants, executors &c.

Wit: Priscilla Jones, Anna Haddock, Elizabeth Crawley.

In a codicil a bequest of twenty pounds is made to Robert Wise, servant to Micajah Perry, for several services done.

Wit: Thomas Lane, Isabella Lee.   Pett, 134.

[Henry Hartwell received the following grants of land in Virginia: 730 acres in James City county, May 13, 1679 (*Virginia Land Registry*, Book No. 6, p. 690); 900 acres in Charles City county, March 30, 1682–3; 1960 acres in Surry county, April 20, 1687; 2½ acres in James City April 20, 1689 (Book No. 7, pp. 234, 595, 901.) He was clerk of the Council of Virginia 1677–1679, and married in or before 1685, ——, relict of Col[o]. William White. In the same year Henry Randolph of Henrico county is recorded as his attorney.

[1] In 1675, according to the York county Va. records, William Hartwell had married the widow of Richard Barnes, deceased. Captain William Hartwell was Justice of the Peace for James City county 1687–8. William, son of Gideon and Martha Macon of New Kent county, Virginia, married, Sept. 24, 1719, Mary, daughter of William Hartwell. John Hartwell patented land in York county, Virginia, in 1642. Harrison Hartwell of Brunswick county, Virginia, was alive in 1728. The name Hartwell is perpetuated as a Christian name in the Harrison, Cocke, Macon and other families of Virginia.

[2] Nicholas Meriwether, "Gent." of Hanover county, Virginia, was granted 400 acres of land in that county, Feb. 18, 1722. (*Virginia Land Registry*, Book No. 11, p. 161.) He and William, David, Thomas, Nicholas, Jr., and Mildred Meriwether received subsequently to and inclusive of the year 1741, numerous and extensive grants of land in the counties of Hanover, Louisa, New Kent, Spotsylvania and Goochland. The descendants of Nicholas Meriwether include the well-known Virginia names of Walker, Rives, Hughes, Nelson and others.—R. A. BROCK.]

FRANCIS WYMAN, of the parish of Westmill in the County of Hertford husbandman, 15 September 1658, proved 14 February 1658. I do give and bequeath unto Jane my wife the full sum of ten shillings of lawful English money to be paid unto her by mine executor presently after my burial. Item I do give and bequeath unto my two sons Francis Wyman and John Wyman wch are beyond sea ten pounds apiece of lawful English money to be paid unto them by mine executor if they be in want and come over to demand the same. I do give and bequeath unto my sister Susan Huitt widow the full sum of forty shillings of lawful English money to be likewise paid to her by mine executor within one whole year next coming after my decease. Item I do give and bequeath unto Thomas Wyman my son all that my messuage or tenement wherein I now dwell with all the other buildings, housen and outhousing thereunto belonging, and all my lands, orchard, garden and yards, with all and singular their appurtenances whatsoever, to him and his heirs forever. All the rest of my goods &c. to my said son Thomas, whom I appoint executor.   Pell, 116.

[Francis and John Wyman, sons of the testator, were among the earliest settlers of Charlestown Village, afterwards named Woburn, Mass. They signed the Town Orders Dec. 18, 1640 (see Sewall's Woburn, pp. 529–30). Francis Wyman was born ab. 1617; m. 1st, Judith Peirce of Woburn, Jan. 30, 1645; m. 2d, Abigail, dau. of William Read of Woburn, Oct, 2, 1650. He was a tanner. He died Nov. 28, 1699, aged 82. Lieut. John Wyman, also a tanner, was born ab. 1621; m. Nov. 5, 1644, Sarah, dau. of Miles Nutt of Woburn. He died May 9, 1684, and his widow m. Aug. 25, 1684, Thomas Fuller of Woburn. See REGISTER, iii. 33–8, for descendants and other details.—EDITOR.]

ANTHONY COPP, of Honeley in the County of Warwick yeoman, 16 January 1653, proved at Westminster 13 June 1654. To my kinswoman Hannah Edwards forty shillings. To Denney my wife five pounds, the which my desire is and so I will and appoint, that she shall, within three years next after my decease, pay or cause to be paid unto my kinsman Thomas Copp. I give and bequeath to my kinsman Richard Heath, for the use of his children, the sum of seven pounds ten shillings, to be paid within one year next after my decease. I give and bequeath to my kinsman Richard Tippin, for the use of his children which he hath by my kinswoman Elizabeth his wife, the sum of ten pounds, to be paid within one year after my decease. I give and bequeath unto my kinsman John Ward the sum of eight pounds, for the use of his children, to be paid within one year next after my decease.

Item I give and bequeath unto my brother William Copp who is in New England the sum of six pounds for the use of his children, the which I devise and will appoint to be sent over or conveyed unto him by my executrix so soon as may be after my decease. I give and bequeath to my brother Walter Copp, for the use of his children, all my lease of the house and land in Honeley wherein Richard Gee liveth and also to his said three children the sum of twenty shillings apiece. I give unto Denney my wife and to her assigns all that my lease and estate and term of years which I have yet to come in the house and lands wherein I dwell in Honeley aforesaid, with remainder among the children of all my brothers to whom I have formerly given legacies before mentioned; that is to say, my cousin Samuel Copps, John Ward for his children, Richard Tippins for his children, Richard Heath for his children, Thomas Copp for his children, Walter Copp for his children and to Mary Busbie for her children, equally to be divided amongst them. And I. do will and appoint and so my will is that my brother Walter Copp and my cousin Samuel Copp and Robert Gardner of Honeley shall have the selling and disposing of the said lease and estate of the house wherein I live and the land belonging thereunto all the residue of years &c. after the decease of Denney my wife.

I give and bequeath unto my kinsman Samuel Copp and unto the said Robert Gardner and Thomas Bakon of —— all that my land, being two closes, lying and being in Haseley in the County of Warwick —— to grant, sell and convey the same for raising of legacies beforementioned.

My brother Walter Copp to be executor, and cousin Samuel Copp, Robert Gardner and Thomas Baken to be overseers.   Alchin, 462.

[William Copp, brother of the testator, settled at Boston and was adm. freeman June 2, 1641. He is probably the William Cope, aged 26, who with Richard Cope, aged 24, perhaps a brother, embarked at London for New England in June, 1635, in the Blessing, John Lecester, master (see REGISTER, xiv. 317). He died March, 1670. "His estate," says Savage, "was in part of that beautiful hill which bore his name." He left posterity.—EDITOR.]

JOHN RAYMENT, in the Ship Friendship of London, on a voyage to Virginia, 2 December 1629, did utter and declare &c. &c. To my kinsman dwelling at Wapping, a servant in my own house, forty shillings. To my mother, dwelling at Poole, ten shillings. To my two sisters, dwelling at Poole, five shillings between them. All the rest to my wife. 2 September 1630, emanavit commissio mariæ Graves als Rayment relictæ etc.

                                                                Scroope, 79.

MARTIN ARCHDALE, citizen and grocer of London 29 October 1597 proved 31 December 1597. To be buried in the parish church of St. Margaret Pattens in London. Sons John, Martin, Robert, Samuel and Daniel. Wife Barbara. Daughters Alice and Sarah Archdale. My good friend Mr Roger Mountagu shall have the order, rule and disposing of my son John, my brother Thomas Archdale shall have the order, rule and government of my sons Martin and Robert, my brother Matthew Archdale shall have the order, rule and government of my sons Samuel and Daniel, and my wife Barbara shall have the ordering, rule and government of my two daughters. My poor sister Elizabeth. My nephew John Archdale, son of Mary Archdale, widow, and his brother Abraham Archdale. My sister Anna Archdale of Oxford widow. The children of my cousin Katherine Browne, daughter of my said sister. My nephew Richard Ripton. The executors to be my son John, when he shall be of the full age of one and twenty years, together with Roger Mountagu, skinner, and my brother Thomas Archdale, draper, citizens of London. A codicil to the above will was subscribed by the testator 12 December 1597.

                                                                Cobham, 114.

MATTHEW ARCHDALE, citizen and draper of London, 14 November 1599, proved 31 December 1599. Five hundred pounds each to Edward More als Archdale, Stredwicke More, Richard Stansfeilde and Mary Stansfeilde. To my cousin Sara Archdale one hundred pounds. To my cousins Mrs. Combs and Mistres Palmer and my cousin Elizabeth Archdale fifty pounds apiece. To my cousin Richard Archdale five hundred pounds. To Edward Browne and his children five hundred pounds. To my brother Thomas one hundred pounds. I discharge my cousin Richard Ripton all the debt he oweth me and I give him five pounds. To my cousin John Archdale of Whetlie thirty pounds. To my cousin Abraham

Archdale forty pounds.   To my cousin Frances Archdale forty pounds and to her other three sisters, Bridget, Margaret, and Barbara, ten pounds apiece. To my cousin Mary daughter of my cousin Combes. To Thomas Beadle ten pounds.   I ordain and make my brother Thomas Archdale sole executor.

Kidd, 95.

THOMAS ARCHDALE, citizen and draper of London, 5 March 1609, with a nuncupative codicil declared about the 14th of November 1611, proved 3 December 1611.   My body to be buried in the parish church of St. Antholins near the body of my first wife.   To my three daughters, Margaret Combe, Sara Sare and Barbara Palmer five hundred marks apiece, one hundred each a year until paid.   One hundred pounds to Archedale Combe, at age of twenty one.   To my grandchild Sara Sare the younger, at her age of twenty years, one hundred pounds.   To my grandchild Jane Sare, at age of twenty years, fifty pounds.   To my grandchild Thomas Sare, at twenty one, fifty pounds. To my grandchild Mary Smyth, at her age of twenty one years, one hundred pounds, so that she be guided and directed by her father and mother, especially touching her marriage.   To the child wherewith my daughter Barbara Palmer is now conceived, if it be a daughter, one hundred pounds, at her age of twenty one; but if it be a son I bequeath the said one hundred pounds to John Palmer, the son of my said daughter Barbara, to be paid at his age of twenty and one years.   To my cousin Abraham Archedale the yearly payment of twenty pounds during the life of the natural mother of said Abraham; also fifty pounds more to be paid to him only by ten pounds a year.   To my cousin Bridget Archedale thirty pounds within six months next after my decease.   To my cousin Richard Ripton forty shillings a year until twenty pounds be paid.   Six pounds thirteen shillings and four pence each to my friend James Colbron and his son Thomas Colbrone.   To my cousin Thomas Archedale, the son of my cousin Richard Archedale, my godson, ten pounds, to be paid at his age of twenty one years. To the two maids which now serve my daughter Barbara five pounds apiece, to be paid unto them the day of their marriage, if they then shall be servants to my said daughter and shall marry by and with the liking and consent of the said Barbara and her husband.   To the poor of St. Antholins five pounds.   To the poor of the parish of Aldermanbury and the parish of Norton in Kent, to each five pounds.   To M[r]. Harlam, pastor of said parish of Aldermanbury, five pounds.   To the poor of St. John's upon Walbrooke forty shillings, and of Whitechapel ten pounds.

My son in law Ady Sare, of the Inner Temple London, Esquire, to be full and sole executor.

Wood, 102.

Thomas Archdale and Mary Clifton marr. 31 Oct. 1568.
Margaret dau. of Thomas Archdale chr. 6 Nov. 1569.
John son of Thomas Archdale chr. 2 Dec. 1571.
Sarah dau. of Thomas Archdale chr. 3 Aug. 1574.
Sarah dau. of Thomas Archdale chr. 1 Apr. 1578.
John son of Thomas Archdale bur. 30 Oct. 1578.
Mary wife of Thomas Archdale bur. 26 Nov. 1578.
Thomas Archdale and Blith Wilfred marr. 29 Dec. 1583.
John Comb and Margaret Archdale marr. 11 Dec. 1587.
Mr. Thomas Archdale from Aldermanbury, bur. 27 Nov. 1611.
Registers of St. Antholins, London.

SAMUEL ARCHDALE 6 June 1617, proved 27 November 1617. Mentions mother Dame Barbara Ayloffe, brothers Martin, Daniel and Robert and sister Sara Archdale.　　　　　　　　　　　Weldon, 113.

ARCHEDALE.

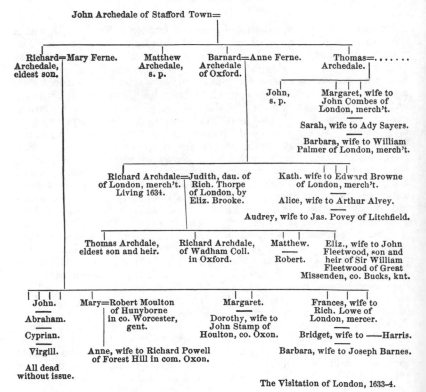

John Archedale of Stafford Town=

Richard=Mary Ferne. Archedale, eldest son.

Matthew Archedale, s. p.

Barnard=Anne Ferne. Archedale of Oxford.

Thomas=....... Archedale.

John, s. p.

Margaret, wife to John Combes of London, merch't.

Sarah, wife to Ady Sayers.

Barbara, wife to William Palmer of London, merch't.

Richard Archedale=Judith, dau. of of London, merch't. | Rich. Thorpe Living 1634. | of London, by | Eliz. Brooke.

Kath. wife to Edward Browne of London, merch't.

Alice, wife to Arthur Alvey.

Audrey, wife to Jas. Povey of Litchfield.

Thomas Archdale, eldest son and heir.

Richard Archdale, of Wadham Coll. in Oxford.

Matthew.

Robert.

Eliz., wife to John Fleetwood, son and heir of Sir William Fleetwood of Great Missenden, co. Bucks, knt.

John.
Abraham.
Cyprian.
Virgill.
All dead without issue.

Mary=Robert Moulton of Hunyborne in co. Worcester, gent.

Anne, wife to Richard Powell of Forest Hill in com. Oxon.

Margaret.
Dorothy, wife to John Stamp of Houlton, co. Oxon.

Frances, wife to Rich. Lowe of London, mercer.
Bridget, wife to ——Harris.
Barbara, wife to Joseph Barnes.

The Visitation of London, 1633-4.

ABRAHAM ARCHDALE of Whately in the Co. of Oxford Esq., 2 August 1631, with codicil of 17 September 1631, proved 14 October 1631. Cousin German Rich[d] Archdale of Dowgate Street, London, merchant. Sisters Margaret Bennett of Oxford, widow, Frances Lowe and Barbara Barnes widow, Anne Powell wife of Richard Powell of Forest Hill, being the only daughter of my sister Mary Moulton. Anne Barnes daughter of my Sister Barbara. The four daughters of my sister Dorothy Stampe, i. e. Margaret Hester, Mary Hall, Elizabeth Stampe and Ursula Stampe. The children of my sister Lowe, viz[t]. Richard Lowe, Mary Pudsey, Elizabeth, Francis and Anne. The two sons of my sister Bridget Blackbourne, viz[t]. William and Richard. Richard Powell, eldest son of my niece Powell. My cousin Thomas Flexney, of Oxford, and his eldest son Francis. My cousin M[rs]. Judith Archdale. Martin and Daniel, sons of Martin Archdale, my uncle late of London, merchant. Dorothy Field, granddaughter of my sister Stampe, and Anne Field, her sister. My uncle Mr. Anthony Ferne of London, gentleman. John Hester son of Margaret Hester. My cousins

M^r. Richard Powell of Forest Hill and Samuel Gardner of the University of Oxon Gent. to be overseers. Richard Archdale sole executor.

16 September 1656 administration *de bonis non*, with the will annexed, was granted to Matthew Archdale, son of Richard Archdale, cousin german, sole executor, &c.   Berkley, 325.

RICHARD ARCHDALE of Cheping Wicombe in the Co. of Bucks : Esq., the last day of May 1638, proved 8 October 1638. My son in law John Fleetwood. My third son Matthew Archdale. My youngest son Robert Archdale. My two grand-children, William and John Fleetwood. My eldest son, Thomas Archdale, his three daughters, Judith, Mary and Susan. My second son Richard Archdale. Household stuff at Whately left unto me by my cousin Abraham Archdale. My brother in law Mr Edward Browne. My cousin Mrs Barbara Rotheram. My cousin Low, James Povey and his sisters Katherine Povey and Jane Povey. My brother in law Mr. Arthur Alvy and my sister Alvy, his wife and his son Bernard Alvy, wife Judith Archdale and son in law John Fleetwood to be executors.
Lee, 120.

WILLIAM ANDROWES of Tottenham, Co. Middlesex, gentleman, conveys, 23 September 1589, to Thomas Archdale, citizen and draper of London, and to Barbara Archdale certain property in Tottenham, referring to Roger Androwes, grandfather, and John Androwes, father of the said William.
Claus Rolls, 31 Eliz.: Part 29.

MARGARET PRESCOTT of the parish of St Thomas the Apostle, London, widow, 1 November 1639, proved 3 January 1639. To my sister's daughter Margaret Parker and her husband Thomas Parker and all their five children. To my son in law Stephen Burton and my daughter Martha his wife. To my son in law William Prescott and my daughter Susan his wife, my son in law John Marvin and my daughter his wife, my son in law Humfry Thornbury, my cousin James Anderton, my cousin Thomas Drinkwater and Elizabeth his wife, my cousin Thornbury and Hester his wife, Mrs Wightman in Cheapside, Mr Cooper my loving pastor and his wife, my neighbor Mrs Kayd, my neighbor Mrs Tore, Mrs Darbyshire, Mrs Olive and her son Gabriel, my neighbor Townesend's son William Townesend and his daughter Joane Townesend, my neighbor Holt, Robert Walpole clerk of the parish of St Thomas the Apostle and Richard Vaughan the sexton, Simon Leeson, my cousin Elizabeth Hooker. My sister Luce Parker to be residuary legatee and executrix.   Coventry, 5.

Administration on the estate of ARTHUR SLADE formerly of the parish of St Nicholas, Deptford, in the County of Kent, but at Portsmouth, New Hampshire deceased, was granted 7 October 1747 to Elizabeth Slade his widow relict &c. Bond of four hundred pounds. Thomas Lawrence of the parish of St Paul's Deptford, gardener, and Isaac Inglefield of the parish of St Nicholas, Deptford, shipwright, bondsmen.
Admon Act Book, P. C. C.

[Is anything known about the above, or his children? He is said to have been a shipwright and Isaac Inglefield his servant.—H. F. W.]

EDWARD SHRIMPTON, of Bednall Green, in the County of Middlesex, merchant, 30 September 1661. A commission was issued 6 November 1661, to Elizabeth Shrimpton, widow and residuary legatee, during the absence of Henry Shrimpton, executor, dwelling in the parts beyond the seas. The will was proved by the executor 18 March, 1662.

To my son Jonathan six hundred & fifty pounds, to be paid him at Boston in New England, presently after my decease. To my daughter Mary Shrimpton (the same sum) at Boston &c. They not to dispose of their portions, nor of themselves in marriage, without the knowledge and advice of my loving brother Mr Henry Shrimpton. To my three sons, Ebenezer, Epaphras and Silas, each four hundred pounds apiece, at their respective ages of twenty-one years. To my daughters, Elizabeth and Lydia, each four hundred pounds, at twenty-one or day of marriage. The two thousand pounds given to my five youngest children to remain in the hands of my brother Henry, to be improved, he allowing my wife, during widowhood, a competent proportion of the improvement towards their education. To the Church of Christ whereof Mr John Sympson is pastor ten pounds. To Mr Wentworth Day, and Mr Richard Goodgroome, each, five pounds apiece. To the Church of Christ which use to meet by Allhallows by the Wall ten pounds. To my wife Elizabeth Shrimpton the residue. My brother Henry Shrimpton to be the executor. Alderman William Peake to be overseer. Wit: William Booker, Thomas Norman.   May, 186.

EBENEZER SHRIMPTON, of the parish of St Katherine Cree Church London, haberdasher, 23 January 1678–9, proved 13 February 1678 by Epaphras Shrimpton, brother & executor. To brother William Benlowes ten shillings and to sister Mary Benlowes his wife, ten shillings; to brother Silas Shrimpton ten shillings; to sister Elizabeth Shrimpton ten shillings; to sister Lydia Shrimpton ten shillings; the rest to brother Epaphras Shrimpton who is to see my legacies and debts paid and funeral discharged, and I make and ordain him to be my full and sole executor.

The witnesses were Ths. Wallslate at Queen hithe gate in Thames St., Robert Tyrrell in Crutchett Fryers, and J^{no} Thrale against Vintner's Hall.
                                                                    King, 25.

ELIZABETH SHRIMPTON, being aged, 6 March 1678–9, proved 15 September, 1682. I forgive my two sons Epaphras and Sylas whatever shall remain unpaid of the money I laid out for binding them apprentices. To my said sons and to my two daughters, Elizabeth and Lydia, whatsoever shall be received of what is due unto me from my cousin M^r. Samuel Shrimpton and from M^r. John Croad. To my daughter-in-law Mary Bingly ten shillings to buy her a ring. My cousin Joseph Bland. My daughter Elizabeth Shrimpton to be executrix.   Cottle, 113.

SAMUEL SHRIMPTON of Boston in the Co. of Suffolk, Prov. of Massachusetts Bay in New England Esq. 5 June 1697. To son Samuel and his heirs my brick messuage or tenement called the Exchange Tavern in Boston &c. and my brick ware house near the Town Dock; also my piece of land at the North End. To my kinswomen Abigail and Elizabeth Bourne of London three hundred pounds apiece, besides their respective legacies left them by their grandfather Shrimpton deceased. To my wife Elizabeth Shrimpton all the rest and residue during the term of her natural life, with full liberty before death to dispose of one thousand pounds thereof to whom and in such manner as to her shall seem most fit, meet and requisite. My said wife to be sole executrix.

Wit: Lydia Watts, Ursula Cooles, Eliezer Moody Sc^r.

On the third day of June in the year 1700 commission issued to Elizabeth Roberts, widow, mother and attorney of Elizabeth Shrimpton widow, recently named executrix &c.   Noel, 89.

LYDIA SHRIMPTON, of the city of London, spinster, 4 February 1682. proved 30 May 1685. To my brother Epaphras Shrimpton one shilling. To my brother Sylas Shrimpton one shilling. To my Sister Mary Bringley one shilling. All my debts and funeral charges being first paid I give and bequeath all the rest of my estate, real and personal, bills, bonds, chattells, dues and debts whatsoever unto my dearest sister M^rs. Elizabeth Shrimpton whom I also appoint to be my sole executrix.

Wit: Agnes Hathorn, Caleb Hathorn, Walt. Himilton.

Cann, 64.

[An attested copy of the will of Edward Shrimpton, of Bednall Green, is recorded in Suffolk Probate Office, Boston, Lib. I. fol. 389, with the Commission out of the Prerogative Court in England, for the probate of wills, from William, Archbishop of Canterbury. This Commission, dated London, July 1, 1662, is directed to John Norton, minister, Simon Bradstreet, Hezekiah Usher and others, merchants. It authorizes Henry Shrimpton to act as Executor to the estate of his brother Edward. An abstract of this Will, proved in Boston, Sept. 6, 1662, with the form of the Oath to be administered to the Executor, is printed in the REGISTER, XI. 170–72.

Thomas Pounsett, of the Parish of St. Stephen, Coleman Street, "merchant taylor," of London, and Mary, wife of said Thomas, "one of the daughters of Edward Shrimpton, late of the Parish of Stepney als. Stebunheath," in the county of Middlesex, gives a power of attorney to her brother, Jonathan Shrimpton, now of New England, merchant, May 19, 1663. See Suffolk Deeds, Lib. IV. fol. 169–171. Also, mortgage deed of estate in Boston, of Edward Shrimpton and his children, Nov. 22, 1663, to William and Hannah Ballantine, ibid, fol. 161.

An abstract of the Will of Henry Shrimpton, of Boston, merchant, brother and Executor to Edward, above, dated 17. 5. 1666, proved Aug. 4, of the same year, is also given in the REGISTER, xv. 76–78. He provides that his "Cousinne, Mary Shrimpton, daughter of my late brother, Edward Shrimpton, Deceased, be paid the remainder of her portion according to her Father's will, with Interest, at sixe in the Hundred;" that, £2000 given the five younger children, "be put out to Interest, and good Security taken for it." He gives £10 "to my sister, Elizabeth Shrimpton, wife to my Brother Edward Shrimpton," as also the same sum to each of the seven children of his late Brother Edward, mentions them all by name.

Samuel Shrimpton's Will is recorded at Suffolk Probate Office, Lib. viii. fol. 102. As also that of Samuel Shrimpton, Jun. (Lib. xv. fol. 167), dated April 21, 1703, proved June 17, 1703. The latter mentions wife Elizabeth, to whom he gives the use of his estate in Suffolk, in right or by force of the Will of his grandfather Henry Shrimpton; his daughter Elizabeth, an only child; uncle Nicholas Roberts, of Boston, merchant, also "my brother Stephen Richardson." Mr. Edward Lyde, of Boston, merchant, executor.

Mary Shrimpton, relict of Jonathan Shrimpton, son of Edward of Bednall Green, administered upon her husband's estate, for the benefit of herself and two children, June 3, 1673. (Suffolk Deeds, Lib. vii. 337, 346, 347.)

The nuncupative will of Bethiah Shrimpton, daughter of Epaphras, and granddaughter of Edward, dated Saturday night, June 27, 1713, mentions, Madam Stoddard, Dr. John Clark, brother Samuel Eliot and his wife, brother and sister Hunt, brother and sister Shrimpton, brother William, sister Hannah, mother, and Humilis Williams. "Said Bethiah died 2^d July current." Ibid. Lib. xviii. fol. 136, 137.—W. B. TRASK.]

WILLIAM YEAMANS of St. Giles in the Fields, Middlesex, yeoman, 24 February 1686, proved 7 May 1687. I give and bequeath to my brother Christopher Yeamans of Madnan's Neck^I in the Queen's County on Long Island in the Province of New York in America, yeoman, the sum of five shillings. And whereas there is the sum of one hundred and twelve pounds fifteen shillings and six pence silver money of New York aforesaid, due and owing unto me from my said brother upon bond, as also the sum of three pounds, with the increase thereof, for goods lately sent to him, I do hereby order and appoint that if he, my said brother, his executors or assigns, do and shall pay unto my executrix the said sum of one hundred and twelve pounds, fifteen shillings and six pence and do also account unto her for the said sum of three pounds &c. then I do give and bequeath unto my said brother twenty pounds like silver money of New York to be equally divided between such of my said brother's children as shall be then living. I give and bequeath unto my sister Anne Bakewell, widow, twelve pence; unto William Gooden ten shillings to buy him a ring. All the rest of my goods &c. to my wife Elizabeth Yeamans, whom I appoint sole executrix.

Foot, 71.

[¹Madnan's Neck is situated in or near Hempstead (Onderdonk's *History of Hempstead, Long Island*, pp. 44–52). See Petition from Madnan's Neck, also one from Christopher Yeamans of the same place to Lieut. Governor Thomas Dongan, about 1683, relative to their meeting-house, in O'Callaghan's *Documentary History of New York*, Vol. 3, pages 211, 212.—W. B. TRASK.]

Sir ROBERT YEAMANS of Redland, Co. Gloucester, Knight and Baronet, 24 January 1686, proved 11 May 1687. To be buried in the parish Church of St. Mary Redcliffe within the suburbs of the City of Bristol as near my first wife as may be. To the poor of Westbury super Trym, Gloucestershire. To my wife Abigail all my messuages &c. in the County of Gloucester for and during the term of her natural life. And after her decease I give to my kinsman Robert Stafford Esq. the tenement or farm in Redland, now in possession of Joyce Beavin, which I purchased of Ralph Sadler Esq. deceased. Other messuages to kinsman Robert Yeamans, now resident in the Island of Barbadoes, son of my late brother Sir John Yeamans deceased, with remainder to John Yeamans of Bristol, brewer, eldest son of my brother Joseph Yeamans deceased, next to Robert, second son of said Joseph, then to George, the third son, then to my right heirs forever. My wife Dame Abigail Yeamans to be sole executrix.   Foot, 71.

[Sir Robert Yeamans, bart., was the second son of Robert Yeamans, alderman of Bristol, who was condemned, by a council of war, for corresponding with Prince Rupert and designing to deliver the city of Bristol into his hand. The two sons of Alderman Yeamans were both created baronets, namely, John, Jan. 12, 1664–5, and Robert, the testator, Dec. 31, 1666. The latter married a daughter of Sir Edward Stafford, knt., but died without issue in 1687. (See Burke's Extinct Baronetage, ed. 1844, pp. 592–4.) The Yeamans family was connected with Carolina as well as with New York and New England.—EDITOR.]

JOHN YEAMANS of the parish of St James within the liberty of Westminster, Esq. February 1747, proved 27 June 1750 by Shute Shrimpton Yeamans. I give all my real and personal estate whatsoever and wheresoever to my only son Shute Shrimpton Yeamans &c. subject nevertheless to and chargeable with the payment of my debts and funeral expenses and also to and with the payment of the sum of four hundred pounds sterling to my niece Mary Vlack, the wife of Mr Johannis de Windt of the Island of St Thomas in America, if living at the time of my decease, otherwise to go to and be divided amongst her children in equal shares &c., and also subject to and chargeable with the payment of one annuity or yearly sum of twenty pounds sterling to Mrs. Elizabeth Stoddard of Boston in New England, mother of my late wife, during her natural life, and of one other annuity or yearly sum of ten pounds sterling to Mrs Mary Stoddard of Boston in New England, sister to my late wife, during her natural life, and of one other annuity or yearly sum of ten pounds sterling to Mrs. Sarah Stoddard of Boston in New England, sister to my late wife, during her natural life, and of one other annuity or yearly sum of ten pounds sterling to Mrs. Mehitabel Stoddard of Boston in New England &c. &c.; hereby recommending to my son and not doubting but that he will be farther kind to the said annuitants as he shall see occasion.

My son to be sole executor. If my said son shall happen to die before me I then give one annuity or yearly sum of two hundred pounds sterling to my daughter Matilda, the wife of my son, during her widowhood. But if she marries again I give her only the sum of one hundred pounds sterling during the remainder of her life; the said last mentioned annuities to my daughter to be issuing and payable out of my real estate in the Island of Antigua.

I give my said real estate in the Island of Antigua and all other my real and personal estate, whatsoever and wheresoever, to George Thomas Esq., Samuel Martin Esq., and Samuel Martin Esq. the younger, all now or late of the Island of Antigua &c., in trust &c. &c.; And as to all my real and personal estate in New England, in trust for and to the use of the said Elizabeth, Mary, Sarah and Mehitabel Stoddard, and the heirs of their respective bodies, to take as tenants in common and not as joint tenants; And in default of issue of their bodies respectively then, as to their respective shares, in trust for and to the use of Eliakim Hutchinson Esq., of Boston in New England and his heirs, if living at the time of my decease, or otherwise in trust for and to the use of the heirs of the said Eliakim Hutchinson.

Wit: H. Maria Byam, Lydia Byam, Elizabeth Mackinen.

219 Greenly.

[See Heraldic Journal, I.—133-4; II.—34.—н. ф. w.]

SHUTE SHRIMPTON YEAMANS of Richmond in the County of Surry Esquire 4 August 1768, proved 30 September 1769. To my son John Yeamans my watch and rings. To my son Shute Yeamans the silver Tureen the large silver cup the three cases of silver handled knives and forks and the silver bread basket. The remainder of my plate vessels and all my books and bookcases to my son John Yeamans. The lease of my house upon Richmond Green with the household goods and furniture therein to be sold. To son Shute the sum of four thousand pounds sterling to be paid unto him at his age of twenty one years. To my servant Sarah Walton twenty one pounds for her great care and attendance on my late wife and daughter in their illnesses. Five pounds to each of my other servants.

I give and devise unto my said son Shute Yeamans and his heirs my farm with the appurtenances called or known by the name of Chelsea farm, situate near Boston in New England in North America and now let to Robert Temple Esquire at the yearly rent of forty pounds sterling. If he die before he shall attain the age of twenty one years then I give and devise my said farm &c. unto my said son John.

I give and devise all my other lands hereditaments and real estate whatsoever in the Island of Antigua in the West Indies, in the provinces of New England and New Hampshire in North America, or elsewhere unto William Berners Esquire of Woolverston Park in Suffolk, William Gunthorpe of Antigua aforesaid Esquire, Samuel Mercer of the City of London Esquire and Mr Thomas Greenough of Boston in New England aforesaid &c. upon (certain) trusts ; —— to the use of my son John and the heirs of his body &c., then to the use of my son Shute and the heirs of his body &c., then to the use and behoof of my aunts Mary Chauncy Sarah Greenough and Mehetable Hyslop of Boston in New England aforesaid and the heirs of their respective bodies &c. as tenants in common and not as joint tenants, then to the use and behoof of my own right heirs forever.

Then follow instructions as to the care and management of the said estates and the investment and disposition of the debts, issues and profits thereof. The said William Berners, William Gunthorpe Samuel Mercer and Thomas Greenough to be executors of the will and guardians of the persons and estates of the said sons until they shall respectively attain the age of twenty one years.

Witnesses Godfrey Kettle, Basinghall Street London. Tim^y Thornhill clerk to Mr Kettle. Howell Powell servant to Mr Kettle. 330, Bogg.

[Richmond

baptized
Mch. 12. 1752 Ann d. of Shute Shrimpton Yeamans Esq. & Matilda
Nov. 16. 1754 Shute s. of   do   & do.

buried
June 15. 1767 Matilda Yeamans
Nov. 17. 1767 Miss Ann Yeamans
Sep. 18. 1769 Shute Shrimpton Yeamans Esq.

J. C. C. SMITH.]

[Henry Yeamans, father of John, the testator, married Miss Shute, her christian name not ascertained. She was a sister of Gov. Samuel Shute, who succeeded Joseph Dudley as Governor of Massachusetts and New Hampshire in 1716. Lieut. Governor John Yeamans, of Antigua, father of Henry Yeamans, according to the family history, had by his wife, previously named Nichols, besides Henry, an elder son John, and a younger, William, also six daughters, whose names are given in the "Yeamans pedigree," page 231, Sumner's *History of East Boston*.

John, the testator, who died in 1749, married Elizabeth Shrimpton, daughter of Samuel Shrimpton, Jun. She was born Aug. 26, 1702, died Dec. 4, 1721. Their only son, Shute Shrimpton Yeamans, born Aug. 20, 1721, died Sept. 10, 1769, married Matilda Gunthorp, had two daughters who died in infancy, as also a son John; and a son Shute, who died under age, unmarried.

Mrs. Elizabeth Stoddard, whose maiden name was Elizabeth Richardson, mentioned in the above abstract of the will as mother-in-law of the testator, married first, Samuel Shrimpton, Jun., who died May 25, 1703. By Samuel Shrimpton, Jun., she had a daughter Elizabeth, who married John Yeamans, as above stated.

Elizabeth (Richardson) Shrimpton, the widow of Samuel Shrimpton, Jun., married Dec. 23, 1713, David Stoddard, son of Simeon Stoddard. The latter had for his second wife, Elizabeth, widow of Col. Samuel Shrimpton. There being three Elizabeth Shrimptons, matrons and maiden, and two Samuel Shrimptons, father and son, each of whom had a wife and one a daughter named Elizabeth, has heretofore led to some complication in the relationship details of certain members of the family.

Mary, Sarah and Mehetable Stoddard were, respectively, daughters of David and Elizabeth (Richardson, Shrimpton) Stoddard. Mary married the Rev. Charles Chauncy, D.D. ; Sarah, Dea. Thomas Greenough; and Mehetable, William Hyslop. The latter were the grandparents of the late Gen. William Hyslop Sumner, of Jamaica Plain. For further particulars, see "Stoddard Pedigree," facing page 226, Sumner's *East Boston*.—W. B. TRASK.]

JOHN WILLIAMS of the parish of St George the Martyr, in the Borough of Southwark and County of Surrey, Esqr (by mark) 25 October 1718, proved 16 December 1718. All my arrears of pay due and owing to me, at the time of my decease, from the crown of Great Britian, as captain of one of the independent companies of foot in North America,—and all my real and personal estate in the County of Cornwall and in the Kingdom of England and in North America, or elsewhere, I give to my loving brother George Williams and his heirs and assigns, whom I do make sole executor. Wit: Robert Elliot, John Gibson, Daniel Prior and R. Hawson.

Tenison, 248.

Sir THOMAS CROOKE of Baltamore, county Cork, Knight and Baronet, of the age of fifty six years or thereabouts, 17 February 1629, proved 7 May 1630. My wife Dame Mary Crooke to have my whole estate left to her sole managing and to remain henceforth as sole executrix, and neither of my two sons, Samuel Crookes nor James Crookes, shall intermeddle with any part of my lands and goods, but shall wholly wait upon their said mother for such supplies of charges for their education as to her shall seem fit, who, I doubt not, will be helpful to them according to her wisdom and ability. I have likewise one daughter, named Judith, divers years since married to Vincent Gooken Esq., who I know need be no chaige to my late tattered estate; notwithstanding, as a token from her dear father, I would have her mother pay unto her ten pounds within a year next after my decease. I have a loving brother called Doctor Helkiah Crooke betwixt whom and me there is an old account of about thirty three pounds; my will is that my executrix shall release that unto him. Another brother called Richard Crooke, who had shewed kindnes to my children in my absence. To him ten pounds, within one year &c. A loving son in law called Arthur Jackson, dwelling in Woodstreet London, from whom and from Mary his wife I have received so many kindnesses unto myself being present at several times and unto my children in my absence that I am not able to requite them; yet, as a friendly gift at parting, I bequeath to him the sum of twenty pounds and to Mary his wife the sum of ten pounds. Another brother called Samuel Crooke, Rector of Wrington in Somersetshire, where divers of my children have had their education for divers years, who hath a wife, my very loving sister, Judith Crooke; to them thirty pounds. My sister Rachel Rosse, wife of Henry Rosse of London, goldsmith, much impoverished, —— & a good old aunt, called Aunt Hudson, —— a yearly pension of forty shillings.

Wit: Helkiah Crooke, Arthur Jackson, Danyell Johnson, the mark of Alexander Hande.

Reg. of Commissary Court of London (1629-34), fol. 27.

ARTHUR JACKSON of London, Clerk, proved 17 August 1666. Wife Mary. Eldest son Joseph, second son John. Messuage in Thredneedle Street. Son John's wife. Eldest daughter Mrs. Elizabeth Hoor. My second daughter Martha Jackson. My grand children (named). An interest in certain lands in Ireland which were formerly my mother's Lady Crooke and now are the jointure of Lady Crooke the widow of my brother Sir Samuel Crooke. The poor of Waldingfield, Suffolk. Mico, 130.

RICHARD RICHMOND, citizen and leather seller of London, 15 April 1684, proved 23 January 1684. To cousin Richaid Rodd, my apprentice, one hundred pounds within one month after the expiration of his term of apprenticeship. To my brother Hounsdon Richmond of St Martins le Grand, victualler, one shilling. To my cousin Christopher Richmond of St.

Martins aforesaid, shoemaker, one shilling. To my sister Anne Jennings of London, widow, one shillings. To my sister Margaret Richmond of Virginia in America, spinster, one shilling. To my cousin Anne Shipton, wife of Joseph Shipton of London, Tallow Chandler, one shilling. To Mary Elsly, my sister, one shilling. To my cousin Christopher Richmond one shilling. To my cousin Katherine Johnson, wife of John Johnson of London, Leather seller, one shilling. My wife Grace Richmond to be executrix and to have my tenements in Cary Lane, in the parish of St John Zacharies, in London (at the sign of the Crown) during her natural life. I desire my wife to make my cousin Richard Rodd her executor.   Cann, 9.

PALMER.—In the last number of these GLEANINGS (*ante*, p. 301–307), a pedigree of the Palmer family and some abstracts of wills were printed. The following additional matter has been kindly contributed by J. Paul Rylands, Esq., F.S.A., of Heather Lea, Claughton, Birkenhead, England.

Admissions to Lincoln's Inn, London.

Midd[x] Joh'es Palmer generosus admissus est in Societatem hujus hospicii 13 April 2 Annæ 1703. Henry Martyn, E. Norman Jun. [sureties.]

Admissions to the Middle Temple, London.

Nov. 29, 1703.   Magister Joshua filius et heres apparens Joshuæ Palmer de Devonsheire Square extra Bishop Gate in comitatu Middlesex Medicinæ professoris admissus est in Societatem Medii Templi specialiter.

Nov. 3, 1707.   Magister Johannes Palmer filius et heres apparens Archdale Palmer de Wanlip in comitatu Leicestriæ Armigeri admissus est in Societatem Medii Templi specialiter.

May 3, 1726.   Magister Johannes Palmer filius unicus Johannis Palmer nuper de Libbery in comitatu Wigorn generosi defuncti admissus est in Societatem Medii Templi.

17 July, 1740.   Magister Johannes Palmer filius tertius Roberti Palmer de Clonmaken in comitatu Limerick in regno Hiberniæ generosi admissus est in Societatem Medii Templi specialiter.

Musgrave's Obituary.

John Palmer, barrister-at-law, died 22 Feb. 1734. Gents. Mag. 107.

John Palmer, of the Middle Temple, juris con: died 23 Dec. 1738. Gents. Mag. 660. Hist. Reg[r]. 50.

Bishop of London: Marriage Licence Affidavit Books.

[Book 1706–8.]   1 Nov. 1708.   Joseph Palmer, of St Margaret's, Lothbury, London, bachelor, aged 25, and Elizabeth Bate, of St Margaret's, Westminster, spinster, aged 22.   To marry at St Martin's in the Fields [but the marriage is not to be found in that register, nor in the register of St Margaret's, Westminster.]

Lord Chamberlain's Records,—Messengers.

[Vol. 249a, folio 12.]   Jo. Palmer pro Mitchell 9 June 1714.

[Vol. 261, folio 12.]   Jn° Hutchins pro Joseph Palmer 29 July 1715.

Prerogative Court, Canterbury.

23 April 1761. Admōn. to Joseph Palmer, late of the Precincts of Whitefriars, London, widower, deceased, granted to Ann Drury, widow, the daughter. [He died December, 1759.]

Joseph Palmer, Esq., Queen's=Elizabeth, daug'r of Thomas Bate, Messenger. Born about 1683. of Ashby-de-la-Zouch, co. Leicester, Died in London, Dec. 1759. Gent. Born 1689, married 1708, died Resided in London & Leices- about 1728. tershire.

Charles Drury, of Not-=Anne Palmer, dau. tingham, Surgeon. & coh. Bapt. at Bapt. at St. Peter's Ashby-de-la-Zouch Church there 19 July, mix. to her father, 1704. Died 14 Jan. 1761. Died 7 May, 1753, aged 48. Bur. 1763, aged 51. Bu-in St.Peter's Church. ried at St. Peter's Church, Notting-ham.

Thomas Kirkland, M.D.=Dorothy Palmer, da. of Ashby-de-la-Zouch. and coh. Born 1723. Bapt. at Ashbourne, co. Married at Packing-Derby, 14 October, 1722. ton, co. Leicester, 3 Died at Ashby, 17 Jan. August, 1747. Died & buried in the chancel 24 Jan. & buried at of the parish church Ashby 28 Jan. 1785. there 22 Jan. 1798. A distinguished physician and author.

QUERY.—Who was Mr. Joseph Palmer, named above?

MARGERY PATE of the parish of St. Pulkers, London, widow, 22 September 1617, proved 2 October 1617. My body to be buried within the church of St. Pulkers near unto my former husband Richard Quille. To my godson John Miller, to Hudson Miller, to Anne Miller wife of Thomas Miller, to my cousin Thomas Miller and to his daughter. To Judith Claxton and her daughter Ann Nicholes. To Elsibeth Pynnocke and to Robert Lide. To James Williams twenty shillings, to Alice Williams, wife unto James Williams twenty shillings. To Alice Quille (certain household goods and wearing apparel). To Elizabeth Albrocke. To Elizabeth Lide, wife unto Henry Lide and to Henry, James, Maurice and Cassandra Lide, children unto Henry Lide. To Roger Williams, son unto James Williams, twenty shillings. To Robert Williams, son of the said James Williams, twenty shillings, and to Katherine Williams, daughter unto the said James Williams, twenty shillings. To Elizabeth and Sarah Webster, daughters of John Webster, and John Webster, his son and the rest of Webster's children. To Edward Goodcoole, Richard Bradley, Elizabeth Younge, widow, and Michael Bolton. Henry Lide of Westminister Esq., to be sole executor and James Williams of St. Pulkers, merchant taylor, overseer. Weldon, 100. (P. C. C.)

JAMES WILLIAMS, citizen and merchant tailor of London, 7 September 1620, proved 19 November 1621. I will and my mind is that, my debts being paid and funeral expenses discharged, all the residue of my goods and chattels shall be divided into three equal parts; one third part whereof I give and bequeath unto my loving wife Alice for her part and portion therein, according to the custom of the city of London. And, for that my son Sydrack and my daughter Catharine, now the wife of Ralph Wightman, citizen and merchant taylor of London, have "binn" by me already preferred and each of them hath received a sufficient portion of my estate, therefore I will that neither of them shall claim or have any customary part or portion of that estate whereof I shall be possessed at the time of my decease. And yet, nevertheless, my will and meaning is that my sons Roger and Robert Williams shall have but one moiety or half part of the other third part of my estate equally between them to be divided, and the

other moiety thereof to remain to such other child or children as I shall
have living at the time of my decease. The other third part of my estate,
which is in my power to dispose, I give and bequeath as followeth, vizt. to
my son Sydrack twenty and five pounds and to my said daughter Catherine
Wightman twenty five pounds, to be paid to each of them severally within
one year next after my decease, and to my said sons Robert and Roger
Williams twenty and five pounds apiece, to be paid unto each of them
severally at his age of four and twenty years. To my godson James Wightman, son of the beforenamed Katherine Wightman my daughter, five pounds
in money, to be paid unto his father for the use of his said son. To Elizabeth Pemberton, Ellen Woolley and Elizabeth Bryan, my god daughters,
to every of them twenty shillings apiece, to be paid to their several parents
or governors &c. To Thomas Nicholson, citizen and currier of London,
ten shillings, to Elizabeth Kinge, wife of Robert Kinge, clothworker,
twenty shillings, and to my kinswoman Alice Harris, now dwelling with
me, forty shillings. To Robert Parke my "Jemmall" ring and to Edward Waterhouse my dagger, knife, chain and girdle. To the poor of
St. Sepulchres without Newgate, London, wherein I now dwell, ten pounds
in money and bread to be distributed amongst them on the day of my funeral or the day after, as follows, vizt. to the poor in Smithfield quarter thirty
five shillings in money and thirty five shillings in bread, to the poor in
Holborn Cross quarter twenty shillings in money and twenty shillings in
bread, to the poor in Church quarter fifteen shillings in money and fifteen
shillings in bread, and to the poor in old bayley quarter thirty shillings in
money and thirty shillings in bread. To the poor of the said parish without
Smithfield Bars twenty shillings in bread. To Alice and Roger Bryan,
children of Henry Bryan, coachmaker, ten shillings apiece. The residue
to my wife Alice Williams whom I do make and appoint sole executrix of
this my last will. And overseers thereof I do make and appoint my
brother in law Roger Pemberton, my said son in law Ralph Wightman,
my kinsman Thomas Morse and the said Robert Kinge, to whom twenty
shillings apiece.

Com. Court of London, Vol. 24, fol. 50.

ALICE WILLIAMS of St. Sepulchres without Newgate, London, widow,
1 August, 1634, proved 26 January, 1634. My body to be buried in the
parish church of St. Sepulchres. To my son Sidrach·Williams one hundred pounds to be paid within ten years after my decease (*i. e.* ten pounds
yearly). If he shall not live to receive the whole one hundred pounds what
remaineth unpaid at his decease shall be paid to such children as he shall
leave behind him.

Item I give to my son Roger Williams now beyond the seas ten pounds
yearly to be paid unto him by my executor for and during the term and
space of twenty years next after my decease. And if he the said Roger
shall not live to receive the same himself fully in such manner as aforesaid
then I will what remaineth thereof unpaid at his decease shall be paid to
his wife and to his daughter, if they survive, or to such of them as shall
survive. And it is my will that my executor shall give security to the overseers of this my will for the due payment of both the said legacies, as well
to my eldest son Sidracke Williams as to my son Roger Williams, in such
manner and form as aforesaid by assignment of the lease or leases (of my
dwelling house and other tenements standing and being on that side of the
way wherein my dwelling house is situated) unto the overseers of this my

will, or to such other persons as they shall think fit and indifferent to be trusted, by such sufficient assurance and conveyance thereof as my said overseers shall think fit and convenient. To my daughter Katherine the now wife of John Davies, clerk, twenty pounds yearly for and during the like term and space of twenty years next after my decease. In case of her death what remains unpaid &c. shall be paid as follows, the one half to the children she had by her former husband Ralph Wightman deceased, or to the survivor of them, and the other half to the said John Davies, if he shall survive, or to his children by my said daughter, or to the survivor of them. Security to be given for such payment out of the lease of the messuage or tenement called the Harrow in Cow Lane, over against my dwelling house on the other side of the way, and of three several tenements backside next adjoining. To my grand child James Williams, son of the said Sidrack Williams, five pounds within four years after my decease. To my grand child Anne Williams my chain of gold, two of my gilt spoons and one of my gilt cups. To my grand child James Wightman two of my silver beakers one wine bowl and two silver spoons. To Dorcas Wightman, his sister, one broad silver bowl and one other silver bowl; and to her sister Rebecca Wightman one other silver bowl and one other broad bowl of silver. To my grand child Elizabeth Davyes one silver salt and two gilt spoons, and to my grand child Hester Davies one beaker, one pot tipt with silver and two spoons. I will and bequeath that my chest of linen, that is to say, the wainscot chest now standing at my bed's feet in my lodging chamber under the window, to be equally divided between my said daughter's five children before-named &c. To my god daughter Alice Ballard my best gown and kirtle, my scarlet petticoat, best petticoat, two best smocks, two best coyfes and forty shillings in money, and to her daughter ten shillings, To her brother Roger Bryan forty shillings. To Alice, the wife of Robert Barthorpp, the ten pounds which her husband oweth me and ten pounds more and my bible and my tawney rug. More to the said Robert Barthorpp and his wife five pounds to buy them blacks for mourning and twenty shillings a-piece to their three children. To my said son Sidracke Williams for blacks for his mourning three pounds and to my said son John Davies for blacks for himself his wife and children ten pounds. To my maid servant now dwelling with me my gown and kirtle with the embroidered lace and ten shillings. To my godson Robert Wolly twenty shillings, and to my other two god sons Tobyas Harvest and John Walker ten shillings apiece. To the poor of St. Sepulchres seven pounds, in bread or otherwise, about the time of my funeral, and forty shillings to be at that time bestowed upon a supper for my tenants at the house over the way called the Harrow. To my said son John Davies, my loving friend and neighbor John May, scrivener, my good friend Robert Kinge, clothworker, and to the aforesaid Robert Barthropp for their pains to be taken for me in assisting my executor as overseers of this my will twenty shillings apiece. All the rest and residue of my goods &c. &c. to my son Robert Williams, he paying my debts and legacies and performing my funeral and I make; constitute and ordain the said Robert Williams my full and sole executor. Wit: Henry Walker, John Collys (his mark), John Thomas, John Hubbard, John May scr.   Com. Court of London, Vol. 27, fol. 12.

RALPH WIGHTMAN, citizen and merchant taylor of London in the parish of Mary le Bow, 27 December 1628, proved 9 February 1628.   To be buried in the parish church aforesaid by my wife Judith deceased. My estate, according to the custom of this City, to be divided into three parts. The one part I give unto my loving wife Katherine Wightman; a second part I give unto my three children now living, James, Dorcas and Rebecca Wightman, and, if my wife should now be with child, to him or her also a part of my second part; and the third part of my estate I give as follows, unto the parish of Inckley* and Wickham in Leicestershire, for the poor thereof, forty shillings, to the poor of Mary le Bow twenty shillings, to my cousin Ezechias Wightman twenty shillings, to my cousin Ralph Prior twenty shillings, to my sister Eaton twenty shillings and to every one of her children now born five shillings apiece, to my mother Williams twenty shillings to buy her a ring, to my brother George's wife ten shillings and to every of his children five shillings apiece, to my brother Robert Williams ten shillings, to my servants with me at my decease five shillings a-piece. And the rest of my third part, the legacies, debts and funeral charges paid, to be divided into three parts; one I give to my wife Katherine, a second part to my son James and a third part to my two daughters. If my wife shall die before my children and all my children die before they come to age, then (by a certain division) to my brother George and his children, my sister Eaton and her children, my cousin Ezechias, my cousin Ralph Prior and my wife's brother and their issue, vizt. my brother Sidrach, my brother Roger and my brother Robert Williams or any of their children living. My wife Katherine Wightman to be sole executor and my brother Sydrach Williams, my brother George Wightman, my brother Roger Williams and my cousin Theophilus Riley to be overseers; and to have twenty shillings apiece to buy them a ring.   Ridley, 18.

A Marriage License was granted to Sydrach Williams, of St. Gabriel Fenchurch Street, merchant taylor, and Anne Pinner of St. Michael ad Bladum (St Michael Querne), widow of Francis Pinner grocer,—at St. Michael aforesaid.—10 Oct. 1621.   B.

[Col. Chester's Marr. Lic. &c.]

Admon. of the goods &c. of Sydrach Williams lately of St. Olave Hart Street, London, but at Barwick in the County of York deceased, was granted 29 April 1647, to John Myster principal creditor.

Admon. Act Book (1647), fol. 46.

RALPH MOORE of St. Alban's, Herts, gentleman, 1 May 1618, proved 28 October 1620. All my goods and chattels &c. to the poor of the parishes of St. Alban's and St. Peter's in the town of St. Alban's. Ralph Pemberton of St. Alban's, gentleman, to be executor. Roger Pemberton of St. Alban's, gentleman, to be overseer. Nicholas and Raphe Cotchett among the witnesses.   Soame, 105.

ROGER STOKES of the town of St. Alban's in the Co. of Hertford, draper, 3 July 1578, proved 4 August 1578. To my father-in-law John Arnold, one of the chief Burgesses of St. Albans, ten pounds. To my father in law John Shadd, late of St. Albans, ten pounds. To my brother Robert Stokes and to Thomas Holden M^r. of Art, the lease &c. of the two tene-ments wherein I now dwell. My brother Robert Stokes to be executor.

The executor, Robert Stokes, having died, Admon. was granted Roger Pemberton next akin.   Langley, 32.

* Otherwise Hinckley.

ROBERT STOKES of St. Alban's &c. M[r]. of Art, 2 August 1578, proved 4 August 1578. To my cousin Roger Pemberton my customary and copyhold lands within the manor of Park, Gorham &c. My friend Thomas Holden of St. Albans. My cousins Frances and Thomas Blackborne. My cousin Thomas Blackborne. To mine Aunt Pemberton an Angel in gold.

Langley, 32.

ROGER PEMBERTON of St. Alban's &c. Esq. 13 November 1624, proved 5 December 1627. To be buried in the parish church of St. Mary Bow, London. Provides for an almshouse for six poor widows, having purchased, for that purpose, a close or meadow or pasture in Bowgate in the parish of St. Peters, in the town of St. Alban's, in mine own and my son Ralphe's name. My three sons John, Robert and Ralphe and my son Wolley and their heirs shall have the placing and displacing of the same widows in the several rooms, they to be above three score years of age and of good honest life and behavior and of civil carriage, two to be of St. Peters two of St. Stephens one of St. Michael and one of Shenley. To my son in law Robert Wolley one signet of pure and fine gold of the value of five pounds, with my arms to be engraven thereupon. To my friend and brother in law M[r]. Francis Kempe one signet of pure and fine gold, to be of the value of five marks, with my arms to be engraven thereupon. To my brothers in law Nicholas Cotchett and Jeremy Odell, to either of them, one hoop ring of gold, of the value of twenty shillings apiece, with this poesie (not the gift but the giver) to be engraven thereon. To my wife and my daughter Tecla Wolley, to each of them a hoop ring &c. with this poesie (my love to you). To each of my daughters in law Katherine Pemberton, Susan Pemberton and Frances Pemberton one hoop ring, with this poesie (keep the golden mean).

Item I give and bequeath unto my cosen and Godsonne Roger Williams the somme of ten pounds of lawfull english money. To my two godsons Ralph Cotchett and Roger Odell twenty shillings apiece. To each of my grandchildren Ellen Wolley and the three Elizabeth Pembertons one hoop ring of pure gold, of the value of thirty shillings apiece, with this poesie to be engraven therein (feare God). My wife and my son Ralph to be executors.

A codicil to this will was made 7 November, 1627, in which are mentioned various other grandchildren (including Robert, son of John Pemberton).

Skynner, 117.

[The above will makes it clear that the Roger Pemberton whom James Williams called "brother in law" and who himself referred to Roger Williams as "cosen" (i. e. nephew) "and godsonne," belonged to a family residing at St. Alban's, Herts., whose pedigree is thus given in the Visitation of Hertfordshire, 1634, published by the Harleian Society in 1886 :—

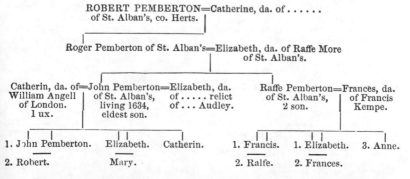

ROBERT PEMBERTON=Catherine, da. of ......
of St. Alban's, co. Herts.

Roger Pemberton of St. Alban's=Elizabeth, da. of Raffe More
of St. Alban's.

Catherin, da. of=John Pemberton=Elizabeth, da.
William Angell | of St. Alban's, | of ..... relict
of London. | living 1634, | of ... Audley.
1 ux. | eldest son.

Raffe Pemberton=Frances, da.
of St. Alban's, | of Francis
2 son. | Kempe.

1. John Pemberton.   Elizabeth.   Catherin.   1. Francis.   1. Elizabeth.   3. Anne.

2. Robert.   Mary.   2. Ralfe.   2. Frances.

Among the Funeral Certificates at the College of Arms is one for the Right Worshipful Roger Pemberton, of St. Alban's, co. Herts, Esq., who departed this life 13 Nov. 1627. The names and matches of his children and the names and ages of his grandchildren are given. His second son, Robert Pemberton, married Susan, daughter of Roger Glover of Beckett or Bewcott, in co. Berks, Esq., and sister of the Rev. Josse Glover of New England, and died at St. Alban's in the Summer of 1628. His will, proved in the Prerog. Court of Canterbury, I expect to give in connection with that of his father in law and other wills bearing on the various alliances of the Glover family.

Admon. of the goods of Robert Pemberton was granted in the Court of the Archdeacon of St. Alban's, 30 September, 1578, to his widow Katherine Pemberton.

. License to marry was granted, 6 May, 1579, to Roger Pemberton of St. Alban's, Herts., and Elizabeth Moores, spinster, of the same —— at St. Anne and St. Agnes, London. The two marriage licenses of his son John may also be found in Col. Chester's Marriage Licenses of London.

Now it so happens that there was a clergyman named Roger Williams living contemporaneously with Roger Pemberton in St. Alban's, to the Rectory of which he was inducted 30 April, 1583. He was also inducted to the Vicarage of St. Peter's, in the same Borough, 1 March, 1592. He must have died before 2 January, 1626, when his (nuncupative) will, made 26 June, 1619, was proved in the Court of the Archdeacon of St. Alban's (Book Dainty, Fol. 166). The witnesses were Andrew Zinzan and James Rolfe Esq^{rs}. and his wife Affradosa. It was to the effect that his wife should have all. Being asked by the said James Rolfe if he would give nothing from her to his kindred, he replied and said no, for he had done well for them already. And then his said wife coming into the Parlor where he lay on his bed, the said Andrew Zinzan and James Rolf being still there present, the said James Rolf said unto her, Mrs. Williams you are beholden to your husband, for his will is you shall have all his goods and estate at his death and will give nothing from you to his kindred, whereunto the said Roger answered and said, in her presence, no, I will give nothing to them from her for I have done enough for them already.

Affradosa, above named, was not his first wife, for I find license granted to Roger Williams, clerk, of St. Alban's, Herts., and Alice Asheton, spinster, of Chishull Magna, co. Essex, dau. of William Asheton, clerk, Vicar of Meldreth in the Diocese of Ely, to be married at Chishull Magna aforesaid, 23 January, 1583–4.—Col. Chester's Marr. Lic.

I trust that I may be allowed a departure from my usual custom of letting the evidence gathered in my gleanings speak for itself, and be permitted to call attention to the significance of a few of the facts in the present case.

The will of Alice Williams, here given, made in the summer of 1634, refers to her son Roger as "now beyond the seas;" she does not say where, she does not even say "in New England." Are there any good reasons for supposing that he was our famous "asserter of religious freedom," as Mr. Savage has called him. How do the known facts tally? Our Roger Williams called himself nearly four score years of age in 1679. Roger the son of James and Alice Williams had an elder brother Sydrach who received license to marry in 1621. It seems reasonable to suppose that he was from twenty one to twenty-four years of age at date of marriage. Allowing a difference of two years between their ages, Roger, his brother, would have been born, say, between 1599 and 1602. So we are not met by any apparent discrepancy in the matter of age. Mrs. Alice Williams mentions, besides Sidrach and Roger, another son, Robert. Our Roger had (according to Savage) a brother Robert. In August, 1634, the Roger spoken of by his mother as "beyond the seas" had a wife and a daughter. At that very time our Roger was beyond the seas, so far as his English relatives were concerned, and with a wife (Mary) and a daughter (Mary), the other children whom he is known to have had being born after that date. Thus far then there seems nothing improbable in the theory that Roger, the son of James and Alice Williams of London, was the very Roger Williams who founded Providence Plantations; on the contrary, to me, I confess, it seems very plausible. What stands in the way? Only TRADITION, which says that he was born in Wales. Tradition, I frankly acknowledge, does not weigh much with me. I will only say that it seems to me as easy to believe that Roger, the son of James and Alice Williams, was born in Wales as that our Roger, who is said to have been at Charter house from 25 June, 1621, to 9 July, 1624, was born there. In fact it would take very strong evidence to make me believe it of either. We have one well known fact, bearing upon this, which Mr. Savage refers to, but with the omission of what I must deem a very important part. I refer to the memorandum written on the back of one of our Roger Williams's letters by Mrs. Anne Sadleir, daughter of Sir Edward Coke, which was as follows:—

"This Roger Williams, when he was a youth, would, in a short hand, take sermons and speeches in the Star Chamber and present them to my dear father. He, seeing so hopeful a youth, took such liking to him that he sent him to Sutton's Hospital, and he was the second that was placed there."

That a Welsh boy of that period should be practising short hand, frequenting the Star Chamber in Westminster and taking notes of speeches delivered there, seems to me absurd on the face of it. Such a statement could only apply, with any show of reasonableness, to a London boy, and then only to one occupying a good position. In Roger, the son of Alice Williams, we find a lad who was closely related to a gentle family, the Pembertons, known in London as well as in St. Alban's; and perhaps in the person of Henry Lyde,* Esq., of Westminster, with whom the father, James Williams, was so closely connected in the management and oversight of Mrs. Margery Pate's estate, we may find the channel of influence by which young Roger Williams got access to the Star Chamber.

In my view of the absurdity of the supposition of Mrs. Sadleir's statement applying to a Welsh lad, I am confirmed by my friend David Jones, Esq. I have his permission to quote what he says about the formerly accepted theory:

"The story, viewed as a whole, is so highly improbable and inconsistent that it falls to pieces upon very slight examination; that is, when you have once begun to suspect its unsoundness. There is of course nothing seriously improbable or preposterous in the supposition that the son of a Welsh farmer, of the reign of James I., should go to a Welsh College at Oxford,† take orders in the Church and afterwards distinguish himself amongst his fellows. The thing has been done over and over again, in a greater or less degree, both during Williams's period and since his day. But to say that a LAD from the midst of the hilly district in mid South Wales should in the reign of James have received in ' his native hamlet' an education fitting him to take down in short hand ' sermons and speeches in the Star Chamber,' and coming to London all unfriended does all this and becomes on friendly terms with great judges of the high courts of law, and to this owes altogether his stepping stone to a University career, is a story which one does not expect to read anywhere outside the covers of the 'Arabian Nights.' At any rate it would answer admirably for a new collection of tales of imagination and marvel. On the other hand there would be nothing marvellous in a clever London youth, of the reign of James, picking up short hand, doing just what Mrs. Sadleir has described *her* Roger Williams as having done, and the clever youth thus getting his ' leg up' on the horse on which he gallops off to the University and so on to the grand highway of life."

Since the foregoing was put into type I have obtained, through the kindness of Archdeacon Lawrence, of St. Albans, the following extracts from the parish register of St. Albans, which begins 17 Nov. 1558:—

BAPTISMS.

Randall Pemerton 19 March 1559.
Ellin Pemberton 22 November 1561.
John Pemberton, son of Robert, 20 June 1563.
Alice Pemberton, daughter of Robert, 18 February 1564.
Elizabeth Moore, daughter of Rafe, 18 March 1564.
Mary Pemerton, daughter of Robert, 1 February 1566.
Sara Pemerton, daughter of Robert, 26 September 1568.
John Pemerton, son of Roger, 15 Dec. 1583.
Robert Wolley, son of Robert, 7 March 1590.

---

* A pedigree of this family may be found in the Visitation of London (1634), published by the Harleian Society (Vol. II. page 66). See also Visitation of Oxford.

† This allusion to a " Welsh College of Oxford" refers to the theory maintained by Prof. Elton, in his life of Roger Williams, that he was the Rodericus Williams admitted into Jesus College, Oxford, 30 April 1624, the theory which, I understand, is not now held by any New England genealogists. With the name Rodericus staring in one's face, a name certainly not interchangeable with Rogerus, the wonder is that such a theory was ever broached.

BURIALS.

Robert Pemerton 15 December 1560.
Joane Pemerton 8 January 1560.
Randall-Pemerton 6 July 1561.
Roger Stokes 4 July 1578.
Robert Pemerton 16 July 1578.
John Pemerton 19 July 1578.
Robert Stokes 5 August 1578.
Florence Pemerton 6 August 1578.
Ellen Pemerton 7 August 1578.
―――― Pemerton 16 August 1578.
Alice wife of Mr. Roger Williams, parson of the parish church of St. Albans,
    3 April 1613.
Mr. Roger Williams, B.D. and parson &c 10 November 1626.

MARRIAGES.

Roger Stokes and Emme Arnold 9 June 1578.
Robert Rawlinson and Mary Pemerton 19 September 1586.
Mr. Roger Williams and Mrs Aphrodoza Moore, widow,* 7 June 1613.

With the help of Mr. A. Parkins, parish clerk of St. Peter's, in the same
borough, I am enabled to publish the following extracts from the register of
that parish, which also begins 17 November 1558 :—

BAPTISMS.

Elizabeth Pemberton, daughter of Roger, 27 December 1585.
Robert, son of Mr. Roger Pemberton, 23 December 1586.
Elizabeth, daughter of Mr. Roger Pemberton, 26 May 1590.
Tecla, daughter of Mr. Roger Pemerton, 27 September 1592.
Ellen, daughter of Mr. Robert Wolley, 15 October 1611.
Roger, son of Mr. Robert Wolley, 12 November 1612.
Robert, son of Mr. Robert Wolleye, 2 August 1615.
Elizabeth, daughter of Mr. Robert Wolleye, 15 June 1618.
Elizabeth, dau. of Rafe Pemerton by Frances his wife, 30 November 1618.
Katherine, dau. of Mr. Robert Wolley by Thecla his wife, 25 July 1620.
Frances, dau. of Rafe Pemerton by Frances his wife, 21 August 1620.

BURIALS.

Mrs. Marie Pemerton, wife of Mr. Rafael Pemerton Esquire, 1 May 1610.
Roger, son of Mr. John Pemerton, 27 July 1611.
Roger, son of Mr. Robert Wollye, 9 December 1615.
Mr. Roger Pemberton Esq. 20 November 1627.
John, son of Mr. Robert Wolley, 31 March 1628.
Mr. Robert Pemberton 29 May 1628.
Martha, daughter of Mr. John Pemmerton, 12 July 1628.
Susan, ―――― of Mr. John Pemberton, 9 November 1630.
Katherine, wife of Mr. John Pemberton, 2 December 1630.
Elizabeth, daughter of Mr. John Pemberton, 21 March 1625.
Mr. Raph Pemberton 11 October 1644.
Mr. John Pemberton 7 January 1644.
Mrs. Elizabeth Pemberton, widow, 15 July 1645.
Anne, daughter of Mr. Ralph Pemberton, 22 March 1654.
Anne, daughter of Mr. Robert Pemberton, 13 May 1658.
Mrs. Frances Pemberton, widow, 25 May 1659.

MARRIAGES.

Mr. Samuel Bedford and Mrs. Frances Pemberton 28 December 1644.

I have also since then received from Mr. Dean a cutting from the Boston
Evening Transcript of Friday, 5 April, 1889, containing an abstract of a paper
read before our society, on the preceding Wednesday, by R. A. Guild, LL.D.,
Librarian of Brown University, on "The Birth, Parentage and Life of Roger

---

* She was widow of William Moore, gent, of St. Alban's, and daughter of Alexander
Zinzan, of St. Michael in St. Alban's, gent (see Col. Chester's Marr. Lic.).

Williams," in which he advances the theory that he was the third son of William Willyams of Roseworthy, near Gwinear, Cornwall, born 21 and baptized 24 Dec. 1602 at Gwinear, and that he had brothers William and Arthur and a sister Margaret.

I trust it is not necessary for me to say that my own attention was drawn to this case long ago, before I learned of that significant clause in the memorandum of Mrs. Sadleir, referring to the short-hand notes taken in the Star Chamber. Bearing in mind what I supposed was regarded by all genealogists as an accepted fact, viz., that our Roger Williams had a brother Robert Williams, and seeing no sign of a Robert in this family, I made up my mind, as I believe every sound genealogist would have done, that I must wait until more light should be thrown on the subject or a better and more promising case appear. So far then as it depended on my judgment the hearing in the case of Roger Williams of Gwinear may be considered as having been adjourned *sine die*. If I had been called upon to render a verdict it would have been the Scotch verdict of *not proven*. Upon receipt of the abstract of Dr. Guild's paper I read it with the most careful scrutiny, again and again, and took pains to consult sundry of my antiquarian friends whose opinions in such matters I valued; but with the same result; allowing the *same* conditions as before the verdict would have been as before, *not proven*. Dr. Guild's method of getting round the obstacle by the assumption that our Roger Williams in calling Robert Williams "brother" meant "brother-in-law" seemed altogether too violent an assumption. I knew of course, every antiquary of experience knows, that instances may be found many instances in fact, where the term brother was used and brother-in-law is to be understood. I have no doubt that several instances may be found in these Gleanings. Ralph Wightman, for example, in his will speaks of *brothers* Sidrach, Roger and Robert Williams. Every one, who sees that, will assume that *brothers-in-law* was meant, and would be justified in such assumption. The same Ralph Wightman speaks of a *brother* George Wightman. Would any one be justified in assuming that, here too, *brother-in-law* was meant? Can Dr. Guild cite a single instance of the sort to support him in such an assumption? And, if so, will he give the particulars and surrounding conditions and circumstances? I can imagine, to be sure, a case where there might be evidence in other ways so overwhelming in its weight as to compel us to have recourse to such an assumption; but I can truly say that I do not recall ever having met with such a case. Has Dr. Guild? Certainly this cannot be called such a case.

But since the receipt of Dr. Guild's paper, Mr. J. O. Austin, the compiler of the Genealogical Dictionary of Rhode Island, has sent me a bit of information which settles the case of Roger Williams of Gwinear, as every genealogist will admit. It seems that the founder not only alluded to Robert Williams as "brother," but in one instance, at least, called him "mine own brother." No one, I suppose, would dream of substituting "brother-in-law" for that expression; and we may therefore consider the claim of Roger of Gwinear as finally dismissed, and judgment entered against the claimant.

Before leaving the consideration of Dr. Guild's paper, let me say that I have to thank him for one item of information which I did not know before, *i.e.* that Roger Williams also alluded to another brother (besides Robert) whom he describes as "a Turkey merchant in London." This may very well apply to Sidrach Williams, whom we already know to have been a merchant taylor of London. I have found, in the course of my investigations (and it is well known by English antiquaries), that it was a very common thing for members of the great companies to be engaged also in other trades and businesses and to be members of other companies. In my examination of the Books of Apprenticeships belonging to the Company of Skinners, some years ago, I found several instances, such as—"William Towerson, Skinner and Merchant Adventurer of Muscovey, Turkey and of Eastland"; "William Cockaine, Skinner and Merchant Adventurer and Merchant of Spaine and Portingale," &c. &c. If the books of the Merchant Taylors' Company are ever examined in the course of this investigation, as they ought to be, I would advise that a very careful search be made, say between 1620 and 1647, for all references to Sidrach Williams, with the hope of finding some such entry as the above.

Dr. Guild makes another statement which seems worth calling especial attention to, viz., that Roger Williams was accompanied to New England by "Thomas Angell, a lad of fourteen, who had been indented as his servant." Savage had already referred to this as one of two traditions, but also added that he "came from London." In connection with all this the following Marriage License becomes interesting :

John Pemberton, citizen and grocer of London, and Katherine Angell, of St. Thomas Apostle, said city, spinster, daughter of William Angell,* of same, citizen and fishmonger of London—at St. Thomas Apostle aforesaid. 19 Jan. 1609-10. B.   (Col. Chester's Marriage Lic.)

Now turn to the Pemberton pedigree, already given, and note the significance of this fact. That very John Pemberton was cousin german to the Roger Williams who was "beyond the seas" in 1634. I suppose we may be allowed to look upon such a coincidence as a genealogical *straw*, may we not?

The question of the wealth, either of James Williams of St. Sepulchre's, London, or of William Willyams of Roseworthy, Cornwall, I do not feel competent to discuss. I have not the data on which to base an opinion, nor do I have any faith that with searching I could find out enough to warrant me in forming an opinion that I should feel justified in making public. I am quite ready to believe that both families were well-to-do.

Let me suggest however to Dr. Guild that he has no right to use the term *heiress* instead of *co-heiress*, as if they were equivalent terms. Alice Williams was, in fact, a daughter and *co-heiress* of Roger Honeychurch. And let me also suggest to the readers of his paper that until we learn, first, what the value of Roger Honeychurch's estate was, and, secondly, how many daughters and co-heiresses there were for this estate to be distributed amongst, it will be useless to attempt to form any opinion about the wealth of Mrs. Alice Williams or to base any argument thereon as to the riches of her son Roger. The terms *heiress* and *co-heiress*, so often found in Heralds' Visitations, merely show that in the lack of male heirs the inheritance of an estate passed to females; and nothing can be predicated as to the value of such an estate. Whether Roger Honeychurch left ten pounds or ten thousand pounds his daughter Alice would still have been called co-heiress. But, allowing that we *knew* the Honeychurch estate to be a large one, it would still be unsafe for any one to pronounce Alice Williams wealthy until the number of co-heiresses should be known. There *may* have been a good many of them, and each single share, consequently, a small one. We read of some rather large families in former times. Some years ago I found, at the British Museum (in Stowe MSS. IX.–70), a declaration made by one Thomas Greenhill, 1 Sept. 1698, that he had been the seventh son and thirty-ninth child of William Greenhill, of Greenhill in Middlesex, by his only wife, Elizabeth daughter of William Dwight, of London. On this account, we are told, he was allowed by the Heralds *(inter alia)* to have the paternal crest (a demi griphon) powdered with thirty-nine mullets *Or*. And, not long since, I heard this story confirmed from another quarter, by a gentleman who had seen a portrait of this very Mrs. Elizabeth Greenhill, on the back of which had been inscribed the statement that she had been the mother of thirty-nine children. Thirty-two of these must have been daughters. Fancy even a large estate divided among thirty-two co-heiresses! By this time, I trust, the reader will have come to a conclusion, with me, that the only value which, with our present information, we can safely attach to the "co-heiress," as applied to Alice Williams, is a purely heraldic one as entitling her lawful issue to quarter the arms of Honeychurch upon their paternal coat.

In regard to the wealth of Roger Williams, himself, too, I do not see sufficient data furnished to warrant me in forming an opinion. The description of his house in Salem is painted in colors so bright as compared with the more quiet and subdued tints used by my friend and colleague, William P. Upham, Esq., that I dare not take it at Dr. Guild's valuation. I learn from this paper that our Roger Williams referred to Chancery suits in which he lost large sums. The examination of Chancery Proceedings may enable us to learn how much he lost there. "His banishment and forced flight in mid-winter" (we are told) "debarring him from Boston, 'the chief mart and port of New England,' was a loss to him, using his own words, 'of many thousand pounds.'" At first this seemed something definite and conclusive; but on looking at it again and noting

---

* For this William Angell, Esq. (as he is styled in pedigree and will), see Visitation of London (Harl. Soc. Pub.), Vol. I. p. 18. He was sergeant of the Catery, &c. His will may be found registered in P. C. C. (Ridley, 83). The will of his son James (Lee, 49) mentions a wife and six children, among whom a son Thomas.

more particularly that first clause, giving the reason for his loss, *i.e.* that he was debarred from the chief mart and port of New England, the question *would* arise in my mind: Did he mean "many thousand pounds" *in esse* or *in posse?* Was it so much money actually owned and then lost, or was it so much money which he had expected to make and by banishment from this "chief mart" was "debarred" from making? I have been left in such a state of doubt that, at the risk of appearing stupid, I have concluded it best to await the result of the Chancery investigation or the discovery and publication of an inventory of his estate before making up my mind on this subject.

I see that the dates of his entrance into the Charter House School and of the Exhibition which he gained there, once considered so well settled and established, are utterly denied in this paper, but no exact dates given in place of them, only a vague statement that he "probably remained there until 1620, after which he studied law with Coke." This, of course, will impose upon some more cautious plodder the task of making a re-examination of the School Register and getting an exact statement of the actual facts in the case, so far as Charter House School is concerned.

At the end of the paper we incidentally come upon another New England worthy of the same name. He it was (at least so says Dr. Guild) who entered into Charter House in 1621 and gained that exhibition in 1624. Six years afterwards he crossed the seas to New England and settled in Dorchester. "Probably" (says Dr. Guild) he was the son of Mr. Lewis Williams of St. Albans, and born in August, 1607. If the newspaper report of this specimen of genealogizing is correct I feel constrained to express my opinion that Dr. Guild does not set before beginners in the study of genealogy as a science an example that I could honestly advise them to follow.

In conclusion let me congratulate all who are interested in the subject upon the extreme probability that at last we have "struck the trail" beyond the seas in the case of Roger Williams. There is a good deal yet to be done in the way of research, and I hope that some one will be moved to carry on the work of investigation among probate records, the books of the Merchant Taylors' Company and the Public Records. If James Williams was apprenticed in his youth to a merchant taylor, the entry of his apprenticeship would undoubtedly disclose the name, occupation or condition and place of abode of his father. In probate records the names of Alice Harris, Thomas Morse and John and Katherine Davies should be hunted for. That will of Mrs. Margery Pate should be studied, &c. &c. I can see plenty of work to be done, and regret that I am debarred from attempting it.

HENRY F. WATERS.

A proof of the above wills and Mr. Waters's first annotations on them was sent to Dr. Guild, of Providence, the author of the paper which Mr. Waters refers to in his later annotations. Dr. Guild sends me the following notes.

1. In a letter to Gov. Winthrop, dated Plymouth, 1632, the Roger Williams of Rhode Island speaks of his conversion in childhood, and of the persecution which he suffered from his family in consequence:—"In Christ Called and persecuted even in and out of my father's house these twenty years." In the case of this Roger Williams of St. Albans, or London, there seems to have been good feeling towards him on the part of the family. The father, James, died in 1620; his brother-in-law, Ralph Wightman, died in 1628; and his mother Alice died in 1634. They all remembered him in their wills, giving to him the same as they gave to his brothers, Sidrach and Robert. In the case of the Willyams family of Cornwall it was without doubt different. This was an aristocratic and wealthy family, included in Burke's "History of the Landed Gentry." Such families had little sympathy with Puritans and Separatists, whom they "persecuted," as the early history of New England fully shows.

2. Our Roger Williams in his "George Fox" (Nar. Club Edition, page 146) speaks of a brother as being a member of the great and wealthy corporation known as the "Levant or Turkey Company of Merchants," whose coat of arms is given by Guillim in his "Display of Heraldry," and whose membership included not a few of the nobility and gentry:—"Myself have seen the Old Testament of the Jews, most curious writing, whose price (in the way of trade) was three score pound, which my brother, a Turkey merchant, had and shewed me."

This Roger Williams of St. Albans had an older brother Sydrach, a "merchant taylor," who died in 1647, and upon whose "goods &c." John Myster the "principal creditor" appears to have been administrator. His brother-in-law, Ralph Wightman, who died in 1628, was also a "merchant tailor." The Roger Willyams of Cornwall had two older brothers, William who succeeded to his father's title and estate, and Arthur who died in 1669.

3. In his "George Fox" (page 413), speaking of judicial oaths, Williams refers to "cases that have befallen myself in the Chancery in England &c. and of the loss of great sums which I chose to bear through the Lord's help (rather) than yield to the formality (then and still in use) in God's worship; though I offered to swear as F. H. mentions they have done, and the judges told me they would rest in my testimony and way of swearing, but they could not dispense with me without an act of parliament." This was probably before Williams left England, which was in 1630, and refers it would seem to the settling of an estate. If the founder of Rhode Island was of the Willyams family, of Cornwall, then his father died in June, 1623, at the age of 84, and he himself became of age in December following. His mother, who was an heiress, died in 1606, and her estate may be supposed to have been divided among her four children, William, Arthur, Roger and Margaret, upon the death of the father. In the case of Roger Williams of St. Albans, the father died in 1621, bequeathing to him twenty-five pounds, payable when he was 24 years of age, and one twelfth of the estate. This would hardly seem to meet the case of "great sums" which the founder of Rhode Island chose to lose rather than take the required oath.

4. The exact age of Roger, the son of James and Alice Williams, is undetermined. Roger, the son of William and Alice Willyams, of Cornwall, was born on the 21st of December, 1602. He lacked, therefore, three months of being 30 years old, when Roger Williams of Rhode Island wrote to Gov. Winthrop, saying that he was "nearer upwards of 30 than 25." Had he been born say in June, 1602, he would have been quite "upwards of 30." If he was born in 1599, as has been generally supposed, then he must have been 25 years of age when he entered college. If, on the other hand, he was born on the 21st of December, 1602, then he entered college (at the beginning of the second term) in just one month and eight days after he had attained his majority. This seems more probable if he had then come into possession of his share of his mother's or father's estate. The usual age for boys to enter college at this early period, it may be added, was fourteen.

5. The Roger Williams of St. Albans and the Roger Williams of Cornwall were both of English birth. The tradition is that the founder of Providence Plantations was a Welshman. This can be readily accounted for if he was born near Gwinear, Cornwall. The ancient Cornish language, says Max Müller, was a Celtic language formed from the Cymric and Gaelic, in which the Welsh dialect was predominant. Being brought up in the neighborhood of Wales, and possessing an ardent Welsh temperament, he would naturally be regarded as a Welshman by those who gave information in 1771 to Morgan Edwards, who has handed down the tradition, and who was himself a Welshman. Williams in his writings frequently refers to England as his native country, but never to Wales.

6. The objection made by some to the Cornwall theory of the birth of Roger Williams, is that he calls Robert Williams his brother, when he may have been his brother-in-law, either as the brother of his own wife, or the husband of his sister Margaret. This, however, is not uncommon, as the readers of the REGISTER well know. In these Genealogical Gleanings Ralph Wightman also calls Robert Williams his brother. It is earnestly hoped that in all these researches and discussions the birth and parentage of the great apostle of civil and religious freedom may be ascertained, as in the case of John Harvard, the founder of Harvard University, beyond doubt or question. .

R. A. GUILD.

The editor of the REGISTER would add a few remarks on Dr. Guild's annotations.

1. I do not think enough is known about the religious sentiments of either of the Williams families to decide which would be most likely to resist the Puritan tendencies of a child.

2. It is possible that one of the sons of William Willyams of Cornwall may have been a member of the Levant or Turkey Company, but if he was I do not

think he would be likely to take such an active part in its affairs as to be styled a "Turkey merchant." Mr. Waters's notes in relation to Sidrach Williams are commended to the reader.

3. The reference to the chancery suit is important, and the Chancery Proceedings may throw light on the parentage of our Roger Williams. Even if it is conceded that the matter related to the settling of an estate, which is not proved, we are not sure by whom the property was left. The time may have been before Williams left England or it may have been later, say during his visit to England in 1643–4.

4. Nothing can be inferred from the respective ages of the two Rogers. One was born in Dec. 1602, and the other was under 24 in 1620, but how much under we do not know.

5. The fifth point is worth noting. But the name Williams is considered of Welsh origin, and this may account for the tradition which cannot be traced back very far.

6. Roger Williams calls Robert Williams his brother in several places, and once he calls him his "own brother," namely in George Fox (vol. 5, of the Publications of the Narraganset Club, page 47), where he says: "Mine own Brother Mr. Robert Williams School-Master in Newport desired to speak," &c. I do no think it necessary to add anything on this point to what Mr. Waters has written.

Though I cannot agree with Dr. Guild in his conjecture as to the parentage of Roger Williams, I am ready to concede to him great praise for his researches, during more than twenty years, into the life of Williams.

The editor would be glad, if space allowed, to transfer to these pages the earliest statements relative to the life of Williams before he came to New England, but he will have to content himself with referring the reader to the books where these statements appear, namely :—Rev. Mr. Hubbard's History of New England, written about 1680 (Mass. Hist. Coll., vol. 15, page 202); Stephen Hopkins's History of Providence, written in 1765 (Mass. Hist. Coll., vol. 19, page 168); Rev. Morgan Edwards's Materials for the History of the Baptists of Rhode Island, compiled in 1771 (R. I. Hist. Coll., vol. 6, page 316); Rev. John Sanford's entries in 1775, on the records of the First Baptist Church of Providence (Benedict's Hist. of the Baptists, vol. 1, pages 473–4); Rev. Isaac Backus's History of New England, with particular reference to the Baptists, vol. 3, published in 1796 (2d ed. vol. ii. p. 489); Mrs. Anne Sadleir memorandum on a letter to her by Roger Williams, written about 1652–3 (Pub. of the Narraganset Club, vol. 6, 1874, pages 252–3). See also Knowles's Memoir of Williams, 1834, page 23; Elton's life of Williams, 1853, pages 9–12; Guild's Biographical Introduction to the Writings of Williams, 1866 (Pub. Narraganset Club, vol. 1), pages 5–9, and Arnold's History of Rhode Island, vol. 1, 1859, pages 47–50.

After the greater portion of the preceding Gleanings and annotations were in type, I received a letter from Mr. Waters calling my attention to two letters by a Roger Williams in the collection of George Alan Lowndes, Esq., of Barrington Hall, Hatfield Broad Oak, England, as reported by the Historical Manuscripts Commission in their Seventh Report (Appendix, page 546). Mr. Waters suggested that these might be by our Roger Williams, and by his advice I procured a tracing of Williams's autograph which I sent to Mr. Lowndes, asking him to compare it with the signatures in the letters in his collection, and if he thought them to be by the same person, I solicited him to furnish copies for printing in the REGISTER. Mr. Lowndes sent me a transcript of the letters, which are here printed. The transcript was accompanied by the following letter:

BARRINGTON HALL,
HATFIELD BROAD OAK, ESSEX,
June 13, 1889.

DEAR SIR:

I have had great pleasure in complying with your request. I have compared the writing of Roger Williams with the copy you sent, and also shown them to an expert, who agrees with me that they are identical.

I enclose you copies of the letters. Mr. Williams, at the time of writing them, was chaplain to Sir William Masham, of Otes, in the parish of High Laver, Essex (where the second letter is dated from). Sir William was the ancestor of Mrs. Masham's husband, who played such a prominent part in the reign of our Queen Anne. Locke, the philosopher, died at Otes, and is buried in High Laver Churchyard. I think it very doubtful whether Roger Williams ever held church preferment in this country (although he mentions in his letter to Lady Barrington that he had had the offer of two livings). Probably his disappointment in love was one of the causes of his emigration.

There is no doubt he proposed to a niece of Lady Barrington, as suggested by his first (undated) letter, and the refusal brought the second, which very much offended Lady Barrington.

Trusting this information is what you require, and if I can answer any further inquiries you may make, I shall be very pleased to do so.

Believe me, dear sir,

Yours faithfully,

J. Ward Dean, Esq.   G. Alan Lowndes.

I think the readers of the Register will agree with me that the internal evidence is in favor of the letters being written by the founder of Rhode Island. This, added to the identity of the hand-writing, I consider conclusive. The letters did not reach me till after Mr. Waters's article was made up, but fortunately I am able to print them here. They will be welcomed as a very important discovery.

These letters have an important bearing upon the question of the parentage of Rev. Roger Williams discussed in Waters's Gleanings. As the writer of the letters had an aged mother living in 1629, it is evident he was not the Roger Williams of Roseworthy, whose mother had then been dead twenty-three years. The writer's expectation of property to be received at the death of his mother does not come far from the sum, ten pounds per annum, which Roger; son of James, actually received. The lowest sum named in the letter is twenty marks per annum. It is evident that the writer was not a wealthy man.

The letters furnish us with the residence of Williams in 1629. It was at High Laver in Essex, not more than a dozen miles from Chelmsford, where Rev. Thomas Hooker preached. This explains why Hooker and Williams were together in their ride to and from Semperingham, as related by the latter in his "Bloody Tenent yet More Bloody," as follows:

"Possibly Master Cotton may call to minde that the *discusser* (riding with himself and one other person of precious memory (Master *Hooker*) to and from Sempringham) presented his *Arguments* from *Scripture* why he durst not join with them in their use of *Common prayer*."—(Pub. Nar. Club, iv. 65.)

Lady Joan Barrington, to whom these letters were addressed, was the widow of Sir Francis Barrington, bart., who died in 1628. They were the parents of Lady Masham. Lady Barrington was a daughter of Sir Henry Cromwell and an aunt of the Protector Cromwell. Knowles, in his Memoir of Roger Williams, says, "It has been supposed that he [Williams] was a relative of Oliver Cromwell, one of whose ancestors was named Williams"; and he cites Baylies's New Plymouth as his authority. But the tradition to which Baylies refers concerned Richard Williams of Taunton, not Roger of Providence. In these letters Williams claims no relationship to Lady Barrington.

Written as the letters were by Williams midway between his leaving Cambridge University and his emigration to New England, they throw much light on a portion of his life concerning which our information has been exceedingly meagre, and they indicate where we should look for further facts. The editor of the Register has asked Mr. Lowndes to communicate any facts concerning Williams which he may find among the manuscripts at Barrington Hall. Perhaps these manuscripts may contain information about the New England emigration.

As both John Hampden, the patriot, and Oliver Cromwell were own cousins of Lady Masham, in whose family Roger Williams was chaplain, no doubt the latter, during his residence at Otes, saw much of these historic personages.   It has been a question how Williams when he returned to England in 1643 obtained access to the leaders of the Parliamentary cause.   But in the case of Cromwell and some of the others he probably became acquainted with them at Otes and Barrington Hall before his emigration to New England.—EDITOR.]

[Without date, written before next letter dated May 2, 1629.]

To his honorable
  good ladie
    Y^e Lady
      Barrington at
        Hatfield Priorie
          these

MADAM

Your Laddiship may wonder at this unwonted absence! & also aske what meanes this Paper deputie! Give me leaue (deare Madame) to say with David, to his brothers in ye field: is there not a cause? A just happily a knowne & open cause, I am sure to yor Lady^{sh} (who as an Angell of God discerneth wisely) a known & open cause.

Many & often speeches haue long fluttered or floune abroad concerning your Ladiships neere kinswoman & my unworthy selfe. What little care I haue given that way (further then I haue harkened after your Ladiships mind) all that know me here doe know. Yet like a rowling snow ball or some flouing streame ye report extends & gathers stronger & stronger which causes me this day to stand behind the Hangings & will not be seen any way countenancing so great a busines wch happily may want strength to bring it forth to see the light. It is ye command of ye God of wisdome by y^t wise King Salomon Establish thy thoughts by councell. I presume therefore to consult (as most of right I acknowledge I ought) with ye soonest with y^r Ladiship, especially considering her loving & strong affection together with ye report, as story abroad.

Good Madame may it please you then to take notice. I acknowledge my selfe altogeather unworthy & unmeete for such a proposition. The neerenes of her blood to y^r Ladiship & godly flourishing branches hath forc't me to confesse her Portion, in y^t regard, to be beyond compare invaluable. Yet many feares have much possest me Longe I have to discover y^t sinceritie & Godlines which makes ye Lord himselfe to like his Creature & must make me if ever I have recciued some good Testimonialls from mine own experience more from others not the least from yor good Ladiships selfe. Objections have come in about her spirit, much accused for passionate & hastie, rash & unconstant, other feares about her present condition it being some Indecorum for her to condescend to my low Ebb there I some what stick: but were all this cleared, there is one barr not likely to be broken & y^t is the present Estate of us both. That portion it hath pleased God to allot her (as I heare) is not for present & happily as things stand now in England shall never be by us enjoyed. For my own part It is well knoune (though I would gladly conseale my selfe) How a gracious God & tender conscience (as Balak said to Balaam) hath kept me back from honour and preferment Besides many former offers & y^t late New England call, I have since had 2 severall livings proferred to me each of them 100£ per annum; but as things yet stand among us I see not how any meanes & I shall meet y^t way. Nor doe I seeke nor shall I be draune on any tearmes to part (even to my last parting) from Oates so long as any competencie can be raised or libertie affoorded. I shall impart the utmost to your Ladiship (more punctually than ever yet to any): beside this meanes I now from hence enjoy little there is yet I can call mine. After the death of an aged loving mother amongst some other Children I may expect (though for the present she be close & will not promise) some 20£ or 20 marks per annum. At hand undisposed of I have some 7 score pieces & a little (yet costlie) studie of bookes. Thus posessing all things I have nothing, yet more than God owes me, or then my blessed Saviour had himselfe.

Poore yet as I am I have some few offers at present one put into my hand, person & present portion worthy. Yet stand they still at dore & shall until the fairest end ye Lord shall please to give to this shall come to light. I have been told to open to your Ladiship the whole Anatomie of this busines. To wrong your precious name and answer her kind love with want would be like gall to all the honey of my life, & marr my marriage joys. The kind affection of your deare Ladiship & worthy niece is of better merit and desert. I shall add for the present I know none in the world I more affect & (had ye Lord been pleased to say amen in those other regards) should doubtles haue fully answered (if not exceeded) her affection.

But I have learned another Lesson to still my soule as a weaned childe & give offence to none. I have learn'd to keepe my studie and pray to ye God of heaven (as oft as I doe pray) for the everlasting peace and well fare of your kind Ladiship, whose soule & comfort is in ye number of my greatest cares. The Lord that hath caried you from the wombe to gray haires crown those gray haires by making your last dayes (like ye close of some sweet harmonie) your rest fruitfull (like Sarah) in old age: out shining all those starrs y^t shine about you: going downe in Peace, rising in Glory in the armes of yor dearest Saviour. To wch everlasting armes he often commits your Soule & yours, who is

ye unworthiest (though faythfull) of all y^t truely serve & honour you.

ROGER WILLAIMS.

To his honorable good
 Lady ye Lady Barring-
 ton at Hatfield
                    these
Otes   May 2^d 1629
MADAME

I am forc't (with ye Seaman) for want of a full gale to make use of a side wind & salute your Ladiship by another, being for a time shut out my selfe I doubt not but your good wisdome & loue haue fairely interpreted my carriage in ye late treatie, & I allso trust, quieted & still'd the loving affections of your worthy niece. We hope to live togeather in the heavens though ye Lord have denied that union on Earth. Dear Madame, Let me beg your christian Pardon if I shall acquaint your Ladiship with a busines of more waight & consequence & much neerer concerning your selfe. I beseech you to reade no further before you resolve to pardon & take with the right hand of love, from the Lord himselfe, a message sent by me, his unworthy Servant. A better hand might better pen it, A better heart more tender of your peace & everlasting good, none y^t know you (if I can) shall carrie toward you.

What I shall now expresse to your Ladiship hath long lyen like fire in my bones Jer 20: 9. I said I should not make mention of his name in this kind to you but his word was in my heart as A burning fire shut up in my bones & I was weary with forbearing & I could not stay.

Good Madame it is not for nothing, y^t ye God of Heaven hath sent such thunderclaps of late and made such great offers at the dore of your Ladiships heart. Distractions about children & their afflictions; deprivall of a deare & tender yoake fellow, weaknesses of the outward & troubles in the inward man, what are they but loud alarums to awake you?

The father of lights be pleased himselfe to show you the interpretation of these dreams, certainly (Madame) ye Lord hath a quarrell against you. Woe unto me if I hold my peace & hide y^t from you, which may seeme bitter at present, it may be sweeter than hony at the latter end. Incouragement to be naked & plaine your Ladiship was pleased to give me at Otes. If ever (deare Madame) when there is but the breadth of a few gray haires betwene you & your everlasting home let me deale uprightly with you.

I know not one professor amongst all I know whose truth and faythfullness to Jesus Christ is more suspected, doubted, feared, by all or most of those y^t know the Lord.

Woe to me if I shall conceale what great thoughts of heart the Lord suffers yet to be & breake forth in his dearest Saincts about you. And yet no hand in this is with me, The God of Heaven & your deare Self only know these secret lines. It hath almost astonisht me (& I trust will deeply affect your Ladiship) y^t not only inferiour Christians but ministers, eagle eyed, faithfull & observant to your Ladiship; after so many yeares of God's patience towards you so long profession, such helpes, meanes incomparable should yet be driuen to sigh, to say little, to suspend their Judgments, to hope but feare & doubt.

I know (deare Madame) your heart is full at these relations, I beseech you (as David said) on me let your thoughts & the burthen fall, but what have these sheepe done? when 2 or 3 or few are excepted: y^t names of so great a number may well be spared.

Three things especially have I often gathered from them. First, feares are y^t the world hath choakt those blessed Seeds y^t have been soune & keepes the fruite from true perfection. 2^{ndly} a strangenes from the faithfull in spirituall societie: This is the fayrest evidence of Adoption. If this Pin breakes all falls. & 3^d a stand or stay in the wayes of holynes young plants of yesterday giving fairer testimonies of greater fruitfulnes.

Deare Madame I beseech you by all those multitudes of tender motherly mercies y^t are in God & exprest to you: by y^t inconceavable patience of the Lord toward you: by ye bowells and blood of ye Lord Jesus by all those sweet cords of love, whereby the blessed Spirit of God hath striven to draw you make a stand and spread my letter (as Hezekiah) before ye Lord in secret.

If ever (good Madame) cry hard & ye Lord help me to cry for you. Let these 2 peticions Psal. 51. 11 & 71. 9 be cleare to you. Rememb: I beseech you Revel 2. 2. 3 ye Church of Ephesus was much esteemed by God, for her works, her labour, her patience her not bearing with those y^t were Evill, for y^t she had borne, & for his sake laboured, and not fainted & yet angry was he & he had something against her: & it was because she had left her first love. The Lord establish my hope for I hope it may be but so with your Ladiship only I beseech you to lay to heart these few considerations.

1. First Job 34. 9 [Qu. 19?]. He with whome we deale excepteth not the

persons of princes nor regardeth the rich more than the poore for they are all the worcke of his hands.

2. When birth greater, maintenance, more ample time longer and means of grace more plentifull, then a great account of the Lord is expected. Luc 12.

3. The Lord will doe what he will with his owne. He owes you no mercy. Exod 33. 19. I will be gracious to whom I will be gracious & I will shew mercy to whome I will shew mercy.

4. Call to mind what a cutt, what a gnawing worme it will be (ye Lord, ye Lord forbid it) if ever you cast up your eye toward heaven, & see so many blessed branches in the bosome of Christ & y^r stock rejected.

5. Slight not I beseech you all these late loud alarums & sharp files with which ye lord hath striven to burnish you Ezech 24.

6. Remember I beseech you your candle is twinkling & glasse neare run ye Lord only knows how few minutes are left behind.   Psal 95. 10. Fourtie yeares was I grieved, then I swore in my wrath they should never enter into my rest.   No heart but a trembling heart can get assurance ye Lord hath not sworne: to y^t heart he hath sworne to be gracious. In y^t Petition my soule follows hard after him & still will I wrastle untill you say, a blessing is come, a blessing of a heart softened & trembling of a Soule gasping after Jesus Christ.   A blessing of Joye refreshing to the faythfull & to him who is ever

> Your Ladiships most faythfull and
> truly ob servant
> ROGER WILLIAMS.

SAMPSON COTTON, of the parish of S^t. Michael Pater Noster in the Royal, London, citizen & draper of London, 17 January 1634, proved 23 July 1635 by Elizabeth Cotton, relict and executrix.   To be buried in the parish church of St. Michael Pater Noster, aforesaid, as near to the place where my loving father M^r. Thomas Juxon was buried as conveniently may be.   All debts paid and funeralls discharged, all my personal estate, &c. according to the laudable custom of the City of London, shall be divided into three equal parts or portions; one third to wife Elizabeth; one other full third part unto & amongst Anne, Elizabeth, Johan, Hester, James, Sarah and Thomas Cotton, the children of me, the said Sampson Cotton, equally &c.; the other third part to discharge legacies & bequests &c.

To my sister Elizabeth Rosewarden, widow, ten pounds per annum during her natural life; at her death, to my said children.   To my sister Anne Fuller, widow, two hundred & fifty pounds at the end of six months after my decease.   To my mother-in-law, Mrs. Elizabeth Juxon, twenty pounds. To my brother Elias Juxon ten pounds.   To my sister Mary Hobbey, widow, five pounds.   To John Hobbey five pounds.   To my cousin Michael Handcorne five pounds.   To Thomas Juxon three pounds.   To Richard Juxon three pounds.   To Philip Bowles three pounds.   To M^r. Worme forty shillings.   To the church warden of S^t. Michael Pater Noster in the royal, whereof I am a parishioner, towards the repairs of the said parish church, five pounds.   To Andrew Vaughan three pounds.   To Richard Sotherne three pounds.   To Edward Lowe three pounds.   To William Outram forty shillings.   To Sibill Maybanke, my servant, twenty shillings. To my cousin Elizabeth Decon twenty nobles currant English money.   All these said several legacies, from Mrs. Elizabeth Juxon unto my cousin Elizabeth Deacon, my will & mind is shall be paid at the end of six months after my decease. To my apprentice Thomas Lightfoote twenty nobles, to be paid him at the expiration of his apprenticeship, if he be then living & shall faithfully and diligently dwell with me and serve my said wife during the whole term of his apprenticeship. To seventy poor men ten shillings apiece after my funeral. My wife to be sole executrix, and my friends, Philip Bowles and Michael Handcorne, overseers.

Wit; Richard Rochdale, scr. and Samuel Ball servant to the said scr.

A codicil, of same date, contains nothing that seems of importance genealogically. Sadler, 82.

[The testator of the above will was the father-in-law of Edmund Sheefe (see the latter's will), and grandfather of Sampson Sheafe of New England. That he did not belong to the same family as the Rev^d. John Cotton of Boston, would seem probable from a tricking of the arms of Sheafe impaling Cotton (1640), in Harleian MS. 1466, fo. 5^b, to which my friend M^r. Eedes called my attention, in the British Museum, and which must apply to this match. These arms are as follows, viz. :—*Ermine, on a chevron gules, between three pellets, as many garbs or*, impaling, *per fesse, argent & azure, a lion rampant counterchanged.*

From this will we get another line of ancestry for Sampson Sheafe and his descendants, viz. : the "famous family" of Juxon.

I have numerous wills and other notes relating to the Sheafe and Juxon families and their alliances.—H. F. W.]

THOMAS JUXON, citizen and merchant taylor of London, 20 October 1620, with codicil dated 6 November 1620, proved 5 December 1620, by Elizabeth Juxon, relict & executrix. To be buried in the parish church of S^t. Michael Pater Noster in the Royal, where I am a parishioner, at the upper end of the aisle on the right hand going into the said church, as near the place where my daughter Katherine was buried as may be. My personal estate to be divided into three equal parts, according to the honorable custom of the City of London. One full third part to my faithful wife Elizabeth Juxon. One other equally just third part unto & amongst my children unadvanced—that is to say—Albone Juxon, Elias als Ellis Juxon, Thomas Juxon, Richard Juxon, my sons, and Sara Juxon, my daughter, the children of me the said Thomas Juxon and the said Elizabeth Juxon my wife (equally). The other third part I reserve for myself to pay legacies &c. Fifty pounds to the church wardens of the church of S^t. Michael Pater Noster in the Royal, towards the repairing of the said parish church and of the windows belonging to the same, by and with the consent and direction of M^r. Angell, M^r. Archdale, M^r. Browne, M^r. Jadwin,[1] M^r. Worsopp, M^r. Cotten and M^r. Rochdale, or any four of them (being vestrymen of the said parish); the said fifty pounds to be paid within one year after my decease and to be expended in three years. To M^r. Woorme, parson of the said church, six pounds thirteen shillings four pence, wherewith to buy himself a mourning gown, or otherwise to be by him, at his own freewill, disposed of.

I do give and bequeath the great ladder & hook, with a pole in it, now remaining in the said church and made and paid for by me, unto the said parish for the help of the parishioners and other neighbors upon occasion of accident of fire (from which need Good Lord defend us and this famous city) and, to the end the same may be safely restored if it shall so happen the same to be lent out of the parish, my will is that the church wardens of the said parish do cause a mark to be set thereupon whereby it may appear unto what parish the same do belong. I give unto the Company of Merchant tailors in London, whereof I am a member, wherewith to make them a dinner on the day of my funeral, twenty & five pounds. To the clerk of the same Company fifty three shillings four pence & to the Bedell of the same Company twenty six shillings & eight pence. Unto Susan Juxon, the daughter of my son Albone, fifty pounds, to be paid unto her at her full age of one & twenty years, or her day of marriage &c. &c.

Item I do give and bequeath unto my son in law Sampson Cotton the sum of one hundred pounds, currant English money; and I do also give & bequeath unto my son Sampson Cotton to and for the use of Anne, Elizabeth, Mary, Joane and Hester, the children of the said Sampson and Elizabeth his wife, the daughter of me the said Thomas Juxon, fifty pounds apiece, currant English money &c. I do give and bequeath unto my son in law Richard Hobby one hundred pounds, and also, to and for the use of Robert, John, Richard, Anne, Rachell and Mary Hobby, the children of the said Richard Hobby and Mary his wife, the daughter of me the said Thomas Juxon, the sum of three score pounds &c. To my son in law William Pitt and Rebecca his wife one hundred pounds; and unto such child as my said daughter Rebecca is now big and goeth withall, ten pounds. And so God bless my sons in law Sampson Cotton, Richard Hobby and William Pitt, their wives and children.

To my son Albone, one hundred pounds. To my son Elias als Ellis one hundred pounds. To Thomas, Richard and Sara Juxon, my children, one hundred pounds apiece. My desire and request unto my said son Sampson Cotton is that he be aiding and assisting unto my said wife in the discharge of the trust which by this my last will I have reposed in her. Provision made to buy mourning for wife, sons & daughters & their children and mourning cloaks for all such as shall be my servants at the time of my decease, and also mourning for my maid servants. And for William Pitt the elder a mourning cloak and for William Marsh, a mourning cloak, or four pounds apiece in money (the two) wherewith to provide them cloaks. Also for to provide forty poor mens gowns to be given unto forty poor men, to wear at my funeral, and no more mourning to be given at my charge either unto my own or my wife's kindred. To St. Bartholomew Hospital, near West Smithfield, ten pounds. To Christ Hospital, near Newgate Market, London, twenty nobles. To my apprentice William Waunderton ten pounds, to be paid him at the end of his apprenticeship if he shall serve my said wife or my son Sampson Cotton the full term of his apprenticehood, truly, dutifully, faithfully and diligently. To all my workmen within my house, viz.: Michael Handcorne, Andrew Vaughan, Richard Southwood, Edward Lowe and Richard Weare, forty shillings apiece. To my said wife ten pounds to this end & purpose, that she shall give and distribute the same unto Mary Hanckinson, my said wife's sister.

To my wife all my lands, tenements &c. in Newbury, and the towns, parishes, fields & hamlets about Newbury, in Berks, &c. My messuage in Colman Street, on the West side of the street, to my son Thomas and tenements in Newbury. My son in law Sampson Cotton & son Ellis Juxon to be overseers.

Wit: Ellis Crispe, Robert Angell, Edward Browne, John Worsopp, John Saal and Richard Rochdale scr.

In the codicil he revokes the bequest of a hundred pounds to Richard Hobby and gives to his loving friend Ellis Crispe, citizen & salter of London, two hundred & fifty pounds at the end of twelve months next and immediately ensuing after that Elizabeth, the testator's now wife, shall after the decease of him the said Thomas Juxon, either marry or otherwise depart this mortal life, which of these two shall first and next happen or come after the decease of the said Thomas. Soame, 116.

[Thomas Juxon was an " adventurer " or member of the Virginia Company of London.
1 Thomas Jadwin, a member of the Virginia Company of London.
John Jadwin patented 650 acres of land on the south side of Rappahannock River, at the head of Sharp's Creek, formerly taken up by John Sharp, Nov. 13, 1658, now renewed Feb. 12, 1662. Va. Land Registry, Book No. 4, p. 566. It appears that a son of John Jadwin, patentee, went into Talbot Co., Md., in 1672. C. C. Jadwin, Honesdale, Wayne Co., Penn., has in preparation a Jadwin Genealogy.—R. A. BROCK, *Richmond, Va.*]

JOHN SCOT of Mattox, Westmoreland County, Virginia, merchant, 28 May 1700, now bound to sea. To my two sisters and their children that I believe is in Ireland, whose maiden names are Jane and Rebecca Scott, one hundred pounds sterling, to be paid by my executor, Gustavos Scott of Bristol. To my brother James's son, named Gustavos, thirty pounds sterling, to be paid out of the money his father and mother "is due" to me. To my brother Gustavos twenty pounds sterling, out of the said money due by sister. And in case the Ship Potomack Galley that I have shipt most of my tobacco on board should miscarry and not get safe home, as God forbid, then my will is the above legacies to be paid but the half part of what I have above named, and the remainder to my wife and children &c. To my son John my plantation I now dwell on, that I bought of Capt. Thomas Mountjoy. If he dies before marriage, or before he cometh of age, the said plantation to go to my daughter Jane and her heirs. To the said Jane the tract of land, five hundred acres on the North East branch of the Potomack River in Maryland, called in the " Paton " Strabane, with remainder to John and his heirs. The plantation of mine at the head of Pope's Creek which I bought from Abraham Field to my wife Sarah;—also the benefit of the plantation I now dwell on until my son John come of age. The rest of my estate equally between my children John, Jane and my wife; and if she be with child then such child shall have one equal share. If my children all die without heirs, remainder to my nephew Gustavos Scott, next to my brother Gustavos. When my son John attains to the age of eight or nine years he shall be sent to England to his uncle Gustavos, to be kept at school there.

My wife Sarah to be the executrix in trust and my kinsman Mr William Graham and Mr. Andrew Munroe[2] the executors in trust to my children until they come of age. My son John and brother Gustavos Scott of Bristol to be executors. A mourning ring to John Hoare, and to his son John, my godson, a thousand pounds of tobacco. To my kinsman William Graham ten pounds (in money) and my watch which I carry to England to be repaired. To M^r. Andrew Munroe my silver hilted sword and belt, a case of pistols and holsters. To M^r. David Wilson a gold ring.

Wit: Nathaniel Pope, Charles Tankersly, James Mason, David Wilson, Thomas Wickers.

Corke 7b^r ye 29th. 1702 My Deare this comes to advise that I thanke God I am safe arrived here and in good health and shall be cleere to Sale this weeke I can heare of noe convoy as yet if there be any hopes of Convoy in any short time I will stay for it. if not I will sayle as soone as I get cleere. our beef stands us 5^s. a bar. more then I can buy for now. fouer of yours I have received which is a great satisfaccon to mee to heare of your health

& wotel doles (*sic*) I pray God continue it to you and send you a safe delivery in his own goode time, I have receivd a Letter from Virginia from Couzen W^m. Graham and the Copy of my Brothers Will which I have sent you & brother Galbraith with a Letter of Attorney by a Publ Notary for I heare the little John is goné for Bristol. So I would have brother and you to take Councill and act as you see fit in for I am whole Executor in the Will next post I will write you more at large my love to brother and sister I hope bathing will prove effectual wth them. I thanke M^{rs}. Long for her and give mine to her againe, and I wish her a good husband, my Deare be sure not to be forgettfull of what I formerly write you from Waterford that is to be kind to yourselfe I will send you by M^r. ffowles some Tongues and Salmon I sent you by Mr Becher S^r. John Duddlestons sonn abroad peece with my kind love to yo^{r}selfe I am yo^{rs} Gust: Scott.

Loving Brother. Inclosed is a Letter to you from W^m. Graham and a power of Attorney by a Not. Publ. from me and a copy of my broth^{rs} to Capt. ffrencklen tell me that M^r. Marten is gone to Bristoll so my desire is that you may take Councill and do in it as you see fitt I doe suppose that Coll^{ll}. Lee has wret to me wch per gues wch may be some direction to you I have no more to Ad, but have dranke yor health in a full glass of good Clarrett with some of yor ffreinds, Give my kind Lo. to Betty & Dolay & Gusay & Wotel Dolay when they comes to Towne and Margaret and the same to your selfe. I rest yor Lo. Brother   Gust. Scott.

Pray sell the little bagg of Indico of mine y^t at yor house and you will oblige yor bro: G: S:

William Galbraith of the City of Bristol Merchant maketh Oath that on or about the Twentieth day of August last past Gustaves Scott of the City of Bristol Mariner, brother of John Scot late of Mattox of Westmoreland County in Virginia Merchant deceased set sail from the Port of Bristoll in a voyage for Cork in Ireland and Montserat and he further saith that on or about the Seventeenth day of October last past this Deponent received by the Post a letter from the said Gustaves Scott from Cork aforesaid with one within on the same sheet of paper, for Elizabeth the wife of the said Gustaves Scott which letter is hereto fixed for the contents thereof this Deponent referreth himself and he saith that enclosed in the said letter there came a copy of the last Will and Testament of the said John Scott attested from Virginia which copy of the said Will this Deponent apprehends by the said letter he the said Gustaves received whilst he was at Cork aforesaid. And this Deponent saith that after his receipt as aforesaid of the said letter from the said Gustaves Scott this Deponent delivered the copy of the said Will to the said Elizabeth Scott together with the Letter aforesaid which Copy of the said Will this Deponent received again from the said Elizabeth Scott and the same was lately delivered by this Deponent or his agent unto M^r. John Hill one of the Proctors of the Prerogative Court of Canterbury. And this Deponent further saith that these said letters are all the proper hand writing of the said Gustaves Scott with whose hand writing this Deponent is well acquainted.   W^m. Galbraith.

Jurat apud Civit̃ Bristoll xiiii° die Decembris 1702 Coram me Tho: Oldfield uũ m͠ro^{rum} Cuȓ Cant̃ Ext̃ȓ.

Decimo nono die mensis Decembris Anno Domini Millesimo septingentesimo secundo Emanavit Commissio Elizabethae Scott ux et Attornatæ lt̃imae Gustavi Scott modo in partibus transmarinis fratris n͠ralis et lt̃imi et unius Executorum nominat̃ in Testamento Johañis Scott nup̃ de Mattox in

Com Westmorlandiæ in Virginia def' heñ etc. Ad Administrandum bona jura et eredita dict defti juxta tenorem et effectum Testiñti ipsius defuncti in usum et beneficium et durante abñia dci Gustavi Scott de bene et fideliter administrando eadem Ad Scta Dei Evangelia Jurat vigore comñis.

Herne, 206.

[² This was probably Rev. Andrew Munroe, who appears among the ministers of the Established Church in 1696. Small patents of land were granted an Andrew Munroe in Northumberland Co., Va., the first of 200 acres, June 8, 1650, in which he is named as one of the "Head Rights." Book No. 1, p. 225, Va. Land Registry.

Rev. John Munroe was a Rector in Northumberland Co., Va., in 1692. The tradition in Virginia is that Andrew Monroe, the ancestor of President James Monroe, was a Major in the Royal Army, and came to Virginia after its defeat. Spencer Monroe, the father of the President, and John Monroe, appear among the signers to "Westmoreland Association," formed in opposition to the Stamp Act, Feb. 27, 1766.—R. A. BROCK.]

JOHN PAGE of Gloucester County in Virginia, designing shortly a voyage for England, 20 April 1709, proved 2 January 1718. To my dear and loving daughter Elizebeth Page all her mother's clothes, rings and jewells and five guineas to lay out on such jewell or ornament as she shall think proper, at the age of twelve years, which will be on the fourth day of November in the year of our Lord one thousand seven hundred and fourteen, and such a certain sum of money besides as with what is due from the estate of Capt. Francis Page[8] and Mrs Elizabeth Page (her mother) deceased, which will appear by my account of the said estates given into the General Court, will make the full sum of three thousand pounds of lawful English money, to be paid her at the age of twenty one years. To my dear and loving daughter Mary Page the full sum of three thousand pounds; that is to say two thousand pounds of the said sum to be paid her three months after the day of her marriage or at the age of twenty one years, which shall first happen, and the other thousand pounds to be paid her at the age of twenty one years, which will be on the twenty eighth day of January in the year of our Lord one thousand seven hundred and twenty seven; also a pair of gold ear-rings set with rubies and rose diamonds, in a shagreen case, and one large gold wedding ring, one gold ring enamelled with blue and another with black, which were her mother's, and the half of all my china ware in my now dwelling house in the said Gloucester County. To my loving daughter in law Martha Page[4] all her mother's rings and jew- ells except the ear-rings and the other three rings already bequeathed to my daughter Mary, and the other half of my china ware &c., and one large common prayer book, with a shagreen cover, plated with silver and clasps, which was her mother's. To my loving son in law Mann Page,[5] upon his arrival in Virginia, a saddle horse such as he shall choose upon any of my plantations, and a large folio Bible with a turkey leather cover, plated with silver and clasps, a silver watch, a silver hilted sword, a "Tortes" shell and silver hilted hanger and belt, and one "Torter" shell and silver handed horsewhip, a crimson velvet housen and holster cape trimed with silver lace, and a silver tobacco box, which were his father's, also five pictures in double lackered frames, now hanging in the parlor of my said dwelling house &c. (viz[t]) of his father Col. Matthew Page, of his mother Mrs Mary Page, of himself and of his two sisters Alice and Martha.

Reference made to a bond to pay the said Mann Page (now under twenty one) to the value of two thousand pounds sterling in negroes, cattle, horses, mares, sheep, hogs, housebould necessaries, working tools &c., and forty hogsheads of prized tobacco upon the plantation of the said Mann Page in New Kent County, which is to be in full payment of what is due to the said Mann Page out of his said father's estate. And whereas it would be a very great hindrance and loss to my said son in law Mann Page to have his plantation in Gloucester County unstockt when they shall come into his hands, therefore my will is that he may have the whole stock of negroes except George and Jemmy two of my carpenters and Doll and Poll two housewenches and their children (together with other stock &c). To my godson South Napier,[6] son of Robert Napier formerly of New Kent County, twenty pounds six months after my decease to buy him a young negro. To my god son Edward Diggs, son of Col. Dudley Diggs, twenty pounds at the age of twenty one years. To my godson Matthew Walker, son of M[r] Joseph Walker of York County, thirty pounds in six months after my decease, to be laid out in purchasing two negro children, which, with their increase, to go to him at the age of eighteen years.

To my son John Page all the residue, both real and personal in England and Virginia or elsewhere, and he to be executor, at the age of eighteen years, which will be on the twenty second day of December in the year of our Lord one thousand seven hundred and seventeen; and until my said son John Page shall attain to the age of eighteen years I appoint my loving friends M[r]. Edward Barkley, of Gloucester County, M[r]. Joseph Walker, of York County, M[r]. Robert Anderson jun[r], of New Kent County, aud M[r]. Richard Wiltshier of Gloucester County, Trustees to see this my last Will and Testament duly executed, and my son in law Mann Page to be joined in this Trust at his age of twenty one.

Wit: Guy Smith cler., John Pratt, Hugh Hughes.

2 January 1718, Deposition of Micajah Perry and Richard Perry, of the parish of S[t]. Katherine Cree Church, London, merchants, and John Page, of York County in Virginia, gentleman, that they were well acquainted with John Page the elder, late of Glocester County in Virginia, but at Bethnal Green in the parish of Stepney in the County of Middlesex, merchant, deceased, and with his handwriting for several years next before and till the time of his death, which happened in the year one thousand seven hundred and ten &c. &c.

The above will was proved by the oath of John Page the executor &c.

Browning, 14.

[3 John Page, son of Matthew the emigrant, married first, Elizabeth, daughter of Capt. Francis Page and his wife Mary daughter of Edward Digges; and secondly, Martha, widow of Matthew Page.
4 Wife of his son John.
5 Son of his second wife.
6 The name Napier is still represented in Virginia. The will of Patrick Napier, "chirurgeon," was probated in York county, Va., April 12, 1669. He mentions wife Elizabeth, son Robert, and daughter Frances.—R. A. BROCK.]

JOSEPH THOROWGOOD (*ante*, page 313). We are favored by Mr. Brock with the following extract from a letter to him by Langdon Cheves, Esq., of Charleston, S. C., relating to the persons and places mentioned in Mr. Thorowgood's will.

The plantation mentioned in that will is situated in St. James's (Goose Creek) parish in Berkeley county, about 20 miles from Charleston. It is still known as "Thoroughgood." It was granted to Joseph Thorowgood by the Lords Proprietors, and after his death passed to William Thorowgood, from whom it passed to Andrew Allen, of Charleston, Esq., and from him by descent to the Deas family. Joseph Thorowgood was, I believe, a son of Sir Benjamin Thorowgood, Knt., Alderman of London.

The John Ashby mentioned was second son of George Ashby, Esq., of Quenby Hall, co. Leicester. He married Elizabeth, daughter of Sir Benjamin Thorowgood, Knt. (above mentioned). *(See Burke's Como. Vol. IV., " Ashby.")* He was active in the settlement of Carolina and was created a " Cassique" under Locke's Constitution.

His son John Ashby, Esq., of Quenby (in St. James's parish, South Carolina), second Cassique, was Receiver General of the Province. His family remained in possession of Quenby until after the war, 1861-1865.

PHILOBERT COGAN of Chard in the County of Somerset, gentleman, 10 February 1640, proved 12 April 1641. To the parish church twenty shillings. To the poor of the town of Chard twenty shillings. To my son Thomas Cogan one gold ring, or ten shillings. To Mary Ludloe, my daughter, one gold ring, or ten shillings. To Elizabeth Endecott, my daughter, one gold ring, or ten shillings. To Martha Holway, my daughter, one gold ring, or ten shillings. To Margaret Cogan, my daughter, three hundred pounds. To Ann Robinson, my daughter, one gold ring, or ten shillings. To Susan Cogan, my daughter, one gold ring, or ten shillings. The rest to Ann my now wife whom I do make and ordain sole executrix of this my last will and testament. To my son Thomas (sundry moveables) after the decease of my said wife. And if he die without issue my daughter Susan shall hold and enjoy my closes of land, meadow and pasture (described). If William Cogan, my cousin, do discharge my said executrix of all such bonds, bills and obligations as I do stand bound with and for him unto M[r]. John Barcroft and Margaret Webb widow then I do give and devise unto him my said Cousin William the sum of fifty pounds. I desire my good friends M[r]. John Hody Gen[t]. and my son in law M[r]. Peter Holway to be my overseers of this my last will and testament.

Evelyn, 40.

[The following pedigree of this family is copied from vol. xi. page 26 of the Publications of the Harleian Society containing the Visitation of Somerset, in 1623. The arms are : Gules, three leaves erect argent.

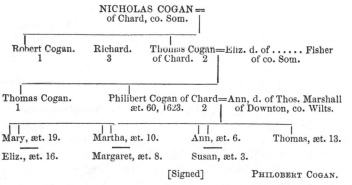

NICHOLAS COGAN ==
of Chard, co. Som.

Robert Cogan.   Richard.   Thomas Cogan=Eliz. d. of ...... Fisher
       1   3   of Chard. 2   of co. Som.

Thomas Cogan.   Philibert Cogan of Chard=Ann, d. of Thos. Marshall
       1   æt. 60, 1623. 2   of Downton, co. Wilts.

Mary, æt. 19.   Martha, æt. 10.   Ann, æt. 6.   Thomas, æt. 13.

Eliz., æt. 16.   Margaret, æt. 8.   Susan, æt. 3.

[Signed]   PHILOBERT COGAN.

H. F. W.

The christian name of the last wife of Gov. John Endicott was Elizabeth. Winthrop in his History of New England, under date of August 18, 1630, has this entry: " Capt. Endicott and ——— Gibson were married by the governor and Mr. Wilson." According to Hubbard's New England, page 165, Roger Ludlow, deputy governor of Massachusetts, was a brother-in-law of Endicott. By the above will of Philobert Cogan, we find that Cogan had daughters, Mary Ludlow and Elizabeth Endicott. I infer that they were respectively the wives of Roger Ludlow and John Endicott. The christian name of the wife of Ludlow is not given in the Ludlow pedigree, by Messrs. Ludlow-Bruges and Scull (REGISTER, vol. 42, page 183; *ante*, page 276). Mrs. Endicott may have been a widow in 1630, when she was married. All of Gov. Endicott's children were by his last wife, and this discovery will be particularly interesting to his descendants.

Whether John Cogan of Boston, Mass., was related to this family or not, I do not know. He appears to have been from Devonshire, as in 1639 he gave Isaac Northcut, of Honiton, a power of attorney to receive any legacy under the will of his mother, widow Eleanor Cogan, of Tiverton in Devon.—(Lechford's Note Book, page 144.) He had wives, Ann and Mary, the latter of whom died 14 Jan. (11 mo.) 1651-2 (REGISTER, x. 71). His last wife was Mrs. Martha Winthrop, widow of Gov. John Winthrop, to whom he was married, 10th March (1 mo.) 1651-2, "p' M' John Endicott Governo'" (REGISTER, x. 222; xx. 144). She was a daughter of Capt. William Rainsborough, and her first husband was Thomas Coytmore (REGISTER, xxxiv. 254; xl. 161; *ante*, page 161). See letter of Rev. John Davenport, where her death is noticed in Mass. Hist. Coll., vol. 30, page 45.—EDITOR.

A coincidence worth examining is the fact that Peter Holwey, of Taunton, England, 1623 (Visitation of Somersetshire, page 57), may have been the husband of Martha Cogan. Possibly her brother Thomas Cogan may have been the Taunton New England settler of 1643, who died 1653 (Savage). May not John Barcroft of Lynn, 1632-3, mentioned by Savage under Bancroft, have been the person named in Philobert Cogan's will?—JOHN COFFIN JONES BROWN.]

THE ANCESTRY OF WASHINGTON.

IN the July number of the N. E. Historical and Genealogical Register I announced some discoveries about the Washington family which I then expected to publish among my Gleanings for that number. Very soon after that announcement I discovered some additional facts so interesting and important, and, apparently, so clearly pointing to the true line of ancestry of our first President that I thought it best, after consulting my friends in England and America, to withhold the matter thus promised until I could add to it these new facts and publish them together, in order that their due relations to each other might be the more apparent. I do not claim to have made an exhaustive study of the Washington Genealogy. That is not my province, as the readers of my Gleanings must, by this time, be well aware. My function rather is similar to that of the prospector who finds the hidden lode of rich ore and makes it known to the miners who may wish to follow up and develop the vein more thoroughly. It is for me to search out and discover the clews and place them in the hands of the specialists who come after, that they may be guided in the right direction and so not waste their efforts in random labor on unfruitful ground. If, in addition, I do occasionally, as in the present case, furnish evidence illustrating a pedigree more at length, it is simply because in my extended wanderings over a wide field I have naturally gathered such facts as have come to my notice and saved them for the general good.

Before entering upon the story of these discoveries let me first state the problem which was to be solved, and refer to one or two attempts which have been made at its solution in the past. The American line of ancestry had been traced back clearly to a John Washington who, with his brother Lawrence, crossed the ocean to Virginia about 1657. The problem was to find their parentage and ancestry in England. It was known that both of them made wills which were proved in Virginia. These wills, or abstracts of them, will I doubt not accompany this paper. *

Sir Isaac Heard, then Garter King of Arms, began in 1791 the discussion of this problem, as I learn from an essay on this subject written by the late Col. Joseph L. Chester, LL.D., D.C.L., and published in the "Herald and Genealogist" (London), September, 1866, and republished in America in "The Heraldic Journal" (Boston), October, 1866, and again in "The N. E. Historical and Genealogical Register" (Boston), January, 1867. From this paper I quote the following extract:

> Sir Isaac took as the basis of his pedigree the Heraldic Visitations of Northamptonshire, in which the Washington family was included. Starting with the well-known fact that the first emigrants of the name to Virginia were two brothers named John and Lawrence Washington, who left England for that colony about the year 1657, he found recorded in the Visitation of 1618 the names of John and Lawrence described as sons of Lawrence Washington of Sulgrave in that county, who had died in the year 1616. The names being identical with those of the Virginia emigrants, and the period at which they lived not altogether inappropriate, Sir Isaac *assumed* their personal identity; and on this assumption constructed his pedigree, deducing the descent of the American President through this heraldic

---

* Nothing can be added to the statement of Bishop Meade, in regard to the wills of the two emigrants, of which documents he gives abstracts. The will of John Washington was then recorded at Westmoreland Court House, "in an old book of wills, though in a somewhat mutilated form." Since then the book has disappeared, probably during the time of the late war. The will of "John Washington, of Washington parish, in the county of Westmoreland, in Virginia, gentleman," was dated February 26, 1675, and proved January 10, 1677. He directs his body to be buried on the plantation upon which he lived, by the side of his wife and two children. He divides a number of landed estates between his second and surviving wife and his children, John, Lawrence and Anne, and also his property in England. He leaves £1000 to his brother-in-law, Thomas Pope; and £1000 and four thousand weight of tobacco to his sister, who had come or was coming over to this country. He makes his wife and brother Lawrence his executors.

The will of Lawrence Washington, of Rappahannock county, dated September 27, 1675, proved January 6, 1677, is presumed to be still on record. Bishop Meade's abstract agrees with the complete copy printed in Welles's book, which latter document is attested by James Roy Micou, Clerk of Essex County, Va. It gives all his property in England to his daughter Mary and the heirs of her body; failing them to children John and Ann. He then mentions his loving wife Jane and her two children, John and Ann, both under age, and the land which came to him in the right of his wife, on the south side of the river, formerly belonging to Capt. Alexander Flemming. Gives two hundred acres of land to Alexander Barrow. Appoints wife Jane, executrix, brother Col. John Washington and friend Thomas Hawkins, overseers.

We now know that John Washington was born prior to 1634, and Lawrence was born in 1635. Hence they were aged respectively about 24 and 22 years in 1657, when they are said to have emigrated to Virginia. Nothing in the wills is decisive of the point whether either or both married prior to their leaving England, but it is more probable than not, and our English friends should be on the look-out for such marriages. In Virginia there may yet be found some dates of grants or purchases of land which will aid in showing their progress there.—WILLIAM H. WHITMORE.

family of Northamptonshire from the still more ancient one of the name in Lancashire. It is but just to the memory of Sir Isaac to say that he himself only regarded the pedigree as a conjectural one, and that he took the precaution to leave on the margin of his own copy a note (which was seen and copied by Mr. Sparks) to the effect that he was not clearly satisfied that the connection of the President with the Sulgrave family was or could be substantiated."

Mr. Bake- in his History of Northamptonshire, followed Sir Isaac's example, but without any reservation. He confidently asserted that John, son of Lawrence Washington of Sulgrave, was of South Cave, co. York, and emigrated to America (from whom, in the third generation, President Washington was derived), and that Lawrence (the brother of this John) was a student at Oxford, 1622, and emigrated to America with his brother.

The above pedigree was accepted by all as authoritative until 1863, when Isaac J. Greenwood, Esq., of New York, threw doubts upon it in a paper communicated to the N. E. Historical and Genealogical Register for July of that year, by suggesting that John and Lawrence, the sons of Lawrence Washington of Sulgrave, were too old to have been the emigrants to Virginia. He also suggested that the Virginians might have been descended from Sir William Washington of Packington, Kn^t., eldest son of Lawrence of Sulgrave.

In Col. Chester's Essay, already referred to, the theory advanced by Sir Isaac Heard and so confidently asserted by Baker in his History, was thoroughly disproved by the array of evidence brought forward which showed that John, the son of Lawrence Washington of Sulgrave, was clearly Sir John Washington of Thrapston, both of whose wives died in England, the latter (Dame Dorothy) outliving her husband; while it is well known that John Washington, the emigrant, buried his first wife (whose name is unknown) in Virginia, and married, secondly, Ann (Pope) whom he appointed executrix of his will, jointly with his brother Lawrence. The children of Sir John, of Thrapston, were Mordaunt, John and Philip. The children of John, of Virginia, were John, Lawrence and Anne. Col. Chester also showed how improbable it was that Lawrence, the brother of Sir John, could have been the Lawrence who emigrated to Virginia, by proving that he was a clergyman of the established church; while Lawrence, of Virginia, simply styled himself "gentleman," a most unlikely thing for him to do, if he were in holy orders.

Col. Chester contented himself with thus completely demolishing the former theory, without setting up a new one in its place; so the original problem was left unchanged. On the American side of the water we had a complete chain running back from the President to the first settler of the name. There the chain, like the vast majority of American pedigrees, was broken short off, at the water's edge. The task which lay before me, on my arrival in England in 1883, was to drag the depths in all directions, with the hope of picking up, somewhere, the lost end of the English line to which the American line belonged. Fortunately I did not come over to hunt for Washingtons alone ; such a task would have seemed well nigh appalling. I was on the lookout for references to every American family of English origin, whatever the name ; and the tedium and monotony of my toilsome search has been relieved by almost daily discoveries, some of exceptional value and importance, like those relating to the Harvard family, the famous Rogers family of New England, the family of Roger Williams, and others of less interest, perhaps, to the general reader, but full of interest, doubtless, to those engaged in the investigation of the genealogies of the special families mentioned in my notes.

At first I gleaned over the whole field for Washingtons and found them in various counties, (e.g.) Yorkshire, Westmoreland, Lancashire, Leicestershire, Worcestershire, Warwickshire, Northamptonshire, Oxfordshire, Buckinghamshire, Berkshire, Hertfordshire, Middlesex, Kent, Surrey, Wiltshire, Devonshire, Essex, Suffolk and Norfolk. In the fall of 1884 or the spring of 1885 I made a very important discovery which led me to limit my field of search, by finding a point on the soil of the mother country to which I could make fast the end of the American line. It appears that upon the death of Lawrence Washington of Virginia, although his will, as I have said, was proved in Virginia, letters of administration on his goods, &c., were granted in England, as follows :—

"Mense Maij 1677 tricesimo die Em^t Com° Edmundo Jones principali creditori Laurentii Washington nuper de Luton in Comitatu Bedford sed apud Virginiā in partibus transmarinis deceden̄ ad adstrand bona jura et credita dict deft de bene etc jurat." Admon. Act Book (P. C. C.).

This was a great step, and it behoved me to make a careful search all around Luton and its immediate neighborhood for further traces. This parish is in the extreme southern part of Bedfordshire, on a kind of tongue or neck jutting into the neighboring county of Herts. For more than four years I have borne this discovery in mind, and in all that time have never let a will made by any one in that part of Bedfordshire or of Hertfordshire pass under my notice without the most careful scrutiny ; and I made known my discovery to most of my English friends, that they might keep their eyes open in that quarter. I had already, to be sure, found an Adam Washington, gentleman, seated at Brent Pelham, Herts, whose father, Adam Washington, citizen and mercer of London, was evidently of the Washington family of Grayrigg in Kendal, Westmoreland, but I had examined the wills relating to them without getting any light about the emigrants to Virginia.

Good fortune, which has so often befriended me in my genealogical work, once more rewarded my plodding toil with bountiful generosity ; and this time she added to the value of her gift by bestowing it through the hand of a friend. It happened in this way. While the official work of indexing certain bonds, once belonging to the Hitchin Registry of the Archdeaconry of Huntingdon, was recently in progress in the Probate Registry, one came to light of which the following is an abstract :

A Bond of John Dagnall, of Grove in the parish of Tring, in co. Herts, Yeoman, and William Roades of Middle Claydon, in co. Bucks., Gen., in the sum of one thousand pounds, dated 29 January 1649 (50), for the administration of the goods &c. of Andrew Knowling, of Tring in the county of Herts., gen., lately deceased, with the will annexed, during the minority of Lawrence Washington the younger, at that time of the age of fourteen years ; also for their faithful conduct as guardians or curators of the said Lawrence Washington &c.

Tring is but twelve miles, or a little more, from Luton,[*] and the two towns are connected by way of Dunstable, and, thence, along the old Icknield Way which runs from Dunstable to the immediate neighborhood of Tring. It was altogether probable then that here was the early home of Lawrence Washington of Luton and Virginia. As I was absent from London at the time of this discovery, my friend took the pains to hunt up the will of Mr. Knowling in order that he might make an abstract of it so as to gratify me with the sight of it upon my next visit at Somerset House. Since then, however, I have made a full copy of this will, which is here given :—

In the Name of God Amen the Thirteenth day of January in the yeare of o[r] Lord god one Thousand Sixe hundred fforty and Nine I Andrew Knowling of Tring in the County of Hertf' gent'·being weake of body but of sound and pfect memory (thanks be giuen to Allmighty God) doe make & ordaine this to be my last will & testam[t] in mann[r] & forme following viz[t] Inprimis I bequeath my soulle into the handes of allmighty God my most mercifull Creato[r] assuredly trusting through the merrittes death & passion of my Lord & only Savio[r] Jesus Christ to enioye eternall life & my body to thearth from whence it came to be decently buried. Item I give to the poore of the Towne of Tring and the upp Hamblettes the some of Twentie Shillings to be paid within one month next after my decease. Item I give to the poore of Willsterne within the said pish of Tring the some of Twenty Shillings to be paid in sorte and mann[r] as aforesaid. Item I give to the poore of Wigginton in the said County of Herts Tenn Shillings to be paid as aforesaid: Item I will give and bequeath unto Lawrance Washing-

---

* See map. Tring is described in the Gazetteer as a parish and market town in Hertford-shire, 28 miles west of Hertford. Acres 7390, houses 667, population 3488 in 1831. It is perhaps best known by the popular, though unfounded rhyme, applied to one of the ancestors·of John Hampden, who was said to have forfeited three manors for striking the Black Prince with his racket when they quarrelled at tennis.
  " Tring, Wing and Ivanhoe,
    For striking of a blow,
    Hampden did forego,
    And glad he could escape so."
Unfortunately neither of these manors ever belonged to a Hampden. (See Notes and Queries, 3rd S., v. p. 176.)
Luton is a town in Bedfordshire, with 15,500 acres and about 6000 population. A glance at the map shows however that Tring and Luton are but a few miles apart and a resident in one town might easily be well known in the other.—WILLIAM H. WHITMORE.

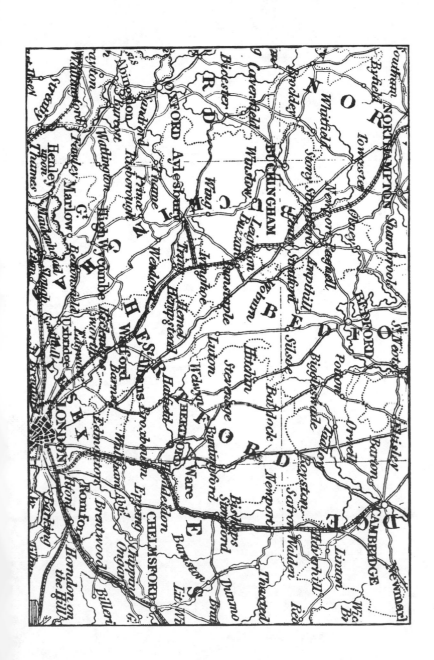

ton the younger (my godsonne) All my freehould Landes and Tenem^{tes} whatsoeu^r lying and being within the pish of Tring aforesaid or else where within the Realme of England. To haue and to hould the same to him and his heires for euer. Item I give and bequeath unto Amphilis Washington my daughter in lawe (& mother of the said Lawrance) the some of Three-score poundes of Curr^t mony of England to be paid her within six months after my decease. Item I give and bequeath unto Elizabeth ffitzherbert one other of my daughters in Lawe the some of ffortye pounds of Curr^t mony to be paid in sorte and mann^r as is last above mencõned. Item I give and bequeath unto William Roades my sonne in Lawe the some of Tenn poundes of Curr^t mony to be paid within sixe months next after my decease: Item I give and bequeath unto the said Elizabeth ffitzherbert all my corne & graine whatsoeu^r now within doores or without. Item I give and bequeath unto the Two daughters of my late daughter in Lawe Susann Bil-ling deceased begotten of her body by her late husband John Billing of Lillington in the County of Buck, Tallowe Chaundler, Tenn poundes apeece to be paid within sixe monthes after my decease And my will is that if either of the said Two children dye before her Legacie shalbecome due and payable Then I will that the Legacie of her dying shalbe paid to the other surviving. Item I give and bequeath unto John Washington, William Washington, Elizabeth Washington, Margarett Washington & Martha Washington (children of the said Amphilis Washington my daughter in Lawe) The some of Eight and Twenty poundes a peece of Curr^t mony to be paid to them att theire seu'all & respective Ages of One and Twenty years, To be putt out in the meane tyme for theire best benefitt & advantage And my will and meaning is that if any of the said ffiue children vizt John, William, Elizabeth, Margarett and Martha Washington shall happen to die before his her or theire Legacie or Legacies shall become due & payable, That then the Legacie or Legacies of him, her or them soe dying shalbe equally divided amongst the rest of them the said five children surviving. Item I give and bequeath unto Susan Emmerton of Tring aforesaid wid̃r̃ the some of ffifty shillings to be paid to her within sixe monthes after my decease. All the rest of my goodes Cattles and chattles & prsonall estate not heerin given and disposed of, my debts and Legacies heerin giuen paid and my fun^rall chardges defrayed I give unto the said Lawrance Washing-ton the young^r my Godsonne whome I make sole and wholle execuo^r of this my last Will and Testam^t And I earnestly desire John Dagnall of Groue within the pish of Tring aforesaid yeoman John Lake of Willst'ne aforesaid Gent' & the said Will͡m Roades and Elizabeth ffitzherbert to take upon them (for the sole benefitt & behoofe of the said Lawrance Washing' myne Execuo^r) The admi'strac̃on of my goodes & Chattles during the minoritie of the said Lawrance Washing' & to see the due pformance of this my said Will, And I doe giue unto them Tenn shillinges a peece All former Wills by me made I doe heerby Revoake & repeale and declare this to be my last Will and Testament. In Wittnes Whereof I the said Andrew Knowling haue heereunto putt my hand and seale the day and yeare first above written.

ANDREW KNOWLING.

𝒜 his m^rke

Sealed subscribed published and
deliu^red in the p'nce of
John ffitzherbert   William Dagnalle
Thomas Norman   James Benning, his m^rke

I B

Itm I will this to be pt of my Will vizt I giue and bequeath unto Wm Knowling beau^r maker in old Bridewell Lond' the soñe of fower pounds to buy him a Ring

<table>
<tr><td>William Dagnalle</td><td>Thomas Norman</td></tr>
<tr><td>James [I B] Benning his m^rke</td><td>John ffitzherbert (testibus)</td></tr>
</table>

Vicesimo nono die Mensis Januarij Anno dñi stilo Anglie 1649 apud Whethampsted p m^rm Gulielmū Dauis in Artibus Magr͂m surrogatū Veñlis viri Johañis Jackson in legibus bacchalaurei Offilis etc. Coñissa fuit Adm͂straco͂ oiū et singlorū bonorū iuriū etc hmōi Andree Knowlinge gen'osi nup de Tryng defuncti unacū testam͂to suo hmōi annexo Johanni Dagnall et Guilielmo Roades in testm͂o prdco nominatis quos dm͂s constituit in Curatores seu Gardianos Laurentio Washington Juniori dc͂i testam͂ti executori etatis 14 aōrū vel circiter ac quibus acceptañ officiū in se Gardianorū seu Curatorū p^rd de bene et fidelr͂ adm'strañd etc. Obligtur dc͂i Johēs Dagnall de Tryng p^rd Yeoman et Guilm͂us Roades de Middle Claydon Coñ Bucks: geñ in 1000^{li}

Through this happy discovery we are at last introduced, in all probability, to the immediate family of the two emigrants to Virginia, their mother, brother, three sisters, uncle, aunts, cousins and grandfather by marriage; for I suppose we may reasonably infer the marriage of Mr. Andrew Knowling with the widowed mother of William Roades, Amphillis Washington, Elizabeth Fitzherbert and Susanna Billing. The name of the husband of Amphillis is not given, but from the fact that the executor and residuary legatee named in the will is called Lawrence Washington the younger, we may also conjecture that his father's name was Lawrence.

A visit to Tring came next in order. There I was most cordially received by the Vicar of that parish, the Rev. W. Quennell, who, having a taste for such investigations and being evidently pleased that I had traced the Washington family to his parish, was kind enough to assist me. The Registers previous to 1634, I found, were not in very good order, and I made a rather hasty examination of them. That beginning 1634 was entitled "A Regester Booke conteaning all the names hereafter Named either Baptized, Married or Buried. Bought by Maister Andreu Knolinge, Richard Hunton" (and others, whose names are given and who are called churchwardens). In it I found the following :—

Baptisms.

Crisames senc our Ladie daye Anno Dom͂ 1635 Layaranc sonn of Layarance Washington June the xxiii^d

Baptized senc our Ladye daye Anno dom 1636 Elizabeth da of Mr Larranc Washington Aug xvii

Baptized senc Mickellmas daye Anno Doñ i64i William sonn of Mr Larrance Washenton baptized the xiiijth daij

Burials.

Andrew Knolling was bur^d this xxith of January 1649.

Edward Fitzherbert bur. the iii of May 1654.

Mrs Washington bur: ye xix of Jan: 1654.

Mr John Dagnall of the Grove bur^d 17 Aug. 1691.

This confirmed my conjecture that the father's name was Lawrence; and, from the fact that the son was called "Lawrence Washington the younger" in Mr. Knowling's will, it is plain that the father was alive when that will was made, in January, 1649–50. I did not find the baptisms of John, Margaret or Martha Washington, and could not therefore determine the age of John Washington at the date of his immigration to Virginia. Fortunately this was settled, near enough, in another way. My next discovery was the following :—

February 1655 The Eighth day L<del>r</del>es of ad<del>c</del>on yssued forth to John Washington the n<del>r</del>all and lawfull sone of Amphillis Washington late of Tring in the County of Hertford de<del>c</del>d to ad<del>s</del>ter the goodes Ch<del>e</del>lls and debtes of the said de<del>c</del>d Hee bceing first sworne truly to ad<del>s</del>ter &c.

Admon. Act Book (P. C. C.), 42.

From this I drew two inferences : first, that Mr. Lawrence Washington, husband of Amphillis and father of John and Lawrence, had predeceased his wife ; and, secondly, that John Washington, to whom the letters of Admon. issued, was the eldest son. As we have seen, Lawrence was baptized in the summer of 1635 and Elizabeth in 1636. John could not have been born later than 1634, and must have been at least twenty-one years of age at the grant of admon., and twenty-three in 1657, the date of emigration.

My next endeavor was to find, if possible, the wills of William Roades, Elizabeth Fitzherbert and John Dagnall. The first, which I soon found, was as follows :—

William Roades (residence not mentioned) 19 September 1657, proved 17 November 1658. To my son John twelve pence and to his wife and two children, William and Anne Roades, twelve pence apiece. To my grand child William Lee twelve pence, and my best bible after my wife's decease. The residue to be divided into four parts, of which one part to my wife and the other three parts to my daughters Hannah, Hester and Sarah Roades. My wife to be executrix.

The will was proved by Hannah Roades, the widow.

Wootton (P. C. C.), 608.

As his place of abode had not been mentioned I called for the Probate Act Book for that year, and found that the testator was of Middle Claydon, Bucks.

The will of Mr. John Dagnall, of Grove, I also found after something of a search, but got no help from it. He only named his immediate family. My search after Mrs. Fitzherbert was a much longer one. At last I came upon the wills of a family of that name, settled in Oxfordshire, which seemed to me worth saving.

Robert Fitzherbert of Begbrooke, Oxon. Esq., 2 August 1636, proved 22 November 1636. Mentions children of brother William Fitzherbert, sister Dyonis Fitzherbert, children of sister Morgan (William, James and Mary), John Fitzherbert, one of the sons of brother Humfrey Fitzherbert deceased, niece Anne Clement, brother Edward Fitzherbert and his children,

John, Edward and Mary, sister Ursula and her children, Thomas, Solymie and Mary, and her grandchild Robert Kente. Thomas Leeke (alias Leake) son of my half brother John Leake deceased.   Pile (P. C. C.), 107.

Edward Fitzharbert of Middleston Stony, Oxon. Gen^t, 10 June 1639. My body to be buried in the parish Church of Middleston Stony, near son Nicholas, deceased. To wife Elizabeth my lease of house and two yards &c. in same parish. Eldest son John, son Edward and daughter Mary Fitzherbert. Brother John Fitzharbert of Bagbrooke Esq. to be executor. The executor having renounced commission issued to Elizabeth Fitzharbert, the widow, 5 May, 1642.   Cambell (P. C. C.), 70.

John Fitzherbert the elder, of Begbrooke, Oxon. Esq., 1 April 1649, proved 25 April 1649. Mentions nephew John, son of brother Edward deceased, also nephew John evidently regarded as heir, nephew Edward and niece Mary Fitzherbert, also children of deceased brother Edward; kinsman Mr. Thomas Hinton and Mr. John Garrett, both of Great Tue, Oxon. The witnesses were John Fitzherbert, Elizabeth Fitzherbert and John Goad, cleric.   Fairfax (P. C. C.), 49.

John Fitzherbert, of Begbrooke, Oxon. Esq., 26 May 1658, proved 23 March 1660. Mentions friends Thomas Hinton of Banbury, Oxon., and John Garrett, of Great Tewe, Oxon., Gen^t; my manor of Begbrooke; wife Anne; my three younger sons, William, Thomas and John (under fourteen); eldest son Francis; daughters Elizabeth and Mary Fitzherbert; father in law Edward Atkins, one of the Justices of the Common Bench.

May (P. C. C.), 44.

My reason for saving these wills was that I guessed Mrs. Elizabeth Fitzherbert might be the widow of Edward Fitzherbert. Her son John was a witness of Mr. Knowling's will. Her son Edward was buried at Tring. (It was her nephew John, however, who inherited the manor of Begbrooke.) This was for a long time only a guess, until, at last, it was converted into a certainty by the following will :

Elizabeth Fitzherbert, of Much Waltham, Essex, widow, 23 February 1684, proved 29 November 1689. She devised all her lands and tenements &c. in Tring, Herts., and the houses and lands called Makins, in Middleton Stony, Oxford, and all her estate and rights &c. in them to John Freeman, of Luton, Bedfordshire, gentleman, and Samuel Marshall of Norstend, Much Waltham, Esq. (in trust) during the joint lives of John Rotheram, of Much Waltham, Esq., and Mary his wife, her daughter, to pay the rents, issues and profits of the said houses in Tring &c. to the said Mary, with other provisions in case of their deaths; and the said John Freeman, of Luton, was to be executor of the will.   Ent (P. C. C.), 154.

Although somewhat disappointed that neither of these wills mentioned the Washingtons and so I was not yet possessed of the positive evidence for which I had been seeking in order to prove beyond a doubt the identity of the Virginians with John and Lawrence of Tring, yet I was, on the whole, satisfied with that of Mrs. Fitzherbert, which, by its mention of Luton, strengthened the probabilities of the case. And I was well aware that the family of Rotheram was a very important one in Luton and its neighborhood (see the Visitations of Bedfordshire), and that through marriages they were connected with Tring as well.

A pedigree of this family of Fitzherbert may be found in the Visitations of Oxford (Harleian So. Pub.).

All this time I was seeking to find an answer to the question, who was this Mr. Lawrence Washington, the father of these children? That he was styled "Mr." on the church Register meant that he was either a clergyman or a person of some importance, and I had a suspicion, which I hardly dared to breathe, that he might be that parson of Purleigh, about whom I have for years had the feeling that if he could only be hunted down we might possibly be able to dispel the mystery enveloping the lineage of Washington. It is perhaps needless to say that I determined to watch most carefully for even the slightest indication of a clew which might lead to the identification of this Lawrence Washington of Tring. First of all, it seemed best to examine with the greatest care all the papers connected with the probate of Mr. Knowling's will, partly for the purpose of making the full copy of that will which I intended to publish *in extenso*, and partly in the hope that I might come upon something or other, not yet known, which would help me a stage further in my research. I found the will, as I have already given it. I found also an inventory of the personal property of the testator, appraised 23 January, 1649, at 534£. 11ˢ. 8ᵈ.

Connected with these papers was a bond of guardianship made by John Dagnall of Grove in the parish of Tring, co. Herts, Yeoman, in the sum of fifty pounds, dated 29 January, 1649 (50), as guardian and curator of the two daughters of Susan Billing deceased, begotten of her body by her late husband John Billing, of Lillington in the co. of Bucks, tallow chandler, the said John Dagnall having been appointed their guardian, &c., for the reason that he was the husband of Elizabeth Dagnall, sister* by the mother to the said two daughters.

It will be noticed that this bond was made on the very same day that the will of Mr. Knowling was produced and Admon. granted, in court at Whethampsted, and the bond was undoubtedly drawn up and signed there.

I then saw a little bit of paper, doubled or folded upon itself, which upon opening seemed about three inches long and from an inch and a half to two inches wide, and covered with writing. Seeing, at a glance, that it was evidently an official memorandum of the issuing of the letters of guardianship and of the oath taken by Mr. Dagnall for the faithful performance of his trust, I did not read it through but at once set about copying it in full, little realizing the start of surprise and gratification I should experience when I should come to the end of what proved to be the most valuable and important bit of genealogical evidence that I ever saw or ever expect to

---

* In the original "Aunte" had been first written, and then a line drawn through it and "sister" written above, with a caret beneath the line.—H. F. W.

see in the course of my gleanings. This little memorandum was as follows :—

M^du qd 29° die Januarij Anno dñi 1649° apud Whethamsted concessæ fuerunt lr̃æ Curatoriæ ad lites duabus filiabus Susannæ Benning defe legatariis in testm̃o hum̃oi Andreæ Knowlinge p recup̃ac̃one legatorū eisdem in dc̃o testm̃o donat̃ et de disposic̃oe eorundē ad usū et commodū dc̃arū filiarū duran earū respē minori aetate et fidelr̃ se gerend̃ etc. et de redd̃o Compt̃o etc Johñi Dagnall de Grove pochiæ de Tring marito Elizabethæ materteræ dc̃arū filiarū iurat̃ etc corā

pñte me Guil: Rolfe   Laurentio Washington
nor̃io pubc̃o   in Art: mag̃ro Surrog̃: Offilis
       etc hac vice
Oblig̃tur dc̃us Johēs Dagnall in 50^li.

It will be noted that Susanna's name in this memorandum is Benning, instead of Billing, a confusion of the two liquid sounds l and n which may be noticed in other languages as well as English. Moreover " *materteræ* " (aunt by the mother) is left uncorrected. The correction, however, was made in the bond, which is in the English language. Probably Mr. Dagnall read it over before signing and noticed the error.

Here we have proof of identification, and of the most positive and conclusive character. There cannot be the least doubt that this Lawrence Washington, M.A., was the husband of Amphillis and the father of her children. He was there in the Archdeacon's Court at Whethampsted, evidently to protect the interests of that wife and those children, who, under the will presented and allowed in court that day, were to receive the bulk of Mr. Knowling's personal estate, while the second son, Lawrence, as the acknowledged heir of his godfather and the executor of his will, was to inherit the real estate of the deceased and all the residuum of the personal estate after the debts, legacies and funeral expenses and other charges should have been settled and paid. There can be but little doubt that this same Lawrence Washington, M.A., who was acting as temporary Surrogate in the Archdeacon's Court on this occasion, was a clergyman ; for that court was an ecclesiastical one, and the office of Surrogate in Testamentary courts was usually, if not invariably, held by a clergyman. The father of these children, then, was a clergyman and a Master of Arts. We have record of only one Lawrence Washington to whom that would apply, namely the fifth son of Lawrence Washington of Sulgrave, brother of Sir William Washington of Packington, and of Sir John Washington of Thrapston. He was student, Lector and Fellow of Brasenose, and in 1631 Proctor of the University of Oxford, and afterwards Rector of Purleigh. The long search after the true line of ancestry of our Washington, begun in 1791, was practically brought to a successful close when that little paper was discovered on Monday, the third of June, 1889.

My next object was to find out, if possible, how it was that Mr.

Lawrence Washington became acquainted with people in Tring, what influences led him thither, and how he came to settle there or in its neighborhood apparently after his ejection from Purleigh in 1643. With that end in view I went to the British Museum and consulted the various Histories of Herts, by Salmon, Chauncy, Clutterbuck and Cussans, reading everything they had to say about Tring and the families seated in its neighborhood; and I made another interesting discovery, and one very much to the point. The manor of Pendley, which is partly within the parish of Tring and partly in the neighboring parish of Aldbury, but with its *caput manerii*, or manor house, in the former parish, held, 10 Edward I., by John d'Aygnel, and thence descending finally to the family of Verney, was sold by Sir Francis Verney to Richard Anderson, Esq., who held a court there, *Anno 5 Jac. I.*, and was knighted two years afterwards. Sir Richard Anderson's wife, Mary, was a daughter of Robert, Lord Spencer, Baron of Wormleighton, owner of the manor of Althorp in Northampton, the great friend of the Washingtons of Sulgrave and Brington, as the old account books preserved at Althorp show* (see Col. Chester's paper already referred to). This was strong corroboration of the other evidence identifying this Mr. Lawrence Washington, if corroboration were needed, and it was also a complete answer to those questions which had been raised in my mind about the influences which brought Mr. Washington to Tring. This Sir Richard Anderson seems to have been by far the most important parishioner then living in Tring, where he died 3 August, 1632, and was buried within the chancel rail of the parish church. His widow, Dame Mary Anderson, afterwards lived in Richmond, Surrey, but was buried at Tring, July, 1658. I examined the will of Sir Richard Anderson, and was gratified to find further evidence confirming my conjecture. It was as follows :

Sir Richard Anderson of Pendly in the county of Hartford knight, 5 October 1630, proved 27 August 1632. To the poor of Bitterly in Shropshire, Norton in Glostershire, Corringham in Essex, Albury, Tringe and Wigginton in Hartfordshire, to each parish five pounds. To the town of Tringe ten pounds to be added and employed, with that money already

---

* It seems proper to state that these extracts from the Althorp documents were first published in 1860 by Rev. John Nassau Simpkinson, then rector of Brington, in Northamptonshire, now rector of North Creake, in Norfolk. This gentleman being greatly interested in the supposed identity of the emigrants to Virginia with John and Lawrence of his parish, wrote a very pleasant story about the Washingtons, and appended many extracts from the household books of Lord Spencer. When Col. Chester utterly upset this theory, Mr. Simpkinson wrote a manly letter to the New York *Nation*, printed 15th April, 1880, acknowledging his mistake. Now, however, that the fact seems established that all the facts collected related to the father and the uncles of our Virginians, it is to be hoped that his book will again meet public favor. Very curiously in that letter Mr. Simpkinson refers to Col. Chester's collections which had been shown to him in confidence, and adds, "that some of these documents seemed to me to supply strong presumptive proof that the emigrants would be found, after all, to have sprung from the Northamptonshire stock, though of a generation below that which was erroneously pointed out." This hint makes one seriously doubt if Col. Chester were wise in declining to print his collections and surmises until he had full proof, and also to hope that these collections will no longer remain secluded from our knowledge until they shall have lost all value and interest by the independent researches of others.—W. H. WHITMORE.

there in stock, to set the poor on work, which money of my own and some others given to that use is in ffeoffee's hands at this time thirty pounds. To my uncle Francis Garaway or, if dead, amongst his children, twenty pounds; to my uncle M^r. John Bowyer and my two cousins, his sons John and Francis, either of them, ten pounds. To my brother in law Mr. Thomas Cowly, now consul at Sante, twenty pounds.

Item I bequeath to Mr. Robinson's two sons, one of Pembrooke College, the other of Albourne Hall, and to my cousin Larance Washington of Brasenose and to Mr. Dagnall of Pembrock College, to each of them forty shillings.

To my wife (over and above her jointure) bedding and household stuff, belonging in my father's time to a house he had in Chiswick, &c. &c. My bigger diamond ring to my daughter Elizabeth. I will and bequeath to my dear and only surviving sister the Lady Spencer of Offley twenty pounds. To the Right Hon. the Lord Spencer, Robert Needham Esq., Richard Spencer Esq., Sir Edward Spencer knight and Sir Thomas Derham knight, my worthy brothers-in-law, ten pounds each. Provision made for second son Robert and third son John, and two younger sons William and Richard (under one and twenty). Eldest daughter Elizabeth, second daughter Mary and third daughter Frances (all unmarried). To five younger daughters, Margaret, Katherine, Penelope, Ann, and Bridgett. Son Henry. My wife Dame Mary. The manor of Corringham in Essex. Cousin Henry Derham gent.   Audley, 86 (P. C. C.).

Nothing could be better than this. Having found Mr. Washington at Tring, or in its neighborhood, I was now able to show through what influence he was led to go there.

Similar questions arose as to the connection of William Roades of Middle Claydon, Bucks, with Tring and its neighborhood, and the connection of the Washington family of Sulgrave and Brington with Middle Claydon; important questions if the hypothesis which I had assumed was correct, viz. that William Roades, Amphillis Washington, Susanna Billing and Elizabeth Fitzherbert, were all step-children of Mr. Knowling and children of ——— Roades deceased, either of Tring or of Middle Claydon. Looking into Lipscomb's History of Buckinghamshire I found that the manor of Middle Claydon passed to the Verney family between 1434 and 1467, in which latter year it belonged to Sir Ralph Verney, knight and alderman of London. But this was the very family which held the manor of Pendley, in Tring and Aldbury, as their chief seat for so many generations until, as I have said, Sir Francis Verney sold it in 1607 to Sir Richard Anderson. The manor of Middle Claydon had been leased in 1535 for one hundred years to the Gifford family and from them to Mr. Martin Lister, who, in 1620, when the lease had but fifteen years to run, surrendered it to Sir Edmund Verney a brother of Sir Francis.

Here then was a promising clew to follow in order to get at the connection between Tring and Middle Claydon, and I thought it well worth the while to hunt for Sir Edmund Verney's will, which I soon found. The following is an abstract :—

Sir Edmund Verney of Middle Cleydon, in the co. of Bucks knight, 26 March, 14 Charles, A.D. 1639, proved 23 December, 1642. My body I will shall be interred in the chancel of the parish church of Middle Cleydon. To the poor of that parish twenty pounds. To my son Thomas Verney, for and during his natural life, one annuity or yearly sum of forty pounds payable quarterly. To my son Henry a similar annuity of thirty pounds. To my son Edmund and every of my daughters, Susanna, Penelope, Margaret, Cory, Mary and Elizabeth respectively, the sum of five pounds. To my cousin Edmund Verney, son of my uncle Urian, an annuity of five pounds, payable quarterly. To my niece Dorothy Leeke twenty pounds.

Item I do give and bequeath unto my servant John Roades of Middle Cleydon aforesaid for and during his natural life an annuity or yearlie sume of ten pounds of lawfull money of England to be paid unto him everie yeare for that tyme at the before mentoned foure fests by even porcons, The first paieht thereof to be made att such of the said fests as shall first come and be next after my decease. To my servant Thomas Chauncy an annuity of five pounds. To my daughter in law Mary Verney, wife of my son Ralph Verney, forty pounds for the buying of her a ring. To my dear mother Dame Margaret Varney all such moneys as are, at the day of the date of this my last will, in her custody and which were not delivered by me or by my appointment unto her to make payment thereof for me. Certain other bequests to wife &c. Son Ralph Verney to be sole executor. William Roades one of the witnesses. Campbell, 129 (P. C. C.).

Can it be doubted for one instant that the William Roades, who witnessed the above will, was the very same person mentioned in Mr. Andrew Knowling's will? or that John Roades, to whom the annuity of ten pounds was left, was one of this family? Was it possible to learn anything more about them? The Camden Society published in 1853 some "Letters and Papers of the Verney Family, down to the end of the year 1639" (John Bruce, Esq., Editor). On page 208 I found that this John Roades was called Sir Edmund's bailiff at Claydon. In 1639 (1st April) Sir Edmund wrote from Yorke to his son Ralph, then at the family residence in Covent Garden, London, as follows: "I thinck my man Peeter and I am parted; if he comes to Lundon bee not deceaved by any falce message; wright privately as much to Roades." The Christian name is not given. On the 21st of June (1639) he writes from camp to his son: "I pray write to Will Roads presently to inquire out some grass for geldings, for I have bought fifty horses and geldings out of one troope, and they will bee at Cleydon about tenn dayes hence. The horses I will keepe att howse till I can sell them." What ever position John Roades may have held, it seems quite evident that in June, 1639, William Roades was bailiff at Middle Claydon. On the 25th of May, 1636, was issued a Warrant from Spencer, Earl of Northampton, Master of His Majesty's Leash, addressed "To all justices of peace, mayors, sheriffs, bayliffs, constables, and all other majesties officers and ministers to whom it shall or may appertayne," authorizing William Roads of Middle Claidon and Ralph Hill of Wendover, servants of Sir Edmund Verney, knight marshal of

His Majesty's household, as deputies and assignees, for the space of six whole and entire years next ensuing, to take and seize to his majesty's use, and in his majesty's name, within all places within the county of Buckingham such and so many greyhounds, both dogs and bitches, in whose custody soever they may be, as the said William Roads and Ralph Hill shall think meet and convenient for his majesty's disport and recreation &c., and also to seize and take away all such greyhounds, beagles or whippets as may anywise be offensive to his majesty's game and disport.

Sir Edmund Verney was in his youth one of the household of Prince Henry. On the 7th of January, 1610–11, he was knighted. In 1613 he was taken into the household of Prince Charles as one of the gentlemen of the privy chamber. In 1622 he was appointed to the lieutenancy of Whaddon Chase, an office in the gift of George Villiers, then marquis of Buckingham and keeper of Whaddon, and an interesting letter to Sir Edmund from Sir Richard Graham, one of the Marquis of Buckingham's gentlemen, relating to this appointment may be found on page 106 of the Verney Papers. In 1623 he visited Madrid with other officers and gentlemen of the Prince's household, Prince Charles and Buckingham having already preceded them on that romantic expedition, undertaken for the purpose of seeing the Spanish infanta. In the service of the prince, as a page, was a Mr. Thomas Washington, whom Col. Chester satisfactorily identified as the sixth son of Lawrence Washington of Sulgrave and Brington, Lawrence, husband of Amphillis, being the fifth. The following extract from "Familiar Letters on Important Subjects, wrote from the year 1628 to 1650 by James Howell, Esq., Clerk of the Privy Council to King Charles I." (tenth edition, Aberdeen, 1713), becomes of interest to us. The letter was dated Madrid, August 15, 1623.

" *Mr. Washington* the Prince's Page is lately dead of a calenture, and I was at his burial, under a fig-tree behind my Lord of *Bristol's* house. A little before his death one *Ballard* an *English* Priest went to tamper with him : and Sir *Edward Varney* meeting him coming down the stairs of *Washington's* chamber, they fell from words to blows, but they were parted. The business was like to gather very illblood and come to a great height, had not Count *Gondamar* quasht it ; which I believe he could not have done, unless the times had been favourable, for such is the reverence they bear to the Church here, and so holy a conceit they have of all ecclesiastics, that the greatest *Don* in *Spain* will tremble to offer the meanest of them any outrage or affront."

Thus we see that Sir Edmund Verney was intimate with one, at least, of the Washingtons and probably with others of the family, as two of them were for a time close neighbors to him, Sir William Washington, at Leckhampstead, and Sir Lawrence Washington, the

Register of Chancery, at Westbury. And there was a connection of the Verney, Washington, Spencer and Fitzherbert families with the Leake* family which is yet to be unravelled. At any rate I think I have presented evidence enough to show how the Roades family may have been connected with Tring and Tring people, and how and where Lawrence Washington the student and Fellow of Brasenose may have made the acquaintance of his future wife. But the same evidence seems to show that it was a match which would not be likely to meet with the approval of the rest of the family, allied as they were to the Villiers, Sandys, Pargiter, Verney and other families then of good social standing ; and, in connection with this, it is worth noting that I have thus far seen no mention of Mr. Lawrence Washington in any of the wills of the family or their connections after this marriage, which must have been soon after the resignation of the fellowship (March, 1632–3).

I now went to the Public Record office and examined the exchequer : First Fruits, Bishop's certificates, Diocese of London (from April, 1630, to April, 1635), and looked over the "Names and cognomens of all and singular Clerks collected, admitted. or instituted to any Benefice, &c., in the Diocese of London, and of patrons, &c., from 12 Sept. 1632, to 16 April," &c., and found the following :

Essex ; Dengy, Decimo quarto die mensis Martii Anno pred Laurentius Washington clicus in Artibus magr admissus fuit ad Rĉoriā de Purleigh Coñ Essexie per pñtaconem Janæ Horsmanden patronissæ pro hac vice.

I also found in the book of compositions for First Fruits the following :

xxij° die martii 1632 Anno Regni dñi nñi nunc Caroli Regis &c. octavo. Essex. Purleigh. R. Laurentius Washington clic comp̄ pro p'rmittis Rĉorie pred ext. ad xxv deĉia inde l'. Obligant' dctus Laurentius, Thomas Beale de Yarkhill in Coñ Hereff geñ et Willũs Smith pochie bte Marie de la Savoy Inholder.

This living he held until 1643, when he was ejected, by order of Parliament, as a Malignant Royalist. This information is given on page 4 of "The First Century of Scandalous, Malignant Priests Made and admitted into Benefices by the Prelates, in whose hands the ordination of Ministers and Government of the church hath been," published by John White and printed by George Miller, by order of Parliament, 17 Nov. 1643. The case of Mr. Washington is No. 9 on the list, and is as follows :

The Benefice of Lawrence Washington, Rector of *Purleigh* in the

---

* The father of Dorothy Leake, called niece in Sir Edmund Verney's will (often referred to in the family letters as Doll Leake), was Sir John Leake, son and heir of Mr. Jasper Leake of Edmonton. Her mother was Ann Turvill, daughter of Geoffrey Turvill, Esq., by Mary (Blakeney). As the widow Turvill afterwards became the wife of Sir Edmund Verney (the elder) of Pendley and mother of Sir Edmund the Knight Marshal, the Lady Ann Leake was the latter's half sister. I have yet to learn who the Penelope Leake was, whom Mrs. Elizabeth Washington of Brington called cousin.

County of *Essex* is sequestred, for that he is a common frequenter of Ale-houses, not onely himselfe sitting dayly tippling there, but also incouraging others in that beastly vice, and hath been oft drunk, and hath said, *That the Parliament have more Papists belonging to them in their Armies than the King had about him or in his Army, and that the Parliaments Armie did more hurt than the Cavaliers, and that they did none at all;* and hath published them to be Traitours, that lend to or assist the Parliament.

In an account of the sufferings of the clergy, by John Walker (London, 1714), I found, in Part II. 395^b, the following remarks upon this case :

Washington, Lawrence, A.M., Purleigh R., one of the best Livings in these Parts: To which he had been Admitted in March 1632, and was Sequestred from in the year 1643; which was not thought Punishment enough for him; and therefore he was also put into the Century, to be transmitted to Posterity, as far as that Infamous Pamphlet could contribute to it, for a *Scandalous,* as well as a *Malignant Minister,* upon these weighty considerations ; That he had said (then follows the extract given above in italics, beginning "The Parliament," &c.)

It is not to be supposed that such a Malignant could be less than a Drunkard ; and accordingly he is charged with frequent Commissions of that Sin ; and not only so, but with encouraging others in that Beastly Vice. Altho' a Gentleman (a Justice of the Peace in this County) who Personally knew him, assures me, that he took him to be a very Worthy, Pious man, that as often as he was in his Company he always appeared a very Moderate, Sober Person ; and that he was Received as such, by several Gentlemen, who were acquainted with him before he himself was: Adding withal, that he *was a Loyal Person, and had one of the best Benefices in these Parts ; and this was the Only cause of his Expulsion, as I verily believe.* After he subjoyns, That Another Ancient Gentleman of his Neighborhood, agrees with him in this Account. Mr. Washington was afterwards permitted to Have and Continue upon a Living in these Parts; but it was such a Poor aud Miserable one, that it was always with difficulty, that any one was persuaded to Accept it.*

We have here the two sides of the story. Whatever judgment we may form as to the charge of being "oft drunk" (which I myself am inclined to reject, or at least view with leniency), we can have no doubt as to his having been a plain and outspoken Royalist. We have the evidence of both sides as to that. How was it, now,

---

* I would here offer a criticism which Mr. Waters may have felt a scruple about making. Col. Chester, in his essay, after quoting this last paragraph, adds, " It is to be hoped that some further trace of him [Rev. Lawrence Washington] may yet be discovered in the neighborhood of Purleigh, where, *putting the usual construction upon Walker's language,* he continued in his profession of a clergyman after the Restoration, and consequently some years after the date of his namesake's emigration to Virginia."

It seems to me, that unless a number of instances can be shown from Walker's book, the usual *construction* would not at all imply that Washington continued to live and serve till after the Revolution of 1660. He was ejected from Purleigh in 1643; if he lived till 1653 or 1654, this would be such a "continuance" as would fully meet Walker's terms.

In fact, Col. Chester was so strongly convinced that Sir John and Rev. Lawrence were not the emigrants to Virginia (an opinion in which all our readers will now concur), that he seems to have over-stated Walker's language, in order to prove that Lawrence was in England after 1657, when his namesake was in Virginia. But it is more satisfactory still to find, as Mr. Waters does, that Rev. Lawrence was dead before 1655; for in a pedigree, as in politics, Stafford's merciless proverb is true, " stone-dead hath no fellow."

W. H. WHITMORE.

with his kindred, friends and connections in that respect? So far as we can learn about them in the records, most of them were on the losing side, as well. To instance a few of them, we have seen that two of his elder brothers, William and John, had been knighted, which rather points that way; the former married Anne Villiers, half sister to the first Duke of Buckingham of that family, the Royal favorite. His eldest son, Henry Washington, nephew of the persecuted parson of Purleigh, was a Colonel in the Royalist Army, and, according to an account which I have seen, Governor of the ever loyal city of Worcester. He was called "late of the City of Worcester" in October, 1649, when he was obliged to "compound" for having been in arms against Parliament. Col. William Legge, who married Elizabeth, one of the sisters of the loyal Colonel, was a notorious Royalist, and endured great hardships on account of it. We have only to look through the Docket of the Signet office to learn how he was betrusted and rewarded by his Royal master. Upon the Restoration, we are told, he was offered an earldom, but feeling unable to support that dignity, spoke in the interest of his son George, who, we know, was created Baron Dartmouth. Sir Lawrence Washington, the Register of Chancery, actually died in Oxford, 1643, while it was held by the King's forces, having gone thither to attend the Royal Seal, as we are informed by Sir John Tirrell of Springfield, knight, who married Martha Washington, his daughter, and who was himself forced to pay a fine of eight hundred pounds in compounding for his own loyalty. Spencer, Earl of Northampton, whose grandfather had taken, for a second wife, one of the Spencer family of Althorp, and whose own mother was also a Spencer, of another branch, was one of the most distinguished of the Royalists, as were all his sons. He was mulcted most heavily for the part he had taken against Parliament, although an attempt seems to have been made to relieve his estates in Bedfordshire, by putting forward evidence to show that his agent collected the rents of these estates not for him, but as agent, really, of Sir John Washington, "by vertue of an extent wch the said Sr John Washington had upon the estate of the said Earle in the said County of Bedford." As to the Anderson family, we have seen that the kinsman and friend of our Parson was knighted. His son and heir, Henry Anderson, was created a Baronet by Letters Patent, dated 3 July, 1643 (see Chauncy's Herts), and we find that he also was obliged to compound for his loyalty in 1646.

I might extend this list, but I think I have given enough to show what the surroundings of our Washington family were in that respect; and I am quite sure I have seen enough myself to lead me to form the opinion that there was quite a nest of Royalists in that part of Herts and Bedfordshire, and I have little doubt that it was largely on that account that Lawrence Washington, the royalist clergyman, was led to seek that neighborhood and stay there. He must have died, as we have seen, before 1655. His wife was buried 19 January, 1654–5, and their children were thus left orphans. Their eldest son, John, was about twenty-three or twenty-four in 1657 ; for it is to be presumed that Mr. Washington did not marry until he had resigned his Fellowship in March, 1632–3 (according to Col. Chester), and Lawrence, we know, was twenty-two in 1657. Supposing them to have been young men of only ordinary enterprise and ambition, with the desire to get on in the world, what chance had they in England at that time, known as belonging to a royalist family, with all, or most, of their friends, to whom, in happier conditions, they might have applied for influence, royalists like themselves, and Cromwell then most firmly seated in his Protectorate? The chances would seem to be utterly against them. No wonder their thoughts turned to Virginia, that transatlantic haven and place of refuge for defeated royalists, which perhaps then first received the name by which it has, since, more than once been called, the home of the Cavaliers in America.

And though without influential friends to help them in old England, had they no good friends to start them in the new world? To this question I think I can give an affirmative answer. Their aunt Margaret, after the death of her first husband, Samuel Thornton, married again, into the Sandys family, one of whom is thus referred to in the following will :

NICHOLAS FARRAR, citizen and skinner of London, 23 March 1619, proved 4 April 1620. My body to be buried in the place where it shall please God to appoint. And for my worldly goods, first, whereas there is lately given a beginning to the erecting and founding of a College in Virginia for the conversion of Infidels' Children unto Christian Religion, my will is that when the said College shall be erected and to the number of ten of the infidels' children therein placed to be educated in Christian religion and civility that then my executor shall give and pay the sum of three hundred pounds unto the Company of Virginia, to ·be disposed of with the advice and consents of Sir Edwin Sandys, now Treasurer of the Company, and my son John Farrar, so as may most tend to the furtherance of that godly work of the College and thereby to the advancement of God's glory. And in the mean while until such time as the said College shall be erected and at least ten of the infidels' children therein placed, until which time I will not that the said three hundred pounds shall be paid or delivered by my executor unto the Company of Virginia, my will is that my executor shall pay and deliver yearly the sum of twenty and four pounds unto the hands of Sir Edwin Sandys and John Farrar, which said sum of twenty and four pounds my will and desire is the said Sir Edwin Sandys and John Farrar shall yearly pay by eight pounds apiece to any three several persons in Virginia, of good life and fame, that will undertake therewith to procure and bring up each one of the Infidels' children instructing them carefully in the grounds of Christian Religion and intreating them in all things so Christianly as by the good usage and bringing of them up the Infidels may be persuaded that it is not the intent of our nation to make their children slaves but to bring them to a better manner of living in this world and to the way of eternal happiness in the life to come.

Soame, 32 (P. C. C.).

This Sir Edwin Sandys, of Northborne (Kent), second son of Dr. Edwin Sandys, Archbishop of York, received the honor of knighthood from King James I. (says Burke), and was distinguished as a politician in that king's and in the subsequent reign. "He was (says an old writer) a leading man in all parliamentary affairs, well versed in business, and an excellent patriot to his country, in defence of which, by speaking too boldly, he, with Selden, was committed into custody, 16 June, 1621, and not delivered thence till 18 July following, which was voted by the House of Commons a great breach of their privileges. He was treasurer to the undertakers for the western plantations, which he effectually advanced, was a person of great judgment, and, as my author saith, *ingenio et gravitate morum insignis.*" He died in 1629.

Alice Washington, another of the paternal aunts of these young men, was married to Robert Sandys of London, eldest son of Thomas, brother of this Sir Edwin. The widow of their cousin, Col. Henry Washington, was, later, married to Samuel Sandys, Esq., another nephew of Sir Edwin. And Sir Edmund Verney had long before sent one of his sons, young Tom Verney, over to Virginia. So it is evident that there was plenty of influence which could be exerted in their favor to assist them in their Virginia scheme.

ADDITIONAL NOTES.

The following notes and abstracts, gathered during the past six years, all relate, more or less, to this family of Washington:

LAWRENCE WASHINGTON of Souldgrave in the Co. of Northampton, gentleman, 18 October 1581, proved 11 February 1584. As concerning my body, which, as it was made of earth, so must it return to dust and earth again, I desire therefore and require mine "exequitor" to cause the same to be inhumate and buried in the parish church of Souldgrave aforesaid, in the South Aisle there before my seat where I usually use to sit, according to his discretion. To Mr. Walter Light a whole sovereign of gold and to his now wife a "ducate" of gold. Towards the amending of Stanbridge Lane twenty shillings. And I will that Roger Litleford shall have the oversight in amending the said lane and bestowing the said twenty shillings. And for his pains in that behalf to be sustained I will him two shillings. And I will to every one of my sons' and daughters' children five shillings apiece, and to every one of my brother Leonard Washington's children six shillings eight pence a piece willed to them by Parson Washington.* Also I give to my brother Thomas Washington's children by his last wife forty shillings. Also I devise to my son Lawrence Washington one goblet parcel gilt, with the cover for the same, and four pounds of currant English money to buy him a salt. And I further will to him one featherbed in the gate-house, one feather bed over the day-house, one coverlet with a blue lining, one coverlet in the gate-house chamber, two boulsters, two pairs of

---

* This may have been Lawrence Washington, junior, presented to the living of Stotesbery (Northampton) by Lawrence Washington, senior, 16 May, 1559 (see Bridge's Hist. of Northamptonshire, I. 203).

blankets, four home made coverlets & four mattresses. Also I give to Lawrence Washington, son to Robert Washington my son and heir apparent, the ring which I usually wear. Also I forgive and acquit my brother Thomas Washington of all such debts and duties as he by any manner of means oweth unto me. And I forgive and discharge John Lagoe, sometime my servant, of all such sums of money as he oweth unto me and of all rents and arrearages of rents due unto me for such lands, tenements or hereditaments as he holdeth of mine, by lease or otherwise, for term of my natural life. And I will to every one of my servants which shall be in service with me at the time of my decease twelve pence. Also I will that the said Robert Washington shall yearly give to my servant Symon Wood a livery coat and forty shillings of currant English money for his wages yearly during his life. And whereas I stand charged by the last will and testament of William Bond, gentleman, for the amending and repairing of Preston Lane and for the repairing of the way between Dalington and the Westbridge at Northampton called Spangstone, I earnestly require my executor and overseers to call upon the said John Balgoye for the amending of the said places, for that I have, long time heretofore, delivered into the hands of the said John Balgaye the sum of ten pounds of currant English money for the repairing of Preston Lane and twenty shillings for the amending of Spangston, for that only use and purpose. Also I will and devise that widow Compton shall have, hold, possess and enjoy for term of her life so much of one cottage as she now possesseth in Sulgrave, so as she well and honestly behave herself during her life, without making or doing any reparations thereupon and without paying any rent therefor, other than one red rose at the feast of Saint John Baptist yearly, if the same be demanded. And my further meaning and intent is that the said Robert and his heirs shall from time to time forever appoint some honest aged or impotent person to inhabit the same cottage for term of life, and that such aged or impotent person as shall not pay to my heirs any manner of rent therefor for term of his life other than a red rose payable as aforesaid, nor shall be charged to repair the same cottage during his or their lives. And my mind, intent and meaning is that if any doubt, ambiguity or controversy shall appear to arise or grow in respect of these presents then I will the same shall be decided and determined by my overseers or any one of them. And of this my last will and testament I constitute, ordain and appoint the said Robert Washington my sole executor, and of the same I make and ordain my well beloved and trusty friends the said William Baldwyn and William Pargiter my overseers, desiring them to call on my executor if any default or slackness shall evidently in him appear, for or towards the performance of this my last will and testament, and for their pains I will to either of them forty shillings. Witnesses, William Baldwin, William Pargiter, Robert Calcott, George Woodward. Brudenell, 5 (P. C. C.).

Northt.　　　　　　　　*Laurence Washington.*

Inq[n] taken at Rothewell in Co. Northt 24th day of August, 26 Eliz. [1584] before Arthur Broke Esq. Escheator, after the death of Laurence Washington gent., by the oath of Henry Moore, William Craddocke &c. &c. Jurors, who say that Laurence Washington was seised in fee of the Manor of Sulgrave with the appurtenances to the Monastery of St. Andrew in the town of Northampton [lately] belonging; also of all the messuages, lands &c. in Sulgrave & Woodford to the same Monastery belonging; also of one close of land &c. [here follows a long list of lands in various places].

He being so seised by an Indenture made the 10th day of Dec. 7 Eliz. [1564] made between himself of the one part and Walter Light of Radwey in Co. Warwick gent. of the other part, in consideration of a marriage afterwards Solemnized between Robert Washington gent. then son & heir apparent of the said Laurence and Elizabeth Light then daughter & sole heiress of the said Walter Light, agreed for himself his heirs & administrators with the said Walter Light, his heirs & administrators that before the Feast of Easter then next following that he (Laurence) would make with certain persons indifferently chosen a firm and sufficient estate in two messuages in the parish of Pattishill with their appurtenances : to hold the same to the use of the said Laurence so long as the said Robert should live; after his death, to the use of Elizabeth Light for life, for her jointure; after her decease, to the use of the heirs male of Robert Washington; for default of such issue, to the use of the heirs male of Laurence Washington, younger son of the said Laurence named in the writ; for default of such issue then to the use of the right heirs of Laurence Washington (the father) for ever.

Robert Washington afterwards took to wife the said Elizabeth who is still alive at Sulgrave.

Laurence Washington (father) died on the 19th day of February now last past; Robert Washington his son & heir was aged 40 years & more at the time of taking this Inquisition.

The Manor of Sulgrave and other the premises in Sulgrave, Woodford & Cotton are held of the King Hen. 8, his heirs & successors in capite by the 20th part of a knights fee, and are worth per ann. (clear) £ 15. 12s. 6d. &c. &c.　　　　　Chan. Inqⁿ. p. m. 26 Eliz. Part 1, Nᵒ. 179.

WILLIAM PARGYTER of Grytworth in the Co. of Northampton, gentleman, 18 January, 26th year of the Reign of Elizabeth &c., proved 30 October 1584. To the church of Grytworth six shillings eight pence. To my son Christopher ten of my beasts, forty pounds of currant English money, after the expiration of one whole year, forty of my ewes that shall be going in my pasture in Stutesbury and forty of my store sheep that shall be going in the fields of Grytworth, to be delivered at any time, upon request, running out of the pen. I do release unto Richard Knight, my son in law, all debts whatsoever which he oweth me. To Ursula Knight, my daughter, one yearly rent of three pounds six shillings eight pence of currant English money, to be paid to her yearly by my son Robert, his heirs, executors or assigns, during the joint lives of the Lady Lawrence and of my said daughter Ursula Knight. To the said Christopher, my son, one dozen of pewter vessell. " Item I doe give & bequeath unto my brother Wasshington his children fourty shillinges to be equally devided amongest them." To my sister Pemerton ten shillings. To my cousin Robert Manley his wife ten shillings. To my cousin Anne Crossewell ten shillings. To my cousin Anne Manley ten shillings. To every of the children of my son in law Crescent Buttery and Richard Knight the sum of forty shillings a piece, to be paid or delivered to them on the day of their marriages. To William, son unto Robert my son, my ring whereon my name is engraven. To Thomas Hancock ten shillings. To John Cowper my servant some of my apparell. To the poor of Grytworth, Laurence Marston and Sulgrave. The residue to son Robert, whom I make my sole executor. And I make and constitute my well beloved and trusty friends William Baldwyn, Walter Light, Robert Washington and Crescent Butterye, gent., overseers.

Watson, 31 (P. C. C.).

CHRISTOFER LIGHTE of Horley, in the Co. of Oxon, gentleman, 16 July 1583, proved 29 October 1584. To be buried in parish church of Horley under the gravestone where my father and mother were buried. My manor of Horley, my manor of Horneton, in Oxfordshire, my messuage and land in Mollington, Warwickshire, &c. &c. to my executors during the minority of Richard Lighte my son. My brother Walter, Johan Halford, my sister, and her children, vizt: Elizabeth Tyson and Ursula Halford. My cousin Robert Pargyter and Christopher Pargytor, and Ursula Knight their sister.

"And whereas I stande bounde by obligation to paye to my Cosen Robert Washington of Sowlgrave in the Countie of Northamptown gentleman, the Somme of one hundred poundes, yf I doe not suffer my Mannors, Landes and Tenementes to discende unto him, my will is that my executors shall paye unto my saide cosen Washington his executors or administrators the saide somme of one hundred poundes w[th]in one yeare nexte after my deathe in full satisfaction and pfourmance of the said Obligaĉon, And in discharge of my promyse and agreement w[th] him made."

Wife Margaret. Five of the children of my sister Halford, viz: Thomas Savage, Elizabeth Tyson, Blanch Halford, Margaret Nicholls and Ursula Halford. I will and do desire my good brother-in-law Mr. William Pargytor of Grytworth, Northampton, and my well beloved brother Mr. Walter Lyght of Radwaye, Warwick, to be executors &c. My father-in-law Mr. Thomas Sheldon and my friend Mr. Ancar Brent to be overseers.

In a codicil the testator says "Whereas William Pargetor one of my exequitors hathe depted from this worlde longe sithence the makinge of my will I doe therefore nowe make and constitute Robert Pargitor, my kynsman, to be one of my Exequitors insteade of the sayde William Pargytor nowe deceased." Watson, 32 (P. C. C.).

Sir JOHN SPENCER of Oldthroppe, in the Co. of Northampton, knight, 6 December, 42[d] Eliz: proved 11 January 1599. My body to be buried in the chancell of Bringhton Church, where my ancestors lie buried, and my funerall to be done in decent sort, not with great pomp according to the order of the world in these days. All my goods &c. to Robert Spenser my loving son whom I do ordain and make sole executor: and do ordain overseers of this my will my honorable good Lord the Lord Hunsden, Lord Chamberlain to the Queen's Majesty, and my loving and assured good brothers Sir William Spencer, knight, Thomas Spencer and Richard Spencer, Esquires, and do devise to them four of my best horses or geldings at their choice. To Lord Hunsden, further, one piece of plate, double gilt, of the value of twenty marks to be made in such sort as it shall seem best to my Executor. To my very loving friend Mr. William Baldwynne of Bifield, Northampton, twenty pounds in consideration of his care and pains in my law causes, and I will my son give him for me a good ambling gelding.

Also I will and bequeath unto Elizabeth Washington the wife of Robert Washington of Great Brinton, in the Co. of Northampton, in regard of her pains about me in my sickness, twenty pounds. To Agnes Fawkner my servant, over and above her wages, forty shillings. To Mr. Procter, parson of Bodington, five pounds or an ambling nag of that price, at his choice. And I give unto Mr. Thomas Campion my minister the presentation of the next Parsonage that shall fall, and if it be not to his contentment then to take that until a better do fall, and then to resign the worst and to take the best, the which I will and command my son to perform. I give to Stephen

French and John Spencer, two of my servants that wait upon me in my chamber, forty pounds to each of them.

Kidd, 95 (P. C. C.).

ROBERT WASHINGTON of Souldgrave, in the Co. of Northampton Esq., 7 February 1619, proved 3 January 1620. My body to be buried in the South Aisle of the church before my seat where I usually sit under the same stone that my father lieth buried under.

I give to my three sons which I had by my second wife, namely to my son Albane Washington, to my son Guy Washington and to my son Robert Washington, the sum of one hundred pounds apiece of currant English money, to be paid unto them and to each of them at their ages of four and twenty years apiece, always provided, and I do mean, that my said three sons shall have the said sums of money aforenamed and at the time aforesaid if they be obedient and will be ruled in the mean space by their mother my executrix and do carry themselves well and as dutiful children to her, but if they, or any of them, be undutiful unto her and will not be ruled by her as it becometh them to be then I will by this my last will and testament that they, or so many of them as shall be undutiful or that will not be ruled by her, shall have but ten pounds apiece at their ages of four and twenty years apiece aforesaid.

Also I give unto three other sons which I had by my former wife, namely to my son Christopher Washington, to my son William Washington and to my son Thomas Washington, the sum of ten shillings apiece. And I do further give unto my son William Washington aforesaid the sum of fifty pounds to be paid unto him out of a debt of four hundred and odd pounds due unto me from the executors or administrators of my son Lawrence Washington deceased, and the said fifty pounds to be paid unto my son William Washington aforesaid as soon as it is recovered from the executors or administrators of my son Lawrence Washington as is aforesaid.

The rest of my goods and chattells unnamed and unbequeathed I give unto my wife Ann Washington whom I make sole executrix of this my last will and testament she discharging my last will and testament and discharging my debts and funerals.

Wit: Thomas Court, scriptor, Christopher Pargiter, John Ireton.

Dale, 5 (P. C. C.).

Of the sons mentioned in the foregoing will, Christopher and William entered Oriel College, Oxford, I think, in 1588, the former fifteen, the latter eleven, years old (as I learn from a memorandum furnished me by J. H. Lea, Esq.). The will or admon. of the son Lawrence, referred to, may be at Peterborough. I have not found it in London. He died at Brington, 13 December, 1616.

ELIZABETH WASHINGTON of Brighton (Brington), in the Co. of Northampton widow, 17 March 1622, proved 12 April 1623. I do give unto John Washington one hundred pounds and four pairs of my best sheets, two long table cloths, two pairs of pillowbeers and four dozen of napkins, four side board cloths, four cupboard cloths and four long towels, one nut to drink in trimmed with silver, one silver beaker to drink in, one silver bowl to drink in, half a dozen of the best silver spoons and one double silver salt cellar, one pewter charger and a plate to it, six of the best platters and six dishes, a pair of andirons and tongs, a fire shovel, a chafing dish, a great brass pot which came from Solgrave, the best standing bed in the great chamber, with all that belongs to it, and half a dozen of Turkey work "quishions" and two long velvet "quishions" and a leather coffer. Item I do give unto Sir William Washington one hundred pounds. Item I do give unto Mrs. Mywse twenty pounds and one silver bowl and one brass pot. Item I do give unto Mrs. Alice Washington twenty pounds. Item I do give unto Mrs. Frances Washington twenty pounds. Item I do give unto my cousin Pill the bed wherein I do now lie, with all that appertains unto it. "Item I doe give unto my Cosen Lawrence Washington who is nowe at Oxford my husband's seal ringe."* Item I do give unto A:me Adcocke twenty five pounds, a pied cow and a pied colt and a yearling bullock, a great brass pott and two great deep platters and two pairs of fine sheets, one pair of pillowbeers and a dozen of napkins, a kettel and a dripping pan. Item I do give unto my cousin Penelope Leake who is now with me ten pounds. And of this my last will and testament I do make and ordain Mr. Francis Mewse my whole executor. And I do desire that all those dues and debts which is now owing by my late husband Mr. Robert Washington may be first discharged and then after them the legacies herein set down performed. And my desire is that my honorable good Lord Spencer would be pleased to be my supervisor of this my last will and testament.

Swann, 33 (P. C. C.).

The following monumental inscription at Brington is copied from Baker's Northamptonshire, Vol. I. p. 93 :

Here lies interred y'e bodies of Elizab: Washington | widdowe, who changed this life for im'ortalitie | ye 19th of March 1622. As also y'e body of Robert | Washington Gent: her late husband second | sonne of Robert Washington of Solgrave in y'e | County of North. Esq. who dep'ted this life y'e | 10th of March 1622. After they lived lovingly together | many yeares in this Parish.†

Sir EDWARD VILLIERS, knight, Lord President of the Province of Munster in the realm of Ireland, 31 August 1625, proved 2 February 1626. I give and devise all my lands unto my dear and loving wife the Lady Barbara Villiers during her life, she to maintain and provide for my children. To my servant Hamond Francklyn two hundred pounds in one year after my decease. If both my self and my wife shall die without any issue begotten of our two bodies that shall be living &c. then my brother Sir William Villiers, Baronet, shall have all my lands &c., and he shall give unto my sister the Lady Elizabeth Butler one hundred pounds to buy her a jewell and to my sister the Lady Anne Washington the sum of five hundred pounds, and to every servant in my service at the time of my death one year's wages and to the poor people of St. Margaret's in Westminster the sum of twenty pounds.   Skynner, 20 (P. C. C.).

PHILLIP CURTIS of Islip in the Co. of Northampton, gentleman, delivered his will nuncupative in the presence of Sir John Washington, knight, and

---

* Qu. Did the sons of Lawrence Washington take this seal ring over with them to Virginia ? If so, what became of it ? Are there to be found any early impressions of it ?

† This is one of the two "Memorial Stones" of which facsimiles were, in 1860, presented to Hon. Charles Sumner by Earl Spencer. Mr. Sumner gave these facsimiles to the State of Massachusetts, and they are now in the State House at Boston. The other stone is that of Lawrence Washington, brother of Robert, who was the grandfather of the presumed Virginia emigrants. He died Dec. 13, 1616.—EDITOR.

Michael Westfield, clerk, 19 May 1636, proved 30 May 1636. To my daughter Katherine Curtis one thousand pounds, at day of marriage or age of twenty one, which shall first happen. Item I give unto my nephew John Washington the sum of fifty pounds to be paid unto him at his age of twenty and one years. Item I give unto my nephew Phillip Washington the like sum of fifty pounds to be paid at his age of twenty and one years. And for my nephew Mordant Washington I leave in trust to my wife. Item I give unto my wife Amy Curtis and to her heirs forever all my free-hold land to be sold towards the raising of my daughters portion &c. And I make her the full and sole executrix &c. Item I make choice of Sir John Washington of Thropston, knight, and Michael Westfield of Islipp, clerk, to be guardians for my daughter. Pile, 55 (P. C. C.).

AMYE CURTIS of Islipp, in the Co. of Northampton widow, 27 June 1636, proved 19 November 1636. My body to be buried in the chancel of Islipp, near unto the grave of my deceased husband. I give towards the repair of the church of Islipp twenty shillings; to the poor there forty shillings: to the poor of Denford twenty shillings.

Item whereas there was given unto my nephew Mordaunt Washington, the eldest son of Sir John Washington, knight, by the last will and testament of his grandmother Curtis deceased the sum of fifty pounds to be employed as [in] the said will is further expressed my will is and I do give unto the said Mordaunt two hundred and fifty pounds more to be employed for his best benefit so soon as my debts be paid and the said money can conveniently be raised, and to be paid unto him at his age of twenty and one years or at the day of his marriage, which shall first happen. Item, whereas my husband, late deceased, gave unto John Washington, the second son of Sir John Washington, the sum of fifty pounds my will is, and I do give unto the said John my nephew the sum of fifty pounds more, to be employed for his best use and benefit, my debts first paid and the money conveniently raised, and to be paid to him at his age of twenty and one years, or at the day of his marriage.

A similar bequest to Phillip Washington, the third son of Sir John Washington.

To my god daughter Amy Hynde twenty pounds. To Michael Westfield, clerk, five pounds and to Mr. Richard Allen of Lowick five pounds. To my neighbor Mrs. Margaret Westfield five pounds. The freehold land given to me by my husband Phillip Curtis, I give unto my daughter Katherine Curtis. My mother Margaret Washington and my brother Sir John Washington to be guardians for my daughter.

Wit: Michael Westfield, William Washington and Phillip Freeman.
Pile, 108 (P. C. C.).

SAMUEL THORNTON, of St. Giles in the Fields, Middlesex, Esq., 9 January 1666, proved 2 May 1666. To my dear wife the sum of four hundred pounds, to my grandchild John Thornton two hundred pounds, to Charles Thornton my grandchild, one hundred pounds, to my grandchild Penelope Thornton one hundred pounds, to my daughter Kirby two hundred pounds, and I make and ordain my dear wife sole executrix.

Wit: Jo: Coell, Eliza: Mewce, Margaret Talbott.

Proved by the oath of Dame Margaret Sandis als Thornton his Relict & executrix named in the will. Carr, 41 (P. C. C.).

Will of Dame Margaret Sandys.

October the eleventh 1673. Into the hands of God the father, the son and the Holy Ghost, three persons but one eternal God, I do commend my soul, and I desire my body may be buried in a private plain decent manner. And that little I have I do desire should be thus disposed of. I do give to my dear sister Mewce twenty pounds and the hangings in our chamber and the silk blanket and my pair of sheets we lie in. I do give to my sister Washington, my sister Sandys and my sister Gargrave ten pounds apiece, which in all is thirty pounds. I give to my nephew John Washington, my dear eldest brother's son, twenty pounds. I give to my son Thornton my Indian gown. I give to my daughter Thornton twenty pounds and the hair trunk in my chamber and the linen in it. I give to my son Kerkby twenty pounds and my Turkey work chairs and the tables and carpets in the Parlour during his life and my daughter's, and after their deaths I give them to Lucy Kerk [Kerkby?] that waiteth on me. I give to my daughter Kerkby twenty pounds and my blue box in my closet and her father's picture in it and all else in the box. I give to my uncle Robert Washington five pounds. I give to young Lucy Kerkby that waits upon me ten pounds and the feather bed, bolster and pillows and blankets and three pairs of sheets she lies in and the wrought sheet and the chairs and stools in my closet and all my other things in my closet. I give also to her and her sisters my wearing linen and my clothes. I give to little Peg Kerkby my silver cup with the cover. I give to little Sam. Thornton my thirty shilling piece of gold. I give to little Nan Dornan a broad piece of gold. I give Sam. Kerby a broad piece of gold. I give to the poor of Soham five pounds. I give to the poor of Fordham two pounds. And I make and ordain my dear son Thornton sole executor of this my last will and testament, desiring him to perform the same and those poor goods I have given that they may have them when I die and the money I have given that it may be paid to every one at the end of six months. In witness whereof I have hereunto set my hand and seal in the presence of the witnesses whose names are subscribed the day and year above written, and what money I have either here or at Haxey undisposed I give two parts of it to John Thornton and one part to Charles Thornton, my son Thornton's sons. And I desire my son that they may have it as soon as it is gotten but the charge of my burying must be taken out of the money I leave.   MARGARETT SANDYS.

Wit: Do: Washington, Elizabeth Mewce, Lucy Kirkby.

Proved 16 November 1675 by Roger Thornton, the Executor.

Dycer, 118 (P. C. C.).

DOROTHY WASSINGTON, relict of Sir John Wassington, knight deceased, 6 October 1678, proved 24 December 1678. My body I leave to my executor's discretion to be laid decently in the grave in the chancel of the church of Fordham, near the place where the body of my dear grand child Mrs. Penelope Audley lies buried. And for that small estate which the lord hath continued to me I bequeath and bestow as followeth. Item I give and bequeath unto my son Mr. Thomas Kirkbey the sum of five pounds and to each of his sons and daughters twenty shillings a piece, to be paid them six months after my decease. Item all the rest of my goods whatsoever, as household stuff, bills, bonds, debts and the like, I give and bequeath unto my daughter Mrs. Penelope Thornton, whom I do make my sole executrix &c.

Wit: Ezech: Pargiter, Hugh Floyde, Sarah Flecher.

Reeve, 148 (P. C. C.).

The three preceding wills seem to show a confusion or mixing up of Sandys, Thornton, Kirkby and Washington. Dame Margaret Sandys was one of the sisters of Sir William, Sir John and the Rev. Lawrence Washington, and had been the wife of Samuel Thornton, Esq., before her marriage with —— Sandys. Dame Dorothy Washington was undoubtedly a daughter of William Pargiter of Gretworth, Esq., by Abigail, daughter of Sir Francis Willoughby of Wollaton, Nottinghamshire, Bart. Her brother Theodore Pargiter's will (1654–1656) has already been published in these Gleanings (*ante*, pp. 84–5). I suppose the "Cosen John Washington" referred to in that will, apparently in Barbados,* was the second son of Sir John Washington of Thrapston, husband of Dame Dorothy. The following will of another brother of this Dame Dorothy Washington seems to prove the connection:

FRANCIS PARGITER of London, merchant, 10 January 1685, sworn to 28th and proved 29 October 1686. To the poor of the parish of Greetworth in the Co. of Northampton, where I was born, the poor of Westhorpe, adjoining to the said parish, the poor of St. Anne Black Friars (and others). To my sister Elizabeth Smith, widow, my sister Abigail Hickman, widow, my sister Phillis Pargiter, my niece Eleanor Pargiter, my nephew Edward Stratford, of Overstone, in the Co. of Northampton, Esq., my nephew Robert Stratford of Baltinglass in the kingdom of Ireland Esq. To such children of my niece Thornton as living, to such children of my niece Friend as living. To my niece Dorothy Marshall, widow, my niece Abigail Hickman.

I constitute and appoint my nephew Thomas Pargiter Doctor in Divinity sole executor of this my said will.

In a codicil, of same date, reference is made to a provision for the testator's nephew John Pargiter.   Lloyd, 137 (P. C. C.).

The mention of the "children of my niece Thornton" evidently refers to Mrs. Penelope Thornton and her children (see wills of Dame Margaret Sandys and Dame Dorothy Washington). This I found confirmed by the will of Mrs. Mewce, a sister of Dame Sandys, as follows:—

ELIZABETH MEWCE in the Co. of Middlesex, widow, 11 August 1676, proved 12 December 1676. My body I commit to the earth whence it came, to be decently buried according to the discretion of my executors. I give and bequeath to my niece Mrs Penelope Thornton fifty pounds and my black shelf and my cabinet with all things that I shall leave therein. I give and bequeath to my niece Thornton's five children, John, Charles, Samuel, Roger and Dorothy Thornton, forty pounds. I give and bequeath to my sister the Lady Washington twenty pounds. I give and bequeath to my

* It may be well to note here that another of the name was in the West Indies. In Gov. Lefroy's elaborate book, "Memorials of the Bermudas," vol. 1, p. 384, he prints a document signed by eighteen of the inhabitants of Smith's Tribe, dated March 30, 1626. The fourteenth name is Laurence Washington.

Again, vol. i. p. 650, at a Council meeting June 20, 1649, "Mr. Axson, Washington and Bethell bayled to answer at next assizes for some words spoken against his majestie." This may or may not refer to the first-named Laurence. But clearly the Bermuda man was not our Rev. Lawrence, who was at this date at Oxford.—W. H. WHITMORE.

sister Mrs. Alice Sandys the sum of twenty pounds. I give and bequeath to my sister Mrs. Frances Gargrave the sum of twenty pounds and my clock and bed and hangings and sheets and all things to my bed belonging whatsoever. To my God-daughter Mrs. Elizabeth Sandys ten pounds. To my niece Mrs. Margaret Stevenage ten pounds and to her two children, William and Mercy Stevenage, five pounds apiece. "Item I give and bequeath to my Uncle Mr. Robert Washington the Summe of five pounds:" to Mrs. Elizabeth Rumball, my niece, five pounds: to my nephew William Pill five pounds: to my niece Mrs. Frances Collins five pounds: to my nephew Mr. Robert Gargrave's five children, Robert, John, William, Elizabeth and Cotton Gargrave twenty pounds apiece and to Elizabeth Gargrave my silver dish and silver porringer and cup and two spoons and all the rest of my small silver things that my note speaks of. To my maid Anne Freestone thirty pounds and her bed that she lieth on, with all things belonging to it, and my suit of purple curtains and the other things in my rooms not mentioned. I do make my two loving nephews Mr. Robert Gargrave and Mr. Roger Thornton executors of this my last will and testament, intreating them to take the care and trouble upon them, and I further desire these my executors, to let that money which I have given to my nephew Thornton's children be put into the hands of their trusty and loving uncle Mr. Francis Pargiter, merchant, to be improved for them till it is demanded, either to put the sons-apprentices or for the daughter's preferment in marriage, &c.

Bence, 154 (P. C. C.).

Mrs. Mewce was another sister of Sir William, Sir John and the Rev. Lawrence Washington, daughter of Lawrence Washington of Sulgrave and Brington and widow of Mr. Francis Mewce of Holdenby in Northampton, to whom she was married, at St. Mary Le Strand, Middlesex, 26 May, 1615. I have not had time to ascertain in what way Mrs. Margaret Stevenage, Mrs. Elizabeth Rumball and Mrs. Frances Collins could be her nieces, nor have I succeeded in finding wills of her two surviving sisters, Mrs. Alice Sandys and Mrs. Frances Gargrave, who were also daughters of Lawrence Washington of Brington and therefore aunts of our presumed emigrants to Virginia. The uncle, Mr. Robert Washington, named in this will, as also in that of Dame Margaret Sandys, was, of course, the youngest son of Robert Washington of Sulgrave, Esq., by his second wife Anne (Fisher), and consequently a grand-uncle of the emigrants.

The pedigree of Mewce of Holdenby may be found in the Visitation of Northamptonshire, 1618–19; by which it appears that Mr. Francis Mewce was eldest son of Nicholas Mewce by Elizabeth, daughter of Edmund Morant of London, and had brothers Edmund and Christopher, and sisters Alice, wife of Richard Ellis of London, Lucy, Maline and Katherine wife of (Humphrey) Hawley of London. The following brief abstract is therefore worth preserving:

RICHARD ELLIES, citizen and haberdasher of London, 15 Aug. 1625, proved 26 Aug. 1625. Property in Rippon and Beverly, Yorkshire. Son

Francis. Daughter Elizabeth. Reference to a bequest made to her by Mr. Nicholas Mewce. Daughters Ann and Mary and the child wife now goeth with. Sister Washington and god daughter Anne Washington. Children of sister Hyde, sister Croft, sister Vessey and brother Goderedge. Rev^d. kinsman Mr. Jeremy Leeche. Aunt Gymber. Sister Hallye. Brother Humfrey Hally. Sister Malin. Brothers Mr. Francis Mewce, Mr. Edmund Mewce and Christopher Mewce. Clarke, 86 (P. C. C.).

Who the sister Washington is, who is mentioned in the foregoing will, I do not know.

The Lady Ann Washington, named in Sir Edward Villiers' will, was the wife of Sir William Washington, eldest son of Lawrence Washington of Sulgrave and Brington, and therefore aunt by marriage to the presumed emigrants. She was a daughter of Sir George Villiers of Brooksby and half sister of the celebrated royal favorite, George, Duke of Buckingham. She was buried at Chelsea, 25 May, 1643. The following is an abstract of the will of her husband :

SIR WILLIAM WASHINGTON of Thistleworth in the Co. of Middlesex, knight, 6 June 1643, proved 1 March 1648. Whereas I am justly indebted unto Elizabeth Washington, my daughter, in the sum of twelve hundred pounds which she lent me in ready money and for payment whereof, at a time shortly to come, I have given her my bond of the penalty of two thousand pounds, my said daughter shall have and retain to her own use, towards satisfaction of the said sum, all that debt of eight hundred pounds, or thereabouts, due unto me upon two Obligations from the Right Honble William, Earl of Denbigh deceased, with the use that shall grow due for the same, and if any part of the said sum of twelve hundred pounds be paid and satisfied unto my said daughter in my life time, or after my decease, out of the overplus of moneys which shall or may remain due or payable unto me or my assigns upon the sale of my manor of Wicke and capital messuage called Wicke farm and other lands thereunto belonging which are now in mortgage to Henry Winn Esq. and John Chappell gent., redeemable upon payment of the sum of eleven hundred forty four pounds at a time now past &c. &c.

And my will and meaning is that, my other debts, which are not many nor great, being satisfied and paid in the next place, then all the residue of the money which shall remain and all my goods, chattles and personal estate whatsoever shall be equally divided amongst all my children that shall be living. And I make and ordain my said daughter Elizabeth sole executrix.

Wit: Rob: Woodford, John Pardo, Thomas Woodford, John Washington. The will was proved by the oath of Elizabeth Washington als Legg, daughter of the deceased and executrix named in the will.

Fairfax, 29 (P. C. C.).

Sir William did not outlive his wife long, for the following entry may be found among the Burials in the Register of St. Martin's in the Fields, Middlesex :—

1643 June 22 Gulielmus Washington *eques auratus*.

From Col. Chester we learn that he was knighted at Theobalds on the 17th January, 1621–2, and that two of his children were baptized at Leckhampstead, in the County of Bucks., and two at St. Martin's in the Fields. The following are the two entries in the Baptismal Register of the last named parish :—

> 1618 November Susanna Washington.
> 1619–20 January 13 Geo. Washington fil. Gulielmi Washington gen^{al} & Annæ ux^r eius unius soror̃ p^{r}nobilis Georgii Marchioñ & Comitis Buckingham.

One of the witnesses of Sir William's will was John Pardo ; and I noticed, in the same parish, the marriage of Guy Washington and Katherine Pardieu, 17 November, 1629. The bridegroom was probably Sir William's young uncle. I noticed too that a Richard Washington, gen., and Frances Browne were married, 27 April, 1627, and had children, Amata, bap. 21 October, 1628, and John, bap. 14 March, 1631–2. Richard Washington was buried 8 January, 1641–2, and Ralph Hall and Frances Washington were married, 17 January, 1642–3. A Philip Washington was buried 26 September, 1643.

Sir William's eldest, and, I think, only surviving son was Col. Henry Washington, the brave and resolute Governor of Worcester, for the King. He was buried at Richmond, Surrey, 9 March, 1663–4, leaving four daughters and a widow, Elizabeth, who was afterwards married to Samuel Sandys of Ombersley, Esq. One of the daughters, Mary Washington, of St. Martin's in the Fields, spinster, made a nuncupative will, 13 January, 1680, leaving everything to her mother, Mrs. Sandys, who renounced, with consent of her husband, and admon., with the will annexed, was granted to Catherine Forster, a sister of the deceased, 5 May, 1681. Abstracts of her will and that of her sister Penelope are given below :

MARY WASHINGTON, spinster, of the parish of St. Martin in the fields in the Co. of Middlesex, 13 January 1680, being in her last sickness whereof she died, with an intent and purpose to make and declare her last will and testament nuncupative and to settle and dispose of her estate, did utter and spake these words following, or the like in effect vizt: I desire that Hannah (meaning her maid-servant Hannah Lewis) may have one hundred pounds out of the money of the King's gift, and the rest I leave to my dear Mother (meaning Mrs. Elizabeth Sandyes), which words, or the like in effect she uttered and declared as and for her last will and testament nuncupative in the presence and hearing of the said Mrs. Elizabeth Sandys her mother, whom she desired to remember what she said to her, and of Katharine Hodges, Katharine Forster and Mary Hall and that she was at the premises of and in her perfect senses and understanding, the same being so done in the house of Mrs. Forster, her place of abode.

Letters issued 5 May 1681 to Catherine Forster, sister of the deceased, to administer the goods &c., for the reason that she had named no executor in the will, Elizabeth Sandys the mother, with consent of her husband Samuel Sandys Esq., expressly renouncing.   North, 83 (P. C. C.).

PENELOPE WASHINGTON of Wickhamford, Co. Worc. spinster, 6 December 1697, with codicil 5 January 1697, proved at Worcester 9 March 1697. To my niece Catherine Foster, spinster, two hundred and fifty pounds, but my mother and executrix, Madam Elizabeth Sandys of Wickhamford, to receive the interest of this money during her life. The said Catherine not to intermarry with any person without the consent of my executrix, being her grandmother. To my other niece Elizabeth Jollett (Gellett) the same sum on similar conditions. To my faithful servant Sarah Tovey one hundred pounds. The residue to my said executrix.

By the codicil all the lands &c. in Bayton and elsewhere in Worc., conveyed unto me by Mr. William Swift deceased and his trustees, to "my deare mother Elizabeth Sandys" her heirs and assigns forever.

Seal—two bars, in chief three mullets.

The above will of Penelope Washington I had the pleasure of receiving quite recently from the Rev. T. P. Wadley, Naunton Rectory, Pershore.

In Add. MSS. 5705 (Brit. Mus.) may be found the substance of a petition from the four daughters of Col. ·Henry Washington, deceased "(transcribed from a book in the Surveyor Gen¹. of the Crown Land's Office, marked K. 1671–72 fol. 368 *ad* 372 inclu.)." They request a grant in consideration of the faithful service done by their father.

Mrs. Catharine Foster, sister of Mary and Penelope Washington, who administered on the estate of the former, was afterwards married to Barnabas Tunstall or Tonstall, of the Middle Temple, Esq., license being granted 9 March, 1686–7. She and her sisters are mentioned in the will of their aunt, Mrs. Susanna Graham, which follows:

SUSANNA GRAHME of Blackheath in the parish of Lewisham in the Co. of Kent 6 October, 1697, proved 30 March 1699. I desire my body may be interred in the parish church of Lewisham. To the Lady Dartmouth twenty broad pieces of gold which are sealed up in a paper with her name upon it. To my niece Mrs. Bilson ten broad pieces (as before) and the sum of one hundred pounds payable out of the arrears of rent which shall be due to me at the day of my death. Besides I give my said niece all the pictures in my little parlour at Blackheath, except my Lady Mordants. To my nephew William Leg Esq. one hundred pounds. To my niece Mrs. Dorothy Heron one hundred pounds. To Mrs. Penelope Washington five broad pieces of gold. To Mrs. Katherine Tonstall five guineas and to Mrs. Gelet, sister to Mrs. Katherine Tonstall five guineas. To my niece Mrs. Musgrave all my plate and china which I have in my house at Blackheath. To my Lord Preston all my furniture and household stuff at Nunnington, except my plate and china, which I give and bequeath to my niece Mrs. Susanna Grahme, his Lordship's sister. To the said Lord Preston his father's picture and my husband's set in gold. To Deborah Sanders all my furniture and household stuff in my house at Blackheath not otherwise disposed of. To my Lord Dartmouth two hundred pounds, out of the arrears of rent, and four hundred pounds which he oweth me, provided always that his Lordship in consideration of the said six hundred pounds settle upon the minister of the parish of Lewisham for the time being and to all future generations such a salary for the reading of prayers once a day at Black-heath as is agreed between us, and I beg and desire of him that the said salary may be so settled according to law that it may be firm to all future ages. To the said Lord Dartmouth all my pictures at Blackheath not otherwise disposed of, with my coach and horses, and five guineas to defray the charges of my funeral. And I constitute and appoint the said Lord Dartmouth sole executor of this my last will and testament.

Proved by the oath of William, Lord Dartmouth.

Pett, 40 (P. C. C.).

In the chancel of the old church at Lewisham, on a grave-stone of black marble, was this inscription : " Here lyeth | Mrs Susanna GRAHME | wife of | Reginal Grahme Esqre | Lord of this manor and second daughter of | Sir William WASHINGTON | who departed this life | the 26th day of February, Anno Domini | 1698 aged 81 years." This Reginald Graham was a citizen and draper of London, and be-longed, I believe, to the royalist family of Graham of Esk and Netherby, in Co. Cumberland. He purchased, 23 May, 1640, of John Ramsay, Esq., the lordship and manor of Lewisham for £1500, and by deed dated 30 May, 1673, conveyed it to George Legge, afterwards Baron Dartmouth, as I learn from the new His-tory of Kent, Hundred of Blackheath (edited by Henry H. Drake). Lord Dartmouth was eldest son and heir of Col. William Legge, a staunch royalist, who received license, 2 March, 1641–2, to marry Elizabeth Washington, of Kensington, Middlesex, spinster, about twenty-two, daughter of Sir William Washington, knight, of the same parish—at St. Faith's. Among the family letters is one of Col. Ed. Cooke to William Legge, Esq., Whitehall, dated Dublin, 10 January, 1662–3. He sends humble service to Legge's lady, his brother and sister Graham, Harry Washington, Dick Lane and all bedchamber backstair friends. Another, from Barbara, Lady Dartmouth, to Lord Dartmouth, 15 December, 1688, says : "it hath pleased God to take away your mother yesterday after a lingering illness . . . . she desired to be carried privatly to the Minorits." One from Sir Harry Goodricke to Lord Dartmouth, dated York, 5 January, 1689–90, expresses the greatest affliction of his wife and himself at the irreparable loss of their dearest mother.

Col. William Legge, who had been a captain in Prince Rupert's Regiment, died at his house in the Minories, 13 October, 1670, aged 63, and was buried in the vault in the Trinity Chapel there, where also his widow was buried, 19 December, 1688, aged 76. Their grandson William, second Baron Dartmouth, was created Viscount Lewisham and Earl of Dartmouth, 5 September, 1711.

———

The following two or three abstracts refer to the Warwickshire branch of this family :

WALTER WASHINGTON of Radway, in the parish of Bishop's Itchington, in the Co. of Warwick, gentleman, being asked 1 January, 1596–7, by his uncle George Warner about the disposition of his estate replied that he would leave all to his wife and children. Commission issued 23 April 1597 to his widow Alice Washington to administer &c.

Cobham, 31 (P. C. C.).

Commission issued 18 September 1646 to Anne Washington, natural and lawful sister of Walter Washington late of Upton, in the Co. of Warwick deceased, to administer his goods &c.   Admon. Act Book (P. C. C.).

Commission issued, 18 September 1646, to Anne Washington, natural and lawful sister of Elizabeth Washington, lately of Tamworth, in the Co. of Warwick, but in Stepney in the Co. of Middlesex, singlewoman, deceased, to administer her goods &c.   Admon. Act Book (P. C C.).

ALICE WOODWARD of Stratford on Avon, 20 Aug. 1642, proved 22 May 1647. To be buried in the church of Stratford near late husband John Woodward gen'. To the poor of Woodstreet Ward. To my son John Washington twenty pounds in six months. Bequests to grandchildren George, Elizabeth, Ann, Thomas and Katherine Washington, the children of the said John Washington, at their ages of one and twenty or days of marriage; also to grandchildren Thomas, Walter and Alice Stanton. Friend Thomas Nash Esq.   Fines, 112 (P. C. C.).

JOHN DANVERS of Upton in the parish of Ratley in the Co. of Warwick Esq., 5 April 1658, proved 2 October 1658. My body to be buried in the parish church of Ratley. I give and bequeath my manor of Upton unto my brother-in-law Richard Swan, my brother George Danvers, my nephew Peter Yate and Ambrose Holbech the younger of Mollington, Warr., until my nephew John Danvers son of my late brother William Danvers deceased, shall attain his age of eighteen years; after that to my said nephew, with remainder to John Danvers, son of my brother George, then to my right heirs. To my brother Henry Danvers the income of five hundred pounds during his natural life, and after his death to Damaras Swann and Susanna Swann, daughters of my said brother Swann and of my sister Dorothy his wife.

Also I give and bequeath unto my brother-in-law John Washington the sum of one hundred pounds &c., and unto Anne Pepys, wife of John Pepys, of Littleton, in the Co. of Worcester, the like sum of one hundred pounds &c., and unto my godson John Washington of Kingston in the Co. of Warwick the sum of fifty pounds &c. (all payable within one year after the decease of the testator). Bequests made to Mary Yate, daughter of Peter Yate, to nephew Edward Yate, to Elizabeth, Hannah and Deborah, daughters of brother George Danvers, to Simon and Anna, children of sister Sibell Edulph, to Elizabeth Danvers, daughter of late brother William, to John and Katherine, the two children of late niece Katherine Goodwyn deceased, to God daughter Anne Tyler, daughter of niece Anne Tyler, to cousin Samuel Tyler and his wife and to brother Henry Browne and his wife.

Wootton, 449 (P. C. C.).

The testator of the above will was the eldest son of George Danvers of Blisworth, Co. Northampton, Esq., son of John Danvers of Cockthorpe, by Dorothy, daughter of Sir Richard Verney of Compton, both in the Co. of Oxford (see Visitation of Northamptonshire, 1618–19). His sister Anne (Danvers) was the wife of John Washington of Radway, son of Walter Washington, whose nuncupative will I have given. The latter's wife was Alice (not Catherine as in some of the pedigrees), daughter of John Morden *alias* Murden of Morton Morell, Warwickshire, by Katherine, daughter and coheir of Richard Marston of Draughton, Northamptonshire. After Mr. Washington's death, his widow Alice seems to have been married to John Woodward, who, I suppose, was the eldest son of Thomas Woodward of Butlers Marston (see pedigrees of Morden and Woodward in Visitation of Warwickshire, 1619). Katherine, daughter of Walter and Alice Washington, was married to Thomas Stanton, son and heir of Thomas Stanton of Woolverton (Woolverdington), Warwickshire. A pedigree of this family is also in the Visitation of Warwickshire.

Commission issued 4 May 1612 to Anne Bateman *als* Washington and Lucy Cheesewright *als* Washington, natural and lawful sisters of Richard Washington, bachelor, in parts beyond the seas deceased, to administer his goods &c.   Admon. Act Book (P. C. C.).

The above relates to a rather remote branch of the family, the said Richard, Anne and Lucy being children of Capt. Thomas Washington of Compton, Sussex (see pedigree). I now come to a nearer and better known line, which furnished a succession of Registrars of the High Court of Chancery, of whom the first was Lawrence, son of Lawrence and brother of Robert of Sulgrave.

License granted to Lawrence Washington and Johanna Sorrell spinster, of High Easter, Essex, to marry there, 16 July, 1576.

License granted to Lawrence Washington of Gray's Inn and Martha Newce, spinster, of Great Hadham, Herts., to marry there, 31 January 1577–8.   London Marriage Licenses.

LAWRENCE WASHINGTON Esquire, Register of His Majesty's High Court of Chancery, 10 August 1619, proved 10 January 1619. I give, will and bequeath all my lands, tenements and hereditaments to my well beloved son Lawrence Washington, his heirs and assigns forever, and all my goods and chattells other than such legacies as I shall give and bequeath to my loving daughter Mary Horspoole, wife to William Horspoole, gent., and to any of her children, and to my loving brother Robert Washington and to my very good loving cousin Sir Justinian-Lewyn, knight, and to the poor of the parish of Soulgrave in the co. of Northampton (and other legacies). I do constitute and make my said son Lawrence sole executor.
                                    Soame, 3 (P. C. C.).

Funeral Certificate of Lawrence Washington, 1619.

Lawrence Washington of Maydeston in Kent gent. and Registrar of his Ma[ties] high Court of Chauncerie second sonne of Lawrence Washington of Sowlegrave in the County of Northampton gent. and daughter of William Pargiter of Gritworth in the County of Northampton aforesaid gent. deceased the 21 day of December 1619 at his house in Chauncerie Lane

and was buried in the parishe Churche of . . . . in Maydeston in Kent aforesayd his body being thither translated on the 24 of the same moneth. He
maried two wyves the first was Martha daughter of Clement Nuse of
Haddam in the County of Hartf. gent. and had issue by her six sonnes and
two daughters viz. Lawrence his eldest sonne and heire who also succeeded
his father in the Office of Register maried to Anne Lewine the da. of
William Lewine Doctor of the Civill Lawe and Judge of the prerogative
Court, Clement his second sonne and Clement his 3ᵈ sonne who dyed both
without issue, Raphe 4 sonne, William 5 sonne, and an other all dyed
before their father. He had also two daughters by the sayd Martha his
first wife the first was Mary maried to William Horsepoole of Buckland
neere Maydeston in Kent gent., the second daughter was Martha maried to
Arthur Beswick sonne and heire apparant of William Beswick gent. of
Spilmandine in the parishe of Horsemandine in the Countie of Kent aforesayd. The second wife of Lawrence Washington deceased was Mary the
daughter of Sʳ Thomas Scott of Scotts Hall in the County of Kent aforesayd
Knight and by her had no issue. This certificate was taken by William
Penson Lancaster Herald the 14 of January 1619 and is testified to be true
vnder the hand of Lawrence Washington the heire of the sayd Lawrence
deceased.

Dr. Howard's Miscellanea Genealogica et Heraldica, 2d ser. vol. 1, p. 173.

Pedigrees of the Newce family may be found in Berry's County
Pedigrees (Herts) and in the Visitation of Hertfordshire (Harleian
Society's Publications). William Horspoole and Mary Washington
were married (by License), 27 May, 1602, at St. James Clerken-
well. He was son of Symon Horspoole, citizen and draper of London.
(See Visitation of London, 1568.)

Commission issued the last of May 1647 to Simon Horsepoole, natural
and lawful son of William Horsepoole late of Great Marlow, Bucks., deceased,
to administer his goods &c.   Admon. Act Book.

Sir JUSTINIAN LEWYN, knight, 8 July 1620, proved 11 July 1620. The
land to descend to his daughter Elizabeth and the lady Elizabeth, his wife,
to have the profits thereof during the minority of her child, towards her
maintenance. The said Lady Elizabeth his wife to be his sole executrix.
Ten pounds to be paid to the poor of this parish, ten pounds to the poor
of Otterden. A hundred pounds to his sister Washington, fifty pounds to
his sister Padgett, a hundred pounds to his sister Isam (Isham), a hundred
pounds to his god daughter Elizabeth Huytt.   Soame, 71 (P. C. C.).

SIMON HEYNES of Towerstone (Turweston) in the Co. of Bucks, Esq.
20 December 1626, proved 17 May 1628. My little nephew and god son
Symon Heynes now in the house with me. As touching my freehold lands
called Millfield, lying in Stuttesbury, Northampton, which I heretofore
purchased of my cousin Lawrence Washington, of the King's Majesty's
in capite, I dispose of two parts thereof in manner as followeth, leaving a
third part thereof to discend to my son Henry Heynes according to law :
one part to my wife, in lieu of her dower, and the other part to my said
son for life &c. I make and appoint my wife executrix and my friends and
kinsmen Lawrence Washington, Esq., and Simon Heynes, Esq., son of
Joseph Heines, overseers.

The wife's christian name is omitted in the Probate.

Barrington, 40 (P. C. C.).

On a mural tablet on the south side of the chancel (Turweston) is inscribed the name of Simon Heynes, Esq., who died April 10, 1628.

Lipscomb's Hist. of Buck., III. 129.

Turweston is the next parish West of Westbury, some time the home of Sir Lawrence Washington.

Sir LAURENCE WASHINGTON of Garsden, in the Co. of Wilts, knight, 11 May 1643, proved 23 May 1643. To be buried in the church of Garsden. My daughter the Lady Tirrell. My nephew Simon Horsepoole. My servants Francis Cliffe, Allen Moore, Thomas Benson and William Freame. My son Lawrence Washington to be executor. To the poor of Garsden twelve pence a week for ever, to be bestowed in bread every Sunday morning, chargeable on my manor of Garsden.

(From the original will.)

The above will is one of the Oxford Wills (so called) which remain unregistered. The Calendars for 1643 and 1644 show many such. The Lady Tirrell mentioned in the will was Martha (Washington), wife of Sir John Tirrell or Tyrrell of Springfield, Essex, to whom she was married June, 1630 (see Visitations of Essex, II. 717). She died 17 Dec. 1670. Her husband was obliged to compound as a royalist in 1645, when he put in the following petition :—

"May it please this honorable Cõmittee to take notice that I was Sequestered for being at Oxford, & the occasions of my goeing thither weare these—Sir Lawrence Washingtõ my wife's father (haueing noe more children besides my wife & one soñe then under age) carried my wife frõ my house att Springfield in Essex to his house at Garsden in Wilts that Midsoñer before the warrs began, & she being with child sent for me about Chrismas after, whereuppõ I pcured a Passe from the Lords & Coñlons of ye Close Cõmittee to travell to her, & about Shrouetide after I got to Garsden, where the King Cõmanded by his Garison in Malmsbury; soone after Sʳ Lawrence went to attend the Seale at Oxford being ill before & at ye tyme of his goeing, but ye disease being quicker uppõ him (for it began wᵗʰ a gentle flux) & his sonne lying there also desperately sick, & his man sending m[e] word he spake of my coñing, for ye settleing his Estate by deed (wᶜʰ accordingly he did) uppõ his sonne & after, uppõ his daughter; I went to Oxford, where Sʳ Lawr. shortly after died & his sonne hardly escaped, & then I returned to Garsden. Then my wife being sick at ye Bath & haueing spent oʳ monys, I went shortly after to Bracly to my Tenant; & then pcureing a Passe frõ my L: of Essex I came to Londõ last January was twelue months & found my estate sequestered & soone after my goods & stock weare sold; & I attended the L: & Coñlons of yᵉ honorᵇˡᵉ Cõmittee for Sequestratiõs till I was heard, & after, aboad in Londõ till Mich: last when haueing no means longer to subsist I repaired to Springfield in Essex to my wife & childrẽ, where I aboad till about 3 weeks since.

I gaue 10£ to the first Propositions. I have payd the 5ᵗʰ & 20ᵗʰ pt to the full, as appears by Certificate of ye Cõmittee at Chelmisford. I haue taken ye National Couenant. I have payd all Rates without distresse, before I was sequestred; & [   ] except 50£ to Habberdashers Hall last Mich: for 20ᵗʰ pt wᶜʰ I hope I am [   ] that my Certeficate saith I haue payd to the Full. My goods haue been sold & stock. My estate in North-amtōsheire lost & utterly spoyled. I had a Passe to goe into ye K: Quarters, & was at Ox: before or when the Ordenance for Sequestratiōs bears date; the occatiō was a greate Concerne unto me, to wit ye setteling Sir Lawr. whole estate by intaile; And my owne land near Bracley. I never boar Arams; nor assisted ye K: Nor kissed his hand whilest I was there."

" Yr humble Servant   " Jo: Tirell"

" 24º April: 1645."

The following inscription was copied at, Garsden by J. Henry Lea, Esq. :

"To the Memory of Sr Laurence Washington K^t lately chiefe Register of the Chauncery of known Pyety of Charity exemplarye A louinge Husband A tender Father A bountifull Master A Constant Relieuer of the Poore and to those of this Parish A perpetuall Benefactour Whom it pleased God to take unto his Peace from the fury of the insuing Warrs Oxon Maii 14to Here interred 24to Año Dñi 1643° Aetat Suæ 64° Where also lyeth Dame Anne his wife who deceased Junij 13to and was buried 16to Año Dñi 1645."

" Hic Patrios cineres curauit filius Urna
Condere qui tumulo nunc jacet Ille pius.

The pious Son his Parents here interred
Who hath his share in Urne for them prepar'd."

Dame Anne Washington, his wife, was a daughter of William Lewin of Otterden, Kent, D.C.L., and sister of Sir Justinian Lewin, an abstract of whose will has been given.

LAWRENCE WASHINGTON of Garsdon in the Co. of Wilts, Esq., 14 January 1661, proved 15 May ·1662. My body to be buried in the chancel of the Parish church of Garsdon. To the poor of Garsdon ten pounds, to be distributed to householders by five shillings to a house, and to the poor of Westamsbury and Bulford, Wilts, ten pounds &c.

"Alsoe I doe giue and devise unto my Cozen John Washington sonne of Sir John Washington of Thrapston in the Countie of Northampton kn^t one Annuitie or yearely Rent of ffortie pounds of Currant English money ffor and dureinge the terme of his naturall life To be issueing and goeing forth out of all my messuages Lands Tenements and Hereditaments and ffarme in Westamsbury als Littleamsbury in the Countie of Wiltes aforesaid To be paid unto him at the ffeasts of Thanunciation of the blessed Virgin St Mary and St Michaell Tharchangell by euen and equall portions the ffirst payment thereof to beginne and to be made at the ffirst of the said ffeasts which shall happen come and be next after my decease and if and as often as it shall happen the said yearely Rent of ffortie pounds to be behinde and unpaid by the space of Tenne dayes next after any of the said ffeasts in the which as aforesaid the same ought to be paid that then and soe often it shall be lawfull to and for the said John Washington into the said Messuages Lands Tenements and hereditaments to enter and distreyne and the distresse and distresses then and there' had found and taken to lead driue take and carry away and the same to impound deteyne and keepe untill the said Annuity or yearely rent of fforty pounds and all the arreares thereof (if any be) shall be unto my said Cozen John Washington fully satisfied and paid."

To Charles Tyrrell, youngest son of Dame Martha Tyrrell of Herne House in the Co. of Essex, one annuity of twenty pounds &c. To my cousin Symon Horsepoole of London, gent., one annuity of thirty pounds &c. To my beloved sister Dame Martha Tyrrell twenty pounds to buy her a ring, and to my nephews John, Thomas and Charles Tyrrell ten pounds apiece and to my niece Martha Tyrrell twenty pounds, to buy each of them a ring. To John Elton of Tedbury, Glouc., physician, for his great care and pains towards me and my family for several years past, forty pounds. To servants (not named). The residue unto Elianor, my wife, whom I make sole executrix &c.   Laud, 73 (P. C. C.).

Dame ELIANOR PARGITER, the relict of Sir William Pargiter late of Gretworth, knight, deceased, 17 July 1685, proved 2 June 1687. My body I desire may be carried in a decent and private way to Garsden in Wiltshire and interred there by my former husband Lawrence Washington Esq[r]. I will and bequeath to my dearly beloved daughter Ferrars my necklace of pearl, being two strings of pearl, which her father gave to me, one saphire ring, which he likewise gave to me, and her father's picture set in gold. To the parish of Garsdon thirty pounds, to be bestowed in decent plate for the Communion Table there, to be kept by the Minister of the place for the time being. To the poor of that parish ten pounds. The residue to my daughter Elianor Pargiter, whom I make, constitute and ordain sole executrix.

Proved by the oath of Elianor Dering *als* Pargiter.
                                        Foot, 82 (P. C. C.).

She was the second daughter of William Guise of Elmore, Gloucestershire. She died 19 July, 1685, according to the monumental inscription at Garsden. Her first husband, Lawrence Washington, Esq., died 17 January, and was buried 11 February, 1661–2.

THOMAS POPE of the parish of St Philip and Jacob in Bristol, merchant, 3 September, 1684, proved 20 October 1685. Being now bound on a voyage to sea &c. To my wife Joanna, for and during her natural life, my messuage and tenement called Noble's corner, and all the lands and appurtenances thereunto belonging, situate in Barton Regis in the County of Glouc. The reversion and inheritance of the same messuage &c. I give and devise to my two sons, Charles Pope and Nathaniel Pope, their heirs and assigns, forever, equally between them as tenants in common.

Item I give and devise to my son Thomas Pope and the heirs of his body lawfully to be begotten all that my plantation, with the lands, servants, cattle, stock and appurtenances thereunto belonging, situate and being at or near Pope's Creek in Westmoreland in Virginia, with remainder to sons Charles and Nathaniel in common . . . My other plantation, commonly called Clift's Plantation, in Westmoreland, on the Potomac River, in Virginia &c. I give and devise to my two sons Richard and John Pope, their heirs and assigns forever. But my wife Joanna shall hold and be endowed of one third part of both my said plantations &c. for the term of her natural life.

Item I make my loving friends and kinsmen Mr. William Hardridge, Mr. Lawrence Washington and Mr. John Washington, all of Virginia aforesaid, and the survivors and survivor of them, guardians and guardian of my said sons Thomas, Richard, John, Charles and Nathaniel for the managing of my said plantations and premises in Virginia. They shall receive and take the rents, issues and profits thereof until my said sons shall attain their respective ages of one and twenty years, and they shall, from time to time, ship and consign the proceeds thereof to my said wife in England during her life, and, in case of her decease, to such other person or persons as shall be guardian or guardians of all or any my children, sons or daughters, to be by her or them from time to time disposed and laid out for and towards the better maintenance and education of all and every my said children.

I make, ordain and appoint Richard Gotley and Charles Jones the younger, merchants of the city aforesaid, executors in trust &c. And to each of my executors and to each of my above named friends and trustees in Virginia I give twenty shillings apiece as tokens of my love. Provision made for three daughters, Mary, Elizabeth and Margaret out of the personal estate (they under twenty-one).

Wit: John Churchman, Wm Meredith, Wm Brayne and John Selwood.

Cann, 124 (P. C. C.).

The Honorable JOHN CUSTIS Esq. of the City of Williamsburg and County of James City in the Colony of Virginia, 14 November 1749, proved at London 19 November 1753. My executor to lay out and expend, as soon as possible after my decease, out of my estate, the sum of one hundred pounds sterling to buy a handsome tombstone of the best durable white marble, large and built up of the most durable stone that can be purchased, for pillars, very decent and handsome to lay over my dead body, engraved on the tombstone my coat of arms, which are three parrots, and my will is that the following inscription may be also handsomely engraved on the said stone vizt.

"Under this Marble Stone lyes the Body of the Honourable John Custis Esquire of the City of Williamsburgh and parish of Bruton formerly of Hungars Parish on the Eastern Shoar of Virginia and County of Northampton the place of his Nativity Aged .... years and yet lived but seven years which was the space of time he kept a Batchelors House at Arlington on the Eastern Shoar of Virginia this Inscription put on this Stone by his own possitive Orders."

And I do desire and my will is and I strictly require it that as soon as possible my real dead body, and not a sham coffin, be carried to my plantation on the Eastern Shore of Virginia, called Arlington, and there my real dead body be buried by my Grandfather the Honble John Custis Esquire where a large walnut formerly grew and is now enclosed with a brick wall, which brick wall it is my will and I strictly charge and require it that the said brick wall be always kept up in good repair very handsomely by my heir that shall enjoy my estate; and if my heir should "ingratefully" or obstinately refuse or neglect to comply with what relates to my Burial in every particular then I bar and cut him off from any part of my estate, either real or personal, and only give him one shilling sterling, and in such case I give my whole estate, real and personal, to the next heir male of my family named Custis that will religiously and punctually see this my will performed, but more especially what any ways relates to my burial in general, and if by any accident the Tombstone and appurtenances should be lost, broke or any ways miscarry in coming in from England, or any other ways whatsoever, in that case my positive will is and I earnestly require it that my heirs or executors immediately send to England for such another stone exactly, with the appurtenances, of the same price, until one shall come safe to hand according to my will and desire.

I give to my dear friend Thomas Lee Esquire, if living at my death, two hundred pounds to buy him any one thing he has a mind to remember me. To my worthy and much esteemed friend John Blair Esq. one hundred pounds, and to Mrs. Mary Blair, his wife, five guineas to buy her a mourning ring.

Whereas my plantation called Arlington, on the Eastern Shore of Virginia is entailed by my Grandfather, the Hon. John Custis Esq., on the heirs male of my body lawfully begotten and for as much as my father, the late Hon. John Custis Esq., had a patent in his own name for two hundred and fifty acres of the said Arlington plantation which my said father has given me by his said will in fee simple, I do entail the said two hundred and fifty acres of land, so given to me, exactly in the same manner as the other three hundred acres contiguous or adjoining to it, and my will is that it always descend exactly in the same manner as Smith's Island and Motton Island, which are firmly entailed on the Heirs male of my body lawfully begotten by the will of my grandfather &c.

And whereas by my deed of Manumission recorded in the County Court of York I have freed and set at liberty my negro boy christened John, otherwise called Jack, born of the body of my slave Alice, now I do hereby ratify and confirm the said deed of Manumission unto the said John otherwise called Jack, and after the death of said John, otherwise called Jack, I give all the estate by me heretofore given to the said John, otherwise called Jack, either by deed or otherwise, to my son Daniel Park Custis to hold to him my said son from and after the death of the said John, otherwise called Jack &c. My will and desire is that as soon as possible after my decease my executor build on the said land I bought of James Morris, situate near the head of Queen's Creek in the co. of York, for the use of the said John, otherwise called Jack, a handsome, strong, convenient dwelling house according to the dimensions I shall direct, and a plan thereof drawn by my said friend John Blair Esq., and that it be completely finished within side and without, and when the house is completely finished it is my will that the same be furnished with one dozen high Russia leather chairs, one dozen low Russia chairs, a Russia leather couch, good and strong, three good feather beds, bedsteads and furniture and two good black walnut tables. I desire that the houses, fencing and other appurtenances belonging to the said plantation be kept in good repair and so delivered to the said John, otherwise called Jack, when he shall arrive to the age of twenty years. I also give him when he shall arrive to that age a good riding horse and two young able working horses. I give to Mrs. Ann Moody, wife of Matthew Moody, if she be living at my death, twenty pounds, to be paid her annually during her natural life. I also give her the picture of my said Negro boy John. It is my will and desire that my said Negro boy John, otherwise called Jack, live with my son until he be twenty years of age, and that he be handsomely maintained out of the profits of my estate given him. I give and devise unto John Cavendish, for the many services he has done me, the house and lot where he now lives to hold the same rent free during his natural life.

All the rest, residue and remainder of my estate, real and personal, be it of what nature or kind soever, or wheresoever lying and being in the whole world, I give, devise and bequeath unto my son Daniel Park Custis to hold

John Washington
of Whitfield.

. c
W

John Washington=Margaret, dau. of Robert
of Warton,
co. Lanc.

Margaret, dau. of Robert
Kitson of Warton, and
sister of Sir Thomas Kit-
son, Kt., and Alderman
of London.

Thomas.

Ellen=James
of W

Elizabeth, wid. of=Lawrence Washington of Northampton=Anne (or Amy), dau of
William Gough of & Gray's Inn, Mayor of Northampton. Rob't Pargiter of Gret-
Northampton. Grantee of Sulgrave 30 H. VIII. Ob. worth, gent. Ob. 7 Oct.
Ob. s. p. 19 Feb. 26 Eliz. (Will.) 1564.

Nicholas.

Leonard=. .

Elizabeth, daugh.=Robert Washington of=Anne, dau. of
and h. of Walter Sulgrave, Esq., æt. 40, ... Fisher
Light of Radway, 26 Eliz. Jointly with of Hanslop, co.
co. Warwick. son Lawrence sold Sul- Bucks.
grave 8 Jac. (Will.)

Lawrence Washington of=
Gray's Inn, Midd'x, Esq.,
Register of High Court of
Chancery. Ob. 1619. (Will.)

Alban (æt. 19 in 1618).
Guy.
Robert (alive 1676).

Mary=Martin Edon of Banbury, co. Oxon.
Margaret=John Gardiner of London.
Catherine.

Sir Lawrence Wash
Westbury, Bucks.,
Wilts., Register of
Chancery. Died in
(Will.)

Lawrence Washington of
Ob. 17 January, 1661-2. (

Lawrence Washington=Margaret, eldest dau.
of Sulgrave and Bring- of William Butler of
ton. Ob. 13 Dec. 1616. Tighes, Sussex, Esq.
Bur. 15 Dec. 1616, at Married 3 Aug. 1588.
Brington. Alive 1636.

Robert, 2d son=Elizabeth, dau. of
Ob. 10 March, John Chishull of
1622-3. Bur. at More Hall, Es'x.
Brington. Ob. 19 March,
1622-3. Bur. at
Brington. (Will.)

Walter Washington=Alice, d
of Radway, Warr. John M
Ob. 1597. of Mor
Morell,
Warr.
1647.)

John Washington of Radway, co. Warr.=Mary, dau. of Geo. Danv

George Washington. Elizabeth. Ann. Thomas.

Sir William Washington=Anne, dau. of Sir Geo.
of Packington, co. Leic., Villiers of Brooksby,
kt. Bur. at St. Martin's Sussex, Esq.
in the Fields, Midd., 22 kt., and half sister of
June, 1643. (Will.) George, Duke of Buckingham.

Sir John Washington=Mary, dau. of Philip
of Thrapston, county Curtis, of Islip, co.
Northampton, kt. Northampton, gent.
= Ob. 1 Jan. 1624-25.
Dorothy (2d wife) dau. Bur. at Islip.
of William Pargiter of
Gretworth, Esq., and
wid. of . . . . Kirkby.
Ob. 1678. (Will.)

Robert.
Richard,
born ab't
1600.

Mordaunt. John. Philip.

Henry Washington, æt. 3, 1618.=Elizabeth, dau. of
Col. in the royalist army; gov. . . . . Remarried
of Worcester. Buried at Rich- Samuel Sandys of
mond, Surrey, 9 Mar. 1663-4. co. Worc., Esq.
Living 1697-8.

George, bap.
13 Jan. 1619-
20.

Christopher.

Elizabeth=William Legge,
Esq. Ancestor
of the Earls of
Dartmouth.

Susanna,
Nov. 1618
Feb. 1698-
at Lewi
Kent. (

Mary Washington (unmarried).
Ob. 1680-81. (Will.)

Penelope Washington (unmarried).
Bur. at Wickhamford, co. Worc., 2
March, 1697-8 (will pro. at Worc., 9
March, 1697).

Katherine, m. first to . . . .
Forster, and secondly to
Barnabas Tonstall of Mid.
Temple, Esq.

Elizabeth

John. Lawrence.

John=Catherine Whiting.

Jane, dau. of Caleb Butler, m. 20 April, 1715=Augustine Washington=Mary
d. 24 Nov. 1728. d. April 12, 1743, æt. 49.

Warner. Henry. 3 daus.

Butler,
d. young.

Lawrence.

Augustine.

Jane,
d. young.

GEORGE WASHING'
b. 11 Feb. 1732;
m 6 Jan 1759.
First President of the
Died *s p* 14 December,

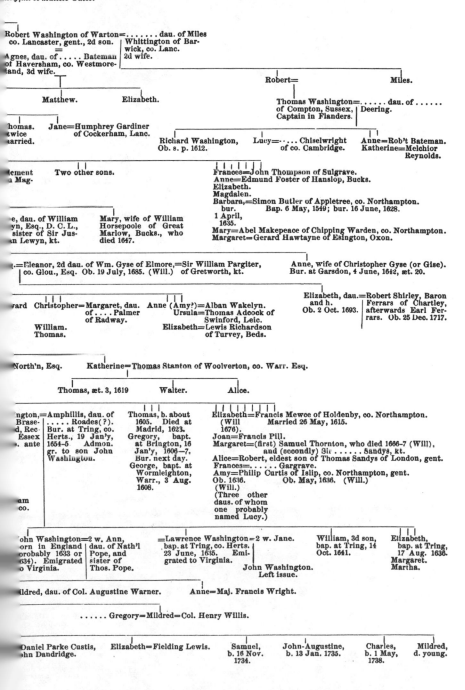

Robert Washington of Warton=........ dau. of Miles
co. Lancaster, gent., 2d son. | Whittington of Bar-
= | wick, co. Lanc.
Agnes, dau. of ..... Bateman | 2d wife.
of Haversham, co. Westmore-
land, 3d wife.

Robert=   Miles.

Matthew.   Elizabeth.   Thomas Washington=...... dau. of ......
                                    of Compton, Sussex, | Deering.
                                    Captain in Flanders.

thomas.   Jane=Humphrey Gardiner
twice   of Cockerham, Lanc.
married.   Richard Washington,   Lucy=-.... Chiselwright   Anne=Rob't Bateman.
                                Ob. s. p. 1612.   of co. Cambridge.   Katherine=Melchior
                                                                                     Reynolds.

lement   Two other sons.   Frances=John Thompson of Sulgrave.
a Mag-   Anne=Edmund Foster of Hanslop, Bucks.
                                    Elizabeth.
                                    Magdalen.
                                    Barbara,=Simon Butler of Appletree, co. Northampton.
                                    bur.   Bap. 6 May, 1549; bur. 16 June, 1628.
..e, dau. of William   Mary, wife of William   1 April,
.yn, Esq., D. C. L.,   Horsepoole of Great   1635.
.. sister of Sir Jus- Marlow, Bucks., who   Mary=Abel Makepeace of Chipping Warden, co. Northampton.
.n Lewyn, kt.   died 1647.   Margaret=Gerard Hawtayne of Esington, Oxon.

..=Eleanor, 2d dau. of Wm. Gyse of Elmore,=Sir William Pargiter,   Anne, wife of Christopher Gyse (or Gise).
  co. Glou., Esq. Ob. 19 July, 1685. (Will.) of Gretworth, kt.   Bur. at Garsdon, 4 June, 1642, æt. 20.

                                                    Elizabeth, dau.=Robert Shirley, Baron
                                                    and h. | Ferrars of Chartley,
                                                    Ob. 2 Oct. 1693. | afterwards Earl Fer-
                                                                     | rars. Ob. 25 Dec. 1717.

.ard   Christopher=Margaret, dau.   Anne (Amy?)=Alban Wakelyn.
                   of .... Palmer   Ursula=Thomas Adcock of
William.   of Radway.   Swinford, Leic.
Thomas.   Elizabeth=Lewis Richardson
                                            of Turvey, Beds.

.North'n, Esq.   Katherine=Thomas Stanton of Woolverton, co. Warr. Esq.

     Thomas, æt. 3, 1619   Walter.   Alice.

.ngton,=Amphillis, dau. of   Thomas, b. about   Elizabeth=Francis Mewce of Holdenby, co. Northampton.
Brase- | ..... Roades(?).   1605. Died at   (Will   Married 26 May, 1615.
.d, Rec| Bur. at Tring, co. Madrid, 1623.   1676).
. Essex| Herts., 19 Jan'y,   Gregory, bapt.   Joan=Francis Pill.
.. ante| 1654-5.   Admon.   at Brington, 16   Margaret=(first) Samuel Thornton, who died 1666-7 (Will),
       | gr. to son John   Jan'y, 1606—7,   and (secondly) Sir ...... Sandys, kt.
       | Washington.   Bur. next day.   Alice=Robert, eldest son of Thomas Sandys of London, gent.
                             George, bapt. at   Frances=...... Gargrave.
                             Wormleighton,   Amy=Philip Curtis of Islip, co. Northampton, gent.
.am   Warr., 3 Aug.   Ob. 1636.   Ob. May, 1636. (Will.)
.co.   1608.   (Will.)
                                                 (Three other
                                                 daus. of whom
                                                 one probably
                                                 named Lucy.)

.ohn Washington=2 w. Ann,   =Lawrence Washington=2 w. Jane.   William, 3d son,   Elizabeth,
.orn in England | dau. of Nath'l   bap. at Tring, co. Herts.   bap. at Tring, 14 bap. at Tring,
.robably 1633 or| Pope, and   23 June, 1635. Emi-   Oct. 1641.   17 Aug. 1636.
.634). Emigrated| sister of   grated to Virginia. | Margaret.
.o Virginia. | Thos. Pope.   John Washington.   Martha.
                                                       Left issue.

.ildred, dau. of Col. Augustine Warner.   Anne=Maj. Francis Wright.

     ...... Gregory=Mildred=Col. Henry Willis.

.Daniel Parke Custis,   Elizabeth=Fielding Lewis.   Samuel,   John-Augustine,   Charles,   Mildred,
.ohn Dandridge.   b. 16 Nov.   b. 13 Jan. 1735. b. 1 May,   d. young.
                                                    1734.   1738.

to him, his heirs and assigns forever. And I do constitute and appoint my said son whole and sole executor. Wit: Thomas Dawson, George Gilmer, John Blair, jun^r.

The above will was proved at a court held for James City County 9 April 1750, Ben. Waller being Clerk of the Court.

On the twenty third day of Sept. 1784 Admōn. (with the will annexed) of the goods &c left unadministered by Daniel Parke Custis deceased &c., was granted to Wakelin Welch, the lawful attorney of Martha Washington, formerly Custis (wife of his Excellency the Honorable George Washington) the relict and administratrix of the rest of the goods of the said Daniel Parke Custis deceased, for the use and benefit of the said Martha Washington, formerly Custis, now residing at Virginia aforesaid, the said Daniel Parke Custis dying intestate.   Searle, 287 (P. C. C.).

Facing this page will be found a folded tabular pedigree which I have compiled to illustrate this article.

[Others of the name Washington than the famed brothers John and Lawrence Washington appear in the annals of Virginia:

"Robert Washington of Wapping in ye p'sh of Stepney and Town of Middlesex, Mariner," executed power of attorney to "Wm Pearson, Chirurgeon," "29th July 1660."

"Edward Washington, convicted of manslaughter and ordered to be burnt in the hand" October 12, 1675.   *Records of General Court of Va.*

The following grants are of record in the State Land Registry:

Major John Washington, Book No. 5, p. 38, 320 acres in Westmoreland Co., M'ch 23, 1664. Major John Washington and Thomas Pope, No. 5, p. 49, 50 acres in Westmoreland Co., Sept. 4, 1667. Major John Washington, No. 5, p. 49, 300 acres in Northumberland Co., June 1, 1664; p. 50, 1700 acres in Westmoreland Co., March 26, 1664. Mrs. Ann Pope alias Washington, No. 5, p. 52, 700 acres in Westmoreland Co., June 13, 1661. Major John Washington and Thomas Pope, No. 5, p. 54, 1200 acres in Westmoreland Co., Sept. 4, 1661. Lt. Col. John Washington, No. 6, p. 349, 450 acres in Northumberland Co., Oct. 10, 1670. Lawrence Washington and Robert Richards, No. 6, p. 60, 700 acres in Stafford Co., Sept. 27, 1667. Lt. Col. John Washington, No. 6, p. 615, 5000 acres in Stafford Co., 1677; p. 183, 500 acres in Rappahannock Parish, Nov. 3, 1673. Richard Washington, No. 8, p. 165, 330 acres in Surrey Co., April 29, 1682; p. 464, 200 acres in Surrey Co., April 20, 1685; p. 88, 772 acres in Surrey Co., Oct. 23, 1690; No. 9, p. 326, 345 acres in Surrey Co., April 25, 1701. John and Arthur Washington, No. 9, p. 371, 742 acres in Surrey Co., 1701.

Neither Robert, Edward, Richard, John or Arthur Washington, appear to have been of the family of John and Lawrence Washington, from the records preserved of these brothers.—R. A. BROCK.

The *Daily Reporter*, Northampton, Eng., August 24, 1889, contains a description of the Washington Slab in Sulgrave Church, and an account of its mutilation about a fortnight before that date by two strangers in gentlemanly attire.

The Washington slab is thus described in the Northampton *Reporter*. Six different brass plates were let into it. The first contained the Washington coat of arms, Argent, two bars gules, in chief three mullets of the second. On each side, in brass, were "effigies of Washington and his wife, and below them on a brass plate of oblong form was the following inscription in three lines:

Here lyeth buried ye bodys of Laurence Wasshingtō Gent & Amee his | wyf by whome he had issue iiij sons & vij daughts w^e laurence Dyed ye day of | an° 15   & Amee Deceassed the VI day of October an° Dñi 1564. |

Under this are representations of the four sons and seven daughters in two groups.

The costume of Lawrence Washington and his children is that of the ordinary attire of civilians of the middle of the 16th century. The father wears a close-fitting doublet, a large loose gown, with demi-canon sleeves purfled with fur, and large broad-toed shoes. The boys wear large doublets, knee breeches, long hose, and shoes like their father; and each has his gyfcière at his girdle. The girls wear close-fitting caps, with gowns reaching to the ankles, and secured round the waist with a band. The brass representing Amy Washington no longer remains. . . . Time has told somewhat on this monument of Lawrence and Amy Washington; and it is also to be regretted, the hand of the thief as well. The head of Lawrence Washington has been knocked off; the brass effigy of his wife has been stolen and taken away bodily; and the enamel with which the coat of arms was colored has crumbled nearly all away, leaving scarce a trace behind. The two portions recently taken away are those representing the 'iiij sons and vij daughters.' Each of these pieces could be covered by a sheet of note-paper."

It is to be hoped that the perpetrators of this dastardly act may be discovered. An abstract of the will of Lawrence Washington and an inquisition post mortem are printed, *ante*, pp. 373-375.

Lawrence Washington of Sulgrave, grandson of Lawrence and Amee Washington, died Dec. 13, 1616, and was buried at Brington. In 1860, as has been stated in the foot-note on page 378, Earl Spencer presented to Hon. Charles Sumner facsimiles of two Washington memorial stones in the church at Brington, which facsimiles Mr. Sumner presented to the State of Massachusetts. One of these stones was that of this Lawrence Washington and the other that of his brother Robert. The inscription on the stone of Robert Washington and his wife Elizabeth is printed on page 378, from Baker's Northamptonshire. Mr. David Pulsifer, in the appendix to his edition of Rev. C. H. Wharton's Poetical Epistle to George Washington (Boston, 1881), gives an account of the presentation of the facsimiles to the State by Mr. Sumner. This account is accompanied by engravings of the two stones. Mr. Pulsifer has loaned us the cut of Lawrence Washington's stone, containing besides the inscription the arms of Washington impaling Butler; and it is printed on the opposite page. Lawrence and Margaret (Butler) Washington were parents of Lawrence Washington, M.A., rector of Purleigh, who, it is believed, was the father of the Virginia emigrants.—EDITOR.

CONCLUSIONS.

A careful examination of the preceding pages will doubtless bring the reader to the conclusion that Mr. Waters has made out a pedigree in the highest degree probable, and lacking absolute certainty only on the two following points. First, having shown that Lawrence Washington of Virginia owned land in Luton, we lack *positive* proof to identify him with the Lawrence baptized at Tring in 1635.

Second, having rendered it almost absolutely certain that the father of the Washington children baptized at Tring, was a clergyman and M.A., we lack *absolute* certainty that he was identical with the Rector of Purleigh.

On both these points we may hopefully expect assistance from our English friends, now that the field of investigation is so contracted. It may be fairly added, that whilst legal evidence on these two points is lacking, the industry and acuteness of Mr. Waters are signally shown in the great amount of circumstantial evidence by him collected, which indeed affords us a moral certainty of the entire correctness of the pedigree.

It is a curious fact that the first pedigree as drawn up by Sir Isaac Heard, should prove to be correct, probably, with the insertion of one more generation. Probability, founded on the persistence of the christian name Lawrence, would lead every genealogist to attempt to connect the Virginia branch with the main line descended from John Washington of Warton and Margaret Kitson. But, in a pedigree, every fact must be susceptible of proof, and Col. Chester is entitled to the highest praise for his successful attempt to prove that the Virginia emi-

HERE·LIETH·THE·BODI·OF·LAVRENCE
WASHINGTON·.SONNE·&·HEIRE·OF
ROBERT·WASHINGTON·OF·SOVLGRA*E*
IN·THE·COVNTIE·OF·NORTHAMPTON
ESQVIER·WHO·MARIED·MARGARET
THE·ELDEST·DAVGHTER·OF·WILLIAM
BVTLER·OF·TEES·IN·THE·COVNTIE
OF·SVSSEXE·ESQVIER·WHO·HAD·ISSV
BY·HER·8·SONNS·&·9·DAVGHTERS
WHICH·LAVRENCE·DECESSED·THE·13
OF·DECEMBER·A : DNI : 1616

THOV·THAT·BY·CHANCE·OR·CHOYCE
OF·THIS·HAST·SIGHT
KNOW·LIFE·TO·DEATH·RESIGNES
AS·DAYE·TO·NIGHT
BVT·AS·THE·SVNNS·RETORNE
REVIVES·THE·DAYE
SO·CHRIST·SHALL·VS
THOVGH·TVRNDE·TO·DVST·&·CLAY

grants were *not* Sir John and Rev. Lawrence, the sons of Lawrence of Sulgrave and Brington, even if it now be shown that they were grandsons.

It is satisfactory, however, to have the pedigree confirmed with this small but vital correction, as it retains the value of all investigations which have been made respecting the Washingtons of Sulgrave, and will continue the interest of all Americans in what had been accepted as the birth-place of the race. Mr. Waters has interposed one more ancestor in the person of the Rev. Lawrence Washington, and we shall doubtless soon learn much more about him.

As Col. Chester's paper of 1866 may not be accessible to all of our readers, we reprint such parts as refer to Rev. Lawrence of Purleigh, especially as Mr. Waters has not cited all of them.

Extract from Col. Chester's " Preliminary Investigation."

" We proceed now to the history of LAWRENCE WASHINGTON, apparently the fifth son of Lawrence and Margaret, and certainly the younger brother of Sir William and Sir John Washington.

Baker was quite correct in stating that he was a student at Oxford in the year 1622. He was of Brasenose College, and matriculated on the 2d of November, 1621. The exact record in the Matriculation Register is as follows: ' Laurent: Washington, Northamp: Gen. fil. an. nat. 19;' *i. e.* Lawrence Washington, of Northamptonshire, whose father's rank was that of a gentleman, and whose own age was nineteen years at his last birthday.

It was not until little more than a year later that the officials commenced entering in the register the christian names and particular residences of the fathers of the students, but in the present instance the above record is almost as satisfactory as it would have been if the other particulars had been given. In the first place, the Washington family of Sulgrave, or Brington, was the only one of the name in Northamptonshire whose sons could be recognized and designated as 'the sons of gentlemen, unless, indeed, the Heralds of that time omitted others, which is not probable. Secondly, there was no other Lawrence Washington at Oxford for considerable periods before and after this date; unless, again, all the officials were guilty of omissions in all the Registers (for the writer has carefully examined them all), which is even more improbable. And, finally, the will of his aunt Elizabeth, widow of his uncle Robert Washington, dated on the 17th of March, 1622-3, among other legacies to his brothers and sisters, leaves him her husband's seal ring, and states that he was then at Oxford.

Lawrence Washington was born, therefore, about the year 1602. He appears to have entered at Brasenose College as early as 1619, but he did not sign the Subscription Book until the 2d of November, 1621, under which date his name also appears in the general matriculation register, in connection with thirty-five others—an extraordinary number, and indicating that from some cause this ceremony had hitherto been neglected. He took his B.A. degree in 1623, and became Fellow of Brasenose about 1624. He is recorded as serving the office of lector, then the principal educational office in the college, from 1627 to 1632 inclusive. On the 20th of August, 1631, he became one of the proctors of the university, filling a vacancy that had occurred by the deprivation of his predecessor by royal warrant. On the 14th of March, 1632-3, he was presented to the then very valuable living of Purleigh, in Essex, and resigned his fellowship. The records of a suit in Chancery, preserved at the Rolls Office, perfectly identify the rector of Purleigh with the fellow of Brasenose and the proctor of the university. He continued at Purleigh until the year 1643, when, according to Newcourt, he was ' ejected by sequestration for his loyalty in the late rebellion of 1642,' and had the honor of being pilloried in the infamous ' Century.' Walker states that he ' was afterwards permitted to have and continue upon a Living in these parts; but it was such a poor and miserable one that it was with difficulty that any one was persuaded to accept it.' The writer has been unable to ascertain the living mentioned; but it is to be hoped that some further trace of him may yet be discovered in the neighborhood of Purleigh, where, putting the usual construction upon Walker's language,* he continued in his profession of a clergyman after the Restoration, and consequently some years after the date of his namesake's emigration to Virginia."

* See foot-note on page 370, *ante.*—W. H. W.

Lastly, this important publication about the Washingtons would be imperfect if no notice were taken of the costly and widely-circulated book, published in 1879, by the late Albert Welles. Many persons have been and will be misled by this utterly false and absurd publication. I will therefore reprint the essential portions of my letter to the New York *Nation* of July 18, 1889.

The English portion was a most ridiculous performance in every point of view, and it is only fair to suppose that Mr. Welles was not in a sound state of mind when he adopted and published this statement. His unnamed English correspondent claimed to have derived his alleged facts from the Common Pleas Rolls, and adds: "The pedigree I now send I can establish by legal evidence."

The object of this pedigree was to show that several generations of Washingtons had been born at Warton, County Lancaster; that a Lawrence W. was born there in 1569, whose eldest son was Leonard W., born about 1595, the father of four sons and one daughter *baptized at Warton* in 1616, 1619, 1622, 1625, and 1627. The two younger sons were said to be Lawrence, baptized 1625, and John, baptized 1627, who were termed the emigrants to Virginia.

I will not waste time in refuting the innumerable blunders of the rest of the pedigree, but deal with the essential point here raised. Col. Chester printed a letter in the New York *World* of March 29, 1879, when he had seen the prospectus of Welles's book. He said:

"I at once recognized an old acquaintance, hawked about London some years ago, the original manuscript of which is in my own possession, and now lies on my table before me, where I keep it for the amusement of my friends. . . . I will simply select the crucial point of it, where it is stated that the two emigrant brothers, Lawrence and John Washington, were sons of Leonard Washington of Warton, and that they were respectively born and baptized in 1625 and 1627. The only possible source from which these two baptisms could be obtained is the parish register of Warton. I have examined the register personally and very carefully, and can declare that no such entries are to be found in it."

At this point I wish to introduce the evidence of the Rev. T. H. Pain, M.A., Vicar of Warton, given in a letter now before me, addressed to the *New England Historical and Genealogical Register*, dated January 25, 1889. He writes:

"I beg to say that I have not been able to find any entry of the baptism of Leonard Washington, said to have been born in Warton about 1595. As to the baptisms of his children, I send the following extracts:

Baptismata Anno Dom. 1616.
Robertus, filius Leonardi Washington, baptiz. octavo die Septembris.
Baptismat. 1619.
Jane, daughter of Leonard Washington, bapd. 4th day of September.
Bapt. Anno Dom. 1622.
Francis, ye sonne of Leonard Washington of Warton, baptized ye 4th day of February.

"*I have not been able to find an entry of the baptism of Lawrence, said to have been baptised at Warton in 1625, or of John, said to have been baptized here in 1627.*"

In the light of these two statements, no one can doubt that the pedigree is a rank and stupid forgery, made by the simple method of fastening upon Leonard Washington two sons of whom he had no knowledge, and without a word of proof.

It seems to me that Col. Chester's statement of the genesis of this forgery may be amusing and instructive. He wrote under date of June 16, 1879:

"If you could see the original, which strangely fell in my hands, you would see how the whole thing was concocted. It was got up some years ago by this ' James Phillippe ' for John Camden Hotten, who died before publishing it, and his successors had too much good sense to carry out his intentions. It is evident that the compiler, after working out an elaborate pedigree, much of which I knew to be false, looked about for a safe place where to put the two emigrant brothers. He finally decided to make them sons of Leonard Washington of Warton. Afterwards, probably thinking that he might be detected, he crossed out this affiliation. But, finding no better place for them, he finally wrote (as an instruction to the printer), ' This is correct.'

" Of course you would not find any proofs of his statements. This distinguished ' genealogist ' never furnishes any. If asked for his authority in any instance, he draws himself up to his full height (6 ft. 4) and says, ' *I* am the authority'; and that is all any one can ever get out of him. . . .

"The 'Common Pleas Rolls' are as well known to every historical student and genealogist as the Heralds' Visitations. Like all similar records, they are more or less valuable, but they rank no higher, if so high, as the 'Chancery Proceedings.' Unfortunately, they are very difficult to search, from being entirely unindexed, and it is this fact of which ' Phillippe' takes advantage. He may almost with impunity say that his authority for a particular statement is a Common Pleas roll, for unless he also gave you, which he never does, the precise year, term of court, number of roll, and number of membrane, it would be almost impossible to test his statement. I spent weeks over these rolls of the period. To say that they are not used by other genealogists is as ridiculous as to say that other genealogists do not look at wills or parish registers or any other common source of information."

Col. Chester proceeds to point out numerous specific errors, and adds :

" I have all the Washington entries of all the Registers in all the places named in the pedigree, and can say without hesitation that they can never have been consulted by the compiler. The whole affair is a mere catchpenny concern, and I am amazed at the impudence of men who can put forth such a concoction and then claim that every statement can be substantiated by legal evidence."

This indignant exposure of the fraud, from the most competent authority, will be sufficient. Every one will regret that Col. Chester did not have the good fortune to bring to a successful conclusion the investigation which he pursued for so many years. But every one will equally rejoice that the work has been accomplished by an American, and will recognize the fact that Mr. Waters has entirely filled the high place which Col. Chester left vacant.—W. H. WHITMORE.]

The following items received since the article was printed in the REGISTER are inserted in this place (see *ante*, pp. 366, 392) :

Nathaniel Pope, Book No. 3, p. 279, 1000 acres on the south side of Potomac river in Westmoreland Co., Sept. 6, 1654.

William Pope, Book No. 4, p. 31, 200 acres in Westmoreland Co., March 11, 1655. [These grantees were probably brothers].

Nathaniel Pope, Book No. 4, p. 51, 1550 acres in Westmore- ⎫
land Co., April 24, 1656.   ⎬ [the same land.]
Thomas, heir to Nathaniel Pope, Book No. 4, p. 51, 1550 ⎪
acres in Westmoreland Co., April 24, 1656.   ⎭

Nathaniel Pope, Book No. 4, p. 63, 1050 acres in Westmore- ⎫
land Co., Nov. 30, 1656.   ⎬ [the same land.]
Nathaniel Pope, Jr., by will, Book No. 4, p. 63, 1050 acres in ⎪
Westmoreland Co., Nov. 30, 1656.   ⎭

Lieut. Col. Nathaniel Pope, Book No. 4, p. 293, 1500 acres in Westmoreland Co., Aug. 31, 1657.

James Pope, Book No. 4, p. 376, 512 acres in Northumberland Co., Sept. 24, 1659.

James Pope, Book No. 4, p. 376, 700 acres in Northumberland Co., Sept. 24, 1659.

William Pope, Book No. 4, p. 406, 200 acres in Nansemond Co., Oct. 30, 1662.

James Pope, Book No. 4, p. 562, 700 acres in Northumberland Co., Feb. 28, 1662.

James Pope, Book No. 4, p. 563, 1000 acres in Northumberland Co., Jan. 28, 1662.

Thomas Pope, Book No. 4, p. 42, 2054 acres in Westmoreland Co., March 23, 1664.

Thomas Pope and Major John Washington, Book No. 4, p. 49, 50 acres in a parcel of islands, number ten, in Westmoreland Co., in the mouth of Cedar Creek, Sept. 4, 1661.

The above abstract of the grants to the name Pope, in our State Land Registry, is transcribed from my Memorandum book.—R. A. BROCK.

A letter has been received from Mr. Waters, dated the 20th of September, in which he states that he had visited Middle Claydon the day previous. He found there a few Roads and Verney items. The most important was the marriage, 4

April, 1668, of John Freeman and Esther Roads of Luton, in the Co. of Bedford. "Esther Roads," he writes, "was of course the daughter of William Roads, and went to her old homestead to be married. John Freeman was the one nominated by Mrs. Elizabeth Fitzherbert as one of her executors and trustees, and we now see the reason. He was her nephew by marriage. And it strengthens *much* the one weak link in our pedigree—the Tring and Luton connection.

"William Roads of Finemore was buried 28 Sept., 1657. This must have been the father of Esther Freeman, and brother of Amphillis Washington."

Mr. Waters suggests that as Fine Moor Hill, about 2½ miles south of Middle Claydon, is near a road connecting the villages of Edgecote and Quainton, the records of those places should be examined.

Amphillis, the christian name of Mrs. Washington, must be very unusual. In the Visitation of Warwickshire it occurs four times, and once in that of Leicestershire. Three of these instances are connected with the Nevill family, and it seems to be persistent in that family.—W. H. WHITMORE.

THOMAS GRAY, of the Borough of Harwich in the County of Essex and Diocese of London, 16 August 1606, proved 29 June 1607. To wife Katherine all my moiety of the messuages, lands & tenements &c in Sutton in the County of Suffolk, late of Robert Miles, of Sutton aforesaid, yeoman deceased, father of the said Katherine; the other moiety, part or purpart whereof one Thomas Wyseman Esq., my brother-in-law, now holdeth. The said property to my wife to hold during her natural life, then to Thomas Gray, my son, and the heirs of his body lawfully begotten; failing such issue then to Susan Gray, Parnell Gray and Katherine Gray, my daughters, and the heirs of their bodies lawfully begotten. If they die without heirs &c. then to the said Katherine, my wife, & her heirs forever. I give & bequeath to daughters Susan, Parnell & Katherine, each one hundred pounds at the age of eighteen years. Wife Katherine to be executrix, Hugh Branham, clerk, to be supervisor and a bequest to him of three pounds for his labor.

Wit: Anthony Branham, Richard Reynoldes and John Moore (by mark.)
Huddleston, 49.

THOMAS GRAYE of Wapping in the County of Middlesex, mariner, 15 November 1626, proved 6 April 1627. Commencing with A Remembrance of what I have in the Ship called the Rain-bow, Anno 1626. Then follow bequests——to the poor of Wapping forty shillings, to my Reverend friend M^r. Sedgweeke, Preacher to the same Hamlet, three pounds, to my sister Katherine Graye five pounds, to my brother Thomas Coytmore fifty shillings, to my sister Elizabeth Coytmor fifty shillings, to my cousin Mary Edglefielde fifteen pounds. All the rest of my goods I give to my sister Parnell Parker, widow, and to her daughter, to be divided between them, whom I make my executrixes. To my loving friend Nathaniel Case thirty shillings, whom I make my overseer.

The will was proved by Parnell Parker, sister of the deceased & power reserved for —————— the other executrix &c.
Skynner, 45.

[See REGISTER, vii. 32 (will of Thomas Coytmor); xxxiv. 253-9 (Gray and Coytmore); and *ante*, 160-71 (Coytemore, Rainborow and Winthrop).—H. F. WATERS.]

JAMES RUSSELL of the city of Hereford, gentleman, 26 December 1611, proved 18 February 1611. To be buried as near my father as may be at the North door of the Cathedral church of Hereford. To the reparations of the church of All Saints ten shillings. To my wife Elizabeth my now dwelling house which I purchased of Walter Hurdeman, gentleman, &c., during her natural life, and at her death to my son Paule Russell and his heirs forever. To my said wife also one other garden which I purchased of William Whitlache, gentleman, during her natural life ——, then to my son Paule Russell. I give and bequeath unto my said son Paule Russell one hundred pounds, within one year after my decease. To my daughter in law Katherine Russell my best double bell salt with the cover. I give and bequeath to James Russell the son of my son Paule Russell one house with the garden which I purchased of my uncle Thomas Mellyn, merchant of Bristol late deceased, and in money twenty pounds to be paid into the hands of his father Paule Russell, within six months after my decease. To my son Edward Russell twenty pounds (within three months &c.) and to every of his children forty shillings apiece. To Anne Russell one of the daughters of my son Henry deceased twenty pounds at her day of marriage or full age of one & twenty. If she die before that, then to as many of the children of my said son Henry as shall then be living. To the said Anne ten sheep remaining in the hands of Thomas Pascall. To Ellinor Russell one other of the daughters of my said son Henry ten pounds, at the age of twenty. To my daughter Katherine Smythe ten pounds and to her son Thomas Smythe my godson ten pounds, which sum of twenty pounds Thomas Smythe, husband to my said daughter, oweth me by bill. I do release James Scryvenor of one bond of four and twenty pounds. To Margaret Shervington of Gloucester, widow, forty shillings. To every of my god children twelve pence. To Philip Symonds my god son ten sheep remaining in the hands of Thomas Pascall. The surplusage more of sheep remaining in the hands of Thomas Pascall I give unto my god daughter Anne Smithe the daughter of Barnabie Smithe. To the poor of the city of Hereford ten pounds. To twelve poor people twelve frize gowns. Towards the reparations of Wybridge twenty shillings, of Mordifords Bridge five shillings. I give to my cousin M^r. Philip Symonds my second black gown. To my brother M^r. Richard Russell forty shillings to make him a ring. To M^r. James Smythe four pounds. The residue to my wife Elizabeth and her I make executrix. The overseers to be my brother M^r. Richard Russell and M^r. James Smythe.

Wit: James Smithe, Richard Russell, Philip Symondes.

Fenner, 12.

PAULE RUSSELL, of the parish of All Saints within the City of Hereford, 3 April 1614, proved 11 July 1614 by Katherine, his widow and executrix. My body to be buried in christian burial where my friends shall think fit. I give and bequeath unto James Russell, mine eldest son, in money the sum of ten pounds, to be paid him by my executrix when he shall accomplish the age of one and twenty years. Item, my will is that all the standards and implements remaining now in and about the house I dwell in shall be & remain unto my son James in manner and form as my father by his last will and testament bequeathed them unto me. Item, I give and bequeath unto my son Paule Russell in money the sum of ten pounds &c. I give & bequeath unto my son Richard Russell in money the sum of thirty pounds, to be paid likewise by mine executrix when he shall accomplish the

age of one & twenty years. To my daughter Elizabeth Russell the sum of
fifteen pounds &c. at the day of her marriage, if she marry with the consent
of her mother and grandmother, or else, when she shall accomplish the age
of one & twenty years. Katherine, my wife, to be sole executrix.
Wit: Richard Russell, Philip Symonds, John Chyne, James Scrivenor,
Thomas Quarrell.   Law, 83.

ROBERT CLARKE of Redriffe, England, mariner, now resident in Boston
in New England, 10 September 1662.   Juxon, 33.

JOHN KEBBY of St. Bennet Fyncke, citizen and Vintner of London, 21
June 1641, proved 18 May 1642, by Joane Kebby his widow and executrix.
To the poor of the parish of Broumfield in the County of Somerset, where
I was born, forty shillings, to be paid unto the church wardens of the said
parish within six months next after my decease. Thomas Castle and
Walter Morrish of the said parish, or their survivors shall have ten shillings
out of the said poor's money. To the poor of the parish of St Bennett
Fynck forty shillings in six months &c.

I give and bequeath unto my brother Henry Kebby, now living in New
England, ten pounds of lawful money of England, to be paid unto him with-
in six months after my decease, in case he shall be then living; but if he
shall be then dead I do then give and bequeath his said legacy of ten pounds
unto his daughter Susan Sellick, if she shall be then living. To my sister
Leave thirty shillings. To my good friend Thomas Harrison of St. Bennet
Fynck fifty shillings. To my good friend William Thomas, servant to Mr.
Marsham, of Milk Street, London, thirty shillings. To my cousin Thomas
Kebby, dyer, forty shillings.—A messuage or tenement in St. Christophers,
near the Royal Exchange, known by the name or sign of the Sun.—My
loving wife Joane to be executrix & residuary legatee.
Wit: Rich. Pepys, Henry Huchenson Scrip. Hen. Huchenson junior.
                                                        Cambell, 60.

WILLIAMS (*ante*, pages 335 and 337).

On the above named pages the Rev. Roger Williams's "George Fox dig'd
out of his Burrowes" (Pub. Nar. Club, vol. v. p. 146) is quoted to show that
Williams had a brother who was a " Turkey Merchant." On page 335 Mr. Henry
F. Waters furnishes reasons for thinking that this Turkey merchant may
have been Sidrack, son of James Williams of London; and on page 337, Dr.
Reuben A. Guild argues that it was more likely to be one of the sons of William
Willyams of Roseworthy. The editor of the REGISTER sent a copy of the
July number containing this matter to the clerk of the Merchant Taylors'
Company of London, asking for entries in the Company's books about Sidrack
Williams and his father James Williams, both freemen of that Company, and
asking also if there was any evidence on the books that Sidrack Williams was
a " Turkey Merchant." He received the following reply :—

                            " MERCHANT TAYLORS' HALL, LONDON, E. C.
                                              31 August, 1889.
  " DEAR SIR:
           In reply to your letter of the 2d inst. I have much pleasure
in forwarding to you the enclosed particulars from our Records regarding
Sydrack Williams and his father.
                              I am, dear Sir,
                                    Yours truly,
       J. W. Dean, Esq.   F. G. FAITHFULL."

Merchant Taylors' Company, London.
re Sydrack Williams.

1620. Feby 20. "Sydrack Williams the son of James Williams* is admitted into ye Freedom of this Company by Patrimony. Witness he is his Sonne Thomas Morse Inholder and Edwd Webster, Merchant Taylor." (Ordinary Court Book 1619–1630, fol. 118.)

* N. B. James Williams was admitted to the Freedom of the Company by Servitude to Nicholas Tresswell on 7 April, 1587. (Alphabetical List of Freemen, 1530–1648.)

Memo. It is known that Sydrack Williams was a Merchant to Turkey, for on 6th March, 1626, he took as an Apprentice one Robert Williams† (son of Jacobi Williams Citizen & Merchant Taylor), and he is described in the Apprentice Book, Vol. IX. p. 233, as a Merchant to Turkey and Italy.

† Admitted to the Freedom on 3 Nov. 1634.

FRANCIS G. FAITHFULL,
Clerk of the Merchant Taylors' Company.

Merchant Taylors' Hall,
London, 31 August, 1889.

STEPHEN SEDGWICK of London, Brewer (*ante*, pp. 259 and 277).

The editor of the REGISTER sent copies of the January and April numbers for 1888 to the clerk of the Brewers' Company, London, and asked him if there was more that one Stephen Sedgwick a member of the Company in the early part of the seventeenth century. He replied as follows:

BREWER'S HALL, ADDLE ST., LONDON, E. C.

DEAR SIR, 4 May, 1888.

I find there were two persons of the name of Stephen Sedgwick members of this Company about the time you mention. The elder was a Liveryman, the younger only took up his Freedom.

Yrs. faithfully,

To John Ward Dean, Esq. WILLIAM C. HIGGINS, *Clerk.*

RAINSBOROW (*ante*, 170):

[It is suggested in the REGISTER for April, 1886, but not directly stated, that WILLIAM³ Rainsborow may have been the son-in-law of Rowland Coytmore. It is quite evident, however, that this must have been WILLIAM² Rainsborow. The former can only have been a boy of about sixteen at Coytmore's death in 1626, while the latter, who married Judith Hoxton, may previously have been husband of Sara Coytmore, named in the will of her grandmother Dorothy Lane, 1605, but not mentioned in the will of her father Rowland Coytmore. I can think of no other way in which Wm. Rainsborow can have been son-in-law of Coytmore, all of whose children and step-children are accounted for, except Sara, who may of course have died young and unmarried.—WM. S. APPLETON.]

ARTHUR SLADE (*ante*, p. 319):

[A note in the April number of the REGISTER asks for information concerning Arthur Slade. His death is recorded on the famous silver waiter of Theodore Atkinson, which is engraved with the names, times of death and ages of 48 persons, who were acquaintances and particular friends of the elder Atkinson. The 11th name on this list is "Arthur Slade, Jan. 12th 1746–64." "He was from New Market. Letters of administration were granted to Henry Keese and his wife Elizabeth. This Mrs. Elizabeth Keese may have been his daughter, but nothing is shown by the Exeter Records of his having a wife or descendants." *Brewster's Rambles about Portsmouth, second series*, pp. 67–68. The only other Slades in Portsmouth within a half century of 1746, so far as known, are Benjamin Slade, and a Slade who was the first wife of William Blunt (son of Rev. John Blunt, of Newcastle. Rev. John was born 1706, and died in 1748. William *seems* to have been his eldest son). Benjamin Slade was taxed in Portsmouth for a small estate, 1739–1743, as living on the north side of Crafford's Lane (not his residence, but a tax limit). As the tax records of this city after 1744 for a number of years are missing, Benjamin may have been here, or at least been taxed here after 1743. The town records show nothing about him (Benjamin) or about Arthur. I mean the town record proper, not the tax lists. I should not expect to find Arthur Slade's name here if Brewster's "from Newmarket" means "of Newmarket," and does not mean a change of residence. The probate records at Exeter will show his residence at the time of his death.

In the correspondence of Theodore Atkinson with Capt. John Thomlinson, agent of the Province in London (IV. N. H. Provincial Papers, page 840), appears the following from Atkinson, under date of Portsmouth, Dec. 10th, 1734 :—

"I am now to acknowledge yours of the 8th of Oct. last by Eggleston and observe what you say relating to Mr. Joans's answer to Col. Dunbar's letter about Mr. Slade, that affair was first mentioned to me by the Coll. with whom I often went into the country, he being obliged often to ride into the woods himself & he found he could by no means trust Mr. Slade he having been bribed by allmost all the goverm^t many towns raising a general contribution among the Logers for him but the Coll. did not dismiss him till he openly Quarrell'd with him & without the least reason for he Lived with the Coll whenever in Town yet he reported everywhere that he was Independ^t & had his Commission from home & hath said within this Ten days 'it is so.' I find nothing about Inglefield in the town records near 1740."

The above will no doubt enable you to find out something further concerning Arthur Slade, who was evidently a person of considerable prominence here.— CHARLES E. BATCHELDER, *of Portsmouth, N. H.*]

THE ANCESTRY OF WASHINGTON.

No. II.

SINCE the publication of the pamphlet on the Ancestry of Washington, contributions of interesting additional matter have been received from various friends and correspondents.

Mr. Blaydes sent some notes which appeared so important that it was thought well to send them to the N. Y. *Nation*, in order that attention might generally be drawn to them. The following is a reprint of the communication to the *Nation*.

To the Editor of the Nation :

SIR : The following very important contribution towards the history of the Washington family has just been received from a well-known English antiquary, in friendly response to the suggestion made by Mr. Whitmore, that the aid of our English friends might confidently be looked for.

Mr. F. A. Blaydes, the editor of the *Bedfordshire Notes and Queries*, writes under date of November 8 :

"Some fifteen years ago, when I was first bitten with the mania for searching registers, I have a faint recollection of finding the name Washington of frequent occurrence on some register that I went through. It was somewhere not far from Luton, but whether Toddington, Chalgrove, or Hockliffe, I cannot now say for certain. However, I forward you a few data, bearing on your work, one being a Washington marriage, which I hope will be of use.

NOTES FROM LUTON, CO. BEDS. REGISTER.

1663 Dec. 22. WASHINGTON, Mary, d. of Mr. Lawrence and Mary, bapt. [Bishop's Transcripts.]

1668 Nov. 20. FREEMAN, Mrs. Mary, d. of Mr. *Thomas* [*sic*] and Mistress Hester, bapt. [Parish Register.]

1675 Jan. 14. FREEMAN, John, son of Mr. *John* [*sic*] and Esther, bapt. [Bishop's Transcripts.]

1660 Jan. 26. WASHINGTON — JONES. Lawrence, *gen.* and Mrs. Mary, married. [Bishop's Transcripts.]

"The will of Edmund Jones of Luton, gent., dated 8 Mar., 1682 (buried in the parish church of Luton, 19 May, 1683), mentions grandchild Mary Washington, to whom he bequeaths 40 shillings. Proved at Bedford 24 June, 1689."

[It will be noted that three of these entries are from the Bishop's Transcripts of the parish records. Mr. Freeman is termed *Thomas* in the first— an undoubted error, whether made in the "Transcript" or by Mr. Blaydes in copying.]

Here we have made known to us the maiden name and parentage of the first wife of Lawrence Washington of Virginia, the dates of their marriage and of the baptism of their daughter Mary, to whom, it will be remembered, her father gave all his property in England by his last will and testament. And it should not be forgotten that it was to Edmund Jones that letters of administration on Lawrence Washington's goods in England were granted.

Two or three years ago I myself went to Luton to examine the parish registers, but, though I reached the place early in the forenoon, it was not until afternoon that I was able to get access to them. I looked rapidly over the entries down to the year 1658, inclusive, and, finding nothing, hurried back to London. At that time, I suppose, everybody believed that Lawrence Washington was married and in Virginia in 1658 and onward. It now seems doubtful when he actually settled there. I have made no thorough examination of the Feet of Fines later than those of the year 1657. They should be searched for ten years further at least. Now that we know the Christian name of his wife, any conveyance of land in or about Tring, made by Lawrence and Mary Washington, would be good evidence to prove that Lawrence of Tring and Lawrence of Luton and Virginia were one and the same. Knowing, too, the place and date of the marriage, it might be worth the while to hunt for the marriage license, with the hope to learn thence his place of nativity. If there are extant in Luton any borough or guild records, we might get help from them. If young Lawrence Washington was apprenticed to any tradesman in Luton, the book of apprenticeships in which his indenture was enrolled would undoubtedly settle the question of his parentage and place of nativity.

I would call attention to the fact that Lawrence Washington of Virginia is now shown to have married his first wife in 1660, which helps us to form an opinion as to his age. Lawrence of Tring must then have been twenty-five years old, which answers very well. Let me also call renewed attention to the interesting and important part played in my story by Mr. John Freeman of Luton, whom we find having children baptized, borne by his wife Hester. It was this John Freeman of Luton whom Mrs. Elizabeth Fitzherbert, aunt of Lawrence Washington of Tring, appointed executor of her will and trustee of her real estate in Tring and Middleton Stony. His wife Hester, we have found, was a daughter of William Roades of Middle Claydon, and so a cousin of Lawrence Washington of Tring. Hither to this parish of Luton, from somewhere in England, came a young Lawrence Washington to marry his first wife, in 1660. Can any one doubt that it was from Tring that he came? If this is granted, my whole case must be allowed; for Lawrence of Luton and Lawrence of Virginia were surely one and the same, while Lawrence of Tring was clearly the son of a clergyman of the same name, and that clergyman can have been no other than the Fellow of Brasenose, whose pedigree was known.

HENRY F. WATERS.

[At the risk of seeming superfluous, I venture to point out that these extracts prove the identity of Lawrence Washington of Luton, whose first wife was Mary Jones, with the emigrant to Virginia. (1.) Because Lawrence died in Virginia and his will was proved January 6, 1677. Administration was granted in May, 1677, to Edmund Jones, principal creditor, on estate of Lawrence Washington formerly of Luton, County Beds., deceased in Virginia. No one can doubt that these entries refer to the only known emigrant.

(2.) Edmund Jones is clearly the father-in-law of Lawrence, and mentions his grandchild Mary Washington. Lawrence Washington of Virginia, in his will, gives all his property in England to his daughter Mary and the heirs of her body, and, failing them, to her half-brother and sister, children of his second wife. This devise, moreover, makes it a moral certainty that Mary was an only child by the first wife, agreeing exactly with what the Luton records show.

(3.) It has been *supposed* that Lawrence came to Virginia with his brother John, about the year 1657. But this rests solely upon Gen. George Washington's statement that such was the family tradition. But George was descended from John, the brother of Lawrence, and, even at that time, a century after the emigration, the two families seem to have drifted apart. There are many Washingtons in Virginia not descended from John, who were not clearly traced even to Lawrence.

Now, Mr. Brock's citations from the Virginia Land Registry show grants to John Washington as early as 1661, in connection with Thomas Pope, but the earliest entry to Lawrence is September 27, 1667, jointly with Robert Richards. *Is there any evidence that Lawrence was here before* 1667?

If Lawrence married Mary Jones at Luton in 1660, and had a daughter Mary in December, 1663, and no other child, is it not a fair inference that the mother died soon after, and that Lawrence then turned his steps towards his brother John, already well established in Virginia, and became resident there about the date of his purchase of land in Stafford county as above cited?

W. H. WHITMORE.]

George E. Cokayne, M.A., F.S.A., Norroy King of Arms, sent notes of matriculation at Oxford (1581 to 1714) of a dozen individuals bearing the family name of Washington, from which we extract the following as bearing especially on this Northamptonshire line.

> 1588, Dec. 6, Christopher, s. of "gent.," co. Northam., 15, Oriel.
> "   " " William   "   "   "   "   11,   "
> 1594, Nov. [—], Lawrence s. of "gent.," Herts., 15, Balliol.
> 1621, Nov. 2, Lawrence, s. of "gent.," co. Nmpton., 19, Brasenose.
> 1638, May 4, Lawrence, s. of Lawrence, Kn^t., London, aged 15,
> S^t. John's.

Of the above list Christopher and William were undoubtedly sons of Robert Washington of Sulgrave (see Pedigree), and Lawrence (1594) was the son of Lawrence Washington, Esq., the Register of the court of Chancery, who then lived in Much Hadham, Herts. He succeeded to the office of Registrar and was knighted. The second Lawrence in the list (who was matriculated in 1621) was the Fellow of Brasenose and father (probably) of the Virginians. The last Lawrence (1658) was the father of Lady Ferrars.

I visited Much Hadham, and, through the kindness of the Revds. S. S. Pearce and E. M. W. Templeman, was enabled to examine Parish Registers, whence I gleaned the following :—

Baptized.

5 April 1579 Lawrence the sonn of Lawrence Washington gent.
4 May 1580 Clement sonn of Lawrence Washington gent.
4 February 1581(2) Mary daughter of Lawrence Washington gent.
22 January 1583(4) (26th Eliz.) Clement sonn of Lawrence Washington gent.

Burials.

28 Sept. 1579 Clement Newce Esquier.
5 May 1580 Clement sonn of Lawrence Washington gent.
26 Aug. 1582 Mistresse Mary Newce widdow.

From the Much Hadham Church Monthly for November, 1889, sent me by the Rev. Mr. Templeman, I learn that Clement Newce, Esq., his father (Thomas) and his grandfather all lived in the house which originally stood on the site of the present mansion in the village known as Much Hadham Hall. I examined the will of Mr. Newce, which was proved 23 November, 1579, but as it was 17 July, 1564 (before the marriage of his daughter to Lawrence Washington), I found nothing that seemed to me worth preserving here. His wife's name was then Mary, and he provided for his burial within the parish church and willed "that a stone be layed upon my grave and that thereon be fixed in plates graved with the pictures of my selfe and my wife and all my children and the armes of London, the mercers' armes, the armes of fflaunders and mine owne armes." These brasses still remain in excellent preservation, and the Rev. Mr. Pearce was kind enough to give me a rubbing of them which he had recently made. The Rev. Alexander Nowell, D.D., Dean of St. Paul's, was rector of Hadham, 1562–1589, and was succeeded by the Rev. Theophilus Aylmer or Elmer, D.D., second son of John, Bishop of London.

From the Rev. Philip Slaughter, D.D., Mitchell's Station, Culpeper Co., Virginia, some notes concerning this branch of the Northamptonshire family have been received, which were written in 1880 by Mr. Conway Robinson, the learned jurist and historian, and printed in 1881. Mr. Robinson states :

It appears as to Lawrence Wasshington of Sulgrave, in Northampton county, that this second son, also named Lawrence, was entered of Gray's Inn in 1571, called to the bar in 1582, had a country residence at Jordon's

Hall, Maidstone, and was Registrar of the Court of Chancery from March 24, 1593, until the end of that reign; that he was in King James' first parliament (1603) a member for Maidstone, and assisted by deputies, continued personally to discharge the duties of the office of Registrar until his death, on Dec. 21, 1619, at his house in Chancery Lane; that he was then succeeded in the office of Registrar by his son Laurence Washington, who was, in 1627, knighted by King Charles the First, and held the office of Registrar until 1643, when he died at Oxford and was buried at Garsden, his residence in Wiltshire.

Lawrence Washington of Maidstone is omitted in the Genealogical Table published by Jared Sparks in his writings of Washington, Edi. 1837, Vol. I. pp. 552, 553.*

My friend Mr. Phillimore also contributes the following paper (sent to the editor).

Mr. Waters's long-looked-for pamphlet has just arrived. None can doubt his wisdom in printing these valuable notes at once, instead of waiting until he had absolute legal proof of the identity of the father of the Tring Washingtons with the Rev. Lawrence Washington, rector of Purleigh. One need not be very sanguine in hoping that this legal proof will soon come. Every scrap of evidence should be at once published, whether dealing directly with the Virginian Washingtons or their collaterals, and this will be a sufficient excuse for sending the following notes:—

P. 31 of Mr. Waters's pamphlet, line 2 from foot (*ante* p. 381, 8th line from top), for *Northampton* read *Nottingham.*†

P. 42 (*ante* p. 392). The Pope family. John Washington the emigrant married Ann Pope. Evidently from the will of Thomas Pope of Bristol, 1685, quoted by Mr. Waters, she was of a Gloucestershire family. As her father was *Nathaniel*, and her brother *Thomas*, it is perhaps worth noting that the will, dated and proved in 1738, of Elizabeth Phillimore of Cam, Gloucestershire, widow of Josiah Phillimore, names Elizabeth and Mary, daughters of her brother *Nathaniel* Pope, and her nephew and niece John and Elizabeth, children of her brother *Thomas* Pope. These Popes were of Cam.

Pages 52 and 53 (*ante* p. 404). Mr. Waters mentions a William Roades of Finemore, 1657, and suggests that as Fine More hill is near Edgecote and Quainton, the records of those places should be searched. But it is more probable‡ that it ought to be identified with a village in Oxfordshire on the borders of Buckinghamshire, five miles from Buckingham, now called Finmere but anciently Finemore. At any rate inquiry about the Roades family should be made there.

In passing the "Lichfield Wills" through the press for the "Index Library," a solitary Washington will has just come to light. It is that of an Agnes Washington, 1547; residence not given in calendar. As far as

---

* It is also omitted by Baker and other writers, but is not omitted in the Visitation of Northamptonshire. As it is not in the president's line of ancestry, it does not affect his pedigree.—EDITOR

† I am obliged to my friend for calling my attention to this error, into which I was led by following copy. The error appears in the Visitation of Northampton, published by the Harleian Society.—H. F. W.

‡ I disagree with my friend entirely. In my first investigations among the maps of the region about Middle Claydon, I noticed both Finemere, Oxfordshire and Fine More Hill, just south of Middle Claydon Park, and the rector of Middle Claydon, with whom I talked it over, spoke of the latter place as near by, through the woods. Since then I have noted on another old map the name Finemore Farm. I have little doubt that investigation will show that this Farm was among the estates of the Verney family. Perhaps those *geldings* were kept there.—H. F. W.

the work has at present gone this is the only will of the name in the Lichfield Registry. But search has not yet extended later than 1562.

W. P. W. PHILLIMORE, 124 *Chancery Lane, London.*

And my young friend Mr. Leland L. Duncan, who is doing admirable work among the records for his own county (Kent), has sent me the following note from

Christeninges in the Parrish of Chisselherst in Kent. 1614.

Lawrence sonne of Lawrence Washington and Anne his wife was christened on ye 24th daie of July in the place at Modinghā,* generosi.

This must have been a son of Sir Lawrence who died young, the Lawrence matriculated in 1638 being several years younger.

HENRY F. WATERS.

[The will of Lawrence Washington, son of the emigrant and grandfather of the President, and the annotations on it by Mr. John C. J. Brown, are printed in these Gleanings (REGISTER, vol. 43, pp. 81–3, *ante* pp. 299, 300). Mr. Brown's suspicions in regard to the Washington pedigree in Mr. Albert Welles's book were well founded, as the researches of Col. Chester and Mr. Waters prove.

Mildred, the widow of the above Lawrence Washington, went to England, and in November, 1700, applied for a grant of probate on the estate of her late husband. At this time she was the wife of George Gale of Whitehaven, Cumberland. Two months later she died and was buried at St. Nicholas', Whitehaven, Jan. 30, 1700–1. The discovery of her will and other records in relation to her by Mr. J. C. C. Smith of Somerset House, London, led to the publication of an interesting article by that gentleman in the Genealogist (London, January, 1883) vol. 7, pp. 1–3, entitled, "New Notes on the Ancestry of George Washington," a valuable contribution to the Washington research.—EDITOR.]

Rev. John Nassau Simpkinson, the rector of Brington, by the publication of his historical novel of "The Washingtons" in 1860, and by his speech at the dinner in London on Washington's birth-day in 1862, revived the interest in the pedigree which has finally been satisfied by Mr. Waters's researches. Mr. Simpkinson was in full and confidential communication with the late Col. Chester, and has kindly informed us that the following facts were in the possession of Mr. Chester, and were discussed by him with his friends.

1. Administration of the goods of Amphilis Washington to her son John.
2. Adm. of Lawrence W., late of Luton, who died in Virginia.
3. The will of Theodore Pargiter, 1656 (the one printed by Mr. Waters, *ante* pp. 84–5).

" Col. Chester was thrown off the scent by the saying of the great President that the emigrants came from a northern county, and latterly he thought he had found the man he was looking for somewhere in the north, Durham, I think, or Northumberland. Of this, however, he would not tell me, reserving himself for an irrefragable proof of his discovery."

Mr. George E. Cockayne, who was Col. Chester's executor, writes that he has not found in the papers left to him the deed which Col. Chester possessed, and which he thought was made by one of the emigrant Washingtons. Mr. Cockayne has also as yet no trace to the law-suit in which Rev. Lawrence W. was concerned when rector of Purleigh; but he has kindly promised to make search therefor.

These facts are worth mentioning as showing how much Col. Chester had found; and, I may add, as a proof that it is perhaps wiser to print facts as fast as obtained, even when not exhaustive of any subject, as thereby the attention of other antiquaries is directed to the deficiencies which their notes may make good.—W. H. WHITMORE.

Bishop Meade's " Old Churches, Ministers and Families of Virginia," vol. 2, pages 167–8, contains an abstract of the will of John Washington, the emigrant. The will is dated February 26, 1675 (that is, 1675–6), and was proved the 10th of January, 1677 (that is, 1677–8). Bishop Meade prefixes this statement:—" I have

* Mottingham.

obtained, by the help of a friend, the will of John Washington, which was recorded at Westmoreland Court House, and whose original is still there in an old book of wills, though in a somewhat mutilated form." Neither the record nor the original will can now be found. Mr. Brock, of Richmond, writes me: " Some years ago, in 1877, in behalf of our lamented friend Col. Chester, I made numerous inquiries for the will of John Washington, of friends and the county court clerks of Westmoreland, Essex, Richmond, Northampton and Stafford counties, without avail and without finding a document with the signature of John Washington. The will has certainly disappeared from the records of Westmoreland county. I have since left no influence untried, but have learned of no trace of the will." Mr. Greenwood, who furnishes us with a copy of the will of Lawrence Washington, obtained in 1873, tried at the same time to get a copy of the will of his brother John, but without success. Mr. Moncure D. Conway, in an article in the New York *Nation*, Oct. 24 last, says: " The Rev. Dr. E. C. McGuire, writing in 1836, says that the will in question was then at Mount Vernon, with the endorsement, ' The Will of Lieutenant Colonel Washington.' Dr. McGuire married a daughter of Robert Lewis, Washington's nephew and private Secretary, and his statement is of sufficient weight to cause the heirs of Judge Bushrod Washington, who inherited Mount Vernon, to institute a general search. For even if the document referred to was a copy of the will, it would be of high value in directing rightly the researches " relating to the Washingtons. Bishop Meade's abstract follows.—EDITOR.]

"In the name of God, Amen. I, John Washington, of Washington parish, in the county of Westmoreland, in Virginia, gentleman, being of good and perfect memory, thanks be unto Almighty God for it, and calling to remembrance the uncertain state of this transitory life, that all flesh must yield unto death, do make, constitute, and ordain this my last will and testament and none other. And first, being heartily sorry, from the bottom of my heart, for my sins past, most humbly desiring forgiveness of the same from the Almighty God, my Saviour and Redeemer, in whom and by the merits of Jesus Christ I trust and believe assuredly to be saved, and to have full remission and forgiveness of all my sins, and that my soul with my body at the general resurrection shall rise again with joy."

Again he repeats the same sentiment, hoping "through the merits of Jesus Christ's death and passion to possess and inherit the kingdom of heaven prepared for his elect and chosen." He directs his body to be buried on the plantation upon which he lived, by the side of his wife and two children. He then proceeds to distribute his property, which he says it has pleased God to give him " far above his deserts." After dividing a number of landed estates between his second and surviving wife and his children,— John, Laurence and Anne,—and also his property in England, he directs that a funeral sermon be preached and no other funeral kept, and that a tablet with the Ten Commandments be sent for to England and given to the church. I think, also, that he directs four thousand-weight of tobacco to be given to the minister, though of this I am not certain, some words being lost. He leaves one thousand pounds to his brother-in-law,' Thomas Pope, and one thousand pounds and four thousand-weight of tobacco to his sister, who had come or was coming over to this country. He makes his wife and brother Laurence his executors.

[The Rev. Edward D. Neill, D.D., in his Address on Washington, delivered at St. Paul, Feb. 22, 1889, says that the above John Washington "married after his first wife's death, the widow of Walter Brodhurst, whose maiden name was Anne Pope." Rev. Dr. Neill, in reply to an inquiry for the evidence, under date of Nov. 23, 1889, writes me as follows :
"Until I receive a letter from Lilleshall, Shropshire, Eng., I cannot prepare such an article as I desire. This much is said to be true. John Washington married the widow Anne Brodhurst, whose maiden name was Pope. Her first

husband's name was Walter; by whom she had several children, one of whom, Walter, lived during his last years at Lilleshall and there died. Walter was the son of William Brodhurst. William when he died left a legacy to his daughter-in-law. If these facts are correct, Walter Brodhurst and Lawrence Washington son of John were half-brothers.

"In Neill's 'Founders of Maryland,' page 139, John Washington, in a letter under date of Sept. 30, 1659,* writes 'I intend to get my young sonne baptized. All yᵉ Company and Gossips being already invited.'

"The young son was probably Lawrence. He had three children by his last wife,—John, Lawrence, Anne."

Mr. Brock of Richmond writes me concerning the Broadhurst connection, that the discovery of the marriage with Broadhurst was made by Col. Chester, in 1880, and Mr. Brock made research in Virginia in relation to the name. He sends the following items:

Walter Broadhurst was a member of the House of Burgesses from Northumberland Co., July, 1653. He died in 1656, leaving bequests to his wife Ann Broadhurst and son Walter. He was a son of William Broadhurst of co. Salop, Gent., England. His will was proved in the Prerogative Court of Canterbury, Nov. 19, 1658.

Walter Broadhurst the elder came to Virginia in or prior to the year 1650. He was granted Oct. 4, 1650, 500 acres of land in Northumberland Co. Va. Land Registry, Book No. 2, p. 249. His son Walter was granted 300 acres, Dec. 9, 1662. Book No. 4, p. 550. Gerard Broadhurst, probably another son, also received the same date 500 acres "near the land of Nath'l Pope." Book No. 4, p. 553.

Mr. Isaac J. Greenwood of New York writes me:

"Col. John[1] W., according to Meade, desires in his will to be buried on the plantation where he lives, by the side of his (first) wife and two children. I understand this old burial ground to have been ½ mile south of the homestead, on opposite side of Bridge's Creek, Westm'd Co. Here also his 2d son Lawrence[2] was buried in 1697, though he had settled in Gloucester Co., on the Pionkatank River, where there is also an old grave-yard. The latter's son John[3] Washington, of the 3d generation, was a vestryman of Petsworth Parish, Gloucester Co., and a letter† of his to Messrs. Cary & Co. of London, dated July 12, 1744, is extant, containing instructions for a tombstone with the arms. In April, 1864, there was exhibited in the "Dept. of Arms & Trophies" of the N. Y. Sanitary Fair, a steel rapier (point broken), with steel hilt apparently set originally with stones, said to have been brought from England by the Washington family and to have been presented by Gen. George Washington to Gen. John Caldwell of Md. (Query,—B. Gen. John Cadwallader?)"

The following copy of the will of Lawrence Washington the emigrant and the brother of John, has been furnished for the REGISTER by Mr. Greenwood.— EDITOR.]

In the name of God Amen I Lawrence Washington of the County of Rappac being sick & weak of body but of sound and perfect memory do make & ordain this my last will & Testament hereby revoaking anulling & making void all former wills and Coddicills heretofore by me made either by word or writing & this only to be taken for my last will & testament. Impᵉˢ I give and bequeath my Soule into the hands of Almighty God hoping and trusting through the mercy of Jesus Christ 'my one Savior and redeemer to receive full pardon & forgiveness of all my sins and my body to the earth to be buried in comely & decent manner by my Executrix hereafter named & for my worldly goods I thus dispose them—Item I give and bequeath unto my loveing daughter Mary Washington my whole Estate in England both real & personal to her and the heirs of her body

---

* The extract from the Maryland records containing this letter was first printed in the Historical Magazine for January, 1867, 2d series, vol. 1, pp. 29–30.—EDITOR.

† Mentioned in an Autograph sale of Messrs. Southgate, Grimston & Wells, No. 22 Fleet St., London, held June 2 and 3, 1830.

lawfully begotten forever to be delivered into her possession imediately after my decease by my Executrix hereafter named. I give & bequeath unto my afores[d] daughter Mary Washington my smallest Stone ring & one silver cup now in my possession to her & her heirs forever to be delivered to her imediately after my decease. I give & bequeath unto my loveing son John Washington all my books to him & his heirs forever, to be delivered to him when he shall come to the age of Twenty one years. I give & bequeath unto my son John & daughter Anne Washington all the rest of m[y] plate but what is before exprest to be equally divided between them & delivered into their possession when they come of age. Item my will is that all my debts which of right & justice I owe to any man be justly & truly paid as also my funerall expenses after which my will is, that all my whole Estate both real and personal be equally divided between my loving wife Jane Washington & the two children God hath given me by her viz.: John & Ann Washington. I give & bequeath it all to them & their heirs of their bodies lawfully beggotten forever, my sonn's part to be delivered to him when he comes of age & my daughters part when she comes of age or day of marriage which shall first happen.

Item my will is that that land which became due to me in right of my wife lying on the South Side of the river formerly belonging to Cap[t] Alexander Flemming & commonly known by the name of West Falco be sold by my Executrix hereafter named for the payment of my debts immediately after my decease. Item my will is that the land I have formaly entered with Capt. W[m] Mosely be forthwith after my decease surveyed & pattented by my Exec[x] hereafter named, & if it shall amount to the quantity of one thousand acres, then I give & bequeath unto Alexander Barron two hundred acres of the s[d] land to him & his heirs forever the remainder I give & bequeath unto my loveing wife afores[d] & two children to them & their heirs forever to be equally divided between them. Item my will is that if it shall please God to take my daughter Mary out of this world before she comes of age or have heirs of her body lawfully begotten then I give & bequeath my land in England which by my will I have given to her, unto my son John Washington & his heirs & the psonall estate which I have given to her I give & bequeath the same unto my s[d] daughter Ann Washington & her heirs forever. Item I do hereby make & ordain my loving wife Jane Washington Executrix of this my last will & Testament to see it performed & I do hereby make & appoint my dear and loveing brother Coll[o]. John Washington & my loveing friend Thomas Hawkins in case of the death or neglect of my Executrix to be the overseers & guardians of my children untill they come of age to the truth whereof I have hereunto sett my hand & seal this 27 of September 1675.

LAWRENCE WASHINGTON   [Seal.]

Signed Sealed & declared to be his last will & testament
   in the presence of us
        Cornelius Wood
        John B. Barron
        Henry Sandy Jun[r].

A Codicill of the last will & Testament of Lawrence Washington annexed to his will & made September 27th 1675. Item my will is that my part of the land I now live upon which became due to me by marriage of my wife I leave it wholly & solely to her disposal after my decease as witness my hand the day & year above written.

LAWRENCE WASHINGTON   [Seal.]

Signed Sealed & declared to be a codicil of my last will & testament
in the presence of us
Cornelius Wood
Henry Sandy Jun[r].

The above named Henry Sandy Jun[r] aged 17 years or thereab[ts] sworn
& examined saith that he did see the above named Lawrence Washington
sign seale & publish the above mentioned to be his last will & testament &
that he was in perfect sense and memory at the signing sealing & publishing thereof to the best of your deponents judgement.   HENRY SANDY.

Iuratus est Henricus Sandy in Cur. Com. Rapp[ac]
Sexto. die Janu'y An[o]. 1677.

℣ Sacrm[l] p[l] probat[d] et recordat[r]
Test Edm[d] Crask Clk. Co.

A Copy   Teste   JAMES ROY MICOU Clk.
Oct. 25, 1873.   Essex Co., Va.

[Rapac Co. from 1653 to '92 was on either side of the Rapac River, extending
for some miles up to the falls above Fredericksburgh.

Col. John Washington settled on the Potomac, Westm'd Co. (Washington
Parish); his brother Lawrence, says Meade, may have settled at first on the
same river and afterwards have located on the Rappahannock river, in the
county of the same name (Littleburne Parish),—not so very far off, as neither
parish was over five miles wide.

1686, Aug. 2.—John Washington, master of sloop Two Sisters, having imported some brandy which had not been landed in England, had informa[tn] lodged
against him in Co. of Adm., for viola[tn] of navigation laws.—Col. Doc. of N. Y.,
xxxiv. p. 40.

Robert Washington writes Congress, from Williamsburgh, Va., 29 July, 1775,
offering his services and speaks of his experience obtained on the Continent
during the last war.—Am. Arch. S. iv.; vol. ii. 1750.

I cannot find his name on the British Army Lists.   I. J. GREENWOOD.

Mr. William John Potts, of Camden, N. J., in the *Nation*, Nov. 28, 1889,
states that in 1874 he discovered in the index of the Surrogate's office in Charleston, S. C., an entry of the will or letters of administration of John Washington, the date of which he and one of the officials supposed to be about
1680. The early wills were in such confusion that he did not attempt to find the
original. The editor of the REGISTER wrote to Mr. Langdon Cheves, of
Charleston, on this subject, and he replied Dec. 12, 1889:

" I acknowledged in my last your letter in regard to administration on
goods of John Washington mentioned in the *Nation* of Nov. 28 (which I had
not seen) as in the Probate Court here. I went at once to the Probate Court
and found the entry in the old index.* But have neither then nor since been
able to find anything more either there or among my own memoranda. All the
early original papers were burnt in Columbia. The only early records now in
the Probate Court are some of the Record Books; they are unindexed (except for
a table of contents), but my mem[a] include a pretty complete index of names up to
about 1700. And I do not think any record of the adm'n now exists in that
office. A good many of the old records are in the State House at Columbia, but
they are almost without indices & not very accessible.

There are two of the old Indices, one evidently copied from the other. They
are bare lists of names with the letter & number indicating the Box or bundle in
which the papers relating to that person's estate were filed and their position in
that bundle. The letters on the bundles indicate in a very vague and uncertain
way their dates; the packages were evidently put up not very long ago, and with
no regard to date, except that papers that had been together, to some degree were
kept so. Frequently the will and inventory are widely separated. I think the
date 1680 far too early (though there is no reason why a 1680 will might not be

* "Washington, John, Inv'ty, F. 43."

in any one of the earlier "single letter" bundles. After entering on the double letters, ' 2 Aˢ' ' 2 Bˢ' &c. the papers run in more regular order.) I judge that the administration on John Washington's estate was granted between 1710 and 1715, probably about 1711. The Record Book for that time is missing."

Mr. William Francis Cregar of Annapolis, Md., has sent me a list of fourteen persons by the name of Pope, who settled in Maryland between the years 1634 and 1683. "Francis Pope," he writes, "was the first to arrive and settled in that part of Maryland which afterwards became Charles County. Nathaniel Pope and wife arrived in Maryland prior to 1648. Settlers on both the Virginia and Maryland banks of the Potomac frequently crossed the river.—EDITOR.

Records of Charles City County Court.—" Robert Washington of Wapping in yᵉ parish of Stepney and Soin[?], Middlesex, Mariner, appoints Mʳ Pearson his attorney; mentions bonds, bills, tobaccos, sugars, houses, chattels, sums of money. 29 July, 1660. Proved at a Court held 3 Dec. 1660.

Records of General Court, James City County.—At a court held 12 Oct. 1675. "Edward Washington indicted for murthering Wᵐ Norcott was found by the petty jury to be guilty of manslaughter, for which he was burnt in the hand."— R. A. BROCK.]

Before these notes are closed let me say that I have in my collections numerous Washington notes, which I have not published as they do not seem to relate to this especial line.   HENRY F. WATERS.

JOHN OXENBRIDGE, preacher of the word of God in Coventry and late minister of Southam in the County of Warwick, 18 September 1617, proved 2 June 1618.

Whereas Mary Oxenbridge my well beloved wife is stated in the conveyance of my house and garden with the appertenances in Bishopsgate Street in Coventry and joined purchaser with me in the same house my will and desire is that the same house and garden with the appurtenances may fully and lawfully be assured and confirmed to my said wife so that she may hold and peaceably enjoy the same as her fee simple for term of her life.— then after her decease the inheritance and the fee simple of the same &c., according to the last will and testament of my daughter Gilbie deceased, may come as of special right to the four daughters now living of my said daughter Gilbie &c. To my said wife all my brass and all my plate and pewter, linen, beddings, and all things thereunto belonging with all other implements and utensils whatsoever belonging to the household except those implements which are named and set down in an Inventory and now remaining in the said house in Bishopsgate Street, all which were bought with the house and so not to be removed &c. To my wife also such and so many of my English books as she shall make choice of. All the rest of my said books I do give to my son Daniel Oxenbridge. Whereas my said son Daniel by an accompt under his hand doth now stand indebted unto me in the sum of six score pounds and upward &c. I do give to his virtuous mother my beloved wife the just sum of six score pounds, to be paid unto her by my said son within four years after my decease, *i. e.* thirty pounds a year. All other debts of my son Daniel, over and above the said sum, I do give to my said son and absolutely remit and free him from being charged with the same forever hereafter. To the poor of the parish of Southam in the County of Warwick twenty shillings within three months &c. To the poor almsmen of Bablake and their nurse eleven shillings &c., *i. e.* to each a shilling apiece. To Hope Gellibrand my grand child a piece of plate worth in value four nobles or thereabouts. What my childrens' children and my great grand children shall have I leave it to the discretion of my said wife.

All the rest to my wife Mary Oxenbridge, and I make her the sole executrix. The overseers to be my son Daniel Oxenbridge and Oliver Bowls. Wit: James Cranford, John Pole.   Meade, 65.

DANIEL OXENBRIDGE of London, Doctor of Physick, 21 December 1641, proved 12 September 1642. To my son Clement Oxenbridge, during the term of his natural life, the annual sum of twenty pounds, to be paid at four feasts or terms in the year, *i. e.* at the Feast of the Annunciation of the Virgin Mary, the Nativity of St. John the Baptist, St. Michael the Archangel and the Birth of our Saviour Christ, by equal portions and to be issuing, during the joint lives of my wife and my said son, out of my lands and tenements in the parishes of St. Stephen, Colman Street, London, and Brodericke in the County of Northumberland, and after my wife's decease then to be issuing out of my said lands and tenements only in the parish of St Stephen, Colman Street. These (latter) tenements &c. I give (charged with the said annual sum &c) unto Katherine my well beloved wife, during the term of her natural life, and after her decease to my son John Oxenbridge and his heirs for ever. All my lands at Brodericke &c (charged as above) I give to my wife Katherine &c., then to my son Daniel Oxenbridge and his heirs forever.

I give and devise unto my said son John and his heirs for ever all my lands in the Sommer Islands. To my wife the messuage or tenement wherein I now dwell, with the appurtenances, situate in St Sythes Lane in London, during so long time of my lease and term therein as she shall happen to live. After her decease the remainder of the lease to my son Daniel. To son Daniel all my part and share in the Tynne Farm, he to pay and discharge the sum of three hundred pounds for which I stand bound unto my son-in-law Mr Edmond Hunt for his wife's portion. I give to my daughter Langhorne ten pounds and to my grand child Daniel Langhorne forty pounds, and to all the rest of my son and daughter Langhorne's children five pounds apiece. To my daughter Fowler ten pounds and to her daughter Katherine ten pounds. Item I give to my cousin (*sic*) Item I give to my daughter Cockroft ten pounds and to her three children five pounds apiece.

My wife Katherine and son Daniel to be co-executors. My brother Sir Job Harby and my three sons-in-law William Langhorne, John Fowler and Caleb Cockroft to be overseers and to receive five pounds apiece.

To Robert Bincks twenty shillings. To my late old servant Thomas Shawe twenty shillings. To the widow Clarke twenty shillings, To my kinsman Thomas Clarke twenty shillings. To my cousin Hoare's wife twenty shillings. To my servants Mary Hart, Mary Hart and my man William twenty shillings apiece. To my well beloved sister the lady Harby my best book in my study which she shall make choice of. The rest to my two executors.

Wit: Isaac Justin, Ric: Preice Scr.

The above will was proved by Katherine Oxenbridge the widow of the deceased, power reserved for the other executor to take out letters.

Campbell, 110.

KATHERINE OXENBRIDGE, 25 March 1651, proved 5 November 1651.

To my son John Oxenbridge two hundred pounds and to his children fifty pounds. To my daughter Humes children two hundred pounds, they having most need, and to her the fifty pounds in my brother Sir Job's (hands) the interest of it to Sir Job's children to buy them rings to remember me by. To my daughter Phillips daughter Betty forty pounds, to her son Daniel forty pounds, neither of them being sure of any portion. To my son Clement two hundred pounds when all is discharged, to his wife the money that her brother has recovered for me. To my son Thom's wife my suit of damask; it is marked with C. O.

I give to the Plantation of New England Ten pounds for to buy books for the Indians to learn to read. To my daughter St John's and my daughter Langton thirty shillings apiece to buy them rings withall. To my daughter Hunt my ring that is set with pearls and all my own wearing clothes. I give twenty shillings apiece to my cousins Conyers, William, Katherine, Dorcas and Thomas.

My sons John and Clement to be executors and Daniel Phillips to be overseer. I give twenty shillings apiece to all my cousins Emitt Darell.

John Oxenbridge renounced executorship.   Grey, 220.

[We have here the will of John Oxenbridge, " a graduate of Oxford in 1572, and a famous Puritan preacher;" that of his son Daniel, " a graduate of Christ Church, Oxford, and a physician of high standing at Daventry," and London; and that of Daniel's wife Katherine, a " daughter of Clement Throgmorton of Hasley, third son of Sir George Throgmorton of Loughton (the family being patrons of Southam) and so descended from Edward III." (Ellis's History of First Church of Boston, page 125–6). John was the grandfather and Daniel and Katherine were the parents of Rev. John Oxenbridge, pastor of the First Church, Boston, Mass., from April 10, 1670, till his death Dec. 28, 1674.

Rev. John Oxenbridge was born at Daventry, co. Northampton; " matriculated at Lincoln College, Oxford, 20 June, 1623, in his 18th year; after was of Magdalen Hall, and continued there a tutor some time, but disquieted with the increased stringency of church ceremonies he went, 1634, to Bermuda and preached, in a few years went home again, but being ejected on the act of uniformity, 1662, took departure for Surinam; thence in short time to Barbados, and in 1669 came hither." (Savage's Gen. Dict. vol. 3, p. 326. See also Mather's Magnalia, ed. 1853, vol. 1, p. 597; Palmer's Nonconformist's Memorial, ed. 1802, vol. 1, p. 299; Wood's Athenæ Oxoniensis; Emerson's and Ellis's histories of First Church Boston.)   Ellis refers to W. D. Cooper's sketch of the Oxenbridges of Sussex and Boston, Mass.   London, 1860.—EDITOR.

The will of John Oxenbridge, proved Jan. 9, 1674–5, is on file at the Suffolk Probate office, and is recorded Lib. vi. fol. 75. The following is an abstract made from the original will :

" Boston in New Engl. ye 12th day of ye first month
in ye year 1673–4.

I John Oxenbridge a sorry man, lesse then ye least of all ye mercies and servants of Christ am ye most weake and worthlesse creature, yet have I bene by ye Lord's hand (even a strong hand upon me) separated to stand before his face in ye ministry of ye Gospel, and in severall places as Barmudas, Great Yarmouth, Beverly, Barwick, Bristol, Eton, and Windsor have I bene led forth in y^t work, and in some measure my Lord hath owned me graciously in all these places. After wch having had my portion wth others of more weight and worth (who had prophecied in sackcloth) to be layd aside from this honorable work in England.   Wherfore I went forth as far as Serenam in desire and hope of serving Christ there, and there I was assaying so to do from 62 at my own great charge in many hazards of my own life, and wth the loss of very dear relations. After those parts were seized by ye Dutch and for a while reseized for ye English by Sr John Harman wth him I went thence to Barbados, and after fruitlesse essays there also (as to publick work) I went in 69. to New England, where now being comfortably fixed by Poynting providences in ye first Church of Boston as pastor thereof, and so in present appearance a period being put to my wasting and weary wandrings and in free mercy receiving an allowance for them I Judge it reasonable to set my soul and house in order."

Daughter Bathshuah Scot for my Executrix. And this I doe in ye sense I have of her naturall affection to me flourishing now at ye last (she showing more Kindeness in ye latter end then in ye beginning) and likewise in confidence of her fidelity to her Sister Theodora, and in all other betrustments. For my Overseers the Honored John Leverett Esq. ye Reverend James Allein, and Mr Humphry Davie.

To my wife Susanna in lieu of all thirds or Dowry, £50 in New England coyn; one bed and bedstead wth curtains; what plate and houshold stuff doth remain of what she had in her former widow hood. Also, what gold rings she hath of mine, not otherwise disposed of, also one silver porringer, one sugar dish, one silver taster wth a funnell, one sweet-meat spoon. Likewise (besides ye bookes she had in her former widow hood) Rogers on Judges and his seaven Treatises, also Thom. Goodwin his child of light. And this small portion of my ruined estate I desire and hope she will accept wth love and satisfaction, as being more then she had from her former husband, m^r Abbot, and more then before marriage wth me was expected or promised, for then she did say she had enough for us both, when by sore losses my estate was much impaired. And I would think in equity she will consider y^t her Annuity of one hundred a yeer will be more then I can leave to my children, and more then she was willing to leave them or me in case of my surviving, for she was not willing to follow ye advise of her chiefest friend Mr Thomas Parris who made ye match between her and me, and he and others did advise to sell her Annuity and purchase in N. E. Which if she had done and cast her estate with mine, it had bene a reasonable thing for her to expect and have ye thirds of mine, but she refusing this, I had not in case of surviving bene one penny ye better for her estate by any thing left to me or mine. Howsoever she hath in ordinary providence (under which we must sett down) she hath sufficient and abundant provision for her, if it be better managed then in her former widowhood, and y^t it may be so I give her in love this faithfull advise till my son Scot's arrivall to make Mr Humphry Davie her Atturney for ye procuring her Annuity, and receive m^ris Kingesmill to her friendly and faithfull care as being more experienced and prudent to order affairs and write letters and accounts for her. To m^ris Kingsmill 3 pound out of my charity bag ye rest in ye bag to be disposed to ye most necessitous brethren and sisters of ye church by ye Deacons thereof. To my daughter Bathshuah Scot my dwelling house in Boston as it is put into my power by Will to doe by Deed of Aug. 22, 1673, she allow her sister Theodora five pound yeerely during ye life of Bathshuah; in case Bathshuah die without issue surviving, then ye reversion to Theodora, she paying fifty pound as a Legacy to ye first Church of Boston; in case Theodora decease without issue, the fifty pound inheritance of the house to be to ye first church in Boston for ye use of ye pastor or teacher for ye time being. To daughter Bathshuah my seale ring, my sugar boxe wth my armes, a fruit dish marked with my own and her Mothers name, also one beaker and 12 spoones so marked, one dish marked D. O. one large tankard marked with my armes, one small tankard marked M. O., one silver porringer, one large salt sellar, 1 wine cup, 1 child's spoon wch was mine in my infancy, 1 silver pensill wth seal lyon, one locket, cornelian ring, one ring beset wth blew specks.

To daughter Theodora all my Tenements in White's ally in Coleman street, London, ye writings whereof were left by me with Mr Kemp of Lombard street, wch houses did formerly yield £35, but ye last lease since ye fire doth agree to £18, and this in Mr John Loder's hand in London, and I desire my Executrix with ye help of my brother Loder y^t Theodora upon ye death of her Grandfather may have her right of ye land in Kent about £10 ye yeer, ye writing whereof was left by Mr Joseph Caryll wth my brother Loder, as also her right in a debt from Mr Killingworth, wch was originally £400, and what other goods or estate w fall to her from her Grandfather.

To daughter Theodora what goods remain of them she brought from England, and also ye value of a fourth part of my estate remaining after debts and legacies payd, only if my estate in Serenam arise to anything y^t she have a young Nigro or two as my Executrix shall think fitt, and ye 4th part aforsayd to be Judg'd by my Overseers.

To Theodora my gilt watch, my gold thimble and whistle, my gold ring wth her name in it, my green emerauld ring wth diamond sparks, a wraught cup wth its covering marked wth my own and her mother's name, one locket, one silver inkhorn marked F. W. one wraught plate wth my own and her mother's armes, also one caudle cup and cover, one large tankard, one silver porringer all marked wth I₁° spoon marked M. H. 1 forked spoon 1 p' of sizers wth silver, 1 cornelian ring, one cornelian bracelet, 1 cristall piece.

To m^r Daniel Hinchman and his eldest daughter, each of them a ring.

To my Son Richard Scot a diamond ring, one of them in Mr Humphry Davie his hand.

To each of my surviving Sisters twenty shillings in gold to buy a ring wth my name in it, and to my sister Ingoldesly I forgive two thirds of what is due to me by bond; and ye like I doe to my Brother Clement Oxenbridge in a bond of £50, and give him a ring as to my Sisters.

To my brother Loder and his wife each a gold ring, and to him, also, Augustin's epitome, and ye platts were left wth m^r Shirley at ye Pellican in litle Brittain. To m^r George Peryer a gold ring. To each of my Overseers a gold ring; to John Leverett my French history, to m^r James Allein Ravanell in 2 volumes, do. m^r Humphry Davie Purchas pilgrim, and to his wife my white amethyst ring. To ye Elders and Deacons of ye first church of Boston twenty pound for ye use of y^t Church.

To my Nigro maid servant Mary fifty shillings to be layd out as my Executrix shall see most for ye good of ye sayd Mary; and to my Nigro boy ten shillings as she sees meet.

To ye publick Library in Boston or elsewhere as my Executrix and Overseers shall judge best Augustins workes in 6 volumes, ye Centuries in 8 volumes, ye Catalogue of Oxford library Tritemius catalogue of ecclesiastic writers. Also Parcus workes in 2 volumes, Pineda upon Job in 2 volumes, Euclids geometry, Willet on Leviticus, Davenant on ye Collosians, Pembles workes, Osiander epit of Centurys in 2 vol.

I leave my Manuscripts to be disposed of by my executrix wth ye advise of my overseers, and in particular ye Plea for ye Dumb Indian, and Colonies to m^r Eliot or any other they shall see meet.

In presence of   JOHN OXENBRIDGE.
Julines Hering
    Ita attest p'
Robert Howard not. publ. Massachusitt Colonie novæ Angliæ.

Mr Robert Howard appearing before Edward Tyng & Major Thomas Clarke Esq^{rs} 9th Jan. 74 made oath &c.

                              Attests FREEGRACE BENDALL Record^r.

Inventory of estate of Mr Jno Oxenbridge.
Taken Jan. 5. 1674, by Anthony Stoddard, Edward Hutchinson, sen^r. Amt. £1715. 14. 8, including his Dwelling house, orchard, Garden, &c. £550. Lib. v. 223.

Susanna Oxenbridge, of Boston, will June 6, 1695. To Mr James Allen Teaching officer of the first Church of Christ in Boston (of wch I am a Member) Mr Mitchils booke on 1' Peter 5. 10. with fowre more att his choice, my Diamond Ringe, one silver forke, two silver framed Spectacles. To his Wife Mrs Sarah Allen, my blacke Prunella Gowne and petticoate, Two Agate Knives, best Silke Stockins and gart^{rs}, Scarlett Coloured Hood, long Silke Girdle, Balsome ball, golden bodkin, one Gold Ringe. To his daughter Hannah and his Son James, I give each of them a gold Ringe, of them I used to weare. To Mr Joshua Moodey, a ring, a paire of my Silke stockings and fowre bookes such as my Executr^{rs} agree upon. To the wife of sd Mr Moodey, my gold Chain I weare about my Necke, my Plush gowne, a Ring & a paire of Silk Stockings, if any left. To Mr Samuell Parris a silver pottinger, and ten pounds, and to his two Eldest children ftve pounds apeice in money. To Mr Peter Thatcher, the piece of gold I wear about my Neck; to him and his wife and his two eldest children, five pounds apiece in money. To Mrs Sarah Davie of Hartford, my Cloth Gowne lined with Lutestring, and black Cloth petticoat belonging to it, my little Bible with Silver Clasps and Case, finest tufted Holland petticoat and Enameled Ring. To Mrs Jerusha Saltonstall and Mrs Elizabeth Davie, I give each of them, a Ring. To Mrs Elizabeth Taylor, daught^r to Mr Humphry Davie, my Gold Seale, a Silver forke and a Ring. To Mr John Davie, a good booke. To Mrs Bellingham, Burroughs of Contentment. To Mr James Allen, Mr Joshua Moodey, Mr Increase Mather, Mr Samuell Willard, Mr Cotton Mather, or those of them that shall be alive att my decease, all the money in a Round painted box, when filled, to bee equally divided among them. To Mr Henry Deering, five pounds; Mr Peter Butler and his wife, three pounds to buy them Rings. To Mrs Hodges, I give Mr Mathew Medes booke, and five pounds money. To the Widows, Armitage, Cart^r and Dinsdale, forty shillings a peice. To Mehetable Hinkely, formerly my servant, I give my changeable silke petticoat, morning wastecoate, white Dimity wastecoate, two paire of my stockins, one black hood. To my servant mayde, twenty shillings. To my kinsman Isaack Taylor, my Geneva Bible, and my Silver box wth a watch in it. To my kinswoman Mary Taylpur, my great Bible and greate Wedding Ringe. To my kinswoman Sarah Gent, my plain blew Bible, and all my Wearing Cloths, with all my Linnen Household goods, bedding, plate not disposed of. Appoint Mr James Allen, Mr Peter Thacher, Mr Pet Butler joynt Executors; as a token of my Love I give to Each, Twenty pound apeice. June 6, 1695. Ezekiel Cheever, Paul Symons, Kath. Welsteed.

[In a Codicil, made Dec. 30, 1695, "finding a necessity of being supported by my Executors therein named, for want of the Incomes of my Estate," she provides, that if there be a sufficient portion of her estate left at her decease, the legacies are to be paid, if otherwise, the aforesaid Legacies, so given, to be utterly null and void.]

Will proved March 25, 1696. Abstract made from the original on file. It is recorded Bk. xi. folio 145. Inventory rendered March 24, 1695-6. Joseph Bridgham, Tho. Clarke, Apprizers. Proved, Boston, April 9, 1696. Jurat Cor. Wm Stoughton.—WILLIAM B. TRASK.]

WILLIAM WHITTINGHAM, late of Boston in Massachusetts Colony in New England, gentleman, 25 March 1672, proved 15 April 1672. To my eldest son Richard Whittingham, to him and his heirs forever, one house, barn, mill house and appurtenances thereto belonging, with twenty acres of arable land, eighty four acres and a quarter of an acre of pasture, in the tenure and occupation of William Pakey &c. in the town of Sutterton, in the parts of Holland in the County of Lincoln. To my son William one dwelling house, barn and appurtenances &c. with two and twenty acres of pasture, two acres and a quarter of arable land, eighteen acres of marsh, now in the tenure &c. of John Trigg &c.; also one cottage and barn, with four acres and a half of pasture and one acre of arable land, in the tenure &c. of Thomas Bayly &c., all lying and being in Sutterton. To my daughter Marie one messuage, or tenement, &c. with nine acres of pasture and six acres of arable land in the tenure &c. of John Wilson &c., with three acres of arable land late in the tenure of Master Baker &c. To my daughter Elizabeth one messuage &c., with eight acres and a half acre of pasture and five acres of arable land in the tenure &c. of John Gidney, with two acres of pasture in the tenure of George Ledman; also one cottage and one acre in the tenure of John Baker, — in Sutterton. To my daughter Martha six acres and a half acre of pasture late in the tenure of William Walker, one cottage and two acres of pasture late in the tenure of Richard Gunn, in Sutterton. All these at their ages of twenty years or days of marriage.

My will and pleasure is that that one hundred and sixty-three pounds due unto my uncle Nathaniel Hubbert, of London, be paid out of the rents and products of the wood and timber standing on the land aforesaid. Reference is made to a bond bearing date 25 March 1667 wherein brother Richard Whittingham, gentleman, stands jointly bound with my said uncle unto Thomas Harris, of the Inner Temple, London, Esq., in the sum of seven hundred pounds for the payment of three hundred and fifty pounds. My debts in London, contracted upon my particular account, or on account of my brother-in-law John Clarke, of Boston in New England, gentleman, to be paid out of the rents &c. of the said lands; together with the annuity due unto my mother, Mistress Martha Eire, for her natural life and to bring up my aforesaid children, till they come to their respective ages &c. All my estate in

company with M[r] James Whetcombe, of Boston in New England, merchant, to be sold for ready money &c.   To my brother John Clarke of
Boston, gentleman, all his proportion of debts contracted by us in company,
by me already paid and ordered to be paid, and all my right, title and interest
of and in the goods and chattels given to me by my father's will.   To James
Whetcombe of Boston aforesaid, gentleman, twenty pounds.   To my cousins
Mary Hubbert and Anne Hubbert, daughters of my said uncle Hubbert,
five pounds each, to buy them rings.   My father-in-law John Laurence of
New York in America, gentleman, William Hubbert, of Ipswich in New
England, my said uncle Nathaniel Hubbert, of London, gentleman, and
John Lewin of London, Esq., to be executors.

Wit: Ben: Downe, Evan Jones, Elizabeth Pogson.

Proved by Nathaniel Hubbert, one of the executors, power reserved for
the others.   Proved 26 March 1678, by William Hubbert, another of the
executors, power reserved for John Laurence & John Lewin.

Eure, 146.

Sententia pro valore Testamenti Gulielmi Whittingham nuper de Masschutes Colonii in Novo Anglia sed infra parochiam Sanctæ Mariæ Le
Savoy in Comitatu Middlesexia decedentis habentis dum vixit et mortis suæ
tempore bona jura sive credita in diversis diocæsibus sive peculiaribus
jurisdictionibus sufficicentis ad fundend jurisdictione in curiae Prerogativæ
Cantuariensis prædicta.—Quod coram nobis in judicio inter Nathanielem
Hubbert unum executorum in dicto Testamento sive ultima voluntate ante
dicti defuncti nominatum partem hujusmodi negotium promoventem ex una
et Martham Eyre matrem naturalem et legitimum et Richardum Whittingham Mariam Whittingham Elizabetham Whittingham et Martham Whittingham liberos naturales et legitimos in specie ac omnes et singulos alios
quoscunq' etc. etc., partes contra quas idem negotium promovetur partibus
ex altera etc. etc., Lecta lata et promulgata fuit hæc sententia diffinitiva
Secundo die juridico post ffestum sive diem Sancti Andreæ Apostoli die
Martis tertio die Decembris Anno Domini Millimo sexcentesimo septuagesimo Secundo etc. etc.   Eure, 157.

[See wills of William and Richard Whittingham, and Mr. Brown's annotations
on them, in the REGISTER, vol. 39, pp. 170–3 (ante pp. 111–114).—EDITOR.

As to this William Whittingham, of Boston, this will gives us little new information.   Savage has already said that he was the son of John W. of Ipswich,
by his wife Martha, sister of Rev. William Hubbard; that he married Mary, dau.
of John Laurence of Ipswich and New York, and that tradition said that he died
in London.   We also know that he had a brother Richard who was thought to
have settled in England, and sons Richard and William, daughters Mary, Martha
and Elizabeth.

In the REGISTER, xi. 26, is an obituary notice of this Mrs. Mary Clark, who
had married secondly, Gov. Gurdon Saltonstall, from the N. E. Weekly Journal
of 1730.   In the REGISTER, vol. 27, pp. 135–139, and vol. 34, p. 34, Mrs. Dall has
made some criticisms, which seem to be in part well-founded.   But I cannot
agree with all her surmises.   It seems to be accepted that Martha, daughter of
John Whittingham and sister of William, the testator, married Dr. John Clark
of Boston, son of Dr. John and Martha (Saltonstall) Clark.   This second Dr.
John, who died in 1690, was the father of Hon. John, William and Samuel.   He
is of course the brother-in-law of John Clark mentioned in William Whittingham's
will.   Mrs. Dall says that this William Clark, brother of Hon. John C., married
his first cousin, Mary, daughter of William Whittingham; but she gives no
authority.   Savage says that William, brother of Hon. John Clark, was born in
1670 and was a representative from Boston in 1720–21 and 1725.   But at all
events he was not the William who married Mary Whittingham, for the will of
this last named William was proved in 1710, and Boston records show that he

died July 26, 1710, aged 62. It is merely a coincidence of names; not so re-markable, when we consider how very many Clarks there were in Boston at that date, all of different families.

As to the remoter pedigree of these Whittinghams, nothing is yet certain. The obituary of 1730 says John was the posthumous son of Baruch W., who was son of William W., the famous Dean of Durham. Mrs. Dall (REGISTER, xxxiv. 35) shows that the family tradition is probably right, in so far that John Whittingham was the son of Baruch W. of Southerton, who was the son of a William W. of the same, but that this William was *not* the Dean of Durham. The lady is of course wrong in tracing Richard Clarke (Copley's father-in-law) to a Francis Clark, as his father was William, nephew of another William C., from the west of England, as will hereafter be shown.—W. H. WHITMORE.]

JOHN SNOOKE of the parish of St. Clements Danes, citizen & merchant taylor of London, 17 August 1665, proved 1 September 1665. My friend Mr William Higginson, in Blackemore Street, in the parish aforesaid, to be one of my executors and my friend Mr Ralph Sedgwick, living in Paul's parish, in Covet Garden, the other. What legacies I do give away in money to be paid out of Sir John Pawlett's[1] one hundred and fifty nine pounds that he owes me, for the which and for my better security, he hath made over to me his plantation in Virginia called Westover, nigh the James River, in the occupation of Captain Otho Southcott, as by the In-denture more plainly doth appear. To my daughter in law, Mary Norrice, widow, in Aldersgate Street, within the first court on the left hand, my biben and my "selde" ring which was her father's which her mother gave me, and my book the which the leaves are guilt. To her daughter Betty ten pounds. To my unkind dafter Elinore Hodgkins twenty shillings, to buy her a ring, she living with my cousin Mr Robert Jacob, at Bow. To his daughters, each of them &c. Cousin Robert Snooke, in Salisbury, shoe-maker. Hyde, 108.

RICHARD SNOOKE, of Southill, in the county of Somerset, in his will, bearing date 14 July, 18th Charles, proved 20 January 1642, mentions cousin Robert Snooke, brother John Snooke and others. Crane, 2.

[¹Capt. Thomas Pawlett was the Burgess for "Argal's Guifte," Virginia, in 1619, and a member of the Colonial Council in 1621. He was granted 2000 acres of land in Charles City county, near that of Capt. Perry, and west of Berkeley, January 15, 1637, based on the "personal adventure" of himself, his brother Chidiock Pawlett and other "head rights." This grant included the noted seat "Westover." Pawlett died in 1643, and bequeathed the land to his brother, Sir John Pawlett, who sold it in 1666 to Theodrick Bland for £175 sterling. The latter bequeathed it to his eldest son Theodrick, who admitted into joint tenancy, his brother Richard. They sold it in 1688 to Colonel William Byrd, the first of the name and family in Virginia, for the consideration of £800 sterling and 10,000 pounds of tobacco and casks. The present building at "Westover" was erected by Col. William Byrd, the second of the name in Virginia. The seat is at present owned and occupied by Major Augustus H. Drewry. A church (of which a grave-yard with tombs indicates the site) and the county buildings near the banks of James river, remained at "Westover" until sometime in the 18th century. Sir John Pawlett was the grandson of Sir Amias Powlett, of the reign of Queen Elizabeth, and a zealous Royalist. He became Baron Pawlett, of Hinton, St. George, and died 20th March, 1649. He was the ancestor of the Lords Powlett. Another of the name of Pawlett appears in the early annals of Virginia. Robert Pawlett was a minister at Martin's Hundred. He was also a physician and surgeon. He was appointed a member of the Council in 1621, but did not accept.—R. A. BROCK, *Richmond, Va.*]

JOHN ALLSOPP of Bonsall in the County of Derby, gentleman, 16 January, 1643, proved 10 February 1646. To be buried in the church at Allsopp in the Dale. To my dear mother Temperance Hopkines fifty pounds which is now remaining in the hands of Anthony Allsopp my eldest brother, as by bond may appear, if she be living: if in case she be dead then the said fifty pounds to go to my two brothers and sister now living in New England, equally to be divided amongst them or the survivor or survivors of them. To my sister Jane Jackson now wife to Mr Roger Jackson of Ashburne in the said County of Derby, gentleman, the like sum of fifty pounds, and also five pounds to be paid by John Gretrax of Bonsall aforesaid the first day of May next ensuing the date hereof. To my grandmother Mrs Jane Allsopp twenty shillings to buy her a ring withall; and likewise I give and bequeath to my loving aunt Mrs Dorothy Hopkinson of Bonsall aforesaid widow all my "lead oare" which I have now lying at Bonsall. To my brother Mr Anthony Allsopp of Allsopp in the Dale aforesaid the sum of ten shillings. For all the rest of my goods and debts now owing which came by my wife Mary Allsopp I give and bequeath unto my said loving wife, after my funeral expenses, debts and legacies being paid and discharged, so long as she shall keep herself unmarried or else she do marry with the good liking and consent of my executors and Jane Allsopp my grandmother. And if in case that she do marry without the full consent and good liking of my executors and grandmother aforesaid then all the said goods and debts which came by my said wife shall be and remain to said two brothers and sister now living in New England aforesaid.

Mr Roger Jackson of Ashborne aforesaid, gentleman, and my said loving Aunt Mrs Dorothy Hopkinson to be full executors.

Wit. Edward Fowler, William Fletcher, John Allen's mark, Richard Bullock. Fines, 34.

JOSIAS ALSOP, clerk, 12 August 1666, pro: 9 Oct 1666. I desire to be buried in St. Clement's Eastcheape Church if I die in London or near it. Of my temporal estate I give two hundred pounds to Mrs Elizabeth Rosseter, my sister in New England, or to her children if she be dead. I give to my brother Mr Timothy Alsop's children fifty pounds. I give to Mr Richard Vigures of Law Litton in Cornwall five pounds, to be bestowed upon a piece of plate and to be sent to him or to any of his children or grandchildren if alive. I give to the poor of Norton Fitz-warren in Somersetshire twenty pounds, to the poor of St. Clement's Eastcheape, London, ten pounds, to be distributed by my very good friends there. I give to Christ's College Library in Cambridge ten pounds to be sent thither privately. I give to Mr Thomas Waplewicke, merchant tailor, in Warwick Lane London, or to his wife, all my clothes, woollen, linen, silk, leather. And I commit to his trust sixty pounds, to be delivered to such poor persons as are named particularly in a letter which will be brought to him written with mine own hand. I give to Doctor Christopher Shute Walton's Hebrew Bible. And I commit to the said Doctor Shute and to mine executor Mr John Prestwood all my other books and papers whatsoever, to be thus disposed of:—first I will that all my papers or paper books marked with this like sign of the Cross (✠) be cast unto the fire and consumed to ashes without suffering any part of them to be read; when this is done I will that the rest of my papers and paper books, and all my other books, be locked up in trunks or boxes and kept for that child of my brother Timothy Alsop's who shall become a minister. And if neither of his sons become ministers I will that they be given to Doctor Christopher Shute to do with them what he pleaseth, upon this condition that he keep to himself the printed books or sell them if he list. As for my papers and written books I will that he promise faithfully to my executor that he will have them all burned at his death. In this particular I expect and require that faithfulness of him after my death which I have found in him all my life time. I give to Mr John Prestwood, merchant, London, fifty pounds, whom I name and make my sole executor, desiring him to bury me cheaply and privately under a tomb stone with my name engraven on it. The remainder of mine estate I give to children born of poor and pious parents that they may be bound out apprentices, in which I desire that the children of Norton Fitzwarren in Somersetshire, if there be any poor ones, may be preferred before any other. Mico, 139.

[The following pedigree of this family, in Dugdale's Visitation of Derbyshire, 1662-3, is re-printed from the Genealogist, edited by Dr. Marshall, vol. 3, p. 63:

Anthoney Alsop=Jane, fil. Ric. Smith
of Alsop   of Coombebridge
in y^e Dale.   in Com. Staff.

John Alsop=Temperance, fil. Will. Gilbert
of Makhauer in Com. Derby.

Anthony Alsop=Ellianor, fil. S^r Jo. Gell
of Hopton.

John Alsop=Katharin, fil. Cope
of ffens Bentley.

Arms. Sable three doves volant argent, beaks and legs gules. *Crest,* A dove close argent, beak and legs gules.

Joseph Alsopp, aged 14, and Thos. Alsopp, aged 20, embarked for New England in the spring of 1635, in the Elizabeth and Ann, Roger Cooper master (REGISTER, vol. xiv. pp. 309 and 314). Mr. Savage supposes them to be brothers (See his Gen. Dict., vol. i. p. 46; vol. ii. p. 528). Joseph settled at New Haven and Thomas at Stratford, Ct. There was also a Timothy Alsop, mariner, at New Haven, 1646. Charles J. Hoadly, A.M., of Hartford, Ct., to whom a copy of the above wills was sent, writes me, "We may probably assume that Elizabeth Rossiter was wife of Bray (or Bryan) Rossiter of Windsor and Guilford."—EDITOR.]

WILLIAM FAIREWETHER, 3 July 1653, proved 2 February 1654. To be buried near my mother and my wife Charitie. "Whereas my wife hath divers times freely declared her minde and earnestlie desired and advised me to preferr my children sayinge shee would haue nothing but desired my children might haue it. In consideraçon whereofe according to her desire I haue alreadie assured unto her use the rentes in Leedes wch I had with her." I give unto my daughter Elizabeth Northend and to her son John Northend, either of them, ten pounds. To my son Thomas five pounds and to his wife forty shillings. To my son William Fairewether my lease of Greenthwait als Granthwait within the parish of Sutton and the forest of Gawtrees late disforested, and all my estate and interest therein with the appurtenances; also my close in Wigginton Lordship &c. To Isabel Swainson my servant fifty shillings. To Marie Wannop ten shillings. To the servant of my son Thomas Howse thirty shillings. To the poor of the city twenty shillings. To the poor of the parish of Martins and Gregories ten pounds. To my son Thomas' daughter Elizabeth Fairewether if she be living at the time of my death ten pounds.

The residue to my son William Fairewether, all my houses Toff's Greene &c. and I make him sole executor.

Wit: Abrah: Askwith & Samuel Saire.   Aylett, 3.

MICHAEL JOBSON of Brantingham, in the co. of York, gentleman, 23 August 1651, pro: 18 November 1651. To be buried in the chancel of the parish church of Brantingham near to my uncle Jobson. To William Swift five pounds sixteen shillings which he is indebted to me. To my sister Swift sixteen shillings a year during her natural life.

Item I give to John Northend, the son of my cousin John Northend, ten pounds which his father oweth me when he shall accomplish the age of one and twenty years. To the poor of this parish ten shillings to be paid on St Thomas' Day before Christmas next, that is to say, to the poor of Brantingham six shillings eight pence and to the poor of Ellerker three shillings four pence. To my cousin Samuel Jobson five pounds to be paid him the three and twentieth day of August in the year of Our Lord 1652. To Richard Thorpe the younger five shillings. To my maid Isabel Aire at Martinmas five shillings more than her wages. To Jonathan and William Newmarch sons of William Newmarch ten pounds apiece when they come to the ages of one and twenty years. Lastly I make my cousin William Newmarch and Ann Jobson my wife sole executors &c.   Grey, 215.

[The wills of William Fairewether and Michael Jobson mention a family of Northend in Yorkshire. Sutton on the Forest and Wigginton are both parishes in the Wapentake of Bulmer, North Riding of co. York, the former 8½ miles N. by W. from York and the latter 5 miles N. from York. The celebrated Lawrence Sterne was vicar of Sutton, which was in the Forest of Galtrees or Gawtrees.

Brantingham is in the Hunsley–Beacon division of the Wapentake of Harthill, East Riding of Yorkshire. Rowley, from which came Ezekiel Northend of Massachusetts, is also in the Hunsley–Beacon division and 4 miles E. N. E. from South Cave, which last named parish is twenty seven miles S. E. from York. There is a chapelry of Ellesker 1¼ mile S. by West from South Cave.

It is fair to suppose then that the Northends mentioned in these two wills were of the same family as the New England emigrant. For an account of the latter's family see Gleanings from English Records, &c., by Emmerton and Waters, puplished by the Essex Institute (Salem, Mass., 1880), pp. 85–88.

HENRY F. WATERS.]

HENRY ISHAM of Henrico County, Virginia, 13 November 1678, proved 5 June 1680. To my half brother Joseph Ryall forty pounds in goods, within twelve months. To Richard Perrin his wife, John Wilkinson his wife, William Byrd his wife, each a gold ring of twelve shillings price. To my honored mother Mrs. Katherine Isham one third part of my personal estate, both in Virginia and England, after the legacies above are satisfied, and to my sister Mrs Anne Isham one third part &c. I give my plantation in Charles City County in Virginia, commonly known by the name of Doggams &c. &c. between my two sisters, Mrs Mary Randolph and Mrs Anne Isham. I bequeath to Mr William Randolph all the rest of my estate both in Virginia and England and appoint him full executor.

Wit: Ja: Tubb, John Wynn, Wilbert Daniel, Hugh Davis.   Bath, 81.

[The family of Isham, now baronets, is one of antiquity and distinction in Northamptonshire, England. Henry Isham, son of Gregory Isham, came to Virginia and became a merchant at Bermuda Hundred; married Katherine, widow of Joseph Royall, and died in Virginia about 1676, leaving issue: i. Henry, the testator, who died, unmarried, in Virginia, his will having been proved in Henrico county, February 1st, 1678–9, the witnesses thereto being also residents of Virginia; ii. Mary, married Colonel William Randolph, of "Turkey Island," the emigrant ancestor of the distinguished Virginia family of the name; iii. Anne, married, 1685, Colonel Francis Eppes, whose probable ancestor, William Eppes or Epes came to Virginia before 1619, and in that year killed Captain Slallinger in "a private quarrel." Mrs. Anne (Isham) Eppes was the ancestress of John Wayles Eppes, member of Congress from Virginia, 1803–11, and 1813–15; U. S. Senator, 1817–19; died near Richmond, Va., Sept., 1823, aged 50 yrs. His wife Maria, daughter of Thomas Jefferson, died April, 1804. In the records of Henrico Co., Va., there is a deed of date Sept. 20, 1678, from Samuel Turke of Gaud Church, Co. of Kent, England, clothier, administrator of Henry Richards, late of London, merchant, deceased, and of John Richards, deceased, "brother" of Henry Richards, conveying to Henry Isham, of London, merchant, in consideration of £140, paid, all goods, monies and tobacco debts in Virginia due to the said Richards, which were left by Samuel Swaan, London, merchant, deceased, in the custody of Henry Isham the elder, merchant, late of Virginia, deceased, father of the aforesaid Henry Isham. Witnesses: John Ruddes [elsewhere spelled Ruds, a shipmaster], John Tubb, Lewis Conner, William Eppes. There is also a similar deed of record dated Sept. 23, 1678. It may be assumed that Henry Isham was then about to leave London for Virginia.

May, 1717. There is of record a deed from Mary Randolph, widow, and Francis Epes and Anne, his wife, conveying to Joseph Royall, Jr., 74 acres in Bermuda Hundred, which was granted to Henry Isham in 1661.

Will of Mrs. Katherine Isham, dated October 10, 1686, proved at December term of Henrico County Court 1686. Bequeaths to grandson, William Randolph, £20 sterling; grandson Henry Randolph, Jr., grand-daughters Elizabeth and Mary Randolph £5 each; residue of money to two daughters Mary Randolph and Anne, wife of Colonel Francis Eppes of Henrico county, and two silver salt-cellars to each; to daughter Mary Randolph her wedding ring, a feather bed and other furniture, and her best silver tankard but one; to her grandson Joseph Royall one servant man and a small silver tankard, and to every child of her son Joseph Royall two silver spoons; to her son Joseph Royall her best silver tankard; to her grandson Richard Dennis a cow and two silver spoons; to her grandson Isham Eppes a negro man Dick; to grandson Francis Eppes her biggest silver tankard but one; to the child of her daughter Anne Epps, "went withall" her large silver porringer and her great silver cup; to her daughter Anne Eppes her seal ring, a pair of silver clasps and a silver bodkin; to grandson Richard Perrin, one feather bed and other furniture; to granddaughter Sarah Royall a heifer; to granddaughters Katherine Farrar, Mary, Sarah and Anne Perrin each two silver spoons; to daughter Sarah Wilkinson and Katherine Perrin wearing apparel; to her loving friend Mary Parker dowlas and sergs [goods for wearing apparel]; to grandson Maiden Maschall a heifer; to son Joseph Royall all of her land. To her executors son Joseph Royall and Francis Eppes her whole crop of corn except to buy gravestones for herself and her deceased husband.

Richard Perrin and John Wilkinson of the abstract were evidently husbands of the half sisters (daughters by the first marriage of his mother with Joseph Royall) of the testator. Hugh Davis, witness, was for some time clerk of Henrico county.

Rev. Henry Isham Longden, St. Michael and All Angels, Northampton, has been making investigations into the connection of the present Ishams of Northampton and the early Ishams of Virginia, with deductions of the present descendants in America of the latter.—R. A. Brock.]

Thomas Grendon of the parish of Westover, in the County of Charles City, Virginia, Gentleman, 23 February 1683–4, proved 4 April 1685. To my wife Mrs Sarah Grendon fifteen hundred pounds sterling out of my personal estate in Virginia; if that be wanting, then to be made up of money due to me in England; or eighty pounds per annum out of the yearly rent of my Real Estate in Furtherly als Fartherly, in the parish of Shenton in the County of Stafford and in Hidefield in the said County.

To William Byrd junior, son of William Byrd Senior, of Henrico County, in Virginia, Esq. To my godsou Nathaniel Simons, son of John Symons of London, upholsterer. To my Goddaughter Susannah Byrd, daughter of William Byrd. To Thomas and Nathaniel Simons sons of John Simons. To my cousin Thomas Jennings of London, merchant, son of Thomas Jennings, late of London, distiller, he paying my aunt, his mother, Mrs Hannah Archer, now wife of Capt. William Archer of Charles City, Virginia, ten pounds per annum. Leases granted, 2 March 1656, by William, Lord Viscount Stafford and Dame Mary his wife, Henry Earle, of Kingston, John Earle, of Thanett Island and the Hon. William Pierpoint Esq. to my late grandfather Thomas Grendon deceased. Friends Mr Robert Coo of London, goldsmith, Mr Thomas Gower of Edmington and Mr Abell Gower of Virginia, the Hon. William Byrd Esq. William Randolph of Henrico County, Virginia, Mr Arthur North and Mr John Harding of London. Wit: Henry Harman, Richard Williamson, John Roach (his sign) Abel Gower.   Cann, 44.

[Lieut. Col. Thomas Grendon was a legatee and probably a nephew of Edward Grendon or Grindon, who in 1623–24 was a member of the Virginia House of Burgesses, and who owned land across the river from Jamestown. He was a son of Thomas Grendon of London, merchant, a burgess for "Smyth's Mount the other side of the water, and Hog Island" in 1632–33, and died at sea in 1684–5. It is a coincidence that the Grendons, father and son, should have married widows respectively of a father and son; Thomas Grendon, the elder, marrying Elizabeth, widow of Thomas Stegge, Senr. of London, and Thomas Grendon, Jr. of Virginia, Sarah, the widow of Capt. or Col. Thomas Stegge, Jr. The Virginia Land Registry has of record an assignment from Captain Wm. Brocas, Thomas Harwood and Christopher East, Chirurgeon of the Gleabe of London, Attorneys for Thomas Grendon of London, merchant, of land sold unto Captain John Browning, lying in Mound's Bay, Va., and held by John Warham, for 3,000 pounds of tobacco, dated April 8, 1638. (Book No. 1, p. 630.)

Will of Thomas Stegge, Sr., dated October 6, 1651, proved July 14, 1652, left estate to his wife Elizabeth and daughter Grace, wife of John Byrd, goldsmith, of London, parents of William Byrd of Virginia, and son Thomas Stegge, Jr.

Will of Thomas Stegge, Jr., dated March 31, 1669–70, proved May 1, 1671, mentioned wife Sarah; mother Elizabeth, then the wife of Thomas Grendon, citizen of London. Lieut. Col. Thomas Grendon went to England in 1676, leaving power of attorney to his wife Sarah, William Byrd and William Randolph. Mrs. Grendon appears to have been a woman of spirit.

In an "Act of Indemnitie and Pardon" passed the House of Burgesses at the February term, 1676–7, among the exceptions to its clemency were "Sarah Grendon, the wife (and now the Attorney of Thomas Grendon) and Edward Phelps who were great encouragers and assistors in the late horrid rebellion, shall have no other benefitt of this present act, but are and shalbe lyable to suffer and pay such paines, penalties and forfeitures not extending to life as by the next grand assembly, or upon a legall tryall before the right honourable the governor and council shalbe thought fitt and convenient."

ii. *Hening's Statute at Large,* p. 371. She married thirdly Edward Braine or Brayne of Charles City county, Va., whose will is dated August 26, 1691; proved September, 1709. Bequeaths to his kinswoman, Elizabeth Johnson, eldest daughter of Frederick Johnson of London, mariner, his plantation in Charles City county, and if she die without issue, to her sister Mary, and in case of her death without issue to her sister Sarah; to Elizabeth Johnson three negroes and other personal property; £12 sterling to buy twelve gold rings to be given to Captain William Byrd, Captain William Randolph, Captain William Perry, Captain John Rudds, to brother James Braine and his wife, to brother Frederick Johnson and his wife, to Mr. John Guy, to Mrs. Hannah Archer, to Mr. William Sutton, to Henry Harman; gold rings of 18 shillings value each to Captain Daniel Llewellyn, Stephen Hudson, Thomas Hughes, Mr. Bannister; gives Jack Kent (doubtless an indentured servant) his freedom after the death of the testator's wife. Gives Henry Harman certain personal property. Gives all the balance of his goods and chattels, plate, rings, jewels, etc., to wife Sarah.

There is of record in Henrico county court, February 10, 1680–1, deposition of Henry Harman, "aged about 33," that he "was living at Mr. Thomas Grendon's in 1676."

Abel Gower was a Justice of the Peace for Henrico county 1677–1685, and High Sheriff in 1681. In 1679 he was listed with "7 tithables" for taxation.

June 1, 1689, will of Abel Gower proved, dated December 25, 1688. Gives wife Jane his plantation for life and then to daughter Tabitha, and if she die without issue to Priscilla and Obedience Branch; his personal property to be divided between his wife and daughters.

March, 1710–11. Petition of Richard Dennis and Mary his wife, heirs at law of Abel Gower, dec'd.

Deed, dated December, 1696, from Jane Gower for a tract of land given her by her father-in-law Christopher Branch of "Kingsland," conveys to John Cocke and Obedience his wife, who was Obedience Branch, daughter of John Branch, dec'd, who was the son of Jane Gower.

October 20, 1700, License granted Robert Grigg to marry Tabitha, orphan of Abel Gower.—R. A. BROCK.]

JOB TOOKIE the elder of Mortlake in the County of Surrey, clerk, 14 October 1637, pro: 21 May 1638. I give to the poorer sort of inhabitants in St Ives in Huntingtonshire forty shillings. To the free school in Uppingham twenty shillings to buy Scapula his Lexicon. To my daughter Rebecca Tookie, being my first born, one hundred pounds, to my daughter Frances Tookie four score pounds, to my daughter Bridget Tookie four score pounds, to my daughter Elizabeth Tookie four score pounds, to my daughter Sara Tookie four score pounds. Item, my will is that all the aforesaid recited legacies bequeathed shall be paid unto the aforesaid legatees out of the profits of my moietie of the office of Registership for the city as they shall arise, which I give and bequeath to my son Job Tookie, with all my right, title and interest unto the same. To my daughters Elizabeth and Sara seven pounds apiece towards their education and bringing up yearly to bo paid at the four usual feasts, that is to say, at the feast of the Annunciation of the Virgin Mary, at the feast of St John Baptist, at the feast of St Michael the Archangel and at the feast of St Thomas the Apostle, until they shall come to the age of one and twenty or the day of their marriage, which comes first, and no longer. To my son Thomas fifty pounds, to be paid unto him within six months after he shall have served his apprenticeship. To my daughter Rebecca one feather-bed. To my son Job twenty pounds, my library of books and my chest of viols and my box of Recorders in the hands of my nephew Thomas Tookie, merchant of London. The rest of my goods &c. in the house, unbequeathed, shall be equally divided amongst my four younger daughters, viz: Frances, Bridget, Elizabeth and Sarah. After the former recited legacies arising out from the office aforesaid shall be paid, then the yearly profits arising out of the said office shall be equally divided amongst my sons and daughters, viz: Job, Thomas, Rebecca, Mary, Frances, Bridget, Elizabeth and Sarah. The residue &c. I give and bequeath to my son Job Tookie, whom I ordain and make the executor of this my last will and testament.

Wit: Rich. Lee, Anna Hassard, Elizabeth Bacon.   Lee, 57.

[I presume that the testator was the minister of St. Ives in Huntingdonshire, whom Palmer in his Nonconformist's Memorial, vol. 3, p. 20 (ed. 1802), states was "turned out of his living for not reading the Book of Sports." If so he was the grandfather of Job Tookie of Marblehead, Mass., whose petition is printed below. See editorial note, REGISTER, vol. 38, p. 81. For a biography of Rev. Job Tookie of Yarmouth, England, son of the testator and father of Job of Marblehead, see the Nonconformist's Memorial, *ubi supra*.—EDITOR.]

At a County Court held the 27 June 1682

Richard Knott, plt:, agst: Job Tookey, deft:, in an action etc. acco: to atachm[t]: dated 24 March 168½: withdrawne. The writ was issued by Moses Mavericke Esq. per curiam for the town of Marblehead and directed to the constable of Marblehead. The return on the back of the writ was made by Elias Henly, constable of Marblehead, who declared that for want of security he had delivered the body of Job Tookie to Benjamin Felton, Goale keeper of Salem. It seems that an agreement had been made between Knott and Tookey (the latter then of Boston) 21 February 1681, under which thè defendant was bound to go in the service of the said Knott on a fishing account for seven months, in consideration of which time and service was to be paid the sum of forty shillings per month in fish as money and was to be found in meat, drink, washing and other necessaries for a fishing voyage, as lines, hooks, lead &c. And the said Knot agreed to pay Samuel Mattockes of Boston the sum of thirty-seven shillings and Mr. Wintworth of Great Island in Pascataqua river seven pounds per order and agreement with said Tookey.

From the evidence of Nicholas Pickett it would appear that when Tookie and he took some ballast aboard Dr. Knott's Ketch the hatches being open "Tookie" ran to a hogshead of rum that stood in the Hold and tooke out the bounge, took the steme of an Indian tobaco pipe which was like a read and drank out of the bounge of the Hogg[h] soe terrible that in a short tyme hee was uncapeable for to doe any bisines.

June the 23th: 82   Doctor Knott came to Goodm̄: Feltons house for a Coppy of y[e] Attachment I hearing his Tongue (may it please y[e] honored Court) callid unto him & desired him to send me my shirt & Drawers Whereupon he came to Goodm̄: ffeltons back Door rayling and reuiling at me most sadly calling of Rogue and Sirrah telling of me he had better at home to wipe his shoes then euer my father was for he said he was an Anny-baptisticall Quakeing Rogue that for his maintainence went up & down England to delude soules for y[e] Diuell w[ch] is no small Greife to me, to Thinke that he has not Onilye abused me in keeping of me in clos Prison almost this fourteen weekes but abuse him whom he neuer knew but was well knowne to be a religuous Godly man by seuerall good Godly people here in New England; likewise his Library w[ch] I brought ouer to This Country Proues him (may it please y[e] honour[d] Court) not to be neither Quaker nor Anny baptist. W[ch] y[e] Reuerend M[r] Allen & M[r] Madder of Boston & y[e] Worshipf M[r] Danford of Cambridge are Sensible of besides a great many Scollers of Cambridge w[ch] bought seuerall of y[e] Bookes pertaining to my fathers Library.

May it please The Honour[d] Court

I beseech you[r] honou[rs] To take this sad miserable and deplorable Condition I am now in; into your honours considerations: in considering in the first place of my Education & bringing up w[ch] was to learning (my great grand father was a Doctor of Divinitye in London in Queen Elizabeths Tyme & Deceased there; my Grandfather was Minester of S[t] Iues (well known by y[e] honoured Gouern[r] Broadstreet as his honour told me himselfe) And likewise by Major Pembleton of Winter hauen* now Deceased) My father (may it please y[e] honoured Court) and M[r] William Bridge Preached Twelve yeares together in y[e] new Church of Great Yarmouth I being his

---

* Evidently Major Bryan Pendleton of Winter Harbor.—EDITOR.

Eldest son he did Intend I should have been a minister And in my Thirteenth yeare of Age sent me to Emanuel Collidge in Cambridge it being y⁰ same Colledge he himselfe was brought up in : But y⁰ prouidence of God ordered it so The Tymes altering; I had been there but a fortnight before my father sent for me home and asked me if I was willing to goe to London to be an Apprentice; My answer was That I was willing to Submitt to his pleasure whereupon he sent me to London & I was Bound an Apprentice to a Whole Sale Grocer in Cheapside; But I had nott been an Apprentice much aboue a yeare before y⁰ Chiefest part of y⁰ Citty was Burnt; my Master sustaining therby so great a Losse as he did by reason his Owne house he liued in & all his Goods and likewise seuerall other houses he had rented out in y⁰ Citty Broke; and was not able to sett up his Trade againe; Wherupon I being uery young desired my father if he pleased That he would giue his Consent that I might goe to Sea; Which request of myne (may it please y⁰ honourᵈ Court) he Consented unto; And bound me an Apprentice for Three yeares to Capt Samˡˡ Scarlett of Boston to serue to y⁰ Sea; Which Tyme I truly served as is well knowne by seueral of Boston; Now y⁰ Debt (may it please y⁰ honoured Court) wᶜʰ Doctor Knott sayes he has Engaged to pay in my behalfe I did not owe it through any Extrauegance but Through y⁰ Prouidence of God having been taken twice and cast away Once since I came out of England; And now lately I accidentally cutt all y⁰ Sinews of my right hand; through wᶜʰ means I was forced to lye lame upwards of six months not being able to use one of my fingers in six months Tyme; That what y⁰ Doctor had for y⁰ Cure of my hand y⁰ Charges I was att for Washing Lodging & Diet it being in so deere a place as it was in Piscataqua River besides the Losse of my Tyme; brought me thus behinde hand; And Therfore I humbly desire youʳ honours to Commiserate my pour & Distressed Condition I am now in; being a Stranger to youʳ honours and likewise to this Towne hauing layn here almost fourteen Weekes in Close prison ; The Lord knowing that there is no one knowes what here I haue suffered since I came in here hauing not now halfe y⁰ strength I had when I came first in here; The Lord knows when I shall recouer my strength againe (but my trust I hope is still in him) besides y⁰ Losse of my most pretious Tyme wᶜʰ can neuer be recalled againe In wᶜʰ Tyme (may it please y⁰ honoured Court) I might haue paid Mʳ Wentworth of Piscataqua his Debt but haue maliciousley been Debarred from it; & kept here by a Writched malicious man falsely wᶜʰ I question not but your Honours plainlye sees it.

Your honours Poor and humble Declarant and Petionʳ Who prayes for yoʳ honourˢ health happinesse and Prosperitye in this Lyfe and in y⁰ World to come lyfe Euerlasting

So prays Your honours humble Petitioner & Seruant

Essex Co. Court Papers, vol. 37, page 150.　　Joʙ Tookɪꜰ

Eᴅᴡᴀʀᴅ Bᴇᴛᴛʀɪꜱ of Oxford, chirurgeon, 29 April 36ᵗʰ year of Charles II. (1684), proved 12 February 1684. To my wife Anne all my two thousand acres of land, and all other lands and tenements whatsoever within the Province of Pennsylvania, or elsewhere, till my daughter Anna shall attain her age of one and twenty years. To my wife the use of my silver tankard and my three silver spoons. Reference to an Indentnre of Lease and Release with Henry Adams of Harwell in the County of Berks, yeoman, and John Adams of Kingston Leisley in the County of Berks, yeoman,—a messuage &c in the parish of Sᵗ. Peter in the Bayly in the City of Oxford. My wife to be executrix.　　Cann, 15.

WILLI'M PENNE of Myntie in the County of Gloucester, Yeoman; 1 May 1590, proved 21 April 1592. My body to be buried within the parish church, chancel or churchyard of Minty where my friends shall think meet. To the poor of said parish twenty shillings.

Item I give and bequeath unto Giles, William, Mary, Sara and Susanna Penn, being the children of my late son William Penn, deceased, twenty pounds apiece, at age of twenty one or day of marriage each. To Margaret Penn, widow, late wife to William Penn my son deceased, ten pounds, to be paid yearly during her natural life, at the Feast of the Annunciation of the Virgin Mary and St. Michael the Archangel, by equal portions, if she shall and do so long keep herself sole and chaste and unmarried. The said Margaret Penn, my daughter in law, and my overseers shall have the whole charge, rule and government of my heir and of all the rest of the children which were the sons and daughters of William Penn, my son deceased, and of all such lands and tenements and hereditaments and of all such goods and chattels as I shall leave at my death till such time as my heir shall accomplish and be of the full age of twenty one years. The rest of all my goods &c I give and bequeath to George ·Penn, being the eldest son of William Penn, my late son deceased, whom I do make my sole executor of this my last will and testament. The overseers to be Mr Robert George of Cirencester and Richard Lawrence of Withingeton in the County of Gloucester Gent, and Francis Bradshawe of Wokesey in the County of Wiltshire Gent.

I further give to Richard Bidle one cow and to his daughter Katherine Bidle one heifer of two years of age. Also I give to my daughter Ann Greene one heifer and to Elizabeth Greene one heifer, each of them to be two years old. I give to William Mallibrooke one yearling heifer. And likewise I lastly give to Alice Shermor my old white mare.

Wit: Francis Bradshewe gent, William Tailer and Richard Munden with others.   Harrington, 31.

Sir WILLIAM PENN of London, Knight, 20 January 1669, proved 6 October 1670 by William Penn. To be buried in the parish church of Redcliffe in the City of Bristol, near the body of my dear mother deceased as conveniently may be. And my will is that there shall be erected in the said church, as near unto the place where my body shall be buried as the same can be contrived, an handsome and decent tomb to remain as a monument, as well for my said mother as for myself, the charges thereof to be defrayed by my executor, hereafter named, out of my personal estate. To my dear wife Dame Margaret Penn, immediately after my decease, three hundred·pounds sterling, together with all my jewells, other than what I shall herein after particularly devise, and the use, during her life,'of one full moiety of all my plate and household stuff and. all such coaches and coach horses or coach mares and all such cows as I shall happen to leave. To my younger son Richard Penn four thousand pounds sterling, together with my fawcett dyamond ring and all my swords, guns & pistols; the said four thousand pounds to be paid him at his age of one & twenty and not sooner. And until he shall arrive at the said age my executor shall pay unto my said son Richard, out of my personal estate, the yearly sum of one hundred twenty pounds, for his support and maintenance, and no longer. To my dear granddaughter Margaret Lowther one hundred pounds sterling. I give unto my two nephews James Bradshaw and William Markeham, to each of them ten pounds sterling. Unto my two nephews John

Bradshaw and George Markeham, to each five pounds sterling. Unto my cousin William Penn, son of George Penn, late of the parish of Brayden in the County of Wilts, gentleman, deceased, ten pounds sterling. To my cousin Eleanor Keene the yearly sum of six pounds during her life. To my late servant William Bradshaw forty shillings, to buy him a ring. To my servant John Wrenn five pounds sterling. To the poor of the parish of Redcliffe twenty pounds sterling. To the poor of St Thomas, Bristol, twenty pounds sterling. To my eldest son William Penn my gold chain and medall, with the rest and residue of all and singular my plate, household stuff, goods, chattels & personal estate not herein before devised, as also the said goods and premisses devised to be used by my said dear wife, during her life, from and after the decease of my said wife. My son William to be sole executor, and I appoint him at my funeral to give mourning unto my said dear wife, my said son Richard, my daughter Margaret Lowther and my son in law Anthony Lowther, the husband of my said daughter, and unto Dr. Whistler and his wife &c. And although I cannot aprehend that any differences can fall out or happen between my said dear wife and my said son William, after my decease, in relation to any thing by me devised or limited by this my will, or in relation to any other matter or thing whatsoever, yet, in case any such difference should arise, I do hereby request and desire and, as in me lyeth, require, conjure and direct my said dear wife and my said son William, by all the obligations of duty, affection and respect which they have and ought to have to me and my memory, that all such differences, of what nature or kind soever they shall be, by the joynt consents and submission of my said dear wife and my said son William be at all times and from time to time referred to the arbitration & final judgment and determination of my worthy friend Sir William Coventry of the parish of St Martin in the Fields, in the County of Middlesex &c.

Wit: R. Langhorne, John Radford, William Markham.

On the margin of the leaf appears the following :—Quinto Aprilis 1671° Recepi Testum oŕile dńi Willimi Penn defti ē Reg^{ro} Curiæ Præogativæ Cantuaŕ ℔ ^{me} Wm PENN.

Testibus Caŕ Tuckyr Ri: Edes. Penn, 130.

I WILLIAM PENN Esq. so call^{e}d Chief Proprietary and Governor of the Province of Pensilvania and the Territories thereunto belonging being of sound mind and understanding for which I bless God doe make and declare this my last Will and Testament My eldest son being well provided for by a Settlement of his mothers and my fathers estate I give and dispose of the rest of my estate in manner following The Government of my Province of Pensilvania and Territories thereunto belonging and all powers relating thereunto I give and devise to the most Honorable the Earl of Oxford and Earle Mortimer and to Will Earle Poulet so call'd and their heires upon trust to dispose thereof to the Queen or any other person to the best advantage and profit they can to be applied in such manner as I shall herein after direct. I give and devise to my dear wife Hannah Penn and her ffather Thomas Callowhill and to my good ffriends Margaret Lowther my dear sister and to Gilbert Heathcote Physician Samuel Waldenfield John ffield Henry Goldney all living in England and to my ffriends Samuel Carpenter Richard Hill Isaac Norris Samuel Preston[1] and James Logan living in or near Pensilvania and their heirs all my Lands tenements and hereditaments whatever rents and other profitts scituate lying

and being in Pensilvania and the Territories thereunto belonging or elsewhere in America upon Trust that they shall sell and dispose of so much
thereof as shall be sufficient to pay all my just debts and from and after
payment thereof shall convey unto each of the three children of my son
William Penn Gulielma Maria Springett and William respectively and to
their respective heirs ten thousand acres of Land in some proper and
beneficial places to be let out by my Trustees aforesaid all the rest of my
lands and hereditaments whatsoever scituate lying and being in America I
will that my said Trustees shall convey to and amongst my children which
I have by my present Wife in such proportions and for such estates as my
said Wife shall think fit but before such conveiance shall be made to my
said children I will that my said Trustees shall convey to my daughter
Aubry whom I omitted to name before ten thousand acres of my said lands
in such places as my Trustees shall think fitt all my personall Estate in
Pensilvania and elsewhere and arreers of rent due there I giue to my said
dear Wife whom I make my sole executrix for the equall benefit of her and
her children.   In Testimony whereof I have set my hand and seale to this
my Will which I declare to be my last Will revoking all others formerly
made by me.   Wm Penn [l. s.]
      Signed sealed and published by the Testator William Penn in the pres-
ence of us who set our names as Witnesses thereof in the presence of
the said Testator after the interlineation of the words above viz (whom I make
my sole Executrix) Sarah West Susanna Reading Thos Pyle Rob^tt Lomax
Robt West.
      This Will I have made when ill of a ffeaver at London with a clear un-
derstanding of what I did then but because of some unworthy expressions
belying Gods goodness·to me as if I knew not what I did I do now that I
am recovered through Gods goodness hereby declare it is my last Will and
Testament at Ruscombe in Berkshire this 27 of ye 3^m called May 1712.
                                              Wm Penn [l. s.]
      Witnesses present Elizabeth Penn Thos Pyle Thomas Penn Elizabeth
Anderson Mary Chandler Jonah Dee Mary Dee.

      Postscript in my own hand as a farther Testimony of my Love to my
Dr Wife I of my own mind give unto her out of the rents in America viz:
Pensilvania &c three hundred pounds a year for her natural life and for
her care and charge over my children in their education of which she
knows my mind as also that I desire they may settle at least in great part
in America where I leave them so good an Interest to be for their Inheritance from generation to generation wch ye Lord preserve and prosper
Amen.   Wm Penn [l. s.]

[1 Mr. Richard Preston, who in the letters of his cotemporaries is styled the
"Great Quaker," immigrated to Maryland in 1650 with Margaret his wife and
Richard, *Samuel*, James, Margaret and Noamy his children, and was in the
same year appointed "commissioner of the North Side of Pautuxent." (Provincial Land Records, Liber A B & H, fol. 139–40.)—Wm. Francis Cregar of Annapolis, Md.]

3 Nov ^ris 1718°

Appeared personally Simon Clements of the Parish of St Margaret
Westminister in the County of Middl^x Esqr. and John Page of George
yard in the Parish of S^t. Edmund the King London Gent. and being severally sworn upon the holy Evangelists to depose the truth did depose and say
as followeth Viz^t: That they knew and were well acquainted with William
Penn late of Ruscombe in the County of Berks Esqr. deceased for many

years before his death and in that time have very often seen him write and subscribe his name to Writeings and thereby became well acquainted with his manner and character of handwriting and having now viewed and diligently perused the codicill wrote at the end of his Will or republication of his Will hereunto annexed beginning thus   Postcript in my own hand as a farther Testimony of my Love to my D^r. wife &c. and ending thus, where I leave them so good an Interest to be for their Inheritance from Generation to Generation wch ye Lord preserve and prosper Amen, and thus subscribed Wm Penn, do verily believe the same to be all wrote and subscribed by and with the proper hand of the said William Penn deceased.

S. Clement   John Page.

Die p^r d.—dicti Simon Clements et Johannes Page Jurat. de veritate p^{r}missorum coram me.   W. Phipps Sur.

Probatum fuit hujusmondi Testamentum apud London cum codicillo annexo coram venerabili viro Gulielmo Phipps Legum Doctore Surrogato Venerabilis ei egregii viri Johannis Bettesworth Legum etiam Doctoris curia prævogativa Cantuar. Magistri Custodis sive Commissarii legitime constituti Quarto die mensis Novembris Anno Domini Millesimo Septingenmo decimo octavo Per Affirmaconem sive Declaraconem solennem Hannæ Penn viduæ Relictæ dicti defuncti et Executricis unicæ in dicto Testam^{to} nominatæ cui commissa fuit Administratio omnium et singulorum bonorum jurium et creditorum dicti defuncti Declaracone prædicta in præsentia Dei Omnipotentis juxta actum Parliamenti in hac parte editum provisum de bene et fideliter administrando eadem per dictam Executricem prius factā etc.

Decimo sexto die mensis ffebruarii Anno Dñi 1726 em^t. commo Johanni Penn Arm^o filio et adstratori cum Testo annexo bonōr etc Hannæ Penn Viduæ deftæe sum vixit Relictæ extricis unicæ et Legatoriæ Residuariæ nominatæ in Testo dicti Gulielmi Penn deftī hēn ad adstrandum bona jura et credita dicti defti juxta tenorem et effectum Testi Ipsius defti per dictam Extricem modo etiam demortuam inadstrata de bene etc jurat.

Tenison, 221.

RICHARD PENN the younger son of Sir William Penn, late of Wansteed in the County of Essex, knight, deceased; 4 April 1673, proved 11 April 1673. To my dear mother Dame Margaret Penn forty pounds yearly during her natural life. To my dear sister Margaret Lowther, wife of Anthony Lowther Esq., fifty pounds to buy a ring or any other durable thing, to wear and keep in remembrance of me. To said brother Anthony Lowther thirty pounds (for the same purpose), also such two of my guns and one pair of pistols as my dear brother William Penn shall appoint. To the poor of Walthamstow in Essex, where I desire to be buried, ten pounds. To George Homond, my servant, ten pounds. My will is that my mother, my brother Anthony and sister Margaret Lowther aforesaid, and her children, my said servant George and the coachman and footmen of my said mother and brother and sister Lowther, and also their coaches shall have mourning in such manner as my dear mother shall appoint. Also I do give unto my loving sister Gulielma Maria Penn the sum of fifty pounds in testimony of my love and affection unto her. And I do hereby constitute and appoint my said dear mother the sole executrix of this my last Will and Testament.

Wit: Richard Newman, George Haman, Michaell Lee.

Pye, 49.

Mense Martii 1681.

Decimo tertio die Em^t. Commissio Gulielmo Penne Armigero filio naturali et legitimo Margaretæ Penne nuρ de Waltham Stow in Com. Essex vid. defunctæ heñtis &c Ad Administrandum bona jura et cred. dictæ defunctæ de bene &c vigori Commissionis jurat.

Admon. Act Book (1682) fol. 31.   P. C. C.

HANNA PENN, widow, the Relict of William Penn late of Ruscombe in the County of Berks Esqr.; 11 September 1718.   Refers to husband's will, bearing date 27 May 1712, and to the Trust created under said will as to the disposal of all his lands, tenements and hereditaments whatsoever, rents and other profits, situate, lying and being in Pennsylvania &c., legacies to his daughter Aubrey aud to the three children of his son William and to their respective heirs, and the conveyance of all the rest of his said lands and hereditaments in America to and amongst his children by the now testatrix, his second wife &c.

All the said lands, tenements and hereditaments and personal estate shall be divided into six (as near as may be) equal parts and portions, whereof I give and bequeath unto my eldest son John Penn and his heirs three sixth parts or one full half, upon condition, and always subjecting the same to that purpose, that he shall pay to his sister Margaret the sum of two thousand pounds &c at her day of marriage or attaining the age of twenty one years, which shall first happen; and the remaining half or three sixth parts thereof I give and bequeath unto my three other sons, Thomas, Richard and Dennis Penn respectively and to their respective heirs, each one sixth part of the whole divided as aforesaid.   And if either of my said children die before attaining to the age of twenty one years the part and portion of such child or children so deceasing shall be equally divided among the survivors.

Wit: Susanna Perrin, Mary Chandler, Hannah Hoskin, Thomas Grove, S: Clement.

On the 16th day of February 1726 there issued forth a commission to John Penn Esq., natural and lawful son and principal legatee named in the Will of Hanna Penn late of the Parish of St. Botolph Aldersgate, London, widow deceased &c to administer the goods &c according to the tenor of the will.   Farrant, 49.

JOHN PENN of Hitcham in the County of Buckingham Esquire; 24 October 1746, proved 13 November 1746.   Personal estate in England to William Vigor of London merchant, Joseph Freame, citizen and banker of London, and Lascelles Metcalfe of Westminister Esq. as executors in trust &c. also all such moneys, goods and effects as shall belong to me in America which, before such time as my death shall be heard of in the City of Philadelphia, shall have been collected and received by any receivers, collectors or other agents there and shall have been actually sent or remitted to any part of Europe or shipped on board any ship or vessel for sending or remitting to any part of Europe or invested in goods, effects or bills of exchange in order to be sent or remitted to any part of Europe on my own account or jointly with my brothers, all the which matters last mentioned and the produce of the same I will shall be paid to my English executors and be considered as part of my English personal estate.   To the same executors all my messuages, land &c in and near to the City of Bristol and in or near to the County of Gloucester,—all to be applied to the payment of the necessary costs and charges in the execution of their trust, the payment of the few debts that I shall owe at my decease, the charges of my funeral and legacies &c.

An annuity to my sister Margaret Freame. One hundred pounds to my servant John Travers, for his faithful service. One hundred guineas to each of my English executors. Legacies to old servants Thomas Penn and Hannah Roberts; to Jane Aldridge wife of Henry Aldridge of White Waltham, Berks. Provision made for the education and maintenance of nephew John Penn. Mention of other nephews and nieces, viz. Hannah Penn, Richard Penn and Philadelphia Hannah Freame, and brother Thomas Penn. To nephew John Penn my share of the mannor of Per-kassie, my tract of Liberty land and my High Street Lot (which private and particular rights respectively I claim under some particular grant or deed made by my late father or under the Will of my late grandfather Thomas Callowhill). To brother Richard Penn all my properties &c in the Province of New Jersey in America (both in the Eastern and Western Divisions of that Province which I claim under the Will of my late father) and my said brother Richard to be executor for such parts of my personal estate as shall be due, owing or belonging unto me in any part of the said Province of New Jersey. My moiety half part of the ffee simple and inheritance of the Province of Pennsylvania and the three lower Counties of Newcastle Kent and Sussex upon Delaware in America &c. &c. to my brother Thomas Penn for life, with remainder &c. to his lawfully begotten sons, in order of seniority; then to brother Richard Penn, with remainder to his sons John and Richard, with remainder to the latter and his male issue, remainder to my niece Hannah Penn only daughter of said brother Richard, and to her male issue &c. &c. The next in the line of entail to be sister Margaret Freame and her issue and niece Philadelphia Hannah Freame &c. The next to be a nephew (of the half blood) William Penn of Cork in the Kingdom of Ireland Esq., then to Springett Penn his eldest son and his male issue, with remainder to Christiana Gulielma Penn, the only daughter of the said William Penn. The next in the line to be a grand nephew (of the half blood) Robert Edward Fell, the only son now living of Gulielma Maria Fell deceased; then a great niece Mary Margaretta Fell, eldest daughter of said Gulielma Maria, then another great niece Gulielma Maria Frances Fell the only other daughter living of the said Gulielma Maria Fell deceased, &c. &c.

Brother Thomas Penn to be the executor for the personal estate in the Prov. of Pennsylvania and the three lower Counties of Newcastle, Kent and Sussex upon Delaware.   Edmunds, 332.

THOMAS PENN of Stokehouse in the county of Bucks Esq. 18 Nov. 1771. Appoints wife Lady Juliana Penn and son in law William Baker of Bayford Bury, Herts, Esq. his executors for the personal estate, except in America. Refers to an Indenture tripartite bearing date on or about 15 August 1751 and made in consideration of his then intended marriage. Bequests to James Hamilton Esq. the Rev^d. Richard Peters and Richard Hockley Esq. all of the city of Philadelphia, of certain lands in Pennsylvania in trust &c. A bequest of twenty pounds per annum to Mr Duffield Williams of Swansea, Glamorgan, mentions sons John and Granville Penn, daughters Sophia and Juliana. Refers to a Family Agreement entered into between the Testator and his late brother on or about 8 May 1732, 31 January 1750 and 20 March 1750. Appoints his nephew Richard Penn, then Lieut.

Govr. of Pennsylvania and Richard Hockley Esq. executors for that Province &c. The will is dated 18 November 1771. Then follow codicils dated 11 July 1772, 18 July 1772, and 23 June 1774. In the first he speaks of having advanced his daughter Juliana in marriage. In the second he bequeaths twenty pounds a year to Mrs Harriot Gordon of Silver Street, Golden Square, and ten pounds a year to Grace Armagh and Mary Clarke. The will was proved 8 April 1775.

Alexander, 166.

[In 1871, James Coleman of London, published a valuable book compiled by him entitled a " Pedigree and Genealogical Notes from Wills, Registers and Deeds of the highly distinguished Family of Penn, of England and America," which should be consulted by the reader of these abstracts. It contains a tabular pedigree from William Penn of Minety, an abstract of whose will is given above to 1871. He was the great-great-grandfather of William^5 Penn the founder of Pennsylvania, through William,^{2} Giles^3 and Sir William^4 Penn. The volume contains the wills in full of William Penn of Minety and William Penn the founder; and abstracts of Penn wills proved at the Prerogative Court of Canterbury, from 1450 to 1700, besides extracts from parish registers and other interesting matter.

A friend writes : "You might call attention to a pamphlet printed in Philadelphia, in 1870, entitled, 'Articles, Wills and Deeds creating the Entail of Pennsylvania and the Three Lower Counties upon Delaware in the Penn Family.' Gilpin's Pedigree of the Penn Family and Keith's 'Provincial Councillors' give facts relating to the descendants of William Penn."—EDITOR.]

RICHARD WATSON of the Parish of St Margaret's, Westminister, in the County of Middlesex, gentleman, 18 April 1685, proved 16 January 1685. Brother in law Theodore Wilkins, of New Rosse, in the Kingdom of Ireland, gentleman, and Elizabeth, Katherine and Michael Wilkins, his children. I give & bequeath unto my late wife's son Robert Boodle, of Rapahanack River in Virginia, the sum of one hundred pounds &c.; but of the said hundred pounds he shall pay unto Mr. John Ward, of the parish St Andrew, Holbourne, in the County of Middlesex, taylor, all such money as is owing to him for a suit of clothes made for him before he went to Barbadoes. To Cicely Brandreth (my late wife's daughter) now the wife of William Brandreth, of the parish of St Margaret's, Westminister, taylor, &c. Mr Thomas Jones, of Westminister, apothecary. Mrs Elizabeth Plumpton, of Westminister, widow, Mrs Elizabeth Arnold, one of the daughters of the said Mrs Plumpton, Mrs Sarah Juxon, another daughter, and Alice Willey, niece of Mrs Plumpton, Ellen Poole, Mrs Plumpton's servant. My godson Hugh Greene, son of Mr Hugh Greene of Westminister, and his mother Elizabeth Greene. Corporal Robert Lloyd in Capt. Littleton's troop. Brune Clench, of St Martins in the Fields, gentleman and Mrs. Katherine Clench, his wife. William Webb, of Bell Yard, King St., Westminister. Madam Rosse. Mrs. Harrard, of King Street, sempstress. Messuages in Bexley, in County of Kent, Willing, East Wickham, Wooledge, Plumsted &c., given and bequeathed to me by the last will & testament of Sir Edward Brett, bearing date on or about 22 December 1682. Sir Edward Brett, Knight, late Sergeant Porter to his Majesty Charles II.

Administration, with the will annexed, granted 16 January 1808 [sic]* to George Hancock, of Basing hall Street, London, gentleman, as a person named by and on the part and behalf of John Smith Esq., limited so far only as concerns all the right, title and interest of him the said Richard Watson deceased in and to a certain capital messuage, mansion House and Farm, with the appertenances situate, lying and being in the parish of

* This entry is on the margin.—H. F. W.

Bexley, in the County of Kent, comprised in a certain term of one thousand years and assigned to the said Richard Watson by a certain Indenture bearing date 14 October 1673 &c.   Lloyd, 9.

WILLIAM FENNINGE of East Smithfield in the County of Middlesex, mariner, bound on a voyage to Virginia in the Abigall of London, 17 January 1620, proved 7 July 1623. To my wife Margaret Fenninge all my estate; but if she die before my return, then to Timothy Bugby, of Stratford-Bow, and Susanna his wife.   Swann, 70.

ROBERT SMITH, citizen and merchant tailor of London, 18 January 1622, proved 1 July 1623. My loving wife and her children, my daughter Mary Peate and her children, the children of my late daughter Judith Sowthacke, her daughter's children and the children of my former wives &c. My daughter Hannah, my only child unadvanced. My late religious, kind and loving wife Alice Smith, moved me to give unto her grand child Edward Parbury her daughter's son, fifty pounds at the age of one and twenty years. I do give to him the said sum of fifty pounds and fifty pounds more, to make up one hundred pounds &c. My said late wife Alice was charged by the last will and testament of her former husband, Mr Edward Peirson, to pay unto Joane Dixon, his daughter, ten pounds yearly. To my cousins Elizabeth Younge and Judith Beale, daughters of my late daughter Judith Sowthack, twenty pounds, to be equally divided between them. To Mary Ofielde forty shillings. To my daughter Susan Morse forty shillings. To my cousin John Sowthacke all my books of "Presidents," Statute Books and other books and papers whatsoever which shall be in the room now used for my office. To my loving father Mr William Palmer, for his pains as overseer, three pounds. To my daughter Hannah Smith and to the heirs of her body lawfully to be begotten, forever, all my lands, tenements, rents, revenues, shares, profits and all other my hereditaments whatsoever, with their appertenances, which I have, shall, may or of right or in conscience ought to have within the country or countries, lands, islands, places or territories called or known by the name of Virginia, in the parts beyond the seas &c. &c.; also in the Barmuthes or Sommer Islands &c., my wife to enjoy the rents and profits during her life. The residue to my wife Judith Smith and my daughter Hannah Smith, one third to my wife and two thirds to my daughter. My said wife to be the executrix. My father, Mr. William Palmer to be overseer; and I desire my daughter Mary Peate and her husband, my former wife's daughters and their husbands and the children and childrens' children of all my said daughters Judith Sowthack, Mary Peate, Mary Ofield and Susan Morse and my late wife's grand child Edward Parbury and all other friends &c. &c., that they will hold themselves contented &c. "I beseech god give them of the deaue of heaven and make them lively stones in the building of the churche of Christ and true members of that bodie whereof the heade is Jesus Christ the lord. I humblie and thankfullie confesse before my heavenly father as Jacobe my greate grandfather accordinge to promise confessed with my staffe came I ouer many Rivers (thoughe not Jordans) I had nothing when I came from my fathers howse my cupp was emptie and now God hath filled it and made it to overflowe he of his grace hath made me able and willinge to give and leave somethinge to others."

Letters of administration issued 24 February 1629 to James Clarke, natural and lawful brother, on the mother's side, of Hannah Smith, natural and lawful daughter of the said Robert Smith deceased &c., the widow and executrix having also deceased.   Swann, 75.

KEBBY (*ante*, page 406):

["Brother Henry Kebby" was of Dorchester, where he married Grizel ——, 8 October, 1657, of course a second wife, by whom he had Sheberiah, born 2 December, 1659; he died 10 August, 1661. Rachel Kebbey died 16 July, 1657. If she were the first wife, her place was soon filled. Henry Kebby's "daughter Susan Sellick" was wife of David Sellick of Boston, who died at Accomack in Virginia in 1654. There were also Kebbys of Boston, whose names are in the ninth Report of the Record Commissioners.—WM. S. APPLETON.]

KATHARINE OXENBRIDGE (*ante*, page 419).

[Peter E. Vose, Esq., of Dennysville, Me., writes to the editor calling attention to the statement, quoted from Ellis's History of the First Church of Boston, that Katherine Oxenbridge, whose will is printed on the page above referred to, was a daughter of Clement Throgmorton. "By my record," he writes, "Daniel Oxenbridge married Katherine Harby, daughter of Thomas Harby, Esq., and his wife Katherine Throgmorton, daughter of Clement Throgmorton, son of Sir George and his wife Katherine Vaux, daughter of Sir Nicholas Vaux and his wife the widow Elizabeth Parr, grandmother of Queen Katherine Parr, which last Christian name probably suggested the name of the daughters of the several succeeding generations." It will be noted that Daniel Oxenbridge mentions in his will his brother Sir Job Harby. His wife also names her brother Sir Job.

We find that Mr. Vose is correct. Mr. Ellis, in transcribing from Cooper's Sketch of the Oxenbridges, has omitted several words. The passage quoted by us should read, "Katherine the daughter of Thomas Harby by Katherine daughter of Clement Throgmorton."

The following account of the brothers and sisters of Rev. John Oxenbridge, children of Dr. Daniel, is given in Mr. Cooper's sketch, which is a reprint of a contribution by him to the twelfth volume of the Collections of the Sussex Archæological Society:

"The second son, *Daniel*, was alive at his father's death, but died before 2d Nov., 1643; he was probably the merchant at Leghorn who left a legacy of £1000 to the Parliament, on which an order was made 7th March, 1643–4, that the amount should be paid by the executor to Mr. Spurstoe, to be applied to the support of the garrison of Wembe, in Shropshire, and that a monument should be raised to his memory; and an ordinance was passed and carried to the Lords on August 7, 1644. The third son, *Clement*, resided at Wimbledon, Surrey; and in 1652 was a commissioner for relief upon articles of war. He was still living as a married man with children when his sister Mary made her will in 1686.

Of the four daughters, *Dorcas* became the wife of Edmund Hunt; *Mary*, who was baptized at Southern 16th August, 1602, married William Langhorne of London, and of Putney, merchant; and the other two married three husbands each, and men of celebrity: *Elizabeth's* first husband was Caleb Cockcroft, of London, merchant, buried at St. Stephen's, Coleman Street, 7th March, 1644–5; the second was ' Cromwell's dark Lanthorn,' Oliver St. John, Sol.-General to Charles I. and Chief Justice of the Common Pleas from 1648 to 1660, who died 31st Dec., 1673; after which his widow took for her third husband Sir Humphrey Sydenham of Chilworthy, near Ilminster, Somerset; she died there 1st March, 1679–80, and was buried at Combe, St. Nicholas; *Katharine* married first George Henley of London; secondly Mr. Phillips, by whom she had one daughter, Katherine, 'who married her stepfather's eldest son, the match being thereby made double.'* This is the lady,—the famed ORINDA,—' who among her sex has distinguished herself by her celebrated poems and letters; she was bred in the school at Hackney, and it must be owned was a woman of the times, and loved poetry better than presbytery '; and her third husband was the parliamentary general, Philip Skippon, whom she survived, and died 1678."

A pedigree of Harbie, signed by Katherine Oxenbridge's brother Job Harbie, will be found in the Visitation of London, 1634, Harleian Society's Publications, vol. 15, page 346.—EDITOR.]

* There is evidently some mistake in regard to the husbands of Katharine Oxenbridge. At the date of her father's will, 1641, she bore the name of Fowler, and all accounts state this to be the maiden name of the celebrated writer, Mrs. Katherine Phillips ("Orinda"), whose husband was James, son of Hector Phillips, and whose father was John Fowler, merchant of London.—See Meyrick's History of the County of Cardigan (1810), pages 101–3; Allibone's Dictionary of Authors, vol. II. p. 1378.—EDITOR.

THE ANCESTRY OF WASHINGTON.

No. III.

A

The following letter appeared in *The Nation* for Feb. 13, 1890:

TO THE EDITOR OF THE NATION:—

SIR: A few facts as to Ann Pope, the widow óf Walter Brodhurst and the second wife of John Washington, the Virginia immigrant, may interest some of your readers.

Her first husband, Walter Brodhurst, was in Virginia as early as 1650, and in 1653 represented Northumberland County in the Legislature. There is a deposition of his, dated August 30, 1655, in which he mentions that he was about thirty-six years of age, and it is known that he was the son of William Brodhurst of Lilleshall, Shropshire, England. Mr. Cralle of Northumberland County, Va., informs the writer that among the old records of that county there is a judgment dated July, 1656, in favor of Walter Brodhurst, and that the next reference to him is in a suit brought on September 30, 1659, by Anne Brodhurst, relict and administratrix of Walter Brodhurst.

In a note on p. 80 of the last (January) number of the *N.-England Historical and Genealogical Register* [*ante*, p. 415], the writer alluded to the baptism in Sept. 1659, of a young son of John Washington, and suggested that he was a child by the second wife—which is a mistake, as at this time she had not married Washington. When the widow Brodhurst became his wife, she had a son, Walter Brodhurst, who went to England and lived and died at his father's birthplace. By John Washington she had a son Lawrence (the ancestor of Gen. Washington), who was buried in 1697, at Bridges Creek, Westmoreland County, Virginia.   EDWARD D. NEILL.

St. Paul, Minnesota.

B

In the Archives of Maryland, vol. ii., edited by W. H. Browne, printed at Baltimore in 1884, we find on page 483 the following data:

In the Maryland House Journal under date of May 20, 1676, is the evidence of Capt. John Allen as to the murder of some Susquehanna Indians. He testified that about the 25th or 26th September (1675 of course), Major Truman commanded the Maryland forces in front of the Indian fort. There was a parley about damage done to Mr. Hanson and others, which these Indians attributed to the Senecas.

Then " came over Col. Washington, Col. Mason and Maj. Alderton, and they likewise taxed them with the murders done on their side," which these Indians also denied. On Monday, the witness " saw six Indians guarded with the Marylanders and Virginians, and the Major, with the Virginia officers sitting upon a tree some distance from them; and after some while they all rose and came towards the Indians and caused them to be bound again, and the Virginia officers would have knocked them on the head, in the place presently: and particularly *Colonel Washington* said, ' What should we keep them any longer? Let us knock them on the head; we shall get the Fort to-day !'

" But the deponent saith that the Major would not admit of it, but was over-swayed by the Virginia officers; and after further discourse the said Indians were carryed forth from the place where they were bound, and they knocked them on the head."

In the debates about punishing Maj. Truman it appeared in extenuation that the execution had " the unanimous consent of the Virginians and the general impetuosity of the whole field, as well Marylanders as Virginians, upon the sight of the Christians murdered at Mr. Hinson's, and them very Indians that were there killed being proved to be murderers both of them and several other Christians." Also that Truman's crime was "not maliciously perpetrated, or out of any design to prejudice the province, but merely out of ignorance, and to prevent a mutiny of the whole army, as well Virginians as Marylanders."

C

Charles P. Greenough, Esq., of Boston, has kindly allowed us to make an abstract of an original deed in his possession.

It is an indenture dated May 2, 1674, between JOHN SHOTTER of Midhurst, co. Sussex, mercer, with his two children John, jr., and Elizabeth, of the one part, and ROBERT WASHINGTON the younger, of Petworth, co. Sussex, currier, of the other part. For £140 Shotter sells Washington the messuage called the Haws (?) in Petworth, now occupied by one Robert Washington the elder, adjoining the beast-market on the west and South street on the south.

We know that Robert Washington of Sulgrave had a son Robert by his first wife, and that he also named a son by his second wife, Robert. Also that in 1676, Mrs. Elizabeth Mewce, sister of Rev. Lawrence Washington of Purleigh, speaks of her uncle, in her will, as then living. *Possibly* this (uncle of the half-blood) will be found to be the Petworth man.

D

In *The Nation* for January 23, 1890, a letter was printed, signed " C.," from which we make the following extracts :

"In connection with this matter, the Washington pedigree, Mr. Frederick D. Stone, the Librarian of the Historical Society of Pennsylvania, has called my attention to the following foot-note on p. 31, vol. i., of Lodge's recently published Life of Washington; it is as follows :

"The well-known account of the Baconian troubles, written by Mrs. Ann Cotton in 1676 (Force's Hist. Tracts, i.), is addressed 'to Mr. C. H., at Yardly, in Northamptonshire,' probably Yardly-Hastings, about eight miles from Northampton, and consequently very near Sulgrave Manor. At the beginning (p. 1) the writer refers to the commander of the Virginians in the first campaign against the Indians as 'one Col. Washington, him whom you have sometimes seen at your house.' This suggests very strongly that John Washington, the first Virginian of the name, was of Northamptonshire, and that he came from or lived in the neighborhood of Sulgrave Manor, and that he belonged to that family."

Here we have comtemporaneous evidence connecting George Washington's great-grandfather with Sulgrave, or at least its immediate vicinity, which, of course, strengthens Mr. Waters's pedigree.

In this pedigree he states the mother of the said John Washington to have been a Roades. It may be worth while mentioning that the records in London of the families of this name throughout England were examined and collected by Col. Chester in the year 1867, as he then informed me by letter. This collection must be still among his papers; if searched, it might throw some light upon the Washington ancestry, at least in its connection with the family of Roades.

This suggestion proves to be probably unfounded. A farther examination of the entire letter of Mrs. An. Cotton, shows that Mr. C. H. had probably lived in Virginia, and we presume that he met Col. Washington there.

This tract, as printed in Force's Collection, vol. 1, was published, "from the original manuscript, in the Richmond (Va.) Enquirer, of 12 Sept. 1804. The writer is Mrs. An. Cotton of Q. Creek. The abbreviation is presumably not for Ann or Anne. It is addressed to Mr. C. H. at Yardley in Northamptonshire. Besides the reference to Col. Washington, "him whom you have sometimes seen at your house," I find the following points.

P. 4, line 22, the people "settled their affections and expectations upon one Esqr. Bacon, newly come into the Countrey, one of the Counsell and *nearly related to your late wife's father-in-law.*"

P. 7, line 12. "The chiefe men that subscribed it at this meeting were Coll. Swan, Coll. Beale, Coll. Ballard, Esq. Bray (all foure of the Councell), Coll. Jordan, Coll. Smith of Purton, Coll. Scarsbrook, Coll. Miller, Coll. Lawrance, and Mr. Drommond, late Governour of Carolina, *all persons with whom you have been formerly acquainted.*"

P. 9. "Brought the Governour a shoare at Coll. Bacon's, where he was presented with Mr. Drumond, taken the day before in Cheekahonimy swomp, half famished, as himself related to my Husband."

P. 10. There was "an Assembly convein'd at the Greene Spring; where severall were condemned to be executed, prime actors in ye Rebellion; as Esqr. Bland, Coll. Cruse and some other hanged at Bacon's Trench; Capt. Yong at Cheekahominy; Mr. Hall, clarke of New-Kent Court; James Wilson (*once your servant*), and one Lieft-Collonell Page (one that my husband bought of Mr. Lee, *when he kep store at your howse*), all four executed at Coll. Read's over against Tindell's point; and Anthony Arnell (*the same that did live at your howse*), hanged in chains at West point, beside severall others executed on the other side James River."

There is also (p. 11) a letter, unsigned, "to his wife A. C. at Q. Creek" dated "from Towne, June 9, '76." He says "but the tother day that I did see N. B. [Nathaniel Bacon] in the condition of a Traitor, to be tried for his life."

In the next succeeding Tract in Force's volume,—a Narrative of these wars in 1675 and 1676,—p. 38, it is said that Bacon's followers were scattered "around, a third parcell (of about 30 or 40) was put into the house of Collonell Nath. Bacon's (a gentleman related to him deceased, but not of his principles) under the command of one Major Whaly, a stout, ignorant fellow."

In the tract preceding Mrs. Cotton's, in Force's volume, entitled "Bacon's Rebellion," we find a few items.

On p. 15 it says, "this young Nathaniel Bacon (not yet arrived to 30 years) had a nigh relation, namely Col. Nathaniel Bacon, of long standing in the Councill, a very rich, politick man, and childless, designing this Kinsman for his heir."

Also on page 25, it seems to say, that young Bacon lived at Jamestown, having "married a wealthy widow who kept a large house of publick entertainment, unto which resorted those of the best quality." I regret to say that Mrs. Cotton is not so easily placed. Mr. R. A. Brock writes from Richmond, Feb. 17th:

"I regret that I have no notes identifying Mrs. Ann Cotton.
There are partial abstracts in our State Library of the records of Henrico and of York Counties.
I find that in the former, at a Court held at Varian, Nov. 1, 1707, it was determined that the Court meet for settling a private dispute at the house of Charles Cotton in Charles City County.
In the latter, Oct. 27, 1660, will of "Elliam" [Ellen?] Wheeler, widow, bequests to her cousins Francis Hall and Mary Hall; to Elizabeth Hooper; to her grandchild Amy Harrison, daughter of Robert Harrison; to her son Nicholas Comins (including a gold seal ring); to John Cotton a gold seal ring.

I find the following grant of land:—John Cotton, 350 acres in Northampton County (formerly granted Oct. 8, 1656, to Nicholas Maddilow and assigned to John Cotton Jan. 28, 1662.—(Virginia Land Registry, Book No. 4, p. 570.)

So in regard to Yardley, we are not entirely sure. There are in Northamptonshire Yardley-Hastings and Yardley-Gobions, and either may be the one intended. The latter is a hamlet in the parish of Pottersbury about 6 miles east from Sulgrave. In 1831 it had 123 houses and 594 inhabitants; but two centuries ago it was of less importance, and was probably undistinguished from the main parish.

Yardley-Hastings is a parish 12 miles north-east from Yardley-Gobions, and 7 miles south-east of Northampton. In 1831 it had 193 houses and 1051 inhabitants. It is close to the border, at the point where Buckinghamshire and Bedfordshire meet, but is separated from Luton, co. Beds., by the whole width of that county.

Our hope now must be that the Northamptonshire antiquaries will endeavor to find out this Mr. C. H. of Yardley, and see if any Washington was resident in that neighborhood.

I do not find in the Visitations of Northamptonshire, for 1564 and 1619 (London, 1887), any family at either Yardley. On p. 185 mention is made of Edward Dorne of Yardley-Hastings. On p. 98 is the pedigree of the Harrisons of Gobion's Manor in the town of Northampton. The later generations in 1618 were

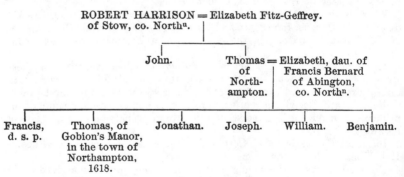

From Bridges' History of Northamptonshire I find that Gobion's manor was about 300 acres "without the east-gate of the city." It was long held by the Turpins, but 5 or 6 Queen Mary, Robert Harrison had it and his son *Robert* (?) succeeded. In 1621 Thomas Harrison sold it to the corporation of Northampton. Another branch of this family of Gobion also owned Yardley-Gobions, but in 1541 that manor was annexed to the honor of Grafton and has descended with that dukedom. It is possible that one of these Harrisons may have settled at either Yardley, after the sale of Gobion's manor.

I believe that the origin of the Virginia Harrisons is unknown. MEADE, i. 310, traces the family to Benjamin Harrison, born in 1645 in Southwark parish, Va., who died in 1712, and says that Mr. Grigsby thinks he may have been the son of Herman H. or of John Harrison governor in 1623. May it not be that the father was one of this Northampton family?

At all events Mr. C. H. of 1676 had been evidently a prominent man in Virginia, and some of the clues given by Mrs. Cotton may aid us in identifying him.

I have already noted that Amphilis seems to be a family name in the Neville family and its relations.

In the Visitation of Bedfordshire, article Faldo, p. 169, I note that Thomas Neville of Cotterstock, co. North[n] (son of William N. of Holt) had Jane married to John Chamberlain, and their daughter Amphilis m. 1, Richard Faldo (who d. 1576), and 2, Thomas Sheppard of Malden, co. Beds. She had a daughter Amphilis Sheppard.

In the Visitation of Northamptonshire I have noted but one instance, viz., on p. 130. Richard Ravenscroft of Maidford in the county, 1619, married Amphilis, dau. of Thomas Lawney of said place. The name is evidently an unusual one, and most probably given only for family reasons.

WILLIAM H. WHITMORE.

E

[Mr. Faithfull, clerk of the Merchant Taylors' Company, London, England, has sent us a copy of a privately printed pamphlet of 48 pages by Major W. Newsome, R. E., published in June, 1879, ten years ago last summer, entitled: "Yorkshire the home of the Washingtons." The author gives his reasons for believing that John and Lawrence Washington were from Yorkshire. Though Mr. Waters's researches lead to a different locality, the genealogical information contained in this pamphlet will be found interesting.—EDITOR.]

Sir EDWARD BRETT of Blendenhall in Bexley parish in the County of Kent Knight and Sergeant Porter to the King's Majesty, 22 December 1682 with codicil of 7 November 1683, proved 17 March 1683. I purchased of Edward Brewster deceased all that the capital messuage or mansion House as called Blendon Hall, situate and being in the parish of Bexley &c. (and other lands and tenements). To the children of Henry Fisher of Greeton, Northampton, gent., by Elizabeth his wife. To the heirs of Stephen Beckingham of Gray's Inn, London, Esq., and Richard Watson of St. Margaret's Westminster, gent. To the several children of my niece Anne Isham, the daughter of my sister Mary Isham, viz.: Richard Wathew, John Wathew, Henry Wathew, Alice Wathew and Sarah Wathew. To the two daughters of my nephew Henry Isham late of Virginia deceased, by Katherine his wife, two hundred pounds apiece, to be paid unto them within twelve months after my decease. To John, Nathaniel and Edward Fisher, sons of the said Henry Fisher. To Alice Grove, of London widow, and my god daughter Anne Grove. To my kinsman Owen Norton of Sherrington, Bucks, Esq. My kinsman Stephen Beckingham of Gray's Inn, Esq., and my kinsman Richard Watson. I give my carpentine cup to my cousin Charles Brett's widow. I give my old cup with the Brett's arms thereupon engraven, and tipt with silver, to my cousin Margaret Duncumbe widow. Reference to a former will bearing date 19 January 1681-2 in which was a bequest to my cousin Charles Brett Esq., lately deceased. My said cousin Mary Brett his widow. Hare, 27.

In the codicil, bequests are made to Robert Norton and others.

[This will of Sir Edward Brett should have accompanied the will of his kinsman, Richard Watson, published in the April number of these gleanings (ante, page 440). Whether the testator was related to the other Bretts whose wills are given in this number I cannot say. According to the late Rev. Frederick Brown, M.A., F.S.A., he belonged to the Brett family of White Staunton, an early pedigree of which family may be found in the Visitation of London, 1568 (Harleian Soc. Pub., i. 47). Robert Brett, citizen and merchant tailor of London, had four sons (see pedigree), of whom William, the second, was of Toddington, Beds., and father of the above testator. Edward Brett, born 1608, married Barbara, only daughter of Sir John Fleming, Kt., and was himself knighted by

Charles I., 31 Aug. 1644, after a gallant charge upon the Parliamentary forces at Lostwithiel, Cornwall, where he "received a shott in his left arm, and having brought his men off, retreated to be drest, when the King called him and took his sword which was drawn in his hand and knighted him on his horse's back."

"Sir Edward Brett died, s. p., aged 75, Feb. 12, 1682-3, and is buried in Bexley Church, Kent, where there is an elaborate monumental inscription recording his military services in behalf of King Charles, and afterwards in the Netherlands, under William, then Prince of Orange."

Henry Isham, whose will has also been given in the January number of the REGISTER (*ante*, page 428), was a kinsman, being the son of Henry Isham deceased, who Sir Edward calls "my nephew," by Katherine his wife.— HENRY F. WATERS.

The two daughters of Henry Isham, mentioned in this will, were Mary, wife of William Randolph of "Turkey Island," and Anne, wife of Francis Eppes. Brett Randolph, grandson of William and Mary (Isham) Randolph, and son of Richard and Jane (Bolling) Randolph, married (in Gloucestershire, England, where he lived and died), Mary Scott of London, and had issue.—R. A. BROCK of Richmond, Va.]

Codicil. I WILLIAM CLAIBORNE of Virginia at present in London, merchant &c., do declare that whereas I some time since made my last will and testament in Virginia aforesaid and appointed executors therein who reside there, I therefore confirm and ratify the same in all its parts and do hereby order, direct and appoint, by way of addition thereto, Mr John Hanbury of London, Merchant, to be my executor here in England in order for him to recover and get in my outstanding debts and effects, and after my decease to remit the same to the order of my other executors in the said will named. 16 May 1746.

This codicil was proved at London 17 July 1746.   Edmunds, 202.

[This William Claiborne was presumably the son of Lt. Col. Thomas Claiborne, b. Aug. 17, 1649; m. ―――― Dandridge; k. by Indians, Oct. 7, 1683, and grandson of Col. Wm. Claiborne, "the rebel."—R. A. BROCK.]

JOHN DODGE of Middlechinnock, 2 April 1635, proved 15 October 1635. To be buried in the church yard there. To the church ten shillings. The same to the poor of the parish. To the minister, for preaching funeral sermon, ten shillings. Wife Margery shall hold and enjoy one tenement in the parish of Halstocke, co. Dorset, containing by estimation ten acres more or less, during her life natural, if my sons Michael and William shall happen so long to live. To wife Margery forty pounds and the bed that I now lie in and the bedstead and all things belonging thereunto. I give and bequeath unto her so much of my other household stuff as shall amount to four pounds, of such kinds as she shall think most needful and useful for her.

Item I give and bequeath unto my son William forty pounds more over and above that portion which I have already given him. To my son Richard one sheep and to take his choice in my whole flock; and to John the son of the said Richard forty shillings. To Mary my daughter twenty shillings and to her son John forty shillings. And my will is that all these goods shall be delivered half a year after my decease.

Item, all the rest of my goods unmentioned I give and bequeath unto my son Michael whom I make and ordain the executor of this my last will and testament.

Witnesses Geo. Parsons, clerk, William Dodge, William Templeman.
Sadler, 101.

[William and Richard Dodge came over to Beverly. Each had a son William. There came a fourth William (son of Michael), who, to distinguish him from his uncle William, and his two cousins of the name, was called William Dodge of Coker, or sometimes Coker William Dodge. Chinnock and Coker are neighboring parishes in the extreme south or southeast part of Somersetshire. Halstock, Dorset, referred to in the will, is just over the line, south of these parishes.—H. F. WATERS.

William Dodge arrived in the "Lyons Whelpe" in 1629, made free in 1637. 16th, 5 mo. 1638 Richard Dodge had 10 acres granted in Salem. 26th, 9 mo. 1638 Richard and William had four score acres granted in Salem between them. Both were first at Salem, then in Beverly.

Richard's first son was John, b. 1631; det. by record of death. William's first son was John, b. 1636; det. by record of death. William Dodge, son of Michael, b. 1635; m. in Beverly, Elizabeth, dau. of Roger Haskell; had two sons and seven daughters, among them a Mighill and Margery.

Richard's will, dated 14th, 9 mo. 1670, pr. 4 mo. 1671, says, "And whereas I haue land in England let to my brother Michael Dodge for foure pound p' annum, I doe hereby acquitt my brother from all dues and demands concerninge the saide rent during my life, but after my decease I giue and bequathc to my wife and my son John the saide rent to be annually paid them during their said lifes according to the tenure of the lease."

In 1692, Capt. Jno. Dodge, Jr., of Beverly, deeds to his cousin William Dodge, 2d, yeoman, 10 acres because of his father William Dodge's [Farmer William, so called] promise so to do providing he should come out to this country.—IRA J. PATCH, of Salem, Mass.]

MARY SHEPPEY of the parish of St. Mary in the Strand, als Savoy, in the County of Midd., widow, 4 June 1624, proved 18 March 1624. To my friend John Brett, of the parish of St. Clement Danes, in the said County, citizen and Merchant Taylor of London, twenty pounds of currant English money, whom I make and ordain full and sole executor of this my last will and testament. I give unto the four children of my son Robert Chapman, late of Newcastle upon Tyne, twenty pounds, to be equally divided and paid unto them, or the survivors of them, at their several ages of twenty and one years or days of marriage, which shall first happen. I give to my daughter Martha Vaughan ten pounds. I give to my grandchild Mary Walford twenty shillings to make her a ring. I give to Mr Nicholas Paye twenty shillings to make him a ring. I give to Captain Thomas Brett twenty shillings to make him a ring. I give to my neighbors Mrs Joan Dannson, ten shillings, Mr Thomas Bratt, twenty shillings, Mrs Anne Pastolow, ten shillings, and Margery Tincombe, twenty shillings, to make each of them a ring. To my god daughter Mary Cunisbie twenty shillings to make her a ring. To my cousin Elizabeth Bacon, widow, ten pounds, to be paid unto her within six months next after my decease, and to Henry, George, Mary and William Bacon, her four children, each of them a piece of gold of the value of twenty and two shillings. To my neighbor Mrs Elisabeth Shaw ten shillings to make her a ring. To my cousin Mrs Clare Bucke twenty shillings to make her a ring. To Symon Gomond forty shillings, to be paid him at his full age of twenty and one years. Further my mind and will is that after my debts, funeral charges and bequests be paid, or so much deducted out of my estate as will pay them at their several times of limitation, that then all the remainder of my estate shall be divided into six just and equal parts, the which, being so divided, I give and bequeath unto the six children of my son in law Richard Waters, late of London, draper, deceased, as namely, I give one part of thereof unto George Waters, one other part unto Margaret Waters, one other part unto Elizabeth Waters the wife of my said executor, one other part unto Martha Waters, one other part unto Lettice Waters and the other part unto Rebecca Waters. And I do nominate and appoint my good friends and neighbors Thomas Bratte and Morris Shawe for over-

seers, and do give to the said Morris Shawe twenty shillings to make
him a ring.   Clarke, 34.

PERCIVAL BRETT of St. Martin's in the Fields, London, 7 May 1638,
proved 24 May 1638.   To the poor of the town and parish of Tenterden.
To the poor soldiers of the town and garrison of Portsmouth.   To my two
god children born and christened in the parish of Tenterden, named and
known by the names of Annis Winchester and Mary Nevill, as I remember.
To John Younge, the son of Dorothy Hodges, born at Coventry and brought
up at one Mr Younge's at the Red Cross in Queen's Street.   To my cousin
Robert Brett of Fayerfield in Kent.   To Richard Brett of Portsmouth.
To Percival Wivill of Portsmouth and to Thomas Wivill.   To my cousin
Beane's wife of Bidenden.   To my eldest brother John Brett, my brother
Thomas Brett and my youngest brother Richard Brett.   To my cousin
Anne Wivill, lately married.   My wife shall have all my lands &c. in the
County of Kent during her natural life.   There is given by bond to me by
my uncle Capt Thomas Brett fifteen hundred pounds to be paid to me after
his decease.   If he be living at the time of my decease I do quit, relinquish
and forgive the debt.   My said uncle to be executor.   Lee, 61.

THOMAS BRETT of St. Martin's in the Fields, Middlesex, 30 November
1638, proved 14 January 1638.   For the disposing of my worldly goods,
as I was never covetous in seeking them so I will leave them without much
curiosity amongst my poor kindred and some few friends.   To my loving
sister only now living one hundred pounds.   To John Brett the son of my
eldest brother John five pounds to buy a piece of plate, and to my loving
cousin his wife the like proportion, and to all their children twenty shillings apiece at ten years of age, and the two other former sons to the
parents to be paid within one year after my decease.   Having given by
deed unto my cousin Robert Wivill two hundred pounds, as well for his
own advancement in marriage as for the better enabling him to relieve his
poor brethren and sisters, I give to the other children of my sister Wivell,
viz. Elizabeth, Alice, Amye, Mary and Percival Wyvill, fifty pounds to be
equally divided amongst them.   To Thomas Wyvill, who hath served me
faithfully some years, two hundred pounds.   To the children of my sister
Nower, viz. John, Joseph, Thomas, Elizabeth and Daniel Nower, three
score pounds, to be equally divided &c.   To my cousin John Brett, dwelling at the Golden Ball in the Strand, five pounds and to my cousin his wife
forty shillings, and to every one of their children twenty shillings apiece at
fifteen years of age.   To the sister of John Brett now married to Symon
Porter three pounds, and ten shillings apiece to every one of her children.
To ten of the poorest and most impotent persons of the parish of Great
Charte in Kent, where I was born and baptized.   To my godson John
Brett, the son of Henry Brett of Great Charte, five pounds.   To my cousin
Robert Brett of Fairefield and his brother Richard Brett of Portsmouth
twenty pounds between them.   To my cousin Robert Brett who lodgeth
in my house forty shillings to buy him a ring.   The perverseness of Tho-
mas Goddyn hath been the true cause of the deferring the execution of my
brother Steven his will.   Refers to a portion due to Mrs Thornhill, being
the legacy of Sir Richard Smith.   Remainder to cousins Thomas and
Richard Brett, sons of my eldest brother John Brett and they two to be
executors.
Codicil 21 December 1638.   Cousin Steven Nower, left out in Will.
A legacy of twenty pounds to him.   Harvey, 10.

RICHARD BRETT of London, haberdasher, 18 September 1643, proved 12 May 1645. I have ventured the sum of five hundred pounds upon the propositions made by both houses of Parliament for the quelling and suppressing of the rebels in Ireland. To my cousins Mildred, Sarah and Mary the three daughters of my brother Thomas. To the eldest son of my brother Thomas. To my Aunt Nowell the wife of Daniel Nowell. To my cousin Pannell, sister of my brother John's wife. To my cousin Whitledge, brother to my brother John's wife living now in London. To my brother Thomas his wife's sister Mrs Wills. To my cousins Robert and Thomas Wivill and their wives. To the wives of my brothers John and Thomas Brett. To my uncle Celhurst [or Colhurst?] and his daughter, my cousin, Mrs Austen. Sundry people living in Tenterden mentioned. Brother John's three daughters. Brother Thomas his three children. Refers to will of uncle Capt. Thomas Brett. To my nephew John Brett, son of my eldest brother John. Rivers, 69.

THOMAS BRETT of Tenterden, Kent, gentleman, 13 November 1646, proved 4 January 1648. To wife Sarah the lease and term of years yet to come and unexpired which I now have of and in the messuage I now dwell in, with the lands thereunto belonging. My seal ring of gold and the great cypress chest now standing in the Hall to my son John Brett. To my servant and kinsman Thomas Brett and Mary his sister five pounds apiece.

Item I give and bequeath to my very loving brother Mr. John Brett, citizen and merchant taylor of London, the sum of ten pounds. And I do hereby make, constitute and ordain the said John Brett, my brother, executor of this my last will and testament. My friends Shemaial Selherst and Mr. Thomas Taylor and my loving brother, Thomas Wills, to be overseers. To all my children. My sister Finche, now wife of Mr. John Finch.

Fairfax, 15.

JOHN BRETT, citizen & merchant taylor of London, 3 July 1684, with memorandum made 9 November 1685, proved 13 January 1685. To my son Matthew Meriton and his wife, each twenty-five pounds within six months after my decease. To my son John Archer and his wife, each (a similar legacy). To my son John Dauling Esq. and his wife twenty-five pounds each, to be allowed out of the hundred pounds that he is indebted to me by a bond. To my son Matthew Meriton and his wife each ten pounds, to buy them mourning. The same to John Archer & his wife, and John Dauling & his wife. To my son John Brett's wife, as a legacy, twenty five pounds. To my servant Susannah Watts, to buy her mourning, four pounds, besides a legacy of ten pounds. To my sister Roulte and my sister Tayler, that was and my sister Marsh, and my sister Sherbrooke, each of them forty shillings. To the three daughters of my brother Thomas Brett Deceased forty shillings each. Unto William Stevens, John Powell, Francis Brand, Matthew Gibbons, each of them forty shillings. To Mr Loves and M^r. Claxton each five pounds. To the poor of the church ten pounds, to be distributed by the two teachers and the deacons to those that have most need. To my cousin Sick's wife and to my cousin Noble, each, forty shillings. To my cousin Bix, widow, forty shillings and also the five pounds that her husband was indebted to me. To my grandson Backwell and his wife and to his children that shall be living at the time of my decease, each of them ten pounds apiece, to be paid to my grandson Backwell for himself and all the rest six months after my decease. To my son John Archer's children ten pounds apiece, to be improved for them until their age of twenty one years. To my grandson Meriton ten pounds when he hath served his apprenticeship. To my grandson Sherbrooke the elder & his wife, and also to his children that shall be living at the time of my decease, ten pounds apiece, all to be paid to their father six months after my decease; and more to my grandson Sherbrooke and his wife ten pounds apiece, in six months &c.; and also the like in case he have any children by his wife: and more to my grandson Dalling when he attains the age of twenty one years, ten pounds, and to his two sisters, each of them ten pounds, to be paid six months after my decease. Unto the widow Browne twenty shillings.

I do give unto my son John Brett the moiety or half part of the lands & tenements and hereditaments lying & being in the Parish of Tenterden, Smalhood, Brencett and Warhorne, being known by the same names or the like, being in the County of Kent; which said lands are in the hands of Richard Marsh, during his wife's life, Kathern, who was the wife of my brother Percival Brett; but, in case my son John Brett have no son, then after his decease I do give the moiety of the aforesaid lands unto my said two daughters Sarah Archer and Elizabeth Dauling, and after their decease to their children.

Item, I do give unto my son John Brett my land that is settled upon me in New England, as appears by a Deed is expressed. As to the land at Eythorne Court, in Kent, the house in Grace Church Parish in which my son lives, known by the name of the Star &c., my will is that the same settlement that was made to my son, upon the marriage of his first wife, shall stand. To my brother Berman three pounds. Other legacies. My son Brett to be executor. Son John Archer and friend ———Blackborne to be overseers. To my sister Archer, in remembrance of my love, forty shillings.　　　　　　　　　　　　　　　　(Signed) JOHN BRET.

Wit: Thomas Browne, Gabriel Glover and Edward Southby.
　　　　　　　　　　　　　　　　　　　　　　　　　　　Lloyd, 1.

1612. "Aug. 9, William Hutchinson, of Alford, co. Lincoln, mercer, and Anne, daughter of Francis Marbury, Minister, by licence." (St. Mary Woolnoth Marriages, page 138.)

1565. Sep. 29, Susanna, wief of William Shorte, grocer, and daughter to Mr. Rogers, late burned in Smithfield. (Ibid. Burials, page 188.)

[The above entries were copied by Mr. Waters from the Registers of the United Parishes of St. Mary Woolnoth and St. Mary Woolchurch Haw, edited by J. M. S. Brooke, M.A. and A. W. C. Hallen, M.A., published in 1886. The first entry supplies the date and place of the marriage of William Hutchinson and Anne, daughter of Rev. Francis Marbury, which Col. Chester when he wrote his valuable account of the Hutchinson and Marbury families, printed in the REGISTER, vol. 20, pp. 355–67, did not find.

If Col. Chester had seen the second entry he might have been spared much labor in proving the family of the proto-martyr. This entry, taken with the pedigree found in the British Museum, constitutes proof positive.—EDITOR.]

WASHINGTON.

A

The will of Alban Wakeline of Henley-upon-Thames, Oxfordshire, Esq., 21 August 1602, proved 10 February 1602, mentions wife Amye, daughters

Phillis, Elizabeth, Mary and Priscilla, unmarried, Hugh Wakeline and his brother George, and his sisters, children of uncle John Wakeline. He appoints his wife executrix, and his friends Robert Washington of Stuttesbury, Esq., Alban Butler of Ashton in the Wales, gent., in the co. of Northampton, and Guy Foster of Hanslowe, in co. Buck., gent., overseers.

Among the witnesses was Lawrence Washington.

Admon. de bonis non was granted 30 April 1624 to Mary Bentley alias Washington, a daughter, &c. Boleyn, 9 (P. C. C.).

John (Bancroft) Bishop of Oxford in his will, 31 August 1639, proved 5 June 1641, enjoins that his body shall be buried in Cuddesdon chancel and desires his chaplains Mr. Fulham or Mr. Washington to preach in Cuddesdon church, and "to make such mention of me as may tend to God's glory." To nephew Kinsman and my niece his wife, cousin-german Elizabeth Isard, widow, and my two brothers, Christopher and Silvester Bancroft.

Evelyn, 80 (P. C. C.).

The following is extracted from a letter received from Mr. J. C. C. Smith:—

Mr. Cave Browne gives me this from Maidstone Register (about to be printed).

Married January 15, 1609–10, Mr. Arthur Beeszicke, gent., and Mistris Martha Washington, gentlewoman.

Laurentius Washington — Mense Januarii 1616. Decimo nono die emanavit Commissio Margarete Washington relče Laurentii Washington nuper de Wickamon in Com. Northampton def heñtis, etc.

The will of Abel Makepeace of Chipping Warden, Northampton, yeoman, was made 16 June 1601 and proved 14 October 1602. He mentions wife Mary, daughters Dorothy and Bridgett, unmarried, three daughters already married, viz. Lucy, Jane and Amye, son Lawrence, and good friends and "cosen" Symon Haynes, gent., Basil Trymnell, gent., Thomas Hollowaye, clerk, George Makepeace and Richard Blason;—also daughter Butler's two daughters. Northamptonshire Wills.

In my notes on the Ancestry of Washington, an abstract of the will of Symon Heynes of Turweston, Bucks., was given (REGISTER, vol. 43, p. 414, ante, p. 389), because in it he mentioned his kinsman Lawrence Washington, meaning, probably, the Register of Chancery. No explanation of that kinship was given. The following pedigree, taken from Harleian MS. 1533 (140 in pencil), shows the connection:

```
           SIMON HAYNES=......, who after married
             Dean of          Dr. May and lastly
        Exeter and Windsor.         Dr. Yale.
     _____|_____                    |
    |                 |                    |
Simon, of Turweston=Amye, dau. and one   Joseph Haynes=Jane, d. and h. of
als. Tarston, Bucks.|  of 3 coh. of        of Barking, | ......Yale of
                    |  Henry Marshall        Essex.    |    Wales.
                    |  of Com. Northᵗⁿ
                    |  and of Elizabeth,
                    |  Aunt to Sir Law-
                    |  rence Washington.
     _____|_____                           |
    |              |                            |
Margaret.       Joane.                      Elizabeth.
```

The will of Thomas Yale, Dr. of Laws (1577–1578), calls Jane wife of Joseph Haynes "niece," and mentions wife Joane. That of Joane Yale, his widow (1585–1587), mentions sons Simon and Joseph Heynes, or Haynes, and William Maye. So we are enabled to fill the blank in the above pedigree, so far as the baptismal name of the wife of the first Simon Heynes is concerned.   HENRY F. WATERS.

B

I might supplement Mr. Conway Robinson's remarks (*ante*, page 411) as to Lawrence Washington, Registrar of the High Court of Chancery, by stating that in 1583 he is styled of "Gray's Inn, co. Middlesex, gent.," during which year he purchased the Manor of Whitacre inferior, co. Warwick, selling it six years later to George Villiers, Esq., of Brokesby, co. Leic. Villiers's dau. Ann afterwards married Washington's grand-nephew. Towards the close of Elizabeth's reign he purchased the Jordan's Hall of Maidstone, Kent, and alienated it later to the Godwins.

From the Privy Council Register, 16 Jan. 1599, it appears that among the lawyers of Chancery, assessed for suppression of the Irish rebellion, was Lawrence Washington, 10 *l*. ster.; and in a Certificate about Privy Seals, co. Middlesex, 1610, among those not having paid are Lawrence Washington of Finchley, near London, and John Washington of Westdreate (Drayton-West).

In a list of monies raised 1626 on Privy Seals in co. Bucks, occurs name of Lawrence Washington ar. of Westbury, 10 *l*.

On a small black marble tomb-stone, on the north side of the east window of the chancel of All Saints, Maidstone, is the following inscription:

Mortalis Morte
Immortalis.

Here resteth the body of Lawrence Washington Esq; of the Family of the Washingtons, antientlie of Washington in the Countie Palatine of Durham: Register of the Highe Court of Chancery xxvii Yeares: He had two Wyvfs, Martha Daughter of Clement Newce of Hartfordshire Esq: and Mary Daughter of Sir Raynold Scott of this Countie Knight: By his First He had 5 Sons and 2 Daughters; Lawrence and Mary, The Eldest only lyving. Lawrence succeeded him in his Office, married Ann Daughter of William Lewyn Judge of the Prerogative Court. Mary married William Horsepoole of this Parish Gentle^m. His other Daughter Martha married to Arthur Beswick Gentle^m. Son of William Beswick of this County Esq.; He having lived A Vertuous & Xtian Life of singular Intiecrity in his place. Being of the age of LXXIII Yeares Died the xxi of December An°. D^ni. 1619. A Faithfull Believer in the Merritts & Mercies of his Saviour. To whose Memorie His Sonne hath erected this Monument.

Though after my Skinne
Worms destroy this Body,
Yet shall I see God in my Flesh.

Church at Garsden

Washington Tablet.

GENEALOGICAL GLEANINGS IN ENGLAND. 455

As is stated his daughter Mary married William Horspoole gent. of Buckland, parish of Maidstone, co. Kent; had children in 1619 : Symon, æ. 15; John, æ. 12; Lawrence, æ. 6; William, æ. 3; Mary; Martha; Elizabeth and Catharine. The other daughter Martha married Arthur, son and heir of Wm. Beswick of Spilmander, co. Kent and Sheriff of the County 1616; she died 1616, leaving daughter Mary.

Lawrence Washington (Jun.), born about 1579, purchased the Manor of Garsden, co. Wilts (3 miles from Malmesbury) of the Moody family. He obtained the grant in reversion of the Registrarship in the Co. of Chancery 16 Apr. 1604, and succeeded his father in that office towards the close of 1619; subsequently he was knighted. Berry, in his Genealogies of Kent, styles him "of Bolingford, co. Wilts." He married Ann, dau. of Wm. Lewyn (or Lovin), LL.D. of Ottringden (Otterden), co. Kent, made Master of Chancery about 1595 : Judge of the Prerog. Co. of Canterbury; Chancellor of Rochester, &c., who died in Ap. 1598, and was interred in St. Leonard in Shoreditch, co. Middlesex. Sir Lawrence died 1643, aged 64, & was buried in Garsden Church; when the church was restored about 1860 the mural monument which, surmounted by the family arms, had stood in the chancel, to left of the altar, was removed to the Rectory, and was exhibited in August, 1862, at the Malmesbury meeting of the Wiltshire Arch. Society. His widow Ann died Jan'y 13, 1645, and was interred in the same ground three days later.

The mansion at Garsden is handsome, old fashioned, built of stone, with walls five feet thick—its timbers chiefly of oak: the family arms carved over the mantel-pieces; and around the building a beautiful garden and orchard. He had children, among them Lawrence and Martha. The following extract, from Records of St. Dunstan's in the West,* London, evidently refers to others of his issue :

Lawrence, son of Lawrence Washington jr., buried 29 Dec. 1617.†

Anne, dau. of Lawrence & Anne Washington, bapt. 29 Aug. 1621.

Lawrence Washington, bapt. 30 Sept. 1622.

Lawrence Washington, Esq., of Garsden, co. Wilts (son of Sir Lawrence Washington, Knt.), was probably the child bapt. at St. Dunstan's in the West, London, 30 Sept. 1622. He was app'd by H. of Com., 7 Nov. 1650, as Sheriff of Co. Wilts, and Inigo Jones's Hist. of Stonehenge, 1655, mentions him as proprietor of that place. He married Eleanor, dau. of Wm. Guise, Esq., of Elmore, Sheriff of co. Glouc. in 1647. His will of 14 Jan. 1661-2 is on record. The widow married Sir Wm. Pargiter, Knt. of Gretworth, co. Northants, who died 11 Aug. 1678, aged 48, leaving dau. Eleanor. She was buried beside her first husband at Garsden, to which church, as Lady Pargiter, she presented a silver flagon, two chalices and a salver. Mr. Washington left an only dau. and heiress Elizabeth, who, in 1671, became the first wife of Sir Robert Shirley, Bart., afterwards Earl Ferrers, and died 2 Oct. 1693; the Earl died 25 Dec. 1717, aged 67, leaving issue.

Martha Washington, dau. of Sir Lawrence W., Knt., married in June, 1630, as his 2d wife, Sir John Tyrell, Knt., of Springfield and Heron, co. Essex, born 14 Dec. 1597, ancestor of the Baronets Tyrell. She died 17 Dec. 1670, and was buried at East Hornden; Sir John died 3 Apr. 1675. He had suffered severely for his loyalty, as is quaintly shown in the Latin inscription on his grave-stone in the south chapel of the church.—ISAAC J. GREENWOOD, *of New York city.*

It happens rather strangely, that on April 26, 1890, there was sold at Libbie's auction rooms in Boston, a deed of Lawrence Washington, the elder, and Lawrence W. the younger, of Maidstone, co. Kent. It was dated June 27, 1614, and related to land in Oxfordshire. The signatures were good, but the seals had disappeared.—EDITOR.

---

* Richard Washington, who had died in Fetter Lane, London, 1651, was buried in this church. He was a Fellow of Univ. Coll., Oxf., where he had taken his B.D. 1633, and was afterwards Provost of Trinity Coll., Dublin.

† This was probably the child baptized at Mottingham July 24, 1614 (*ante*, page 413).— EDITOR.

C

The natural interest which all Americans must feel in every detail of the family and connections of our great first President has been powerfully stimulated by the able paper of Mr. Henry F. Waters, in the October number of the REGISTER (*ante*, pp. 352–403), which has finally, let us hope, settled the vexed question of the origin of John and Lawrence Washington, the Emigrants of Virginia, and it now seems in order to adduce every scrap of evidence bearing on the descendants of John Washington of Whitfield, the founder of the line, for preservation for the use of the future writer of the Genealogy of the Family.

As is well known, Sir Lawrence Washington, Knt., the second Register of the High Court of Chancery of that name, and the nephew of Robert Washington of Sulgrave, the Ancestor of the Virginia line, acquired by purchase the estate of Garsdon in Wiltshire from the Moodys to whom it had been granted by King Henry VIII. as a reward to one William Moody, his footman, for saving his life on the occasion of an accident which befel him in the hunting field.* The family seem in fact, as will be shown, to have been in this neighborhood for upward of a hundred years (1570–1685) and perhaps still earlier than the former date.

In the year 1887 the writer spent some weeks in Malmesbury and vicinity engaged in genealogical researches, and twice visited the Church at Garsdon where the Rev. Dr. Gray, the Rector, afforded him every facility for the investigation of the monuments existing there.† The principal of these is the mural monument of Sir Lawrence Washington, Knt., the first owner of Garsdon Manor of the name, who died in 1643, and which was cited by Mr. Waters in his paper. This once splendid memorial of gilt and painted freestone, surmounted by an oval shield of the Arms of Washington and Lewyn and with an inscription cut on a black marble slab surrounded by a wreath, was taken down during the destructive "restoration" of the edifice in 1855 and has never been replaced. The marble slab was used as a barrow plank by the masons and broken in two, and the fragments of the whole lay neglected for years in a corner of the building until at length, in 1877, some enterprising disciple of Artemus Ward literally carried off the whole bodily with the intention of exhibiting it in America, and had actually reached Southampton with his plunder, when Dr. Gray, who had then just been inducted to the living, discovered the desecration, pursued him and compelled its return. The broken parts of the slab are now united and protected by a strong oaken frame, pending the proper restoration of the monument to its place on the chancel wall.‡

The other four are floor tombs in the Chancel covered with large inscribed slabs of black marble, without armorial bearings, but each has a similar pattern of an urn engraved beneath the inscription. The first three of these are very distinct, but the last is so heel worn that it was only with the greatest difficulty that the writer was able to clearly indentify the fragments given. All are now well protected by strips of husk matting.

To the | Memory of Sr | Laurence Washington | Kt lately chiefe Register of the | Chauncery of known Pyety of | Charitye exemplarye A louinge | Husband A tender Father A boun- | tifull Master A constant Relieuer of | the Poore and to those of this Parish A | perpetuall Benefactour Whom it pleased | God to take unto his Peace from the fury | of the insuing Warrs Oxon Maij 14ᵗᵒ Here | interred 24ᵗᵒ Ano. Dni. 1643° Ætat Suæ 64° | Where allso lyeth Dame Anne his wife who | deceased Junij 13ᵗᵒ and was buried 16ᵗᵒ Ano | Dni. 1645.

Hic Patrios cineres curauit filius Urna
Condere qui tumulo nunc jacet Ille pius.

* Aubrey's Collections for Wilts, p. 25.—Garesden.
† It is greatly to be regretted that the Parish Registers have perished previous to 1737, and that the fragmentary Bishop's Transcripts at Salisbury yield absolutely no entries of the name.
‡ The Arms in the shield, shown in the accompanying illustration, are as follows:—Quarterly, 1 & 4, argent, two bars and in chief three mullets gules (*Washington*) ; 2 & 3, —— ? a cross patonce between four cinquefoils or (—— ?) ; surcharged with a crescent or. Impaling per pale gules and azure three bucks' heads couped or (*Lewyn*).

The pious Son his Parents here inter'd
Who hath his shar⌣ in Urne for them prepar'd.

Here Lyeth ye Body of Lavrence | Washington Esqr the only Son | of Sr Lavrence Washington who | Departed this life Jan 17 was | Bvried Feb 11 Ano. Dni. 1661 and | Inclosed By Elinor his Wife | April 18 Ano. Dni. 1663 | Ætat Suæ 39.

En mercede virum Pensatum muner[a d*]igna
Prospicit ille suis diua supersta sibi

Behold how duty well perform'd is paide
His Sire he him here his deerst hath laide.

[*Sacrum Me†*]moriæ Annæ Filiae | Lavrentij Washington Eqvitis | Et vxoris Christopheri Gise | Hic Sepvltæ Jvnij 4to An: Do: | 1642 Ætat Svæ 20.

Here lyes ye body of Dame | Elienor Pargiter 2nd Daughter | of Wm. Guise of Elmore in ye | County of Gloucester Esqr | First married to Lawrence | Washington Esq. afterwards | to Sr Wm. Pargiter of Gritt | worth in ye County of North | Hampton Kt. Who departing | this life the 19th Day of July in | the Year of Our Lord 1685 | ordered her remains to be | deposited here in hopes of | a blessed Resurrection.‡

```
- - - - - - - -   - - - - |  - - - ce the Bod - - - of Lawrence | - - - - - - - & D - me
Jone  - - -  wife | - -  - - - r - e  - - - - ington | - - -  - - - - - -.
- - ha  - - - - ing  - - -  - -  - -  - -  - - - |
- - - - - e  You S - - a - - - -  - - - - - |
W - - -  Wan - - a -  - cil  - - - ilot - |
- - - - - - -  ma  - -  m  - - - -.                         §
```

Malmesbury Abbey Parish Registers.

Searched from 1590 to 1650.

1601. July—George Washington & Johann Hatt were maryed the 20th daye.
1625. May 2—George Washington buried.
1640. Buried the same daye (*i. e. April* 28)   (*blank*) servant to Sir Lawrence Washington of Garsden whose legg was taken off by Mr. Phillips, Chirugeion.

Will of Henrye Washington of Malmesburie, dated 2 Julij 1570; no Probate act or date of probate given; To be buried in parish Churchyard

---

* Obliterated.
† Covered by the corner of a pew.
‡ A splendid set of Communion Silver, which was presented to the Church by Lady Pargiter in 1684, is still preserved and in perfect condition. It consists of four pieces, engraved with the monogram I H S in a halo with emblems of the Crucifixion and with the following inscription:
    "This was given by the Lady Pargiter to Garsdon Church, shee was formally Wife to Lawrence Washington, Esq., who both lye buried here."
It is said that this plate owes its escape from the almost universal spoliation of the time of the Commonwealth to the superstition of the peasants of the neighborhood, who believed that a Demon, or other "unco'" being was confined in the box which contained it, and their fears being, fortunately, greater than their curiosity, it remained untouched and forgotten in a garret until the latter part of the last century, when it was restored to its former use.
§ Comparison with the Malmesbury Registers, hereafter cited, will enable us to construct this last mutilated inscription with certainty as follows. (*Beneath this Pla*)cc the Bod(*ies*) of Lawrence (*the son*) & D(*a*)me Jone (*the*) wife of (*Geo*)r(*g*)e (*Wash*)ington (*are buried.*) The same authority shows us that its period (there is no trace of a date on the slab) must be placed between 1601 and 1625, probably within a year or two of the former date, thus carrying back the connection of the Washingtons with Garsdon to the first decade of tho 17th century.

of St. Pouls of Malmesburie; To daughter Elyn Washington "my presse, a fether bede & a flocke bede & payer of fine sheyts & payer canvas shetes, a fine diaper metclothe, 2 coffers, 8 platters, 4 sawsers & 3 Candelstickes, the beste Chaffeyn dyshe, a latin Bassen, a Cistren & a Querne, mi beste Crocke, 2 Salt Sellers, my beste Couerlet & Bolster"; To cosin Alls Halle 2 Pottingers, a sawser & a candelsticke; Wiffe Agnis to be Residuary Legatee and Executrix; Supervisers Williā Shellard & Rauffee meale.

Consistory Court Sarum, Vol. I. fo. 32.

It seems to the writer highly probable that the above Henry and George Washington were the unnamed sons of Lawrence Washington, the Mayor of Northampton, younger brothers of Robert of Sulgrave and Lawrence (the father of Sir Lawrence of Garsdon) and therefore the uncles of the latter; their presence in the neighborhood (Garsdon is on the outskirts of Malmesbury and only about two miles distant) having no doubt caused their nephew to settle here. An examination of the Feet of Fines in the Public Record Office would perhaps give the exact date at which Garsdon was purchased from the Moodys, which is said to be 1640, but the last entry found in the Malmesbury Registers shows the Washingtons in full possession of the estate in the first month of that year, and it is likely that it was acquired earlier than has been supposed.

The Manor House of Garsdon, the former residence of the Washingtons, is not far from the Church on the Malmesbury road. The greater part of the mansion has perished, and what remains is now occupied as a farm house—it is the property of the Earl of Suffolk, whose residence, Charlton Park, is near Malmesbury. The Coat of Arms of the Washingtons which was above the door was " appropriated·" by a former tenant on his removal some 35 years since, and is now built into a farm house a few miles distant.

The Rector, Dr. Thomas S. Gray, is most anxious to restore the mural monument to its former condition and location, and is likewise planning the erection of a " Washington Memorial School" in the parish. It is greatly to be hoped that the interest excited by Mr. Waters's brilliant discovery may enable him to carry out this long cherished design, and our wealthy and patriotic Americans should be among the first to lend a helping hand to the good work.—J. HENRY LEA of Cedarhurst, Fairhaven, Mass.

D

I venture to contribute the following information, which seems to indicate that two John Washingtons emigrated to Virginia about the same time, and, as is so often the case in genealogies, there might be some danger of confusing one with the other.

In the records of Surry County, Virginia, we find that John Washington was betrothed in 1658 to Mary Flood, widow, whom he afterwards married. She had previously married a Mr. Blunt, and after Mr. Washington's death she married Charles Ford, so she must have been a very attractive woman. By Mrs. Flood he had one child, Richard Washington, who sold land in 1678 and died in 1725. He married Elizabeth Jordan, who died in 1735. She was the daughter of Arthur Jordan, who died in 1698. The children of this marriage were : George, Richard, John, William, Thomas (died in 1749), James, Arthur, Elizabeth (married Samson and Robert Lanier), Priscilla, Faith and Mary. The estate of Mr. John Washington was about three miles below the present town of Claremont, on the banks of the James River, and about nine miles above Jamestown.

We also find in the records that a Thomas Wrenn, who died in 1775, speaks of his daughter Rebecca Washington. The gentlemanly Clerk of the Court tells me that a Mr. Washington still lives in Isle of Wight County, just over the border from Surry, who is no doubt descended from the first John Washington.

Some of the papers on which I base this communication are as follows :—

" Be it known unto all men by these presents that whereas a contract of matrimony is agreed upon between me John Washington and Mary Flood, widow, and the said Washington from divers good causes and considerations me thereunto moving, doe before the celebration and solemnization thereof, by these presents engage and oblige myself, my heirs, executors, administrators or assigns, to give and deliver, or cause to be given and delivered unto Robert Stanton, Clerke, feoffe in trust, one mare filly of one year old, to and for the sole use and behoof of Thomas Blunt, son of the said Mary, his heirs, executors, administrators and assigns, with male and female increase forever, which said mare filly is to be delivered as abovesaid the day that the said Thomas Blunt shall attain to ten years of age, in Surry County, and further I the said John Washington do hereby oblige myself to acknowledge this my real and voluntary act and deed in the next court to be holden for the county of Surry, and to have it recorded accordingly in the said County records. Witness my hand and seal. Dated the 15th day of 9ber stile Anglia, anno Domini 1658. JOHN WASHINGTON

Signed, sealed and delivered in the   [sealed with red wax.]
presence of us   John Flood
Ben. Sidway   Edmund Shipham
Jno. Allann   Thos. Flood."

Charles Ford had a patent, 19 May, 1638, bounded north by James River, southerly by the woods, easterly by land of John Flood, westerly by Sunken Marsh. He died intestate, the land escheated to the King and was granted by the Governor to Thos. Blunt and Richard Washington, orphans and sons in law unto the said Charles Ford.

Blunt and Washington sold 140 acres to John Gorring on 1 March, 29th year of Charles II. (1678).

THOMAS M. CLEEMANN, 2135 Spruce Street, Philadelphia, Pa.

Mr. Cleemann referred us to A. S. Edwards, Esq., Clerk of Courts, Surry Court House, Va., for confirmation of the statements. A proof of the foregoing note was sent to Mr. Edwards, who has most kindly read and revised it. He adds that "Benjamin Sidway, one of the witnesses, seems to have married the widow of Benjamin Harrison, the first of that name in Virginia. January 16, 1652, Benj. Sidway, by order of the Court, conveyed certain land belonging to Peeter Harrison, orphan of Benjamin Harrison. Then Benj. Sidway and Mary his wife convey certain lands in their own right; and in 1687-8 Mary Sidway by will disposes of certain property to her two sons Benjamin Harrison and Thomas Sidway. Thomas Flood was guardian of Benjamin Harrison, who died in 1712." Mr. Edwards also adds that Mary Sidway in her will also devised a horse to her granddaughter Hannah Harrison. Benjamin Harrison, the Speaker, &c., who died in 1712, by his will devised £400 to his daughter Hannah, which helps to identify those persons.

We have already (ante, p. 446) quoted Meade on the origin of the Harrisons. The first Benjamin (Speaker, &c.) was born in 1650. Mr. Edwards seems to make it certain that his father was a Benjamin also.—WM. H. WHITMORE.

E

In preparing the **Institutions of the Archdeaconry of Bedford** for the press, I came across the following re Washington, which may be of interest.

1642, Aug. 12, Wm. Pargiter, clk., inst. to Rectory of Carlton, Patrons, Sr. John Washington, Knt., and Robert Pargiter, pro hac vice.

According to the pedigree in Mr. Waters's pamphlet, Sr. John Washington m. for his 2nd wife Dorothy, d. of Wm. Pargiter of Gretworth.

What became of this Wm. Pargiter I have not yet ascertained, as the next institution in point of time is wanting.—F. A. BLAYDES of Bedford, England.

GEORGE POPHAM.—

IN the name of the Allmighty, being Father, Son and Holy Ghost three parsonnes and one God eternall I make my Will and Testament and is that my soule I betake into the handes of my saide God and Saviour twenty poundes to my Nephew Edwarde Popham wth me in voyage ffyve poundes to Thomas Oxnan my servaunt all the rest unto the above Lettice Maior whome I make my sole executrix. In witnes whereof I hereunto have subscribed the laste of Maie one thousande six hundred and seaven.

GEORGE POPHAM.

The halfe lyne blotted was myne owne doing.

George Popham.   Windebancke, 112.

Proved 2 December 1608.

[Capt. George Popham, the testator, was president of what is called the Popham Colony, and died there Feb. 5, 1607-8. His nephew, Edward Popham, whom he names, was a son of his brother Alexander Popham. See Visitation of Somersetshire, vol. 11, of the Harleian Society's Publications, pp. 87-8.—ED.]

SIR JOHN POPHAM cf Wellington, Somerset, Knight, chief justice of all Pleas, 21 September 1604, proved 17 June 1608. Wife Amye. Son and heir Sir Francis Popham, knight, and his daughters. Sara Popham one of the daughters of Ferdinando Popham, my nephew, deceased. Amye Mallett the child of my daughter. My five daughters Penelope Hannam, Elinor Warre, Elizabeth Champernowne, Katherine Rogers and Mary Mallett. John Horner, my daughter Horner's son. George Rogers my godson. My trusty friends and cousins Edward Popham of Huntworth and James Clarke Esq. Grandchild Amye Pyne (separated from her husband). Sons in law John Mallett, Sir Richard Champernowne knight, Thomas Horner, Edward Rogers and Roger Warre Esq.^rs

Then follows Sententia, in which the executrix and relict is called Anna.

Windebancke, 58.

[Sir John Popham, Knt., the testator, was a son of Alexander Popham. He was born in Huntworth, Somersetshire, 1531, and died June 10, 1607. A biographical sketch of him, by James P. Baxter, will be found in "Sir Ferdinando Gorges and his Province of Maine," edited by Mr. Baxter, and published by the Prince Society, vol. i. pp. 72-3. His elder brother, Edward, was the father of the preceding Capt. George Popham, and of Ferdinando Popham, who is named in the will. See Burke's History of the Commoners, vol. ii. pp. 196-201, and Visitation of Somersetshire, *ubi supra.*—EDITOR.]

Sir GEORGE SOMERS of Barne, in the county of Dorset, knight, intending to pass the seas in a voyage towards the land called Virginia, makes his will 23 April 1609, proved 16 August 1611. He makes bequests to the poor of Whitechurch and of Lyme Regis, Dorset, to John and William Somers, sons of his brother John, Toby Somers, another son and Mary Somers, a daughter of said brother John. Nicholas Somers, eldest son of Nicholas Somers deceased, and his brother Matthew Somers, to release their rights in all the testators lands and tenements in Whitechurch, Marshwood and Upway and to have, after the death of wife Dame Joan, certain tenements &c. in Lyme Regis, to the said Matthew Somers the capital messuage and farm called or known by the name of Waybay House, situate and being in the parish of Upway, and other lands. Brother John Somers, of Lyme Regis, to be sole executor, and Richard Hodie, gentleman, James Heywood, gentleman, and Baldwin Sanford to be overseers. The witnesses were Thomas Moleins, John Boylden and Henry Corbinne.

Then follows an inventory of household goods.   Wood, 71.

[Sir George Somers, the testator, an experienced naval officer, who was one of the original patentees for colonizing Virginia, was born at Lyme Regis in 1554, and died in the Bermudas, Nov. 9, 1610. He was shipwrecked on these islands in July, 1609. The vessel was lost, but all lives were saved. He built two small barks, in which he and his company reached Virginia in the following spring. There being a famine in Virginia, he returned to the Bermudas for provisions, but died there. The islands were named the Somers Islands for him. See a biographical sketch by R. A. Brock, in the Virginia Company of London, vol. i. p. 114, in the Collections of the Virginia Historical Society.—EDITOR.]

JACOMYN STERMYN of Wisbeche, within the Isle of Ely, in the County of Cambridge, widow, 23 April 1613, proved 11 December 1613.

I give to Mr. Blackston vicar of Wisbeche twenty shillings "soe as he doeth att my ffunerall expound some portion of Holy Scripture to the instruccon of the people."

To my brother William Lynde my messuage in King's Lynn, Norfolk, with free ingress and egress, in, by and through a certain entry there unto a street there called the Checker. My kinsman William Lynde of Leverington. My kinsman William Vaughan and Anne now his wife. My kinsman Robert Lynde. My brother in law Richard Blancke. Thomas Byrde the younger of Wisbeche and Stermyn Byrde, his son. Thomas Deysborough of Elme and every one of his children. My kinswoman Margaret Taylor, the wife of Robert Taylor. Robert Attlebridge the son of the said Margaret. Alice the wife of James Pemberton and Hellen Abott. My kinsman William Lynde of Leverington to be executor.

Capell, 118.

MARY MAYPLETT of London, widow, 7 December 1646, proved 10 April 1647. Imprimis I give and bequeath unto my daughter Mary Gorton, wife of Samuel Gorton living in New England, all the money which her said husband Samuel Gorton doth owe me, and a breed of cattle which he hath of mine. Item I give and bequeath unto my said daughter Mary the sum of ten pounds of ·wful money of England to buy her mourning; to be paid by my executor within one year next after my decease. To my daughter Elizabeth Ham and to her husband William Ham the like sum of ten pounds, between them, to buy them mourning. To my sister Elizabeth Freeman, widow, six pounds to buy her mourning. To my grandchild Samuel Chapleine, son of my said daughter Elizabeth Ham by her former husband, the sum of twenty pounds, which I have lent to the Parliament upon the public faith, and all the interest, profit and increase that shall accrue and arise thereof. To Mrs. Joane Joyner twenty shillings. To Mrs. Elizabeth Warrington ten shillings. To Mrs. Elizabeth Swann, widow, ten shillings. The residue to my son John Mayplett, whom I make and ordain sole executor.

Fines, 69.

[We have here the Christian, and probably the family name of the wife of the famous Samuel Gorton of Warwick, R. I., author of Simplicity's Defence against Seven Headed Policy.—EDITOR.]

EDWARD HANBURY of old Brentford in the parish of Ealing alias Zealing, Middlesex, —— 1646, proved 26 April 1647. To be buried near the body of my late wife. To the poor of new and old Brentford. To wife Mary my two acres and a half of arable land (freehold) in new Brentford field, which I purchased of Mr. Illingworth. My two youngest sons, Luke and Peter, which said Peter is now in America beyond the seas. My eldest son Thomas. My daughter Elizabeth Ivory, wife of Luke Ivory of old Brentford. William Moore, one of the sons of John Moore of new Brentford, coalseller. A cottage and land, which land I purchased of my kinsman Thomas Nuball deceased and now have builded upon the same. Peter Hanbury the youngest son of me the said Edward now inhabiting beyond the seas in New England. My kinsman John Moore of New Brentford.   Fines, 66 (P. C. C.).

AN Inventory of what Adventure and necessaries I carry to the East Indies with me in the Rebecca Mr. Buckam Master, primo ffebruarii Anno 1644. Then follows a list of books, clothing, bedding and other miscellaneous goods, as well as money &c. The following appears:

In my uncle's hands at New England 11.00.00. Mr. Fra. Cooke's Bill for 2.00.00.

Things sent to and left at my father's house.

I owe unto my father 100.00.00. What money I shall receive of Mr. Maurice Thompson or leave in his hands in case I die at sea.

(signed) NATHANIEL BRADING.

Then follows his will, in which he mentions his father Mr. William Brading of the Isle of Wight in the parish of Godsall.

Whereas my uncle Mr. Richard Kent of the parish of Newbury in the Colony of New England hath by his letters being in the custody of my abovesaid father made me an assurance of the inheritance of his estate after his decease I do therefore in case of his decease bequeath that portion of estate whatsoever it shall be unto my brothers James and Joseph Brading and my sister Ruth Brading. To my sister Ruth a diamond ring which I left with her at parting and also my picture which I have at present with me. To Capt. John Smart, Gov. of the plantation of Madagascar and Mr. Robert Willet minister of the said plantation. To brothers James and Joseph my library and to my mother Mrs. Helen Brading my large picture that I left at home, as also five pounds to buy a ring.

Dated in Augustin Bay in the Isle of Madagascar this sixteenth of November Anno Dñi 1645. Proved 1 July 1648.   Essex, 115.

[Two persons by the name of Richard Kent embarked for New England in the Mary and John of London, March 26, 1634 (REGISTER, vol. 9, p. 267). Both settled at Newbury, Mass. Richard Kent, sen., malster, who died in 1654, left a family. Richard Kent, Jr., m. 1st, Jane——, and 2d, Mrs. Joanna Davison, but Coffin records no children. I presume that it was the latter who was uncle to Nathaniel Brading, as a person with children would not be likely to promise to make a nephew his heir. A James Brading, perhaps the brother of Nathaniel, was at Newbury in 1659, whence he removed to Boston. His daughter Elizabeth was the first wife of Edward Bromfield.—EDITOR.]

THOMAS ALDERNE of London, merchant, 21 April 1656, proved 20 June 1657. To be buried in the church of Hackney as near my late mother in law, Mistress Rowe deceased, as may be. Two hundred pounds and no more to be expended in and about my funeral. My estate to be divided into three parts, one third to my wife (Dorothy), one third to my children and the other third to be disposed of by myself. My manor of Monnington Stradle. My farms called Old Hill and Hunderton in the parishes of Vowchurch, Madley and Clehunger. My houses in the city of Hereford. Alice Greene, widow, hath a moiety of the said manor of Monnington Stradle during her life. My moiety of the manor of Orgars-wick &c., in the County of Kent purchased by me and Col. Beale of Robert Hammond. My brother Edward Alderne, Doctor of Laws. My kinsman Francis Griffith. My sons Thomas, Owen and Edward. My nephew John Greene. My daughter Dorothy.

To son Owen my part of the Saw mill with the land and appurtenances thereunto belonging in New England beyond the seas purchased by me and Col. Beale of Richard Leather and John Becks. My two messuages in Capell Court in Bartholomewe Lane near the Royal Exchange, London. My brother Daniel Alderne. My kinsman Jonathan Dryden. My sister Greene and her two daughters Frances and Elenor. My sister Clarke and my brother Clarke and his three children. Mary, Frances, Constance, Robert and Henry, children of my cousin Martha Dryden. My brother Charles. The poor of Master John Goodwin's church. My father and mother Rowe. My sister Sarah Rowe. My brothers Samuel and Joseph and my sister Hannah Rowe. My brother Carleton and his wife. My brother Ellis Crispe and his wife. My brother George Brett and his wife. My brothers Tobias, Samuel, Edward and Rowland Crispe. My aunts Salmon and Hodges. My kinsman and servant Edmond Alderne. My friends Major Cor^{ll} Disborowe and his lady. My servants in the Victualling Office. The four children of my late master, James Russell deceased. My said father in law Col. Owen Rowe. Mistress Russell the executor of my said late master. Ruthen, 218 (P. C. C.).

[The following extracts from the Hackney Register of Burials have been furnished me by my friend Mr. Eedes:

1657. April 9, Capt. Thos Alderne of Darleston.
1658. Sept. 7, Mrs. Dorothy Alderne from Darleston.

The Richard Leather, named in this will, must be Richard Leader. His name and that of John Becx will be quite familiar to those acquainted with the history of the Iron works at Saugus.—H. F. WATERS.

Richard Leader while in England Oct. 5, 1653, sold one quarter of his saw-mill at Pascataqua to John Becx of London, another quarter to Richard Hutchinson of that city, and another quarter to Col. William Beale and Capt. Thomas Allderne. On the 14th of Feb. 1655, Leader pledged the remaining quarter to Edward Hutchinson, Jr., attorney for the said Becx, Hutchinson and Allderne. See the York Deeds, Bk. I. fol. 74-5. See also sketch of Richard Leader by Dr. C. E. Banks in Tuttle's Capt. John Mason, pp. 92-4.—EDITOR]

RICHARD WHITEHEAD of Windsor upon Connecticut River in New England in the parts of America, 26 April 1645, proved 26 June 1645. Whereas there is or was lately due and owing unto my daughter in law Mary Lewes the sum of one hundred pounds, being a portion given unto her by my wife, hereafter named, whilst she was sole and unmarried, which money was entrusted with my brother in law Hugh Hopkins and by him, by and with the consent of my said wife and daughter, delivered unto me for the use of my said daughter etc. I do therefore hereby give and bequeath unto the said Mary Lewes the sum of thirty pounds, in ready money or goods to be transported over to her, to her liking, towards the satisfaction of her said portion; and I do give and confirm the gift and delivery of several goods and chattels unto her towards further satisfaction thereof, which my wife hath already delivered unto her, which goods etc. were of the value of thirty pounds more. And I give and bequeath unto the said Mary Lewes, and her heirs forever, my messuage or tenement, with the backside, orchard and garden and all edifices and buildings upon the same built and standing, lying in Knoll in the county of Warwick in the kingdom of England, and now or late in the tenure, use or occupation of Thomas Miles and John Shakespeare or one of them, which said messuage is known by the sign of the Crown; which said premises I conceive are of the value of forty pounds more, which I give towards further satisfaction of her said portion.

To wife Mary Whitehead and her heirs and assigns forever all my lands, tenements and hereditaments lying in New England, also my goods, cattle and chattels upon condition that she shall pay and satisfy unto my said daughter in law Mary Lewes so much more money as will satisfy unto her and fully make up her said portion of one hundred pounds. To my brother John Andrewes of Clifton thirty pounds to secure him for the five pounds a year lying upon his lands due to my brother Edward Whitehead for his life. To John and Edward Whitehead, sons of my said brother Edward, twenty pounds to be equally divided between them when they shall attain their several ages of one and twenty years. To Joane Whitehead, daughter of my brother Matthew Whitehead, twenty shillings. To John Andrewes, son of my brother John Andrewes of Clifton twenty shillings. To my sister Joyce Fisher forty shillings and to her son Richard Fisher forty shillings and to her daughter Mary Fisher forty shillings. There is a demand made by my kinswomen Hannah, Sarah, Rebecca and Abigail Higgins of some part of their mother's portion unpaid to their father, which I am confident was fully satisfied and paid: yet that there shall be no clamor about the same and upon condition that they shall acquite all demands concerning the same I do hereby give them twenty shillings a piece. To my friend Mr. Thomas Fish of Wedgeneckt Park five pounds in part of recompence for my diet and great charge and trouble that I have put him to. To my maidservant Dorothy Underwood ten shillings. I hereby constitute and ordain the said Mr. Thomas Fish and my said brother John Andrewes executors and John Rogers, Edward Rogers, Matthew Edwards and William Smith of Langley to be overseers.

Wit: Fran: Eede, Hester Fishe, Cr: Fishe, Michael Perkins.

Proved by John Andrews, power reserved for Thomas Fish.

Rivers, 87.

[Savage, under *Whitehead*, says that Richard of Windsor " served on the jury at July Court, 1640, married Mary, widow of William Hopkins, and no more is known of him; but his wife was living in 1670 with her dau. Lewis." Under *Hopkins* he says, " William, Stratford, 1640, an assistant 1641 and 2, but it is unknown whence he came, when he died, or what wife or children he had. Perhaps it was his daughter Mary who after his death, in virtue of a contract of marriage made by her mother Mary, wife of Richard Whitehead of Windsor (who was living 1670), with William Lewis of Farmington, 1644, became wife of William Lewis, son of the bargainer. If so we might infer that our Connecticut magistrate was then dead, and his widow who married Richard Whitehead was named Mary." It is shown in the above will that Richard Whitehead had a wife Mary, a brother-in-law Hugh Hopkins, and a daughter-in-law Mary Lewis, and this no doubt was the wife of William Lewis, Jr., of Farmington. Lewis married for a second wife Mary, daughter of the famous schoolmaster Ezekiel Cheever (REGISTER, vol. 33, page 192). His son by the 2d marriage, Ezekiel Lewis, gr. H. C. 1695, was a teacher in Westfield and Boston, and afterwards a successful merchant in Boston. (REGISTER, vol. 8, pp. 47–8; Hill's Old South Church Catalogue, pages 324–5.)—EDITOR.

Windsor records show but little trace of " Goodman " Whitehead:—he had, in 1640, a lot 10 rods wide on what was known as " The Island," directly opposite the lot of Henry Wolcott, and about 15 rods south of the road to the Island, on west side of street; died early—and his wid. sold the place to Thos. Orton, who, in 1665, sold (with dwelling) to Simon Wolcott. This location was among the " best families " of Windsor—the Wolcotts, Phelps, Loomises, etc.—inferentially, then, his social status was high.—HENRY R. STILES, M.D., of Hill View, N. Y.

On page 55, vol. i. of the Colonial Records of Connecticut, the name of Richard Whitehead appears in the list of " The Jury," July 2, 1640. He probably failed to bring in to the recorder his land for record, as none is entered in the Land Record under his name; but Henry Wolcott the younger has a lot bounded north by Goodman Whitehead, and Christopher Wolcott has a lot bounded south by Richard Whitehead, under date of 1640. The same lot, without date, is sold to Thomas Orton by Mary Whitehead, widow. On the map of the first settlers of Windsor, in volume 2 of the Memorial History of Hartford County, the lot of Whitehead appears between the lots of George Phelps and H. Wolcott, Jr.

Mr. Whitehead's name does not appear in Matthew Grant's record of births, marriages and deaths.—JABEZ H. HAYDEN, of Windsor Locks, Ct.]

MARGARET HARRISON of Battersea, Surrey, widow, 10 December 1641, proved 4 March 1641. Kinswoman Johan Wiggins, wife of Thomas Wiggins the elder. To her children, that is to say, Mary, Samuel, Sarah, Francis, Martha and Edmund, at one and twenty or day of marriage. To Anne Husband at one and twenty. To Anne White and her daughter Elizabeth Cox both of Martin, John Hester of Shiplack, Goodwife Husbands, and to Alice Andrewes in New England five pounds. To Thomas Andrewes his five children, Thomas, John, Samuel, Nathaniel and Elinor ten pounds apiece. My son in law Robert Heyborne and Katherine his wife. Son Richard Floyd's two daughters Sarah and Martha and the child my daughter goeth with. Twenty poor widows of Henly upon Thames. Son Thomas Andrewes to be executor.

Richard Andrewes one of the witnesses.		Cambell, 34.

MARGERIE VERNON of St. Martin's, Ludgate, London, widow, 4 May 1654, proved 3 May 1656. My body to be buried as near unto my late husband Edward Vernon as may be. To my son in law, Francis Vernon now or late in New England in the parts beyond the seas the sum of five pounds sterling. To my daughter in law, the wife of William Methald my Turky grogerom gown, my mohair petticoat and my best hat. Of the money due unto me from the Commonwealth upon the public faith the sum of forty shillings to my said daughter Elizabeth, to her husband the said William Methwald twenty shillings, to his daughter Bridget Methwald twenty shillings. To my son Robert Potter five pounds. To my daughter Mary Vernon a seal ring, &c. My son Robert Potter and my daughter Mary Vernon to be executors.		Berkley, 149.

MATHEWE WHIPPLE the elder of Bocking, Essex, clothier, 19 December 1616, proved 28 January 1618.

My capital messuage or tenement, with the yards, gardens, orchards, members and appurtenances, situate in Bradford Street in Bocking, now in the occupation of me the said Mathewe, from and after my decease shall remain to Mathewe Whippell, mine eldest son, upon condition that he shall pay or cause to be paid to my son John Whippell fourscore pounds within three months next after my decease, and to my daughter Jane thirty pounds within six months, and to my daughter Elizabeth thirty pounds within twelve months, and to my daughter Mary thirty pounds at one and twenty or day of her marriage, and to my daughter Amie thirty pounds at one and twenty or day of marriage, upon reasonable demand made by the said Jane, Elizabeth, Mary and Amye. To my daughter Amce (?) six silver spoons of the better sort, two high latten candlesticks, my biggest brass pot and three pounds six shillings and eight pence. To my daughter Johane forty shillings. To my daughter Jane two silver spoons, two pewter platters of the greater sort, one pewter candlestick, one half headed bedstedle, my best flock bed, a flock bolster, a coverlet and a pair of blankets. To my daughter Elizabeth two silver spoons, one pewter candlestick, two pewter platters of the greater sort, a half headed bedstedle, next the best, a flock bed, a flock bolster, a coverlet, a pair of blankets and the little chest which was her mothers. To my daughter Mary two silver spoons, two pewter platters and a pewter salt, a trundle bedsteadle, a flock bed, a flock bolster, a coverlet, a pair of blankets. To my daughter Amye two silver spoons, two pewter platters, a pewter salt, a trundle bedsteadle, a flock bed, a flock bolster and a pair of blankets. To my son John a joyned table and frame standing in my old parlor (and other movables). To my sister, wife of Richard Rathbone twenty shillings. To Hercules Stephens ten shillings. To my grandchildren Hercules Arthur, Margaret Arthur, Henry Caldham and Anne Caldham six shilling eight pence apiece. To the poor of Bocking twenty shillings. All the rest to my son Matthew, sole executor.

Parker, 2.

JOHN AMIES of Bockin 7 April 1647, proved 16 April 1647. To wife Mary Amies four hundred pounds and that dwelling house wherein we now dwell, being situate in Bocking aforesaid, paying to my mother yearly and every year during her natural life six pounds; and after the death of my mother I give it to her wholly during her natural life; and after her decease and my mother's I give it to my son John Amies and his heirs forever. To wife Mary my house now in the occupation of Richard Everd and Richard Jobson, during her life, and then to my son John. To my son John three hundred pounds at the age of one and twenty years or day of marriage. To daughter Mary Amies two hundred and fifty pounds at eighteen years or day of marriage. To daughter Elizabeth Amies (the same). To my dear mother as a token of my last love ten pounds. To my brother William, as soon as it shall please God he take a dwelling house, my clock and case. To my son John Amies all my books and manuscripts to be carefully kept for him. To my wife all the furniture in best chamber except that which is my mother's.

Item I give the piece of cloth at home unto Mr. Rogers, John Whiple and a jerkin cloth of it to Mr. Norton of Ipswich, N. E. I desire that my wife would buy for my uncle Skynner and my brother Samuel Hasell, each of them, a gold ring with a death's head on it, at her pleasure, as the last token of my love. My wife Mary to be sole executor and my uncle Skynner and brother Samuel Hasell to be supervisors. Houses and lands in Church Street in Bocking.

Fines, 75.

JOHN HAWKINGS of Brayntree, Essex, Gen[t]. 3 September 1633, proved 18 October 1633. To wife Sara messuages lands and tenements in Tolleshunt, Bushes, Salcott, Wigborough and Verley which I late had and purchased of Sir Edward Bullocke, knight, Francis Steele and Elizabeth his wife, John Hewes and Elizabeth his wife, formerly the wife of —— Steele, John Osborne (and others), for and during her natural life; and the messuage wherein I dwell in Brayntree and the two little tenements adjoining unto the churchyard of Brayntree so long as she shall keep herself a widow and unmarried after my decease. To eldest son John messuages and lands in Barking (and other parishes). To son Robert messuages and tenements in Old Newton, Suffolk. To son Abraham the messuage wherein I dwell (and other lands and tenements). To my daughter Sara six hundred pounds at her age of eighteen and again at the age of one and twenty. To my daughter Margaret five hundred pounds at eighteen and again at one and twenty. To my daughter Mary messuages, etc. in Bradwell next the sea. To my daughter Judith messuages, etc., in Finchefield, Essex. To my brother in law John Kent one hundred marks for 'his care and pains to be taken as one of the executors. To my loving friend Mr. Collins of Brayntree forty shillings to buy him a ring, and also four pounds per annum during his ministry there. To my mother Mary Hawkins, widow, sixteen pounds a year, etc. To my friend William Lingwood twenty pounds. To my sister Kent and my sister Edes thirty shillings apiece to make them rings. To my brother Francis Hawkins, my sister Archer and my sister Whipple forty shillings apiece as remembrances from me. To my cousin Tomson, my aunt Woodward and my aunt Goodaye ten shillings apiece. Loving friends and neighbors Adrian Mott and Joseph Loomys also mentioned. Joseph Loomys one of the witnesses. Russell, 87.

[The three preceding wills relate undoubtedly to the family of Whipple in Ipswich, Massachusetts, descended from two brothers Matthew and John. A very brief extract of the will of Matthew Whipple the elder was given in Emmerton and Waters's Gleanings (Essex Institute, 1880).—HENRY F. WATERS.]

The last will and testament of Mr. THOMAS SPENSER 22 June 1648, proved 23 August 1648. To my eldest son John Spenser all my means in New England, paying to his eldest sister Penelope Spenser, or to her husband John Treworthy, or to her heirs and his. twenty pounds a year for five years, etc., and paying his mother Penelope Spenser five pounds a year during her life. For my means here in England I do bequeath my lease of Waddam called Russells *alias* Bamsters, in the parish of Chertsey, equally divided between Thomas and Rachel, paying their mother during her life fifteen pounds a year and at her decease ten pounds a year falling unto her son Thomas Spenser and the other five pounds a year unto her daughter Rachel Spenser. I bequeath my wages and liveries due to me for my ordinary place of the Guard and Service unto the King's Majesty unto my wife and four children, divided equally amongst them. My brother Nicholas Kidwell to be my executor. My daughter in law Anna Fylliall.
Essex, 124.

Marriage License granted to Thomas Spencer, gen[t], of the City of Westminster, bachelor, 30, and Penelope Filliall, of the City of London, 30, widow of Westerne Filliall, draper, deceased,—at St. Peter's, Paul's Wharf,—24 Sept. 1623. B.   (Col. Chester's Mar. Lic.)

[This Thomas Spenser must have been a brother of John Spencer whose will, bearing date 1 August 1637 and proved more than eleven years afterwards at Salem, Massachusetts, mentioned a nephew John Spencer, whom he constituted his heir, a brother Thomas Spencer, a cousin Ann Knight, a cousin Gardner, a brother Nicholas Kidwell and a sister Rachel Kidwell. This will gives us the baptismal name of the wife of John Treworthy, who (says Savage) was married at Newbury 15 January, 1646. I note a connection between the Chadbournes and both the Treworthy family and the Spencer family of Piscataqua. Some of our friends in Maine may assist us here.—HENRY F. WATERS.]

NICHOLAS KYDWELL of Kingston upon Thames in the County of Surrey, gen[t]., 25 July 1676, proved 16 September 1679. To my only daughter and child Rachel the wife of John Gatton my messuages, etc. in the said parish. And forasmuch as my said son in law hath been very unnatural and unkind to my said daughter his wife wherefrom differences have arose between them so that for several years last past they have not lived together as man and wife should have done, my will etc. is that James Davison the elder of Berwell Court in the said parish gen^t., Thomas Spencer of the town of Plymouth in the County of Devon Dr. in Physick, John Hayes of Kingston upon Thames gen^t. and Thomas Mellersh of Monersh Surrey gen^t., or any two of them, shall have full power during the life time of the said John Gatton and with the consent and approbation of my said daughter to sel and let all or any of the messuages, etc., and the rents etc. thereof to receive and take up without the consent, knowledge or any power of or from the said John Gatton, in trust (then follows the disposition of the trust). My sister Rachel wife of John Hayes.   King, 117.

WILLIAM KINGE of Ipswich, shipcarpenter, 30 March 1655 and sealed 9 April 1655 (no probate act noticed). He calls himself aged and full of days, and yet is "bound on a voyage to sea." He mentions grandchildren William, Thomas, Mary, John, Joseph, and Jeremy Sandwell, sons and daughters of his son in law Sandwell and his wife deceased, niece Elizabeth Hichman, widow, and grandchildren, the children of son in law Thrumble and his wife now living in New England. He appoints his son in law John Thrumble, now resident in New England, supervisor, etc.

Wills of Arch. of Suff. (Ipswich), 1650–60.

ISAAC LEE late of Rappahanock River in America, mariner, but now of Stepney, Middlesex, 18 November 1726, proved 3 November 1727. To my honored mother Sarah Lee of America, widow, oue of my best negroes, such as she shall choose. To my brother Richard Lee of America the next best negro, such as he shall choose. To my brothers John Lee and Hancock Lee all my estate, such as land and houses in America, to hold to them and the survivor of them when they shall attain the several ages of twenty one years, and to the male heirs of their bodies. If they die without issue male then to my brother Richard Lee and the issue male of his body. Failing such then to the daughter or daughters of my said brothers John and Hancock Lee during their natural lives, and after their decease to my sisters Anne Eustace and Elizabeth Lee. If they die without issue then to the daughters or daughter of my brother Richard Lee. Other provisions. I hereby nominate and appoint Coll. Robert Carter and my brother Richard Lee of America executors &c. relating to all my estate and effects in America, and William Dawkins of London, gen^t. relating to my effects in England.   Farrant, 267.

[The testator of the above will was a descendant, doubtless, of Col. Richard Lee of Virginia, whose own will was entered for probate in the Prerogative Court, as shown by the following extract, but not registered.]

Mense January 1664 juxta etc. Decimo die probatum fuit Testamentum Richardi Lee nup de Stratford Langton in Com. Essexiæ sed apud Virginiā in ptibus transmarinis ar. defunct heñtis etc. Juramént Thomæ Griffith et Johis Lockey duoř execuť etc. Reservata potestate similem coñinem faciend Johi et Richō Lee alť Execuť.

Admon. Act Book, P. C. C.

[The published Lee genealogy gives the descendants only of Richard and Hancock Lee, second and fifth sons of Col. Richard the emigrant. The testator, Isaac

Lee, may have been the son of Francis, William or Charles, the remaining sons. I know not of another instance of the Christian name Isaac among the descendants of Col. Richard Lee. Hancock Lee married twice; first, Mary, daughter of William Kendell of Northampton County, Va., and second, Elizabeth, daughter of Col. Isaac Allerton of Virginia, who was a grandson of Isaac Allerton the Mayflower emigrant. Isaac Lee, the testator, may have been named for Isaac Allerton.—R. A. BROCK, of Richmond, Va.]

WILLIAM PINDAR, clerk, parson of Mottisfount in the County of Southhampton, and parson of Horneford Stocke, Essex, 15 September 1625. The poor of Mottisfount, Lockarleigh and East Deane. The poorest among my parishioners of Harneford Stock. Kinsman Mr. Thomas Pratt, clerk. My nephew John Shingleton *als* Lea of London, carpenter, and his two sons John and Michael.

Item I give unto Thomas Shingleton *als* Lea now at Virginia, the brother of John Lea, carpenter, ten pounds currant moneys of England, to be paid unto him within two years after my decease. The children of George Shingleton *als* Lea, my nephew, late of Plymouth deceased, namely Robert and John Lea, at twenty-one, and their mother. My wife Cicely shall, during her natural life have my house in Southampton, in English Street in the parish of All Saints, called corner tenement, wherein Richard Tirrill now dwelleth, for her dwelliug house; she to pay yearly unto Elizabeth Davis the sum of three pounds at two payments, according to the will of Mr. John Cornish deceased, and keep the said messuage in good and sufficient reparations tenant like. Her children &c. To Edmond Freke forty pounds, John Emerye ten pounds and to Sara and Mary Emery five pounds apiece at twenty-one. Samuel Pindar my grandchild, son of my natural son Michael Pindar late of Winchester deceased Esq. and his sister, my other grandchild, Elizabeth Pindar. My wife's children Edmond, William Freke, Mrs. Sara Slatire, Alice Emory and Martha Freke. My godson William Slatire.

On the 16th of February 1626 Commission issued to Sara Pindar mother añd guardian of Samuel Pindar, grandson of the deceased, to administer the goods and effects during his minority for the reason that the deceased had not named any executor at all.   Skynner, 13.

LAWRENCE LEY of St. Martin, Ironmonger Laue, London, merchant, 28 December 1624, proved 29 April 1625. My brother Humphry Richards; my brother John Ley; my friends Thomas Matthew, Nathaniel Wright, Rowland Trulove and Richard Somersall. My wife Effie to be executrix. Eldest son Isaack and youngest son Jacob.

Item I give and bequeath all my lands, tenements and hereditaments whatsoever within the kingdom or continent of Virginia, in the parts beyond the seas, unto my said son Isaack and to the heirs of his body lawfully begotten, with remainder to son Jacob and his heirs and next to brother John Ley and his heirs and finally to my right heirs forever,
                                                        Clarke, 37.

JONE MAPLISDEN, wife of Peter Maplisden of Westminster, gentleman, 6 December 1656, proved 20 December 1656. To Mrs. Mary Van Winterbecke wife of Michael Van Winterbeck, of Fleet Street, jeweller, fifty pounds to be raised and paid out of and by the sale of all my lands, tenements and hereditaments in or near Romford in Essex. To Jane Bird, sister of the said Mary, fifty pounds (as before). To Laurance Gibson, now servant to the said Michael Van Winterbeck, one hundred pounds. To sister Ann

Gibson fifty pounds. To Michael, Mary and Susan, children of the said Michael Van Winterbeck, ten pounds apiece. To Anne and Frances, daughters of Anne Clarke, widow, ten pounds apiece. My husband, Peter Maplisden, to be executor. To my brother John Smith of Chichester ten pounds per annum, half yearly during his life. To Ellen, the daughter of my sister Gardiner, ten pounds and to my kinsman, John Lee of Virginia, the sum of one hundred pounds within three months after he shall come in person and demand the same, and not before. To my niece Magdalen, wife of —— Dudley of Darking in Surrey, a little plain silver cup, a gold hoop ring and fifty pounds in money, and to all her children that shall be living at my decease ten pounds apiece as they shall accomplish their several ages of one and twenty years. To Tobias Markham of St. Giles Cripplegate five pounds and to my nephew William Smith ten pounds. To my husband's three children, Elizabeth, Dorothy and Susan Maplisden, ten pounds apiece.

Mem. these words " in the tenure or occupation of Nathaniel Beadle or his assigns " being interlined in the twelvth line of the first sheet.

Berkley, 439.

RICHARD LEE of St. Michael Bassishaw, London, merchant taylor, 22 December 1666, proved 4 January 1666. My worldly goods either in this land and elsewhere in any foreign nation, as Barbados, Virginia, or any other place, all to and for the use of my two youngest children, Richard Lee and Grace Lee, only my son Richard to have my bible in quarto over and above his half share of my goods and estate, and also my ring with a carnelian stone engraven with this figure, a boy blowing a bubble. To my kinsman Mr. Thomas Roe late of St. Bride's, London, forty shillings to buy two rings for him and his wife. To my kinswoman Elizabeth Sims twenty shillings to buy her a ring. To my maid Elizabeth Wright five pounds. To my son in law John Guy one shilling. And to the rest of my children beyond the seas twelve pence apiece if the same be demanded. To my loving friends Samuel Stone, Richard Cocke and William Rudd twenty shillings apiece; the said Samuel Stone and Richard Cocke to be joint executors and William Rudd to be overseer.

Carr, 7.

SAMUEL LEE at this present time inhabitant of Abbots Langly in the County of Hartford, gen^t. 3 December 1685, proved 13 April 1692.   All my lands, tenements and hereditaments whatsoever, be the same freehold or copyhold, unto Nathaniel Hulton of Hornsey, gen^t., and Edward Horsman of Lincoln's Inn, gent., in trust to raise four hundred and fifty pounds to be given and paid to my wife Martha if surviving and also, out of the rents and profits to pay the usual interest of that sum yearly during her life, in lieu of dower, otherwise the said Martha shall not take or have any benefit of or by this my will.   As for the overplus of the money raised and such of the estate as shall not be sold the same shall be paid, conveyed and divided unto and amongst my four daughters, now at this present through God's mercy alive and in health, Rebekah Lee, Anna Lee, Lydia Lee and Elizabeth Lee, to be paid and conveyed unto them respectively at their respective ages of one and twenty years or days of marriage.

To my daughter Rebekah my manuscripts in Divinity if she be not disposed in marriage before this will take effect.   To Anna, Lydie and Elizabeth all my manuscripts in Natural Philosophy, Chimistry or Physick, or of any the Liberal Arts and Sciences, and all the printed books in Chymical

Physick, to be divided equally, share and share alike, the eldest choosing first, excepting one manuscript book in Octavo, large, with black covers, in the first leaf thereof is found written " (Experimentorū Liber III) " which I give and bequeath to my daughter Elizabeth.

The said Nathaniel Hulton and Edward Horsman to be executors.

In the Probate Act Book the testator is called " nup de Abbotts Langley in Com. Hertford sed in regno Galliæ Gen..defti." Fane, 70.

[There can be no doubt that I have found here the will of Mr. Samuel Lee of Bristol, New England, written just before he set sail from England and proved after his death in a French prison, he having been captured and carried into St. Maloes while on his voyage home in 1691.—HENRY F. WATERS.

In the notes to Sewall's Diary, vol. i. pp. 148–150, I collected some facts relative to the daughters of Rev. Samuel Lee. It seems certain that

REBECCA	married	John Saffin	of	Boston.
LYDIA	"	{ John George	"	"
		{ Rev. Cotton Mather	"	"
ANNE	"	Henry Wyrley	"	New Bristol.
ELIZABETH.				

I noted a letter dated in 1728, from Dr. Isaac Watts to Mrs. Katherine Sewall, daughter of John George and Lydia Lee. Therein he says, " Mr. Peacock, who married your eldest Aunt, was my intimate friend. Mrs. Bishop and Mrs. Wirley were both my acquaintance." It seems probable that Elizabeth, the fourth daughter, married a Bishop. Rebecca seems to have been the oldest daughter, and as she was the third wife of John Saffin and quarrelled with him, it seems very probable that after his death in 1710, she married Mr. Peacock. I do not see the reason why Samuel Lee is termed " gentleman " in his will—as he was a clergyman, Oxford-bred, and a tutor and proctor there.—W. H. WHITMORE.]

GEORGE PLUMMER of St. Michael, Crooked Lane, citizen and barber surgeon of London, 6 March 1646, proved 29 April 1647. To daughter Emme Plummer fifty pounds and also ten pounds out of money due unto me by and from James Gooday, captain and commander of the ship Arabella now in the parts beyond the seas. Son in law William Watts and my daughter Mary, his wife. Granddaughter Anne Allen. Grandchild Thomas Plummer. Grandchild Raphael Shemmonds whom I have brought up ever since he was born. My brother Richard Plummer. My wife Em Plummer to be sole executrix. Fines, 72.

RICHARD JAMES of Romford, Essex, innholder, 20 July 1639, proved 12 April 1647. I do will and give unto my brother Edmund James, now beyond the seas, the sum of forty shillings to be paid unto him by my executrix. To my daughter Elizabeth James two hundred pounds at her age of twenty and one years. The other daughters of my wife Rebecca Jefferson and Beatrice Jefferson. My wife Mary to be sole executrix. The overseers to be Mr. John Fenninge of Romford, woolen draper and Mr. Robert Grafton, butcher, my brother in law.

A codicil added 7 October 1642. To my cousin and godson Richard James now or late of Glensford ten pounds.

Another codicil 17 July 1644. Ten pounds more to my said cousin and godson. Fines, 74.

[Edward James was granted 350 acres of land in Rappahannock river, Va., 30 miles up on the North side, May 22, 1650. Book No. 2, p. 219.—R. A. BROCK.]

RICHARD SEYMOR of St. Mary Savoy *als* Strand, Middlesex, gen. 13 April 1641.

I give and bequeath unto my loving wife Mr^{is}. Jane Seymor, for and during the term of her life, the interest, benefit and profit which shall be made, raised and received of and for the sum of six hundred pounds which is owing to me by the persons hereafter named, vizt. the right Hono^{ble} the Earl of North^{ton} four hundred pounds, the Earl of Peterborough one hundred pounds, Mr^{is}. Margaret Washington my wife's mother fifty pounds and my wife's brother in law Mr. Francis Muce fifty pounds. All the securities for the said moneys shall be made in the name of my loving nephew Lawrence Swetnam gen^t., whom I do desire to pay the said interest money to my said wife from time to time as he shall receive the same during the term, etc. To my son Spencer Seymer all my goods, chattels, moneys, leases, bonds, bills, debts and other things whereof I am possessed, he to be executor of this my will and my said nephew Mr. Lawrence Swetnam to be guardian to my said son during his minority. Richard, Arthur, Robert and Stephen Squibb my nephews, sons of my brother in law Mr. Arthur Squibb. I humbly beseech and desire the right Honble. the Earl of Northampton, my noble lord and master, and my brother in law Arthur Squibb Esq., one of the four tellers of the Receipt of H. M. Exchequer at Westminister, to be supervisors of this my last will, etc.

On the last day of May 1641 commission issued to Lawrence Swetnam, guardian named in the will, to administer the goods etc. of the deceased according to the tenor of the will during the minority of Spencer Seymor the executor named, etc.   Evelyn, 62.

[This will makes known to us a sister of Lawrence Washington, M.A., Rector of Purleigh, of whom hitherto we have been entirely ignorant. And it shows that his mother, Mrs. Margaret (Butler) Washington, was still alive in 1641.— HENRY F. WATERS.]

JOHN LANE.—In the name of God Amen: the seaventh day of August in the Thirteenth yeare of the Raigne of our Soveraigne Lord King Charles the Second over England etc. Annoq̃ Dñi one Thousand Six hundred Sixty one I John Lane of Rickmersworth in the County of Hertford yeoman being of a good and perfect memory (praysed be God) knowing death certaine but the tyme and hower very vncertaine being weake and sick in body doe make this my last will and Testament in manner following. And ffirst of all I give to the poore people of Rickmersworth aforesaid ffifty shillings of good and lawfull money of England To be distributed amongst them where most need is within one Moneth next after my death At the discretion of myne Executo^r hereafter herein named Item I give and bequeath to Rebecca Baker my daughter ffive pounds of like good money And to my kinsman Job Lane sonne of my brother James Lane deceased I give and bequeath the sume of Thirty pounds of like good money And to my kinsman Thomas Lane sonne of my brother Symon Lane deceased I give and bequeath ffifteene pounds of like good money And to Jahasell Lane sonne of my brother Jeremiah Lane deceased I give and bequeath the sume of Tenn pounds of like good money And to Mary Lane my kinswoman daughter of the said Jeremiah I give and bequeath the like sume of Tenn pounds of like good money All which said Legacies And severall sumes of money soe bequeathed I will shall be paid to them and every of them within Six Moneths after my death by myne Executo^r hereafter herein named   Item I give and bequeath vnto my kinswoman

ffrances the now wife of Richard Lovett Tenn pounds of like good money
to be paid vnto her Twenty shillings a yeare dureing Tenn yeares next
ensueing after my death.   Item I give and bequeath to Judith Lovett y⁰
wife of Henry Lovett yᵉ like suṁe of Tenn pounds of like good money to
be paid vnto her Twenty Shillings a yeare dureing Tenn yeares next ensueing after my death.   Item I give and bequeath unto my said kinsman
Jahasell Lane The bedstedd in my Parlour whereon I now lye with all
bedding and furniture of Bedding thervpon or therwithall now vsed And
if my·said daughter Rebecca or the Bayliffe of the Lord of the Mannoʳ of
Rickmersworth shall take away the said Bedstedd or any other bedding
thervnto belonging for the Herriotts to be due att my death Then my will
is that my Executoʳ shall give the full price or valew sett upon them for
Redemption therof or if not to be redeemed shall give him the full price as
they shall be valued att in ready money Item I give unto the said Jahasell
Two paire of sheete And one Brasse Porrage pott with a Notch in it.
Item I give vnto my sd kinswoman Mary Lane Two paire of sheets and
one Dozen of Table napkins And my long Table cloth with a fringe att end
of it and one short table cloth   Item I give will and bequeath Three
Hundred of Spray ffaggotts to the poore people of Millend to be delivered
to them thensueing winter next after my death att the discretion of myne
Executoʳ herein hereafter named The said poore people that live betweene
James Edlins and Eves house to have the said ffaggotts and none else And
if any new erected Cottage be made or sett up within the liberty aforesaid
hereafter and any more poore shalbe therby added and increased such
poore shall have noe share in the said ffaggotts And my will is that Three
Hundred of such like ffaggotts shall be given to such poore and continued
for one and twenty years next after my death and not longer And concerning Mary Hall which is now with me I doe will that my Executoʳ herein
named shall take fatherly care of her And shall provide and manttayne her
with meate drink and apparell in decent manner for and during the terme
of three years next ensueing after my death Item I give and bequeath unto
James Lane brother to the said Job, Tenn pounds of like good money to be
paid to him within Six Moneths next after my death by myne Executoʳ
Item I give and bequeath vnto my kinswoman Martha Lane daughter of
Jeremiah the like suṁe of Tenn pounds of like good money to be paid to
her within six moneths next after my death by myne Executoʳ. Yf it
happen that my kinsman Thomas Lane shall dye before his Legacie become due then The ffifteene pounde Legacie shalbe paid to his wife, yf shee
dye then to his children And if my kinsman Job dye before his Legacie
shall become due then the thirty pounds Legacie shalbe paid to his wife if
shee dye Then to his children And if any of the other Legatoʳˢ That are
single persons and unmarried happen to dye before their Legacie or
Legacies shall become due Then my Executoʳ shall pay such Legacie of
him or her soe dying to the next brother or sister att his owne discretion
Item all the rest and residue of my goods and chattells whatsoever vnbe-
queathed I give and bequeath unto my kinsman John Lane whome I name
and appoint Executoʳ of this my last will and Testament In witnes wherof
I the said John Lane the Testator have hereunto sett my hand and seale
the day and yeare ffirst above written.   John Lane. Read published and
declared subscribed and sealed by the Testatoʳ In the pʳsence of Paul Ives
Alice Shrimpton her marke John Hobs his marke.   Laud, 7.
[Proved January 13, 1661.]

[This will adds somewhat to our knowledge of the family of Job Lane of Malden, concerning whom we printed much in the REGISTER, XI., April and July, and also in Vol. XVII., 266. At these citations will be found evidence that Job Lane had an older brother John, brothers James and Edward, and uncles Henry, George and John. The will of this uncle John is herein-before given, and we can sum up the record of that generation as follows :—

   i.   Henry, prob. d. s. p.
   ii.   John ; dau. Rebecca Baker.
   iii. James ; sons John, Job, James, and Edward.
   iv.   Simon ; son Thomas.
   v.   Jeremiah ; son Jahasel, daus. Mary and Martha.
   vi.   George.

It seems reasonable to suppose that John Lane, "kinsman" of the testator and executor of his will, is John, brother of Job, although not specifically termed a son of James, Sen.

In the REGISTER for April, 1888, the late Rev. James P. Lane writes about the descendants of James Lane, brother of Job.—W. H. WHITMORE.]

JOHN HOOKER of Marefield in the county of Leicester gentleman, 1 January 1654, proved 26 November 1655. To my cousin William Junnings his five children now living one hundred pounds, and to his wife fifty pounds and to himself fifty pounds. Item I do give unto my cousin Samuel Hooker, student in New England, the sum of one hundred pounds. To my cousin Elizabeth Erricke one hundred pounds and also to her daughter Abigail five pounds. To my cousin Alice Burton ten pounds. To my cousin Rebecca Webster five pounds. To my cousin Catherine Coge (?) ten pounds. To William and John Iunings (?) the two sons of John Iunings (?) of Chilcott in Denbighshire twenty pounds betwixt them, and to Elizabeth and Dorothy the two daughters of the said John Juñings ten pounds. To my cousin John Hooker, student in Oxford twenty pounds. The children of my sister Frances Tarlton of London ten pounds amongst them all. To the poor of the parish of Tylton and Halstead two pounds. All the household goods and commodities appertaining to the house shall continue in it and go along with the house unremoved. Item I do nominate and appoint my said cousin William Junnings of Marefield the executor of this my last will and testament.

(In the Probate Act the name of the executor is given as Jennings.)

Aylett, 403.

[This is the will of a brother of the Rev. Thomas Hooker, the first minister of Hartford, Ct. Mather in his Magnalia (Book iii. Part 1, Appendix ; edition of 1853, vol. i. p. 333), says of Thomas Hooker that he "was born at Marfield in Leicestershire, about 1586, of parents that were neither unable nor unwilling to bestow on him a liberal education." Rev. Edward W. Hooker in his life of Thomas Hooker, Boston, 1850, p. 9, gives the date of his birth July 7, 1586. Savage in his Genealogical Dictionary changes Mather's Marfield to Markfield, which is the name of a parish a short distance northwest of Leicester. He finds that the parish register of Markfield "for a few years before and after is totally deficient," and that "the family name does not appear at all in the register." He therefore doubts Mather's statement. But Marefield, which is a short distance to the northeast of Leicester, was the birthplace of Thomas Hooker. The Rev. George Leon Walker, D.D., in a contribution to the Memorial History of Hartford County, vol. i. p. 277, retains Mather's spelling of Hooker's birthplace, but locates it correctly." "The little hamlet of Marfield," he says, "is one of four tithings or towns which make up the parish of Tilton and contains but five houses, having had six at the time of Hooker's birth." Miss Mary K. Talcott, in a contribution to the same work (vol. i. page 245), says that, Rev. Thomas Hooker was a "son of Thomas Hooker or Hoker of Marfield in the parish of Tilton, grandson of Kenelm Hooker of Blaston, who was the only son of Thomas Hoker or Hoker of Blaston, co. Leicester, whose will, dated Sept. 2, 1559, was proved Jan. 27, 1561-2, by Cecilia Hooker his relict and executrix. It is supposed that this Thomas Hooker held some stewardship or like office under the Digby family who possessed estates in that part of Leicestershire. Kenellime Digby, Esq., is a witness, and is named as supervisor of the will. Kenelm or Kenellyme Hooker undoubtedly received his name from Kenelm Digby." Miss Talcott adds : " Thomas Hooker, father of Rev. Thomas Hooker, occupied in 1586 land in Frisbye and Gaddesby, co. Leicester. The parish register of Tilton records the burial of ' Thomas Hooker of Marfield, July 24, 1635,' and administration of his estate was granted to his eldest son, John Hooker, in the Archdeacon's Court at Leicester, Jan. 11, 1636–7; and he is there described as ' Thomas Hooker of Marefield, in the parish of Tilton, gentleman.' The Tilton register, under date of April, 1631, gives the burial of Mrs. Hooker, wife of Mr. Hooker of Marfield; probably the wife of Thomas."

Samuel Hooker, named in the will as a " student in New England," and John Hooker, as a " student in Oxford," were sons of Rev. Thomas Hooker. Samuel graduated at Harvard College in 1653. At the date of the will he was a Fellow of the College. He was settled in 1661 as the minister at Farmington, Conn., where he died Nov. 5 or 6, 1697, aged 62. See sketch of his life in Sibley's Harvard Graduates, vol. i. pp. 348–52. John Hooker, brother of Samuel " in 1660," according to Miss Talcott, " became vicar of Marsworth in Buckinghamshire, and in 1669 was presented by Sir Edward Pye, bart., to be rector of Leckhampstead in the same county. He died in 1684 and was buried at Marsworth."—EDITOR.

WASHINGTON.—

[The following extracts from the Warton Parish Register were kindly furnished me by Miss Fanny Bland, Orton, Westmoreland, England, a lady of antiquarian and genealogic tastes :
Married, 1573, —— Washington and Jennet Jackson.
Baptized, 1584, Elizabeth Washington.
Married, 1583, Lawrence Washington and Alice Godsalf.
Baptized, 1586, Ann Washington.
    "   "   John Washington.
    "   "   John Washington.
    ".   1593, Mary, daughter of Lawrence Washington of Warton.
    "   1597, Ann,   "   "   "   "   "
    "   1600, Robert, sonne   "   "   "   "   "
Buried, 1613, the wife of John Washington in the Church.
Baptized, 1619, Jane, daughter of Leonard Washington.

Miss Bland also sends me the following from *The Sedbergh and District Parish Magazine for the parishes of Sedbergh, Cantley, Cowgill, Dent, Garsdale and Howgill.* No. 26. Feb. 1890.

" THE PARISH REGISTER." *Symond Washington, yonger.* " D " is not an original part of Simon's name, but after " n " it crops up occasionally as an excrescence. Compare the " d " in the word " expound," in the surname " Simmonds," in the Sedberghian " he fell i' soond " = " he fell into a swoon."

On the first occurrence of a male Washington it may be appropriate to note that a century of Washingtons (1564 to 1665) are commemorated by initials and dates on a flat stone at the East end of the Church. Judging from the threefold occurrence of " S. W." among them, it may be supposed that Simon was a favorite name in the family. An adjoining stone, now (alas!) almost illegible from scaling, records that it is " erected in further Memory of the an[tie]nt Fam[ily] of the Washing[ton]s of [Gate]side in Howgill." What gives its interest to these Washingtons is the probability that they belong to the family from which the famous George Washington, the first President of the United States, sprang."—R. A. BROCK.]

HOLLIS.

I HAVE long felt it a pious duty to look up the Hollis and Holworthy families, and ever since I first came here I have been gradually picking up items about them in Wills. It has occurred

to me that one or two numbers of my Gleanings especially devoted
to these and other benefactors of my old college* would be proper.
I now send some Hollis matter. The Hollis family were cutlers by
trade though Drapers by company. A pedigree and notice of the
family may be found in Morant's Essex, Vol. II. p. 167. A letter of
Thomas Hollis the great benefactor is printed in the REGISTER,
Vol. II. p. 265. See also Memoir of Thomas Hollis, London,
1780.—H. F. WATERS.

[The following is a brief genealogy of the Hollis family :
"Thomas Hollis, of Rotherham in Yorkshire, a cutler, came to
London during the civil wars. His wife's maiden name was Ann
Whiting. They had sons, Thomas, Nathaniel and John, and a
daughter Mary. Thomas died without issue. Nathaniel had several
children, of whom only one, by name Thomas, survived him.
This Thomas was the second benefactor of that name, and was the
father of another benefactor, mentioned in the Harvard College
Records. as Thomas Hollis, Esq., of Lincoln's Inn. John Hollis
had a considerable family of children, of whom the most important
were Timothy and Isaac. All these men, with the exception of
Thomas Hollis of Rotherham, appear in the College Records as
benefactors. In these notes, the three benefactors who bore the
name of Thomas Hollis will be distinguished as 1st, 2d and 3d.
Robert Thorner was an uncle of Thomas Hollis 1st.—(See Morant's
Essex, 2 : 16, and Memoirs of Thomas Hollis (3d), I. pp. 1 and 2.)"
—EVARTS B. GREENE, of Harvard University, Cambridge, Mass.†]

THOMAS SMITH, citizen and cutler of London (aged) 21 November 1674,
proved 6 May 1675. To wife Anna for term of her natural life my capital
messuage or tenement &c in the parish of Walthamstow in Essex, except
the little tenement wherein John Tompkins now liveth. And afterwards
the reversion &c of the same to my son John Smith and the heirs of his
body lawfully begotten. To my said son John my messuages &c in Dunmowe, Essex, with condition that my said son John, his heirs or assigns, or
some of them, shall and do within the space of three months next after my
decease pay, or satisfy, or cause to be paid or satisfied, unto my foresaid
wife Anna the full sum of four hundred pounds in performance of a contract
made between us at and before marriage. I give and bequeath unto my
eldest son Thomas fifty pounds, to my youngest son William fifty pounds,
to my grandsonn Thomas Smith, son of my second son John, one hundred
pounds, and to my brother Thomas Thorowgood twenty shillings (to buy
him a ring). I give to my sister Frances Tompkins her dwelling free in
the house wherein she now liveth during her natural life, and to her now
husband after her decease, so long as he shall live a widower. To my
brother Valentine twenty shillings (for a ring), to my kinswoman Frances
Burrough five pounds. Twenty shillings each to my sister Margaret Ellis,
to my sister Elizabeth, to my brother Thomas Hollis, to my sister Frances

* Few of our readers need to be told that the *alma mater* of Mr. Waters is Harvard College. He was graduated in the class of 1855. See REGISTER, vol. 39, page 325.—EDITOR.
† This and other annotations to which Mr. Greene's name is affixed, have been
kindly contributed by Evarts B. Greene of Cambridge, Mass., a member of the Harvard
Seminary in American History.—EDITOR.

Tompkins and to my sister Susan. To my sister Katherine twenty shillings a year, to be paid out of my lands in Walthamstowe. The residue to my executrix and executor equally. Wife Anna to be the executrix and son John the executor. Dycer, 52.

Robert Thorner of Baddesley, in the co. of Southampton, gen^t, 31 May 1690. To my wife Rachel Thorner five hundred pounds absolutely &c in case she have no child by me; but if she have any child by me then I give the said five hundred pounds only for the term of her natural life; and after her decease I give the same to such child. To said wife my tenement and lands at Pitton in the co. of Wilts, during her natural life; and after her decease I give the same to Ellis Langford, son of Harry Langford, now in Jamaica, if he be then surviving; and if not, then to Edward Langford of London, goldsmith. To my sister Katherine Begon the interest or use arising upon one hundred pounds for the term of her natural life, to be paid to Mr. John Filer of Litton, in Dorset, to be by him paid and given towards my said sister's subsistence. And after her decease I give the said sum of one hundred pounds to the grandchildren of my said sister (equally). To my niece Mary Thorner of Blackfriars, London, three shillings per week for the term of her natural life. To Thomas Durman, my wife's brother, two shillings and four pence per week; to Margery Durman, my wife's sister, ten pounds. To Mrs. Elizabeth Legay, daughter of Mr. Isaac and Katherine Legay, of Weststoake, near Chichester, Sussex, one hundred pounds, if living and unmarried two years after my decease, or if then married with her parents' consent and good liking. To my reverend pastor Mr. Nathaniel Robinson of Southampton twenty pounds; to his daughters Mrs. Elizabeth and Mrs. Anne Robinson ten pounds each to buy a piece of plate in remembrance of me. To Isaac Watts,* son of Isaac Watts of Southampton, clothier, ten pounds to be paid to his father for his use. To the eldest son of Robert Beare of Southampton, five pounds. To Robert Hawkins, son of Richard Hawkins of Blackfriars, London, ten pounds. To Mr. John Filer, minister, and Mr. Richard Meadway of Litton, Dorset, twenty shillings each to buy rings. To William Sprackett, now of Taunton, twenty pounds. To Mrs. Elizabeth Belchamber, of Twickenham near London, ten pounds. To Hester Davis, wife of John Davis of Titchfield, five pounds. To Mrs. Cuell of Winchester ten pounds. To Mrs. Margaret Noyes and Mrs. Cooper, widows, and Jonathan Batchelor and Jonathan Tremaine, all of Southampton, five pounds each. To the Congregational church in Southampton to which I belong two hundred pounds, for and towards the maintenance of a minister or pastor among them, to be improved at interest or else laid out in the purchase of lands. To the officers of the said church all my interest in the house above the Bar in Southampton built for a meeting place for the congregation there attending, so long as it shall continue to be used as a meeting place. And in case the same be not used as a meeting place then immediately from and after such disuse I give and bequeath the same house and appurtenances unto Mr. Nathaniel Robinson, if living, or in case of his decease before the expiration of the lease, to his daughter Mrs. Elizabeth Robinson, and in case of her decease &c. to the second son of Isaac Watts aforenamed for the remainder thereof.

* Was not this the famous Dr. Watts, who was born in Southampton July 17, 1674, and who was therefore in his sixteenth year at the date of this will? His father, Isaac Watts of Southampton, at one time kept a boarding school there.—H. F. W.

" Item I devise give and bequeath unto Harvard College in New England whereof Mr. Increase Mather is now President, the sume of ffive hundred pounds to be paid unto the President of the said Colledge and imployed for the propogateing of learning and piety which sume I appoint my Executors or Trustees or their Successors to pay out of the Revenues of my Lands in London soe soone as it shall be raised out of the neate proceedes thereof after the expiraĉon of Sʳ Peter Vandeputts Lease according to the limitaĉons and directions and in manner and forme hereafter expressed. Item I devise give and bequeath all my reall estate in Messuages Lands Tenements and appurtenances scituate and being in the city of London being at present of the value of eighty pounds per Annum and after the Lease of the same to Sʳ Peter Vandeput be expired may be of the value of ffoure hundred pounds per Annum (be it more or lesse) unto Mr. Bennett Swaine citizen and ffishmonger of London, Isaac Watts of the Towne and County of Southampton clothier Thomas Hollis jvnʳ of London cutler and John Brackstone of the Towne and County of Southampton clothier To hold the said Messuages Lands Tenemᵗˢ and appurtenances unto them the said Bennett Swayne Isaac Watts Thomas Hollis junʳ and John Brackstone and to their Successors and Assignes to be appointed as is hereafter declared for ever. In Trust nevertheless for the use and uses hereafter menĉoned & expressed That is to say Tenne pounds per Annum forever out of the neat proceeds issues and profitts of the said Lands to be equally divided betweene my said Trustees yearly and soe from time to time to continue to their successors in the said Trust for their own proper use and uses cleare of all charges and disbursements as a recompence for their dischargeing the Trust in them reposed in receiveing the rents issues and profitts of my said Lands and disposeing of the residue thereof according to this my Will which said Tenne pounds per Annum being allowed and my other Legacies aforemenĉoned paid alsoe my debts and ffunerall expences and other charges first paid and discharged I appoint the first five hundred pounds which shall arise out of the residue of the neate proceeds rents issues and profitts of the said Lands to be for the dischargeing of the Legacie aforemenĉoned given to my child in case my Wife hath any such child by me then the same to be imployed and disposed of for the maintenance education and portion of such child in manner as aforesaid. And after payment of the said ffive hundred pounds for my child (if any such be) Then I appoint Twenty pounds per Annum of the remaineing neate and cleare proceeds issues and profitts of the said Lands during the continuance of the Lease now in being by which the said Lands are demised to be paid and imployed towards the maintenance of a ffree Schoole in the parish of Litton in the County of Dorsett to teach the Male children of the said parish to read write cast accompt and grammar from the age of six yeares to fifteene The Schoolemaster to be nominated by my Trustees and the remainder of the neate issues and profitts of the said Lands the foregoing legacies menĉoned being first allowed I give to the binding out apprentices to Mechanicall labouring trades such poor children and youth as are of pious and sober persons of the said Parish of Litton the Towne of Dorchester towne of Southampton and City of Sarum to every child five pounds for placeing out apprentice and five pounds more for a stock to sett up at the end of their apprenticeshipp which I will only to such persons of the said places as are sober and industriously inclined in the judgment of my Trustees. And for the more exact direction of my Trustees in this affaire I appoint that if the said Lands determined to this use as aforesaid shall amount to ffive hundred pounds received in Land by my said Trustees Then the same to be disposed the one fourth parte thereof to the children of Litton & the other three fourth partes thereof to the children of Dorchester and the second five hundred pounds soe to be raised and received as aforesaid to be disposed to and for the children of Southampton And the third ffive hundred pounds in like manner to and for the children and youth of Sarum and soe successively as money shall be raised and received in such severall sūmes of ffive hundred pounds to be disposed in manner and for the uses aforesaid for the placeing and setting up of the children of sober persons of the places aforenamed. The said children and youth being accordingly qualifyed as farre as may be discerned by my Trustees during the continuance of the said Lease by which the said Lands are now granted And after the expiraĉon of the said Lease then I devise and appoint one hundred pounds certaine per annum out of the rents issues and profitts of the said Lands (the tenne pounds per annum to my Trustees and my other Legacies aforemenĉoned first being paid) to be imployed to the uses aforesaid that is to say One fourth parte of the said one hundred pounds per Annum towards the ffreeschoole at Litton and the other three fourth parts thereof to the placeing and setting up of children of the places aforenamed to be raised received and disposed of in like manner as aforesaid and soe to continue forever to the end of time And the overplus of the rents and profitts of the said Lands above the said tenne pounds per annum to my Trustees and their Successors (my other Legacies aforesaid and the said one hundred pounds per Annum above menĉoned I devise the first five hundred pounds that can be raised thereof after the aforesaid Lease be expired to be for the discharging the Legacie aforemenĉoned to Harvard Colledge in New England to be paid to the then President thereof for the uses aforesaid And after payment of the said ffive hundred pounds Then I devise the remaining overplus which shall arise as aforesaid out of my said Lands to be imployed for the building of Almeshouses within the Towne and County of Southampton for the maintenance of poore widowes each widow to be allowed two shillings per weeke and her house room the same to be purchased built and maintained when a convenient sūme of money is raised by the revenues aforesaid for performing the same and soe to be maintained and increased in number from time to time forever according as moneys shall arise as aforesaid out of the said Lands And I doe nominate appoint and ordaine them the said Bennett Swayne Isaac Watts Thomas Hollis jun[r]. and John Brackston to be equall joynt and sole executors of this my last Will and Testament."

Proved by Thomas Hollis and Bennett Swayne 8 December 1690 and by Isaac Watts and John Brackstone. 4 June 1691.   Dyke, 211.

[Under the record of a meeting of the Corporation held Dec. 24th, 1691, the provisions of Thomas's will, having reference to the College, are cited as above. On this page is entered a memorandum made at a later period, giving parts of a letter from Henry Newman, as follows. The letter is dated June 10th, 1710.

" I have enquired after Mr. Robert Thorner's legacy of £500 . . . . . I compared the abstract you sent me out of the College register, & found them agreeing with the will." He gives the names of the trustees at that time, among them, John Hollis, who succeeded Bennet Swaine, deceased (see College Book, IV. and V. p. 3, beginning at the back). On the same page is the following memorandum : " Mr. Thorner's lease will expire A.D. 1769, says Mr. T. Hollis (nephew), in his letter, Aug. 5, 1734."

In 1728, a copy of the will was received from Thomas Hollis 1st. A memorandum by Wadsworth at this time suggests doubts as to the value of the leases mentioned (College Book, " Wills, Gifts and Grants," p. 18). The full amount of this legacy was not paid until 1775. In 1774, Timothy Hollis, then one of the trustees, announced that he was ready to pay £100 at once and the remainder of the legacy before the new year. In the winter of 1774–5, an order was drawn on Hollis for the remainder, which he had already declared himself ready to pay.—(See Hollis Letters, p. 83, and Harvard College Papers, 2 : p. 31.)—EVARTS B. GREENE.]

THOMAS HOLLIS the elder, of the parish of St. Mary in White Chapel, Middlesex, and citizen and draper of London, 27 January 1713, proved 23 September 1718. To wife Ann Hollis one hundred pounds and the furniture of the chamber wherein we usually lodge. My annuity of twenty-five pounds payable out of Her Majesty's Treasury for the term of ninety nine years (by virtue of Tally or order bearing date 16 Oct. 1708) to my son Thomas Hollis in Trust for my said wife so long as she shall happen to live, and then to my son Thomas. To said son Thomas one hundred pounds. To my granddaughter Mary Winnock fifty pounds. To the seven children of my son John Hollis, namely Isaac, Samuel, Jacob, Timothy, Hannah, Ann and Elizabeth, seven hundred pounds, to be equally divided and paid to them at their respective ages of one and twenty years or days of marriage. To my grandson Thomas Hollis two hundred pounds. My annuity of fifty pounds payable out of Her Majesty's Treasury (by virtue of Tally and order dated 26 Oct. 1706) to my said grandson Thomas Hollis, in trust for Nathaniel Hollis son of me the said Testator and father of my said grandson so long as he shall happen to live, and after that in trust for my grandson William Ladds for the whole remainder of the term (ninety nine years). Another annuity of forty five pounds to my said grandson in trust for my said son Nathaniel and next to the said Thomas. Another annuity of fifty pounds to my said son John in trust for my daughter Mary Ladds, for her own separate and peculiar use and maintenance exclusive of her husband who shall not intermeddle with the same, and after her decease in trust for my granddaughter Mary Rennalls, daughter of the said Mary Ladds. A bequest to a cousin Hannah Hutton and her children (except James and Elizabeth her two eldest children). To the children of a late sister Hannah Brunt, to the children of a late sister Mary Gold of Derbyshire, to a cousin Daniel Sheldon, a cousin Ann Ramskar, to William Creswick and his sister Elizabeth Creswick, to friends Mr William Woolaston and Mr. Robert Rennalls.

Sons Thomas and John Hollis to be the executors. A codicil made 11 January 1716–17, in which he calls himself Thomas Hollis the aged and refers to a decay in the sight of his wife Anne, provides for a trust for the use of a cousin Dorothy Malin, widow, and her two daughters &c.

Tenison, 178.

[For an account of Thomas Hollis, the elder, see "Memoirs of Thomas Hollis (3d), pp. 112." In the REGISTER, Vol. 2 (1848), p. 265, is printed a letter from Thomas Hollis 1st, dated Aug. 25th, 1719, in which he alludes to the death of his father. He was a generous benefactor of numerous charitable and religious institutions. He died in London in 1718, aged 84 years.—EVARTS B. GREENE.]

THOMAS HOLLIS, senior of St. Mary, Whitechapel, Middlesex, and citizen and draper of London 6 January 1723, proved 26 January 1730. Five hundred pounds or more to be laid out and expended for mourning and other such purposes. All my freehold messuages &c in Ash and Winoxverge near Sandwich, Kent, now in occupation of Thomas Minter or his undertenants, unto Richard Solly (second son of my nephew Richard Solly deceased) and his heirs forever. And my mind and Will is that his uncle

John Solly of Feversham, grocer, do manage and take care of the same in trust for him until he shall arrive at his age of twenty-one years. My messuage or tenement in the parish of St. Laurence Pountney to my nephew Thomas Hollis (son of my brother Nathaniel Hollis) also my freehold lands &c. in Pollox Hill, Bedford. I give to Thomas Hollis (son of my nephew Thomas Hollis) three thousand pounds to be paid to his father in trust for him until he arrive at the age of twenty-one years. To my brother Nathaniel Hollis one thousand pounds and also two hundred pounds per annum for life. To my brother John Hollis two thousand pounds and I hereby ratify and confirm the settlement or provision which I have formerly made for the benefit of the children of my said brother John Hollis (five, named, Isaac Hollis, Timothy Hollis, Mary Winnock, Hannah Edwards and Elizabeth Ashurst). To nephew William Ladds, merchant, one thousand pounds. To niece Mary Reynolds, wife of John Reynolds, one thousand pounds, and to her daughter my cousin Mary Reynolds one thousand pounds. To my said cousin the furniture of my chamber at Tottenham and her mother Ladd's picture. To Elizabeth Williams, wife of John Williams, daughter of my late uncle John Hollis of St. Alban's deceased, one hundred pounds. One hundred pounds apiece to each of the children of my said cousin Elizabeth Williams, over and above what I have already advanced and given. One hundred pounds apiece to the two children of my late cousin Dorothy Moor deceased, viz. Hannah Malyn and Elizabeth Malyn, over and above what I have already advanced and given. To Joshua Hollis, covenant servant to John and Thomas Hollis cutlers, three hundred pounds. To Elizabeth and Ann Hollis, children of my cousin Thomas Hollis of St. Alban's, cutler deceased, three hundred pounds, to be paid into the hands of their brother, the said Joshua Hollis. To my said brother John Hollis one hundred and thirty-four pounds four shillings and ten pence in the stock commonly called the Orphan's stock in the Chamber of London, in trust to pay the dividends &c unto my cousin Hannah Hutton Senior during her life and next among her children. And I give and bequeath unto the proper use of my cousin Hannah Hutton, wife of James Hutton senior, two hundred pounds, and to her son George Hutton one hundred pounds. To Elizabeth Edmonds, daughter of my said cousin Hannah Hutton, fifty pounds. To my brother John and my nephews Thomas and Timothy Hollis one thousand pounds in trust for such purposes as I have or shall direct them. To my brother John and his son Isaac Hollis fifteen hundred pounds in trust for such purposes as I have already or hereafter shall direct them by writing under my hand. To the President and Governors of Christ Church Hospital London five hundred pounds for the placing of poor boys out unto masters in apprenticeship, they permitting my executor to nominate two boys to be taken in qualified according to the rules of the House. To the President and Governors of St. Thomas's Hospital, Southwark, five hundred pounds for the use of the poor of the same. To the President and Governors of the Corporation for the poor of the City of London, or the New Workhouse in Bishopsgate Street, five hundred pounds. To John Noble and Edward Vallin, gentlemen, five hundred pounds on trust to distribute the same for and upon such trusts &c. as I have or shall direct. To the Deacons of the French Church in Threadneedle Street one hundred pounds, to be distributed amongst the poor of the said church. To the Deacons of the Dutch Church in Austin Friars one hundred pounds for the poor in like manner. To the Church Wardens of the parish of Trinity Minories, where I lately

lived, twenty pounds to be distributed amongst the poor housekeepers therein,
and thirty pounds more &c. To John Browne and John Wadsworth of
Sheffield in Yorkshire one hundred pounds upon trusts to give the same
unto such of the poor laboring workmen of Sheffield as I have formerly
dealt with and other poor people in Sheffield and its neighborhood. To
Thomas Halford and John Henn of Birmingham in Warwickshire fifty
pounds upon trust to distribute the same amongst such of the poor cutlers,
both short and long, and other workmen of Birmingham as I used to deal
withall. To Charles Osborne of Wolverhampton in Staffordshire the like
sum of fifty pounds to distribute amongst such poor workmen there as I have
usually dealt with. To Mr. John Towers near Aldgate one hundred
pounds for the use of the Society for Reformation of Manners in London
for the encouragement of so useful a work. To Mr. Jeremiah Hunt one
hundred pounds for his own use, and the further sum of one hundred
pounds for the use of his son Benjamin Hunt.

I do hereby name and appoint my aforesaid nephew Thomas Holis, son
of my said brother Nathaniel Hollis, to be my successor in the Trusts committed to me as executor to and Trustee of my late uncle Robert Thorner &c.

" And Whereas I have at Sundry times remitted diverse sums of money
to the Treasurer of the Corporation of Harvard Colledge in New England
for service I have appointed or shall hereafter appoint in that Colledge and
the Corporation are become Obliged to me and to my Executors under their
seal for the true performances of my orders and paying and distributing of
the Annual Increase or Interest that shall arise therefrom Now I do hereby
appoint my Executor Thomas Hollis my Trustee concerning the same, and
I order that he have the same powers in nominating and confirming the
Professors and the Students that are on my ffoundation which I might
claime in all things according to the Power I have reserved or shall reserve
to my self And I give him Power to appoint his successor in the same
Trusts after him in like manner to Supervise as much as may be and to call
for Accounts and in case of Imbezlement contrary to my orders to put the
Obligations in suit and to Inforce them in all times coming."

All the residue of personal estate to said nephew Thomas Hollis (son of
my said brother Nathaniel Hollis) and I make and ordain him full and sole
executor. Wit: Josiah Maber, Wm Limbery, Humfrey Buck.

A codicil, dated 6 July 1730, provides for bequests of " fifty pounds to
Mr. J. Maber who now lives with me " and fifty pounds apiece to your servants.   Isham, 10.

[The clause of the will relating to Harvard College is given as above in the
Hollis Book, p. 24.

In Newman's letter of June, 1710, already quoted, to the college authorities, is
the following very interesting clause : " Mr. Thomas Hollis, one of the Trustees
at the Cross Daggers in Little Minories, desires his will may be inquired for after
his death. About the year 1718, an effort was made to divert Hollis's gifts to the
College at New Haven. In this design, Cotton Mather, then on bad terms with
the college authorities, took a prominent part. The gist of this episode is given
in letters quoted by Quincy in his history of Harvard College, 1 : p. 527, 528. In
his letter to Increase Mather, Aug. 25th, 1719, already referred to, Hollis speaks
of having sent over produce to the amount of £300 for the benefit of the college,
and adds : " I have thôts living or by will to order over to you a large parsel
[of] goods, the produce to be added for same uses to the sum you now have in
hand."

The " diverse sums of money " remitted at " Sundry times to the Treasurer
of Harvard Colledge " may be found noted from time to time in the records of
the Corporation for this period. His first gift was that just mentioned. On

May 24th, 1720 (Coll. Book, IV. and V. p. 66), the following vote was recorded : " Voted that the thanks of the Corporation be rendered by Mr. Pr's'd't & Mr. Coleman to the worthy Mr. Thomas Hollis of London, for the further valuable donation he has been pleased to make to the College, and is already in part arrived." The gifts made by Hollis up to 1775 are summarized in the following extract, from the formal acknowledgment given by the Corporation in response to the request of Hollis.—(See Coll. Book, IV. and V. pp. 105, 106) :

"Whereas it hath pleased Almighty God to inspire Mr. Thomas Hollis, merchant in London, with most pious and generous designs for yᵉ honour of our great and glorious Lord & Saviour & for yᵉ good of mankind & hath in particular disposed him to execute some of those designs in ample & most beneficial donations to Harvard College aforesaid, Insomuch yᵗ there hath already flowed into yᵉ Treasury from yᵉ bountiful hand of yᵉ said Mr. Thomas Hollis to yᵉ value of three thousand six hundred & seventy pounds, thirteen shillings & an half penny . . . . he hath transmitted statutes date January yᵉ tenth 1722 which are lately come to yᵉ hands of yᵉ said Pres'd't & Fellows of Harvard College, wherein he directs yᵗ . . . . . . yᵉ Increase or produce of yᵉ same be applied to yᵉ ends following, yᵗ is to say, eighty pounds per Annum, part thereof for a Salary & support for his Professor of Divinity, ten pounds apiece per annum to ten scholars, more or fewer according to yᵉ produce yᵉ money shall make per Annum." It is interesting to note in this connection that one of the first scholars on the Hollis foundation was Samuel Mather, a grandson of Increase Mather.— (See Letter of Hollis in " Hollis Letters, 9.") The Divinity Professorship was founded in 1721. Various letters on this subject, which passed between Hollis on one side, and the President and Mr. Colman, a Fellow, on the other, are reprinted in Quincy's History, 1 : 529–540. The first reference in the college records to this subject is in the College Book, Nos. IV. and V., under date of April 25th, 1721. There was a prolonged discussion on the subject of the new Professorship (q. v. Quincy, 1 : 529–540, where a large number of these letters are reprinted from the College archives), of which we find frequent record in the College books. Hollis showed throughout this discussion a liberality of spirit remarkable in those times. Hollis, it must be remembered, belonged to the Baptist denomination, though affiliating to some extent with the Independents in London (see his letter to Increase Mather, REGISTER, 2 : 265). In his regulations for the Divinity Professor, the only theological test required was " that he declare it as his belief that the Bible is the only and most perfect rule of faith and manners." The Overseers amended by striking out the words " and most," and substituting for " Bible" the " Scriptures of the Old and New Testament."—(See Hollis's Book, pp. 3 and 4 ; Records of Overseers, 1 : 21, 22.) In January, 1721-2, Edward Wigglesworth was elected the first " Hollissian Professor in Harvard College."—(Coll. Book IV. and V. p. 74.) In the winter of 1726-7, Hollis transmitted £1127 to found a Professorship of Mathematics and Natural Philosophy, and in the following year presented the college with a valuable set of philosophical apparatus. Aside from these larger gifts, he proved his constant interest in the College by sending, from time to time, valuable collections of books for the library.

On learning of the death of Hollis, the Corporation, at a meeting held April 21, 1731, passed the following vote (see Hollis Book, p. 23) :

" Having lately received yᵉ tidings of yᵉ death of our worthy and generous benefactor, Thomas Hollis, Esq., of London, who departed this life yᵉ 21ˢᵗ of January last *—Voted yᵗ a copy of yᵉ sermon preached in yᵉ College Hall on yᵗ sorrowful occasion by yᵉ Revⁿᵈ Doctor Wigglesworth (his Divinity Professor) be desired in order to its being printed."

The clause in the will reserving to his successors the same right of approving the nomination of scholars and professors on his foundation, which he had reserved for himself, created some difficulty. The Corporation called the attention of his nephew and executor to the clause in the original orders which in the case of the scholars and the divinity professor limited the right of appointment to the founder himself, and in the case of the mathematics professor continued it only for his immediate successor. Hollis averted any possible friction by generously waiving all claims to exercise such rights (Hollis Book, pp. 23-25).—EVARTS B. GREENE.]

* This I presume gives us the precise date of death of Thomas Hollis, namely, January 21, 1730-1. I have not found it correctly given elsewhere.—EDITOR.

THOMAS HOLLIS, citizen and draper of London 8 February 1732, proved 17 June 1735. To be buried near the body of late dear wife. To honored father Nathaniel Hollis five hundred pounds. Reference to Trusts "I have for him from my grandfather" and to will of late honored uncle Thomas Hollis. Bequests to the Revd Jeremiah Hunt, cousins Elizabeth Creswick and William Creswick of St Albans, to the eldest child of cousin Sarah Taylor late of Sheffield deceased, to Mr John Browne of Sheffield, to cousin John Hammersley of Deptford, to cousin Margaret Hall of Staffordshire, to cousin Sarah Harrison of Nottingham, to Mr. Charles Osborne of Woolverhampton, to John Barnesley of Birmingham, Thomas Holford of Birmingham and Thomas Trulock, to cousin Timothy Hollis, cousin Daniel Parker of Enfield, Middlesex, and cousin Hannah Malin, to the congregation at Pinners Hall whereof the Rev^d. Mr. Jeremiah Hunt is pastor, to John, Thomas and Ann Williams children of cousin Elizabeth Williams, to Elizabeth Hollis daughter of late cousin Thomas Thomas Hollis of St. Albans, to poor workmen or their widows of Birmingham, and of Woolverhampton and Bilson, to the French Church in Threadneedle Street and the Dutch church in Austin Friars, to Mr. John Hollister the lease of the house wherein I now dwell in Mansell Street in Goodmansfields during the remainder of the term. All the real estate and the residue of the personal estate to son Thomas when he should attain the age of twenty-one years; but if he should die before attaining the said age then to cousin Isaac Hollis for and during his natural life, next to his heirs male, next to cousin Timothy Hollis and to his heirs forever. Mr. John Hollister, of Charterhouse Street, and my friend Thomas Trulock to be executors.

"And I do hereby nominate and appoint the said John Hollister to be my successor in the Trusts mentioned in the Will of Mr. Robert Thorner, in which I was appointed to succeed in the Room and Stead of my said late uncle Thomas Hollis deceased, and do desire the other Trustees who shall be living at my decease with all convenient expedition to Invest Instate Convey and Transfer the legal estate and Interest in the Lands and Tenements devised in Trust by the Will of the said Robert Thorner to the said John Hollister joyntly with themselves upon the Trusts in the said Will in such manner as Council shall direct, That so the said John Hollister may be capable and fully impowered to act in and perform the said Trusts in conjunction with the other Trustees according to the Directions of the said Will." Wit: W^m. Limbery, W^m. Wright, James Spence. Ducie, 124.

[Thomas Hollis 2nd in a letter of February 3rd, 1731-2, enclosed two bills for £350 each, the income of which was to be applied in adding £20 each to the salary of each of the Hollis professors. At the same time he enclosed a letter from his father, Nathaniel Hollis, announcing a gift of £350 for the support of two students, preferably Indians (Hollis Book, pp. 26, 27). In 1732, he presented the college with several philosophical instruments, including a "new-invented machine called an orrery, showing ye daily and diurnal motion of ye sun, earth and moon." (Hollis Book, p. 29.)—EVARTS B. GREENE.]

JOHN HOLLIS of St. Mary Matfellon alias White Chapel, Middlesex, and citizen and draper of London 21 March 1733, with codicil dated 12 December 1735, proved 13 January 1735, Messuages, lands &c. in Boreham and Hatfield Peverell, Essex, and all my part, share and dividend of the messuages, lands, &c in the parish of St. Mary Magdalen, Bermondsey, Surry, late of my father in law Edward Sandford deceased, after the death of my mother in law, to wife Hannah Hollis for and during the term of her natural life, next to son Isaac Hollis and the heirs of his body lawfully begotten next to son Timothy Hollis and the heirs of his body lawfully begotten, next to my grandson Hollis Edwards forever. Messuage in Old Street, St. Giles without Cripplegate, now in the possession of my cousin Cover (*sic*) widow, to son Isaac, upon condition that he permits and suffers my said cousin Cover to dwell in said messuage rent free during the term of her natural life. To said son Isaac my freehold messuage in Pettycoat Lane, St. Buttolph without Aldgate. Other bequests ; among them to the five sons of daughter Ann Solly, to the children of daughter Hannah Edwards, to the children of daughter Elizabeth Ashurst, to cousin Hannah Hutton, wife of James Hutton senior, to cousin Ann Loyd, the sawyer's wife, to cousin Elizabeth Williams, widow, to cousin Robert Ruslin, etc.

Son Timothy Hollis to be successor in the Trusts mentioned in the Will of Mr. Robert Thorner, in which I was appointed to succeed in the room and stead of Bennet Swaine deceased. To the French Church in Threadneedle Street, the parishes of White Chapel, Trinity Minories, Sheffield, Birmingham, Woolverhampton and Wallsall, to the Scotch Society at Edinburgh for Propagation of Christian Knowledge. Wife Hannah to be executrix.

Derby, 9.

[At a meeting of the Corporation held Oct. 21, 1724, " Professor Wigglesworth laid before them a letter from the worthy Mr. Thomas Hollis, merchant of London, informing them of a very valuable gift of books from his brother, Mr. John Hollis, merchant of London." Coll. Book IV. and V. p. 99.

Two of the sons of John Hollis, Isaac and Timothy, were also benefactors. On p. 81 of College Book, "Hollis Letters," is a letter from Isaac Hollis, apparently to some one of the college authorities, referring to a sum of £500 which he had sent over for the education of Indian boys, and expressing his intention of sending an additional amount. The letter is dated 1746-7.

Timothy's name appears in the Donation Book for a subscription of £20 to the College. He succeeded his father as trustee of the Thorner will, and it was by him that the final payments were made. The records of the Corporation (Coll. Book VII. p. 32) state that in Feb. 1732, Timothy was appointed an agent for the College in London.—EVARTS B. GREENE.]

NATHAMIEL HOLLIS of Peckham, Surrey, gen^t. 10 July 1735, proved 3 February 1738. My body to be buried in the burying ground in Bunhill Fields and no more than forty pounds laid out about my funeral. To my grandson Thomas Hollis and his heirs forever all my freehold estate in Guilford, Surry, now or late in the occupation of . . . . Luff and Anne Standish. To my wife Frances Hollis my leasehold estate in Deptford, Kent, for life, then to said grandson Thomas Hollis. Reference to a Trust in hands of John Reynolds and William Ladds and another in hands of Josiah Maker* of London. To my brother John Hollis and his wife ten pounds apiece for mourning. To my kinsman John Hamersly of Deptford, shipwright, ten pounds. To my kinsman William Creswick of St. Albans, cutler, my cousin Elizabeth Creswick, my kinsman John Edmunds, my nephews Isaac Hollis and Timothy Hollis, and others. Henchman, 33.

FRANCES HOLLIS of Peckham, Surry, widow, 8 February 1738, proved 9 May 1739. To my sister (not named) twenty shillings. All the rest to my grandson Thomas Hollis. Mr. Josiah Maber to be sole executor.

Henchman, 104.

HANNAH HOLLIS of St. Mary Matfellon *alias* White Chapel, Middlesex, widow, 12 October 1738, with a codicil dated 8 March 1739, proved 19 May 1740. To my daughter Mary Winnock, widow, five hundred pounds.

* Qu. ? This perhaps should be Josiah Maber.—H. F. W.

To such child or children of my son Isaac Hollis as shall be living at my decease One hundred pounds apiece. To the children of my daughter Hannah Edwards living at my decease one hundred pounds apiece. To such of the five sons of my daughter Ann Solly as shall be living at my decease. one hundred pounds apiece. To the daughter of my daughter Elizabeth Ashurst one hundred pounds. To my cousin Hannah Hutton one hundred pounds. To my cousin Robert Ruslin one hundred pounds and one hundred pounds in trust for the separate use and benefit of his sister Susanna Row and her children, without the intermeddling of her husband. To Mrs. Grantham, another sister of Robert Ruslin, one hundred pounds. To another sister of his named Cover fifty pounds. To my brother Nathaniel Hollis and his wife ten pounds apiece for mourning. To my cousin William Ladds and his wife ten pounds apiece for mourning. To my cousin John Reynolds and his wife, to my brother Samuel Sandford, to my sister Mary Leader, my sister Ruth Collyer, my cousin . . . Turner and his wife, my cousin Benjamin Woodhouse, to the Rev^d Mr. Needham of Hitchin, Mr. Gill, Mr. Samuel Wilson, Mr. Samuel Price, Mr. Denham and Mr. Jolley, ministers, ten pounds apiece. The residue of my estate I give and bequeath unto and among my children, Isaac Hollis, Timothy Hollis, Mary Winnock, Hannah Edwards, Anne Solly and Elizabeth Ashurst. My sons Isaac and Timothy to be executors. Browne, 144.

[Will of Thomas Hollis 3d, clause relating to Harvard College taken from Harvard College Papers, 2 : 31.

" I give to the College instituted for promoting Learning at Cambridge in New England, Five hundred pounds to be laid out in books for the use and benefit of that College" (cited in a letter from Thomas Brand Hollis to John Hancock giving notice of the death of Hollis. Dated Pall Mall, May 28th, 1774.)

Thomas Hollis 3d was, with the exception of the first Thomas Hollis, the most liberal benefactor of the family. His gifts are well summed up in the following passage taken from the College Donation Book, p. 79.

" This gentleman began to honor the College with his notice a short time before the destruction of Harvard Hall. As soon as he was made acquainted with this event, he subscribed £200 sterling to the apparatus and the same sum to the library. . . . He hath at different times enriched the Library with a very large number of curious, valuable and costly books. The whole amount of his benefactions amounts, it is supposed, to more than fourteen hundred pounds sterling."

Note.—Hollis Hall was named January 13th, 1764, with elaborate ceremonies, by Francis Barnard, then Governor of Massachusetts. (Coll. Book VIII. p. 112).

Specially useful sources of information relating to the Hollis family and their gifts, are the Hollis Book (No. VI. of the College series); the Hollis letters bound in volumes entitled " Hollis Letters " and " Hollis Letters to Leverett "; the Donation Book; the " Memoirs of Thomas Hollis " (in three folio volumes). Quincy's History of Harvard College gives much interesting matter on this subject gathered from the College Papers.—EVARTS B. GREENE.]

WASHINGTON :

ROBERT PARGITER of Grytworth in the Co. of Northampton, 4 February 1557, proved 31 January 1558.

To be buried within the Church of Gritworth in St. Katherine's aisle there. To the mother Church of Peterborough four pence. Towards the reparation of the church of Gritworth six shillings eight pence. To my son William Pargiter twenty pounds in money and my best gown. To my son George Pargiter ten pounds in money and my second gown. To the same George one shod cart, one plough, with all " Irne " ware belonging to the same plough, and two harrows ready pointed. To the same George five horses or mares to the number of five towards a team and all harness belonging to the same, sixty sheep out of all my sheep as they shall happen to run out of the pen, three kyne, three breeders, whereof two breeders to be of one year old and the other of two years old, and two hogs; all which goods to be delivered to the same George at the discretion of my executors. To Edmunde my son five pounds in money. To every one of my "childers" children three shillings four pence. To every one of my godchildren if they will demand it twelve pence. To every one of my servants that shall happen to be in my service at my departure one quarter's wages over and above their covenant wages. I will that Anne my wife shall have and enjoy all my lands and tenements and all other my possessions, with all profits and commodities thereto belonging, whatsoever they be, lying and being within the towns and fields of Gritworth and Laurence Marson, during her natural life, and that she shall have and enjoy my lease of my farm in Grytworth which I do now hold of the Right Honorable mylord Windsor by indenture, during her natural life, paying the annual rent therefor. My son William and Anne my wife shall have my farm in Shattiswell in the Co. of Warwick, which I hold by indenture of Sir Thomas Pope, knight, during my years therein, to be equally divided and severed betwixt them. After my decease my son William shall pay yearly out of my lands in Stuttisbery to Anne my wife forty shillings, that is to say every half year twenty shillings by even portions. I give and bequeath to my daughter Mary Molle four marks of good and lawful money, to be paid to her every year a mark during four years. Other bequests of household goods to son George. The residue to Anne my wife and my son William Pargiter, whom I do ordain and make mine executors.

Item. I ordain and make Lawrence Wasshington my son in law to be the supervisor of this my last will and testament and he to have for his labor and pains to be taken therein forty shillings. In witness hereof I the said Robert Pargiter to this my last will have subscribed my name in the presence of Lawrence Wasshington, John Tymes, Richarde Duglys, John Bethome and Richarde Kenche wth other.   Welles, 26.

[The pedigree of Pargiter of Greatworth in the Heralds' Visitation of Northamptonshire, 1564, shows that this Robert Pargiter was son of Richard Pargiter by Anne, dau. of Richard Coles of Preston in the same County. His own wife Anne was a daughter of John Knight of Carlton. The will of his son William (A.D. 1584) has already been given in my notes on the Ancestry of Washington. The will of his father I found at Northampton, among the wills proved there 1510–1520. My notes of it are very meagre, chiefly owing to the sad state it was in.]

Ric. ₽gyt^r of Grytworth 7 Nov.—, proved —— ——. The children of Robert Pynkerd. My daughter Jone Pynkerd. Edmund Pargyter the son of——. My wife Annes. My sons Edmund and Robert Pargyter. Wills of the Archd. of Northampton.

[The following items have recently been given me by a friend who had an opportunity to take a look into the Churchwardens' accounts of the Parish of Tring.]

Lawrence Washington rated in the year 1665 for £ 1
      "   "   "   "   1666 " £ 2

[This new information tallies admirably with our recently formed hypothesis that Lawrence Washington of Luton and Virginia did not remove from his old home until 1667 or a little before that year.]

An Elegie upon the death of Mr. Tho: Washington the Princes page who dyed in Spayne 1623.

Hast thou beene lost a moneth? and can I bee
Compos'd of anything but Elegie?
Or hath { this / the } Country taught my soule to feele
Noe greife, where hearts are made of Spanish steele?
Or am I hyred not to magnifie
Ought that my Countrey breedes? els how could I
Bee silent of thy { losse / selfe, } who liue to see
Now nothing but thy goodnes left of thee.
If I forget thee thus, let my scorn'd herse
Want a true mourner and my tombe a verse.
May I unpittied fall, unwisht againe
And (to sume uppe all curse) fall sicke in Spayne.
A Curse wᶜʰ had'st thou scap't, noe aire had bin
So cruel to haue strucke thee at eighteene.
But as some purer ayres, they say, endure
Noe poisonous breath, but either kill or cure
What ere infects it, so againe 'tis true
Unles you poyson this it poysons you.
You must breath falshood heere and trechery,
For undisguised fayre simplicity
Agrees not wᵗʰ { this / the } soyle, noe more then thou
Lou'd youth, { wᶜʰ to that basenes could'st not bowe / who could'st not to this basenes bow. }
Therefore infection when it could not seize
Thy soule or manners, { throwes / cast } into disease
Thy body, to see if distemp'red bloud
Could make thy troubled soule lesse pure, lesse good.
But noe rude Feauer, ruder { Argazile, / Alquazile, }
No Jesuit, noe Deuil could make thee feele
Distemper in thy soule, though Hell combin'de
To strike at once thy body and thy minde.
Thy most { distemp'red / distracted } thoughts and wildest blood
Haue sence, yet to discerne their ill from good,
And hate that Barbarisme that durst increase
Thy { dolour by distemp'ringe / dolours with disturbing } thy last peace.
Now if there be a curse which thou hast not Madrid / Madrith } already, may it fall as hott
As are thy noone tides on thee, w { doe / dost } nurse
Those Moores which are thy scandall and our curse.
Though thy infectious ayre { denyes / deny } him breath

Yet (for shame) / For shame yet } giue him liberty of death.
Doe not inuent so new a cruelty
Not to giue leaue to what thou killst to dye.
But { thy / hee } faire soule is fled now farre aboue
The reach of all their malice { or / and } our loue,
Where { she / he } shall { haue / find } noe Spaniards to molest
Or { interrupt her / intercept his } everlasting rest.
Only the Case { wᶜʰ / that } couered { his / that } rich mind,
His body, he hath left with us behind.
And that is challenged (as Patroclus bones
By two armies) soe) two religions
Lay clayme to this: so once the Deuil did striue
For Moses dead { who / wᶜʰ } was not his aliue,
And though his soule could not be touch't by him
{ He / Yet } would haue thank't the Angel for a limbe.
But this hath found a graue, though still must
Greiue that such choice unvaluable dust
Should dwell so long, so ill imprison'd, there
Till he be wak'd with summons to appeare
When that last { hunts up / judgment } shall call at his doores.
How white shall he appeare amongst those Moores,
Those sullied sunburnt soules, of { the selfe / that } same dye
And tincture of the place where they shall frye.
Yet heere we leaue the treasure which they keepe
Whil'st we haue nothing left us but to weepe
The losse whereof the { friend / man } that hath true sence
Knowes both their Indies cannot recompence.
O you who henceforth shall desire to seethe
Or stew yourselues in Julie at { Madrid / Madrith }
Hope not your temperance or your youth can cure
Or guard your goodnes frô a Calenture.
T'was his disease, the purest and the best
Is made a sacrifice for all the rest.
Resigne your innocence before you part
From your own Countrey, leaue behind your heart
If it be English, bring noe vertues hither
But patience, heere other vertues wither,
And you shall find it treason at the shore
For any man to bring such traffick o're.

Let it be { henceforth counted a / counted as henceforth for } mis-
hap
To see Spayne anywhere but in a Mapp.
Let Shipwrack't men like rockes auoyd
{ this / the } shore
And rather chuse to perish then come o're
To saue themselues upon this cost, the
wombe
Of fraud and mischeife and of good the
tombe.
Yet now it holds a guest which euery age
Will inuite strangers { unto / to a } pilgrimage.
Thy reliques Washington may bring
againe
Me and my curses once more { backe to / into }
Spayne.
Who had forsworne it ; but if ere I come
I'le come a Pilgrim to weepe o're thy
tombe.

HIS EPITAPH.

Know'st / Knew'st } thou whose these ashes were.
Reader thou would'st weeping sweare
The rash fates err'd heere as appeares
Counting his vertues for his yeares.
His goodnes made them ouerseene
Wᶜʰ shew'd him threescore at eighteene.
Inquire not his disease or paine
He dyed of nothing els but Spaine
Where the worst Calentures he feeles
Are Jesuits and { Argaziles / Alquaziles }
Where he is not allow'd to haue
Unlesse { by stealth / he steal't } a quiet graue.
He needs noe { ..... / other } epitaph or stone
But this—heere lies loued Washington
Writes this { in / with } teares in that loose dust
And euery greiued beholder must
When he weighs him and knowes his
yeares
Renew the letters with his teares.

[The foregoing verses I found in two separate manuscripts in the British Museum, viz. Add. MSS. 12496 and 15227. The former was purchased at the Strawberry Hill sale, 30 Apr. 1842 (Lot 84). It has the bookplate of Mr. Horatio Walpole and contains an inscription showing that it was bought at the sale of Sir J. Cæsar's MSS. Dec. 1757 (Lot 54) for 1. 8. 6. It was evidently a collection of MSS. (with a few printed proclamations, &c.) made by Sir Julius Cæsar, knᵗ., Master of the Rolls. At least many of the documents had certainly belonged to him. The last half dozen seem to refer entirely to Virginia. One (f. 433) appears to be a form of policy for settling and governing Virginia, and is entitled " Mr. Capt. Bargraves project touching Va. 8 Dec. 1623." Another (f. 435) by Jo. Martin, is styled The manner how to make a Royal Plantation. Another (f. 439) by the same, The manner how to bring the Indians in Subjection. A letter (f. 449) from John Martin to Sir Julius Cæsar, written 8 March 1626, at Martin Brandon, refers to the arrival of cousin Richard Martin, and names Capt. Prinne. It is signed " Your Honnors ever faithfull brother in law at Command—Jno. Martin." Another (f. 452) is the King's Com. for settling a Government in Virginia, 15 July, 1624. The Verses upon Thomas Washington begin fo. 364 and are endorsed " Epitaphiall Verses uppon the death of young Mr. Washington Prince Charles his page in Spaine in anno 1623."

The second MS. (Add. 15227) is a little duodecimo volume of miscellaneous poems and metrical translations in manuscript, m any of them epitaphs, some humorous. The two copies differed somewhat. I have given the two readings where these differences seemed worth noting. The upper reading is from MS. 12496, and the lower from MS. 15227.

The connection between Sir Julius Cæsar and his "Bro. Martin" as he calls him, is explained by the marriage, 26 Feb. 1581 (2) of Julias Cæsar, doctor of laws and one of the advocates of the Arches, and Dorcas Lusher, widow. Gen. license granted 23 Feb. 1581-2 (Diocese of London). She was a daughter of Sir Richard Martin, knᵗ., Lord Mayor of London, and widow of Richard Lusher, genᵗ. She died Monday, 16 June 1595, and was buried in the Temple Church. This I learn from my friend R. G. Rice, Esq.—HENRY F. WATERS.]

ELIZABETH SANDYS of Wickamford in the Co. of Worcester widow, 21 December 1698, with codicil bearing date 24 December 1698, proved 20 February 1698. I nominate and appoint my cousin John Sandys, now or late of Loveline, executor, and give him all my messuages, lands, tenements, etc., at Bayton or elsewhere in the Co. of Worcester purchased of Mr. Swift or his trustees in the name of my late daughter Penelope Washington, but in trust to sell and dispose thereof to the best value and to raise money for a portion for my granddaughter Elizabeth Jarlett, now with me, and to educate her in such a manner as to my said executor shall seem meet and convenient and at her age of one and twenty years or marriage, to pay to her her said portion.   And I appoint him guardian desiring him to breed her up in the Protestant Religion.   And if he depart this life before her said age or marriage then I appoint Mr. Francis Bromley trustee and guardian to her.   I give to my executor fifty pounds as a legacy.   To my daughter Tunstall ten pounds.   To my daughter Jarlatt ten pounds.   To my granddaughter Katherine Forster two hundred and fifty pounds, besides the two hundred and fifty pounds her aunt Washington gave her if she should please me.   To Mr. Francis Bromley my great silver cup and cover. To my faithful and kind servant Mrs. Mary Hall one hundred pounds (and other personal property).   Twenty pounds for a communion carpet and pulpit cloth for the Church of Wickamford.   Remainder of personal estate to my said granddaughter Jarlatt.   If she refuses to be educated or become a Papist I give her only a fourth part of what I hereby before have given or intended for her, &c.

In the codicil is a bequest to " my " son in law Capt. Sandys, of a sealed ring which my dear brother Packington constantly wore.   To my daughter in law Mrs. Sandys a large table diamond ring.   To Mr. Martin Sandys, their son, a gold watch and gold case to it.   To my god daughter Mrs. Devorax her grandmother, my lady Sandys' picture set in gold.   To my niece Mrs. Bradshaw her grandfather, Sir John Packington's picture set in gold.   To Mrs. Tomkins her grandmother's picture set in an enamel ring. To my god daughter Mrs Tomkins a pair of gold sleeve buttons.   To my granddaughter Mrs. Forster a pair of diamond earrings and a fine gold watch that was her aunt's &c.   To my granddaughter Mrs. Jollott all my plate which I have not disposed of.   Pett, 32.

[Elizabeth Sandys was first wife of Col. Henry Washington, the trusty defender of the ever faithful city of Worcester, who was a nephew of the Rev. Lawrence Washington, and a cousin of John and Lawrence.   She afterwards became the wife of Samuel Sandys Esq., of Ombersley, co. Worcester.—H. F. W.]

NICHOLAS SPENCER of Cople, Bedfordshire, Esq[re] 10 January 1625, proved 17 February 1625.   My body to be buried with mine ancestors in the parish church of Cople.   To the poor of the parish ten pounds. Reference to indentures bearing date 6th of this instant January and made between the said Nicholas Spencer of the one part and Sir Oliver Luke of Hawnes, Beds., kn[t]., Sir Myles Fleetwood of London kn[t]., Thomas Ellmes of Norton in the Co. of Northampton Esq[re] and William Ellmes Esq[re] son and heir apparent of the said Thomas Ellmes, of the other part.   Certain manors demised to them and they to pay unto Mary Spencer, my wife, two hundred pounds per annum, and to pay such debts as I do now owe.   To my four daughters, Alice, Mary, Christian and Rose Spencer, two thousand pounds, i.e. five hundred pounds each.   And after debts paid and the said two thousand pounds raised they are to assign and set over to my youngest son Robert such of the lands &c., as are situate in Eaton Socon, Mogerhanger and Blanham, and the residue of said manors, lands and premises unto Nicholas Spencer my eldest son, upon whom part of the said manors are already entailed, etc.   To my brother Arnold Spencer fifteen pounds. To my brother Edward Spencer ten pounds.   To my sister Margaret Spencer ten pounds.   To my sister Cicely Spencer twenty pounds.   To my sister Rose Spencer twenty pounds.   To my godson John Spencer, second son of my brother George, twenty shillings.   To my niece Mary Gibbins, daughter of my sister Gibbins, fifty shillings.   To my cousin John Cokaine of Cople twenty shillings.   To my cousin Dorothy, his daughter, my god-daughter, ten shillings.   To my cousin John Cokaine of Hollowaie twenty shillings.   To Mr. Greenough forty shillings.   To Mr. Thomas Watson of Cardington, clerk, ten shillings to buy him a book.   (Other small bequests.)   To my mother Mrs. Spencer three pounds.   To my said father in law Thomas Ellmes Esqre and my brother in law William Ellmes Esqre (and others) twenty shillings apiece.

In a codicil he refers to his brother John, as John Spencer of Woodend in the parish of Cople, gen^t., and to Elizabeth Wynne (evidently the wife of the said John).   A legacy to John the son of the said John.

Hele, 24.

CHRISTIAN ELMES of Green's Norton, in the Co. of Northampton, widow, late wife of Thomas Elmes of Green's Norton Esqre lately deceased, 12 October 1632, proved 5 May 1635.   Eldest son William Elmes of Lileford, Northampton Esqre.   Second son Thomas Elmes of Warmington.   Third son Anthony Elmes of Fawsely.   My goods at Casswell Dairy house and my house at Norton.   Grace Elmes the wife of Anthony and daughter of Sir Robert Bevill of Chesterton, Hunts., kn^t. of the Bath.   The lands descending to my son Anthony cannot feed or depasture any more but 2500 (sheep) at five score to the hundred, nor in my father Hickling's time nor in my late dear husband's time there were at any time more kept or could possibly be kept, &c.

To my eldest and well beloved daughter Mary Spencer of Cople, Bedfordshire, widow, one hundred pounds.   My daughter the Lady Martha Dacres, the wife of Sir Thomas Dacres of Chesthnut, Herts., kn^t.   My third daughter Elizabeth Hawford, wife of William Hawford of Wellam, Leic., Esqre.   My fourth daughter Alice Fountaine, wife of Thomas Fountaine of Hampton, Northampton, Esqre.   My youngest daughter the Lady Frances Hesilrigge, wife of Sir Arthur Hesilrigge of Nosely, Leic., Bar^t.

Sadler, 53.

NICHOLAS SPENCER of Cople, Bedford, Esq., 10 April 19th Charles, proved 13 March 1644.   To eldest son William Spencer my mansion houses etc., in the Counties of Bedford and Huntington.   To my other sons, Michael, Robert and Edward Spencer five hundred pounds each.   To my daughter Mary Spencer eight hundred pounds, upon consideration nevertheless that if Mary my now wife shall survive me and be living one whole year next after my decease then my said daughter Mary shall have seven hundred pounds and no more ; and if my wife shall be living two whole years my daughter Mary shall have six hundred pounds and no more (and so on).   And if my wife shall be living seven whole years my said daughter shall have one hundred pounds and no more.   I do nominate Sr William Botler of Bidnam, Beds., kn^t., Walter Rolt of Clifton, Beds., Esq., Gaius Squire of Eaton Socon, Beds., Esq., and Robt Howgall of Willington, Beds., Clerk, executors of this my last will and testament, to each of whom I bequeath twenty shillings to buy him a mourning ring.   To each of my brothers and sisters ten shillings, to buy them rings, and also to each of my brothers and sisters in law.   My son William shall have his education at the Grammar School until he is fit for the University, and then to remain there until he shall go to the Inns of Court.   My son

Nicholas to be likewise educated at the Grammar School until he be fit for the University and then there to remain. My other two sons Robert and Edward to be educated in a fitting way to be tradesmen and bound apprentices.   Rivers, 52.

WILLIAM SPENCER of Cople, Beds., Esq., 18 January 1683, proved 2 June 1686. I do confirm unto my dear mother, the Lady Mary Armiger, late wife of my father Nicholas Spencer Esq. all such joynture which was settled upon her for her life by my said father. Brothers in law Oliver Luke of Cople Woodend and John Luke of Cople Woodend, in the parish of Cople. Wife Elizabeth Spencer shall receive two hundred pounds yearly out of my messuages, lahds &c. for and during her life. After her death the said messuages to descend to my eldest son by her and his lawfully begotten heirs males, remainder to next son &c. Failing such I give the reversion and remainder unto my loving brother Nicholas Spencer Esq. now in the County (sic) of Virginia for life and then to his eldest son William Spencer, my beloved nephew. Legacies to niece Judith Luke, to John Ventris of Campton, Beds., and others. Household goods at Codham Hall. My Essex lands. Matrum Spencer, second son of my said brother Nicholas Spencer.
A codicil bearing date 19 March 1685.   Lloyd, 88.

NICHOLAS SPENCER of Nominy in Westmoreland Co. in Virginia 25 April 1688, proved 15 January 1699. To my son William Spencer, now in England, all the lands, houses and tenements unto me in England appertaining or belonging, either as I am now the only surviving son of my father Nicholas Spencer Esqr. deceased and also as heir to my brother William Spencer Esqr. dec'd, or by the last will and testament of my said brother William Spencer, the lands &c lying in the town of Cople in Bedfordshire. I also give to him my lands in Barford and in Blunham and in St. Neets in Huntingdonshire and at Codham Hall, Essex. To my wife, Mrs. Frances Spencer, during her natural life, all my lands, houses and tenements in the Neck of land called Kingcopsco (sic), i.e. all the lands I bought of Mr. Richard Wright and of Mr. James Hardige and the lands I bought of Richard Awburne, formerly William Newberrie's lands; then to my son Motrom Spencer and his heirs forever. To my son Nicholas all my lands lying at the head of Nominy, being the lands I bought of Mr. Foster and Mr. Hawkins and the lands I bought of Mr. Manley, as also the lands I took up, relapsed, from Tho. Dies. To my son John all the right and title I have or may have unto the land lying near Pope's Creek, escheated in the name and to the use and benefit of my son John; also all the lands I bought of Mr. William Horton and Capt. John Lord and the land I bought of Jacob Reny and the lands I bought of Mr. John Froadsham, the Survey of all the last aforesaid lands lying near unto Coll^o Wm Peirce's lands and dwelling seat.
"I give and bequeath unto my son Francis Spencer and his heirs for ever that moiety of five thousand acres which upon a division shall fall to my lott, being a tract of land lying and being in joint tenancy between Capt. Lawrence Washington and myself, with condition that noe advantage of Survivorship shall be taken of either side."
To my dear and beloved wife all her jewels and wearing apparell. To my son Motrom Spencer five hundred pounds sterling, to be paid him at his age of one and twenty by my son William out of the rents of my lands

and houses in England.   As to my personal estate in Virginia, be it plate, household goods, cattle, horses and sheep, as also my English servants, Negro slaves, tobacco and grains of all sorts, as also my tobacco debts and money debts due to me in Virginia, my debts and legacies being first paid, I do will and bequeath unto my beloved wife, Mrs. Frances Spencer, my son Nicholas Spencer, my son John Spencer and my son Francis Spencer to be equally divided between them, but to remain entirely together, and no division made thereof until all my debts and legacies be fully satisfied and paid with the present year's crop, &c.

I nominate and appoint my son William Spencer executor of my last will and testament of all my estate in England, and my wife Mrs. Frances Spencer, my son Nicholas and my son John Spencer executors as to my estate in Virginia: and I nominate and appoint my singular good friends Coll. Isaac Allerton of Matchotick, Capt. George Brent of Stafford Co. and Capt. Lawrence Washington, Feoffees in trust &c. giving forty shillings to each of them, to buy mourning rings, and to Coll. Isaac Allerton my riding horse called Hector.

Wit: George Luke, Thomas Hobson junior and Nathā Webster.

Letters issued 15 January 1699 to John Rust of All Hallows Lombard St., silkman, to administer the goods &c according to the tenor and effect of the above will.   Noel, 14.

MOTTROM SPENCER of Nomini in Westmoreland Co. in Virginia 24 October 1691, proved 15 May 1703.   To my dearly beloved wife Mrs. Jane Spencer all the right and title I have to five hundred pounds sterling left me by my father's will payable out of the estate of my well beloved brother William Spencer of Cople in the Co. of Bedford Esqr., and also three hundred pounds sterling with the interest thereof now due and what shall become due unto me to the time of my decease, which said three hundred pounds 1 require my mother, Mrs. Frances Spencer, to pay unto my wife. If my said wife should depart this life before me then I will, give and bequeath unto my beloved brother William Spencer Esqr whatever I had willed, given or bequeathed unto my wife.   I also give and bequeath a mourning ring of one pound price to my sister Mrs. Lettice Barnard, another of the same value to my brother William and another to my Aunt Anne Armiger.   My wife Mrs. Jane Spencer to be executrix.

Wit: Richard Kitchiner, Lettice Barnard, Will: Saueige.

Decimo quinto die mensis Maii Anno Dñi millimo septingentesimo tertio emanavit commissio Capitaneo Willimo Spencer ffratri et Legatario nominato in Testamento Mottrom Spencer nuper Vexillarii in Legione Domini Comitis Essexiæ in pōa Sancti Ægidii in Campis in Comitatu Midd. deffi heñtis &c. ad adstrand. bona jura et cređ dc̄i def juxta tenorem et efftūm Testamenti ipsius deffi (eo quod Jana Spencer Relicta et Execut in dict testament nominat̄ oneri Executionis dicti Testamenti expresse renunciaverit) &c.   Degg, 135.

Christofer Washington of Soulgrave in the co. of Northampton, gentleman, gave bond 7 June 1619, as one of the creditors of William Mole, late of Mixbery, co. Oxon., gentleman, deceased, to administer the goods and chattels &c of the deceased, with Edward Mole of Fulwell, in the parish of Mixbery, gentleman, as his fellow bondsman.   Admon. Bonds, Oxon.

[This I suppose was the son of Robert Washington of Sulgrave and brother of Lawrence Washington of Sulgrave and Brington.   Mixbery is next to Westbury, the home for a time of Sir Lawrence Washington.—H. F. W.]

[In April, 1890, I received from Rev. R. M. Samson, Head Master of Hawkshead Grammar School, Lancaster, England (which School was founded by Edwin Sandys, Archbishop of York in Elizabeth's time), a copy of the record in the Archbishop's Bible which is kept at the School house, and I herewith enclose a copy from the lower part of the page (the upper part being a record of the births of the Archbishop's children), and you will notice the frequency of the names Washington, Spencer, Meuce, Anderson, etc., as godparents of these Sandes children. Now as Robt Sandys, the eldest son of Thomas Sandys, 4th son of the Archbishop, was married to Alice Washington, sister of Sir William, Sir John and Lawrence Washington, I am inclined to think most of the children mentioned in the record were the children of this Robert Sandys (the name is variously spelt Sandys, Sandis, Sandes, Sands). The deep interest the Sandys family in England took in the settlement of America—both Virginia and New England, and also later on in Connecticut and New Jersey, coupled with the marriages of the Sandes and Washington family—may make the record of some use to you, particularly if read in connection with Mr. Waters's note in the REGISTER for October, 1889.

The names marked? Mr. Samson had much difficulty in making out and may not be correct; they are Doheres, Wem, Paraster—which latter may be Pargiter.

JAMES T. SANDS of St. Louis, Mo.]

Penelope Sandes was borne
ye 9th April 1629 beinge
Thursday about 7 at night

God Father Sir John Washington
God Mothers Ye Lady Penelope Spencer
    Mrs Margaret Washington

Thomas Sandes was borne
ye 14th of M^ch 1629 beinge
Sunday about 5 in the morning

God Fathers Thomas Sandes Esquire
    Francis Meuce Esquire
God Mother Y^e Ladye Washington

Richard Sandes was borne
ye 29th April 1631 beinge
Friday about noone

God Fathers Richard Spencer Esquire
    Francis Meuce Esquire
God Mother Mrs Elizabeth Spencer

Francis Sandes was
borne ye 20th of Aprile
1636 being Friday about
Eleven at night

God Father Francis Meuce Esquire
God Mothers Mrs Margaret Washington
    Mrs Elizabeth Washington deputy
    for the Ladye Washington

Elizabeth Sandes was borne
ye 23 of July 1633 beinge
Tuesday about 6 in the morning

God Father Arthur Samuel Esquire
God Mothers Mrs Elizabeth Spencer
    Mrs Elizabeth Meuce

Susannah Sandes was borne
ye 14th of August being Thursday
about midnight (the date of
year is not given)

God Father Simon Adams, Clarke
God Mothers Mrs Margaret Washington
    Mrs Anne Doheres?
    deputy for Mrs Susan Wem?

Robert Sandes was borne
ye 24th of May 1636 beinge
Wednesday about 6 at night

God Fathers Robt Spencer Esquire
    Robt Paraster ? Esquire
God Mother Mrs Margaret Anderson

Edwin Sandes May 6th
between 4 & 5 at night
    Gemelli borne 1637
Myles Sandes May ye
7th between 8 & 9 at night

God Fathers John Bulins deputy for
    Sir Myles Sandes

    Richard Seymer Esquire
God Mother Mrs Elizabeth Meuce

Roger Williams (*ante*, pp. 327–344; 406, 407.)

[Readers of the letters of Roger Williams printed in the Register for July, 1889 (*ante*, pp. 341–344), have doubtless felt a curiosity to know the name of the lady whose hand the future founder of Rhode Island sought in vain about 1629. Having found what I thought to be a clew to the mystery, I sent a query to the editor of the London "Notes and Queries." It appeared in the issue of that periodical July 5, 1890, as follows:

"Whalley.—A list of the manuscripts of George Alan Lowndes, Esq., of Barrington Hall, co. Essex, in the 'Seventh Report of the Historical Manuscripts Commission,' Appendix, contains this entry:—

"' (No. 156) 1628, July 28 [22], Screaveton.—Ryc. Whalley to Lady Joane Barrington, baronettess, at her house Hatfield in Essex.—On a report of the death of her husband, Sir Francis, he condoles with her. Asks that his daughter (her niece) may still remain with her. Sends the third and last volume of Mr. Parkins's works.'

"Can any reader of 'N. & Q.' tell which of Mr. Whalley's daughters this was? The pedigree of Whalley, in the 'Visitations of Nottingham,' 1569 and 1614, Harleian Society's Publications, vol. iv. p. 118, shows that he had two daughters, Elizabeth and Jane, the former of whom married William Tiffin, of London, mercer. The famous Roger Williams, the founder of Rhode Island, then chaplain to Lady Barrington's son-in-law, Sir William Masham, of Otes, solicited of her, about the year 1629, the hand of her niece; but the niece's name is not mentioned in the correspondence on the subject, which is printed in the *New-England Historical and Genealogical Register*, vol. xliii. (1889), pp. 315–20, from a copy furnished by Mr. Lowndes, the owner of the original letters. I have queried whether it was not the niece mentioned in Mr. Whalley's letter whose hand Williams aspired to. A brother of Miss Whalley, Major-General Edward Whalley, one of the king's judges, came to New England and died here. Jane, the youngest daughter of Richard Whalley, named in the pedigree, married Rev. William Hooke, a graduate of Oxford University, who was vicar of Axmouth, in Devonshire, but as early as 1639 came to New England. He preached a few years at Taunton, in Plymouth colony, and from 1644 to 1656 at New Haven, Conn. He then returned to England, and was private chaplain to Oliver Cromwell. Some letters of Mrs. Jane Hooke to friends in New England are printed in the 'Massachusetts Historical Collections,' vol. xxxviii. pp. 260–68. If this was the niece of Lady Barrington whom Roger Williams wished to marry—and I think it not unlikely that it was—though one clergyman failed to obtain her hand she became the wife of another."

Soon after the article appeared, I received the following letter from Samuel Rawson Gardiner, Esq., LL.D.:

"South View, Wedmore Road, Bromley, Kent, July 8, 1890.

"Dear Sir:

It will hasten matters if I reply directly to your inquiry headed '*Whalley*' in 'Notes and Queries.' The Barrington correspondence is now in the possession of the British Museum, and Whalley's letters are in Egerton MSS. 2,644.

"The letter which you quote is of July 22, not July 28, and is at folio 275. It affords no indication of the name of the daughter, but from another letter I gather that it was Jane. In a letter dated Nov. 15, 1623 (folio 204), Whalley writes to Lady Joan:

"'And for my daughter Jane for whom I ought ye at Bartholomew tide 20^1.'

"From a letter of July 4, 1622 (folio 202), I gather that Elizabeth was already married. Whalley says he has been arrested by Tyffyn, 'who was a dogge to my daughter and hath performed neither to her or her daughter whatt he was bound unto.' Believe me, yours sincerely,

Samuel R. Gardiner.

John Ward Dean, Esq., Boston, Mass., U. S. A."

It is reasonable to suppose that Lady Barrington's niece, whose hand Williams sought, was in some way under the care of that lady. We find that Jane Whalley, in all probability, resided in her family about the time that Williams made his proposal; and we know of no other niece of hers who did. From the facts stated, there is little reason to doubt that Jane Whalley was the lady in question. She and her husband, the Rev. William Hooke, came to New England, and for some years lived at Taunton, not many miles from Providence, the home, if my theory be correct, of her former lover.

The mother of Jane Whalley was Frances Cromwell, a sister of Lady Barrington; of Elizabeth, mother of John Hampden; and of Robert Cromwell, the father of Oliver Cromwell, Protector of England.—EDITOR.]

THE present instalment of Gleanings is a continuation of the wills of benefactors of Harvard College and their families.

HENRY F. WATERS.

HOLWORTHY.

JOHN MAN of the town and county of Pool, merchant, 8 July 1577, proved 13 June 1578. Son William and his children. Sons John, Edward, Thomas and Bartlemewe. Late wife Amy Man. Daughter Amy Pitt. Daughter Cicely Havilonde. Daughter Edith Lewen. Daughter Agnes Wickes. Stephen and Richard Whetacre, sons of my daughter Edith Lewin. My three sons in law John Crooke, Christopher Wickes and Christopher Havilonde. John Crooke of Southampton, merchant. One of the witnesses was a Christopher Wickes. Langley, 28.

ROBERT KECHIN, merchant, one of the aldermen of the City of Bristol, 19 June 1594, proved 10 January 1594. (The name also appears as Kitchin and Kitchen.) Body to be buried in the parish of St. Stephen's in Bristol near the place where first wife Johane was buried. To Robert Havyland, son of Matthew Havyland, of Bristol, merchant, three tenements and a garden in Hallyes Lane, with remainder to William Havyland, then to John Havyland, sons of the said Matthew. My capital messuage or mansion house wherein I now dwell, situate in Snale Street in the parish of St. Warborough, Bristol, to be sold at best price and the money received therefor to be employed for the best benefit relief and "sustentacõn" of the poor; but my wife Justyne shall have and enjoy the use of the said house and of the furniture in it during her natural life. Qther bequests to the sons of Matthew Haviland, to brother Matthew Ketchin, to sister Agnes, to Robert Ketchin of London, merchant, being the son of brother Richard, to brother Thomas, to nephew Thomas Ketchin son of brother Matthew, to Niece Agnes daughter of Matthew, to niece Elizabeth wife of John Friend of Bristol, hooper, to niece Margaret Ketchin daughter of brother Matthew, to niece Elizabeth Ketchin daughter of brother John, deceased, to Jane Ketchin his other daughter, to niece Marrian Nottingham wife of John Nottingham of Bristol, to Robert Nottingham son of John Nottingham of Bristol "hullion" and of Marryan his wife, and to William their younger son, to Abel Kitchen. John Barker, Matthew Haviland, John Rowberoe and Abel Kitchen to be executors and trustees. The residue to the relief of the poor in Bristol and in Kendal, Westmoreland. Scott, 2.

ANNE COLSTON of Bristol, widow, 13 July 1603, proved 28 February 1603. Body to be interred in St. Nicholas Crowd in the City of Bristol in the place where the "corps" of my mother or my good husband Mr. Richard Hentley lieth, if I decease in Bristow or within twenty miles thereof. My brother Mr. Robert Dowe in London. Mrs Bridget Dowe late the wife of my late deceased nephew Thomas Dowe. My nephew Sir William Smith of Essex, knight, and the lady his good wife, John, Clement and Edward Smith brethren of Sir William. My cousin Mrs. Rose White wife unto Mr. Francis White, preacher in Rochester, and her son John Peck. My cousin Henry Reynoldes, minister. Elizabeth Buttry sometime the wife of William Buttrie, my sister's son. My cousin Mrs. Mary Awstell wife unto Mr. Awstell of Grey's Inn, gen^t. My nephews Bush Welles and John Welles. My cousin John Mothe's children that he had by my cousin Elizabeth his first wife, being daughters to my brother Welles, long since deceased. Grace Robinson wife to a preacher of that name and her sister Martha Smith daughter unto Robert Smith, which he had by my cousin Susan, my sister's daughter. My cousin Alice Threder's daughter, I know not her name. Philip Poyntell son unto William Poyntell deceased, who dwelt sometimes in Presteyne. Raphe Pointell's children, being fatherless, who was a tailor sometimes in London. Mr. Matthew Haviland's three eldest sons, Robert, William and John. Matthew Haviland and his sisters Anne and Mary Haviland. Brynt Gulliford, son unto Mr. Robert Gully-ford preacher of God's word and one of the prebends in the College. Samuel Gulliford, my godson, brother to the said Brint. Ellen Atkins of Bristol widow (one dozen silver spoons, six of them Apostle spoons and six with maiden heads). Her daughter Anne Atkins my god daughter. Alice Bull daughter of Robert Bull deceased, being my kinswoman. Charity Longe wife of Edmond Longe of Bristow, comfit maker. Anne Aldworth, daughter unto Simon Aldworth of Reading, Berks., whom he had by his first wife Mary Aish. Mr. Matthew Haviland to be executor. My loving daughter in law Mrs. Joice (sic) Haviland his wife. Cousin Mrs. Mary Awstell, sister of Bush and John Welles. Cousin Mr. John Mothe, gold-smith in cheapside London. Thomas Wilcox son unto Thomas Wilcox and Rebecca his wife both deceased. His sisters Anne, Margery and Rebecca Wilcox. Andrew Patch, clerk of Alhollon. Edward Colston son unto Richard Colston. My Cousin Mr. Crescent Buttry dwelling at Lawrence Marson, gentleman (a ring with a death's head and two letters under the same—A: R:). Cousin Dewberry wife unto —— Dewberry dwelling in Reading. To " Alice Thredder's daughter I know not her name she is to be harde of aboute Straford Dowe, her mother's brother dwelleth in Stratford aforesaid, one William Poyntill an old man if he be livinge, the said Pointill was verye young when he came firste to Stratford, his ffather and mother contynued to their old age in that place and had manie children. I saie to the saide Thredder's daughter I giue a gowne and a peticoate of mine such as may serue for a poore woeman's wearinge, a fustian wast coate, two good smockes, thre good kercheifes, if she live; I hope she shall be harde of." Mr. Robert Redwood of this city. Mrs. Redwood for her brother Robert Farrar's wife. Mrs. Langley widow, with whom I kneeled in the church about twenty three years. Anne Colston wife of Richard Colston. Vincent Colston's wife. Elizabeth Colston the wife of Robert Colston. Others. Harte, 28.

THOMAS PITT of Bristol, merchant, 1 May 1613, proved 5 August 1613. To my son William Pitt one lease for the term of his natural life, of my tenement without Temple Gate within the Liberty of the city of Bristol, which is now in the possession of George Tyce, innholder, called the Sara-cen's Head, and one lease of a tenement which I lately built without Temple Gate, now in the occupation of Thomas Arthur Esq., he to pay to

Robert Pitt, the son of my said son William, ten pounds yearly, after the said Robert shall accomplish the age of twenty two years. After the death of the said William these two tenements to the said Robert. My son William shall give his sons William and Robert ten pounds apiece at the age of sixteen years. To my daughter Alice Northen one silver-gilt ale cup and the sum of forty pounds within two years after my decease to bestow upon her children at her will and pleasure, and in the meantime four pounds every year for the use thereof. To my daughter Anne Merrick one silver-gilt ale cup and to my son in law John Merrick twenty pounds within eight months to be equally divided between my daughter Ann Merrick's three children, vizt. Ann Waters, Mary Waters and Robert Merrick. To my daughter Mary Owen a silver gilt ale cup and to my son in law Robert Owen twenty pounds within eight months to be divided between my daughter Mary's three children: Robert, Mary and Joane Owen. To my cousin Mr. Matthew Havyland, alderman, a ring of gold to the value of twenty shillings. To my kinsman William Pitt, draper, another. My kinsman Edward Batten. My friend Mr. Samuel Davies to preach my funeral sermon. My daughters in law Mary Marlowe, Cicely Gunning and Elizabeth Batterton. My kinswoman Mary Robinson. Son William Pitt to be executor and trusty friend and neighbor, Thomas Callowhill to be overseer.

Capell, 75.

MATTHEW HAVYLANDE of Bristol, merchant and one of the aldermen of the City, 2 March 1619, proved 22 May 1620. Body to be buried in Warborrowes churchyard, even in the grave in which my wife Joyce was laid in, and to be buried without a coffin if I may. To grandchild Matthew Havylande, son of Robert, my son, the farm and buildings in Hawkesbury, Glouc., which I bought of M^r. John Vizar and his father (and other lands). Provision for the maintenance of son William during his natural life. Grandchild Bartholomew Havyland, son of the said William. Son John to have certain estates in Somerset. To my son Matthew my eighth part of the Prisage wines coming to the Port or Creeks of Bristol, during the lease thereof granted, on condition that he shall pay unto Tacie my wife fifty pounds yearly during her life. To my said son Matthew my house and tenement in Smale street (sic) wherein M^r. Thomas Colston now dwelleth (and other property). Son Robert's children, Matthew, Mary, Florence, Jane and Elizabeth. Daughter Anne Lorte's children, Sampson and Joyce. Reference to bond of their father, Sampson Lortt.

I give and bequeath unto my daughter Mary Holworthies children, Matthew, Mary, Richard, Anne and John, one hundred nobles, to be paid unto them as they shall accomplish the full age of twenty years or days of marriage. To my son in law Mr. Richard Holworthie the like sum of one hundred nobles, to be paid within one year after my decease, praying him to be one of the overseers of this my last will. To my sister Elionor Helye five pounds in money and a gown. To Mr. Farmer minister of Warborrowe's church five pounds to make him a gown. To M^r. William Yeaman preacher (the same) so as he will preach at my funeral and his text to be on the twelfth chapter of Ecclesiastes and seaventh verse. Son Robert and his heirs shall pay yearly forever out of my lands called the Grange, in or by Kingswood, Wilts, four pounds unto the Mayor and Commonalty of the city of Bristol to the end and purpose that in the common gaol of the said city called Newgate shall be preached yearly for ever twelve sermons. My kinsmen Mr. William Pitt draper and Mr. William Pitt merchant and Edward Batten gen^t. to be overseers.   Soame, 43.

MATTHEW HAVILAND of Bristol, merchant, 16 May 1623, proved 29 April 1624. To Mr. John Farmer minister of God's word in the parish of St. Warburge five pounds. To my niece Joyce Lorte, daughter of Sampson Lorte, late of Bristol merchant, one hundred pounds and my estate in the messuage wherein Charles Hammond, mercer, lately dwelled, situate near the "Crowde" door of St. Nicholas church, with my lease and writings concerning the same, and also ten pounds which Richard Fownes, the son of Mr. Thomas Fownes of Plymouth, merchant, is to pay me at the day of his marriage. To the said Joyce Lorte and to my niece Mary Holworthy, one of the daughters of M^r. Richard Holworthy, merchant, all my household stuff &c. now remaining in the now dwelling house of the said Richard Holworthy. To my nephew Matthew Haviland, son of brother Robert, my household stuff &c. in the now dwelling house of the said Robert at Haukesberry, Glouc. To my kinsman Peter Helye of Bristoll, whitetawer, five pounds. To William Brimsdon, soapmaker, twenty marks. To John Vizer of Owlepenn, Glouc., gen^t. twenty nobles. To my brother in law Mr. Richard Holworthy, of Bristol, merchant, twenty pounds in token of my hearty love and affection.

Whereas my dear father Matthew Haviland, late of the city of Bristol, alderman, deceased, did give and bequeath unto me five hundred pounds and appointed that I should yearly pay unto Mrs. Thasia Haviland, his then wife, fifty pounds per annum during her natural life, for her better security I do deposite and leave in the hands of the said Richard Holworthy four hundred pounds and authorize and appoint my brother Robert to pay unto him one hundred pounds more to make up the five hundred in regard that my said brother oweth me a more sum. And the said Richard Holworthy shall keep the said five hundred and in consideration of the forbearance and benefit thereof shall yearly pay unto the said Thasia during her natural life the sum of fifty pounds per annum. And after her decease he shall distribute and dispose of the said five hundred pounds in manner and form following: that is to say, to Matthew Holworthy, Mary Holworthy, Ann Holworthy, Richard Holworthy and John Holworthy, children of the said Richard and Mary his late wife, my sister deceased, the sum of two hundred pounds to be equally divided amongst them, vizt. to each one of them the sum of forty pounds apiece. To Prudence Holworthy and Thomas Holworthy, two other children of the said Richard, twenty pounds to be divided between them. To each of the children of brother Robert, namely Matthew, Mary, Florence, Jane and Elizabeth Haviland, forty pounds apiece. The residue to my brother in law Mr. Richard Holworthy whom I do constitute, make and ordain my sole and only executor.

Byrde, 29.

THOMAS FOWNES of Plymouth, Devon, Esquire, 15 June 1637, proved 13 June 1638. To the Mayor and commonalty of Plymouth one hundred pounds, to set poor people on work and keep them from idleness. Reference to a like gift made by Mr. John Gayre. A gift to the new Hosp. of Orphans Aid near Plymouth church. To the poor of Bristol. Elizabeth wife of William Stephens of Bristol, merchant, and Mary Longe, daughter of Mary Longe my sister deceased. Every of the daughters of Judith Amades my kinswoman (Francis Amadas their father). The daughters of Humpry Fownes deceased. Warwick Fownes my kinsman (elsewhere spoken of as of London, merchant), kinswoman Johan the wife of John Rogers and her children. Diones Cotten's son which she had by John Cotten deceased. Susan Walker (*sic*) and Johane Walter, daughters of my sister Susan Walter, and Thomas Walter her son. My farm and barton at Whitley. Richard Hawkins and his wife in my service. My kinsman Richard Longe of Bristol, merchant, and his children. My daughter Prudence, now the wife of John Waddon, and her children. To my daughter Mary, the wife of Richard Halworthy six hundred pounds, which shall be for her and the children that she hath by Richard Halworthy. To my daughter Johan the wife of Hugh Gayer deceased, six hundred pounds, two hundred for herself and a hundred apiece for her children. James Yard, my godson, son of my aunt Yard lately deceased, and John Yard, her son. To Richard Fownes the son of Richard Fownes deceased my tenement in Tavistock. To my son John the tenths, tithe and sheafe of the parish of St. Budiox during my term and estate therein to come. To son Thomas messuages &c. in Plymouth called the Pump Close, by the pump near the new "key." To my two daughters Elizabeth Yard and Susan Kellond all the apparel and rings which were their mother's, my late wife deceased. Certain Jewels and rings that were Julian Fownes deceased (wife of Richard Fownes deceased) I give unto her two sons Thomas and Richard Fownes. To my son John all the barton of East Whitleigh and the manor of Honiknowle. Provision against his proving a wasteful young man keeping riotous company and spending and consuming his estate in drunkenness and idle courses. Son Thomas Fownes. Thomas and Richard sons of Richard Fownes deceased (called grandchildren). The two daughters of Francis Fownes deceased. The poor of Milbrooke in Cornwall. Abraham Sherwill now preacher at St. Budiox. My messuages &c. purchased by me and my heirs from my cousin Warwick Fownes lying in the parishes of Ilsington and High Week, Devon, and two pieces lying near the Lady Well. To Thomas Fownes my grandchild, son of Richard Fownes deceased, my manor of Lipson. I lately built and erected a Messuage, Hospital and Alms House near the great Hill in Plymouth, containing thirteen rooms. John, Thomas and Susan Kellond the sons and daughter of John Kellond. Edward Deacon, merchant, son of Edward Deacon deceased, and all his children. Prudence Martyn the daughter of Edward Deacon deceased and wife of Francis Martyn and all her children.

Sons John and Thomas to be joint executors.   Lee, 84.

RICHARD HOLWORTHIE, merchant, one of the aldermen of the city of Bristol, 10 October 1643, proved 9 December 1645. I have conveyed my dwelling house in Small street to my wife for her life. My eight children. To the mayor and commonalty of Bridgewater, Somerset, where I was born, fifty two pounds. My daughter Launce and her son. To William Launce. My daughter Cam. My daughter Croft. All my grandchildren. My brother Nicholas Holworthie and his children. My sister Mallet and her children. My cousin Robert Kitchen. To my son Matthew Holworthie my rich scabbard which I had when I was mayor. My son Thomas Holworthie. Wife Mary to be executrix and my friend Mr. Richard Long, alderman, and my son in law Mr. James Crofte and my loving friend Mr. William Yeomans gen*. to be overseers. The residue to be divided into ten equal parts whereof my wife shall have two and my eight children, Matthew, Richard, John, Thomas, Joseph, Nathaniel, Samuel and Sarah, to have each one. Reference to a gift made by father in law Mr. Fownes to his grandchildren my four younger sons and my daughter Sarah. To brother Robert Haviland five pounds.   Rivers, 147.

THOMAS HOLWORTHY of Bristol, gen., 3 April 1654, proved 5 June 1654. Copyhold tenements in Rowberow, Somerset. Son Thomas, brother-in-law James Crofte, merchant, and three of his children, Richard, Anne and Mary Crofte. Wife (not named). Alchin, 491.

WILLIAM LAUNCE, clerk, Rector of the parish church of St. Edmund the King and Martyr in Lombard Street, London, 13 January 1664, proved 21 January 1665. To be buried in the chançel of that church. Sister Elizabeth Forsithe, widow, and her daughter Elizabeth Forsithe. William Launce, Matthew Launce, Prudence Launce, Mary Lang and Ann Parker, the sons and daughters of my brother James Launce. My said brother James and Anne his wife. Zurishaddai Lang, Doctor in Physick, the husband of the said Mary Lang. Mico, 11.

The 28th of August 1665.

Brother MATHEW HOLWORTHY for the moneys of mine you have in yor hands That is Two hundred ffour scoar nine pounds five shillings and Eleauen pence I would desire you to pay my daughter Mary Lang the sume of ffowerteene pounds of the interest moneys first due and the next interest moneys due to make up those moneys in yor hands 3 hundred pounds. (Then follow gifts and bequests.) Son William Launce. Son Matthew Launce. Daughter Ann wife of William Parker living at Surinam. Son John. Daughter Prudence Launce.

This was signed "Your loveing Sister Anne Launce." Mico, 130.

NATHANIEL HOLWORTHY, gentleman, 29 January 1667, proved 20 February 1667. I do appoint my brother Mr. James Croft senior to be my sole executor and Mr. John Speed to be his overseer. My body to be buried in the parish church of St. Wasbrowes (sic), near to my father Mr Richard Holworthy, and I do appoint forty pounds to bury me and for funeral charges, at my brother Crofte's discretion. To my sister Mrs. Prudence Croft ten pounds "to morne." To my brother James Croft, ten pounds to mourn. To my sister Sarah Holworthy fifty shillings. To my sister Holworthy in the College Green fifty shillings. To my cousin Thomas Holworthy fifty shillings. To my cousin James Croft junior five pounds. To my cousin Mary Croft five pounds. To my cousin Ann Croft five pounds. To my cousin Hoppen forty shillings. To my cousin Thomas Cam forty shillings. To my cousin Arthur Cam forty shillings. A piece of gold of twenty shillings to Mr. Jones, the minister, to preach my funeral sermon. To Mr. Palmer the minister a piece of gold of twenty shillings. To Mr. Yeamons forty shillings. To Mrs. Sarah Yeamons twenty shillings. The best watch I give to my cousin James Croft junior and my other watch to my cousin Mary Croft. To Mr. Yeomans' son, William Yeomans ten shillings. To be paid to Mr. Cox in the Hurstreet twelve pounds for a debt. All what I have at sea, God sending it well home, I give to my cousins James, Mary and Anne Croft. To Anne Smith ten shillings. To Rachel Lewis ten shillings. To Mr. John Speed forty shillings. Hene, 19.

In the Probate Act Book for 1668 the testator above named is called lately of the city of Bristol.

Mense Januarii 1677. Vicesimo nono die emt Como Dño Matheo Holworthy miti marito ltimo Mariæ Holworthy nup põæ stæ Margaretae Lothbury London deftæ heñtis etc. Admon. Act Book, 1678.

Mathew Holworthy of Hackney, Middlesex, knight, 9 May 1677, proved 28 November 1678. To my wife Susanna Holworthy, over and above her jointure and other settlements made unto her and for her use, three hundred pounds and all her jewells and ornaments of her body for ever, and the use of all my plate and furniture and goods of my house during her natural life. And after her decease I do give the same unto my son Matthew forever. I do further give unto my said dear wife full power to sell the fee of my now dwelling house in Hackney, with all the ground and appurtenances thereto belonging, and to retain unto herself, to her proper use, one third part of the moneys that shall be made thereof. The other two third parts thereof I do give and bequeath unto my son Matthew and to his heirs forever.

"Item I doe giue and bequeath unto the Colledge or university in or of Cambridge in New England the summe of one Thousand pounds to be paid and made over to the Governors and directors thereof to be disposed of by them as they shall judge best for promoteing of learning and promulgation of the Gospell in those parts. The same to be paid within Two yeares next comeing after my decease."

There shall be land bought to the value of six hundred pounds near my manor of Sporle in Norfolk and the yearly rents and profits thereof shall be given and paid unto such ministers as shall be fitly qualified for the ministry and known to be of a good life and conversation and shall, every Lord's day, preach two sermons in the Church of that parish at the usual hours. The sum of two thousand pounds shall be given and disposed of in and to such charitable uses as shall be directed in and by a Schedule hereunto annexed or by any other writing under my hand writing. To the poor of the town of Sporle twenty pounds. To the poor of the parish of Hackney twenty pounds. To Edmond Channell nineteen pounds thirteen shillings, to Cisly Binner thirty six pounds, six pence (reference made to a book of accounts), to John Burrow the debt he oweth unto me and all my house goods that are in the keeping of his brother Robert Burrow and all those sums of money owing unto me by several bonds of his brother Thomas Burrow. To all and every of my nephews and nieces ten pounds, I say ten pounds to each of them. To my sister Mary Madocke eight pounds per annum during her natural life, to commence from the next day after my death. To my sister Croft six pounds per annum. I do order and will that six pounds shall be paid every year unto Mr. Thomas Gouge to promote his labour in instructing the Welsh as long as he shall continue in that pious work. Three hundred pounds to be paid unto such ministers as my executors shall judge deserving and to need supply, not exceeding ten pounds unto any of them singly. To my son Matthew all the remainder of my estate, both real and personal, to him and his heirs forever, he paying to every other child begotten me the sum of three thousand pounds to each of them, as soon as any of them shall have attained unto the age of twenty one years, and shall also pay unto every and each of them forty pounds per annum during the life of my dear wife, for their maintenance and breeding up, and after her decease shall allow and pay unto every and each of them one hundred pounds per annum for their maintenance and greatening of their portions, until they shall have attained their respective ages of twenty one years and the receipt of their respective portions of three thousand pounds hereby given and bequeathed. My manor of Sporle shall stand engaged for the payment thereof. Provision made in case of death of issue. To my nephew George Holworthy, to enjoy during his natural life, my manor of Sporle, with Great Palgrave, Norfolk, and after his decease to his next heir male (lawful) &c., remainder to his brother John Holworthy, remainder to my nephew John, son of my brother John Holworthy. If my said son and every other child of mine shall all depart this life without issue, then the remainder of my personal estate to the children, then living, of my brother Richard Holworthy deceased, of my brother John Holworthy, of my sister Mary Madocke and of my sister Anne Lauuce, in equal parts &c. My father Henry Henly Esq. and my wife Susanna to be my executors and guardians of my son.

Administration was granted 17 August 1704 to Matthew Holworthy Esq., the son, on the goods &c. left unadministered by Henry Henly Esq., and Dame Susanna Holworthy, now also dead.   Reeve, 41.

JOHN HOLWORTHY of London, merchant, 23 February 1683, proved 1 December 1687. Mentions wife Anne, refers to agreement made with her father deceased, before marriage, mentions also son John Holworthy, friend Sir Thomas Jenner, Recorder of London, daughter Ann Holworthy, Provision in case she marries Luke Robinson of Gray's Inn, Middlesex, Esq. Mrs. Anne Horsnell, her son and daughter. Cousin Sarah Ramsden wife of Michael Ramsden. Sister Madox. Mr. John Foche in Cannon Street, scrivener. Christ church Hospital.   Foote, 151.

SAMUEL PENOYER of London, merchant, 29 June 1652, proved 12 May 1654. To my brother William Penoyer and to his wife Martha ten pounds apiece, to buy them mourning. Twenty pounds to poor godly families which shall be in want, to be disposed of by my said sister Martha Penoyer. To the children of John Butler and David Butler, dwelling in Herefordshire, twenty pounds, to be paid to my brother William Penoyer for the use of the said children. To Master Brookes the minister six pounds and to Master Fraiser the minister five pounds to buy them mourning. The residue of my goods, chattels and personal estate to my wife Rose Penoyer, whom I make and ordain full and sole executrix; and for overseers I nominate and appoint my loving friends Master Richard Hill, Master William Hobson, Esquires, and Master William Penoyer Esquire, and I give and bequeath to them ten pounds apiece. Touching my lands, tenements and hereditaments, I give and bequeath to my wife Rose, for and during her natural life, my manor of Tharfield, Herts., and all my lands &c. in Acton, Middlesex, and all my adventures for lands in Ireland; and after her decease I give and bequeath the said manor, and lands &c unto Thomas Adams Esq., Thomas Cullam Esq., and Alderman of London, Christopher Pack Esq. and Alderman of London, Andrew Rickards Esq. and Alderman of London, Robert Lowther and Samuel Vassall Esquires, John Rogers, Robert Winch, John Taylor and James Russell, members of the Company of Drapers of the City of London, upon this trust and confidence and to this intent and purpose, that they shall pay and dispose of the first three years' rents &c after the decease of my said wife to such uses and in such manner as my said wife by her last will, or by any other writing under her hand and seal, shall direct and appoint. And if after the first three years next after my wife's decease my brother William and Martha his wife, or the survivor of them, shall happen to be in want and poverty and shall make such his, her or their want and poverty known to the said Company at any Court of Assistants, then the said trustees shall, after the first three years' rents &c paid and disposed of as aforesaid, pay or cause to be paid unto my said brother William, during the natural lives of him and his wife Martha, one hundred pounds per annum, and to the survivor of them fifty pounds per annum during the life of such survivor. If any of my collateral cousins on my father's side or mother's side (not exceeding the second degree from any of the brethren or sisters of my father or mother) shall stand in need of money to place them forth apprentices the said trustees shall out of the said rents pay or disburse the sum of fifty pounds for the putting forth apprentice of every such collateral cousin of mine to some godly man to be brought up in some honest and lawful trade, and shall pay such cousin one hundred pounds for and as a stock if he or she shall live till the expiration of his or her apprenticeship and shall be of honest life and conversation. Provision made for the putting forth of other, fatherless, children of fourteen years of age &c. There shall be paid to Richard Butler, student in the University of Cambridge, out of the rents &c. of my lands in Acton an annuity of six pounds per annum for ten years next after my decease. Twelve pounds per annum for a lecture to be yearly preached on Thursday or Friday for ever in the meeting-place or church called St. Stephens within the city of Bristol. Provision made in case wife bring forth a son or daughter before or after my decease.

Alchin, 388.

WILLIAM PENNOYER Esq., citizen and cloth-worker of London, 25 May 1670, proved 13 February 1670. Having attained to a competent worldly estate and having no children, being desirous to make provision for Martha, my dear and loving wife, daughter of John Joycelyn, late of Hyde Hall in Sabridgeworth in the county of Hertford, Esquire deceased, and others of my kindred &c &c. Then follow sundry bequests for the poor &c. To Mr. William Bridge the elder at Great Yarmouth ten pounds, to Mr. William Greenhill of Stepney twenty pounds, to Mr. William Hooke twenty pounds and to his two sons, John and Walter, ten pounds apiece. Others named, including Sir William Thompson, Maurice Thompson Esq. and John Jolliffe Esq. To my brother Joscelyne Esq. ten pounds. To Samuel Desborowe Esq. twenty pounds and to Rose his wife (the late wife of my brother Samuel Pennoyer deceased) twenty pounds. To Elizabeth Cheese, my near kinswoman, now wife of John Cheese of Ashford near Ludlow, three hundred pounds, to be wholly at her own dispose, and to John Cheese her husband fifty pounds. To my kinsman Pennoyer Cheese, son of the said Elizabeth, two hundred and fifty pounds, to his brother Samuel Cheese two hundred pounds and to Elizabeth Cheese their sister two hundred pounds, the sons at two and twenty and the daughter at like age or marriage. To Thomas Edes (eldest son of my kinswoman Isabel Edes) fourscore pounds and to each other of the children of the said Isabel, one hundred pounds apiece. Samuel and Richard, two of her sons, to be placed apprentices. To David Butler of Dorson, Hereford, yeoman, fourscore pounds and to his two daughters fourscore pounds apiece. To Evan Butler of Cusopp, Hereford, seventy pounds and to his son Walter, now at New England, and to each other of his children threescore pounds apiece. To Thomas Butler, son of Thomas Butler late of Cusopp deceased, sixty pounds and to his own sister Elizabeth twenty pounds, and to their sisters, Mary, sixty pounds, and Jane, seventy pounds. To William Butler, late of the city of Hereford, twenty shillings. To Toby Butler, one of the children of John Butler, late of Dorson deceased, sixty pounds, to William, another of the children, fifty pounds and to their brother Thomas Butler, apprentice to one Williams a taylor, seventy pounds. To their sister Mary one hundred pounds. To Katherine Butler *alias* Roberts, sister of the aforesaid Evan Butler, five pounds to be paid to her own hands. All and every of the said several persons of the sirname of Butler being of my kindred. And to all of them and to all other of my own kindred and my wife's kindred, except John Hyat, stiller, I forgive all such sums of money as any of them shall owe unto me at my decease.

Item. I will and order that the sum of eight hundred pounds, ster. shall be laid out in the best goods and merchandizes fit for New England, which I suppose to be woollen cloth and other woollen commodities and linen, all which I desire may be bought and provided by Mr. Henry Ashurst, draper, Mr. John Langley, Mr. John Jolliffe aud Mr. Benjamin Albyn, or any two of them, and my executors to allow them two p cent for their pains and no more; and I order the same to be sent over to the Corporation for the Propagation of the Gospel in New England and the parts adjacent in America, to be secured for the purposes hereinafter mentioned;—to the intent and purpose that the value of eight hundred pounds ster., in goods and commodities of that country, may upon sale thereof be delivered to Robert Pennoyer of Stamford in New England for the equal use and benefit of himself and each of his children; and further to the intent and purpose that what shall be made thereof above the said eight hundred pounds value in the commodities of that country shall be and remain to his sister Elianor Reading and her husband Thomas Reading and all their children equally and indifferently. To my kinswoman Anne Cruse, the wife of Richard Cruse, near Dorson, seventy pounds and to her son one hundred pounds. To William Pennoyer, late servant to Mr. Michael Davison, one hundred pounds, if living at my decease. To the poor of Great St. Hellens, London, one hundred pounds. Sundry other bequests and provisions.

And for and concerning my other messuages, lands tenements and hereditaments in the said County of Norfolk,* let to Robert Moore at the yearly rent of forty and four pounds per annum. My will is that out of the rents and profits thereof ten pounds per annum shall be paid for ever to the Corporation for Propagation of the Gospel in New England and that with the residue thereof two Fellows and two scholars forever shall be educated, maintained and brought up in the college called Cambridge College in New England, of which I desire one of them, so often as occasion shall present, may be of the line or posterity of the said Robert Pennoyer, if they be capable of it, and the other of the colony now or late called "Newhaven" Colony, if conveniently may be. And I delare my mind to be that eight years or thereabouts is a convenient time for education of each scholar respectively, and about that standing others to be taken in their places, which nevertheless as to time I leave to the Master and Governors of the said College. Provision for the continuance of the trusteeship. A bequest to Mrs. Row, mother of Mr. Samuel Crispe. Duke, 25.

[Walter Butler, son of Evan Butler of Cusop, Herefordshire, named above as being in New England, was probably the Walter Butler who in 1672 was one of the 27 purchasers of Horseneck in Greenwich, Ct. He was a legal voter of Greenwich in 1688, but his name does not appear in the town lists for 1694-5; though a Thomas Butler is found in that list. (See Mead's History of Greenwich, Ct., pages 67, 71 and 79.) The christian name Walter occurs in the Butler family of New London, Ct., at a later date. (See Caulkins's History of New London, page 342.)

* In or near Pulham St. Mary, according to a description in a previous clause of the will.

Robert Pennoyer of Stamford in New England, named above, was an early settler of Stamford, Ct. He had a son Thomas born there in 1658. Several parcels of land were assigned him soon after the settlement of the town. (See Rev. E. B. Huntington's History of Stamford, page 59.) It is supposed that he was the Robert Pennaire aged 21 years who with Thomas Pennaire aged 10 embarked at London for New England, Sept. 8, 1635. (See REGISTER, vol. 2, page 399.)—EDITOR.]

MARTHA PENNOYER of London, widow, relict of William Pennoyer late of London Esq. deceased, 16 July 1672, proved 2 July 1674. To brother Edward Jostlin one hundred pounds and to his daughter Anne Jostlin seventy pounds. To my niece Susan Gwin twenty pounds and to her three children now living twenty pounds apiece (they minors). To John Jostlin son of Mr. Thomas Jostlin minister twenty pounds. To my cousin Susanna Lansdell seventy pounds. Five shillings weekly, for ten years, to my cousin Elizabeth Davies, the wife of Benjamin Davies, to be paid into her own hands. Her two children (not named). To my cousin Andrew Cater, minister at Hide Hall, twenty pounds and to his brother Henry Cater twenty pounds. To their sister Cater ten pounds and to the daughter of the said Henry Cater ten pounds. Bequests to poor and distressed people and families. My cousin Jane Courtman of Colchester and her four children (sons and daughters). John Davies, merchant, and his son John. Isabel Edes of Ullinghall, Warwickshire. Anne Cruse wife of Richard Cruse, of Clifford in the Co. of Hereford. Others. Bunce, 3.

ROSE DISBROWE of Elsworth, Co. of Cambridge, widow, late wife of Samuel Disbrowe Esq. (aged and indisposed &c.). To brother Joseph Hobson Esq. ten pounds to buy him mourning—other property—and my great bible for the term of his life, and, after his decease, to sister Mrs Sarah White. To sister Mrs Elizabeth Hobson five pounds and to her granddaughter five pounds. To sister the Lady Bolton ten pounds to buy her mourning. To sister Sarah White the first year's rent of my estate in Ireland after my decease, which said estate was given unto me by my late dear husband Mr Samuel Pennoyer, merchant and citizen of London—and certain jewells &c., which are to go to her daughter Mrs Rebecca Lloyd and her other two daughters. To sister Mrs Ann Hudson and each of her own sons and daughter. To my brother M^r. George Robbins a ring. To nephew M^r. William White the elder the second year's Irish rents. To Mr William White the younger and to Mrs White his wife. To my nephew Mr Samuel Browne and my niece Mrs Elizabeth Browne. To Dr Fryer and my niece his wife and her children. I further give unto my said niece Fryer her grandfather Bolton's locket for life, and after her decease unto Anna Maria her daughter; also six napkins marked R: L: To John Fryer. To my niece Mrs Elizabeth Pomfret. To my niece Mrs Hannah Aldrich the elder. To my niece Mrs Sarah Pastor. To my niece Mrs Rebecca Lloyd and her daughter Rose Lloyd. To Hannah Aldrich the younger, now dwelling with me. The third year's rent of my estate in Ireland, after my decease to be equally divided between the children of my nieces Aldrich, Pouter, Pomfret, Fryer and Lloyde. To Mrs Mary Sherwood the elder and her daughter Fryer. To Mr George Sherwood her husband. To Mrs Dudgein and Mrs Sarah Baker. To my son Christopher Mills Esq. and to his lady. To my grandson Samuel Mills Esq. and to his lady. To said grandson his grandfather's ring with his coat of arms upon it. To Matthew Hallworthy Esq. my grandson and to his lady my granddaughter. To said granddaughter her grandfather's picture set in gold and if she die without heirs of her body my grandchild Samuel Mills Esq. shall have the same after her decease. To Mrs Hannah Aldridge the younger. To Mrs Dye the elder and her daughter Mrs Ann Dye. To brother Joseph Hobson Esq. my own father's picture and my husband Lacey's picture. To my sister Mrs Sarah White my Lady Arman's picture, and my father Lacey's picture. To the Reverend Mr James Disbrowe my nephew. To my cousin Sarah Kiniston.

Dated 28 June 1698. Codicil dated 4 March 1698. Sworn to 25 March 1699. Proved 21 April 1699. Pett, 56.

[Mrs. Rose Disbrowe died March 4, 1698, in her 83d year, and her husband Samuel Disbrowe died Dec. 10, 1690, aged 75. See inscriptions at Elsworth in the REGISTER, vol. 41, pages 360–61 (*ante*, p. 251). The will of Samuel Disbrowe is printed on page 355 of that volume (*ante*, p. 245).—EDITOR.]

WILLIAM HOBSON of Hackney, Middlesex, Esq., 13 November 1661, proved 13 March 1661. Aged and very infirm. Personal estate very small and inconsiderable. Daughter Anne. Son Joseph. Christ's Hospital. The poor of St Martin Ludgate. The poor of Great Glen where I was born. The poor of Hackney. The Company of Haberdashers.

"Also I give to my daughter Desborow Tenne Pounds to buy her a peece of Plate." To my daughter Bolton the like sum. My daughter Sarah White the wife of Jesper White. My daughter Ward. The two children of my daughter Bannister at eighteen or days of marriage. My daughter Sarah White's four children at eighteen or days of marriage. The six children of my daughter Rebecca White, late deceased wife of William White, the sons at twenty-three and the daughters at one and twenty years or days of marriage. My sister Alice Wickes. My daughter Mary Sherwood. Farm in Hendon, Middlesex. My manor of St. John in Jerusalem in Hackney. My sons in law William White and Patience Warde. Son Nathaniel. Grandson William White. My son in law George Robins. My son in law Thomas Moore. My son in law Alderman William Bolton. My loving friend Robert Yarway. Nathaniel and Anne to be under guardianship. Laud, 38.

"Laus Deo in London the fower & twentith August one thousand six hundred thirty six."

EDWARD FOORD citizen and leather: of London and merchant adventurer of England. To be buried in the choir of the Church of Aldermanbury, it being the parish where my house standeth and my residence most is. According to the laudable custom of the city of London I divide my estate into three parts, one third to my dear and loving wife, one third to my child, and the other third I dispose of in legacies, being in my own power so to do. I conceive that my mansion house in Aldermanbury, with my two tenements adjoining, may amount to as much within 500£ as my third part. I give the inheritance of all three houses to my son Daniel Foord, he to pay to his sister Rebecca Foord, my second daughter, one hundred fifty pounds, and to his three younger sisters, Hannah, Elizabeth and Hester Foord, each fifty pounds and to his brother Edward, which was born before I ended this my last will, one hundred pounds more than his child's part. These are to be paid them at their several days of marriage or twenty one years of age. To wife Hannah her free dwelling in my mansion house in Aldermanbury, only allowing twenty pounds per annum to my son Daniel towards his breeding at schools abroad. Other provisions for

wife and son Edward. My wife to pay six pounds yearly to Doctor
Staughton, my minister, during his life or abode in Aldermanbury, and
after him the next minister that shall succeed him if the said minister be
chosen by the parish and comes in with their good liking. To my brother
William Foord of Kynver a lease which I hold of Mr. John Whorwood,
known by the name of Wilkinson's lands, at Compton. To my brother
Humfrey Foord ten pounds and to my brother and sister Eaton five pounds
to buy them rings, and to my godson William ten pounds when he shall be
put to apprentice. To my brother Daniel Gouer fifty pounds, to be paid
him when he hath done with his creditors, to help him in the world. To
the parish of Kynver where I was born. To sundry ministers, companies
and charities.

"Also I give towards the erectinge a free schoole in New England, if
anie such worke be done, that the Companie doth owe me, wch is in true
right fiftie poundes; and yet I gave fifty poundes towardes the worke, which
I value at nothing; and yet I am content to give tenn poundes more
towardes a free schoole, there to educate youth, yf anie such thing bee done."

I forgive Henry Moseley a debt of seven pounds which he oweth me.
To Mrs. Susanna Bland forty shillings, being doubtful I borrowed a bill
of store of her husband, John Bland, and do not remember I paid him.
The rest of my estate, debts and funeral charges paid, I desire may
be divided, one half to my wife and the other half to my son Edward.
I entreat my brother Humfrey Foord and my dear friend Mr. Daniel Hod-
son to assist my wife whom I make sole executrix. To my said friend
Daniel Hodson ten pounds.

Three lines added 13 September 1639 to explain that daughter Mary
Foord, being advanced in marriage 11 July last to Mr. Tho: Bunch, with
whom testator gave a thousand pounds present and promised two hundred
pounds more the 11 July 1641, is to have no more than that till all her
sisters and younger brother have as much as she, and then to divide equally.

Acknowledged by the testator as his will 13 September 1639. Proved
by the widow 6 January 1641.   Cambell, 2.

FRANCIS BRIDGES of Clapham, Surrey, citizen and salter of London,
28 May 1642, proved 23 June 1642. To loving sister Elizabeth Benson
twenty pounds and to her four children, William Risby, Elizabeth Pennington, Sara Thorne and Judith Risby, fifty pounds apiece. Bequests to
cousin german Oliver Huntley, and to Humfrey Huntley, son of cousin
William. Cousins John Barton, Constance Clayton, and Susan Wheeler.
Wife's mother Susan Carpenter and brother in law Gabriel Carpenter.
Sister in law Mary Bicke. Cousin Mr. Charles Offspring, minister. Mr.
Francis Taylor parson (at present) of Clapham and Mr. John Arthur our
now lecturer. Mr. Pemberton, minister. Mrs. Mary Washborne, widow
(the elder). Wife's kinsman Samuel Bonner. Wife's cousin Elizabeth
Harris. Samuel and Sarah Remnant, the two children of William Rem-
nant.

"Item I give and bequeath unto Mr. Wells, Mr. Hooker, Mr. Peters
and Mr. Syms (Ministers of New England) the soffie of fiftie poundes
towards the enlargement of a colledge in New England for students there.
Alsoe I give unto the said ffower New England Ministers Twenty Poundes
to bee disposed towardes the clothinge of the poore in New England according as they in their discretions shall thinke fitt."

Bequests to the poor, to the city of London, to Christ's Hospital &c.

Four messuages in St. Sythes Lane, London, now or late in tenures or occupations of Mr. Remnant, Mr. Simpson, Mr. Mosse and Mr. Heath. The manor and Lordship of Lachington Barnes *als* Purleigh Barnes in Essex. Mr. Daniel Pennington living in Bow Churchyard. My brothers in law Gabriel Carpenter, William Beeke, Thomas Walker and Henry Bonner. My mother Carpenter. Sister Bicke and her husband. Wife Sara to be executrix. Cambell, 80.

NATHANIEL HULTON, citizen and sadler of London, 29 July 1692, proved 13 March 1693. Bequests to James Greene the younger, son of James Green my son in law, Richard Green another son, John Greene, another son, Margery Greene, a daughter and Elizabeth, their sister. To Joseph Scriven. To the poor of Newington Green, where I now live. To wife Elizabeth, for life, my copyhold messuage, at Newington Green, newly erected and built with brick, where lately was standing an old messuage commonly called or known by the name of the Green Dragon, and after her decease I give the said tenement to William Hulton, son of my late kinsman William Hulton deceased and his lawful male issue (entailed), then to Joseph Hulton, son of my late kinsman Adam Hulton deceased and his lawful male issue, next to my right heirs. To the widow and the daughter of said kinsman Adam Hulton, these two legacies to be paid into the hands of my kinsman Samuel Haward. Thomas Crompton son of my late kinsman Adam Crompton deceased, and to his two daughters. The daughter of my kinsman George Crompton. My kinsman John Hill. Nathaniel Hill son of Edmund Hill deceased. My kinswoman Elizabeth Hill. My sister Elizabeth Dickins widow of John Dickins deceased. My kinswoman Ann Pimlott. Mary Pickford wife of Mr. Pickford and her seven children. My kinsman Robert Dickings.

A codicil bearing date 23 March 1692, mentions son in law Thomas Horrocks, and his wife, daughter in law Jane Perry and others.

Another codicil dated 1 January 1693 contains the following bequest:—

" I give and bequeath to Mr. Encrease Mather Minister of the Gospell in New England the Summe of One Hundred pounds of Lawfull money of England for the use of the Colledge there of which hee is president."

Bequests to Bridewell Hospital, to Christ Church Hospital and to daughter Jane Perry. My body to be interred at Bolton in Lancashire near father and mother. Box 54.

SAMUEL HOLDEN of London, merchant, 29 December 1733, with codicil bearing date 16 November 1738, proved 18 June 1740. My body to be buried in my vault in St. Bridget's churchyard with all that privacy that is consistent with decency, without bearers or more to attend my corpse than are necessary. I give and bequeath to poor congregations what I have remaining of Mr. Baxter's Works in the same manner as those disposed of in my life. To the Society for Propagating Christian Knowledge in the Highlands of Scotland one hundred pounds. To each of the directors of the Bank of England and each of the Assistants of the Russia Company a gold ring. To the Revd Doctors Harris, Grosvenor and Watts, each a gold ring. To my good friend Matthew Shiffner fifty pounds for mourning for himself and wife. To Joseph Fawthrop twenty pounds for mourning, and rings to such other of my friends as my wife shall see fitting. The rest and residue of my personal estate I give and bequeath to my dear wife Jane Holden, to my daughters Priscilla, Jane and Mary Holden,

share and share alike.   To Jane my wife, during her natural life or widowhood, all the rents, profits and emoluments of my estate in the co. of Derby
for her sole use and benefit; and after her decease or marriage, which may
first happen, to my daughters Priscilla, Jane and Mary Holden, each one
third part; and at the decease of any of them the same to be divided by
the survivors; and after the decease of all to the children of Priscilla, or in
default thereof to those of Jane, or in default thereof to those of Mary
Holden.   If all should die without children and my wife Jane Holden
should survive them then the residue to be at her disposal.   My said wife
to be sole executrix and my friend Joseph Fawthrop, merchant, trustee for
the fulfilling of the same, willing the legacies of my children to be paid
them at the age of twenty one years or at marriage.

(Codicil) My will further is that what my estate may exceed sixty
thousand pounds (exclusive of land) be distributed in charitable uses at the
discretion of my wife and children, such as promoting true Religion, I
mean Sobriety, Righteousness and Godliness, without regard to any party
or denomination, either here or in New England, the relief of industrious
poor and of those who are aged and friendless or in such other ways as
have the greatest tendency to the promoting the honor of God and the good
of Mankind.

18th June 1740, personally appeared John Lewis Hansen of St. Peter le
Poor, London, merchant, and Henry Shiffner, of the same, gentleman, &c.
and deposed that they were well acquainted with Samuel Holden late of
Roehampton, in the Parish of Putney, in the co. Surrey, deceased, for several years next before and until the time of his death, which happened on
or about the twelfth day of this instant June, as these deponents are informed and believe, &c. &c.   Browne, 172.

WASHINGTON NOTES.

It was announced on the cover of the January REGISTER that the will of Col.
John Washington, the emigrant ancestor of President Washington, had been
recently found.   Both the original will and the original record of it were found
at about the same time in different places.   Mr. Moncure D. Conway of New York
city, in a communication to the New York *Nation*, Oct. 24, 1889, says: " The
Rev. E. C. McGuire writing in 1836 says that the will was then at Mount Vernon "
(see REGISTER, vol. 44, p. 79, *ante*, p. 414), and he suggested that search be made
among them.   It was among these Mount Vernon papers preserved by Mr. Lawrence Washington of Alexandria, which last winter were temporarily deposited
in the National Museum at Washington, D. C., that the curator of the Museum,
Mr. A. Howard Clark, discovered the original will.   The papers were withdrawn
from the Museum in February last, to be sold at auction.   Joseph M. Toner,
M.D., of Washington, has made an exact copy of this will from the original.
The wills of Lawrence Washington the emigrant, brother of Col. John;
of Lawrence Washington, son of John the emigrant; of Augustine Washington, son of the preceding and father of the general; and of Lawrence
Washington, the general's half brother, are also extant and Dr. Toner
has copies of them.   The five wills are promised to us by him for the
next number of the REGISTER.   The will of Augustine has never been printed.
There is, as part of the same record, a copy of the Deed of Roger Gregory and
his wife Mildred (Washington) Gregory—aunt and god-mother of George,—to
Augustine Washington, her brother, of the Little Hunting Creeke, now Mount
Vernon, Estate which she inherited from her father Lawrence Washington, son
of John the emigrant.   The recitals in this deed to Mildred's brother Augustine
the father of George, makes clear the kinship of the Washingtons and also the
claim of title to the Mount Vernon estate.

The record of the will was discovered, about the same time as the will itself, by Mr. J. Warren Hutt, clerk of the county court of Westmoreland, Va., in his office. Mr. Isaac J. Greenwood caused searches to be made in this office in 1873 and in 1889, and Mr. Conway made a search there personally in the latter year. They were all unsuccessful. But the search was not abandoned, and in December, 1890, the old original record book of Westmoreland county, embracing the proceedings of the courts, patents, assignments of patents, deeds, fiduciary acts, depositions, etc., after having been thrown aside, was accidentally discovered. In this volume the will of Col. John Washington was entered. Mr. Hutt promptly notified Messrs. Conway and Greenwood of the discovery, and sent them copies of the will. Mr. Conway had the will printed in the *Nation* for Dec. 18, 1890, and Mr. Greenwood sent his copy to the editor of the REGISTER. The record is much mutilated, and there are many breaks in the copies furnished by the clerk. It was no doubt from this record that Bishop Meade got his brief notes of the will, which he says was much mutilated. The original will, fortunately, can all be made out.

Mr. Conway has written an article on the Washington family for Harper's Magazine, which will appear in the May number. It will be richly illustrated. The author visited England last year and collected much interesting material. His personal researches have resulted in finding important evidence in favor of Mr. Waters's theory, which will appear in his article. We shall lay it before our readers in our July number. Mr. Conway's article cannot fail to be interesting and trustworthy.

Mr. James Greenstreet has contributed to "The Genealogist" for January, 1891, page 145–7, an article entitled "The Ancestry of General Washington," in which he makes known to us some of the unpublished discoveries of Col. Chester, relating to the ancestry of Washington. Mr. Waters will print this article in the next number of his Gleanings. Mr. Whitmore expressed the feelings of Col. Chester's American friends, when he wrote in the REGISTER for October, 1889 (vol. 43, page 424, *ante* p. 403), in his annotations of Mr. Waters's article : "Every one will regret that Col. Chester did not have the good fortune to bring to a successful conclusion the investigation which he pursued for so many years."—EDITOR.

RICH⁴ RUSSELL of the city of Hereford the elder, gen¹, 16 August, 1627, proved 13 June 1628. My body to be buried at the West door in the parish of St. Jones in the city of Hereford as near to the grave as may be of Jane Russell my late wife deceased. To my cousin Bridget Parry wife of Charles Parie, gen¹. To Elizabeth Russell daughter of Paul Russell deceased. To Katherine Scroope the daughter of my sister Winifred Scroope. To my said sister Winifred Scroope. To the four sons of my cousin Robert Russell of Whitefilde in the Co. of Hereford, deceased, viz¹ Hugh (his eldest son), William, Robert and Richard Russell. To the four daughters of the aforesaid Robert Russell, viz¹ Alles, Mary, Winifride and Bridget Russell. To Frances Bridges the grandchild of Jane, my late wife deceased. To my maid servant Anne Jeffres and Jane Jeffres, my late servant. To my cousin William Russell senior. To my cousin Richard Ravenhill junior and to my sister Ellenor Ravenhill. To Mr. Charles Parrie, to Mary, wife of James Scrivenor, to Mr. James Lane and his wife Katherine Lane. To Francis Lyde. My cousin James Scrivenor. Edward Russell of London. Ann Holland wife of Richard Holland, tanner. James Russell of London, girdler. Richard and James Ravenhill the sons of Richard Ravenhill junior. Thomas Quarrell of the City of Hereford mercer. Richard Russell of Caldicote. Elizabeth Griffitts wife of William Griffitts sadler. Katherine Roath wife of William Wroath. Katherine Smith wife of Thomas Smith of Wesson gen¹. Anne wife of Hopkin Protheroath. The three sons of Paul Russell deceased, viz¹ James, Paul and Richard Russell. My four godchildren, viz¹ Richard Smith of Wesson,

Roger Simons, Bartholomew Taylor and Elinor Quarrell. The poor of every ward in the City of Hereford. The five children of my cousin Hugh Russell deceased. Residue of personal estate to Frances Bridges and Anne Jeffres equally. My executors to be my loving kinsman William Russell the elder, gen^t, and Francis Lyde, goldsmith.

Barrington, 63.

MARY EYTON of St. Stephens, within the city of Bristol, widow 30 April 1645, proved 20 April 1646. To be buried in St. Stephen's Church near my late husband William Eyton deceased. To my dear and loving mother fifty pounds (and certain silver &c). My brother Richard Robinson. I give and bequeath to my kinsman Mr. James Russell the other of those two cups which were my grandmother's and which my said mother shall refuse, and also twenty pounds in money to make him and his wife rings. I give and bequeath to my cousin Mr. Paul Russell twenty pounds of lawful money of England as a token of my love. I give and bequeath to my god daughter, my cousin Mr. Richard Russell's daughter, twenty pounds &c. as a token and six silver "Postell spoons," which were her great-grand-mother's. To my cousin Elizabeth Derricke twenty pounds, my cypress chest (and other things). I give and bequeath to my cousin Mr. James Russell's daughter my best suite of Holland of laid work and fringed. I give and bequeath to my cousin Richard Russell's daughter Catherine my best suite of diaper, two pair of sheets and a pair of pillowbeeres and a side board cloth laced round and wrought round. To my cousin Elizabeth Bampton ten pounds, and her husband shall not have anything to do therewith, but it shall wholly be at her disposing. To my god daughter Elizabeth Fox forty shillings. To my cousin Hiscocks, his daughter, my god daughter, forty shillings. To my cousin Millen's two daughters, my late husband's god daughter and mine, Catherine and Mary, fifty pounds equally to be divided between them, so that they do not molest, trouble, sue or vex in the law mine executrix for either of their legacies given them by my said husband William Eyton deceased. To my godson Hugh Kelly five pounds. To Mary Reade dau. of William Reade. To Dorothy Eyton my cousin John Eyton's daughter. My cousin Elizabeth Dearges living in London, daughter of Edward Russell, and her two children. My kinswoman Mary Hathway, daughter of Thomas Hathway and Margaret his wife, to be residuary legatee and executrix. None of her kindred by her father's side shall have anything to do with my gifts to her.

Twisse, 45.

[In Oct., 1889 (See REGISTER, Vol. 43, pp. 425–6, *ante* p. 405), I gave abstracts of the wills of the father and grandfather of Richard Russell of Charlestown. The two preceding wills also refer to him. According to Wyman's Genealogies and Estates of Charlestown, Richard Russell, son of Paul, of Hereford, born 1611, apprenticed at Bristol, England, 4 Oct. 1628, arrived 1640 with wife; both admitted to the church 23.3.1641. He was a merchant, representative, Councillor, Speaker, Treasurer and Assistant. He married, first, Maud Pitt, who died 1652, and, secondly, Mary Chester, who died 30 Nov. 1688, aged about 80. He died 14.3.1676, in the 65th year of his age. In his will, made 29.5.1674, he mentioned wife Mary, her three daughters and seven grandchildren, Whiting, son James and his family, daughter Roswell and her son, daughter Graves and her children, sister Mrs. Elizabeth Corbet of Bristol, sister Sarah Russell of Bristol, sister in law Mary Newell and her sons Joseph and John, James Cary and others. He bequeathed one hundred pounds to Harvard College and made large bequests to the town and church. The "sister-in-law Mary Newell" mentioned by him is recorded as "relict of Andrew Newell of ye City of Bristol, merchant," and "daughter of William Pitt, Sheriff of the City of Bristol." For notes on the family of Pitt of Bristol see previous number of Gleanings, relating to the Holworthy family.—HENRY F. WATERS.]

JOSEPH MAYE of the Strand, in the county of Middlesex, gentleman, 5 (?) March 1631, proved 15 February 1635. To the poor of the parish of Savoy forty shillings. To my sister Susan ten pounds. To my sister Ellen a ring of twenty shillings. To my cousin Benjamin Cheland (sic) five pounds. To my cousin Thomas Moyne thirty pounds, my brother Nathaniel's son, to be given him at the discretion of my executor, or if he die in the wars four years after to his "dafter" thirty pounds.

"Item I give to my cozen Cornelius Maye fyve pounds, to be paid him as his Uncle Phinees Maye doth thinke fitt. But if he dye at sea I only give his sonne that was borne in Virginea." Item I give to my cousin Mathyas children to be ordered by my executor. To my cousin Thomas Collynes five pounds and to all his sisters a ring of twenty shillings apiece, and a ring to his wife of like price. To my cousin William Collyns and his wife a ring of twenty shillings apiece. To my Jane Primrose five pounds and to her sister Elizabeth Maye forty shillings. To the young man that dwelleth at Tavistock* called Joseph Maye. To a goldsmith wife called Mary Ratcliffe in Exon. Others. My brother Phynies Maye to be executor, &c. In witness whereto I set my name and seal 10 July 1632. Item to Manuell Maye my kinsman, Joseph Maye. Let my brother Phinees remember better Mathias children and my cousin Thomas Maye. A ring to my brother Collyns. A ring to my cousin John Beare and to my cousin John Sherman. 20 November 1635.

A codicil (made on death bed about 20 Nov. 1635). His cousin Benjamin Cleveland† should have but forty shillings, whereas is expressed in the said will x^{lb} (? v^{lb}). His cousin John Sherman should have nothing. His cousin Joseph May of Tavistock should have nothing.   Pile, 9.

PETER RANDOLPH of Chatsworth in the county of Henrico Esq. 4 May 1767, proved 21 Oct. 1768. To my dear wife Lucy the land and plantation known by the name of Chatsworth, with all the slaves, horses and stocks of all kinds thereon at the time of my death, and all my household furniture, plate, linen and china, likewise my chariot and horses for and during her natural life, to be in lieu and satisfaction of her dower. And that she may be the better enabled to support herself and entertain my children I likewise give unto my said wife fifty pounds sterling during her natural life in case she thinks fit to demand it of my executors; and also that the house may be supplied with provisions from my plantations in as plentiful a manner as was in my lifetime &c. To son William all the estate bequeathed unto his mother, after her death, and my tract of land in Chesterfield County called Skin Quarter, with all the slaves, stocks and horses thereon, and the tract of land I purchased of Robert Munford lying on Stanton River, with all the slaves &c. To my son Beverley my tract of land in Cumberland County known by the name of the Fork, and two tracts of land on Roanoke River which I purchased of Thomas Nash, containing about thirteen hundred acres &c. To my son Robert three tracts of land on Roanoke River, that is to say, the land which I purchased of Col° Bannister, that which I purchased of Thomas Douglas, lying on Dan River and the land I purchased of Hampton Wade, lying on Stanton River, the whole being about three thousand acres &c. To daughter Ann Fitzhugh three hundred and fifty pounds. My two acres of land in Chesterfield opposite to Chatsworth to my three sons, in common, for the accommodation

---

* A line run through "dwelleth at Tavistock."—H. F. W.
† See Cheland above.—H. F. W.

of th'eir servants, slaves and horses, to bring down tobacco to the ware-
house. Residue to son William. Col. Archibald Cary, Col. Richard Ran-
dolph, John Wayles and Seth Ware Sen 'to be executors.
Wit. : Carter Braxton, John Hylton and Anthony Hay.
In the Probate Act he is called the Hon. Peter Randolph, late Surveyor
Gen¹ of H. M. Customs for the Middle Western District of North America.
Secker, 393.

[See Bishop Meade's Old Churches, Ministers and Families of Virginia, vol. I.
pp. 138–40.—EDITOR.]

SIBELL FRYER of New Sarum, widow of John Fryer of the same city,
innholder, 29 December 1635, proved 23 February 1635. To my grand-
child Margaret Brook who now lives in house with me twenty pounds at
her age of eighteen. My late husband's son George Fryer.
Item I give unto John Bennett, now in New England, five pounds if he
be living, and unto Mary Sharpe daughter of my husband's eldest daughter
I give five pounds. To the two eldest daughters of my daughter in law
Mary Owen five pounds apiece, at fourteen. To my two daughters in law
Julyan Sharpe and Mary Owen ten pounds apiece. To my daughter Ann
Jempson ten pounds in regard of a promise made unto her of satisfaction
for putting her life out of a leasehold which is settled on my daughter
Margaret. All the rest to my two daughters Margaret Good and Anne
Jempson whom I ordain &c. sole executrixes.
Wit: Ambrose Hewes, Mary Godfrey, William Jemson, Robert Good,
William Derbie.   Pile, 19.

[There was a John Bennett in that part of Salem afterwards set off as Marble-
head, who had a grant, in 1638, of four acres " upon John Peaches Necke."
William Keene and Nicholas Liston had grants of land on the same neck, which
now goes by the name of Peach's Point, and is the summer home of Messrs.
George W. Benson, Benjamin W. Crowninshield, and others.—HENRY F.
WATERS.]

RICHARD SPENCER of London, genᵗ, 17 March 1645, with a codicil
bearing date 29 May 1646, proved 8 June 1646. To Thomas Spencer,
son of my brother Thomas Spencer, all my copyhold lands and tenements by me purchased of the creditors of Walter Marston, situate in
Kingsbury Street near St. Albans, in the co. of Hertford, in the parish
of St. Michael. To Daniel Spencer of London, grocer, son of my
brother John Spencer deceased, all those eight messuages or tenements
&c. lately by me purchased of John Gearing, grocer, from and after the
decease of Margaret Greene of London, widow, situate in the parish
of St. Margaret Lothbury in London. To Sarah Bland and Hannah
Bland, daughters of my sister Katherine Bland deceased, and to Elizabeth
Tomlyns, widow, daughter of my brother Jarrard Spencer deceased, my
messuage or tenement situate in Grace Church Street, near the great Inn
called the Crosse Keys, late in the tenure of William Toone or his assigns,
to be equally divided between them, by the rents, issues and profits thereof
during their natural lives. And after the decease of the said Elizabeth
Tomlyns and Hanna then I give and devise the said messuage and tenement unto the said Sarah Bland and her heirs forever. To the said Daniel
Spencer all my lands and tenements in the counties of Kent and Essex, he
to pay unto Anthony Spencer and Jarrard Spencer, sons of my brother
Thomas Spencer deceased, and unto the two children of Margaret Spencer
deceased, now in or near London and at the disposing of Elizabeth Carter
their aunt, the sum of thirty pounds yearly during their natural lives, i. e.

ten pounds per annum to the said two children or their guardians in their minorities, or the survivor of them, and ten pounds apiece to the said Anthony Spencer and Jarrard Spencer, to be paid unto them and their guardians by half yearly payments as the rents of the said lands and tenements shall grow due after my decease.

Item I give and bequeath unto Jarrard Spencer, Thomas Spencer, Michaell Spencer, sons of my brother Jarrard Spencer deceased, the sum of fifty pounds apiece, and unto the children of William Spencer, son of my said brother Jarrard Spencer deceased, to be divided between them equally, the sum of fifty pounds, to be paid unto their guardians, and within two years next after my decease.

To Thomas Martyn and Mary his wife, now dwelling with me, the remaining term to come in my dwelling house and the hangings and pictures in the two rooms thereof, with all partitions in the upper rooms of it or elsewhere. To Edward Terrey vintner, my kinsman, one hundred and thirty pounds which he oweth me by bond. And I bequeath unto him and Elizabeth his wife, my sister's daughter, thirty pounds, within three years &c. The rest to Daniel Spencer whom I make and ordain sole executor.

Wit: John Norburie, William Norburie. Twisse, 79.

[In the June Term of Essex Co. Court (Salem), 1671, in a trial of the case of John Ruck, Administrator, *versus* Joseph Armitage, the following paper was put in:

"Boston: in New England ye 19 Jan'y, 1648.

Att thirty dayes sight of this my seacond bill of exchange (my first & third of the same teñour & date not being payed) pay unto Mr. Thomas Ruck, haberdasher, att the Seauen Starres on London Bridge, or to his assignes, the some of thirty pounds sterly & is part of the Legacy gyuen mee by my Unckle Richard Spencer & the payement hereof shalbee your discharge for soe much at day, pray you make good payement & place it to acco.: I say pay £30 : 00 : 00."

(Signed) " MICHAELL SPENSER."

"The dyrection is—To my Louinge Cousen Mr. Danyell Spenser Grocer in Friday Streete in London."

This bill was protested by Joshua Mainett, Notary and Tabellion publick of London, who reported that "the said Danyell Spencer answered that hee will pay noe monneyes nor haue to doe with the sayd bill of exchange."

The above case was referred to the arbitration of Capt. Roger Spenser and Christopher Lawson.

I find that Michael and Jarrard Spencer were both at Lynn, for a while, and that Timothy Tomlin owned land next to the latter. HENRY F. WATERS.]

JOHN STYLE of Stebonheath *als* Stepney, Middlesex 26 October 1685, with a codicil referring to a former will bearing date 25 March 1680; proved 30 July 1686 and again 31 August 1686. To Elizabeth Nurse thirty pounds and to Frances Walshall seventy pounds, to be abated to them upon their paying the sum of six hundred pounds, remainder of mortgage chargeable on Glassenbury house in Smithfield. To Mr. Matthew Meade, sometime minister of Stepney, twenty pounds, to Dr. Ainslow of Spittlesfields ten pounds, to Seth Powell of Barnard's Inn, London, gent., ten pounds. To my sister in law Mrs. Elizabeth Short twenty shillings to buy her a ring. To her son Peter Short five pounds. To Mrs. Lisle forty shillings to buy her a ring. To Mrs. Mildmay, daughter to Mrs. Brewster four pounds. To Mrs. Taylor, wife of Mr. Taylor of Barking, ten pounds. To Mr. Graves, sometime minister of Stepney, five pounds. To —— Henderson, my god daughter, five pounds. To William Burrough of Staple Inn, London, gent., whom I do make whole and sole executor, forty pounds; and he shall, from time to time, when required, give a true account of the management to the above named Seth Powell, whom I make overseer. To my servant Elizabeth Vere all the household goods.

Lastly I give to my nephew George Burrough of New England, clerk, all my books and all other my estate whatsoever or wheresoever not before devised, which shall, from time to time and in such manner as he and the said Mr. Powell shall desire, be consigned or remitted to him by my said executor, or else the said legacy of forty pounds to him given shall be void.

In the codicil he confirms the devise made in the earlier will to Richard Hoare, citizen and goldsmith, of the capital messuage in West Smithfield known as the Glassenbury house, together with four messuages in Cock Lane, St. Sepulchre's, and gives to Mr. Austin Brewster forty shillings to buy him a ring.   Lloyd, 101.

[George Burrough, named as a nephew in the above will of John Style, was " the most prominent victim of the witchcraft fanaticism of 1692." Accounts of him will be found in Sibley's Harvard Graduates, vol. 2, pp. 323–34; and Upham's Salem Witchcraft, vol. 1, pp. 255–68, vol. 2, 140–63, 296–304, 480, 482, 514; besides in various other books. Sibley says that he wrote his name Burrough " in Sewall's receipt book for a bill of exchange drawn on his ' cousin-german Wm Burrough of London.'" This William Burrough is probably the person whom Mr. Style appoints his executor. The Rev. George Burrough wrote his surname, Burroughs in the latter part of his life, as is shown in the facsimile of his autograph in Upham's Witchcraft, vol. 1, p. 280. In the Roxbury church record it is spelled Burrows. He was admitted to full communion in the church at Roxbury, April 12, 1674, and had a daughter Rebecca baptized there the same day, and a son George baptized Nov. 25, 1675. It is probable that he was a son of "Mrs Rebecca Burrows who," according to the Roxbury church records, " came frō Virginia yt she might enjoy God in his Ordin. in N. E." and who, Nov. 29, 1674, was " recommended & dismissed, she going for England." (REGISTER, vol. 33, p. 239.)

George Burrough was graduated at Harvard College in 1670, and was a preacher at Casco, now Portland, Maine, as early as 1674. Here he resided when the place was destroyed by the Indians, Aug. 11, 1676. He preached at Salem Village, now Danvers, from November, 1680, to March, 1683. As early as June, 1685, he returned to Casco, which settlement was again destroyed by the French and Indians, May 20, 1690. He then went to Wells, where he was preaching when the witchcraft excitement broke out. He was apprehended at Wells, May 4, 1692, and carried to Salem, where he was tried for witchcraft and condemned. He was executed on Gallows Hill, August 19, 1692.—EDITOR.]

EDWARD SAMMES of London, grocer, proved 26 February 1635. To wife Bennett one third of my whole estate according to the laudable custom of the city of London. One other third to my children unprovided, vizt Martha, Elizabeth, Edward, John and William. To daughter Margaret, already preferred in marriage, forty shillings to buy her a ring, and to her husband Edward Parker forty shillings to buy him a ring. Copyhold lands in Barking, Essex, and lands in Mark's Teye, Feering and Aldum which I bought of my cousin Doctor Sammes to my wife for life; afterwards the lands in Barking to son Edward, remainder to son William. To Edward the houses and lands at Maldon, Essex, given me by Mrs. Anastace Wentworth. To son John the lands bought of Dr. Sammes, with remainder to William and then to Edward. To son Edward the reversion of a copyhold lying in Royden near Dysse in Norfolk. To my loving cousins Dr. Sammes and his wife forty shillings apiece, to buy them rings; to my brother in law Dr. Wright and his wife, each forty shillings &c.; to my brother in law Nathaniel Wright and his wife, each forty shillings &c.; to Mr —— Browne preacher of St. Ellen's four pounds and to my cousin Stone preacher in New England five pounds. To Mr. Thomas Stock and his wife forty shillings.   Pile, 21.

[Edward Sammes, the testator, was a son of Henry Sammes of Totham in Essex, and his pedigree is found in the Visitation of London of 1633 (Harleian Society's Publications, vol. 17, p. 224). He married Bennet, daughter of John Wright of Rumford in Essex. His eldest son Edward was 12 years old in 1633. There are pedigrees of Sammes, evidently the same family, in the Visitation of Essex, 1634, Harleian Soc. Pub., vol. 13, pp. 482-3. The cousin Stone named was, I presume, Rev. Samuel Stone of Hartford, Ct.—EDITOR.]

ANNE TOWERS of Maydstone, Kent, widow, 29 October 1653, proved 21 March 1654 (English style). To the poor of the parish of Maidstone five pounds, to be distributed at the discretion of My brother Mr Thomas Taylor of Maidstone. To my daughter Mrs. Dorothy Hathway of Maidstone, widow, that house &c. wherein John Chantler liveth, the which I lately bought of Mr. Matthew Morse. To my said daughter Hathway my house and lands, together with my parsonage tythes in Barsted, Kent, all which are in the tenure and occupation of William Wells of Barsted. But my daughter Hathway shall pay to my dear mother Mrs. Dorothy Taylor of Maidstone, during her natural life an annuity of ten pounds per annum. Provision made for John Taylor, eldest son of brother Mr. Taylor, and for his brothers. Provides also for the payment of one hundred pounds to my daughter Mrs. Anne Sañis, wife of Mr. John Sañis of Coggeshall in Essex, clerk. Also for the supplying of my sister Mary Chambers with necessaries and for the better education and putting out of her children.

My daughter Dorothy Hathway to be executrix and brother Mr. Thomas Taylor and kinsman Mr John Turner of Maidstone to be overseers.

Christopher Gorham and Thomas Meriam witnesses.   Aylett, 342.

[Mr. John Sams, mentioned in the will of Anne Towers, came to New-England in 1640, according to Savage, and settled in Roxbury. He held land in that town which, in 1642, after his removal, was taken by execution to satisfy a debt of £50. 18s. due Gov. Thomas Dudley (Suffolk Deeds, Lib. I. fol. 37-8, 81). Calamy says that he had his education in New-England. He was appointed Vicar of Kelvedon in Essex, Sept. 9, 1647, by the Committee for Plundered Ministers. He was still at Kelvedon in 1650, as appears by the Parliamentary return of that year. He succeeded Dr. John Owen as Vicar of Coggeshall in the same county as early as 1653. On the 11th July, 1654, Deborah, daughter of Jo. and Anne Sames, "vicar," was baptized there. He was ejected from Coggeshall under the Bartholomew act. Afterwards he set up a separate meeting in that place, of which he died pastor. He was buried at Coggeshall, Dec. 16, 1672. His funeral sermon was preached by Thomas Lowry from Isaiah lxiii. 1, 2. (See Beaumont's History of Coggeshall, pp. 62 and 141; Davids's Annals of Evangelical Non-conformity in Essex, pp. 363-5; Calamy's Ejected Ministers, vol. II. p. 305; Palmer's Non-conformists' Memorial, ed. 1778, vol. I. p. 498.)— EDITOR.]

FRANCIS BENSKIN of St. Martin in the fields, Middlesex, Esqre 26 September 1691, proved 2 January 1691. To loving friends Edmund Wyatt of Maidstone, Kent, Serg^t at Law Richard Bings the elder Esqre, Edmund Ogar Esqre and Thomas Whitfield, Scrivener, &c. all that my messuage &c. in Oxendon Street, St. Martin's, wherein I now dwell, for the term of years I have to come in the same by virtue of a Lease &c. in trust, to suffer my dear wife, Frances Benskin, to take and receive to her own use the rents thereof during her natural life, if she keep herself a widow, except one room up one pair of stairs forward and the furniture thereof, which I give and dispose to the use of my daughter Frances Benskin &c. And after the decease or marriage of my said wife then they shall permit and suffer my said daughter and the heirs of her body and, for want of such issue, my son Thomas Benskin and the heirs of his body, and, for want of such issue, my son Henry Benskin and the heirs of his body, and, for want of such issue, my cousin Edward Benskin, his executors, administrators and assigns, to take and receive the rents &c. of my said messuage to her, his and their use successively. All my plate to my wife. Eight hundred pounds to my daughter at her age of twenty years. Five hundred pounds to my son Thomas, payable out of a certain mortgage or estate in Leicestershire granted unto me and my son Thomas by John Platts and Theophilus Bernard. To my son Henry Benskin of Virginia two hundred pounds within one year. To my kinsman Edward Benskin twenty pounds.

Fane, 3.

[For will of Henry Benskin see *ante* p. 106, REGISTER, Vol. 39, p. 165.— H. F. W.]

WILLIAM SPENCER of Cheriton 14 August 1596, proved 20 September 1596. To my daughter Joanna fifty pounds, to be put out for her use (by the advice of my wife, Mr Richard Burden, parson of Tysted, Mr. Stephen Bacheler, minister of Whenoell [Wherwell?], my brother John Spencer, and John Osgood, my wife's brother), until her age of eighteen years or day of marriage. To my second daughter Alice Spencer two and forty pounds, to be put out according to the order aforesaid. To my daughter Anna Spencer forty pounds to be put forth accordingly. To my mother my sealing ring. To my eldest son John Spencer fifty pounds, whom I commit to the tuition of my mother during her life, and after her to my wife again, and his portion to be put out for his use according to a godly course until he be of the age of one and twenty years. To my son William forty pounds, to be employed as the rest before until he come to one and twenty years of age. To Mary Peto six pence. To my brother John Osgood my best suit of apparell with my rapier and dagger. To my sister Elizabeth Osgood forty shillings. To my brother Robert Osgood and to Richard Osgood and to Peter Osgood twelve pence apiece. I give a certain little gold ring to my brother John Spencer. To my mother in law ten shillings in gould. To my brother Thomas Spencer two shillings. To all my brothers and brothers in law their children four pence apiece. . The rest of my goods to wife Margaret whom I ordain and constitute sole executrix; and do appoint Mr Richard Burden, Mr Stephen Bacheler, John Osgood and John Spencer my overseers. To my cousin Carpenter ten pounds. My cousin Edw: Spicer and William Lydall owe me &c. Others. Stephen Bachiler one of the witnesses.

Drake, 67.

[Margaret, wife of William Spencer the testator, was probably a daughter of Peter Osgood, either of Upper or of Nether Wallop, Hants, whose will, dated January 26, 1585-6, was proved Feb. 21 (see REGISTER, vol. 20, page 23). Peter left a daughter Margaret, and also sons Robert, Richard, Peter and John and a daughter Elizabeth. Spencer makes bequests to persons of these names as his brothers and sister. "Robert Osgood, son of Peter and named in his will, was that Robert of Wherwell (a parish adjoining the Wallops) whose will dated Aug. 25, 1630, was proved Nov. 17 of the same year." Osgood Field, F.S.A., who contributed to the REGISTER the article above referred to, supposes the John Osgood, who settled at Andover, Mass. (and who according to his will was born July 23, 1595), was a son of Robert and grandson of Peter Osgood.—EDITOR.]

EDMUND ALLEYN of Hatfield Peverell, Essex, Esq^{rs} 19 February 1615, proved 27 September 1616. To be buried within the chancel of the parish church of Hatfield Peverell under the gravestone of my great grandfather Gyles Leigh. To wife Alice all the plate, implements of household and other moveables she brought unto me at our intermarriage, and one carpet of needlework which I bought of my cousin Alabaster Wentworth &c. The rest of my goods &c. to my wife during her natural life, and after her death to be divided into three equal parts, one to be at the free disposition of my said wife another to my son Edward Aleyne, my daughter Elizabeth Castell and my daughter Mary Hall and the last third to remain to such charitable uses as hereafter shall follow. To son Robert Castell, gen[t], my manor or farm called Bowers, in Woodham Walter, Essex, he to pay unto my six grand daughters, Martha Alleyne, Constance, Martha and Elizabeth Castell and Margaret and Martha Hall, one hundred marks apiece at their days of marriage or ages of one and twenty, and to my son Edward's three sons, Edmund, George and Robert, towards their education &c. twenty pounds a year, and to his own sons, Robert and Edmund Castell twenty marks a year &c., and to Susan the wife of Josias Franke one hundred pounds within one year after the death of her said husband Franke. To son Edward, my manor and farm of Plomborough in Hockly Essex. Provision made for the stipend and allowance of the Vicar of Hatfield, and my cousin John Stable (or Stuble) now incumbent, to hold his lands free of tythe during his abode there in the ministry. To Mr. Buckley ten pounds and to Mr. Bachelour five pounds. Other clergymen named. A bequest to Edmund Franke, son of Josias.

Stephen Bacheler was one of the witnesses.   Cope, 87.

[Edmund Alleyne of Hatfield Peverell, the testator, was a grandson of John[1] Alleyne of Thaxted in Essex, and his wife Margaret, daughter of Giles Leigh of Walton, in Surrey. His father John[2] married Margaret Alabaster. Edmund married Martha, dau. and co-heiress of John Glascock of Powers Hall, Witham in Essex. She died June 5, 1593. He died Sept. 12, 1616. His eldest son Edward was created a baronet, June 24, 1629 (See Wotton's English Baronetage, London, 1741, vol. 2, pp. 150-1, and Harleian Society's Publications, vol. 13, pp. 133-4 and 333-4). His other children were John, Henry, Elizabeth who married Robert Castell, Mary who married —— Hall, Ann and Agnes.

John Stable was presented to the living of Hatfield Peverell, Aug. 8, 1605. "Edm. Alleyne, Gen." was the patron. (See Newcourt's Repertorium, vol. 2, p. 313.)—EDITOR.]

MATTHEW WYNGE of Banbury, Oxon, taylor, 9 August 1614, proved 15 November 1614. To be buried in the church yard there. To the poor of Banbury ten shillings. To eldest son Fulk the lease of the house in which I now dwell and twenty pounds in money. To second son Thomas thirteen pounds. To third son John forty shillings. To son in law Robert Chamberlain ten pounds. To daughter Johanne twenty shillings. To the children of eldest son Fulk, viz[t] Anne, Dorcas, Mary, Matthew. To John the son of my second son Thomas. To Debora Wynge the daughter of my third son John, and to John, his son. To John Nicholls son of John Nicholls my son in law. To William Wynge the son of my fourth son James. To Thomas Chaumberlayne son of Robert Chaumberlayne my son in law. To the children of Richard Gullins, John, Thomas and Phebe. Sons Fulk and Thomas to be executors.   Lawe, 111.

JOHN WINGE late of the Hague in Holland, clerk, now living in St. Mary Aldermary, London, 2 November 1629, proved 4 August 1630. Certain lands (freehold) in Cuckston and Stroud, Kent, shall be sold as soon as conveniently may be and the money thereof arising shall be, with all my other goods &c. divided into two equal parts, the one to be had, received and enjoyed unto and by my loving wife Debora and the other part or moiety to be equally and indifferently had, parted, divided and enjoyed unto and amongst all my children, share and share alike, except unto and by my daughter Deborah whom I have already advanced in marriage. Wife Deborah to be executrix **and** Edward Foord of London, merchant, and Andrew Blake of Stroud in Kent, yeoman, overseers.

Scroope, 73.

[The following extracts from Q. R. Miscell, 560 (Licenses to pass beyond the Sea, Eliz. to Car. I.), were made in the Public Record Office two or three years ago:]

xxii° Junii 1624, Debora Wynge xxxii years old, wife of Mr. Jn° Winge preacher resident in Vlishing wth her two children, vizt Steephen iii yeares old and Debora Winge xiii yeares old vrs. ib'm.

(Q. R. Miscell, 560–2.)

[This will, taken in connection with what I printed in the REGISTER in October, 1884, and January, 1885, seems to give the Wing Pedigree as follows:
Matthew[1] Wing, of Banbury, died 1614, had sons:
    Fulk,[2] had son Matthew.
    Thomas,[2] had son John.
    John,[2] had son John.
    James,[2] had son William.

Rev. John[2] Wing, "pastor of the English Puritan Church at Middleborough in Zeeland," married Deborah, daughter of Rev. Stephen Bacheler, and died at London in 1630. He had:
    Deborah,[3] b. 1611.
    John,[3] b. 1613 or thereabouts, of Yarmouth.
    Stephen,[3] b. 1621, of Sandwich.
    Daniel,[3] of Sandwich.
    Matthew,[3] had a son John, who died young.
The will of Rev. John, here given, enables us to expunge entirely Savage's reference to a first John W. of Sandwich. He did not come, but his widow Deborah (Bachiler) did, with her children. As she was born in 1592, it is certain that she was not the "old goody Wing" buried at Yarmouth in 1692, as we must not create a centenarian. — W. H. WHITMORE.]

23 Junii 1631, Steephen Bachiller aged 70 yeres, resident at South Stonham in Com. Southampton et uxor Hellen of age xlviii yeeres, vrs fflushing to visite their sonns and daughters, and so to returne within two moneths.   xxv° Junii 1631, Ann Sandburn of age 30 yeres, widowe resident in ye strand, vrss. Vlishing.   (Q. R. Miscell, 560–22.)

[This reference to Rev. Stephen Bachiler is very interesting, as it proves the correctness of the reports as to his great age. This wife Helen, aged 48 years in 1631, is of course the one who came here with him, and who is termed by Winthrop in 1641 "a lusty, comely woman." As Bachiler's daughter, Deborah Wing, was a mother in 1611, she was born in 1590 to 1595. Mrs. Helen Bacheler, born in 1583, could not be her mother, and was therefore a second wife. In the article printed in the REGISTER for October, 1873, on the Daltons and Batchellers, I copied a letter from Stephen B. son of Rev. S. in 1685, speaking of his uncle Francis Mercer's will, his cousin Thomas M. (who was son of Peter M.) and cousin Pryaulx. Perhaps Mr. Waters will hereafter find these Mercers.—W. H. WHITMORE.
See also the preceding wills of William Spencer and Edmund Alleyn.—ED.]

WASHINGTON :—

The following article by Mr. James Greenstreet on "The Ancestry of General Washington" appeared in "The Genealogist" for January, 1891:

It is due, I think, to the memory of Colonel Chester that it should be known he long ago travelled over much the same ground as that which Mr. H. F.

Waters has made public in his recent pamphlet; and which he speaks of (p. 8),*
unwittingly, as though it had been hitherto an untrodden track. As far back
as 1864, Colonel Chester was aware of the connection with Luton; and on p.
74 of his Washington notebook, in the College of Arms, the Admon. of 30 May,
1677, [re-] "discovered"† by Mr. Waters, in 1884 or 1885, will be found duly
set out.

Following the same chain of facts as Mr. Waters has since done, Colonel
Chester likewise went to the Tring Registers, but unfortunately only by proxy;
and, still more unfortunately, he rested contented with the information sent to
him by that proxy. Had Colonel Chester gone to Tring and examined the
books himself, in all probability Mr. Waters would have been entirely forestalled twenty years back.‡ On page 35 of his notebook, the Colonel has copied
a letter he received from Tring, from which it will be seen that he never knew
the Registers there actually chronicled the baptism of a Lawrence, son of the
Rev. Lawrence Washington.

"From same [Rev. C. J. Robinson, curate of Great Berkhampstead, Herts],
May 16, 1864.

"'I have searched carefully the Par. Reg^rs of Tring, co. Herts, from 1580 to
1710. The only entries of the name of Washington which I could find are
these:

'1641. Oct. 14, William, soun of Mr. Larrance Washenton.'—
Baptized.
'1654–5. Jan. 19, Mrs. Washington.'—Buried.
' No occurrence of the name is to be found among the Marriages; but I should
add that the Registers have been ill kept, and there are many gaps in them.'"

Since the publication of Mr. Waters's pamphlet, I have been able to identify
the Chancery suit referred to by Colonel Chester in 1866—see Mr. Whitmore's
additions to the pamphlet, at p. 50.§

Chancery Proceedings, Charles I., Bills and Answers, Bundle WW 35, No. 43.
Washington *versus* Browne.

Bill of complaint [exhibited "20 Oct. 1640"] of "your daylie oratour Lawrence Washington, of Purleyn [*sic*], in the Countie of Essex, cl[erk, That]
whereas your said oratour, in or about the moneth of July in the eight yeare of
his Maties raigne that now is, was indebted vnto John Browne, of the Citty of
Oxford, in the summe of sixtie & nyne pounds & eighteene shillings, or
thereabouts, And for security of payment thereof, at a day betweene him &
your oratour agreed upon, your oratour did enter into an Obligacion to the said
John Browne, of the penaltie of one hundred & ffortie powndes, or thereabouts,
condicioned for the payment of the said summe of sixtie nyne pownds, eighteene
shillings, or thereabouts, at a day now past, W^ch said Bond the said John
Brown[e] left in the hands of one Mr Haruey, of London, And appointed your
oratour to pay the moneyes as they grewe due & payable . . . to the said M^r
Haruey . . . And your oratour did . . . pay unto the s^d Mr Haruey, to his

---

* REGISTER vol. 43, p. 382, *ante* p. 355.—EDITOR OF REGISTER.

† Surely Mr. Greenstreet does not mean that Mr. Waters ought to have called his finding this admon. a "re-discovery" when neither he nor the public had any knowledge of
a previous discovery. Mr. Waters had no opportunity, as far as he knew, of seeing Col.
Chester's collections and learning what he had found.—EDITOR OF REGISTER.

‡ We think that Mr. Greenstreet is hardly warranted in saying that, "Had Colonel
Chester gone to Tring and examined the books himself, in all probability Mr. Waters
would have been *entirely* forestalled twenty years back." Mr. Greenstreet seems to ignore
one of the most important discoveries made by Mr. Waters, namely, that memorandum
written on the day of the probate of Andrew Knowling's will, showing the presence in
Court of Lawrence Washington, M.A., acting as surrogate and therefore a clergyman. If
that paper or some other equally conclusive evidence had not been discovered, the pedigree
of George Washington would have been left still shooting in the air. We appreciate as
highly as anyone the rare skill of Col. Chester in genealogical research and the success
with which his labors were so often crowned. His editorial work on the Harleian Society's
volumes, particularly that on the Registers on Westminster Abbey, which shows a wealth of
antiquarian learning; his Life of John Rogers; his contributions to the REGISTER and other
periodicals; and his vast genealogical collections in manuscript, now in the College of
Arms, are a lasting monument to his memory. The Washington collections are very extensive. To Col. Chester is due the credit of having solved problems that had baffled the
ablest antiquaries.—EDITOR OF REGISTER.

§ REGISTER vol. 43, p. 423, *ante* p. 401.—EDITOR OF REGISTER.

the said Browne's use, severall summes of money, at severall tymes, in part of satisfa[ction of the said] bond . . . And your oratour further sheweth, that, about seaven yeares since, one Mr Parr, now Bi[shop of the Isl]e of Man, and one Mr Atherton Burch, having a Chamber ioyntly betweene them in Braz Nose Colledge, in Oxford aforesaid, they the said [Mr Parr and] Mr Burch did, at their ioynt charges, furnish the same Chamber . . . And in & about such furnishing thereof did ioyntly expend about ffortie pownds, that is to say, each of them twentie pownds a peece . . . And afterwards the said Mr Parr being to leaue the said Chamber and Colledge, And your oratour being to succeed him in the same Chamber, hee the said Mr Parr did contract & agree wth your oratour, and therevpon your oratour . . . did buy of the said Mr Parr all his interest, part & share of all & every the said goods and furniture . . . but tooke no particular Inventory thereof . . . And, after that, your orator finding other particular goods & furniture to bee more fitting & convenyent for his particular use, did bring into the said Chamber severall other goods and chattells . . . of the value of fffteene pownds, or thereabouts . . . Now so it is, may it please your good lordshipp, that your oratour having some occasion to take a long journey from Oxford & and [sic] to be absent from thence some tyme, and and the said Mr Burch then dying in the said Chamber, wherein all the said goods furniture were, whilst your oratour was absent, The said John Browne, pretending that the said Mr Burch was somthing indebted to him, the said Browne, and hee takeing, or pretending to take or have Administracion of the goods of the said Mr Burch, did not onely enter upon, and take and carry away all the said goods and furniture wherein the said Mr Burch and your oratour had ioynt interests, but also all the goods and chattels whatsoever wch were the particular and sole estate and goods of your said oratour, and wherein neither the said Mr Burch nor the said John Browne had any colour of interest, and whereto they, nor either of them could lay any clayme or title," &c.

Answer of John Browne the defendant, sworn 20 Oct. 1640—Sets out that the complainant, being indebted to him 69l. 16s., entered into an obligation dated 20 July 1632, subsequently buying goods of him to the amount of 6l. 0s. 2d.,* "and shortly after left his fellowship and aboade in the Vniuersity of Oxon." The complainant has paid to the said Mr. John Harvey several sums on account, namely, about May 1633, 40l., and, about May 1636, 10l., but never paid any more either to Mr. Harvey or the defendant.

I have to express my obligation to Mr. G. E. Cokayne, F.S.A., Norroy King of Arms, for kind permission to make use of Colonel Chester's MS.

———

Mr. Moncure D. Conway contributed to the New York *Nation* for March 19, 1891, an elaborate article, entitled, "The Earliest Washingtons in Virginia," in which he shows that a branch of the Washington family was settled in Virginia as early as 1636, a patent for land having been taken out by Arthur Washington in that year. He may have been the ancestor of the Surrey County Washingtons noticed in the REGISTER for July, 1890 (vol. 44, pages 307–8, *ante* pp. 458–9), among whom Arthur was a favorite name. No connection has been traced between this family and the Westmoreland County Washingtons. Much interesting matter about the various families of Washington is found in the article.

The illustrated article by Mr. Conway on "The English Ancestry of Washington," announced by us in our last number (*ante*, p. 511) as to be published in Harper's Magazine, appeared in the number for May, 1891. Since the publication of Mr. Waters's discoveries in the REGISTER for October, 1889, *ante* pp. 352–403, Mr. Conway has visited England and gathered material bearing on the subject

———

* The items of this later bill are:—"Sixe elnes and a hal[f of] . . . for two shirts, and the making of them. One paire of worsted hose. Strapps for bootes. One paire of graye hose. One cloake bagge. Seaven yards of phillissety. ffive yar[ds and a ha]lfe of homes. One elne and a quarterne of canvas. One yard and an (*sic*) half of thick cotton. Two yards of hayes cotton. Half an ounce of silke, ffoure d[ozen] . . . ns. One dozen of ribband points, buckram, pastbord & claspes. Three quarternes of large ffringe. One skinne for pocketts. One half elne of loopelace. . . . of belliepeeces. Half a quarterne of taffaty. Two yards of tape. One paire of worsted hose, and one yard and a halfe of eightpennye ribband. One paire of roses. Six elnes and an (*sic*) halfe of holland, and making two. . . . . . Two fine holland bands, and three paire of cuffes and strings."

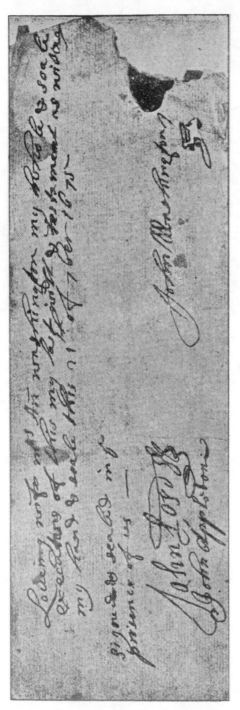

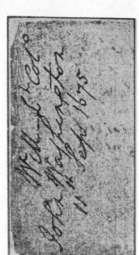

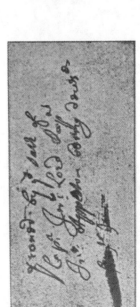

Signatures to the Will of Col. John Washington. See page 526.

Seal to Release.
See page 533.

of his article. He was also allowed by George E. Cokayne, M.A., F.S.A., the friend and executor of Col. Joseph L. Chester, LL.D., D.C.L., the use of the Washington *collectanea* of that distinguished antiquary contained in a thick folio volume. Mr. Conway is now a believer in the theory of Mr. Waters. In the Harper article are given the main points of the evidence in relation to the Ancestry of Washington. One new fact of great importance is that Lawrence Washington, rector of Purleigh, had a wife living in 1649, as shown by the order of the "Committee on Plundered Ministers," August 15 in that year, that "Mr. John Rogers, minister of the sequestered rectory of Purleigh in Dingey Hundreds do pay the fifth part of the tithes and profits of said Rectory unto Mrs. Washington, according to a formal order of ye Com. of Plundered ministers." On September 20th the Committee "Ordered that Mr. John Rogers and Mrs. Washington be heard on Wednesday in the sessions." On the last page of the book this decision of the Committee is recorded: "fifth part of Purleigh ordered to the plundered Rector's wife." Mr. Conway was also discoverer of the fact found in the original will, that Col. John Washington the emigrant had a sister Martha, as already announced in the REGISTER. Both of these new facts strengthen the position taken by Mr. Waters.

Mr. Conway's contribution to Harper's Magazine is very interesting, particularly to those who have a curiosity to know all they can about the homes of the emigrant ancestor of President Washington, and of his kindred. Very graphic descriptions of the localities are given. The illustrations like all those in Harper are of a high order of merit. They consist of views of the churches of Tring and Luton, and the baptistry of the latter; brasses in St. James Church, Sulgrave; Gen. Washington's seals; and fac-similes of the autograph of Col. John Washington, and of entries in the Tring parish registers. As Harper's Magazine has a large circulation in England, we hope this article will meet the eyes of antiquaries in the localities with which Lawrence Washington and his wife Amphillis were connected, and that they will try to discover the records of Mr. Washington's marriage and death; the record of the baptism of his son John; the name of the living which the rector of Purleigh held after that living was sequestered, and other evidence bearing on the Washington pedigree.—EDITOR.]

I hope that Mr. Conway's article will inspire the clergymen near Tring and Luton to examine their records for mention of Lawrence Washington's marriage. The circumstantial evidence of the marriage of Rev. Lawrence Washington to Amphillis Rhodes is very, very strong, but not conclusive. The proof is still to be found. The fact is that a Lawrence Washington, M.A., was in January, 1649–50, acting in the court at which a guardian was appointed for one of the children of Amphillis Washington. Until some evidence is produced we must hold that this Lawrence Washington, M.A., is identical with the rector of Purleigh. We cannot, however, yet say that Lawrence Washington, husband of Amphillis, was a clergyman, though the baptisms at Tring call him "Mr." It is not *impossible* that some cousin and namesake of the Rev. Lawrence of Purleigh, was the husband, and persuaded him to be present at the court and act as surrogate. This is highly improbable; but coincidence and circumstantial evidence are not clear proofs. Therefore until new evidence is obtained, the Washington pedigree is not to be taken as wholly proved.—W. H. WHITMORE.

[THE following may be relied upon as authentic transcripts of the wills of the American ancestors of George Washington. They possess interest to the genealogist and historical student, and are presented in the following order: First, the emigrant John Washington—the great-grandfather of the General. Second, Lawrence Washington, also an emigrant, and brother of John. Third, Lawrence Washington, son of John and nephew of Lawrence the emigrant. Fourth, Deed of release from Roger and Mildred (Washington) Gregory to Augustine Washington. This Mildred Gregory was daughter of Lawrence Washington and sister of Augustine Washington, and the aunt and god-mother of George Washington. Mildred inherited from her father Hunting Creek plantation now "Mount Vernon," which she and her husband by this deed conveyed to her brother Augustine. Fifth, Augustine Washington, son of Lawrence and grandson of John. Sixth, Lawrence Washington, son of Augustine Washington, half-brother of George and great-grandson of John the emigrant and patentee of the Hunting Creek plantation.

The will of John Washington has been copied from the original when it was in a better condition than it is at present, and every word I believe is correctly interpreted. The other wills are from certified copies of probated wills on record. The deed of Roger and Mildred Gregory is copied from the original document. They are submitted as sources of history without further explanaiton or comment.—J. M. TONER, M.D., of Washington, D. C.]

WILL OF JOHN WASHINGTON THE EMIGRANT.

In the name god amen, I John washington of washington parish in y⁰ Countie of westmerland in Virginia, genᵗ. being of good & perfect memory, thankes be unto Almighty god (for it) & Calleing to remembrance the uncertaine estate of this trans[itory] life, & that all flesh must yeild unto death, when it shall plea[se] god for to Call, doe make Constitute ordaine & declare this my last will & testament in maner & forme following, revoaki[ng] & anulling by thes presents all & every testament & testam[ents] will or wills heirtofore by me made & declared ei[ther] by [oath] or by writing & this to be taken only for my last will & testament & noe other, & first being hartily & sorry from the bottome of my hart for my sins past, most humbly desireing forgivenes of the same from the Almighty god (my saviour) & redeimer in whome & by the meritts of Jesus Christ, I trust & beleive assuredly to be saved & to have full remission & forgiveness of all my sins & yᵗ my soule wᵗʰ my body at the generall day of ressurriction shall arise againe wᵗʰ Joy & through the merrits of Christ death & passion, posses & inherit the Kingdom of heaven, prepared for his ellect & Chossen & my body to be buried on y⁰ plantation wheirr I now Live, by the side of my wife yᵗ is already buried & two Children of mine & now for the setling of my temporall estate & such goods Chatles & debts as it hath pleased god far above my deserts to bestow uppon me, I doe order give & dispose the same in maner & forme followeing—

first I will yᵗ all those debts & duties yᵗ I owe in right or Consience to any maner of person or persons wᵗsoever shall be well & truly Contented & payd or ordained to be payd by my executors—herein after named—

Imprimis I give & [be]quea[th] unto my eldest [son Lawrence Wash-] ington yᵗ seat of land wheiron Henery flagg liveth [wᶜʰ I bought of John] watts & Robert Hedges, being by patten seven hundre[d] ac[res] it being by my father pope made over to me & my heirs Lawfully begotten of my body—

Item I give unto my soñ Lawrence washington my watter mill wᵗʰ all appertinances & Land belonging to it a' the head of Rosiers Creik to him & his heirs for ever, reserveing to my wife her thirds dureing her Life—

Item I give unto my soñ Lawrence washington yᵗ seate of Land wᶜʰ I bought of Mʳ Lewis marcum being about two hundred & fifty acres, at the mouth of rosiers Creik on y⁰ northwest side, wᵗʰ all the houseing their unto belonging to him & his heirs for ever reserveing to my wife her thirds dureing her Life—

Item I give unto my soñ Lawrence washington yᵗ seate of Land at upper machotick wᶜʰ I bought of Mʳ Anthony Bridges & Mʳ John Rosier, being about nine hundred acres to him & his heirs for ever, reserveing to my wife her thirds dureing her life—

Item I give unto my soñ Lawrence washington my halfe & share of five thousand acres of Land in Stafford County wᶜʰ is betwixt Coll Nicolas spencer & myselfe wᶜʰ we [are engaged] yᵗ their shall be no benifit taken by survivour ship to him & his [heirs] for [ever].

Item I doe give unto my soñ John washington yᵗ plantation wheiron I now Live wᶜʰ I bought of David Anderson & yᵗ plantation next to Mʳ John

Foxhall y^t I bought (wch was Ric^d Hills) to him & his heirs for ever & y^t seate of Land of about four hundred acres wch lyeth uppon ye head of Rappahaneck Creik & adJoyning uppon David norways orphants Land the Land being formerly John whetstons & sold to me to him & his heirs f[o]r ever reserveing to my wife her thirds of the afoare sayd Land dureing her life—

Item I give unto my son John washington y^t seate of Land wch Robert foster now Liveth on being about three hundred acres to him & his heirs forever, Likewise I give unto my sayd son John washington y^t seat of Land wch Robert Richards Liveth on wch I had of my bro: Lawrence washington being about three hundred & fifty acres to him & his heirs for ever reserveing to my wife her thirds of the two sayd tracts of La[n]d dureing her life—

Item I give & bequeath unto my daughter An washington y^t seate of Land y^t tract of Land y^t Tho: Jordan now liveth on being about twelve hundred acres to her & her heirs for ever, Likewise I give & bequeath unto my sayd daughter that tract of Land wheiron John frier now Liveth being about fourteen hundred acres after M^r fricke hath his quantity out of it to her & her heirs for ever reserving to my wife her thirds of the two above seates dureing her Life.

Item I give unto my sayd daughter, wch was her mothers desire & my promise, y^t Cash in ye new parlour & the Diamond ring & her mothers rings & the white quilt & the white Curtains & Vallians—

And as for the rest of my personall estate after my debts & dues are sattisfied Justly, wch I desire should be sattisfied out of my Cropps, which I doe not question but will be far more than I doe owe (thanks be unto god for it) theirfore it is my desire y^t my estate should not Come to any appraisement, but I order & bequeath a followeth y^t is to say that their shall be a Just Inventory & List taken of my personall estate y^t I am possessed of & for to be devided in quantitie & quallitie by three men of Judgement wch I request the Court to nominate, into foure [par]ts to be equall & proportionable devided in quantitie & qualitie the one fourth part I give to my Loveing wife in Kind in Lew of her dower or Claime, & one fourth part to my son Lawrence washington in Kind, & one fourth part to my son John washington in Kind, & one fourth part to my daughter An washington in Kind to them & either of them severally & their heirs for ever & it is my will y^t if either of my above sayd Children should happen to dy, before they obtaine the age of one & twenty years or day of marriadge then the Land of y^t Child y^t Dyeth to be the eldest son then Liveing, & if both my sons should dy then the Land to be my daughter An, & as for the personall estate if any of my three Children should happen to dy, before they Come of age or day of marriadge, then it is my will that the two surviveing Children should equally devide the personall estate of y^t Child y^t is dead betwixt them & theirs for ever

Item I give & bequeath after all my legacies payd out w^t mony I shall have in England my son Lawrence washington

[Ite]m my desire is y^t their may be a funerall sermon preached [at ye Ch]urch & that their be no other funerall Lest y^e [fun]erall exceid four thousand pounds of [Tobb]^{co}.

Item I give unto the Lower Church of washing[ton] parish [y]^e ten Comandements & the Kings armes wch is my desire should be sent for out of w^t mony I have in England

Item it is my desire y^t w^t estate I shall dy possessed should be Kept Intire wth out devideing untill all debts & dues be payd & sattisfied

Item I give unto my bro: Lawrence washington four thousand pounds of tobb^{co} & Caske—

Item I give unto my nephew John Washington my godson eldest soñ to my bro: Lawrence w[as]hington one young mare of two years old—

Item it is my desire y^t when my estate is devided in quantitie & qualitie into four equall parts, & y^t my wife hath taken her fourth part, y^t then every Childs part should be put out uppon their owne plantation or plantations theire for to [be] managed to the best advantage, for the bringing up & educating o[f each Chil]d acc[ordi]ng to the proffit of each Childrens share—

Item it is my desire y^t my wife should have the bringing up of my daughter Añ washington untill my soñ Lawrence Comes of age or her day of marriadge & my wife for to have the managdement of her part to my daughters best advantadge

Item I doe give to my bro: Thomas Pope teñ pounds out of y^t mony I have in England

Item I doe give unto my sister marthaw washington teñ pounds out of y^t mony I have in England & w^t soever else she shall be oweing to me for transporteing her self into this Country & a years accomodation after her Coming in & four thousand pounds of Tobb^{co} & Caske—

Item it is my desire y^t my bro: Thomas Pope have the bringing up of my soñ John Washington & for to have the managdement of his estate to my soñs best advantadge untill be of age of one & twenty years or day of marriadge—

finally I doe ordaine & appoint my bro: m^r Lawrence washington & my soñ Lawrence washington & my Loveing wife m^{rs} Añ washington my whole & soale executors of this my last will & testament as witness my hand & seale this 21th of 7ber 1675.   JOHN WASHINGTON.

signed & sealed in y^e   proued by ye Oath of
   presence of us—   Cap^a Jno Lord Cap^a
   John Lord   Jno Appleton Being deces^d
   John Appleton

[The following endorsement is on the back of this will in the hand-writing of General Washington:

Will—Lt Col^o
John Washington
11th Sep^t 1675.

This further endorsement but in a different hand is also on the back:—" Recorded in ye County records of Westmoreland Co ye 10 Jan'y 1677."—J. M. T.

The original of the above will of John Washington, the emigrant ancestor of President Washington, was preserved among the General's papers at Mount Vernon. After the sale of the estate in 1858 to the Ladies' Mount Vernon Association of the Union, the papers and other relics were removed by the owner. Some of them were exhibitd at the United States National Museum at Washington, for a few weeks, last winter, but were removed in February last to be sold. A catalogue was prepared and printed, and on Tuesday, Wednesday and Thursday, April 21st, 22d and 23d, 1891, the collection was sold at auction in Philadelphia by Thomas Birch's Sons. The relics brought very high prices. This will was sold to Mr. Collins for $700. The original of the release of Roger and Mildred Gregory here printed was in the same collection. The relics sold were owned by Messrs. Lawrence Washington, Bushrod C. Washington, Thomas B. Washington and J. R. C. Lewis.

Much search has been made for about a dozen years for this original will of the Virginia emigrant, John Washington. In 1878 Mr. James Coleman, the well known genealogical bookseller in London, advertised for sale a deed of

GENEALOGICAL GLEANINGS IN ENGLAND. 527

certain real estate in London, from John Washington of London, citizen and draper, and Margaret his wife one of the daughters of Henry Harwood, gent., to Robert Abbott, citizen and scrivener. The deed was dated June 5, 1657. A deed of a John Washington, dated 1657, probably this one, came about 1878 into the possession of the late Col. Joseph L. Chester, who conjectured that this John Washington might be the Virginia emigrant, selling his property before leaving England, and as he knew his ancestry, he wished to procure an autograph of the emigrant, or a tracing of one, to compare with the signature to the deed. He wrote to Mr. Robert A. Brock of Richmond, Virginia, to the editor of the REGISTER, and to others in this country, asking them to assist him in procuring one. Mr. Brock had search made in the Westmoreland County Court House for the will, but neither the original nor the record was to be found there. Bishop Meade in his Old Churches, Ministers and Families in Virginia, published in 1857 (vol. 2, page 167), had printed an abstract of the will which was obtained from the papers at that Court House. This abstract must have been made from the record, as we now know that the original will was then in the possession of the family. But even the record book could not then be found in the office; and it was not discovered till last December, when Mr. J. Warren Hutt, the clerk, found it. He at once sent a copy to Mr. Moncure D. Conway and another to Mr. Isaac J. Greenwood. (See REGISTER, vol. 45, pp. 164–5, ante, pp. 510–511.) Mr. Conway communicated his copy to the New York Nation in which paper it was printed December 18, 1890. Mr. Greenwood sent his copy to the editor of the REGISTER. The record was much mutilated, portions of it being missing. Before Mr. Greenwood's copy of the record could be printed, the editor was informed of Dr. Toner's copy from the original, in which the missing portions are all found; and he has now the pleasure of laying it before his readers with other interesting Washington documents. The date on the original will looks like 21th, and the recorder read the figures 21; but Gen. Washington's minute is "11th Sept 1675." The record gives the date of probate "10th Jana: 1677."

This is the first time a perfect copy of the will has appeared in print. A facsimile of the original was taken by the National Museum in Washington, and another is given in Messrs. Thomas Birch's Sons' sale catalogue, from which we have had photo-engravings made of a few lines of the closing portion with all the signatures; of the minute of the probate of the will; and of the endorsement by President Washington. The fac-similes are given in the engraving facing page 523.—EDITOR.]

THE WILL OF LAWRENCE WASHINGTON, EMIGRANT.

In the name of God, Amen.

I, Lawrence Washington, of the county of Rapp^ak, being sick & weak in body, but of sound and perfect memory, do make & ordain this, my last will & testament, hereby revoking, annulling, & making void all former wills and Coddicills, heretofore by me made, either by word or writing, & this only to be taken for my last will & testament. Imp^rs I give and bequeath my soul into the hands of Almighty God, hoping and trusting through the mercy of Jesus Christ, my one Savio^r and redeemer, to receive full pardon & forgiveness of all my sinns, and my body to the earth, to be buried in comely & decent manner, by my Executrix hereafter named, & for my wordly goods I thus dispose them. Item,

I give and bequeath unto my loving daughter, Mary Washington, my whole estate in England, both reall and personall, to her & the heirs of her body, lawfully begotten, forever, to be delivered into her possession imediately after my decease, by my Executrix hereafter named. I give and bequeath unto my afores^d daughter, Mary Washington, my smallest stone ring & one silver cup, now in my possession, to her & her heirs, forever, to be delivered to her imediately after my decease. I give and bequeath unto my loveing son, John Washington, all my bookes to him & his heirs, forever, to be delivered to him when he shall come to the age of

Twenty-one yeares. I give and bequeath unto my son, John, & daughter, Ann Washington, all the rest of my plate; but what is before exprest to be equally divided between them, & delivered into their possession when they come of age.

Item, my will is, that all my debts which of right & Justice I owe to any man be Justly & truly paid, as allso my funerall expenses, after which my will is, that all my whole estate, both reall & personall, be equally devided between my loving wife, Jane Washington, & the two children God hath given me by her Viz^t John & Ann Washington. I give & bequeath it all to them, & the heires of their bodies, lawfully begotten, forever, my sonn's part to be delivered to him when he comes of age, & my daughter's part when she comes of age or day of marriage, which shall first happen.

Item, my will is, that that land which became due to me in right of my wife, lying on the south side of the river, formerly belonging to Capt. Alexander Flemming, & commonly known by the name of West Falco, be sold by my Executrix hereafter named, for the payment of my debts, immediately after my decease.

Item, my will is, that the land I have formerly entred with Capt. Wm Mosely, be forthwith after my decease, surveyed & pattented by my Exec^r hereafter named, & if it shall amount to the quantity of one thousand acres, then I give & bequeath unto Alexander Barrow, two hundred acres of the s^d land, to him & his heires, forever, the remainder I give & bequeath unto my loving wife afores^d, and two children, to them & their heires, forever, to be equally devided between them.

Item, my will is, that if it shall please God to take my daughter Mary out of this world before she come of age, or have heirs of her body, lawfully begotten, then I give & bequeath my land in England, which by my will I have given to her, unto my son, John Washington & his heirs, & the personall estate which I have given to her, I give & bequeath the same unto my daughter, Ann Washington & her heires, forever.

Item, I do hereby make & ordain my loveing wife, Jane Washington, Executrix of this my last will & testament, to see it performed, and I do hereby make & appoint my dear and loveing Brother Coll^l John Washington, & my loveing friend Thomas Hawkins (in case of the death or neglect of my executrix), to be the overseers and guardians of my Children untill they come of age to the truth whereof I have hereunto sett my hand & seale, this 27th of September, 1675.

LAWRENCE WASHINGTON   [Seale].

Signed, sealed & declared to be his last will & testament,
  in the p^rsence of us,
     Cornelius Wood.

  Signed,
 John B. Barrow
 Henry Tandy, Junr.

A codicill of the last will & testament of Lawrence Washington, annex^t to his will, & made September 27th 1675.

Item, my will is, that my part of the land I now live upon, which became due to me by marriage of my wife, I leave it wholly & solely to her disposall after my decease, as witness my hand, the day & year above written.

LAWRENCE WASHINGTON   [Seale].

Signed, sealed & declared to be a Codicil of my
    last will & tastmt in the p[r]sence of us.
        Cornelius Wood,
        Henry Tandy, Jun[r].

The above Henry Tandy, Jun[r], aged 17 yeares, or thereab[ts], sworn &
examined, saith, that he did see the above named Lawrence Washington,
sign, seale & publish the above mentioned, to be his last will & testament,
& that he was in perfect sence and memory at the signing, sealing & publishing thereof, to the best of your deponents Judgment.

                                HENRY TANDY.

Juratus est Henricus Tandy, in Cur Com) Rapp[ak] Sexto die, Jany, An[o]
1677, p Sacram) pr[d]   proba[t] et rec-dah[r].
                           Test
A Copy   Teste   EDM[d] CRASK, Cl Cu[r]
    JAMES ROY MICOU,
        Clerk, Essex County Court, State of Virginia.

WILL OF LAWRENCE WASHINGTON, SON TO JOHN WASHINGTON.

In The Name of God amen I Lawrence Washington of Washington
Parish in the County of Westmoreland in Virginia Gentleman, being of
Good and perfect memory thanks be unto almighty God for it & calling
to mind the uncertain Estate of this Transitory life & that all Flesh must
yield unto death when it shall please God to call me, doe make constitute,
ordain & Declare this my last Will and Testament in manner and form
following, revoking and annuling by these presents all and every Testament & Testaments, will or wills heretofore by me made and declared
either by word or writing & this to be taken only for my last will and
Testament and none other, and first being heartily sorry from the bottom
of my heart for my sins, most humbly desireing forgiveness of the same
from the Almighty God my saviour & Redeemer in whome by the merits
of Jesus Christ, I Trust and believe assuredly to be saved and to have full
remission & forgiveness of all my sins and that my soul with my body at
the General day of Resurrection shall rise again with joy, and through the
Merits of Christs Death and passion, possess & Inherit the kingdom of
Heaven prepared for his Elect & Chosen and my body to be buried if
please God I depart in this County of Westmoreland by the side of my
Father and Mother & neare my Brothers & Sisters & my Children, and
now for the setling of my Temporal Estate and such goods Chattles &
Debts as it hath pleased God far above my desarts to bestow upon me I
doe ordain give and bequeath the same in manner and form following:

Imprimis I will that all those Debts and dues that I owe in right or
Concience to any manner of Person or Persons whatsoever shall be well
contented & paid or ordained or demanded to be paid by my Executors or
Ex[tx] hereafter named.

Item I give and bequeath to my well beloved friends M[r] William Thompson clk & M[r] Samuel Thompson, each of them a mourning Ring of Thirty
shillings Value each ring; Item I give and bequeath to my Godson Lawrence Butler one young mare & two Cows: Item I give and bequeath to
my Sister Anne *Wirtts* children, one man servant a piece of four or five
years to serve or Three Thousand pounds of Tobacco to purchase the
same, to be delivered or paid to them when they arrive to the age of

Twenty years old. Item I give and bequeath to my Sister Lewis a morning wring of forty shillings price. Item I give my Cuz: John Washington Sen: of Stafford County all my wearing apparel: Item I give unto my Cozen John Washingtons Eldest Son Lawrence Washington my Godson one man servant of four or five years to serve or Three Thousand pounds of Tobacco to purchase the same; to be paid him when he comes to the age of Twenty one years old: Item I give to my godsons Lawrence Butler & Lewis Nicholas that tract of Land adjoining upon Meridah Edward's and Daniel White, being Two hundred and seventy five acres of Land to be equally divided between them and their heirs forever: Item I give to the upper and Lower Churches of Washington parish, each of them a Pulpett Cloth & Cushion: Item it is my will to have a Funeral sermon at the Church, and to have none other Funerall to exceed Three Thousand pounds of Tobacco. Item it is my will after my Debts & Legacies paid, that my personal Estate be equally divided into four parts: my loving wife Mildred Washington to have one part, my Son John Washington to have another part, my Son Augustin Washington to have another Part and my Daughter Mildred to have the other part: to be delivered to them in specie when they shall come to the age of Twenty one years old: Item I give to my son John Washington, this seat of Land where I now live, and that whole tract of Land lying from the mouth of Machodock, extending to a place called the round hills, with the addition I have' thereunto made of William Webb and William Rush to him and his heirs forever. Item I give and bequeath unto my Son Augustine Washington all the Dividend of Land that I bought of Mʳ Robert Lesson's Children in England Lying in Mattox, between my Brother & Mʳ Baldridge's Land where Mʳ Daniel Lesson *formerly* lived, by Estimation 400 acres to him and his heirs forever, as Likewise that Land that was Mʳ Richard Hilts; Item I give and bequeath unto my said Son Augustine Washington, all that Tract of Land, where Mʳ Lewis Markham, now lives after the said Markham's & his now wife's decease, by Estimation 700 acres more or less to him and his heirs forever. Item I give and bequeath my Daughter Mildred Washington all my Land in Stafford County, lying upon hunting creek, where Mʳˢ Elizabeth Minton & Mʳˢ Williams now lives by Estimation 2500 acres to her and her heirs forever. Item I give my water mill to my son John Washington to him and his heirs forever. Item it is my will and desire if either of my children should die before they come to age or day of marriage, his or her personal Estate be equally divided between the two survivors and their Mother; Item it is my will and desire if all my children should die before they come of age or day of Marriage, that my Brothers children shall enjoy all their estate real, Except that Land that I bought of Mʳ Robert Lesson's children, which I give to my loving wife and her heirs forever, and the rest as aforesaid to them and their heirs forever; Item I give my personal Estate in case of all my childrens death as above said, to be equally divided between my wife and Brothers Children, my wife to have the one half; Item I give that Land which I bought of my Brother Francis Wright, being 200 acres lying near Storkes Quarter, to my Son John Washington and his heirs forever. Item It is my desire that my estate should not be appraised but kept entire and delivered them as above given according to time & my Children to continue under the care & *Tution* of their Mother till they come of age or day of marriage, and she to have the profits of their estates, toward the bringing of them up and keeping them at school; Item I doe ordain and appoint my Cozen John Washington of Stafford and my friend Mr Samuel Thompson my Executors, and my loving wife Mildred Washington my Executrix of this my last will & testament. In Witness whereof I have hereunto set my hand and Seale this 11th day of March Anno Dom 169$\frac{7}{8}$.

LAWRENCE WASHINGTON [Seal].

Signed Seald Declared & pronounced in presence of us,
> Robt Redman,
> George Weedon,
> Thomas Howes,
> John Rosier.

Westmoreland Sct:—

At a Court held for the said County the 30th day of March 1698.

The Last will and Testament of Lawrence Washington Gent desc. within written was proved by the oaths of George Weedon, Thomas Howes, & John Rosier Three of the witnesses thereto subscribed, and a probate thereof Granted to Samuel Thompson Gent one of the Executors therein named, and the will ordered to be recorded.

Teste   JAMES WESTCOMB C. W. C.

A Copy

Teste   J. WARREN HUTT, Clk.

of the County Court of Westmoreland C^o. V^a.

RELEASE OF THE HUNTING CREEK OR MOUNT VERNON ESTATE.

This Indenture made the Seventeenth Day of May in the thirteenth year of the Reign of Our Sovereign Lord George by the grace of God King Defender of the Faith &^{c} and in the year of our Lord God One Thousand seven hundred Twenty six Between Roger Gregory of Stratton-Major. Parish in King and Queen County Gent of the one part and Augustine Washington of Washington Parish in Westmoreland County Gent of the other part Wittnesseth that the said Roger Gregory and Mildred his wife for divers good causes & conciderations him thereunto moving but more Especially for and in Concideration of the sum of one Hundred & eighty pounds Sterling money of Great Brittain,—to him in hand paid at and before the Ensealing and Delivery of these presents the receipt wherof the said Roger Gregory and Mildred his wife Doth hereby acknowledge and himself therew'th to be Fully Satisfied and contented and Paid and thereof and every part and Parcel thereof doth fully and absolutely acquit Exhonerate and Discharge him the Said Augt Washington his Heirs Execu^{rs} and Adm^{ts} and every of them by these Presents Hath Granted, Bargained Sold Remised Released Alienated, Entfeeofted and confirmed and by these presents Doth Grant Bargain Sell Remise Release Alien Entfeeftee confirm unto the said Augt Washington his Heirs Execu^{rs} Adm^{ts} and Assig^s for ever. He being in the actual Possession thereof by virtue of a Lease thereof made by the said Roger Gregory and Mildred his wife bearing Date the Day before the Date of these Presents and by virtue of the statute for transfering usses into Possession all that certain tract or Parcel of Land situate Lying and Being in the Parish of Overwharton—in the County aforesaid, Being by Estimation two thousand

& Five hundred acres a moiettie or half of five thousand acres formerly
Lay'^d out for Coll° Nicholas Spencer & the father of Capt Lawrence Washington and Bounded as followeth Begining by the River Side at the Mouth
of Little Hunting Creek and Extending up the Said Creek according to the
several courses and Meanders thereof nine hundred Eighty and Six Poles
to a mark'^d A Corner Tree standing on the west side the South Branch
being the main branch of the said Hunting Creek From these by a Lyne
of mark'^d trees west Eighteen Degrees South across the Woods to the
Dividing Lyne as Formerly made Between Madam Francis Spencer and
Capt Lawrence Washington and from thence W'^{ly} the said Lyne to y^e
River and with the River and all the Courses and Meanders of the said
River to the Mouth of the Creek afor'^{sd} Together with all Houses Out-
houses Gardens Orchards Fences Meadows Pastures Feedings Woods
underwoods Swamps marshes Way'^s Waters Watercourses and all other
Emoluments Herediteriments and appertenances to the Said granted
Premisses belonging or in any wise appertaining with all the Estate Right
Title Interest Claim and Demand Whatsoever of him the said Roger
Gregory or Mildred his wife of in & unto the said granted Premisses and
every part therof w'^{by} the appurtenances to the said granted Premisses and
reversion and remainder yearly and other rents and Profits of the Premisses
and every part and Parcell thereof To have and to hold the said two
thousand & five hundred acres of Land together w'th all the Rights Titles
Benefitt Property Interest, Claim and Demand whatsoever of in and to the
said Lands & Premisses hereby granted sold demised released & confirmed
and mentioned or intended to be herein granted Bargined Sold Remised
Released & Confirmed and every part and Parsel thereof w'^h their and
every of their appertenances unto the said Augustine Washington his Heirs
forever to the only Proper use and behoof of the said Augustine Washington and his heirs and assignes forever to be holden of the chief Lord or
Lords of the fee or fees of the Premises by the Rules & services for the
same due & accustomed to be paid and the said Roger Gregory and Mildred
his wife for themselves their heirs Exec^{trs} and Adm^{trs} Doth covenant and
w'^{ly} the said Augt Washington his Heirs & Assig^s by these Presents that
the said Roger Gregory and Mildred his wife now is and standith Right-
fully seised of and in the said two thousand & five hundred acres of Land
and Premises w'th their appertenances of a good sure perfect & Indefeasable
Estate in Fee simple and now hath good Rightful powers and Lawful
authority to grant and convey the said Land & Premises unto the said
Augustine Washington and his heirs according to the purport True intent
and meaning of these Presents and that it shall and may be Lawful to and
for the said Augt Washington his Heirs and assg'^s from time to time and
at all times forever hereafter Peaseably & Quietly to have hold Possess
ocupy & enjoy the said two thousand & five hundred acres of Land w'th
their and every of their appertenances w'thout the Lett Suit Trouble
molestation or Interuption of him the said Roger Gregory & Mildred his
wife their Heirs Execu^{tors} Adm'^{tors} or Assigns or any of them or any other
Person or Persons Lawfully claiming or to claim from by or under them
or either of them and the said Roger Gregory & Mildred his wife for
themselves their heirs Execu'^{trs} & Adm'st Doth covinent and agree to and
w'th the said Augustine Washington his heirs & Assig'^s by these presents
that he the said Roger Gregory and Mildred his wife their Heirs Execu'^{trs}
Adm'^{trs} and assig'^s shall and will at any time or times hereafter During the
space of   years next Ensuing the Date hereof upon the request and

at the Charges in the Law of the said Augs^t Washington his heirs or assig'^s do make and Execute or cause or procure to be done made or Executed all and every such further and other act and acts conveyance & conveyances in the Law whatsoever for the further and better conveying and assuring the said two thousand & five hundred acres of Land & Premises with their appurtenances unto the said Augustine Washington his heirs and assig'^s forever as by the Counsell Learned in the Law of the said Augustine Washington his heirs or assigns shall be Reasonable Devised advised or required Soe as the Parties Required to do the same be not compelled to travell above Fifty miles from the place or places of their abode for the doing thereof Wittness whereof the Parties to this Indenture have Interchangeably hereunto set their hands and seals this Day and year first above written—

Rog^r Gregory [ ]

Mildred Gregory [ ]

Sign'd Seal'd & De^l In Presence of

    Wm Aylett J^r

    John Washington

    Lawz Butler

[Immediately below the text and signatures of the Indenture is recorded in the same hand-writing the following]—

The corses of Spencers Land and mine on Little Hunting Creek beginning at ye mouth of Little Hunting Extending up ye s^{'d} Creek 986 poles thence by a marked Line of trees W 188—÷- cross ye main wood, a mapel standing on ye E. side of ye main brantch of Dague run 720 p thence Down ye said Brantch & Creek 1128 p p^c to ye mouth of ye s^{'d} Creek thence along ye river to ye begining.

[Endorsed in Genl Washington's hand-writing]—

Rog^r & Mild'^d Gregory'

Release to

Augus^t Washington

17th May 1726

[Beneath this endorsement is the following of a probable current date with the execution of the Indenture.]

Merandom thos Leews & Reles was acknowledged at ye Jeneral Court by Rodger Gregory & Mildred his wife in Aprill 1726.

[The document is written on two large sheets of paper fastened together with wafers. To each signature is attached, in sealing wax, an impression of a seal which may be heraldic but cannot be called so with confidence. The design is a bloodhound on scent, who stands on what may be a wreath, but perhaps is only meant for a support to his feet. A photo-engraving of this seal will be found in the illustration facing page 523.]

Will of Augustine Washington, Father to General George Washington.

In the name of God, Amen.

I Augustine Washington of the County of King George—Gentleman being sick and weak but of perfect and disposing sence and memory, Do make my last will and Testament in manner following hereby revoking all former will or wills whatsoever by me heretofore made.

Imprimis;—I give unto my Son Lawrence Washington and his heirs forever all that plantation and tract of Land at Hunting Creek in the County of Prince William containing by estimate, two thousand and five hundred acres with the Water Mill adjoining thereto or lying near the same and all the Slaves, Cattle and Stocks of all Kinds whatsoever and all the Household Furnature whatsoever now in and upon or which have been commonly possesed by my said son, together with the said plantation track of Land and Mill.

Item,—I give unto my son Augustine Washington and his heirs forever all my lands in the County of Westmoreland except such only as are here-inafter otherwise disposed of together with twenty five head of neat Cattle forty hogs and twenty sheep and a negro man named Frank besides those negroes formerly given him by his mother.

Item,—I give unto my said son Augustine three young working Slaves to be purchased for him out of the first profits of the Iron Works after my desease.

Item,—I give to my son George Washington and his heirs the land I now live on which I purchased of the Executors of Mr Wm Strother deceased. And one, one moiety of my land lying on Deeps Run and ten negro Slaves.

Item,—I give unto my son Samuel Washington and his heirs my land at Chotank in the County of Stafford containing about six hundred acres and also the other moity of my land lying on Deeps Run.

Item,—I give unto my son John Washington and his heirs my Land at the head of Maddox in the County of Westmoreland containing about seven hundred acres.

Item,—I give unto my son Charles Washington and his heirs the land I purchased of my son Lawrence Washington whereon Thomas Lewis now lives, adjoining to my said son Lawrence's land above devised. I also give unto my said son Charles and his heirs the Land I purchased of Gabriel Adams in the County of Prince William containing about seven hundred acres.

Item,—It is my will and desire that all the rest of my negroes not herein particularly devised may be equally divided between my wife and my three sons Samuel, John and Charles, and that Ned, Jack, Bob, Sue, and Lucy may be included in my wife's part, which part of my said wife's, after her decease I desire may be equally divided between my sons George, Samuel, John and Charles, and the part of my said negroes so devised to my wife I mean and intend to be in full satisfaction and in lieu of her dower in my negroes. But if she should insist notwithstanding on her right of Dower in my negroes I will and desire that so many as may be wanting to make up her share may be taken out of the negroes given hereby to my sons George, Samuel, John and Charles.

Item,—I give and bequeath unto my said wife and my four sons George, Samuel, John and Charles, all the rest of my Personal Estate to be equally divided between them which is not particularly bequeathed by this will to my wife and it is my will and desire that my said four sons Estates may be kept in my wife's hands until they respectively attain the age of twenty one years, in case my said wife continues so long unmarried but in case she should happen to marry before that time I desire it may be in the power of my Executors to oblige her husband from time to time as they shall think proper to give security for the performance of this my last will in paying and delivering my said four sons their Estates respectively as they come of age, or on failure to give such security to take my said sons and their estates out of the custody and tuition of my said wife and her husband.—

Item,—I give and bequeath unto my said wife the crops made at Bridge Creek, Chotank, and Rappahanock quarters at the time of my decase for the support of herself and her children and I desire my wife may have the liberty of working my land at Bridge Creek Quarters for the time of Five years next after my decease, during which time she may fix a quarters on Deeps Run.

Item,—I give to my son Lawrence Washington and the heirs of his body lawfully begotten forever that tract of Land I purchased of Mr. James Hooe adjoining to the said Lawrence Washington's land on Maddox in the County of Westmoreland which I gave him in lieu of the land my said son bought for me in Prince William County of Spencer and Harrison and for want of such heirs then I give and devise the same to my son Augustine and his heirs forever.

Item,—I give to my said son Lawrence all the right title and interest I have to in or out of the Iron Works in which I am concerned in Virginia and Maryland provided that he do and shall, out of the profits raised thereby purchase for my said son Augustine three young working slaves as I have herein before directed and also pay my daughter Betty when she arrives at the age Eighteen years the sum of four hundred pounds which right title and interest on the condition aforesaid I give to my said son Lawrence and his heirs forever.

Item,—I give to my said daughter Betty a negro child named Mary daughter of Sue and an other named Betty daughter of Judy.—

Item,—It is my will and desire that my sons Lawrence and Augustine do pay out of their respective Estates devised to them one half or moity of the debts I justly owe and for that purpose I give and bequeath unto my said two sons one half of the debts and owing to me.—

Item,—For as much as my several children in this will mentioned being of several venters cannot inherit from one another in order to make a proper provision against their dying without issue It is my will and desire that in case my son Lawrence should die without heirs of his body lawfully begotten that then the land and Mill given him by this my will lying in the county of Prince William shall go and remain to my son George and his heirs but in case my son Augustine should choose to have the said lands rather than the lands he holds in Maddox either by this will or any Settlement. Then I give and devise said lands in Prince William to my said son Augustine and his heirs on his conveying the said lands in Maddox to my said son George and his heirs. And in case my said son Augustine shall happen to die without issue of his body lawfully begotten, then I give and bequeath all the said lands by him held in Maddox to my son George and his heirs and if both sons Lawrence and Augustine should happen to die without issue of their several bodies begotten then my will and desire is that my son George and his heirs may have his and their choice either to have the lands of my son Lawrence or the lands of my son Augustine to hold to him and his heirs and the land of such of my said sons Lawrence or Augustine as shall not be so chosen by my son George or his heirs shall go to and be equally divided among my sons Samuel, John and Charles and their heirs share and share alike and in case my son George by the death of both or either of my sons Lawrence and Augustine should according to this my intention come to be possessed of either their lands then my will and desire is that said lands hereby devised to my said son George and his heirs should go over and be equally divided between my sons Samuel, John and Charles and their heirs, share and share alike and in case all my children by my present wife should happen to die without issue of their bodies, Then my will and desire is that all the lands by this my will devised to any of my said children should go to my sons Augustine and Lawrence if living and to their heirs or if one of them should be dead without issue then to the survivor and his heirs. But my true Intent and meaning is that each of my children by my present wife may have their lands in fee simple upon the contingency of their arriving at full age or leaving heirs of their bodies lawfully begotten or on their dying under age and without lawful issue their several parts to descend from one to another according to their course of descent and the remainder of their or any of their land in this clause mentioned to my sons Lawrence and Augustine or the survivors of them is only upon the contingency of all my said children by my present wife dying under age and without issue living, my sons Lawrence and Augustine or either of them.

Lastly,—I constitute and appoint my son Lawrence Washington and my good friends Daniel McLarity and Nathaniel Chapman—Gentlemen Executors of this my last will and Testament.—

In witness whereof I have hereunto set my hand and Seal the Eleventh day of April 1743.

AUGUSTINE WASHINGTON   [L. S.]

Signed sealed and published
in the presence of us

    Robert Jackson
    Anthony Strother
    Jas Thompson

Provided further that if my lands at Chotank devised to my son Samuel should by course of law be taken away then I give to the said Samuel in lieu thereof a tract of Land in Westmoreland County where Benjamin Wicks and Thomas Finch now live by estimation seven hundred acres.

Item—I bequeath to my son George one lot of land in the town of Fredericksburg which I purchased of Col John Walton also two other lots in the said town which I purchased of the Executors of Colo Henry Willis with all the Houses and appurtenances thereunto belonging.—

And whereas some proposals have been made by Mr Anthony Strother for purchasing a piece of land where Matthew Tiffy lately lived now if my Executors shall think it for the benefit of my said son George then I hereby empower them to make conveyance of the said land and premices to the said Strother.

In witness whereof I have hereunto Set my hand and seal this eleventh day of April 1743

AUGUSTINE WASHINGTON   [L. S.]

Signed sealed and Published
in the presence of us

    Robert Jackson
    Anthony Strother
    Jas Thompson

At a court held for King George County the 6th day of May 1743
The last will and testament of Augustine Washington Gent'n deceased

was presented into Court by Lawrence Washington Gent'[n] one of the Executors who made oath thereunto and the same was proved by the oath of Anthony Strother and James Thompson admitted to Record

A Copy   Teste

HARRY TURNER—Clerk

WILL OF LAWRENCE WASHINGTON, HALF-BROTHER TO GEORGE WASHINGTON.

In the name of God Amen, I Lawrence Washington of Truro parish in Fairfax County and Colony of Virginia Gent, Knowing the uncertainty of this transitory life, and being in sound and desposing mind and memory do make this my last Will and Testament, hereby revoking and disannulling, all other wills and Testaments by me at any time heretofore made.

Imprimis my will and desire is that a proper vault for Interment may be made on my home plantation wherein my remains together with my three children may be decently placed, and to serve for my wife and such other of the family as may desire it.—

Item my will and desire is that my funeral charges and respective debts be first paid and discharged, out of such of my personal Estate as my Executors hereinafter to be be named Shall think best and most advisable to be disposed of for that purpose.—

Item my will and desire is that my loving wife have the use benefit and profits of all my Lands on Little Hunting and Doegs Creeks, in the parish of Truro and County of Fairfax with all the Houses and Edifices during her natural life, likewise the use labour and profits arising from the one half of all my Negroes, as my said wife and Executors may agree in dividing them, negro Moll and her issue, to be included in my wife's part of the said Negroes.   I also devise that my said wife may may [sic] have the use of the Lands surveyed on the south fork of Bull Skin, in the County of Frederick, during her natural Life.   But in case of my daughter Sarah dying without issue before her said Mother then I give and devise my said Bull Skin tract, to my said wife, to her and her Heirs for ever.—

Item it is my will and desire that all my Household goods, and furnature with the liquors be appraised and valued by three persons to be chosen by my wife and Executors and that my wife have the liberty to choose any part of the said Household goods, and furnature to the amount of a full moiety of the whole sum which they shall be appraised to.   Which part I give and bequeath to her and her heirs for ever; the other moiety to be sold and the money arising applied towards the payment of my debts.—

Item   What I have herein devised and left to my wife I intend to be in Lieu, and instead, of her right of Dower, provided my wife according to her promise, sells her several tracts of Land near Salisbury Plains, and applys the said money to the discharge of my debts due at the time of my death; But in case of her refusal then my will is that all my Household furnature be sold, and the whole amount to be applied towards the discharge of my debts—

Item   I give and bequeath to my Daughter Sarah and the heirs of her body lawfully begotten forever after my just debts are discharged all my real and personal Estate, in Virginia and the Provence of Maryland not otherwise disposed of.   But in case it shall please God my said Daughter, should die without issue, it is then my will and desire my Estate both real and personal, be disposed of in the following manner

First I give and bequeath to my loving brother Augustine Washington and his heirs forever all my stocks, Interest and Estate in the Principio, Accokeck, Kingsbury, Lancashire, and N° East Iron works in Virginia and Maryland reserving one third of the profits of said works to be paid to my wife, as hereinafter mentioned, and two tracts of Land lying and being in Frederick County which I purchased of Col Cresap and Gerrard Pendergrass.—

Second I give and bequeath unto my loving brother George Washington and his heirs forever, after the decease of my wife all my lands in Fairfax County with the improvements thereon, and further it is my will and desire, that during the natural life of my wife, that my said brother George shall have the use of an equal Share and proportion of all the Lands hereafter given and devised unto my brother Samuel, John and Charles.—

Third I give and bequeath all those Several tracts of Land which I am possessed of and claim in the County of Frederick (except the tract on the south Fork of Bull-Skin, bequeathed to my wife and the two tracts purchased of Col Cresap and Gerrard Pendergrass devised to my brother Augustine) unto my brother Samuel, John and Charles, reserving as above an equal proportion for my brother George provided they Samuel, John or Charles pay or cause to be paid unto my and their sister Betty Lewis the sum of One hundred and fifty pounds.—

Fourth my will also is that upon the death of my or all of my said Brothers George, Samuel, John and Charles, dying without lawful issue, such Lands as was given them or any of them in case of my said Daughter's demise as aforesaid, to become the property and right of my brother Augustine and his heirs.—

Fifth my further will and desire is that after the demise of my said wife the Negro woman Moll and her increase be given unto my said brother Augustine his Heirs Admors &c. and likewise give him an equal proportion with his other brothers, of the other part of the Negroes, and personal Estate upon their paying my said wife One Hundred pounds sterling, my intent and meaning is that the said one hundred pounds sterling be paid by my said brothers, to my said wife immediately or soon after it may please God to remove by death my said Daughter—

Item I further give and bequeath unto my loving wife during her natural life, one full third part of the profits from the share I hold in all the several Iron works both in the Colony of Virginia and Maryland to be paid unto my said wife from time to time by my Executors immediately upon notice given them by the partners residing in England of the annual amount of the profits to be paid either in bills or cash at the current exchange as she shall choose—

Item I give unto my brother John Washington, Fifty pounds in lieu of the Land, taken from him by a suit at Law Capt Maxmn Robinson, after my debts are paid.

Item my will and desire is that my two Tracts of Land one joining my wife's Tract, near Salisbury plain, the other on a branch of Goose Creek being three hundred and three acres, my two Lots in the town of Alexandria with the edifices thereon and my Share and Interest in the Ohio Company, all be sold by my Executors and the money applied toward discharging my debts. also my arrears of half pay, which Col° Wilson the agent or Mr Stuart his kinsman, and clerk be addressed for and the money applied to the same use.

Item whereas the purchasing Negroes and Land may greatly tend to the advantage of my Daughter, I therefore fully empower my Executors to lay out the profit of my Estate, or any part thereof in Lands and Negroes at their discression, *i. e.* I mean such part of the Estate as I have devised to my Daughter Sarah which said several purchases in case of her disease, without issue shall be deemed and counted personal Estate, and be accordingly equally divided among my brothers as above provided.—

Item I also desire my just suit of Complaint at Law depending against Gersham Keyes of Frederick County for breach of trust be effectually prosecuted by my Executors.—

Item it is furthermore my will and desire that all my estate be kept together till the debts are discharged.—

Item I give to my wife, my Mother in Law and each of my Executors a mourning ring.—

Lastly I constitute and appoint the Honb^e William Fairfax and George Fairfax Esqr'^s my said Brother Augustine and George Washington, and my esteemed friends Mr Nathaniel Chapman and Maj^r John Carlyle Executors of this my last will and testament, whereof I have hereunto set my hand and Seale this twentieth day of June one thousand seven hundred and fifty two in the 26th year of his Majesty King George the Second's reign.—   LAWRENCE WASHINGTON   [Seal].

Signed Sealed & published
in the presence of us
            Wm Waite
            Jno North
                his
            Andrew W Warren
                mark
            Joseph Gound

At a court held for Fairfax County September the 26th 1752 This last will and testament of Lawrence Washington Gen^t deceased was presented in court by the Honb^e William Fairfax and George William Fairfax Esqr^s John Carlyle and George Washington Gen^t four of the Executors therein named who made oath thereto according to Law, and being proved by the oaths of William Waite, John North and Andrew Warren three of the witnesses is admitted to record.—

And the same Executors performing what is usual in such cases, Certificate is granted them for obtaining a probate in due form.

                        Test   JOHN GRAHAM C.
            A Copy   Test   Wm MOSS C.
    Copy   Test

        F. W. RICHARDSON—Clerk

URSULA TRYE of Fordham in the co. of Essex, spinstèr, relict of Thomas Trye of Breadstone in the parish of Burkley and county of Gloucester esq. deceased, 7 January 1656, proved 5 December 1664. To my beloved son William Trye five pounds and my wedding ring only as a token of my love. To my grandchild Thomas Trye five pounds. To my daughter Margaret Trye fifty pounds and my bed and boulster, with a pair of down pillows and a pair of blankets and a green rug and all the rest of the furniture belonging to it that is at Overbury (and sheets, table cloths &c.). To my daughter Elenor Trye twenty pounds (and sundry damask table cloths, napkins &c) and my crimson satin mantle and all my needlework that is in

my trunk at Overbury, and all my wrought covers for chairs and stools
and two long cushions of cloth of gold and two long cushions of Needlework wrought with coloured silks at New Parke &c. To my daughter
Susanna Vickeridge five pounds (and sundry sheets, napkins &c). To my
daughter Anne Bulkley five pounds and a pair of pillow beeres wrought in
black silk and a cupboard cloth wrought with white work edged about with
bone lace, and a flaxen board-cloath marked with my own name, a long
towell and a half dozen flaxen napkins marked with "Em and Tee." To
my grand child Try Vickaridge twenty shillings and all my books at overbury, and to his three brothers Slauter, John and William Vickaridge ten
shillings apiece. To my grandchild Margaret Vickaredge my two least
gilt spoons and to her sister my silver spoon. To my grandchild Edward
Bulkley twenty shillings and to his two brothers John and Thomas Bulkley ten shillings apiece. To my grandchild Margaret Bulkley my great
gilt spoon. To the poor twenty shillings. My daughter Elenor Trye to
be executrix.
      Wit: John Bulkley, Ann Bulkley.   Bruce, 140.

      ELIANOR TRYE of St. Lawrence Lane, London, spinster, 24 November
1691, proved 1 March 1691. A messuage I bought of one Mary Dauice, (?)
spinster, situated in Breadstone in the parish of Barkley in the county of
Gloucester, for one hundred and five pounds, I do hereby give and devise to
my nephew Thomas Trye. To my sister Susanna Vicaredge of St. Lawrence Lane, London, relict of John Vicaredge, gent. deceased and to my
nephew John Vicaredge of St. Lawrence Lane, gentleman, all my messuages &c in Broadway, Worcester, and other property, in trust, to pay
legacies &c.
      To my niece Elizabeth Fawkner two hundred pounds. To my nephew
Edward Bulkley the elder two hundred pounds. To my nephew Thomas
Bulkley, gone into New England, one hundred and fifty pounds. To my
niece Susanna More one hundred pounds. To my niece Elizabeth Vicaredge one hundred and fifty pounds. To my nephew Thomas Bulkley's son
John, or what child he shall have living at my death, fifty pounds at the
age of sixteen years. To my nephew John Vicaredge one hundred and
twenty pounds. To my nephew Sheldon Vicaredge eighty pounds. To
Frederick, son of said Sheldon, twenty pounds. To my nephew Thomas
Vicaredge one hundred pounds. To my nephew Charles Vicaredge one
hundred pounds and to his three children, Charles, John and Thomas, each
twenty pounds. To the three children of my nephew Trye Vicaredge,
deceased, Try, Susanna and Elizabeth Vicaredge, vizt to the son thirty
pounds, and to the two daughters forty pounds each. To Everard Fawkner, son of my nephew Everard Fawkner, twenty pounds. To little John
More, son of my nephew John More, twenty pounds. To the poor of
Broadway, Worcester, six pounds. To Dr. Annesley my worthy pastor
three pounds. To the Lady Frances Pickering twenty shillings to buy
her a ring and to her Ladyship's son Gilbert Pickering Esqre twenty shillings to buy him a ring. To my cousin Anthony Trye of Passenham and
his wife twenty shillings apiece. To my sister Auice Bulkley twenty
shillings to buy her a ring. To my cousin Joseph Bulkley's son Edward
twenty shillings to buy him a ring. To my cousin Cassandra Lewis twenty
shillings to buy her a ring. My brother John Buckley did repose a trust
in me and my sister Wroughton deceased to dispose of diverse goods and
jewels in a schedule annexed to a certain indenture mentioned to be made

between my said brother Buckley, sister Wroughton and myself, bearing date 29 June 1665, which goods do belong to my sister Anne Buckley's children. I have delivered all those mentioned goods, plate and jewels and money to Edward, Thomas, Elizabeth and Joseph Bulkley as will appear by receipts under every one of their hands. Reference also to other articles of agreement made between said brother Bulkley and Ann his wife, myself and several others, bearing date 5 July 1658, and to others, dated 30 June 1665, between said brother Bulkley and myself. To sister Susanna Vicaredge my diamond ring with five diamonds set round upon the ring, my gold locket with a death's head and E.A. upon the locket, my silver freezed cup with a cover and my coat of arms upon the cup (and certain wearing apparell and other goods). To my nephew Thomas Trye my gold seale with two coats of arms upon it (and other things). To my niece Elizabeth Fawkner my large diamond jewell set in a racket, being in all, small and great, fifty-nine diamonds in that jewell (and other things of value). To my niece Susannah More my gold watch with a studden case and gold chain to it, my diamond bracelet, being ten diamonds set in gold, my diamond locket with M.S., seventeen diamonds in it (and other things of value). To my niece Elizabeth Vicaredge my best pearl necklace, being three strings of pearls, my diamond ring with thirteen diamonds in it. To my nephew Fawkner's son Everard a silver porringer with T.W. upon it, and a gold medal inamelled and a coat of arms upon it and two heads of white agates. To my nephew John Vicaredge my silver goblet cup embossed and my coat of arms upon it. (Other valuable objects given to various relatives) My sister Susanna Vicaredge and my nephew John Vicaredge to be trustees and executrix and executor. All my china that is at Lawrence Lane, also my pictures, to my sister Vicaredge and her two daughters Susanna More and Elizabeth Vicaredge. My red china tea pot 1 give to my niece Elizabeth Fawkner. Reference to a bond with nephew Edward Bulkley.

Fane, 46.

JOHN BULKELEY of the Precincts of St. Katherines (near the Tower, London) gen[t] 11 October 1689, proved 28 January 1689. My body to be buried half an hour before sunset if in the Winter, or when the days are shorter than the nights; but if in the Summer, or when the days are longer than the nights, it shall be at the furthest by six a clock in the afternoon. To wife Avis thirty pounds over and above what was settled upon her before our intermarriage and the possession and use, during her natural life of all those rings, necklaces. jewells &c which she had before our intermarriage or hath been by me since given unto her, willing with all and desiring that her best diamond ring be immediately after her decease given (taken by) or delivered to my loving daughter Elizabeth the now wife of Everard Falkener, grocer.

Bequests to sister Mrs. Elenor Trye, to brother and sister Vicaridge and to their children, to the eldest son of my late nephew, Trye Vicaridge, to three brethren in New England, viz[t] Edward, Gersham and Peter, to sons of deceased brother Thomas, to nephew Edward Bulkeley here in England and to nephew Thomas Trye son of late brother in law Mr William Trye.

The land at Ringshall, Suffolk, settled upon me and my heirs, after my wife's decease shall be sold and of the proceeds two hundred pounds paid to son Falkener, in full of his wife's portion, and the remainder divided between my two sons Edward and Thomas Bulkeley. My son Edward, my wife Avis and my daughter Elizabeth Falkener to be joint executors

Dyke, 2.

[Mr. John Bulkly of Fordham in the co. of Essex and M'ris Anne Try of Odell, married, March 19, 1650. (Parish Registers of Odell in Genealogia Bedfordiensis, by F. A. Blaydes.)—H. F. W.

Rev. John Bulkeley, M.A., born 1619-20, H. C. 1642, was the son of Rev. Peter Bulkeley, of Odell (Woodhill), Bedfordshire, and of Concord, Mass., by his first wife, Jane Allen, of Goldington. He returned to England soon after his graduation, and was settled as a minister in Fordham, Essex, where the baptisms of a son and daughter are recorded by his own hand. Having been ejected from his living in 1662, he removed to "Wapping in the suburbs of London," and there practised as a physician till his death, probably in January, 1689-90. (Sibley's Harv. Grad. I. 52; Bulkley Family, p. 64.) He married, first, March 19, 1650[-1], Anne Trye, who probably died before June, 1665; secondly, Avis or Auice ——. His children by Anne Trye were: Edward, John, Thomas, Margaret (born before 1656) and Elizabeth. John, who with Margaret died before 1689, was probably the father of the Joseph Bulkeley mentioned by Elinor Trye among her sister Anne's children; though as John evidently died before his father, it is curious that Joseph is not mentioned in John Bulkeley's will. But, unless both John and Joseph married much younger than men usually did even in those days, this Joseph could scarcely have been the "cousin Joseph Bulkley" whose "son Edward" is mentioned in Elianor Trye's will. It is, however, difficult to see who else it could be. Thomas, who was in New England in 1691, had John (less than sixteen in 1691, died before 1720), and Thomas, who was in the East Indies about 1720. Elizabeth married Everard Fawkner (died 1707), and died 1720. She was probably a second wife, with a stepson Everard who died before his father. (See REGISTER, 1888, p. 272; or ante, p. 281, for Elizabeth Fawkner's will.)

The "nephew Edward Bulkeley here in England," of John Bulkeley's will, and the "cousin Edward Bulkeley" with wife Sarah and daughter Elizabeth (less than twenty-one in 1720) of Elizabeth Fawkner's will, may have been the son of Hon. Peter[3] Bulkeley (Rev. Edward,[2] Rev. Peter[1]) perhaps, brought by his father to England in 1676, and left in his uncle John Bulkeley's care. (Ante, pp. 285-6; REGISTER, 1888, pp. 275-6.) As he was the eldest son of the eldest son, it seems not at all improbable that his English relatives should have agreed to provide for him. The expression "my nephew Edward Bulkley the elder" in Elianor Trye's will might seem to imply that John's son Edward had himself a son Edward, who might then be supposed to be the "cousin" mentioned by Elizabeth Fawkner. (See ante, p. 277, note by Mr. Waters.) But it is very unlikely that of all her nephews and nieces she would call only one by the name of "cousin"; and the expression, "the elder," was probably used simply to distinguish John Bulkley's son, born about 1651, from his cousin and adopted brother of the same name, born 1668-9.

The children of THOMAS (died before 1656) and URSULA (died 1664) TRYE, seem to have been: WILLIAM T. (died between 1656 and 1689) who had son Thomas; MARGARET T. m. —— Wroughton (?), and died between 1665 and 1691; ELIANOR T. died unmarried, 1691-2; SUSANNA T married before 1656 JOHN VICARIDGE (who died between Oct. 11, 1689, and Nov. 24, 1691), and had eldest Trye V., born about 1648, died between 1656 and 1689 (had Trye, Susanna and Elizabeth, all living in 1691); Slauter V. died between 1656 and 1691; John V.; William V. (had Frederick); Thomas V.; Charles V. (had Charles, John and Thomas); Margaret V.; Susanna V. married John More (who had John, perhaps by a former marriage) and Elizabeth V., unmarried in 1691. Of these, Trye, Slauter, John, William, Margaret, and probably Susanna, were born before 1656; and Trye, Slauter, William and Margaret apparently died before 1691.

The use of the word "spinster" in Ursula Trye's will is very curious. ("Bachelor" is sometimes used of a widower.) The Mrs. Hester Vicaridge mentioned with her son the "chyrurgeon," in Elizabeth Fawkner's will, was perhaps the widow of the younger Trye Vicaridge.

St. Laurence Lane runs north from Cheapside to Cateaton St.; the Church of St. Laurence Jewry is opposite its northern end. The Precincts of St. Katherines have been swallowed up by St. Katherine's Docks.—EMMA F. WARE, of Milton, Mass.

In reference to the use of the term spinster, see REGISTER, vol. 13, page 284.—EDITOR.]

MARY NEEDHAM of Hampsted in the co. of Middlesex, widow, 12 April 1660, proved 20 March 1661. To the poor of the parish of Hampsted forty shillings. To my son John Needham and his heirs my brick messuage or tenement now in the occupation of the said Mary, in Hampsted, and also two other cottages with the appurtenances in Hampsted in the tenure &c. of John Bosier and Richard Webb, and two little closes to the said messuages belonging now in the tenure of John Spicer and all my other messuage &c. in Hampsted. To my son Benjamin all that messuage &c. wherein the said Benjamin now dwelleth, situate and being in Ave Mary Lane in London, together with all the goods, implements and necessaries expressed in a scedule annexed to his lease by me formerly made unto him, subject and chargeable nevertheless with the payment of two hundred pounds of lawful money of England to my son Edmund Needham, now resident in New England, by ten pounds thereof yearly, and if the said Edmund happen to die before all the said two hundred pounds shall be fully run out &c. then the residue thereof unpaid at the time of his decease to be paid and satisfied unto his son Daniel Needham &c. To son Benjamin the lease of the messuage in Ave Mary Lane called by the name or sign of the White Horse which I hold from the Company of Stationers of London, on condition that he pay to my daughter Barnes, wife of Thomas Barnes Esq. twenty pounds, to my daughter Katherine Needham fifty pounds, to my daughter Anne Coles wife of Mr. Coles fifty pounds, to Elizabeth Brent, my grandchild daughter of my late daughter Mary Brent, threescore pounds, to my grandchild Richard Brent twenty pounds, and to my son John thirty pounds.

To my sons Thomas Barnes, John Needham and Benjamin Needham eight pounds apiece for mourning for them and their wives, and to my daughters Katherine Needham and Anne Cole and her husband and my son in law John Brent and Elizabeth his daughter four pounds apiece for mourning. The residue to John and Benjamin equally and they to be executors. Commissary C^t. of London (1660-4) fo. 128.

[Edmond Needham settled in Lynn, Mass., where he died in June, 1677. His wife, Mrs. Jone Needham, is said to have died 24 October, 1674, aged about 64 or 65 years. Mr. Needham's will, made 26. 4. 1677, was proved 29, 4. 1677. He refers to his wife as not living, and mentions son Ezekiel and his two children, son Daniel and his five children (John, Ezekiel, Judah, Mary and Elizabeth), daughter Hannah Diven and her two children (Hannah Armitage and John Diven) both minors, son-in-law Samuel Hart's children (Samuel, Joseph, Abigail and Rebecca Hart), and son-in-law Joseph Mansfield's children (Joseph, John, Elizabeth Wheate and Deborah Mansfield). He refers to John Mansfield as a boy " which I have brought up ever since his childhood, till now he is about 15 years old." He also mentions Samuel Hart's daughter-in-law, born of his wife's first husband, Elizabeth How, but now by marriage Elizabeth Chadwell.

Then follows an Inventory, at "mine owne valuation," in which is entered " my clock yt strikes and another watch and larum that does not strike—5£." " Debts in old England in sufficient bonds and most abell mens hands, as the Company of Merchant Adventurers and another looked at as a great rich cittizen fit for an Alderman of London, though they doe what they can to deceaue us, that is to say my Brothers and sisters, to whome they owe us aboue 3000^{li}—600.00.00. But for this debt in old England, y^t is somthing uncertaine what my two Atturneys in England, being my two brothers, may gett for mee and themselues, with somthing that may be comeing both to themselues and me, I desire to leaue it to my children in the best order as I can amongst them." (Prob. Reg., Essex Co., Mass.)—H. F.W.]

PETER RANDOLPH (*ante*, pp. 513-4).

[Peter[3] Randolph, son of William[2] and Elizabeth (Beverley) Randolph, and grandson of William[1] Randolph of "Turkey Island" and his wife Mary, daughter of Henry and Catherine Inham of Bermuda Hundred, married Lucy Beverley. They had issue:—i. William,[4] married Mary, daughter of Sir William Skipwith: ii. Beverley[4] of "Green Creek," governor of Virginia, married Martha Cocke: iii. Robert[4] of Fauquier, married Elizabeth Carter of Shirley; iv. Anne,[4] married William Fitzhugh. The executor, John Wayles, was the father-in-law of Thomas Jefferson, and the witness, Carter Braxton, was the signer of the Declaration of Independence.—R. A. BROCK, Richmond, Va.]

SILVESTER (*ante*, pp. 16–9):—

[Mr. N. Darnell Davis, of Georgetown, Demerara, contributed to *The Argosy* of that city, March 21, 1891, a letter which he found among the Tanner Manuscripts in the Bodleian Library. It is endorsed "A Ltr from Barbados, by y[e] way of Holland show[g] ye condicon of honest men there," and is dated "this 19–9 August 1651." The writer had signed his name Gyles at the foot of the letter, but had afterwards drawn strokes through the signature. The surname is not given, but Mr. Davis supposes the writer to be one of the family of Silvester then settled in Barbados; and the wills of Peter, Giles, Constant and Nathaniel Silvester, at the above references, strengthen this opinion. The letter is addressed to "My most honored and loving Father."

It relates principally to his business and the oppressive measures of the King's officers towards him and other Parliamentarians. "They had granted," he says, "a generall pardon, or rather oblyvion, thorough the whole yland: & now since they haue made an engagement for every one to take it, and some not takeing it, went away pryvately from the Yland. This people because they could not come to their desyre, they went & broke their Act of Oblyvion; & sequestred 52 gallandt plantations, who are as mutch worth as all ye Yland besydes: & lay heavy taxations upon us dayly, all ye way they device to ruine us, they are redy by day or night to doe it; they have taken 25 of my servants & made souldiers of them. I am to pay every month for 8 men & a half, besydes those 25 men, to every mañ 180 lb p[r] month which is in all 1530 lb. of sugar p[r] month, and for my brother going without his ticket, he was fyned 5000 lb of sugar more, which I was constrained to pay immediately after his going."

The writer mentions brothers Constant and Nathaniel; uncles Nathaniel Arnold, Elyas, Elysha; aunts Lydia Thorp, Marey, Pelham, Aunt Susanna. He says: "My brother Nathaniel is not come from New England yet. I have not received any letters neither of him, nor of my brother Constant, who went away on Good Freeday last. One y[t] came from Boston in New England last, tould me that he spoke with both of my brothers there, & y[t] my brother Nathaniel would come p[r] y[e] next ship y[t] come for these parts."

Mr. Davis prints references to Silvesters from the Calendars of State Papers (Colonial). He also prints from Col. Chester's Marriage Licences, this entry: "Sylvester, Giles, of St. James, Duke's Place, London, merchant, bachelor, 30, and Anne Burrell, spinster, 18, daughter of Sir Redmayne Burrell, knight and bart. of Dowsby, co. Lincoln, who consents—at Great St. Bartholomew, London, 13 January, 1662." It is not unlikely that this Giles Sylvester was the writer of the letter, and that he was also the person an abstract whose will is printed in the REGISTER, vol. 37, page 384 (*ante*, p. 16), who left a widow Anne.—EDITOR.]

MARY MATHER of London widow, 29 April 1699, with a codicil dated 7 November 1699, and another dated 11 May 1705, proved 6 March 1705. To my cousin Mr. John Holmes and unto his wife and unto my cousin Mrs Elizabeth Mather twenty shillings apiece to buy them rings. I give twenty five pounds to my brother in law Mr. Increase Mather, his executors or administrators; twenty five pounds unto Mrs. Katherine Darby, daughter of Mr. Samuel Mather deceased, or her children as my executor thinks fit. I make and constitute Mr. Nathaniel Gwillym to be executor and give him ten pounds for his pains and trouble. The rest to be divided into four parts, one of which equal parts I do give and bequeath to Mr. Wareham Mather son of Mr. Eleazar Mather deceased, one other to Mr. Samuel Mather son of the aforesaid Mr. Increase Mather, another to the said Mrs. Katherine Darby or her children. The remaining fourth part shall be divided unto four equal shares, one of which I give to my sister Mrs. Hannah Lobb another to her son Mr. Nathanael Lobb another to my cousin Mr. Isaac Polewheel and the fourth or last to and among all the children of my cousin Mr. Stephen Lobb which shall be living at such division and distribution. In the first codicil five pounds is directed to be given to Mr. Wait, minister at Chessen (*sic*) and five pounds to Mr. Carlile of Tiballs, one half the books to be given to Mr. Wareham Mather and the other half to Mᵣ Samuel Mather, to Mrs. Priscilla Gardner five pounds and to Mrs. Prudence Green three pounds. The second codicil recites that Mrs Green is dead, wherefore the above legacy is to go to her two daughters. Mr. Samuel Mather to have all the books and to pay Mᵣ Warham Mather one hundred pounds. Mr. Mather's picture to N: Gwillym. To Mr. Samuel Mather his uncle's watch. Eedes, 66.

[Mrs. Mary Mather was the widow of Rev. Nathaniel Mather, son of Rev. Richard Mather, of Dorchester, Mass. He was graduated at Harvard College in 1647. A few years later he went to England, and in 1655 obtained the living of Harburton in Devon. In 1656, Cromwell presented him to the living of Barnstaple in the same county. In 1662, he was ejected under the Bartholomew act. He then went to Holland and was minister to the English congregation at Rotterdam. About 1672, he succeeded his brother Samuel as pastor of the Congregational church at Dublin. In 1688, he succeeded John Collins (H. U. 1649) as pastor of a Congregational church in Lime Street, London. He was also a lecturer at Pinners Hall. He died July 26, 1697, aged 67, and was buried at Bunhill Fields. A Latin inscription on his tombstone, written by the celebrated Dr. Isaac Watts, is printed in the American Quarterly Register, vol. 8, page 332. Biographical sketches are printed in Sibley's Harvard Graduates, vol. 1, pp. 157-61: Palmer's Nonconformists' Memorial, vol. 1, page 339; and H. E. Mather's Lineage of Rev. Increase Mather, pp. 55-7. According to the last-named work, he married Maria, daughter of Rev. William Benn.—EDITOR]

Memorand. That TIMOTHY ALSOP late of the parish of St. Mary Somerset in London Esq., lying sick of the sickness whereof he died and having a desire to make his will and to dispose of his estate, did, on or about the five and twentieth day of July one thousand six hundred and sixty four, being in perfect mind and memory make and declare his last will and testament nuncupative in manner and form following vizᵗ. The said Timothy called to his wife Martha Alsop and said, my dear I have a few words to say, that is the agreement in marriage jewells and other things I leave to thee my dear. I hope there will be for my daughter Betty twelve or fourteen hundred pounds. I hope there will be for my daughter Prudence ten or eleven hundred pounds. I give to my brother Josias Alsop fifty pounds. I give to my sister in New England one hundred and fifty pounds to be paid within a twelve month. I give to poor ministers five and twenty pounds. To the poor of the parish five pounds. And further said I do declare these things to be my last will and testament, and therefore take notice of it and write it down. Which word or words to the same effect he so declared and spake in his perfect mind and memory with intent they should stand for and be his last will and testament nuncupative in the presence and hearing of the said wife and other credible witnesses.

Commission issued 19 August 1664 to Martha Alsop his widow to administer according to the tenor and effect of this will. Bruce, 94.

[The will of his brother Josias Alsop was printed in the REGISTER for 1890 (vol. 44, p. 91; *ante*, p. 426). The "sister in New England" we may suppose to be Mrs. Elizabeth Rosseter, named in the will of Josias —H. F. W.]

JOHN CAFFINCH now of Tenterden, Kent, and late of New Haven in

New England, 14 October 1658, proved 19 January 1658.   My will is that my wife Sarah Caffinch and my three daughters Sarah, Mary and Elizabeth Caffinch which were coming for England about a year since should have and enjoy my house and land in Tenterden which I lived in before I went into New England, with four parcels of land thereunto belonging, as by the writings contains eleven acres with a barn and stable and orchard and garden thereto adjoining, with a shop at the church gate in the Butchery which John Church useth and another shop in the butchery that was bought of John Lewis, belonging thereunto; also another house at New Rumney, with a slaughter house and stable and garden thereunto belonging which Goodman Pinke butcher now liveth in.   If my wife and children should never come to enjoy this estate then I do give and bequeath it unto the two daughters of my well beloved brother Samuel Caffynch late of Tenterden deceased, Lydia and Sarah Caffynch; and if they die before they come to twenty years of age or day of marriage then my kinsman Samuel Caffynch, son of Jeremiah Caffynch late of Biddenden deceased, whom I make executor, shall have, possess and enjoy it.   To Lydia and and Sarah Caffynch, before mentioned, the house barn and land called Igenden Farm in Tenderden, and a house at the Church gate &c. &c.   I make Mr James Skeets and Mr Richard Burchett overseers of this my last will.   My will is that all such lime and tiles as are at my house in Tenterden where my sister now liveth shall be employed about repairing of the said house.   And there will be due from sister Caffynch for rent of the house ten pounds.   This shall be laid out in repairing the said house.   Pell, 19.

[John Caffinch was one of the original proprietors of Guilford, Ct., 1639. He was of New Haven 1643.   He had children: Sarah, bap. March 9, 1650–1; Mary, bap. July 9, 1654; and Elizabeth, bap. Feb. 8, 1656–7.   His brothers. Samuel and Thomas, resided also at New Haven; the latter having died early in 1647, leaving his brother John executor.   (See Savage's Genealogical Dictionary, Ralph D. Smith's History of Guilford, and New Haven Colony Records.) —EDITOR.]

JOHN SAYER of Wapping, Middlesex, mariner, 2 May 1651, proved 12 May 1655.   To wife Mary the household stuff &c that was hers before our intermarriage.   Houses in Gun Alley and Cross Alley.   Son Samuel, daughter Rebecca Bolt.   Grandchild John Richardson, grandchild William Richardson.   Daughter Martha Searle.   Sisters Anne Sayer and Katherine Sayer.   Grandchild John Lee.   The house wherein Aske the matchmaker dwells, situate in or near Radcliffe Highway I give to my sister Katherine Sayer for life, rent free.   Grandchildren Sarah, Rebecca, Hannah, Mary and Ruth Wormlayton.   Grandchildren Andrew and John Bolt.   Daughter Martha Searle, Daughter Sarah Wormlayton.

I give to my cousin Master Matthew Haviland five pounds, to my cousin Davis and his wife twenty shillings apiece, to my sister Lock thirty shillings, to my son Thomas Harrison and his wife twenty shillings apiece, to my wife's sister thirty shillings, to my own brothers' and sisters' children twenty shillings apiece, to my son Burton and his wife twenty shillings apiece &c.   Son Edward Searle.   Son Fulk Wormlayton.   Son Richard Bodilee.   Son Andrew Bolt.   Aylett, 107.

SARAH ANDREWES of St Leonard's Shoreditch, Middlesex, widow, 20 September 1669 proved 28 September 1669.   I give and bequeath unto my loving brother Matthew Haverland (sic) clerk my diamond ring to wear in remembrance of me.   To my loving sister Constance Haverland my silver watch as a token of my love. To my loving cousin Samuel Bayley of London mercer the sum of ten pounds. To my cousin Rebecka Sprint widow ten pounds. To my friends Ellinor, Basill and Rebecca Cotterill twenty shillings apiece to buy them rings. Refers to a lease from the City of London of a parcel of land in the parish of St. Dyonise Backchurch London, whereon I have erected and built a brick messuage or tenement now in lease to one William Phillips citizen and apothecary of London at forty pounds per annum. Refers to will of late husband Richard Andrews, citizen and Scrivener of London. My loving brothers and cousins Samuel Sprint, clerk, Zachariah Sprint, clerk, Richard Sprint, clerk, and Samuel Sprint, bookseller. Sister Barbara Barnes of Hackney widow. Cousin Benjamin Andrews. Coke, 101.

MATTHEW HAVILAND of London, clerk, 6 April 1667, proved 4 February 1670. Refers to a certain instrument or conveyance dated 30 April 1663 between me the said Matthew, Constance my wife and Fulke Wormelayton of Wapping, Middlesex, distiller on the one part and Lewis Roberts of the city of Gloucester gen^t Benj. Albin, citizen and skinner of London and Samuel Baylye citizen and cordwainer of London on the other part, as trustees for sundry uses therein expressed, concerning an interest in a certain lease of pasture ground called one hundred acres near Bridgewater, Somerset. After the decease of my wife they shall permit my sister Mary Davyes of London, widow to receive the clear issues and profits thereof for two years and then they shall sell the lease and divide the proceeds among the children of my four sisters, the said Mary Davyes, Florence, late wife of Robert Culme of Bristol, Jane, late wife of William Torry of New England, and Elizabeth late wife of George Offield late of Bristol aforesaid, gen^t, by even and equal portions. My wife shall enjoy the goods &c. which were sometimes the goods &c. of my late dear father Mr. Robert Haviland of Hawkesbury, Gloc. for life; then to Elizabeth, Hannah and Sarah Davyes, daughters of my said sister Davyes, and Elizabeth Culme daughter of my said sister Culme. To my cousin Thomas Offield ten pounds. Other legacies. To the said Thomas my embroidered beard brush. To my brother in law Mr. Samuel Sprint all those books that I lent him, and to my cousin Richard Sprint all those books I lent him. To my brother in law Robert Culme, to my loving aunt Mrs Elizabeth Guise and her daughters, my cousins Anne and Elizabeth, and my sister in law Mrs. Sarah Andrews widow and my sister in law Mrs Anne Sprint twenty shillings apiece. Duke, 21.

[Rev. Matthew Haviland was rector of Trinity Church, London, from which he was ejected under the Bartholomew act. (See Palmer's Nonconformists' Memorial, vol. 2, page 647; Newcourt's Repertorium, vol. 1, page 556). He was born about 1608, and was the son of Robert and Elizabeth (Gyse) Haviland. of Hawkesbury, Gloucestershire. He was descended from ——^{i} Haviland, of the Isle Guernsey, through Christopher,[2] of Poole, Dorset; Matthew,[3] mayor of Bristol, and Robert,[4] above, his father, who, according to the Visitation of Gloucestershire, 1623, had five children : " Mathew Haviland, 15 yere old 1623, Mary, Florence, Jane, Elizabeth." The four daughters are named in their brother's will. Jane is called " late wife of William Torry, of New England." (See Visitation of Gloucestershire, Harleian Society's Publications, vol. 21, page 78. See also wills of the testator's grandfather, Matthew Haviland, and of his uncle, Matthew Haviland, both merchants of Bristol, ante, pp. 498, 499. The grandfather, in his own will, names two wives, viz., Joyce deceased, and Tacie then living. According to the Visitation of Gloucestershire, he had a wife Mary, who was a daughter of Robert Kitchen.)—EDITOR.]

" WILLIAM TORRY of Combe Seynt Nichãs in the dioc. of Bathe and Welles," 7 October 1556, proved 18 June 1557. My body to be buried in the church yard of Combe St. Nicholas. To the Church of St. Andrew in Welles twelve pence. To the Church of Combe St. Nicholas six shillings eight pence. To Elizabeth Screvyn my servant a chilver sheep. To John Morys my servant a chilver sheep. To every of my children ten sheep. To Alexander Nobyll twelve pence. The residue of my goodes not given " nother " bequeathed I give and bequeath to Thomasyn my wife, whom I make and ordain sole executrix. William Gollopp and Thomas Torrye two of the overseers.   Wrastley, 18.

HENRY COOKNEY of Hawkechurch, Dorset, 13 May 1593, proved 23 January 1601. To Robert Cookney, John Cookney, " dryller," William Michell, the middle, Avice Hussey, John Stephens, Gregory Smithe and George Wilkins twelve pence apiece. I give towards the reparations of the Church of Hawkechurch twelve pence. To William my son ten pounds and to Jone my daughter ten pounds. To Thomasine my daughter ten pounds and a cow which is with her uncle William. To every of my godchildren two pence apiece. The one half of all the residue of my goods and chattels I give unto my youngest daughter; and do ordain Emmett my wife to be my whole executrix. Also I appoint my brothers Philip Torry, William Torry and John Cookney overseers, and do give every one of them twelve pence apiece.

John Bowditch one of the witnesses.   Montague, 1.

The last day of August 1604 PHILIP TORRY late of Wadbrook in the parish of Hawkechurch, Dorset, husbandman &c. did make his last will and testament nuncupative in this manner and form following, or the like in effect, vizt. To his son William Torry he did bequeath ten young sheep and not any other chattle or goods whatsoever. He bequeathed all the rest of his goods to Margaret his wife and Dorothy his daughter. And last of all he appointed his forenamed son William Torry the sole executor of his last will and testament. Witnessed by Henry Holcombe and John Cookeney with others. Proved 23 February 1604.   Hayes, 12.

PHILIP TORREY of Combe St. Nicholas, Somerset, husbandman, 16 April 1621, proved 27 June 1621. To be buried in the church yard of Combe. To the relief of the poor of Combe three shillings four pence. Anne Torrey mine eldest daughter shall have threescore pounds when she shall accomplish the age of sixteen years, to be paid my overseers who shall take the government of it until she shall accomplish the age of one and twenty years. To her the biggest brass pan to be delivered unto her at the time of her marriage and not before. To Mary Torrey my daughter twenty pounds at sixteen to be held (as before) until she is twenty one, and the second brass pan. To Sarah Torrey my daughter three and thirty pounds six shillings eight pence at sixteen (as before), and the second best brazen pot. To James Torrey my son thirty pounds at 16 (as before), and one silver spoon when he is one and twenty. To Philip Torrey my son twenty pounds, at 16 (as before) and he shall be put an apprentice unto some trade so soon as he is able, and also I 'do give him one silver spoon to be delivered unto him when he is one and twenty years old. I do give unto William Torrey my son the biggest brazen pot, the furnace kettle, the best table board the cupboard with this condition that his mother shall have the use of it so long as she doth keep herself widow and dwelling in the house. To

Joseph my son ten pounds. All the rest to my wife whom I make sole executrix. My father William Torrey my cousin John Fry, John Richards, Robert Sellecke and Thomas Lumbert to be overseers, and I give them five shillings apiece. Proved by Alice Torrey the widow. Dale, 56.

[All of the foregoing Torrey wills, with the exception of that of Henry Cookney, were gathered by me early in October, 1884. I was accompanied in the search by the late Hon. Alphonso Taft, then U. S. Minister to Austria or Russia, who kindly gave me, not long after, the following abstract of a will found by him in the District Registry at Wells.—H. F. W.]

ALICE TORREY of Bettam in the parish of Combe St. Nicholas, Somerset, widow, 24 April 1634. To be buried in church yard of Combe. To the parish church iii⁸ 4ᵈ and the poor of the parish vi⁸ viij ᵈ. To son James Torrey so much of mine own estate as to make his father's bequest and his sister Marie's by 3 score pounds, and the same to be paid unto him within three months after my decease. A similar bequest to son Philip Torrey, to be paid unto him when he shall attain the age of one and twenty years and not before. To Joseph Torrey a similar bequest of three score pounds. To my servant Jone three pounds. To Samuel, the son of my son William, one book, in the house, of Mʳ Perkins' works. I give to him also one ewe and lamb the best of all my flock. All the rest of my goods not given nor bequeathed, my debts and legacies paid and my funeral discharged, I give and bequeath to William Torrey my son, whom I do make whole and sole executor, and for my son's assistance in the performance of this trust I do intreat Mr. Joseph Greenfeild my cousin John Blake Henry Dunster and Hugh Sheppeard to be my overseers, for the good of my children.

Wit. Henry Dunster and *signum* Johañ ł Clarke.

Memo: 13ˡⁱ 10⁸ due from my brother in law Thomas Lumbard.

[The seal seemed to be a chevron between three crescents.—H. F. W.

The four sons of Philip and Alice Torrey emigrated to New England about 1640. James settled in Scituate, where he married Ann, daughter of Elder William Hatch, Nov. 2, 1643. He died there July 6, 1665, leaving a large family, many of whose descendants are now living. Philip settled in Roxbury, where he married, Oct. 1, 1647, Mary, widow of John Scarborough, and died May 12, 1686. It is not known that any of his direct descendants are now living.

Joseph owned land in Weymouth in 1642, and was a resident of Rehoboth in 1643, and was prominent in the affairs of the Newport settlement from 1656 to the time of his death, 1676. He had one daughter, name unknown. William married Agnes, daughter of Joseph Combe, of Combe St. Nicholas, March 17, 1629; she lived not more than a year, and he married second, Jane Haviland, referred to in the will of Matthew Haviland in these Gleanings; she died 1639, leaving two sons, Samuel and William. He soon married a third wife and emigrated to New England, taking his two sons. They settled at Weymouth. Here six children were born. Capt. William Torrey was a leading man of his time, was many years clerk of the Deputies, and occupied many positions of prominence in the Colony. He died at Weymouth, June 10, 1690.

In a letter to the writer, dated Nov. 6, 1884, Hon. Alphonso Taft, referred to by Mr. Waters, says: "The line as I find it is, William, who died in 1557, leaving a will; Philip, his son, who died in 1604, leaving a will; William, his son, who survived his son Philip, but the date of whose death we have not; Phillip, who died in 1621, leaving a will naming his four sons who emigrated to America."

Mr. Taft also furnished from the Bishops' Register at Wells the following for Combe St. Nicholas:

"1608   William the son of Philip Torrie was baptized 21 day of December.
"1608   Agnes daughter of Joseph Combe was baptized the 4 of January.
"1629   William Torry was married unto Agnes Combe the 17 day of March.
"1639   Jane the wife of William Torry was burried the 27 day of April Anno. 1639."

Savage mentions Naomi Torrey who married Richard Sylvester at Weymouth in 1632, and says she was "probably sister of William." From the will of Phillip this would appear not to be the case, yet Samuel, son of Capt. William, in his will in 1707, mentions John Lowle (who was probably a grandson of Naomi) as "his kinsman." It would seem, therefore, that Naomi was a relative of William.—H. A. NEWTON, *of North Weymouth, Mass.*

Mr. Newton, of North Weymouth, the writer of the above note, furnished to Mr. John Torry, of Scranton, Pa., author of the Torrey genealogy, published in 1885, the matter in that book relating to the English ancestry of the New-England Torreys. (See REGISTER, vol. 40, page 236.) Mr. Newton had previously procured from England abstracts of most of the above Torrey wills.—EDITOR.

The foregoing wills seem to establish a pedigree of Torreys, viz.: 1, Philip, who died in 1604; 2, his son William, whose death is not yet found; 3, Philip, who died in 1621, leaving a widow Alice, and the four sons, who are undoubtedly the emigrants. The affidavits cited by Savage are recorded in Suffolk Deeds, vol. viii. p. 392, and are as follows:

"Phillip Torrey aged fifty nine years or thereabouts heeretofore of Combe St Nicholas in the County of Somersett within the Realme of England, there liveing untill the yeare sixteene hundred & forty, yeoman, in that yeare removeing to New England with William Torrey & Samuell his son, both of the s^d Comb St Nicholas with whome hee lived for severall years & beeing arived settled & hath ever since lived in Roxbury in the County of Suffolk in New England afors^d On his corporall Oath deposed that hee well knew & was acquainted with the s^d William Torrey the Father & Samuell Torrey his sonn all the whiles hee lived in Comb St Nicholas afores^d in old England & ever since hee came to New England and to this day, being in their company on his Oath affirms them to bee the same William Torrey & Samuell Torrey, father & sonn, aboves^d, haveing severall opertunities in each yeare to see & confer with them, ever since, they being both in good health this day, being the fifth of March 1673–4.

Taken upon Oath March 5th 1673–4, by Phillip Torrey, before us,
Richard Russell
Thomas Danforth"

"George Fry aged fifty eight years or thereabouts heretofore of Comb St. Nicholas in the Realme of England, husbandman, liveing there untill the yeare sixteene hundred & forty, in that yeare removed & came in the same shipp to New England with William Torrey & Samuell Torrey his sonn, both of the s^d Comb St Nicholas, & being arrived in New England setled & ever since have lived in Weymouth in the County of Suffolk in New England afores^d. On his Corporall Oath deposed that in old England for severall yeares untill the yeare abovesaid he was well acquainted with & knew William Torrey the Father and Samuell Torrey his sonn & ever since untill the day of the Date hereof, they & hee this deponent having lived in one Towne vizt in Weymouth in New England aboves^d & beeing with them in Boston in New England they are both in good health this day being the fifth of March 1673–4.

Taken upon Oath in Boston March 5th 1673–4 by George Fry, before us
Richard Russell
Thomas Danforth"

The reference in the will of widow Alice Torrey to her brother-in-law Thomas Lumbard, and the fact that her husband, in 1621, made Thomas Lumbert one of his overseers, may lead to the discovery of the ancestry of that family.

Thomas Lombard or Lumbard came here in 1630, according to Savage, with children including Bernard, who was born in 1607 or 1608. Both went to Scituate and thence to Barnstable. Deane (Hist. of Scituate, pp. 307–8) calls Bernard Lumbard "one of the men of Kent," and says that Richard L. was in Scituate in 1640, returning to Tenterden, Eng., on the strength of Elder Nathaniel Tilden's will. But that document (*ibid*, p. 355) does not bear this out, since it gives "to wife Lydia the income of my Stone house, with the lands in Tenterden in Kent, in which Richard Lambeth now dwells," etc. Certainly Lumbard or Lumbart is not the same name as Lambeth, nor even an easy corruption therefrom.

The will of Alice Torrey gives a much more promising clue for the origin of Thomas Lombard, as her brother-in-law would be the exact contemporary of the emigrant; and his success in settling here might well induce his presumed nephews to come over ten years later. It is rather strange that Philip Torrey in his deposition does not call William and Samuel Torrey, respectively, his brother and nephew, at a time when the avowal of the relationship would seem to greatly increase the value of his affidavit.

In the will of widow Alice Torrey, she makes Henry Dunster one of her overseers, and he witnesses. Mr. Newton has a memorandum from the Bishop's office at Exeter, of a marriage license granted 8 May, 1627, to Henry Dunster of Willsworthy and Anna Torry of Whitstaunton, co. Somerset. Our president of Harvard, Henry Dunster, was, however, born in Lancashire, and I merely note the coincidence of names.—W. H. WHITMORE.]

WILLIAMS (*ante*, pp. 3, 8):

[At the above references, Mr. Waters, in his GLEANINGS, gives abstracts of the wills of Jane Williams of Whetenhurst, Glouc., a sister of Richard Williams of Taunton, N. E., and that of Benjamin Williams of Stoke, near Guildford, Surrey, a nephew of Richard and Jane.

Upon the publication of these abstracts, Ex-Gov. Joseph Hartwell Williams of Augusta, Me., a descendant in the 7th generation from Richard Williams of Taunton, undertook to prosecute the investigation by correspondence, and obtained very gratifying results, which he gives in an article contributed by him to the *Maine Historical and Genealogical Recorder* for January, 1889 (issued December, 1890), pp. 255–62. We make the following extracts:

" In the Consistory Court of the Bishop of Gloucester was found the will of Samuel Williams, dated Sept. 26, 1668, proved in 1669. He was apparently a clergyman, for he gave to his son Benjamin his ' Book of Marters' and ' Perkins Works,' and to his son Nathaniel his ' Written Sermons.' He also mentions his ' brother,' James Adams (his wife's brother), his brother Richard Williams and his sister Elizabeth Williams, the Adamses again, and his cousins (nephews and nieces) the four Hall children.

" Next was discovered the will of William Williams of Synwell, a hamlet in Wotton-under-Edge. It was dated Sept. 26, 1618, and proved in the same year. It names sons Samuel and Richard, daughters Ann or Anna, Elizabeth and Jane. These are the same names as in the other wills, except that it is here found that the name of Mrs. Hall was Ann. The witnesses were William Martin, Robert Trotman and Francis Wright, the two former of whom are named as overseers. These are well-known names of families of high standing. The executor was Richard Tyndall (or Tyndale) of North Nibley, a relative of William, the translator of the Bible, who suffered martyrdom in Flanders.

" An examination of the register of the parish of St. Mary the Virgin in Wotton-under-Edge in Gloucestershire, brought to light the baptisms of the following children of William Williams: 'An,' daughter, Dec. 2, 1599; Richard, son, Jan. 28, 1606; Jane, daughter, March 19, 1608.

" There is also the record of the burial of William Williams, Sept. 29, 1618, and of Elizabeth Williams, Nov. 19, 1630. It was at first supposed that this Elizabeth might have been the mother of Richard; but as no wife is mentioned in the will of William, this is scarcely probable. Susanna Williams was buried Jan. 11, 1610, and she may have been the wife of William.

" The records show that Samuel Williams married Alice Knight, a widow, in 1637; that their son Samuel was baptized in 1638, their daughter Hannah in 1640 (died 1645), and their son Nathaniel in 1645; that the mother died in 1661, and the father in 1669. Samuel, Jr., died young, and the record of Benjamin's baptism has not been found."

An early genealogical manuscript, preserved in the Williams family, states that the wife of Richard Williams was " Frances Dighton, sister to Catharine Dighton, who was married to Governor Thomas Dudley." Gov. Williams finds corroboration of this statement. He finds a record that,

" February 11, 1632, Richard Williams was married to Frances Deighton of Gloucester in the Parish of Witcombe Magna."*

He finds also the will of John Deighton, father of the above Frances, dated Jan. 31, 1639, proved May 21, 1640, which " mentions his eldest son John, his

---

* Richard and Frances Williams had two children born to them while living in Gloucester: John, bp. March 27, 1634, and Elizabeth, bp. Feb. 7, 1635–6. Both died young.

eldest daughter Jane, his daughter Frances Williams, his daughter Katherine Haighburne, and his daughter Damaris, who was made residuary legatee." The following inscription found in St. Nicholas Church, Gloucester, we quote from the same article:

" Here lies interred the bodies of John Deighton of this city, gent., and Jane, his wife, daughter of Edward Bassett of Uley, by whom he had issue three sons and four daughters. He spent all his time in the study of chirurgery, and attained to great knowledge therein. He died 16 May 16[40], and she 23 April, 1631."

The registers of the same church show the christenings of his daughters, Frances, baptized March 1, 1611, and Katharine, baptized Jan. 16, 1614.

Katharine Deighton, baptized Jan. 16, 1614-5, married Samuel Hagburne or Haighburne. They came to New England and settled in Roxbury, where the husband died Jan. 24, 1643. An abstract of his will is printed in the REGISTER, vol. 2, pp. 261-2. She married 2d, Gov. Thomas Dudley, April 14, 1644, who died July 31, 1653. She married 3d, Nov. 8, 1653, Rev. John Allin of Dedham, who died Aug. 26, 1671. She died three days after, August 29. She had children by all her husbands. Gov. Joseph Dudley was one of her sons.

See also the address of the Hon. Josiah H. Drummond of Portland, Me. (also a descendant of Richard Williams), at the Quarter Millenary Celebration, June 4 and 5, 1889, of the founding of Taunton, Mass., pages 112 to 117 of the printed proceedings, where some of these and other facts relating to the Williams family are given.

Mr. Drummond contributed to the *Maine Historical and Genealogical Recorder*, April, 1889 (published Feb. 1891), pages 362-6, an article on the Dighton family, with particular reference to the descendants of Samuel and Katharine (Dighton) Hagburne. The will of Samuel Hagburne names " my brother Lugg." Mr. Drummond gives reasons for believing that this was John Lugg of Boston, who had a wife Jane, supposed by him to be Katharine Dighton's sister of that name.—EDITOR.

JOHN BEST, the son of Rowland Best of Twining, in the Co. of Gloucester, yeoman, and the son and heir of the said Rowland, deceased, do here declare this my last will and testament 18 June 1666, proved 4 May 1667. I give to John Best the younger, the son of John Best of Twining, and to his heirs, my lands which I purchased of Thomas Darke of Twyning 1654. I give to William Hancocke of Twyning gen^t, the son of William Hancocke of Breedon's Norton Esq. my part of a lease granted by the Dean and Chapter of Christ Church, Oxon of the Rectory and Parsonage of Twyning to Edwin Baldwin and John Porttman of Twyning for one and twenty years, the said John Porttman for himself, John Best, John Adams, Thomas Sparry and William Deaves &c. To Mary Hancocke, the wife of Richard Hancocke twenty pounds, a feather bed and bolster, a pair of sheets, a pair of blankets and my best coverlid. To William, Richard, Charles, John, George, Rowland and Septimus Hancocke, being the seaven sons of the said Richard Hancocke and Mary his wife, unto each of them twenty pounds apiece at their ages of one and twenty. To Thomas Best of the Kings home near unto the city of Gloucester, gardener, and seven of his children, vizt Thomas the younger, John, Edward and Samuel Best, Joane, Dorothy and Elizabeth Best, unto each of them ten pounds. To Susanna Hancocke, the wife of Richard Hancocke of Twyning, ten pounds. To Hester Best the daughter of the aforesaid Thomas Best of the Kings home, fifty pounds. To Anne Darke, the wife of Thomas Darke of Twyning, five pounds. To Charles Hancocke, gen^t. of the Middle Temple in London, ten pounds. To Thomas Best's two daughters of Breedons Norton, Avice Best and Mary Best, ten pounds apiece. To William Hancocke, the son of Edward Hancocke of Twyning, ten pounds. To Thomas Savidge and Richard Savidge, of the city of London, vintners, ten pounds apiece. To Richard Wittmore my servant forty shillings. "Item I give and bequeath unto Richard Lea, the sonne of Collonell Richard Lea, tenn pounds. Item I give and bequeath unto ffrancis Lea another sonne of Collonell Richard Lea, tenn pounds and my silver Tankard." To Elizabeth Richards widow, the wife of John Richards, carpenter, deceased, five pounds. To William Hancocke, the son of Thomas Hancocke of the city of Worcester, clothier, five pounds. To the poor of Twyning eight pounds. To John Best of Crombe, clerk, ten pounds. To John Best of the Stone seven pounds which he oweth us. To Sara Hancocke of the city of Worcester forty shillings. To George Best, the son of John Best of Twyning the remainder of my lease of a close of four acres in Twyning. To John Best of Twyning the younger, the son of John Best of Twyning the elder, all my goods &c unbequeathed: and I make him sole executor.   Carr, 58.

[Who can doubt that the "Collonell Richard Lea" mentioned in the above will was Col. Richard Lee of Virginia? His sons were named John, Richard, Francis, Hancock and Charles, a very significant array of baptismal names considered in connection with the names in this will. The pedigree of the family of Hancock of Twining (co. Glouc.) may be found in the Visitation of the County of Worcester, 1682–3, published 1883 (Walter C. Metcalfe, F.S.A.). It is perhaps needless to say that I shall bear the names of Best and Hancock in mind in connection with this problem. I have already secured a few notes about the Hancock family, and found evidence of a connection between Shropshire and Worcestershire in the will of one John Best in 1631.—H. F. W.]

December 1656. JOHN SPENCER. On ye thirtieth day issued forth Letters of Ad⁰ⁿ To Anne Fillioll Spinster ye sister by ye mothers side of John Spencer late att Jamaica in ye part beyond ye seas, Batchelor deĉd. To Administer all & singuler ye goods chělls and Debts of ye sayd Deĉd Shee being first sworne truely to administer &c., Penelope Spencer ye mother Thomas Spencer ye brother & Rachell Spencer the sister havcing in due forme of Law renounced ye sayd Adĉon of ye sayd deĉds goods. As by ye Acts of Court may appeare.   P. P. C. Admons 1656, folio 316.

[This is John Spencer, nephew and heir of John Spenser of Newbury, whose will, dated August, 1637, was proved at Salem, March, 1649. In Austin's Rhode Island genealogy, the nephew is mentioned as possibly identical with John Spencer of Newport (1661) and East Greenwich (1677). Circumstantial evidence pointed to this connection, and the work of Spencer genealogy, now in progress, has strongly favored it. Hence the importance of the discovery to Spencer family history.

Some other items about this line of Spencers in addition to those supplied in the will discovered last year by Mr. Waters (see REGISTER, Oct. 1890, vol. 44, page 391, ante p. 467), are the following.

The records of burial of the two brothers, John and Thomas, appear together in the parish register of Kingston-upon-Thames, co. Surrey, England, under date, 1648, June 28 and 29 respectively.

The neighboring parish of Chertsey has the baptisms of Thomas and Penelope's children. Their marriage took place Sept. 25, 1623, as recorded in register of St. Peter's, Paul's Wharf. Penelope's maiden name was Jernegan. She was baptized at Shalford, co. Essex, Oct. 24, 1591. (See Jernegan pedigree, in which her name appears in Suckling's Suffolk.)

A "Parliamentary Survey" made in 1650, of Russells alias Banisters [?] Farm, mentioned in the will of Thomas Spenser, is preserved at the Public Record Office in London.

The professional life of Thomas Spenser, younger son of Thomas and Penelope, was spent in Plymouth, co. Devon. He was a physician.

Some references to him may be seen in "The Western Antiquary," published at Plymouth in Devonshire.—RAY T. SPENCER.

The preceding admon. and notes were furnished me by Mr. Spencer of 18 Bedford Place, Russell Square, London, England.—H. F. W.]

SYLVESTER (*ante*, pp. 16–19, 544):—

[In the Proceedings Mass. Hist. Soc., Second Series, vol. iv. pp. 270–291, are twenty-six letters from members of the family of Sylvester, written between 1653 and 1683, several of them from Giles Sylvester in Barbados; communicated by Robert C. Winthrop, Jr., A.M., from the Winthrop Papers.—EDITOR.]

WILLIAMS, DIGHTON AND LUGG (*ante*, pp. 551–2):—

[Hon. Josiah H. Drummond, of Portland, Me., in his article previously referred to on the Dighton family in the *Maine Historical and Genealogical Recorder*, vol. 6, pp. 362–6, prints the following extract from a deed dated Feb. 11, 1713–14, sworn to March 4, 1713–14, and recorded in the Registry of Deeds for Bristol County, Mass.:

" EASTER MARSHALL, a widow four score years of age, living in Norton, whose maiden name was Hester Lugg, dau. of Mr. John Lugg and Jane Lugg his wife, who lived near the city of Gloucester in Great Britain, for and in consideration of the care which her son-in-law, John Hall of said Norton, hath for many years past taken of her in her old age, and that he continueth to take the like care of her, and hath obliged himself to provide for her all things necessary for her comfort during her natural life, and for other good causes and considerations especially moving," etc.   Gives all her rights, etc. in the estate of her honored father and mother, John Lugg and Jane Lugg, deceased, and in any other estate of her kindred and relatives which might come to her in Great Britain or New England, to her son-in-law John Hall, whom she appoints her attorney.

This proves that John Lugg and his wife Jane of Boston, came from the vicinity of the city of Gloucester, England, and with other known facts leaves little doubt that Jane Lugg, was a daughter of John Deighton and a sister of Frances wife of Richard Williams and of Katharine successively wife of Samuel Hagburne, Gov. Thomas Dudley and Rev. John Allin. Messrs. Lugg, Hagburne and Williams probably came from Gloucestershire to New England about the same time.

John Lugg settled at Boston.   His lands are recorded in the Book of Possessions (Record Commissioners' Second Report, part ii., second edition, page 29). They were on the southerly side of the present School street, on or near where the easterly end of the Parker House now stands.   His wife Jane was admitted to the First Church, Feb. 10, 1638–9 (Winsor's " Memorial History of Boston," vol. i. p. 572).—After his death his widow married Jonathan Negus.   On the 27th of October, 1647, Negus was " granted the inheritance of the house and ground of John Lug to the value of 20li that he may dispose of the same towards the education of his five children " (Mass. Col. Records, ii. 198).

Besides Esther, the maker of the deed, who must have been born in England, John and Jane Lugg had three children, born in Boston, where their births are entered on the town, and their baptisms on the church, records.   They were Elizabeth, b. 1638–9; Mary, b. 1642, and John, b. 1644.   Esther Lugg married 1st, James Bell.   For a record of their children see REGISTER, vol. 16, pp. 327–8. He was killed by the Indians in 1676, while laboring in the field in that part of Taunton now Raynham (Baylies's Memoir of Plymouth Colony, part 3, p. 192). His widow Esther married Richard Marshall, Feb. 11, 1676–7 (REGISTER, vol. 17, p. 236).   Of the children of James and Esther Bell, Mary, b. July 7, 1669. married July 19, 1693, Joseph Hall, ancestor of Capt. John W. D. Hall of Taunton, secretary of the Old Colony Historical Society.   Another daughter Esther, b. Aug. 15, 1672, married Dec. 14, 1692, John Hall of that part of Taunton which afterwards became Norton and then Mansfield.   He is the son-in-law mentioned in the deed.   For these facts I am chiefly indebted to a letter of Capt. Hall and the article by Mr. Drummond in the *Maine Historical and Genealogical Recorder*, vol. 6, pp. 362–6.

An article on the family of Williams of Wooton-under-edge appears in the *Gloucestershire Notes and Queries* for July, 1891, vol. v. pp. 92–6.   In the same magazine, Sept. 1891, vol. v. pp. 135–6, is an article by Mr. Conway Dighton of Cheltenham on the Deightons of Gloucestershire.—EDITOR.]

[The following wills of members of the Gyse or Guise family of Gloucestershire (See Heraldic Visitation of that county) will prove of interest through their mention of Washingtons and also of Haviland, with whom the Holworthy family and the Torrey family of New England were connected.—H. F. W.]

JOHN GUYSE of Elmore, Glouc., gen^t. 31 March 1614 proved 24 October 1614. To brother William Guyse the younger one hundred pounds. To my sister Havyland for life the use of fifty pounds and after her decease the principal to my brother William Guyse the younger. To brother Charles Guyse thirty pounds. To my sister Perrye twenty shillings, not that I love her less than any other but because God hath blessed her husband with so good an estate that she hath less need than the rest. The rest of my goods &c. to brother William Gwyse the elder whom I make my executor.   Lawe, 98.

WILLIAM GUISE of the City of Gloucester Esqre, 22 July, with a codicil 30 December, 1640, proved 31 May 1641. To the poor people of that city ten pounds to be distributed amongst them within three months. To my beloved brother Sir William Guise, knight, twenty shillings to buy him a ring. To the Lady Elizabeth his wife and my kind sister whom I have ever found loving to me and mine the like sum of twenty shillings to buy her a ring. To my dearly beloved wife my house at Gloucester wherein I live and the garden for one and thirty years, if she live so long. To my daughter Anne Guise towards her marriage portion three hundred pounds. To my daughter Elizabeth Guise three hundred pounds towards her marriage portion; these portions to be paid them at their several days of marriage or several ages of twenty and one years. To my servant Joyce Neale my wife's kinswoman ten pounds within one year. All the rest to my wife Elizabeth whom I make and ordain sole executrix of this my last will and testament "hartely praying her by that true and unfained love that wee have borne each to other and the mutuall comfortes wee haue enioyed each from other both to our soules and bodies, to haue a care of those o^r daughters the pledges of our unfained love and as shee hath hitherto dunne soe to continewe to breed them upp and instruct them in the feare of God soe shall wee all I hope one day meete againe to our everlastinge comforte in the kingdome of Heaven."
   The codicil is as follows:—I give to my kind brother Hauiland and sister and my nephew Matthewe Haviland to each of them twenty shillinges to buy them a ring. Item, I give to my trusty servant Richard Merrye forty shillings. Item I give to my servant Edward Wheeler forty shillinges. To my servant Richard Hancock the horse that his mother gave me when he came to me. To my servant Anne Nashe twenty shillings.
   In presence of Robert Haviland and Matthew Haviland.
                                                    Evelyn, 60.

WILLIAM GYSE, of Elmore (Glouc.) Esq. 10 November 1650, proved 14 September 1653. To be interred in the parish church of Elmore near my father. To my wife Cissely all my plate, household stuff and goods of what quality and sort soever, and one lease which my father (Sir William Gyse) purchased of Mr. Ockald for three of my brothers lives, vizt. George, Anthony and Edward Gyse, one of which lives is since deceased, viz. George &c. Other leases to her. To my eldest daughter Elizabeth Horton twenty shillings to buy her a ring. To my second daughter Ellinor Washington twenty shillings to buy her a ring to remember me. To my third daughter Frances Codrington twenty shilling &c. And I desire to have this poesy engraven in the inside of all their rings— *Vive ut Vivas.*— All the rest to my eldest son Christopher Gyse whom I make sole executor.

Brent, 41.

[A pedigree of the Havilands may be found in the Visitation of Gloucestershire (Harl. Pub. vol. 21, p. 78). Jane, daughter of Robert Haviland by Elizabeth (Gyse) was the wife of William Torrey of New England. See Haviland and Torrey wills, REGISTER, vol. 45, pp. 150–3; 298–302 (*ante*, pp. 496–9, 546–51).—H. F. W.]

WASHINGTON.

JOHN WOODWARD of Quinton, in the Co. of Gloucester, gen[t], 21 April 1612, proved 13 May 1612. My body to be buried in the parish church of Stratford upon Avon near to the grave there of my deceased father Richard Woodward gen[t]. To William Abraham, my godson, son of Richard Abraham of Quinton, Bucks, gen[t], my messuage or tenement in Stratford wherein Frances Woodward my mother now dwelleth.

Item, I give and bequeath unto Thomas Washington gen[t], my wife's brother-in-law, all that my pasture ground and meadow in Quinton, Glouc., for the term of one thousand years, he paying yearly unto Alice my wife, during her natural life one annuity of twenty pounds heretofore by me granted unto her, issuing forth of the said lands. To John Lane son of Nicholas Lane gen[t], five pounds. To John Perkins my servant ten pounds.

My wife Alice to be sole executrix and my uncle Thomas Woodward gen[t], my brother-in-law Richard Murden gen[t] and Nicholas Lane gen[t] to be overseers.

Fenner, 42.

[This John Woodward was the one who married Alice the widow of Mr. Walter Washington of Radway, Warwickshire (see the Washington Pedigree). Her will (1642–1647) has already been published (REGISTER, vol. 43, p. 412, Oct. 1889, *ante* p. 387). The above testator belonged to the family of Woodward of Butlers Marston (see Visitation of Warwickshire, Harl. So. Pub. pp. 119 and 227), being a son of Richard Woodward of Stratford upon Avon, and Frances, daughter and heir of Paiot. His wife Alice was a daughter of John and Katherine Morden *alias* Murden, of Morton Morell, Warr. (see same Visitation, p. 319).—H. F. W.]

CATHERINE CURTIS of Islipp in the Co. of Northampton "gen[t]," 6 December 1622, proved 17 June 1626. My body to be buried in the church of Islipp. To Mordant Washington, my godson and grandchild, the sum of fifty pounds to be employed and laid out for his best benefit and to be paid unto him, with a true account of the profits and gain thereof, when he shall come to the age of twenty and one years, and if he depart this life before his age of one and twenty years then my executor shall pay the aforesaid sum, with all profits by it made, unto the next child of my natural daughter Mary Washington when it shall come to the age of twenty and one years, whether the said child be a son or a daughter. I give to my natural son Philip Curtis and to my daughter Curtis his wife, to the first begotten by them the sum of fifty pounds, whether it be son or daughter, to be paid at the age of twenty and one years. I give unto my natural daughter Mary Washington the sum of thirty pounds. All the rest of my goods, moveables and chattels unbequeathed, my debts and mortuary paid and my body reverently brought to the grave, I give unto my natural and well beloved son Philip Curtis, my sole executor of this my last will and testament.

Michael Westfield was one of the witnesses.

Hele, 92.

[Mrs. Catherine Curtis was the mother of Mary, who was the first wife of Sir John Washington of Thrapston, knight (see the Washington Pedigree) and of Philip Curtis, who married Amy, one of the sisters of Sir John and of the Rev. Lawrence Washington, rector of Purleigh. The wills of Philip Curtis and his widow, Amy Curtis, have been already published (See REGISTER, vol. 42, pp. 403, 404, Oct. 1889; *ante*, p. 378-9).—H. F. W.]

RANALD GRAHME of Nunington, co. York, Esqr, 14 November 1679, with a codicil dated 25 May, 1680, proved 2 December 1685. Body to be buried within the parish church of Nunington. To my nephew Sir Richard Grahme of Netherby, co. Cumberland, Barr^t and to the Honorable the Lady Anne Grahme his wife the sum of fifty pounds betwixt them, to buy them mourning, and I do hereby recommend Charles Grahme, now eldest son of the said Sir Richard Grahme, to the care and kindness of my dearly beloved wife. Item, I give and bequeath unto Sir Richard Grahme of Norton Conyers in the Co. of York, Barr^t, and his now wife twenty pounds apiece to buy them mourning. To my nephew James Grahme, privy purse to his R. H. James, Duke of York, and to Dorothy his now wife twenty pounds apiece to buy them mourning, and I do hereby release to my said nephew James Grahme all such debts as he oweth me upon any account whatsoever. To Sir Henry Goodricke, knight and Barr^t, and to his now lady, my niece, twenty pounds apiece to buy them mourning, and moreover I give unto his said lady, my niece, my onyx ring which she formerly gave me. To my nephew Col. George Legg, and Barbara his now wife, and to his mother Elizabeth Legg and to William Villiers Legg, my godson, twenty pounds apiece to buy them mourning, and also to Susanna Wilson and her husband twenty pounds between them to buy them mourning. To the said Col. George Legg my diamond ring with four great stones in it set around with small diamonds, to hold, use and enjoy for the term of his natural life, and after his decease I give and bequeath the same to the said William Legg, his son, my godson, forever. To Sir John Churchman twenty pounds to buy him mourning. To Katherine Foster late wife of Captain Foster ten pounds to buy her mourning. To my sister Sands twenty pounds to buy her mourning and to her daughter Elizabeth Washington one hundred pounds. Also I do hereby give and bequeath unto Mrs. Penelope Washington and Mrs. Mary Washington ten pounds apiece to buy them mourning. To Mr. Thomas Jackson one hundred pounds and ten pounds more to buy him mourning. I do hereby release unto Edward Carleton the twenty pounds he oweth me and I do give him thirty pounds more, and five pounds more to buy him mourning. To Richard Grahme once my groom four pounds per annum payable quarterly during my wife's life. To Archibald Johnston once my butler twenty pounds and to John Grahme once my servant five pounds to buy him mourning. To the now Lord Bishop of Oxford, the now Lord Bishop of Exeter, to the Lord Chief Justice North and to his brother Dr. North, to Richard Allestry Dr. in Divinity and Provost of Eaton College, to Dr. Barwwick, to Sir William Wyld of London, Barr^t, Sir John Coell, Sir William Turner, Sir Robert Clayton, John Morris Esq., Matthew Johnson Esq., Col. Richard Grace, Mr. Charles Usher, Mr. George Usher, Mr. John Cooke, Mr. Broughton, Mr. Fothergill, Nathan Tilson, Mr. Christopher Conyers of Clifford's Inn, Mr. Robert Blanshard and Francis Child, to each of them a ring of the value of twenty shilling. To Christopher Story four pounds to buy him mourning. To my cousin Richard Grahme, principal of Clifford's Inn, London, one hundred pounds, and twenty pounds more to buy him mourning. To my cousin Jane Smith and her sister Sara Gregory five pounds apiece to buy them mourning. To old Dicke Grahme (annuity). To the poor of Nunington, West Ness and Stangrave, York, of Lewsham, Kent, and of St. Margaret's, Westminster. To William Charleton of Hasleside, Northumberland, and Elizabeth his wife, my niece. To Dame Mary Musgrave, widow, my niece, and to her son Sir Richard Musgrave of Heyton, Cumberland, and his sisters Frances and Catherine. To Sir Cuthbert Heron of Chipchase, Northumberland, and his lady, my niece, and their son Cuthbert. To Winifred Fisher who was the daughter of my master William Lathum, who was very kind to me when I was his apprentice. To my worthy friend Col. Edward Villiers. To Philadelphia Eston daughter to Peter Ladore my friend. To my nephews Fergus and Ranald Grahme and my niece Margaret Fenwicke. To my nephew William Grahme the sum of two hundred pounds, to be paid him within six months next after he shall be instituted and inducted vicar of the parish church of Lewsham, Kent. For the use of the poor in the parishes of Arthewrett and Kirk Andrews, Cumberland. To Ranald Grahme, coachman to my nephew Sir Richard Grahme. My little nephew Charles Grahme, son and heir apparent of my nephew Sir Richard Grahme of Netherby.

I make and ordain my worthy friend John, Lord Bishop of Rochester, my dearly beloved wife Susanna Grahme and Sir Richard Grahme of Netherby executors of my will &c., and desire my said nephew Col. George Legg and the said Richard Grahme of Clifford's Inn to be aiding and assisting to my said executors.   Cann, 150.

[The above testator belonged to a great border family of whom the Grahams of Esk, of Norton Conyers and of Netherby were branches. His wife Susanna, whose will has already been given (see REGISTER, vol. 42, p. 410, Oct., 1891; *ante*, p. 385), was a daughter of Sir William Washington (see the Washington Pedigree), a sister of Col. Henry Washington, governor of the "ever faithful" city of Worcester and a niece of the rector of Purleigh.—H. F. W.]

WILLIAM LEGGE of the parish of little Minories Esq. maketh his will as followeth, viz.: to his son William Legge 2000[li] at 21 years, to his daughter Susan L. 2000[li] at 18 years or marriage, they in the meantime to be maintained out of profits at discretion of executors, his son George Legg and Elizabeth his wife Executors, Harry Norwood Esq. and George Wharton Esq. trustees. Written according to the directions of the said Testator and approved by him in the presence of G. Wharton, H. Norwood, John Chambers.

A nuncupative codicil of the same day, declared that, as the real estate in Ireland was settled upon his son George in marriage, it was concluded needless to mention it in the Will. His sisters, being three, he recommended to his son George, who declared he will do as his father hath done formerly. He said he had several legacies to poor kindred, but, being desired to declare those legacies, he named no person, his spirits being spent and faint. Dated 11–8ber, '70, proved 18 February 1670.

On the 18th day of November, A.D. 1700, commission issued to the Lady Barbara, dowager Baroness Dartmouth, relict of George late Baron Dartmouth deceased, one of the executors named in the above will, to administer the goods &c of the said Col. William Legg deceased, left unadministered on account of the death of the said Baron Dartmouth, and for the reason that Elizabeth Legg, relict and the other executor, had departed this life.   Duke, 23.

Dear & Loving Sister,   Virginia, June yᵉ 22ᵈ, 1699.

I had the happiness to see a Letter which you sent to my Aunt Howard, who died about a year and a half ago; I had heard of you by her before, but could not tell whether you were alive or not. It was truly great joy to hear that I had such a relation alive as yourself; not having any such a one by my Father's side as yourself. My Father had one Daughter by my Mother, who died when she was very young, before my remembrance. My Mother had three Daughters when my Father married her, one died last winter, and left four or five children, the other two are alive & married and have had several children. My Mother married another man after my Father, who spent all, so that I had not the value of twenty shillings of my Father's Estate, I being the youngest & therefore the weakest, which generally comes off short. But I thank God my Fortune has been pretty good since, as I have got a kind and loving wife, by whom I have had three sons and a daughter, of which I have buried my daughter and one son. I' am afraid I shall never have the happiness of seeing you, since it has pleased God to set us at such a distance, but hoping to hear from you by all opportunities, which you shall assuredly do from him that is,

Your ever loving Brother
till death
Jnᵒ Washington.

If you write to me direct yours to me in Stafford county, on Potomack River in Virginia. Vale.

To Mrs. Mary Gibson, living at Hawnes in Bedf's. These sent with care.

[The above very interesting letter has been sent me by Mr. Worthington C. Forde (97 Clark Street, Brooklyn, N. Y.) It has first been published in his collection of Washington Wills (Historical Printing Club, Brooklyn, N. Y., 1891), as a foot note on page 25. Mr. Ford tells me that it is a copy, sent to the President, and it is undoubtedly genuine. It was evidently written by the son of Lawrence Washington, the immigrant, to his half sister Mary, daughter of Lawrence by his first wife (Mary Jones). It adds to our knowledge her married name. She was in all probability, the wife of Edward Gibson, Vicar of Hawnes, who died 11 May 1732, æt. 71.—M. I. (See Genealogia Bedfordiensis, by Frederick Augustus Blaydes, printed at the Chiswick Press, 1890). The father of Mr. Gibson, of the same baptismal name and likewise Vicar of this parish, was buried 25 April, 1690. He died 22 Apr. æt. 73. Mary Hazelden of Hawnes, in her will, dated 16 June, 1679, mentions her nephew Edward Gibson, minister at Hawnes, and his daughter Mary Butler, and sons Edward, John and Seth. To her niece Margaret, wife of Edward Gibson, she gave all her lands, plate and apparel, and constituted her sole executrix. The Register of Baptisms shows that the second Mr. Edward Gibson had a wife named Mary. This wife, Mary (Washington?), probably died before her husband, if I draw the correct inference from his will, which I found in Prerog. Ct. of Cant. (Bedford 163), executed 6 Jan. 1723, and proved 17 June, 1732. He calls himself "minister," mentions brothers John and Seth, the latter to be executor. Mother deceased. Granddaughter Mary Pemberton (her father deceased). Sons Edward and George. In 1732, at date of probate, George was of St. Martin's in the Fields, Midd., and Edward was of Hawnes.

I would suggest that the "Aunt Howard" of the letter, was the Martha Washington whom Col. John Washington, her brother, mentions in his will as having come to Virginia.—H. F. W.

Since the above copy was received from Mr. Waters, the letter of John Washington, June 22, 1699, has been annotated by Mr. Ford and printed in the New York *Nation*, October 15, 1891.

Hawnes, now spelled Haynes, is a parish in the hundred of Flitt, Bedfordshire, about four miles north east of Ampthill.—Editor.]

In the New York *Nation* for July 16, 1891, the editor quotes from a correspondent, who, we are informed, is Mr. N. Darnell Davis of Georgetown, Demarara, to the effect that the original manuscripts on which Walker's Sufferings of the Clergy is founded are preserved in the Bodleian Library, Oxford. " There are about 25 or 30 volumes in all. Of these some seven are of a biographical nature, consisting of letters from persons who gave facts set forth in the printed work." Mr. Davis being interested in the question of Washington's ancestry made a rapid glance over these volumes, which are not indexed, in the hope of finding the letter which gave a good character to Rev. Lawrence Washington of Purleigh, and possibly learning the name of the small living which he was allowed to hold. But he was unsuccessful. The next month Mr. Waters visited Oxford and examined the books with a better result, as is shown in a communication from Mr. Whitmore in the *Nation* for October 8th last; as follows :

" Following up the suggestion made in the *Nation* for July 16, 1891, that the manuscript authorities for Walker's ' Account of the Sufferings of the Clergy' were in the Bodleian Library, Mr. H. F. Waters has recently examined the volumes with gratifying results. He writes under date of Sept. 1, 1891 : ' This afternoon I came upon the chief letter upon which he [Walker] evidently depended for his information about the sequestered rector of Purleigh.' This letter, he adds—' was in worse order than anything I had been looking at. It, and two or three accompanying papers, had evidently suffered from dampness, and had been eaten, I think, by flies, perhaps by mice. The letter was probably written in 1706 (judging from the dates of those near it), but where from or by whom, there was nothing on the face of it to disclose at first sight. It was devoted to the cases of Mr. Cherry, Mr. Washington, and Mr. Wright of Witham. He spoke of Mr. Cherry, as having ' dwelt 20 miles from me.' A little further on he writes : ' The first visitation our diocesan made here at Easterford Kelvedon Mr. Cherry preached,' etc. Then comes this reference :

" ' I doe not remember that ever I knew or heard of Mr. Washington after he had been sequestered, but there was then one Mr. Roberts a neighbor of mine who was owner and patron of a parish so small that nobody would accept of his church (but with difficulty) and Mr. Roberts entertained Mr. Washington, where he was suffered quietly to preach. I have heard him and tooke him to be a very worthy pious man. I have been in his company there, and he appeared a very modest sober person, and I heard him recommended as such by several gentlemen who knew him before I did. He was a loyal person, and had one of the best benefices in these parts, and this was the onely cause of his expulsion as I verily believe.'

" Mr. Waters adds that against both paragraphs—viz., those relating to Mr. Cherry and to Mr. Washington—Walker had written, ' See last paragraph in this ——. J. W.' Turning to the last paragraph, where dampness and flies had done the most mischief, Mr. Waters could make out only the word ' Braxted.' A reference to Morant's ' Essex' showed that Braxted Parva was just such a poor, mean living, and that the patron was Thomas Roberts. The Visitation of Essex shows the Robertses to have been there for four generations in 1634. A comparison of handwritings showed that the writer of this letter was the Henry Ayloffe who wrote another letter in the same collection, under date of March 26, 1706, annotated by Walker as ' Esquire and Justice of the Peace.' As Morant says that the Ayloffes had their chief seat at Braxted Magna, this letter seems to be of the highest authority. There was a Henry Ayloffe, third son, born about 1630, according to the visitation of Essex, in 1634, who seems to be the writer. The early register of Little Braxted seems to be lost, but probably further search will give more particulars about Lawrence Washington there."*

Soon after this discovery, Mr. Waters was informed by his friend, Miss Walford, an experienced genealogist, of her discovery of the place and date of the burial of Rev. Lawrence Washington, as follows :

" 46 Gt. Coram' St., Russell Square, W.C.,

" *Dear Mr. Waters,*   15 Sept. 1891.

While searching the Register of the parish of All Saints, Maldon, Essex, I found the following entry which I am sure will interest you :

---

* The present rector of Little Braxted, the Rev. Ernest Geldart, has written to Mr. Whitmore that the old registers prior to 1730 are lost. The Roberts family is extinct, Thomas dying in 1680, when the estate passed to the Ayloffes.

'Mr. Lawrence Washington buried January 21, 1652.'
I therefore send you a note of it at once, hoping that you will make whatever use you please of it.   Yours very truly,

EMMA M. WALFORD.

Henry F. Waters, Esq."

Mr. Whitmore after announcing this discovery continues: "Maldon is but three miles north from Purleigh, and is an old and comparatively large town, the natural abiding place of anyone interested in Purleigh. The inference is irresistible that we have at last discovered the death of George Washington's last English progenitor. I may here add that Little Braxted is about six miles north from Maldon, lying just to the east of Witham. From Purleigh to Braxted is less than nine miles in an air line."

Mr. Whitmore notes that in the library of Mr. Samuel G. Drake was sold a book by that John Rogers, minister of Purleigh, who was ordered to pay Mrs. Washington a portion of the tithes (See REGISTER, vol. 45, p. 240; *ante*, p. 523). This book contained some autobiographical items, and he thought they might have some reference to Purleigh and asked if that or another copy could be found.

In a communicatian to the *Nation*, Oct. 22, 1891, Mr. Worthington C. Ford states that he has found a copy of the book inquired for in the library of the New York Theological Seminary, New York city, and he gives some interesting facts about the author derived from that volume. Nothing, however, is found relative to his predecessor, Lawrence Washington. This John Rogers was a son of Rev. Nehemiah Rogers of Messing, and a grandson of Rev. Vincent Rogers of Stratford Bow, traditionally descended from the martyr. He was father of John Rogers, a merchant of Plymouth, who was created baronet Feb. 21, 1698, and was ancestor of the late Lord Blachford. The book in Mr. Drake's catalogue bore the title " Ohel or Bethshemesh; a Tabernacle of the Sun," &c. Mr. Ford states that there is no printed title in the book he quotes from, but there is a written title, " Dod or Chartran, the Beloved," &c., and that " Ohel or Bethshemesh" is the heading of one division of the work. Col. Chester, in his life of John Rogers the martyr, pp. 287-8, gives both titles in his list of the author's works.

Another communication from Mr. Whitmore is printed in the *Nation* for Nov. 5, as follows :

" *To the Editor of the Nation :*

"" Sir: Since an English writer has seen fit to refer to the Rev Lawrence Washington of Purleigh as ' a drunken parson,' I have found great consolation in looking over the ' Annals of Evangelical Nonconformity in Essex,' by the Rev. T. W. Davids (London, 1863). The author has considerable to say about the Episcopal ministers who were expelled from their livings in 1643, doubtless for their loyalty, but ostensibly for other causes. He quotes the evidence in many cases. He cites (p. 246) the charge against Washington as a tippler and often drunk, but he also quotes the same charge against many others. I notice these cases: T. Punter (p. 232), Thurman (p. 233), Fairfax (p. 233), Hurt (p. 238), Turner (p. 239), Southen p. (239), Chamberlain (p. 242), Frost (p. 243), Staples (p. 245), Washington (p. 246), Lake (p. 247), Heard (p. 249), Laud (p. 249), N. Wright's curate (p. 250), Darnell (p. 251), Hull (p. 253), Brinsley (p. 341), Bird (p. 349), Beard (p. 350), Man (p. 380), Benson (p. 417), Nicholson (p. 422), Billio (p. 512), Deersley (p. 515), F. Wright (p. 518).

" Here there are twenty-five cases, where clergymen were deprived, in which this same charge of drunkenness is made. Considering the social habits of the time, and the fact that most of these, if not all, were also accused of excessive attachment to the cause of Episcopacy and monarchy, is it not evident that the charge is a mere pretext, and that Mr. Washington does not deserve to be singled out for opprobrium and judged according to recent standards or morals?

" From Mr. Davids's book I glean one or two interesting points. Thus he states (p. 302) in regard to Braxted Parva, " The return in 1650 is ' Mr. White was presented, but he hath left it about three years, and Mr. Roberts provides for the supply of the cure.' Lands. MSS. 459." Again (p. 156) he says of the Rev. Nehemiah Rogers of Messing, that he was sequestered at Bishopsgate in 1643 and at Ely in 1645. " He continued to preach, however, for three years at Little Braxted, for upwards of six at St. Osyth, where he is found in 1650, and ultimately became rector of Doddinghurst, where he died."

"It would seem, then, that Mr. Roberts had given this 'poor living' first, about 1645, to Nehemiah Rogers; then, about 1647 or 8, Mr. White was presented, but in place of him Lawrence Washington took it. It is certainly very curious that it was John Rogers, son of Nehemiah, who expelled Washington from Purleigh (p. 272), and that the latter was thrown upon the same charity which had supported Rogers's father. As Nehemiah and his son seem to have been on opposite sides, I presume that there was no retaliation in this.

"If, by any happy chance, the family papers of the Robertses of Little Braxted have been preserved, we may yet learn something of this patron of distressed clergymen. The first of the name at that place was Thomas, auditor to Henry VIII. His son was Clement, whose son Thomas married Alice Hobson and was alive in 1612. Then came Thomas, the owner in 1634, whose son Thomas was aged sixteen. As the father then had ten children, it seems probable that he deceased before the Civil War, and that it was the young man who was the friend of Nehemiah Rogers and Lawrence Washington.

"In 1660, among the signers of a petition to Gen. Monk, calling for peace and amnesty (Davids, p. 323), are Sir Benjamin Ayloffe of Great Braxted and Thomas Roberts of Little Braxted.

"Mr. Davids quotes as authorities Cole's MSS., Landsdowne MSS. 459, Add. MSS. 15660, 15669, and 15670, also Journals of the House of Lords, Journal of House of Commons, and State Paper Office files. He seems to say that many of the original papers in regard to these sequestrations are preserved. If so, we may yet find the petition of the wife of the rector of Purleigh, and learn her Christian name, or we may get a signature of the Rev. Lawrence Washington. Col. Chester's references, as quoted by Mr. Conway, are Harl. MS. 6244, in regard to the petition for tithes; and Pub. Rec. O. Charles I., W. 58, No. 29, as to the chancery suit.   w. h. w."

The English writer referred to by Mr. Whitmore is a correspondent of the London *Notes and Queries*, July 11, 1891, page 23, who writes under the signature of "Vernon." Among other things, Vernon speaks of some deeds which she had lately copied, one of which "puts beyond a doubt" that Sir John was the eldest son of Lawrence Washington of Sulgrave. This confirms a suspicion of Mr. Waters, which he communicated to me some two years ago. "Vernon" is Mrs. Vernona I. C. Smith of Barnes, Surrey, England, as appears by her letter to the *Nation* for November 26. In that letter she states that the documents relating to the Washingtons, referred to by her in *Notes and Queries*, have been sent to an American friend. I hope that this gentleman will give the substance of them to the public in due time.

The Rev. Edward D. Neill, D.D., of St. Paul, Minn., has contributed to the *Nation*, Nov. 19, 1891, further details relative to the family of William Brodhurst of Lilleshall, Shropshire, whose son Walter's widow, née Ann Pope, was the second wife of John Washington (*ante*, pp. 414, 443). The baptisms of the children of the second Walter Brodhurst, half-brother of Lawrence Washington, are given by Dr. Neill, from the parish register at Lilleshall, as are the inscriptions on the tombstones of two of them.

It will be remembered that Col. Chester at one time was very anxious to obtain a copy of the signature of John Washington, the emigrant, to compare with that of John W., of London, on a deed dated in 1657, as was stated by Col. Chester in the *New York World* March 29, 1879, and repeated by us in the REGISTER, vol. 45, p. 203 (*ante* p. 527). By the expressions which he used, it was understood that this deed was in Col. Chester's possession, and his executor, Mr. Cockayne, has kindly made thorough but futile search for it. By a letter received recently from Mr. James Coleman, of Tottenham Terrace, London N., it seems that he advertised this deed in his catalogue, vol. xii. No. 119, for 1877. He sold it to Col. W. Newsome, R. E., before Col. Chester arrived; but, as it had not been delivered, Col. C. was able to make an abstract and to trace the signature. Col. Newsome, in 1879, printed privately a tract entitled "Yorkshire as the Home of the Washingtons." (See REGISTER, vol. 44, p. 200; *ante*, p. 447.) He cites this deed, without saying that he owned it. From the catalogue kindly furnished us by Mr. Coleman we copy the description. It was a deed, dated 1657, signed by John Washington, citizen and draper, and Margaret his wife, one of the daughters of Henry Harwood, gent., to Robert Abbott, citizen and scrivener, relating to houses near Fleet Bridge, London. Newsome adds the precise date of the deed, June 5, 1657, and states that Margaret was one of six children, the others being Thomas, Henry, Frances, Martha and Mary Harwood; and that their mother was named Martha. It seems that Col. Newsome's papers are not at present accessible; but now that we know that Col. Chester had only an abstract and a tracing of a signature, these may possibly be found in his papers. The admissions to the Drapers' Company, if still preserved, should show the parentage of this London man. Of course, we can now refer to the original signature of Col. John Washington of Virginia, on his will. A facsimile of this signature will be found in vol. 45 of the REGISTER, facing page 199 (*ante* p. 522). Col. Chester stated in the *New York World* that he knew the history of the London John Washington.

Two pamphlets on the genealogy of the Washington family have lately appeared, the titles of which will be found in the Book Notices in this number. One, by Col. Thornton A. Washington of Washington, D. C., gives the descendants of the elder emigrant John Washington in the line of President Washington, and continues it in the line of the president's eldest full brother, Samuel. The other is by Rev. Horace Edwin Hayden, M.A., of Wilkes-Barre, Pa., and is devoted to the descendants of the younger emigrant Lawrence.—EDITOR.

THE last will and testament of RICHARD GREGSON deceased the 21 August 1640, proved 31 August 1640. My dead body to be buried in the church of St. Augustins St. Austin's Gate as near and as conveniently as I may unto the bones of my deceased wife. To Ephraim Udall of this parish forty shillings. To my father in law Mr. Nicholas Hurt and unto Mrs. Dorothy his wife and to my dear and loving brother Mr. Henry Gregson and unto Edith his wife, to Mr. William Dickins, Mr. John Goddard, Mr. Robert Lewis and Mr. Thomas Haford, to every several person thus named twenty shillings apiece. To George Gregson that liveth in Paternoster Row five pounds. To my servant Anne Hill all the money that she oweth me (to be made up twenty shillings). To Mary Arnold my now nurse ten shillings.

I give and bequeath unto my kinsman Thomas Gregson, my now partner, and to his wife Mary and to Mr. Thomas Horne twenty shillings apiece and to Thomas Gregson in New England twenty shillings. To Nichõ my eldest son whatsoever shall be recovered of Roger Stephens and George Burtun or from either of their estates &c. The remainder of my estate shall be equally divided unto my aforesaid son Nicholas, John, Thomas, Anne and Elizabeth, equal shares, part and part alike. To my now partner Thomas Gregson fifty pounds in full satisfaction of what money he doth pretend he hath lent unto my cousin Thomas Gregson in New England and unto me his natural uncle. To my cousin Richard Gregson of Bristol one judgment confessed by one Samuel Oldfield unto Thomas Gregson, which the said Thomas assigned to me; also one deed or indenture made over by one Roger Clisant, vintner, of Bristol concerning two houses in that city &c. My son Nicholas to be sole executor, my father in law Mr. Nicholas Hurt, my brother in law Mr. Roger Hurt, my natural brother Mr. Henry Gregson, Mr. John Goddard citizen and grocer of London, my first cousin Mr. William Dickens gen^t, Mr. Robert Lewis, citizen and grocer, and Mr. William Baker an attorney at the King's Bench, to be overseers.

Coventry, 116.

[Thomas Gregson or Grigson of New Haven, Ct., according to Savage (vol. 2, pp. 315-6), "came from London to Boston 26 June, 1637, in company with Gov. Eaton and John Davenport, was one of the chief men, an active merchant and an Assistant of the Colony, first treasurer and first commissioner for the union with the other N. E. colonies, lived on the east side of the harbor, sailed in January, 1646, for London with Lamberton and ' divers other godly persons' of whom nothing was ever heard, the little vessel having no doubt foundered." (See Winthrop's New England, ed. 1853, vol. ii., pp. 325-6; Johnson's Wonder

Working Providence, pp. 124, 214–5; and Mather's Magnalia, ster. ed., vol. i. pp. 83–4.) He left a widow Jane, who lived to June 4, 1702, one son Richard, and, it is said, eight daughters.

His son Richard[2] Gregson settled at Bristol, England, and *his* son William[3] of London had a son William[4] also of London, who March 26, 1736, conveyed to Rev. Jonathan Arnold of New Haven, land in New Haven, formerly the property of his ancestor, Thomas[1] Grigson, for building and erecting a church thereupon. On the 26th October, 1768, William[5] Grigson of Exeter, a great-great-grandson of Thomas, quitclaimed the property to Trinity Church (Ibid. 57. The deeds are printed in the Collections of the New Haven Colony Historical Society, vol. 1, pp. 76–8. See also pp. 48–53, and vol. ii. p. xix.)— EDITOR.

Mr. Thomas Gregson — (name pronounced as if spelled Grixson), New Haven, one of the first comers, "came," etc., as in Savage. Freeman 18 Feb. 1639–40, truckmaster 23 Oct 1640, deputy 29 Oct 1640, treasurer May 1641, commissioner 6 Apr 1643, magistrate 26 Oct. 1643, oath of fidelity 1 July 1644. Sailed to procure patent in Jan. 1645–6.

Inventory taken 2 Nov. 1647, presented 7 Dec. 1647: Land in 1st Div. West-meadow £16,5; land on further side of W. Meadow £5,15; 21A Meadow £21; Dwelling house and home lot £48; little house and barn £35. Estate Dr. to Mr. Stephen Goodyear, Mr. John Evance, Henry Lindelle, Mr. Wm Hawkins, Mr. Davenport, Mrs. Lamberton, Mr Malbon, Edward Wigglesworth, Thomas Wheeler, Mr. Butler, Mr. Ling, Mrs. Turner, £126,3. Estate Cr. by Philip Leeke, Burwood of Stratford, Adam Nichols (an adventure in the *Susan* to Barbadoes), Jno. Gregory, £18,7. Real Estate, £246; Personal Estate, £225,19. Total, £490,6. Clear Estate, £364,3. Prized by Matthew Gilbert and Richard Miles. (Page 12, vol. I., part 1, New Haven Prob. Rec.)

Distribution, 2 Apr. 1716, to heirs of only son Richard, heirs of Mrs. Anna Daniells, heirs of Susanna Crittenden, heirs of Rebeckah Bowers, heirs of Sarah Whitehead, daughter Phebe Russell. Page 397, vol. iv., New Haven Prob. Rec.

He left a widow Jane, who died 4 June 1702. Her will, dated 5 Feb. 1691–2, "being aged and weak," "to be buried by her executrix and dear relatives," to "daughter Anna Daniel, my house and homelot and the remainder of my upland not yet disposed of at my farm on the east side of New Haven harbor (about 30A.), unless some of the children of my son Richard Gregson in England come over" (in which event such child is to have them after her death); "and to daughter Anna Daniel my meadow at my said farm for life, then to her daughter," to "daughter Mary in England 30A of my Third Division near the Sperries' farm," "also to daughter Anna Daniel 6 or 7A of meadow near West-field for life, then to those of the children that need it most," to "grand-child Ruth Frisbie of Branford 14A of my East Side farm also 15A of said farm to daughter Susannah Crittenden," to "daughter Phebe, 40A in the Third Division," to "grandchild Elizabeth Winston, 8A of meadow and 10A of the Third Division," to "grandchild Joanna Thompson, 9A of Third Division and 5A in the Quarter by the west lane after my daughter Daniel's decease," to "grandchild Rebecca Thompson, 6A meadow at Westfield (so called) now in her possession and 10A of Third Division," to "great-grandchild Elizabeth Glover that now lives with me, 9A in the Neck," to "the four children of my daughter Whitehead, 6A of Third Division each," daughter Daniel to have all movables in the house and be executrix. Witnesses: Wm. Peck and John Jones. Codicil (verbal) made a short time after the will. 6A of meadow to daughter Daniels and after her death to *her* daughter Joanna and her children, viz. 3A at South End and 3A at the West Side, also 3A of meadow at South End to daughter Susanna Crittenden. Witness Hannah Falconer Witnesses sworn in Court 30 July 1702. (Page 298, vol. ii., New Haven Prob. Rec.).

Inventory taken 4 Aug. 1702. House and homelot £80, meadow on the West Side cove £24, meadow on the East Side £30, land on East Side untaken up £15, Third Division land £27. Total £198. Debts unknown. Prized by Thomas Tuttle and Nathaniel Boykin.

Distribution to Mrs. Ruth Frisby alias Hoadly, Joanna Thompson, Mrs. Susanna Crittenden and Mrs. Mary Wyke. (Page 223, vol. iii., New Haven Prob. Rec.)

Anna is also called Hannah in the town record of her marriage, and in July, 1649, Hannah and Rebecca Gregson are witnesses in a trial. I have arranged the children as follows:

i. RICHARD, was seated in 1656. Returned to England and lived in Bristol.
ii. ANNA, m. [1651] Stephen Daniels.
iii. REBECCA, m. Rev. John Bowers.
iv. SUSANNA, m. 13 May 1661, Abraham Crittenden,
v. SARAH, m. (1) 12 Dec. 1667, John Gilbert; m. (2) 9 May 1676, Samuel Whitehead.
vi. MARY, bapt. 26 Jan. 1639–40, returned to England; m. ———— Wyke.
vii. PHEBE, bapt. 15 Oct. 1643; m. (1) 1673, Rev. John Whiting, of Hartford; m. (2) 1692, Rev. John Russell, of Hadley.
viii. ABIGAIL, bapt. 23 Feb. 1644–5.

FRANCIS B. TROWBRIDGE, of New Haven, Ct.]

JOHN MAPLETT of the city of Bath, Somerset, Doctor in Physick, 13 April 1670, proved 7 February 1670. I give and bequeath unto my dear sister Mrs. Mary Gorton of New England the sum of twenty shillings, and to each of her children I give the sum of ten shillings apiece. I give and bequeath unto my dear sister Mrs. Elizabeth Ham of London, widow, the sum of twenty shillings. To my dear daughter Anne Maplett the sum of four hundred pounds to be paid her at the day of her marriage if so be she marry with her mother's good liking and consent, otherwise only five pounds. To her younger sister my daughter Elizabeth the sum of three hundred pounds (on same condition). To my aforesaid daughter Anne Maplett all that portion of land and houses in Bristol brought to me by her mother at our marriage, being formerly part of the estate of her brother Mr. Walter Williams (after the decease of her mother). To my wife my house in Bath with the tenement and gardens thereto belonging all lately bought of Mr. Thomas Fisher, to be her own forever and at her sole disposal. She to be sole executrix. Signed, declared and published 31 July 1670. Duke, 24.

[This will was found long ago and forgotten. It should have accompanied the will of Mrs. Mary Mayplett, the mother of the testator, published in the REGISTER for October, 1890 (vol. 44, p. 384, <i>ante</i>, p. 461). Mrs. Gorton's husband was the famous religious disturber, Samuel Gorton.—H. F. W.]

SYMON WINGE of St. Clement's Danes, tailor, 28 July 1625, proved 6 February 1626. To my wife Rebecca one hundred pounds due unto me from Mr. Bryam Palmes of ———— in the Co. of Northampton gen^t, and sixteen pounds due unto me by Mr. William Palmes gen^t. and six pounds owing me by Mr. Stafford Palmes and six pounds and a crown due unto me from Sir Archball Dugles. To Jane my daughter forty pounds owing unto me by Mr. Samuel Heale of Fleet in Devonshire gen^t. and five pounds ten shillings due and owing me by Mr. Holmes of Carshalton in Surrey gen^t. and also four pounds due unto me by Henry Arthur of Ivybridge gen^t. and forty-two shillings owing me by Mr. Edward Rosse the younger of Ashwell in Rutland and five pounds due unto me by Mrs. Dennys for rent. To my sister Bridget Smithe twenty shillings. To my godson Henry Croswell ten shillings. To my brother John Winge ten shillings if he be living. To John Cathin of Barroe in Rutlandshire five shillings. To my said daughter seven and twenty pounds owing me by bond and fourteen pounds owing me upon books by Thomas Grove of ———— in Wiltshire gen^t. To my brother Matthew my cloth hose and canvas doublet. To my sister Elizabeth ten shillings. To my uncle Stevens and his wife twenty shillings. To Thomas Cooper one of my executors my writing deske. I do make John Meader of St. Andrew's Holborn, tailor, and Thomas Cooper of Clifford's Inn gen^t. my sole executors and to each of them forty shillings. Skynner, 24.

JOHN BURNELL, citizen and clothworker of London, 15 December 1603, proved 16 August 1605. My body to be buried in the parish church of Stanmore the Great. My goods &c to be valued, appraised and divided into three equal parts, according to the ancient and laudable custom of the city of London. The first part to my wife Barbara for so much due to her by the said laudable custom. The second part I devise and appoint to my five children amongst them equally to be divided; and the third part I reserve to myself and to my executrix towards the payment of my funeral charges and of such legacies as I have herein devised. Then follow sundry bequests to the poor and to his guild &c. To wife Barbara one thousand pounds. To eldest son John one thousand pounds. To brother in law Tevis Cruse, remaining in Dantzic, a ring of gold with a death's head thereon of the value of four pounds. To my brother Mr. John Cage and to my sister his wife, each of them, a mourning gown. To my cousin Richard Cage his son a mourning cloak, and to his wife a mourning gown. To my brother in law John Swifter, mercer, and Curdela his wife, to each a mourning gown. "Item, I give to my son in law Thomas Morley and Katherine, his wife, my daughter, to each of them a mourning gowne." To my son in law Richard Ball and Ann his wife, my daughter, to each of them a mourning gown. To my cousin Barbara Russell, widow, a mourning gown and forty shillings yearly, during life. To my cousin Salomon Coke six pounds, thirteen shillings four pence and a mourning cloak. To my cousins Mary Church and —— Willowbee of Dover, widows, forty one shillings apiece. To Mr. Willowbee, parson of Stanmore, a mourning gown. To sundry servants. To Hilson Swifter, my wife's sister's son, five pounds. To my good friend Mr. Robert Cogan a ring of gold with a death's head worth three pounds. To Elizabeth Morley, my goddaughter and grandchild, fifty pounds in money and unto Katherin Morley, sister of the said Elizabeth, forty pounds, and unto Ann Morley, another sister, forty pounds, to be paid them at their several ages of seventeen or at their several days of marriage. To Katherin Ball, another of my grandchildren, forty pounds in money. To my wife Barbara my manor of Stanmore the Great in the co. of Middlesex, in as large and ample manner and form as I now enjoy the same by virtue of an assignment thereof made unto me by and from John Koyn Esq. and Katherine his wife, with remainder to my son John &c. To my son John my copyhold messuage or tenement and eight acres of land in Stanmore now in the tenure or occupation of Ann Bluitt, widow, or her assigns, and thirty acres in my own occupation. To son Thomas the copyhold tenement &c. called Fiddell's (with certain land). To son William for ever my lease of two messuages &c in Stanmore the less, and freehold and appurtenances in Hendon. The remainder to be divided among my three sons, John, Thomas and William, and my two daughters, Katherine wife of Thomas Morley and Ann wife of Richard Ball. The seven hundred pounds each which I have given to my two sons in law, in marriage with my daughters, shall be considered parcells of my daughters' portions. My wife Barbara to be executrix and my brother in law Mr John Cage and my sons in law, Thomas Morley and Richard Ball to be overseers. Thomas Morley one of the witnesses.   Hayes, 58.

In a codicil made 28 March 1604, reciting certain statutes or recognizances, indentures of covenants, indentures of defeazance and obligations or deeds obligatory, he appoints his friend Thomas Gourney of London, Esq. sole executor for and concerning the said statutes or recognizances, &c. Proved 2 December 1605.   Hayes, 85.

JOHN BURNELL, citizen and clothworker of London, 18 February 1621, proved 23 January 1622. My estate to be divided into three parts according to the custom of London, one of which I give and bequeath unto my loving kind and faithful wife, as her due per the said custom. One other third to be divided equally amongst my children then living, and the other third part I give and bequeath as followeth. Then follow certain legacies and bequests to the poor of Barking parish (if dwelling there at the time of my death) to be bestowed in seacoles at the fittest season of the year and reserved in store for them till the winter and then sold to the needy at cost price. To poor children at Christ's Hospital and the poor in St. Bartholomew's and St. Thomas' Hospital, the poor in Ludgate and the two compters in London, the poor of Stanmore magna " where I was born" &c &c. To wife Ann, eldest son John, eldest daughter Barbara Burnell, second daughter Ann Burnell, third daughter Katherine Burnell, fourth daughter Elizabeth Burnell and son Thomas Burnell. To my virtuous and loving mother Barbara Burnell " for the remembraunce of a sonne which whilst he liued truely honored her and desired nothinge more then her quiet peace and good, and her loue againe was noe lesse towardes me and mine." To my brother Thomas Burnell. To my brother William Burnell. To my sister Katherine Morley and my sister Ann Ball (her husband deceased). To good wife Hall of Stanmore and her children. To Philip Hill of London, widow, and Winefrith Lyle. My brother and sister Morley. My servant Edward Josselin, goodman Fleminge, Mr. Edward Abbott our vicar of Barking. To my mother in law Jone Brownerigg a diamond ring, the first gift I gave her daughter my wife. My mother in law Ann Wealch. My wife Ann and my brother Thomas Burnell to be executors and the Right Worshipful and my especial kind friend Sir Thomas Coventry* knight, II. M. Attorn. Gen. and my brother in law Thomas Morley to be overseers.

Swann, 7.

BARBARA BURNELL of Great Stanmore, Midd., widow of John Burnell, merchant, deceased, 27 June 1631, proved 18 January 1631. Aged and weak. To be buried in the parish church of Stanmore as near the body of my late husband as conveniently may be. To Christ's Hospital, St. Thomas Hospital, St. Bartholomew's Hospital and the poor therein. To the four prisons of Ludgate, Newgate and the two Compters in London and the poor therein. To the Co. of clothworkers of London, they to provide for a distribution of twelve pence a week in bread to the poor of the parish of Stanmore every Sunday in the year, and one pennyworth thereof to the parish clerk of Stanmore, and to pay the said parish clerk of Stanmore two shillings " to thintent" that he shall keep the monument of my said husband and myself now standing and being in the church of Stanmore clean without dust, also to provide four pounds six shillings in woollen cloth to make yearly six waistcoats and six safeguards for six poor women, and five pounds a year to a poor scholar of Oxford who intendeth to profess divinity. To my brother Swister and his daughters each a mourning gown and to Barbara his daughter, my goddaughter three pounds to make her a ring. I give to my son Morley in money twenty pounds and to my daughter, his wife, my silver bason and ewer parcel gilt, my three gilt bowles, my broadest " shole" to lay spoons on, parcel gilt, my porrenger, parcel gilt, and my silver sugar box and the spoon used to it &c. To my daughter

---

* His brother in law (See Pedigree of Sebright in the Harleian Society's Visitations of Essex, Vol. 13, p. 289).—H. F. W.

Ann Ball &c. I give to my son Morley and his wife and to my daughter Ball and their sons and daughters, mourning cloaks and gowns. I also give to my two daughters Katherine and Anne my wearing linen &c. To the children of John Burnell my late son deceased five hundred pounds. My executor to sell my "shoverfeet" to set glasses on, my twelve apostle spoons, my spout pot, my little "haunce" pot (& certain other silver &c) to the utmost value he can. To sons Thomas and William (certain articles of silver &c). To cousin Thomas Freeman and his daughter Barbara. To my cousin Gates, my cousin Robinson, my cousin Young and my cousin and the children which I shall be godmother and great-godmother unto and the children which I am or shall be great-grandmother unto and not godmother. To my sons Thomas and William all my linen at my son Morley and my daughter Ball's several houses in London. To Thomas Morley, son of my son Morley, to Barbara Ball, my daughter Ball's daughter, and to Thomas Burnell, son of my son William, thirty pounds apiece. To all the children of my sons and daughters. To Elizabeth, now wife of my son William. Thomas and James Morley, sons of my said son Morley. My son Thomas Burnell to be executor and my son Morley overseer.   Audley, 7.

[In my GLEANINGS for 1884 (REGISTER, vol. 38, p. 419, *ante*, p. 79), I gave an abstract of the will of Thomas Burnell of this family, who referred to his nephew John Morley as "resident in New England." I have no doubt that this reference is to John Morley of Charlestown, although he had been dead about five months when the will of his uncle Thomas Burnell was written. In his own will, proved 2d 2d mo. 1661 (Middlesex Prob. Reg. Mass.) he mentions wife Constant, sister Mrs. Ann Farmer and mother Mrs. Katherine Morley deceased, and devises housing and lands in the manor of Cheshunt, Herts, England, to his wife for her life and then to his sister Mrs. Farmer.

The following pedigrees, taken from the Visitation of London (1633, 34, 35), Harleian Society Publications, vol. 17, p. 111; vol. 15, p. 123, show his lines of ancestry, both paternal and maternal.

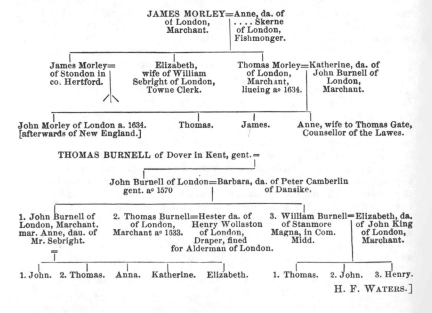

H. F. WATERS.]

MANY readers of Waters's "Genealogical Gleanings in England" have made inquiry as to the significance of the surnames appended to the abstracts of the several wills printed in this series of articles. The answer is that the names indicate the volumes where the wills are to be found. Instead of the volumes of the registers of wills of the Prerogative Court of Canterbury being numbered, as those of our own Probate records are, they are labelled and referred to by surnames. The editor of the REGISTER asked Mr. Waters to write out for publication in his "Gleanings" an explanation of this plan. He said he would willingly do so, but that his friend J. Challenor Covington Smith, Esq., superintendent of the literary department of the Probate Registry, Somerset House, London, could give a fuller and more reliable statement, and advised the editor to invite Mr. Smith to prepare such a paper. That gentleman, who has taken much interest in Mr. Waters and his researches as well as in the REGISTER, consented to do this, and has prepared the following paper which gives much valuable information concerning the principal Probate registry of England.—EDITOR.

Will-registers of the Prerogative Court of Canterbury.

From time immemorial these MS. books have been labelled with, and identified by, names—not numbers nor dates. The inaccuracy, and consequent inconvenience, inseparable from the use of numerals for such purposes sufficiently show the advantage of (and perhaps the reason for) the method adopted in the prerogative office.

No doubt it was found impracticable to adhere rigidly to any particular plan in selecting names for the successive volumes, but at any rate the designations were, from whatever cause, chosen on different systems at different periods.

With the exception of book "Crumwell," the 54 earliest registers bore the names of the testators whose wills happened to occur first in the respective volumes.

Register "Crumwell" (1536–40) took that title from Thomas Crumwell,* at that time the King's Vicegerent in ecclesiastical (including of course testamentary) matters. This volume is, in many respects, distinct from the main series, and there is a strong presumption that it represents a jurisdiction which the Vicegerent claimed and exercised, independent of the Archbishop's prerogative.

From and after the 55ᵗʰ volume ("Peter") the registers down to 1650 are still, with a few exceptions, named from the first will occurring in the book, but it had become customary to place in that position the will of either a peer, a knight, or some deceased official of the court.

---

* His surname is repeatedly thus spelt in the preamble to this register, though it is usually written "Cromwell" and mis-pronounced accordingly.

From 1651 to 1840 the names given to the yearly registers were taken arbitrarily from the lists of wills proved during the respective years, such names being usually those of persons distinguished in the State, Church, Army, Navy, Law, etc., but the nomenclature during the latter part of the period in question was derived in large proportion from the surnames of proctors and other officials of the Prerogative Court.

It is to be borne in mind that when in process of time the number of wills proved in the year became too large to allow of the transcripts being bound in one volume, the same distinguishing name was applied to the whole of the volumes, few or many, pertaining to the particular year.

From 1384 to 1840 inclusive there are 1938 of these bulky volumes; at the extinction of the ecclesiastical court (Jan. 11, 1858), the number had increased to 2263; and at the end of 1888 the total was 2821.

These few notes are to a great extent founded upon information collected some time ago by Mr. George H. Rodman and very kindly placed at my disposal.

J. C. C. Smith.

In the spring of 1891 Mr. Smith prepared a table giving the numbers of the Calendars, the names of the Registers and the years included in the several Registers. He had a few copies printed for the use of himself and his friends. By his permission we reprint the table below :

No. of Calr.	Date.	Name of Register.	No. of Calr.	Date.	Name of Register.	No. of Calr.	Date.	Name of Register.
	1384. } 1452. }	Rous		1533-36.	Hogen		1569.	Sheffelde
				1537-39.	Dyngeley		1570.	Lyon
	1401-23.	Marche		1540-41.	Alenger	4	1571.	Holney
	1423-49.	Luffenam		1541-43.	Spert		1572.	Daper
	1454-62.	Stokton		1544-45.	Pynnyng		1573.	Peter
	1463-68.	Godyn		1546-47.	Alen		1574.	Martyn
1	1471-80.	Wattys		1548-49.	Populwell		1575-76.	Pyckering
	1479-86.	Logge		1550.	Coode		1576.	Carew
	1487-90.	Milles	3	1551.	Bucke		1577.	Daughtry
	1491-93.	Dogett		1552.	Powell		1578.	Langley
	1493-96.	Vox		1553-54.	Tashe		1579.	Bakon
	1496-00.	Horne		1554-56.	More		1580.	Arundell
	1500-01.	Moone		1556.	Ketchyn		1581.	Darcy
	1501-03.	Blamyr		1557.	Wrastley		1582.	Tirwhite
	1504-06.	Holgrave		1558.	Noodes		1583.	Rowe
	1506-08.	Adeane		1558-59.	Welles		1583-84.	Butts
	1508-11.	Bennett		1559.	Chaynay		1584.	Watson
	1511-14.	Fetiplace		1559-60.	Mellershe		1585.	Brudenell
	1514-17.	Holder		1561.	Loftes		1586.	Windsor
2	1517-20.	Ayloffe		1562.	Streat		1587.	Spencer
	1520-22.	Maynwaryng		1563.	Chayre		1588.	Rutland
	1523-25.	Bodfelde		1564.	Stevenson		1588-89.	Leicester
	1525-28.	Porch		1565-66.	Morrison & Crymes	5	1590.	Drury
	1529-30.	Jankyn					1591.	Sainberbe
	1531-33.	Thower		1567.	Stonard		1592.	Harrington
	1536-40.	Crumwell		1568.	Babington		1593.	Nevell

No. of Calr.	Date.	Name of Register.	No. of Calr.	Date.	Name of Register.	No. of Calr.	Date.	Name of Register.
	1594.	Dixy	19	1654.	Alchin	69	1713.	Leeds
	1595.	Scott	20	1655.	Aylett	70	1714.	Aston
	1596.	Drake	21	1656.	Berkley	71	1715.	Fagg
	1597.	Cobham	22	1657.	Ruthen	72	1716.	Fox
	1597-98.	Lewyn	23	1658.	Wootton	73	1717.	Whitfield
	1599.	Kidd	24	1659.	Pell	74	1718.	Tenison
	1600.	Wallop	25	1660.	Nabbs	75	1719.	Browning
6	1601.	Woodhall	26	1661.	May	76	1720.	Shaller
	1602.	Montague	27	1662.	Laud	77	1721.	Buckingham
	1603.	Bolein	28	1663.	Juxon	78	1722.	Marlbro'
	1604.	Harte		1664.	Bruce	79	1723.	Richmond
	1605.	Hayes	29	1665.	Hyde	80	1724.	Bolton
	1606.	Stafford	30	1666.	Mico	81	1725.	Romney
	1607.	Hudleston	31	1667.	Carr	82	1726.	Plymouth
	1608.	Windebanck	32	1668.	Hene	83	1727.	Farrant
	1609.	Dorset	33	1669.	Coke	84	1728.	Brook
	1610.	Wingfield	34	1670.	Penn	85	1729.	Abbott
	1611.	Wood		1671.	Duke	86	1730.	Auber
7	1612.	Fenner	35	1672.	Eure	87	1731.	Isham
	1613.	Capell	36	1673.	Pye	88	1732.	Bedford
	1614.	Lawe	37	1674.	Bunce	89	1733.	Price
	1615.	Rudd		1675.	Dycer	90	1734.	Ockham
	1616.	Cope	38			91	1735.	Ducie
	1617.	Weldon		1676.	Bence	92	1736.	Derby
	1618.	Meade	39	1677.	Hale	93	1737.	Wake
	1619.	Parker		1678.	Reeve	94	1738.	Brodrepp
	1620.	Soame	40	1679.	King	95	1739.	Henchman
	1621.	Dale	41	1680.	Bath	96	1740.	Browne
	1622.	Savile	42	1681.	North	97	1741.	Spurway
8	1623.	Swann	43	1682.	Cottle	98	1742.	Trenley
	1624.	Byrde		1683.	Drax	99	1743.	Boycott
	1625.	Clarke	44	1684.	Hare	100	1744.	Anstis
	1626.	Hele	45	1685.	Cann	101	1745.	Seymer
	1627.	Skinner	46	1686.	Lloyd	102	1746.	Edmunds
9	1628.	Barrington	47	1687.	Foot	103	1747.	Potter
	1629.	Ridley	48	1688.	Exton	104	1748.	Strahan
	1630.	Scroope	49	1689.	Ent	105	1749.	Lisle
	1631.	St. John	50	1690.	Dyke	106	1750.	Greenly
10	1632.	Audley	51	1691.	Vere	107	1751.	Busby
	1633.	Russell	52	1692.	Fane	108	1752.	Bettesworth
11	1634.	Seager		1693.	Coker	109	1753.	Searle
	1635.	Sadler	53	1694.	Box	110	1754.	Pinfold
	1636.	Pile		1695.	Irby	111	1755.	Paul
12	1637.	Goare	54	1696.	Bond	112	1756.	Glazier
	1638.	Lee		1697.	Pyne	113	1757.	Herring
13	1639.	Harvey	55	1698.	Lort	114	1758.	Hutton
	1640.	Coventry		1699.	Pett	115	1799.	Arran
	1641.	Evelyn	56	1700.	Noel	116	1760.	Lynch
14	1642.	Cambell	57	1701.	Dyer	117	1761.	Cheslyn
	1643.	Crane	58	1702.	Herne	118	1762.	St. Eloy
	1644-45.	Rivers	59	1703.	Degg	119	1763.	Cæsar
15	1646.	Twisse	60	1704.	Ash	120	1764.	Simpson
	1647.	Fines	61	1705.	Gee	121	1765.	Rushworth
16	1648.	Essex	62	1706.	Eedes	122	1766.	Tyndall
	1649.	Fairfax	63	1707.	Poley	123	1767.	Legard
17	1650.	Pembroke	64	1708.	Barrett	124	1768.	Secker
	1651.	Grey	65	1709.	Lane	125	1769.	Bogg
18	1652.	Bowyer	66	1710.	Smith	126	1770.	Jenner
	1653.	Brent	67	1711.	Young	127	1771.	Trevor
			68	1712.	Barnes	128	1772.	Taverner
						129	1773.	Stevens
						130	1774.	Bargrave

No. of Cal^r.	Date.	Name of Register.	No. of Cal^r.	Date.	Name of Register.	No. of Cal^r.	Date.	Name of Register.
131	1775.	Alexander	154	1798.	Walpole	177	1821.	Mansfield
132	1776.	Bellas	155	1799.	Howe	178	1822.	Herschell
133	1777.	Collier	156	1800.	Adderley	179	1823.	Richards
134	1778.	Hay	157	1801.	Abercrombie	180	1824.	Erskine
135	1779.	Warburton	158	1802.	Kenyon	181	1825.	St. Albans
136	1780.	Collins	159	1803.	Marriott	182	1826.	Swabey
137	1781.	Webster	160	1804.	Heseltine	183	1827.	Heber
138	1782.	Gostling	161	1805.	Nelson	184	1828.	Sutton
139	1783.	Cornwallis	162	1806.	Pitt	185	1829.	Liverpool
140	1784.	Rockingham	163	1807.	Lushington	186	1830.	Beard
141	1785.	Ducarel	164	1808.	Ely	187	1831.	Tebbs
142	1786.	Norfolk	165	1809.	Loveday	188	1832.	Tenderden
143	1787.	Major	166	1810.	Collingwood	189	1833.	Farquhar
144	1788.	Calvert	167	1811.	Crickitt	190	1834.	Teignmouth
145	1789.	Macham	168	1812.	Oxford	191	1835.	Gloucester
146	1790.	Bishop	169	1813.	Heathfield	192	1836.	Stowell
147	1791.	Bevor	170	1814.	Bridport	193	1837.	Norwich
148	1792.	Fountain	171	1815.	Pakenham	194	1838.	Nicholl
149	1793.	Dodwell	172	1816.	Wynne	195	1839.	Vaughan
150	1794.	Holman	173	1817.	Effingham	196	1840.	Arden
151	1795.	Newcastle	174	1818.	Cresswell			
152	1796.	Harris	175	1819.	Ellenboro'		Registers from this date	
153	1797.	Exeter	176	1820.	Kent		are labelled with *year* only.	

ADMINISTRATION CALENDARS. No. 1, 1559-90; No. 2, 1591-1600; No. 3, 1601-8; No. 4, 1609-14; No. 5, 1615-30: No. 19b, 1653-4; No. 23b, 1658.

ADMINISTRATION ACT BOOKS complete from 1559, except that 1662 is lost.

ORIGINAL WILLS begin 1484, but are very sparse to about 1524. Fairly complete from about 1600.

PROBATE ACT BOOKS begin November, 1526. Wanting from October 1538, to October 1547, and the years 1650, 1653, 1654 and 1662.

COUNTIES are not indicated in Will Calendars previous to 1631.

DATES IN THIS LIST are given in "historical" or "new" style throughout.

We append an index to the preceding table.

Dycer, 1675.	Holney, 1571.	Nevell, 1593.	Sheffelde, 1569.
Dyke, 1690.	Horne, 1496.	Newcastle, 1795.	Simpson, 1764.
Dyer, 1701.	Howe, 1799.	Nicholl, 1838.	Skinner, 1627.
Dyngeley, 1537.	Hudleston, 1607.	Noel, 1700.	Smith, 1710.
Eedes, 1706.	Hutton, 1758.	Noodes, 1558.	Soame, 1620.
Edmunds, 1746.	Hyde, 1665.	Norfolk, 1786.	Spencer, 1587.
Effingham, 1817.	Irby, 1695.	North, 1681.	Spert, 1541.
Ellenboro', 1819.	Isham, 1731.	Norwich, 1837.	Spurway, 1741.
Ely, 1808.	Jankyn, 1529.	Ockham, 1734.	St. Albans, 1825.
Ent, 1689.	Jenner, 1770.	Oxford, 1812.	St. Eloy, 1762.
Erskine, 1824.	Juxon, 1663.	Pakenham, 1815.	St. John, 1631.
Essex, 1648.	Kent, 1820.	Parker, 1619.	Stafford, 1606.
Eure, 1672.	Kenyon, 1802.	Paul, 1755.	Stevens, 1773.
Evelyn, 1641.	Ketchyn, 1556.	Pell, 1659.	Stevenson, 1564.
Exeter, 1797.	Kidd, 1599.	Pembroke, 1650.	Stokton, 1454.
Exton, 1688.	King, 1679.	Penn, 1670.	Stonard, 1567.
Fagg, 1715.	Lane, 1709.	Peter, 1573.	Stowell, 1836.
Fairfax, 1649.	Laud, 1662.	Pett, 1699.	Straham, 1748.
Fane, 1692.	Langley, 1578.	Pile, 1636.	Streat, 1562.
Farquhar, 1833.	Lawe, 1614.	Pinfold, 1754.	Sutton, 1828.
Farrant, 1727.	Lee, 1638.	Pitt, 1806.	Swabey, 1826.
Fenner, 1612.	Leeds, 1713.	Plymouth, 1726.	Swann, 1623.
Fetiplace, 1511.	Legard, 1767.	Poley, 1707.	Tashe, 1553.
Fines, 1647.	Leicester, 1588.	Populwell, 1548.	Taverner, 1772.
Foot, 1687.	Lewyn, 1597.	Porch, 1525.	Tebbs, 1831.
Fountain, 1792.	Lisle, 1749.	Potter, 1747.	Teignmouth, 1834.
Fox, 1716.	Liverpool, 1829.	Powell, 1552.	Tenderden, 1832.
Gee, 1705.	Lloyd, 1686.	Price, 1733.	Tenison, 1718.
Glazier, 1756.	Loftes, 1561.	Pyckering, 1575.	Thower, 1531.
Gloucester, 1835.	Logge, 1479.	Pye, 1673.	Tirwhite, 1582.
Goare, 1637.	Lort, 1698.	Pyne, 1697.	Trenley, 1742.
Godyn, 1463.	Loveday, 1809.	Pynnyng, 1544.	Trevor, 1771.
Gostling, 1782.	Luffenam, 1423.	Reeve, 1678.	Twisse, 1646.
Greenly, 1750.	Lushington, 1807.	Richards, 1823.	Tyndall, 1766.
Grey, 1651.	Lynch, 1760.	Richmond, 1723.	Vaughan, 1839.
Hale, 1677.	Lyon, 1570.	Ridley, 1629.	Vere, 1691.
Hare, 1684.	Macham, 1789.	Rivers, 1644.	Vox, 1493.
Harrington, 1592.	Major, 1787.	Rockingham, 1784.	Wake, 1737.
Harris, 1706.	Mansfield, 1821.	Romney, 1725.	Wallop, 1600.
Harte, 1604.	Marche, 1401.	Rous, 1384.	Walpole, 1798.
Harvey, 1639.	Marlbro', 1722.	Rowe, 1583.	Warburton, 1779.
Hay, 1778.	Marriott, 1803.	Rudd, 1615.	Watson, 1584.
Hayes, 1605.	Martyn, 1574.	Rushworth, 1765.	Wattys, 1471.
Heathfield, 1813.	May, 1661.	Russell, 1633.	Webster, 1781.
Heber, 1827.	Maynwaryng, 1520.	Ruthen, 1607.	Weldon, 1617.
Hele, 1626.	Meade, 1618.	Rutland, 1588.	Welles, 1558.
Henchman, 1739.	Mellershe, 1559.	Sadler, 1635.	Whitfield, 1717.
Hene, 1668.	Mico, 1666.	Sainberbe, 1591.	Windebanck, 1608.
Herne, 1702.	Milles, 1487.	Savile, 1622.	Windsor, 1586.
Herring, 1757.	Moone, 1500.	Scott, 1595.	Wingfield, 1610.
Herschell, 1822.	More, 1554.	Scroope, 1630.	Wood, 1611.
Heseltine, 1804.	Morrison & Crymes,	Secker, 1768.	Woodhall, 1601.
Hogen, 1533.	1565.	Seager, 1634.	Wootton, 1658.
Holder, 1514.	Montague, 1602.	Searle, 1753.	Wrastley, 1557.
Holgrave, 1504.	Nabbs, 1660.	Seymer, 1745.	Wynne, 1816.
Holman, 1794.	Nelson, 1805.	Shaller, 1720.	Young, 1711.

The will of JOHN BAKER. To my son Hugh Baker and the heirs of his body lawfully begotten all my house and lands in Essex after my wife's decease, and for want of such issue to my son John Baker and the heirs of his body lawfully begotten, and for want of such issue to my daughters

Sarah Copping and Mary Baker and the heirs of their bodies lawfully begotten, and for want of such issue to my sister Jane Gilbert of New Haven in New England and to her heirs forever. To my daughter Sarah Copinge one shilling, she having had a full child's portion already. To my three children hereafter named five hundred and fifty pounds, viz: to Hugh Baker one hundred and fifty, to John Baker two hundred and to Mary Baker two hundred pounds. To my friends Mr. George Appletree, clothworker, and Mr. Joseph Holden, haberdasher, both of St. Bride's parish, the sum of ten pounds apiece. The rest to my loving wife Jane Baker, whom I appoint executrix and my friends Mr. George Appletree and Mr. Joseph Holder (*sic*) of Bride's parish executors. Dated 4 December 1661 and proved 13 June 1664. In the probate act the name of the last executor is given plainly Joseph Holden.   Bruce, 75.

[Who was the Jane Gilbert of New Haven mentioned in this will? Could she have been Jane, daughter of Hugh Rossiter, who married Thomas Gilbert of Taunton, Mass.? Her death, June 1, 1691, is found on record at Taunton. (See REGISTER, vol. 17, p. 35.) I have seen no evidence that she ever resided at New Haven.—EDITOR.]

NATHANIEL BULCKLEY whiles he lived of the parish of St. Michael Bassinghall London made and declared his testament and last will nuncupative in manner and form or to the effect following; videlicet being moved to make his will and being asked who should be his executor answered that his father Edward Bulckley Doctor of Divinity should be his executor,— being then and there present M[r] Dod preacher and William Baker servant to M[r] Alderman Hallidaye. Proved 4 December 1602.   Montague, 82.

[A brother of the testator, the Rev. Peter Bulkeley, came to New England in 1635, and was settled as the first minister of Concord in 1637. See REGISTER, vol. 31, pp. 153–9, and Bulkeley Family, by the Rev. Frederick W. Chapman, 1874, pp. 24–38. See also for Bulkeley, REGISTER, vol. 42. pp. 272–7, *ante*, pp. 281–287.—EDITOR.]

GILES DE BUTT of Hackney, Middlesex gen[t] 8 February 1631, proved 14 March 1632. To my brother in law Mr. Peter Bonny ten pounds and unto my kinsman Enoch Lynde likewise ten pounds, with mourning apparel to them and their wives and children. To Mathew Lynd son unto Enoch Lynd if in case he continues his study and shall follow it so long till he proceeds Master of Arts, then at his going out Master I do give him twenty pounds. To my brother Josse de Quester I give ten pounds for mourning. To my two cousins Jean and Clays Velinges to either of them I give forty shillings to make either of them a ring for a remembrance of me. To my cousin Susan Terray now the wife of Maruschall and to Susan Dangnow now the wife of Cooper I give to either of them, five pounds. To the minister of the parish where it shall please God that I shall be buried forty shillings. To my maid servant Susan who now hath dwelt with me about ten years I give ten pounds to be paid her at her day of marriage. To Margaret our maid servant if she dwell with me when I die four pounds. To the poor of St. Andrew Hubbard in East Cheape five pounds. To the poor of Hackney five pounds. To the poor of the French congregation five pounds. To the poor of the Dutch congregation forty pounds. Other bequests to the poor in various hospitals and prisons. To John Hou[lt] my son in law five pounds for mourning. To my wife Anna de Butt my capital messuage in Thames Street called the three Tuns now or late in the occupation of Mrs. Mary Hearewyn widow and her son in law Timothy van Vlettend, Dutch minister, and Jeremy Loveland, merchant, and others, so long as she shall live sole and unmarried. But if she choose to marry my son James shall have and enjoy one half the rents and profits &c. during my wife's life time, and at her death I give all my capital messuage and tenements, houses &c. to my son. To my said son James my two houses in Tower Street which I have bought of William Perkins, called the Roll of Tobacco, and now in the occupation of John Carden, haberdasher of hats and caps and William Hyde a tailor. "And whereas I hold by lease from the parishioners of the, parish of St. Andrew Hubart in East cheape a Messuage or Tenement wth the appurtenances and beinge in Bottellane in London and now in the occupation of my kinsman Mr Enoch Lynde" I do will and appoint that my wife shall have hold and enjoy the said messuage and the clear yearly rent thereof during so long of the term to come in the said lease as she shall be living. My wife and son James to be the executors of this my last will, and for overseers I name and appoint Mr. Matthew de Quester Esq. and Mr. Robert Cudnor and my kinsman Enoch Lynde praying them to assist my said executors with their good counsel and advice. Reference to a gift my son was to have by the death or decease of his sister Anna wife of John Hoult my son in law.   Russell 23.

[The Visitation of London 1633, 1634, 1635 (Harl. So. Pub.) vol. I. p. 210, under Cudnor, shows the match of Robert Cudner and Susan, da. to Matthew Dequester, and on page 228 of the same volume we find the pedigree of De-Quester. By this will we get hold of some clews pointing to the connections of the Lynde family and learn where M^r. Enoch Lynde lived. Bottellane I suppose to be Botolph Lane near Billingsgate. Incidentally, too, we learn a little more about "Doomsday," Sedgwicke's connections (see my Gleanings, ante, p. 259). Timothy van Vlettend, the Dutch minister, suggests Timotheus Van Vleteren, the son in law of W^m. Sedgwicke, and Mrs. Mary Hearewyn, widow, the mother-in-law of van Vlettend, who occupied the Three Inns in Thames Street, may have been the relict of Mr. James Harewin at whose death Timotheus Van Vleteren became the possessor of six hundred pounds, three hundred of which passed through Mr. Sedgwicke's hands, perhaps through a marriage with the widow Hearewyn or Harewin.   HENRY F. WATERS.]

MARY PENNINGTON "Att my house att Woodside in Amersham parish and County of Bucks. this Tenth day of the third moneth called May One thousand six hundred eighty," but signed and sealed 5 July 1680, proved 11 October 1682. Refers to personal estate "which I had before marriage to my deare husband Isaac Pennington which he made over for my use by a deed before marriage to my cousin Elizabeth Dallison." I have taken upon me the debts of my husband by administering after his death.

As for my daughter Penn though she be very near to me and hath deserved well of me in her own particular and upon her worthy father's account yet she hath a large proportion of this world's substance and these my latter children have not any thing but what I give them, the Lord having seen it good to strip their dear and pretious father and left him without a capacity to do anything for them, and if so my estate not being great I can only signify my naturalness to my dear daughter Penn and hers by some little things for them to remember me by, and I do believe the witness of God in her will answer to the righteousness of it. To my son William Pennington five hundred pounds sterling, the one hundred pounds to bind him to so some handsome trade that hath not much of labor, because he is but weakly, and the other four hundred pounds to be paid him at the age of twenty two years. To son Edward Pennington the like sums upon the like conditions. To my daughter Mary Pennington thirty pounds a year till she marry, and if she marry three hundred pounds sterling. To my dear son William Penn fifty pounds sterling and to my friend Thomas Elwood the like sum. To my cousin Mary Smith, wife to William Smith, fifty pounds. I give twenty pounds towards a meeting house when friends of Chalfont meeting think it convenient to build one. To Martha Sampson two pounds a year for life. To Martha Cooper *als* Heywood three pounds a year for life. To my daughter Gulielma Maria Penn her choice of a suit of damask except that suit marked $_I P_M$. To her son Springett Penn my great platt with the Springett's and my coat of arms upon it and the silver two eared cup made in the fashion of his mother's golden one. To her daughter Letitia Penn my silver chafin dish and skimmer with a brasile handle and that large nun's work box and a little basket of nun's work and a purse and a girdle of black plush and a black straw basket which her father brought me out of Holland &c. &c. To my son William Pennington my dear husband's watch. Other bequests to son Edward Pennington and daughter Mary, to cousin Mary Smith the elder and her daughter Mary. To son John Pennington my house and land at Woodside and all my husband's houses in Kent (upon conditions). Reference to will of my mother the Lady Prewed "that is annext to my fathers Sir John Prewed," also to "my mother's sister the Lady Oxenden." I would have my son John Pennington lay mee in friends burying ground at Jordans very neare my deare and precious husband Isaac Pennington. My son John to be executor and my dear son William Penn and my loving friend Thomas Ellwood to be overseers.   Cottle, 121.

[The following notes and pedigree illustrating this Springett–Penn connection, furnished me by my friend Capt. Attree, R.E., deserve to be entered here.
                                                            H. F. WATERS.]

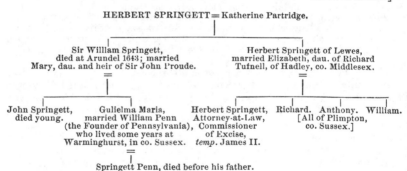

HERBERT SPRINGETT = Katherine Partridge.

Sir William Springett, died at Arundel 1643; married Mary, dau. and heir of Sir John Proude.

Herbert Springett of Lewes, married Elizabeth, dau. of Richard Tufnell, of Hadley, co. Middlesex.

John Springett, died young.

Gulielma Maria, married William Penn (the Founder of Pennsylvania), who lived some years at Warminghurst, in co. Sussex.

Herbert Springett, Attorney-at-Law, Commissioner of Excise, *temp.* James II.

Richard. Anthony. William. [All of Plimpton, co. Sussex.]

Springett Penn, died before his father.

William Penn's connection with Sussex commenced in 1676, when according to Cartwright, Warminghurst was sold to him. He married in 1672, before he bought Warminghurst, Gulielma Maria, the daughter of Sir William Springett, who was killed at the Siege of Bramber. A daughter of Penn was buried in the Friend's meeting house, still in existence, in a bye-lane near Conyhurst Common, in the parish of Thakeham, and the grave can be pointed out. Penn always attended service in this Chapel, which is still conducted by the Society of Friends, and there is a congregation of about seventy every Sunday.

Warminghurst was sold in 1644 by Sir Thomas Haselrige and Sir Thomas Williamson and their wives to Henry Bigland, of Grays Inn, Esq., by whom it was sold in 1676 to William Penn, Esq. In this deed he covenants to secure the premisses discharged of all manner of tythes other than a yearly payment of 2ᵈ per acre due and payable by custom as a modus to his Rector. In 1702 Wm. Penn, Esq. sold them to James Butler, Esq., in whose family they continued till 1789, when they were allotted to Ann Jemima, eldest daughter of James Butler, Esq., wife of Rev. Robert Clough, by whom they were sold in 1805 to Charles, late Duke of Norfolk, and now form a part of the settled estates of the dukedom.

Copied from the Sussex Archæological
Collections by F. W. T. Attree
Capt. R.E.

[See Penn wills in these GLEANINGS, *ante*, pp. 434–440; also an article on the Penn family by James Henry Lea in the Pennsylvania Magazine of History, vol. 14. pp. 50–63; 160–181; 281–296.—EDITOR.]

THOMAS BRETT of the City of Westminster genᵗ, 13 August 1636, proved 29 August 1636. To be buried in the church of Stepney near my father, if I die in or near Westminster. One hundred pounds I owe to one Mʳ Johnsonne of whom I purchased certain lands at Higham in the County of Kent. To the poor of the parish of Petame, St. Margaret in Westminster and Stepney (if I be buried there). To Anne Irish, my wife's sister. To Henry Irish and his son Thomas. To my Aunt Stone and every one of her children. To James Stone the younger and his children. To my cousins Wonslyes and to my cousin Renold's children. To my cousin George Gosnoll and his son. To Mʳ Lewis his daughter, my godchild, five pounds if he pay me my former rents due. To all my tenants at Tower Hill. To my wife Ellinor Brett my two houses on the Millbank in Westminster in one of which Mʳ Bowll lately dwelt and in the other we ourselves. To my said wife one annuity or rent charge of three-score and ten pounds of lawful money chargeable upon all my lands &c in Kent, Essex and Middlesex and at or near the Tower of London (that land of mine at Feversham in the County of Kent only except). To my sister in law Mary, during her natural life, one annuity of forty shillings by the year (chargeable as above). To my brother Robert Brett all my lands tenements &c (chargeable as above), upon condition that if he marry and have issue male that he settle upon his first son and his heirs all my lands &c at Feversham and upon his second son all my lands &c in the County of Essex and upon his third son all my lands &c at Stepney.

"Memorand I the Testator doe hartilie desire yow my loveing Brother which now I onely trust and to whome I leaue this porcon of my goodes which the Lord hath lent mee, that yow truely loue my wife and lett nothing but death make yow leaue her, nay when yow dye, if it be before my wife lett her not be forgotten. And yow my wife I desire yow to loue my brother and lett none of his writinges be kept back from him that he maie be enabled to pay these my smale Legacyes, for by my death both of yow wilbe enabled to geue (if yow please) greater Legacyes. The Lord my god that hath blessed mee and hath soe many and sundry wayes shewed mee fauors blesse yow both And think not yow much Brother that yow have soe little Nor yow my loveinge wife that yow haue noe more; That which the Lord hath lent mee in his grace and bountifull mercy I leaue to yow twoe as I haue setled it in my will: I brought nothing into this world nor I shall I carry anything with mee as yow see. Therefore liue in peace, and the God of peace bee with you THO: BRETT."

Pile, 92.

JOHN PARKER of London, haberdasher, and of the parish of St. Pancras, Soper Lane, London, 7th and 14th May 1639, proved 27 August 1639.

For my burial place I cannot tell whether I shall die in England, at sea or beyond the seas, but if I die in my own country then I desire to be buried in St. Pancras Church in Soper Lane and in my good wife Bridget's grave if it conveniently may be. Of my goods &c. one third part of three equal parts, to be divided, shall be and remain to and amongst all my children, that is to say, Bridget, Sara, Johanna, Mary and Elizabeth. Reference to mutual agreement with wife Joane before marriage, made between William Drake Esq. and Francis Drake gen[t], my said wife's brethren, of the first part, my said wife, by the name of Joan Drake, of the second part and me, the said John Parker, of the third part, dated the eight and twentieth day of May in the tenth year of our now Sovereign Lord and King Charles. Have settled, by my deed in the hands of my brother in law Mr George Smith, all my houses in Saun (Swan?) Alley near Coleman St. London on my wife and do now settle upon her my houses which I purchased of M[r] Storye in Highgate. Moreover I give and bequeath unto her my lease of Highgate house where we dwell &c. My will is to lend to my brother Joseph Parker twenty five hundred pounds upon condition that he become bound with my brother William Jollye of Leeke and some other sufficient man to the Chamber of London for securing of this foresaid twenty five hundred pounds to be paid to my children that shall be at age or married after the death of my life[?] &c. &c. Reference to brother Smith: and cousin John Dethicke. "My daughter Bridgett (whome I had by my first wife)." My daughter Sarah, "the eldest daughter by my now wife." To my loving brother Marke Parker three hundred pounds, to be paid to him one hundred pounds within a year after my decease, and one hundred pounds within two years and the other hundred pounds within three years if he be living; if not it shall be distributed equally amongst his children. To him also, if he outlive my wife, forty pounds per annum, to be paid him out of the rents of my houses in Swan Alley near Coleman St. Houses in Soper Lane "where my brother Joseph and I now dwell." To my sister Hannah Ese fifteen pounds every year, and to George Ese, her husband, if he outlive my sister, eight pounds per annum during her life. To my sister Bamford forty pounds and to her son Joseph Coulson twenty pounds towards the binding him forth to an apprentice.

Item I do give and bequeath to my brother James and to his son John Parker two hundred and fifty pounds. To my sister Elizabeth one hundred and fifty pounds. To my cousin Joane Jeffery fifty pounds, to be paid at day of marriage or one and twenty years of age. To John Ese my sister Hanna's son, when he shall have served his apprenticeship. To Rebecca Ese, my sister Hanna's daughter, now dwelling with me, one hundred pounds to be put forth to interest for her. To Mary, my sister Hannah's daughter, and to Francis and Joseph, also her sons, twenty pounds apiece. To Mark, James and Samuel, three other of her sons, twenty pounds apiece at eighteen. To my mother Drake ten pounds for mourning and twenty pounds more. To my brother William Drake fifteen pounds, to buy him and his man mourning, and as much to my brother Francis Drake. To my cousin John Parker the counsellor ten pounds to buy him mourning. To M[r] Barnarde of Gray's Inn, to M[r] John Dethicke and his wife, to M[r] Goodyer and his wife, if they be in England, to buy them mourning, ten pounds, and as much to my loving friend M[r] Bayley. Other bequests to sundry clergymen and servants and for the use of the poor.

"Item I doe give & bequeath three hundred Pounds to bee employed in the takinge up out of the streete or out of the Bridewelle twelve fatherles and motherles boyes and eight girles from seaven yeares old and upwards and for the furnishing them with necessaries and paying for their passage to New England and for their being bound apprentices to some such as will be carefull to bring them up in the feare of God and to maintaine themselues another daie. And my will is that my brother James should take his choise out of these, of three of them if hee need soe many for his owne use. And whereas formerly I menčoned two hundred and ffiftie Pounde, given him and his sonne, and named One hundred for him and one hundred and ffiftie Pounds for his sonne John Parker, my meaninge is that if his said sonne should dye yet the said one hundred and ffiftie pounds should bee paid to him for the use of the rest of his Children."

Other bequests to apprentices and servants &c &c. Item I do give and bequeath to two such godly ministers as are without any pastoral charge fifty pounds and these to be chosen by my wife and my executors to this purpose that they shall employ themselves to the reading and perusing of those six books wherein I have written of my own life, man's misery, God's mercy and of charity, which said two ministers I desire should employ themselves in collecting my scattered meditations unto some order and method, I mean so many of them as they shall conceive God may receive some glory and my children may receive some comfort and edification thereby: and my will is that when they are collected unto some good method that then they shall be transcribed into a fair legible hand and bound up in a book and so many children as I have so many copies to be written, which shall be given them as they attain to years of discretion. And for these books &c I do allow ten pounds.

To my brother Jeseph's daughter Elizabeth thirty pounds when she cometh to age. To my brother (George) Smith's daughters and sons, viz. Robert ten pounds, Joane ten pounds, Margaret ten pounds and Mary, my god-daughter, twenty pounds, at their several marriges or when they shall be one and twenty.

My brother Joseph Parker and my brother in law Mr George Smith to be executors and my brother Mark Parker (if he be in England) and friend John Dethicke and cousin John Parker the counsellor my overseers.

Harvey, 142.

JOSEPH PARKER citizen and skinner of London and of the parish of St. Pancras, Soper Lane in London, 15 October 1642, proved 3 December 1644. To be buried in Pancras, Soper Lane, as near to my most dearly beloved brother John Parker as I may be. To wife one third part and to Elizabeth my only daughter one third part of my estate. To my deceased brother John Parker's five daughters two hundred and fifty pounds, to whose father I was much bound for his great care and true affection always towards me. i.e. cousin Bridget, the eldest, fifty pounds, cousin Sarah, the second, cousin Joanna the third, cousin Mary the fourth and cousin Elizabeth the fifth and last fifty pounds each. To my beloved brother Mark Parker's children sixty pounds. My brother John by his will gave me one hundred and fifty pounds upon condicon to become bound and to pay my sister Hannah Elce fifteen pounds every year during her life and after her death to pay her husband George Elce eight pounds per annum. My brother Mark Parker (now residing in Rotterdam in Holland) to continue the payment. To my brother and sister Bamford (in another place written Bramford) and to her only son Joseph Colson. To my brother James Parker in New England and his children. To my sister Elizabeth Shuckford. To John Elce son to George Elce my brother in law, and to Joseph, Francis, Mark, James and Samuel and to Rebecca and Mary, my sister Elce's two daughters. To the town of Leicester where I was born, to be distributed among knitters of stockings. My poor kindred of the Kowleyes and Warrens children. My cousin John Parker of Gray's Inn and his son Mark Parker. To William Salmon and Russell Allsopp. To my cousin Mary Hull. Her husband referred to. To Sarah Jackson wife of Thomas Jackson. My wife Anna Parker and daughter Elizabeth to be joint executors, and my brother Mark Parker, my brothers William and John Jolly my brother Patrick Bamford, by brother George Smith and my cousin John Dethicke overseers.   Rivers, 21.

SIR FRANCIS DRAKE of Bucklond in the County of Devon, Knight, — August, 37th Elizabeth, proved 17 May 1596. Being now called unto action by her majesty wherein I am to hazard my life as well in the defence of Christ's Gospell as for the good of my Prince and Country. To the poor people of the town & parish of Plymouth forty pounds. To Dame Elizabeth, my wife, furniture &c. in my mansion house of Buckland and (a certain estate) for life: then to my brother Thomas Drake. To Thomas, also, a certain messuage or tenement in the High Street, within the Borough of Plymouth, now in the tenure or occupation of the said Thomas, to hold for four score and ten years, if the said Thomas Drake, Elizabeth his wife and Francis and Elizabeth, their children, or any of them, so long do happen to live.

A later will made 27 January, 38th Elizabeth. I Francis Drake of Buckland Monachorum, in the County of Devon, Knight, General of her majesty's Fleet, now in service for the West Indies. To my well beloved cousin, Francis Drake, son of Richard Drake, of Eshire in the County of Surrey, Esq., one of the Quiries of her majesty's stable, my manor of Yarckombe in the County of Devon &c forever. The said Richard Drake and Francis Drake, his son, their heirs executors or administrators, to pay or cause to be paid unto Thomas Drake of Plymouth in the County of Devon, gentlemen, two thousand pounds within two years after my decease. To Jonas Bodenham, gentleman, my manor of Sampford Spyney in Devon. My said brother Thomas Drake to be executor. The former will shall stand. Proved by Francis Clarke, Not. Pub., procurator of Thomas Drake, brother and executor of the deceased.   Drake, 1.

[Sir Francis Drake, the celebrated admiral in Queen Elizabeth's reign, was a son of Edmund Drake, vicar of Upchurch in Kent. See his pedigree in Vivian's Devonshire Pedigrees, page 299.—EDITOR.]

FRANCIS DRAKE, of Esher in the County of Surrey Esq., 13 March 1633, proved 7 May 1634. Whereas my son William delivered me the legacy of one thousand pounds which William Tothill, my late father in law, did demise unto my daughter Joane Drake, and with three hundred & fifty pounds, part thereof, I did soon after purchase of Sir John Lidcot a parcell of land called Rayswarren, in the names of her and myself, she is to have the land and also the one thousand pounds entire, &c. To my daughter Mary Drake, the only child that I had by my late wife Philadelphia, one thousand marks to be well employed for her benefit, until her marriage or full age. If she die, then to my son Francis Drake.

My wife to have the education of my said daughter Mary, and I desire her and my said son Francis and my daughter Johan to have a special care of my daughter Mary's good education. I have settled several things on my son William in my life time; it hath pleased God largely to provide for him otherwise; nevertheless he is to have half the pictures in the gallery at Esher (and other property). To my wife (among other things) the lease of my house in Fewter al̃s Fetter Lane in London, and to Joshua White, her son, twenty pounds. To every other of my sons that shall be living at my death five pounds apiece. To my cousin Henry Drake of Childay thirty pounds, now in his hands. To John Drake, my cousin William Drake's son, twenty pounds to be sent unto him in New England, in commodities such as my executor shall think fit. To my cousin Banner, the midwife, in London, ten pounds. To John Long, my first wife's cousin, ten pounds, to be paid him when he comes out of his apprenticeship. My faithful servant Thomas Cheesman and his wife and John Timberle and all my other servants. To Johanna Hooker, who is now in New England, thirty pounds at her day of marriage. To Amye and Joane, the two daughters of my said cousin William Drake, ten pounds apiece. To my dear friend Mr John Dodd, minister, for all his great kindness shewed to me and mine, ten pounds, and to Mr. Speed, minister of the word at Eshere, ten pounds, and to Mrs Owen, his mother in law, ten pounds. Thirty pounds to poor godly people, three parts whereof to be given in Eshere, Walton, West Moulsey. To Doctor Gough of the Blackfryars, London, and Richard Sibbs, Doctor of Divinity, ten pounds apiece, and they to be overseers. To my son Francis Drake all my interest in the Rectory & Parsonage of Walton upon Thames and West Moulsey in the County of Surrey. To Mr Cooke, now vicar of Walton, the Easter Book. To Mr Malthouse the small tithes of West Moulsey and to him my manor of Walton, after the death of his brother William. My said son Francis to be executor. To my cousin John White of the Middle Temple, London, Esq., fifty pounds; he to be joint executor with Francis and to give him his best direction and assistance.

Wit: Joseph Glover, George Billingehurst, John Steedman.

Seagar, 43.

[Francis Drake of Esher, died March 17, 1633. He was the son of Richard Drake of Esher, equerry to Queen Elizabeth. See his pedigree in Vivian's Devonshire Pedigrees, page 293. John Drake (son of his cousin William), who was in New England in 1633, was probably the John who came here in 1630 and finally settled in Windsor, Conn., where he died, Aug. 17, 1659. See Stiles's Ancient Windsor, page 183, and Savage's Genealogical Dictionary, vol. 2, p. 70.

The Johanna Hooker named as being in New England, was probably Joanna, daughter of Rev. Thomas Hooker of Hartford, Conn., who married Rev. Thomas Shepard of Cambridge, Mass.—EDITOR.]

ELIZABETH JADWIN, of the parish of St. Mary Newington, Surrey widow, 18 January 1637, proved 4 March 1638. I give to John Jadwin, the son of Robert Jadwin, a silver gilt wine cup. I give to my sister Sibill Wright my best apron and a gold ring with a sand colour stone in it. I give to my grandchild Jadwin Dunscombe twenty nobles of lawful money of England to make up the proportion of marks given to him by his grandfather the sum of twenty pounds. I will and bequeath unto my goddaughter Elizabeth, the daughter of William Sharrowe, a wainscot chest and all that is in it and likewise a silver gilt tankard, and unto Susanna, the other daughter, a man candlestick and six plate trenchers, and likewise I give to her a silver gilt wine cup and that which is in it. I give and bequeath unto John Malthus and his wife, to each of them twenty shillings for rings and to his wife my best ruff. To my servant Mary Stephenson forty shillings and two smocks and two aprons. To Joane Curryen, the servant of my sister Sibill Wright, one smock and one flaxen apron. To my son in law Robert Jadwin three towells and one dozen napkins and one table cloth. I do forgive and release unto my son in law Thomas Dunscombe and to my daughter Hannah his wife all such sum and sums of money, debts, duties and demands whatsoever which they or either of them do owe unto me by any ways or means howsoever, whether as being executrix to my late deceased husband Thomas Jadwin or otherwise howsoever. I give to my daughter Hannah Dunscombe half my household stuff. The rest and residue I give and bequeath to my daughter Susanna the wife of William Sharrowe and I do will and ordain likewise William Sharrowe and his wife full joint coexecutors of this my last will and testament, willing them te see my debts be paid. I likewise give twenty shillings more to Mary Stephenson to make up the forty shillings before three pounds. I give one pair of sheets to my son in law Robert Jadwin. I give to my kinswoman Elizabeth Cole twenty shillings and likewise to my kinswoman Dorothy Cooke twenty shillings. I bequeath twenty shillings to my cousin Thomas Sherly for a ring.   Harvey, 44.

[In GLEANINGS (*ante*, pp. 289, 290) I gave an abstract of the will of Thomas Jadwin, husband of the above testatrix, who was one of the "adventurers for Virginia." On page 6 of the second volume of The Visitation of London A.D. 1633, 1634 and 1635 (Harl. So. Pub.) may be found what I presume to be a pedigree of this very family, as follows :—

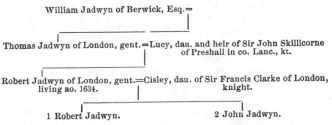

William Jadwyn of Berwick, Esq.=

Thomas Jadwyn of London, gent.=Lucy, dau. and heir of Sir John Skillicorne of Preshall in co. Lanc., kt.

Robert Jadwyn of London, gent.=Cisley, dau. of Sir Francis Clarke of London, living ao. 1634.   knight.

1 Robert Jadwyn.   2 John Jadwyn.

Mrs. Elizabeth Jadwyn was evidently a second wife of Thomas Jadwyn and step-mother of Robert Jadwin, whose son John I suppose it to have been who patented 650 acres of land on the south side of Rappahannoc River, Virginia, 13 Nov. 1658 (see REGISTER, vol. 43, p. 305, *ante*, p. 347).—H. F. WATERS.]

WILLIAM GLOVER of Dedham in the County of Essex, clothier, 26 January 6th James, proved 5 May 1609. To brother Thomas Glouer all the houses, lands &c, which my father Thomas Glover, lately deceased, gave to me; my said brother Thomas to pay out, &c., four hundred pounds, as hereafter specified, viz. to my brother Edward Glover one hundred pounds within one year after my decease, to my brother John Glover one hundred pounds within two years &c., and to my sisters Anne Cole & Susan Beuersham one hundred each. I give to the poor of Dedham ten pounds, to be paid into the hands of Henry Sherman the elder and Robert Alefounder, to be employed to the uses abovesaid. To Mr Rogers preacher of Dedham ten pounds, within one year. To M[r] Sage, minister of Dedham, three pounds in a year. To Joseph Morse of Dedham forty shillings, in one year &c. To my cousin Margaret Nicholson, my sister's daughter, fifty pounds, at her age of twenty years. To Thomas & William Nicholson, the sons of my late sister Margaret Nicholson, four score pounds (i.e. forty pounds apiece); they to have nine pounds ten shillings a year until they shall accomplish their several ages as aforesaid. Margaret, the same, until her age of seventeen. To John Pye of Dedham forty shillings, in one year &c. To my cousin Anne Howell, forty shillings, in one year &c. To M^ris Dove of Stratford three pounds in one year &c. To Mr Beadle, minister Wooluerston, three pounds in a year &c. To Samuel Salmon my sealing ring and two pairs of my best jersey stockings, one of the two pairs to be those that are at Mr Gooutches, Mr Cardinall's son at Norwich, which lie there to be changed. To the daughter of Habbacuck Page, late of Dedham deceased, forty shillings, to be given into the hands of Mr Ravens within one year after my decease. My sister Ann Cole's husband. To Thomas Wood, where I now lie, forty shillings, and to his wife forty shillings. I give unto my Aunt Anger five pounds in one year &c. To the widow Morse, in the Valley, twenty shillings in one year. The residue to my three brethren, Thomas, Edward & John Glouver. My brother Thomas Glover and Samuel Salmon to be executors.

Wit: Samuel Neall, John Wood, Edward Downes.   Dorsett, 39.

JOHN WOOD of Stratford in the County of Suffolk, yeoman, 10 January 1615, proved 2 February 1615. My wife Bridget shall peaceably enjoy during her natural life my two tenements or messuages in Dedham in the County of Essex, now in the occupation of John Pye and John Pope; also thirty pounds in money (and certain furniture, household stuff &c). My son John is to have my land in Clafton.* To Abigail Wood, daughter of my son Thomas by his first wife, forty pounds. To my son John's two eldest children, John and Mary, twenty pounds apiece at age of seventeen years. To my grandchildren Robert and John Alefounder,† sons of my daughter Elizabeth, five pounds apiece at age of seventeen. To Mr. John Rogers, now preacher at Dedham, forty shillings. And to my cousin Samuel Ward, now preacher at Ipswich, forty shillings. And to my cousin Nathaniel Ward, his brother, forty shillings. And to Mrs Dowe of Stratford, widow, thirty shillings. All these four last legacies to be paid within six months after my decease. All the personal property not otherwise bequeathed, to son Thomas: and he to be executor.

Wit: Josua Ward, Robart Browne, Richard Pamer.   Cope, 17.

[Samuel and Nathaniel Ward named in this will were sons of the Rev. John Ward of Haverhill. Their aunt Abigail is said by Candler to have married Samuel Wood of Dedham (see my memoir of Nathaniel Ward, 1868, p. 128, and Mr. Muskett's article on Ward of Suffolk and America, REGISTER, vol. 41, p. 282). An abstract of the will of the first named of them, Rev. Samuel Ward, town preacher of Ipswich, is printed in these GLEANINGS, ante, page 19. A sketch of his life will be found in my memoir of N. Ward, pp. 135–62. The second brother Nathaniel, was the Rev. Nathaniel Ward, of Stondon Massey and Shenfield in Essex, England, and Ipswich, Massachusetts. He was the author of the Simple Cobler of Aggawam, and compiler of the Massachusetts Body of Liberties. A memoir of him by the present editor of the REGISTER was published in 1868, by Joel Munsell of Albany, N. Y., in an octavo of 213 pages.—EDITOR.]

GEORGE RAYMOND the elder of Ipswich, grocer, 10 April 1617, proved 17 June 1617. To the poor of Bocking and Branktree twenty shillings (each). Wife Jane Raymond. Sons Jeremy, George, Thomas, John,

* Probably Clackton in Essex is meant.
† In a pedigree of Alfounder at Herald's College, Visitation of Essex, 1664 (D. 21.), 1 find that Robert Alfounder of East Bergholt married Elizabeth, dau. of —— Wood of Rivenhall.   H. F. W.

James and Richard. Daughter Priscilla wife of John Leaver of Ipswich, clothier. Daughter Mary wife of Moses Shill. Grandchildren George, Elizabeth and Priscilla, children of John; James, George and Samuel, children of James; John, George and James, children of George; Priscilla and George, children of Thomas; George and Mary, children of Jeremy; and Christabell and George, children of Richard. Brother Allen. Others named. To Mr Samuel Warde forty shillings.

"And whereas yt hath pleased God to put into the harte of Mr Warde our preacher to stirre up this Corporaçon for the erecting of A Librarie wch being furnished wth all kinde of bookes can not but grately further the advancement of God's Glorie his worshippe and religion amongest us I doe will and bequeath fower pounds of lawfull English monie to bee paid within one yeare next after my decease ou^r & aboue the xx s I haue allreadye payd towardes the supplie of that good work begunne."

Archd. of Suff. (Ipswich) B. 50 L. 292.

[The fact that Rev. Samuel Ward, town preacher of Ipswich (see preceding note), incited the corporation of Ipswich " for the erecting of a Librarie" is new to me.—EDITOR.]

EDWARD WARDE of Little Wrathinge, Suffolk, yeoman, 9 January 1620, proved at Ipswich 7 March 1620. To my wife Judeth my house, orchard and garden, with the skepps of bees therein, during her natural life, so as she shall leave one upper chamber, furnished for mine executor, who soever he be, viz. one bed and all things thereunto belonging, called Joseph's chamber. To my son Nathaniel Warde forty pounds and my best riding cloak. To my son Leonard (?) fifty pounds and my best cloak, when his apprenticeship shall come forth. To Lydia, my daughter, thirty pounds. To Mary, my daughter, twenty pounds. To Rebecca Warde, my daughter, forty pounds. To Susan, my daughter, ten pounds. Son Thomas Ward to be sole executor. To son Edward Ward after his time shall come forth &c.   Consistory C^t Norwich. B^k Williams 60.

(Mem. Perhaps for "Leonard," above, we should read Edward.—H. F. W.)

[Edward Warde, the testator, was I presume the brother of Rev. John Ward of Haverhill, named by him in his will, which is printed in full in my memoir of N. Ward, pp. 130–1. See Muskett's Candler's pedigree in the REGISTER, vol. 41, p. 284. The will of his daughter Susan, widow of Robert Brown, follows this.—EDITOR.]

SUSAN BROWNE of Ipswich, widow, 22 March 1626, proved 24 April 1627. To Mr Samuel Warde, Preacher of the Tower parish in Ipswich the sum of five pounds &c in two years, in full discharge and satisfaction of whatsoever money is now due unto him and unpaid from or by Robert Browne, my late husband, deceased. To Elizabeth Browne daughter of my brother in law William Browne. My sister in law Mary Browne. My sister Mary Cutting. My mother Judith Warde. My sister Rebecca Warde. My brother Edward Warde to be executor and residuary legatee.

Consistory C^t Norwich Book Travers.

EDWARD WARD of Ipswich in the Co. of Suffolk, hosier, 18 November 1646, proved 10 February 1646. I give unto my two sons, Edward and Samuel Ward, the sum of two hundred and ten pounds a piece, to be paid to either of them when they shall accomplish the full age of four and twenty years. I give unto my kinswoman Abigail Smart the sum of ten pounds, to be paid within one year next after my decease. I give unto Richard Lockewood my cousin the sum of five pounds, to be paid unto him

at his full age of four and twenty years, provided that he doth faithfully serve and dwell with my wife the remainder of the time he is bound
unto me. I give unto Elizabeth my wife all the remainder of my temporal
goods &c. And I do ordain and make George Raymond of Ipswich
clothier and·John Denton of the same town hosier my executors. My son
Samuel to be put to some trade as the said George Raymond, with the
consent of my wife, shall see most meet.   Fines, 35 (P. C. .C.)

[Edward Ward, the testator, was a nephew of Rev. John Ward of Haverhill
and probably son of Edward Warde of Little Wrathinge, whose will is given
above. The testator married Elizabeth Dale, who survived him and married
Thomas Griggs. See REGISTER, vol. 41, p. 284. Mr. Griggs's will is given
below.—EDITOR.]

RICHARD GRIGGES of Ipswich, Suffolk, tallow chandler, 11 October
1654, proved 3 July 1655. To my brother William Griggs twenty shillings. To my cousin Mary Grigges, his daughter, three pounds. To my
cousin John, his son, five pounds. To my brother Robert thirty pounds.
To my brother Edmund thirty pounds. To my brother John ʼGreene five
pounds. To my sister Mary Greene five pounds. To my cousin Mary
Greene five pounds. To my cousin Anne Greene five pounds. To my
cousin William Greene five pounds. To my cousin Damaris five pounds.
To Rebecca Greene five pounds. To my cousin Alice Greene five pounds.
To my cousin Edward Ward the sum of six pounds. To my cousin Samuel
Ward the sum of five pounds. To my sister Elizabeth Grigges ten pounds.
To Bridget Riches five pounds. To William Hawkins five pounds. To
my brother Thomas one hundred pounds, and one two and thirtieth part
of the ship John and Susan of Ipswich and one sixty-fourth part of the
ship Humility of Ipswich. My brother Thomas Grigges to be executor.
                                                    Aylett, 76.

THOMAS GRIGGS of Ipswich, Suffolk, apothecary, 18 October 1665,
proved 12 October 1666. Wife Elizabeth. Tenement in parish of St.
Mary at the Tower. Thomas Griggs, son of my brother Edmund Griggs
of Buxhall, and his heirs. My close of land in the parish of St. Peter's,
called Windmill close. John and Mary Griggs children of brother Edmond. John Griggs son of brother William. Damaris Greene daughter
of my brother John Greene. Rebecca Dale wife of Samuel Dale of Burst-
hall. Anne Nelson wife of Charles Nelson of Hadleigh. Alice and Mary
Greene, both of Lynsye, Suff., spinsters. My sister Mary Greene. Dorothy Daines the daughter of my loving friend Doctor John Daynes. My
brother in law Capt. Daniel Dale. Brother Robert Griggs.
I give and bequeath unto ——— Ward, son of my late son in law Samuel Ward late of London dec'd., fifteen pounds at his full age of one and
twenty years. My messuages, lands and tenements in Bergholt and Raydon, Suff., which I have in reversion after the death of Mrs Mapelthorpe,
which were given unto John Sicklemore Esq. and me, the said Thomas
Griggs, by Abigail Markham als Marchant of Ipswich widow, as by her last
will and testament bearing date 4 April 1656. My brother Edmund
Griggs to be executor and brother John Greene of Lynsey supervisor.
                                                Mico, 144 (P. C. C.)

[Thomas Griggs was the second husband of Mrs. Elizabeth (Dale) Ward.
See preceding note.—EDITOR.]

JOHN WARD of St. Clement's parish, Ipswich, Suffolk, Clerk, 15 April
1662, proved 29 April 1662. All my debts to be paid out of my personal

estate. What remains to be equally divided betwixt my children that are unmarried, they paying out thereof to my daughters Mary and Susan, which are married, to each of them ——. Joseph Wayte of Sprawton, clerk, to be sole executor.

Consistory C^t Norwich (Bundle for 1662) N° 230.

[The testator, Rev. John Ward, was a son of Rev. John Ward of Haverhill, and a brother to Revs. Samuel and Nathaniel, before noticed in these annotations. He was a member of the Westminster Assembly. A sketch of his life is printed in my memoir of N. Ward, pp. 162-5.—EDITOR.]

JOHN SYM of Leigh in Essex, Clerk, 19 March 1637, proved 5 June 1638. To Sarah the wife of Richard Tabore ten shillings. To my well beloved brother Mr Thomas Younge, vicar of Stowmarket, Willett's Synopsis papismi &c. To my cousin Mr Ward of Hadleigh my best casock. To my cousin Mr John Knightbridge of Chelmsford twenty shillings. To my cousin Elizabeth North twenty shillings and to her husband ten shillings. To my dear and loving wife Sarah six and thirty pounds to distribute amongst her children. And she shall have all the goods &c remaining that she brought with her unto me. To goodman Jonathan Wire twenty shillings. To my son John Sym & his heirs all that messuage &c called Gould's, in Leigh. If he die before he accomplish the age of twenty one years I do will and give the said tenement to my loving daughter Elizabeth the wife of John Fowler, citizen of London, she to pay two hundred pounds to Sarah my wife. I give to my said son John the gold ring that Mr Wilson gave unto me, with all my plate and library of books &c. I give to my daughter Elizabeth Fowler a gold ring and a silver toothpick that were her mother's. To Josias Wheeler of Stowmarket ten shillings and to the son of William Wheeler in Woodham Ferris twenty shillings and to Sarah the daughter of Thomas Wheeler ten shillings. If my son and daughter die without either of them having heirs of their bodies lawfully begotten or not having first disposed of by will or otherwise of said Gould's &c. then the overseers shall sell the said tenement to the best value they can and of the price thereof to have twenty pounds apiece for their pains, besides allowances for their other charges, and divide the remainder into three equal parts, whereof I will one to the children of my wife Sarah, another to the children of Elizabeth North, wife of Stephen North and the children of Josias Wheeler of Stowmarket, of William Wheeler of Woodham Ferris and of Thomas Wheeler of Leigh. The third part I will to the children of my brother Patrick Gardner and of my sister Christian Ramsey and of my cousin Henry Sym in the Carrse of Gawrie in Scotland, by the means of my brother Mr Thomas Young to be delivered. I appoint Sarah, my dear and loving wife to be full executrix and intreat my well beloved brother Mr Thomas Younge and my well beloved sons in law John Fowler and John Barfoote and John Straight, son in law to my beloved wife Sarah, to be overseers.

Consistory C^t of London, Book Allen Leaf 356.

[The marriage license of Mr. John Symes, as well as that of his kinsman Mr. John Ward of Hadleigh, I have given in my Collection of Extracts from Marriage Licenses granted by the Bishop of London, recently printed.—H. F. W.

The Rev. John Ward of Hadleigh, named in this will, came to New England and was the minister at Haverhill, Mass., from 1645 till his death, Dec. 27, 1693. The reference to him in this will may furnish a clew to the name and parentage of his mother, the wife of Rev. Nathaniel Ward the Simple Cobler.—EDITOR.]

ROBERT BOLTON of Ipswich in the Co. of Suffolk, Doctor of Physick,

17 December 1646, proved 22 January 1646. I will that eight hundred pounds shall be disposed of and laid out by my executrix for the use and benefit of William Bolton, my son, within two years after my decease, in manner and form hereafter expressed, viz: I do desire my brother in law Joseph Ward, Cl., my brother in law Richard Golty, clerk, and my cousin John Symondes, clerk, &c to be a means to procure a purchase of certain lands and tenements for the sum of eight hundred pounds, to be settled and assured unto and upon the said William Bolton & the heirs of his body lawfully to be begotten, and, for want of such issue, the remainder to Deborah Bolton, my daughter, her heirs and assigns for ever. I give and bequeath to the said Deborah my daughter all that messuage &c in Earl Stonham, in the Co. of Suff., which I late had of the grant and demise of Ambrose Goodwin Esq. and other my lands &c in Earl Stonham. To the said Deborah also one hundred pounds to be paid unto her at her age of eighteen years. I give unto my mother Mrs Deborah Ward the sum of ten pounds, to be paid within twelve months next after my decease. To the said Joseph Ward, Richard Golty and John Symondes, to every of them forty shillings for their care and pains &c. To the poor of the parish of St. Mary Tower wherein I now dwell forty shillings. The rest of my goods and chattells, rights and credits, lands and tenements, shipping, parts of ships and personal estate I give unto Anne, my loving wife, whom I make and ordain executrix.

John Symondes one of the witnesses.   Fines, 8 (P. C. C.)

[Dr. Robert Bolton, the testator, was a step-son of Rev. Samuel Ward, town preacher of Ipswich. Joseph Ward, clerk, named by him was his half brother, and was rector of Badingham in Suffolk. Richard Golty, clerk, rector of Framlingham in Suffolk, was the husband of Deborah Ward a half sister of the testator. See Muskett's Candler pedigree, vol. 41, p. 283.—EDITOR.]

ANNE WARD of Stratford, in the County of Suffolk, widow, 16 October 1634, proved 7 November 1634. To John Ward, my eldest son, twenty pounds of lawful money of England, which, together with the legacy left him by his father's will, doth make one hundred and three score pounds to be paid unto my said son when he shall be of the age of two and twenty years. To my son Samuel Ward fifty pounds of like lawful money, which, together with the legacy given him in his father's will, doth make one hundred and fifty pounds to be paid him at the age of two and twenty. To my two sons John and Samuel all my plate, linen, brass and pewter, to be equally divided between them, the one part to be kept and reserved in the hands of Mr. John Clarke of Colchester, to be given to my son John Ward when he shall be of the age of two and twenty years, unto whose care I do also commend the tuition of my said son in his minority; and the other part to be kept and reserved in the hands of John Barker of Stratford, clothiers to be given to my son Samuel when he shall be of the age of two and twenty years, unto whose care also I do commend the tuition of my said son in his minority. I give unto my two sons John and Samuel Ward all that my fourth part in the ship called the Unity of Manitree and all my stock therein, and also my eighth part of the ship Johnes of Manitree &c. and all the profits that shall be raised by means of the said ships, to be reserved and kept by my executors to be equally divided between my two sons, to either of them his part when he shall be of the age of two and twenty. If both sons die before they come to that age my executors shall give and bestow one hundred pounds amongst my husband Barker's kindred and one hundred amongst my own kindred, where they shall see most need, and one hundred amongst my husband Ward's kindred &c.   To Mr. Samuel Linsell, minister of Stratford forty shillings, to Mr. John Rodgers, lecturer in Dedham, and to Mr. John Eedes minister of Lawford forty shillings. To the poor of Stratford forty shillings.

I do make and ordain John Clerke of Colchester in the County of Essex, chirurgeon, and John Barker of Stratford in the County of Suffolk, clothier, to be my executors &c., and I give them ten pounds apiece for their pains; and my friends Mr. Samuel Linsell and Mr. John Eedes supervisors.

Seager, 105.

[Mr. John Ward, one of the sons of this Mrs. Anne Ward, was a resident of Ipswich, in New England, as we learn from his will, dated 28 December, 1652, now among the Essex County Court Papers (III. 46). It was sworn to in court 25—1 mo. 1656 by Mr. Robert Payne, to whom it was sent sealed up with a letter. The following abstract may be of value in connection with the mother's will: To my cousin Nathaniel Ward, son of my uncle Nathaniel, the house and land given me by my father in his will, lying in Mersey in County Essex in old England. To my said uncle the rents and profit of that tenement since I made Edmund Sharman of Dedham last my attorney. To my cousin Ward's of Wethersfield two youngest sons twenty pounds apiece when of age of one and twenty years. To my cousin John Barker's eldest daughter Anne Barker twenty pounds. To Samuel Barker, my cousin John Barker's son, ten pounds (it is to be understood John Barker of Boxted in Essex). To my mother's poor kindred ten pounds, which I do desire my cousin John Barker to distribute. To my cousin Samuel Sharman's two youngest sons ten pounds apiece, this is to be understood my cousin Sharman that died some X years since in Boston in New England, to be paid them at one and twenty or to those that have now the care of them. Ten pounds to my cousin Philip Sharman of "rood" Island. My books and chirurgeon's chest to Thomas Andrews of Ipswich. Linen to cousin Nathaniel Ward when of age. Twenty pounds to Robert Payne and he to be executor. The remainder to Harvard College.

Wit: Richard Shearman and Thomas Spale (by mark).

This was evidently written in Boston, if I may judge from the names of the witnesses. The testator was called John Ward of Ipswich chirurgeon 19 Nov. 1651, in Vol. XII. 63, of Essex Court Papers.

The John Clerke of Colchester, chirurgeon, whom Mrs. Anne Ward appointed one of the joint executors of her will, was undoubtedly the John Clarke of Boston and Newbury, chirurgeon, referred to in the Memoir of Nathaniel Ward, p. 194.   HENRY F. WATERS.

See also REGISTER, vol. 22, pp. 31-3.—EDITOR.]

JOHN WAYTE of Meesden in the County of Hertford clerk, 17 June 1664, proved 27 May 1669. I give unto Joseph Wayte, my nephew, clerk, all my goods and chattels whatsoever, all my ready moneys, bonds, bills, debts due unto me, plate, pewter, linen apparell, all my books, manuscripts, chests &c. and make him sole executor.   Coke, 65.

JOSEPH WAITE of Sproughton in the County of Suffolk, clerk, 7 June 1669, proved 11 September 1671. To my dear and honored mother Mistress Judith Laurence ten pounds to be paid within one year after my decease. To my loved sister Mary Laurence forty pounds at day of her marriage or within one whole year after the same. The rest of my house and lands, goods and chattels &c. to my dearly beloved wife Margaret, the house and lands in Framlingham for and during her natural life and after her decease to my cousin Master Samuel Golty of Ipswich clerk and to my loving brother Master Thomas Whiting of Hadleigh, draper, as trustees. This house and land which cost me in purchase five hundred and three score and five pounds is to be sold and the proceeds divided by even and equal portions to each of my natural brothers and sisters then surviving in old

England or in New, or to the heirs of each of them. Five pounds apiece to my executors. Wife Margaret to be sole executrix.
Witness: John Richardson, John Livermer.   Duke, 117.

MARGARET WAITE of Ipswich, widow, 1 April 1675, proved 5 August 1675. To my mother, Mrs. Judith Lawrence, twenty pounds, and to my sister Mary Lawrence eighty pounds. To my nephew Lawrence Smyth one hundred pounds. To my brother Mr. Samuel Smyth of London five pounds. To my other three brothers, Mr. Robert Howe, Mr. Thomas Whitinge and Mr. John Whitinge, five pounds apiece. To my cousin Thomas Lawrence in Bedfordshire five pounds. To Mrs. Margaret Huthinson of Lee near London and her sister Mrs. Sarah Reed in Lincolnshire five pounds apiece. To my niece Sarah Lungley of Milford ten pounds at one and twenty.
"Also I geve to soe many of the brothers and sisters of my dear husband as shalbe livinge att my deccase in old England or new the sume of forty shillinges apeece to buy them somethinge for a small remembrance of me, and to my cousin Joseph Wait, Hellen Aldus and Mary Wait, to each of them five poundes." To my good friends Mr. Samuel Golty and Mr. Benjamin Browning of Ipswich five pounds apiece. To Mary, wife of Robert Goodrich of Woodbridge and Elizabeth, wife of John Cope of Ipswich forty shillings apiece. To the widow Raymond of St. Peter's parish, Ipswich, twenty shillings. To Mrs. Raymond and her daughter Russell forty shillings. To eight ministers (named)—servants named. To Samuel Greene of St. Clement's and his wife. My executors to be Mr. Samuel Golty of Ipswich and Mr. Thomas Whitinge of Hadleigh.
In a codicil made 25 May 1675 she calls herself widow and relict of Joseph Waite of Sproughton, clerk, and refers to a judgment obtained in Town Court of Colchester against William Stockton of Ipswich, gen[t], in the sum of two hundred pounds in the hands of John Trewelove of Sproughton; assigned and set over unto Richard Truelove of Sproughton, gen[t]. The said Richard Truelove is appointed executor as to it.
                                   Suffolk Wills (Ipswich)
                                   Book Fanconberge, Leaf 140.

[Joseph Waite, whose will and that of his wife Margaret are here given, was a brother of John Waite who settled at Malden, Mass., and of Mary, wife of Robert Lord of Ipswich, Mass. See a letter of their sister, Mrs. Susan Redington, in the REGISTER, vol. 31, p. 161. See also REGISTER, vol. 32, pp. 188–96; vol. 41, p. 283. —EDITOR.]

NATHANIEL WARD, rector of Pitsey, Essex, clerk, 20 February 1687, proved at Chelmsford 11 May 1688. To wife Elizabeth house and fifty-five acres of land called Felmoores in Pitsey during her life. To daughter Ward four score pounds, to be paid after decease of my wife, out of said house and land. The said house and land, so charged, after the decease of my wife I give to my son Samuel Ward and to his heirs forever upon condition he pay the fourscore pounds to his sister so soon as the lands shall come and descend unto him. All the rest of my goods, chattels and personal estate whatsoever I give to my loving wife Elizabeth Ward and I do nominate and appoint her to be sole executor &c.
                            B. Parrett (Archd. of Essex), L. 138.

EDMUND GOLTYE, of Ipswich in the County of Suffolk, merchant, 13 December 1614, proved 13 May 1615. Wife Susan, James Tillott mch[t],

William Carr and Isaac Dey, clothier, shall have, hold and enjoy all my lands and tenements in the parish of St Matthew in Ipswich and Branford in said County for twelve years, for payment of debts and of legacies following:—to daughter Susan one hundred and fifty pounds at age of twenty or on day of marriage, to daughter Elizabeth one hundred and fifty pounds at age of twenty or day of marriage, to son Myles Goltye one hundred pounds at age of twenty four years. Sons Richard and Edmund. To wife lands, tenements &c. in Bocking, Ashe, Hemyngston and Gosbeck for life, and after her death then to eldest son Richard and his heirs. To son Edmund, after the aforenamed debts and legacies shall be duly paid, my houses, lands and tenements in Ipswich and Bramford. (Mem. His son Richard seems to have been in Pembroke Hall, Cambridge, at the time).

Rudd, 47.

[I have references to other wills and records relating to the Wards and their connections which I hope to present soon. My friend, the Rev. W. E. Layton, whose friendly attentions to me during my visit to Ipswich and kind assistance in examining the parish registers there I shall always recall with gratitude, gave me the following copy of an inscription to the memory of the famous Town Preacher of Ipswich. HENRY F. WATERS.]

Mr. Samuel Ward minister olim hujus ecclesiæ & eximius concionator Gyppovicensis, ad Clavem denatus, apud nos sepultus est Martij 8° 1639.

MARK MOTT Rector of Raigne parva in the County of Essex Doctor of Divinity, 18 December 1630, proved 1 April 1631.

I give to the library of St. John's College in Cambridge Alexander Halles his somes in three volumes in folio and Lyra on the Bible in six volumes in folio and Altissodocensis and Occam on the Sentences and Pelbartus on the Sentences in four volumes in 4to. Item I give unto my father Mr Mark Mott my book called Mr. Downeham's Directions to a godly life. To my brother Mr Robert Woolriche twenty nobles and to my sister Sarah his wife three stoned pots tipped with silver, and to John Mott my brother a watch. To my sister Alice Mott ten shillings and to my sister Katherine Mott a silver toasting iron a silver grate a fruit dish of china and six sallet dishes three saucers and six porrengers of China and all my stone pots and dishes and my other stuff of stone. To my worthy neighbor Mr Doctor Barker my Turkey grogram gown, my wrought satin cassock and my tippet, a pair of gloves and a girdle. And to my faithful friend John Clarke of Copford Hall twenty shillings to put into a ring. To my cousin Alice the wife of John Draper of Felsted four sallet dishes of china. To my cousin Dorothy the wife of John Taylecott* two porengers of china. To my son Henry Mott an English Bible in 8vo and another bible in folio of the old translation. To my daughter Frances a bible in quarto of the old translation. To my daughter Dorothy an English Bible in quarto of the new translation. To Mr Thomas Dyke of Horam in Sussex twenty shillings to make him a ring. To William Dyke of Faunt in Sussex twenty shillings to make him a ring. To the poor people of Rayne six pounds thirteen shillings and four pence to be disposed of for their good by mine executors within six months next after my decease. And to the church of Rayne a green cloth carpet for the communion table fringed at the ends with green silk fringe and a green cloth for the pulpit fringed round with silk fringes. To Jane Hamersly my servant thirteen pounds six shillings

---

* This was Caylecott in the record. My friend Mr. Smith, at my request, examined the original will and found that it should be as above. H. F. W.

and eight pence to be paid her within one year next after my decease. To Leonard Greene twenty shilling and a mourning cloak. To my man Thomas Pullin forty shillings and a mourning cloak and my suit of serge which I late made. To Thomas Mott my brother John Mott's son my best cloak. To Mark Mott my brother Adrian Mott's son my cloak that is faced with velvet to the bottom and lined on the back and also my silk wrought cassock of stitched grogram with the satin sleeves a budge gown and all my manuscripts paper books and written papers. Item I give to my cousin Mr Samuel Collins vicar of Braintree my mourning cloak and to Mr Samuel Wharton vicar of Felsted my longest mourning gown and my chamlet grogram cassock. To my good friend Mr Doctor Aylet and his wife either of them twenty shillings to buy them rings. And I give more unto her a bason and ewer of china a bowl two fruit dishes .six sallet dishes and six saucers all of china. To Mrs Smith the elder of Cressing Temple my silver box with the case of counters of mill six pences in it. To Elizabeth the wife of Mark Mott my son in law my great guilded standing cup with a cover to it and three china poringers. To Mercy Mott my daughter my down bed with the bolster to it three down pillows a feather bolster my best pair of blankets my best coverlet a pair of my best laced curtains my cyprus chest and all my needle work vallence belonging to my best bed all my needle work covers of stools and stools which are in my best chamber a needle work side board cloth two needle work cushions for the windows in my best chamber an outlandish cabinet standing in the same chamber a furniture of damask linen and all her mother's childbed linen. To my daughter Frances all things wrought with needlework in my great parlor with the stools there and covers belonging to them my best featherbed two feather bolsters a pair of pillows a pair of blankets & an arras coverlet. Item I will that all my linen unbequeathed shall be divided by mine executors amongst my five daughters, part & part alike. Item I give to George Paske of Rayne forty shillings to be paid him within three months next after my decease and a suit of old apparel & an old rug gown and all the residue of my goods cattle chattels books plate money & debts whatsoever herein not bequeathed my debts legacies and funeral charges with the expenses about my will first paid deducted & allowed I give to my executors to sell & dispose of and the money thereof coming to be equally divided amongst my five daughters. Item I devise unto my eldest son Henry Mott from and after the accomplishment of his age of 21 years & to the heirs of his body lawfully begotton all that my copyhold land containing by estimation eight acres lying in Romford in le Reeden in the county aforesaid until the said Henry shall refuse to convey and assure at the request costs and charges of my other children respectively the lands tenements and hereditaments hereafter given and bequeathed unto my said other children in such manner and form as the said lands are respectively given to them by this my last will and testament. And in case the said Henry Mott shall refuse to make any such conveyance or assurance then I will and bequeath the said copyhold land unto my son Mark Mott and the heirs of his body lawfull begotten. To my second son Mark Mott from and after the accomplishment of his age of 21 years & to the heirs of his body lawfully to be begotten all my lands called Rochfords with the appurtenances in Bocking and also my copyhold lands called Goddings with the appurtenances in Brayntree. I give to my daughter Mercy Mott from & after the acccomplishment of her age of 21 years or her day of marriage, which shall first happen, the one moiety, in two parts equally to be divided, of my two farms whereof one is called Old Hall, the other Watkins & the moiety of a meadow called Bawdes Meade & of another meadow called Round Mead adjoining to it, being copyhold, all lying in much Hadham, Herts. To my daughter Frances Mott, at 21 or day of marriage, the other moiety (of the two farms & meads). To my daughter Dorothy Mott, at 21 or day of marriage, one full third part of my manor or Lordship of Great Birch & lands &c part & parcel thereof, situate &c in Great Birch, East Thorp. Layer Bretton, Copford, Stanway or elsewhere in Essex. To my daughter Hannah Mott, at 21 or day of marriage, one other full third part of said manor. And the other full third part of the same manor I give to my daughter Mary Mott at 21 or day of marriage. If any of my said five daughters happen to die before accomplishing said age or day of marriage then her part shall be divided equally among the rest of my said daughters then living. If all my said children die without issue, lawfully begotten, then I will and bequeath my said lands called Rochfords & Goddings unto my brother John Mott during his natural life and after his decease to his son Mark Mott & to his heirs forever. And my said Manor of Great Birch unto my brother Adrian Mott during his natural life, and after his decease to his son Mark & his heirs forever. And my said farms called Old Hall & Watkins with Baudes Mead & Round Mead unto my sister Sara Woolrich during her natural life & after her decease to the heirs of her body & for want of such issue to remain to my right heirs. And my said lands in Romford to remain to my said cousin Samuel Wharton & Martha his wife during their natural lives & after their decease to the heirs of the body of the said Martha & for want of such issue to remain to my right heirs. And I do appoint the said Samuel Wharton & my said brother Adryan Mott to be executors of this my last will & I do give to each of them for their great pains & care that they are to take for the performance of this my will twenty pounds apiece, charging them as they will answer before God at the dreadful day of judgment to see my will faithfully performed without partiality or respect of any person or persons whatsoever. And I do nominate the said Mr Dr Barker & my said father Mark Mott my said brother Robert Woolritch & the said John Clark of Copford Hall overseers. And I do nominate assign & appoint the said Samuel Wharton & my said brother Adryan Mott to be several guardians of my said children, they to receive the rents & profits in manner and form following (that is to say) that my said cousin Samuel Wharton shall have all the said lands & ten^{ts} in much Hadham called Old Hall Watkins Bawdes Mead & Round Mead, and receive the rents and profits thereof, that my brother Adryan Mott shall have the rest of my manor land & tents & receive the rents & profits thereof. And my said children shall be bred up in good education & nurture. And I do will & charge my son Henry Mott of my blessing that he suffers and permits the said Adryan Mott to be his guardian & to receive the rents & profits of all the lands in Sussex which are descended or fall to him by his mother. And that his said guardian shall allow unto him sufficient & liberal maintenance out of the said rents & profits of the said lands in Sussex until the said age of one & twenty years. And the said guardians shall severally allow unto the said other children out of the rents & profits sufficient & liberal maintenance until their several & respective ages &c.

My son Mark Mott shall have for his education & maintenance out of my said lands in much Hadham ten pounds yearly until such times as the lands called Rochfords & Goddings shall happen to come into his hands & possession or the hands & possession of his guardian.

And thus revoking all former wills by me formerly made I pronounce this to be my last will and Testament being written in five sheets of paper & have set my hand to the last of them & my seal to the label that fasteneth them together this eighteenth day of December Anno Dñi 1630 Anno regni Dñi Regis Caroli Sexto.   MARKE MOTT
in the presence of us Emanuell Stocke Henry Josslen William Hañiond. Proved 1 April 1631

    Book Allen (Consistory Court of the Bishop of London) Leaf 81.

THOMAS FITCH of Bockinge, Essex, clothier, 11 December 1632, proved 12 February 1632. To the poor of Bocking three pounds. To my eldest son, Thomas, that chief messuage wherein I now dwell in Bocking and the messuage adjoining, now in the occupation of the said Thomas, and all the lands tenements &c which I purchased of William Collin in Bocking, and the lands and tenements in Bocking which I lately purchased of Edward Peppen genᵗ and his wife and John Amptill and his wife and the barn in Bocking by Panfield Lane which I lately purchased of Thomas Trotter, upon condition that he pay my sister Stracy twenty shillings yearly during her natural life. To my son and his heirs the messuage in Bocking late of Richard Usher deceased and which I lately purchased of Paul Usher and Peter Kirby and Ursula Bond, widow, and the little garden or orchard in Bocking now in the occupation of Richard Skinner or his assigns, and the tenement in the occupation of Thomas Laye in Bocking by Panfield Lane and the great orchard adjoining which I purchased of Mr Thomas Trotter, to enter upon the same at his age of one and twenty years. To my son John two hundred pounds at one and twenty.

"Item I give to my sonne James one hundred pounds to be paid him when he shalbe a batchelor of Art of two yeares standinge in the uniu'sity of Cambridge, for I desire he should be bredd up a scholler, And I also give him and my minde is that he shall have thirtie pounds a year paid him by my Executrix out of my lands and teñts. from the tyme of his admission to be a scholler in Cambridge until he be or have tyme there to be a master of arts." To my sons Nathaniel and Jeremy, to either of them a moiety and half part of the farm messuage, Lands and tenements, both free and copy, lying and being in Birch or elsewhere in Essex, which I lately purchased of William Brock, genᵗ, to be equally divided between them, and they to enter upon the same at their several ages of one and twenty. My executrix shall lay out six hundred and fifty pounds within one year after my decease and shall purchase with the same as much lands and tenements within the County of Essex as the same will buy in a frugal and good manner, to be assured to the use of my two younger sons Samuel and Joseph. And my wife Anne shall have the lands and tenements in Birch, which I have given to Nathaniel and Jeremy, and the lands &c to be purchased for Samuel and Joseph until these four sons shall severally accomplish their ages of sixteen years &c. To my three daughters Mary, Anna and Sara three hundred pounds apiece, whereof two hundred pounds apiece to be paid at their several ages of eighteen, and the other hundred at one and twenty. To my loving friends Mr. Hooker, Mr. Nathaniel Rogers, Mr. Daniel Rogers and Mr. Collins twenty shillings apiece as a token of my love. To son Thomas my great oil cistern of lead, so as he give and deliver to my son John the little cistern of lead for oil which I late bought and gave to Thomas. To my brother John Malden and my sister his wife twenty shillings apiece. To Henry Stracy my kinsman five

pounds.   To my brothers John Reeve and William Stacy (Stracy?) forty
shillings apiece and to my brother Jeremy Reeve twenty shillings as a
token of my love.   The residue to my wife whom I make sole executrix,
she to enter upon a bond of two thousand pounds to my said brothers John
Reeve and William Stacy (Stracy?) with condition to prove this will within
two months after my decease and to pay all the legacies and perform all
things contained therein.   My said brothers to be supervisors.
    W. Lyngwood one of the witnesses.   Russell, 20.

JOHN MANSFEILDE Esquire 13 July, 1601, proved 31 July, 1601.   I do
make my executors my loving friends David Waterhouse and John Preisley
of the Inner Temple Esquires.   And my will and mind is, as concerning
my lands, tenements, goods and chattels whatsoever, that first by sale or
otherwise, as my executors can best, my debts be satisfied.   And, after that
and funeral charges and other parts of this my will performed, my will and
pleasure is that my son John Mansfeilde shall have two parts in six, to be
divided, of my clear estate.   And my house at Malton and the residue of
my clear estate to be equally betwixt Elizabeth my wife and my three
daughters, Elizabeth, Anne and Martha divided; for Armyn my will is
that Mr Pytt, or such as have the interest, should according to true meaning assure it to Mr David Waterhouse or such as he shall appoint, upon
condition for the payment of such moneys as is due to him, and that, after
two hundred pounds a year thereof be assured to Robert Hemyngway and
Bryan Crowther and their heirs, paying above the fourteen hundred and
fifty pounds already by them paid according to the articles between them
and me, the surplusage, as well of money as lands, equally to be divided
betwixt me and Mr Waterhouse, according to our agreement; for the
"Mylnes" at York and Stamford Brigg mills assured to Master Steven
Waterhous and Mr. John Mylner the true meaning is that the one moiety
should go, after debts paid, to me and my heirs and the other to Mr. Waterhouse and his heirs; for the land at Huton conveyed to Mr. Steven Waterhous and his heirs my will is that, by sale or otherwise thereof, satisfaction
be made of my debts and what shall remain to go to wife and children according to this my will.   And whereas divers other lands and leases, goods and
chattels are in the hands of other men to my use and in trust, only at my
disposition my will is that all such be conveyed and delivered unto my said
executors for the performance of my will in manner and form aforesaid.
And as concerning legacies to be given by me my will is first that out of
my lease at Sytterington, lately taken of Her majesty, there be assured
unto Mrs Gregorie, for her great pains and care taken in this my sickness,
ten pounds yearly during her life, if the lease so long continue, and twenty
pounds in money.
    Further additions &c.   First the tuition of my children and their estates;
my will is that Mr David Waterhouse shall have the tuition and government
of my son John and of his estate during his nonage.   Item, my will is that
Elizabeth my wife shall have the tuition of Elizabeth my daughter, putting
in good security to my executors for her portion and education.   Item, my
will is my sister Mrs Hassell and my sister Wilkinson shall have the tuition
of my other two daughters and their portions, they putting in good security
to my executors for their portions and education.   Item I give to my
brother Rafe and my three sisters, each of them, five marks for a remembrance.   Item my will is that my executors shall pay unto Mr Bonde, to
whom my nephew John stands prentice, twenty pounds by year for the two

first years he shall employ him in his trade beyond seas, not doubting but the said master Bonde shall make him free according to our agreement. Item I give to each of my servants menial, as well here as in the country, five marks apiece.   Woodhall, 47.

[I think there can be little doubt who this was. He was the father of Mrs. Ann Keayne and of Mrs. Elizabeth Wilson. His son John, I recollect, speaks in his will, which I have seen but cannot now lay my hand on the extract I made from it, of property in Yorkshire which he inherited.—H. F. WATERS. Cotton Mather in his Magnalia, edition of 1853, vol. 1, page 305, calls the father of Mrs. Elizabeth, wife of Rev. John Wilson of Boston, Mass., " Sir John Mansfield, master of the Minories and Queen's Surveyor," and her brother John Mansfield, in a petition June 25, 1661, says that his father " was a rich man, a justice of the Peace and a knight." REGISTER, vol. 6, page 156. It is evident, however, that he was not knighted.—EDITOR.]

I RICHARD WYLLYS of hole mynde the xxiiii day of January in the yere of our lord God m^c vc xxix—proved 11 May 1532. My body to be buried in the church of Fenny Compton, before our Lady in the chancell. To said church six shillings eight pence. To the three orders of freres within the shire of Warwick and the city of Coventry forty shillings, every of them to say for my soul one trentall of masses. To the mother church of Coventry in recompense and satisfaction of my misstything, no tything, tythen forgotten, of all other trespasses. wrongs and injuries that I have done to the house and mother church of Coventry and the prior and monks there, serving God at any time in my life, twenty shillings. To the church of Napton and parish of the same twenty shillings, in satisfaction of such trespasses as I have done with my cattle to them within the said parish. To the Church of Priors Marston &c ten shillings. To the church of Priors Hardwick &c six shillings eight pence. To the township and parishes of Nether Shuckburgh six shillings eight pence. To son Richard Willys forty pounds which I owe him of his marriage money. To every one of my daughters that is single unmarried the day of my decease twenty pounds. I will that Joane my wife have all my lands in Lodbroke and three messuages in Napton, for term of her life; and after her decease I will that my son William and his heirs have them. To Joane Shendon widow in recompense of my offences to her done twenty shillings. The residue of all my lands and tenements I will that my son William have them to him and his heirs according to his inheritance in the same. To John Clyffe and his wife ten sheep. To John Kynge ten sheep. The residue of my goods &c to Joane my wife whom I make sole executrix. And I make William Willys, Richard Willys, and Sir John Sowtham supervisors.   Thower, 15.

AMBROSE WILLIS of Fenicompton in the County of Warwick, 8 June 32^d of Elizabeth, proved 21 November 1590. Reference to grant made to wife Amie at time of marriage. To son Richard all the goods &c in my pasture in old Hodnell, and my household stuff in Fenicompton and half the money I now have in my house. My son Richard and his wife (if he marry) and the children of his body lawfully begotten to be provided competent meat and drink at the charges of Amye my wife according to her ability. To John, Margaret and Alice Edes children of John Edes of Loxelie ten pounds to each, to be paid by Amye my wife and Richard my son by equal portions. To my servants, six shillings eight pence. To every cottage house in Fenicompton twelve pence. Towards the reparations of the church in Fenicompton twenty shillings. To Robert Porter forty shillings. To Elizabeth Butcher so called the younger six shillings eight pence. To my godson Thomas Pomfrett twenty shillings. To my godson Ambrose Makepeace ten shilling. To the rest of my godchildren, each one twelve pence. The rest of my goods to Amie my wife whom I make sole executrix. And I make overseers my brothers in law John Edes and William Makepeace and for their pains I give to every of them twenty shillings. Drury, 81.

RICHARD WILLES of Fenny Compton 10 June 1597, proved 16 June 1597. My mother, by the agreement of my two grandfathers before marriage, is to have the manor or farm of Fenny Compton, where she now dwells, during her widowhood, and if she marry again then to have only an annuity of six pounds thirteen shillings four pence. I do confirm the same & give to her, only during her widowhood the one half of my pasture at Hodnell and half my sheep there and that household stuff my father gave me by his will. Through negligence my wife's jointure hath not been by writing limited. She shall have in lieu thereof my farm at Nafton now or late in the tenure of my uncle Richard Willes or his assigns &c. Other bequests to wife. I give and bequeath to my son William my said farm at Napton (my wife's interest always excepted) during his life and after his decease to the heirs male of his body lawfully begotten, and for default of such issue, to my son George and the heirs male of his body lawfully begotten, and for default of such issue to my son Richard and the heirs male of his body lawfully begotten, and for default of such issue to the right heirs of me the said Richard. To my daughter Judith three hundred pounds, to be paid her in money at the eighteenth year of her age or within three months after her marriage if she marry between fourteen and eighteen years of age. And if my wife be now with child and it live I give it also, whether it be son or daughter, three hundred pounds in money, to be paid when it shall come to the age of eighteen years. To John Paine five pounds. To every cottager whom my executors shall think fit ten shillings apiece. To every servant in the house six shillings eight pence. But to William Heyword, for his good service, twenty shillings. Towards the reparation of the chancell of Fenny Compton, wherein I desire to be buried, forty shillings. The residue of my lands and goods I give to my son George whom I make executor of this my last will and testament and I constitute and appoint Mr Hollway, vicar of Cropreddy and my cousin Richard Triste of Maidford, my mother and brother Eides overseers of this my last will and testament and also guardians of my said executor and give to each of them a gold ring of twenty shillings in value. I give my nurse Turner five pounds.

Commission issued 16 June 1597 to Hester Willes, relict of Richard Willes defunct, to administer during the minority of George Willes, son and executor. Cobham, 65.

RICHARD WILLIS the younger of Fenny Compton in the Co. of Warwick gent. 7 December 1639 proved 8 May 1640. To my brother Mr. William Willis of London, gen^t two hundred pounds out of my lands and tenements in the lordships of Napton upon the Hill and Ladbrooke and Southam. I give and bequeath to the heirs of my body lawfully begotten or to be begotten all my lands and tenements whatsoever, lying and being in Napton and Ladbrooke and Southam aforesaid, and for want of such issue I give and bequeath the said lands &c to my nephew Mr. George Willys and to the heirs of his body &c upon condition that there be paid to my brother William Willys aforesaid out of the same lands &c the sum of two hundred pounds aforesaid; and for want of such issue of the said George Willys then to my heirs forever. I give to my brother Mr George Willis and to my sister Mrs Mary Willis his wife ten shillings apiece, and to my two nieces Hester and Amy Willys four pounds apiece and to my nephew Samuel Willis four pounds. I give to my brother in law Mr Thomas Guilder and to my sister Judith Gilder his wife twenty shillings apiece, and to every one of their children twenty shillings apiece to buy every one of them two silver spoons apiece of ten shillings price apiece. To my brother in law Mr John Ekins and to my sister Mary Ekins his wife twenty shillings apiece and to every one of their children twenty shillings apiece (as above). To my brother in law John Rutter and to my sister Elizabeth Robertes and to my sister Mary Millington and to my brother Thomas Harris ten shillings apiece, and to my sister Anne Powle three pounds and to my cousin Thomas Powle her son twenty shillings and to my cousins Richard, Edmund and Bridget Harris, children of the said Thomas Harris by Bridget his wife late deceased, four pounds apiece. To my sister in law Anne Smith and to Hester her sister ten shillings apiece. To my cousin Margaret Grant twenty shillings. To Mr James Sutton Rector of Fenny Compton three pounds and to Mary Sutton his wife three pounds and to their children Samuel and Hannah Sutton ten shillings apiece and to their son Thomas Sutton twenty shillings. To Mr. Nathaniel Cotten of Adson forty shillings. To my loving and careful surgeon Richard Dighton of Gloucester gen^t three pounds for his love, pains and faithfulness towards me in my weak state and lameness. To the Inhabitants, Churchwardens and Overseers of the Poor of Fenny Compton twelve pounds. To those of Napton four pounds. To Persis Veares ten shillings to Richard Westbury and his wife five shillings apiece, to Mary Barroes five shillings, to Elizabeth Clarke widow five shillings, to the children of Mary Willys widow twenty shillings to be equally divided amongst them, to Edward Petifer and his wife five shillings apiece, to my cousin Luce Robertes twenty shillings, to John Basse and his wife five shillings apiece, to Robert Hastinges five shillings if living; if deceased then to his wife, to Simon Paine and his wife five shillings apiece, all these being poor inhabitants of Fenny Compton, and to every one of my household servants five shillings apiece. To Mr Sutton and Mr Cotton above named forty shillings apiece to be bestowed in cloth for mourning cloaks to be worn at my funeral. I make my brother William Willis and my nephew George Willis joint executors.

Coventry, 57.

GEORGE WILLYS of Hartford upon Connecticot 14 December 1644 proved 9 February 1647. I give all my buildings, lands, tenements and hereditaments in Hartford bounds and at Tuxus Sepos unto my beloved wife Mary Willys and unto my son Samuel and his heirs &c. To my son George all my buildings and land upon the West side of the great river in the bounds of Wethersfield; now in the hands and occupation of divers men, provided he do come over into New England and settle himself and family here according as I have wrote him by letter dated the 28th of October past (a copy whereof is among my papers superscribed with my own hands) and provided that he make payment and send over hither in goods according to the tenor of the said letter to the value of three hundred pounds, it being my will that if he attend the terms propounded by me in the letter aforesaid he shall enjoy and there shall be made good to him what I have offered and tendered to him in my said letter, which is the buildings and land aforesaid, as also one hundred pounds to be paid him in corn and cattle within three months after his arrival here, reserving only twenty pounds a year out of the said lands which my will is he shall pay to my beloved wife Mary Willys during the term of her life. But in case my son do not attend my advice in transplanting himself and family into these parts or perform the conditions propounded by me as afore then my will is that the buildings and lands aforesaid shall be and remain at the whole dispose of my beloved wife Mary Willys. My son George shall enjoy and possess my lands and buildings at Fenny Compton in Old England according to a deed made to him by my ffeoffees, and the heirs of his body after him, and in the case of the want of such heirs then to fall to my son Samuel and the heirs of his body, next to the right heirs of me. To my daughter Hester four hundred pounds whereof two hundred pounds shall be paid at the day of her marriage. To my daughter Amy three hundred and fifty pounds, whereof one hundred and fifty pounds shall be paid at the day of her marriage. To my son Samuel all my land upon the East side of the great river within the bounds of Witherfield, he paying to my daughters Hester and Amy forty pounds apiece six years after my decease. To my friends Mr Fenwicke, Mr. Haines, Mr Hopkins, Mr Welles, Mr Webster, Mr Whyting, Capt. Mason, Mr Hooker, Mr Stone, Mr Warrham twenty shillings apiece as a token of my love. To Mrs Huett five pounds out of the debt due to me from her deceased husband and to Mr Smith five pounds out of the debt he oweth and to William Gibbins ten pounds out of Mr Smythe's debt. I make my wife sole executrix.

Witnesses Edwa: Hopkins, William Gibbins.

A codicil made 22 February 1644 discloses that Samuel was under twenty-one years of age.

And the codicil made 4 March 1644 contains bequests of twenty nobles to the poor of Hartford, five marks to the poor in Weatherfield, forty shillings to the poor of Winsor and forty shillings to the poor of Tunxus Sepos, to be paid in country commodities.   Essex, 28.

SAMUEL TOMLINS, minister of Northaw in the County of Hertford, 23 July 1661, proved 11 October 1661. To my son John my house in Northaw, which I purchased of Mr Price, and my lease of two tenements in Thredneedle Street, which I hold of Emanuel College, Cambridge, and my lease in Colman Street, which I hold of the mercers. To my daughter Haworth I have already given for her portion the sum of four hundred pounds: moreover to my grandson Sam: Haworth the sum of one hundred pounds. To my daughter Martha five hundred pounds. To my poor sister Carter the sum of twenty pounds. To my sister Ingrā forty shillings. To my cousin Thomas Willus I give all my sermon notes. To my cousin Martha Washbourne I give the sum of ten pounds. To my good friend Mr Leman the elder I give a mourning ring which was given me at the funeral of Mrs Bety Crafts. To my neighbor Henry Marsk five shillings. To Richard Noone five shillings. To goodwife Longe five shillings. To my son John my watch. To my daughter Martha my books & great bible. To son Haworth and my brother Edward Tomlins, each twenty shillings (for rings). To my brother Timothy's son Samuel ten shillings. My son John Tomlins to be executor.   May, 165.

[Edward and Timothy Tomlins, the two brothers named in Mr. Samuel Tomlins' will, were probably the two who came to Lynn, where also settled

Capt. Robert Bridges, whose wife Mary was a grand-daughter of Robert and Mary Washborne, the parents of Sara the wife of Mr. Samuel Tomlins. (See Gleanings from English Records, &c., by Emmerton and Waters, pp. 13–16.) To Lynn also came Mr. Thomas Willis of Thistleworth (Isleworth), school-master, who married Mary, daughter of —— Tomlyn of Gloucestershire (according to the pedigree of the Willis family). His wife was probably, therefore, a sister of Samuel, Thomas and Timothy Tomlyn. He had a grant of five hundred acres in Lynn, which was afterwards sold to Isaac Hart by the Rev. John Knowles (of Watertown) and his wife Elizabeth, the daughter of Mr. Willis. A reference to the pedigree, a portion of which I append, shows this match. I have taken it from the Visitation of Warwickshire, 1619 (pub. by the Harl. So. vol. 12), p. 311.

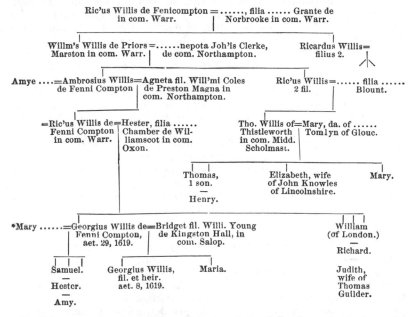

In this connection it seems well to insert the following extracts from the parish registers of Hackney, which were given to me long ago by my lamented friend the late Mr. Joseph Eedes.

Baptism. Aug. 16, 1632. Sarah d. of Samuel Tomlins, Curate of Hackney & Sarah his wife.

Dᵒ Mar. 3, 1635-6. Samuel s. of Samuel Tomlins, minister, & Sarah his wife.

Dᵒ Nov. 14, 1640. Henry s. of Calibute Downning & Margaret his wife.

Burial. Jan 21, 1633-4. Sarah d. of Samuel Tomlins, Curate of Hackney.

Dᵒ Sept. 29, 1635. Sarah Tomlins a child.

Marriage. Apr. 1, 1611. George Downinge & Jane Rockwood.

Dᵒ Dec. 4, 1651. Mʳ John Salmon & Mʳˢ Ann Downing.

Dᵒ Jan. 5, 1653-4. John Wright of Sᵗ Martins Ludgate London, haberdasher & Eliz. Downinge da. of Dʳ Downinge late of Hackney.

* In a future contribution I intend to furnish evidence as to the family connections of Mary, the last wife of Governor Wyllys of Connecticut.—HENRY F. WATERS.

Marriage.   Mar. 4, 1655–6.   George Farmery of Hackney, late of Hor-
thorpe Co. Linc. gent. & Margaret Down-
ing of Hackney.

JOHN ABINGTON of London, merchant, 14 January 1692. All just
debts to be paid whether contracted in England, Maryland or elsewhere,
especially the money due to Mr. Richard Harrison of Maryland which I
have in my hands of his. I give to Do[r] Mick. Parney, my brother in law,
all debts due to me from him. To my sister Mirriel Parney, wife of Do[r]
Parney aforesaid, the living at Stoake near Bristol, which is made over to
me for a debt and now in the possession of William Worrell. To their
daughter, my niece Mirriel Parney fifty pounds within six months. To
my niece Mirriel Abington one hundred pounds sterling. To Mrs. Alice
Nelmes one hundred pounds sterling for her separate and distinct use, to
be paid to herself; and my executors to pay to her own hands one hundred
and fifty pounds per annum for distinct and separate maintenance of herself
and the maintenance, education and bringing up of her two sons, John and
Charles and that she now goeth with. Other bequests to them. If the
said Mrs. Nelmes shall receive and enjoy the estate left her by her father
in Ireland and which she is now in suit with her brother for (then a different disposition of these bequests). To my godson John Abington, son
of William Abington deceased, fifty pounds at one and twenty. To Mr.
John Pellett, for his assistance to my executor, fifty pounds.

My will is that my land in Maryland, negroes, servants, all stocks and
debts be sold so soon as that can be done and the produce equally divided
into so many shares as the children of Mrs. Alice Nelmes shall then have
living of the three she is supposed and now to have, that is John, Charles
and one she is now big with, each to have his equal part. The remainder
to my kinsman Mr. John Abington whom I make executor.

Witness: Fenton Bynnes, Henry Dennett, Thomas Freeman.

Commission issued 21 July 1694 to Mirriel Parney, a sister, and Mirriel
Abington, a niece on the brother's side and legatees named in the will of
John Abington late of the parish of St. Faith the Virgin deceased &c. for
the reason that John Abington, executor named in the said will, hath expressly renounced &c. Catherine Countess dowager of Carnwarth in the
Kingdom of Scotland, late the wife of Samuel Collins Doctor in Medicine,
sister of the same deceased, hath also renounced &c.

Commission issued 1 April 1698 to William Isatt, the lawfully appointed
guardian of John and Charles Nelmes, minors &c. for their use and benefit
&c., the letters granted as above having been recalled.   Box, 148.

[A pedigree of the family of Abyngton may be found in the Visitations of
Gloucestershire, 1623 (pub. by the Harl. Soc.), pp. 194, 195, and on page 196
may be found the entries of baptisms, marriages and burials of members of this
family, taken from the registers of the parish of Dowdeswell. From a note we
learn that John, eldest son of Anthony Abyngton of Dowdeswell, Esq., married
Mirriell, daughter of Richard Berkeley of Stoke, Esq., by Mary his wife,
daughter of Robert Rowe and sister of Sir Thomas Rowe, kn[t], Chancellor of
the Most Noble Order of the Garter.   HENRY F. WATERS.]

JAMES ALLEN of Kempston in the County of Bedford, blacksmith, 7
January 1656, proved 20 January 1657. To my son Roger Allen, now
living in New England, the full sum of thirty pounds and to his children
ten pounds to be equally divided amongst them within six months after my
decease. To my daughter Joane the now wife of Abram Dowlittle living
now also in New England the full sum of ten pounds and to her children

ten pounds, to be equally divided amongst them within six months after my decease. To my son William twelve pence and to his daughter Elizabeth ten shillings at the age of sixteen. To my daughter Martha Parkes five pounds and to each of her sons, Matthew and John, twenty shillings apiece. To my daughter Martha also one safe cupboard, one mattress, one pair of sheets, one green chair, one green stool, one barrell, one feather bed and one feather bolster, (the last two) in case my daughter Joane comes not to demand the same within two years. To Richard Parkes husband unto Martha Parkes, half a crown. To my daughter Mary Warren's children, Mary, Rebecca and Margaret Warren and James Warren, three pounds apiece at sixteen years of age. To her other four sons, William, John, Thomas and Henry Warren, forty shillings apiece. To my son John Allen that messuage, house and out house, with the close adjoining, lying in Kempston Woodend and one close called "nyne Leyes." And the remainder to my son John, whom I make executor &c. and I appoint my two trusty and well beloved friends John Ampps of Kempstone and William Ridgeley of Newport Pagnell overseers, to each of whom twelve pence. Witness: Edmund Allen, Luke Pickeringe, the mark of Sara Witt.

Wootton, 36.

[Roger Allen or Alling of New Haven is said to have married Mary, eldest daughter of Thomas Nash. Their son James, born (it is said) 24 June, 1657, was the third minister of Salisbury and married Elizabeth, daughter of the Rev. Seaborn Cotton of Hampton.

Abram Doolittle was of New Haven and the father of a large family.

HENRY F. WATERS.]

JOHN ALEXANDER of St. Olave Southwark, Surrey, bound to Carolina in the good ship Edward Francis, whereof Thomas Man is master &c., and son and heir apparent to my father Robert Alexander of the town of Manchester in the County of Langton *als* Lancashire, 12 September 1698, proved 27 July, 1700. To brothers Robert, Charles and my youngest brother, to each of them one shilling, to my sisters, to each of them one shilling. To my wife Jane Alexander all my estate in reversion, now in possession of my father, containing one house, barn and orchard with about seventy acres of land belonging, in a place called Middle Wych in the County of Chester, after the decease of my said father, to her use and behoof during the term of her natural life and to my heirs born of her body for ever. If wife should die without issue then the said estate to Ann Nicholls of St. Olave, Southwark, widow, and her heirs and assigns forever, they to pay to Thomas Manning of St. Olave, son of Thomas Manning of Weldon, Northampton, thirty pounds, and to Joseph Manning of St. Thomas, Surrey, son of the said Thomas Manning of Weldon, fifty pounds. The residue &c to my said wife.

Noel, 94.

WILLIAM ALLEN, late of Grimston, Norfolk, but now of London gen^t,— March 1647, proved 28 April 1648. To the town of Grimston the sum of twenty pounds towards a free school there, upon condition that the said town, or inhabitants thereof, shall within the space of two years next after my decease really and legally establish the same for the free teaching of the inhabitants' children of Grimston in Religion and learning; and in case it be not so settled within that time my will and mind is that the said sum of twenty pounds be equally divided between my brother Bozoune Allen and my sister Birtham for her life only and then to her child or children, to be used and employed according to the discretion of my executor. To the poor of the parish of Grimston five pounds and to the poor of Sedgford forty shillings within a year after my decease. To my worthy friend and kinsman Sir John Thoroughgood my diamond ring and to his good lady and wife the picture in my chamber. To the virtuous wife of Mr. Thomas Thorrowgood my watch in remembrance of my love. To my brother Birtham my seal ring. To the two daughters of my land lady, Elizabeth and Chrysagon, each of them, twenty shillings. To my cousin Thomasine Wace fifty pounds to be paid her at her day of marriage in case she shall marry with the good liking and approbation of my executor, if not then to be divided between the children of my brother Bozoune and my sister Birtham. The residue of my estate equally to my said brother and sister. If my brother Bozoune shall, for want of a surrender, claim or challenge my copyhold lands as heir at law then my sister Birtham shall have and receive as much of my personal estate as shall be equivalent to the said copyhold lands.

My friend and kinsman Mr Thomas Thoroughwood, clerk, to be my sole executor and I bequeath to him ten pounds to buy him a gelding and all my books. Certain debts to be forgiven (as indicated in a special note).

A codicil to be added to the last will and Testament which was made (we are told) towards the end of March 1647 makes bequest of a ring set with nine diamonds to the Lady Thorrowgood, twenty shillings each to the wife of the executor and to the wife of William Girling, clerke, to be laid out upon two death's head rings. Whereas in my last will and testament I have given and bequeathed two legacies to the two daughters of Elizabeth Lane in Chancery Lane, widow, my mind now is that both these legacies shall be paid to Chrisagon, the younger of the said two daughters. To the poor sort and the best disposed people in Kensington forty shillings, to be distributed upon the day of my funeral. To my servant Freeman one black cloth suit of clothes and a cloke and jacket. To Robert Turner, servant to Sir John Thorowgood one black suit of clothes and boots. To Peter Meutys on eleven shillings piece of gold. To Mrs. Jane Proctor, kinswoman and servant to the Lady Thorowgood my silver seal with a stone in it. To Katherine Simons and Edward Bush, servants in the house, each five shillings, and the like to Richard White. Dated 14 April 1648.
                                                            Essex, 63.

[The Bozoune Allen, named by the testator as his brother, was, perhaps, Bozoune Allen of Hingham, Mass., who came from Lynn in Norfolk (REGISTER, vol. 15, p. 27) about six miles from Grimston, where William Allen formerly resided. Bozoune Allen came to New England in 1638, with a wife and two servants, in the Diligent of Ipswich, John Martin, Master. He was prominent in civil and military affairs. He removed to Boston, where he died Sept. 14, 1652. An abstract of his will is printed in the REGISTER, vol. 5, pp. 209-10. The trouble occasioned by his being chosen captain of the Hingham company is narrated by Winthrop in his History of New England, vol. 2, pp. 221-36. See also Savage's Genealogical Dictionary, vol. 1, p. 29, and Whitman's History of the Ancient and Honorable Artillery Company, 1842, pp. 158-60.

A pedigree of Sir John Thorogood, whom the testator calls his kinsman, is found in the Visitations of Essex, edited by W. C. Metcalf, Harleian Soc. Pub. vol. 14, pp. 607-8.—EDITOR.]

ISAAC AMYAND of Charleston in the Province of South Carolina in North America, gentleman, but now in London, 26 August 1738, proved 20 December 1739. To my good friend Thomas Corbett of "Charles Town" aforesaid my desk and book case and all my books, to be delivered to him immediately after my death. To my good friend Childermas Croft of the town and province aforesaid my gold watch, immediately after my decease. I appoint Gabriel Manigault of Charleston esquire executor of my will &c. bequeathing to him all that I possess in the province of South Carolina at the time of my decease except what I have herein before disposed, in trust to sell the same as soon as conveniently may be after my decease and after paying funeral charges and just debts, remit the produce of such sale to London to be paid and delivered to my dear and honored uncle Claudius Amyand, Sergeant Surgeon to. His Majesty, of the parish of St. Martin in the Fields Esq. upon trust that he will invest the same in three per cent annuities, payable at the Bank of England, and pay the income of my dear mother Justina Amyand of Aberstwith in the Principality of Wales. Upon her decease he shall pay one moiety of the principal trust estate to my cousin Claudius Amyand, eldest son of my said uncle and the other moiety to the rest of my uncle's children, share and share alike. All my estate in England to my uncle to be applied in the same way. My said uncle to be executor as to my estate in England.   Henchman, 250.

Johane Andrewes, widow, of the Tower hill, All Saints Barking, 19 February 1594, proved 14 January 1597. My body to be buried in the choir of All Saints Barking hard by the body of my late husband Thomas Andrewes. To my son Launcelot Andrewes my best salt with the cover, being silver and gilt. To my son Nicholas one hundred pounds. To my son Thomas Andrewes, servant unto Mr. William Cotton, draper, one hundred and thirty pounds (and other bequests). To my son Roger one hundred pounds. To my daughter Marie Burrell, wife of William Burrell of Ratclif, shipwright, fifty pounds. To Andrewe Burrell, their son, one hundred pounds. To my daughter Martha Andrewes one hundred pounds over and above the two hundred pounds she is to receive of me as executrix of the last will &c of my husband, Thomas Andrewes, her father. To Alice Andrewes, wife of William Andrewes, my brother in law, five pounds. To Thomas Andrewes, second son of Matthew Andrewes, my brother in law, by his first wife, five pounds. To my brother in law William Andrewes and Richard Ireland, sometime my servant, my one third part of the ship called the Mayflower of the burden of four score tons or thereabouts, equally between them, upon condition that they shall aliene or sell the same and that the said Richard Ireland shall follow, attend and be master of the same ship as he hath followed, attended and been master of it heretofore. To Joane Butler, late wife of Robert Andrewes, my brother in law, my hooped ring of gold and to Agnes Butler, her daughter by my brother Robert Andrews my "gimous" rings. To Emma Fowle, my cousin germain five pounds.   Lewyn, 5.

[The Launcelot Androwes or Andrewes mentioned in this will was the learned Bishop of Winchester, about whose ancestry a short paper will be found in the Transactions of the Essex Archæological Society, New Series, Vol. i. p. 55.
                                        Henry F. Waters.]

John Andrewes now resident in the island of Barbados 30 November 1648, proved 11 February 1649. To Mr. Francis Smith, clerk ten pounds in one twelve month after my decease. To my loving mother Mrs. Mary Elliott ten pounds sterling to buy her a ring. To my sister Deborah Fenn, wife to Mr. Robert Fenn, of Boston in New England, mariner, fifty pounds sterling money. To Thomas Sprigg one thousand pounds of good Muscovado sugars, or thirty pounds sterling. To his wife Maudline five pounds sterling to buy her a ring. To Morgan Powell one thousand pounds of

sugar or thirty pounds sterling.   To his wife Elizabeth five pounds sterling
to buy her a ring.   The rest of my personal estate, my debts and funeral
expenses being first paid, I give and bequeath unto my brother Samuel
Andrewes, whom I hereby nominate, ordain and appoint the sole executor
of this my last will and testament, and my loving friends Morgan Powell
and Thomas Sprigg, above named, tutors and guardians to my said executor.
And in case my said executor decease before he accomplish the age of
twenty one years then I give and bequeath unto the said Morgan Powell
one hundred pounds sterling and to his wife twenty pounds sterling and
to Thomas Spriggs one hundred pounds sterling and to his wife twenty
pounds sterling.   All the rest and residue of said estate, debts and funeral
expenses paid, I give and bequeath unto my said sister Mrs. Deborah Fenn
and her children, except one hundred pounds sterling which I give and
bequeath unto Mrs. Mary Elliott the wife of Henry Elliott and (my?)
natural mother.
One of the witnesses was an Arthur Dudley.   Pembroke, 20.

[Deborah Fenn appears as one of the members of the church in Salem, Mass.,
A.D. 1639.—(See Felt's Annals of Salem.)   HENRY F. WATERS.]

ROBERT FENN of Wapping, mariner, 1 June 1655, proved 4 January
1655.   I give and bequeath unto Mary my beloved wife all that estate
which I had in marriage with her as is in New England in the parts beyond
the seas.   To my loving friend Master Thomas Bell merchant twenty
pounds of lawful money of England and to Susan his wife ten pounds of
like money.   To my loving friend Robert Leuett, woodmonger, and
Penelope his wife twenty shillings apiece to buy each of them a ring to
wear in my remembrance.   To Thomas Hawkins, my wife's son by Thomas
Hawkins her former husband, ten pounds, and to Abigail and Hannah, her
daughters, five pounds apiece.   To Elizabeth, Mary and Sarah, her daughters by her said former husband who (are?) now married, twenty shillings
apiece.   The rest to be divided into five parts, one part whereof I give to
the said Mary, my wife, and the other four fifth parts to my children,
Sampson, Robert, Deborah and Elizabeth Fenn equally, provided that if my
wife shall be with child by me and such child shall be born alive then my
estate shall be divided into six equal parts &c.   My wife Mary and Master
Thomas Bell to be sole executors.   Berkley, 18.

[Robert Fenn, a captain from London, by wife Deborah from the church at
Salem, had Robert, baptized June 16, 1644; Deborah, born Jan. 15, 1645–6.   It
seems from the preceding will of John Andrewes of Barbados, that his wife
Deborah was his sister.   After the death of his wife Deborah, he married, June
26, 1654, Mary, widow of Capt. Thomas Hawkins of Boston.   She survived him
and married, Feb. 27, 1661–2, Henry Shrimpton.   See Savages's Genealogical
Dictionary, vol. 2, p. 152.—EDITOR.]

HENRY ANDERSON, mariner, now residing in Bantam on the island of
Java major, 18 August 1675, proved 12 February 1675.   To the Worshipful Henry Dacres one hundred ryalls of eight for to buy mourning.
To Capt. William Lymbery two hundred ryalls of eight and my two servants Maccaser and Humphry.   To Mr. Joseph Ward one hundred dollers.
To Mr. John Spery, my late purser, two hundred dollers and all my wearing
apparell and house moveables, excepting my plate, jewells and gold buttons,
and do allow of his accompt drawn up with me, desiring my overseers to
pay him the balance thereof immediately after my decease.   To the Council
of Bantam (that is to say) Mʳ John English, Mr. Albinus Willoughby, Mr.

Robert Marshall and Mr. Abel Payne, to each of them thirty dollars to buy mourning. To Mr. Francis Bowyer thirty dollars to buy mourning. To Mrs. Margaret English, Mrs. Ann Ward and Mrs. Mary Bowyer, each, thirty dollers to buy mourning. To the Worshipful Matthew Gray, in Surat, five hundred rupees. To Mr. Philip Gyffard, in Surat, three hundred rupees. To my loving cousin John Bennet, of Bombay, mariner, one thousand rupees. To my servant Kisnaw fifty dollers. These legacies to be paid out of my estate in Bantam and Surat. To the poor of Great Yarmouth in England fifty pounds sterling. I do desire that my body may be opened and my heart taken out and sent in a silver box to Bombay, to be buried there, in the same tomb where my wife lies interred,—and my body to be buried in the English Factory in Bantam, my overseers there causing a small tomb to be built over it at their discretion. One thousand rupees to be employed for the keeping in repair my tomb at Bombay. My friends Capt. William Limbery, Mr. Joseph Ward and Mr. John Spery in Bantam to be my assigns and overseers, to take care of what estate I have in Bantam and the South Seas, and the Worshipful Matthew Gray and Mr. Philip Giffard of Surat to take care of what I have in Surat or parts adjacent.

The rest of my worldly estate I give and bequeath as followeth; to my loving father, John Anderson of Boston in New England, shipwright, the one quarter part, to my loving brother David Anderson of Charles Town in New England, mariner, one quarter part, and to my brother Jonathan Anderson, shipwright, my sister Emm Brackenbury, wife to John Brackenbury, mariner, my sister Katherine Mary Philips, wife to John Philips of Charlestown, in New England, mariner, my sister Mary Anderson and my sister Johanna Anderson the remaining half part, to be divided equally amongst them, share and share alike. My father John Anderson, and my brother, David Anderson, to be sole executors.

Proved by David Anderson, with power reserved for John Anderson when he should come to seek it.   Bence, 10.

JOHN ANDERSON of Boston in New England, shipwright, 25 September 1677, proved 20 February 1677. To my beloved wife Mary Anderson my dwelling house, garden and the shops standing before and near adjoining, with the collarage under said shops, during the term of her natural life, and the use of my wharves. After her decease I give and bequeath unto my grand child David Anderson one half of my said dwelling house, next the street, twenty feet in breadth and all the land and wharf on the same breadth running in length from the fence late in the occupation of Mrs. Elizabeth Freake, down to the lowermost part of the hollow wharf, if he live to attain unto the age of one and twenty years; but, if not, then said part to return unto my children then surviving &c. The other half to be disposed of for payment of legacies. To my four daughters, Emme Brackenbury, Katherine Philips, Mary Linde and Joanna Newman, each, seventy five pounds in money, to be paid out of my shipping and my part of the estate given me by my son Henry, that is yet to come out of England. To wife fifty pounds out of that estate left by said Henry in England. That chain of gold of mine that is whole to my two daughters Emme and Katherine, equally, the other chain being by me already disposed of. To my six grand children fifteen pounds apiece, in money. To John Brackenbury all my carpenters tools and other building gear, besides the fifteen pounds in money. My outward wharf, forty feet in length, and all the rest of my estate to my executors, John Phillips, my son in law, and Mary Anderson, my wife.

Wit: Nathaniel Greenwood and Thomas Kemble.　　Reeve, 10.

[John Anderson, shipwright, of Boston, died Sept. 28, 1677. Will proved here Oct. 1, 1677. His wife Jane died May 4, 1654, and he married, Jan. 3, 1654–5, Mary Hodges of Charlestown, who survived him and made her will Nov. 6, 1689, which was proved March 14, 1692–3. His children were: 1, Henry (whose will is given above); 2, David; 3, Emma, married 1st, July 17, 1655, John Brackenbury, 2d Joseph Lynde; 4, Katharine, who married July 19, 1655, John Phillips; 5, Mary, married 1st Thomas Lynde the 3d, married 2d, July 27, 1682, Rev. Thomas Shepard, married 3d Samuel Hayman; 6, Samuel, died July 10, 1655, at Boston; 7, Joanna, born Dec. 25, 1655, married —— Newman; 8, Ann, born May 5, 1657. See Wyman's Charlestown, vol. 1, pp. 20–21, Savage's Dictionary, vol. 1, p. 51.—EDITOR.]

RICHARD TOPPING of Solbery, in the county of Bucks, 20 August 1657, proved 9 April 1658. My body to be buried in the burying place of Solberie if it please God it may be so. I give unto my son Richard Topping forty shillings, to be paid to him at the day of my death. Item, I give and bequeath unto four of my children which I have in New England twenty shillings apiece, conditionally in case the venture of goods which I sent into New England come well over, otherwise but ten shillings apiece, and that to be paid them if they do come over into this land. To my daughter Lidia twenty shillings, to be paid unto her when she is at the age of one and twenty years or the day of her marriage, which shall come first. To my two younger sons Joseph and Benjamin five pounds apiece to bind them apprentices and five pounds apiece to be paid them when they be at the age of one and twenty years. All the rest of my goods unbequeathed I do give unto my wife whom I do make my whole executrix.

Witnessed by Bernard Buckner, Thomas Hickman (by mark) and Thomas Emerton.　　Wootton, 128.

[Richard Topping and his wife Judith joined the Boston church, November, 1633. He was adm. freeman, March 4, 1633–4. His wife died, and he subsequently married Alice —— who joined the Boston church, April 17, 1647. See Savage's Dictionary, vol. 4, p. 255.—EDITOR.]

CHRISTOPHER BEALE of East Jurleigh, Kent, taylor, 31 May 1651, proved 20 June 1651. To my daughter Ann now wife of George Climpson twenty shillings in one year after my decease. To my daughter Margaret now living in New England ten shillings in one year &c. To my daughter Elizabeth ten pounds in lieu of eight pounds which her uncle Robert Beale gave her, to be paid within one year next after my decease. To my youngest daughter Katherine four pounds which she oweth me and one shilling more. To my two sons, Christopher and Thomas Beale, all my messuages in East Furleigh and all my goods and chattels, equally to be divided.　　Grey, 108.

JOHN BOLLES of St. James, Clerkenwell, Middlesex, esquire, 1 July 1665, proved 9 May 1666. To my wife Frances a yearly sum or annuity of fifty pounds, to be paid quarterly on the feast days called Candlemas Day, May Day, Lammas Day and Martinmas Day, by even and equal portions, to issue forth of the rents and profits payable out of and from the houses in Claire Street and Holles Street in the parish of St. Clement Danes. And my will and mind is that if she will make a full and general release &c. of her claim &c. to my personal estate then I give her one hundred pounds due and owing unto me by Col. John Booker and my cousin William Leeke in Nottinghamshire. I also give her upon such release one silver tinkard two silver porringers one silver salt which have my arms upon them, four silver spoons, my two Turkey carpets, six Turkey work chairs, leather carpet, my oval table, my countor or cabinett, the chair and cushion whereon and wherein I use to "sett on" standing and being in my Dining room three Irish work chairs with my wainscot box of drawers standing in my lodging chamber &c. &c.

I give unto my brother Joseph Bolles living in New England three hundred pounds, to be paid out of the money I have put out by Alderman Hanson or Mr Hawkins his partner or deputy. My will is that all deeds, orders, decrees and other writings concerning the manor of Osberton in Com. Nott. and the houses in Shoreditch or of any other lands which I lay claim unto or which are in my custody shall be sought out from amongst my other writing books and deeds and faithfully delivered unto my said brother Joseph (if he be dead to his eldest son) to his heirs and assigns. To my old servant Elizabeth Hanmer formerly called Elizabeth Eastment, who hath lived with me almost ten years and hath been true and faithful unto me and careful and diligent for and about me in all my affairs, sicknesses and weaknesses, if she continue and be with me at the time of my death, all my whole term and interest in a Brew house and two other dwelling houses next adjoining, situate &c. in Mercer Street in the parish of St. Martin in the Field, now in the tenure and occupation of Thomas Lacke brewer (together with sundry household stuff enumerated). John Sparrow of the —— Temple Esquire and Joseph Clarke of Clifford's Inn gent to be the executors, and I give to each of them five pounds per annum for four years. I remit to my tenants of my said houses in Clare and Holles Streets the moiety of fees or dues payable unto me once yearly, as Turkeys, goose, capons, neates tongues and marrowbones or the moiety of the value thereof in money, as their respective leases is expressed. And the other moiety I give and appoint my executors to make a dinner therewith once every year during the continuance of my term or lease or the life of my said wife, which shall first happen. And I desire that all my said tenants and their wives, my wife and the said Elizabeth my servant may be thereat if they will or may when and where my executors shall think good. The remainder or overplus of the rents arising out of the said houses or any part of my personal estate not given and bequeathed otherwise by this my will I give unto Elizabeth Hanmer formerly Elizabeth Eastment if then living, but if not the same to be equally divided to and amongst my sister Elizabeth her eldest son my cousin Thomas Sharrow and Marmaduke Ascough or to the longest liver of them respectively during the continuance of the lease. To Anthony Marbury, Doctor of Physic, all my physic books and ten pounds in money. To Captain Francis Stacy living on Tower Hill all my books written by Jacob Behme, Teutonick Philosopher and Cornelius Agrippa &c. And I make the said Capt. Francis Stacy overseer. To my cousin Savage, widow six pounds and a silver porringer and two silver spoons.   Mico, 71.

[Memorandum.—The name once written Sharrow is to be found two or three times written Sparrow.   H. F. W.]

SARA BROWNE of the city of Gloucester, widow, 8 October 1643, proved 17 December 1646. My body to be buried in the Cathedral Church of Gloucester and to my burial a funeral sermon to be made by some godly preacher, and Mr. Holford to perform it if he be then living and may be had; if not then Mr. Marshall. To him that shall perform it I give three pounds. My lease which I lately took of the Dean and Chapter of Glou-

cester of the manor and farm of Churcham in the County of Glouc., with
my lease of the rectory and parsonage of Churcham shall remain, as I have
assigned the same, unto Gregory Wilshire my son, John Harris of London,
Thomas Pury, one of the aldermen of the city of Gloucester, and James
Wood of the same city, gentleman, upon trust to pay my debts and legacies
&c. Provision made for daughter Hester Browne and grandchild John
Browne, her son and to his male issue &c. My grandchild Hester, the
new wife of John Harris, before named, and Sarah Browne, her sister. To
Gregory Wilshire, son of my said son Gregory and to Sarah and Anne,
daughters of my said son. To my grandchild Lawrence Wilshire. To
my grand child Thomas Browne. To my son Gregory my lease, right, interest and estate of the scite of the manor of Maysemore, within the city.
To the said John Harris, the husband of my said grandchild Hester Harris,
my lease &c. of a great brewhouse in the said city. To my great grandchild John Harris the lease of a house near the "fforraigne" Bridge in the
said city, if he die then to William Harris, his brother. Fifty pounds to
Lawrence Harris his brother and my godson. To my kinswoman and servant Hanna Prior one hundred pounds. To my grandson Lawrence
Wilshire one hundred pounds.

Item, I give unto Sarah, the wife of William Barnes, late of Barton
Street in Gloucester, now inhabiting in New England, the sum of twenty
marks of lawful money of England, for the use of the said Sarah, my grandchild, and for the benefit of her children if she shall have any. To my
grandchild Hester Wilshire one hundred pounds. To my grandson Gregory
Wilshire, son of my late son Lawrence, one hundred pounds. To my
grandchildren Joane, Christopher and Margaret Wilshire, children of my
said son Lawrence, deceased, one hundred pounds apiece. To the four
children of John Mayo of Batchford, Somerset, fifty shillings apiece, and
to the two sons of Lawrence Mayo, late of this city, deceased, fifty shillings
apiece. To Sarah Holtshipp, wife of Francis Holtshipp, my god daughter,
ten pounds. To Hester, her sister, now wife of Hugh Griffin, five pounds.
Whereas there was by me left in the hands of my cousin John Mayo of
Charfield, Glouc., gentleman, late deceased, twenty pounds, the profits to be
paid unto Anne Mayo, the relict of my brother Francis Mayo, now both
deceased, my will is that ten pounds of this shall be and remain unto Anne
Mayo, her daughter, and the other ten to the two children of Margery
Mayo, my brother John's daughter. To the Master, Wardens and Frater-
nity of Weavers of this city ten pounds. To each of my servants that shall
serve me at the time of my death (except Hanna Prior) forty shillings
apiece. My brother Abraham Mayo shall have the yearly rent of six
pounds out of a messuage &c. in Eastgate Street in the said city. To
Dennis Wise and her daughter Ellinor Wise five pounds apiece. To Mr.
Nanfan Gibson of Glouc. three pounds. To Joane Singleton, now wife of
Lawrence Singleton, alderman, five pounds. To Ester Bath, wife of
Samuel Bath, five pounds. To John Taylor, son of Richard Taylor, five
pounds. To my kinsman William Mayo, an attorney at Law, five pounds.
Bequests to various parishes, hospitals &c. To my daughter in law,
Margaret Wilshire, widow (certain bedding &c). To my grandchild
Hester Harris two chairs embroidered that were my best chairs in Barton
Street, together with four low stools. To my daughter Hester Browne
two chairs, one of crimson velvet, the other of cloth of gold, with the stools
belonging to each of them. Provision made for putting forth three poor
boys apprentices yearly, of the ages of fourteen or sixteen and not under
fourteen. My son Gregory to be executor.   Twisse, 181.

THOMAS TOMLINS of Bartholmew the Great, citizen and grocer of London, 10 July 1665, proved 26 September 1666. All my debts to be paid &c. I give and bequeath unto my loving brother in law Francis Camfield, citizen and grocer of London, all that my plantation or dividend of land situate and being in Mockjacke Bay, in the parish of Ware in the county of Gloster in Virginia, which said plantation &c., containing by estimation three hundred acres or thereabouts, was by me the said Thomas Tomlins some time since purchased of the said Francis Camfield, to me and my heirs. And whereas I the said Thomas Tomlins do still and at this time remain in a very great part indebted unto the said Francis Camfield for the said plantation and the servants, goods, stock, cattle and other the appurtenances then thereunto belonging, and the said Francis having no writing obligatory under my hand for the same, therefore I the said Thomas, as well for the satisfaction of the aforesaid debt as for other reasons me thereunto moving do (as in conscience I ought) by this my last will and testament absolutely give and bequeath as aforesaid unto Francis Camfield all that plantation &c. &c. and also all my share in a certain water mill situated upon Crane Creek, in said parish of Ware. To my loving sister Lettice Draper, wife of my brother in law Matthew Draper, my copyhold or customary house or tenement, and land in Wormeley, in the county of Hertford, provided if shee see cause to sell the said copyhold that then she shall pay unto my cousin Judith Millsopp, her daughter, ten pounds. To my brother Jonathan Tomlins three pounds as a token of my love unto him. To my brother Samuel Tomlins twenty two shillings in gold, as a token &c. To brother John Tomlins thirty pounds. To my sister Patience Camfield two and twenty shillings in gold, as a token &c. To my sister Judith Pope two and twenty shillings. To my little cousin Jacob Camfield, son of brother Francis Camfield, two and twenty shillings, as a token &c. and all my school books. To my cousin Hanna Camfield twenty two shillings, my mourning ring and my silver cup. To my loving aunt Joane Willinge (?) twenty shillings, as a token of my love &c. To my kinswoman Judith Butcher five pounds in twelve months. To my kinsman Hugh Vessey twenty shillings as a token &c. To my friend Katherine Bingham twenty shillings &c. Remainder to Francis Campfield whom I appoint executor and, in case of his death, my sister Patience Camfield.

Wit: John Armiger, Richard Camfield, John Phillies.   Mico, 136.

[See will of Rev. Samuel Tomlins and annotations, *ante*, pp. 598-9.—EDITOR. There is a grant of record in the *Virginia Land Registry* to Robert Tomlin of 350 acres on the south side of the Rappahanock river, between the lands of Thomas Brice and Epaphroditus Lawson. Head rights : —— Burkitt, William Eleans, George Blackgrove, —— Browne, Miles Rich, Jane Willis, April 27, 1654. Book No. 3, p. 222. The name Tomlin has been locally prominent. Harrison B. Tomlin, Esq., of King William County, served for a number of years in the Virginia Assembly, first in the House of Delegates and latterly in the State Senate.—R. A. BROCK, *of Richmond, Va.*]

LANCELOT ANDREWES, Bishop of Winchester 22 September 1626, with codicils dated 1 May 1626, proved 26 September 1626. Bequests to the poor of Allhallows Barking where I was born, St. Giles without Cripplegate where I was Vicar, St. Martin's within Ludgate, St. Andrew's in Holborne and St. Saviour's in Southwalk where I have been an inhabitant; to the Master, Fellows and Scholars of the College or Hall of Mary Valence, commonly called Pembroke Hall, in Cambridge (a thousand pounds to found two fellowships and also the perpetual advowson of the Rectory of Rawreth in Essex); to brothers' and sisters' children, vizt. William, son of brother Nicholas, deceased, the children of brother Thomas deceased (his eldest son Thomas, his second son Nicholas, his youngest son Roger, his eldest daughter Ann, married to Arthur Willaston and youngest daughter Mary), the children of sister Mary Burrell (her eldest son Andrew, her sons John, Samuel, Joseph, James and Lancelot, her daughters Mary Rooke and Martha), the children of sister Martha Salmon (her son Thomas Princep by her former husband Robert Princep, her sons Peter and Thomas Salmon, her daughter Ann Best); to kindred removed, as cousin Ann Hockett and her two sons and three daughters, cousin —— Sandbrooke, cousin Robert Andrewes and his two children, cousin Rebecca, to my father's half sister Johan (her first husband's name was Bousie) and each of her two children, and more kindred I know not. To Peter Muncaster son of Mr. Richard Muncaster my schoolmaster. To Mr. Robert Barker lately the King's Printer (whom I freely forgive those sums wherein he stands bound to my brother Thomas deceased) and his two sons Robert and Charlès, my godsons. To my godson Lancelot Lake. To the poor of All Saints Barking by the Tower, Horndon on the Hill, Rawreth (and other parishes) &c. &c. My executor to be Mr. John Parker, citizen and merchant taylor of London, and overseers to be Sir Thomas Lake, Sir Henry Martin and Dr. Nicholas Styward.   Hele, 109.

[See will of Johane Andrewes, the testator's mother, and notes, *ante*, page 603.—EDITOR.]

RICHARD STREET of Winterborne Kingston (date not registered) proved 23 November 1626. My body to be buried in the Churchlitten of Winterborne Kingston. To the parish church there two shillings. To the poor of Kingston forty shillings. To my brother John Streete's children ten pounds, equally to be divided among them. To my sister in law Agnes Streete forty shillings. To my brother Nicholas Street's children three pounds apiece, being seven in number. To the singers which shall sing my knell five shillings. To the church of Sturmister Marshall forty shillings. All the rest of my goods, moveable and unmoveable, not before given nor bequeathed, my legacies being first paid, I give unto my brother Nicholas Streete, whom I make my whole executor.

Wit: Thomas Woolfris, Henry Basan, Agnes Jones.   Hele, 117.

[See Mr. Lea's article on the Street family, REGISTER, vol. 46, pp. 257-67.—EDITOR.]

ROBERT WATSON of Bengeworth, 21 July 1563. To daughter Agnes my copyhold in nether Geeting in Cottesolde for term of the lease which is in the keeping of my brother Thomas, with eight score sheep upon the ground, and forty pounds at day of marriage. Her grandfather Thomas Haye, my brother John Watson, my brother Thomas and my brother William Watson shall have the govenment of her. To Dorathie my wife's daughter forty marks. To brother John Watson the obligation of twenty pounds that my brother Veners oweth me. To my brother Thomas Watson the obligation of one Bowiar clotheman of Cambden. To brother William Watson the obligation of Thomas Munne of Evesham, he paying to Thomas Haye of Bengeworth three pounds. To my brother James the obligation of twenty pounds that my brother William Horwood oweth me. To my sister Fraunces twenty pounds. To the child my wife goeth with, if a manchild the house by inheritance in the husband end the which my father gave me for four score years (and cattle &c) and the wardship of him

I commit to my three brethren. If a woman child my wife shall give it forty marks at day of marriage. To my seven sisters seven silver spoons. To my father Haye twenty shillings. To my brother Veners twenty shillings. To my brother Smyth twenty shillings. To Thomas Horwood twenty shillings. To my brother William Horwood twenty shillings. To my brother Howse twenty shillings. To my brother Robert Haye twenty shillings. To others named. The residue to Radigune, my wife. whom I make my executrix.

Admon. granted 20 November 1564 to Radigunde his widow and John Watson Clerk, Archdeacon of Surrey and Thomas Watson brother of deceased &c.   Stevenson, 31.

ALICE SMYTH, widow, late wife to William Smith of Stratford upon Avon, linen draper, 28 April 1584, proved 28 May 1585. I ratify and confirm the gifts and legacies made by my late husband in his last will and testament. If my eldest son William Smith will perform and let a lease of the new house in Stratford unto his brother John for the full term of sixteen or seventeen years then he, the said William shall have all the glass and wainscot belonging to said house and fastened upon the walls thereof, or else the same glass and wainscot be indifferently praised and sold by my executors and bestowed between the rest of my children. My debts first paid I give to my daughter Margett, towards the advancement of her marriage and above the legacy given by her father, ten pounds which was bequeathed unto me by my brother the late Bishop of Winchester. I constitute and ordain my sons in law William Say and July Bradshaw my executors, to whom I give ten shillings apiece. I request my brothers Mr. William Watson and Mr. Richard Venar, Mr Thomas Harward to be overseers and assistants unto them. The residue to be equally divided amongst my children.

A codicil made 1 July 1584 bequeaths to son in law Mr William Say a gilt bowl with a cover bequeathed to testatrix by her brother John, Bishop of Winchester. To daughter Alice Bradshawe the featherbed whereon I lay, which was her father Savage. To the poor of Evesham, Bengeworth and Stratford.   Brudenell, 26.

THOMAS WATSON of Stretton in the co. of Glouc. gen^t. 20 June 1567, proved 15 February 1570. My body to be buried in the church of Stretton before the seat which my wife kneeleth in. To wife Mary in full recompence of her dower and in full performance of the condition of the obligation that I was "bounded" to her father upon marriage with her all my free and copyhold tenements, the manor of Stretton and all the demains there &c. &c., during her natural life, she to keep court yearly in some place within the said manor for good order of the tenants. Other lands described in Wilts and Glouc. Provision made for son Thomas and daughter Anne Corett under twenty two years of age. To Richard Watson, my cousin six pounds thirteen shillings four pence. To the son and daughter of Thomas Watson which were with my uncle, parson of Hathropp, with their legacies of my said uncle's, five pounds apiece. My wife Mary to be sole executrix. The overseers to be my brother Archdeacon Watson, my brother William Watson, my cousin Sir John Watson, Chanter of Holy Cross, my cousin Lloyd, William Webbe of Dolman's Lane and Mr. John Rede.   Holney, 5.

JOHN WATSON, Bishop of Winchester, 23 October, 25th Elizabeth, proved 22 June 1584. My body to be buried in the body of the Cathedral church of the Trinity of Winchester. To the Corporation of All Souls College, Oxford, forty pounds. To the Corporation of the University of Oxford twenty pounds. To poor scholars in that University one hundred marks, to be delivered within a half year after my death by the discretion and appointment of my cousins William Saye, Symon Trippe, of the parson of Winchfelde, William Harward and of mine executors or any three of them. An exhibition of four pounds a year for five years to five poor scholars of that University. To the poor of Winchester and of the Soke there twenty pounds. To the poor of Evesham, where I was born, ten pounds. To the poor of Bengeworth five pounds. Forty pounds for a stock to set the poor of Evesham on work, by the discretion of the Bayliffs of Evesham and of my brother William. To my brother William Watson one hundred pounds &c. To John, his eldest son. To Thomas, his second son. To William, his youngest son. To my cousin Trippe and his wife. To Nicholas Beane and his wife. To William York and my cousin Ancret his wife. To Agnes Watson, my brother Robert's daughter. To my cousin William Saye. To my sister Smithe ten pounds and a gilt bowl with a cover, and to every one of her children (not otherwise provided for by this my testament or before my death) ten pounds. To William Smithe her son, the elder, that is with me, twenty marks. To William Smith, her son, now scholar in the College, twenty marks. To my brother William Harward and my sister his wife a silver bowl and ten pounds, and to every one of their children ten pounds. To my brother and sister Venor. To Thomas Venor of the College of Winchester. To Richard Venor. To my brother Thomas Harward and my sister his wife a silver bowl and ten pounds. To their son Thomas and the other of my brother Thomas Harward's children. To my brother and sister Howse, their son John and their other children. To my brother and sister Hopper, their son Robert and their other children. To Robert Heye, a prentice in London, son of my sister Heye deceased and to John Heye, her son, now child in the College. To my cousin John Watson, parson of Winchfeld, and his brother Henry. To my cousin John Watson one of the brothers of Saint Cross. To William Harwarde, Prebendary, one of my gowns.

A codicil dated 22 January 1583 refers to brother William Howse &c. and Leonard Paige that married my brother's daughter, to Thomas Watson of Stratton and others.

Other codicils were appended of no special genealogical importance.

Watson, 1.

JOHN SMYTH of Stratford upon Avon in the County of Warwick, ironmonger, 12 April 1612, proved 24 April 1613. My body to be buried in the parish church in the South Aisle next adjoining to my son Henry. To eldest son Thomas, after decease of Alice my wife, my dwelling house in which I now dwell. To son Richard the land I bought of cousin William Smyth, my brother Richard's son, that is the two grounds that Thomas Knight doth hold of me and all that Richard Hathewey the baker holdeth of me and a little house now in the occupation of Thomas Lawne by the Meare side. To William Smyth my son, after the decease of Alice my wife the two tenements which I have in Ship Street, now in the occupation of William Tasker and Richard Augworth. To my son John my tenement in Swine Street now in occupation of John Pytes the taylor and the tenement which I have in the Rothermarket, now in occupation of the widow Peare. To my son Robert my tenement in Bridge Street now in occupation of Richard Hatheway the baker. To my son Francis all that my tenement which I have in the High Street now in the occupation of Philip Rogers the pothecary. To Alice Smyth, my daughter, my tenement in Bridge Street, now in occupation of Alice Younge widow, and twenty pounds. To Margaret Smyth, my daughter, my tenement in Wood Street, now in occupation of one widow Rearkes, and twenty pounds. To daughter Ellioner the little piece of ground which I have in the home now in occupation of John Sheffield and twenty pounds. To the poor &c. Remainder to wife Alice, sole executrix. My cousin Richard Vewens, my brother Henry Walker, my cousin Thomas Harrowed (*sic*) and my cousin John Wendres to be overseers.   Capell, 33.

FRANCIS SMITH of Stratford in the county of Warrwick, mercer, 15 April 1623, proved 27 May 1625. To the poor of Stratford six pounds. To wife Alice my house wherein I dwell, with the shop and other buildings belonging, and my house in that street in Stratford called by the name of Wood Street, with barn and close, to hold the said houses &c. during the terms of years yet to come and unexpired. If she die before the expiration of such term, I give and bequeath these premises to my daughter Mary. To wife Alice also four yards of land, three of which lie in the Common Field of Stratford and one in Shottry fields. I give her also the house wherein John Coles now dwelleth, in Stratford, with the Close adjoining, for life, and after her decease to the said Mary Bysbie my daughter. I give to Francis Smith, son of my brother William, twenty pounds a year, to be paid to the use and bringing up of the said Francis, at school, or otherwise for his maintenance until he shall accomplish the age of twenty and one years. I also give him two hundred pounds, at his full age of twenty one. To Thomas, son of my said brother William Smith, twenty pounds and to Mary and Alice Smith, his daughters, twenty pounds, to be paid to the said Thomas, Mary and Alice when they shall accomplish their several ages of twenty and one years. To Francis Smith, son of my brother Roger, one hundred pounds within one year after my decease. To Thomas Smith, son of brother Roger, one hundred and twenty pounds, within a year and six months &c. To Mary and Ann Smith, daughters of said brother Roger, forty pounds each at twenty and one. To Margaret, the daughter of my brother Henry Smith, forty pounds within one month after the decease of my wife Alice. To my sister Joane Brunt forty shillings, to be paid yearly during her life. To my sister Margaret Smith twenty shillings yearly &c. To William Chandler, now in Oxford, son of William Chandler, and to Richard Castle, son of Richard Castle, to each ten pounds. I give fifteen pounds to buy Winicot stone and Shottery gravel to make a "Cawswaie," provided the inhabitants of Stratford do pay for the carriage of the same stone and gravel and to bring it to the place of the said "Cawswaie," at their costs and charges. I give also twenty nobles to make up and perfect that "Cawswaie" in Bishopston which I have begun, beginning at the upper end and so to the hedge (on similar conditions). I give to John Cole and his wife the little house &c. now in his tenure, during their lives &c. paying to the chamberlain of Stratford two shillings yearly, which shall be distributed among the almsfolk in Stratford. My wife Alice and my daughter Mary shall yearly abate forty shillings unto William Deane of that rent which he is to pay for that messuage &c. which

he holdeth now in Bausall Street in said county, which said messuage &c.
shall remain to Alice my wife during her life and, after her decease, to
Mary my daughter and to Alexander Bysbie, her husband, during their
lives &c, and next to Richard Smith, son of my brother Roger Smith.
Reference made to Mr. Wilson, vicar of Stratford. I give and bequeath
unto my servant maid Margaret Rogers the sum of three pounds, to
my servant maid Margery Carless forty shillings, to Mr. Richard Ward,
minister &c. in Hatton, forty shillings, to the two children of the
said William Deane, vizt. William and Mary, each of them five pounds
within ten years &c., to Hannah, daughter of Thomas Hawkes of Stowe,
ten pounds in five years, to Mr. Francis Auge, now alderman in Stratford,
my best gown, to my brother Henry Smith my ring, to Francis Smith, son
of my brother William, all my silver plate (the best piece only excepted)
at the decease of my wife, to Mary Carter of Hookenorton, Oxfordshire,
and her two children twenty two pounds, to the said Mr. Thomas Wilson,
our vicar, forty shillings for his pains to be taken to preach my funeral
sermon.

My wife and daughter to be joint executors and Mr. Daniel Baker, my
brother Henry Smith and Richard Castell to be my overseers.

Clarke, 52.

[The will of William Smythe of Stratford upon Avon, mercer, proved at
Worcester, 10 May, 1626, has already been given in my notes on the Ancestry
of John Harvard (REGISTER, vol. 40, pp. 364–5, *ante*, pp. 181–2).

HENRY F. WATERS.]

ALICE SMITH of Stratford upon Avon in the county of Warwick and
diocese of Worcester, "being aged and crasie in my bodie" &c. 15 July
1632, proved 28 June 1633. My body to be buried in the parish church
of Stratford near the body of Francis Smith, my dear husband. For my
worldly estate &c., I give unto Mary Willis the whole furniture of the new
chamber as it now standeth and I give her my wedding ring and the best
silver bowl and a trunk with these linens in it, a pair of flaxen sheets, a
long flaxen table cloth and a square table cloth, a pair of Holland pillowbeares, a dozen flaxen table napkins and a towel. I give unto Samuel
Willis my grandchild one hundred pounds to be employed by my executor
for his use, by purchase or otherwise, when he shall come to the age of
four years till he shall come to the lawful age of one and twenty years. I
give unto Joane Gibbard, my sister, twenty pounds. I give unto Daniel
Gibbard, her son, forty pounds, within three months after my decease, and
to Hannah Gibbard, her daughter, twenty pounds at the age of one and
twenty years, to Sarah Gibbard, her daughter, twenty pounds (as before),
to Elizabeth Gibbard, her daughter, twenty pounds (as before) and to
Mary Trappe, her eldest daughter, forty pounds in one year &c. To the
children of Christovell Brookes, my sister, first to Anthony Brookes, for
the good of himself and his children, forty pounds, to Baldwin Brookes, for
himself and his children, fifty pounds, to Elizabeth Deane, for her and her
children, three score pounds, forty of which her husband oweth me. I give
unto my sister Anne Hauckes, her children, first to Mary Haukes forty
pounds at one and twenty, to Hannah four score pounds (as before), and to
Sara forty pounds (as before). I give unto Sara Ferneley, my brother
John Ferneley's daughter, forty pounds at one and twenty or day of marriage. If any of these die before their portions grow due such portions
shall be given to Samuel Willis my grandchild. To Mr. Thomas Wilson,
our vicar, three pounds. To Mr. Robert Harris three pounds. To Mr.

John Jackson, my friend, three pounds.   To Mr. John Trapp, my kinsman, three pounds.   To Mr. Symon Trapp, our curate, forty shillings.   To the poor of Stratford six pounds.   I give forty shillings towards the repair of the°great bridge in Stratford.   To the poor of Stowe in the Woold three pounds.   To Mary Carter, my old servant, five pounds.   To Alice Williams, Elizabeth Hauckes and Alice Cooles, which were my servants, three pounds, i.e. twenty shillings apiece.   To Richard Castle, Baldwin Brookes, John Brookes and Richard Hunt, that were my servants, twenty shillings apiece to carry my body to the burial.   I will that my executor bestow twenty pounds upon a banquet for my friends that shall accompany my body to the burial.   All the rest of my goods and chattels whatsoever unbequeathed I give to George Willis of Fenny Compton, gen^t, my loving son in law, whom I ordain and appoint the sole executor of this my last will and testament.
  John Jackson a witness. Russell, 56.
  Commission issued 9 February 1647 (8) to George Willis, son of George Willis of Hartford in New England in the parts beyond the seas deceased, to administer his goods etc. according to the tenor of his will, during the absence of Mary Willis, the relict. Prob. Act. Book, 1648.

[Mary, daughter of Francis and Alice Smith,—who is named in the wills of her father and her mother, in the former as Mary Bysbie, wife of Alexander Bysbie, and in the latter as Mary Willis—was the second wife of Gov. George Wyllys of Hartford, Conn., who came to New England from Fenny Compton, co. Warwick, and settled at Hartford, Ct., in 1638.   He was an assistant of the colony in 1639, deputy governor in 1641, and governor 1642.   He died March 9, 1644-5.   His will, dated Dec. 14, 1644, codicils Feb. 22, 1644-5 and March 4, 1644-5, is printed in full in the Colonial Records of Connecticut, edited by J. Hammond Trumbull, vol. i., 468-72.   He names wife Mary, sons George and Samuel, and daughters Hester and Amy.   Land in Fenny Compton is mentioned.   His pedigree is printed in the REGISTER, vol. 22, page 186; vol. 46, page 329; and *ante*, page 599.   See also Savage's Dictionary.   EDITOR.]

JOHN SMITHE of Stretford upon Avon, in the County of Warwick, vintner, 5 November 43^d year of Elizabeth, proved 4 July 1603.   To wife Margaret the use of the chamber over the parlour, called the new chamber.   All the rest of the house to Raphe Smithe, my son, to his use, provided he use himself well and kindly to his mother.   After her death all of it to him provided he give to my daughter Helena Herson ten pounds in one year after his entrance, or do assure unto her my garden ground in Henbury Street, with the timber thereon; for want of heirs male, next to Hamlette Smithe and the heirs male of his body &c.; then to John Smithe & the heirs male of his body.   To John Smithe, my son, the lease of Hare's house and of my ground in the Bridgetown.   To my daughter Elizabeth Smithe the lease of my house in Sheepe Street.   To my daughter Anne Smithe ten pounds.   To my brother Hamlet Sadler my gown and my black doublet and my hat lined with velvet.   To the two sons of my daughter Elizabeth forty shillings apeece to bind them apprentice.   Remainder to Margaret my wife whom I make executrix.   And I desire the Right Worshipful Sir Edward Greeuill (Grevil), my brother Francis Smithe and my loving friend Peter Ruswell to be overseers.   To my brother Richard Walker my medley jerkyn and my medley breeches.   To Barnaby Sadler ten shillings.   To Hamlet Smithe my son ten pounds.
  Wit: Richard Byfeild, ffrancis Smithe, Hamnett Sadler. Bolein, 64.

[Richard Byfield, who probably wrote as well as witnessed the above will, was the grandfather of Nathaniel Byfield of New England.   Hamnett Sadler also witnessed Shakespeare's will. HENRY F. WATERS.]

ROGER SADLER of Stretford upon Avon in the County of **Warwick**, baker, 14 November 1578, proved (with codicil of 15 November), 17 January 1578.   My body to be buried in the parish church of Stretford nigh the seat where I did accustomably use to sit and serve God in, or elsewhere, at the discretion of my friends.   To the poor, at my burial, five pounds.   To my brother Skidmore of London and my sister, his wife, two star Royals in gold.   To my cousin Ridley and his wife two pieces of gold, being three pounds ten shillings apiece.   To my cousin Alice Sadler that is with my cousin Ridley twenty pounds in money, at the age of eighteen. If she die before that then it shall be equally distributed among her brethren and sisters, vizt Hamnett, Jane and Margarett.   To my brother Robert Sadler a coat, a pair of hose and twenty shillings.   To my brother Richard Sadler's children six shillings eight pence apiece.   To my brother Thomas Sadler's children ten shillings apiece.   To my brother John Walker's children ten shillings apiece, and to Elizabeth Walker, his daughter, twenty pounds within one year after my decease or else at the day of her marriage.   To Francis Auge of Bishopton two kine and to every one of his (five) children ter shillings apiece.   To John Cooke's children of Alder Marston six shillings eight pence apiece.   To Elizabeth Jackson that dwelleth with me four pounds six shillings eight pence, in one year or at day of her marriage.   To my cousin John Smythe's children twenty pounds; i.e. to Elizabeth Smithe six pounds thirteen shillings four pence, to Elynor Smythe six pounds thirteen shillings four pence and to Rafe Smythe, his son, six pounds thirteen shillings four pence.   I give and bequeath unto Hamnett Saddeler three tenements &c. which I have in Church Street, together with the lease of my house wherein I now dwell after the decease of Margaret my wife.   This house I give to my wife during her natural life to hold according as the lease thereof maketh mention.   To my cousin John Smythe the lacke or lease which I have of one yard land and a half in the old town field, after the crop for this year is taken off the same.   And he shall have my team of horse, being six in number, and all my carts, ploughs, harrows and gears thereto belonging, he paying for the same to my executors ten pounds in money.   To my friend Robert Gibbs of Stretford twenty shillings.   To my cousin Alice Higginson's children, to be equally divided amongst them, six shillings eight pence.   To sundry servants.   The residue to my wife Margaret and my cousin Hamnett Sadler whom I make and ordain to be my executors, and I desire my friends John Walker of Syllehull and Richard Ange of Stretforde, baker, to be my overseers, to whom I give six shillings eight pence apiece.

Then follows a list of Debts due from and to the testator.   Among the latter appear the names of Richard Hathewaye *als* Gardyner, of Shottery, William Coxe, of Syllehull, and Edmonde Lambarte and —— Cornishe for the debt of Mr John Shaksper (five pounds).   In the codicil he bequeathed to the children of Thomas Jones *als* Giles, i.e., Richard, Stephen and Ellen Jones *als* Giles, three pounds six shillings eight pence, to be equally divided among them, and to Nicholas Holder, son of Humfrey Holder, three pounds six shillings eight pence.   Bakon, 1.

WILLIAM Cox of Southwarke, Surrey, in the parish of St. Olave's Gen^t, 1 July 1633, proved 7 November 1633.   My body to be buried in the parish church of St Olave's, Southwark, if I depart this life within twenty miles of London.   To my loving mother ten pounds to buy her blacks to wear at my funeral.   To my sister Nashe seven pounds for the like use.

To my brother Edward Cox, with that he oweth in the book, five pounds, as also my sealed ring. To my sister Streete seven pounds to buy her blacks &c. To my brother Thomas five pounds for blacks for himself and man, to say, three pounds ten shillings and thirty shillings. To my brother George Nashe three pounds, for blacks &c. To my uncle Thomas ten pounds if so be with conveniency my wife cannot keep him. To my cousin Matthew Cox three pounds. To Thomas, my man, and to my maid, Anne Young. To my cousin Alexander Cox and Matthew England, parish clerk. To my good comforter in health and sickness, Mr Moreton, preacher of God's word, and to Mr. Osney, my loving friend and preacher, &c. My will is whichsoever preacheth to have twenty shillings more so as he wear a gown and hood. To various friends, among whom "my good friend Richard Kiddar of East Grinstead." The three drums and fife for that day ten shillings apiece. To my servant William Mullin forty shillings to buy him a black cloak. To the Company of the Clothworkers five pounds to buy them a cup. To one hundred aged poor men of St. Olave's twelve pence apiece on the day of my funeral. To the repair of the church provided that my colours may hang up in some convenient place of the church. To the building of the Armory, if it be not builded before my death, provided my arms be set up in glass, at my own proper costs, in the middle window of the Armory. My will is that all the garden men and other of my band so accompany my corpse with black ribbons, as a soldier, to the ground, receiving a blanket before they go in the vestry house and schools. My dear wife Ann to be sole executrix.

Signed and sealed 12 September 1633 in presence of William Molins, Thomas Haruard, Elizabeth Dunstervile. Russell, 108.

[As a Thomas Harvard was a witness to the above, there can be little doubt that the testator was the William Coxe, citizen and clothworker of London, to whom John Harvard's brother Thomas was apprenticed. (See REGISTER, vol. 42, pp. 173–4, ante, pp. 266–7.) But the above will also shows an interesting connection between Southwark and Stratford upon Avon through the mention of George Nashe as a brother. A reference to the Visitation of London (Harl. Soc. Pub.), Vol. II. p. 121, will make it pretty clear that this George Nashe belonged to a Stratford family. And the pedigree of Nash given in the Visitation of Warwickshire (Harl. Soc.), p. 147, discloses a double connection of William Cox with this family. His sister Mary had become the wife of George Nash, while he himself married Anne Nash, a niece of George Nash and sister of the Thomas Nash whose marriage connected this family with Shakespeare. There seems to have been a colony of Stratford families settled there in Southwark, and it is not at all improbable that Shakespeare was a frequent visitor at the house of John Harvard's mother. HENRY F. WATERS.]

SUSANN COXE, of St. Olaves in the Borough of Southwarke in the County of Surrey, widow, 12 January 1634, proved 12 June 1638. To my son Edward Coxe, now living within the realm of Ireland, fifty pounds which he oweth me upon bond, which I delivered unto him at his last being in London, which is about five months past. To my grandchild Edward Coxe, his eldest son, my lease of a tenement situated in Candleweeke Street in the parish of St. Mary Abchurch, now in the tenure, use or occupation of one —— Richardson, clothworker, the yearly rents &c. to be kept to and for the use and behoof of the said grandchild until he shall attain the full age of one and twenty years. To the rest of son Edward's children five

---

* In this connection let me correct the Latin which the English correspondent of the New York *Nation* (April 8, 1886) gives in his extension of the abbreviated original. For *par Octo Annos* (as he gives it) read *pro Octo Annis*.

pounds apiece. To my daughter Mary Crowe the wife of George Nash the lease which I took of Mr. John Bruton deceased, with all the time and term of years now to come and unexpired. To Edward Nash, her son, ten pounds. To Mary Nash, her daughter, five pounds. To her daughter Susann Braborne five pounds. To my daughter Margery, now the wife of William Rowsewell, one hundred pounds, being part of her portion promised &c. I give to my said daughter Margery all those goods and household stuff which were late her husband Streetes, which I bought of him for a valuable sum of money, to him in hand paid before his death. To Susan Coxe, daughter of my late son Robert Coxe deceased, twenty pounds, at day of marriage. To Hester Monsey forty shillings, at day of marriage. To my son William Coxe his wife twenty shillings to buy her a ring. To my cousin Alexander Coxe thirty five shillings which she oweth unto me. To Mr. Oseney, minister, for preaching my funeral sermon, forty shillings. To the poor of St. Olave's, Southwark, five pounds. To the vestry men of my said parish and their wives six pounds for a supper. I make my loving sons in law, Mr. George Nash and Mr. William Rowsewell, executors, to whom I do give the residue of my goods and estate unbequeathed (the lease of Matthew Kinge's house excepted).

Memorandum—that the said Susan Coxe, after the making of her will, within written, and in the time of her sickness whereof she died, about two or three days before her death, which happened on or about the sexteenth day of May, 1638 &c. willed and bequeathed the same (*i.e.* the lease of Matthew Kinge's house) unto her grandchild Edward Coxe, eldest son of her son Edward Coxe, " to goe for his breeding upp and placeing abroad." The witnesses to this last were Mary Nash and Jane Nashe.

Lee, 72.

ANTHONY NASSHE of Old Stretford, in the County of Warwick, gen[t]., 20 August 1622, proved 2 December 1622. To wife Mary six hundred pounds, household stuff and plate &c. To son John Nasshe five hundred pounds. To my daughter Coxe in token of a remembrance, forty pounds, within twelve months after my decease; but if she die before her legacy be due unto her, then to William Coxe, my son in law, twenty pounds. To son Thomas Nasshe that little land I have, viz[t], a messuage or tenement lying in new Stretford commonly called the Bear, and one other messuage &c. adjoining next to a messuage being the land of William Cawdry on the West &c. My son Thomas to be executor.   Savile, 111.

THOMAS NASH of the New place in Stratford upon Avon, in the County of Warwick, Esquire, 25 August 1642, proved 5 June 1647. My body to be buried in the church of Stratford. To Elizabeth, my wife, the messuage in Chapell Street now in the occupation of one Joane Norman, widow, and a meadow in old Stratford called the square meadow, near unto the great stone bridge, now in the tenure &c. of one William Abbotts, innholder, (and other lands, among which the tythes of corn, grain, blade and hay yearly coming, growing, renewing &c. or to be had or taken out of or within the manor or lordship of Shottery). To my kinsman Edward Nash, gentleman, son and heir of my uncle George Nash of London, gentleman &c. after my wife's death all that messuage &c. To my sister Anne Wither, now wife of Anthony Wither, Esquire, for life all the rents &c. of a messuage &c. in Haselor, Warr., called the Parsonage House, and the rente &c. of a tenement in Henley Street, Stratford now in the tenure &c. of John Hornby, blacksmith, and of another messuage &c. in a place called the Moore's town's end, now in the tenure &c. of one Thomas Such, and of a messuage &c. in High Street, near the High Cross there, now in the tenure &c. of John Copland, and of a messuage in Chappell Street, now in the tenure &c. of one Nicholas Ingram, and of two cottages by the water side &c. and of a close near the great stone bridge called the Butt close. To my said kinsman Edward Nash and to his heirs and assigns forever one messuage or tenement, with the appurtenances, commonly called or known by the name of the New Place &c. in the street called Chappell Street, and four yard lands in the common fields of Stratford and a messuage in the parish of——in London called the Wardropp, and all the messuages, lands &c. which I have and hold in mortgage of William Broade and Frances his wife, Thomas Broade and Francis Broade, in Barton in said county, and, after the decease of my sister Anne Wither the Rectory and Parsonage of Haselor (and the other lands and tenements before mentioned). To the poor of Stratford ten pounds. To Mary Ashby, widow, my kinswoman twenty pounds, in consideration whereof she shall release all her right &c. which she may claim unto any my messuages, lands &c. unto my Kinsman Edward Nash &c. whom by this my will and testament I make my heir. To William Ashby, her son, forty pounds. To Katherine, her daughter, forty pounds. To Marie, daughter of Marie Bushell deceased, my kinswoman, twenty pounds. To Elizabeth Underhill, another of her daughters, twenty pounds. To Anne Greene, the daughter of John Greene, gen^t., deceased, twenty pounds at her age of one and twenty or marriage. The residue to wife Elizabeth whom I make full and whole executrix and I appoint and entreat my loving friends Edward Rawlins, gen^t., William Smith and John Easton to be overseers.

In a codicil dated 4 April 1647 he made requests (among others) to his mother Mrs. Hall fifty pounds, to his cousin Braband fifty pounds, to the children of Elizabeth Underhill, wife of Nathaniel Underhill, thirty pounds, to Elizabeth Hathway fifty pounds, to Thomas Hathway fifty pounds, to Judith Hathway ten pounds, to his uncle Nash and his aunt, his cousin Sadler and his wife, his cousin Richard Quiney and his wife, his [cousin] Thomas Quiney and his wife, to each of them he gave twenty shillings to buy them rings; and he willed that the inheritance of his land, given to his cousin Edward Nash, should be by him settled, after his decease, upon his son Thomas Nash and his heirs. Fines, 127.

JOHN LANE son of Nicholas Lane, gen^t, of Stratford upon Avon in the County of Warwick —— at Cyprus Salinis 15 August 1638, proved 12 December 1638. I have been sometime resident abroad in my profession of a merchant employed, and am now, God permitting, resolved to take my passage for England upon the ship Unicorn, who hath lately "bin" here taken in goods and now is departed for the Scale of Aleppo, called Scandona alias Alexandretta, and there to receive her full lading when she returneth hither and so goeth to England. Goods consigned to Mr. Henry Hunter, merchant, resident in London, ladin from this place on the good ship Eneas, Master William Goddard, and the aforesaid ship Unicorn, Master Edward Johnson, per bills lading and Invoice copy &c. I herewith send unto my uncle Mr. George Nashe of London, woollen-draper, or his executors or assigns &c. I give unto my cousin Alce Staunton, daughter unto Thomas Staunton, gentleman deceased, one hundred pounds. To my uncle George Nashe and Edward Nashe for their pains herein, to buy them or either of them a ring, the sum of fifty pounds. The rest wholly and solely to my

mother Katherine Lane of Stratford upon Avon for her life or during her
widowhood.   After her death or. at her day of marriage the said estate to
go wholly to my brother Richard Lane, now apprentice in London, or, if it
should please God to call him away, to my aunt Busshell and Aunt Greene,
their children, as next heirs.   This is my real and true intention and that
my said uncle George Nashe or Edwarde Nashe his son would see and
oversee this my last will and testament &c.   I ought to put this same into
a better form for avoiding lawyers quirks &c.   Lee, 182.

[The will of Richard Quiney has already been given in my Gleanings (*ante*,
pp. 197 and 198), where will also be found a pedigree of Quiney.   His father
Richard Quiney, Bailey of Stratford, was buried 31 May, 1602, and his brother
Thomas married Judith Shakespeare.—HENRY F. WATERS.]

The last will and testament nuncupative of JOHN HALL of Stratford upon
Avon in the county of Warwick gen^t, made and declared 25 December
1635.   To my wife my house in London.   To my daughter Nash my house
in Acton.   To my daughter Nash my meadow.   I give my goods and
money to my wife and to my daughter Nash to be equally divided betwixt
them.   Concerning my Study of books I leave them (said he) to you, my
son Nash, to dispose of them as you see good.   As for my manuscripts I
would have given them to Mr. Boles if he had been here; but forasmuch as
he is not here present you, my son Nash, burn them or do with them what
you please.   Witnesses hereunto Thomas Nash, Simon Trapp.

On the 29th of November 1636 Commission issued to Susanna Hall,
the relict of the said deceased, to administer his goods &c. according to the
tenor of the above will &c. no one having been appointed executor &c.

Pile, 115.

[One may wonder, on reading the above, whether, among the manuscripts
referred to in this will, there may not have been some writing of Shakespeare's,
some unfinished play perhaps.   He gave New Place to his daughter Susanna
Hall.—H. F. WATERS.]

DAME ELIZABETH BARNARD, wife of Sir John Barnard of Abington
in the county of Northampton, knight, 29 January 1669, proved 4 March
1669.   I have limited and disposed of all that my messuage &c. in Stratford upon Avon called the New Place and that four yard land &c. in
Stratford Welcombe and Bishopton in the county of Warwick (after the
decease of the said Sir John Bernard and me the said Elizabeth) unto
Henry Smith of Stratford, gen^t and Job Dighton of the Middle Temple,
London esquire, "sithence" deceased, upon trust to sell the same for the
best value they can get, and the money thereby to be raised to be employed
and disposed of as I shall signify &c.   My cousin Edward Nash Esq. shall
have the first offer or refusal thereof, according to my promise formerly
made to him.   To my cousin Thomas Welles of Carleton, Beds, gent. fifty
pounds within one year.   If he die before that, then to my kinsman Edward
Bagley, citizen of London.   To Judith Hathaway, one of the daughters of
my kinsman Thomas Hathaway, late of Stratford, the annual sum of five
pounds, after the decease of Sir John Bernard and of me.   To Joane, wife
of Edward Kent, one other of the daughters of the said Thomas Hathaway,
fifty pounds, within one year &c. and if she should die before that then to
Edward Kent the younger her son.   To Rose, Elizabeth and Susanna,
three other of the daughters of Thomas Hathaway forty pounds apiece &c.
To my kinsman Thomas Hart, son of Thomas Hart, late of Stratford, my
messuage or Inn situated in Stratford upon Avon called the Maidenhead,
and to his heirs &c., failing such, to George Hart, his brother &c.

Penn, 35.

[Dame Barnard was the widow of Thomas Nash, daughter of John and Susanna Hall and grand-daughter of Shakespeare. She was buried, 17 February, 1669. Her father, Dr. John Hall, was buried 26 November, 1635, and her mother, Mrs. Susanna Hall, was buried 16 July, 1649.—HENRY F. WATERS.]

JOHN SADLER of St. Stephen's Walbrooke, London, grocer, 11 December 1658, proved 3 January 1658. My body to be buried in the church of St. Stephen's &c. if I happen to die in the said parish or in the parish of Hogsdon in Middlesex, unless it happen I die in the parish of Fifield in Essex, then to be buried there or in Stratford upon Avon in the county of Warwick, then to be buried within a vault in the said parish church where my late wife was lately buried. I give and devise all my land, messuages &c. in Stratford or elsewhere in said county unto my two sons in law Master John Wilby, Doctor in Physick, and Master Anthony Walker, now minister of Fifield in Essex, upon trust &c. twenty pounds a year to be expended for the breeding and education in learning of John Wilby, son of the said John Wilby, and twenty pounds &c. for the breeding &c. of John Walker my other grandchild (these during the term of eighteen years). The residue &c to my son John Sadler for his natural life, with remainder to his male issue. To my daughter Ellen four hundred pounds. To my daughter Anne four hundred pounds.

To my son John Sadler all my lands, tenements &c. and several plantations in Virginia, in the parts beyond the seas, called Martins Branden and Merchants hope and my stock of male cattle there in those parts. My female cattle I give to the lawful minister of the said parts and place or parish there and twenty pounds worth in goods which I will shall be delivered to Master Charles Sparrowe and the chiefest of the parishioners of the said parish of Martins Branden, for and towards the repairing and amending of the church and parsonage house there. Refers to advances made to daughter Elizabeth, wife of Master Walker, and to daughter Isabel Wilby deceased. Bequests to grand children Elizabeth, Isabel and Katherine Wilby and Margaret and Elizabeth Walker. Forty shillings to nephew Adrian Quyney. To cousin John Lilborne and his wife and Master John Wolmer senior of Stratford, to each of them twenty shillings. To cousin Margaret Jones of Stratford and cousin William Baker of the same place, to each five pounds. Other bequests. My two sons in law to be executors.

Pell, 7.

[The following grants of land are of record in the *Virginia Land Registry :* John Sadler and Richard Quoyoring, merchants, and William Barber, mariner, 1250 acres in Charles City county, May 30, 1635. Book No. 1, p. 320. John Sadler and Richard Quoyoring, merchants, 1140 acres in Charles City county, June 11, 1644. Book No. 2, p. 200. Charles Sparrowe and Richard Tye, 2500 acres in Charles City county, August 12, 1650. Book No. 2, p. 248.—R. A. BROCK.]

ADRIAN QUINEY, citizen and grocer of London 4 February 1692, proved 14 August 1693. My body to be privately and decently buried with my father, mother and brother in the church of Stratford upon Avon, the place of my nativity. To my brother Thomas Quiney and sister Sarah Cooper, each one rent charge of six pounds per annum during their natural lives, to be issuing out of my lands, tenements and hereditaments situate and lying in Shottery in the county of Warwick. To my said brother Thomas Quiney one another rent charge of twenty pounds per annum during the life of my brother William &c. To my nieces Sara and Elianor Cooper forty pounds. To my nieces Mrs. Barbara Harvey and Elianor Richardson

and her husband twenty shillings apiece to buy them rings. To the grandchildren of every of my sisters and all my cousin Jermans rings of ten
shillings apiece. To my loving brother in law Mr. Edward Pilkington and
to my kind brother in law Richard Pile Esq. and my sister Mrs. Elizabeth
Pile, his wife, and to my brother Thomas and my sister Sara Cooper and
my friend Mr. Charles Hills and my kinsman Mr. William Baker five
pounds apiece to buy them mourning. To Sarah Kirkham, daughter of
Jane Kirkham, ten pounds at one and twenty or day of marriage, forasmuch
as the said Jane hath attended on my poor distracted brother William
Quiney for above twenty years past &c. &c. In consideration of the faithful service done and performed by the said Jane Kirkham for me, ever since
the death of my brother Mr. Richard Quiney, I give her twenty pounds.
To my cousin Elianor Parker of Henly in Arden, widow, forty shillings.
To my cousin Margaret Wright ten pounds. To Honora and Isabell Lilburne, daughters of my nephew George Lilburne, ten pounds apiece at one
and twenty or days of marriage. To my said nephew George Lilburne and
Honora his wife ten pounds apiece. To my cousins Robert Harvey and
Richard Cooper (whom I make executors &c.) all my lands, tenements &c.
in Shottery and Kylands Hill in the county of Warwick, or elsewhere in
said county, to the use, in part, of the said Robert Harvey and Barbara
his wife and the heirs of their bodies &c. and in part of the said Richard
Cooper &c.   Coker, 129.

JOHN SADLER late of London grocer, now of Hunsdon Herts, 2 January
1698, with a codicil dated 12 January 1698, proved 16 November 1716.
I give and devise unto Sir Charles Ingleby knight, Sergeant at Law, and
his heirs, to the use of him and his heirs, all those my two parts, the whole
into four parts to be divided, of all those copyhold messuages, lands, tenements and hereditaments held of the manor of Newington Barrow als High-
bury, in the parish of Islington Middlesex, heretofore surrendered to the use
of this my will, and all that my messuage or tenement situate and being in
St. Lawrence Lane in the parish of St. Mary le Bow in the said city of
London, with the appurtenances, late in the possession of Thomas Parker,
now in the possession of the widow Freeman or her assigns; the said Sir
Charles and his heirs yearly to pay to my wife Elizabeth during her natural
life one annuity or yearly rent charge of thirty pounds of lawful money (in
quarterly sums).

And I devise unto the said Sir Charles Ingleby and his heirs all that my
moiety of a certain plantation in Virginia at or near James River, containing by estimation six thousand four hundred acres or thereabouts, called
Martins Brandon, and also all that my moiety of one other plantation, at or
near the said river in Virginia, called or known by the name of Martins
Hope, containing one thousand nine hundred acres or thereabouts, upon
trust that the said Sir Charles Ingleby and his heirs do and shall pay or
cause to be paid unto my daughter Elizabeth Sadler. and her assigns one
moiety or half part of the clear yearly rents issues and profits of my said
shares of the said plantations in Virginia for and during the term of her
natural life; and, in case the said Sir Charles Ingleby or his heirs shall
think fit to sell the said moieties or shares of the said plantations, then as
to one third part of the money arising by such sale my will is that the same
shall be in trust for my said daughter her executors, administrators and
assigns. And I give to my wife the whole benefit, advantage and term of
years yet to come of and in the house I now dwell in and all my plate,

furniture and household stuff of what nature and kind soever. And my will is that my executor, herein after named, shall remise, release and forever quitclaim unto Thomas Jackson, my tenant in Virginia aforesaid, all actions, suits, debts, and demands whatsoever for or upon account of any rent or arrears of rent or any fine or income for what lands or tenements he holds of me in the plantations aforesaid, or either of them. I give to Mr. Charles Spencer five pounds, to Mr. Charles Stafford five pounds. All the rest and residue of my estate, as well real as personal, after my debts paid and funeral expenses defrayed, I give and bequeath unto the said Sir Charles Ingleby, whom I make sole executor.

The codicil contains nothing of importance genealogically and does not refer to the estate in Virginia. Fox, 215.

JOHN FERNE of London yeoman, 2 December 1619, proved 7 January 1619. Having freehold lands and hereditaments in Virginia, the "Sommer Ilands" and elsewhere, I do will, give, devise and bequeath the same as followeth: I give and bequeath to my three sons John, James and Daniel Ferne all those my lands and hereditaments, with all profits which I have, in Virginia in the parts of America. To son Daniel my lands &c. in that part of America called the "Sommer Ilandes," and my freehold lands, tenements &c in Harrow on the Hill, Middlesex. To John fifty pounds, to James fifty pounds, to my daughter Bridget, wife of John Newark, to whom I have already given a sufficient portion, over and above the same portion, the sum of five pounds sterling, to the two sons of Richard Lisney a book of Mr. Greeneham's works, now amongst my books in the house of my said son James, to son Daniel my chest plated thick with iron and three locks and keys to it, and my two oaken chests and desk, being all in the house of my said son James. The residue to son Daniel whom I make sole executor. Soame, 8.

STEPHEN APTHORPE of Gamlingay in the County of Cambridge yeoman, 5 January 1615, proved 28 February 1619. To Annys my wife the sum of ten pounds yearly to be paid her during her natural life, for and towards her better maintenance, and all my household stuff in the house (except one cupboard). My said wife shall have her being and dwelling in my house which I lately bought and purchased of one Maldenn for and during her natural life, without paying anything therefore to my heir or executors, and my executors shall yearly during her natural life give, bring and deliver at the said house to and for my said wife two sufficient loads of wood to burn. I give and bequeath to James Apthorpe, son of Edward Apthorpe, my son, the said house wherein my wife is to have her dwelling during her life, and the two closes thereunto belonging, and also the house which I purchased of one Bradshawe. I give to Edward Apthorpe, another of my son Edward's sons, that ground or close which I purchased of one Bett, with the barn thereon standing, and the close which I purchased of one Mr Jacob, and also the close which I bought and purchased of one Botterell. To my godchild Stephen Apthorpe, the youngest son of the said Edward my son, my three closes lying at the Brook End in Gamlingay. To Elizabeth, daughter of the said Edward my son, the said cupboard before excepted. To Stephen Apthorpe, one other of my godchildren and eldest son of my son John Apthorpe, all that my messuage or inn called the Cock in Gamlingay, and the close thereunto belonging and one rood of meadow lying in West Meadow. To John Apthorpe, second son of my said son John, all my copyhold land and meadow in Gamlingay. To Thomas Apthorpe, his third son, those five acres and three roods of arable land, lying in the fields of Gamlingay, which I bought and purchased of one Nicholas Baxter, and seven roods of meadow which did sometimes belong to the Bell "which was latelie brent" in Gamlingay, whereof one acre lyeth at Black ditch in Gramesmeadow and the other three roods in West meadow. Of the debt of four score pounds due unto me from my son John I give thirty pounds thereof to John, his second son, at eighteen years of age, and thirty pounds to Thomas, his third son, at his age of eighteen. The other twenty pounds shall be divided between my executors, Edward and John Apthorpe, my sons.   Soame, 15.

EDWARD APTHORPE of Gamlingay in the County of Cambridge, yeoman, 15 May 1643, proved 31 July 1645. I give to my son James Apthorpe five shillings in money. To my son Edward the like sum of five shillings. To my son Stephen the sum of ten pounds of lawful money. To my son Christopher five pounds. To my daughter Elizabeth, wife of John Philips, five shillings. To my daughter Anne Apthorpe one hundred pounds. To my brother John Apthorpe five shillings. To my cousin Anne Peeter six shillings and eight pence. To the poor people of Gamlingay forty shillings to be distributed amongst them by mine executrix. The residue to my wife Elizabeth whom I do make to be sole executrix &c.   Rivers, 92.

. NICHOLAS EAST of Stanford within the parish of Southill in the County of Bedford, yeoman, 12 April 1649, proved 13 June 1649. [Mem. The probate act reads, incorrectly, 1646]. To my wife Agnes East the bedstead and bedding now in the custody of William Rudd, her youngest son, and my cottage nigh Shefford's bridge wherein Ralph the glover now dwelleth, for and during her natural life, and after her decease unto my son Nicholas East, his heirs and assigns, forever. I give unto John Rochford and to Margaret Squire forty shillings apiece, being my first wife's children. I give and bequeath unto my three daughters, Agnes Abthorp (sic), Elizabeth Barly and Mary Thurgood, fifty pounds apiece, and to their children twenty pounds to be equally divided amongst them, as well to those which are already born as also to those which shall be born during my life. To James Apthorp, William Barly and John Thurgood, my sons in law, the first and next gift and disposition of the rectory or parish church of Clifton in the County of Bedford in trust and confidence that they or the longest liver of them shall bestow the same with all the rights and members thereunto belonging upon my son Nicholas East, if he doth survive Isack Bedford, the incumbent; if otherwise, then on some learned man whom they shall think fit and worthy of the same. To my poor brother William East my wearing apparell and in money three shillings four pence, to be paid him quarterly during his life. To my son John Thurgood gen[t], whom I make whole executor of this my last will and testament the residue of my goods &c. Whereas I did will, give &c. to my three daughters fifty pounds apiece I do thus alter and change the aforesaid legacy to my said three daughters viz[t]. I give unto the said Agnes Apthorp, Elizabeth Barley and Mary Thurgood one hundred pounds to be equally divided amongst them.
                                                                Fairfax, 92.

JOHN APTHORPE of Gamlingay, Cambridge, yeoman, 19 March 1646, proved 10 May 1648. To my grandchild Stephen Apthorpe my grandchild, son of Stephen Apthorpe, my son, ten pounds. To Anne, daughter of my said son Stephen, twenty pounds. To Mary, daughter of my said son Stephen, ten pounds. To my son John forty pounds. To my grandchild John Apthorpe, son of my said son John, fifteen pounds. To Stephen, son of my said son John, fifteen pounds. To Elizabeth, daughter of my said son John, twenty pounds. To Katherine, daughter of the said John, ten pounds. To Annis, daughter of the said John, ten pounds. To my son Thomas Apthorpe thirty pounds and to his son John ten pounds. To my sister Annis one shilling per annum, to be paid her so long as her now husband, Laurance Peter, and she shall live both together. And in case she shall fortune to overlive her said husband then I give unto her the sum of twenty shillings per annum during her natural life. To my said son Thomas all that my messuage or inn and close adjoining in Gamlingay called by the name of the Cock &c. &c. My son Stephen Apthorpe to be sole executor. Essex, 68.

SIMON APTHORP of Gamlingay, Cambridge, yeoman, 8 December 1653. Wife and son John to be executors. Daughters Alice, Elizabeth, Hanna and Sarah. Sons Stephen, Thomas, Simon and Edward. Alchin, 152.

[There is a long pedigree of the Apthorp family in William Cole's Collection for Cambridgeshire (fols. 180–189), Add. MS. 5812, Brit. Mus.—H. F. W.]

JUDITH PARKER widow, 5 May 1649, proved 24 May 1649. I bequeath twenty pounds unto Thomas Shepherd, son of Thomas Shepherd of Cambridge in New England, and ten pounds apiece unto Robert Parker and Sarah Parker, son and daughter of Thomas Parker of Needham Market. And if money be not made of my goods in so large a manner as is expected then I bequeath but five pounds unto Sarah Parker the abovesaid. Also I give unto Sarah Westhrope, the wife of Richard Westhrope, one feather bed, one boulster, one pair of blankets, one half part of my wearing linen and a bedsted. Similar bequests to the widow Carter, the widow May, "my kinswoman" Sarah Westhrope and Elizabeth Wiseman widow. I appoint Robert Manninge of Ipswich executor. If it should please God to cause my estate to perish either at Sea, by coming over, or otherwise then the parties abovesaid to remit and not to require those abovesaid legacies. Memorandum—I give John Doubble sen[r]. and John Doubble jun[r]. half a crown apiece. Fairfax, 61.

ELIZABETH HARWOOD of Bednall Green in the County of Middlesex, widow, 5 August 1686, proved 11 April 1687. Interested in a brewhouse, with its appurtenances, situate, lying and being in the parish of St. Leonard Shoreditch, now in the occupation of William Goodman. One moiety or half part of said brewhouse to my daughter Elizabeth Sedgwick and the other moiety to my daughter Hannah Manwaring. I give and bequeath all that my one sixth part of the profits, product and proceed of such goods which my late husband sent beyond seas, which is expected to be returned for England, unto my three sons John, Jacob and Joseph, equally to be divided amongst them, share and share alike, upon this condition nevertheless that they shall pay out of the same unto my brother Samuel Usher the sum of five pounds. Whereas my late husband by his said will did give unto my grandchild Elizabeth Manwaring two hundred pounds to be paid her at her age of seventeen years; now in case she shall die before she shall attain the said age my will and mind is that the said two hundred pounds shall be put out at interest for the benefit and separate maintenance of my said daughter Hannah Manwaring &c., and after her decease to such child or children of my said daughter as she shall have living till they come of age; then to pay to such child &c. the principal sum. To my son John one silver tankard with his father's arms engraven on it and my largest wrought silver server and my late husband's seal ring and two large silver spoons. To my son Jacob my largest silver tankard and my lesser silver wrought server and two large silver spoons. To my son Joseph my next biggest silver tankard, one plain silver plate and two large silver spoons. All the rest of my silver plate, jewels, rings and all my household goods of what nature or kind soever I give and bequeath to my said two daughters Elizabeth Sedgwick and Hannah Manwaring, equally to be divided between them. Whereas my brother Hezekiah Usher of New England did by his last will and testament give me a legacy of one hundred pounds which is not yet paid me I do give the same to my daughter Hannah. I give to my said sons and my said daughters and my son in law Ralph Manwaring, to my good friend Isaac Dafforne, to my grandchild Samuel Sedgwick and to my grandchild Elizabeth Manwaring ten pounds apiece, to buy mourning. My son Jacob to be sole executor. Foot, 49.

[The above testatrix was the widow of John Harwood whose will has already been given in these Gleanings (REGISTER, vol. 42, pp. 64–5, *ante*, pp. 256–7). H. F. WATERS.

Hezekiah Usher, called by the testatrix her brother, was of Cambridge, Mass., 1639, and removed in 1645 to Boston, where he was a bookseller. He was admitted a freeman of Massachusetts March 14, 1638-9. "He was the agent for the Society for Propagating the Gospel among the Indians, and it was through him that types and paper were procured by which Green of Cambridge printed the great Indian Bible in 1660–1663. He went to London for this purpose in the winter of 1657-8." He died May 14, 1676. In his will he mentions brother John Harwood and sister Elizabeth Harwood. An article on the Usher family is printed in the REGISTER, vol. 23, pp. 410-13. See also Historical Catalogue of the Old South, 1883, edited by Hamilton A. Hill, A.M., page 216; Paige's History of Cambridge, Mass., pp. 673-4; and Savage's Genealogical Dictionary, vol. 4. pp. 362-3.—EDITOR.]

WILLIAM WEST of Eaton in Bucks, yeoman, 21 July 1686 proved 14 June 1687. My copyhold or customary messuages &c. in the parish of Upton in said county, held of the Lord or Lady of the manor of Upton cum Chalvey &c. to my son Thomas West. My freehold messuages &c. in Upton, Datchett, Stoke Pogis and Horton, Bucks, and in Bray, Berks, to my said son Thomas. My leasehold messuages &c. in Eaton and Upton to my said son. I give and bequeath unto my grand daughter Margaret West, daughter of my son William West deceased, who lived several years in Virginia (and died there as I am informed) the sum of fifty pounds. To my grand daughter Mary West, daughter of my said son William West deceased, fifty pounds to be paid at her age of eighteen years. To my grand son William West (son of my said son William deceased) fifty pounds at the age of eighteen years. If any of these grandchildren shall not, in person, come into England and make it appear that he or she is truly the child of my said son then the said legacy shall not be paid. To my grand son Thomas West, son of my said son Thomas, fifty pounds at one and twenty. To my grand daughter Anne West, daughter of said Thomas, fifty pounds at eighteen or day of marriage. To Edward West and William West, sons of my late brother Francis West deceased, five pounds apiece. Other bequests. Thomas West to be sole executor. Foot, 88.

[A genealogy of the West Family of Virginia is printed in *The Critic*, a newspaper published in Richmond, Va., Feb. 3 and 17, 1889.—EDITOR.]

FRANCIS SPENCER of St. Giles without Cripplegate, London, citizen and brewer of London, 7 April 1636, proved 24 October 1636. My son Thomas Spencer shall, immediately after my decease, have, hold and enjoy, to him and his heirs forever all my houses, lands, tenements and hereditaments &c. in Hitchin, Herts., which for the most part I have already estated him in. To my three daughters, Susan, Elizabeth and Agnes, each, three score six pounds, thirteen shillings and four pence, at one and twenty or day of marriage. Other provision for son and daughters. The residue to wife Margaret whom I make and ordain full and sole executrix. And I appoint my uncle Richard Spencer, citizen and haberdasher of London and brother Daniel Spencer, citizen and grocer of London, to be overseers. One of the witnesses was Richard Milton, scrivener. Pile, 106.

[The testator of the above will must have been akin to Michael and Jarrard Spencer of New England. (See my Gleanings in REGISTER, Vol. 45, p. 232, *ante*, p. 515.) The widow having died administration was granted, on the above date, to Thomas Marler, Arch-deacon of Sarum, brother of the executrix. As to the witness it will be borne in mind that John Milton was the son of a London scrivener.—HENRY F. WATERS.]

MARGARET SPENCER, late wife and executrix of Francis Spencer of Goulding Lane in the parish of St. Giles Cripplegate, London, ale brewer, 21 September 1636, proved 31 October 1636. My body to be laid in the parish church of St. Giles, close by my said last husband. All my goods to Thomas Roberts and Mary Roberts, my son and daughter at 21 or days of marriage. My brother Thomas Marler of Lydeard, Wilts, clerk, to be sole executor. Pile, 104.

JEREMIE LANE of Rickmersworth in the County of Hertford, yeoman, 30 September 1646, proved 2 June, 1647. I give and bequeath to Martha my wife for and during the term of eight years next ensuing, if she so long live, for and towards the education, maintenance and bringing up of my children, all my messuage, lands, tenements and hereditaments &c. in the hamlet of West End in the parish of Rickmersworth. And if she die before the expiration of said term then I give and bequeath the same, to the purpose aforesaid, to my son John Lane and to my brother John Lane for such part of the said term that then shall be to come and unexpired. After the said term of eight years I give and bequeath the one moiety of the said messuage &c. to my eldest son John Lane and the heirs of his body lawfully begotten or to be begotten; and, for default of such issue, to remain to Josias my son and the heirs of his body lawfully to be begotten; and, for default of such issue, to remain to Jahasiel my son &c. &c. and then to remain to the right heirs of me the said Jerome Lane forever. Provision made for daughters Mary and Martha. Wife Martha to be executrix. Wit: Jo: Androwes, John Lane, *signum* Alice Shrimpton *ux.* Johis Shrimpton. Fines, 121.

[This was the Jeremiah Lane referred to as "deceased" in the will of his brother John Lane. (See my Gleanings in REGISTER, Vol. 44, pp. 395-6, *ante*, p. 472.) He was therefore an uncle of our Job Lane of Malden, Mass.—HENRY F. WATERS.]

JOHN BIGGE of St. Mary Mattfellon *als* Whitechapel, Middlesex, citizen and tallow chandler of London, 30 January 1635, proved 2 September 1636 by the widow Joane Bigg. To wife Joane my freehold messuage &c. which I lately purchased of Mr. Allen and joined my said wife purchaser with me, the same is now in the tenure and occupation of Thomas Neale, wholesaleman, and situate in the Mynories, in the parish of St. Buttolph without

Algate; also two tenements in the occupation of one Brookes, comfitmaker, and Edward Vollentine, whitebaker, near the Saracen's Head in the parish of St. Katherine Creechurch *als* Christ's Church, within Algate, London, these two for life; and, after her decease, to my brother Thomas Bigg of Wilhamstead, Beds., yeoman, and his lawful issue, with remainder to my sister Susan Ward and her lawful issue, then to my brother Henry Bigg of Virginia, beyond the seas, taylor, and his lawful issue, then to the poor of the three parishes hereafter named, viz[t], St. Katherine Creechurch *als* Christ Church within Algate, St. Buttolph's without Algate and St. Mary Matfellon *als* Whitechapel. Other bequests to wife and sister Susan Ward, brother Thomas Bigg, sister Mary Cowper, wife of Edmond Cooper of Houghton Conquest, Beds., yeoman, brother Henry Bigg, godchildren (not named), my late wife's sister Anne Pickett of Causam (Caversham) near Reading and her children, a servant named William Lake, a maidservant named Dorothy Smith, and Richard Barnett, an apprentice. To William Wyer and Anne Wyer, son and daughter of William Wyer of St. Martin in the Fields, gentleman, ten pounds apiece at twenty one. To Francis (Frances) Rogers of Virginia, spinster, ten pounds at her age of one and twenty years. The residue to wife Joane whom I make &c. sole executrix, and I make Thomas Cane of Whitechapel, tyler and bricklayer, and Thomas Jeffery of the same, citizen and girdler, overseers.   Pile, 99.

DANIEL WILLIAMS of Hoxton, near London, Doctor of Divinity, 26 June 1711, proved 6 November 1716. I desire my body may be privately buried in the new Burying Ground near the Artillery Ground, where a vault shall be purchased and a good tomb erected, therein any of my and wife's relations may be buried or, in want of such, any good ministers as the place will permit room for them. Instead of her marriage settlement (of four hundred pounds a year) my wife shall enjoy for her natural life the ground rents I bought in and near Queens Street in Westminster from one Sutton, amounting to one hundred and nine pounds or thereabouts per annum, and the interest of one thousand pounds which remaineth in Mr. Benj. Sheppard's hands (over and besides the other thousand pounds in his hands which I order him to pay her in a year after my decease as what I covenanted to do), also my dwelling house in Hoxton with all gardens &c., also the two Peverils and whole estate in Essex which I bought of Daniel Tanfield Esq[r]. which is about one hundred and fifty pounds per annum, also Totham in Essex, whereof one Sewell is tenant, which at the time of our marriage was let at forty five pounds per annum, but now reduced to thirty eighty pounds (and other property). I give to her for life all the jewells and plate, except my large bason which I leave to Mrs. Wyn, as having been her father's, and my largest silver tankard, which I give to my cousin Richard Meredith Esq[r]. My repeating clock I give to Mr. John Evans. At the death of my wife my jewells, plate &c. shall be equally divided, one half to my daughter Mary Sheppard the other to my daughter Elizabeth Barkstead. The thousand pounds in Mr. Sheppard's hands shall, at her death, be thus distributed. To my daughter Mary Sheppard three hundred and fifty pounds, or if she be dead, to her husband and children. To my daughter Elizabeth Barkstead three hundred pounds, to my son Francis Barkstead two hundred pounds, to my wife's sister Stannet fifty pounds, to young Daniel Loften fifty pounds. I also give my son Benjamin Sheppard, my daughter Mary Sheppard, my daughter Elizabeth Barkstead and son Francis Barkstead ten pounds apiece to buy them mourning. My brother and sister Roberts, and the survivor of them, shall during his or her natural life possess all that my estate in Burton and Cross Howel &c. in Denbighshire, which I bought of Mr. Smith, he and she paying yearly six pounds to Mr. Kenrick or other the Presbyterian dissenting minister in Wrexham and ten pounds a year to such a man as they shall appoint to teach twenty children to read and write and instruct them in the principles of religion, but I forbid them to make any waste by cutting down any young trees or timber.   I give and bequeath to my said brother all my wearing apparel, and to the family of our kindred the Sackvils one hundred pounds, to be distributed among them to such and in such sums as my said brother and sister shall judge fit, and not otherwise.   Whereas my cousin Richard Edwards deceased owed me three hundred and forty five pounds principal, besides as much more on trading profit, and I have administered to him, my will is that the said principal, when recovered, shall be to my cousin Hugh Edwardes, the father of the said Richard, and his children, and I remit to Dorothy Edwards, the widow of the said Richard, all the interest and profits due, and assign the administration to her.   To Mr. John Welsh, to be paid to the Societies for reformation of manners, one hundred fifty pounds.   To Walter Stephens and Joseph Damar Esqr, living in Dublin, one hundred pounds for the education of youth &c unless I pay this in my life time.   To Mr. Joseph Boys of Dublin, the minister, one hundred pounds and to the poor of Wood Street congregation, whereot I was once pastor, forty pounds.   One hundred pounds to be paid to Dr. Duncan Cumming, in Dublin, to be lent by him so that the widow Mrs. Sara Hartley may have the interest of it during her life and after death the said one hundred pounds to be paid to the widow Mrs. Barrington, daughter of Mr. Benj. Pratt.   I also remit and forgive my cousin Richard Meredith Esqr the several sums of money due from him to me and give to that son of his which beareth my name one hundred and fifty pounds, and to my cousin Elizabeth West, sister of the said Richard, one hundred pounds. Five pounds apiece to servants for mourning.   To my kinsman Hugh Edwards one hundred pounds.   To Mr. Samuel Pomfret the minister thirty pounds.   To Mr. John Evans my colleague fifty pounds and the lease of a house in Plumbtree Street which I bought of Mrs. Hannah Fox als Bradley.   To the poor of Hand Alley Congregation fifty pounds.   To poor French refugees one hundred pounds.   To the poor of Shoreditch twenty pounds.   Five pounds apiece to Mr. Cook of Clare in Suffolk, Mr. Stephens of London, Mr. Lorimore, Mr. Hunt of Newport, Mr. Rastrick of Lin in Norfolk, Mr. Kempster, all ministers except the last, and the same to one Mr. Cordell, a minister about Cambridgeshire, and Mr. Benjamin Robinson, Mr. Chandler of Bath and his brother (all ministers), as also to Mr. Isaac Bates of Hackney.   Four pounds apiece to the following ministers' widows, vizt, Mrs. Taylor about Wem, Mrs. Evans about Oswestry, Mrs. Naylor about St. Helens in Lancashire, Mrs. Wine, Mrs. Hardcastle, Mrs. Gosnal, Mrs. Webb of Fromley (the two last known to Mrs. Jacomb).   I forgive Mr. Toms half of what he owes me.   I forgive Mr. Lyford what he owes me and give him five pounds.   I release my cousin Katherine Taylor of Wrexham of what she is indebted to me, and I authorize my executors to release Mr. William King, the baker in London, of what he stands bound to me, which from the respect I bear to the parents of his wife I lent and am willing to forgive, with all the interest due thereupon, the same, if she survive him, I forgive his said wife and give her also five pounds.   I forgive Mrs. Dicksy the nine pounds she oweth me.   I give to my cousin

Stephen Davies, minister at Banbury, ten pounds and forgive what he oweth to me. I give to Mr. Hull, a tinman in London, twenty pounds and to Anne Jerom fifty shillings. I give the reversion of an estate in Elsley in Cambridgeshire, after the death of the widow Mason, now possessor of it to St. Thomas Hospital and the Workhouse in Bishopsgate Street, London, the rents and profits to be equally divided between them for ever (valued to me about fifty five pounds per annum). I give all my houses in Burnham to Robert Metham Senr for the use of the Presbyterian Meeting there. I give to the College of Glasco, whiles the present Constitution of the Church of Scotland continueth, my house and land in Barnet, Herts, set now at forty five pounds per annum, and the reversion of my lands in Totham, Essex, after my wife's death, as also one hundred pounds in money, my trustees and assigns to appoint and nominate, from time to time, four South Britain youths to be students at Glasco, who shall receive six pounds per annum from the said College, and also three South Britains who, after they are commenced Masters of Arts in said College, shall receive ten pounds apiece per annum for three years, or otherwise two at fifteen pounds apiece. More Exhibitions to be added as the yearly profits will afford. Provisions made in case Prelacy or the Episcopal Hierarchy or Popery shall be established in North Britain. To the Society in Scotland for Propagating Christian Knowledge one hundred pounds, and also, at the end of one year after they have sent three qualified ministers to abide in foreign infidel countries, all my lands and tenements in and about Catworth in Huntingtonshire (set at about sixty eight pounds per annum).

I give to Mr. Jos. Thompson and the rest of the Society for New England an estate in Essex called Tolshant Becknam manor, which I bought of Mrs. Hannah Fox *als* Bradley, after her death, as long as the said Society or Corporation shall continue, upon condition that sixty pounds per annum shall be allowed between two well qualified persons as to piety and prudence to be nominated successively by my trustees to preach as itinerants in the English plantations in the West Indies and for the good of what Pagans and Blacks lie neglected there, and the remainder be paid yearly to the College of Cambridge in New England, or such as are usually employed to manage the blessed work of converting the poor Indians there, to promote which I design this part of my gift. But if my trustees be hindered from nominating the said itinerants under the pretence of any statute in New England or elsewhere I give the said three score pounds per annum to the said College in New England, to encourage and make them capable to get constantly some learned Professor out of Europe to reside there and shall be of their own nomination in concurrence with the ministers of the Town of Boston in the said New England. And if the foresaid Society or Corporation shall happen to be dissolved or deprived of their present privilege my will is and I hereby give the said manor, with all the profits and advantages, to the said Town of Boston, with the ministers thereof, to benefit the said College as above and to promote the conversion of the poor Indians.

To my cousin Stephen Davies, minister at Banbury, and to the heirs male of his body, lawfully begotten, and, for want of such, to my son Benjamin Sheppard and the heirs male of his body &c. next to Mr. John Evans, my colleague and his heirs male &c., then to Dr. Edmund Calamy and his heirs male &c., then to the Magistrates and City of Edinburgh in North Britain all the contigent remainders which respect Glasgow or the Society in Scotland &c., as also all that is due to me for the remainder of the term of ninety nine years from the Exchequer, my interest in the Thames Water, my estate in and about Travallen and Gregsford which I bought of the Merediths and that near Holt bought of Mr. Weaver, and the estate in Burton and Cross Howell which my brother and sister Roberts are to enjoy for life, as also what I bought of Mr. Maddocks, near Clare in Suffolk, with all the lands and houses settled on my dear wife for life, except Totham as before disposed of, and all other real estate of freehold, in trust that Mr. William Lorimer, Doctor Oldfield, Doctor Edmund Calamy, Mr. William Tongue, Mr. Mat. Henry, Mr. Benjamin Robinson, Mr. Zachariah Merrol of Hamstead, Mr. John Evans, my colleague, Mr. William Harris, Mr. Thomas Reignolds, Mr. Isaac Bates, Mr. Jeremia Smith, Mr. Read (ministers of the Gospel), Mr. John Morton, linen draper, Mr. Edmund Farringdon jun[r], Mr. William Adee, Mr. Jonathan Collier, my son Mr. Benjamin Sheppard, my son Mr. Francis Barkstead, Mr. —— Archer, Mr. Richard Watts, Mr. Isaac Honiwood, Mr. George Smith, son to Mr. Thomas Smith &c. shall act as my trustees (for various purposes). One of them is for a preacher of the Gospel, being a protestant and skillfull in the Irish Tongue, as an itinerant to preach in Irish where he can find an opportunity for it in Ireland, to be nominated and approved by Walter Stephens Esq., Dr. Duncan Cumming, Mr. Joseph Boys, Mr. Nathaniel Weld, in or near Dublin; another for the support of Welsh young men to preach the Word of God in Wales.

As to my library my will is that duplicates and useless books and unfit to be set in a public library be given away to such as they may be useful to and want them. The residue I appoint for a public library whereto such as my trustees appoint shall have access for the perusal of any book in the place where they are lodged. I ordain my executors, with the advice of my trustees, to purchase some or other freehold edifice in some cheap and convenient place without or within the walls of the City of London (as a Throwsters workhouse or the like) with one room for a single person whom they my Trustees shall from time to time trust to keep the said books, whereof two catalogues shall be kept, one by the Keeper of the Library, one by such as the Trustees shall name of their own number (wherein any other person's gift of books may be inserted, under them the names of such donors as shall add to the said Library). And the said Trustees shall pay ten pounds per annum to the said Library Keeper (a young preacher seems fittest for it). If no fit edifice can be procured then a small piece of ground shall be bought and a building erected for this purpose (not pompous or too large) &c.

The executors having renounced admon. was granted to Jane Williams the widow.

Admon. de bonis non was granted 5 March 1739-40, to Francis Barkstead, the widow having died (but in this record her name is given as Anne). Hugh Roberts had also died.   Fox, 218.

[The Library thus provided for was the well known non-conformist library, now, I believe, at 16 Grafton St., Gower St. The Inscription at Bunhill Fields describes him as "Dan[lis] Williams S. T. P. Wrexhamiæ in Comitatu Denbigensi inter Cambro-Britannos nati," &c. The date of his burial (or death) "vii. Kal. Feb. Anno ætatis suæ LXXII. Christi MDCCXVI."—H. F. W.

The Society for New England, represented by Mr. Joseph Thompson, named in Dr. Williams's will, was the society under whose patronage John Eliot printed his Indian translation of the Bible. For a sketch of its history see REGISTER, vol. 39, pp. 299–301. See also vol. 36, pp. 157–61; vol. 39, pp. 29–30; pp. 179–83; vol. 42, pp. 329–30; vol. 45, p. 248.—EDITOR.]

NICHOLAS BAKER of the parish of St. George's in Marylard one of his Majesty's plantations in America, 28 February 1753, proved 7 January 1766. My debts and funeral charges paid all the rest of my worldly goods &c. I give to my brother John Baker of Gray's Inn Lane, St. Andrew Parish, gardner, during his natural life, he making no waste &c., and after his decease to my sister Elizabeth Baker of St. Andrew's and Gray's Inn Lane.

Then follows an Inventory of his estate in America, bequeathed by the aforesaid will to John Baker and Elizabeth his wife: vizt twc hundred acres called Nicholas Baker's Choice, or the rich Bottom, now in possession of John Taylor of the parish of St. George's in America (and certain live stock). Tyndall, 3.

THOMAS ALDWORTHE of the city of Bristol, alderman and merchant, 22 November 1598, proved 5 March 1598. My body to be buried in the Gauntes church in St. Augustine's Green. I give four pounds towards the reparation of the church of St. Warborough and to the new works adjoining to the same. To my wife Margerie two hundred pounds, within one year after my decease, and three hundred ounces of my plate, and one hundred pounds yearly during her natural life (and other property). To my brother Richard Aldworthe of London twenty pounds, and to my cousin Robert Aldworthe, his son, two hundred pounds, and three tankards of silver and gilt for a remembrance. To John Aldworthe, my brother Richard's son, two hundred pounds, and to his two daughters Margerie and Elizabeth, ten pounds each at day of marriage. To Elizabeth Aldworthe, my brother Richard's daughter, twenty pounds. To Richard Tovye. To Thomas Aldworthe of Wantinge, Berks., tanner, ten pounds. Thomas Wright, my godson, Robert Younge, the youngest child of John Younge deceased. My brother in law Mr John Webb. John Collimore, draper. Jeromie Ham, town clerk. To my friend Robert Redwood ten ounces of plate. To Thomas Aldworth, vicar of Congresbury, twenty five pounds. My cousin Joan Harris of Oxford and her two brethren. My cousin Markes Smithe in Berkshire and his two sisters. To Thomas Aldworthe, " the whooper," ten pounds. To certain almshouses, prisons and hospitals. To certain servants. I make my beloved Thomas Aldworth als Darbridg, who espoused Marie the daughter of Walter Williams, draper of this city of Bristol deceased, my full and whole executor &c. I give to the same Thomas Aldworthe als Durbridge the fee farm of my now dwelling house in Smale Street &c. And I desire my well beloved brother in law John Webb, my cousin Robert Aldworthe and John Aldworth, merchants, and Mr. Doctor Francis James to be my overseers &c. Kidd, 25.

MARGERIE ALDWORTHE of Bristol, late the wife of Thomas Aldworthe of the same city, alderman deceased; 19 May 1602, proved 26 June 1602. My body to be buried near to the place where my husband is buried. To the Hospital of Queen Elizabeth in Bristol. To Thomas Cullimor, son of Humprey Cullymor my brother, late of Sodbury, Gloc., deceased. To Alice Corye, daughter of John Corye late of the parish of Redcliffe in Bristol deceased. To John Corye her brother. To Margery and Elizabeth Aldworth, children of John Aldworth, of Bristol, merchant. To certain children of John Cullymor late of Bristol, merchant, deceased. To Alice Parker daughter of John Parker of Sodbury and to Anne Parker, another daughter. To Melcha Hare and Anne Ven, daughters of my brother James Cullymor. To Humprey Collymore, son of John Collymore of Bristol deceased. My brother Aldworthe of London. My cousin Mr. Robert Aldworthe. My sister Webbe. My friend Mrs. Redwood. My cousin Jane Davies. My sister Aldworthe of London. My cousin Robert Aldworthe's wife. My cousin John Aldworthe's wife. My brother John Webbe of Bristol, alderman, I make executor, and my cousin John Aldworthe and Robert Redwoode overseers. Montague, 47.

JOHN ALDWORTH of Bristol, merchant, 18 December 1615, proved 14 February 1615. My body to be buried in the Gauntes Church at St. Austines Green. Towards the reparation of said church ten pounds. To my daughter Elizabeth Aldworth five hundred marks, being three hundred and thirty three pounds, six shillings and eight pence. To my daughter Martha Aldworth five hundred marks &c. To my sister Elizabeth Crockhay fifty pounds and to her daughters Elizabeth and Sarah Crockhay fifty pounds. To Elizabeth Aldworth, daughter of my brother Thomas Aldworth, sometime vicar of Congresbury deceased, fifty pounds. To Elizabeth Poodie, daughter of my sister Mary Podie deceased, fifty shillings. I give unto Giles Elbridge, sometimes servant to my brother Robert Aldworth, the sum of ten pounds in money. To my poor cousin Richard Wright of Bristol, mercer, ten pounds. To my cousin the wife of Richard Redwood five pounds. To her sister Mary, wife of Thomas Turner, baker, five pounds. To the poor tuckers and "sheeremen" in Bristol, most needing, the sum of ten pounds to be distributed amongst them at the discretion of my two overseers. To Robert Younge, son of John Younge, merchant, deceased, ten pounds. To his mother, Philip Ivye, my cousin, to her own use, five pounds. To my maid servant, Bridget Sweeper, five pounds. To my two brothers in law, Francis and Edward Knight, to each of them thirty three shillings and four pence, to make either of them a ring in token of my love towards them. All the rest of my goods and chattles (my debts and legacies being paid and funeral expenses discharged) I do give and bequeath unto my son Francis Aldworth, being now in the parts beyond the seas, whom I do ordain and make whole and sole executor of this my last will and testament, to see all my debts and legacies performed within six months after my decease (if possible it may be) or else within one whole year at the utmost. And I do make, ordain and appoint my well beloved brother Robert Aldworth executor in trust until my said son Francis shall accomplish his full age of twenty and one years; and for his pains I give him fifty pounds. And I appoint my brother William Challoner and my son in law Philip Ellis to be overseers, and give to each of them five pounds and ten shillings. Cope, 19.

FRANCIS KNIGHT, one of the aldermen of the city of Bristol, 8 August 1616, proved 12 October 1616. To son Francis all my lands &c. in the city and County which were purchased by myself and not any of those lands which were my last wife's and which came by her. My son's wife Katherine. My son Edward. My daughter Martha Challoner, wife of William Challoner of Bristol, merchant. John Knight, son of my said son Francis. Francis Aldworth, son of John Aldworth late of said city merchant deceased. Francis, Bridget, Robert and John Knight, children of my son Edward. Robert and Francis Challoner, two of the sons of the said William Challoner and Martha his wife Martha, Joane, William, Thomas and Bridget Challoner children of the same William and Martha. My brother Robert Aldworth and his wife. To my sister Challoner a

mourning gown and one of my wife's best rings. Frances Knight, daughter
of my brother Matthew Knight, and John Knight, his son. My nephew
Thomas Knight. The rest of my brother John Knight's children, sons and
daughters. My sister Benntlye's children. I do hereby forgive, release
and discharge unto my cousin William Mallatt all such sums &c and debts
which he oweth unto me for the debts of his predecessor William Townsend or for himself. I forgive Elizabeth Bentley her debts. I forgive
Margaret Wallis widow, her debts. I give unto my cousin Richard Knight
my Book of Martyrs and Peter Martyr and all other books which he hath
in his keeping. My son Edward to be sole executor and my brother in
law Robert Aldworth John Egglesfield and my son in law William Challoner to be overseers.   Cope, 112.

WILLIAM CHALLONER of Bristol, merchant, 19 June 1620, proved 27
November 1620. My body to be buried in such place as to my wife and
my mother shall seem best. To wife Martha five hundred marks. My
mother Joane Challoner to be paid threescore pounds per annum during
her life. Three tenements in Back Street Bristol now in the holding of
John Veale John Worgan and George Benson. To my son Robert my
great house wherein I now dwell upon the back of Bristol (and other lands
&c). And I hope my wife will according to the trust reposed by her father
leave unto my son Robert her lands at Chew. The said Robert hath ten
pounds given him by his grandfather Knight and twenty pounds by his
grandfather Challoner. I hereby give him so much as to make it up an
hundred and fifty pounds, which I will shall be paid him, fifty pounds thereof
when his uncle and master Mr. Robert Aldworth shall think fit for him to
go to sea, and the other hundred at his age of one and twenty. My son
Francis is to have the great house in Ballard Street in Bristowe wherein
my father Knight dwelled. Son William Challoner. Son Thomas Challoner. Daughters Joane Challoner and Bridget. My brethren Richard
Challoner, Thomas Cleybrooke, Walter Harflett, Charles Chute, Francis
Knight and Edward Knight and their wives. Thomas Colston of Bristol
merchant hath married my daughter Martha. Wife to be executrix.
                                                      Soame, 98.

FRANCIS ALDWORTH of Bristol, merchant, 23 August 1623, proved 26
January 1623. My body to be buried in the Gaunts Church in St. Augustine's Green within the suburbs of the City of Bristol as near my father
there as conveniently it may. To the said church ten pounds. To the
poor in the almshouses within the said city and suburbs ten pounds. To
the poor shearmen and tuckers in Bristol ten pounds. To my sister Martha
Aldworth my two messuages &c. in Congresbury, Somerset (and other
bequests). To Robert Elbridge Martha Elbridge and John Elbridge,
children of my sister Elizabeth Elbridge, and to the child wherewith she
now goeth, equally between them, all that my part of the prisage or prize
wines which I have and hold by Indenture of lease for all the years and
term which I have to come in the said lease, to be received yearly by my
executors to increase a stock or portion for the said children, to be kept to
their use until they shall accomplish their several ages of 21 years or be
married. To my said sister Elizabeth Elbridge two hundred pounds within
two years after my deceese. To my kinswoman Elizabeth Crockhay fifty
pounds. To my kinswoman Elizabeth Aldworth twenty five pounds and
to my kinswoman Elizabeth Poodye fifty pounds. To every of the chil-

dred which Edward Knight, my kinsman now hath living five pounds apiece. To my friend William Lyons twenty pounds. The residue to my most dear and loving uncle Robert Aldworth of the aforesaid city merchant, one of the aldermen of the same city, whom I make, appoint and ordain whole and sole executor. . Byrde, 3.

[The will of Giles Elbridge, father of John and Thomas Elbridge, was one of the Oxford Wills (so called) of 1643-4, *i.e.* it was proved at Oxford but not registered, owing to the unhappy state of affairs in England at that time. I have to thank my friend Mr. J. C. C. Smith for the following notes taken from the original, which was evidently a draft, made probably at the bedside and never formally written out, but put in just as it was written.—H. F. WATERS.]

Feb. 24-5, 1643, Giles Elbridge m^{r}cat^r. his body to be laid in S^t. Peter's Crowd appoynted to y^t purpose "Son John executor" to Thomas and Aldworth his sonnes that ye monies to them att age of 21 yeeres given by their unckles John & Frauncis Ald 400^{li} apeece   to Martha & Eliz: his children by his former wife 400te *ut supra* apeece within 6 moneths next after his decease   to John his son & to his heirs & ass forever the sugarhouse the tenīte late in tenure of George Paine in St. Peters Churchyard Bristol & his farme of Natton wth the apptenances Hend to him his heires & ass forever.   to —— dau. of my son Robert £50 in money at 21 the rest of his estate &c. John   Wit. Thomas Colston Nath. Cale Rowland Searchfeild Hum. Yeamans
   Copia vera   Collacone inde fca 4 March 1643 *per nos* (then follow the names of the above witnesses)
                pr. 19 Mch. 1643 at Oxford.

[A further account of his descendants in New England must be sought for in the records of the town and parish of Marblehead and those of Essex Co. at Salem. The families of Russell, Greenleaf and Gerry* were connected with them. My own notes showing these connections are unfortunately in Salem.
                                        HENRY F. WATERS.

Gyles Elbridge, the testator, was one of the patentees of the Pemaquid grant. On the 29th of February, 1631-2, the President and Council of New England granted to "Robert Aldworth and Gyles Elbridge of the City of Bristol, merchants," twelve thousand acres of land "near the River comonly called or known by the name of Pemaquid," and also one hundred acres for every person transported thither by them. The patent is printed in the Report of the Massachusetts Commissioners on the Land Titles of Lincoln County, Maine, May 20, 1811, pp. 33-9, and in Ancient Pemaquid by J. Wingate Thornton in the Collections of the Maine Historical Society, vol. 5., pp. 207-14, the latter copy having been verified by the notarial copy preserved in the library of the American Antiquarian Society. Mr. Thornton, on page 226 of the above work, calls Gyles Elbridge a nephew of Mr. Aldworth, and states that Aldworth died in 1634 and the patent then became the property of Mr. Elbridge, at whose decease and that of his eldest son John it passed to the second son Thomas about the year 1647.

As early as 1650 Thomas Elbridge was in New England and had his residence at Pemaquid. Here he made grants of lands, held courts, tried causes and punished offences. On the 10th of December, 1650, he mortgages to Abraham Shurt the island of Monhagan by a deed in which he describes himself as "Thomas Elbridge of Pemaquid in N. E. merch^t." On the 1st day of February, 1651-2, he sold to Capt. Paul White one half of "the patent and plantation of Pemaquid." The deed is printed in the Report of the Massachusetts Commissioners before quoted, pp. 41-5. On the 3d of September, 1657, he sold

* It was from Elbridge Gerry, a descendant, that the political term "Gerrymander" (pronounced with the hard sound of G, not, as our English friends call it, "Jerrymander") got its name.—H. F. W.
See an article on the Gerrymander in the REGISTER, vol. 46, pp. 374-83.—EDITOR.

the other half to Nicholas Davison of Charlestown, who had previously purchased the half sold to Paul White. In the deed Elbridge describes himself as
" Thomas Elbridge son of Giles Elbridge of the city of Bristol in Old England,
and executor of the last will and testament of John Elbridge late son and heir
of the said Giles Elbridge," adding " my late brother John Elbridge by his last
will and testament, bearing date the eleventh day of September in the year of
our Lord one thousand six hundred forty and six did devise, give and bequeath
unto me the said Thomas Elbridge, my heirs and assigns forever all that tract,'
&c. This deed and other conveyances relating to this property, including the
patent, are recorded in the Suffolk Deeds, which are now printed. See Liber
I., fol. 131; Lib. II., fol. 69; Lib. III., fol. 46–57. Rebecca, wife of Thomas
Elbridge, released her dower to half of the property Sept. 5, 1657. Mr. Elbridge
was a resident of Pemaquid as late as May 18, 1672, when he signed the petition
of that date to Massachusetts colony to be taken under the government of that
colony. (Maine Hist. Collections, vol. 5, page 240.) The Massachusetts commissioners in their report May, 1811, in considering the right at that time to the
property, says: " It is contended by the present claimants that this Grant is a
joint tenancy and that Giles Elbridge survived Robert Alsworth [Aldworth] and
became sole proprietor of the whole, and that John Elbridge, eldest son of
Giles, afterwards died, and by his will devised the whole to Thomas Elbridge,
the second son of Giles, and that so the present claimants derive their title
down through him" (Report, page 9). From these Aldworth and Elbridge wills
I infer that Gyles Elbridge married Elizabeth Aldworth, daughter of John Aldworth, a brother of Robert Aldworth, alderman of Bristol, his partner. If this
be so he was a nephew of the latter only by marriage.—EDITOR.]

JOHN ELBRIDGE of St. Peters within the city of Bristol, merchant, 11
September 1646, proved 16 October 1646. My body to be buried or
interred by my fathers and ancestors of good fame and memory in the vault
or arched dormitory for that purpose built and erected in the upper end of
the South Aisle of the parish church of St. Peter's aforesaid. Refers to
last will of father, bearing date 25 February 1643 (*stilo Anglicano*) wherein
he willed, devized and bequeathed unto me, under his hand and seal, by
the name of John Elbridge, divers lands, tenements, houses and hereditaments &c situate &c within the City and County of Bristol, the counties of
Somerset, Gloucester or elsewhere, as also in New England within the
confines and continent of America, who also therein willed and bequeathed
divers and sundry legacies unto my brothers, sisters and others, which are
not yet paid. To my brother Thomas Elbridge my whole manor of Chell-
wood, in the county of Somerset, with the capital messuage or tenement
thereto belonging &c. &c. To my said brother Thomas that tenement or
tenements on the North side of the churchyard of the parish of St. Peter's
aforesaid and on the South East side on the river Avon, most commonly
known as the Swagar House. Refers to Royal Patent and grant of New
England bearing date 3 November 18th of His Majesty's reign and an Indenture and deed by the President and council bearing date 29 February
1631, demising "unto my Auncestors of good memory, viz[t]. Robert Aldworth and Giles Elbridge of the Cittee of Bristowe marchants " &c. one
great continent of land consisting of twelve thousand acres, be it more or
less, situate &c. in New England &c. all which are now come unto me by
virtue of my deceased father's will, as being sole executor thereof, the
surviving heir and eldest son now living. I do hereby devise, will, give
and bequeath unto my said brother Thomas Albridge (*sic*), his heirs and
assigns for ever, all that said continent of land of twelve thousand acres, be
it more or less, and all and every part of the new Plantation there, with
all castles, forts, edifices, buildings, messuages, houses, out houses, tenements, cottages, rents, reversions of rents, suits, services, mounds, walls,
woods, underwoods, rivers, runlets, cricks, ponds, fishings &c. &c. to him

and his heirs forever. I give to my brother Aldworth Elbridge and his lawfully begotten heirs my farm known as Natton Farm, in the parish of Ayshchurch, Gloc. To my sister Martha Cudley, widow, and the heirs of her body lawfully already and hereafter to be begotten a certain newly erected messuage &c. (by my uncle Robert Aldworth one of the aldermen of the city of Bristol) wherein George Payne, merchant, lately lived, adjoining the East end of the parish church of St. Peter's &c. [This sister afterwards called Martha Cugley.] To my sister Elizabeth now the wife of thomas Moore, merchant, ten pounds, as a remembrance of my love. To my cousin Elizabeth Payne, daughter of George Payne of the city of Bristol, merchant, and Elizabeth his wife, twenty pounds. To my friend John Berriman, merchant, as a remembrance of my love, fifty pounds, desiring him to be helping and assisting unto my executors in the discovering of my estate, where it lieth and wherein it consisteth. Sundry bequests to the poor. To Mr. Robert Pritchard, clerk, the minister of the parish church, forty shillings. My brother Thomas and my friend Mr. Nathaniel Cale, of Bristol, soap boiler, to be joint executors, the latter of whom I desire by reason of the ancient true love and respect he hath always born unto my deceased father and myself, by way of trust, in the absence of my said brother, being now beyond the seas and in his minority, to undergo the same and immediately after my decease to take upon him the execution thereof, for which I give and bequeath unto him as a legacy and token of my love my great double gilt bowl to the end that none of my creditors in their several and respective debts neither any of my brothers or sisters, in their particular legacies willed and bequeathed by my deceased father, more especially Mr. Thomas Barker, his children, and the administratrix of Mr. Thomas Tucker, clerk, lately deceased, that they nor any of them be not protracted, deferred or delayed &c. &c. I desire my loving friends Mr. William Colson and Mr. Rowland Searchfield, merchants, to be overseers. I give to my niece Elizabeth Cugley twenty pounds.

This was proved by Mr Nath¹ Cale, power reserved for Thomas Elbridge, brother of the deceased, when he should come to seek it.   Twisse, 148.

URSULA BOVEY of London, widow, wife of Ralph Bovey of London Esq. 25 April 1643, proved 3 April 1647. Lands in Shorne, Kent. Son Ralphe Bovey. Brother Mr. Richard Aldworth. Sister Mrs. Sara Charke's younger children. My lands in Sillhill, Warwick. My daughter Anne Davies, wife of Mr. Priamus Davies of Coxhall, Hereford.   Fines, 63.

MICHAEL PINDAR citizen and fishmonger of London 11 October 1646, proved 19 May 1647. My wife, Mary Pindar shall have and enjoy one third part of all my goods &c., which of right is due to her by the laudable custom of the City of London. My children, Michael, Henry, Richard and Paul Pindar shall have and enjoy one third &c., which of right is due to them &c. My executrix not to spend above twenty pounds about my burial. To my son Michael one hundred pounds over and above his orphanage part, to be paid to him out of my third part at his age of one and twenty years. To my son Henry sixty pounds (as above). To son Richard fifty pounds (as above). To Paul forty pounds (as above). I nominate and appoint my wife Mary my sole executrix and my father in law Richard Aldworth of Bristol, alderman, and my brother Robert Aldworth of Lincoln's Inn Esq. overseers. ffr. Neale a witness.

Fines, 100.

ELIZABETH NEVE of the town and county of Southampton, widow, 22 August 19th of Charles, proved 20 February 1645. My body to be buried in the church of Holy Roods in a vault within the said church or where it shall please God to dispose. To ten poor people, men and women, that shall be thought to have most need and such as have lived in the fear of God and in good order and brought up their children to work and do appertain to the French Church within Southampton, to each of them as followeth, to the men dublet and house and to the women gowns, and gowns to the poor men instead of dublet and hose as it shall be thought most convenient. My will is that the cloth be a sad russett of home made cloth, of coarse wool of six pence a pound, and each of them a pair of stockings and a pair of shoes; and my will is that this be continued by the space of twelve years next ensuing my death once every two years during the said twelve years. I give unto twenty poor people that are in need the sum of three shillings apiece, to be paid at my funeral to such persons as shall be thought meet to partake hereof. Mr. White, the minister of Otterborne, forty shillings. My will is that forty shillings a year be given to some faithful minister that shall be settled in this town of Southampton or Winchester for the space of twelve years.

Item, I give to the children of Thomas Dummer and Susanna his wife, my beloved daughter of Chicknell, in manner as followeth, vizt to Thomas Dummer, his son, the sum of thirty pounds of currant money, to Hester Dummer, his daughter, the sum of thirty pounds of money, to Jane Dummer, his daughter, thirty pounds, to their daughter Mary Dummer the sum of thirty pounds, to their daughter Anne Dummer the sum of thirty pounds &c. To John Hersent the elder his wife forty shillings by the year till the children Peter and John shall be of age of twenty and one years. To Jane, the daughter of John Hersant the elder of Southampton, three pounds in three years after my decease. To the children of my daughter Elizabeth Carman as followeth, to her son John Carman and to Elizabeth Carman their (sic) daughter, fifty shillings apiece, to be paid to them at the end of seven years after my decease, if one die the survivor to have the legacy pertaining to the deceased. To my grand daughter Elizabeth Yong, to raise some portions for her children if it please the Lord to send her any, two hundred pounds. To my grandson William Yonge, her brother, one hundred pounds. My will is that of all the legacies given to my kindred the two last mentioned be first paid. To my goddaughter Margaret Hersent three pounds. To John Hersent the younger forty shillings. To my son Carman's three children which he had before he married with my daughter forty shillings apiece. All the rest of my goods &c. I give and bequeath unto my beloved daughter Susanna Dummer and Thomas Dummer her husband whom I make &c. my true and lawful executors. And I ordain and appoint my trusty and well beloved in Christ Jesus John Hardye, Minister of God's Holy word in the parish of Fursby and sometimes preacher of God's Word within this —— to be overseer.   Twisse, 57.

ELIZABETH, Viscountess Campden, dowager (late wife of the Right Hon. Baptist, late Lord Viscount Campden deceased) 14 February 18th Charles, proved 11 August 1645. My body to be buried by my late husband in that Chapel where he lieth buried in the parish church of Campdon, in the County of Gloucester. To the companies of Mercers and Merchant tailors of London. To the Church wardens and certain parishioners of St. Lawrence Jewry. To certain parishioners of St.

Mary Magdalen, Milk Street (among whom Mr. Richard Aldworth and Mr. Martin Pindar) and to the church wardens of that parish. To the Churchwardens and certain parishioners of Kensington. To the poor of Campden town and Burrington in Gloucestershire and of Brooke in Rutlandshire and of Watford in Herts. To my son in law Edward, Lord Viscount Campden, and my daughter Julian, his wife. My house near the lower end of Milk Street. My grandson Henry Noell Esq., second son of the said Edward, Lord Viscount Campden. My grand daughter the Lady Elizabeth Capel, wife of the Right Hon. Arthur, Lord Capell, and sole daughter and heir to Sir Charles Morison, Knight and Baronet deceased, and my great granddaughter Elizabeth Caper (*sic*) her daughter. My son in law Sir Edward Alford, knight. My grand son Baptist Noell Esq., son and heir apparent of the said Edward, Viscount Campden. The daughters of my grand daughter, Elizabeth Chaworth deceased. My grand daughter the Lady de la Fountaine, now wife of Sir Erasmus de la Fountaine knight, and daughter of the said Edward, Viscount Campden. My grandson the Lord Chaworth. The children of my late brother Mr. Hugh Maye; Charles May, son of my late honorable brother Sir Humphrey May, knight, deceased, late Vice Chamberlain to his Majesty. Henry, Robert, Richard, Algernon and Baptist May, other sons of Sir Humphrey. Nephew Richard Bennett Esq., Nephew Thomas May of Raw-meare, Sussex, Esq. My brother Thomas May Esq. My nephew Adrian May. Nephews Thomas and Humphrey Bennett, sons of my late sister Bennett. Brother in law Sir William Heyrick, knight. My nephews Robert Heyricke and Henry John Heyricke and my two nieces Martha Heyricke and Elizabeth Heyricke, these four. John Heyricke my nephew (now clerk to my cousin Sergeant Rolles). My nephew William Heyricke. My nephew Richard Heyricke. My niece Dorothy Lancashire, widow, and her children (my said nephew William Heyricke their uncle). My niece Anne Rowse, one of the daughters of my brother Richard May Esq. deceased. My niece Alice Leighton, another of his daughters. (Sundry other relatives, among the Mays, named). My niece Farrington, one of the daughters of my brother John May deceased. My niece Dorothy Cowley, widow, and her two sons. I give and bequeath to my cousin Richard Aldworth, eldest son of my late nephew Richard Aldworth deceased, four hundred pounds sterling, to be paid him within one year next after my decease. To all the younger children of my said nephew Richard Aldworth deceased six hundred pounds sterling, to be paid unto their eldest brother, my said cousin Richard Aldworth, in one year, he to pay two hundred pounds thereof to his now sister at her age of eighteen or day of marriage, and the residue to his younger brothers in equal parts as they shall accomplish their several ages of one and twenty years: To the three children of my niece Andrewes deceased. To John Taylor, my kinsman, and his children. To Mr. Challoner and his wife, being grand daughter to the Earl of Mulgrave. My kinswoman Lady Crooke, late wife to Judge Crooke deceased. To Alice Hinckson, widow. To Edward Bates, son of Mary Marshall, and grandson of the said Alice Hinckson. Elizabeth Wilson and Mary Marshall, both of them daughters of the said Alice Hinckson.

Rivers, 109.

[Elizabeth, Viscountess Campden, dowager, the testatrix, was the widow of Baptist Hicks, created Baron Hicks of Ilmington, co. Warwick, and Viscount Campden of Campden, co. Gloucester, May 5, 1628, with remainder, failing issue male, to his son-in-law, Edward, Baron Noel, husband of his eldest daughter, Julian Hicks. Her husband died in 1629, *s.p.m.* (See Nicholas's Synopsis of the Peerage, ed. 1825, vol. 1, p. 6.) For her descendants through her daughter Julian, see Burke's Extinct Peerage of Great Britain (ed. 1846), pp. 398–9; Collins's Peerage (ed. 1741), vol. 2, pp. 428–32; (ed. 1779), vol. 4, pp. 45–53. For account of Sir William Herrick, named in the will, see Herrick Genealogy by Dr. Lucius C. Herrick (Columbus 1885), pp. 8–11, where portraits of him and his wife Joan, daughter of Richard May, are given.—EDITOR.]

CICILY HOOKE of Bristol, widow, 31 August 1660, proved 17 October 1660. My nephew Humphrey Hooke Esq. to be sole executor. I desire to be buried in the parish church of St. Stephens in Bristol near my late deceased husband Humphrey Hooke Esq. deceased. To my daughter Creswicke sixteen hundred pounds. To her children (named). My daughter Hellier (the same amount) and to her son Thomas Richardson, her son Humphrey Hellier and her daughter Sarah Hellier. My grandchild Mary Peterson. My grandchild Mary Wasborow. To my grandchild Sarah Elbridge one hundred pounds. My grandchildren William Hooke, Mary Hooke and Thomas Hooke. And to Mary Aldworth, daughter to my grandchild Dorothy Aldworth, fifty pounds. My grandchild William Cann. Florence Hooke daughter of my grandson Humphrey Hooke. My brother in law Mr. Edward Hooke. My sister Mrs. Alice Gostlett. My sister in law Mary Dixon. My kinswoman Cicily Tiley. My two daughters Elizabeth Creswicke and Sarah Hellier. My grandson Humphrey Hooke to be sole executor.   Nabbs, 187.

[In Suffolk Deeds, Liber I., folio 15, is recorded a mortgage, Nov. 23, 1640, from Thomas Dexter of Lynn, to Humphrey Hooke, alderman of Bristol, and others, of Dexter's farm in Lynn. In the same volume is recorded a deed, April 24, 1650, from William Hooke of Salisbury, Massachusetts, to Samuel Bennet, of land which was given him by an arbitration between Thomas Dexter and him or his father Humphrey Hooke. Francis Hooke of Kittery is called by Savage a son of Humphrey Hooke, alderman of the city of Bristol. Francis Hooke married Mary, daughter of Samuel Mavericke, whose Description of New England is printed in the REGISTER, vol. 39, pp. 33–48. A petition of Mary, wife of Francis Hooke, Feb. 13, 1687, about Noddle's Island, is printed in the REGISTER, vol. 8, p. 334.—EDITOR.]

ELIZABETH HAYWARD of Crickley, Gloucestershire, widow, 29 April 1657, with a codicil dated 15 August 1658, proved 7 June 1659. I give to my granddaughter Elizabeth Elbridge the rents &c. of a parcell of meadow or pasture ground in Crickley aforesaid, in the parish of Badgworth in said county, for the term of fifteen years, and after that I give the same ground (called great Darksfield) to my grandson James Cartwright. My grandson John Cartwright. My daughter Isabel Cartwright. My son in law Mr. James Cartwright. My kinsman Anthony Webb of Charleton Kings. My brother in law Samuel Maunsell of Charleton Kings, gen^t. My grandson Thomas Cartwright.   Pell, 398.

SIR THOMAS HOOKE of Lincoln's Inn, Middlesex, Baronet, 1 December 1677, proved 3 January 1677. To wife Dame Elizabeth Hooke the use of household stuff in my house called Tangier Parke in the County of Southampton. Lands &c in the counties of Norfolk, Warwick, Derby, Gloucester, Somerset and Monmouth to son Hele Hooke for life. In trust to Sir William Thomson and Robert Thomson to support and preserve certain contingent estates. My three daughters, Elizabeth, Mary and Ann. Lands and tenements &c. in Cornwall. Stocks of the East India Company, London. Lands, tenements &c. in Devon. I give to my son Hele Hooke my study of books and the diamond ring I usually wear, which I bought of Mr. Winge. Sir William Thomson of London, knight, and the Lady Thomson, his wife, father and mother of my said wife. I give to my sister Dorothy Aldworth fifty pounds. To my niece Mary Aldworth three hundred pounds and to my nieces, Elizabeth, Dorothy and Ciceley Aldworth, two hundred pounds apiece—all at their days of marriage or ages of twenty one years. To my sister Mary Scrope fifty pounds. To my niece Mary Scrope three hundred pounds, to my nephew Thomas Scrope three hundred pounds to my niece Elizabeth Scrope two hundred pounds and to my sister Scrope's other two youngest daughters two hundred pounds apiece. I make and appoint the said Sir William Thomson and Robert Thomson Esq., brother of the said Sir William, executors &c. My manor of Frampton upon Severne, Glouc. To my nephew Thomas Aldworth one hundred pounds at sixteen. I give my brother Jackson twenty pounds to mourn. To my sister Alford twenty pounds to mourn and to Col. Alford her husband ten pounds to mourn. To Dr Goodwin Dr. Owen and Mr. Collins two hundred pounds to be disposed of as they shall see good. To my cousin Michael Pindar twenty pounds. To my sister Aldworth one hundred pounds for her tenderness to me in my sickness. Reeve, 4.

RICHARD ROGERS the elder, citizen and goldsmith of London, now dwelling in Edlmeton (Edmonton) Middlesex, 5 July 1578, proved 21 May 1579. My body to be buried in the parish church of Edlmton. My cousin Richard Rogers, citizen and goldsmith of London, to be residuary legatee and executor. My friends the Right Worshipful Sir Rowland Haywarde knight, citizen and Alderman of London, and Robert Hayes of Ennfield, Middlesex, gentleman, to be overseers. To my brother Roger Rogers of Nest Cliffe, in the county of Salop, for the term of his natural life, all my messuages, lands &c in the parish of Nesse Strange in the said county, my two water mills, the one a corn mill the other a "walke mill" &c. in Oswestry. After his decease I give the same to my cousin Roger Rogers, the son of my uncle Thomas Rogers, and the heirs male of his body lawfully begotten; and for default of such issue, to my cousin John Rogers, brother to the said Roger, my uncle's son &c. To Richard Higley, son of John Higley, my house &c. in Erdston, in the parish of Riton, in Salop. To Richard Vaugham, the son of Vaugham, my house &c. in Wickie. To Cutbert Crackplace and Johan his wife, for term of their lives and the life of the longest liver of them, my four gardens, now made into six gardens in an Alley called —— without Bishopsgate London (and another garden) paying unto my nephew John Rogers of London, grocer, his heirs and assigns, twenty shillings at the four terms of feasts of the year. I give to the said John Rogers, grocer, the reversion of the said five gardens, now made into seven. To Jane Flemminge, wife of William Flemminge of London, currier, for term of her natural life, all the rest of my gardens in St. Buttolph's without Bishopsgate, London, and the reversion of them to Bridget and Jane Flemminge, the daughters of the said William Flemminge. To William Cowell and Luce his wife (for life) my tenement in Finch Lane, London wherein they now dwell, and the reversion of it to John Rogers grocer &c. To my said brother Roger Rogers and Elizabeth his wife (for life) my tenement &c. in the maze of Cleweth, and also another tenement in Oswestry, with the reversion of them to John Browne son of William Browne of Nesse Strange. To Dorothy Rogers, the daughter of my cousin John Rogers, (a tenement in Oswestry). Certain annuities to Isabel Rogers, Katherine Rogers and Jane Rogers, daughters of my uncle Thomas Rogers. Annuities to Dorothy Rogers and Margaret Rogers, daughters of John Rogers of Wafford (Walford?), to Richard Higley, son of cousin John Higley and to Thomas and Roger Higley, two other sons, to Katherine Vaugham, youngest daughter of John Vaugham of Willcott, and others. Six and thirty shillings and eight pence to be distributed amongst the poor people of Basse Church, by the discretions of my uncle Thomas Rogers, John Rogers his son, John Shelford and John Higley. The same sum to the poor of Nesse Strange by the discretions of John Vaugham of Willcocke and Roger Rogers of Nesse Cliffe &c., by the hands of my cousin John Rogers of London grocer. A bequest to Anne Higley, daughter of nephew John Higley. To my cousin the said Richard Rogers, goldsmith, my freehold lands and tenements &c. in Edlmton and Tottenham. Money and bread to be given away and a sermon to be preached. A gift to the company of Goldsmiths for poor decayed workmen. My dwelling house and shop in West Cheap, London. To the said John Rogers grocer my Alley called Fishmongers Alley and three tenements in Tower Street London. To my cousin Jane Swanne my tenement without Bishop's gate now in occupation of Godfrey Swayne. I forgive my son in law Thomas Leake all debts &c.   Bakon, 22.

WILLIAM ROGERS of London, goldsmith, being at this present time greeved in body &c. 1 December 1625, proved 24 March 1625. To my loving kinswoman Sara Poore, wife of Stephen Poore, butcher in the Borough of Southwark, twenty pounds. To Thomas Poore, her son, twenty pounds and to Sara Poore, her daughter, twenty pounds. To Mary Barnett, a grandchild of my deceased brother John Rogers, thirteen pounds six shillings eight pence at eighteen. To my kinswoman —— Barnett, her mother and a daughter of my brother John, three pounds six shillings eight pence. To my god daughter Martha Swann a silver and gilt cup of the full value of three pounds six shillings eight pence. To my landlady Mary Rogers forty shillings. To my brother Richard Rogers a ring of gold having an agate stone set in it. To my kinsman Jesper Draper a ring of gold having an onyx stone set in it, and to my kinswoman Anne Draper, his wife, a ring of gold having a diamond stone set in it. To my kinsman Stephen Poore a ring of gold having a white "spyke" stone set in it, and to Sarah Poore his wife a ring of gold having a diamond stone set in it. To my kinswoman Lydia Rogers a ring of gold having a ruby and "emrodd" stone set in it. My kinsman Jesper Draper, citizen and grocer of London, to be sole executor, and my kinsman Stephen Poore to assist him.
                                                          Hele, 37.

RICHARD ROGERS Esq., Comptroller of his Majesty's Mint, within the Tower of London, 22 June 1636, proved 8 September 1636. My body to be buried within the parish Church of St. Michael in Crooked Lane, London, near the place where Sir William Walworth knight, deceased, lieth buried, in the North side of the Chancel, if with conveniency it may be, or else in the middle Aisle near my wife's pew. After payment of my debts and funeral charges the remainder of my personal estate to be divided into three equal parts, according to the ancient and laudable custom of the city of London, whereof one part to my wife Joane, one other third to my son Edward Rogers and my daughter Anne wife of Jasper Draper equally, the other third part I reserve unto myself for payment and performance of legacies &c. To my said daughter Ann (besides other gifts) one gold ring of Crown gold with a death's head in it, of the value and price of forty shillings, to wear for my sake. I release to William and James Hewson their obligations of fifty three pounds and ten shillings apiece. To my cousin Mary Russell, wife of —— Russell, ten pounds, with which her husband shall not meddle, but my executors shall therewith buy or take a chamber for her. To Mary Barnard, daughter of my said cousin Mary Russell, thirty pounds at her age of twenty one or day of marriage. To my kinsman Abraham Rogers five pounds and a mourning cloak of forty shillings price, and to my kinsman John Rogers ten pounds and a gown and a hood of fifty three shillings, four pence price. To my grandchild Richard Rogers fifty pounds at twenty one, to my grandchild Edward Rogers one hundred pounds at twenty one. To my granddaughter Lydia Rogers, daughter of my said son Edward, one hundred pounds at twenty one or day of marriage. And the said Edward Rogers, being their father, shall employ his said three children's legacies to the most benefit and advantage of his said three children that he can or may untill they shall attain to or accomplish their full ages of twenty and one years or be married. Mourning gowns to my wife Joane and my goddaughter Sarah Edmonds and to my son Edward and Lydia his wife and their four children (and others). To my son in law William Hewson and to his two sons the said William and James, black cloth for mourning garments. The same to my cousin William Stanley and his wife Joane. My cousin —— Poore and Sarah his wife and their son. I also give to their said son, being my godson, six silver spoons of the value and price of thirty three shillings and four pence. To my cousin Robert Swann and to his daughter which was lately married to a grocer, black cloth for mourning gowns &c. To my son in law Ephraim Paget, black cloth &c. and a ring of Crown gold with a death's head on it. Black cloth to Mr Haselwood, clerk of the Co. of Goldsmiths and to Mr. Robinson Beadle of the same Company. To my deputy and good friend Mr. Henry Coggan, my cousin William Gearinge and to —— his wife and their son Richard Gearing, my godson. To my cousin Elizabeth Androwes, wife of George Androwes black cloth &c. To my cousin Dorothy Bowler and her two sisters, Elizabeth and Ellen Broome and to my cousin John Broome of Great Nesse, Salop, black cloth &c. and to his son Andrew Broome, servant to the Right Hon. the Lord Strange To my son Edward my sealing ring with a saphire in it. To the Governors of Christ's Hospital to the use of the poor children harbored within the same hospital. I will that there be bestowed the sum of eight pounds in wine and cakes on the day of my burial, on the Governors of Christ's Hospital (whereof I am a member) and on the Livery of the Company of Goldsmiths (whereof I am a brother) and on my neighbors and friends that shall attend or accompany my body to the grave. To the poor of sundry parishes (named) —— of little Nesse wherein I was born. Certain poor to come decently in mourning gowns and black hats to accompany and attend my dead body to the ground. One hundred pounds to be bestowed in a dinner to be made ready and provided in the Hall of the Company of Fishmongers of London for my neighbors, friends and kindred which shall attend or accompany my dead body to the ground on the day of my burial, whereof thirty and five couple to be of the better sort, amongst which I will and appoint the deputy of the Bridge Ward in London and his wife to be one couple. My dwelling house in Thames Street in London, &c shall be valued and apprized. Reference to will of uncle Richard Rogers deceased as to certain freehold lands in Edmonton. I make my son Edward Rogers and my son in law Jasper Draper and his wife Ann, my daughter, full executors and my cousin William Stanly and my son in law Ephraim Pagett overseers.

I give and bequeath my lands, tenements and hereditaments in Virginia, in the parts beyond the seas, to my son Edward Rogers for and during the term of his natural life, and after his death I give the same to my grandchild Richard Rogers to hold to him, his heirs and assigns forever.

Pile, 97.

JOANE ROGERS of London, widow, 6˙ December 1640, proved 7 July 1646. My body to be buried within the parish church of St. Michael Crooked Lane, near my late husband Richard Rogers Esq., Comptroller of H. M. Mint. My kinsman William Goldsmith. My cousin and god daughter Elizabeth Andrewes. My cousin William Goldsmith's wife Barbara. George Andrewes, husband of my cousin Elizabeth Andrewes. Their children Elizabeth Andrewes, Margaret Andrewes, Mary Andrewes and William Andrewes (minor). My cousin William Gerie. My cousin Richard Gerie. My cousin Elizabeth Gery, wife of William. To William Gerie, brother of Richard at one and twenty. My cousin Henry Edmondes. My daughter in law Anne Draper. My cousins William Stanley and Joane Stanley. My kinsman Valentine Markham and his wife. My kinsman William Husson. My cousin Mary Russell. To Henry Cogan a piece of plate of ten pounds, to be delivered to him at the age of one and twenty years. My cousin Warman once my servant. My good friend Henry Cogan Esq. Comptroller of His Majesty's Mint to be sole executor.

Twisse, 113.

HUMPHRIE HIGGINSON of Ratcliffe in the parish of Stepney *alias* Stebonheath in the county of Middlesex, gentleman, 23 February 1665-6, proved 22 March 1665. My will is that my brother Christopher Higginson, now resident upon my plantation called Harupp in Virginia, be maintained upon and out of the same during his natural life. And for the remainder of my estate, real or personal, in England, Virginia or elsewhere, I give, devise and bequeath unto my beloved wife Elizabeth Higginson whom I name, constitute and appoint to be my sole and only executrix of this my last will and testament.

Wit: Thom: James, Anne Freomonger, Sarah Cooke.   Mico, 46.

26 February 1672-3. Mem. That Elizabeth Foster, late wife of Henry Foster, in Virginia late deceased, did, the day and year above written, make her last will, as follows; she did nominate and appoint her mother Elizabeth Higginson, widow, late wife of Humphry Higginson, to be her only and sole executrix. Wit: Thomas Hasellwood, Mary Higginson, John Bettes M.D. Proved by Elizabeth Higginson 14 March 1673.

Bunce, 35.

RICHARD MARTIN of Chatham, Kent, shipwright, 20 May 1659, proved 6 June 1659. I give to my son Richard Martin, who is now in New England as I suppose, my house, with the ground and yard &c. which I have in Ipswich in the Co. of Suffolk, on the backside of the church in St. Clements parish, which said house &c. I give unto my said son Richard in lieu of all debts &c. due or owing by me unto him, he paying out of the said house &c. unto my daughter Martha Martin, (now, being married, Martha Heath) and to my daughter Margaret Martin, to each of them, or their heirs, five pounds within one week after his first coming to take, possess and enjoy the said house &c., but if he never comes then the said house

&c. shall be, after the death of my executrix, taken, possessed &c. by and between my said two daughters. To my daughter Anne, commonly called Hannah Martin, after the death of my executrix, my house wherein I now dwell &c. in Chatham, she paying out unto the eldest child of my daughter Martha ten pounds in seaven years after the death of my executrix, and my daughter Anne shall pay unto my daughter Margaret ten pounds in one year &c. I make my wife Rose Martin sole executrix and I give her my house in Chatham during her natural life, and also my house in Ipswich during her life if my son Richard do not come to demand it. Pell, 389.

RICHARD TEW of Newport in Rhode Island, in New England, yeoman, and now of St. Leonard's Shoreditch, Middlesex, 19 January 1673, proved 27 March 1674. Being desirous to settle my affairs and concerns which I have in old England, my native country, according as I have already done in new England, do hereby declare &c. I give to my brother John Tew of Tossiter (Towcester) in the County of Northampton, Doctor in Physick, twenty shillings to buy him a ring to wear for my sake. The rest of my goods &c. now in old England I give unto my son Henry Tew of Newport in Rhode Island &c. yeoman; whom with my said brother John, I appoint executors; and I appoint my loving friends Edward Wharton of Salem and Joseph Nicholson of the said Rhode Island to be overseers.

Bunce, 40.

AGNES CLARKE of Ayshill, Somerset, widow, 20 October 1647, proved 10 May 1648. My body to be buried in the churchyard of Ayshill near unto John Clarke my deceased husband. To the poor of the parish and to the church. I give and bequeath unto William Harvey, the son of Thomas Harvey deceased, my kinsman now in New England, eighteen pounds, being parcel of thirty five pounds which is owing unto me by Richard Parker of Ayshill upon his bond, which sum is to be paid as soon as it can be recovered if he shall come to demand it any time within four years, but if he come not then my will is that William Harvey the son of James Harvey shall have the said money at such time as he shall be of lawful age to give a discharge. I give to the said William son of James Harvey fifteen pounds parcel of the said thirty five pounds, when of age; and my desire is that Richard Harvey, John Witherall and Richard Crabbe shall put it forth to use to the best benefit of the said William Harvey. I give to John Wytherall the elder of Cudworth twenty shillings and to Mary, wife of Francis Moore of Bicknell twenty shillings. I give and bequeath unto William Harvey in New England all my household stuff during his life if he come to claim it, and after his decease to remain in the house to the use of James Harvey, his brother, and the said James to make use of it until William, his brother, shall come to claim it. I give to Ellen Vyle the wife of Robert Vyle the elder of Strotten my best coffer. To the two children of John Vyle of Donniett to each a pewter platter. To William Clarke of Sommerton and to my goddaughter Deanis Nicholls, to each twenty shillings, to be paid them within one year &c. by John Clarke of Donnyett out of the ten pounds he oweth me. The other eight pounds I give to the said John Clarke and Katherine his wife. To my kinswoman Edith Mitchell of Churchstock twenty shillings. To Elizabeth wife of Richard Harvey, Lucrece wife of William Curtis and Deanes Nicholles, my said god daughter, twenty shillings apiece. To Elizabeth Dyke servant of the said Richard Harvey ten shillings. To Deanes Hayball two shilling six pence and to Anne wife of John Pitman twelve pence. The residue to my kinsman Richard Harvey whom I make sole executor. Essex, 86.

[Savage gives two persons by the name of William Harvey who were then in New England at that time. One was of Boston, and had by wife Joan children Abigail b. 1640, Thomas b. 1641, Experience b. 1644, and Joseph b. 1645. A person of this name, probably the same, by wife Martha, had children William b. 1651, Thomas b. 1652, and John b. 1653. He died Aug. 15, 1658, and his widow married Henry Tewksbury, Nov. 10, 1659. The other William Harvey was of Plymouth, married Joanna, 1639; removed to Taunton; was rep. 1664 and 13 years after. Query: May not the Plymouth man be the same as thé Boston man and the Taunton man be a different person?—EDITOR.]

THOMAS WILSON the elder, sometimes citizen and clothworker of London but now resident at Ryecroft in the parish at Rawmarsh and county of York, 25 February 1657, proved 14 February 1658 (English Style). My body to be buried in the church or chancel of Rawmarsh. My lands in Hunslett in the parish of Leeds, amounting in value, as now leased, to the yearly rent of thirty six pounds, to my son Thomas Wilson and Agnes his wife, for their natural lives and the longer liver of them, and after their decease to the heirs of his body lawfully begotten; and for want of such issue I give it equally to my two neices or grandchildren, Mrs. Alice Smith wife of William Smith, now citizen and mercer of London, and Mrs. Dorcas Clarke, wife of William Clarke, in the county of Lincoln gen^t and their children. To the school of Rawmarsh for the better maintenance and encouragement of the schoolmaster there for the time being and for the teaching and instructing of seven poor children of the parish and for keeping the school in good repair, three pounds six shillings eight pence yearly to be paid out of the rent of Ryecroft by the tenant or occupant whosoever he shall be. I give to Robert and Mary, children of Thomas and Anna Jessop, ten pounds apiece to be paid to Thomas Jessop, their father. To the poor of Rawmarsh forty shillings yearly. John Dobson and his wife and children shall have ten shillings &c.

I give to my cousin George Brownell of London twenty pounds to be paid him out of the rents of Ryecroft &c. I give unto my cousin Thomas Brownell of Portsmouth, Rhode Island in New England and to his children twenty pounds to be paid either to him himself, if he shall come over to receive the same or else to such person or persons in his behalf as he shall lawfully assign to receive the same. To Mary daughter of Thomas Jessop twenty pounds. To Mary, daughter of George Brownell ten pounds at day of marriage if with the father's consent, if not then to her father. To my kinswoman Mrs. Anne Hall of Nottingham ten pounds. To Thomas Jessop the younger ten pounds, and it is my mind and will concerning him if he prove ingenious and capable of learning that he be sent to the University of Cambridge to study Divinity, and, to that end for his encouragement and towards his maintenance there, that he have ten pounds a year &c. for the term of seven years next after his going thither. To my kindred Grace Hall, Elizabeth Brooke, Jane Hall, George Hall and Lancelot Waterhouse six shillings and eight pence apiece, if they take it as a free gift without any other respect or condition. To Mr. Richardson ten shillings. To his wife five shillings. To Gervas Sheppeard two shillings. To George Wright, Elizabeth Webster, and Edward Wright two shillings apiece. Remainder to my son Thomas and the heirs of his body lawfully begotten and to be begotten forever; but for want of such issue I give it to Thomas Jessop the younger and his heirs forever, with respect to be had to the rest of his brethren and sisters for their better subsistence and maintenance in the world. My son Thomas and Thomas Jessop the elder to be joint executors.   Pell, 109.

[Thomas[1] Brownell of Portsmouth, R. I., died 1665; m. Ann; she died 1665. He was Freeman 1655. Name on record in Portsmouth, March, 1647. They had: 1, Mary,[2] b. 1639, d. Jan. 12, 1739; m. Robert Hazard, of Thomas and Martha. 2, Sarah,[2] b. ———, d. Sept. 6, 1676; m. June 1, 1658, Gideon Freeborn, of William and Mary. 3, Martha,[2] b. May, 1643, d. Feb. 15, 1744; m. 1st, Jeremiah Wait, of Thomas; m. 2d, Charles Dyer, of William and Mary. 4, George,[2] b. 1646, d. April 20, 1718; m. Susanna Pearce, Dec. 4, 1673, of Richard and Susanna. 5, William,[2] b. ———, d. 1715; m. Sarah Smiton, of William and Sarah. 6, Thomas,[2] m. Mary Pearce, d. 1732, of Little Compton. 7, Robert,[2] b. ———, d. July 22, 1728; m. Mary. 8, Ann, b. ———, d. April 2, 1747; m. Joseph Wilbur, of William. All the above is from Austin's Genealogical Dictionary.

From Portsmouth Town Records.

Thomas Brownell, of William, Sarah, (daughter of William Smithron, dec.), his wife, b. May 25, 1674. Sarah Brownell, of Thomas and Sarah, b. Nov. 25, 1675. Martha Brownell, of Thomas and Sarah, b. May 24, 1678. Anne Brownell, of Thomas and Sarah, b. June 4, 1684. According to Austin's account, Sarah Smiton was married to William Brownell, son of Thomas. I have no data which will elucidate this discrepancy, but have great confidence in Austin's authority.—HENRY E. TURNER, M.D., of Newport, R. I.]

JOHN KEMPSTER of Plaistow in Essex, citizen and glass seller of London, 7 March 1686, proved 6 June 1687. To Elizabeth, my now wife, five pounds. To my grandson John Whiston and his heirs &c. a certain annuity or rent charge payable unto me on every St. Matthew's day from the Company of Tallow chandlers London, and also the lease of my house in Leadenhall Street, now in possession of Robert Fleetwood, glass seller, or his assigns, ten pounds a year being allowed him until he attain the age of one and twenty years to find him clothes &c. according to my contract with Mr. Humphrey Owen, his master, with whom he is now apprentice. My house in Plaistow wherein I now live, purchased in the name of my said grandson, I leave to him. Loving friends Humphrey Owen of Wapping, deal merchant, and Philip Peroy Sen[r], citizen and fishmonger of London, to be overseers. House in Leadenhall Street now in possession of Mary Glover, widow. My daughter Mary Whiston. To my brother Thomas Kempster five shillings. My brother Edward Kempster and nephew Walter Kempster. To John the son of my sister Anne Bendry twenty shillings and to my cousin Elianor Greeneway twenty shillings, and to her daughter Elianor Bendry twenty shillings, and to my cousin Elizabeth Dun twenty shillings.

Whereas my cousin John Wilkins of Boston in New England is indebted unto me in a certain sum by bond payable with interest and in a further sum for goods sold my will is that he, paying the principal money due upon the said bond and discharging the said book debt also within one year and a day next after my decease, shall be acquitted and discharged of all interest due on his bond to the time of my decease. To my cousin Thomas Kemble, now apprentice to a boxmaker, in Birchin Lane, twenty shillings. To the poor of the parish of Westham within the precinct of Plaistow twenty shillings. To my cousin Edward Withers of London, carpenter, five pounds. To my son in law James Whiston of London, Exchange broker, five pounds. To my friends Thomas Ainger, citizen and apothecary of London and Philip Perry junior of London gen[t], each of them five pounds, which said Edward Withers, James Whiston, Thomas Ainger and Philip Perry junior I do hereby make, constitute and appoint executors &c.　　　　　　　　　　　　　　　Foot, 79.

[John Wilkins of Boston, named in this will, was probably the John Wilkins, a native of Wiltshire and a glassmaker by trade, having served an apprenticeship in London, who came to Boston, and not long after was married to his only wife, Mrs. Anstis Bissett, whose maiden name was Gold. He was one of the original inhabitants of the town of Bristol in Plymouth Colony (now in Rhode Island), admitted Sept. 1, 1681. He died in that town between 1704 and 1711. For accounts of himself and his wife by Mr. Harrison Ellery of Chelsea, see the Newport Historical Magazine, January 1884, vol. 4, pages 189–91. The following item from the Marriage Licences of London, edited by Mr. Joseph Foster, page 134, evidently refers to the first marriage of Mrs. Anstis Wilkins: "Bissex, Thomas, of Stepney, Middlesex, tailor, and Enstice Goold, of same, spinster— at Trinity, Minories, London, 15 July 1661."—EDITOR.]

JOB TOOKIE (of St. Giles without Cripplegate, London, says Prob. Act Book) 10 June 1669 proved 6 May 1671. To my dear wife Anne Tookie four hundred pounds before any other legacies be paid whatsoever. To my eldest daughter Rebeccah Tookie fifty pounds. To youngest daughter Sarah Tookie fifty pounds. To my two sons Job and Jonathan Tookie and to my three daughters Rebeccah and Hannah and Sarah Tookie, to every and each of them one hundred pounds (that is to say) to my sons as soon as they respectively shall have served out the full time of their several apprenticehoods, to my daughter Rebeccah as soon as debts oweing to unto me can be conveniently called in of that value over and above the four hundred pounds afore mentioned given to my executrix, and to my daughters Hannah and Sarah Tookie as soon as they, and as they, attain the age of one and twenty years. To my sister Mary Bendish, my brother Thomas Tookie and my brother Edward Bendish of Norwich, and to my sisters Rebeccah Tookie, Frances Tookie and Bridget Detleifson, to each of them a gold ring of ten shillings value. Wife Anne to be sole executrix.

Duke, 69.

ANN TOOKIE of London widow 12 May 1671, proved 1 December 1673. To son Jonathan one hundred pounds to be paid him at his age of one and twenty years; to my daughter Rebecca the like sum of one hundred pounds; and to my daughters Hannah and Sarah one hundred pounds at their respective ages of one and twenty years or days of marriage respectively first happening. To my son Job the sum of five pounds in money over and besides such books wh. I have already given and delivered to him. The rest to daughters Rebecca, Hannah and Sarah, equally. Daughter Rebecca to be sole executrix.

Pye, 166.

[In the REGISTER for January, 1890 (vol. 44, pp. 96–8; *ante*, pp. 431-3), was printed with annotations the will of the grandfather of our Job Tookie of Marblehead. These wills are those of his father and mother.—H. F. W.

A petition of Job Tookie to the Essex County Court, in 1682, in which he gives a detail of the events in his life, is printed in the REGISTER, vol. 44, pages 97–8; *ante*, pp. 432-3. It appears from one of the accompanying documents that he brought to this country his father's "Library" and that part of it was disposed of to the Rev. Messrs. Allen and Mather of Boston and Mr. Danforth of Cambridge.—EDITOR.]

JACOB JESSON of London, merchant, 30 September 1682, proved 17 August 1686. Refers to marriage agreement with present wife Mary. I give, will and devise unto Mr. George Scot and Mr. Richard Lloyd, my executors all my lands, messuages &c at Yarmouth in New England in trust, they to sell my lands and tenements in Plymouth Colony in New England to such persons as John Walley of Boston in New England, whom I have authorized to sell the same, shall sell or agree to sell and the money that shall be raised by the sale thereof shall be reckoned as part of my personal estate and shall go to my children. I give and bequeath to my honored mother Dorothy Jesson twenty pounds to buy her a ring and five pounds to buy her mourning. To my father in law Richard Glover five pounds to buy him mourning. To my brother Nathaniel Jesson twenty pounds to buy him a ring and five pounds to buy him mourning. To my brothers in law William Grosvenor, John Glover, Gabriel Glover, Richard Thomas and James Cocks five pounds apiece to buy them mourning. To my sisters Rebecca Thomas, Elizabeth Cocks, Sarah Grosvenor and Elizabeth Jesson* five pounds apiece to buy them mourning. To the said Sarah Grosvenor five pounds to buy her a ring. To Madam Lydia Martin *als* Stevens at Westminster twenty pounds if she survives me or else to her heirs. To my loving brother in law Mr. Jn° Walley of Boston five pounds of New England money. To my niece Elizabeth Walley, the daughter of my brother in law Thomas Walley deceased twenty pounds in New England money, to be paid to her upon the attaining to the age of twenty one years or day of marriage. To my loving friend Tho: Taylor, minister, now living on or near Gaslick Hill in London ten pounds and to my cousins William and Josiah Bird five pounds apiece. To my uncle Samuel Short and to my aunt Rebecca Cooper and unto my cousin Stephen Newton twenty shillings apiece to buy each of them a ring. To Thomas Jacomb Doctor in Divinity five pounds. To my executors fifteen pounds in trust to give the same unto such poor ministers as they shall think fit. To the parish of St. Andrew Undershaft where I now dwell five pounds for the churchwardens to distribute as they shall think fit. Forty pounds to be paid to such persons as my sister Rebecca Thomas shall direct and appoint, and the same amount to such as my sister Elizabeth Cocks shall appoint. The rest to my children.

My friends Mr George Scot, citizen and fishmonger of London and Mr. Richard Lloyd, citizen of London and by calling linendraper, to be executors.   Lloyd, 108.

[Of the above Jacob Jesson, Savage says that he was a merchant in Boston and agent of his brother Abraham, an ironmonger of London. He was a member of the Artillery Co. 1673. It is to be hoped that some of my Boston friends will show just who the testator's brothers in law, John and Thomas Walley, were.   HENRY F. WATERS.]

[These wills give us the following facts. Dorothy[1], widow of —— Jesson, had children:

    Nathaniel,[2] survived his brothers.
    Jacob.
    Abraham, who had three children.
    Rebecca, wife of Richard Thomas.
    Elizabeth, " " James Cox.
    Sarah, " " William Grosvenor.

Of these, Jacob Jesson was in New England, and undoubtedly was twice married. His first wife, as will be shown, was Elizabeth, probably a daughter of Rev. Thomas Walley; his second wife, Mary, was evidently a daughter of Richard Glover. These marriages are clearly pointed out by his mention of brothers-in-law John and Thomas Walley, John and Gabriel Glover. I find on the Boston records that Jacob and Elizabeth Jesson had: Jacob, b. Dec. 18, 1670; Abraham, b. July 14, 1672; Jacob, b. Sept. 16, 1674. As neither of these children is mentioned in Mrs. Dorothy Jesson's will, it is fair to presume that they died young and that their mother also died here. I find by Suffolk Deeds, viii. 266, that 25 March, 1671, Abraham Jesson of London, ironmonger, made his brother Jacob J. of Boston his attorney. This power of attorney was witnessed by John Lawrence, Jr., Christopher Clarke and Isaac Addington; Clark verified

* This Elizabeth Jesson must be his niece, daughter of Abraham J.—w. h. w.

it here 1 July, 1671, and Addington did so Dec. 4, 1673. In 1674 Jacob Jesson bought land on Rawson's lane from Edward and William Rawson. He sold the same Jan. 10, 1676, to William Hubbard (Suff. Deeds, xiii. 81) and as no wife joined therein, I have no doubt that she was dead, and that he was going home. I find that Feb. 16, 1685, Major John Walley and wife Sarah, of Bristol, Plymouth County, mortgaged a wharf and other property in Boston to Jacob and Nathaniel Jesson of London, for £246 (Suff. Deeds, xiii. 445). This mortgage he paid in full Aug. 17, 1694 (Suff. Deeds, xvi. 394) to William Stoughton, attorney for Nathaniel Jesson and John Petit, executor of Jacob Jesson.

I do not find the marriage of Jacob Jesson and Elizabeth Walley at Boston, presumably in 1669 or 1670, but it seems that her father, Rev. Thomas Walley, came to Boston in 1663. It is also possible, as Rev. Thomas had been rector of St. Mary's, Whitechapel, London, that Jesson had known the Walleys in London and had married there, coming to New England to join his wife's relatives.

I will now proceed to the Walley family, concerning which much confusion exists in printed accounts.

There were two contemporary John Walleys in Boston, both members of the Old South. One was John, son of Rev. Thomas, a major, judge, &c.; the other was a very reputable citizen. In regard to this latter John, I find that Boston town records show that John Walley m. Elizabeth, dau. of late Robert Wing, 3 April, 1661, and they undoubtedly were the parents of six children between 1662 and 1679; viz. John, b. Aug. 27, 1662; Elizabeth, b. May 8, 1665; Elizabeth, b. July 28, 1667; Samuel, b. Feb. 1, 1670; Thomas, b. Feb. 26, 1672; Samuel, b. Aug. 4, 1679.

Then we come to probably another John and Elizabeth four years later, and I presume the Old South Catalogue is correct in saying that this was John Jr., and his wife Elizabeth was dau. of the second John Alden, and that she remarried in 1702 Simon Willard. Their children were:

> Sarah, b. Aug. 25, 1684; d. June 29, 1690.
> Abiel, b. Aug. 30, 1686.
> William, b. Dec. 23, 1687.
> John, b. July 19, 1689.
> Elizabeth, b. May 4, 1693.
> Sarah, b. April 17, 1695.

So far this seems all clear and probable. There were also in Boston, John Walley and wife Sarah, who had John, b. 7 Nov. 1677, and Hannah, b. 23 July, 1680. I see every reason to suppose that this was our Major John Walley, who was of Art. Co. 1671, and removed to Barnstable about 1683, and thence to Bristol where he was in 1685. Nor do I see that he had any other wife than Sarah Walley, Old South, Dec. 1672. His wife Sarah, who was alive in 1685, d. Nov. 10, 1711, and was buried on the 15th, as Sewall says (ii. 326). He also says, "Nov. 29. Mrs. Hannah Walley died last night aged better than 30 years." This agrees with the above birth of the daughter in 1680; and under date of Dec. 1, Sewall says, Mrs. *Sarah* Walley buried, evidently a slip of the pen, and possibly strengthening our surmise that Hannah was daughter of Sarah.

It seems highly probable that Major John Walley's first child, John, died early, and that at Bristol he had the four who survived him. His will of Feb. 4, 1712 (Suff. Wills 17, p. 402) mentions son John Walley, two daughters Elizabeth and Lydia Walley, dau. Sarah Chancy, widow [of Rev. Charles C.] and her four children, viz. Charles, Mary, Isaac and Walley. He also mentions his late brother Thomas, and late sisters Hannah Alleyn and Mary Crocker.

I do not trace the documents of Major John, because a very good account is given in Freeman's Cape Cod, i. 291. But the will enables us to correct Savage's account. Rev. Thomas[1] Walley of London is *supposed* to have been the son of Robert of London, whose will is dated 1651, and grandson of John Walley, printer, of London, recorded at Whitechapel. He had sons John[2] and Thomas,[2] and daughters Sarah wife of Samuel Alleyne, and Mary wife of Job Crocker.

Thomas[2] Walley, Jr., m. Hannah Baker and had Thomas,[3] who d. *s. p.*; Hannah,[3] who m. William Stone, and secondly James Leonard; and Elizabeth, wife of Edward Adams, cordwainer. Thomas,[2] d. in 1672, and his widow m. Rev. George Shove of Taunton.

I am surprised that the maiden name of Major John[2] Walley's wife is unknown, but it is not improbable that he married in England.—W. H. Whitmore.]

DOROTHY JESSON of Bethnall Green in the parish of Stepney *als* Stebon-heath, Middlesex, widow, 20 December 1690, proved 6 October 1693. To my son Nathaniel Jesson twenty pounds. To my daughter Rebecca Thomas twenty pounds. To my daughter Elizabeth Cox twenty pounds. To my grandchildren Abraham, Elizabeth and Rebecca Jesson, son and daughters of my late son Abraham Jesson deceased, five pounds apiece. To my grandson Glover Jesson and to my grand-daughters Mary and Elizabeth Jesson, the children of my late son Jacob Jesson deceased, five pounds apiece. To Messrs Robert Braggs, Senior, Matthew Meade and Richard Lawrence fifty shillings apiece. To my friends Mr. John Pettit, citizen and merchant tailor of London, and James Pettit, citizen and mercer of London, ten pounds apiece. To the widows Butler, Wells and Moone twenty shillings apiece. To poor widows of Bethnall Green and Dog Row forty shillings. To poor widows of St. Mary Matfellon *als* Whitechapel three pounds. To my grandchildren Dorothy Cox and Rebecca Thomas all my linen which is locked up in the trunk marked with W. T. To Anne and her sister, daughters of William Biddle of Dallinson, in Co. Stafford, my third part of a parcel of land called Daywork in Dallison. Whereas I, the said Dorothy Jesson, do stand possessed of and in one messuage or tenement with the appurtenances situate in Lombard Street in the parish of St. Nicholas Acons in London, called or known lately by the sign of Rose and rebuilt by Henry Pinson, citizen and merchant tailor of London upon the Toft, soil and ground whereon a messuage which was burnt down in the late dreadful fire which happened in London stood, and now in the occupation of John Price, Barber &c. I bequeath the same to the said John and James Pettit upon trust to pay one half the clear rents and profits to my daughter Rebecca Thomas and the other half to my daughter Elizabeth Cox. The residue of my goods &c. to my son Nathaniel and my said daughters equally. Coker, 159.

JOHN COKE of Dorchester, in the County of Dorset, mercer, 23 April 1641, proved 26 October 1641. To the poor of the parish of Holy Trinity in Dorchester ten shillings. I give unto John Coke my son the moneys and goods that are in Mr. Smithe's hands in New England and ten pounds more. The ten pounds given unto him by his late grandfather Mr. Vawter shall be paid out of a debt due unto the said Mr. Vawter by William Savage Esq. and Francis Matthews Esq. To my son Samuel Coke ten pounds over and above the sum given unto him by Mrs. Elizabeth Strode deceased, late daughter of Sir Richard Strode knight. Son Thomas Coke shall be placed apprentice &c. My daughters Elizabeth and Debora Coke. My wife Elizabeth. My friends Thomas Gollopp the elder Esq., Gilbert Iron-side clerk, Bachelor in Divinity, James Gould of Dorchester, merchant, Edward Bragg of the same place, woollen draper, and Richard Scovile of the same place gen^t. Evelyn, 127.

COMFORT STARR of the town of Lewis in the County of Sussex, clerk, 21 June 1709, proved 20 December 1711. I give unto my son Josiah Starr (who is now beyond Sea at Bermudas) my silver tobacco box which hath a coat of arms upon it and all my five silver spoons marked with these letters thus placed c ; g; also a silver salt and a little silver cup marked with the same letters, in manner as before expressed. I give unto my two sons Josiah and John Starr all my pewter and linen that is marked with the same letters, to be equally divided between them. I give all my Latin, Greek and Hebrew books to my son Josiah Starr and all my English books and manuscripts to my son George Starr, excepting the bible which I ordinarily use and nine pieces of Mr Cary upon Job, which I give to my son John Starr. I give my son Josiah (besides all he had of me when I set him up at London) one hundred pounds. To my son John twenty five pounds, which with the three score and fifteen pounds he hath had of me since I came to Lewis makes up the full sum of one hundred pounds, and to his children Elizabeth, Comfort, Thomas and Sarah five pounds apiece. Moreover my mind and will is that my sons Josiah and John lay no claim to any moneys put out in my name upon mortgage or bond which belong to their brother George, if there be any sum or sums abroad that may be made appear to be given to him or his mother for his use by his grandfather or grandmother Finch of Dover or by his Aunt Hartman of Lewis or any other. I give to my said son George one hundred pounds and also twenty pounds which my aunt Hartman desired me to pay him at my decease. I give unto my three sons Josiah, John and George Starr my messuage (now made two tenements) with the shops, yards, backsides, gardens and appurtenances, lying and being in Ashford in Kent, for ever, after their mother's (my present wife's) decease, and not before. I give also to my said three sons those two pieces or parcels of Land containing by estimation ten acres, more or less, called Yondersfields in Shadoxhurst near Ashford. I make my dear and loving wife Anne Starr sole executrix. Young, 267.

[Comfort Starr was a graduate of Harvard College in the class of 1647. He was born at Ashford in Kent, in the year 1624, and came to New England with his father in 1635. In 1650 he returned to England, and was minister at Carlisle in Cumberland, but was ejected in 1662. He died Oct. 30, 1711, in his 87th year, at Lewes, in Sussex, where he was pastor of a church. He was the son of Comfort Starr of Cambridge, Duxbury and Boston, who died Jan. 2, 1658-9, and whose will is printed in the REGISTER, vol. 9, pp. 223-4. Sketches of the life of the testator will can be found in Sibley's Harvard Graduates, vol. 1, p. 162, and Palmer's Nonconformists Memorial, ed. 1802, vol. 1, p. 378.—EDITOR.]

THOMAS BANCKES citizen and barber surgeon of London, 15 October 1595, proved 17 May 1598. My body to be buried in the parish church of St. Michael in the Querne. Forasmuch as my eldest son Richard Banckes hath unnaturally and undutifully forsaken his native country and natural parents and in the course of his life hath brought great grief and sorrow to me and to his mother and in regard of his want of compassion towards us hath justly deserved to be holden and reputed as a lost son I do therefore will and devise all my lands, tenements and hereditaments to my son John Banckes. My movable goods and chattels &c. shall be divided, according to the custom of the City of London, into three equal parts, whereof one part I give and bequeath to Joan my loving wife and an other third part I will to be divided amongst my children, whereof as many of my said children as are already advanced shall every one of them have, out of the same third part, so much for their full and further advancement as shall make up their portions, according to the custom of the City, equal with the residue of my said children not yet advanced, saving that my said son Richard shall be utterly secluded out of this my last will and testament and hold himself to his advancement already received, without partaking with the residue of my children in any of my estate, either of inheritance, goods or chattels. The other third part, being by the custom of the said City in my free and voluntary disposition, I do ordain &c. to bear, perform and pay the charges of my funerals and other the ordinances, legacies and payments hereafter limited, bequeathed or devised. Then follow certain bequests of mourning gowns &c. to individual friends, servants &c: To my godson Richard Deane son to my daughter Mary Deane twenty pounds, to my daughter Katherine Some twenty pounds, to my daughter Mary Deane twenty pounds, to my daughter Elizabeth twenty pounds, to my daughter Susan twenty pounds, to my daughter Joan twenty pounds, to my daughter Sarah twenty pounds, over and above their said portions rising unto them by the custom of the said City of London. I do also forgive unto my brother William Banckes all such sums of money as he doth owe me, and five pounds to be equally divided amongst his children. A similar bequest to brother Christofer Banckes and his children, and to brothers Snowe and Seybrooke, and four pounds to be divided amongst their children, all of them. To my brother Thomas Pettit three pounds. To eight poor scholars of the University of Cambridge, whereof two of them to be of Trinity College, eight decent suites of black apparel, viz. doublets, hose and stockings, to be delivered them at or against their proceeding and going forth Bachelors of Art. To the relief of the poor children harbored in Christ's Hospital, to sundry companies and the poor of sundry parishes. My wife Joan and son John to see to the due execution of this my last will and my two sons in law Bartholomew Some and Richard Deane to be the overseers. Then follows a list of such as were to receive rings &c. A codicil was made 25 March 1598, providing for additional bequests, among which to loving friend Master Robert Cogan, Treasurer of Christ's Hospital, a gown of black cloth, to nephew William Banckes a cloak of black cloth, to Susan wife of Gregory Hargrave a gown of black cloth &c.   Lewyn, 48.

JOHN BANCKS citizen and mercer of London, 20 May 1630, proved 30 October 1630. My body to be buried in the Chancel of St. Michael's the Querne in the Ward of Farrington within, in the same grave wherein my dear and loving parents, with my two most dear beloved wives, lie buried. One half of my personal estate I give and bequeath to Anne, my dear and only daughter, to be paid unto her at her age of twenty and one years or her day of marriage. Eight thousand pounds allotted for her portion. Bequests to various city companies, to the children of my sister Mary Deane deceased, the children of my sister Susan Draper and of my sister Joane Titchborne. My sister Dame Catherine Barnardiston. To William Banckes, Richard Banckes, Thomas Banckes, George Banckes and Mary Banckes the children of my uncle William Banckes deceased, Christopher Banckes, Mary Banckes (a maid) Anne Banckes which married John Bigges, and Alice Banckes, all the children of my uncle Christopher Banckes deceased. To my daughter Anne a great chest with guilded leather which hath nineteen iron bars over the cover, with all things in it, as plate, linen, chains, jewels, rings, with all things in it of what nature or condition so ever, to her own use forever, as my gift, without any accompt to be made &c. For the more decent and comely performance of my funeral, according to my degree and place, I do allot and allow to be spent thereon the sum of two thousand marks. (To sundry poor, among which) the poor of the parish of St. Michael Basingshawe where I am a parishioner. To the parson, churchwardens and parishioners of St. Michael's the Querne, where I was born, a fair great flagon pot of silver, with the mercers' arms on it, of the value of twenty five pounds sterling; and another like it to the parish of St. Michael Bassingshawe. To thirty of my kindred and dear friends rings of gold of three pounds each ring, likewise one hundred rings of gold, to kindred and friends, of forty shillings each, and further one hundred rings of gold, to familiar loving friends, of twenty shillings each. William Banckes a minister, the eldest son of my uncle William Banckes deceased. To Mary Banckes, my uncle William's daughter, and to her five children. To the four children of Alice Banckes deceased (she was the wife of one Holman) vizt. John her son and Alice, Anne and Elizabeth her daughters. My uncle Christopher's daughter Mary, an ancient maid. My aunt, Anne Banckes, late wife of my uncle Christopher. The four children of my aunt Seabrooke, vizt Thomas her son, her daughter Frances and her six children, another daughter Margaret and her five children, and another daughter Martha and her three children. Joane Snowe daughter of my aunt Snowe deceased. The three children of my brother in law Charles Evans deceased, vizt Thomas, Elizabeth and Jane. John and Anne Evans the children of my brother in law William Evans deceased. My two sons in law Richard and John Hassells. Richard and Anne Pountyes the children of my brother in law John Pounteyes. Samuel and Mary Husbandes the children of my sister in law Mary Husbandes deceased. The children of my sister Mary Deane vizt Joane Mildemaye, wife of Mr. Robert Milemaye, Mary Deane wife of ———— Goodwin, my god daughter, Sarah Deane wife of William Rolfe, and Catherine Deane, my sister Mary's youngest daughter. My sister Joane, wife of Robert Titchborne, and her daughter Catherine Titchborne, my god daughter, wife of Edmond Monioye, and her other children, Johanna, Elizabeth and Robert Titchborne. At this present my goddaughter Katherine Titchborne is great with child and looketh every day, by the blessing of God, to be delivered. To Susan ffoge the wife of Raffe ffoge, the daughter of my sister Susan Draper, the sum of fifty pounds and also to John ffoge her son fifty pounds more. My sister Susan Draper the wife of Edward Draper, girdler, and her two daughters Susan ffoge and Mary Draper. Sundry friends and servants named. My brother in law Robert Titchborne of London, skinner, I make sole and absolute executor, and my brother in law Sir Richard Deane, knight, Sir Robert Densie, Baronet, Anthony Withers, mercer, Clement Mosse, under chamberlain of the City of London, and Hamblett Clerke, free of the Fishmongers and one of the ancient clerks in the Mayor's Court, overseers. Then follows a list of names of kindred and friends who are to have the thirty gold rings (among them Sergeant Towse, my brother in law, Edward Monioye my cousin, Robert Goodwine my cousin, Richard Glide my cousin, Luke Jackson my cousin). Then the names of several preaching ministers in London which have no livings the which my will and mind is shall have five pounds each (among them Mr Elliott, under Mr Worme, Soperlane, Mr Damport, under Mr. Walton, Canninge (Cannon) Street). Then the names of those who were to have rings of forty shillings each (among them Dr Johnson Mrs Wightman's father, Robert Johnson her brother, John Hasell my brother in law, Ralfe ffoge, my cousin, and uxor, Thomas Thomas, my cousin, and uxor, John Banckes of Gray's Inn counsellor). Then a list of friends who were to have rings of twenty shillings each (among them Thomas Stampe, my sister Alkin's man, Anthony Stoddard, beadle (and others) parishioners of St. Michael the Querne). Scroope, 84.

[Raffe ffoge named in this will may have been the Salem man.—H. F. WATERS.
Sir Richard Deane, the brother-in-law of the testator, having married Mary, daughter of Thomas Banckes whose will precedes this, was, according to Fuller's Worthies of England, vol. 1, page 524, the son of George Deane of Much Dunmow in Essex. He was a freeman of the Skinners Company, and was Lord Mayor of London in 1628. He was knighted at Greenwich, May 31, 1629. See Book of Knights, by Walter C. Metcalfe, page 190.—EDITOR.]

JOHN GACE of Stortford in Herts. tanner, 29 August 44th Eliz., proved 20 September 1602. My body to be buried in the parish church of Stortford. To the use of the poor there fifteen pounds, to the intent and purpose only that continually afterwards there may be relief provided to and for them according to the quantity thereof. It shall be paid in one year after my decease to James Morley, gen[t], Thomas Perye, gent., John Miller the elder and "maister" Thomas Miller, all now inhabitants of the same town etc. If it happen that they and every of them be dead or removed from the town before that time then the said fifteen pounds to be paid to the Churchwardens and Overseers of the poor &c., to buy and purchase a piece of ground in fee simple, in or near this town, to be let to farm and the rents and profits bestowed upon the poor. Before such purchase is made to give to the poor fifteen shillings yearly, which is after the rate of twenty years purchase of the land. I give to Agnes my wife the house wherein I dwell and the messuage &c. which I bought of Edward Hurlykin of Sabridgeworth, lying and being in Thorley Street within the parish of Thorley for eight years; also the one half and moiety of all my householdstuff, utensils and implements of household, to be equally divided between her and mine executor. I give her also one hundred marks, with all her apparel, and four silver spoons which were hers before I married her. And she shall have the meadow which I hired of Widow Bowyer of Stortford &c. and my beasts and swine and all the hay which I have lying within the Castle yard or house therein, in Stortford. To the daughter of my sister Agnes called Judith, twenty marks at one and twenty. To Elizabeth Wheelwright my sister in law ten pounds, in six months after my decease.

Item, I do give and bequeath to George Dennyson, in consideration of the discharge of a legacy given to him by his father, forty pounds, in six months &c. To Edward Dennyson, one of my wife's sons, brother to the said George, ten pounds. To William Dennyson, one other of my wife's sons, forty shillings. To Elizabeth Crouch, my wife's daughter, five pounds. To Robert Smith of Mallendyne, Essex, butcher, twenty pounds. To Richard Paine of Stortford, shoemaker, twenty tanned hides. Nathaniel Gary of Stortford, shoemaker, shall be discharged of all such debts &c. which are due and owing unto me, amounting to four pounds or thereabouts. John Marden of Stortford, shoemaker, shall be discharged of eight shillings eight pence. To Edward Hurlekyn of Sabridgeworth, shoemaker, thirty shillings yearly during his natural life, payable quarterly. To Elizabeth Cocket my servant six pounds thirteen shillings four pence. To Francis Gates of Pelham, Herts., yeoman, twenty marks. If the widow Northage and George Ilgare of Stansted Mountfitched, Essex, or either of them, do take order to pay to mine executors sixteen pounds in full discharge of a greater debt which the said George Ilgare doth stand bound to pay to me, for the discharge whereof the said George hath certain copyhold land to him surrendered, then the said widow Northage shall be discharged of all such debts which she oweth unto me. The residue of my goods &c. I give and bequeath to my brother Miles Gace of Hempsted, Herts., whom I make executor, and I entreat James Morley and Thomas Perry to be overseers.

Wit: James Morley, Thomas Perry, Edward Well, George Abbot.

Montague, 61.

[John Gace, the testator, was the step-father of William Denison of Roxbury, Mass., whose mother Agnes, widow of John (?) Denison was married to Mr. Gace, May 1, 1584. See J. L. Glascock's Pedigree of Denison in the REGISTER, vol. 46, pp. 352. For the Denison pedigree, see also REGISTER, vol. 46, pp. 127-33 and 275-6.—EDITOR.]

ROGER RAYNER of Burnham Abbey, Bucks., farmer, 12 July 1682, proved 14 October 1682. My body to be interred in the parish church of Burnham and thirty pounds to be spent in and upon my funeral. To my loving sister Anne Rayner three score pounds. To my loving brother John Rayner three score pounds. To my kinsman Jacob Rayner twenty pounds. To my kinswoman Rachel Rayner ten pounds. To my kinsman Thomas Rayner five pounds. To my kinswoman Anne Spooner five pounds. To my kinsman John Rayner of New England five pounds, to be paid at any time within a year and a day after my decease if he shall within the said time make his personal appearance to my executor, otherwise the said five pounds shall be paid unto my said kinsman Jacob Rayner. To my four servants now dwelling with me twenty shillings, to be divided equally among them. The rest to my uncle Thomas Rayner whom I make sole executor. Abra. Spooner one of witnesses.   Cottle, 121.

[John, Thomas, Jacob and Rachel Rayner were well known names in my boyhood, belonging to the family of Rayner of North Reading, Mass., descended out of Charlestown.—H. F. WATERS.

The John Rayner of New England named in this will cannot be Rev. John Rayner of Plymouth and Dover, who d. in 1669; nor his son John. It may be John of Charlestown, Captain of the ketch Dolphin, who m. in 1681. See Wyman's Genealogies.—W. H. H.]

WILLIAM CROSSE of St. Clement Danes, Middlesex, tailor, 31 May 1621, proved 26 July 1621. My body to be burried in the church of St. Clement Danes near my mother. To the poor of said parish ten dozen of bread to be distributed among them at the day of my funeral. To my son in law Robert Simpson, at one and twenty, the hundred pounds I stand bound to Doctor Poe. If he die before that then forty pounds of it to my wife and the other threescore pounds to my two children, Thomas Crosse and Elnor Crosse, at their several ages of one and twenty. To Thomas all that tenement and malt house which I purchased of Thomas Jarrett, situate &c. in Dartford, Kent. To Elnor a messuage in Dartford purchased of Mr. Swarland, minister. If either of said children die before coming of age, then I devise, give and bequeath unto the children of Robert Okes, my brother in law, had by a former wife, and also his children by my sister Agathie, ten pounds, part and portion alike. To daughter Elnor twenty pounds, one of my silver beakers and six silver spoons. The rest to wife Alice whom I make sole executrix; and I appoint my friends John Glasse and Robert Chippe overseers.   Dale, 65.

RICHARD BALDWINE, citizen and girdler of London, 9 June 1634, proved 23 July 1634. To my dear father and mother one hundred and twenty pounds; to my mother a ring with a death's head, worth twenty shillings. To my brother in law Thomas Dudsbury twenty five pounds. To my brother John Baldwine thirty pounds. To my brother in law Thomas Ward twenty pounds. To my brother in law Thomas Butcher twenty five pounds. To Mrs. Wood, widow, lying at Mrs. Lynnes, four pounds. To Mrs. Savill, at Mr. Benbowe's four pounds. To Mrs. Ward, widow, at a smith's house in Coleman St., forty shillings. To Mr. Cadman, a setter, three pounds. To Dr. Layton forty shillings. To the poor of Chesham, where I was borne, forty shillings. To the minister that shall preach at my funeral twenty shillings. To Urian Oakes and Anne, servants in the house where I lodge, ten shillings apiece. To Mrs. Hawes, widow, in Iremonger Lane, twenty shillings. To Mr. John Vicaris, a minister, late prisoner, twenty shillings. To poor distressed ministers, at my executor's discretion, three pounds. To my uncle Richard Baldwin twenty shillings to buy him a ring with a death's head. Towards the maintenance of a Lecture at Tooke on the Hill, for four years, four pounds, by twenty shillings a year. (Others mentioned.) My friend Henry Shawe, merchant tailor, and Henry Poole girdler, to be executors. Reference to a partner in trade, named George Thwaites. My stock dispersed in debts beyond seas and in other places. Wit: Thomas Benbowe, Vryan Okes, Rich: Preice and Henry Colbron, ser. Seager, 70.

[Richard Baldwin, the testator, was the son of John Baldwin of Chesham, Bucks. See REGISTER, vol. 38, p. 168, in Col. Chester's Family of Baldwin.— EDITOR.]

JOANE LENNYS of St. Antholin, London, widow, 25 April 1643, proved 22 January 1644. There is due and owing unto me by the King's Majesty three hundred pounds, for which I have spent much money in endeavoring to obtain. I give to my cousin Richard Evans, citizen and cutler of London, three pounds thereout, and to his son Richard Evans, my godson, forty shillings, and to his daughters Jane Evans and Anne Evans forty shillings apiece. I give thereout to my daughter in law Elizabeth Collinwood in Ireland twelve pence and unto such child or children as she had by my son Raphe Collenwood twelve pence apiece. The residue and remainder of the same moneys and all other my goods &c. I wholly give and bequeath unto my grand children Urian Okes and Jone his wife and Israell Collinwood and Mary Stonier his intended wife, vizt the half part thereof unto the said Urian Okes and Jone his wife and the other half part to the said Israel Collenwood and the said Mary. And whereas the said Urian Okes hath received of Mr. Jacobson, brewer, for my use, three score and ten pounds, in case the same shall be recovered back again my grandchild Israel Collenwood shall bear an equal part of the loss or damage that the said Urian shall sustain. The sum of twenty pounds to be expended about my funeral charges. The said Urian Okes and Israel Collenwood to be executors, and my cousin Richard Evans overseer. Rivers, 28.

[The foregoing wills of Crosse, Baldwin and Lennys show the existence of a family named Okes, or Oakes, in London, among whom the baptismal name of Urian is to be found.
From the Registers of St. Antholin (published by the Harleian Society) I extract the following :—
Raphe son of Israell Collingwood chr. Mar. 28, 1597.
Israyell Collingewood bur. Oct. 2, 1603.
William Collingwood & Bridget Collingwood marr. Jan. 16, 1616.
Jone dau. to William Collingwood chr. Nov. 2, 1617.
Israel son to William Collingwood chr. Feb. 7, 1618.
Urian Oakes & Joan Collingwood marr. Nov. 14, 1637.
Urian Oake bur. Nov. 6, 1661.
The Registers of St. Michael Cornhill also contain references to the Lennis family and to the Oakes family. Baptisms of children of an Edward Oakes are there given.
I should look therefore among the London records for the family of our Urian Oakes of Harvard College. HENRY F. WATERS.]

EDWARD OAKES, Doctor of Physicke in the parish of St. Peter ad Vincula, 6 October 1665, proved 13 October 1665. All my worldly goods &c. whatsoever I give unto my well beloved wife Elizabeth Oakes, whom I constitute and appoint sole executrix.
Wit: Mary Linis, Nathanee White. Hyde, 120.

EDWARD PECK, Sergeant at Law, 11 July 1675, proved 1 June 1676.
My body to be buried near my wife and children.   Two hundred pounds to
my brother Stannard, to be by him disposed of to such one or more of his children as he shall think fit.   To my brother Thexton three hundred pounds
(for a similar disposition among his children).   To brother Thexton the
further sum of two hundred pounds, for disposition among my sister Malt-
ward's daughters.   To my brother Osbert's eldest daughter two hundred
pounds and to his youngest daughter fifty pounds.   All these legacies to be
paid, without interest, within three years after my death.   To Francis
Agar of London, gen^t, and to my servant Richard Webster five hundred
pounds upon trust to be expressed in a writing to bear even date with these
presents.

Item, I give to Mr. —— Oakes of Cambridge in New England one hundred pounds per annum for so long time as my son Edward shall continue
to live with him and be governed by him, and no longer, whereout he is
first to reimburse himself whatsoever shall be coming or due to him any
wise relating to my said son.   And he is to take care that the residue
thereof be not disposed of in vicious courses.   I give to the said Richard
Webster fifty pounds.   (To sundry servants.)   I make William Peck, my
eldest son, my sole executor.   To my dear daughter I give two hundred
guineas.

A codicil made 11 July 1675 refers to the trust &c.   Bence, 116.

SIR THOMAS MOWLSON, knight and alderman of London, 6 July 1636,
proved 8 December 1638.   For so much as I have no child, after my debts
be paid, all the residue of my goods &c shall be divided into two equal
parts, according to the laudable use and custom of the City of London;
whereof one half I do give and bequeath unto Dame Anne my loving wife
for her customary and widow's part, to her due and appertaining by the
custom of the said City.   Bequests to the children of Doctor Barker, which
he had by my sister Kendricke's daughter.   The children of William
Pitchford.   Thomas Pitchford my god son.   Cousin John Robotham of St.
Alban's, his wife* and two sons.   Cousin Arthur Turner, his wife and three
children.   The poor of St. Christopher where I dwell.   Mr. Samuel Rogers,
minister or curate.   The Company of Grocers.   My brother John Mowlson
and his wife.   My cousin John Stevens and his wife.   My cousin Robert
Gurdon and his wife.   My cousin Elizabeth Barnes.   My cousin Elizabeth
Higham, daughter to Sir Richard Higham.   My Lady Thornton and her
husband.   My cousin Pickrell and her husband.   My cousin Keightley
and her husband.   My cousin Smith and her husband.   John Harvye and
his wife.   My cousin Samuel Harvy and his son that is my God son.   Sir
Gilbert Gerard and his lady and his son Thomas that is my God son.   My
cousin William Gerard and his wife.   My cousin John Gerard and his
wife.   My cousin Meavis and her husband.   My cousin Misemoye and her
husband and his son my godson.   My cousin Isabel Gerard.   The Right
Hon. the Lord Keeper and his Lady.   My old Aunt Aldersey.   My cousin
John Aldersey, her son.   The Lady Capel.   Sir Norton Knotchbold and
his Lady.   My cousin Crane and his wife.   My cousin Margaret Aldersey,
widow.   My cousin John Kendricke, his wife and children.   My cousin
Chapman and his wife and my cousin Massam, widow.   My cousin Mekin,
widow.   Sir Nicholas Raynton and his Lady.   Sir Robert Parkhurst and

* She was Penelope, daughter of William Pichford.   Her dau. Elizabeth was married to
Thomas Aldersey.

his Lady. My cousin Smith of Haggerston, widow, and my cousin Palmer, her sister. Mrs. Wackefeild, widow of Edward Wackefeild. My cousin John Aldersey of Spurstowe and his wife, and his son Thomas, my godson. My cousin Edwardes and his wife and his son Thomas, my godson. My cousin Tilston of Huxley and his wife. My cousin Raph Egerton. My cousin Anthony Radcliffe and his wife, and his son Thomas, my god son. My cousin Parsons of Milton and his wife. The company of Merchant Adventurers of England. Twenty poor ministers. Bowles my beadle and Peter Ives. The schoolmaster who is, or shall be, appointed to teach scholars in the chapel at Hargrave (which I caused to be built at my own charge), and the minister there. My nephew Thomas Mowlson, son of brother John. Houses and lands in Broxson in the County Palatine of Chester, which I bought of John Dod.

In a codicil made 16 November 1638 he mentions cousins Stretton and wife, Mr Wilson our curate, and others. Another codicil was added 5 December 1638. Lee, 180.

DAME ANNE MOULSON of St. Christopher's, London, late wife of Sir Thomas Moulson, Knight and Alderman of London, 11 August 1657, proved 2 November 1661. My body to be buried in the vault within the parish church of St. Christopher's wherein my late husband was buried. My nephew Sir Gilbert Gerrard of Harrow on the Hill, Middlesex, Baronet, and his Lady, and my cousin Mr Francis Gerrard, his eldest son. My godson Gilbert Gerrard eldest son of my said cousin Francis. Gilbert Gerrard, second son, Thomas Gerrard, third son, and John Gerrard, the other son of my nephew Sir Gilbert Gerrard. My cousins Mrs Kempe, Mrs. Mary Gerrard and Mrs Katherine Gerrard. My cousin Mr. Tristram Conyers and my cousin Mrs. Winifred Conyers, his wife. My nephew Mr Anthony Radcliffe of Buckinghamshire, eldest son of my brother Mr. Edward Radcliffe deceased. Thomas Radcliffe, eldest son of my said nephew. My niece Mrs Katherine Parsons, widow, sister to my said nephew Anthony Radcliffe. Her three sons and four daughters which she had by her late husband Mr. Parsons. Anne Broome and Anne Peacocke grandchildren of my said niece Katherine Parsons. Mr. Peacocke, woollen draper, late of Watling Street, and his wife. My niece Meux widow, late wife of Bartholomew Meux &c. Mr. Cary Mildmay otherwise Harvey of Marks in Essex, and my niece Dorothy, his wife. His son Mr Francis Mildmay. Mrs. Harvey, late wife of Mr. John Harvey deceased. James Harvey son of Samuel Harvey deceased. My niece Mrs. Kightly of Aldborrowhatch, widow. Her son Edward Kightley and her daughter Mrs Barners. Mr. John Stephens and his wife, another of my niece Kightley's daughters. Mr Thomas Stephens, eldest son of Mr. John Stephens by Anne his late wife, daughter of my late husband's brother. Arthur Barnardiston son of Mr. Barnardiston which he had by my niece the Lady Thornton. The eldest daughter of my said niece the Lady Thornton, by the said Mr. Barnardiston, who is lately married to one Mr Fowler, a minister. Roger Thornton, son of my said niece, and his wife. My nephew Mr. William Gerrard of Ashton Clinton, minister, and his wife. My niece Mrs. Joyce Gurdon, widow, and her two sons Mr. James and Mr. John Gurdon. Mr. Leeds and my cousin Elizabeth his wife. Mr. Philip Smith, who formerly married my niece Mrs. Mary Harvey, and his daughter Mary who is married to one Mr Knight. My sister Moulson, widow of Mr. John Moulson of Cheshire. Mr. Holcroft of Ham in Essex, eldest son to

Sir Henry Holcroft deceased, and to my kinswoman his wife. Mrs Anne Turner, widow of Sergeant Turner deceased, and her son Mr. Edward Turner, Counsellor at Law, and her son in law Mr. Colthrop and his wife. My kinswoman Mrs Reynalds, widow, and her brother Rocker, a minister, whom she lives with. Mrs Sawne my kinswoman, daughter to my cousin Mrs. Massam deceased. Mrs Sawne's eldest daughter, lately married to one Mʳ Madison.

A codicil was added 27 September 1661. Another was written 8 October 1661. In the latter she mentions, among others, cousin Mr. Holland, minister.   May, 185.

[Those who were sufficiently interested in the article on the Exhibitions of Harvard College in the REGISTER, July, 1892, to read the note to the Lady Mowlson gift, page 234, will remember that in that note it was suggested that Lady Ann Mowlson, the founder of the Scholarship, might prove to be the widow of Sir Thomas Mowlson, who was Lord Mayor of London in 1634. All that was known of her was her name and that she was a widow in 1643. It will be observed that in the above abstract of the will of Sir Thomas, we have a codicil dated December 5, 1638, while the will was probated December 8, 1638. The bequest to " Dame Anne, my loving wife," furnishes the name of his widow. That Lady Ann, the relict of Sir Thomas Mowlson, was alive in 1643, is shown by the execution on her part in 1657 of a will and in 1661 of two codicils, which were probated November 2, 1661. For the bequest to Anthony Radcliffe, eldest son of her brother Edward Radcliffe, it may be inferred that her maiden name was Radcliffe.

The questions which it was hoped that an examination of the wills of Sir Thomas and Lady Mowlson would answer, were three. Was her name Ann? Was she alive in 1643? Was she a widow at that time? The researches of Mr. Waters enable us to say that the Lady Ann Mowlson, who in 1643 founded the first Scholarship at Harvard College, was probably the widow of Sir Thomas Mowlson, at one time Lord Mayor of London.

ANDREW MCFARLAND DAVIS,
of Cambridge, Mass.]

JOHN DODDRIDGE of Bremeridge, Devon, Esq. 20 January 1658, proved 20 June 1659. If I happen to die within thirty miles of Cheshunt, Herts, my body may be carried thither and there interred in the Vault of my honored father in law Sir Thomas Dacres of Cheshunt, knight, as near the body of my very dear virtuous and truly loving wife Martha, the youngest daughter of the said Sir Thomas Dacres, as conveniently may be, who hath promised me a burying place there according to my great desire. But if I happen to die within thirty miles of the town of Barnastaple, Devon, then I very much desire that my body may be carried to Barnstaple and buried as near the body of my dear virtuous and loving wife Jane as may be. Bequests to the town of Barnstaple, for the poor there, to the aldermen of Bristol (forty pounds) for a piece of plate with my coat of arms engraven upon it and this inscription *Ex Dono Johanni Doddridge Recordatoris Civitatis* Bristoll. To the poor of Ilfarcombe, Fremington and Southmolton. My most dear wife Judith. My dear sisters Mistress Elizabeth Crossing, Mistress Dorothy Lowring and my nephew Master John Martin. My father in law John Gurdon Esq. and my loving brothers John Hele Esq., Thomas Dacres Esq., Robert Gurdon Esq., Master John Martin, Master Richard Crossing, Master John Lowring, Master Joseph Jackson and my friends Master Robert Aldworth, Master Edward Watts and Master Richard Sherbrook.

I give and bequeath unto the College in New England towards the maintenance of scholars there the yearly sum of ten pounds forever, issuing and going forth out of my Rectory of Fremington in the County of Devon.

Also I give and bequeath unto the Trustees for the maintenance of select scholars at the University, according to the model drawn up by Master Poole and other godly ministers, the like yearly sum of ten pounds &c.

My cousin Dorothy Watts wife of Master Edward Watts, Sarah Walker daughter of Thomas Walker minister of Assington, Suffolk. Cousin Roger Hill one of the Barons of the Exchequer. My manor of Abbotts bury in Porbury, in the County of Somerset. My niece Jane Martin.

Pell, 380.

[The bequest of John Doddridge to Harvard College is noticed in the REGISTER, vol. 46, page 235, by A. McFarland Davis, A.M., in his Exhibitions of Harvard College.—EDITOR.]

THEOPHILUS GALE of Stoke Newington, Middlesex, Gen^t, 25 February 1677, proved 25 June 1679. To my sister Mrs. Katherine Northcott fifty pounds. To my kinswoman Sarah Rows, daughter of John Rows deceased, fifty pounds, to be paid at day of marriage or age of twenty one. To my cousins Thomas and John Rows, sons of John Rows deceased, also to my cousins John Goddard the younger, Thomas Goddard, Edward Goddard, Ann, Mary and Susanna Goddard, to each twenty shillings. To my friends Dr. Thomas Goodwin, Dr. John Owen, Henry Dorney of London, John Collins, James Baron, John Berry of Barnstaple, Bartholomew Ashwood of Axminster, Joseph Swaffield of Sarum, Henry Coue of Southampton, Joseph Hallett of Exon, Giles Say of Southampton, Mr. Conway at Malsbury, Mr. Dent by Hungerford, John Troughton at Bicester, Mr. Rowswell by Calne, Mr. James of Stanes, Mr. James of Wapping, Mr. Catsness of Wapping, Stephen Lobbe of London, Mr. Reinolds on Bunhill fields, Dr. Samuel Annesley of London, Thomas Dauson in Spittle fields, Mr. Veale of Stepney, Samuel Lee of Newington Green, Edward Terry of Stoke Newington, Mr. Crowch in Little Morefields, Mr. Gilson, Mr. Hayworth of Ware, Mr. Baker of London, Mr. Henry Berry late of Crediton, Thomas Jollie at Pendleton in Lancashire, George Larkham at Tassantire in Cumberland, Col. Kelsey of London, brewer, Major Reynes of London, Mr. Bens of Islington, brewer, to each of these five pounds. To Isaac Eures Esq. of London a piece of plate to the value of two pounds. To Nathaniel Overton and Robert Pauceforth, to each three pounds.

All the rest and residue of my estate, both real and personal &c., as also all my books and manuscripts I give and bequeath unto the above mentioned Dr. John Owen, Samuel Lee, John Collins, John Troughton, Edward Terry, Mr. Crowch, Col. Kelsey, Henry Dorney, Robert Pauceforth and Nathaniel Overton, to be disposed and employed by them, or any three of them, joyntly, for the maintenance, education and benefit of such poor scholars or other charitable uses as they in their discretion shall judge fit and most agreeable to my mind and will; and they shall have the sole and free disposition of the said residue &c., without being accountable or called in question &c.; and if any person or persons shall sue, call in question or to account the said Dr. John Owen (and the others) my will is that neither such person or persons nor any in whose behalf he or they shall so call in question these said persons, Sam: Lee and the rest, or either of them, shall have any part of my estate or benefit by this my will. And I make and ordain the said Dr. John Owen (and the others) my executors.

Memorandum, whereas my sister Northcott owes me about one hundred pounds upon Bond and about forty pounds that I lent her to carry on the house above withall I received for my scholars diet over and above what I have given her in my will I desire the interest of what she owes me may be foreborne until she be in a capacity to pay it. Also my desire is that she have all my gold and rings, excepting those pieces of gold and rings that shall be disposed of by me. Mem^dum if Mr. Moreland be not mentioned in my will I desire he should have five pounds. Also Mr. Giles Say of Southampton six pounds to make up what is mentioned in my will so much. My will and desire also is that Mr. Henry Dorney may have twenty pounds more added to what I have given him in my will. And that my library be also given and disposed to the Colledge of or in New England where Mr. Oakes is head, except those philosophical books which are needful for students here. Robert Paunceforte of Gray's Inn, in the Co. of Midd., Gen^t made oath to the above. King, 70.

[The library of Theophilus Gale was received by Harvard College, and for many years constituted more than half of the college library. It was burned with the rest of the college library January 24, 1764. See Quincy's History of Harvard University, vol. 1, pp. 184, 185 and 543, and vol. 2, p. 481.—EDITOR.]

WILLIAM BOLTON of Harrow on the Hill, Middlesex, clerk, 8 April 1691, proved 22 February 1691. To my cousin Susanna Fisher ten pounds. All the residue and remainder of my estate whatsoever, my debts and funeral charges being first paid and discharged, I give unto my son and heir, Archibald Bolton, for his education in the time of his minority and afterwards to such uses as he shall think fit, but in case my said son Archibald shall depart this life during the time of his minority then I give and bequeath what shall remain after his decease unto my brother Henry Bolton in Virginia and to his heirs and assigns forever. I make my trusty and well beloved friends Robert Payn of the Charter House, London, Esq. and Thomas Robinson of Harrow on the Hill, gentleman, sole executors. Fane, 22.

NATHANIEL BRADDOCK, citizen and mercer of London, 10 July, 1635, proved 31 May 1636. Bound on a voyage to Virginia in the parts beyond the seas, in the good ship called the Marchant Hope of London. My brother in law John Rooke standeth bound unto me for payment of three score pounds the First of January next ensuing the death of my father John Braddocke. Out of this sum I give to John Rooke, son of said John, twenty pounds, which his father shall put out and employ for the most use and benefit of the said John Rooke his son, until he attain to the full age of one and twenty years; then the twenty pounds, with the benefit and increase, to be paid unto the said son. To John More son of my brother Valentine More other twenty pounds out of the said three score, at one and twenty years. In the meantime my executor to pay to my sister Susann Moore, mother of the said John Moore, thirty and two shillings per annum towards the maintenance of the said John. To my brother John Braddocke five pounds out of the said three score pounds, and five pounds more thereof I give to my sister Rebecca Braddocke. The residue of the said three score pounds to my brother in law John Rooke if he take upon himself the execution of this my will. All my other goods I give to my brother John Braddocke and my sisters Sarah Rooke, Rebecca Braddocke and Susan Moore. Pile, 51.

EDWARD BRADLEY of the City of Philadelphia in the Province of Pensylv^a, glazier, 22 March 1743-4, proved 8 November 1746. I do nominate and appoint my dear and loving wife Esther and my trusty friends Ebenezer

Kinnersley and Thomas Leach, both of the said city, shopkeepers, to be the executrix and executors of this my last will and testament for and concerning my estate in Pensylv^a and elsewhere (Great Britain excepted). Whereas the said Ebenezer Kinnersley is indebted unto me in the sum of thirty pounds, this Currency, or thereabouts now I do release him of the aforesaid upon this condition only, that he undertake the burthen of executorship without any further consideration or reward for his trouble therein; and I do give unto the said Thomas Leach thirty pounds Pensylv^a Currency for his trouble as an executor; and I do give and bequeath unto my said dear and loving wife Esther particularly all my negroe slaves, namely, York, Daphne, and the child Gin, with all my plate, household furniture and the sum of seven hundred pounds currency aforesaid in cash, or such bonds or securities to the amount thereof as she shall choose; also the moneys that become due unto me for the land I lately sold unto William Haw, and also my mare, chase and harness thereto belonging, and all my right to the stable which I took of Thomas Howard. Moreover I give and devise unto her, my said wife, Esther, my messuage or tenement, and lot of ground thereto belonging situate in Front Street in the said City, between the messuages and lots of Robert Strettle to the North and George Shed to the Southward, together with the appurtenances and all those yearly rent charges in or near Elbow Lane which I purchased of Joshua Carpenter, amounting to the yearly sum of twelve pounds, eight shillings and four pence or thereabouts. As for and concerning the rest and residue of all and singular my lands, tenements, rents and hereditaments I do hereby direct and authorize my executors for my estate in Pensylv^a, or such of them as shall undertake the executorship there, or the survivors or survivor of them to make sale thereof for the best price that can reasonably be gotten and out of the moneys thence proceeding, with what more can be recovered or made of my goods and chattels, it is my will that by and out of the same and out of my effects in Great Britain there shall first be raised and paid the sum of one hundred pounds sterling apiece to my brothers, Thomas Bradley and Joseph Bradley and my sister Ann Shepherd, and, in the next place, the sum of thirty pounds sterling apiece to my two nephews, namely, Edward Shepherd (my said sister's son) and William Bradley (the son of my brother Joseph) which two nephews I do nominate to be my executors for my estate and effects in Great Britain. And lastly as concerning the surplusage, if any, I do hereby give and devise the same unto her my said wife Esther, her executors, administrators and assigns for ever.

Wit: Pr Turner, C. Brocden, Robt Strettle.

The will was proved by the oath of Edward Shepherd, to whom administration was granted, power reserved of making the like grant to William Bradley, the other executor, when he should apply for the same.

Edmunds, 318.

WILLIAM WADE late of Westham, Sussex, yeoman, bound to Pennsylvania in America, 24 August 1682, proved 28 October 1682. I do order and appoint Philip Ford living in London, in Bow Lane, merchant, to be my executor and do give him ten pounds and do allow him reasonable charges. I do give unto my brother Edmund Wade five pounds. To my brother Thomas Wade five pounds. To my brother Edmund's eldest son Edmund Wade one hundred pounds. To his younger son Thomas Wade all my estate in goods in Pennsylvania, paying every servant both men and maids five pounds apiece when they have served their times out. To the meeting at Asen five pounds, at Mascall Picknols and Moses French and Samuel Web's disposing, and what remains over in England to be equally divided between my two brothers Edmund and Thomas Wade, except the hundred pounds I have in Sosiets (*sic*) stock, my will is that it should be divided between my brother Edmund Wade's two sons, Edmund and Thomas.   Cottle, 124.

SARAH SEWARD of Bristol, widow, well stricken in years, 12 July 1681 proved 2 December 1682. My body I commit to the earth to be decently interred in St. Thomas Churchyard within this city, as near as may be to the corpse of my late deceased mother there. To my elder son John Seward and to his wife Hester ten pounds, so as they buy them mourning apparel and wear it at my funeral. To the said John one hundred pounds in money, in one year after my decease, if he be then living, but not else. My executors shall in twelve months pay into the chamber of Bristol two hundred and fifty pounds, to remain at the usual interest by them given, for the benefit of my five grandchildren, Sarah, Hester, John, James and Thomas Seward, children of my said son John by his said wife Hester, to be paid, fifty (with its interest) to each at one and twenty. To my eldest daughter Bridget Williams five pounds, to be paid into her own hands within ten days after my decease, my intent being that it shall not be liable to satisfy any debt due by her husband nor that he shall have any thing to do therewith. I give her five pounds more to buy her mourning apparel to be worn at my funeral. My executors also to settle on her an annuity of twenty pounds, cleer of all taxes, charges, deductions and reprizes, to be paid into her own hands (in quarterly payments); and her husband shall have nothing to do with it &c. Another annuity or yearly sum of ten pounds to be settled on my grandson James Williams, son of my said daughter Bridget; but if my said grandson shall either be beyond sea or cannot come to receive his said annuity in person my executors shall detain the same till he doth return from sea or can come to receive it in person, it being my intent that his father nor wife shall have any benefit by this my bequest and that if my said grandson dies in the life time of my executor all arrears of this his annuity shall accrue and be paid to him my said executor. Certain wearing apparel and household effects to said daughter. To said grandson James Williams ten pounds within ten days after my decease. To my daughter Sarah Hasell five pounds, for mourning to wear at my funeral, and five pounds more as a token of my love. And I forgive her the fifty pounds which I lent her late husband William Hasell. To her son William Hasell twenty shillings, and the reason why I give him no more is because I intend to give fifty pounds towards the placing of him apprentice; but to her son John Hasell I give nothing because he is beyond sea, never likely to return for England. To her other five children, Richard, James, Sarah, Mary and Katherine Hasell fifty pounds apiece, to be paid at their respective ages of one and twenty years. To my daughter Mary Seward five pounds (for mourning) and five pounds as a token of my love; and the reason why I give her no more is because I have promised to give her three hundred pounds for an increase of her portion on her intermarriage with Robert Dowding, and if said marriage takes place in my life time I give the said Robert Dowding five pounds for mourning. To my son James Seword my lodge and garden on St. Michael's Hill, Bristol, in or near the Royal Fort, being city land, and all my term &c. to come therein. To my daughter Rebecca Seword two hundred pounds and five pounds more (for mourning).

Ten pounds to ten poor householders of Bristol, and forty shillings in bread to other poor. To Mr. Nicholas Penwasme, minister of St. Stephens, forty shillings, and to Mʳ Thomas Palmer, minister of St. Walburge twenty shillings. All the rest to my said younger son James Seword, whom I constitute sole executor.

Francis Yeamans, Richard Hollester and Richard Yeamans among the witnesses. Cottle, 150.

JONATHAN CAY, Rector of Christ Church parish in Calvert County in the Province of Maryland 24 June 1718, proved at London 19 October 1738. I give my body to the ground to be decently interred by my executrix, with as little charge as possible. To my loving brother, John Cay, all my books, those only excepted which shall be chosen by my executrix, as hereafter mentioned. I give to my wife Dorothy any twenty books which she shall choose out of mine; the remainder to my brother as already mentioned. All the rest &c. of my goods, chattels &c. I give to my wife whom I constitute sole executrix.

Wit: Phillis Clodius, Frederick Clodius, Owen Ellis.

Under the above was written " *Copia Vera* p Gabriel Parker, Depᵗʸ Comʳʸ, Calv't County." Then follows a statement showing that this will had been proved in Maryland 6 June 1737. Brodrepp, 229.

EDMONDE YORKE of Cotton End in the County of Northampton, yeoman, 18 November 1614, proved 17 April 1614[?]. My body to be buried in the churchyard of Hardingston. I give to Nathaniel, my eldest son, a certain bowl called the "mazzar," to be delivered unto him after the decease of Katharyne my wife, over and above the goods heretofore given unto him, as by certain writings thereof made betwixt me and the said Nathaniel may appear. I do give to Barthêw (Bartholomew) my second son twenty pounds to be employed as a stock for the keeping of him. And when he shall be able to employ the same, in the judgment of my overseers, the same money shall be delivered unto his own hands (some bedding also to him). " I doe geue and bequeathe unto my daughter Dudley one guilt bole." To my daughter Greene one silver bowl. These to be delivered unto them after the decease of Katherine my wife.

" Itm̃. I doe geue to my three grandchildren, that is to say to Samuell Dudley and Abygaill Greene forty shillinges apeec and one silver spoon a peec and to Anne Dudley twentie shillinges and one siluer spone to be deliuʳed unto them at their seuʳall ages of one and twentye yeares or before if my wif shall thinke fytt." To Abigail Hills my servant three shillings and four pence and to every of my servants that shall dwell with me at my decease two shillings apiece. To Mr. Flud, Mr. Foster and Mr. Rushbrook ten shillings apiece. To the poor in West Cotton six shillings eight pence and to the poor in East Cotton six shillings eight pence. I do also give six shillings and eight pence towards the repair of the Cawsye leading from my house to Northampton. To Samuel Osmonde and to Joseph Boyes five shillings. All other my goods and chattels, whatsoever and wheresoever they be, I give unto Katherine my wife and Joseph my son, whom I do make full executors. And I do constitute and appoint Robert Tanfield, Thomas Dudley, William Sharpe and Lewes Thomas my overseers. Wit: by Stephen Henchman and others. Northampton Wills. Book 8, 137.

The will nuncupative of Katherine Yorke late of Northampton, widow, was declared about the 21 day of June, A.D. 1633, in the presence of Mr.

Thomas Ball, vicar of All Saints in Northampton, Mr. Bullivant, parson of Abbington, and William Turland, and proved 24 August, 1633. She gave all her goods whatsoever to John Marston of Northampton, baker, in consideration of what she owed unto him and for the dicharge of ten shillings which she owed to Mr. John Lawe of Northampton, and eight shillings to Thomas Houghton of the same.

The inventory, returned by Mr. Marston, amounted to £6, 3s, 3d.
Northampton Wills, Book F., 117–118.

[It looks as if I had found the will of the father of Gov. Thomas Dudley's wife. From the parish registers of All Saints, Northampton, I gleaned the following:
"Nov. 1608, Samuell filius Thome Dudley baptizat. fuit xxx° die.—H. F. WATERS.
Dorothy, the first wife of Gov. Thomas Dudley, died at Roxbury, Mass., Dec. 27, 1643, aged 61 years. *See* REGISTER, vol. 10, page 130, and History of the Dudley Family, by Dean Dudley, Part I., page 79.—EDITOR.]

SARAH BINDING of Chertsey, Surrey, widow, 17 July 1687, proved 3 September 1687. My six acres of copyhold land, in Chertsey Eastmead, late the lands of Robert Wye of Chobham and now in the occupation of Peter Preist, I give and devise unto my daughter Abigail Dyke now the wife of Jeremiah Dyke of London; and also my copyhold messuages and the brook land thereunto belonging at Andrew News in the same parish of Chertsey, now in the occupation of Richard Goodenough, John Janeway and John Bristow; and my messuage of freehold, with the gate room or yard and one garden plot, with two closes of arable land, at Andrew News, now in the occupation of Elizabeth Starke widow, I give and devise unto my said daughter.

And whereas the Co. of Vintners in London stand bound to me in a bill obligatory in the penal sum of two hundred pounds, for the payment of one hundred pounds principal, with interest, as by the said bill, dated 27 February 1685, doth and may appear, I will and bequeath the said hundred pounds, with what interest shall be due for the same from the time of my decease until the said hundred pounds shall be paid unto my daughter Sarah Buckley, the wife of Mr. Richard Buckley of Boston in New England. And whereas John Warner of Adlesdon in Chertsey doth owe unto me one hundred and fifty pounds upon a surrender of his house and lands in Aldesdon, the surrender being in the hands of Richard Jordan and Maurice Crockford, two of the customary tenants of the manor of Chertsey Beomond, I give and bequeath one hundred pounds thereof unto my grand daughter Sarah Ireland the wife of Mr. Richard Ireland, chirurgion. And whereas my son in law Mr. Jeremiah Dyke doth owe unto me three hundred pounds, upon a Bond dated 8 June 1682, I do give and bequeath two hundred and fifty pounds thereof to be equally divided between five of my said son Dyke's children, Peter, Dorothy, Sarah, Lucy and Eleanor Dyke, to each of them fifty pounds apiece. Out of my other estate I give and bequeath to my niece Mrs. Bird Blackwell ten pounds, to my son Ireland and his wife twenty pounds for mourning, to my son Collier and his wife twenty pounds for mourning, to my great grandchild Sarah Ireland five pounds, to my great grandchildren Daniel Collier and Sarah Collier five pounds apiece, to my loving friends Mr. Thomas Clowes and his wife, each of them, a ring of twenty shillings, to Elizabeth Slarke twenty shillings, to Joice Rimell the elder twenty shillings, to the poor of Chertsey foure pounds. I give to my daughter Abigail Dyke my jewell of Diamonds, to my grand daughter Sarah Ireland my ring set with three stones and my best carpet in my parlor and Gerrard's Herbal. I give to my grandson Jeremiah Dyke my crystal watch and one shilling in money. The residue to my son in law Mr. Jeremiah Dyke and Abigail his wife, whom I make and ordain executors &c. Foot, 112.

[Richard Buckley, of Boston, was perhaps a relative of Joseph Buckley who had a son Richard (see Savage).—EDITOR.]

JOHN BURNAPP of Aston, Herts., clerk, 30 March 1653, proved 10 March 1653. My body to be buried in Aston Chancel as near unto my deceased wife as conveniently may be. To the poor of Aston three pounds, to be distributed amongst them within one month after my decease. I will and give unto my son Thomas two hundred and fifty pounds which, my will is, shall be laid out by my executor, with the advice and approbation of the overseers of this my Will, in merchantable commodities and wares and so sent into New England to my said son Thomas at three several times, when it may be done most safely within four years. But if through the troubles of these times my said overseers shall conceive that the said commodities and wares, so willed to be sent to my said son Thomas, or any part thereof, may not be safely conveyed to him then my will is that so much of the said two hundred and fifty pounds as shall not be laid out and sent to my said son Thomas, as is aforesaid, shall be laid out in land or otherwise by my said executors for the use of my said son Thomas and his heirs according as my said overseers or the survivor of them, or the heir of the survivor of them, shall direct and think fitting. I give to my old "sarvant" Margaret Hunt five pounds of currant money, and I will my son John to be helpful and kind unto her. I give unto my sarvant Thomas Thorpe twenty shillings and to my sarvant James Humfrey ten shillings and to my sarvant Mary Cann ten shillings of like currant money. I give unto all the children of my brother Thomas Burnapp and of my deceased brother Abraham Burnapp and of my sister Perry twenty shillings apiece. I do nominate and desire my loving friends Nathaniel Dodd of Bemington in the said County of Hartford, Clerk, and Henry Chauncy of Yardly, in the County of Hartford aforesaid, Esquire, to be overseers of this my last will and to do their endeavors for the performance of my will herein, as is aforesaid; and for their love and pains therein I give and bequeath to each of them forty shillings to buy them rings. My said son John to be the executor.

Wit: Henry Chauncey, John Humberston, the mark of Thomas Thorpe. Alchin, 193.

[For an account of the Burnaps of New England, see Savage's Genealogical Dictionary, vol. I, pp. 303–4.—EDITOR.]

JOHN TOWSEY, 10 March 1698–9, proved 19 September 1709. I do give and bequeath unto Mrs. Abigail Henchman, widow, dwelling at this present in Boston in New England the sum of three hundred pounds currant money of New England, provided she be remaining in the state of widowhood at the time when this my ·last will and testament shall be in force and of good effect. The rest of my estate and goods of what kind soever I give unto my brother Thomas Towsey and his heirs forever, whom I constitute and appoint to be the whole and sole executor of this my last Will and Testament.

Wit: Abraham Adams, Abigail Adams, John Soames. Lane, 229.

[Abigail Henchman named in this will was the widow of Hezekiah Henchman of Boston, who died May, 1694 (Savage).—EDITOR.]

WILLIAM BURNET, Governor of New York and New Jersey, subscribed and sealed at New York 6 December 1727, proved 9 July 1730. As to my body I will that it be buried at the Chapel of the Fort at New York, near to my dearest wife Mary and one of my children, in a vault prepared for them, in case I die in the Province of New York, but if I die elsewhere, in the nearest church or burying ground, or in the sea, if I should die there, well knowing that all places are alike to God's allseeing eye; and I hereby direct that I be buried in the most private manner and with the least expence that may be, and after the manner of any Protestant Church that may happen to be nearest to the place of my decease. Whereas I have some estate in Holland and some estate and effects in England I require my executors hereafter mentioned, or one of them, to give full powers to my brother in law David Mitchel and to my sister Mary his wife, or to the survivor of them, to sell and dispose of all my share and interest in any estate and effects which I shall die possessed of in England and Holland and of my share in the produce of my father's History yet to come, and to apply the whole to the satisfying all that remains due to the estate of my late brother Gilbert from me, and when that is done my executors are likewise to send over all my books and pamphlets to my said brother and sister in England, to be sold by them and the produce applied in the same manner till the said debt and the interest thereof be fully paid, and if that is not sufficient then to desire an account from my said brother and sister of what remains due thereon and to send that over as soon as may be to them out of the sale of my effects or estate, real or personal, in America till the said debt be fully discharged, my brother Gilbert having with the utmost generosity and affection supplied me with all that I wanted to discharge my other incumbrances when I left England, as my brother Mitchel had in like manner done, with the same generous friendship; but I have had the satisfaction to pay him already.

Item, I order that my son Gilbert Burnett be taken care of by my executors and sent over, provided with all conveniences within six months after my decease, to the care and guardianship of my said brother and sister Mitchell, or the survivor of them, who are to take care of his education out of the estate in England which shall belong to him after my decease; and they are likewise to take care that all my estate or effects in England or Holland, after my said debt to my brother Gilbert is paid, be applied, if any remainder there be, to the use of my said son Gilbert, to whom therefore, because already well provided in England, I leave no part of my estate or effects in America, except the gold and silver medals bearing the images of King (George?) the first, of the Princess Sophia and of King George the Second and the gilt tea table plate, both which were given to my father by the said Princess Sophia, late Electoress Dowager of Brunswick, which medals and plate I leave to my said son, and after him to my male heirs forever, who are hereby charged to keep the same as a perpetual memorial that my father's faithful services to the Protestant Succession in that Illustrious House were well accepted before their accession to the Throne of Great Britain, as they have been since amply rewarded by King George the First to my father's children. As to mourning to my servants I leave that to the discretion of my executors. My debts and legacies beforementioned being first paid I do hereby give full power and authority to my executors hereinafter mentioned, and to the survivor of them, and to the executors or administrators of the survivor of them, to grant, bargain, sell, convey and assure every or any part or parts of all my estate, real and personal, in fee or for life or for years, as to them shall seem most expedient, and to make, execute and acknowledge all such deeds, writings and acts as shall be necessary for that purpose, but, nevertheless, upon this special Trust and confidence that the moneys or profits arising by sale or otherwise of the premises be applied and given to and for the use of my children, William, Mary and Thomas, by my late dearest wife Mary Vanhorn, in the proportions following, to witt, in three equal shares among them while they all three continue alive and under the age of twenty one years, but in case of the death of any of my said children then the share of the dead child to be shared equally by the surviving children aforesaid. My will is that all such parts of my estate that shall happen not to be sold shall, when my eldest son of my aforesaid three children by my last wife comes of age, be valued, each part thereof particularly by the persons empowered to sell them and if all my said children be then alive then my will is that my said executors or the survivor of them &c., do give, grant and convey to the said William such part and parts of my real and personal estate as will amount in value to a full third part of my said estate, and that the profits of the shares of my other two children be applied to their use till they respectively arrive at the age of twenty one years, and then their shares respectively to be given to them in the same manner as William's share is hereby directed to be given to him &c. &c. I do hereby appoint Abraham Vanhorn and Mary his wife, and the survivor of them, and the executors or administrators of them, executors of this my last will and testament and guardians of my said three youngest children.

(signed) W. Burnett

Wit: Iˢ Bovin, John Haskott, Stephen Deblois. Auber, 183.

[Gov. William Burnet, the testator, was a son of Gilbert Burnet (the historian), bishop of Salisbury, and was born at the Hague, March, 1688, and died at Boston, Mass., Sept. 7, 1729, being at that time governor of Massachusetts. He had previously been governor of New York and New Jersey. His daughter Mary married Hon. William Browne of Salem, Mass., where she died August 1, 1745. Her husband in his will (extracts from which have been furnished us by George R. Curwin, Esq.), directs that his body be buried in "the tomb of my ancestors in Salem," and that it "be laid nearest to the body of my dear, my beloved, my affectionate, and my constant wife, friend and companion, Mary the daughter of Governor Burnet, deceased." Notices of the Browne family of Salem, including the son-in-law of Gov. Burnet, are printed in the REGISTER, vol. 20, page 243.—EDITOR.]

JAMES TOOPE of Ratcliffe, Midd'x., mariner, bound out to sea in that good ship called the Turkey Merchant whereof Capᵗ John Kempthorne is Commander, for Smyrna, 6 September 1675, proved 5 October 1682. To my kinsman Nathaniel Toope, son of Robert Toope of the parish of Stonehouse, Devon, ropemaker, twenty shillings, within six months after my decease. To Elizabeth Toope, daughter of the said Robert, five pounds (in six months &c.). All the rest of my estate, whether real or personal, I do wholly give and bequeath unto my loving wife Eleanor, whom I make &c. sole executrix. And I desire my loving brothers Edward Carter of London, merchant, and Richard Burley of Ratcliffe, mariner, to be the supervisors or overseers of this my last will &c. Cottle, 124.

EDWARD CARTER of Edmonton, Middˣ, Esquire, 18 October 1682,

proved 29 November 1682. My body to be interred in the parish church of St. Dunstan's in the East in London, in the middle aisle under the stone laid for my daughter Anne Place, and as near to the grave of my former wife Mrs. Anne Carter, buried there, as conveniently may be. I give all my messuages, land and tenements in Edmonton and my third part (the whole in three parts to be divided) of and in all those messuages, tenements, lands and hereditaments in Chalfont St Peters, Bucks, and all other my messuages, lands, tenements &c. whatever within the Kingdom of England and all that my Plantation in Virginia called Brice's Plantation, lying on the North side of Rappahannock River, now in the possession of my Agents, assigns or overseers there, with all the stock, servants, negroes, housing, buildings, edifices, materials, implements, utensils, goods and chattels whatsoever belonging to or used with, in or upon the said Plantation, and my other Plantation in Virginia, called Monasco Plantation, lying also on the North side of the said river &c., to my son Edward Carter, and the heirs of his body; remainder thereof to my eldest daughter Elizabeth Carter, and the heirs of her body; remainder to my daughter Anne Carter and the heirs of her body; and for want of such heirs to my wife Elizabeth Carter and her heirs for ever. (Provision made in case wife should sell these plantations.) And I do here make it my desire to my said dear wife that she will not sell or dispose of the said plantations, stock or goods unless she finds urgent occasion for so doing. And I make my said wife guardian to all my said children, Edward, Elizabeth and Anne Carter, until they severally attain their respective ages of twenty and one years, she to maintain, bring up, educate and instruct my said children in the fear of God and in a decent, suitable manner agreeable to their respective fortunes. As to my other lands in Virginia and my land in Maryland I give and bequeath the same as follows; my tract or dividend of land in the County of Upper Norfolk in Virginia, in Bennett's Creek, in Nansemond River, where I formerly lived, and my other tract in the said County, at or near the head of the said Creek, containing about five hundred acres, and my other tract, near the mouth of the Nansemond River, formerly in the occapation of Coll. Thomas Busbidge, together with another tract or dividend in the Province of Maryland, called Werton, part whereof was lately in the occupation of Wm Salisbury deceased, be sold by my executrix for the payment of my debts and the better maintenance and education of my said children. All the residue of my estate shall be put out at interest and improved for the benefit and advantage of my said two daughters, Elizabeth and Anne Carter. My wife to be executrix. Cottle, 128.

JOHN OLYVER of the City of Bristol "marchant." My body to be buried in the parish church of St. Stephens within the City of Bristol. I give and bequeath to my son Robert Olyver all my lands and tenements within the County of Gloucester and in the parishes of Wickwarr, Cromholde and Yate, the which I lately purchased of Alexander Neale of Yate, to have and to hold to him and his heirs male forever upon condition that the said Robert and his heirs do pay unto my youngest son, Henry Olyver, during his natural life, out of the said lands &c., the sum of twenty pounds currant money yearly. In default of such issue male of my son Robert I will that the said lands &c. do come and descend to Thomas my son, and to his heirs male, upon the like condition; and for want of issue male of Thomas, then to John my son &c. and so from one to another to the last. All the lands and tenements within the City of Bristol that were sometimes the lands and tenements of my father Thomas Olyver and all that I myself purchased within the said City I give and bequeath in manner and form following. First my Capital messuage in Corn Street that lately I purchased of Richard Kalke gen[t] and the tenement that Robert Fryer dwelleth in I give to Thomas my son and to his heirs forever. I give to John my son my tenement on the back wherein lately William Colston dwelt. I give and bequeath my three tenements in Reckliffe (Redcliff?) Street, wherein Richard Wodson dwelleth, John Dolphin and Thomas Holbin, baker, dwelleth, unto James my son and to his heirs forever. I give my tenement in St. Thomas Street, called the White Lion, and three little other tenements and a garden and two stables to Thoby my son. I give to Henry my son the garden and lodge in Marsh Street that I lately purchased of Mr. Kelke. I give to James my son my tenement that I dwell in, situate in Balland Street, paying to the company of Taylors within the City of Bristol forty shillings per annum, as by their writing appeareth. I give to Mary my daughter the profits and commodities that shall grow and increase upon my part of the lease of "presage" for three years. The rest of the years unexpired, after three years, I will that Thomas and John my sons shall equally have and enjoy. I give to James one hundred pounds and to Thoby one other hundred pounds. My land in long Ashton, in the County of Somerset, I give to my well beloved wife Elizabeth Olyver and to her heirs forever. I give to the Church Wardens of St. Stephens forever one little tenement in Fisher Lane wherein Manfield lately dwelt, to the use of the said parish &c. All the rest of my goods &c. I give to Elizabeth my wife, whom I make and appoint executrix, whom I do desire that she will give to my mother Margaret Coxe, widow, during her natural life, five pounds per annum sterling. And I do intreat my good friends Mr. John Webbe, now mayor, Thomas Coventrye Esq. and Mr. John Barker to be overseers of this my last will; and I give to every of them a gown apiece, to solemnize my funeral.

This will was proved at London 6 February 1597 by the oath of Thomas Lovell, Not. Pub., attorney for Elizabeth the relict and executrix named in the will. Lewyn, 21.

[John Oliver, the testator, was a son of Thomas and Margaret (Alkyn) Oliver of Bristol. He married Aug. 28, 1577, Elizabeth Rowland. He died in January, 1597-8, and his widow, whose will is given below, married Feb. 18, 1599-1600, Jerome Ham. Their son James, born 1588, died 1629, married Frances Cary. They were the parents of John Oliver, born in Bristol, Eng., in 1615, came to New England in 1639, settled in Newbury, and died about 1642. See Ancestry of Mary Oliver, by William S. Appleton, Cambridge, 1867, where much information about this family of Oliver will be found with wills, extracts from parish registers and tabular pedigrees.—EDITOR.]

RICHARD COLE of the City of Bristol, alderman, 16 June 1599, proved 17 July 1599. My body to be buried in the church of All Saints, Bristol, where my first wife lieth, in the North Aisle. My manor, lands, tenements &c. in Nailsey, Somerset, and in Connisbury (Congresbury?) and Weeke St. Lawrence, Somerset, I give to my wife, and also my house in which I now dwell in Bristol, and my grounds, orchard and gardens in Lewens mead in the parish of St. James in the suburbs of Bristol, known and called by the name of the Friars or Gray Friars &c., and my two store houses on the Key in Bristol, one in the tenure of Mr. John Hopkins, merchant, and the other in the late tenure of Elizabeth Ham late wife of John Olyver, merchant, in the parish of St. Stephens; all during her natural life. And after her decease I give them to Richard Cole, son of William Cole, son of Thomas Cole my brother, which son Richard he had by his first wife, the daughter of John Ashe merchant. For lack of issue of the body of the said Richard Ccle I give them to his father William Cole and his lawful issue, failing which, I give the house wherein I now dwell in the High Street and the Friars aforesaid to Richard Boulton, son of John Boulton of Bristol, merchant; and my house and land in Nailsey to Alexander Bainham son of Henry Baynham of Yeate, Gloucester; and my manor of Saniford in Somerset to Richard Cam, son of Arthur Cam, which he hath by my brother Thomas Cole's daughter Fortune; and I give to Nicholas Murford, son of Thomas Murford of Bath, which he had by my sister's daughter Mary, my tenement called Dandris, now in the tenure of William Yonge (and two other tenements, both which are in Connysbury, Somerset); and I give to all the sons of John Sarney of Wickwar, Gloucester, which he had by my sister's daughter Yedith, all the rest of my lands undisposed in Connysbury; and to Thomas White, son of Thomas White of Bristol, merchant, my house in Marsh Street, Bristol. A ring which hath a Saphire Stone, which Mr Chester gave me, I give to Anne Cole, William Cole's wife. A conditional bequest to Thomas Knight, son of Edward Knight, which he had by my sister's daughter Alice. William Spratt my first wife's brother. Joice Fisher, wife of William Fisher, my sister's daughter (John Fisher his father). Brother Thomas Cole. To Anne, wife of William Cole, a gold ring with a saphire stone, which ring her grandmother Mrs. Chester gave me. To George Goughe, son of Henry Goughe, a ring of gold which his grandfather Robert Smith gave me. To Alice Hopkins, daughter of Thomas Hopkins, a ring which her grandfather Robert Rowlande gave me. To my cousins Gyles Dymery and Nicholas Dymerie twenty shillings each and a black cloak. My cousin Morris Cole's children. The rest of Thomas White's children. My cousin Mr. George Snigg, Recorder of Bristol. My brother Edward Carre of Woodspring, gentleman. Andrew Patche sexton of All Saints. My cousin Arthur Cam. Arthur Hibbens.   Kidd, 64.

ELIZABETH HAM, wife of Hierom Ham of the City of Bristol gen^t, late wife and executrix of John Olyver of the said city merchant, 24 December 1619, proved 30 October 1628. I give unto my daughter Mary Gryffith one sixteenth part of the " prysadge " lease and unto my son Henry Olyver the other sixteenth part of the same prysadge lease ·I now hold, which prysadge lease I did put my husband Hierom Ham in trust to buy for me and to be disposed of at my pleasure. If my said daughter Mary Griffithe shall decease and depart this life before the end of the said lease then the profit and benefit of the time then remaining shall come to her children, to be divided by equal portions, that child only excepted which shall then be "interested" in the living in Redland. More I give unto her one feather bed one bolster and two pillows, marked with two letters for her name, and my best Arras coverlet, the great Cypres chest, a neddle work chair, with the two stools, one of the gilt chairs and all my wearing apparel &c. To my grand child William Griffith the great spruce chest in the higher gallery and my green carpet. To Mary Griffith my grandchild my dozen of Apostle spoons. My will is that my son Henry do pay, out of his said sixteenth part of the prysadge lease, unto my husband Jerom Ham ten pounds yearly during the lease (if he so long shall live), only the last two years excepted to him the said Henry. More, he shall pay unto my son Thomas Rowland (only the last two years excepted) ten pounds yearly (if the said

Thomas so long shall live); and if the said Thomas shall happen to depart this life before the end of these years given him then my will is that what years shall be then to come shall remain to his children that hath no portions left them by their grandmother Redwood. More, my will is that the first ten pounds payable out of his sixteenth part of prysadge lease unto my son Thomas Rowland shall be given unto Mary Oliver, the daughter of my son James Oliver, as my gift. And my will is that my son Henry Olyver shall leave in my executor's hands the said sixteenth part of the prysadge lease so given him, for the assurance of the payment of the said ten pounds yearly to the said Hierom Ham and the ten pounds yearly to the said Thomas Royland: and if the said sixteenth part, so given the said Henry, shall at any time not amount to the sum of forty pounds by the year then each of them shall stand to their part of the loss accordingly. And if it happen my son Henry Olyver depart this life before the end of the years given him then whatsoever is given him by this my will shall remain to his children, John, Thomas and Hierom Oliver, to be divided them by equal portions. The rest of my plate and household stuff not given I give unto my husband Hierom Ham, and my will is that until my funeral and the hundred pounds due to the chamber for Robert Rowland and what else I shall owe be paid none shall receive or demand any portion out of the prysadge. And I do ordain for my executors my husband Hierom Ham and my son in law John Griffith. Agreed unto by me Hier^m Ham.

Administration, according to the tenor of the will was granted to William Griffith, grandson of the deceased, for the reason that John Griffith, one of the executors named in the will, had died before accepting the duties of executorship.   Barrington, 92.

[See notes on will of her first husband, John Oliver, which will be found on page 671.—EDITOR.]

THOMAS COOKE the elder of Pebmershe, Essex, yeoman, 30 August 1621, proved 26 November 1621. To the poor of that parish five pounds. To the poor of Alphamston and Lamarshe in Essex twenty shillings (i.e. ten shillings each). Those bequests to be distributed by the discretion of the minister and the most chiefest inhabitants of either parish. Five pounds more to the poor of Pebmershe as an increase of the stock of twenty pounds given to them by Mr. Hugh Clapham, sometime the minister of the same parish, to purchase a house or lands &c. To Thomas Cooke my grandchild my messuage &c. called Goddard's & all my lands &c. which I late purchased of John Hilton gen^t and Mary his wife, situate &c. in Gestingthorpe and Little Mapelsted, Essex, now in the occupation of John Clark or his assigns. To my brother Lawrence Cook and Robert Cook, during their natural lives, to either of them forty shillings apiece yearly. To Thomas Wiscowe the younger, my sister's son five pounds. To every of the children of my brother John Cooke deceased, my sister Wiskowe and my sister Sawen deceased and my brother Lawrence, not before nominated and bequeathed unto, twenty shillings apiece. To George Cook my grandchild all such my estate, interest and term of years which I have yet to come in lands &c. in Lamarshe, Essex, which I late had by demise and grant of one Robert Becle of Lamarshe. I do forgive unto Edmund Reade my son in law the three score pounds due unto me by his bill of 1 December 1606. To my daughter Elizabeth, now his wife, three score pounds in one year after my decease. To my said daughter Elizabeth and to Margaret her daughter, now wife of John Lake, and to Susan now wife of my

son Thomas, to every of them one spur Riall of gold apiece. To Samuel
Reade my grandchild forty pounds and every of the residue of my daughter
Reed's children unmarried, ten pounds apiece, to be paid within one year
after my decease unto them or their father for them.   To every of the
children of Thomas Cook, my son, twenty pounds apiece.   The residue &c.
to Thomas Cooke, the younger, my son, whom I make sole executor. If he
refuse then I make Edmunde Reade my son in law sole executor.   I give
to Martha Reade, now wife of —— Epps of London, my grandchild, ten
pounds, in one month after my decease.   To Johane Gilott, my late servant,
twenty shillings.   To Maryon Edwards, Clement Chaundler and Elizabeth
Hayward five shillings apiece, and to William Scott George Smith and
Samuel Medcalf three shillings four pence apiece, and to Thomas Maninge,
Thomas French and Richard Goodwyn two shillings six pence apiece.
    Wit: George Coo, Robert Willm̃s and Thomas Smithe.   Dale, 94.

[This will, which I communicated very briefly to the Mass. Historical Society
in January, 1890, was a welcome find as confirming my supposition that Elizabeth, wife of Edmund Reade of Wickford, was daughter of Thomas Cooke of
Pebmarsh. (See Ancestry of Priscilla Baker, p. 105.) Her descendants in this
country are many. The Cooke pedigree may be seen in Visitation of Essex,
Harleian Society, vol. xiii., p. 383.—WILLIAM S. APPLETON.]

THOMAS COKE of Pebmersh, Essex, Esquire, —— January 1679, proved
24 November 1682. My desire is that my body may be decently buried
without pomp or ceremonies in the churchyard of Pebmersh, between the
graves of my dearly beloved and entirely loving wives, Elizabeth and
Judith; and, being so buried, my will is, and I do hereby require mine
executors to cause three graves (together with my son John's on the North
side of his mother's) to be raised with good brick, and a large stone to be
laid upon them. I do give and bequeath (as an addition to the provision
for the aged poor people of the parish of Pebmersh) ten pounds, to be paid
when the house and croft in Little Henny shall be sold, and the money
thereof arising shall be laid out on a purchase of some house or houses near
the Church, or some piece of land in or near the parish, to be employed for
the more comfortable relief of the aged poor according to the intention of
the first donors, at which time and for the effecting whereof I do appoint
mine executors to pay the said ten pounds.   And I do also give five pounds
more to be distributed among the poorer sort of well disposed people of the
said parish.   I do give to John Scot and ·Abigail his·wife three pounds
apiece, to Edward Abraham three pounds and to Mary his wife six pounds,
and to my servants which shall be with me at my death ten shillings apiece.
To every of my brothers' and sisters' children twenty pounds apiece, Thomas
Bennett taking reasonably for the mare my son had of him or else I do
give unto him but ten pounds.   To Mr. Brinley Mr. Ely and Mr. Crow
three pounds apiece, and eleven pounds more to be distributed among such
other poor ministers as are turned out of their living because they conform
not, such as known to my nephew Grandorge.   I do give unto Joseph Coke
my brother seven pounds and all my wearing clothes, which are fit for
his condition, and to his wife three pounds.   To Mrs. Arrowsmith, Mrs.
Parsons and Mrs. Horton all such linen as was Mr. Percivall's, their father,
in his life time and are now remaining.   To my daughter Elizabeth her
mother's bible, that she may improve it as she did, and also all things in
my best parlor chamber.   To Joseph Coke, my brother, fifteen hundred
pounds, to be paid out of my whole estate, for the redeeming of Huntshall
&c, upon this condition, that if my son and daughter Parsons and their

trustees shall release unto him and his heirs all the right, title and interest which they have in my said farm called Huntshall in Pebmershe &c., then this bequest of fifteen hundred pounds to be void and of none effect. And I do then give Huntshall &c. unto my said brother Joseph for life, and after his decease to his son Thomas and his heirs for ever, paying unto his sisters here in England twenty pounds apiece and to his brother and sister in New England also twenty pounds apiece, to be paid unto them within one year after he shall be twenty and one years old. And if my son Parsons or my daughter, or their trustees, shall refuse to release unto them the said Huntshall then my will and meaning is, and I do hereby give and bequeath unto my said brother and his son and heirs the houses and lands bought of Turner and Wistow and other freehold which I purchased, together with all my leasehold lands and copyhold lands to him and his heirs for ever, hoping they will not endeavor to cross what I know was my dear father's desire and is here accordingly declared to be my will. To Mr. Trussell thirty shillings and to his son Thomas ten shillings. For the payment of my debts and legacies and my son's just debts I do give to be sold by mine executors all my pieces of meadow in Lumer Road Meadow, my farm in Gestingthorpe, called Goddards, and the farm wherein George Radleigh now dwelleth, in Pebmersh, both free and copyhold, with all my stock, goods and chattels without the house &c. And, my debts and legacies being all so paid and Huntshall well and surely settled upon my brother Joseph and his son Thomas and his heirs as above is provided, I do give and bequeath all the residue of my real and personal estate unto Elizabeth my daughter during the term of her natural life, and after her decease the goods and personal estate to her children as she shall please, and all the land and real estate &c. to her son John Parsons, my grandchild, his mother allowing him good maintenance for his liberal education, and he (when he shall enjoy the lands) paying to his sister Anthonia three hundred pounds and to the rest of his mother's children which she may hereafter have one hundred pounds apiece. To Anthony Parsons my son (if he will accept of it) my best fur coat and what book he pleases. My other fur coat I do give unto Joseph my brother, if living at my decease; if not, then to John Scott. I do give my Polyglott Bible to my nephew Grandrige, and my watch and half a dozen of my books to my cousin Samuel Read, and my law books unto my nephew John Bennett.

Lastly, I do hereby ordain, make, constitute and appoint my well beloved daughter Elizabeth Parsons, my cousin Samuel Read, my nephew John Bennett and my nephew Isaac Grandridge to be executors &c., requiring them to pay all my debts and legacies and also all my son's just debts, that a blessing may be upon what I shall give and leave unto them.

The will was proved by John Bennett, of the other executors Samuel Read and Isaac Grandorge renouncing and Elizabeth Parsons being dead.

Cottle, 128.

THOMAS THATCHER of Beckington, Somerset, 8 January 1610, proved 13 June 1611. To certain poor persons in the parish of Beckington whom I particularly named to my executrix twenty shillings, to be divided to the said poor persons by the discretion of my overseers. For the better relieving of my uncle John Thatcher my executrix shall deliver into the hands of my brother Clement Thatcher a cow which now is in the custody of my brother in law Robert Keenell that, by the discretion of my brother Clement, she may be employed to the use of my said uncle during his natural life, and after his decease the said cow to remain to the use of his children. My executrix shall, in like manner, deliver into the hands of my brother Clement one other cow, color black, for the better relieving of my aunt Elizabeth Thatcher, the use of it to her for life, and then to remain to the use of my said uncle John's children.   To William Hillman twenty shillings.   To Thomas Griffin ten shillings.   To Thomas Bembury ten shillings. To my maidservant Mary Wattes twenty shillings.   To Hester Thatcher, my brother William's daughter, one flock bed and one bolster, and one sheep.   To Ezra Thatcher, my brother William's son, one sheep.   A conditional bequest to John Gallington son of brother in law John Gallington.

Item, my will is that if my brother Anthony Thatcher (who now is in the "seperation") do join in the profession of true religion with any true church, that then my executrix within one whole year after he shall so have joined himself, either with the reformed Dutch church, in which country he now liveth, or shall return into England and join with us, shall pay unto my said brother five pounds, which in token of brotherly affection, I give unto him.   'The rest of my goods I give to Anne my wife whom I make executrix, and make my friend Toby Walkwood and brother Clement Thatcher overseers.   Wood, 60.

CLEMENT THATCHER of Merston Bigot, Somerset, yeoman, 13 January 1629, proved 4 May 1639.   I give to the Church of Froome and Merston six shillings eight pence, to be eqally divided, and to the poor of Froome five shillings and to the poor of Merston five shillings.   To my son Clement forty pounds, to be in the custody of Bridget my wife until he comes of the age of one and twenty, she, the said Bridget continuing in my name, and not otherwise, it then to be ordered and disposed by my overseers.   I give unto Thomas my son twenty pounds and to Hannah my daughter twenty pounds and to Mary and Joane my daughters twenty pounds apiece.   To William Thatcher my kinsman five pounds and to his sisters Alice and Jane forty shillings apiece.   To Thomas Thatcher my kinsman Hatton twenty shillings.   To all my God children an ewe and a lamb, or six shillings eight pence in money, at the discretion of my executor.   To my brother Gallington's children an ewe and a lamb apiece and to my brother William Thatcher's children an ewe and a lamb apiece, and to my brother Anthony, which is beyond sea, forty shillings, and to his two children ten shillings apiece.   To Thomas my son my chattel lease of the house in the field and five acres of ground thereunto belonging.   Two other chattel leases in Filton and Mr Cable's land, that which was lately in the tenure of Elizabeth Hipstonn, shall remain to Clement my son &c.   Wife Bridget to be executrix and brother William Thatcher and brother John Gallington overseers.   Harvey, 92.

PETER THATCHER of the City of New Sarum, Wilts, clerk, 1 February 1640, proved 5 August 1641.   I give and bequeath to Peter Thatcher and Thomas Thatcher, two of my sons, the sum of thirty five pounds in money, which was sent over to New England to buy goats, and is in the hands of my brother Anthony Thatcher.   Also I give and bequeath to my said two sons twenty pounds which is due to me from my said brother for keeping his child.   Also I give to my said two sons the several sums of thirty and one pounds and fourteen pounds, being in the hands of my brother in law Christopher Batt.   All which said several sums of money to be equally divided between my said two sons.   And my will is that my said son

Thomas shall have his legacy paid as conveniently as may be after my decease, and my said son Peter to have his legacy paid when he shall have served out his apprenticeship, and not before. And in the meantime to be managed by my overseers. To my son Peter my great brass pot and Mr. Henry Aynsworthe's works and Mr. Rogers his seven Treatises. To Anne Thatcher, my daughter, fifty pounds and all her mother's childbed linen. To Martha and Elizabeth Thatcher, my daughters, to each of them fifty pounds. The said legacies given to my said three daughters shall be paid unto them when they shall respectively attain to their several ages of twenty and one years or be married, which of them shall first happen. To John Thatcher, my son, fifty pounds, to be paid to him when he shall have served out his apprenticethip or shall have attained to his age of twenty and three years. All these four last mentioned legacies of fifty pounds shall be paid out of the moneys specified in a writing now in the hands of Mr. Francis Dove. I give to my last nominated four children, Anne, Martha, Elizabeth and John, ten pounds each, to be paid at the times limited for the payment of their other legacies; and if my said daughters, or either of them, shall marry before they shall respectively attain to their several ages of twenty and one years without the consent of my overseers, or one of them, then such of them as shall so marry shall have only this last legacy of ten pounds, and their other legacies of fifty pounds to be divided among the survivors of them, at the discretion of my overseers. I give and bequeath to Samuel, Paul and Barnabas Thatcher, my three youngest sons, to each of them fifty pounds, to be paid to them when they shall respectively attain to their several ages of twenty and three years. And it is my will that the benefit and commodity to be made of all the said legacies given to my said children shall be bestowed and employed by my overseers for and towards the education and maintenance of my said children until their legacies shall respectively grow due and payable in such sort as my said overseers shall think best and fittest for them. (Provision made in case of the death of any child.) I give to my two brothers John and Anthony, to my wife's four sisters, Elizabeth, Margory, Mary and Dorothy, and to my sister Anne Batt, to each of them five shillings, to make them rings, as a remembrance of my love to them. To my servant Edith Davis forty shillings, to be paid within one month after my decease. All the rest of my goods, debts, chattels, plate, implements of household, household stuff and books (except such of my books as I shall give and dispose of by a note or schedule hereof to be annexed to this my will, and reserving to my children the plate which was severally given to them at their births or since). I give and bequeath to Alice Thatcher, my loving wife, whom I also ordain and make sole executrix &c, and I desire my very loving friend, the said Francis Dove, and my loving brother in law Richard Alwood to be the overseers of this my last will and testament, to whom I give five shillings apiece in token of my love.

Wit: Nathaniel Conduit, John Ivie jun[r].

Then follows a long list of books (chiefly theological) " Giuen to my sonn Thomas Thatcher theis books following." Evelyn, 112.

[In the collections of Licenses to pass beyond the sea, Eliz. to Car I. in the Public Record office, I have found the following entry:

"Primo die Octobris 1631. Anthony Thatcher of age 65 years dwelling in Leyden, et uxor Clarey Thatcher, 38."

A pen has been drawn through this entry, but on the margin is written, " Wm Cooke dwelling in Bermondsey street test" against it; and there is also written against it in the margin the word " Stet."—H. F. WATERS.

A word as to the record spelling of Peter Thacher's surname. There can be no doubt that the signature of the original will was spelled as he invariably spelled it, so far as is known, without the middle " t." The writer has in his possession photographs of original signatures of his, so spelled, and the records of his parish are full of his signatures, so spelled. He was settled in 1616 over the Parish Church of Milton, Clevedon, Somersetshire, and an inscription upon a stone in the wall of that church to the memory of his deceased child, *John*, contains the name THACHER. Why, then, it may be asked, did the scrivener who wrote the will, or the clerk who recorded it, spell it otherwise. Unquestionably from carelessness in one or both. A distinguished historian and antiquary, in Winsor's " Memorial History of Boston," has spelled the name both ways, in the same article, on the same page. Anthony, brother of Peter, always spelled his name, also, with one " t."

The leaders of St. Edmunds Parish in Salisbury were Puritans, and a disagreement having arisen, in consequence, with their minister, Hugh Williams, he resigned in 1621 or 1622. These leaders having fixed upon Mr. Thacher as Mr. Williams's successor, he was invited to that parish by repeated, urgent votes of the vestry. He finally resigned the vicarage of Milton Clevedon, and Feb. 23, 1622–3, he was instituted rector of St. Edmunds, Salisbury, by the then Bishop of Sarum, JOHN DAVENANT, who favored the Puritans. He continued rector, to the great acceptance of his parishioners, until his death, Feb. 19, 1640–1. He was harassed, more or less, during this period, by Archbishop Laud, because of his Puritanism.

It has been generally supposed that the Anthony named in the wills of Thomas and Clement as their brother, and as being out of the realm, was the same Anthony, brother of Rev. Peter, who is mentioned in his will. The writer, however, for various reasons, doubts the correctness of this hypothesis, notwithstanding a pedigree of the Thacher family, furnished many years since by officials of the College at Arms in London, to the late Hon. J. S. B. Thacher of Natchez, Miss., assumes Thomas, Clement, Peter, and the Anthony of Peter's will, to have been brothers. The extract from the Public Record Office in London, which Mr. Waters appends to his abstracts of the three wills, places the matter, it seems, beyond controversy. We there find, Oct. 31, 1631, an Anthony Thacher, 65 years of age, dwelling at Leyden, with his wife *Clarey*. Now Anthony Thacher, brother of Rev. Peter, so celebrated for his graphic and pathetic description of the awful shipwreck on Thacher's Island, Aug. 15, 1635, when he and his wife were the sole survivors of the vessel's crew and passengers, numbering twenty-three, and who was afterwards one of the three founders of Yarmouth, Mass., never had a wife " Clarey." His first wife, Mary, died at Salisbury, July 26, 1634, while he was serving his brother Peter as curate at St. Edmunds, which office he held several years. (In the record of his wife's death, in the parish register, he has the title of " Clerk" or clergyman.) *Elizabeth Jones* became his second wife only six weeks before she embarked for New England, on or about April 6, 1635, with her husband and four of his children, one (Benjamin) having been left behind in the care of his brother Peter, because of his tender age. They were accompanied by Thomas, then 15 years of age, son of Peter, afterwards first pastor of the Old South Church of Boston, and who preferred a tramp through the woods from Ipswich, the place of embarkation, to the water trip, having, says *Cotton Mather*, " such a strong and sad impression upon his mind about the issue of the voyage, that he, with another, would needs go the journey by land." (See 1 Mag. 442. Hartford ed. of 1820.) Anthony died Aug. 22, 1667, aged about 80 (see Freeman's History of Cape Cod), which would require his birth to have occurred in 1587. He could hardly have attained that age, however, as Peter, for good reasons, believed to have been the elder, was born in 1588. If we assume that Anthony was eighty in 1667, he would have been forty-four in 1631, when the Anthony of the Public Record Office was sixty-five. Anthony, the brother of Peter, had received a good education, wrote a very handsome hand, and expressed himself with ease, correctly, with force and perspicuity, and sometimes, eloquently. Yet the most persevering researches have failed to discover the place of his education. It has been surmised that he may have received his education from his brother Peter.

It will be observed that in neither of the wills of Thomas and Clement is there any reference to a brother Peter, or a sister Anne, which can hardly be accounted for if the two latter, indeed, bore such relation to the two former.

The *John Thacher*, son of Peter, named in his will, being the second son of that name, was interred Sept. 1, 1673. Administration was granted on his estate Nov. 10, 1673. He was a *chirurgeon*. All the children named in the will, except *Samuel, Paul* and *Barnabas*, of whom the testator speaks as his " three youngest sons," were the children of his first wife, Anne, whose burial is recorded March 26, 1634. In those days baptism usually succeeded the birth within a day or two, and sometimes took place on the day of birth. Martha was baptized Nov. 30, 1623; Elizabeth, Jan. 29, 1625-6; John, Feb. 3, 1627-8. Mr. Thacher was married to his second wife, *Alice Batt*, a sister of Christopher Batt, named in his will as his "*brother in law*," about April 14, 1635. The record of this marriage has not been discovered, but the *marriage allegation*, recorded in the Diocesan Register at Salisbury, is as follows:

" April 14, 1635. Personally appeard Richard White of St. Thomas, in Sarum, Grocer, and he craves License for marriage between Peter Thacher, Clarke, Master of Arts, Parson of St. Edmunds, in Sarum, and a widower, and Alice Batt of St. Edmunds, in Sarum, Spinster, aged 30 years, or thereabouts, and alleged that, to his knowledge, there is noe impediment, either in respect to consanguinity, affinity, former contract, or otherwise, but that they may lawfully marry together, and that her parents are both dead, and of the truth thereof he offereth to make faith."

Francis Dove, the author of the inscription on Peter Thacher's tomb, signed " F. D.," was one of his principal parishioners, and a Churchwarden of St. Edmunds during the greater part of his incumbency. Francis Dove was of the order of the *gentry*. He was held in the highest esteem in Salisbury, and was a man of pure morals and of sterling integrity. He was twice mayor of that metropolitan city. His brothers, John and Henry, also in turn held that responsible office. Francis was the " very loving friend" of his minister, and married his widow, Alice (Batt) Thacher, Oct. 19, 1641. The " loving brother in law," Richard Alwood, appointed with Francis Dove " overseers " of the will, married Elizabeth Batt, a sister of Alice, Jan. 29, 1640-1. Mr. Thacher deceased Feb. 19, 1640-1.

Alice and Elizabeth Batt were sisters of Christopher Batt, above mentioned. The testator also speaks of his " sister Anne Batt," to whom, with his " wife's four sisters, Elizabeth, Margery, Mary and Dorothy," he gives five shillings each, " to make them rings as a remembrance of my (his) love to them." The fact that he calls Anne, wife of Christopher Batt, his sister—said Christopher being his brother-in-law—has led to the belief that she was his own sister. But as Christopher was the brother of Mr. Thacher's wife, and thus the former became the latter's brother-in-law, and as there is no evidence, outside of this will, that Mr. Thacher ever had a sister Anne, and as it appears by the record at St. Edmunds that Christopher Batt married another person, it has been inferred that the testator called Anne Batt his *sister* out of courtesy merely. In the Bishop of Sarum's Books, under date of Oct. 10, 1629, there is recorded an " allegation of marriage" between Christopher Batt, tanner, aged 26 years, and Anne Baynton, Spinster, aged 26 years. October 12, 1629, there is found in the Parish Register of St. Edmunds a record of their marriage. There is no evidence that said Christopher was married a second time. The record of the births of his children tends to show that their mother was Anne (Baynton) Batt. He emigrated to New England with his family in 1638. His wife Anne survived him.

The will of *Paul*, one of the three youngest sons of Peter Thacher, baptized July 22, 1638, interred Sept. 16, 1678, and that of the son of Paul, *Anthony Hillary Thacher*, baptized Nov. 4, 1671, interred Nov. 25, 1692, allowed and recorded in the court of the Sub Dean of Sarum, are now to be found in Somerset House, London. Paul inherited from his mother a large real estate.

PETER THACHER, of West Newton, Mass.

See also the article on the Thacher Family, by Samuel Pearce May, Esq., in the REGISTER for April, 1889, page 171.—EDITOR.]

RICHARD ALLWOOD of New Sarum, Wilts, haberdasher, 20 May 1644, proved 22 March 1644. After my debts have been paid and the charges of my burial defrayed the remainder of my estate I give &c as follows. To the four children of my late sister Alice Turner forty shillings apiece, to be paid unto the men children when they shall be bound apprentices and to the daughters when they shall attain to their several ages of twenty and one years or days of marriage, which shall first happen. To my brother Gabriel Currons forty shillings. To the poor knitters of the Parish of Christ church in the County of Southampton twenty shillings, to be distributed in bread amongst them according to the discretion of my overseers. I give ten pounds to be distributed yearly for ten years together next after my decease unto such Godly ministers as they shall get to preach in the said parish church upon Ascension Day in every year. To the poor of the parish of Ringwood, in Southampton, twenty shillings, to be distributed amongst them in bread. To my loving friend Mr. William Pape forty shillings. To my daughter Dorcas one hundred pounds, and also all the goods and chattels which are belonging unto me and that are in the hands of my brother Mr. Edmond Batter in New England, to be conveyed over according to the discretion of my said overseers, and half my trunk of linen and one silver bowl and a silver cup. I give and bequeath unto my brother Mr. Christopher Batt the sum of five pounds. And whereas I do conceive that Elizabeth my wife is now with child my will and meaning is and I do hereby give and bequeathe unto such child, if it shall be born alive, the sum of one hundred pounds and two silver bowls, to be paid and delivered unto him or her when they shall attain to the full age of twenty and one years, or sooner if to my said wife it shall seem meet. And in case the said child shall happen do die before it shall attain to the full age of twenty and one years then my will and meaning is that some part of the said sum of one hundred pounds shall be disposed for the use, benefit and behoof of my said daughter Dorcas according to the discretion of my said executrix. The residue of my goods &c. I give and bequeath unto the said Elizabeth my wife, desiring her, out of that estate that I have herein bequeathed unto her, to allow unto my mother in law ten pounds a year so long as she shall live, to be paid quarterly unto her &c. And I make, ordain &c. the said Elizabeth my wife the sole and only executrix and my loving friend Mr. Humfrey Ditton the elder and my brother Mr. Francis Dove overeers of this my last will &c., and for their pains therein to be taken I do hereby give and bequeath unto them ten shillings apiece to buy them rings.

Rivers, 54.

[The testator Richard Allwood, the brother-in-law of Peter Thacher and of Christopher Batt, had it seems another brother-in-law in New England, namely, Edmund Batter, who was a man of some account in Salem. He owned and occupied a narrow strip of land on the north side of Essex Street running from Washington Street (where his house stood) back to North Street.—H. F. WATERS.]

BENNETT SWAYNE the elder of the City of New Sarum, in the County of Wilts, gent, 3 December 1630, proved 27 January 1630. My body to be interred in the parish church of St Edmond's, within the said city. To the same church ten shillings and to the poor within that parish forty shillings. To the poor within St Martin's parish forty shillings, vizt twenty shillings to the poor of that parish within the precincts of the city and the other twenty shillings to the poor of Milford that are within the same parish and without the liberty of the city. To the poor of Laverstocke parish ten shillings. To my old servant Greenway ten shillings and to my servant Graye and his fellow five shillings apiece. To my maid servant Emms Brachem and man servant Thomas Battyn twenty shillings apiece and to my servant William Knowlton five shillings. To my sister Sibbell Mitchell five pounds, to be paid unto her within six months next after my death. To my daughter Jane Swayne one hundred and fifty pounds in money and her mother's drinking bowl tipped with silver, to be paid and delivered unto her at her age of one and twenty years or day of her marriage, which of them shall first and next happen. To my daughter Jone Swayne one hundred and fifty pounds and one silver bowl, to be paid and delivered (as to her sister Jane). To my son Richard Swayne one hundred and fifty pounds and one silver bowl, to be paid and delivered at his age of one and twenty. To my daughter Rebecca Swayne one hundred and fifty pounds and one silver bowl, to be paid and delivered (as to her sisters). To John Swayne my eldest son ten quarters of good seed barley at or before the five and twentieth day of March now next coming. To my daughter in law Anne Swayne, my son John's wife, my double gilded salt having a top and a bottom. To my said son John my signet ring. To my daughter Christian Pewde, the wife of William Pewde, ten pounds in money and my gilded stone cup, and unto William, Martha and Andrew Pewde, her children, to each of them three pounds six shillings and eight pence apiece, which I appoint shall be paid unto their father for their uses within twelve months next after my decease. To my daughter Margaret Batt, the wife of Thomas Batt, twenty pounds in twelve months &c. To the said Margaret Batt my silver teen. To my said son Richard Swayne & the heirs of his body lawfully to be begotten the lease of my house in Gilderland Street which I bought of Robert Holmes gen^t and all the term and estate which I have thereof and therein yet to come and unexpired; but if he die without lawful issue before his said age of one and twenty I give the said lease unto my said daughter Jane Swayne &c., remainder to my right heirs forever. I give the lease of the messuage in Winchester Street, wherein I now dwell, and all the term of years therein yet to come, with all the glass, wainscot and benches in and about the same, unto the said John Swayne my son and his lawfully begotten heirs, remainder to my son Bennett Swayne, next to my son Richard Swayne. But my wife Bridget shall hold and enjoy the said messuage &c,—during the term of her life, if she shall so long remain a widow, paying the rent thereof to the Dean and Chapter of the Cathedral Church of Sarum and keeping the same in reparations and in tenantable manner. The residue of my goods &c. I give to Bridgett my wife and Bennett Swayne my son, and I make them sole executors. And I do nominate my loving brother in law Andrew Pewde gen^t Thomas Harwood gen^t, John Vyninge, John Barrowe the elder and William Bowles gen^t overseers, and I do give to each of them in token of my love twenty shillings apiece to make each of them a ring.

Wit: Thomas Kynton *als* Matthew, William Bowles, William Widnoll and Richard Tuck.   St John, 8.

[Rebecca, daughter of Bennet Swayne the testator, came to New England and died at Ipswich, Mass., July 21, 1695. She married 1st, Henry Byley; 2d, John Hall; 3d, Rev. William Worcester; and 4th, Deputy Gov. Samuel Symonds. For a pedigree and other facts concerning the Swayne family, see Appletons' Ancestry of Priscilla Baker, pp. 132–7.—EDITOR.]

HENRY BILEY the elder, of the City of New Sarum in the County of Wilts gen^t, 18 October 1633, proved 23 June 1634. To the parish church of S^t. Edmond's twenty shillings, and twenty shillings more to the poor of the same parish. To the Mayor and Commonalty of the City three pounds six shilling eight pence, to be employed in the working house within the said city towards the setting of the poor there at work. To my grandson

Henry Biley ten pounds in money and my bedstead and one of my great chests and my square table board and my cupboard which are in my great chamber, and my cupboard in my hall, and the cupboard and tableboard in my kitchen, and one of my silver beakers, and my biggest brass pot, save one which is to the Lymbeeke, and my biggest brass kettle, and my second tyled house or standing in the Row by the Corn-market, next to the "pillowry," and all my vats &c. &c. in and about my tan-house &c. To my grandson John Biley twenty pounds, to my grand daughter Mary Biley ten pounds and a silver beaker, to my grandchildren Edward, Elizabeth and William Biley ten pounds apiece, to my grandson Christopher Batt, son of Thomas Batt, gen[t] deceased, twenty pounds in money and my uppermost tyled house or standing in the Market-place near to M[r] Thomas Elliott's house there, to my grandson Thomas Batt, son of said Thomas deceased, twenty pounds, to my grand daughters Mary and Dorothy Batt, daughters of said Thomas deceased, fifty pounds each, to my great grandchildren Christopher, Anne and Jane Batt, children of said grandson Christopher Batt, forty shillings each, and forty shillings to my great grand daughter Elizabeth Batt, daughter of said grandson Thomas Batt. Forty shillings to my servant John Hulett. To my grand daughter Alice Batt, daughter of said Thomas deceased, one hundred pounds in money and my bowl of silver and gilt having a "Poesy" about it and my biggest brass pot and lymbecke thereto used &c. To my granddaughters Elizabeth and Margery Batt fifty pounds each. My grandsons Christopher Batt, and Henry Biley and grand daughter Alice Batt shall have, hold, use, occupy and enjoy all my lands and tenements in Wellowe and my dwelling house, tan house, orchards and gardens in New Sarum and on the West side of the river Avon and all my stock of money, bark, hides, leather &c., and shall receive and take the rents and profits towards the maintenance and keeping of my wife and family &c. My son Henry Biley to be executor and friends Thomas Hill and Michael Mackerell and grandson Christopher Batt over-seers.   Seager, 60.

[See REGISTER, Vol. 42, p. 308; and annotations on wills of Thomas, Clement and Peter Thacher, *ante* pp. 677–9, and Richard Alwood, p. 680.—EDITOR.]

GRACE HEATH of London, widow, 16 December 1654, proved 16 February 1654. My body to be buried in the parish church of S[t] Stephen's, Coleman Street, where I do now dwell. To my loving cousin Bennett Swaine and his children one hundred pounds, each one of them to have an equal and ratable part thereof. To my cousin Rebecca Worster and her two children (videlicet) John Hall and Rebecca Byly one hundred pounds, to be parted and divided as aforesaid. To my cousin Henry Byly one hundred and fifty pounds, to my cousin Elizabeth Cousins ten pounds, to my cousin Elizabeth Barrett twenty pounds, to Master William Taylor, preacher, ten pounds and to his wife twenty shillings to make her a ring to wear in remembrance of me, and to his four children ten shillings apiece to make them rings. To Master George Griffeth of London, merchant, ten pounds and to his wife twenty shillings and to his son and daughter ten shillings. To Master Osburt Fowler and his wife twenty shillings apiece, to make them rings. To the poor of St. Stephen's Coleman Street ten pounds. To my son in law Thomas Heath twenty pounds and to his wife twenty shillings to make her a ring. To my son in law John Heath twenty pounds and to my son in law Jeffery Heath the lease of my now dwelling house in Coleman Street, upon condition that he do and shall yearly, during the term of my said lease pay unto mine executrix the clear yearly payment and sum of ten pounds. I give to the wife of the said Jeffery Heath twenty shillings to make her a ring. The residue of my estate I give and bequeath unto my loving sister Bridget Swayne, widow, and I do make and ordain my said sister Bridget Swayne full and sole executrix and my loving friends Master William Taylor and Master George Griffeth overseers.

The testatrix made a codicil to the above will, Thursday 18 January 1654. Among other things she appointed her cousin Bennett Swaine to be co-executor with her sister Bridgett Swayne. The will (with its codicil) was proved by Bennett Swayne, power being reserved to make the like probate and grant the like administration unto Bridgett Swayne, the other executor, when she should come and in legal manner desire the same.

Aylett, 40.

JOHN HALL of London, goldsmith, 13 April 1691, proved 6 May 1691. I will and bequeath all my household goods, household plate and my wearing jewells and my wearing rings to my most dear and entirely beloved wife, Elizabeth Hall, excepting such things which by me or my said wife have been given to my dear daughter Elizabeth Hall to furnish her closet. To my said wife fifty pieces of gold of the value of fifty pounds sterling, all my messuages &c. in St. Nicholas Lane and Abchurch Lane in the parishes of St. Nicholas Acon and St. Mary Abchurch, London, and the lease thereof granted by the Master and Wardens and Brethren and Sisters of the Guild or Fraternity of the blessed Mary the Virgin of the Mistery of the Drapers, London, unto my late uncle James Hall deceased, of whose last Will and testament I am executor, &c. To my wife all my messuages &c. which are held by lease of the Governors of St. Thomas Hospital in Southwark, which late belonged to Mr. Samuel Lynne deceased, late father of my said wife; and I do hereby ratify and confirm the settlement by me formerly made on my said wife Elizabeth Hall, of the copyhold or customary messuages &c. in Islington, Middlesex, and another settlement made by Indenture dated 12 October 1686, by Fine and Recovery, wherein contained two messuages in St Nicholas Lane and Lumbard Street, in the parish of St Nicholas Acon, are limited to the use of me and my said wife and after our deaths to the use of my daughter Elizabeth. To my said daughter my messuages &c. in Candlewick *als* Cannon Street, in the parish of St. Clement's Eastcheap, London, now or late in the tenure of John Fryer, which was heretofore bought of Mr. Joseph Curtis and others by my uncle James Hall deceased and since his death is descended on me and my heirs. To the said Elizabeth my messuage &c. in St Olave's Southwark, held by lease of the Co. of Drapers. To my said daughter my Poole's two volumes of English Annotations, Littleton's Dictionary, my Quarto Bible of the old translation, fine paper, printed 1582, all Dr Manton's, Dr Goughes, Bishop Hall's and Mr. Charnock's works and "Foxes Martriologie" in three volumes, which are in my Library. I give to my cousin Robert Hale, my sister Rebecca Hale's son deceased, my five volumes of Poole's Synopsis Criticorum, Ainsworth's Annotations and Mellificium Theologicum. All the rest of my library I give to my said wife Elizabeth. I give to my ever honored mother Rebecca Hall *als* Symonds twenty pounds, in full of all demands, and to my maid servant Ruth Creswell five pounds. I give to my uncle Mr. Bennett Swayne and to my aunt Swayne, his wife, and to my cousin Anne Slaughter, my said cousin Robert Hale, my aunt Rotherforth, my aunt Mary Oliver, my cousin Sarah Evans, my cousin Mary Akerod, Mr. Samuel Layfield, my cousins Humphrey Hall of Hertfordshire, Daniel Hall of Gravesend, Dorothy Leadford and Sarah Soutton ten shillings apiece to buy them rings. I give forty shillings to the poor of the parish of Islington, where I now live, to be distributed as the Vestry shall think fit. The Residue of my goods &c. I give to be equally divided and parted between my said most dear and beloved wife Elizabeth Hall and my said daughter Elizabeth Hall. Reference to a deed of Settlement of a messuage in St Nicholas Lane on the East side thereof, in the parish of St. Martin Orgars &c. Wife Elizabeth to be sole executrix and my cousin Mr. Bennett Swayne and Mr. Samuel Read of London, merchant, to be guardians to my said daughter until she shall attain her age of one and twenty or be married, she not to marry without the consent of her mother. I give to my said cousin Bennett Swayne six pounds and to the said Samuel Read three pounds.

Among the witnesses was a Robert Hall.   Vere, 81.

[The records of old Norfolk County, Massachusetts, which are now lodged in Salem Court Houses, contain considerable information about the Byleys and Halls. I find that Mrs. Rebecca Hall, widow, was making a conveyance to Henry Ambrose, carpenter, as early as 18 Nov. 1647. By the death of her former husband, Mr. Henry Byley, she had become possessed of certain lands in Salisbury (Mass.). These she made over to her two children Henry and Rebecca Byley, as part of their portion, at the time of her marriage with Mr. John Hall.

Mr. John Hall was maried to Mrs Rebecca Bylie by ye Worship. Mr Symon Bradstreet the 3^d day of April 1641.

John Hall the sonne of Mr John Hall and Rebecka his wife was borne the 18th of the 1st mo. 1641–2.

Mr William Worcester was married to Mrs Rebecka Hall the 22^d of the 5th mo. 1650.

John Hale married Rebecca, daughter of Henry Byley of Salisbury, 15 December 1664. Their daughter Rebecca was born 28 April 1666, and their son Robert was born 3 November 1668. The latter was graduated at Harvard College 1686, and lived and died in Beverly. He took a high position in the affairs of his town and county, and also of the Province. Years ago I saw in the rooms of the American Antiquarian Society at Worcester, Massachusetts, among the papers probably received from the executor of the Will of the Revd William Bentley, D.D., some interesting memoranda and letters which had evidently belonged to Robert Hale, Esq., and which threw additional light upon his family connections in old England.

The reference made by John Hall of Islington to the will of his late uncle James Hall, deceased, led me to hunt for that will, with the following result:]

JAMES HALL of St Clement East Cheap, citizen and draper of London, 16 November 1665, proved 19 November 1686. My body to be decently buried in the chancel of the parish church of St. Clament's East Cheap, and my executors shall lay out and expend two hundred pounds upon my funeral and shall give thereat to five and thirty poor men, to appear with black gowns, twenty shillings apiece, and two hundred rings, of ten shillings price each ring, to so many persons to be invited to my funeral. I give my three messuages &c. in Lumbard Street and in St Nicholas Lane, in the parish of St Nicholas Acon, commonly called or known by the several names or signs of the Flying Horse, the Hen and Chickens and the Golden Lion, now or late in the several tenures &c. of Henry Bourne, David King and of one Dodsworth, unto my loving mother Sarah Wraxall of London, widow, for and during the term of her natural life only, and after her decease then unto my nephew John Hall of London, merchant, and to the heirs male of his body lawfully to be forgotten, remainder to my cousin Humphrey Hall, eldest son of my uncle Thomas Hall &c., then to my cousin Daniel Hall, youngest son of my said uncle Thomas, and to his heirs forever. I give my messuage &c. in St. Nicholas Lane in the parish of St. Martins Orgars, commonly called or known by the name or sign of the Red Lion, now in the tenure &c. of William Clarke, to my said nephew John Hall and his heirs forever (conditioned on payment of certain legacies). I give my three messuages &c. in Lamb Alley without Bishopsgate, in the parish of St. Buttolph Bishopsgate, unto Aldermen William Hooker, grocer, John Jefferies, baker, Thomas Ward, apothecary, William Richards, clothworker, Benoni Honywood, merchant taylor, Thomas Trayton, draper, Thomas Grave, innholder, Thomas Meadow, draper, Harvey Seale, butcher, and John Lee, goldsmith, citizens of London and inhabitants within the said parish of St. Clements, East Cheap, forever, upon Trust that they shall, by and with the yearly rents and profits of the said three messuages &c. maintain and kept a Lecture, to be preached upon every Wednesday in the afternoon in every week from the Feast day of St. Michael the Archangel to the Feast day of the Annunciation of the blessed Virgin Mary, in every year successively forever, in the parish church of St. Clement East Cheap aforesaid by some godly and learned minister of God's word, to be from time to time chosen and appointed thereunto by the inhabitants of the said parish, to be assembled at their Vestry for that purpose &c. Provision made for the succession of the Feoffees. I give and bequeath unto my said mother Sarah Wraxall one hundred pounds of lawful money and twenty pieces of old gold, ten of them being two and twenty shillings each piece and the other ten being twenty shillings each piece, and all my plate (except two silver and gilt spoons hereafter mentioned). To my cousin Sarah Bewley, daughter of my sister Sarah Berry, fifty pounds. To my friend Mrs Anne Williams at the sign of the Ship in St. Clement's Lane, widow, ten pounds to buy her a tankard. To the poor of certain parishes. To St Bartholomew's Hospital forty pounds, to be disposed at the discretion of my cousin Mills, treasurer thore. To Christ's Hospital fifty pounds. To the three prisons viz* Ludgate and the two Compters, towards the relief of poor debtors, ten pounds to each prison. To my two executors eight yards and a half of fine black cloth, of twenty shillings the yard, for mourning, and unto my said mother Sarah Wraxall fifty pounds for mourning for her self and her servant, and unto my said sister Sarah Berry twelve pounds for mourning for herself and servant &c. The residue I give to my said nephew John Hall and I make my said nephew John Hall and my friend Robert Mordant executors.

8° Septembris 1686. Personally appeared Samuel Layfield of St. Michael Cornhill, London, goldsmith, aged forty years or thereabouts, the husband of Mary Oliver, niece of James Hall late of London, draper, deceased, by Mary his sister, and did depose that he went to visit James Hall deceased &c. on Tuesday the tenth of August last past, who was then very dangerously ill at his house, in Lamb Alley in the parish of St. Buttolph Bishopsgate, and there he staid and watched with him in his chamber until three of the clock in the morning, about which time the said James Hall departed this life, and this deponent assisted in the laying forth his body, and about five or six of the clock in the said morning he did send for Mr. John Hall, the said deceased's nephew, and he came thither about six of the clock and he immediately sent for Mr. Thomas Fige and Mr. Edward Johnson, two of the deceased's neighbors, and he the said Mr. John Hall did not go up the stairs into the said deceased's chamber until they the said Mr. Fyge and Mr. Johnson came, and then they went up all together and there agreed to search amongst the said deceased's writings for a Will, and

this said deponent took out of the pocket of the breeches which the said
deceased did usually wear and were then in his said chamber a bunch of
keys and a watch, one of which keyes belonged to a trunk which stood in
the chamber, which they unlocked (having searched two small trunks before) but in that trunk there were several writings of concern, a bag of
money with a ticket upon it to be fifty pounds, a purse with a quantity of
gold in it, being ninety nine guineas, and two broad twenty shilling pieces,
in which said trunk there was also found, wrapt up in a paper upon which
were endorsed these words The Last Will and Testament of James Hall,
made the sixteenth day of November 1665, to be delivered to his executors
Mr. John Hall and Mr. Robert Mordant, or one of them, which paper
seemed to have formerly sealed but at the said finding was unsealed, which
being opened they found eight sheets of paper fixed together on the top
with red tape, and a seal thereupon, which was immediately, in the presence
of all the said four persons perused and read, and they did observe and take
notice that the words James Hall were subscribed to the bottom of every
of the said sheets and they also took notice of the several obliterations (then
follows a list of such obliterations).   And they did observe that by the
numbers of the sheets there were two wanting, vizt the 6th and 7th, but those
that were so found the said Mr. John Hall took into his custody and locked
up the said trunk again, and the said Mr. Hall also kept the key thereof,
and immediately thereupon they searched and rummaged all trunks, boxes
and other places where they could imagine any other will might be placed
or laid because that which they had found was of so ancient a date.   And
this deponent doth further depose that by the order of the said Mr. John
Hall he did remove the said trunk, wherein the said money was, and the
said sheets &c., and also two other little trunks to his own house, for better
security, and there locked them into his closet, the said trunks being locked
and the said Mr John Hall having the keys in his custody, as aforesaid.
And that, on or about the nineteenth of the said month of August the said
Mr. John Hall and this deponent looking over the remaining papers in the
said trunk, which had not been opened since the bringing the same to his,
this deponent's, house, and there, towards the bottom of the said trunk,
they found two other sheets numbered 6 and 7, with several obliterations
and blottings, torn at the top and at the bottom, and that the said eight
sheets, so fixed together as aforesaid, and the said two sheets " soe loose
obliterated and torne," and annexed to this his deposition, were at the time
of finding thereof as they now are.   Then follows a deposition (of the same
general purport) made by Thomas Fyge and Edward Johnson jointly 8
September 1686.   Lloyd, 43.

[The above will, which is undoubtedly the will referred to by John Hall as
that of his uncle James, seems to place this family.   In the Visitation of London (1633–4–5), may be found the following pedigree of Hall, of Bishopsgate:
James, the fourth son of John and Sarah Hall, was evidently the testator of
the will of which I have just given an abstract.   His mother, Sarah, had probably remarried —— Wraxall; his brother John (the second son) was the one who
went to New England and married the widow Rebecca Byley, by whom he had
the son John who afterwards came to England and lived and died at Islington.
Sarah, the eldest daughter of John and Sarah Hall, had married —— Berry and
had a daughter Sarah married to —— Bewley.   Mary, the fourth daughter,
married —— Oliver and had a daughter Mary, wife in 1686 of Samuel Layfield.
Their cousins Humfrey and Daniel Hall, sons of Thomas and Benet Hall, seem
to have been living in 1691, the former in Hertfordshire and the latter at
Gravesend.   In a future number I hope to give other wills referring to John
Hall of Islington, and also to New England.   HENRY F. WATERS.]

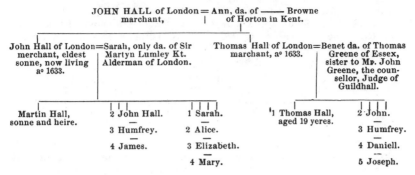

JOHN HALL of London = Ann, da. of —— Browne
marchant, | of Horton in Kent.

John Hall of London = Sarah, only da. of Sir
merchant, eldest | Martyn Lumley Kt.
sonne, now living | Alderman of London.
aº 1633.

Thomas Hall of London = Benet da. of Thomas
marchant, aº 1633. | Greene of Essex,
sister to Mr. John
Greene, the coun-
sellor, Judge of
Guildhall.

Martin Hall,
sonne and heire.

2 John Hall.
—
3 Humfrey.
—
4 James.

1 Sarah.
—
2 Alice.
—
3 Elizabeth.
—
4 Mary.

¹1 Thomas Hall,
aged 19 yeres.

2 John.
—
3 Humfrey.
—
4 Daniell.
—
5 Joseph.

CICELY HILL of London, widow, 7 August 1621, proved 14 September
1621. I give to the daughter of my late deceased sister Alice, dwelling in
Manchester in the County of Lancaster, twenty shillings and two of my
gowns, two petticoats, a kirtle and two aprons. To Effie Clyffe my cham-
lett pettycoate. I give and bequeath to Hanna Jadwyn, the daughter of
Thomas Jadwyn, scrivener, twenty shillings. .To Dorothy Marden twenty
shillings. To the three maiden children of Mr. George Johnson, citizen
and merchant tailor of London, ten shillings apiece.- To Mary, Ann and
Hester, the daughters of my cousin Peter Hynde, citizen and embroiderer
of London, ten shillings apiece. I give to Elizabeth Jadwin the wife of the
aforesaid Thomas Jadwyn, ten shillings. To my brother James Radley
forty shillings. To my cousin Thomas Harrison of Manchester twenty
shillings. To my cousin John Harrison, his son, twenty shillings. To my
good friends Mrs. Alice Bridgitt and to the aforesaid Thomas Jadwyn ten
shillings apiece. I give to Mrs. Owen ten shillings. To William Johnson
ten shillings. To the wife of William Latham ten shillings. To George
Latham their son my featherbed, flockbed, boulster and rugs. To Catherine
Madoxe, daughter of the said George Johnson, ten shillings and all my
pewter. To Mr Edward Steney clerk ten shillings. To Mr. Young, curate
of the parish where I now dwell, ten shillings. To the poor of the parish
ten shillings. Tothe eldest son of my deceased sister Alice twenty shillings. To my kinsman William Radley forty shillings. To Winnifred
Latham daughter of William Latham ten shillings. To Rebecca Sayers
ten shillings. The residue to my cousin Peter Hynde and Katherine Johnson, wife of George Johnson, whom I make executors.   Dale, 77.

WILLIAM LYNN, citizen and carpenter of London, 20 July 1678, proved
10 June 1680. My body to be buried in the parish church of St. Thomas
the Apostle, Southwark. To my wife Mary the lease of my ground called
The Timber Yard, bearing date 1 January 1658; the said lease given me by
the last will of my father, Samuel Lynn deceased, held of the Governors of
the Hospital of St. Thomas and situate in the parish of St. Thomas the
Apostle in Southwark, aforesaid. I give her also the lease of the house I
now dwell in (in the same parish) held of John Hall and Elizabeth his
wife of Islington, Middlesex, gent. To my eldest son William Lynn my
moiety of four messuages &c. in Church Yard Alley near Fetter Lane, he
to pay twenty pounds to my daughter Mary Lynn, fifty pounds to my son
Samuel and one hundred pounds to my son John. To my daughter Elizabeth Lynn my messuage &c., now divided into two tenements, in Tooly
Street, in the parish of St. Olaves, Southwark, she to pay fifty pounds to

my daughter Mary and one hundred pounds to my son Richard Lynn.   My
wife Mary to be sole executrix and my trusty and well beloved friends Mr.
John Reve and my brother Mr. John Hall of Islington to assist my executrix.   A codicil dated 15 December 1679.

John Hall one of the witnesses.   Bath, 82.

[The John Hall of Islington here called brother was the goldsmith whose will
was given in the January number of the REGISTER (*ante*, p. 683). The following wills also relate to his family and their connections, as a reference to the
pedigree of the family in the Visitation of London (Harleian Soc. Pub.), will
show.   HENRY F. WATERS.]

JOHN HALL the elder, citizen and draper of London, 16 January 1617,
proved 19 December 1618.   My body to be buried in the parish church of
St Nicholas Acon in London where I now dwell and have remained nine
and fifty years and more, I praise God.   To my son John my three messuages or tenements in Lumbard Street and St Nicholas Lane, whereof one
is in the tenure of Edmond Tennant, citizen and clothworker of London,
another in the tenure of Richard Mills, draper, and the other in the tenure
of Benjamin Buckstone, grocer; with remainder to my second son Humfrey
Hall, and next to my third son Thomas.   My wife Anne shall have her
full third part of the rents of the said three messuages during her natural
life.   To my son John my garden and a fair tenement thereon builded, in
the parish of St Buttolph without Bishopsgate, in an Alley there called
Lambe Alley.   To my son Thomas &c. a yearly rent charge of thirty three
shillings four pence, in Pulborow, given and bequeathed unto me by the
last will of Thomas Hall of Horsham Sussex, gen^t, deceased.   To the said
Thomas all other my lands &c. in Sussex.   My goods to be divided into
three parts, of which one part to my wife Anne.   Another part to my son
John, for that I have advanced all the rest of my children long sithence and
have not given any advancement or child's portion unto the said John.   To
my son in law Richard Bate and Anne his wife, whom I have already fully
advanced, I give four pounds, to my son in law Daniel Gossege and Alice
his wife the like legacy of four pounds, to my son in law Miles Corney and
Gartred his wife, the like legacy, to my son Humfrey the like legacy, to
my son Thomas the like.   To my son Anthony whom I have advanced and
satisfied his child's portion since his full age, forty shillings and to my son
Daniel Hall the same.   To Elizabeth daughter of Richard Bate four pounds
at one and twenty or day of marriage.   My son John to be full and sole
executor and my son Humfrey Hall and my son in law Daniel Gossege to
be overseers.

By a codicil dated 22 October 1618 he gives to cousin John Englishe
four pounds and to cousin Mary Kettelye four pounds for a remembrance.
                                                        Meade, 127.

THOMAS HALL citizen and haberdasher of London, 6 March 1634, proved
14 April 1635.   My body to be buried in the church of St Nicholas Acon.
My worldly goods (my debts being paid and funerals discharged) to be
divided into three equal parts, according to the custom of the City of London; one third thereof to my wife Bennett Hall, another third to my children and the other third I give and devise &c.   To my brother Daniel
fifteen pounds if my other brothers will give him so much to set him free.
If not then I give him five pounds.   To my kinswoman Anne Lewis forty
shillings.   To Mr. John Jones, the parson of St Nicholas Acon forty shillings for a sermon at my funeral in the said parish, where I desire to be

buried by my father and mother. The residue to my wife and children half to her and half to them (other bequests omitted). I make my wife Bennett Hall sole executrix and my brothers M[r] John Greene and M[r] John Hall my overseers. My land in Enfield Middlesex to my eldest son Thomas and his heirs. Sadler, 36.

SIR MARTIN LUMLEY knight, citizen and Alderman of London 1 September 7th Charles, A. D. 1631, proved 15 July 1634. To Sarah Hall, the daughter of my son in law John Hall and Sarah his now wife, the daughter of me the said Sir Martyn Lumley, four hundred pounds at such time as she shall be married, upon the condition that it be with the consent and approbation of my son and heir Martin Lumley. To my sister Elizabeth Archer ten pounds to buy her some token and I also give her mourning to wear at my funeral. To my sister Alice Woodrove two parts of my now wife's gold chain, in three parts being divided; that is to say so much thereof as was my late deceased wife's and her sister's chain. To sundry poor. To M[r] Vowcher, parson of S[t] Peters in London, whereof I am a parishioner, five pounds, and I give him mourning to wear at my funeral. To M[r] Walker, preacher of God's word, ten pounds. To my son in law John Hall and my daughter Sara his wife and all their children mourning to wear at my funeral. To my cousin Inge and her husband mourning. To M[r] Kertridge and his wife and M[r] Hailes and his wife mourning to wear at my funeral. To Richard Rochdale ten pounds and mourning. To Frances Booren, wife of John Booren one annuity of five pounds by the year during her natural life. To Edward Litton one annuity of three pounds for life. To Judith Raymond the like annuity. The residue to my son and heir Martyn Lumley, whom I appoint full executor &c. Twenty pounds yearly rent charge on the messuage wherein I did late dwell, in the parish of S[t] John the Evangelist, called the Black Boy, to the church wardens of S[t] Helen's Bishopsgate Street, for the establishing and settling of a lecture or a sermon forever to be preached in the said church of S[t] Helen's upon the Tuesday in every week weekly and in the evening of the same day, from the feast day of St. Michael the Archangel unto the feast day of the Annunciation of our blessed Lady S[t] Mary, to the honor and glory of God and comfort of the auditory; the said churchwardens to pay it unto a good and godly, religious divine in consideration of his pains to be taken in preaching such sermon or lecture. The said sermon or lecture always to begin about five of the clock in the evening. Another yearly rent charge of four pounds out of the aforesaid messuage to be distributed annually amongst the poor householders inhabiting within the said parish of St. Helen's. To my daughter Sarah wife of John Hall one hundred pounds a year for life. Other provisions for Sarah Hall the grand daughter.

A codicil 23 March 1631. To my grandchildren Martin Hall, John Hall, Humphrey Hall, James Hall, Alice Hall, Mary Hall and Elizabeth Hall, the children of the said John Hall by my said daughter Sarah, his now wife, fourteen hundred pounds, or two hundred pounds apiece to Martyn, John, Humphrey and James at their several ages of one and twenty and to Alice, Mary and Elizabeth at one and twenty or days of marriage. To my grandchild Prudence Lumley daughter of my son and heir Martin Lumley by Jone his late wife deceased, one hundred pounds wherewith to buy her jewels.

Another codicil 30 June 1634. My kind and loving wife Dame Mary Lumley shall have the use of all my mansion and dwelling house wherein

I now dwell, in Wood Street London for one year &c.   Other provisions and bequests.   Christ's Hospital, whereof I am President.   To Mr Hall the sword bearer twenty nobles.   To widow Perkins five marks.   To Richard Lumley fifty pounds.   Seager, 65.

[A pedigree of this family (under the name of Lomley) may be found in the Visitation of Essex, 1634 (Harleian Soc. Pub.), vol. 1, p. 436. His daughter Sarah, after the death of her husband John Hall, became the wife of Abraham Wraxall, as is shown by her will which here follows.   HENRY F. WATERS.]

SARAH WRAXALL of St. Bartholomews the Little, near the Royal Exchange in London, widow, late wife and relict of Abraham Wraxall, late of Fleet Street, London, gen. deceased, 8 July 1665, proved 14 December 1668.   Calls herself of great age.   My body to be buried in the Parish Church of St. Hellens in Bishopsgate Street, London, as near to my father Sir Martin Lumley, late of London, alderman deceased, as may be.   To my daughter Sarah Berry, wife of Thomas Berry of London gen^t, twenty shillings (and sundry wearing apparell &c.).   To my daughter Elizabeth Radham, wife of John Radham of Northumberland, five and twenty pounds of lawful money of England, which I will, after her decease, shall be paid and distributed to and for the use of her child and children.   To my daughter Mary Oliver, wife of Richard Oliver, five and twenty pounds, to be paid and distributed to and for the use of her child and children.   To my grandchild Sarah Bewley, wife of John Bewley, twenty shillings.   To my grandchildren Edward, Dorothy and Sarah Blackwell, children of my late daughter Alice Blackwell late wife of Gervas Blackwell who now is a linen draper in Newgate Market, twenty shillings apiece.   To my grandson John Hall, merchant, twenty shillings.   To my maid servant Kath. Bridges three pounds.   To one (———) Long, daughter of Mrs Bourne, ten shillings.   (To others.)   I desire that Mr Merriton, the minister and now pastor of St. Michael Cornhill London, may preach my funeral sermon, and I give him forty shillings.   I give a silver pot with two ears (and other pieces of plate) to my son James Hall, draper in Cannon Street, all of which plate are in and about my lodging chamber.   The residue to my said son James whom I make sole executor &c.   To my daughter Sarah Berry my wedding ring with a diamond in it.   Hene, 162.

HUMPHREY HALL citizen and girdler of London 29 December 1641, proved 21 November 1648.   By deed bearing date 24 December (this instant month) I have assigned and conveyed unto Richard Bateman, William Bateman and Anthony Bateman, sons of the Worshipful my good friend Robert Bateman the Chamberlain of London all my estate and term of years in my two tenements situate in the parishes of St. Nicholas Acon and St. Mary Abchurch London, to me demised by lease by my late father John Hall deceased, upon sundry trusts.   To my daughters Elizabeth Barnes and Sarah Griffith five pounds.   To my wife Mercy Hall one annuity of fourteen pounds issuing out of the said two tenements in London.   To Mary Townley now the wife of Mr. Lawrence Townely of Norwich, who was heretofore the wife of my son John Hall the yearly rent of ten pounds payable out of the rents of the said two houses.   Twenty pounds per annum for the use of the poor in the Hospital that I have built at Brandon *alias* Brandon Ferry in Suffolk.   My desire and direction is that my brother Danyell Hall, whom God hath in his mercy chastized by taking from him his estate, may during his life be reader of divine service to the poor of the Hospital and to receive his convenient dwelling in the said

Hospital, with four pounds per annum as Curate. Reference to brother John Hall and to testator's dwelling house at Brandon. Essex, 165.

[A reference to the pedigree of Hall of London will show what relation the testator of the above will bore to our John Hall of Hampton, and to John Hall the goldsmith of Islington. HENRY F. WATERS.]

THOMAS SNOWE of East Camell, Somerset, 6 August 1583, proved 5 October 1583. My body to be buried in the churchyard of East Camell. Son Robert (a minor). Son William (a minor). Wife Jone. Daughter Jane. Daughter Susan. Daughter Edith (due her under her grandmother's will). Son John Snowe.

One of the witnesses was Peter Thatcher, minister. Butts, 2.

GEFFREY BIGGE of Patney, Wilts, clerk, 15 October 1630, proved 3 May 1632. I give to Mr. Peter Thatcher a little to help his too small stipend for his painful and profitable ministry in the parish church of St. Edmunds in Sarum, the sum of five pounds, to be paid within half a year after my decease if he shall be then incumbent there. My son in law Joseph Bate and my son in law John Dove. My daughter Anne Bate and her son Joseph Bate. My daughter Elizabeth Dove and her eldest daughter Anne Dove. My wife Hester Bygge. The children of my brother Edmund Bygge (saving Edmond and Richard). To Mr. Edward Gough the Concordance that my Reverend and loving father gave me at his decease. My loving friend and neighbor Mr. John White, vicar of Chirton. My nephew Richard Bigge. My brother Edmund Bigge of Wilfford Clerk.

Witnessed by John White clerk and the probate granted by Peter Thatcher clerk, by virtue of a Commission. Audley, 55.

[The above two wills I thought worth saving as of interest to the Thachers of New England. HENRY F. WATERS.]

MARGARET CHEESEMAN of St. Mary Magdalen Bermondsey widow, 15 January 1679, proved 21 July 1680. My overseers shall disburse, expend and lay out for my funeral expenses and charges fifty pounds. To the poor of this parish five pounds. To all the children of my very loving kinsman Mr Lemuel Mason the elder in Virginia that shall be living in Virginia at the time of my decease ten pounds apiece, to remain in the hands of my executors until they shall attain to their several ages of one and twenty years or days of marriage. To my Cousin Elizabeth Theleball, now living in Virginia, five pounds. To all her children living at time of my decease five pounds apiece. To John Matthews, living in Virginia, who was brother by the mother's side to my late granddaughter Anne Cheeseman deceased, five pounds and a diamond ring which formerly was his sister's. To my kinswoman Anne Gayney twelve pence. To my god daughter Margaret Mason, who lives with me, one hundred and fifty pounds and the lease of my house and all the plate I had of John Harrison. The rest of my plate I give to the children of my said cousin Lemuel Mason as followeth (i.e.) to Alice Mason a great beaker, to Elizabeth a tankard, to Anne a tankard and to Abigail, Mary and Dynah all the rest of my plate, to be equally divided &c, and to Lemuel Mason the younger my best great ring. Five pounds apiece to Mr John Samuel, Mr. Thomas Gladwin, my said cousin Margaret Mason and Mrs. Mary Childe widow; and they to be overseers of my will. All the residue to my kinsman Mr Lemuel Mason in Virginia; and he to be executor; and my said god daughter Margaret Mason to be executor in trust only for the use and benefit of the Lemuel her father. Proved by Margaret Mason. Bath, 92.

[Lieut. John Chisman was of Elizabeth City in 1624 then aged 27, he had come out in the Flÿinge Hart in 1621, and with him was Edward Chisman, probably his brother, aged 22, who came in the Providence in 1623* and, in the last named year, a Thomas Chisman was also of Elizabeth City.† Lieut. Chisman had a patent for 200 acres of land on South side of Elizabeth River in 1626‡ & was still living in 1635§ & was probably the same John Chisman who, 9 Nov. 1646, is witness to an agreement between Lieut Francis Mason & William Dounman.||

William Gany was of Elizabeth City in 1624, aged 33, he came out in the George in 1616, his wife Anna, aged 24, came in the Bona Nova in 1620, their daughter Anna was born in Virginia before 1623¶ query if not the legatee of 12 d. in the will? Henrie Gany, aged 21, who came in the Dutie in 1619, is in the roll of servants of Francis Mason in the same Muster.** It is noteworthy that Alice & Margarie Gany where among the first names in Lieut. Francis Mason's list of Head Rights.††

But the most interesting portion of this valuable will lies in the clue which it affords to the probable English home of the Mason family and their connections. Elizabeth Theleball, as the writer has shown,‡‡ was the daughter of Lieut. Francis Mason & sister of Col. Lemuel Mason; the Ganey connection, before indicated, is made certain & the daughter Margaret accounted for. Thomas & George, sons, & Frances & Mary, daus. of Lemuel Mason, are not mentioned by name in the will, but were of course included in the gift of £10 to all the children " now living in Va."§§

The Registers of St. Mary Magdalen, Bermondsey, now in course of publication in the Genealogist, will no doubt afford information of very great value in this connection. They have at present, however, only reached the year 1604.|||| J. HENRY LEA.]

DENNIS HOLLISTER of the City of Bristol, grocer, 1 September 1675, with a codicil bearing date 6 July 1676, proved 21 July 1676. To my only son Dennis Hollister and his heirs forever my corner house and shop which I bought of Richard Jones, in the parish called Mary Part in Bristol, in which I now dwell, except a certain pavement over the kitchen, the full breadth of it one way and about half the breadth the other way, which shall be forever to my other house next adjoining, bought of James Hughes and Thomas Haynes, for an outlet and to preserve the lights of the said house from being stopped up. I give him also two low and ten high turkey work chairs with red leather cases standing in the Parlor (and other furniture). To my daughter Hannah Callowhill, wife of Thomas Callowhill, during her natural life, my new house, lately built in a place called the Fryars Orchard in the parish of Jamessas in the suburbs of the city of Bristol and my stable in the Fryars and my houses or tenements there, bought of Henry Lloyd, wherein one Nehemiah Hollister and one Jeane Partridge, widow, now dwell, and my warehouses and lofts bought of William, Robert and Thomas Challoner, in Peter's Parish near the East end of the Burying yard there; and after her death these warehouses to go to my grand daughter Sarah Callowhill, her eldest daughter, and to her heirs, with remainder to my grand daughter Hannah Callowhill. The houses and tenements bought of Henry Lloyd to go to my grand daughter Bridget Callowhill, with remainder to her sister Hannah. And the new house to go to Thomas Callowhill if he survive his wife, to hold for life, and then to my grandson Dennis Callowhill, his eldest son, with remainder to Thomas Callowhill, second son of my said daughter Hannah &c. To my daughter Lydia Jordan, wife of Thomas Jordan my new house lately built at Frampton Cot-

* Hotten, p. 252.　　　† Ibid. p. 185.　　　‡ Ibid. p. 274.
§ Note 25 in Head Rights, Reg. Jan. 1893, p. 70.
|| Lower Norf. Ct. Rec., Book iv., fo. 18b.　　　¶ Hotten, p. 256.
** Ibid. p. 251.　　　†† Head Rights, Reg. Jan. 1893, p. 63.
‡‡ Ibid, note 18, p. 68.　　　§§ Ibid, note 31, p. 70.
|||| Genealogist, vol. vi.–ix. and in progress.

terill, Gloucestershire, and all lands and pastures thereunto belonging, which I lately bought of Humphrey Hooke, knight. This for her natural life and then to her husband Thomas Jordan, for life, and next to my grand daughter Bridget Jordan, my daughter Lydia's eldest daughter, and a portion to my grand daughter Lydia Jordan. To my daughter Mary Hollister my new house bought of James Hughes and Thomas Haynes, in Mary part Street (and the outlet or pavement before referred to), and other property. To my daughter Phebe Hollister half of my Inn called the Whitehart, in Broad Street, one fourth part of which was my wife's inheritance and one fourth I lately bought of Anne Yeomans deceased, and one other fourth part I lately bought of Edmond French, son and heir of Elizabeth French also deceased, and the other fourth part I lately bought of Henry Rowe and Judith his wife, which said Judith, Elizabeth, Ann and my wife were the daughters and coheirs of Edmond Popley, merchant deceased. To my said daughter (among other things) "my lesser silver belly pott." To my kinswoman Lydia, that lately served me and is now become the wife of Edward Hackett, one hundred pounds over and above what I have already given her towards her marriage portion. To "my Beloved ffriends George Fox, William Dewsbery, Alexander Parker, George Whitehead and John Storye ten pounds apiece and unto Thomas Brigges, John Wilkinson of Westmoreland, James Porke, Steeven Crispe and John Wilkinson of Cumberland five pounds apiece as a token of my love to them and the service they have done for the Lord and for his people, and to the intent none my claim any right to any of these legacyes last mentioned to whom I intended it not I do declare and my Will is that it be payd only to that Geo: Fox, Will. Dewsbery, Geo: Whitehead, Alex: Parker, John Story, John Wilkinson, Tho: Bridges, James Porke, Steven Crispe and John Wilkinson who hath often lodged at my house and eaten bread at my table and one well knowne to my Executors" &c. Bequests to Thomas Goulding of Bristol, grocer, and his wife Mary, and to John Love of Bristol and his wife Magdalen. To each of my natural brothers and sisters children that survive me, except Samuel Hollister, son of my brother Thomas, and Nathaniel Tovie, the only son of my sister Margery Tovie deceased, who, because they are ill husbands and are like to mispend it, my will is not to give it to either of them but to Samuel Hollister's wife, for the benefit of his children and to Nathaniel Tovie's children that are living in England at the time of my decease. To Nem Dawson, widow, Joane Pillerne, widow, Margaret Price, widow, and to Mary Evans, widow. My servant Joseph Smith. My daughter Phebe shall possess and enjoy my house and lands called Old Fields, at Urcott in the parish of Almesbury Glouc[r], held by lease of Edward Browne. My son Dennis Hollister and my two sons in law Thomas Callowhill and Thomas Jordan to be joint executors and Alexander Parker, George Whitehead, Walter Clements and John Story to be overseers.

Witnesses I. Chauncy, John Eckly, Rich. Hawksworth.

In the codicil he bequeaths to his grandchildren Hannah, Thomas and Elizabeth Callowhill a messuage at Westerleigh, with the lands thereunto belonging, held of the Dean and Chapter of Welles. He speaks of his grand daughter Lydia Jordan as "dead." He names Samuel Hollister, son of his brother William, Dennis Holllister son of Abel Hollister, Samuel Hollister, grandson of brother William and son of Jacob Hollister, Thomas Speed, and others.   Bence, 91.

ANNE YEAMANS of Bristol widow 2 November 1664 proved 1 December 1668. My son William Yeamans to be full and sole executor, conditionally, and if he fails to fulfill the conditions then my sons in law John Haggat Esq. and Thomas Speed merchant. I, as executrix of the last will of my late husband William Yeamans, gent deceased, have paid the two hundred pounds which my husband gave to and amongst the children of my daughter Speed. Now I give to every one of her children, as well by Robert Yeamans as by Thomas Speed, which shall be living and unmarried at the time of my decease, the sum of ten pounds apiece, that is to say, to such of them as she had by the said Robert Yeamans to the children themselves, and to such of them as she had by Thomas Speed to their father to their use. My husband gave to my son Haggat's children John, Mary and Nathaniel, ten pounds apiece. This to be made up twenty pounds apiece. To the rest of the children of my said son Haggatt ten pounds apiece. To the daughter of my son William Yeamans ten pounds besides what hath " bin " given to her by my said husband. My husband gave to his grandchildren Matthew, William and Joyce Warren ten pounds apiece, and William " sithence " deceased, whereby his legacy is ceased, I desire that ten pounds apiece may be added to the said legacies of the said Mathew and Joyce, of my gift, to make them up twenty pounds apiece. I give to Anne and Mehetabell, the two other children of my daughter Warren, ten pounds apiece. I give to the (. . . .) children of my son Prigge ten pounds apiece. To my grandchild John Morgan ten pounds, to my daughter Joyce Warren and Sarah Prigge five pounds apiece, to my son in law Thomas Prigge five pounds, to my son William ten pounds and to his wife five pounds more as a token of my love. To my cousin Francis Yeamans five pounds. To my sister Jones forty shillings, and eight pounds to be divided amongst such of her children as my executor shall think meet. To my kinswomen Mary Topleafe, Susan Rider, Elizabeth Owen and Alice Collins and to my kinsmen Thomas Yeamans and John Yeamans, sons and daughters of my brother in law Edward Yeamans, forty shillings apiece and to Anne Owen, the daughter of my cousin Owen, forty shillings. To my sons Haggatt and Speed ten pounds apiece and to my said son Haggatt all that long green carpet and all those leathern chairs which I formerly delivered him to use in his forestreet parlor. To my kinswoman Mary Hagatt all that great cypress chest which standeth in her father's best forestreet chamber, provided that her father shall have the use and occupation thereof during his life. To my sister in law Johane Tomlinson forty shillings. To my cousin William Yeomans and my cousin his wife, my cousin Anne Curtis, my cousin Mary Westfield, my cousin Bethshua Speed and my cousin Elizabeth Milner forty shillings apiece, as tokens of my love, and to Richard Speed twenty shillings. To all the daughters of my brother Robert Tomlinson forty shillings apiece. To the children of my cousin Elizabeth Milner fifty pounds. To Mary Haggatt, the daughter of Richard Haggatt gent deceased, forty shillings. Five pounds to be distributed amongst the poor of the parish of Stapleton. I desire to be buried in the parish of Stapleton as near my husband as conveniently may be. My son William to be executor.   Hene, 162.

WILLIAM ROTHWELL of the City of New Sarum, Wilts., gent, 16 April 1633, proved 13 May 1634. To my sons Stephen, Robert, Henry and William Rothwell ten shillings apiece. To my daughter Mary Rothwell two hundred pounds, to my daughter Elizabeth Rothwell one hundred pounds and to my daughter Martha Rothwell one hundred pounds, to be paid at their several ages of one and twenty years. To the children of my son Stephen now living (except Margaret, Elizabeth and Mary) twelve pence apiece and to the children of my son William now living twelve pence apiece. To my kinsman John Giles ten shillings. To my kinsman Jane May ten shillings. To my first wife's kinswoman, sometimes called Bridgett Swayne, ten shillings and to Agnes Tuggie, widow, ten shillings, to be paid unto them within six months next after my decease, if they shall be then living, and not otherwise. The residue &c. to my wife Mary Rothwell, whom I make my full executrix, and I appoint my loving friends Maurice Aylerugge, woollen draper, and Humfrey Ditton, mercer, overseers, and give them ten shillings apiece for their pains which they shall take in this behalf.   Seager, 46.

BENJAMIN FEN Senior of Milford in the Colony of " Conecticott " in New England, 14 September 1672, proved 1 February 1674. I do give and bequeath unto my eldest son Benjamin Fen, as an addition to his portion that he hath already received, to the value of three hundred pounds and upwards, that farm that I formerly bought of Mr. Samuel Bach, late of New Haven, lying on the East side of East River, consisting of eighteen acres of meadow, more or less, with all the upland that is laid out thereto, he paying, or causing to be paid, thirty pounds towards the purchase, as was agreed upon, besides what he hath already paid. To my second son Samuel Fen my dwelling house that I now inhabit, within the town of Milford, with housing, uplands and meadows belonging, with that piece of upland and meadow that I bought of the Indians, above Pagasick, called Plum meadow, and the uplands adjacent thereto. To my youngest son James Fen my house in New Haven, with the warehouse and all the land belonging thereto, on this side East River, and that parcel of meadow belonging to the house, on the other side of the River, and all my right &c. in that farm that the Hon. General Assembly gave to me. To my three eldest daughters, Sarah, Mary and Martha, besides what they have already received for their portions, twenty pounds apiece, to be paid within one year after my decease out of my estate in New England. To my youngest daughter Susanna Fen, for her portion, one hundred and twenty pounds, to be paid at eighteen years old or day of marriage. To my grandchild Benjamin Fen, son to my eldest son Benjamin, the house, orchard and land formerly Joseph Fenn's, in the town of " Norawake." To all the rest of my grandchildren respectively I do give one ewe sheep to each of them. My will is that my grandchild Benjamin should enter and possess his house and lands at Norawake at the end and period of the lease that it's now let for. My two youngest sons Samuel and James shall come to enter and possess their legacies at their accomplishing of the age of one and twenty years, but, in case my dear and loving wife should see it her way to dispose of herself in marriage before then, it's my will that they should enter upon the one half of their housings and lands at eighteen, and at one and twenty the whole but their mother's third. To my son Samuel my dwelling house, lands and meadows in the parishes of Chiddington, Masworth, Ivingho, Wing, all of them in Buckinghamshire, given to me by the will of the late deceased Agnis Seare of the same parish and Shire. My said son, if he comes to the full possession of it at one and twenty, to pay to his brother James forty pounds at one and twenty and to his sister Susanna twenty pounds at one and twenty, and twenty pounds to his eldest brother Benjamin within five years after his entrance and possession. All the residue, whether in New England or old, I give to my wife Susanna Fen and I make her executrix. My will is that within five years after my decease she pay to each of my three eldest daughters, Sarah, Mary and Martha, ten pounds apiece, to be laid out in old England in pewter and brass for money pay and sent over for their several and respective uses, they bearing the charge of transportation and the danger of the seas. I entreat my honored, loving friends Mr. James Bishop of New Haven, Mr. Robert Treat. Thomas Wheeler and Daniel Buckingham to lend and afford their best help, council and advice as overseers &c.

Wit: Robert Treat, Ephraim Sanford.   Dycer, 14.

[Benjamin Fenn settled in Dorchester as early as 1638, and soon after removed to New Haven and to Milford. He had two wives, of whom the first was Sarah, daughter of Sylvester Baldwin, and the second, whom he married March 12, 1664, was Susannah Ward. He died in 1672. For other details see Savage's Genealogical Dictionary, Vol. 2, p. 152.—EDITOR.]

THOMAS CALLOWHILL of the city of Bristol, linen draper, 28 November 1711, proved 24 December 1712. My now dwelling house in St. James within the suburbs of the city. I stand possessed of a remainder of a certain term of one thousand years granted to me by Edward Baugh, white tawer, since deceased, interested also in the remainder of another term of one thousand years lately granted to me by Edward Baugh jun[r], and in the residue of another term of a thousand years lately granted to me by my daughter Hanna, —— the last described as three several messuages &c. on the South side of a certain messuage called the Quaker Meeting House, in or near a certain place called the Fryers, and now or late in the several tenures &c. of Simon Barnes Daniel Kindall and William Timbrell.   I gave the same parcels of ground, messuages &c. to my kinsman Brice Webb of the said city linen draper and Charles Harford of the city aforesaid merchant upon trust, to permit the same premisses to be held and enjoyed and the rents, issues and profits thereof to be had, received and taken by my wife Hanna *als* Anna, for and during so much of my said several terms respectively to come as she shall live, and, after her decease, by my grand daughter Margaret Penn, daughter of Hannah Penn my daughter by William Penn, Esq[r] her husband, as long as she shall live, next by my grandson John Penn for all the rest of the several terms to come.   By deed indented bearing date the seven and twentieth day of this instant month I have conveyed to Brice Webb and Charles Harford, linen drapers, and Richard Champion, merchant, divers messuages, lands &c. within the said city, the Co. of Somerset and other places in England and in Pennsylvania to divers uses, limitations and appointments therein mentioned and contained, with power of revocation. I hereby ratify, confirm and allow the same deed.   Provision for granting to grand daughter Margaret Penn certain premisses in Broad Meade, in the parish of St James, part of my wife's jointure, with remainder to grandson John Penn. I have an interest in the Province of Pennsylvania as a security for one thousand pounds sterling due to me from the said William Penn, interested also in a messuage &c. in Caldecott, Monmouth, as a security for one hundred and sixty pounds due from Mary Herbert, spinster, sole heir of Francis Herbert Esq[r] deceased.   Other investments also described.   And I am also interested in one sixteenth part of certain Packett Boats now sailing or trading for the Port of Bristol to New York and other places in America, in partnership with Brice Webb, Richard Champion and others. All these interests I give to Brice Webb and James Peters upon trust, to pay to the said William Penn and Hanna his wife, and the survivor of them, the yearly sum of twenty and six pounds, clear of all taxes and charges, during their natural lives (and for other purposes described). Provision for Thomas Penn, another son of Hanna Penn. My brother Walter Duffield is bound to me by two several obligations, one of 12 January 1694, for payment of twenty five pounds, and interest, and the other, of 13 August 1674, for payment of fourteen pounds ten shillings. He to be freed from the payment of all but twenty five pounds. My sister Elizabeth Javeling to be conditionally discharged of certain bonds. I give and bequeath unto my neices Elizabeth Javelin, Duffield Javelin, Sara Gurnay and Mary Gurnay one piece of gold apiece of the value of twenty three shillings six pence. My wife Hanna *als* Anna to be sole executrix and the said Brice Webb and Charles Harford overseers.

On the 19th of October 1738 issued forth a Comⁿ to John Penn Esqr the natural and lawful son and adm^r with the Will annexed of the goods of Hannah Penn widow deceḍ. (whilst living) the natural and lawful daughter and only child and adm^x with the will annexed of Thomas Callowhill late of the City of Bristol widower deceḍ. to administer the goods &c.

Barnes, 231.

GEORGE SMITH of London, gen^t, 10 January 1658, proved 11 February 1658. Lately freed from a dangerous illness. To Anne Cox, sister to my beloved wife deceased, for her convenient subsistance, ten pounds per annum, payable quarterly. To Margaret Thorpe, another of my wife's sisters, five pounds per annum, payable in like manner. To Elizabeth Thorpe, daughter of the said Margaret ten pounds. To John Thorpe fifty shillings that he oweth me. To my wife's niece Elizabeth Chapman three score and five pounds, besides thirty and five pounds which I have in my hands in trust for her and owe unto her, all which maketh the sum of one hundred pounds. To Frances Cheney another niece of my wife, ten pounds. To my cousin Bridget Audley, daughter of John Hoddesdon Esq. deceased, five pounds. To my cousin Mary Gosslin forty shillings to buy her a ring. To Judith Sandford, late wife of John Sandford, sometime my tenant, fifty shillings. To my beloved cousin Christopher Hoddesdon of Lee Gardens, in Hornchurch Essex, Esq., ten pounds to buy a piece of plate. To Martha Hoddesdon, his daughter, forty pounds. To Thomas, his younger son, forty pounds. To Christopher Hoddesdon, son of Thomas Hoddesdon, gentleman, deceased, four pounds.

Item I give unto the three daughters of my beloved brother Master Thomas Walley, now Pastor of the Church of Whitechapel in the Co. of Middlesex, as followeth; to Hannah Walley the eldest I give forty pounds, to Elizabeth, the second I give thirty pounds, to Mary the youngest daughter I give fifty pounds. I give unto Master Thomas Wally, my beloved brother, Pastor of Whitechapel, twenty pounds to buy a piece of plate. To Thomas Gilling, my dearly beloved wife's son, one hundred pounds, but with this proviso, that he be a truly humbled and reformed man to settle himself in some honest way of livelihood, not else to be paid him to waste and riot to the dishonor of God, as he hath done his former estate, and for the discovery of his reformation and abandoning all his lewd and wicked company I commit to the judgment of my executors and overseers &c., and if they find not a real change in him my will is that my executors shall only pay unto

him six pounds per annum interest for the hundred pounds, but if he, the
said Thomas Gilling, through his "deboistnes" shall happen to die that
then the said hundred pounds shall be paid to my two cousins Elizabeth
Chapman and Frances Cheney, to each of them fifty pounds. To Master
Dicklosse clerk of the Church of Whitechapel ten shillings and to sexton
ten shillings. To the poor of Master Wally's congregation three pounds.
To Margaret Thorpe, before named, and to her children (wearing apparel).
To Mrs. Elizabeth Silverwood, wife to Capt. John Silverwood, forty shil-
lings to buy a ring and to his three daughters each ten shilling (for rings),
and to his two sons, each ten shillings to buy what they please. And I
make, ordain &c. my beloved and trusty friend Capt. John Silverwood of
St. Giles Cripplegate, London, gentleman, my lawful executor &c., and my
truly beloved friends and brethren Master Abraham Jesson and Master
Trustran May to be overseers, both of them being members of Master
Wallye's church, and I give each of them fifty shillings to buy rings.
    Wit. Robert Parrott, Lenye Mountgomery.
    Then follows a paper beginning——This is a perfect Accompt of ffrances
Cheyney and Rebeccah Cheyney of monies which I George Smith tooke
into my hands as Guardian to improve for them. — — — Memorandum,
that Richard Cheney died the last day of October One thousand six hundred
fifty and one. The goods was not praised till the tenth day of November
one thousand six hundred fifty two, but by reason of the contravery which
was not divided till the twenty second day of March one thousand six hundred fifty two, about which time I received of Frances Cheney's money one
hundred and twelve pounds seventeen shillings three pence, which I used
to her best advantage, at six pounds in the hundred, till about the third of
May one thousand six hundred fifty five I lost fifty pounds of her money
and the interest by one Thomas Gilling, which, notwithstanding I think I
was not bound neither by Law nor conscience, yet I have made it up, both
principal and interest, at six pounds in the hundred, which next March is
six years, and is, in all, the sum of one hundred forty eight pounds seven
shillings three pence, due at or about Lady (day?) one thousand six hundred
fifty nine.
    Memorandum That Frances Cheney's mother received all her dividents
for her, I received none—GEORGE SMITH.
    Then follows a somewhat similar account with Rebecca Cheyney, by
which it appears that testator lost by one Captain Bushell ten pounds and
interest, which however he made up unto her. — — — Received of my
sister Cheyney about January 1654 or 1655 for a divident a seventh part
of two year's rent for Inglefield, due to Rebecca 16. 00. 05½. (Then follow similar receipts.)   Pell, 95.

    [As the testator of the preceding will called Mr. Abraham Jesson brother,
and Jacob Jesson of New England, who called Mr. John Walley of Boston,
Mass., brother-in-law, had a brother Abraham Jesson, the following will is
worth saving.—H. F. WATERS.
    See Mr. Whitmore's notes on the Jesson and Walley families in the January
REGISTER, pp. 104-6 (ante, pp. 648-50).—EDITOR.]

    ABRAHAM JESSON, of Bethnoll Greene in the parish of Stebonheath als
Stepney in the County of Middlesex, ironmonger, 26 October 1666, proved
14 February 1666. To my wife Dorothy Jesson the yearly rents, issues
and profits of all my lands &c. called by the names of Stenfields and Cowper's Crofts, lying and being in Wedensbury in the Co. of Stafford, late in
the tenure of John Tuncks or Thomas Edwards, which I purchased of

Francis Perry of Wedensbury mercer (and of other estates there). This during her natural life, she making no waste &c. After her death they are to go to my eldest son Abraham Jesson (with other estates near Woolverhampton and in the City of Worcester &c.). One of the tenements in Worcester is described as a tavern called the Myter and another as a tenement called the Cross Keys. To my son Jacob Jesson and his heirs all that messuage, tenement or dwelling house situate or being in White Chapel, Middlesex, commonly called or known by the name or sign of the Sythe and Dripping Pan, now in the tenure or occupation of John Ward, ironmonger, which I purchased of Samuel Abraham. I give to my son Jacob seven hundred and sixty pounds &c., to be paid unto him when and so soon as he shall accomplish his full age of one and twenty years. To my son Nathaniel Jesson eight hundred pounds at one and twenty. To my daughter Rebecca Jesson seven hundred pounds at one and twenty or day of marriage. To my daughter Elizabeth Jesson seven hundred pounds at one and twenty or day of marriage. To my friends Mr George Scott and Richard Loton Esq. twenty pounds apiece and to my friends Mr. John Harwood, Mr. Nathaniel Taylor, Mr. Samuel Short and Mr. Myles Cooke fifty shillings apiece for rings. To my loving sister Rebecca Cowper twenty five pounds. To William Bird the son of Henry Bird and of my said sister Rebecca, twenty shillings. To Josiah Bird, son of the said Henry and Rebecca, five pounds. To Elenor Newton, the wife of Stephen Newton and the daughter of the said Henry and Rebecca, five pounds. To Sarah Cowper, daughter of the said Rebekah, five pounds at one and twenty or day of marriage. Other bequests. My friends Mr. George Scott, grocer, Richard Loton Esq. and my son Abraham Jesson to be executors, and my friends Mr. John Harwood, Mr. Nathaniel Taylor Mr. Samuel Short and Myles Cooke overseers.

A Codicil was added 20 January 1666, in which he bequeathed his then dwelling house in Bednall Green, lately bought of Mr. John Speering and Katherine his wife, to his wife Dorothy for life and then to his son Abraham.   Carr, 22.

The following is a brief abstract of the will of Abraham Jesson, the eldest son of the preceding testator, and brother of Jacob Jesson of New England.

ABRAHAM JESSON of London, ironmonger, 1 December 1678, proved 22 September 1680. Wife Elizabeth. Grazeley farm near Woolverhampton Co. Stafford. Dwelling houses in or near Clarkenwell, Middlesex. Son Abraham. Messuage in the City of Worcester. Tenement called the Cross Keys in Bradderdine near Worcester. Daughter Mary Jesson. Stanfeild's Leasow in Wedensbury in Co. Stafford &c. Daughter Elizabeth Jesson. Lands in Wedensbury held, occupied and enjoyed by Richard Smith, locksmith, in the right of Anne, his wife, relict of George Jesson deceased. Daughter Rebecca Jesson. Messuages in or near Bednall Greene, Stepney, Middlesex, late in the tenure of my honored father Abraham Jesson deceased, now in the tenure of my honored mother Dorothy Jesson &c. Children all under age. My brother Jacob Jesson and his wife Mary. My sister Rebecca Thomas and her husband. My sister Elizabeth Cockes and her husband. My mother in law Mary Basse and her husband. My brother Francis Barkested and his wife Jane. My brother John Barkested. Jeremiah Basse, Mary Basse, Esther Basse. My Aunt Rebecca Cowper, William Bird, Ellinor Newton, Joseph Bird, Samuel Short, John Tomkins and Miles Cooke. My nephew James Cockes.

Brother Nathaniel Jesson. Wife and said brother Nathaniel to be joint executors.

The will was proved (as above) by Elizabeth Jesson, power reserved for Nathaniel Jesson.

Commission issued 15 March 1689 to Francis and John Bakstead lawful guardians of Abraham, Elizabeth and Rebecca Jesson, minor children of the deceased to administer (during their minority) the goods left unadministerd by Elizabeth Jesson deceased, Nathaniel Jesson, the brother, renouncing.

Commission issued 19 July 1697 to Abraham Jesson the son, who had come to his full age.   Bath, 118.

JOHN SMITHIER of Arlington in the parish of Buybury and County of Gloucester, yeoman, 16 February 1618, proved 31 October 1626. All my lands of inheritance &c to John Smithier, e!dest son of my son John Smithier deceased, next to my cousin (sic) Henry Smithier, his brother, then to my niece Johan Powell, then to my niece (sic) Thomazine Smithier, daughter of said son John deceased, then to my cousin John Custis als Cliffe, then to my cousin Henry Custis als Cliffe, then to my right heirs forever. I give and bequeath my lease of Camdens unto my son in law Edmond Custis als Cliffe and to his son John Custis and to the survivor or longest liver of them, the said John to pay, during the natural life of the said father, towards the maintenance of Elizabeth, his sister, twenty shillings yearly, and after the decease of his said father, if he survive, forty shillings yearly during his own natural life. Bequests to Thomas Howse, son of my daughter Anne Howse late of Colne Rogers deceased, to Richard Howse, his brother, to my cousin William Howse, their brother, to James Howse, their brother, to Margaret Howse, their sister, and to Bridget Howse, their sister. I give to John Custis als Cliffe and Henry his brother, the sons of Edmond Custis now of Cirencester, ten pounds apiece. To William Custis, their brother, thirteen pounds six shillings eight pence and my best shirt. To Nicholas Custis, their brother and to Edmond Custis, their brother, each, thirteen pounds six shillings eight pence. Bequests to Elizabeth and Mary Custis, their sisters. To my sister Jones forty shillings. Thomas Smithier and his children. Richard Smithier. Matthew Smithier and his children. Ellianor Peirson and her children. William Smithier of Northletch. Mary Powell, the daughter of my niece Joane Powell, and Elizabeth, her sister. My cousin Joane Powell to be sole executrix.

A codicil was written 12 November 1619, modifying some of the bequests made in the will.   Hele, 133.

[The foregoing will I deem well worth saving, associating together, as it does, the family name Custis and the place name Arlington.   HENRY F. WATERS.]

MATHEWE SILLESBYE of the town of North'ton in the County of North'-ton gen^t 18 April 1662 proved 19 February 1662. To my worthy friend Salothiell Lovell of Northampton Esq., George Norwood of Nothampton, gen^t., and Lawrence Wollaston of the same town gen^t and to their heirs and assigns for ever all that my messuage, two yard land and close, with their and every of their appurtenances now in the occupation of Nathaniel Basely, within the town fields and parish of Duston in the County of Northampton, as also one close of pasture situate in St. James End, within the same parish, called Dove house close, and another close called Crowthorp close lying on the West side of Dallington Moor, within the parish of Dallington, and my meadow ground called Fleaten Holme within the parish of Hardingstone, and my hook of meadow called Bull's Hooke, lying in Cotten Marsh within the parish of Hardingston, and my yard land and close in Millton *als* Middleton Malsor in the said County, upon this intent that they shall with all convenient speed, immediately after my decease, make sale all my said lands and premises above mentioned for the best price they can get, and with the moneys raised shall pay and discharge all my debts, and the remainder shall be towards the payment of my legacies &c.   I give to my son Matthew Sillesbye the messuage &c. wherein I now live, situate in the Drapery, in the town of Northampton, as also the tenement in the possession of Samuel Gibbs, next adjoining to the same, and a piece of ground, lying my backside, which I purchased of the town, being part of my walk there.   And I give him two hundred pounds over and above what I have already given him.   I give to my daughter Elizabeth four hundred pounds, to my daughter Rebecca three hundred pounds, to my son Samuel all my freehold land at Wellingborrow (my son Matthew to make surrender of the same).   Also I do give unto the said Samuel my messuage in Northampton in the occupation of my sister Cricke, near the great Conduit there, and a messuage called Collingtree wood House and the three pasture grounds adjoining, and six acres of arable land within the parish fields of Road.   And I give him one hundred pounds.   I do give and bequeath unto my son Nathaniel Sillesbye my messuage or tenement called Thrupp wood House, with the several closes and little wood ground thereunto adjoining, lying and being in the parish of Roade, and six acres of arable land in the fields of Roade near unto the Hide there.   And I give unto my son Nathaniel all my books, for my earnest desire is that if it shall please God to make him capable that he be bred up a scholar.   I give unto my sister Martin five pounds.   I give to my said trustees one messuage or tenement &c. in Bridge Street, in the occupation of Edward Martin, another messuage or tenement in a place called the New Lane, now in the occupation of Daniel Sanders, another tenement in the Horse Market, in the occupation of Edward Horne, and an orchard or garden in St. John's Lane, in the parish of All Saints, and a close of ground in St. Edmond's End, in the parish of St. Giles, both in the occupation of George Davies, upon this special trust that they shall convey the said messuage &c., now in the occupation of Edward Martin, to some honest person or persons in trust for my said sister Bethia Martyn during her life, and after her decease in trust for Thomas Martin her son and his lawful issue, failing such to my right heirs for ever; and, as for the other messuages, orchard and close, that they shall permit my said sister, during her natural life, to receive the rents &c. to her own proper use and behoof; and after her decease they shall convey the fee simple of the said messuages or tenements, orchard and close of ground &c. unto the Mayor, bailiffs, and burgesses of the said town, and to their successors for ever, to the intent and purpose that they shall fit and prepare the said messuage in the Horse Market for the comfortable habitation of two poor widows or widowers of good honest life and reputation, natives of the said town of Northampton, and more especially of the parish of All Saints, to be elected and chosen by the Mayor and Aldermen for the time being, or the major part of them and all the rents &c. of other the said premises to be granted as aforesaid to be equally divided between the said two poor people, for the time being for ever.   I give and bequeath unto my aunt Clarke if living ten pounds, to my aunt Ungley if living five pounds, to my sister Harper fifty shillings, the rest of my goods, &c. to my son Samuel and my two daughters Elizabeth and Rebecca.   Juxon, 29.

[The above abstract was taken from the registers of the Prerogative Court of Canterbury, Somerset House, Strand, London. A copy of the same will is also preserved in the Probate Registry at Northampton. The testator was baptized in All Saints' Church 17 February 1610(11), being a son Mr. Matthew Sillesbye, the elder, a scrivener who was chosen Mayor of Northampton 1631 and was buried (in All Saints') 29 March 1639. The son seems to have followed closely in his father's footsteps, for he too was a scrivener and was Mayor in 1649-50. The signatures of both of them may be found in many of the wills now preserved in the probate registry of Northampton and are so much alike that it would puzzle an expert to distinguish them apart. The elder Matthew was probably an apprentice of Mr. George Coldwell, common clerk of Northampton about A.D. 1596, and afterwards Mayor.

The property in Horsemarket left by Mr. Matthew Sillesbey (the younger) for the habitation of two poor widows or widowers, is described as follows in a case between Thomas Chadwick, of Northampton gen^t, petitioner, and the Mayor, Bailiffs and Burgesses of the said town of Northampton and the parishioners of All Saints' Parish in the same town, defendants, under date Saturday 26 April 1684.* The petitioner calls himself tenant by lease of a toft, piece or parcel of ground, with the backside or garden and the appurtenances, situate and being on the west side of Horsemarket, on which said toft stood formerly a messuage or tenement burnt down and demolished by the late dreadful fire which happened in said town of Northampton, a tenement lying on the North formerly called the Three Tuns and certain parish land lying on the South; which said messuage or tenement, soe burnt down as aforesaid is in the front twenty and five foot in the length, with the garden or backside belonging to the same, and was and now is, parcel of the lands given by the last Will and Testament of Matthew Silesby, late alderman of the said town of Northampton deceased, towards the maintenance of two poor widows, to be appointed by the Mayor and Aldermen of the said town of Northampton. The other property in dispute was the parish land next adjoining on the South. The Petitioner was allowed to rebuild and hold by lease for ninety-nine years &c. This would seem to furnish evidence as to the age of the present building now devoted to that charity (No 35 Horsemarket). Through the courtesy of Mr. Samuel Hull I was enabled to ascertain that the estate in the New Lane (*i.e.* Newland) was sold in 1866 for £470 and the proceeds (less expenses) invested in Consols (£482 15s. 6d.). The gentleman who bought this property built two houses thereon, now numbered 27 and 27A on the west side of Newland. The land in St. John's Lane was sold to the Bedford Railway Co. for £312 10s. I believe the Bedford and Northampton Railway Station stands on the site. The front part of the close in St. Edmund's End was sold off in 1869 to the Grammar School Trustees, who built the School House thereon, and the back part is rented (at £10 per ann.) as a playground for the school. The proceeds of the sale of the front part (£665 10s.) was invested in Consols. (£715 11s. 6d.) I understand that the income of the Fund now supports three widows, two of them in the Horsemarket house.

Contemporary with the elder Matthew in the same parish of All Saints', and undoubtedly a brother, was a Henry Sillesby, sometimes styled linen draper and sometimes mercer, the baptisms of whose children (Matthew, John, Robert, Henry, Mary, Elizabeth, Samuel, and Thomas) are to be found in the Registers of that parish. In his indenture of apprenticeship (1593), enrolled in vol. xiii. of the Town Records, he is described as a son of Robert Sillesbye of Duston. Another contemporary was Anthony Sillesbie of Duston, whose will was proved 13 September, 1623. The name of his brother Henry appears as a witness. Still another was their brother William Silsbie of Harleston, whose nuncupative will was proved 15 April, 1626. Henry Sillesby was one of the bailiffs in 1622. His wife (and the mother of all his children) was Mary Randes (married 20 April, 1602, and buried 22 October, 1632). Their son Henry (baptized at All Saints', 20 May, 1613) seems to have emigrated to New England, and finally settled in Lynn, Massachusetts, where he died. From him are descended a family of Silsby, more or less scattered throughout New England, and the influential and highly respectable family of Silsbee of Salem, Massachusetts, one of whom, Mr. Edward A. Silsbee, is now visiting Northampton in search of the

* Book of Records of the Commissioners appointed by Act of Parliament for the better and more easy Rebuilding of the Town of Northampton, A.D. 1676.

traces of these ancestors of his who were flourishing in Duston and Northampton nearly three hundred years ago. HENRY F. WATERS.

From Northamptonshire Notes and Queries, vol. v , 1892, p. 104.

The foregoing was communicated to Northamptonshire Notes and Queries last Fall, while I was visiting Northampton with my friend and townsman, Mr. Edward A. Silsbee, whose guest I was.

The following are brief abstracts of the wills of William and Anthony Silesby, above referred to. HENRY F. WATERS.]

The words of WILLIAM SILSBIE late of Harleston deceased that he spake a litle before his death Beinge demanded whether he would make a will he answered noe, but he would leaue all unto his wife to bringe up the Children And as touchinge William his eldest sonne if he would be ruled by his mother, then his desier was that he should haue halfe wth her Otherwise if he were not ruled by her he should haue but only that five pounds that was given unto him by his Aunt in the p^{r}sence of George Nelson & Richard Knight & others.

Decimo quinto die Aprilis Anno dñi 1626 corā dño Cane cõmissa fuit ad^o cū hmõi testam^{to} annex —— Silsbie eius relictæ et princ^{ti} legataŕ in cođ nominat de bene etc Jurat saluo etc
Inventarii Suma lvi^{te}iis

Book AV (1621–28) 270. Northampton Wills.

Will of ANTHONY SILLESBIE of Duston in the Co. of Northampton, husbandman 23 July 1623, proved 12 Sept 1623

My body to be buried in the church or church yard of Duston.

I will & bequeath to Anne my wife ten pounds of good & lawful English money and my wool, being fourteen fleeces and some of last year's wool and the bed I lie on with the furniture and a chest and halfe my householc stuffe throughout and two beastes, vid, a brown cow and a red cow and eighteen sheeps. Item my will is that if my wife will sever from my son in diett while she is now p^{r}sent or removing from hence shall return again that she shall have a quarterne land (she paying the proportionable rent for it) to be dressed by Robert my son as he doth his own, and to be brought home for her and she to have convenient place for it and the cattle belonging to it as also for her own dwelling.

I give & bequeath to my dau. Sarah Harrise an hive of bees, which they shall choose. I give to my grand children Rebeccah & Sarah Sillesbie two lambs which my son Robt shall choose as also two coverlets the better to Rebeccah the other to Sarah. I give and bequeath to Willm Sillesbie my brother & Jane Smallbone my sister two strikes of Barley apiece, to be delivered to them at the feast of St. Michael the Arch-Angel next ensuing the date of presents. I give & bequeath to my sister Howett a strike of barley to be delivered at the same time.

The rest of my goods unbequeathed, my burial discharged & my debts paid, I give & bequeath to Robert Sillesbie my son whom I make my sole executor of this my last will & testament.

In witness whereof I have to these presents set my hand Date the 23th day of July 1623.

my overseers { my brother Henrie Sillesbie
              { my brother in law Nicholas Whiting

Wit: John Coles
Henrie Sillesbye
Edmund James

The mark of
Anthony Sillesbie.

[By the kind permission of the town clerk, William Shoosmith, Esq., to whom I was introduced by Sir Henry Dryden, Bar^t, I made a rather extensive examination of the town records and documents in his keeping, and gathered a lot of interesting notes about the Sillesby family and other names of interest to New England genealogists. I have to thank Mr. Shoosmith and his sons for the great kindness shown by them during and after this search.—H. F. WATERS.]

[In the Book of Inrolments of Apprentices, Indentures and Admissions to the Freedom of the town of Northampton (1562–1727), I found the following:]

M^d that HENRY SILLESBYE (sonne of Robert Sillesbye of Duston in the Countie of North^n) by Indenture baring date the ffirste daye of Maye in the fyve and thirtith yeare of the raign of our sou^{r}aign Ladye quene Elizabeth etc. hathe putt himselfe apprentice wth Lawrence Ball of the towne of Northampton, grocer, and Margaret his wyfe at the trade of a grocer ffor the terme of eight yeares, to begynne at the daye of the date of the same Indenture. The saide Henry Sillesbye doth coveñnte to doe the saide Lawrence Ball and Margarett true and diligent service during the saide terme. And the said Lawrence and Margarett doen coveñnte to teache the saide Henry Sillesbye the said trade of a grocer, to fynde him all things necessarie during the terme, and to geve him at thende of his terme double apparell etc.

Irr Primo die Decembris A^o xxxvi^{to} rñe Elizabeth etc. 1593.

1622. Richard Woolleston, mayor, and Henry Sillesbye and William Brookes bailiffs, *a Festo die Sancti Michaelis Archangeli anno dñi 1621 An 10q regni dñi ñri Jacobi Regis nunc Anglie etc. vicesimo etc usque ad eundem festum anno Revolut.*

I found also, during the Mayoralty of William Knight (1626–7) an Inrolment of an Indenture whereby Robert Sillesby, son of Henry Sillesbye of Northampton, Linen draper, put himself apprentice with Thomas Cowper the younger, of the said town, Ironmonger, to be instructed in the trade of an ironmonger for the term of nine years from the date of the Indenture, which was 29 September last past.

In the time of Laurence Ball, mayor (1641–2) Thomas Sillesby, son of Henry Sillesby of Northampton, mercer, by indenture dat. 14 October, put himself apprentice to Edward Burgins of the said town, barber, for eight years.

Among the Admissions to Freedom (beginning A.D. 1606) I found the following:

Georgius Randes nup. appr. Henrici Sillesbie, mercer, et iur. natali admiss. fuit decimo die Junii A^o 1612 et solvit —— iij^s iiij^d.

In the Mayoralty of Richard Wollaston (1622–3), (Henry Sillesby one of the bailiffs,) John Luck lately apprentice of Matthew Sillesby, scrivener, was admitted to Freedom 14 March, 22 James, and paid ten shillings. Also, Richard Dudley, apprentice of John Shingleton, 24 May 1623, and paid ten shillings. Again—Daniel Washington, taylor, *per concessū colloquii admiss. fuit xxvi^{to} die Septembr. a^o p^{r}dco et solvit*—x^{li}.

Later, I found the following:—

Johēs Sillesbie filius Henrici Sillesbie iure natali admiss. fuit xx^o die Julii 1631, *et solvit*—iij^s iiij^d.

Still later:—*Robertus Sillesby filius Henrici Sillesby, Lynnendra$\wp$ Jur. natali admiss. fuit xviij^o die Novembris Anno Dñi 1636, et solvit*—iii^s iiij^d.

Thomas Silsbie filius Henric. Silsbie dēfi iure natali admiss. fuit xxiij^o die Aprilis 1646, et solvit—iij^s iiij^d.

In a Book of Orders of Assembly (from 1616 to 1744) appears the following:

At an Assemblie of John Harbert, maior of the towne of Northampton, the Aldermen his brethren, lat. maiors of the same towne, the bailiffs, all those that have been bailiffs and the fourtie & eight Burgesses of the Com. Councell there assembled in the Guild hall the sixteenth day of Aprill in the Sixth yeare of the Raigne of our Sou'aigne Lord Charles now King of England &c. 1630, It is agreed and ordered that Henrie Sillesbie shall haue a leasse of a part of Cap lane, now in his occupation, excepting passage for the heires of George Coldwell dec., for xxi years from the feast day of the Annunciation last, upon the Rent of viii^{li} yearlie upon Coveñuts as shalbe thought fit.

At an Assembly 12 October 1635 I noted the election of Mr. Matthew Sillesbie one of the Auditors and Henrie Sillesbie Constable of the Checker Ward.

1637. It is agreed and ordered that Mr. Sillesbie, late Mayor of this town, who hath disbursed some moneys about the placing of poor boys apprentices in the time of his Mayoralty, shall have paid him the iiij^{li} vi^s viii^d he hath laid out.

Among the Leases and Conveyances possessed by the Town I found one in which Henry Travell of Coventry, gen^t assigned and Surrendered, 24 April 1622, all his estate &c. in and to the moiety of Gobions Manor (formerly belonging to the Harrisons) to Thomas Cowper, the then Mayor of Northampton, Henry Chadwick, Raphael Humphrey, Abraham Ventris, Thomas Bradforde, Thomas Martyn, Edward Collis, William Knight, Richard Woollaston, Thomas Guttridge, John Harbert, John Fisher and Henry Syllesby, who have purchased the inheritance and reversion of the whole manor.

1621. Counterpart of a conveyance from the Mayor, Bailiffs and Burgesses of Northampton to Henry Sillesby of Northampton, linendraper, and John Scryven of the same, shoemaker, for £53–6–8, of a messuage, tenement and backside lying in the "Checkerwarde," on the E. side of the street or place called "the Cheker," sometime in the occupation of Thomas Burges, since in the tenure of Thomas Crasbrooke and now in the occupation of Margaret Ball widow, and abutting on the Street called the "Cheker" on the W., the land of said Margaret Ball on the S., a tenement of Joseph Brian gen^t, called "the Holy Lambe," now in the occupation of Anthony Smith, on the N. and the land, sometime of John Brian the elder deceased and now of Edward Burrows and Elizabeth his wife, on the E. &c. &c. dat. 20 December 1621. Two seals attached.

1645. Counterpart of a Conveyance from the Corporation to Samuel Coldwell of Northampton, gen^t (in consideration of £15.5^s) of a piece of ground, part in the parish of All Saints and part in the parish of St. Sepulchre's, abutting upon a certain lane called "Sylver Street" and the land of the heirs of Abraham Ventries deceased and land of the said Samuel Coldwell and land belonging to the Hospital of St. Thomas in Northampton on the N. E. parts and a certain lane leading from the backside of an Inn called "The Lyon" leading to the Castle Hill and the land of one [—] Harris and the land of the heirs of Thomas Pilkington deceased on the S. and W. parts &c.; —— which said piece of ground was sometimes a lane long since enclosed by the said Mayor, Bailiffs and Burgesses, called "Cap Lane," and was sometimes in the tenure of George Coldwell, Gentleman, deceased, and late was in the tenure and occupation of Henry Syllesby, also deceased, and now in the occupation of one Nathaniel Benbow. Conveyance made absolute. Dat. 10 May 1645.

I examined the Registers of All Saints and extracted the following entries (among others):

Baptisms.

May 1603.   Mathewe filius Henrici Sillesby baptizat. fuit xv° die.
April 1605.   Nathaniell filius Mathei Sillesby bapt. xxviii° die.
Dec. 1607.   Bethiah filia Mathei Sillesby bapt. fuit primo die.
   "   "   John filius Henr. Sillesby bapt. fuit xxvij° die.
Sept. 1610.   Robert filius Henrici Sillesby bapt. fuit xxv° die.
Feb. 1610.   Mathew, filius Matthei Sillesby bapt. fuit xvij° die.
May 1613.   Henricus filius Henrici Sillesby, m͏ʳcer, ꝑ Mariã uxorē eius bapt. fuit eõd. die (i.e. xx° die).
Oct. 1615.   Abdiell filius Mathei Sillesby et Katherine, uxor. xxix° die.
Jan. 1615.   Mary filia Henri Sillesby, Lynnendrap ͏ët Marie uxõr. eius bapt. fuit xxviij° die.
April 1618.   Samuel fil. Matthei Sillesbie, Script., ꝑ Katherin uxor. eius bapt. fuit xij° die.
Sept. 1618.   Elizabeth filia Henrici Sillesby, linendraper, ꝑ Maria xx° die.
Dec. 1621.   Thomas filius Mathei Sillesby, scrivener, et Katherin xvi° die.
Sept. 1622.   Samuel filius Henrici Sillesbie et Marie uxor. eius bapt. fuit octavo die.
Feb. 1625.   Thomas filius Henrici Sillesbie, Linendraper, et Marie uxor. eius xij° die.

Marriages.

April 1602.   Henry Sillesbie et Maria Randes nupti fuer xx° die.
Oct. 1631.   Edward Martin et Bethaia Sillesbie iij° die.
Sept. 1635.   Matthew Sillesby et Eliz. Gray primo die.

Burials.

July 1578.   Robert Sylbye sepultus fuit eodem die (i.e. vicesimo octavo).
Feb. 1609.   Parvulus, Mathei Sillesby sepultus fuit vi° die.
Sept. 1622.   Samuell filius Henric. Sillesbie sepultus fuit xxiiij° die.
Oct. 1624.   Agnes filia Henrici Sillesby—quinto die.
Oct. 1632.   Mary uxor Henry Sillesby sepulta fuit xxij die.
March 1639.   Mr. Matthew Sillesby sepultus fuit xxix die.
May 1642.   Anne uxor Mr. Henrici Sillesby sepulta fuit xxiiij die.
Sept. 1643.   Mrs. Katherine Sillesby sepulta fuit xij die.

On my return to London I was able to make notes of the following wills of members of this family.

SAMUELL SILLESBY, Fellow of Queen's College in Cambridge, 18 October 1650, proved at London 9 November 1650.   I give unto my sister Bathiah Martin, wife to Edward Martain of Northampton fifty pounds and unto her two children Thomas Martin and to John Martine the sum of ten pounds apiece, all which sum of seventy pounds my will is shall abide in the hands of my executors hereafter to be named, to be laid out for the use and benefit of my said sister and her two Children, according as they my said executors shall in their judgments and conscience shall think best for the advantage and benefit of my said sister and her said two children.   I give to my brother Thomas Sillesby, M^r of Arts of Christ Church in Oxford, all my books and papers and clothes, with every other thing belonging to my chamber and study at Queen's College in Cambridge and the furniture of my chamber or whatsoever is mine in the Gallery thereto belonging, and what else I have lent to any in Cambridge or elsewhere (money only excepted). I give thirty pounds to Queen's College in Cambridge, whereof ten pounds is for the use of the Library, especially for the buying of those Greek fathers, in their own language, as yet are wanting there, and the other to be distributed to the poorest and most improving and pious scholars in the said College, according to the judgment of the President and Fellows of the said College. I give to my cousin Tymothy Rushbrooke and Ellenor his wife all the money which formerly I have lent them, together with a lease of theirs which is in my custody, which, my will is, shall be restored unto them. I give to the young " scholeboy of my Cozen Iues, shoomaker in Northampton " five pounds for his better education in learning. My will is that five pounds be laid out in plate to be given as a memorial of my true affection to my very good friend Mr Ofspring. I give to Judith Ball forty shillings, who hath attended me in my sickness. The rest of all my estate, my funeral charges and the legacies aforesaid being first paid and discharged, I give to my two brothers Matthew Sillesby and Thomas Sillesby to be equally divided between them, whom I appoint executors of this my last will and testament.

Wit: Charles Ofspring, Jeremiah Whittaker.   Pembroke, 190.

1650, Oct. 21, Samuel Sillesby, vice-president of Queen's Coll. Cambr., bur.   Registers of St Antholin, London.

In the year 1644, according to an old parchment register of Queen's College, " Mr Sillesby (was) chosen Proctor for ye yeere ensuing, beginning at Michaelmasse next, by ye Consent of ye President and maior part of ye fellowes." The President at this time was Edward Martin D.D. On the 11th day of June 1644 the Earl of Manchester, under the authority of an Act of Parliament, appointed nine new fellows, to fill vacancies that had been created in April. Among these new Fellows was Samuel Sillesby. Another was William Ames. We are informed that all these new Fellows were from Emmanuel College, except John Hoare and Samuel Glover, who were from St Catherine's Hall. Mr. Sillesby was then styled Master of Art. He also obtained the degree of B.D.

His brother Thomas was entered at Queen's Coll. as a Pensioner 15 November 1644. Tutor Mr. Sillesby. B A. 1647–8.

I have not examined the Oxford records to find traces of him there. His will is as follows:

Memorandum that THOMAS SILLESBY of West Thurrock in the County of Essex, deceased, on or about the eighth day of September 1653 &c., did utter and speak these words following, or the like in effect, vizt, I give unto my brother Matthew Sillesby the moiety or one half part of all my estate; and I give unto my sister Bethia Marten and her children the other moiety or half part of my estate; and my will is that my said sister shall only have the benefit and increase of the said moiety &c. during her natural life; and after her decease that the same moiety &c. be equally divided between her two children, and that the same legacy given to my said sister and her children shall remain in the hands of John Sandford Esq. to their use, and she to have the yearly use thereof during her life, for her more comfortable maintenance: and my will is that my said sister's husband, in regard of his ill husbandry, shall not receive or intermeddle with any part of the said legacy given to my sister and her children: and I make and appoint my brother Matthew Sillesby my sole executor and John Sandford Esq. and John Ashon my overseers: which words, or the like in effect, he the said Thomas Sillesby uttered and declared as and for his last will and testament nuncupative in the presence and hearing of the said Mr. John Sandford and Elizabeth Dickens, whom the testator desired to take notice thereof.

The above will was proved by M[r] Matthew Sillesby the sole executor, who in the registered probate act is wrongly called son of the deceased.

Brent, 28.

M[d] the x[th] day of June in the xij[th] yere of the reigne of o[r] Sau[r]aine Lady Quene Elizabethe etc.—Chadde Browne the sone of Arthure Browne of Melcheborne in the Countie off Bedford yoman hathe put himself ap'rentice w[th] Leon[r]d Omston of North'ton Curriar, ffrom the day off the makinge hereof unto the ende and terme off eight yeres. And Leon[r]d to him eu[r]y quarter iiij[d] (*sic*). And it is farther agreed that after the vij yeres be doone the seide Chadde Browne shall s[r]ue the viij[th] yere as a Jorenyman and ffor that yeres seruice shall giue the saide Chadde Browne ffyve marks off mony and doble apparrell for hollyday and workinge day.

[The above name, well known to New England genealogists, caught my eye as I was examining the book wherein is contained the Inrolments of Indentures of Apprenticeship and Admissions to Freedom now preserved among the archives of the town of Northampton. The Indentures of apprent:ceship begin with the early years of the reign of Elizabeth; the Admissions to Freedom begin A.D. 1606. Among the latter I found the following interesting items referring to another well known name:—]

1617–18   Egideus Corey, maulster, p concessū colloquii admiss. fuit decimo die Martii et solvit—x[li].

[This entry had a cross against it on the margin, but the next year appeared the following:—]

1619–19   Gyles Corey maulster, p concessū colloquii i admiss. fuit xxij° die Januarii et solvit—x[le].

[I considered it not a bad day's work when I found two such names as those, to say nothing of others which I hope to present to the readers of my "Glean-ings." HENRY F. WATERS.

Mr. William H. Whitmore announced these discoveries in relation to Brown and Corey, in the New York *Nation*, March 9. In relation to the apprenticeship of Chad Browne, he says: "The year is A.D. 1570, and the apprentice was doubtless fourteen years old. It is well known that a Chad Browne came" to Boston "in 1638, in the ship Martha, when his oldest son John was eight years old"; that he settled at Providence the same year; "that he and his son and grandson were successively elders in the Baptist church, and that the liberality of his descendants is commemorated in Brown University. It is hardly probable that the apprentice, Chad, was the emigrant, as he would have been over seventy when his son was born. Coincidence of names makes it highly probable that the apprentice was father of the emigrant. As the general work of Mr. Waters for the REGISTER does not allow of special searches, will not some of the graduates of Brown contribute the necessary funds to investigate the clue so that Mr. Waters may do for their founder what he has done for Harvard."

In relation to the admission to freedom of Giles Corey, Mr. Whitmore re-marks: "Here we seem to be on the track of the father of that stout-hearted victim of the Salem witchcraft, Giles, who was born about 1616." We trust that both clues will be followed.—EDITOR.]

WALTER LIGHT of Radway, within the parish of Busshopper Itchington and County of Warwick, gentleman, 16 March 1596, proved 22 April 1597. My will is that my body shall be buried in the chancel of the parish church of Radwaye aforesaid, near where my wife lieth, with such convenient funerals as shall seem good to my executor. I give to the mother church of Litchfield twelve pence. I give towards the repair of the parish church of Radwaye ten shillings and towards the repair of the church of Chadshunte three shillings fourpence. To the poor in Radwaye twenty shillings, to be distributed by the discretions of my well beloved friends Richard Hill, vicar there, and my executor. Whereas my cousin Robert Washington maketh demand of divers things which he saith was given by his grandmother, in recompense and discharge thereof and of my further good will I do give to him ten pounds, to be paid within one year next after my decease. I give unto Christopher Washington my kinsman five pounds, to be paid to him within one year after my decease, as before. To my kinsman William Washington five pounds, to be paid in like sort. To Thomas Washington my kinsman five pounds, to be paid at his age of twenty and one years. To Amy Wakelyn, my kinswoman, seven pounds, to be paid to her within one year after my decease. To Ursula Adcocke, my kinswoman, ten pounds, to be paid in like sort and manner. To Walter Nicholls my godson five pounds, to be paid to him when he shall come to the age of twenty and one years. I do forgive Thomas Savadge, my kinsman, of Kyneton, all such debts as he doth owe me either by bill, bond or otherwise. I do give to all my servants that shall fortune to serve in house with me at the time of my decease, as well men servants as maid servants, to every of them three shillings four pence, to be paid to them at the end of their term. Furthermore I do give to every of my god children three shillings four pence.

Moreover whereas I have taken upon me to be executor unto my brother Mr. Christopher Light and have executed the same till this time, by means whereof there are divers sums of money come into my hands more than is laid out, to the value of one hundred and fifty pounds or thereabouts, of which said sum there is ten pounds in the hands of Mr. Edward Yorke, which I delivered to John Eborne and have no writing to show for the same, now my will is that if Richard Lighte, son of the said Christopher, to whom if he shall live to the age of twenty and one years I am to make accompte of the said money, do accept and allow of all such bills, reckonings and charges, as well about his pretended wardship as other wise, as I have left in writing and is true that I have paid, and do accept of the said sum which shall appear by those reckonings to be due unto him in full discharge of all things to him by me due or payable or which I may be charged with as executor unto his father, without and contrariety or suit in law against my executor or executors, whomsoever they shall be, and do lawfully and sufficiently by his deed in writing discharge and acquit my said executor and executors of and from all debts, "dueties" and demands which were due by me unto him the day of my decease, then I do, of my own free gift, give and bequeath unto my said kinsman Richard Light all such plate which came and yet is in my hands which was his said fathers, and also such fine linens which be in a coffer in my house at this present, which were also his fathers, if he live to the said age of twenty and one years, then and upon performance of the premisses to mine executors according to this my will to be delivered to him and not otherwise. But if he shall contend in law or not accept of the said sum, as before, or refuse to allow of such bills and reckonings as my said executor or executors shall offer unto him, or not make unto him or them such discharge as is afore said, or if he shall die before his said age of twenty and one years, then my will is that the whole legacy or legacies to him by me given as aforesaid shall be utterly void and of no validity.

And also whereas my kinsman Lawrence Washington hath procured and gotten administration, after the decease of his brother Walter Washington, of the goods and chattels which were his said brothers, so that it is yet doubtful what the Law will determine of two leases of the farm in Radwaye (wherein I now dwell) the state whereof was in the said Walter Washington at the time of his decease, which leases in truth I always did mean and intend that he the said Walter and his wife and children should have and enjoy, by means whereof I rest uncertain what to give to my daughter Alice Washington the late wife of the said Walter Washington and to her two children John and Katherine Washington until the matter be decided either by law or other ways who shall have the said leases. Wherefore I do by this my last will and testament give and commit all my goods and chattels whatsoever to my well beloved friend John Murden of Ratley in the County of Warwick, who is natural father to my said daughter Alice Washington and grandfather to the said children, to the end and intent that when it is determined either by law or other ways what will become of the said two leases that then the said John Murden shall make such distribution, as well of the said leases as of all my other said goods and chattels and other things aforesaid, my debts and legacies being discharged, between my said daughter Alice and her children, according to the discretion of the said John Murden; which I mean shall be in discharge of certain covenants and agreements which were made between me the said Walter Lighte and the said John Murden at the marriage of his daughter unto my kinsman Walter Washington. And of this my last will and testament I do constitute and make my said friend John Murden my sole executor and my well beloved cousin George Warner and my very good neighbor and friend Richard Aillmy overseers. And I give to either of them forty shillings.

Cobham, 33.

[As this family of Light were ancestors of our Washington, I give the following abstracts of wills which I have gathered from time to time. Let me, meanwhile, improve the opportunity by calling renewed attention to the error which slipped into the pedigree of Washington presented by me in 1889. Robert of Sulgrave married first, Elizabeth, daughter of Walter (and not Robert) Light.

HENRY F. WATERS.]

THOMAS LIGHT of Horley in Oxfordshire 6 January 1520, proved 30 January 1520. My body to be buried in the church of St Awdrey in Horley. To the high altar of the same church, for my tythes negligently forgotten, six shillings eight pence. To the same church a cope and a pair of vestments of black velvet. I will have a priest singing in the same church for me two years next ensuing for the Welth (sic) of my soul and Christen souls. I will that there be bought at London a great marble stone to lie upon me and my wife both after her decease, and therein to be graven I and my wife in brass with all our children. To the mother church of Lincoln three shillings four pence. To the church of Hornton three shillings four pence. To the church of Rotley three shillings four pence. To the church of Rodway three shillings four pence. To Thomas Blencow and Joane my daughter six pounds thirteen shillings four pence. To every one of their children ten sheep. To John Warner and Anne my daughter six pounds thirteen shillings four pence. To every one of their children ten sheep.

To Master William Pargetour my Curate, to pray for me, six shillings eight pence. I wolle (*sic*) that John Parsons, an old servant of mine, that he remain still servant with my wife and my son Christofer, and after that he is no longer able to do service I will that he remain still in my house and to have meet and drink, or else six pence a week as long as he liveth and be at his pleasure. I will that Agnes Warden, an old woman in my house, be ordered after the same manner as John Parsons. To Joane Heckes, a maid servant of mine, six shillings eight pence. To Thomas Horsman and his wife of Horneton ten shillings. To every of my godchildren one sheep. To Richard Mall my godchild ten sheep. I make mine executors my wife Agnes Lyght and my son Christopher Lyght. I make overseers Thomas Blencowe and William Malle of Adderbery. I bequeath to Thomas Blenecowe (*sic*) for his labor in this cause twenty shillings. To William Mall other twenty shillings and my best gown. All the rest of my goods not bequeathed, my debts paid, and also the lease and occupying of my farm for the years that be to come, and of all the pastures and other profits that I have within the Lordship of Halse within the County of Northampton I will that my wife and my son Christofer have them and occupy them jointly together, to the use of them both, as long as my said wife liveth; and after the decease of my wife I will that my son Christofer shall have them and he for to dispose for both our souls after his discretion. William Pargytur Curate and Vicar there of Horley a witness.

Maynwaring, 4.

AGNES LYGHT, widow, of the parish of St Lawrence Marston, 20 November 1523, proved 15 December 1523. My body to be buried in the church of St. Lawrence Marston. To the mother church of Lincoln four pence. To the church of Lawrence Marston for my "leyston" and to the reparation of the church twenty shillings. To the church of Hornton six shillings eight pence. To every one of my godchildren that be not married a sheep. To every one of my "childers childern" four sheep. To two children of William Malle, every one, four sheep, and to his daughter a cow. To Agnes Lyght my daughter my red saye cloth. To Thomas Lyght my great chest. To Margaret Blenckowe (certain household effects) and a cow. To Julian Malle, daughter to William Malle, and to Ellynor Warner (household effects). To the son of William Malles wife four sheep. To Richard Burton vicar of Horley six shillings eight pence, to pray for my soul and my husband's soul in his "bedroll." Thomas Brynknell Doctor of Divinity, overseer of this my will, to have to the profit of St John's of Banbury, six shillings eight pence and four sheep. The residue of my goods to Thomas Blenckowe and William Malle, the which I have ordained and made my executors, that they dispose them after their will for the wealth of my soul. Edmunde Pargytor priest, one of the witnesses. Bodfelde, 15.

CHRISTOFER LYGHTE 28 March 1546, proved 9 November 1546. My body to be buried in the parish church of Horley, if it be my chance to die there, as near to my father's grave as may be conveniently. To the high altar of the same church, for my tythes negligently forgotten, twelve pence. Towards the reparations of the said church forty shillings. "Item I will that every christian creature wthin the Parrishe of Horley and euery other man wooman and childe that dothe thethur resorte at the day of my buriall haue euery of theyme ij^d to pray for my soule, and euery priste that is at my buriall to haue viii^d and his Dynner." "Item I will to haue a priste to celebrate and to pray for my soule, for the soules of my ffather and mother, Thomas and Agnes, and other my freendes and for Xpeñ soules the space of one hole yere and to have for his stipende v^li vi^s viij^d." I will that Christofer Lighte my son have my whole manor of Horneton and my land there called Avenettes, Little Horneton and Waralles &c. with proviso that he grant to his brother Walter and his heirs male one annuity of five pounds sterling to be paid yearly out of the said manor of Horneton. The said Christofer to have more, my moiety of the manor of Horley and the lands appertaining, within the towns and fields of Horley and Molington. I give to Walter Lighte my son my house at Salton's corner within the town of Horley that William Peter now dwelleth in, to have and to hold to him and his heirs male forever. I give to Thomas Light my son all my lands and tenements in Banbery and in Banbery parish, to him and his heirs male forever. Provision for entailing. To Christopher my lease of the manor of Horley, my lease of the parsonage of Horley and my leases of Weescotte (also called Wescotte) and Knight Hardwick, with proviso that he keep for the use of his mother, during the time of Mr. Compton's lease of Wescotte and Hardwick, three score wether sheep in the fields of Horley and Horneton and twenty ewes and twenty hog sheep in Wescotte and six kyne "other" at Westcotte or in Horley field and a nag, to be kept as he keepeth his own, certain household stuff to the sons and to Agnes Pargetour and Johan Savage. And I will that both my daughters have each of them a cow and twenty couples "so that I separte this worlde betwene carrying tyme and sammas." To a poor child called Thomas Hayes six pounds thirteen shillings four pence. To certain others and to servants in the house and to godchildren. I will that Mr. Crocker have my best ring. I will that my brother Nicholas Woodwarde of London have for a remembrance five gilt spoons which he hath in his own keeping. The residue to my sons Christopher Lighte and Walter Lighte whom I make mine executors, willing and desiring my brother Robert Pargetor and my cousin Parson Box to be overseers &c., and I give them for their pains and labors in so doing three pounds six shillings eight pence.

One of the witnesses was John Crocker gen^t.   Alen, 19.

The following pedigree of this family is taken from the Visitation of Oxfordshire (Harleian Soc. Pub.) p. 141.

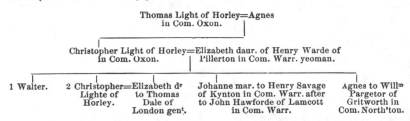

Thomas Light of Horley=Agnes in Com. Oxon.

Christopher Light of Horley=Elizabeth daur. of Henry Warde of in Com. Oxon. | Pillerton in Com. Warr. yeoman.

1 Walter.   2 Christopher=Elizabeth d^r   Johanne mar. to Henry Savage   Agnes to Willm
   Lighte of   to Thomas   of Kynton in Com. Warr. after   Pargetor of
   Horley.   Dale of   to John Hawforde of Lamcott   Gritworth in
                 London gen^t.   in Com. Warr.   Com. North'ton.

In the name of God Amen I MARTHA HAYWARD of the County of Stafford being sick and weak of body but of perfect sence and memory, thanks be given to God therefor Doe make and ordaine this my last Will & Testament

Impr^s I give and bequeath my Soul to God and my body to the Earth to be buryed in Christianlike and Decent manner att the disposition of my Exec^rs hereafter named and as for what worldly Estate it hath pleased God to bless me wth all I give devise and dispose of in the following manner & forme

Item I give and bequeath unto my two cousins John and Augustine the sons of my coz^n Lawrence Washington of Westmoreland County one negroe woman named Anne and her future increase and in case of their deaths before they come of age then I give the s^d negroe to the afores^d Lawrence Washington & his heirs forever.

Item I give unto my cozen Lawrence Washington son of Mr John Washington of Westmoreland County one mallatto girle named Suka to him and his heirs forever.

Item I give and bequeath unto my cozen John Washington son of the said John Washington of Westmoreland county one mallatto Girle named Kate to him and his heirs forever.

Item I give and bequeath my cozen Nathaniel Washington, son of the said John Washington one Negroe boy named John to him & his heirs forever.

I give and bequeath unto my Coz^n Hen: Washington son of the said John Washington one negroe boy named George William to him & his heirs for ever.

Item I give and bequeath unto my kinsman Mr John Washington of Stafford County one negroe woman named Petty and her future Increase to him & his heirs forever.

Item I give and bequeath unto my kinsman Mr Rich^d ffoot two thousands pn^{ds} Tobbacco to him & his heirs for ever.

Item it is my will & desire that my Ex^{trs} wth all convent^t speed after my decease doe procure and purchase for each of my two sisters in Law vizt Mary King and Sarah Todd a servant man or woman as they or either [of] them shall both like haveing att least four or five years to serve wch I doe give to them and their heirs forever.

Item I give and bequeath to my afores^d cozins the sons of my two coz^{ns} Lawrence and John Washington of Westmoreland County to Each of them a feather bedd and furniture to them and their heirs forever.

Item it is my will and desire that my Exec^{trs} with all Convent^t speed send to England to my Eldest sister Mrs Elizabeth Rumbold a Tunne of good weight of Tobacco, & the same I give to her and her heirs forever.

Item it is my desire that my said Executors Doe likewise take freight send for England to my other sister Mrs Marg^t Galbut [Talbut?] a Tonne of good weight of Tobbacco which I give to her and her and her [sic] heirs forever.

Item I give and bequeath unto Mr Wm Pruckner [?] of the County of York my gold signett.

Item I give and bequeath unto Ca^{pt} Law: Washington and his wife, Mr John Washington of Stafford County and his wife, Mr John Washington of Westmoreland County and his wife, Mary King, Sarah Todd and Mary Wheatley, each of them a gold of twenty shillings piece To be procured with all Convent^t speed after my decease.

Item I give and bequeath unto Samuel Todd son of Wm. Todd a heiffer about three years old.

Lastly after all my just Debts are p^d all the rest of my Estate whatsoever and wheresoever I doe give and bequeath unto Capt Lawrence Washington, Mr John Washington of Westmoreland County, & Mr John Washington of Stafford County to be Equall[y] Divided between them and I doe hereby [   ] Constitute and ordaine the afores^d Lawrence Washington & John Washington of Westmoreland County Execut^s of this my last will & Testament. In Witnesse whereof I have hereunto sett my hand and & ffixed my Seale this 6th day of May annoq^e Domi 1697.

MARTHA HAYWARD.

Signed, sealed and delivered in the presence of us : Geo. Weedon, Sarah Kelly, Sarah X Powell, her marke, John Pike.

Proved and Recorded the 8th of December, 1697.

 Vera copia Teste

  J. Perry

   D. C. Cur. Com. Stafford.

[The above will of Martha Hayward, sister of John Washington the emigrant ancestor of President Washington, was found among the Washington MSS. in the United States Department of State, by Mr. Worthington C. Ford of Brooklyn, N. Y., who communicated it to the New York *Nation* in a letter dated Nov. 8, 1892, which appeared in the *Nation* Nov. 17, 1892. Mr. Ford. in his letter, shows the importance of this will as evidence in favor of Mr. Waters's theory of the Ancestry of Washington.

In the *Nation*, Dec. 22, 1892, appears a letter from Mr. Ford, dated December 1st, in which he quotes from a communication to him by Mr Waters, as follows :

" It is certainly (apart from its great value for the light it throws upon the American family) the greatest discovery that has been made since I found that memorandum upon which my theory of the solution of the Washington problem (*i.e.*, as to the English connections) was chiefly founded.

" That theory undertook two tasks : first, to identify the Virginians, John and Lawrence Washington, with the eldest sons of Lawrence and Amphillis Washington, named in the will of Andrew Knowling of Tring; secondly, to identify Lawrence, the husband of Amphillis and father of the Virgianians, with Lawrence, the Fellow of Brasenose College and Rector of Purleigh. When the theory was published we did not know that there was any evidence existing to show that the parson of Purleigh was married. Probably (as it appears) Col. Chester knew; but, if so, his knowledge died with him. Then Mr. Conway, looking up documents referred to in Chester's MSS., came upon evidence which established the fact that Lawrence Washington of Purleigh had a wife living as late as the latter part of September, 1649. Afterwards Miss Walford found the burial of Mr. Lawrence Washington at Maldon (the date being 21st of January, 1652). This was undoubtedly the burial of Lawrence of Purleigh, who had been holding a poor and miserable living a few miles from Maldon, to which there was no parsonage attached. He was, therefore, in all probability, making Maldon his headquarters. With these new facts it seemed evident that nothing really stood in the way of eventually establishing a complete parallelism between the two. On the one side we had Lawrence, the husband of Amphillis. undoubtedly M..A., in all probability a clergyman, married probably in 1633 (if we may judge from the age of his eldest son), deceased between 1650 and 1655; on the other side, Lawrence of Purleigh, M A., a clergyman, married probably in 1633, when he gave up his Fellowship, and dead in 1652.

" In addition, I was able to prove an interesting connection between Lawrence of Purleigh and his family and Tring and Middle Claydon, the homes of Amphillis and her brother. Then the negative testimony was of tremendous value. Not another Lawrence, with all our searching, could be found, except the Purleigh man, who could meet the conditions; and now more than three years have elapsed, and we can still make the same assertion. M.A's do not grow on every bush. The records of Oxford have been ransacked, and we can pronounce it impossible to find there another Lawrence Washington, M.A. (other than the parson of Purleigh) ; and those at Cambridge have been so well examined that we can declare it altogether improbable that one will be found there. And nowhere else can we look for that other Lawrence Washington, M.A. In fact, there was no other—so you may imagine I felt quite sure that whatever evidence should turn up would be in confirmation of my theory, or certainly not opposed to it.

" Take the case of that sister of the two brothers in Virginia. We did not know what her name was until the will of her brother John was brought to light. According to my theory, she must have borne one of three names—Elizabeth, Margaret, or Martha. If any other, then the worse for my theory. We learned from that will that she was Martha, who, according to my theory, was the youngest sister of John, and he, as the youthful head of the orphaned family, would be likely to assist his youngest sister. Then came your discovery of that letter written in 1699 by John Washington of Stafford Co., referring to an Aunt

Howard. Of course, this must be that Martha whom we have been discussing. Now comes your last discovery, showing us that this Aunt Howard (or Hayward, for they are one and the same) was that Martha Washington, the youngest sister of the two Virginians. And she mentions sisters in England. Here would be another danger to my theory if that had been a weak one. That theory demanded that Martha's sisters should be two in number, and named Elizabeth and Margaret. Note the obliging way in which Mrs. Howard says ' my *eldest* sister, Elizabeth ' and ' my *other* sister, Margaret,' and the married name of the eldest caps the climax. The naming of Mrs. Elizabeth Rumbold clinches the matter. It is the keystone of the arch we have been building, securely binding the two sides together. When we find Mrs. Mewce, the known sister of Lawrence of Purleigh, calling Mrs. Rumbold ' neice,' and Martha Howard, the sister of John and Lawrence of Virginia, calling her ' sister,' we can no longer doubt the descent of our Washington from Lawrence Washington, the Rector of Purleigh."

The editor of the REGISTER trusts that further evidence bearing on this subject will be found in England or in this country.]

JOHN BREWER citizen and grocer of London 4 September 1631, proved 13 May 1636. I do will that after my decease my body be buried without any mourning apparel or gowns given to any but those of mine own household. To my dearly beloved father Thomas Brewer eight pounds yearly and every year so long as he shall happen to live after my decease (payable quarterly). I do will and bequeath unto my son John Brewer my plantation in Virginia called Stawley Hundred *als* Bruers Borough, only the third part of the profits thereof arising during the life of Mary my wife I do give unto her, as also the third part of all my goods and chattels besides which is also due unto her by the custom of the City of London. To my son Roger Brewer and my daughter Margaret Brewer forty pounds apiece, payable at day or marriage or age of one and twenty. To my brother Thomas Brewer forty shillings and to each of his children ten shillings, in one year after my decease. The residue to my said three children John, Roger and Margaret, to be equally divided between them, and I make them executors, but as they are now young and not able of themselves to manage and dispose of those things that belong unto them I do hereby authorize and appoint my dearly beloved wife, Mary Brewer, and my loving uncle Mr. Roger Drake, citizen and clothworker of London, not only overseers but also full and absolute guardians unto my said children. If my son John happen to die before he attain the age of twenty and one years then my plantation to go unto my son Roger and his heirs forever. And if both my said sons happen to die before they attain the age of twenty and one years then my said plantation to descend half to my daughter Margaret and half to my wife. To each of the said guardians forty shillings to buy each of them a ring for a remembrance of me.

Administration was granted to the widow Mary Brewer *als* Butler, the testator being said to have lately died in Virginia. Dale, 66.

GEORGE COLE of Dorchester, Dorset, merchant, 29 March 1659, proved 20 May 1659. I give and bequeath unto my trusty and loving wife Anne Cole six hundred pounds, she to give bond for repayment of one hundred pounds to be equally divided amongst my younger children in case she marry again. To said wife all my household stuff and utensils of household. To my eldest son, John Cole, and his heirs all that my lands and real estate lying and being in New England in America and also the sum of five hundred pounds in money, with what I have already given him towards the same therein included. And I give unto my said son all my study of books. In case he renounce his right in the said lands within eighteen months after my decease, then to enjoy his equal part and share in all the residue of the said estate with my younger children, over and above the said five hundred pounds. I give all my other estate in moneys, credits, debts, bills, bonds, accompts, goods of merchandize and other estate whatsoever unto my younger sons, George, Stephen, Jacob and Symon, and to my four daughters, Elianor, Anne, Mary and Sarah Cole, to be equally divided amongst all, except my son George Cole, who, my will is, shall have one hundred pounds less than my other younger children in respect of the moneys already bestowed with him in Apprenticeship. My will and desire is that the house for which I have lately contracted in this town be forthwith paid for out of my said estate last before mentioned (the said sums of six hundred pounds and five hundred pounds before devised being first satisfied). My wife shall hold and enjoy the said house for and during her natural life and the reversion I give to my said son John and his heirs, he paying (after the decease of my wife) one hundred pounds to my younger children &c.   Wife Anne and son John to be executors, and friends Mr. John Bushead the elder, Mr. John Heysome, Master Dawbeny Williams and Master Erasmus Baker overseers. To the poor of St. Trinity parish five pounds and five pounds to the poor of St. Peters . nd All Saints. A plot of garden mentioned as near the Guildhall. Elinor Cole one of the witnesses.   Pell, 267.

SIR PETER COLLETON of the parish of St. James, Middlesex, Bar[t], 12 January 1693–4, proved 24 April 1694. My body to be decently buried without pomp or solemnity and to be accompanied to the grave by my own family only. To my son John all my manors, lands, tenements and heredi- taments &c. in England, and my lands, tenements and plantations in the Island of Barbados and in Carolina, and my eighth part or share of the Province of Carolina, with all its dominions, royalties and jurisdictions, to have and to hold to him and the heirs of his body, lawfully begotten, when he shall come to the age one and twenty years. In the mean time my lov- ing brother in law Col. John Leslie of the Island of Barbados and Katherine Colleton my daughter and Mr. William Thornburgh of London, merchant, or such of them as shall be within the Kingdom of England at the time of my death, shall have the guardianship, care and tuition of the said John Colleton and shall receive the rents, issues and profits of the premises till he come to the age of one and twenty years; and I appoint them executors &c., in trust for the sole use and benefit of the said John, until he shall arrive at the age aforesaid, when he shall be my only executor. If he should die without issue before then I leave all my lands &c. in England and Carolina to my brother James Colleton and the heirs male of his body lawfully begotten.   To my daughter Katherine Colleton one thousand pounds and my Tally for three hundred pounds lent by me and paid into their Majesties' Exchequer in the name of the said Katherine and my share and dividend thereof by virtue of an Act of Parliament made in the fourth year of their Majesties' reign entitled an Act for granting to their Majesties certain rates and duties of Excise upon Beer, Ale and other liquors, for securing certain Recompences and Advantages, in the said Act mentioned, to such persons as should voluntarily advance the sum of ten hundred thousand pounds towards carrying on the War against France. To Anne Colleton, my younger daughter, fifteen hundred pounds at one and twenty or day of marriage, and fifty pounds a year in half yearly payments. To Charles Colleton, my natural son, a rent charge of thirty pounds a year, in quarterly payments out of my lands and tenements in the County and City of Exon. To Elizabeth Johnson daughter of William Johnson and Elizabeth Johnson heretofore my wife one thousand pounds. To Barbara Thacker one hundred pounds in four months after my decease. If the said John Colleton die without issue (lawful) before coming to the age of twenty one then all my personal estate shall be equally divided between my two daughters Katherine Colleton and Ann Colleton and the said Elizabeth Johnson. And in such case, and not otherwise, I give to the said Charles Colleton three hundred pounds. If the said John die without lawful issue male before coming to age and the said James die without lawful issue male &c. then all my real estate shall come to my right heirs &c. Anthony Weldon of the Middle Temple, Esq., and John Hothershall of Guiddy Hall, Rumford, Essex, Esq. to be overseers. The son proved the Will 31 January, 1700. Box, 72.

EDWARD COLLINGTON of St. Saviour's, Southwark, Surrey, joiner, 24 February 1659, proved 27 July 1660. To my loving wife Perrin Collington the lease of my house, with all the profits thereof, during the term not yet expired, if she shall so long live or continue a widow. In case of her marriage or death before the expiration of said lease it shall go to my grandchild, Edward Brookes, if then living, if not then to his sister Sarah. I give to my daughter Sarah ten pounds, in twelve months after my decease. To her eldest daughter, called Sarah, ten pounds either at day of marriage or at twenty four years of age.

Item—I give unto my daughter Isabell in New England ten pounds, that is to say five shillings unto my daughter Isabell and nine pounds fifteen shillings, the remainder of the ten pounds, to be divided amongst her children. I give to my cousin Mary Collington five pounds, in a twelve month. To my cousins William and Sarah Collington ten shilling apiece in a year. In case my cousin Mary die before the year be expired the five pounds given unto her shall be equally divided between my cousins William and Sarah, and in case the said William and Sarah die then it shall go to my brother Robert Collington and his wife. To my said brother Robert and his wife five shillings each. I make my wife Perrin Collington whole and sole executrix and my friends Mr. George Ewer and Mr. John Winnington overseers. Nabbs, 109.

WILLIAM GREGORY, of the town and County of Nottingham gen^t, 18 June 1650, proved 5 February 1651. I give and bequeath unto George Gregory, my grandchild, eldest son of my son John Gregory, all those my three Water Corn mills, two houses or tenements, eight crofts, tofts, closes or pingles and eleven acres of land arable, meadow or pasture, be the same more or less, to the said mills or tenements belonging, which I purchased with the said mills, situate &c. in Lenton and Radford in the County of Nottingham; and all my tythes or tenths of hay &c. in the fields and territories of Lenton and Radford &c., to the said George Gregory and the heirs male of his body lawfully begotten and to be begotten, and for want of such issue to Philip Gregory, second son of the said John, remainder to Francis Gregory, third son, then to Edward Gregory, fourth son and last to my right heirs. To Philip all my fourteen selions or leyes of meadow or pasture ground, containing by estimation seven acres, in the town of Notts. aforesaid at or upon a place there called the little Rye Hills and a close of five acres I purchased of John Heywood, in the town of Notting-

ham aforesaid, near a place called St. Anne Well, to the said Philip &c.,
then to Francis then Edward and lastly to my right heirs. I give to my
brother Henry Gregory twenty marks if he live six months after my decease, and to every child of his body lawfully begotten (except my cousin
Perry, his daughter) that shall be living at the end of six months after my
decease, five pounds, to be paid within twelve months after my decease.
I also give and bequeath the sum of four pounds to be paid towards
the charges of fetching of the said legacies, given as aforesaid unto my
said brother Henry and his children, they being now, as I am informed,
in the parts beyond the seas called New England. I give and bequeath to
my said Cousin Perrie, my said brother Henry's daughter, the sum of ten
pounds, to be paid within six months after my decease. To my brother
John Gregory, if living six months next after my decease, fifteen pounds.
To Philip Gregory, Francis Gregory, Edward Gregory, Elizabeth Gregory,
and Anne Gregory, children of my said son John, to every of them one
hundred pounds, as they attain to their several ages of eighteen years. To
each of the children of my nephew John Gregory twenty shillings, six
months after my decease. To Elizabeth the wife of my said son John
Gregory and to my said son Francis Gregory and Anne his wife, to every
of them twenty shillings in six months &c., to buy each of them a gold
ring. To my cousin William Baylye of Grimston, in the County of Leicester, three pounds and ten shillings and to every one of his children six
shillings eight pence in three months &c. To James Chadwick Esq. and
to my brother Alderman James to either of them a piece of gold of twenty
and two shillings, in six months &c., to buy either of them a gold ring. To
my honored friends Col. Francis Pierrepont Esq. and Col. John Hutchinson Esq., in six months &c., forty shillings each, to buy either of them a
gold ring. To my much esteemed good friend Huntington Plumptree Esq.,
in six months &c., a piece of gold of twenty two shillings to buy him a gold
ring. To my loving friends Nicholas Charleton Esq., John Mason gen^t,
William Flamsteede gen^t, and to my god daughter Mary Edge, in six months
&c., twenty shillings apiece to buy each of them a gold ring. To Mr.
Walter Edge and Mrs Edge his wife and to Mr. Randolphe Miller, William
Jackson, Adam Jackson and John Jackson, in six months &c., ten shillings
each. To Thomas Widoson ten shillings. The rest of my lands to my
wife Anne. The residue of my goods &c. to my son John whom I constitute sole executor.   Bowyer, 30.

VALENTINE LUDWELL of Wells in Somerset, 2 June, 9th of James, proved
9 May 1623. To St. Andrews Cathedral of Welles twelve pence. To
the poor people of St. Cutberts in Welles three shilling and four. To my
son Thomas twenty pounds in one year, my best bed, with the covering
sheets and blankets thereunto belonging, my best brasen crock, my best
pan of brass, three platters, three porrengers and three saucers of " Tynne,"
and one of my candlesticks of copper. To Ellinor my daughter one little
vessel called a skyllet of brass, one pottenger, one saucer and candlestick
and ten shillings in money. The residue of my goods, chattels and debts
I give unto Christian my wife, whom I make my sole and whole executrix.
Wit: Thomas Jenkins the elder, Thomas Jenkiens, William Jenkins,
Elizabeth Poulen.   Swann, 49.

THOMAS LUDWELL of Bruton in Somerset, gen^t, 10 November 1676,
proved 17 January 1678. The whole interest of all the money I am possessed of in London to be paid to my dear mother during her natural life,

excepting two hundred pounds sterling out of the principal, to be paid to my dear friend Mrs. Margaret Hayes of Hallyport, near Maidenhead, and these legacies following, vizt to Mr James Hayes of Hallyport ten pounds, and to John Jefferyes, Mr. Edward Leman and Mr. John Browne (my executors in trust) to each of them ten pounds, and to the poor of Bruton ten pounds. After the decease of my mother the principal sum shall be equally divided between my four sisters, Mary, Margaret, Sarah and Jane. I give unto my brother Philip Ludwell and to his heirs forever all my lands and other estate in Virginia. If he die before me, then I give all my land in Virginia to his son Philip and my personal estate to be equally divided between him and his sister Jane, except thirty pounds sterling which I order to be paid to the Vestry of Bruton Parish in Virginia, to be employed towards the building a church; and I do appoint Major Theophilus Hone Capt. Thomas Thorp and Mr. Henry Hartwell my executors in trust for Virginia part of my will, giving each of them, out of that estate, five pounds.   King, 7.

ROBERT LUDWELL of Brewton in Somerset, mercer, 16 November 1678, proved 14 February 1678. Have settled upon wife the tenement wherein I now live, called Roper's tenement, with two pieces of meadow lately Mr Jarvis', situate in Brewton, and the tenement in Stoke Hollway, in the County aforesaid, which I hold of Sir Stephen Fox. My wife to enjoy all this for life, the remainder being settled on eldest son Robert. I nominate and appoint my brother John Ludwell of Wadham College in Oxford, Doctor of Physick, and my brother Thomas Ludwell the executors of this my last will and testament. To my son James Ludwell all such estate as I have or claim, after the decease of my mother, of and in two grounds in Brewton, the one called School House Close and the other Rye Ash, my son James to hold them when he shall attain the age of one and twenty. To son John three acres in the North Field of Brewton at his age of one and twenty, and all such benefit and advantage that may happen unto me from any of the estate of my brother Thomas Ludwell by the will of my father. To son Lewis Ludwell two hundred and fifty pounds at one and twenty, and all the benefit &c. that may happen unto me from any estate of my brother John Ludwell by the will of my father. To my daughter Christian Ludwell two hundred pounds at one and twenty or day of marriage. A similar bequest to daughter Mary. A broad twenty shilling piece of gold to each child. To brother Thomas Ludwell my black gelding and hair camlet cloak. To brother in law James Albyn my best hat if he please to accept it.   King, 20.

CHRISTIAN LUDWELL of Brewton in Somerset, widow, 24 April 1691, proved 19 February 1695. All the personal estate &c. either of mine own or my late husband's Robert Ludwell properly belongs to my six children by virtue of their father's last Will &c. and I give them all my right, title and interest &c. and appoint my brothers in law John Ludwell of Oxford, Doctor of Physick, and Thomas Ludwell of Brewton, mercer, my executors. I give to my daughters Christian and Mary Ludwell all my rings and wearing apparel.   Bond, 16.

AUGUSTIN LYNDON, late of Boston in New England and now of the parish of St. Paul, Shadwell, Middlesex, shipwright, 10 April 1699, proved 29 August 1699. To my beloved son Josias Lyndon, now or late of Rhode Island in New England, and to the heirs of his body forever all those parts

and proportions of my house and lands near the Town Dock in Boston in
New England which I bought of John Scotto and Mahittabell his sister,
and all other of my estate in New England.   To Anne Bellamy, for life, a
tenement in Plough St., St. Mary Whitechapel, now in possession of Mr.
Sparke, she paying the ground rent of fifty shillings per annum; afterwards
to my cousin John Johnson, joiner.   To him also all my messuages &c. in
St. Mary Whitechapel, provided if my son Josias or my grandson Samuel
Lyndon come over at any time the said John shall pay my said son or
grandson twelve pounds for clothing him and paying his passage back again.
John Johnson to be sole executor.   Pett, 136.

GRACE TYLER the now wife of John Tyler of Colchester, Essex, say-
weaver, 24 May 1647, proved 19 July 1647.   All that my copyhold messuage or tenement given me in and by the last will and testament of James
Aldous, late of Dennington in the County of Suffolk, carpenter, my late
husband deceased, together with all and singular the lands, meadows, pastures and feedings thereunto belonging &c., shall be sold within one whole
year next after my decease by mine executors &c., together with Richard
Aldous of Winkfield, Suffolk, yeoman &c. as expressed in the will of my
said late husband, and the moiety of the money raised by such sale shall be
disposed of as follows:—To Sauina Mouser, my sister, ten pounds within
one month after said sale.   All the residue of the said moiety of the money
so raised shall then be put out and improved for the benefit and commodity
of my said husband John Tyler during his natural life, and the profits &c.
paid to him every half year.   After his decease I give all the residue of
the said moiety as follows, vizt to my sister Elizabeth Brock of Dedham in
New England five pounds within a half year after the decease of my said
husband, and to John Brock, Elizabeth Brocke and Anne Brock, the children of my said sister Elizabeth, ten pounds to be equally divided amongst
them, within one half year &c.   To Sauina Mouser my sister and to
Samuel Smith, Richard Smith, Sauina Smith, William Mouser and Henry
Mouser, the five children of the said Sauina my sister, thirty pounds to be
equally divided amongst them within one half year &c.   To John Burgesse,
eldest son of my late sister Sibilla Burgesse deceased, five pounds within
one half year &c.   To James Burgesse, Peter Burgesse, Sibilla Burgesse
and Elizabeth Burgesse, the children of my said sister Sibilla, ten pounds,
to be equally divided amongst them &c.   And, with my husband's consent,
I will that the residue of my goods and household stuff shall be equally
divided and parted amongst the said four children of my sister Sibilla, immediately after the decease of my said husband.   All the gifts, legacies and
sums of money herein formerly given shall be paid at or in the South porch
of the parish Church of Winckfield aforesaid.   I appoint my cousins John
Browne of Brundish and William Younges of Cratfield, Suffolk, to be executors.   All the overplus or surplusage of the aforesaid moiety remaining
shall be equally divided and parted amongst the children of Elizabeth
Brocke and Sibilla Burgesse my sisters and Sauina Mouser my sister.
Consented to by John Tyler husband of the abovenamed Grace Tyler.
                                                              Fines, 165.

GERVASE PARTRICH citizen and cordwainer of London, 11 June 1647,
proved 20 August 1647.   I give and bequeath unto my loving wife Katherine Partrich, for life, all my messuages, lands and tenements in London
and the towne and parishes of Barking, Essex, and Leneham, Kent, she

keeping the same in good reparacions during that time. After her decease my messuage or tenement, with the yard, garden, orchard, &c., in Axe Street in the town of Barking, now in the tenure of William Kensum, butcher, which I purchased of Robert Knaresborough, and also those my two parcels of land containing by estimation five acres of land called Culverhouse Crofts lying at Loxfoord gate, Barking, now in the tenure or occupation of Richard Reeue of Barking, shall remain, come and be unto my brother Ralph Partrich, clerk, for life, and after his decease I give, will and appoint the same unto and amongst the two daughters of my said brother Ralph, viz⁺ Mary the wife of John Marshall of Leneham, Kent, mercer, and Elizabeth, the wife of Thomas Thatcher, clerk, equally to be parted and divided between them. After the decease of my said wife my messuage, with garden and orchard, called Davie's house, and the two closes called Pinnell's, at or near Great Ilford in Barking, now in the tenure of William Payne, shall remain and come unto my brother Randolph Partrich of the town and port of Dover, Kent, apothecary, for life, and after his decease to and amongst the three sons of my said brother (that is to say) John, James and Samuel Partrich, equally to be parted and divided amongst them. After my wife's decease my messuage, with the outhouses &c., in North Street, Barking, and my piece of land near Loxford Bridge, in Barking, which I purchased of Robert Knaresborough, shall remain and come unto Robert Partrich and Elizabeth Partrich, the two children of Gervase Partrich, citizen and haberdasher of London, deceased, equally to be parted and divided &c. After my wife's decease my messuage, with barn, stable, yard &c., in Leneham, Kent, which I purchased of Benjamin Brooker, and that my piece of meadow called Millmead in Leneham shall remain and come unto my sister Elizabeth Fydge widow, late the wife of David Fidge of Feversham, Kent, Kerseymaker, deceased, for life, and, after her decease, to three of the children of the said David Fidge and Elizabeth his late wife (that is to say) James, Jeremy and Mary Fidge. After my wife's decease my messuage &c., in All Hallows the Less, London, the which I purchased of Michael Lowe Esq., shall remain and come unto James Partrich, citizen and vintner of London, son of my brother James Partrich late of Leneham deceased. After my wife's decease my messuage or tenement and garden &c. in Heath Street Barking, which I purchased of Nicholas Webling and Triamore Sparke, shall remain and come unto Mary Fidg, the daughter of my said sister Elizabeth. I give and bequeath unto my masters, the Company of Cordwainers of London, for a dinner or supper to be made for them on the day of my funeral, ten pounds. To Matthew Tarleton and Daniel Pen, beadles, of the said Company, twenty shillings apiece. I give and bequeath unto my kinswoman Anne Gillowe, the wife of Francis Gillowe, gen⁺, five pounds. To my kinswoman Edith Richardson, to be paid into her own hands, forty shillings. To Edward Richardson forty shillings. To Dorothy Nayler, Nicholas Plowman and Elizabeth Plowman forty shillings apiece. To Mrs. Anne Carter, widow, forty shillings. To my friends William Frith, citizen and draper of London, and William Newbold, citizen and cordwainer of London, forty shillings apiece in token of my love. To Francis Gillowe and Thomas Floyd sometimes my servants, forty shillings apiece. To Mr. William Lichfield and Mr. William Geare, citizens and cordwainers of London, thirteen shillings and fourpence apiece. To Rachel Granger, the daughter of Judith Granger deceased, forty shillings. To Gervase Michell twenty shillings. To Bridget Ingland, my now maid servant, fifty shillings. To the poor of the parish of St. Margaret Moses in London forty shillings. To Joan Aynsworth ten shillings. I make my brother Randolph Partrich of Dover, apothecary, sole executor, and give him five pounds for his pains. The residue of my goods &c. to my wife Katherine, in full satisfaction of such part of my personal estate as to her may appertain and belong by the custom of the City of London.   Fines, 172.

WILLIAM HADDOCKE, planter, now bound on a voyage to Virginia, 4 October 1648, proved 27 August 1649. My brother Richard Haddocke, girdler, standeth bound and engaged for me by obligation, dated 29th September last, unto John Corey, stiller, for the payment of forty six shillings sterling, at the end of ten months now next coming, or within ten days next after the arrival of the ship William and Anne from her now intended voyage to Virginia first happening; and also by one other obligation, dated the [?] of the date hereof, with condition of the payment of eighteen pounds to William Lucke, Mr of the said ship, at the return thereof from Virginia, or at the end of nine months now next coming, which shall first happen. I have left in the custody of William Whitbye at Virginia an order of Court for the recovering and receiving of all such moneys and portion as is yet due and unpaid to me for my last wife's portion. By my Letter of Attorney I have given full power unto Arthur Purnell of Virginia to receive, keep and dispose for my use all my goods, chattels, debts and estate whatsoever in Virginia. I stand indebted to Ellen Ady, spinster, for the sum of twelve pounds. I give to my said brother Richard all my goods and estate whatsoever in Virginia or elsewhere for the payment and discharge of the said debts and obligations. The remainder to go to my said brother.
Wit: Thomas Huger, Matthew Burchfield and James Windus Scr.
Fairfax, 122.

JOSEPH COLLYER the elder, citizen and grocer of London, 21 August 1648, proved 28 September 1649. To the poor of St. Saviours Southwark, where I dwell, ten pounds. Twenty pounds to be distributed to ten or twenty poor Godly Christians, as my executors, in their discretions shall think fit. To my brother Abel Collyer twenty pounds. To my niece Elizabeth Bourne, the daughter of my sister Elizabeth Bourne, ten pounds. To my sister Judith Warner ten pounds. To my sister Rhoda Dorton, ten pounds. I give to my sister Mary Browninge in New England the sum of ten pounds. To my sister Dorcas Slingsby thirty pounds, by three pounds per annum, for the space of ten years. If she dies before the expiration of the said ten years it shall be disposed towards the bringing up of her youngest child. Fifty pounds to be distributed amongst the children of my brother Abel and my sisters. Whereas I had threescore pounds in money of my sister Rachaell, now the wife of Richard Parnell of Epsham, unto which I added one hundred and therewith purchased a house and lands in Epsham wherein my said sister and her husband have dwelt and enjoyed about ten or twelve years and have not paid any rent (the said house being worth ten pounds per annum) I do hereby remit unto the said Richard and Rachaell all the rent that is past and will that they shall or may hold the said house and land during her life, paying only forty shillings per annum unto my son Joseph. And I give my said sister Rachaell ten pounds. Reference to a grant made to testator, 19 May 1647, by Marlyon Rithe of Chipstead Surrey, gent, of a house and farm called Storracks, containing by estimation one hundred and three acres (evidently a mortgage as security for payment at my now dwelling house in Southwark of five hundred pounds 27 March 1654). On the redemption of the said messuage I give three hundred pounds to my son Samuel (to be paid at one and twenty) and the other two hundred pounds to my sons Joseph and Benjamin. To Joseph and Benjamin the lease of my dwelling house in Southwark &c. and of my garden house near the upper ground in St. Saviours. To sons Joseph, Abel and Samuel all my household stuff and plate which I was possessed of before I was last married, to Elizabeth my now wife. To the said Elizabeth one third of my personal estate &c., and all the household stuff and plate which was her own before our intermarriage. To my daughter in law Anna Harris ten pounds at one and twenty or marriage. To my niece Susan Warner, daughter of my sister Judith Warner, ten pounds if unmarried at the time of my decease. To the two daughters of my daughter Savage, Hannah and Elizabeth Savage, one hundred pounds, fifty pounds each, at one and twenty or marriage. The residue to my four children Elizabeth Savage, Joseph, Benjamin and Nathaniel Collyer, equally to be divided amongst them. Fairfax, 136.

HENRY SMITH of Wraysbury, Bucks., 1 August 1681, proved 24 October 1682. My body to be buried in a decent manner. I do give unto my daughter Martha Camock five shillings. To my daughter Mary Lord in New England five shillings. To my daughter Rebecca Lee five shillings. To my son Elisha Smith five shillings. To my daughter Elizabeth Smith, not yet disposed of in marriage, I do give fifty pounds, to be paid at the time of her marriage, if she survive after her mother. I do, out of that dear and tender love I bear unto my beloved wife, Mrs. Anna Smith, give and bequeath all and singular my goods, chattels, leases, debts, ready money, plate, rings, household stuff, apparel, brass, pewter, bedding and all other my substance whatsoever, movable or immovable, quick and dead, of what nature, quality or condition the same are or be, as well in my own possession as in the hands and possession of any other person whatsoever, to her own proper use and behoof, whom I do hereby ordain and appoint to be my only executrix.

xxiv° Octobris 1682. Which day appeared personally Cuthbert Walker of the parish of St. Gregories' London, haberdasher, aged about fifty, and Rebecca Lee, of Wraysbury in the County of Bucks., widow, aged about thirty years,.one of the daughters of the deceased, being severally sworn upon the Holy Evangelists deposed that they were well acquainted with the within named Henry Smith, the testator deceased, and with his manner or character of handwriting, and having perused the will within written and the name Henry Smith thereto subscribed believe the same to be all wrote with the proper handwriting of the said deceased. *Jurati coram* Rich Lloyd Surr. Cottle, 123.

BRIAN JANSON of London Esq. 5 November 1634, proved 13 December 1634. The poor of the parishes of St. Margaret Moses and of Becconsfield. My body to be interred in the chancel of the parish church of Ashby leegors in the Co. of Northampton. My son in law Robert Thorpe to be sole executor, and I give unto him and Anne his wife all my lands in Oxfordshire which I had in trust for me of and from one Whytinge, and all my other lands, tenements &c., and my interest in lands &c. in Ireland belonging to the Company of Drapers in London, and my share out of the rents due for the same.

Commission issued 9 December 1664 to Henry Janson grandson of the deceased to administer, according to the tenor of the will, the goods &c. not fully administered by Robert Thorpe the executor, now also deceased.

Seager, 116.

MARY GODDARD of St. Bennett Fincke, London, widow, 12 March 1635, proved 6 July 1638. My body to be buried as near unto my pew door in said parish church as conveniently may be, in such decent manner as my executor shall think fit for my degree. To Mr. Roger Warfield, minister and curate of the said parish of St. Bennett Fincke, and to the poor of the said parish. To my cousin William Campion Esquire, the son of Sir William Campion, knight, all my lands &c. in Thawite (?) Suffolk. The Lady Elizabeth Campion, the Lady Ann Campion and Mrs. Barbara Springett. My cousins Elizabeth Campion, daughter of Sir William Campion, and Elizabeth Campion daughter of Sir Henry Campion. My two cousins Henry and Edward, sons of the said Sir William. Bryan Janson son of my cousin Mr. John Janson, and Anne Janson, daughter of my said cousin Mr. John Janson. Mrs. Elizabeth Campion daughter of Mr. Edward Campion. My friend Mr. Eleazar Hudson M.D. My cousin Francis Stone. My two brothers in law John and Christopher Goddard and their sister Susan Dawes. Mrs. Fenton widow, and her daughter Wright, and her daughter Sara. Mrs. Rose Parker, widow, and Mrs. Mary Webbe, widow. Mr. Henry Huchenson scrivener and Mercy his wife. My faithful and painful servant Susan Dawes. Lee, 91.

THOMAZINE J:ANSON the relict of John J:anson of London Esquire deceased, 27 December 1658, with codicils (the last dated 29 December) proved 18 February 1658. My body to be decently interred within two days after my decease, at Katherine Creechurch, in the chancel near my friends. To my sister the Lady Katherine Oldfield, for mourning, ten pounds. To my nephew William Oldfield Esquire, and his wife, son to the Lady Oldfield, for mourning, twenty pounds. To my nieces Elizabeth and Sarah Oldfield, the children of my brother Joseph Oldfield deceased, twenty pounds, to be equally divided &c. To my sister Martha Smith twenty pounds and to her husband, for mourning, ten pounds. To my niece Katherine Oldfield a ruby ring which was my mother's. To my son in law Bryan J:anson Esquire one hundred pounds, within a year. To my nephew Robert Winch five pounds. To Daniel and Rebecca Winch, the children of my niece Thomasine Winch deceased, ten pounds apiece. To Susan, Mary and Thomasine Harrington, the children of my nephew Isaac Harrington deceased, thirteen pounds.

I give to Judith Towser of New England, daughter to my nephew Thomas Smith deceased, ten pounds, but in case the said Judith Towser should die before it be due them I give it to her child or children. I give to John Wryeth, Samuel Wryeth, Mary Wryeth, the children of my niece Mary Wryeth deceased, thirty pounds, to be equally divided amongst them, but in case any one of them shall die before his or her portion shall become due and payable then I give the part of him or her so dying to their brother Marlion, son to my said niece Mary. If any two of them die I give their parts to the survivor and the said Marlion (equally). To John, Samuel, Ebenezer, Martha, Mary and Rebecca Wyeth, the children of my niece Thomazine Wyeth deceased, threescore pounds (equally &c.). To John Barlee and his wife and daughter, for mourning, twenty pounds. To Master William Taylor, minister of Coleman Street, London, five pounds, and in case he preach my funeral sermon I give him forty shillings more. To Master Thomas Gouge, minister of St. Sepulchres Church near Newgate, five pounds. To Master Bates, Minister of Dunstan in the West, three pounds and to Master Peirce, the Lecturer there, forty shillings, unless I give it to them in my live time. To Master Samuel Winston, Minister of Everdon in Northamptonshire, five pounds. To the poor children of Ledgers Ashby in Northamptonshire ten pounds,· to be disposed of at the discretion of my son J : anson and the churchwardens for the education of the same children. (To other poor and to servants). To John, Mary and Abigail Shorte, the children of my nephew Thomas Shorte deceased, thirty pounds (equally &c.). To Eusebas Shorte,· daughter to my nephew John Shorte deceased, ten pounds, but if she die before it be due to go to her sister ―――― Shorte. I will that the legacies given to the aforesaid Harringtons, Wryeths, Wyeths, John Shorte and Thomas Shorte's children shall be disposed for putting them forth to be apprentices or to be paid at their respective ages of one and twenty years or days of marriage &c.

Item I give unto my niece Elizabeth Winthropp (sic) of New England, daughter unto my sister Sarah Glover deceased, the sum of ten pounds, but in case she dies before it be paid to her hands then to go to her child or children. Item I give unto Adam Winthropp, nephew unto the aforesaid Sarah Winthropp and son to my niece Elizabeth Winthropp deceased, the sum of ten pounds. To my nephew Richard Stapers five pounds to buy him a ring. I will that my executors or overseers do invite those persons unto my funeral which are set down in a Roll of paper bearing date with this my will, and in case they come upon such invitation to give unto each of them a gold ring of ten shillings price with the poesy in them as those have that have by me at my death (sic). My kindred and friends which are likewise mentioned in a paper bearing date also with these presents, to have rings sent unto them by my executors or overseers of the same value before mentioned. And I do make, constitute and ordain my son in law Thomas Essington of Brightwell Hall, Suffolk, Esq. and my nephew Thomas Oldfield, of Exon, Devon, merchant, executors &c., and my friends Master Robert Winch, silkman in Cheapside London, and Master John Barlee of Fleet Street leather seller, overseers.

Then follows a list of those invited to the funeral: Mr. Bates and his wife, Mr Christopher Wryeth of Clements Inn, Mr George and his wife, Dr. Reynoldes, Minister of St. Laurence Church, and his wife, Mr. Taylor and his wife, Mr. Robert Winch and his wife with their son Daniel and daughter Rebecca at the Cross Keys in Cheapside, Mr. George Cooper and wife in Billiter Lane, the minister of Creechurch and the clark, Mistress Lee, widow at Dowgate and her son and daughter Reeve, Mrs. Kempe and her eldest son Mr. William Kempe, linen draper on Cornhill, Mrs. Sarah Robinson, in case she be then resident at Mr. Barlee's house, Mr. Drew and his wife, soap boiler, living in Thames Street near Dowgate, Mr. Lant, merchant, and his son, if in town, Mr. Jackson, minister of Faith's under Paul's Church, and his wife, Mr. John Watson and his wife in St. Clement's Lane without Temple Bar, my own servant or servants, Mr. Barlee's man and maid servant, Mr. Needler and his wife, Minister of Fryday Street, Hannah Monford.

Next comes the list of kindred and friends who were to have gold rings sent or delivered unto them: Bryan J:anson Esq. and his wife and their five children and Mistress Robinson their kinswoman, Mr. Samuel Winston, minister of Everdon, and his wife, Mr. Smith, minister of Ashbey Ledgers and his wife, Thomas Essington Esq. and his wife, with their four children, brother Smith and sister, with their grandchild Mistress Jea at Stepney, the Lady Katherine Oldfield at Elsam in Lincolnshire, William Oldfield Esq. and his wife, with the rest of the Lady's children (*videlicet*) Mrs. Katherine, Mrs. Margaret, Mrs. Mary, Mrs. Elizabeth, Master Goodwine and wife, Mr. Blouut and wife and Mr. James Oldfield, Mr. Richard Stapers at Kensington and his friend Mr. Hughett, Mrs. Thomas Oldfield, Mrs. Elizabeth Oldfield at Mrs. Sarah Oldfield's, at Mr. Richard Crossing's (*sic*), my executors, Mr. William Greenhill minister at Stewney, Thomazine Smith of Welton daughter of George Walker of Ashby deceased, Mr. Samuel Oldfield of Staple Inn, Mrs. Williams my son J:anson's mother in law, Mr. John Barlee and his wife and their daughter Dorothy.

On the codicil of later date she bequeaths her gold watch to her daughter in law Mrs. Anne Essington, her diamond ring to her daughter Mrs. Mary J anson, wife unto her son Bryan J:anson, her cabinet which was her mother's to her niece Elizabeth Oldfield of Exon, daughter to her brother Joseph Oldfield, her sable muff to her niece Katherine Oldfield, ten pounds to be equally divided between Paul and James Poole, the children of her cousin Elizabeth Poole deceased, for the putting of them forth to be apprentices or to be paid at their ages of one and twenty. To Sarah, Mary and Thomazine Harrington ten pounds more than what is expressed in the will, to be equally divided &c. To John, Samuel and Mary Wryeth ten pounds more (equally &c.) and a conditional additional bequest to Marlyon Wryeth. To John, Samuel, Ebenezar, Martha, Mary and Rebecca Wyeth twenty pounds more (equally &c.). To John, Mary and Abigail Short ten pounds more. To Eusebas Short three pounds. To Mr. John Barlee's man and maid servant forty shillings apiece and to the Sexton of St. Dunstan's in the West ten shillings.   Pell, 95.

[The following will imparts a value to the following collection of wills which I have gathered at different times the last few years, on account of their evident connection with each other, as shown by the recurrence of some name or names common to all or a part of them.   HENRY F. WATERS.]

RICHARD WALTER, citizen and girdler of London, 4 March 1587 proved 16 March 1587. By the laudable custom of the City of London my wife Elizabeth is to have one third part of my goods after my debts and funerals are paid and borne. I further give unto her, out of my own third part, five hundred pounds and the lease of my house upon London Bridge which I now dwell in and my interest and term of years yet to come of my garden and house within the mint in Southwark, and all my lands, tenements &c. in Hartford. Having at this time but only one son whose name is Nathaniel I not only will and devise unto him the third part that to him belongeth by the custom but also, out my third part, five hundred pounds more, to be employed and bestowed upon such lands, tenements &c. as my well beloved cousin William Walter the elder, my well beloved brother in law Thomas Kempe, John Feeld, preacher, George Cheston, preacher, Richard Dennam of the Bridge and William Clayton of the same, my very good friends. And if my said son should die without lawful heir of his body, then forty pounds a year thereof shall be employed by my said friends towards the building of a school-house in Thingdon, in the Co. of Northampton, where I was born, and after it is built and paid for then the forty pounds a year to be employed towards the maintenance of the schoolmaster and usher appointed for that purpose. Of the residue one fourth part shall be conveyed to the Governors of St. Thomas Hospital in Southwark for the use of the poor there for ever, another fourth to the Governors of Christ Hospital, London, for the use of the poor there for ever, another fourth part to the Governors of St. Bartholomew's Hospital, for the poor there forever, and the other fourth part to the Governors of Bridewell in London for the poor there forever. During the minority of my said son my said trustees shall collect and receive the profits and cause my son to be brought up in the fear of God &c. and of the residue that shall remain in their hands at his full age make an account to him and deliver the same into his hands, he giving them a sufficient discharge. If I shall have any more children living at the time of my decease, or my wife "privyment or grosement Incent with childe" and after delivered then so much of the said third part as shall so appertain to such child or children shall be paid unto it or them according to the custom of the said City, and the five hundred pounds shall also be divided between Nathaniel and the rest of all my children. Bequests to certain preachers, poor scholars at the Universities &c. &c., to the company of girdlers, whereof I am a member (to help five honest, poor men of that Company). To my cousin Belderbye and his now wife. To my brother Edmond Walter. To Mr. Christofer and his wife and Mrs. Wrothe, her daughter. To my neighbor Mr Taylor and his wife and Mr. Rumneye, their son in law, and his wife. To my grandfather Gardner. To my mother Moore. To my brother Kempe and his wife. To my brother Ofield and his wife. To my sister Margaret Moore. To my brother Walker (sic) and his wife. To my brother Walgrave and his wife. To Thomas Bulbman and his wife. To my brother Henry Walter and his wife. To my sister Waxham. To my brother Dawes and his wife. To my cousin William Walter. To my friend William Clayton. To Richard Northcote. To Mary Bagford. To my cousin Mary Gibbes. To John Heyton. To William Heathe of Bath if his sister Johane, my servant, do not marry with Mr Prowde. To Humfrey Basse. All these legacies to my kindred and friend to be paid within three years. To my cousin John Walter, son of my brother Edmond. To Abigail Walter, daughter of my cousin William Walter, and to the residue of his children. To the children of my brother Henry Walter. To the rest of my sister Dawes' children (except Mary Gibbes). To my cousin Belderbrie's children. To the rest of my cousin Garrette's, by his first wife (except Belderbie's wife). To Katherine Bell daughter of my sister Waxham. To Robert Bell my servant. To Nathaniel son of Richard Northcote. (Others named). My wife Elizabeth to be sole executrix.

One of the witnesses was Robert Washborne. Rutland, 20.

JOHN MOORE of Ipswich, Suffolk, merchant 27 October 1587, proved 2 May 1588. Refer to deed of 27 May 22^d Elizabeth, between said John Moore on the one part, and Thomas Kempe my son in law, on the other part, by which one moiety of my manor of Little Brisett, after the deaths of me, the said John, and Joane now my wife, was to go to the said Thomas Kempe and Anne his wife &c. John Kempe, son of said Anne. To wife Joane my capital messuage and mansion house in Ipswich, for her life, and afterwards to Roger Ofield, my son in law and Thomasine his wife, my daughter. To Margaret Moore my daughter. My messuage &c. called Topsfield Hall in Hadley, Suffolk, to wife, for life, and then to Joane Walker and daughter &c. My executors shall sell all my tenements &c. in Little Waldingfield, Much Waldingfield &c. which I lately had and purchased of Isaac Wincolde gen[t] and Mary his wife (for payment of legacies). To my daughter Mary Walgrave fifty pounds, to be paid to her within one year after George Walgrave gen[t], her husband shall accomplish the full age of one and twenty. I am bound to pay unto Richard Walter of London, merchant, my son in law, four hundred pounds, the residue of nine hundred pounds which I gave him in marriage with Elizabeth Walter my daughter, his wife. My executor shall pay it. To my brother Ralfe Moore twenty pounds and to John Moore his eldest son fifty pounds. To every one of the six children my brother Ralfe now hath five pounds, at one and twenty or days of marriage. Bequests to the Bailiffs and Portmen of Ipswich for the poor. To the repair of the church of Beccles. To Mr. Negose now minister of Lighe in Essex. To Mr. Warde pastor of the Tower Church in Ipswich. To Mr. Carter pastor of Bramford, and others. I make and ordain Robert Derehaugh gen[t] my cousin Robert Barker and Samuel Smithe of the said town of Ipswich my brothers in law supervisors and Joane my wife sole executor.

Wit: Thomas Knapp and George Downeinge.   Rutland, 36.

ELIZABETH WALTER of Christ Church next unto Algate, London, widow, 4 December 1588, proved 23 December 1588. Reference to last will of late husband Richard Walter deceased. I his executrix. His only child Nathaniel Walter. My said son is very young. I most earnestly intreat my loving brother and sister Kempe that they would take upon them the care and charge of his bringing up. I lately bought and purchased to me and my heirs of my loving mother Joane More and my sister Margaret Moore a messuage or mansion house &c. in Ipswich, Suffolk, in which my father John Moore did inhabit and dwell. I give it to my mother to have and enjoy for life, and, after her decease, to my said son Nathaniel and his heirs, with remainder to my sister Kempe, my sister Walker, my sister Owfeld, my sister Waldgrave, my sister Margaret Moore and their heirs forever, as next and coheirs unto me the said Elizabeth Walter. I give to my son my ring of gold which was my late husband's seal of arms, and all my plate whatsoever, as all my pots of silver, bowls, goblets, salts, spoons of silver, parcel and double gilt, and also one stone pot garnished with silver gilt, excepting only my silver casting bottle, double gilt, when he shall accomplish his age of twenty and one years. Other gifts to son and mother and sisters. To my brother Kempe, my brother Walker, my brother Owfeild and my brother Waldgrave, each a ring of gold of the price of thirty shillings. To my loving grandfather Gardyner a ring of the price of fourty shillings. To my uncle Robert Barker and my aunt his wife, each a ring of the price of thirty shillings. To my uncle Samuel Smith and mine aunt his wife, each a ring of thirty shillings. To mine aunt Crane a ring of the price of thirty shillings. To my brother Henry Walter a ring of thirty shillings. To sister Waxam, my sister Dawes and my cousin Gibbes his wife, each a ring of thirty shillings. To my cousin William Walter of Wimbleton and his wife, each a ring of thirty shillings. To Mr. Robert Taylor of the Bridge and his wife, each a ring of forty shillings. Rings of twenty shillings each to Mr. Rumney and his wife, Mr. Clayton and his mother, Mrs. Greene, Mrs. Johnson dwelling on the Bridge, Mr. William Chambers' wife, Mr. Richard Norcott and his wife and Mrs. Hixon. To M[r] John Eaton a ring of thirty shillings. To and amongst my uncle Samuel Smithe's children one hundred pounds, at one and twenty or days of marriage. Forty pounds amongst my uncle Raphe Moore's children.

Ten pounds amongst my uncle Godfrey Moore's children. Ten pounds to my cousin John Gardener and five pounds to my cousin Steven Gardyner, each at twenty and six years. Ten pounds to my cousin Margaret Gardyner and five pounds to my cousin Judith Gardener, each at one and twenty or day of marriage. Other bequests to nephew John Kempe, nieces Elizabeth Walter and Elizabeth Owfelde, William Walter son to brother Henry Walter, cousin John Walter (and sundry preachers and others). I give to Mr. Downing, Schoolmaster of Ipswich, ten pounds, to Mr. Catlyn, a student in the University of Cambridge ten pounds. Fifty pounds to be employed for and towards the maintenance of a Godly, learned preacher in the parish of St. Laurence in the town of Ipswich. Three hundred pounds for the relief of such vertuous preachers of God's Word as presently do or hereafter shall stand in any need or be in poor estate &c. Four hundred pounds to be employed either in purchasing lands or tenements to be conveyed unto the Master, Fellows and Scholars of Emanuel College in Cambridge to maintain scholars and fellows studying and professing Divinity &c. Fifty pounds towards the relief of Godly poor widows and fatherless children in London and Ipswich, fifty pounds for the relief of poor and godly householders in London and Ipswich, one hundred pounds for the relief of poor and godly strangers and foreigners that live either in London and Ipswich to enjoy the freedom of their conscience, and twenty pounds for the relief of poor prisoners in London and Ipswich. To Mr. Stoughton and Mr. Carter, ministers of God's Word in Suffolk, each five pounds. To Mrs. Crane, widow, three pounds, so that she shall continue the hearing of the Word in public assemblies. To one Inglishe, a Frenchman, five pounds. (To others). To the poor in the Hospital in Ipswich ten pounds. My executors to be Mr. Robert Wrighte, preacher of Ipswich, my loving brother Thomas Kempe and Mr. Charke, preacher.

The Probate Act shows that the Christian name of Mr Charke was Robert.   Leicester, 15.

MARGARET GARDENER of Ipswich, Suffolk, spinster 5 April 1596, proved 26 April 1596. To my brother John Gardener five score pounds of money. To my two cousins Mary and Susan Hunting forty pounds betwixt them. To my aunt Thomasin Smith ten pounds. To my cousin Susan Winkoll, daughter of Thomas Winkoll, ten pounds at twenty or day of marriage. The rest of her sisters. To Mr. John Burges, preacher of Ipswich, forty shillings. To my uncle Stephen Gardener five pounds, now in the hands of my grandfather John Gardener. To Eliazer Dunkon, M.D. forty shillings. To Thomas Hunting of Ipswich, merchant, forty shillings. To Thomasine Diser, the daughter of my aunt Dyser, forty shillings. To Thomasine Lawraunce the daughter of my aunt Lawrance forty shillings. To Samuel Maddocke the son of my uncle William Maddocke forty shillings. To the poor of St. Nicholas and St. Mary at the Elms, Ipswich, forty shillings. To Annis Runting, now servant with my uncle Hunting, fifteen shillings. My uncle Edward Hunting and my cousin William Bloyes to be my executors.

Wit: Edmond Barker and Robert Barker.   Drake, 23.

JOHN GARDYNER, visited by the hand of God, in Saphia 23 July 1601, proved 21 October 1601. My body to be buried in Saphia. I left with my cousin Roger Owffield, about Christides was seven years, as will appear by a bill of his hand in my power in Morroccus, two hundred and thirty pounds sterling: more for one hundred pounds sterling which my sister Margaret

Gardener at her death bequeathed me, the which how long it is since my aforesaid cousin received it I refer to his own declaration: more for my wages since I went into Italy about his affairs, being upwards of seven years, at one hundred marks sterling money (after thirteen shillings four pence per mark) the year; which he always promised me, as it will appear by his letters in my portmantua, which my good cousin his wife hath in her power, and that it should be always better unto me than the wages I should have of my Mr. Stone, which was the abovesaid sum, as he himself (I mean my cousin Owffield) is not unacquainted with: more some sixteen thousand ounces Barbary money, the King allowing me for Thomas Pate's chests of drugs, and some other odd things of my own, as pictures and other drugs out of Italy, the Alcaide, Azus, for the King, offering me ten thousand ounces and at his last speech with me promised me twelve thousand ounces to be got as I can: for the said chests of drugs of Thomas Pate's my will is that he be allowed after eighteen ounces the pound sterling, free of all charges, whereof I have sent him home one thousand ounces long since. I desire that John Wakeman and William Bolderoe may make up the accompt, which is very plain. I remember not that I am indebted unto Christian, Moor or Jew, but only to Mr. Gore's house for odd toys of John Walter's son: for a cloth that Sir Sampson Cotton demandeth, Nicholas Ensworthe received it of him and must answer him for it. I do will and ordain John Skerroe and William Belderoe with full authority to pay and receive what shall any manner of way to me belong. William Bolderoe's wages and charges to be paid out of my cousin Roger Owffeilde's estate. Bequests to sundry individuals and to the poor of Moroccus and Sus. To my grandfather John Gardner two hundred pounds, and one hundred pounds to his son Stephen Gardner, and if my grandfather should be deceased the whole to come to his son and his heirs. To my uncle John Maddock fifty pounds. One hundred pounds to be distributed by my cousin William Bloyes and my uncle Edward Huntington either upon our poor kindred in Ipswich or otherwise, as they shall think good. (To other individuals). The residue to my cousin Roger Owffeild his wife and children.

Commission issued 21 October 1601 to Roger Owfeild, cousin and legatee named in the will.   Woodhall, 69.

ROGER OWFEILDE citizen and fishmonger of London, 26 November 1608, proved 1 December 1608. My goods to be divided into three parts according to the laudable custom of the city of London, whereof one third part I leave unto Thomasine, my well beloved wife, to her own proper use. Another third part I give and leave to and amongst all my children, Samuel, Joseph, Elizabeth, Mary, Martha, Abigail, Thomasine, Hanna, Sara and Rebecca. A marriage to be had between Hewytt Stephens (sic), merchant, and my daughter Elizabeth. Of my own third part I give unto Thomasine my wife one thousand marks. To my son Samuel Owfeilde one thousand pounds. To my son Joseph one thousand pounds. To my said daughter Elizabeth Owfeild for increase of her portion and better preferment, if the said marriage do not take effect between her and the said Hewytt Stapers (sic), the sum of five hundred pounds. To my mother in law Jone Moore fifty shillings, to make her a ring. To every one of my wife's sisters and to every one of their husbands forty shillings apiece to make them rings. To my brother in law Robert Washebourne five pounds. I remit and forgive my brother John Owfeilde of Asheborne in the County of Darby all such debts and sums of money as he oweth me. Reference to a purchase of lands in Asheborne and to John.Owfeilde's wife and sons John, Roger and William and daughters Elizabeth and Anne. To Richard Owfeilde, one of the sons of my late brother William Owfeilde deceased, forty pounds and to Elizabeth Temple, daughter of my said brother William Owfeilde, thirty pounds. To the five children of my late sister Dorothy Washebourne deceased, Daniel, Elizabeth, Mary, Anne and Dorcas, ten pounds apiece, to Daniel as soon as may be conveniently and to the daughters at one and twenty or days of marriage. To certain preachers and others. To poor students at Cambridge and Oxford, and to poor ministers. To poor householders in London that do fear God. To the poor of Ashborne and the erecting of an Almshouse there. For the support of a Lecturer in the parish of St. Catherine Cree church. To the Company of Fishmongers in London. To the relief of poor children harbored in Christ's Hospital, of poor impotent people in St. Bartholomew's Hospital and the poor of St. Thomas Hospital Southwark. The residue to my children, Samuel, Joseph, Elizabeth, Mary, Martha, Abigail, Thomazine, Hanna, Sarah and Rebecca. Reference to the marriage to take effect between the said Hewyt Stapers and my daughter Elizabeth. Wife Thomazine and sons Samuel and Joseph to be sole executors.

In a codicil of same date he bequeaths his messuage and Inn called the Spread Eagle in Gracious Street *als* Grace Church Street, London, to son Joseph Owfeild. Windebanck, 111.

ABELL MAKEPEACE of Chipping Warden in the county of Northampton, yeoman, 16 June 1601, proved 14 October 1602. My body to be buried in the church of Chipping Warden. To that church four pounds. To the poor in Warden four pounds, to be paid in eight years, ten shillings a year at Christmas. To my daughter Dorothy Makepeace two hundred pounds, one hundred at day of marriage and one hundred that day twelve month next following, and her wedding apparel. To my daughter Bridget two hundred pounds and her wedding apparel (paid in the same way). Reference made to three daughters already married, viz[t] Lucy, Jane and Amye. To my son Lawrence Makepeace eight hundred pounds to be paid him at the age of four and twenty years, and all my lands and rents which I late purchased of Robert Catesbye and Hugh Catesbye, gen[t], he paying to my wife Mary Makepeace, during her natural life ten pounds at two feasts in the year, viz[t] the Annunciation &c. and St. Michael &c. Other bequests to him. He to be sent to the Inns of Court. I desire that he may live as a modest student without wasteful or idle expenses. I most heartily pray and intreat my good friends and cousin Symon Haynes gen[t], Basill Trymnyll gen[t] Thomas Hollowaye, clerk, George Makepeace, Richard Blason to be my overseers and to help to assist my wife and my son, if it please God they can, by their good counsel and advice. To my daughter Butler's two daughters ten shillings apiece and to my godson Abel Nycolls twenty shillings. To my godson Abel Makepeace ten shillings. To Abel Warde five shillings. To Richard, son of Thomas Makepeace three pounds. Bequests to John Phippes, Elizabeth Bradford and Mary Lester. Wife Mary to be sole executrix.

William Harris, William Parsons and John Heathe wit.

Northampton Wills, W. 306.

THOMAS CAMPIAN of Althrop in the Co. of Northampton, clerk, 2 August 1613, proved 17 November 1613. My body to be buried in the parish church of Brington. I do give to my sister An Robertes ten pounds. I do give unto her son Valentine Robertes five pounds and to her daughter five pounds. I do give unto all the rest of her sons, Thomas excepted, twenty shillings apiece. I do give unto my sister An Blan (?) twenty shillings. To the poor of Overson twenty shillings. To Francis Write, my brother, forty shillings. To Edward Write, my brother, twenty shillings. To the poor of Brington parish forty shillings. To my Aunt Lane of Boughton ten shillings. To Mrs. Segrave twenty shillings. To Mr. Butler, Mr. Corbet, Mr. Pill, Mr. Patrick, Richard Carter, Thomas Dodridge, John Nichols, Richard Warwick, Hugh Cranfield, Peter Mackernes, Alexander Tayler and William Tarleton, to each of them two shillings and six pence apiece to buy them gloves. To the rest of my Lord's yeomen about Althorp eighteen pence to buy them gloves. To George Hollis of Daventree twenty shillings. To the poor of Wick Dive and Wick Ham forty shillings. To the maidservants of Althrop eighteen pence apiece to buy them gloves. I do give to Mrs. Jane Wasshington and Elizabeth Kelly, to each of them two shillings and six pence to buy them gloves. To Mr. Ryall of Pasman (Passenham?) my best gown furred with "Cunny." To Mr. Phillipps of Whilton my best sleeved cloak. I do give to Mr Robert Wasshington my embroidered chair. To all my god children twelve pence apiece. All the rest of my goods and substance unbequeathed I do give to Thomas Robertes, my nephew, whom I do make my sole executor. I do appoint Mr. Robert Wasshington and Mr. Phillipps overseers of this my last will.

Debts owing to the testator. Imprimis Mr Lawrence Wasshington 35^s. It. Mr Jerome Lambert of Wickham 30^s, Mr. Andry Ward of West Haddon 5£, William Witmell of Cosgrave 26^s 8^d, Old Foster the plumer of Northampton, 13^s 4^d: —10£ 5^s.

Witnesses to this will

Wm̃. Phillipps   Northampton Wills, T. 121.

Robert Wasshington

MARY MAKEPEACE of Sulgrave, in the Co. of Northampton, widow, the last day of July 1621, proved 16 January 1622. My body to be buried in the church or church yard of Sulgrave. To the church of Sulgrave ten shillings and to the poor ten shillings. To my three daughters Amy Edens, Dorothy Pultney and Bridget Colls, to every one of them five pounds apiece. To my daughter Makepeace, my son's wife, one piece of gold of thirty shillings. To my daughter Trimnell one piece of gold of fifteen shillings. To my daughter Butler one piece of gold of fifteen shillings. To Mary Nicolls the bed in the blue chamber, with all things belonging thereto, as mattress, two bolsters, a pair of blankets, two pairs of sheets, one pair of pillowbeers; one table cloth one dozen napkins one towel and ten pounds. To Mary Pultney two pairs of sheets, one pair of pillowbeers, one table cloth, one dozen of napkins one towel and five pounds. To Mary Colls one pair of sheets, one pair of pillowbeers, one dozen napkins and one towel. To Frances Makepeace my embroidered stamell chair and the stools belonging to it and a pair of sheets, a pair of pillowbeers, one table cloth, one dozen napkins and a towell. To Abel Makepeace, Abel Nicolls, Michael Pultney and Abel Colls, to every one of them an apostle spoon. To every one of my children's children to whom I have not bequeathed anything five shillings apiece.

It. I give to my [*sister Humfre and my sister Butler to either of them]

---

* The words in brackets were interlined, the following having been scratched through, viz.: "thre sisters to every on of them."

ten shillings apiece. To Alis Glover, my servant, ten shillings. To my daughter Bridget Colls my Holland sheets and pillowbeers after that I am brought to the ground and am buried my will is that she shall have them so long as she hath use for them and after my will is that she give them to Mary Colls her daughter. The rest of my goods ungiven and unbequeathed I give unto Lawrence Makepeace my son whom I make my sole executor, he to see my body reverently brought to the ground and my legacies performed. And I would intreat my good and loving cousins Mr. William Pargiter of Gretworth and Mr. Christophèr Pergiter of Sulgrave to be overseers, to whom ten shillings each. None of these legacies to be paid till two years after my death.

John Trelawny, Elizabeth Court and Jane Pargiter wit.

Northampton Wills, P (1617–20), 147.

THOMAS LEESON of Sulgrave in the County of Northampton, gentleman, 13 August 1614, proved 27 September 1614. My body to be buried in the parish churchyard of Sulgrave near my late wife. Bequests to son Thomas Leeson, daughter Susan and son in law William Steavens. I give and bequeath to my daughter Jane Pargiter one of my best silver spoons, the press and the "courte cubbarte" which standeth in my chamber and a wainscot chest. My daughter Elner Leeson wife to my son Arther Leeson. My sister Bridget Haynes wife of Thomas Haines of Mollington. Every one of my children's children. My servant Alice Page. The rest to my son Arther Leeson, whom I make and ordain sole executor. And I do ordain and constitute my well beloved friends Mr Thomas Courte, vicar of Sulgrave, and Mr. Robart Wasshington of the same, Esquire, to be overseers, and to either of them I give two shillings for their pains.

Northampton Wills, Book S., 96.

THOMAS WATKYN of Watford in the County of Northampton, 30 September 1630, proved 22 October 1630. My will is the ten pounds that I owe to my brother Waterhowse should be paid unto him; —— that five and twenty shillings should be paid to the widow of Samuel Lemm (?) if she be living, but if she be dead then my will is that it be paid to her executors, if any can be found, and for default of them to be paid unto any of her poor kindred, but if none of them can be found then the money to be distributed to the poor according to the discretion of my executors —— that the sword which I have, or five and twenty shillings in money should be delivered to the executor of Richard Wolfe, sometimes vintner on Lambath Hill near Old Fish Street London, but if no executor can be found then my will is that the said sword and money be delivered to Thomas Wolfe, the father of the said Richard Wolfe, dwelling at Norton by Dainntre, to take either five and twenty shillings or the sword at his discretion. To the poor of Long Boughby thirty pounds, to be disposed of for their benefit, according to the discretion of my cousin Gifford Watkyn, or his deputy, within one twelve months after that the said money shall be paid into his hands &c. And the money shall not be put out to usury after the rate of eight in the hundred &c. I give and bequeath unto my uncle William Hale and my aunt Roase to each of them five pounds to buy them rings, as a small token of my love and thankfulness unto them for their especial care of me from my youth, whom I pray God eternally to bless. To my cousin Richard Walcott five pounds to buy him a ring. To my cousin John Watkyn ten pounds to buy him a nag. To my cousin Gifford Watkyn of Watford forty pounds. And whereas he saith he oweth me ten pounds I freely forgive it him.   To my cousin Elizabeth Watkyn, his wife, twenty pounds.   To my cousin Elizabeth Watkyn, his daughter, ten pounds.   To Abigail Watkyn, his sister, forty shillings.   To Wenifride Reeve, his sister, forty shillings.

Item   I give and bequeath unto Mr. John Ireton of East Hadden forty shillings to buy him a ring.   To Katherine Ireton, wife unto the said John Ireton, forty shillings to buy her a ring.   To my god daughter Elizabeth Ireton, his daughter, forty shillings.   Item I give and bequeath unto Mrs. Anne Washington mother unto ye aforenamed Katherine Ireton forty shillings to buy her a ring.   To Mr. Bourne, minister of East Hadden, forty shillings.   To Mr. John Stringer and Mary his wife, to each of them forty shillings, to buy them rings.   I give and bequeath three hundred pounds unto my sister Eliza Waterhowse her children, which money I will shall be paid out of my lease of Long Boughby, so soon as it shall arise out of the profits of my land, provided always that the King's rent be first paid out of the profits of my land before this or any other legacy whatsoever.   My will is that these former legacies which I have given and bequeathed shall be paid out of the profits of my lease at Boughby, in order as they are set down, unless my brother William Watkyn do otherwise agree with the parties.   The remainder of my Lease shall be wholly to the benefit and behoof of my brother William or his assigns.   And I constitute and appoint him sole executor.   I appoint and desire my cousin Richard Walcot of London and my cousin Gifford Watkyn of Watford overseers for the performance of this my last will and testament.

Northampton Wills, Book OE, 1626–30, 273.

[The pedigree of Watkyn is to be found in the Visitation of London, 1633–4, while that of Ireton, showing the connection with Watkin, appears in the Visitations of Northamptonshire (Metcalfe).   Catherine Washington was the youngest (probably) of the children of Robert Washington of Sulgrave by his second wife Anne (Fisher).   Her brother Robert was living at East Haddon, and, most probably, her mother also, who is referred to in the above will.—HENRY F. WATERS.]

ROBERT ALDWORTH merchant, one of the aldermen of the city of Bristol, 30 August 1634, proved 12 January 1634.   My body to be laid in Christian burial in the vault in mine own aisle in the church of St Peter in Bristol where my late loving wife Martha lieth buried.   I give to and for the beautifying of the church of Wantwich in Berks twenty pounds.   To the Mayor and Aldermen of the City of Bristol twenty pounds for the benefit of the Gauntes Hospital in the suburbs of Bristol and of the poor children therein.   To poor tuckers and shermen within the city twenty pounds.   To the poor in all the almshouses in Bristol twenty pounds.   To my sister Elizabeth Crockhay wife of Benjamin Crockhay, merchant, yearly during her natural life, fifty pounds, to be paid to her own hands for her own proper use and maintenance.   To my kinswoman Martha Barker, yearly for life, an annuity of twenty four pounds; and after her decease there shall be divided equally amongst her children then living the sum of three hundred pounds, those under eighteen to have their parts payable at that age.   To my sister's daughter Sara Crockhay thirty pounds at the day of the "solempnization" of her marriage, or within two years next after my decease.   To every of the children of my kinsman Edward Knight, living at the time of my decease, five pounds apiece, to the sons at twenty one and the daughters at eighteen.   To my kinsman John Ballow of London, merchant, once my servant, twenty pounds.   To my late servant

Thomas Neathway, merchant, ten pounds. To every of the children of Erasmus Aldworth, mariner, living at time of my decease, five pounds apiece. To William Lyons, once my servant, ten pounds. I give and bequeath to the six children of my kinsman Giles Elbridge, merchant, that is to say, Robert, John, Thomas, Aldworth, Martha and Elizabeth, the sum of one hundred pounds apiece, to be paid, the sons, at one and twenty and the daughters, at eighteen. Bequests to godson Rowland Tucker, son of Thomas Tucker, clerk, to Abel Lovering, clerk, to servant Rowland Searchfield. To my kinsman Thomas Aldworth of Wantwich (Wantage?) twenty pounds. I give and bequeath unto Abraham Shurt, my servant, if he live till my decease and shall return to Bristol, the sum of two hundred pounds, to be paid within two years next after my decease. To my kinsman George Payne, who married my kinswoman Elizabeth Crockhay, twenty pounds. To Matthew Morgan, carpenter. To my godson Robert Aldworth, son of Richard Aldworth, mercer, ten pounds, at one and twenty. To Elizabeth Mericke the daughter of Elizabeth Mericke, twenty pounds. To the poor of St. James in Bristol ten pounds and the same to the poor of St. Philip. A provision for the poor in the Almshouse of St Peter's.

The residue to my well beloved kinsman Giles Elbridge, merchant, whom I do make and ordain to be full and sole executor of this my last Will and Testament, confidently believing and assuredly persuading myself that, as I have found him always true, honest and careful in the managing of my businesses and in his employment in mine affairs in my life time, so he will be as honest and careful in the payment of my legacies and performance of this my last Will and Testament after my decease, according to my true meaning. I give to my said kinsman Giles Elbridge and to his heirs forever my house wherein Job Willowby dwelleth on the Bridge in Bristol.

Among the witnesses were William Yeomans and Francis Yeomans.

Sadler, 3.

[Abraham Shurt, mentioned in this will, was probably the settler at Pemaquid, Me., of this name. See note on page 58 of the "Trelawney Papers," edited by Hon. James Phinney Baxter. His name often appears in early colonial history. — EDITOR.]

ALDWORTH ELBRIDGE of the City of Bristol merchant, now bound upon a voyage for the West Indies, 1 September 1653, proved 10 July 1680. To my cousin Thomas Moore twenty pounds. To my cousin Elizabeth Cugley twenty pounds. To my sisters Martha Cugley and Elizabeth Moore twenty shillings apiece to buy them rings. All the rest of my moneys, goods, debts (or legacies or what estate soever) due unto me from the will of my uncle Robert Aldworth, merchant, deceased, or from the will of my father Giles Elbridge, merchant deceased, or from the will of my brother John Elbridge, merchant deceased, my debts and legacies being paid and funeral expenses discharged, all the rest of my estate I give and bequeath unto my brother in law Thomas Moore, whom I do hereby nominate and appoint to be my sole executor.

Admon. with the will annexed was granted (as above) to Thomas Moore, nephew by the sister of the deceased, Thomas Moore, the executor named in the will, having died during the life time of the deceased testator.

Bath, 95.

[See Aldworth and Elbridge wills already published (REG. Vol. 46, pp. 440–5; *ante*, pp. 632–637.)—H. F. W.]

FRANCES GUY of St. Mary Spittle, Middlesex, widow, 20 June 1680, proved 5 August 1680. I give and bequeath unto my loving brother William Clutterbuck of Boston in New England and Elizabeth his wife twenty shillings each to buy them rings. To my niece Frances Ding ten pounds. To my nephew William Bing and his wife each ten shillings to buy them rings. To my sister Bing and her husband and their two sons Bartholomew and George twelve pence apiece. The rest to my friend John Heyth of the place and Co. aforesaid, M.D. whom I have appointed executor.

Bath, 107.

[I would suggest that there may have been a confusion of the two names Bing and Ding in the above. I copied them as I found them written in the Register. Any one especially interested can at any time, on the payment of the proper official fees, have the original will examined to see if the registered copy is correct.   HENRY F. WATERS.

For an account of William Clutterbuck, named in this will, see Wyman's Charlestown Genealogies and Estates, vol. 1, page 223.—EDITOR.]

HENRY SMITH of Stratford upon Avon in the County of Warwick, gentleman, 4 February 1638, proved 18 November 1650. My body to be buried in the church of Stratford near the place where my loving wife Anne Smith was buried. To the poor of Stratford five pounds. To my son in law William Hicks and Anne his wife lands in the townfields of Bishopton and the "meddowing" and grass thereunto belonging lying in the meadows of Shottery, Welcome and Hampton which was sometime the land of one Rogers and by me purchased of Mr. Nicholas and John Lane. To the said William and Anne the closes in Bishopton and the tenements standing therein, with the barn of five bays standing next to Simon Hornes, all in the holding of Robert Howes. To Thomas Dighton and my daughter Margaret his wife my messuage &c. in Bishopton with one other new barn of five bays, also certain land and pasture sometimes younges land &c. in Bishopton and certain meadowing and grass in Shottery, Welcome and Hampton, also my yard land &c. in the common fields of old Stratford and Hampton meadow. To Henry Smith, son of brother Roger Smith, three score pounds. To the eldest son of my nephew Francis Smith, son of said Henry, ten pounds, and to the two younger sons of said Francis ten pounds, vizt five pounds apiece. To Richard Smith, his brother, ten pounds. To Anne Smith, their sister, ten pounds, and to Mary, their sister, twenty pounds. To the wife of Francis Smith, my brother William's son, five pounds and to their children five pounds more. To Thomas Smith, brother of said Francis, ten pounds. To my sister Joane Brent twenty shillings and also forty shillings more yearly, to be paid quarterly during her life. To my god daughter Elizabeth Ainge, daughter of my cousin Francis Ainge, three pounds. To my god daughter, the daughter of William Hickes, twenty shillings. To my old servant Elizabeth the wife of William Bradley forty shillings. To my servant Margery Grove forty shillings. Other servants. To Joane wife of Arthur Brogden, butcher, twenty shillings yearly for life, to pay her house rent. I give and bequeath, will and devise unto Thomas Dighton, my son in law, and to my said daughter Margaret his wife and to the heirs of their bodies lawfully begotten, or to be begotten, for evermore all the close or inclosed grounds, with the appurtenances and hereditaments thereunto belonging, by me lately purchased, situate, lying and being in the liberties of Welcome, in the said County of Warwick, to this intent and purpose, that they shall cheerfully and lovingly, as occasion shall be offered, entertain and bid welcome to the house I now live in my said son William Hickes and his said wife and children and my said kindred at London. To my son Hickes and Anne his wife the messuage &c. in old Stratford now in the tenure and holding of one Mr Fluellin.

Pembroke, 189.

[See wills of other members of this family already published (REG. Vol. 46, pp. 419-23; *ante*, pp. 611-615). HENRY F. WATERS.]

NATHANIEL BURROUGH of Limehouse in Stepney, Middlesex, merchant, 13 December 1681, proved 23 March, 1682. My body to be interred at the discretion of my executrix. And for my temporal estate, goods and chattels (my debts and funeral charges first paid) I give the same in manner following. I give unto my son George Burrough of New England the sum of twenty pounds of lawful money of England. I give unto Anne Wheeler of Limehouse, widow the sum of ten pounds and also all such debts as are justly due unto me from any person or persons whersoever. And I do nominate and appoint the said Anne Wheeler sole executrix of this my last will.

Drax, 32.

[Here we have the will of the father of George Burrough who was tried for witchcraft, condemned, and hung 19 August 1692, on Gallows Hill, Salem (see REG. Vol. 45, p. 233; *ante*, p. 516). HENRY F. WATERS.]

EDMOND ASPINALL, at Priaman, 31 December 1615, proved 20 September 1617. I give unto my friend William Leightonn, late the Secretary to the Right Honorable East India Company, twenty five pounds according to a note set down in their book at my departure from England. I give unto William Aspinall of Blackwell Hall, clothier. all the remainder due unto me in the hands of the Right Hon. East India Company of my wages due in England. I would entreat Mr. John Myllerd and Mr. John Sandcroft to make sale (of certain oriental goods) and to send the proceeds thereof unto Mr. Francis Sadller, Sec. to the R^t Hon. E. I. Comp., and to Mr. Atkinson, servant to the said Comp., also the proceeds of my apparel and other goods whatsoever; out of the which I give unto Mr. Atkinsonne six pounds and unto Mr. Sadler forty shillings; the remainder of all those goods I give unto the youngest daughter of my brother James Aspynall of Merley in the Co. of Lancaster, gentleman. I give unto Mr. John Sandcroft one diamond ring and unto Mr. John Myller, one ring with nine rubies. Also I give unto Thomas Brighous one "Tapsell chist" of clothes, unto Robert Burdon one gown. I desire Mr. John Myllerd and Mr. John Sandcroft to send to Mr. Sadller and Mr. Atkinsonne the rest of my wages due here unto me, either in goods or per exchange as they shall think fitting.

Also what I have set down in a former will, made at my coming out of England, my will is that, according to the said, the said land mentioned therein may take effect and for debts standing out due unto me I desire John Halsted of Merlle do enjoy and recover one debt due unto me by Sir Robert Young, knight, and one debt due unto me by Larence Halsted of London, merchant, for four pieces velvet he had of Henry Nowell of mine; all other debts, as well beyond the sea as in England, I freely give unto the abovesaid William Aspinall.

Commission issued to William Aspinall of Standinge, Lancashire, a cousin, James Aspinall, the brother, renouncing.

Weldon, 83.

WILLIAM AMBROSE, clerk, of Stepney, Midd., 10 February 1637 proved 18 June 1638. Ten pounds for and towards a stock to set some poor people in Stepney on work, for their better relief and succor. To my cousin, Timothy Aspinwall, Perkins' two volumes now in my study and twenty shillings. To my wife's sister Margaret Bouch three pounds. To the children of my uncle Thomas Aspinwall, Samuel, Peter, Elizabeth, Thomas and the rest, I give five pounds to be paid out of such moneys as are due to me in Lancashire. And to Peter Aspinwall I give the money I formerly lent him. To Mrs. Jane Goldman, late wife of Mr Doctor Goldman dec'd., my death's head ring in which her husband's and my name are written and two twenty shilling pieces, as a remembrance of my thankfulness. To Mr Henry Glover an angel, my striking clock and my cypress standish. To Mr Torbock an angel. To Mr Edgworth twenty shillings. To Mr Robert Goldman my standish set with pearls and to Mr Cullam a ring. To my cousin Thomas Aspinwall (certain household stuff) and five pounds to be paid out of moneys due me in Lancashire. I will that such moneys as are due to me by any in Lancashire, except John Bird's moneys, be divided amongst the children of my brother Peter Ambrose. The residue to be divided into two portions of which one to my wife Ciceley Ambrose and the other to my brother Peter Ambrose and his children. And I make my said brother Peter, Mr Henry Glover and my wife Cicely executors. To Dr. Douglasse twenty shillings and my best standish and to my cousin Jirehiah Aspinall a twenty shilling piece.

Thomas Aspinwall was one of the Witnesses.   Lee, 79.

CICELY AMBROSE of Stepney *als* Stebonheath, Middlesex, widow, 26 June 1639, proved 8 July 1639. To the poor of Stepney to increase their stock five pounds. To twenty poor widows two shillings and sixpence apiece at my funeral. M^r Dr. Douglasse and his wife and Mr. Edgworth his curate. George French, clerk. Twenty shillings apiece to my cousin Harman's children, my cousin Heughe's children and my cousin Webster's grandchildren. To William Ryall, now in New England, my sister's son, I give ten pounds and to Jane Browne, my brother Browne's daughter, five pounds. To Peter Ambrose, my late dear husband's brother, I bequeath the twenty pounds I am bound to give him at my death and ten pounds more to his two children. Likewise to the said Peter Ambrose I give my sealed ring. To Cicely Joanes, my god daughter, living at the Bankside, forty shillings. To my cousin Thomas Heughes forty shillings. To my cousin John Webster forty shillings. To my cousin Thomas Harman thirty shillings, to buy them rings. To John Perkins, son of Mrs. Perkins of Poplar ten pounds. To John Swanley, to buy him a piece of plate, five pounds. Gifts to Ellen Camball, in Painter's Rents, George Goldman, my cousin Sarah Cropp, George Heyward, grandchild to Mr. Collymore, George March, George Hall, Mr. Fletcher, Mr. Glover, Mr. Hopkinson the bookbinder in Aldgate parish and Mary wife of Walter Holloway. To Abraham Adams the four pounds in his M^{rs} hande if it please God to take me before his return. To my loving sister Margaret Bouch I give forty pounds and I do make and constitute my said sister the sole and alone executrix of this my last will and testament.

Wit: George French and Thomas Norton.

Commissary Court of London, B. 28 (1639–42), fol. 67.

[This mention of William Ryall or Royall as the testator's sister's son may help to locate the place in England from which he came. An account of him and his descendants, by Mr. Edward Doubleday Harris, will be found in the REGISTER, vol. 39, page 348.—EDITOR.]

TIMOTHY ASPINWALL, Lecturer at St. Michael's in Coventry, 30 January 1643, proved 24 May 1645. Have "bin" afflicted in body and not yet recovered. I give all my books, moneys, plate, chattels, leases, bonds, bills, annuities or legacies due or that may be due to me &c. by my father's will or any others, and all goods &c. in mine own possession or in the possession of any of my brothers or other friends for mine use, unto my dearly beloved wife Katherine Aspinwall, who by her carriage, goodness and unwearied pains about me in such a long and tedious sickness hath deserved much more at my hands than I can give her. Next unto God Almighty, with whom I chiefly trust my beloved wife I commend her to the love, advice and care of her mother and brethren, from amongst whom I received her, from whom I have received such natural love and sweetness that I doubt not but the beams of their love with all unite much more upon their deserving sister, to yield her their best advice and comfort. My friend Mr. Mackworth, or any others who have been my friends, I desire may be also hers and that none of my own kindred do offer to hinder any legacy by me given or devised to her &c. &c. I make her my sole executrix.

Rivers, 69.

PETER AMBROSE of Toxteth, Lancashire, gen^t, 22 December 1653, proved 10 January 1653. The poor of Ormeskirke, of Toxteth Park, of Much Crosby, of Orrell &c. Sarah Webster, my wife's sister, and her children. Sarah Borth. To Ellen, late wife of Richard Dicconson of Eccleston, daughter of Peter Aspinwall, late of Ormeskirke, ten shillings. My cousins John, William, Richard and Elizabeth Ambrose, sons and daughters of Thomas Ambrose late of Ormeskirke. Isaac, Thomas, Mary, Anne, Elizabeth and Rebecca, sons and daughters of Thomas Ambrose now of Ormeskirke. Anne Robinson sister of the last named Thomas Ambrose. Three of the youngest children of Henry Ellison, late of Wannertee. Also my will and mind is and I hereby give and bequeath to Joshua and Daniel Henshawe, late sons of William Henshawe, late of Toxteth aforesaid deceased, who are now in New England, so much money as shall make up what already hath "ben" by me laid forth for them and expended for them for their voyage to New England and otherwise, the sum of thirty pounds, to be paid them at such time as they shall have attained full age and shall give a sufficient discharge for the whole thirty pounds. Sarah Warreckes widow. Alexander, James and Ellen Warrecks, sons and daughters of John Warrecks late of Toxteth. They to quitclaim all title to a certain messuage &c. in Toxteth Park called Wharrocks Tenement, now in my possession and in possession of Richard Johnson of Everton, which he holdeth in right of his wife; which messuage &c. was heretofore bargained to me by the said John Wharrocks and the said Sarah his wife, administratrix of the said John. My wife Judith. Her former husband's estate in the County Palatine of Chester and the County of the City of Chester &c. Her son John Bird. Joshua and Nehemiah Ambrose my sons. Nehemiah my younger son. My freehold inheritance in Walton in the County of Lancaster. To Joshua Ambrose my elder son that capital messuage &c. called Wautree House or Wautree Hall &c. (copyhold). Thomas Bannester *als* Rose, reputed son of Joseph Rose. Wife Judith and younger son Nehemiah executors. Proved by Judith Ambrose the relict, power reserved for Nehemiah Ambrose, the other executor, when he should come in and legally demand the same.   Brent, 394.

[William Henshaw, named in this will as the father of Joshua and Daniel Henshaw in New England, was the son of Thomas Henshaw of Derby in Lancashire. See tabular pedigree in the REGISTER, vol. 22, p. 115.—EDITOR.]

JAMES FLETCHER, citizen and haberdasher of London, of the parish of St. Lawrence in the old Jewry, being very aged &c., 13 January 1654, proved 22 May 1656. My body to be in fitting and decent manner interred in the parish church of St. Lawrence aforesaid, as near the body of my dear wife late deceased as conveniently may be. And my mind and desire is that my funeral be kept and celebrated at Haberdashers Hall or else Brewers Hall (which I had rather) and my body to be thence brought in the day time, and not in the night, to the desired place of burial, accompanied with such friends and acquaintances as my executors, hereafter named shall think fit to invite and four score poor people in gowns; for defraying of which charges I do appoint the sum of two hundred pounds. To my sister Alice Fletcher of Ormskirke, spinster, two hundred pounds, not doubting but that she will give and bestow the same at her death unto and amongst her sister's children and grandchildren which shall have most need and best deserve the same. I give and bequeath unto my nephew William Aspinall, minister of God's word in Lancashire two hundred pounds. Whereas I have heretofore disbursed and paid several sums of money for my nephew Thomas Aspinall and he now oweth me by bond or otherwise two hundred and fifty pounds I do freely forgive the said debt &c. Certain adventures in Ireland to nephew Richard Aspinall. Fifty pounds each to the four daughters of my loving sister Elizabeth Aspinall late deceased. The children of my sister Mary (which I take to be three). The children of my sister Jane deceased, vizt Alice Barton of Ormeskirke and Catharine Morecroft of Ormeskirke, in Lancashire. To my half sister Jennet Hunt one hundred pounds, with which her husband is not to intermeddle. All her children. Towards the maintenance or augmentation of the maintenance of the freeschool in Ormeskirke (where I was born) one hundred pounds. To the poor of Ormeskirke five pounds, to be distributed by my nephew William Aspinall, Richard Zouch, Miles Barton, Richard Morecrofte and my cousin Hugh Cooper. To the poor of St. Lawrence (where I now live) three pounds. Jane Cumberbatch, widow (my late wife's near kinswoman) now resident with me, and her children John, James and Elizabeth. My cousin Elizabeth Stone. Richard Fletcher of Ormeskirke and his son Miles Fletcher now dwelling at Islington, and his son James Fletcher. Hugh Fletcher, another of his sons. Christopher, son of my cousin Love. Abraham Drye who married my cousin Jane Barton. The son or daughter of my niece Margaret Fletcher who married one Stone in Cheshire. My niece Anne Fletcher. Hugh Fletcher my nephew's son. Mrs. Dorothy Hatt wife of Mr John Hatt, attorney. The grandchildren of my late sister Elizabeth Aspinall, of my late sister Mary deceased and of my late sister Jane deceased. My late wife's friends and poor kindred. The town of Bretherton where she was born. Cousins John, Ellen, Alice and Margaret Haddock. Cousin Richard Sharples and his wife and daughter. Cousin Ellen Crossen and her two children. Richard Rose and his sister Jane and their two younger sisters. Cousin John Hough and my cousin William Hough. Her mother. Her cousin Porter. Others of her friends and kindred.

My cousin William Aspinall's children. To my cousin Mrs. Elizabeth Stone my silver can marked with these letters T : S E:. Mary Laurence, my uncle Miles' his grand daughter. My kinswoman Abraham Drye's wife of Orsett and her children. Dorothy, the daughter of my cousin Jane Dry of Orsett. John Barton son of Miles Barton. My kinsman Thomas Aspinall of Chester now oweth me by bonds one hundred pounds, whereof I give fifty pounds to Jame [sic] Aspinall son to the said Thomas by his now wife (at 21), and twenty five pounds to Elizabeth Eden (who now dwelleth with me) and the remaining twenty five pounds to Jane Sutch daughter of my kinsman Richard Sutch of Ormskirke. All those two messuages (in St. Lawrence old Jewry) now in my own occupation and in the tenure of John Wells, I give and devise unto my loving nephew William Aspinall, minister of God's Word in Lancashire, for and during the term of his natural life, and after his decease to Peter Aspinall, eldest son of the said William, and to the heirs male of his body &c, remainder to my nephew Thomas Aspinall of Chester &c. then to the right heirs of the said William Aspinall forever. Another messuage to kinsman Silvester Sutch. Other two messuages to kinswoman Jane Comberbatch, for life, then to Silvester Sutch and his heirs forever. The two messuages given to cousin William Aspinall shall be chargeable with the payment of two several annuities, to my sister Alice Fletcher, spinster, ten pounds for life, and to my sister Jennet Hunt, wife of Thomas Hunt, five pounds for life (both by quarterly payments). I am interested in several messuages in the minories without Aldgate. My two kinsmen Thomas and Samuel Aspinall sons of my nephew Thomas Aspinall of Chester (under 24). My niece's son Henry Moorcroft now of Ormskirke. My cousin Hugh Fletcher now (as I conceive) in the Barbados Islands. My cousin Jane Fletcher son of Miles Fletcher of Islington. John Fletcher, brother of the said James. Others. All the rest of my estate, real and personal, to the poor of Ormskirke. My very loving and cordial friend Mr. John Hatt, attorney, and my loving kinsman Mr William Aspinall, minister &c. to be my executors and my cousin Thomas Aspinall and John Hough (sometimes my servant) to be my overseers. Berkley, 140.

[The foregoing half dozen wills must be considered by all New England genealogists a very valuable group of wills, as they show the English connections of the families of Ambrose, Aspinwall, Henshaw, Ryal (Royal), &c. The wills of William and Ciceley Ambrose I have had by me a great many years, hoping to come across that of the brother Peter Ambrose referred to. Fortunately I was saved from the trouble of a direct search for it by the kindness of our friend Mr. William S. Appleton, who found it and gave me the reference.

HENRY F. WATERS.

P.S. I find that there was a Nicholas Haspinall, rector of Stepney 30 May 1652.

H. F. W.

There were two early New England immigrants by the name of Aspinwall. William came in 1630 and settled at Charlestown, removed to Boston, was banished as a supporter of Mr. Hutchinson, lived awhile in Rhode Island and New Haven, and about 1643 returned to Boston, where he was clerk of the writs and member of the artillery company. He returned to England, and published at least two books, besides reprinting Cotton's "Abstract of Laws" for New England with a preface. Savage says that his wife Elizabeth was "somehow sister of Christopher Stanley, more probably of his wife Susanna, who became wife of Lieut. William Phillips."

The other emigrant, Peter Aspinwall, came here from Toxteth Park, and settled first at Dorchester, and finally in Muddy River, now Brookline. An article on him and his descendants, by Mr. Edward A. Bowen, is printed in the REGISTER for July, 1893.—EDITOR.]

DAME KATHERINE BARNARDISTON wife of William Towse Sergeant at the Law, 25 February 8th of Charles, proved 19 March 1632, confirmed by sentence 2 March 1633.   At time of marriage of the said Dame Katherine with the said William Towse she had assigned certain goods &c. unto Richard Deane, now citizen and alderman of London, by the name of Richard Deane citizen and skinner of London, John Banckes citizen and mercer of London and Robert Tytchborne citizen and skinner of London, upon Trust &c. to this intent &c. that the said Dame Katherine might at any time devise, give, bequeath and dispose the same at her will and pleasure. This with the full consent of her now husband.   Reference to the present dwelling house of the said Dame Katherine and her husband as at Witham in Essex.   To William and Nathaniel Matthew if dwelling with me &c. six pounds for blacks.   To other men and women servants.   To Mrs. Nicholls of Witham for blacks five pounds.   To Katherine Banckes, George Banckes' daughter, three pounds.   To the Lady Fishe and her daughter Barnardiston Fishe and her man, for blacks, fifteen pounds.   To Mary Banckes, my uncle Christopher Banckes his daughter, for blacks, five pounds.   To Alice Banckes her sister for blacks five pounds.   My desire is that my body be decently kept till my funeral and if George Dunn be then living that he does then "imballe me" as he did my late brother Banckes, not diminishing or opening any part of my body by any means, allowing him linnen of all sorts and for his pains and charge otherways and for blacks I allow him twenty pounds.   To my husband's grandchild William Towse five pounds and to his daughter Towse eight pounds.   And to his grandchild Margaret Towse eight pounds.   To my son Skott and his wife thirteen pounds and to Mary Skott my god daughter five pounds.   To my son Warrine and his wife and his eldest son fifteen pounds.   To my daughter Mary Griges six pounds.   To Sir Richard Deane and his lady &c.   To my nephew Mildmey and his wife.   To my nephew Rollfe and his wife.   To my nephew John Goodwine and niece Goodwine.   To my brother Titchborne and my sister and their children unmarried.   To my sister Draper and her husband and Mary Draper.   My nephew Moungay and his wife.   My nephew Smyth and his wife.   To my nephew Fogge and his wife and his son.   My nephew Waller and his wife.   Sir Nathaniel Barnardiston and his lady and eldest son and daughter.   My son Arthur Barnardiston.   My son Thomas Barnardiston and his wife and daughter Katherine.   My cousin Thomas Soame of London.   My cousin Austine and his wife and daughter Mary.   Christopher Banckes and his wife. Richard Banckes.   Thomas Banckes.   George Banckes.   John Bigg and his wife and eldest daughter and eldest son.   To ten poor scholars of Cambridge, four of them to be of Trinity College.   The parish of S[t] Michael's in the Querne London where I was born.   The poor of Witham.   The poor of Hadstock where my father was born.   The poor of Little Bradley where my first loving husband was born.   The poor of Could church in the parish where I dwelt.   Other parishes named.   My husband, Sergeant Towse and my brother Sir Richard Deane to be overseers.   A nephew Rolfe mentioned.   Bartholomew Bigg eldest son of John and Anne Bigg. Susan Fogg and Mary Draper, daughters of my sister Susan Draper. Provision for three scholarships at Katharine Hall, Cambridge.   Ralfe Fogg the husband of my niece.   John Fogg her eldest son.   My late husband, Sir Thomas Barnardiston buried in the parish church of Ketton, Suffolk.   Present husband to pay a certain yearly sum to his daughter the Lady Elliott.   Kinswoman Mary Raugton the elder, and her sons Thomas and Christopher. Cousin Thomas his wife at London. Cousin Thomas his wife's sister at Maulden. Kinsman William Pettitt and John Pettitt his brother. Kinswomen Mary, Margaret and Alice Pettitt. Kinsman —— Addams. Niece Water. I give her my great bason and ewer, my two great flagons and three candlesticks and one dozen plate trenchers, being all silver, which were given me by her father, my brother. To niece Rolfe my silver chafer, to niece Goodin my other silver bason and spout pot and my half dozen of silver plate trenchers which are unmarked. To niece Mildmay my three silver fruit dishes parcel gilt and my silver morter and pestel and my diamond chain &c. To sister Draper three little oxe eyes (and other silver). To Christopher Banckes my silver Colledge Pot (and other silver). To husband a diamond wedding ring. To son Thomas Barnardiston my sergeant's ring. To niece Mountjoy my silver stuffkirtle &c. An immense lot of other silver &c given to kindred and friends.

Russell, 25.

[See Bancks wills published in January number, pages 107–10 (*ante*, pp. 652–654). Note that our Ralph Fogg had an elder son John. H. F. W.
Wootton's Baronetage, London, 1741, vol. 4, p. 399, says that Dame Catherine Barnardiston was the second wife of Sir Nathaniel, evidently a mistake for Sir Thomas Barnardiston, and died *s.p.* 3 March, 1632, *i.e.* 1632-3. The children of Sir Thomas Barnardiston by his first wife Mary, daughter of Sir Richard Knightley, were: 1, Sir Nathaniel; 2, Thomas; 3, Arthur; 4, Stephen; 5, Thomas; 6, John; 7, William; and several daughters, of whom one married Sir William Fish, knt., and another, Hannah, married Sir John Brograve.—EDITOR.]

ELIZABETH BINGHAM of St. Martin le Grand, London, in the parish of St. Leonard in Foster Lane, spinster, on or about the second or third days of November 1636 declared her will, nuncupative, proved 20 May 1637. She gave and bequeathed to her master, James Lindell five pounds, to her Mrs., Mary Lindell five pounds, to Joshua Lindell five pounds, to Caleb Lindell five pounds, to Thomas Benn five pounds, to Susan Smith three pounds, to Margaret Harvyy fifty shillings. And she did give and bequeath to Francis Butcher threescore pounds. Her estate was in the hands of Mr. Thomas Boyland, gen\t. The remainder to him. Which words, or to the same purpose, she uttered and spake in the presence and hearing of Mary Lindell, Susan Smith and Joane Swanstone.

Commission issued (as above) to Francis Butcher, the principal legatee, to administer the goods &c. according to the tenor of the will, no executor having been named, and sentence was passed to establish the will, in a case between Francis Butcher, on the one part, and Thomas Bingham, Elizabeth Browne *als* Bingham and Bridget Bingham, next akin. Goare, 74.

[It will be readily believed how gladly I saved the above reference, as showing the English home of the well known Salem family of Lindall, from which some of our good Bostonians, as well as Salemites, derive their descent.
HENRY F. WATERS.]

JOHN BRADSHAWE of Westminster, Middlesex, brewer, 3 November 1606, with codicil added 20th of the same month, proved 6 March 1606. Wife Elizabeth. Eldest son and heir. My brewhouse and other my houses in Westminster. My wife shall have the government of my five younger children. I have now two sons scholars in the University of Cambridge. To each of my clerks, the master brewer Pasco, Margaret and goodwife Person, my nurse, twenty shillings apiece, and to all the rest of my servants, both men and maids that have "bene" with me by the space of one year last past, ten shillings apiece. I desire mine executors to deal kindly with Henry Wood, one of my ancient clerks, and that he might still continue his place and that my executors pay unto him yearly the sum of five and thirty pounds for his service therein whiles he possesseth the said place. To my mother Emson twenty pounds and to her two sons Thomas and William Empson ten pounds apiece.

Item, I give and bequeath to Nathaniel, Benjamin, Ephraim, Josuah and Elizabeth Child and to Abigail Warren, all the children of my sister Warren, forty shilling apiece. Fifty pounds (five pounds apiece) to ten ministers, vizt Mr. Egerton, Mr. Wilcockes, Mr. Wotton, Mr. Bamford, Mr Jacob, Mr. Hopkins, Mr. Smith, Mr. Bradshawe, Mr. Lewes and Mr. Witheman. Whereas I have in my hands ten pounds of one Fortune, a kinswoman of mine, and certain stuff in a chest that did belong unto her my will is that notwithstanding the said Fortune is dead yet that mine executors pay the said money and deliver the said stuff to the next of kin to the said Fortune on the mother's side. To Evan Bridgett, my kinsman, five pounds. I make and ordain my beloved and Christian friends George Pope of the Inner Temple, London, Andrew Wilmore of Stratford Bow, Midd., gentleman, William Fynch of Watford, Herts., tanner, Andrew Ellam and Symon Gereing of London, merchants, my joint executors, to whom, in token of my love, I hereby give and devise five pounds apiece over and above such charges and expences they may be at &c. I earnestly entreat them to continue the trade of brewing in my said brew houses (in Westminster) and to maintain my other stocks for the term of four years after my decease, and, because some of mine executors be "unexpert" in that course and dwell far from my said brew houses and other stocks, my request and desire is that the disposing and managing of the said businesses may be principally acted and effected by my brother Simon Gereing, one of my said executors, and for his pains he shall have forty pounds yearly, with his house room, meat and drink for himself, his wife and children as long as as he shall inhabit there and take upon him the special charge and care of the said brewing and continue faithful in effecting my will therein. Direction made for yearly balance sheets. Property to be divided when youngest son Abraham comes to the age of one and twenty years. Ten pounds a year for four years to be paid to sister Ellen Rowe for her proper maintenance. Further conditional bequest to her. Reference made to "my" five sons (not named). Again a reference to "my" seven children. Anne Geringe one of the witnesses.

In the codicil he refers to his dwelling house as over against his brew-house in Westminster. He calls Henry Wood one of his chief clerks, "my cozen." He desires to be buried in the new churchyard as near as may be to Mr Rogers, sometime my faithful pastor at Stratford Bow.

Hudleston, 25.

[The names of Benjamin, Ephraim and Josuah Child are so suggestive of one of the New England families of that name that I have felt it my duty to preserve the foregoing will. The will of Simon Geering of Lachlade, Co. Gloucester, registered in the same volume (Hudlestone, 46), mentions a son Symon and a son John as of London, a daughter Elizabeth Evans, and others.

HENRY F. WATERS.]

ZACHEUS BREEDON of Croulton, in the County of Northampton, clerk, 10 December 1662, proved 1 October 1663. The poor of Croulton. To my son Zacheus Bredon the close of pasture in Apeley Guise, Beds., called Woods Close, and a cottage thereunto adjoining &c., he paying to Margery

my wife five pounds yearly during her life, in lieu of Thirds. To my son
John Breedon twenty pounds to be by him employed in the best manner
and for the best advantage to and for the only use, benefit and behoof of
my daughter Elizabeth Sedgwicke, and to be at her own dispose during her
life and also for her disposing thereof to such of her children as she shall
please after her death, and her husband to have no right or title thereunto
or to intermeddle with the same. To my said son Zacheus the messuage
in Aspeley Guise now or late in the tenure of Francis Coleman &c. I
give him also all and every of my books in Hebrew, Greek and Latin. To
John Johnson my son in law and my daughter Martha his wife two cows
commons &c. in Aspeley Guise. To my said son in law and his wife
Martha and to my son in law William Richardson and my daughter Lydia
his wife a messuage &c. in Aspeley Guise, to be held jointly. To my son
Robert Breedon three hundred and fifty pounds. To my son Charles
Breedon ten pounds, I having formerly given him three-hundred and fifty
pounds to set up his trade. The lesser of two pastures in Aspeley Guise
to my wife Margery; and of the greater of the two I give one half to my
son Thomas Breedon and the other half to my son John Breedon, upon
trust that he shall sell the same for the best price that can be had and the
one half of the money so raised to have and keep to his own use and the
other half to employ for the benefit of my said daughter Elizabeth Sedgwick &c. The residue to wife Margery and she to be executrix and my
brothers Robert Lawson and Charles Michell to be overseers, to whom, for
their pains, twenty shillings apiece.

Ric. Kent a witness. Juxon, 117.

ROSE BRUMPSTED of St. Martin in the Fields, Middlesex, spinster, 18
August 1665, proved 12 July 1666. To the poor of St. Martin's forty
pounds, to be distributed as my brother in law Mr John Breedon, Mr. Robert
Burgh and Mr Samuel Maurice shall think fit, none having under ten shillings. The poor of Kew Green. My god daughter Rose Preston, Charles,
Thomas and Elizabeth Robinson. To Mr Charles and Mr. Robert Breedon,
to the use and for the benefit of such children of Mr. Stephen Sedgwicke
when and as they shall think fit, forty pounds with what proceeds or advantage can be made thereof in the mean time. To my god son Robert Breedon
all those goods or adventure and advantage thereby arising which I lately
sent to New England and came safe to the possession of his father, Captain
Thomas Breedon. To my good friend Mr Francis Throckmorton five
pounds out of the money he owes me on bond. Mr. Dodington, clerk, and
Mr. St John, clerk. To my worthy good friend Mr. Volentine, clerk, to
distribute to such of his children as he shall think fit, fifty pounds, out of
and as soon as my executors shall receive five hundred pounds (or satisfaction for the same) remaining still due to me by obligation from Col. William Legg, and not otherwise. To my honored friend Mrs Markham twenty
pounds she had of me for a friend. To my worthy good friend Mr John
Markham, for the use of his daughter Mrs. Mary Markham, fifty pounds
(on the same conditions as the bequest to Mr. Volentine). To my good
friends Mr. Stephen Sedgwick and his wife, Mr. Zacheus Breedon, Mr.
Charles Breedon, Mr. Johnson and his wife, Mr. Richardson and his wife,
young Mr. Thomas Breedon, Mr. Sampson Harborne, Mrs. Elizabeth
Evans, Mrs. Burgh, Mrs. Maurice, Mrs. Wakefield, cousin Helme and his
wife, Mrs. Fenney and his wife twenty shillings apiece, or rings to that
value. To my dear nephew Thomas Brumpsted, the eldest son of my

[brother] Brumpsted, two hundred and fifty pounds, and to my other dear nephew, Charles Brumpsted, brother of the said Thomas Brumpsted, the like sum of two hundred and fifty pounds, to be paid unto them, with interest and proceeds thereof, from the time of my death when and as they shall attain his or their several and respective ages of one and twenty years &c. To my worthy good friends Mrs. Elizabeth Griffith, Mrs. Elizabeth Leigh, Mrs. Elianor Bust and Mr. Maurice Griffith rings to the value of twenty shillings apiece. To my said nephew Thomas Brumpsted one table diamond ring that was his grandfather Harborne's and to my said nephew Charles Brumpsted one silver plate and eight spoons. I make and constitute my said brother in law Mr. John Breedon, Edward Edkins, Esq. Mr. Edward Noell executors and give to them for their care and pains ten pounds apiece, and ten pounds apiece more for mournings. I make Mr. Robert Burgh and Mr. Samuel Maurice overseers and give them for their pains fifty shillings apiece. To my brother Brumpsted and my sister Breedon ten pounds apiece for mournings and to my said nephews ten pounds between them for mourning. The residue to my executors in trust for my said nephews &c. And I earnestly desire, according to their late dear mother's chiefest care, that both my said nephews be brought up and instructed, in their youth, in the fear and love of God &c.

Wit: Peter Griffith, Rich: Flexney, Robt Breedon.

Commission issued, 12 July 1666, to Thomas Brumpsted, senior, natural and lawful father and lawfully appointed guardian of Thomas and Charles Brumpsted &c. to administer &c., the executors first renouncing.

Mico, 111.

JOHN BREEDON of Pangbourn, Berks. Esq., 24 March 1684, with a codicil dated 5 July 1685, proved 21 October 1685. To my wife Mary, for life, my annual or fee-farm rents issuing out of divers lands, tenements and hereditaments in the County Palatine of Durham, which rents I have settled in reversion, after the several deceases of my self and my said wife, upon my loving nephew Mr. Thomas Brumpstead and his heirs. To my said loving wife also one hundred and fifty pounds per annum, issuing and payable out of my estate in the Strand and Hartshorn Lane, St. Martin's in the Fields, Middlesex, now in lease unto my loving brother Robert Breedon for the remainder of a term for one and twenty years at the rent of three hundred and twenty pounds per annum. To wife for life also my manor of Pangbourne &c and all my other estate in Berks., except the house or toft of ground adjoining &c. late in the occupation of one Spencer. And my desire is that my wife do live in my mansion house of Beare Court in Pangbourne, &c., my said wife to make a release to my nephew Mr Thomas Brumpsted and my cousin Mr Zacheus Sedgwick of all her dower and thirds &c. To my cousin John Breedon, son of my nephew Elkanah Breedon deceased, my said manor of Pangbourne and all other my estate in Berks. from and after the decease of my said loving wife, except as aforesaid (with provisions for entail), remainder to John Breedon, one of the sons of brother Thomas Breedon by his now wife, next to Zacheus Breedon, another son of brother Thomas, then Robert Breedon, another son of brother Thomas, and lastly to my right heirs for ever. In case my nephew John Breedon, son of my cousin Elkanah Breedon, shall happen to die without issue, whereby the estate aforesaid shall descend to John, Zacheus or Robert Breedon, sons of my brother Thomas Breedon, or to any other my right heirs, that then and in such case I do charge the said estate with the payment of two thousand

pounds to Mrs. Mary Breedon, daughter of my said [brother?] Thomas Breedon and now wife to one M^r—— Elmore in the Kingdom of Ireland, which
sum is and shall be in full discharge of the trust reposed in me by the last will
and testament of my nephew Elkanah Breedon and a discharge of a mortgage of houses in the Strand and Hartshorne Lane for securing the said
sum. To John, son of the said Elkanah Breedon that farm &c. called Old
Stockhouse in Rickmersworth, Herts., now in the occupation of James
Weedon, heretofore purchased of Mr Fotherley of Rickmersworth in my
name in trust for the said Elkanah his father, subject nevertheless to the
payment of seventy pounds per annum unto Mrs Bridget Brasier, formerly
wife to the said Elkanah Breedon, as part of her jointure during her natural
life. To my said wife Mary and my nephew Mr Thomas Brumpsted and
my cousin Zacheus Sedgwicke, whom I appoint executors, my rectory or
parsonage of Rickmersworth which I hold by lease of several lives of the
Bishop of London (and other estates &c) in trust that they pay to my
nephew Charles Brumpstead five hundred pounds which I owe him by
obligation &c. as one of the executors to his father. To John, Zacheus
and Robert Breedon, sons of my brother Thomas, five hundred pounds
each, payable out of my estate as aforesaid. To my nephew Charles
Brumpstead one thousand pounds, one half within five years and the other
half within six years after my decease. To my brother in law Mr Richardson, to be divided amongst all his children (except his eldest son William)
seven hundred pounds in six years &c. I do further give to my said brother
William Richardson three hundred pounds which he oweth me &c. To
the children of my brother Zacheus Breedon, clerk, one thousand pounds,
to be divided amongst them equally, vizt Grace, Elizabeth, Jane, Margaret,
Thomas, Martha, Lydia and Mary Breedon, one hundred twenty five pounds
apiece. Ten pounds per annum to be paid to the wife of William Richardson jun^r for and towards her separate maintenance, during her natural life,
if she continue separate, and her husband not to intermeddle with the same.
To my very loving nephew Mr. Zacheus Sedgewicke one thousand pounds
in seven years &c. and he to have the right to will it in the mean time.
To my executors that parcel of ground in Pangbourne late in the occupation of —— Spencer, containing half an acre more or less, which I have
enclosed with a flint wall and on which I have built a messuage or tenement containing one hundred feet in length and fifteen feet in breadth,
which I hereby direct and appoint shall be for a free school house and
habitation for a schoolmaster forever. Provision for an endowment of forty
pounds a year for the said school (for twelve boys) &c. &c. Brother
Zacheus Breedon minister of Southmorton. To my nephews Stephen Sedgwick, Francis Sedgwick and Robert Sedgwick ten pounds apiece for to buy
them mourning. And ten pounds apiece also to my brothers Thomas,
Zacheus and Robert Breedon and my brothers in law Mr William Richardson and Mr. Johnson ten pounds apiece for mourning. The residue to my
cousin John Breedon, son of my cousin Elkanah Breedon.

In the codicil reference is made to the death of his wife Mary since the
will was written. He now gives to brother Thomas Breedon Esq. and to
Mary his now wife the yearly sum of one hundred pounds for life.

Commission issued 2 March 1697 to John Breedon Esq. grand-nephew
of the deceased, to administer &c., Thomas Brumpstead and Zacheus Sedgwicke, executors, having deceased. Cann, 117.

[To one posted as I have been in the records of Boston and of Suffolk County,
Massachusetts, the name of Captain Thomas Breedon comes up like that of an

old friend. And most unexpectedly too there turn up, in his company, a lot of other old friends in the persons of Stephen, Francis, Robert and Zacheus Sedgwick, who have all appeared in previous pages of my Gleanings. See REGISTER, vol. 42, pp. 67–9, 184 *(ante,* pp. 259–61, 277). HENRY F. WATERS.]

ANNE COGGESHALL of Castle Hedingham, Essex, widow, 16 April 1645, proved 10 November 1648. I give unto my son John Coggeshall, now dwelling in New England, my house and lands at Sibble Hedingham, now in the occupation of Nathan Browne and George Germin, with this proviso that the said John Coggeshall shall no way molest my executors for the forty pounds received by appointment from him, being a legacy given him by his uncle John Batter. But if he shall molest my executors then this demise shall be void and he shall have only twenty shillings; and then I give the said house and lands unto Henry Raymond (the son of Richard Raymond deceased) my grandchild. To my grand child Anne Raymond, eldest daughter of said Richard, forty pounds. Of the seventy two pounds lent to the Parliament upon the Public Faith twenty pounds to my grandchild Henry Raymond, and fifty pounds to be divided equally between my eight grandchildren, John, Anne, Mary Jos (*sic*) and James Coggeshall, the children of my son John, before mentioned, and John, Richard and Elizabeth Raymond, the children of Anne Raymond my daughter. The remainder of said money I give to my executor. I give my watch to my daughter Anne Raymond for life and afterwards to my grandchild John Raymond. A bequest to grandchild Anne Raymond. To my aunt Morphew forty shillings. My daughter Anne to be sole executor.

Wit: Vere Harcourt, Henry Carew, John Belgroue.   Essex, 171.

[For an account of John Coggeshall of Newport, R. I., see address of Hon. Henry T. Coggeshall in the Rhode Island Historical Magazine for October, 1884, vol. v., pp 144–72; for his descendants see genealogy by Mr. C. P. Coggeshall in the same volume, pp. 173–90.—EDITOR.]

SIR THOMAS DALE of London, knight, 20 February 1617, proved 15 January 1620. For the disposing of such worldly substance as it hath pleased God to bestow upon me, forasmuch as I do find the same to be scarcely sufficient for the convenient maintenance and stay of living of my dear and loving wife, Dame Elizabeth Dale, I do therefore give and bequeath all my plate money, household stuff, goods and chattels whatsoever unto my said dear wife &c. whom I do also make and ordain the sole executrix &c., and I do desire the Right Hon. Henry Earl of Southampton and my loving brother in law Sir William Throckmorton, kn^t, and Bar^t and my loving friends Sir Thomas Smythe, knight, and Sir William Cooke, knight, to be overseers.   Dale, 1.

DAME ELIZABETH DALE, widow, late the wife and sole executrix of Sir Thomas Dale knight, deceased, her will made 4 July 1640, proved 2 December 1640. My will and mind is that out of my estate in the hands of the East India Company and out of my estate in Virginia my just debts shall be paid. To my niece Mrs. Dorothy Throckmorton five hundred acres of land in Virginia, with the appurtenances. To Edward Hamby, son of Mr. Richard Hamby all my land, with the appurtenances, in Charles Hundred in Virginia and all my estate and interest therein. To Richard Hamby, son likewise of the said Mr. Richard Hamby, all my land &c. in Shirley Hundred in Virginia. To Hanna Pickering, my old servant, one hundred pounds. All my lands and tenements, goods chattels &c. both in

England, Virginia and elsewhere, my debts and legacies being paid and performed, and all charges of prosecution and recovery deducted, shall be divided into two equal parts. The one moiety of the same I give to the children of Sir William Throckmorton, knight and Baronet deceased, and William Samborne, to be disposed at the discretion of my executors, and the other moiety I give to my worthy, deserving friends Mr. Richard Hamby and Mr. William Shrimpton, whom I do make and ordain sole executors. I give to my nephew the Lord Viscount Scudamore a ring of ten pounds price.   Coventry, 162.

[Sir Thomas Dale, whose will and that of his widow are here given, was one of the early governors of Virginia. His wife was Elizabeth, daughter of Sir Thomas Throckmorton. For an account of Sir Thomas Dale, see Mr. Alexander Brown's Genesis of the United States, vol. 2, pp. 869-74.—EDITOR.]

WILLIAM GRAY of Harrow on the Hill, Middlesex, yeoman, 27 January 1647, proved 4 January 1648. To my son John Graye twenty pounds. To son Henry twenty pounds. To son Isaac that cottage or tenement, now or lately in the occupation of Michell Anderson, lying and being in Hobgoblins Lane near Sudbury Green in the parish of Harrow on the Hill &c., being freehold &c. To my daughter in law Susanna Gray, the wife of my son William, five pounds as a token of love to her. To my grandchild Abraham Gray, son of William, forty shillings, and to Josiah forty shillings and to Rebecca, daughter of my son William, all my pewter, and to his youngest daughter, Priscilla, all my brass, as one pot one kettle &c. To my sister Rose Wight five pounds out of a greater sum she oweth me, which five pounds I give her as a token of my love unto her. To my cousins Thomas Ashwell and Mary his wife five pounds, to be distributed amongst their three children, as a token of my love. To Elizabeth Carde that three pounds that is in the hands of John Page of Aperton, yeoman. To William Peache son of John Peache of Greenford twenty shillings, to be deducted out of a greater sum his father John Peache oweth me. I make my son William Gray of London, merchant taylor, full and sole executor and give unto him all and singular my moneys, cattle, chattels, goods and lands, and whatsoever is mine that is not yet heretofore disposed of &c. I further will that the five pounds I give my sister Rose Wight, after her decease shall be given to Thomas Ashwell's children.
                                                        Fairfax, 12.

[The first two sons named in the foregoing will were doubtless the John and Henry Gray who were found in Fairfield, Connecticut, A.D. 1643 or thereabouts (see will of William Gray, their brother and eldest son of the foregoing testator, ante,, p. 264).   HENRY F. WATERS.]

SYMON SMITH of Stepney, formerly citizen and merchant of London, aged fourscore and two years, 3.October 1665 proved 2 January 1665. To my loving wife Martha, with whom I have lived fifty five years in wedlock all my goods and household stuff and my rents in Seething Lane and Stepney for her better maintenance during her life, she having twenty pounds annuity settled on her by her mother Mrs. Thomazine Oldfield, deceased, and twenty pounds annuity settled on her by Mr George Payne. I give her also my tenement in Robinhood Lane in Poplar. To my grandson Thomas Smith fifty pounds. To my grand daughter Thomazine Jaye fifty pounds and to her husband James Jay twenty pounds. To her son Symon Jaye twenty pounds and to his brothers James and John Jaye ten pounds apiece. To the five children of my cousin William Seaman that married my niece Judith Pearce, the daughter of my sister Katherine Pearse deceased, fifty pounds, to be equally divided unto them.

Item I give and bequeath unto my cousin Judith Toozer, the wife of Richard Toozer, the daughter of my son Thomas Smith, now at New England, the sum of fifty pounds, to be equally divided to and amongst her children. To my daughter Emma Smith the wife of my son Symon Smith, my executor, twenty pounds. To ten poor families in Stepney and five poor families in St. Olave's Hart Street. To my son Symon, my executor, all my rents in Seething Lane and Stepney, after his mother's decease, to be employed towards the maintenance and education of his children and raising of portions for them, share and share alike. To poor prisoners &c. My friends Mr. William Greenhill and Mr. Henry Barton to be overseers.

Owing to me by Squire Dennis Gawde, his majesty's victualler of the Royal Navy, on account of my wharf and buildings at Deptford, the lease whereof I have sold him for 1600£, whereof he hath paid me 500£, so there remains due to me 1100£.

Among the debts of the testator was one to Samuel Elliott's estate, as his guardian, 300£.   Mico, 14.

[The will of Thomasine J:anson, already published (see REGISTER, vol. 47, p. 282, *ante*, p. 724), shows clearly enough to what family Mr. Symon Smith's wife Martha belonged and her relationship to the Glovers, the Winthrops and the other families mentioned in the group of wills presented in that number of the REGISTER. In Savage's Gen. Dict. (vol. iv., p. 320), will be found some account of Richard Tozer. Mr. Savage suggests that Simon Tozer of Watertown may have been a son of Richard. This is now rendered more probable by the discovery of the foregoing will, which shows that Simon was an ancestral name. I would add that, so far as my observation goes, Tozer seems to be a Devonshire name.

Since gathering the above I have come upon the following will, which, by its mention of Robin Hood Lane in connection with the fact that the testator had an "uncle Mr. Symon Smith," becomes of importance to all interested in this Tozer family of New England.   H. F. W.]

JOHN ELLIOTT (will drawn in his own hand writing) 1663, proved 3 February 1663. I nominate and appoint Mr. Henry Johnson and Mr. Robert Mordant and my uncle Mr. Symon Smyth my full whole executors &c., and, in case any of those three shall die, to take in his room Mr. Richard Whittall. To my son Samuel Elliott all my land and "housen" at Sibelliningame (Sibell Hedingham?), called by name of Brookehouse, and my house in Robin Hood Lane and twenty hundred pound in money. To my son John thirteen hundred pounds. To my daughter Mary Elliott thirteen hundred pound. To my daughter Hannah Elliott ten hundred pound. To my daughter Margaret Elliott ten hundred pound. And as for my household stuff and plate and linen, which is six hundred and eighty pound, I desire it may be equally divided amongst them, part and part alike, either in goods or money, as my executors shall see to be best for their good; the particulars I have in my book or journal in my study at Ilford. Further, it is my will and desire that if my son Samuel Elliot should die before he come to the age of twenty one years all the land and housen I give to my son John Elliott, and the money and goods as did belong to him to be equally divided among the other four, part and part alike; and if John should die &c. &c. then their estate in land and goods to be divided and sold and parted among my three daughters, part and part alike. Provision also in case of death of any of the daughters before marriage or age of twenty years. Ten pounds to the poor of Poplar. Ten pounds to the poor of Ilford and ten pounds apiece to each of my executors.

Die Mercurii 3ᵗˡˢ Februarii 1663, etc. · Which day &c. personally appeared Mary Elliott, spinster, aged seventeen years or thereabouts, being the daughter of John Elliott late of Barking in Essex deceased, Henry Osbaston, clerk, of Little Ilford, Essex, aged forty five years, or thereabouts, John Lovell of Barking, Essex, genᵗ, aged sixty four years or thereabouts, and George Fenney of Stepney, Middlesex, mariner and did severally depose &c.

By the deposition of the daughter it appears that her father died 28 January 1663, English Style. On the other hand Messrs Osbaston and Lovell and Mary Elliott herself did depose that upon Wednesday in the evening, being the twenty seventh day of February 1663, they were with the said John Elliot at his house in Ilford, who had the said day received a hurt and was in one of the lower rooms of the house. Again, George Fenney and Mary Elliott deposed that upon Friday morning the twenty seventh of February 1663, being the next morning after his death the will was found in a screetore in the closet &c. Bruce, 14.

[The above is the strangest muddling of dates I think I ever met with. I venture to suggest the following as the correct statement of the events as they occurred. He received his hurt on Wednesday the twenty seventh day of January, 1663, and his friends were with him that evening; he died the next day, (Thursday) 28ᵗʰ January; they found his will on Friday morning, 29ᵗʰ January 1663, being the next morning after his death; and they all made their depositions and probate was granted Wednesday 3ᵈ February 1663. HENRY F. WATERS.]

SAMUEL ROBINSON of Boston in New England, merchant, 13 January 1661–2, proved 20 April 1664. To my honored father Thomas Robinson, to be paid forthwith after certain advice of all my debts fully satisfied, whether in England or elsewhere. To my brothers Thomas, James and Joseph and to my sister Mary Robinson, each ten pounds, to be paid as my legacy to my father aforesaid. To my cousin Mary Rocke in consideration of my conjugal love to her and her great love to me, manifested by her care and pains in my sickness of me, the one third part of all my estate after my just debts paid and satisfied; and my legacies are to be paid out of the other two thirds of my estate. To Ann Ervell, my father's servant maid, four pounds. To John Noyes and Elizabeth Lugg, each twenty shillings, to be paid within two months after my decease. I appoint my honored father and my brother John Robinson executors of this my will and my uncle Joseph Rocke and my loving friend Mr. Peter Oliver overseers, to each of whom I give and bequeath twenty shillings apiece.

Wit: John Clarke, Thomas Bumsteed, Anthony Checkley.
Bruce, 36.

[This enables us to correct Savage. Thomas of Boston and Thomas of Scituate were one and the same. And Joseph Rocke, it seems, had a daughter Mary. HENRY F. WATERS.]

CHARLES LIDGETT, late of Boston in N. E., but now of the City of London Esq., 9 April 1698, proved 16 May 1698. Before and at my marriage with my dear wife Mary I confessed a judgment of six thousand pounds, or some other considerable sum, to her father William Hester of the Borough of Southwark, soapmaker, since deceased, "defeasanced" for the payment of three thousand pounds sterling to my said wife at my death. I give my said wife all my lands, tenements &c. in New England and all my other estate, real and personal, except what is hereinafter given to my brother in law John Hester of the said Borough of Southwark, soapboiler, for the present support and maintenance of my children. My said wife shall first pay and satisfy herself the said sum of three thousand pounds and then the overplus of my said real and personal estate shall be paid to and equally divided amongst my three children, Peter, Charles and Ann, whom I do heartily recommend to the care and kindness of my said brother in law, their uncle, John Hester, until my said wife shall send for them or dispose of them. And whereas I expect some money or effects to be suddenly remitted from New England I do hereby order the same, when they arrive, to be paid and delivered to my said brother in law for the support and maintenance of my said children, and do make my said brother in law executor of all my goods and chattels in England until my said wife shall arrive from New England, and I do hereby recommend my said wife to the advice and kindness of Mr. Francis Foxcroft of Boston in New England, in whose justice and friendship I have always had great satisfaction; and lastly I do make my said wife full and sole executrix of all my goods and chattels in New England and also of my goods and chattels in England, after her arrival here.

Wit: Tho: Richards, Jn° Joursey, Wᵐ Wharton.

The will was proved by John Hester at the date already given, with power reserved for Mary Lidget, the relict of the deceased, when she should come to demand it. She took probate 24 May 1701.   Lort, 126.

[Charles Lidget was a son of Peter and Elizabeth (Scammon) Lidget. See Savage and REGISTER, XIII., 133.—EDITOR.]

ELIZABETH SMITH of Taunton, Somerset, widow, 7 March 1653, with a codicil dated 31 March 1654, proved 17 July 1654. My kinswoman Elizabeth wife of Lawrence Richardson of Taunton, who liveth with me. Joane Westouer the younger who liveth with me. Johane Westouer the elder who liveth with me and Jane Williams of New England. The said Johane Westouer the elder, my kinswoman. I give to the aforesaid Jane Williams (the wife of William Williams of New England) my sister's daughter, (certain articles of apparel) and six diaper napkins marked with R: S: E:; to Elizabeth Williams (the daughter of the said Jane Williams) a piece of gold of eleven shillings. To my kinswoman [?] Jonas Westouer of New England a piece of gold of two and twenty shillings. To my kinsman John Westouer of London a piece of gold of twenty shillings. To Judith Westouer (wife of Richard Westouer of Taunton, my kinsman) and the three children of the said Richard, who dwell with him. Johane Westouer the younger, who liveth with me (the daughter of the said Richard) Richard, Gabriel and Jane Westouer, her brothers and sister.   Alchin, 247.

[William Williams, named in this will, was of Hartford, Ct. as early as 1645. He was a cooper, born about 1625; married Nov. 20, 1647, Jane Westover, and died Dec. 17, 1689. His widow died Dec. 25, 1689. They had 9 children. See Memorial History of Hartford County, vol. 1, p. 276. There was a Jonas Westover at Windsor, Ct. in 1649, who removed to Kellingworth. See Savage's Genealogical Dictionary.—EDITOR.]

WILLIAM WALTHAM *als* Mason of London, genᵗ 19 May 1600, proved 7 January 1606. Brother Richard and his children, married and unmarried. Mr. William Gilbert, preacher. My cousin Mr. Richard Worne, preacher and parson of Hemm Magna. My cousin Mayo. My cousin Thurnall. My cousin Joseph Haynes the elder and my cousin his wife. My godson

Symon Haynes, son of the said Joseph. My cousin Joseph Heynes the younger, his son, and my cousin Thomas Haynes, the youngest son of the said Joseph. Elizabeth, Jane, Mary and Margaret, the daughters of my said cousin Joseph Haynes the elder. My cousin Mr. Symon Heynes dwelling in Lurston in Berkshire and my cousin his wife. Henry Heynes their son and Jone Heynes their daughter. My cousin Mr. William Mey, preacher in Carlyle and my cousin his wife and Mary their daughter. My cousin William Wall gen^t and my good cousin Mrs. Joane, his wife. My good cousin Mr. Doctor Farrand and my cousin Mary Farrand, his wife. My cousin Edward Orwell and my cousin Richard Farrand and their children. My cousin Jone Hill, wife to Mr. Jonas Hill gen^t. My god daughter Mary Hill. My cousin Mr. John Tedcastle, and my good cousin his wife. My cousin William, the son of my said cousin John Tedcastle, my godson. My loving sister Elizabeth Harte, widow, and her children, William John and Henry Harte. My godson William Harte, son of the foresaid William Harte. My loving cousin Alice Hart, wife of my said cousin William. Every one of the children of my sister Luce, late the wife of John Hogge.

Item, I give to every one of the children of Alice ffirman, my sister deceased, five marks apiece, to be paid upon every one of their acquittances, which I will shall be sufficient discharges for the same. My sister Margaret Prannell, wife of Robert Prannell. My cousin Henry Prannell, son of my said sister, and his brother, my cousin George Prannell. My brother in law George Bagset, and his son George, by my sister Agnes his wife. My cousin Randall Fenton and my cousin his wife. My brother Richard to be sole executor.   Hudleston, 4.

Rose Mason als Waltham late of Shimplinge. widow, 10 April 1610, proved 9 January 1610. To William Mason als Waltham, my eldest son, twenty pounds and one double bell salt of Silver, six new silver spoons, one of my silver vessells called a beaker and my two small " pownced " cups of silver. To my son John Mason his debt of fifty five pounds due to my late husband, and when he shall return again from beyond the seas ten pounds shall be given unto him within six months after his return. To my son Richard one silver goblet or bowl of silver pounced, two great knopped silver spoons and ten pounds of current money at twenty one. To my daughter Rose wife of Roger Mayhewe ten pounds. To my daughter Margaret wife of John Thurnoll of Stansfield ten pounds. To the children of my daughter Margaret the twenty pounds appointed unto them out of the sale of the tenement in Cavendish by my late husband Mr. Richard Mason als Waltham at their several ages of twenty one, part and part alike. To my daughter Bridget ten pounds and two of my apostle spoons. A similar bequest to youngest daughter Rebecca. To my brother Henry Lesse, Clerk, towards his maintenance, thirteen pounds six shillings eight pence. The legacies given to my son Richard Mason, daughters Bridget and Rebecca and brother Henry Lessey shall be delivered into the hands and custody of my brother in law John Fyrmyn, clerk, and of William Gilbert, Clerk, my son in law, within six months next after my decease to the several uses of them. I give unto Thomas James my son in law the sum of forty shillings, to be paid unto him when he cometh to the age of one and twenty. Son William Mason to be my sole executor.

Wit: John Fyrmyn, Christopher Firmen, Edward Stallon, and signum Roberti Everad.   Wood, 4.

JOAN ETHERIDGE, wife of William Etheridge, of Burley in the parish of Ringwood in the County of Southampton, yeoman, 3 January 1712, proved 1 March 1715. Makes reference to an obligation of four hundred pounds bearing date 16 May 1695, given under said husband's hand and seal before the day of marriage. To my kinsman Thomas Heath of the town and County of Poole five pounds sterling, one silver caudle cup, one silver spoon marked I ᴳ I, my truckle bed and bedstead &c. To my kinswoman Elizabeth Post, wife of Ben: Post of London one red rug &c. To my kinswoman Joan Wice my small silver tankard marked I ᴳ I. To my kinswoman Francis Stoakes, wife of Henry Stoakes of Rederiffe London, (certain apparel). To my daughter in law Mary Fizwell, widow, formerly the wife of my son James Gilbert five pounds. To my kinswoman Mellicent Fisher, widow, part of my wearing apparel. To my cousin John Fisher one broad piece of gold, one feather bed, bolster and bedstead (now in the possession of my kinswoman Mellicent Fisher) &c. To my kinswoman Margaret Morris one broad piece of gold (and other things). To my cousin Joan Nickleson one broad piece of gold &c. To my kinsman Josiah Nickleson my biggest silver salt marked I ᴳ I &c. To my cousin Elizabeth Nickleson one broad piece of gold and one silver spoon. To my cousin Elinor Jones my large fringed chest of drawers cloth. To my cousins John and Mary Jones, each of them a silver spoon. To my kinswoman Mary Rolles, widow, one broad piece of gold &c., and to my cousins Mary and Elizabeth Rolles, each a small silver salt and one silver spoon, and to my cousin John Rolles one silver spoon. To my kinswoman Elizabeth Phippard one piece of Spanish gold &c. and my map of Virginia. Other bequests to cousin Mellicent Smith, cousin John Smith, cousin Cicely Clark, widow, and others. Residue to kinsmen Nicholas Diamond of London, merchant, and Thomas Nickleson of Poole, merchant, who are appointed executors. In codicil, of same date, she makes bequest (among others) to the Men's Monthly Meeting of Friends in Poole. She gives to John Phippard Senior her book of Martyrs, to cousin Joan Wice William Dewsberry's Book, to Jeremiah Colborne Stephen Crisp's journal and Robert Barclay's Apology, to cousin John Fisher Wᵐ Penn's No Cross no Crown. To my cousin Eliz: Phippard Wᵐ Penn's Journal, to cousin Mell. Smith Eliz: Bathurst's Book.   Fox, 48.

JOHN DENNISON of Stortford in the County of Hertford, Genᵗ, 7 January 1676, proved 21 March 1676. I give and bequeath unto Edward Brograve, son of Henry Brograve genᵗ, all that messuage and farm situate in Southminster in the Co. of Essex, together with the lands and pasture ground thereunto belonging, now in the occupation of William Chamberlain, to have and to hold forever. I give unto my loving father George Dennison and his heirs forever all that my messuage and farm, with the land and pasture ground thereunto belonging, and all other messuages and lands in Southminster aforesaid, now in occupation of Jonas Mincks and other tenants, not herein before bequeathed. I give all my Clothes and Cravatts to Richard Osborne. I give unto Susan Gyver my sleeves and all my linen. I give my gelding unto William Powell and I do make the said George Dennison, my father, sole executor.

Chelmsford Registry
Com. Court of Essex and Herts.,
Book Heydon (1676–80), Leaf 29

[" 1676, Mr. John Denison yᵉ son of Mr. George Denison, Jan. 10ᵗʰ." Burials at Bishops' Stortford. REGISTER, vol. 46, p. 354.—EDITOR.]

GEORGE DENNISON of Bishops Stortford, Herts, tanner, 30 Nov. 1678, proved at Stortford 24 January 1678. I give all my lands at Pigotts, in said parish, which I purchased of Mr. Robert Wolley, unto my cousin William Powell until Anne Read (the daughter of my cousin Anne Read widow) shall attain unto the age of one and twenty years. Then the said land to belong to said Anne Read and her heirs forever. To my sister Anne Powell, for life, my messuage or tenement called the Anchor &c. lying and being at Puckeridge in the parish of Stondon, and after her decease I give the said messuage &c. to my cousin William Powell and his heirs forever. I give to Constance Plash, the wife of Richard Plash, my cottage &c. in Braughin, Herts. I give the lease of the lands held of the widow Eve unto William Powell, he paying the rent. To my brother Thomas Goose ten pounds which he owes me. To William Powell my mare. To my cousin Anne Read widow my gelt colt. I appoint Matthew Wolley of Stortford gen^t my sole executor.

Heydon (as above), Leaf 212.

[For a pedigree of the Denison family see REGISTER, vol. 46, pp. 352–4. See also Autobiography of Gen. Daniel Denison, Ibid. pp. 127–33.—EDITOR.]

RICHARD FOULDGER of St. Lawrence Essex, yeoman, 20 June 1678, proved at Chelmsford, 19 July 1678. To wife Margaret twenty pounds, for to be paid 29 September 1679. To the child which is now in her womb twenty pounds for to be paid likewise 29 Sept. 1679. I give and bequeath to Hopestill Munnings my son the full sum of twenty pounds, for to be paid at the age of one and twenty years, and the child to be brought up at the charge of my executor till he come to that age. To my son Rich Fouldger twenty pounds, at one at twenty &c. I nominate and ordain my loving brother Takehced Munnings for to be my sole executor &c.

Book Heydon (as above), Leaf 154.

THOMAS SMYTH of London, merchant, 17 October 1663, proved 12 January 1663. I give the one moiety of all that my messuage or tenement &c. in Smithfould in the Co. of Lancaster to Anne, my dear and loving wife, for and during the term of her natural life; and the other moiety I give to my eldest son Thomas Smith, for and during the term of his natural life; afterwards to the heirs of the body of my said son. All my goods, chattels &c. shall be divided into three equal parts, one part whereof I give to my said wife and the other two parts as follows. To my son in law John Wiswall, his wife and children, five pounds apiece. To my son Thomas Smyth all the profits he hath had of the house and ground in Smythfould for this eighteen or nineteen years last past, and to him and his children five pounds apiece. To my son in law John Cliffe and his children forty shillings apiece. To my daughter in law Bridget Smith and her children ten pounds apiece. To my son in law James Wilson, his wife and children forty shillings apiece. To my son Adam Smith, his wife and children forty shillings apiece. To my son Samuel Smyth, his wife and children ten pounds apiece. To my son Jonathan Smyth twenty pounds. To my son Abiel Smyth thirty pounds. To my sister Ellen Bowker ten pounds, if living at time of my decease. To my cousins Samuel Borsett and Abiel Borsett three pounds apiece. To my brother Abraham Hilton, his wife and children forty shillings apiece. To my brother Richard's children, living at my decease, twenty shillings apiece. To the poor of Little Hulton, Lancashire, fifteen pounds. All my children and grandchildren in and about London and in Lancashire shall have mourning. To my servant Jane Rowson five pounds and mourning. To Ellen Boulton mourning. One hundred or one hundred and twenty shall have rings at my funeral. The residue to my two grand daughters Mary and Lydia Smyth, which are the daughters of Bridget Smyth aforementioned, and to all my grandchildren living at the time of my decease, which are the children of my son and daughter John Wiswall and Margaret Wiswall in New England, to be equally divided among them. I make my son Thomas sole executor and I desire my loving friend Mr. Henry Ashurst of Watling Street, London, woollen draper, and my loving son in law James Wilson to be my overseers. Samuel Smith and James Smith witnesses.

Bruce, 8.

[The above will I was quite prepared to find, sooner or later, for I brought over with me the recollection of a letter which I had seen in the Massachusetts State Archives years ago. It was written by Thomas and Ann Smith to John Wiswall and his wife, their daughter, and is to be found in Vol. 57, No. 4 of the State Archives. I hope some good antiquary, possessed of sufficient leisure, will have the goodness to append a copy of it to this note. I recall that a reference was made to Wiswall's son Munninge. HENRY F. WATERS.
The letter of Thomas and Ann Smith referred to by Mr. Waters, is dated "May the 11th 1660," and is printed in the REGISTER, vol. 7, pp. 273–4. Reference is made to goods sent from Mr. and Mrs. Smith to Mr. and Mrs. Wiswall by Mr. Woodgreen in the ship Prudent Mary. In the trunk containing the goods was a letter dated April 18, 1660. A packet from Mr. [Henry] Ashurst for Henry Webb was also enclosed. Mention is made of your brother Cliffe, sister Wilson, brother Adam, brother Jonathan, and brother Abiel, and of Mr. Glover, Mr. Withington and Mr. Waldo. Reference is made to the drowning of "your sonn Munnings." This was Mahalaleel Munnings, drowned Feb. 27, 1659–60. An abstract of Munnings's will is printed in the REGISTER, vol. 10, pp. 176–7. For a genealogy of the Wiswall family see REGISTER, vol. 40, pp. 58–62. A deposition of John Wiswall, Jr., is in vol. 18, p. 70.—EDITOR.]

THOMAS SLAYNE of Kings Linne in the County of Norfolk merchant, 20 November 1648, proved 7 June 1649. My body to be buried in the churchyard of Margarets in Lynne, by my dear and loving wife deceased. To my eldest son John Slayne my house and garden &c. wherein my son in law Daniel Goodwin, merchant, now dwelleth, bought of Henry Robinson and Lawrence Collins, being near Margarets church in Kings Linn. To my son John Slanye my warehouse in Kingstaire Lane, bought of Mr. James Grennaye, mariner, provided he let my loving daughter Sarah Lynge, wife of Thomas Lynge, merchant, take and enjoy the rent of the tenement wherein one Sparrow now liveth, being part of the house before bequeathed him, during her natural life. I give to the daughters of my son John Slayne the eight acres of pasture ground both of Sampson Cleathers lying in South Lynn abutting upon Hardwick Common, and the tenement and close bought of Thomas Dunham in the parish of Roumton, my said son to take the rents as long as he liveth and after his decease both to be sold for the portions of his said daughters, to be equally divided amongst them. I have been offered one hundred eighty five pounds for both. To my said son John ten pounds. To my son Thomas Slayne and his heirs forever all the free and copyhold land and dwelling houses, barns, stables, orchards &c. in Islington bought of Thomas Smith of Herefordshire wherein one Howling now dwelleth and payeth twenty pounds per annum. The whole farm is about thirty three acres; he to enjoy the same at four and twenty. To my said son Thomas, at twenty four, the messuage with fourteen acres of ground &c. bought of Robert Sparrowe of Watlington, clerk, now in the occupation of Thomas Palmer, lying in Terrington St Johns. I give to my said son Thomas Slayne my mansion house wherein I now dwell in Kings Linn, in the street called Woollmarket, bought of Beatrice Waters, with the malt houses, warehouses, yards and gardens belonging, to enjoy the same after the decease of my wife Mary Slayne, and the iron cradles and other household stuff in the same, he to pay unto my daughter Mary Slayne fifty pounds of currant money, if she be living; but if not then he to pay ten pounds apiece to my daughters or their children, vizt, Joane King ten pounds, Annie Goodwyn ten pounds, Anne Hudson ten pounds, Sarah Linge ten pounds, and to my daughter Slayne, wife of John Slayne ten pounds, all for the use of their children; to be instead of twenty five pounds given him by my brother William Atkyn deceased and of ten pounds given him by his dear mother. To my youngest son Samuel Slayne my lands in Terrington or elsewhere, copy and free, being about fifty five acres and a half bought of William Champney of Lynn, merchant, and the six acres and three roods &c. in Terrington, bought of Thomas Adamson, clerk, and the piece of pasture ground in Terrington, bought of Dorothy Robbinson lately containing two acres and one rood, to have and to hold the same at the age of twenty and four years. To my daughter Amye Goodwyn twenty younds, to my daughter Anne Hudson twenty pounds, to my daughter Sarah Linge twenty pounds, and to my daughter Slanie wife of John Slanye twenty pounds, for the use of their children. Other bequests to them. To my wife Mary Slanye one hundred and fifty pounds and one third part of my brass, linen and pewter, the other two thirds to be divided equally between my daughters, vizt Amye Goodwin, Anne Hudson, Sarah Linge and my daughter Slanye. My wife shall have and enjoy all her own household stuff that is in the house which was her own before I married her. I give to my daughter Sarah Linge the sum of twenty five pounds which was the gift of her uncle Mr. William Atkin. I give to her also that which I promised her husband in marriage and which he now hath the possession of, the mansion house &c. in South Lynne wherein one Leonard Bowes now dwelleth, bought of one William Furnish.

I will and desire that the sum of forty pounds be paid to my daughter Joane Kinge according to a bond entered to her husband before marriage for payment of fifty pounds, according to the condition of the said bond; there being ten pounds paid of it in New England already, so there is forty pounds remaining if my said daughter be living at my decease; and if she depart this life before my decease then my desire is that her children may have the said forty pounds. To my daughter Amye Goodwyn twenty five pounds, the gift of her uncle Mr William Atkin. To my daughter Anne Hudson (a similar gift of her uncle). My daughter Kinge hath had her part, and John Slanye and William Slanye. To the children of John Newborne dwelling in Essex forty shillings apiece. To my sister Hodgekyn twenty shillings to buy her a ring. To John Jackler and Mary Jackler, the two children of my wife twenty shillings apiece to buy rings. To four of the poorest people in Snailwell where I was born five shillings apiece. To Mr. Horne twenty shillings and I desire him to preach at my funeral. I make my son in law Thomas Linge of Kings Lynne, merchant, and my friend Thomas Moore of Wisbitch executors and my friend Mr John May, alderman, overseer.   Fairfax, 82.

JAMES GOFFE of Clements East Cheap in London, citizen and leatherseller of London, 17 January 1656, proved (with Codicil of 18 January) the 4th February 1656. Upon marrying with my dear and loving wife Anne Goffe I did settle and convey upon her for life, in case she did survive me, my farm and lands in New Alresford, Southampton, of the yearly value of four score pounds or thereabouts. I give her five hundred pounds besides, she not to claim any further part, either by law or by the Custom of the City of London. Of all the rest my four children, James, Elizabeth, Mary and Deborah, shall have one full third part, according to the Custom of the City of London (personal estate). And the rest I leave as follows &c. To wife the lease of my house at Peckham, Surrey, and the goods, household stuff and furniture in said house, except the wrought cabinet and the several things in the same, which I give to my three daughters, only my watch therein, which I give to my son James. To wife certain goods in my now dwelling house in Cannon Street, except goods &c. in the shop &c. To son James my farm &c. in Alresford, Co. Southampton, after the decease of my wife. To son James, towards his education and breeding abroad till he shall attain his full age of sixteen years, the yearly sum of fourteen pounds out of the rents &c. of my farm called Shuttlehurst, Sussex. To my eldest daughter Elizabeth, for and towards her maintenance and education, the lease of my farm which I hold of William Marsh in Prittlewell Essex, taken in the name of my brother Nicholas Ady (for me). I make my loving brothers Major General William Goffe, Nicholas Ady, and Edward Bovery executors &c. and give them five pounds ten shillings apiece to buy them diamond rings therewith, to wear for a loving remembrance of me. In the codicil he refers to a former wife and gives to Elizabeth the chest of drawers that was her own mothers.   Ruthen, 63.

[Major-General William Goffe, the Regicide, mentioned as his brother by the testator, came to New England with his father-in-law, Col. Edward Whalley, a cousin of Oliver Cromwell, the Protector, and died here. See Stiles's "History of Three of the Judges of King Charles I."; and "Letters and Papers relating to the Regicides," in the Collections of the Massachusetts Historical Society, 4th series, vol. 8, pp. 122 to 225. The traditionary story of Gen. Goffe's appearance in an attack by the Indians on Hadley, where he was then concealed, and leading the soldiers to repel the assault, is conclusively disproved by Hon. George Sheldon in the REGISTER, vol. 28, pp. 379–391. Gen. Goffe was a son of Rev. Stephen Goffe, a Puritan divine, rector of Stanmer, Sussex, England.— EDITOR.]

MILDRED HITCH of London widow, 11 February 1657, proved 23 March 1657. To my brother in law Maurice Hitch ten pounds. To William Hitch, his son, ten pounds, and to William Hitch, his son, grandchild of the said Maurice, ten pounds. To my kinsman John Hitch ten pounds and to his son John Hitch ten pounds. To my sister Bridget Bennett an annuity or yearly sum of five and twenty pounds to be issuing and payable out my lands, tenements &c. in Chilworth in the parish of Milton in the County of Oxford. To my niece Martha Andrewes wife of John Andrewes forty pounds, to be paid into her own hands by my kinsman William Gibbs or my executor. To my niece Martha Andrewes an annuity of four pounds sterling per annum for fifteen years if she lives so long. To the said John Andrewes and his eldest son five shillings and to his sons Ezekiel and Francis Andrewes five pounds apiece. To my kinsman William Gibbs five shillings as a remembrance. To my kinswoman Clemence Gibbs, daughter of the said William, one hundred pounds at one and twenty or day of marriage. To my kinswoman Mary Johnson of New England, formerly by the name of Mary Hazard, twenty pounds. To every of them, John Hazard, Rebecca Hazard and Hannah Hazard, children of my said kinswoman Mary Johnson, by a former husband, twenty pounds apiece. To my kinswoman Anne daughter of John Peircevall five pounds. To Mary late wife of John Peircevall five shillings. My friend Mrs. Elizabeth Hardwin wife of Master Grace Hardwin. To Anne Hitch, sister of my executor, five pounds. To my kinsman and servant Thomas Hitch, living with me, all the rest and residue and I make him full and sole executor, and my friends Thomas Staines and Grace Hardwin, waxchandlers, overseers. To the said Thomas Hitch my messuage &c. in Hensley, Oxon. One of the witnesses was a Grace Hardwick. Wootton, 115.

ELIZABETH KENT of Sunning, Berks, widow, 16 September 1679, proved 8 June 1680. I give and bequeath unto my brother Carey Latham of New England five pounds; and if he should die before it be paid the five pounds I give to his eldest son. To my cousin Jesper Latham of London, stonecutter, five pounds (with the same proviso). To my cousin Christopher Smith of London, gold wyer drawer, five pounds; and in case of his death before it be paid the said five pounds to his wife. To my brother John Latham his son's daughter five pounds. To my brother Pagett Latham his son's son five pounds. To my son John Kent of London, merchant, my silver tankard. To my grand daughter Ruth Kent my silver porringer and spoon. To my grandson John Kent my wedding ring. To my grandson Walter Kent my great bible. To the wife of my cousin Jesper Latham my East India gown lined with yellow. To my sister Elizabeth Latham my "mantow" gown lined with black and a petticoat. To my brother Carey Latham my father's picture. To the wife of my cousin Christopher Smith my silver bowl and one of my best green petticoats. To Mrs Anne Goffe (certain household stuff). To eight poor widows of Sunning town two shillings six pence apiece. To my god daughter Hannah Pearcy five pounds. To my godson Henry Young twenty shillings. To my godson Richard Newland ten shillings. To my god daughter Elizabeth Breach and my god daughter Small, daughter of Thomas Small of Burway, ten shillings each. To my sister Mrs Katherine Hunt all the residue of my moneys and goods &c., and she to be my whole and sole executrix.

Ralph Pearcy a witness. Bath, 82.

[Carey Latham, called a brother by the testator, resided at Cambridge as early as 1639. He had a wife Elizabeth. He removed to New London, Ct., and died in 1685. See Paige's Cambridge, page 398.—EDITOR.]

WALTER KELWAY of Chelmsford, Essex, 1 October 1650, proved 28 February 1650. To my wife Joanna all the movable goods which she brought with her to me, and certain household stuff (including a wicker chair), also a parcel of land in Writtle and three score pounds of money. He calls her "my faithfull yokefellowe." Certain property to be sold or disposed of for the best advantage of my three daughters in New England, namely my daughter Margaret Mountague, my daughter Melcas Snow and my daughter Mary Lane, by equal portions. Reference to grandchildren now in New England and to grandchildren now born in old England. My grand child Elizabeth Kelway. My grand child John Roper. As for my two houses which I have in Rayleigh in Essex, which by right belongs to my two daughters Ruth Caunte and to my daughter Mary Lane of Boston in New England, for which two houses I have taken order that my two daughters shall yield up all their right that they have in the two houses to me to dispose of them, and then, if I can sell them in my life time, I will

the moneys for which they be sold it shall be divided into three parts and shall be for my three daughters in New England before mentioned; but if I cannot sell the two houses in my life time then it must rest to be disposed of by my daughter Mary Lane after my death, and she must take the two houses for her portion if no more will fall to her share. But yet in the meantime I give and do bequeath to my three daughters in New England twenty pounds apiece. To my grandchildren in New England already born before this 1 October 1650 four pounds apiece. To my grandchild Elizabeth Kelway, the daughter of my son Jonathan Kelway deceased, for her better bringing up, twenty pounds, and three pounds of this twenty the mother of the child has already received, and twenty shillings more every quarter shall the mother of this my grandchild receive &c. To my grandchild John Roper four pounds. To the poor of Chelmsford and Moulsham. Wife to be executrix and Mr. Richard Holbrough to be my overseer.
One of the witnesses was a Sarah Kellum. Grey, 26.

[The reference to the above will was given me by our friend Mr. W. S. Appleton. H. F. W.]
Since Mr. Waters has mentioned my name, I will add that I noted this will in 1888, and lately asked him to include it in the "Gleanings," as possibly interesting to three families in this country. According to Savage the three daughters were evidently the wives respectively of Griffin Mountague, Thomas Snow and William Lane.—WILLIAM S. APPLETON.]

CHARLES FROTHINGHAM of Birchhanger Hall in the Co. of Essex, gentleman, 24 July 1652, proved 22 May 1656. To wife Margaret twenty pounds (over and above the benefit of the two hundred pounds during her life in her brother Rant's hand) and the annuity of forty pounds a year for life. To son Charles my leases of the manor and mill of Birch hanger. To son Christopher two hundred pounds at four and twenty. If he die before attaining to that age then it shall go to my eldest son and executor. To second son Stephen a yearly sum of twenty pounds for life &c. To daughter Anne Evans, wife of William Evans an annuity of twenty pounds for life. To grandchild Charles Evans ten pounds to bind him an apprentice. To my sister Elizabeth Frothingham five pounds. To Bridget Frothingham twenty shillings. To Peter Frothingham twenty shillings. To Katherine Stampe, wife of Martin Stampe living at Heddington near Oxford, twenty shillings. To my two sisters in Yorkshire five pounds apiece if it be demanded. To my friend Robert Abbott of London, scrivener, five pounds and to his wife twenty shillings for a ring, as a token of my love. To Stephen Rant of Quie (Quy) in Cambridge, clerk, twenty shillings in token of my love and respect. To my cousin Mr Goldsmith twenty shillings. To my friend Richard Tisdale, taylor, in Gray's Inn Lane ten shillings. To my brother John Frothingham, if living, ten pounds, to be paid when he shall demand the same. The residue to my son Charles Frothingham, whom I make executor, and I desire my said brother Stephen Rant and my friend Robert Abbott to be overseers &c. Berkley, 181.

[The recurrence of the name Peter Frothingham in the above will made me deem it worth preserving. HENRY F. WATERS.]

TOBIAS FELLGATE being in Westover in Virginia and having been for the space of eight days or thereabouts, sick in body and so then continuing, but of sound and perfect memory, being requested by one Mr Jeremy Blackman and others then present, made his will April 1635, proved 23 April 1635. To his eldest son William Fellgate one hundred and fifty pounds, to be paid upon demand. To his daughter Sarah Fellgate two hundred and fifty pounds, to be paid at her day of marriage and if she died before she were married (*sic*) then the said legacy to be paid to the said William his son. If William should die before demanding his legacy then he bequeathed the said one hundred and fifty pounds unto Sarah his wife. And if both children died then the said two hundred and fifty pounds to come to his wife. To Mrs. Elizabeth Minifie dwelling in Virginia ten pounds. To a youth called Tobias of Berry forty pounds. Wife Sarah to be sole executrix and William Fellgate and Mr Greene his overseers.

The witnesses were Jeremy Blackman, Peter Swyer, James Jones and Robert Page, in the presence of Salomon Smith. Sadler, 38.

JOHN DERSLEY of Stepney, Middlesex, shipwright, 2 June 1634, proved 19 January 1634. To my reverend friend Mr. Richard Sedgwicke, preacher of God's word in Wapping, five pounds. To the poor of the hamlet other five pounds. My wife Frances shall hold and enjoy the tenements and gardens in Wapping which I hold by five several leases, according to the agreement between her and me upon our marriage. This for her life; and after her decease I bequeath to my son Thomas my interest in my now dwelling house &c. which I hold of Mrs. Heard and my interest in the garden which I hold of one Tibballs, and my interest in the tenements in Gun Alley in Wapping now in the several occupations of John Hughes, widow Clawson, goodman Minstrell, goodman Salter, goodman Webb, goodman Bromage and one Mills. To son John, after my wife's death, my interest in the Gun Tavern in Wapping and in the tenements now or late in the occupation of John Taylor and the shops under it and in the two tenements in the plank yard &c. I am part owner in divers ships and vessels. Composition money to be paid for the houses dock and wharfs &c. now in the occupations of John Dersley and Thomas Hawkins, out of the sale of some of the shipping. Of the rest of my shipping, tackle, furniture &c. I give one moiety to my wife and the other to my two sons. The rest of my goods &c. to my wife and sons. As touching the disposing of my freehold lands, tenements &c. in the several occupations of my son John Dersley and the said Thomas Hawkins, lying between the tenement o Sir John Winter, in the occupation of John Brady, on the West and a tenement of the Hospital of St Thomas in Southwark, in the occupation of one Dogget on the East, one third thereof I give to my wife Frances for term of life, in lieu of her dower, and the other two parts I give to my two sons.

And my will and mind is that the assurances of my said freehold lands &c. which are to be made upon the said composition shall be taken in the names of my son Ting and of Mr Syse and Gibbs and others, according to a book and directions already drawn by my counsel to the uses specified in this my will. I make the said Frances my wife sole executrix and my friends Thomas Wright of Ipswich and my brother Robert Risley overseers. And whereas I have demised to Thomas Hawkins a plank yard &c. for which he pays me twenty pounds per annum, I give the said plankeyard to my wife and my two sons. I give to my overseers five pounds apiece, to my sister Bowle forty shillings, to Captain Edward Johnson my watch, to my brother Bowle my seal ring, to my son William Ting and Anne his wife fifty shillings apiece, to Thomasine Humfrey the sawyer's wife twenty shillings. Son Thomas under twenty one. Sadler, 4.

JOHN JOHNSON of Chart next Sutton Valence, Kent, gentleman, 5 November 1627, proved 12 November 1627. I stand seized of forty acres of woodland ground in Hollingborne Kent and three score acres of arable and pasture land in Chart. My wife Katalyna Johnson now with child. I give and bequeath unto my brother Edward Johnson, gen^t, twenty pounds, in one year after my decease. To my sister Rose Chylld ten pounds, in one year and a half &c. To her four children, vizt Thomas, Dorothy, Robert and Elizabeth Chyld, to every of them thirty shillings, in one year and a half &c. To my brother Robert Johnson's four children, John, Elizabeth, Robert and Katherine Johnson forty pounds, to be equally divided &c. when they shall [have] accomplished their ages of eighteen years apiece. To wife Katalyna for her jointure, out of my lands, six score pounds by the year.

Item, I geeue and bequeath unto my sister Susanna Locke's fower children, viz. Ann, Mary, Susanna and Margaret, to euery of them the sum of five shillings. To my sister Elizabeth Asquew's two daughters two shillings and six pence apiece. The child my wife now goeth with. To my said wife the household stuff which I now possess and was sent down into Kent unto me and my said wife by my mother in law Ann Cole. To her also my brown nag with the side saddle. To my brother in law Alexander Chyld forty shillings to make him a ring. I do in duty which I do bear unto Thomas Johnson, my father, make him my said father, Thomas Johnson, my sole executor, and he shall bestow one hundred pounds upon my funeral and my brother Alexander Child shall help to manage the same business. If my father do happen to depart this life before my child, if it be a man child, do accomplish the age of eighteen years then my brother Edward Johnson shall take and have the executorship.

A codicil added 6 November 1627 (affecting the jointure).

Proved by the father, Thomas Johnson; but on the 8th of June 1630 probate was granted to Edward Johnson, by reason of the death of the father.   Skynner, 113.

THOMAS JOHNSON of Chart next Sutton Vallence in the County of Kent, gentleman, 21 January 4th Charles, proved 8 May 1630. To be buried in the church of Chart near unto the body of my deceased wife. The poor of Chart. My son Robert Johnson. John, one of the sons of my said son Robert. Robert, Elizabeth and Katherine, other the children of my said son Robert (at their several ages of one and twenty years). Item, I give to my son Edward Johnson twenty shillings, to be paid within four years after my decease. Item, I give to my daughter Rosanna Childes ten pounds, to be paid also within four years &c. To my said daughter Rosanna's children, Thomas, Robert, Dorothy and Elizabeth, vizt to Thomas five pounds, to Robert forty shillings, to Dorothy ten shillings and to Elizabeth forty shillings, to be severally paid unto them at their several ages of one and twenty. My servant John Hide. My servant Elizabeth Goldwier. To my son in law Alexander Childe forty shillings to make him a ring. To my grandchild Stephen Johnson, the son of John Johnson late deceased, twenty shillings, at one and twenty. The residue to my son Thomas Johnson, whom I do make, constitute, ordain and appoint the sole executor of this my last will and testament, and I hereby give and bequeath unto my said son Thomas my messuage or tenement, and the lands thereunto belonging &c. in the parish of Yaldinge, Kent, and called or known by the name of Pickfishe, and all other my messuages, lands &c. in Kent.

Sententia pro valore &c., 8 May 1630, &c., *in judicio inter Thomam Johnson, filium naturalem et ltimū. et executorem* ρmoveñ. *ex una et Edwardum Johnson, filium nālem et ltimū. eiusdem defuncti, partem contra quam hōi. negotium promovetur, necnon Johannem Fish notarium pubcum. curatorem ad lites Stephano Johnson nepoti ex filio* &c. Scroope, 47.

WILLIAM LOCK of Wimbledon, Surrey, gen^t, 10 June 1661, proved 7 June 1664. Certain houses, with their appurtenances, standing and being in the parish of St. Savior's Southwark given and bequeathed by Mr Roger Cole, my father in law, to Susanna, my well beloved wife, and her children. My three eldest daughters, Hannah, Susanna and Margaret, I have bestowed in marriage. I shall leave an estate in land for my son Thomas and by this my will provide for my daughter Elizabeth. To my daughter Sarah Lock five brick tenements and another house, known formerly by the name of the Gaden House, all standing upon the ground given by Mr Roger Cole. To my daughter Jane Locke two houses next the Thames, in the said parish, now or late in the tenure of Mr. Robert Bowes or his assigns. To my wife Susanna that parcel of land with four brick tenements thereon built, commonly called the Beane Acre, in Lambeth, Surrey, she to give two hundred pounds to my daughter Elizabeth, towards a portion for her. And I also give and bequeath to my wife all other my personal estate &c., she paying my debts and legacies and discharging my funeral; and I make my said wife Susanna full and sole executrix. To the poor of Wimbledon three pounds.

On the margin is written—"7 Junii j664 Recepi testament originat. Su: Lock." (This signature is evidently in her own handwriting).

Bruce, 37.

JANE LOCKE one of the daughters of William Lock, gen^t, deceased, having one hundred pounds in money at my own dispose, make my last will and testament 19 March 1669, proved 25 October 1670. I give and bequeath the sum of twenty pounds to my dear and hono^{ble} mother Mrs. Susanna Lock. I give and bequeath the sum of ten pounds to my brother Mr Thomas Lock. I give and bequeath the sum of twenty pounds to my sister Mrs. Hannah Bragne. I give and bequeath the sum of ten pounds to my sister Mrs. Margaret Willoughby. I give and bequeath the sum of twenty pounds to my sister Mrs Elizabeth Lock. I give and bequeath the sum of five pounds to be divided between the two children of my sister Willoughby, that is to say, to Francis and Susanna fifty shillings apiece. I give to Susannah Lock and Hanna Lock, children of my brother, twenty shillings apiece and also to the children of my sister Stephenson, Susanna and Mary, twenty shillings apiece. I give the sum of five pounds to be paid to some poor, honest people as my brother, Mr Thomas Bragne shall see fit, desiring him to distribute it. I also give the sum of forty shilling to be distributed to the poor of the parish of Wimbledon at the discretion of my executrix. Lastly I give and bequeath the little remainder of my hundred pounds, not herein given, to my dear mother Mrs. Susanna Lock, whom I, with her leave, make full and sole executrix of this my last will and testament.

Penn, 136.

[The four preceding wills have a value as bearing on the connections of our Deputy Governor, Francis Willoughby. The two Johnson wills may also acquire an additional interest hereafter if we are so lucky as to trace any connection between them and our famous Captain Edward Johnson and Dr. Robert Chyld, who were both men of Kent. HENRY F. WATERS.]

HENRY PEYTON of Lincoln's Inn, Middlesex, Esq. 10 December 1655, proved 6 May 1656. To my faithfully loving and dearly beloved wife Katherine four thousand pounds and the lease of my house wherein I now dwell in Chancery Lane, which I hold of Magdalen College in Oxford, and all my estate, right, title and term of years therein to come, for her better support and livelihood. To my daughter Mary Peyton one thousand pounds at eighteen or day of marriage. To my sons Vallentine, Laurance and John five hundred pounds apiece within four years after my decease. To my sons Sandis Peyton and Charles Peyton eight hundred pounds apiece, to Sandis at six and twenty and to Charles at one and twenty: and my executrix to allow to my son Charles thirty pounds a year for his education and maintenance at school, out of the proceeds of his said portion, until he shall accomplish his said age. To my daughters Margaret Raven and Bridget Humphry a hundred pounds apiece, to buy them and their husbands mourning. To Mistrese Mary Bateman, my wife's sister, one hundred pounds, in one year, but her husband to have nothing to do with it or any part of it. To my grand children John Raven, Henry Raven and Edmund Humphry fifty pounds apiece, at eighteen years of age respectively, and to Katherine Humphry, daughter of my said son and daughter Humphry, fifty pounds, at eighteen or day of marriage. To my brother Master William Peyton twenty pounds, to buy him and his son William mourning, and to my cousins William and Henry Peyton, sons of my brother Edmond, ten pounds apiece, to buy them mourning or rings to wear for my sake. The rest of my estate to my wife Katherine, whom I make and ordain to be sole and only executrix.

Wit: William Bampfeild, Philip Bamfeild.   Berkley, 145.

GILES DAVIS of Chippinge Sodbury, Co. Gloucester, yeoman, 5 January 1640, proved 27 May 1641. Wife Margaret. Two daughters Mary and Anne. My loving father Tobias Davis and loving brother Robert to be executors of my will and guardians of my children. William Ellery one of the witnesses.   Evelyn, 60.

[This, I think, is the only will in which I have found the name of Tobias Davis, well known in New England. Understanding that Mr. J. H. Lea was taking notes of the name I gave the reference to him, and called attention to the mention of Tobias as a christian name. Afterwards I learned from him that he could not get any more light on the question of a possible connection of this family with our Roxbury family of Davis. The will of Robert Davis of Little Sodbury was proved 1680 (Bath, 78). In both cases the signature was written Davis, although in the copy of the above will it was written Davies.
                HENRY F. WATERS.]

WILLIAM WEARE of Tregonye, Cornwall, yeoman, 8 January 1619, proved 20 May 1623. To be buried in the churchyard of Cubie. To the church of Cuby. To my daughter Margery, wife of Arthur Eustis twenty shillings. To my daughter Margery's four children, vizt Arthur Lyppingcott, Richard Lyppingcott, Maude Lyppingcott and Johane Lyppingcott, two shillings and six pence apiece. To Otes Tillam als Jeles the like sum. The residue to Susan Weare, my now wife, whom I make full and whole executrix.

Wit: John Williams and Philip Cooke.   Swann, 38.

[The foregoing will, also, I have preserved for the reason that it contains the only reference, thus far, to a Richard Lippincott which I have found in my researches here.   HENRY F. WATERS.]

PHILIP HAMPSON, citizen and merchant tailor of London, 2 June 1654, proved 4 July 1654. My body to be buried in the parish church of St. Michael Queenhithe London. To Samuel Hampson, my eldest son, one hundred pounds, at twenty one, together with fifty pounds more of the debts now owing me by Sir William Killigrew, if the same debts shall be had and received. To Jonathan, my youngest son, one hundred and twenty pounds at twenty one, and fifty pounds of the same debt &c. Household effects to each.

Item, I give and bequeath unto my daughter Beatrice Josselyne the wife of Abraham Josselyn the sum of five pounds and uhto the said Abraham Josselin I give ten shillings and all such debts and sums of money which he oweth me except one of thirty one pounds that he oweth me upon bond. I give and bequeath unto Abraham Josselin and Philip Josselyn my grand children five pounds apiece, to be paid unto them when and as they shall severally and respectively attain unto the age of twenty one years. To my daughter Hannah Philipps twenty shillings and to Hugh Philipps her husband ten shillings and to Hugh Philipps my grandchild five pounds at twenty one. To Anne Webb my wife's kinswoman five pounds at her day of marriage. To my sister Mary Delfe twenty shillings. To my sister in law Elizabeth Talbott twenty shillings. To John and Nicholas Hampson, the two sons of my late brother Richard, ten shillings apiece, if they come and demand it, and to Margaret and Anne daughters of my said late brother Richard twenty shillings apiece. To my brother Mr Robert Bedford of Coventry and my friend Mr Henry Madocks, dyer, my overseers &c, twenty shillings apiece as a remembrance of my love unto them. The rest to my wife Anne whom I make sole executrix. Alchin, 41.

[Abraham Josselyn of Hingham, Mass., supposed to be a son of Thomas of the same place, had a wife Beatrice (See Savage's Dictionary). It is not known whether this family is related to Henry Josselyn, "the first and only loyal Chief Magistrate of Maine," whose pedigree with an account of himself will be found in the REGISTER, vol. 40, pp. 290-4. — EDITOR.]

JOHN FRY of Combe St Nicholas, Somerset, gen^t, 2 January 1635, proved 20 November 1638. To be buried in the parish church of Combe St Nicholas. The children of my sisters that are now living. My wife Dorothy. My kinsman Robert Chute and Julyan, his wife. My servant John Luffe. Lands in Combe St Nicholas lately purchased of Edward Rossiter, gen^t, deceased. Brother in law John Richards. Cousin David Yea.

Lee, 166.

[George Frye of Weymouth, Mass. was from Combe St. Nicholas and March 5, 1673-4, being then about 58 years old, testified in relation to William Torrey and his son Samuel who were of Combe St. Nicholas and came in the same ship with him in 1640. See Suffolk Deeds, viii. 392, and Gleanings in the REGISTER, vol. 45, page 302 (ante, p. 550). John Frye of Newbury and Andover, Mass. from Basing, Hants., who came to New England in the Bevis of Hampton in 1635, is not known to be related to George. A tabular pedigree of his descendants is printed in the REGISTER, vol. 8, pp. 226-7.—EDITOR.]

JONAS DE PEISTER, born at Ghaunt, at present dwelling at London, son of late Jooas de Peister, also of Gaunte, 5 December 1638, proved 29 December 1638. "Findinge myself weakned with an Ague." Wife to be executrix. Poor of the Dutch Congregation. Poor of the Congregation at Haerlem. My cousin William de Peister that dwelleth with me (at 24). Peter de Peister, brother of William, "because he is sickley." Elizabeth de Key, my niece, daughter of my sister Mary, begotten by Jacob de Key,

the son of Michael. George Barker, serving with me. Our daughter
Anne. Wife, if with child. At death of child or children and marriage of
wife to my right heirs, vizt, John, James and Lieuen de Peister the children
of Joos de Peister, the children of Mary de Peister. My wife's brothers
Peter and Josias Crosse. I most friendly require my brother James and
Lieuen de Peyster and first my father in law William Crosse, Mr. Nicholas
Corselis, cousin William de Peister and George Barker for to be overseers
of this my testament. [Among the names of witnesses was that of George
Parker (not Barker). The widow's name not given in Probate Act.]

Lee, 172.

PRISCILLA HARRIS of Northam, Devon, spinster, 11 January 1650,
proved 12 September 1651. The poor of Northam and of Barnestable. I
give and bequeath unto my sister Agnes living in New England twenty
pounds and to her children thirty pounds, equally to be divided amongst
them. My sister Mary Gribble. My dwelling houses in Budporte in
Barnstable. My cousin Priscilla Baker. My cousin Bartholomew Stra-
bridge. My brother Richard Harris his daughters. My cousin Rebecca
Harris. My sister Philip Greade. My master and mistress Leigh and
their son in law Mr. John Berry. My brother in law John Gread and
sister Philip his wife. Mr. William Berry and his sister Honor. The rest
of their brothers and sisters. Bartholomew Shapton the younger and his
two sisters and brother John Shapton. My master William Leigh. Brother
Richard Harris to be sole executor.   Grey, 173.

JOHN COOKE of Sprowston, Norfolk, yeoman, 29 January 1650, proved
13 November 1654. To my wife Elizabeth all my houses and lands in
Norwich, which I bought of Erasmus Alesson, clerk, lying and being in the
parish of St. George, Colgate; also two closes in Burston for her natural
life. To Dorothy wife of Edward Potts of Cambridge all my houses &c.
after the decease of my wife Elizabeth, subject to certain legacies. To
Elizabeth Parlet wife James Parlitte of Hingham ten pounds, to Anne the
wife of Edmund Pitts in New England, if she come to demand it, ten
pounds, to Mary Pitcher daughter of Isaac Pitcher the elder, of Hingham,
ten pounds and to Sarah (another daughter) ten pounds. To Isaac Jyssoppe
(Jessopp?) son of Thomas Jyssoppe the elder my two closes in Burston he
to pay to his brother's four eldest children five pounds apiece at eighteen
years of age. Wife Elizabeth executrix.   Alchin, 270.

JOHN SMITH of Southwold, Suffolk, gentleman, 4 November 1650, proved
8 February 1650. To John Smith, my eldest son, at his age of four and
twenty years, the house called the Lyon in Southwold, he to pay out of it
ten pounds apiece to my daughter Anne and my son Robert and to my
daughter Mary. My request is Mr. Harrison should give a release of the
Lyon according to his promise, otherwise that the two hundred pound
bonds due to me from him should be prosecuted for the good of my children.
To my daughter Anne, after the decease of my wife, those houses that
were lately Webb's and Cockerell's, and my wife shall pay out of those
houses three pounds every year during her life to my daughter Anne. To
my daughter Phebe the house upon the Common after the decease of my
wife. To my son Robert the house in the Lane that was lately Pinne's,
after the decease of my wife. To my daughter Mary the house that was
lately Mason's after the decease of my wife. To my wife all my movable
goods, stock, shipping, for the payment of my debts and for the bringing up

of my children. And after her decease my daughter Anne shall have out of the same ten pounds, my daughter Phebe ten pounds, my son Robert twenty pounds and my daughter Mary twenty pounds. I give and bequeath unto my wife a house and all debts in estate in New England during her life, and after her decease to be equally divided amongst my children. To my sister Phebe Smith a gold ring and twenty shillings. I make my wife Hellen Smith executrix and desire M[r] Thomas Spurdance my son in law and Mr. William Smith my cousin to be supervisors. Grey, 39.

CLAREE THATCHER of Woolsackaller in Hounsditch, St. Buttolph's without Aldgate, London, widow, 9 April 1656, proved 19 April 1656. To my loving sister Mary Langham, wife of Richard Langham, twenty gilders sterling money. To my loving friend and brother in the faith Anthony Trayford, five pounds of lawful money of England. To my nurse Margery Beale forty shillings. To Elenor Shilcock twenty shillings. To my daughter Sarah Hancocke, wife of Robert Hancock of Amsterdam, silk dyer, the sum of five shillings and no more. All which legacies my desire is shall be paid unto the several and respective legatees aforesaid within six months next after the death or departure out of this mortal life of me the said Claree Thatcher. I give, will and bequeath unto Mary Moody daughter of James Moody of Stepney, mariner, a debt of forty shillings due unto me from her said father. All the rest and residue of my goods &c. to my loving son Humble Thatcher, whom I ordain and make sole executor &c.
    Wit: Ralph Grafton, William Cock, John Butler Scr.
                                                      Berkley, 128.

[I would suggest that the testatrix of the above will was the widow of Anthony Thatcher referred to by his brother Thomas as "in the Seperation" (see REG. vol. 47, p. 131, ante, p. 676). The rather odd name Clarcy (Claree), the bequest of twenty "gilders," the reference to a friend as a "Brother in the fayth," and to a son in law as "of Amsterdam," all seem to show this. Let me say, too, that I have had the references to those Thatcher wills already printed, for nearly ten years, and only refrained from publishing them long ago for the reason that I felt so extremely doubtful as to the identity of Anthony Thatcher. I could not believe that the Anthony Thatcher who was "in the Seperation" was our man who was wrecked off Cape Ann.
                                                      HENRY F. WATERS.]

JOHN BURTON of London, gen[t], 7 December 1626, proved 23 June 1627. I give and bequeath my manor of Barons in Essex and all messuages, lands, tenements &c. thereunto belonging, situate in the parishes of Purleigh and Haseley, Essex, unto my son William Burton for life, and then to the heirs male and female of his body &c., next to John Russell &c., then to Henry Rawlinson, clerk &c. And for default of such issue &c. I give the half part of the said manor, messuages, lands &c. to the Company of Vintners, and their successors forever; and the other moiety I give and bequeath for and towards a yearly maintenance of such preachers which shall from time to time preach at "Powles Crosse" London, and also for a yearly maintenance of the poor of St. Brides als Bridget, London, equally to be divided. Other bequests to son William (including a messuage or tenement called the Three Tuns, on the Bankside, Surrey). Also my sword and inlaid musket and bandileers and my horsemans pistol and all my Latin and French books, together with my Prayer book which my father left unto me as my whole legacy. To wife Elizabeth my lease of certain tenements on the millbank at Westminster, and of a lease of certain cellars under the long Armory in Milk Street (and other property). To my brother in law William Handcorne five pounds (for a ring) and to his two daughters twenty pounds apiece, at sixteen or days of marriage. The Company of the Vintners ten pounds to buy them a cup in form of a Tun, with a burr on the top of it.

Item, I do give and bequeath unto the Knot of my cousins, vizt Mr. Henry Fryer, Mr. Windevor, Mr. Mavericke, Mr. Symon Younge, Mr. John Burton in Gracious Street, London, Mr. Paul Chapman, Mr. Thomas Wentworth, Mr. Walter Meeke, Mr. Lowe, Mr. Haughfen, Mr. Richard Hewlett, Mr. Carre Coventry, Mr. Richard March and Mr. Andrew Burton, four pounds to pay for a supper for them to meet together. To every one of my said cousins ten shillings apiece to buy them bandstring rings to wear in remembrance of me. Two hundred pounds to the said John Russell if he live to the age of one and twenty years. To Mr. Felix Wilson of the White Friers, London, forty shillings (for a ring); also to Mr. George Vernon and his wife. My wife's now daughter by her former husband. My son William to be sole executor and the said Mr. Henry Fryer, Mr. Felix Wilson, Mr. Edward Wendover, Mr. Symon Younge citizen and embroider of London, Mr. John Lane of London haberdasher, Mr. Andrew Burton of Gray's Inn and Mr. Thomas Wentworth the younger overseers.

Commission issued 23 June 1627 to Elizabeth Burton the relict to administer during the minority of the executor, who took upon himself the executorship 22 May 1640.   Skynner, 60.

[The above will and that which follows contain the only references to the name of Maverick which I have noticed during my examination of probably more than a quarter of a million wills in England.   HENRY F. WATERS.]

MOSES MAVERICK, on board the good ship Phæneas and Margaret, 6 January 1678-9, at 9 or thereabouts of the clock at night, proved 23 July 1679, by Elizabeth Downing *als* Dunning. To my landlady Mrs Elizabeth Downing the sum I owe her (seven pounds eight shillings), and a ring of the value of one " Ackye " and a half. To Mr Thomas Nelson the sum of five pounds I owe him and a ring of two " Ackyes " and a half. A ring of same value each to Mrs Deale and her two daughters. To my father and mother, brothers and sisters, each of them, one ring of the value of one " Acky " and a halfe. To every officer in this said ship Phineas and Margaret a ring of the value of two " Ackyes " and a half. To Mrs Ligh two rings of that value. To Robert Hall one ring of the value of two " Ackyes." Upon sundry occasions to myself best known I make my landlady Elizabeth Downing my heir and executrix and to see this will performed within ten days of the arrival of the ship at London.   King, 88.

[The Probate Act Book gives me no help as to his former place of abode.   H. F. W.]

JOHN LOWERS of Darnth, Kent, husbandman, 8 June 1645 proved 5 February 1650. I give and bequeath unto Thomas Lowers half my part of Roxly Wood, which I hold, and my sister Scudder and Henry Scudder her son, of Mr Bugings in lease, paying yearly for that part the sum of four pounds ten shillings during the full term thereof. To my sister Scudder's sons, Thomas, Henry, William and John Scudder, twenty shillings apiece and to her two daughters, Elizabeth and Martha Scudder, ten shillings apiece, to be paid within one year after my decease by my executor. To my cousin Thomas Lowers twenty shillings within one year &c. Wife Mary to be full executor and John Umphrey of Darnth yeoman and Thomas Lowers of Dartford husbandman to be overseers.   Grey, 27.

[Since our Thomas Scudder of Salem (1648) had children named John, Thomas, Henry, William and Elizabeth, I can not but think I have found traces of his family in the above will. If that should turn out to be correct, the following will should also be saved. H. F. W.]

WILLIAM SCUDDER of Darenthe, Kent, yeoman, 27 July 1607 proved 4 November 1607. My body to be buried "solempely," according to the custom of the church of England, within the parish churchyard of Darenthe, as near as may be unto my father's grave. To wife Margery all my lands and tenements whatsoever and whereever, during only her natural life. After that to Parnell Scoodder, my eldest daughter, my lands in Dartford and Wilmington now in the tenure &c. of James Pinden, with remainder to Mary Scudder, my youngest daughter. To my two next daughters, Margaret and Joane Scudder, my messuage of tenement called Frog Lane (with mault houses &c. belonging), now in the tenure of John Ellis &c. in Sutton at Hone. To daughter Mary a parcel of land called Pricles Meade (six acres or more) in Sutton at Hone, with remainder to Parnell, my eldest daughter. And if they two both happen to die without issue &c. then to my other two daughters. If all my four daughters shall happen to die without heirs of their bodies lawfully begotten then I give Parnell's portion to Henry Scudder, son of John Scudder, my natural brother deceased, and to his heirs forever. The lands and tenements bequeathed my daughters Margaret and Joane I then give to Henry and Thomas Scudder, sons of my natural brother Henry Scudder deceased, equally to be divided. The land bequeathed to Mary I give to John Scudder, the son of Henry Scudder my natural brother deceased &c. To my eldest daughter, Parnell, one hundred and twenty pounds. To my second daughter, Margaret, fifty pounds. To my third daughter Joane fifty pounds. To my fourth daughter, Mary, one hundred pounds. These to be paid at their respective ages of one and twenty years or days of marriage. To Judith West daughter of Will: West six pounds at age of eighteen. If she die before that then three pounds of it to Thomas Austyn of Darenthe and the other three pounds to my executrix. To John Johnson the elder ten shillings; to John Johnson the younger twenty shillings; both of the parish of Wilmington. To the children of Will: Gascoine begotten of his wife Bridget Walter twenty shillings. To the poor of Darenthe twenty shillings, of Sutton at Hone ten shillings and of Horton Kyrby ten shillings. The rest to Margerie my wife, whom I ordain full and sole executrix &c., desiring and entreating my trusty and well beloved cousins and neighbors Robert Walter, John Humfrey and Thomas Scudder to be overseers and assisters &c., and, for their care &c., I give them twenty shillings apiece.

Hudleston, 85.

HENRY ATKINS (without date) proved 6 November 1630. To my niece Margaret Wildon sixty pounds at the one and twentieth year of her age, and if it please God to call her out of this life before she come to age it is my will that the said legacy be given to my nephew George Wildon, her brother. To my nephew George twenty pounds at one and twenty, and if he die before he attain to those years my will is that it be given to my niece Margaret Wildon his sister. To Jane Pate ten pounds. To the three under cooks in the kitchen, to each of them ten shillings. Small bequests to Mr Ralph Catlyn, Mr Francis Patrick, Mr. George Neale, Gilbert the butler and Elizabeth Kemball. To the poor of Northampton ten shillings. To Edward Lawrence one silver porringer and one silver spoon. To Mrs.

Elizabeth Mewce two silver dishes, two saucers, one silver bowl, one silver gilt salt, five spoons, one down bed, one down bolster, one down pillow, one pair of Holland sheets, one Holland pillow beer. I give to Mrs. Francis Washington the sum of twenty pounds. To William, the Keeper of Althorpe Park, my bedfellow, forty shillings. To Edward, Mr. Mewce his man, ten shillings. To William, Mr. Mewce his man, ten shillings. And I make my loving and worthy friend Mr. Francis Mewce my sole executor.

These words were spoken by the Testator the night before his death, while he was in perfect memory &c.

Northampton Wills, OE. (1626–30), 298.

THOMASINE OWFIELD of London, widow, 16 June 1637, proved 9 November 1638. My body to be decently buried in the parish church of St. Katherine Cree Church *als* Christ Church in London, as near to the body of my late deceased husband Roger Owfield as conveniently may be. To my son Samuel Owfield all my lands &c. in Lincoln which I purchased of the Right Hon. the Earl of Hertford. A provision for children of daughter Elizabeth Staper. To my son Joseph Owfield eight hundred pounds, my seal ring of gold (and some silver plate). To John Janson, eldest son of my daughter Thomasine Janson, one hundred pounds at one and twenty. To my daughter Rebecca Geering's child, if she have any, one hundred pounds. To the four sons of my daughter Martha, wife of Symon Smith, six hundred pounds, after the decease of their mother, viz: Samuel and Thomas one hundred pounds each and John and Symon two hundred pounds each. To Samuel, (eldest son), and Thomas Smith one hundred pounds each in six months after my decease. To my grandchild Elizabeth Smith one hundred pounds at one and twenty or day of marriage. To Thomas Wyeth my grandchild one hundred pounds to be employed for the use of his daughter Thomasine Wyeth, daughter of my grandchild Martha Wyeth deceased. To my daughter Thomasine Janson, wife of John Janson, my cabinet. To John Short, eldest son of my late son in law John Short deceased, sixty pounds and to his brother Thomas Short forty pounds. To the four children of my daughter Abigail Harrington deceased, late wife of Francis Harrington, likewise deceased, eight hundred pounds. To my executors two hundred pounds for the use and benefit of Francis Harrington, to Isaac two hundred pounds, to Abigail two hundred pounds and to Mary two hundred pounds.

Item I give and bequeath unto Roger Glover, eldest son of my daughter Sara Glover deceased, the sum of one hundred pounds, to be paid him at the age of one and twenty years, and to Elizabeth Glover, eldest daughter of Sara Glover deceased, the sum of fifty pounds, and to Sara Glover, youngest daughter of Sara Glover deceased, the sum of fifty pounds to be paid unto them at the age of one and twenty years or days of marriage, which first shall happen. To Richard Staper, eldest son of Hewit Staper, three hundred pounds, to Samuel Staper two hundred pounds, to Josua Staper two hundred pounds, to Benjamin Staper two hundred pounds. To certain ministers (including Adoniram Bifield). To the two children of my niece Martha Valentine deceased, forty pounds, *i.e.* to the eldest daughter Ann twenty pounds and to the other daughter twenty pounds, at one and twenty or days of marriage. To my son in law John Geeringe ten pounds to make him a ring. To John Owfield, my kinsman in Billiter Lane, and his wife ten pounds apiece to make them rings. To sundry servants and others and to the poor in Hospitals and elsewhere. Sons Samuel and

Joseph to be executors. I give unto the Wor^ll Company of Fishmongers as a remembrance of my hearty love and good affection unto them the sum of twenty pounds to be spent at a dinner amongst them upon the day of my funeral or at some other convenient time, at their pleasure. To Richard Staper, eldest son of my daughter Elizabeth Staper, the lease of my house at Istleworth which I bought of John Juxon, he to permit his mother to dwell in it so long as she shall live, if she like to dwell there, she paying the rent &c. And my express will and desire is that my executors do bury me in the afternoon without any heralds. Lee, 142.

[This will binds the Walter, Moore, Gardiner and Owfield wills on pages 726 –31 to that of Thomasine J: anson (*ante*, p. 724) already given. The following wills relate more closely to the Glover side of the connection.— H. F. W.]

ROBERT GOODWIN citizen and salter of London, 4 August 1610, proved 16 October 1610. To my son Peter Goodwin (certain household fixtures &c.) a pair of brass andirons a fire shovel and a pair of tongs all of brass, a pair of bellows, the boards being of Cipres wood, one table and a court cubbard of Walnut tree, another court cubbard with three cubbards in the same, six wainscot stools, a picture of the ten virgins and my own picture. To my son John Goodwin (certain household goods) and (a similar bequest) to my daughter Mary. To son John three hundred pounds within three months after he shall be made a freeman of London or shall have attained to the age of six and twenty years, which first shall happen. To my daughter Mary, wife of Richard Jennye, eight pounds a year. To the poor of the Dutch church five pounds.

Item I give and bequeath unto my son in law Roger Glover forty shillings to make him a ring; also I give unto him a mourning gown. Item I give and bequeath unto Susan Glover a white pepper box of silver. Item I give and bequeath unto Ellen Glover two gilt spoons. To Anthony Guy a debt of forty shillings which he oweth unto me by his bond. To Richard Jenny, my son in law a debt of thirty one pounds which I paid to Ballard for him and also another debt of ten pounds which I paid to Sir John Wattes for him. To the Company of Salters, whereof I am a member, that shall accompany my body to the church, ten pounds to make them a dinner at Salters' Hall. Item I do give and bequeath unto my daughter Glover a mourning gown and forty shillings to make her a ring. Other bequests to children and other individuals. My son Peter Goodwin to be my full and sole executor and my friend John Highlord to be overseer.

Wingfield, 91.

ROBERT PEMBERTON of the Borough of St. Albans in the County of Hertford, gentleman, 25 May 1628, proved 3 July 1628. Lands in Shenley, Herts, in the tenure of Henry Sharpe, and my messuage and fields in Shenley in the tenure of William Carter, and my fields &c. in Shenley late in the tenure of William Harris shall be sold by my brother in law John Glover of Lincoln's Inn, Middlesex, Esq. and by my brother Raphe Pemberton gentleman, now mayor of the Borough of St. Albans within convenient time after my decease for and towards the payment of such moneys as is now or hereafter shall be due unto my father in law Roger Glover of Bewcott in the Co. of Berks Esq., upon a Mortgage of my houses and tenements in Bow Lane in the parish of St. Mary le Bow London, and unto Roger Marsh for the discharging of the debts which shall be due unto him for the Mortgage of certain lands in Shenley Herts. Any overplus shall go towards the performance of this my will &c. My wife Susan shall have one hundred pounds yearly out of my messuages &c. in Bow Lane, for and during her natural life.   And the rest of the rents &c she shall take and receive during all the time she shall remain sole and unmarried, until my eldest son Roger shall accomplish the full age of twenty and one years, for and towards the maintenance of my three children Roger, Robert and Elizabeth (and for certain other specified purposes).   Then follow elaborate provisions for the children.   Reference to a debt due from Randolph Willey citizen and vintner of London and one due to Mr. Valentine Moretoft of London, and debts due to testator beyond the seas &c.   To the poor of St. Peters in St. Albans of Shenley and of St. Mary le Bow, London.   To Mr. Jeremy Leech, parson of St. Mary le Bow one ring of gold, with a death's head, of the value of twenty shillings.   To my well beloved father in law Master Roger Glover the like ring of gold of the value of thirteen shillings and four pence, and to my brother in law John Glover the like ring of the value of thirteen shillings four pence.   To my dear mother Mistress Elizabeth Pemberton, widow, and to my loving brother John Pemberton and Katherine his wife, and my loving brother Raphe and Frances his wife, and my loving brother in law Mr. Robert Woolley and Tecla his wife, each of them the like ring of the value of thirteen shillings four pence apiece.   Rings to wife, to cousin Ellen Woolley, to son Robert to daughter Elizabeth and to Robert, son of brother Mr. Robert Woolley. To son Roger my ring bequeathed unto me by my father Mr. Roger Pemberton deceased.   Son Roger to be executor and brothers John Glover and Raphe Pemberton to be overseers.   Barrington, 69.

[Robert Pemberton, the testator, was a son of Roger Pemberton of St. Albans by his wife Elizabeth dau. of Raffe Moore, and was a cousin of Roger Williams. His father's will printed on p. 331 mentions him, though he is omitted in the pedigree, copied on the same page from the Visitations of Hertfordshire of 1634.   Robert Pemberton, the testator, was baptized at St. Albans, Herts., Dec. 23, 1586, and was buried there May 29, 1628.   His sisters were also baptized there, namely, Elizabeth, Dec. 27, 1585, prob. d. young; Elizabeth, May 26, 1590; and Tecla, Sept. 27, 1592.   Of these, Tecla m. Robert Wooley.
Mr. Watkins, in his article on the Pemberton Family, vol. 46, pp. 392-8 of the REGISTER, supposes Ralph Pemberton, born about 1609, who is regarded as the ancestor of the Pemberton Family of Pennsylvania, to be "Ralfe" mentioned in the Pemberton pedigree above referred to as the son of Raffe and Frances (Kempe) Pemberton; but from information he has since received, he is convinced that the supposition is erroneous, the father of Ralph, the Pennsylvania emigrant, being named William.— EDITOR.]

ROGER GLOVER of London Esq. 9 January 1633, proved 7 August 1634. Daughter Elizabeth Glover to be full and sole executrix.   Reference to a mortgage made to testator by son in law Robert Pemberton, of certain houses in Bow Lane for the sum of eleven hundred and forty five pounds principal lent to the said Robert at the time of the said mortgage, on which testator has recently received eight hundred and fifty pounds.   If the executor shall receive the remainder of the principal money which is unpaid and the forbearance of the eight hundred and fifty pounds which is already paid me, during the time it was in the hands of my son John Glover and Mr Ralph Pemberton then she shall reconvey the said houses unto the heirs of the said Robert Pemberton my late son in law.   "And if neede shall soe require I desire my eldest sonne Josse Glover to ioyne wth my said executor in the reconvayinge of the said houses the wch I trust hee will not deny in regard hee hath given me a release " &c.
I give my household stuff and plate unto my two daughters Elizabeth and Sarah to be divided equally between them at the time of either of their

marriages and my will is that my wife shall have the use of the said plate &c during her natural life &c. Reference made to a bond of son John Glover for the payment of twelve hundred pounds to Sir William Hewitt (which he did not pay) and for the payment of five hundred pounds to my daughter Sarah and five hundred pounds to my son Ralphe after my decease. The lease of my house in Drury Lane to my daughter Sarah.

Whereas I have disbursed threescore and sixteen pounds for and towards a ship called the Coslet for which ship I have a bill of sale, my will is that my son Roger be presently furnished with one hundred twenty four pounds more to make up the same two hundred pounds towards setting out of him and the said ship, and my will is that the said ship be insured during this voyage &c.   Seager, 78.

ELIZABETH GLOVER of the parish of Anne Blackfriars London 4 May 1643, proved 7 May 1643. To my brother Francis Collins and my sister Sara Collins ten pounds apiece. To my mother Mrs Anne Glover ten pounds and my pair of brass andirons that are at Amy Collins's house and a cap pan of Brass to them. To my three nieces Elizabeth, Sara and Anne Collins, daughters of my said sister Sarah Collins, one hundred pounds apiece. To my niece Elizabeth Pemberton fifty pounds (and certain goods). To my nephew Robert Pemberton fifty pounds. To my brother John Glover and his wife ten pounds apiece. To my said brother John Glover, for the use of his son Charles, my nephew and godson, thirty pounds of lawful English money. I do will that if my nephew William Moretoft shall live to the age of one and twenty years then I do give him thirty pounds, but if he shall die before he attain to that age then I do will the said legacy last mentioned to my said Nephew Robert Pemberton. To my uncle Roulte, to the Lady Abigail Darcy, to Mr. Morris and his wife, to Mr. Coppinger, to Mr. Dunton and his wife, Mr. Smyth and Mr. Miller and their wives and to Sir Edward Leech and his lady, to each of them a ring enamelled, with a death's head, of the price of forty shillings for each ring. To the poor of Istleworth five pounds. To Dr. Gouge forty shillings. To my said sister Sara Collins all my linen and woollen clothes, to dispose of them all to her own proper use &c. To my nurse Cushion twenty shillings, besides her wages. I make and ordain my nephew Roger Pemberton sole executor, to whom I give one hundred pounds. The rest &c. to my niece Elizabeth Pemberton.   Crane, 38.

JOHN GLOVER of Lincoln's Inn Middlesex " Petter " Barrister, 23 October 1648, proved 19 October 1649. I devise my manor of Water Newton, with the appurtenances, in the Co. of Huntingdon and all my lands, tenements &c. in that county unto Gamaliel Catlmer of Lincoln's Inn Esq., Richard Broughton of the Middle Temple gen^t, my nephew Robert Pemberton of Lincolns Inn gen^t, and certain estates in Whaddon and other towns in Cambridgeshire to be conveyed to my said three friends by William Vaughan of Gray's Inn gen., my late servant, in whose name they stand as my trustee. All these upon trust to allow my wife to take the profits of her jointure, to pay for the maintenance and education of my eight children in such proportion as my wife shall think meet. And there shall be raised for the portions of my seven younger children as follows, to every of my three younger sons, Charles, John and Richard, five hundred pounds apiece, to be paid them at their respective ages of one and twenty. To every of my four daughters as follows; to Elizabeth one thousand pounds, to Dorothy one thousand pounds, to Sara six hundred pounds and to Deborah five hundred pounds, at their respective ages of twenty years or days of marriage. The inheritance of certain estates in Highgate which I have purchased to be surrendered to my wife. And whereas my brother in law Mr George Griffith did heretofore pretend that I was indebted to him I do clear my self and, to give my mother in law and others satisfaction, protest before God that I owe him not one penny. My friend and kinsman Philip Smith Esq. hath in his hands and keeping an ancient Statute of Sir John Whitbrookes for which I have paid many years since one thousand pounds, for the debts of my said brother in law. Lands in Surrey to descend to my eldest son Francis Glover. I make my wife executrix. By a codicil he relieves his wife of the trouble of acting as executrix and appoints his son Francis executor, and I wish him to take administration of the goods &c. of my brother Richard Glover deceased.

Fairfax, 150.

[The name of the testator's wife does not appear in the above will, and the change of mind as to the executorship prevents our learning it through the Probate Act. But he is known to have married Joane, one of the daughters of Francis Dorrington of London, merchant, for whose pedigree see the Visitation of London (1633–34), Harleian Society's Publications, vol. 15, p. 235. Her mother was a daughter of Simon Horspoole.   H. F. W.]

ANNE GLOVER of St. Stephen, Colman Street, London, 5 July 1650 with codicil made 22 January 1651, proved 26 June 1654. My body shall be carried to Milton Hervy in Bedfordshire and buried in the parish church near unto my dear and loving husband Francis Barty in decent and comely manner. To my nephew William Portington, the son of my sister Judith Portington, the lease of my house the which I hold of the Right Hon. the Earl of Bedford, in the Strand &c., paying the lord's rent, which is eight pounds a year; also the lease of my house in Colman Street. Other gifts to him. I give also to my nephew Portington one hundred and fifty pounds of the money due to me out of Ratcliffe from John Glover, the which made over to me for fifty pound a year that his father in Beckett he sold, the which my husband Glover made over to me out of Beckett for part of my jointure, being part of my jointure he made in Ratcliffe fifty pound a year which was to be paid yearly by his father's executor to me as long as I lived; for want of payment the whole is forfeited to me, which is my jointure. To Sir Thomas Hartopp five pounds to make him a ring. To my niece Dorothy one dozen of gold buttons enamelled and six of them with rubies and six with diamonds. To my niece Mary Hartopp a dozen gold buttons set with rubies &c. (They have them already). To my nephew William five pounds to make him a ring. Gifts to sister Rodd and niece Rodd. To Sir John Rolt my Arras hangings, five in number, and my best cabinet. To his lady a dozen and a half of gold buttons set with three diamonds apiece. To my daughter Dorothy my pointed diamond ring. To my daughter Elizabeth Glover my gold bracelet set with diamonds. To my niece Judith fifty shillings. To her sister Susan and Margaret ten pounds apiece, to be paid to their brother (Judith to be in his hand). To Elizabeth, Mary and Anne Ebbs. To my servant Robert Darnton ten pounds of the money due to me at Ratcliffe from my son John and John Glover grandchild to my husband Roger Glover. To my niece Baynam twenty pounds due to me from the House of Parliament. My daughter Seward's children. My daughter Knightbridge. My son Anthony

Knightbridge. My niece Elizabeth Rolt. My nephew George Fitz Jeffery. My son John Glover the heir of Ratcliffe &c. My son Collins' children. Sarah Prophet. To my nephew Sir John Rolt the third part of the money due to me from my grandchild John Glover and John Glover that their father did tie over for the fifty pound a year to have been paid to me yearly, but was paid but one year. Cousin Robert Tanisse. My three nephews Thomas, Walter and Richard. My nephew William Portington.

In the codicil she says "whereas heretofore Josse Glover Clerke surrendered the Reverc̃on of certaine Coppiehold Messuages, Tenements and hereditaments with their appurtenances holden of the Mannor of Stebonheath (which I have in Joyncture) to the use of my brother Thomas Rolt Esquire, Nevertheless upon condic̃on that the said Josse Glover and his should pay me fiftie pounds a yeare duringe my life &c." Reference to John Glover, son and heir of said Josse Glover. Aylett, 156.

FRANCIS GLOVER of Westminster, Middlesex, gentleman, 12 October 1659, proved 16 July 1666. Reference to will of late father John Glover of Lincoln's Inn, utter barister, lately deceased (about 1648) and his devise to Gamaliell Catline of Lincoln's Inn Esq. and others, in trust &c. To my wife six hundred pounds, and also forty pounds to buy her mourning. To my sister Skynner one hundred pounds, seven years hence, if her husband's late eldest brother's child be then living, otherwise not to be paid. Twenty pounds to be paid to my sister Skynner and her husband over and above the one hundred pounds. Twenty pounds between my sister Sarah and Deborah. Ten pounds to my brother John and ten pounds to my brother Richard Glover. And ten pounds to my cousin John Glover, Doctor of Phisick. Twenty pounds to my cousin Pemberton and thirty pounds to my brother Church and his wife. Ten pounds to my Aunt Ferraro in Yorkshire. Twenty pounds to be laid on my burial and three pounds to the minister that preacheth my funeral sermon. The overplus to my brother Charles Glover. I make him executor and my cousin Robert Pemberton and my brother Church overseers.

Decimo sexto die mensis Julii Anno Domini Millesimo Sexcentesimo Sexagesimo Sexto Emanãt Cõmissio Theodoræ Glover Relctæ dict: defuncti habentis dum vixit et mortis suæ tempore bona jura sive credita in diversis Diocess. sive Jurisbus Ad Administrand. bona jura et credita ejusdem defuncti juxta tenorem et effectum Testamenti ipsius defuncti, Eo quod Carolus Glover, Executor in dicto Testamento nominat., antequam onus Executionis in se acceptasset, ab hac luce etiam migrau'it etc.

Mico, 117.

CHARLES GLOVER, late of Princes Street in the parish of St. Giles in the Fields, Middlesex, declared his will nuncupative or by word of mouth on or about 4 December 1663; he the said deceased speaking while Jane Glover, his wife, at the same time with several of his friends and acquaintances were then present, said I give my whole estate to my wife for the good of my children.

Adm̃on. with the will annexed was granted to his widow Jane Glover 15 December 1663. Juxon, 145.

Mense Augusti 1684. Vicesimo primo die Em̃t Com̃o CAROLO GLOVER ffratri nr̃ãli et lt̃im̃o Richardi Glover nup de Virginia sed sup alto mari in nave vocata The Maryland vidui defuncti haben̄ etc.

Mense Novembris 1684. Undecimo die em^t Com° Carolo Glover, nepoti
ex fratre Richī Glover, nup de Virginia in ptibus transmarinis sed iñ nave
vocata The Maryland vidui defuncti habeñ etc. ad adstrañd bona jura et
credita dicti defuncti p Carolum Glover fratrem nrālem et ltiñium dicti
defuncti modo etiam demortuum inadministrat etc.

Admon. A. B. 1684.

Whether the following will refers to the same family I am unable to say.

MARY GLOVER of the City of London, widow, 21 March 1660, proved
2 July 1661. To my daughter Bennett Glover now of Virginia in parts
beyond the seas, twenty shillings. I give unto her my two mourning rings,
now in the custody of my daughter Anne Glover, if she the said Bennett
shall fortune to come over the seas and to this City of London to receive
and enjoy the same rings herself. To my son Richard Glover ten pounds
to put him forth an apprentice, at the care, discretion and good liking of my
loving brother Mr. Isaac Perkins, minister of God's Word. To my said
son Richard (certain household stuff).

Item, my will and mind is that all such moneys, goods, commodities and
other things now due or hereafter to be due to me as Adventure or as part
of my late husband Richard Glover's estate from beyond the seas, and also
all benefit and profit to be recovered and received of the debt now due to
me from Thomas Cooper, shall be both equally had, parted and received by
my son and daughter Richard and Anne Glover, part and part alike. The
residue to my daughter Anne Glover. I do desire, nominate and appoint
my very loving cousin John Watson full and sole executor.

Among the witnesses were Henry Cope and Elizabeth Cope. Proved
by John Watson.   May, 111.

[With reference to the family of Mr. Josse Glover, the following notes taken
some years ago from the Suffolk Court files (with the kindly assistance of my
friend Mr. William P. Upham, who called them to my notice) ought to
be preserved; and no better occasion has ever occurred than now when I have
given so many wills bearing on the ancestry of Mrs. Sarah Winthrope, Mrs.
Elizabeth Winthrop and Mrs. Priscilla Appleton, daughters of Mr Glover, and
the parties concerned in the suit about the estate of Dr. John Glover, the son
of the Revd Josse Glover. Some account of him, by the way, will be found in
Munck's History of the College of Physicians.   HENRY F. WATERS.

See REGISTER, vol. 13, pp. 135–7, and vol. 30, pp. 26–8, for notices of Rev.
Josse Glover; also Miss Anna Glover's Glover Memorials and Genealogies
(Boston, 1867), pp. 560–72.—EDITOR.]

JOHN GLOUER sonn of Mr Josse Glouer & Priscilla his wife died intestate (in London 1668) seized of a farme at Sudbury leaueinge one only
Sister Priscilla the wife of Jo: Appleton who in her right claimeth the Inheritance of the said Land as his next heire the said Glouer dyinge with
out Ishshewe.

This said Mr. Josse Glouer by a former venter had two daughters Sarah
ye wife of Mr Deane Wintrop & Elizabeth the wife of Mr Adam Wintrop
deceased Leaueinge Issue Adam Wintrop now liueinge, neither of wch aut
to claime any part of the said Land of Josse Glouer beinge but of the halfe
bloud at the least & for other reasons:

1 Because John Glouer enjoyed these Lands in his Mothers right his
ffather beinge neuer possessed of them and the said daughters Sarah &
Elizabeth cannot claime any right by descent from a Mother in Law: nor
halfe sisters claime as particulars wth a sister of the whole bloud.

2 Because y⁰ said Sarah & Elizabeth had large portiones bequeathed them by there ffather Mr Josse Glouer wch they also receiued, but y⁰ s^d Priscilla the wife of Jo: Appleton receiued not her portion giuen by her ffather but lost thereof 150^{lb}

3 Because uppon y⁰ marriage of y⁰ said Priscilla wth Jo: Appleton: there was a Couenant made that if y⁰ s^d Priscilla died wthin a yeare the said Glouer should enjoy halfe her estate which was to be retornd to him & no Concideratione had of the other sister by the same Reason: were there no other might the said Priscilla expect the sole benifit of the Estate dyinge wthout Issue intestate & therefore humbly prayeth the assistance of this Court to put her into a Legall possession thereof by granting the s^d Jo: Appleton: her husband Administration: or by any other meanes wthin there wisdome they shall thinke meet

witnesse my hand John Appleton

Vera Copia Attest

p Edw: Rawson Secret

In the Case wherein Capt John Appelton is p̃t: ãgt: Thomas Danforth as Administrator to Dr. John Glouer deceased, the said Thomas Danforth doth owne & confes in Court, that Mrs Priscilla Appelton the wife of the said Capt: Appelton is the reputed daughter of Mr Josse Glouer, Mrs. Elizabeth his wife, & that the aboue named Dr. John Glouer was her reputed Brother, & that the said Dr. Glouer was seized of a farme neere Sudbury & that for many yeares, before hee died, & that hee the said Dr. Glouer, sold a part thereof, & the remainder as Atturney to Dr. Glouer, tho said Thomas Danforth leased it out to the tennant that is now in possession of it:

This is owned in Court & Attested to bee true:

Capt John Appleton et ux. Priscilla v. Tho⁸ Danforth adm^r Est of John Glover dec'd. Attachment dated 3^d Nov. 1668. Midd^x Co.

Court held at Charlestown 15 Dec. 1668.

Copy of letter.

Louing Brother   I am sorry that Providence hath soe ordered it, that I could not see you. I am sorry that you gave such a release, but now it cannot be helpt. I am now come out of Scotland my Grandmother being dead. I am to pay a great deale of moneys before I can enjoy my Estate if it should please the Lord to take mee out of this world. I shall take sume course that you may understand how my busines is here for it is my desire that my sister youre wife should haue all that I haue both in old & new England. I pray giue mee an Account how my Estate is there &c concerning priuate matters.

I rest youre very affectionate Brother till death
J: GLOUER

London March: 5
1655

Superscribed   Directed to Capt: John Appelton of Ipswich. Extracted out of a letter on file, & is a true Copie so farr as it refers to the Case in question

As Attests   Tho: Danforth, R.

15: 10: 1668:   By mee Tho: Danforth

Vera Copia Tho. Danforth: R:

Vera Copia Attest : p Edw. Rawson Secret.

Att a Generall Court held at Boston: 22: May: 68   The Court granted
Mr Hugh Peters ffiue huudred Acres.   To Mr Thomas Allen ffive hundred
Acres: in regard of Mr Harwards Gift: To Mrs Glouer six hundred Acres.
To Leift Sprage one hundred Acres, having borne difficulties: &c.
   That this is a true Copie taken out of the Court Booke of Records
                                   As Attests   Edw. Rawson Secret.
Vera Copia Attest'
         p Edw. Rawson Secret.
   From Papers in a suit concerning the estate of Dr. John Glover—taken
from the files of Suffolk Co. Court.

PETER SOHIER (translated out of the French) Will made 3 April 1576
proved 30 July 1576.   Wife Anne de la Fontaine *alias* Wicarte.   Property
on this side as on the other side of the sea.   My children (not named).
My administrators and executors to be Anna de la Fontaine *alias* Wicarte,
my wife and bedfellow, my brother Matthew Sohier, presently dwelling at
Southampton, and my brother in law Erasme de la Fontaine.
   Commission issued to Matthew Sohier, Erasmus de la Fontaine, Cornelius
Sohier and Thomas Fountaine to administer &c. during the minority of
Anne, Mary and Peter Sohier, children of the deceased, for the reason that
Matthew Sohier and Erasmus de la Fountaine, executors, had renounced
and Anna the relict and other executor had died.   Carew, 19.

MARY SOHIER born of Andwerp, at this present dwelling at London,
widow of late Augustine de Beauliou (?) (translated out of the French) will
made 10 March 1602 (stile of England) proved 11 February 1603.   One
hundred and fifty pounds in my hands appertaining unto John, Paul and
Peter le Clercq, children of the honest John le Clercq my son in law, which
he had by Susan de Falloyse my deceased daughter, and the which sum
hath " bine " by the testament and last will of late James de Falloise, my
son, bequeathed unto the said children and of which he hath given me the
use during my life.   The poor of the French church in London.   The
children of Samuel de Falloise my son (at five and twenty or estate of
marriage).   I make the said John Le Clercq, my son in law, sole executor.
                                   Dean and Chapter of St. Paul's
                                            Book C, Leaf 194.

MATTHEW SOHIER the elder, son of late Matthew, merchant, born of
Valenchienne, at this present dwelling in this city of London &c (translated
out of the French) will made the last day of February 1593 (stile of England) proved 17 October 1605.   My body to be buried and put into the
ground after the Christian manner of the reformed churches.   The poor of
the French Church in London.   The poor of the parish where I dwell.
To my nephew Daniel Resteau son of John Resteau, my brother in law,
all the linen which Catherine Resteau, my wife deceased, hath had of her
mother.   To Nicholas Cuper, merchant dwelling in London, one silver cup
of a Dolphin fashion.   To James de Valloise one silver cup of au Eagle
fashion upon the olive tree.   Mary Coppine, daughter of late William
Coppin and Mary Sohier, daughter of late Peter Sohier, my nieces.   John
and Cornelius Sohier, my brothers deceased.   Mrs. Woudrien Sohier, my
sister, and her children.   My sister Mary Sohier.   The kindred of late
Catherine Resteau my wife deceased.   John Resteau, her brother, my sole
executor.   Mr. Augustine de Beaulieu, merchant dwelling at London, and
the abovesaid Nicholas Cuper to be assistants.   Hayes, 67.

MARY SOHIER, the relict widow of late Francis de Behaulte deceased, in his life time merchant dwelling in London, her will made 10 May 1614 proved 15 July 1614. The poor of the French Congregation in London. Alice Coyfe, sometime my maid servant and now wife of John Franck. My cousin Cornelius Spyrinck, Magdalen de Behaulte, my sister in law. Jane Sohier my sister, wife of James Godscall, merchant. Adrian Mary, bookseller, my son in law. My son John de Behaulte. To him his father's sealing ring of gold whereon is engraven his father's arms and those two cushions whereon are wrought the said arms. My daughter Elizabeth de Behaulte at one and twenty or marriage. William Langer my grandson, the son of Leonard Langer and the late Mary de Behaulte, my daughter deceased. My brother in law James Godscall and Daniel Van Harinckhoeck, merchant, his son in law, to be my executors and my brother in law John du Quesne and my said cousin Cornelius Spirink overseers. Proved by Daniel Van Haringhooke, one of the executors, James Godscall, the other, renouncing. Lawe, 85.

THOMAS HALL of the Precinct of St. Katherine's near the Tower of London, citizen and turner of London, 7 October 1662, proved 9 May 1663. I give to my loving son Joseph Hall my freehold lands and tenements in Tilbury, Essex, which I lately bought of Henneage Featherstone, of Gray's Inn Middlesex, esquire, upon condition that he pay unto my executrix within two years next after my decease, six hundred pounds for and towards the payment and discharge of the debts which I shall owe at my decease and of such legacies as I have, by this my last will &c, given and bequeathed unto the several persons named. To my eldest son Timothy Hall one hundred pounds (having already given him above five hundred pounds) to be paid by twenty pounds a year yearly during five years. To my youngest son Thomas Hall one hundred and fifty pounds, by ten pounds a yearly until the same sum shall be satisfied and paid. To my son Joseph my lease which I hold from the Co. of Fishmongers of my shop and house in the Precinct of St. Katherine's, and one moiety and equal half part of the wares, wood and working tools in my said dwelling house. The other half of said wares &c. I give to my executrix towards the payment of my debts and legacies. To my grandson Joseph Hall, son of the said Joseph forty pounds at one and twenty. To the eldest child of my son Timothy twenty pounds at one and twenty or marriage. To my two sons Timothy and Joseph my lease of one thousand years of lands in Tilbury, Essex, with the messuages &c, thereby demised; they to pay out to my cousin Anne Smith and my sister in law Aveline Lister, and the longest liver of them, sixteen pounds a year, that is to say to my cousin Anne Smith for life and, after her decease, to my sister Aveline Lister for life, if she shall survive the said Anne. To my said cousin and sister twenty shillings each, to buy them rings. To Mr. Samuel Slator thirty shillings and to Mr. Richard Kentish twenty shillings to buy each of them rings. To sister Elizabeth Cox forty shillings, and I release unto her, if living at the time of my decease, the ten pounds which she oweth unto me by bond. To my brother David Hall in Gloucestershire ten shillings and unto my brother John Hall in New England ten shillings and to my Aunt Hall at Gravesend twenty shillings. To the poor of St. Katherine's forty shillings. To my wife Judith my lease which I hold from the Master, Brothers and Sisters of the Hospital of St. Katherine's and the messuage &c. therein demised, in St.

Katherine's, and my lease of a tenement at the Tower ditch side and all the rest of my goods &c., and I make her full and sole executrix.

Juxon, 65.

Here follow some other wills of Halls connected with New England.

SAMUEL HALL of Langford, Essex, gen[t], 13 November 1679, proved 25 January 1680. To my wife Sarah the whole profits and rents of my dwelling house and lands in Langford and all the rents and profits of my land in Bentley in the Co. of York during her natural life. I give her all my goods and movables and all debts owing to me in New England or upon any bonds or mortgages whatsoever. I give the five acres of meadow in Bentley, York, which I purchased of Roger Perkins of Doncaster, apothecary, (by deed of 1 Feb. 1676) to the use of the poor of that parish for ever, and have settled by a deed to feoffees in Trust, bearing date 10 January 1677 to the use of the poor of Bentley cum Arksay and Stockbridge. I give unto John Hall of Islington in the County of Midd[x], gen[t], and to his heirs forever all my messuage and land &c, in Langford Essex that I purchased of John Ponder gen[t] deceased upon condition that within one year after my wife's decease shall make sale of the messuage and lands that I have devised and given to him and his heirs, to pay all the legacies that I have bequeathed in this will &c within one year after my wife's decease. To my cousin Daniel Hall of Doncaster and his two sons Thomas (*sic*) thirty pounds equally to be divided amongst them. To Daniel Hall's wife five pounds to buy her a gown. To Daniel Hall's brother's wife and her children thirty pounds equally to be divided amongst them. To my wife's sister Beatrice Graves fifteen pounds. To her two daughters, Halvester's wife and Henrietta, ten pounds each. To her son Francis Graves and to her youngest son five pounds each. To her son Ralph Graves one shilling if it be demanded. To my cousin John Hall of Stockbridge five pounds in full satisfaction of all his right, title, interest and demand whatsoever which he may challenge or demand out of all or any part of my lands, goods, credits and debts whatsoever. To three of his sisters ten pounds equally to be divided amongst them. To my cousin Richard Nicholson twenty shillings to buy him a ring. To his two daughters ten pounds equally to be divided amongst them. To my cousin Mary and my brother Richard Hall's and her children fifteen pounds to be equally divided amongst them. To Samuel Cocking, son of Joseph Cocking deceased, my wife's brother, fifteen pounds. To John Ellis his children ten pounds equally to be divided &c. To my cousin Nathaniel Revell twenty shillings to buy him a ring and my best wearing suit. To my cousin Thomas Bradford of Doncaster twenty shillings if he be living when my other legacies are paid. To my adopted cousin M[r] John Hall of Islington twenty pounds and to his daughter Elizabeth twenty pounds to be paid to her upon the sale of my land and to be improved by her father for her sole use until she shall marry. To twenty silenced ministers ten pounds. To my cousin Hall's wife one great silver spoon and ten shillings to buy her a mourning ring. To my cousin Richard Hall of Bentley and his eldest daughter and Robert Hall, his brother, each of them twenty shillings. To Mrs. Robinson ten shillings to buy her a mourning ring. To her daughter Mrs. Hickford ten shillings to buy her a mourning ring. To my friends Mr. John and Mr. Thomas Freshwater each ten shillings to buy mourning rings.

I give out of my estate unto Boston in New England and other towns in that Colony that hath most suffered by the wars and by that late great happening in Boston one hundred pounds, fifty pounds to Boston and the other fifty pounds to the poorest that suffered by the wars, to be sent over for those uses at the will and discretion of my executor, as money can be raised out of my estate. To Elizabeth Thompson, Joseph Peachey and John Thompson, each half a crown to buy their gloves. To John Bearblock ten shillings to buy him a ring. To the poor of Great Totham, Little Totham, Heybridge and Wickham Bishop, each parish, twenty shillings, to be given to their most aged poor by their officers. To the poor of Malden twenty shillings. To the poor of Langford four pounds, the said four pounds to be laid out in cloth for them. I make my wife and Mr. John Hall of Islington joint executors. Commissary of London, Essex, Herts. Book Heydon, L. 375.

["1682 Mr. Samuel Hall, some time a resident in Massachusetts, had died at Langford near Malden, Essex County, England. He bequeathed £100 to those, who lost by the great fire in Boston and by Indian wars in this Colony. Mr. John Hall of Islington, near London, was his executor, who sent an order to his mother, Mrs. Rebeccah Symonds of Ipswich, to dispose of the bequest. She gave to individuals who had suffered by Indians, as follows:—£8 to Martha Graves; £10 to Moses, of Newichiwanack, son of the Rev. William Worcester; £5 to Frances Graves of Ipswich; £3 to Martha Coy, fled to Boston, widow of John Coy of Brookfield, slain; 33s. to Susannah, widow of Thomas Ayres, also slain."—(Felt's History of Ipswich, p. 62.)

Rev. Dr. Felt probably compiled this account from papers now in the American Antiquarian Society's Library, the substance of which is given by Mr. Abraham Hammatt in his Early Inhabitants of Ipswich, pp. 130.

Samuel Hall, the testator, came to New England about 1633. In that year he, with John Oldham and another person, set out on an exploring expedition and went as far as the Connecticut River. They returned Januaay 20, 1633-4, having endured much misery. Mr. Savage thinks he may have returned to England and have come back in the spring of 1635, aged 25, in the Elizabeth and Ann. He was at Ipswich in 1635, and his name with that of John Hall is on the original list of townsmen of Salisbury, 1640. He was a member of the Artillery Company, 1638. The date of his return to England I do not find. (See Savage's Dictionary, vol. 2, p. 337; Rev. David B. Hall's Halls of New England, pp. 720-1; Hammatt's Early Inhabitants of Ipswich, pp. 129-31; Winthrop's New England, vol. 1, p. 123 (146 new ed.); Hutchinson's Massachusetts, vol. 1, p. 43, first ed., p. 46, third ed.; Hubbard's New England, pp. 169-70).

The will of John Hall of Islington, the executor of Samuel Hall, and some facts concerning him, will be found in these GLEANINGS, ante pp. 683-4. His pedigree is printed, ante p. 687.

The will which follows is that of the testator's widow.—EDITOR.]

SARAH HALL of Langford, Essex, widow, 8 November 1680, proved at Chelmsford 25 January 1680. My body I bequeath to the Earth until the General resurrection at the last day to be decently buried by my loving and much respected friend Mr. Henry Robinson, minister of the parish of Langford, at his discretion, in the parish church of Langford in linen. I give up and resign all my right, title &c. in my deed of gift which my late husband Mr. Samuel Hall sealed unto me of the house and land &c. in Langford called Custaynes and Springers (containing twenty two acres more or less) to pay off my husband's legacies. If not enough then it shall be made good out of my own personal estate. I give five and twenty pounds to be expended about my funeral. To my friend Mr. Henry Robinson, minister of Langford twenty pounds. To Samuel Cockin, my brother Joseph's son, and his two children (now dwelling in Hull) forty pounds and two silver spoons, i.e. twenty to him and ten to each of his children and one of the spoons to each of the children. To Mrs Mundaye's daughter of Boreham,

Essex, spinster, ten pounds and unto Mrs Mundaye, her mother, forty shil-lings. Gifts to Mr. Heckford of Langford, to Mr Thomas Freshwater of Heybridge, to twenty nonconformist ministers or their widows, now living in Essex, the latter (ten pounds) to be paid into the hands of Mr. Martyne Carter the elder of Maldon, hoyman, to be by him disposed of (in sums of ten shillings apiece). To the poor of certain parishes. I give my customary cottage in Langford called Foster's Garden to the parish of Langford for the use of the poor of the parish. Tó Mrs Robinson of Langford my thumbring &c. To Daniel Hall of Doncaster forty shillings to buy him four rings, one for him, one for each of his two sons and one for his son's wife. To my brother in law William Graves of Bentley ten pounds. To twenty of the poor nonconformist ministers, or their widows, in or about the City of London. To John Hall of Bentley, my late husband's kinsman in Yorkshire, five pounds. To Henrietta Graves, my kinswoman, of Lon-don, twenty shillings.

And lastly I do constitute and appoint my loving friends Mr. Thomas Glover, a New England merchant, living in St. Clement's Lane near Lum-bard Street London and Mr. John Hall of Ilington (Islington?) to be joint executors. Item, my further mind and will is that after my debts and legacies are paid and all other charges defrayed I do give the overplus of my estate to be left in the said Mr. Thomas Glover's hands, to be laid out in cloth for the use of the poor of Newbury, Hampton and Amesbury in New England to be equally divided amongst them, part and part alike.

Memorandum before the sealing and delivery hereof. I do give to Mrs Robinson my silver tankard and I do give a small trunk of linen to be sent to my sister Beatrice Graves at Bentley in Yorkshire for her use.

Book Heydon, L. 483, Com. of Lon-
don for Essex and Herts.

[Thomas Glover, a New England merchant mentioned in this will, was, I presume, Thomas, son of John Glover of Dorchester, Mass., who at the age of three years was brought to New England by his father. He returned to Eng-land, and died in the parish of St. John, Hackney, London, Oct. 6, 1707, aged 80 yrs. and 9 mo. (See Miss Anna Glover's Glover Memorial, pp. 81-95). His will is printed on pp. 90-4 of that work.—EDITOR.]

NICHOLAS MORETON, minister of the word of God at St. Saviours South-wark in the Co. of Surrey, 29 May 1640, proved 18 August 1640. To my wife Elizabeth Morton her third part of those tenements at Shipyard near Chain Gate in Long Southwark that descended upon her by the death of her late father Mr. Nicholas King; also the rents of the two leases I hold at St. Katherine's Hospital near the Tower of London, forty pounds a year, during her life. Except two pair of sheets to each of my sons I give her all my household stuff. I give her fifty pounds in money, with all her own apparel, plate, jewels, except one silver salt, the late gift of my sister in law Margaret King to Nicholas Morton, my young son, and a piece of plate to each of my other sons at her own discretion. To Charles, John and Nicholas Morton, my three sons, I give to each of them thirty pounds a year, to be paid them or their guardians by half year payments during the widowhood of my said now wife Elizabeth, or, when she marrieth, by quarterly payments. Upon the marriage of the said Elizabeth all her estate, right, claim, use and possession of any and every part of my estate, as my executrix or otherwise, shall wholly cease and be void and remain only to the use of my children, except those above-named legacies to her bequeathed by this my will. Upon the death of either of my children in his minority his estate shall descend upon the survivors. Or if it happen that they all die in their minority, if my said wife continue a widow at that time, then one third of their estate shall fall to her and the other two parts to be bestowed upon and amongst the children of my brother William Morton of Coventry, or such of them as shall then be in England; or if they be not in England then to the two daughters of my late sister Joane Smith of Long Wharton or to Agnes Slyman, my sister Slyman's daughter, or the survivor or survivors of them.

I appoint my said beloved wife Elizabeth Moreton my executrix of this my last will and my loving father in law Mr. Thomas Kestle of Plendevie (Pendevie?) by Wadebridge in Cornwall and my good friend M[r] Pitt of Clifford's Inn, gen[t], my executors in trust. I appoint M[r] Rich&rd Tuffnaile of St. Olave's Parish in Southwark, brewer, and Mr. Philip Parker of Crutched Fryers, London, merchant, to be overseers of this my last will, desiring my said wife to present them, my father in law and friends, with a ring to each of them as a poor token of my love.

Mrs Margaret King was one of the witnesses.　　　　Coventry, 115.

[Rev. Nicholas Moreton, the testator, was the pastor of John Harvard, the founder of Harvard College (REGISTER, vol. 39, pp. 284; *ante*, p. 134). He is mentioned in the will of Thomas Harvard, 1638, brother of John (*ante*, pp. 128 -9), and in that of John Sedgwick, 1638 (vol. 38, p. 207; *ante*, p. 48).

Rev. Charles Morton, the eldest son of the testator, was educated at Oxford University, B.A. Nov. 6, 1649, M.A. June 24, 1652, was rector of Blisland 1656, from which living he was ejected for non-conformity in 1662, removed to the parish of St. Ives and preached privately to a few people of a neighboring parish till the great fire of 1666, when he established an academy at Newington Green, where DeFoe was his pupil. In July, 1686, he came to New England, and was pastor of the church at Charlestown from Nov. 5, 1686, till his death April 11, 1698, aged 72. He was vice-president of Harvard College (with the founder of which institution he had been doubtless acquainted) from June 4, 1697, till his death. "He was grandson by his mother's side, of Mr. Kestle of Pendavy, Cornwall, and was born in his house about the year 1626." (See Drake's Dictionary of American Biography, p. 640; Palmer's Non-conformist's Memorial, ed. 1778, vol. 1, pp. 273–5; Frothingham's History of Charlestown, pp. 193–6; Wyman's Genealogies and Estates of Charlestown, vol. 2, pp. 687-8; Budington's First Church of Charlestown, pp. 106-9, 222, 224; Foster's Alumni Oxonienses (1500–1714) p. 1038). Another son of the testator, Nicholas Morton, was also a graduate of Oxford University (see Foster's Alumni Oxonienses (1500–1714), p. 1039).—EDITOR.]

PETER PRYAULX of the town and County of Southampton, merchant, 15 November 1643, proved 31 December 1644. The poor of the English Church of Southampton. The poor of the French church there. The poor of St. Peter Port in the Isle of Guernsey. To my son Peter Pryaulx the fee simple of a house and garden I have near unto littles (*sic*) gate; lease of my now dwelling house next to the Star in Southampton &c., according to what I have conditioned with M[r] Peter Seale before the marriage of his daughter to my said son. I give him my great gilt bowl which his grandmother gave me, together with my scarlet gown an[d] my two other black gowns. To Jeane Pryaulx, Mary Pryaulx, John P.yaulx and Jacob Pryaulx, the four children of my said son, one hundred pounds apiece, at one and twenty or day of marriage; and these sums shall remain in the hands of M[r] Paul Mercer and William Pryaulx, two of my executors, to be put forth to the best profit &c. To my son William Pryaulx two hundred pounds that I stand bound by bond unto Henry Stone and others at

the making up of the marriage with Jeane Stone, his wife. To his son
Peter Pryaulx and his daughter Frances Pryaulx each a hundred pounds
(as above), to remain in the hands of Mr Paul Mercer &c. To my son
Robert five hundred pounds. To my son John eight hundred pounds, and
the patronage of the parish church of Elsteed. To my son Paul seven
hundred pounds and my house, land and copse in the tything of Bitterne,
according to the Custom of the manor. Anne and Jacob Fortery the two
children of Jacob Fortery merchant of London. Reference to contract of
marriage of my daughter Elizabeth, late wife unto the said Jacob Fortery.
To my daughter Frances Pryaulx a thousand pounds &c. My wife desired
me, at her death, to give unto her son Peter her best diamond ring, to her
daughter Elizabeth her best rose of diamonds, to her daughter Frances her
other rose of diamonds, to her son William her best saphire, to her son
Robert her other saphire, to her son John her emeraud, and to her son
Paul her ruby, and for her three wine bowls (parcel gilt) one to William,
one to Robert and one to her daughter Elizabeth. Other provisions. I
make Mr Paul Mercer, my loving brother in law, and Peter Pryaulx and
William Pryaulx, my sons, my joint executors &c. I give to my said
brother Mercer twenty pounds to be bestowed in a piece of plate to his
own liking, in remembrance of me. My overseers to be my son Robert
and my son John.   Rivers, 12.

DANIEL MERCER of St. Olave, Southwark, Surrey, dier, 28 August
1650, proved 6 September 1650, by Peter Hublon, one of the executors,
and by Paul Mercer, the other executor, 2 May 1651. To the poor of
St. Olave twenty pounds sterling. To my cousin Cooper, minister of the
said parish, five pounds. To Mistress Woocock forty shillings. To my
cousin Francis Batchellor three score pounds sterling, to be paid him at
his age of one and twenty years. To my brother Peter Mercer three score
pounds, to be paid unto him by my brother Paul Mercer as he shall see
occasion and in his discretion think fit, and not otherwise. To my brother
and sister Johnson I give ten pounds, between them to be divided. To my
wife Sarah all such goods, leases and estate as were her own when I married her, besides her children's portions, to be assigned over to my wife to
her children's use and benefit. I give her also five hundred pounds out of
my own neat estate, she to secure my executors from such debts as she or
her former husband did owe. To my brother Paul Mercer and my brother
in law Peter Hublon, whom I make sole executors &c., five pounds apiece.
To my son Daniel my messuages &c. in Sussex which I lately purchased
of John Middleton gentleman. The rest to my children Elizabeth and
Benjamin Mercer and such other child or children as my wife now goeth
with. Provisional legacy to brother Peter Hublon and sister Luparte and
their children and to my own kindred, brothers Paul, Peter and Francis
Mercer, my sister Priaulx children, my sister Blanchard, my sister Johnson, my sister Strowde and my sister Batchellor's children.
                                                   Pembroke, 147.

PAUL MERCER of Southampton, merchant, 6 June 1661, with a codicil
dated 7 June, proved 9 September 1661. To be buried in Godshouse
Chappell within Southampton town. Thirty cloth mourning gowns to be
distributed amongst thirty poor men and women inhabitants of said town,
every gown being worth near upon thirty shillings apiece. To Mr. William

Bernard, vicar of Holywoods church five pounds.   To the common poor of the English and French churches gathered in said town one hundred pounds. For a remembrance to John, Jacob and Paul Pryaulx, Mary the wife of John Lamport, Elizabeth, Catherine and Thomasine Pryaulx, the son and daughters of late Capt. Peter Pryaulx, my cousins, to each of them the sum of ten pounds at one and twenty years of age.   To my sister Elizabeth Blanchard, for a remembrance, my second best diamond ring.   And as concerning the hundred pounds (principal) due by her son John Stroad, his obligation dated 2 February 1645, my will is that out of it he shall pay unto Francis Mercer, my brother and executor, thirty pounds and another thirty pounds unto Jane and Elizabeth Godsall the daughters of his sister Jane, now the wife of John Hill, or the survivor of them, at twenty one or days of marriage.   The remainder of the said John Stroad's debt is hereby discharged and acquitted him forever.   To my sister Judith Johnson, widow, a yearly annuity of twenty pounds during her natural life; and to her daughter Mary the relict of late James Chipchase, my niece, and after her decease to her child or children equally to be divided, the sum of two hundred pounds.   To her sister Jane, the relict of late Gideon de Lawne, my niece, and after to her child or children my jewel of pendent diamonds &c, valued at one hundred pounds, with one hundred pounds in money.   To my brother Peter Mercer, during his natural life, a yearly pension of forty pounds, providing that the legacy given him by the last will of our deceased brother Daniel Mercer shall remain properly for my use as my own and proper goods.   As for his only daughter Hester, now the wife of Thomas Cary, my dear niece, I having already fully paid and satisfied her debts &c. —(reference to her contract of marriage dated 12 May 1660), she shall have two hundred pounds &c.

Item, I do give to her brother my nephew Thomas Mercer, and after his decease to his children or child begotten in wedlock, the sum of fifty pounds. To Susan and Anna Mercer, the daughters of my deceased nephew William Mercer, one hundred pounds equally to be divided &c.   And if anything can be produced by their mother Susan Mercer, widow, from her late deceased husband's debtors it shall be (after decease) equally divided by her three children, named Paul, Susan and Anna Mercer, upon an account of a judgment of eleven hundred pounds by their said mother acknowledged heretofore unto me.   To the children of my brother Francis Mercer, clerk, named Peter, John, Francis, Jane and Hester Mercer, to every one of them one hundred pounds at twenty one or days of marriage &c.   To the four children of my deceased brother Daniel Mercer, for a remembrance, five pounds apiece at twenty one.

Item, I give unto "my niepce Anna de (sic) daughter of late Nathaniel and Hester Bachiler now the wife of Daniel du Cornet of Middlebrough, merchant," as a marriage portion, three hundred pounds current Flemish money or, in lieu thereof, one hundred and four score pounds current English money, at my executors choice.   To her three younger brothers, my nephews, named Francis, Nathaniel and Benjamin Bachiler, two hundred pounds, to be equally divided amongst them or the survivors of them.   I give unto the grandchildren of my deceased sister Anna, begotten on the body of my late "niepce" Mary the wife of late John Bachiler, viz⁵ unto their eldest son, named John Bachiler, sixty pounds, unto his sisters Mary, Anna and Margaret Bachiler and unto their brother Paul Bacheler six hundred, to be by them four equally divided (they under twenty one years of age).   To Hester Mansbridge, the relict of late Richard Mansbridge, for a

remembrance, thirty pounds; and I acquit and discharge her of all debts
&c. which she or her late husband owe to me; and if she happen to decease
before me my will is that her daughter Hester Cushing, or her child or
children lawfully begotten on her body, shall have and enjoy the above
mentioned legacy bequeathed unto her above-named mother.   Certain servants.   The residue to my dear brother Francis Mercer, Clerk, and his forever, whom I make the only executor &c.; but in case he shall happen to
decease before the accomplishing and perfecting of it then my desire is that
my dear nephews Dr. John Pryaulx and Paul Pryaulx of London, merchant, with Mr. Henry Pitt and Mr. Joseph de la mott of Southampton,
merchants, or any three or two of them, will be pleased and are hereby
empowered and authorized to accomplish and perform the contents of this
my present will &c., as being selected to be my overseers.
     In the codicil he provides that in case his clear estate should not amount
to three thousand two hundred pounds, proportional deductions and abate-
ments should be made on the legacies (pious uses, Hester Cary and Anna
du Cornet's sums excepted).   May, 142.

[Mr. Waters deserves the sincere gratitude of every descendant of Rev.
Stephen Bachiler in America for filling so conclusively the provoking gap between the minister and his grandson, Nathaniel Bachiler, senior, of Hampton,
N. H., besides furnishing other valuable information.
     No one can examine these Mercer and Pryaulx wills in connection with the
letter referred to by Mr. Waters (see REGISTER, vol. 27, p. 368), without feeling
sure that the father of Nathaniel Bachiler, senior, of Hampton, was Nathaniel,
the son of Rev. Stephen Bachiler, and that the mother of Nathaniel Bachiler,
senior, of Hampton, was Hester Mercer.   The following will show the connection between Rev. Stephen Bachiler and Nathaniel Bachiler, senior, of Hampton, N.H. :

1. REV. STEPHEN[1] BACHILER, of Lynn and Hampton, b. 1561 in England; he
     m. (1) ———— ————; he m. (2) Helen ————, who was b. 1583, d. about
     1641; he m. (3) in 1647 or 1648, Mary ———— : he d. 1660, at Hackney,
     now a part of London, Eng.   Their children were :
         i.   THEODATE, m. Christopher Hussey; d. 20 Oct. 1649.
2.   ii.   NATHANIEL.
         iii. DEBORAH, b. 1592; m. Rev. John Wing, pastor of the English Puri-
               tan Church at Middleburgh, Zealand.
         iv.   STEPHEN, b. 1594.
         v.   ANN, b. 1601; m. John Sanborn.

2. NATHANIEL[2] BACHILER, m. Hester Mercer.   Their children were :
         i.   STEPHEN, of London, Eng. in 1685.
         ii.   ANNA, m. Daniel DuCornet of Middleburgh.
         iii. FRANCIS.
         iv.   NATHANIEL, of Hampton, N. H., b. 1630; d. 19 Jan. 1709-10.
         v.   BENJAMIN.
     Perhaps another daughter married Thomas Wenborne.
                              C. E. BATCHELDER, of Portsmouth, N. H.]

     FRANCIS MERCER, clerk, rector of Godmanston, Dorset, 25 January
1667, proved 31 January 1668.   To be buried in the Chancel of the parish
church of Godmanston.   Frances the daughter of William Highmore, my
god daughter.   To John Pryaulx, Doctor in Divinity, my beloved nephew,
all the books belonging unto me that are remaining in his custody.   To my
beloved son in law Robert Browne Esq. the pictures of Sir Robert Browne
and Dame Frances his lady and of Mrs. Ann Browne the daughter of the
said Sir Robert.   To Mr. Richard Capeline of Southampton, merchant, Sir

Walter Rawleigh his History of the World and to his wife my great gold ring with a death's head cut in the stone, therein set, and to Mrs Sarah Capeline, their daughter, I give my desk, as also my round and long table boards which I left in the custody of her father at my removal from his house in Southampton; all which I bequeath unto them as remembrances from their friend. My son Francis Mercer shall annually pay fifteen pounds unto or for the use of Katherine, my wife, during the time of her natural life. I give thirty pounds to the children or child of my son Peter Mercer, another thirty pounds to the children or child of my daughter Jane now the unhappy wife of Edward Furber, another thirty to the children or child of my daughter Esther now the wife of John Willis and another thirty to the children or child of Francis Mercer my son. My will and desire is that the annuity of forty pounds per annum which was bequeathed to Peter Mercer, my brother, by the last will of Paul Mercer, my late brother, to be paid unto him by ten pounds quarterly during his natural life, shall be well and truly performed by my executors, and at or within forty days after the decease of the said Peter, my brother, and the determination of his said annuity, I give and bequeath the sum of six hundred sixty and six pounds to be divided and distributed to and amongst the children of Peter, Jane, Esther and Francis aforesaid, my sons and daughters. Other bequests to Jane and the others. My wife Katherine shall have the use of such household stuff of mine as did belong unto her before my marriage with her or hath since been given unto her by Robert Browne Esq., her son. Other bequests to her. Reference to sums lent to son Peter in his necessity. To son Francis (among other things) the picture of my mother and her wedding ring of gold and one other gold ring having a coat of arms cut in the stone that is set therein, my silver seal of arms, my steel glass, my best gold weights, my agate picture, the picture of Henry the Fourth, the late French King, the pictures of my late brother Samuel and of two gentlewomen, with all the cases that belonging to them; and to Abigail, his wife, my case for rings, with a small ring of gold with a death's head therein. To Edward Furber, my son in law, my black cloak of proof serge, my black pair of boots, my cart and wheels and harness and pigs-trough. Certain jewels and silver to daughter Jane. Bequests to son John Willis and daughter Esther (among which) a silver tooth-pick with a claw of a bird set therein, my eye-cup of silver, my clock and the plummets thereof and twelve small pictures, in frames, of Moses and the prophets. To son Peter (among other things) the picture of my father and the case thereof. The residue to my sons and daughters, Peter, Jane, Esther and Francis (equally). Mention of trusts under the will of brother Paul Mercer deceased. My son Francis Mercer of the City of Sarum, Wilts, ironmonger, to be my executor and my approved friends John Pryaulx, Doctor in Divinity, and Canon of the Cathedral Church of Sarum, and Robert Browne of Blandford St. Mary Esq., my son in law, to be overseers. Published and declared 20 August 1668. Coke, 8.

[It is evident that John, one of the sons of the above Francis Mercer, had predeceased his father. The following is a brief summary of his will.]

JOHN MERCER of London, mariner, bound on a voyage to Bantam in the East Indies in the good ship or vessel called the Constantinople Marchant, 26 January 1662, proved 23 March 1663. To my loving father, Francis Mercer, five pounds. To my loving brother Francis Mercer twenty pounds.

To my very loving brother Captain Robert Browne ten pounds to buy him a ring to wear in my remembrance. To the rest of my brothers and sisters living at the time of my decease twenty shillings apiece to buy them rings &c. To my friend Clem^t Witham, scrivener, forty shillings (for a ring). To my very loving mother Katherine Mercer forty pounds. To my loving sister Anne Mead, wife of Josuah Mead all the rest-and residue of my estate; and I make the said Anne my sister sole executrix; but if she die before me then I make Anne Meade, daughter of my said sister, executrix and I bequeath to her all my goods so given and bequeathed unto her said mother. And I appoint my said brother Josuah to be aiding and assisting unto his said daughter in the executing of this will.   Bruce, 32.

[The foregoing Pryaulx and Mercer wills are sent in reply to the friendly challenge of W. H. Whitmore (see REG., vol. 45, p. 237; *ante*, p. 520). One must refer also to the REGISTER for October, 1873, page 368, and read that letter referred to by my friend W. H. W.   HENRY F. WATERS.]

MARGERY ANGUR (or Augur) of London, widow, 3 January 1653 proved 9 October 1658. To my son John Angur forty shillings. To my son Nicholas Angur now residing in New England (certain household goods) and also one messuage &c. in Plastowe in Westham, Essex, formerly given unto me by Mistress Mary Guilliams &c. If Nicholas happen to die before such time as he should return into England then my daughter Hester Angur shall have the aforesaid messuage &c. To Ann, the wife of my son John Angur my little gold ring with a Bristol stone in it. And all the residue I leave to my said daughter Hester whom I make sole executrix, and I appoint my brother Gabriell Bynnion, citizen and tallow chandler of London, overseer.   Wootton, 540.

[Nicholas Auger of New Haven, Ct., 1643, was a physician and trader. He swore allegiance August 5, 1644. He made a will Sept. 20, 1669. He had a sister Esther Coster and a brother John probably then in England, who had a son Nicholas. He had also a relative Robert, probably a nephew. His inventory dated Feb. 26, 1677-8 amounts to £1638. Mrs. Hester Coster, to whom he left the larger part of his estate, died at New Haven, April 5, 1691. After her death Robert Auger "the next of kin resisted probate of her will containing some bequests for the 'support of religion and learning'; but he met with not success."
See, for other facts, Savage's Genealogical Dictionary, vol. I., page 79, and Rev. Stephen Dodd's East Haven Register, p. 102.—EDITOR.]

PARNELL FEAKE of St. John Zachary in London (nuncupative) 25th or 26th October 1593, proved 8 November 1593. She lying sick in her house did declare to her three daughters, Margaret, Judith and Anne Feake, being attendant upon her, that her mind and will was that William Feake her son should have the disposition of all whatsoever she had. And she did also declare unto them that she had locked up all that she had in a chest, saving that which she willed should be bestowed at her funeral, and willed and charged her daughters that they should deliver the key of the said chest unto her son William. And that her said son William should bestow so much of her goods upon every of her said daughters and her son James as he thought good. And made the said William Feake her son sole executor of the said her will. And also made William Feake, her husband's brother, Mr Padmere and Robert Padmere overseers.

Nevell, 80.

WILLIAM FEAKE the elder, citizen and goldsmith of London, 7 May 1595, proved 19 May 1595. To be buried in the parish church of St. Edmund the King in Lumbard Street, London, where I am a parishioner, at my pew door. To twenty poor men of the poorest of my Company of Goldsmiths twenty gowns of twenty shillings price apiece and twelve pence apiece for their dinner. To ten other poor men ten gowns of like price and twelve pence apiece for their dinner. To every of my brethren's children now in London and every of my men and women servants a cloak or gown. My goods &c. (after debts paid and funerals discharged) to be divided into three equal parts, according to the ancient and laudable use and custom of the City of London, one part whereof I give to my beloved wife Mary, the second part I give and bequeath unto and amongst Thomas, John, Edward, Sarah and Rebecca, my children (minors). The third part I reserve unto myself to be disposed of &c. To poor prisoners in seven prisons, the hospitals, poor and towardly scholars in Cambridge the Goldsmiths' Company &c. A house for six poor men or women at Wighton in Norfolk where I was born. Poor goldsmiths' widows. The Governors of Bridewell. To James, Parnell, Mary, Margaret, Judith and Anne, the children of my brother James Feake deceased, ten pounds apiece. I have heretofore given to some of the children of my brother Edmond Feake ten pounds apiece. I do now give to every of his other children (saving Anne Feake now dwelling with me) ten pounds apiece. To the same Anne sixteen pounds, besides the four pounds I have in my hands and received to her use of the gift and bequest of her mother's brother. I have already given to some of my sister Jygg's children forty shillings apiece. I now give forty shillings apiece to every of her other children. I have heretofore given to some of the children of my brother John Angell forty shillings apiece. I do now give the like sum to every of his other children. I have heretofore given unto some of the children of my brother William Angell forty shillings apiece. I now give the like sum to every of his other children. Three pounds six shillings and eight pence to every of the children of my brother Simon Feake to whom I have not already given the like sum. To my son James Feake three hundred pounds, he entering into bond to my executrix to pay unto my son William and Mary his wife, during their lives and the life of the longer liver of them, ten shillings weekly. To my son in law Thomas Barneham and Mary his wife two hundred pounds. I hold for divers years yet to come, by virtue of two several leases, one from the Goldsmiths Company and the other from Mr. Younge, grocer, all my now dwelling house in Lumbard Street and three tenements in Birchen Lane. My wife Mary shall hold and enjoy my said now dwelling house for life and then the remainder of the years to come in the said dwelling house and three tenements I give and devise unto the said James Feake, my son. My wife shall at her own charges keep and maintain my son Thomas at his learning and study in the University until he shall attain the age of thirty years. She shall put out my son John apprentice to some honest merchant fearing God and of good trade and credit and for his better preferment shall deliver out with him one hundred pounds. My son in law Thomas Barneham standeth bound to me by obligation to pay to my son Edward two hundred pounds at his age of one and twenty, and my son James is likewise bound to pay two hundred pounds to my son John at his age of one and twenty. The residue to wife Mary whom I make sole executrix. I give to her my messuage in Lumbard Street called or known by the name of the sign of Noah, now in the occupation of Noah Farmer, goldsmith, and my two tenements, divided into three, being in St. Swythens Lane, which I bought of Mr. Nicholas Herrick, to hold for life, the remainder to my son Thomas, then to my son William, then to my son James, next to my son John, next to my son Edward, lastly to my daughters Mary, Sara and Rebecca.

Commission issued 20 May 1625 to Judith Feake, relict and administratrix of James Feake deceased, while he lived executor of the will of Mary Feake deceased, while she lived relict and executrix of William Freake likewise deceased, to administer the goods &c. of the said William, according to the tenor of his will not fully administered by the said Mary Feake his relict.   Scott, 34.

ROBERT FEAKE, citizen and goldsmith of London, 4 July 1612, proved 10 July 1612. To my son James Feke a hundred and twenty pounds, to be put forth to and for his use and behalf until he come to the full age of twenty and one years. To my brother William Feake twenty shillings. To my sister Ann Bullocke ten shillings. To my sister Elizabeth Gregorye ten shillings. To my sister Susann Feke ten shillings. To my sister Audlea Feke ten shillings. My man Anthony Bradshawe. To my brother in law William Sales and my brother in law William Audlea twenty shillings apiece for to buy them rings for a remembrance. They two to be overseers. All the residue &c. to my loving wife that now is, Judith Feke, whom I do make full and sole executrix.

Wit: Walter Awdlerey, William Sales, William Sayles junior.
                                                                                        Fenner, 65.

MARY FEAKE of London, widow, the late wife and executrix of William Feake late citizen and goldsmith of London deceased, her will made 9 March 1618 (*Stilo Angliæ*) proved 23 August 1619. To be buried in the church of St. Edmond the King in Lumbard Street, London, near to the place where my late husband lieth buried. Every of my sons and daughters and their wives and husbands, and every of their children. Sarah Bullock my servant. The poor prisoners of eight prisons. The hospitals. Other poor and needy people. The parish of Wighton in Norfolk, where my husband was born. The Company of Goldsmiths. The Governors of Bridewell. My son James Feake. My son Edward Feake. To the latter twenty acres in Horne, Surrey (called the Moores) which I lately bought of one Nicholas Hurling. Son John Feake to have the messuage known by the sign of the Noah, in Lumbard Street and the two tenements (divided into three) in St. Swithins Lane which I bought of my son Thomas Feake. To John, for life, certain property in Godstone *als* Walcombstead, Surrey (a messuage called Maynard's &c) which messuage and lands I late bought of my son in law William Smythe of London, mercer; after his decease I give the said messuage &c. to my grandchild Samuel Feake, son of my said son John, remainder to Judith Feake, daughter of the said John and lastly to the right heirs of the said John for ever. To my son James those two messuages in Lumbard Street now in the several tenures or occupations of Anthony Bradshaw and Robert Davies, goldsmiths. To every of the children of my son John twenty pounds apiece. To my daughter Rebecca Bournford six hundred pounds and certain goods of my daughter's late husband, sold unto me by the late Sherriffes of London, by force of an Extent. The said Rebecca to occupy the house in Bow Lane which I hold of the Company of Goldsmiths, and after her decease I bequeath the said lease unto Samuel and Henry Bournford, her children. To Alice Feake, daughter of my son James, one hundred pounds. To my son in law William Smithe three hundred pounds upon condition he shall pay to my son William Feake, during his natural life, twenty pounds a year. To Katherine Smith, the daughter of the said William and Sara Smithe his wife, one hundred pounds. My daughter in law Mary Feake, wife unto my said son William. Reference to a daughter Barnham. Reference to the now dwelling house of son James Feake in Lumbard Street.

Item, I give to James Feake and Robert Feake my grandchildren, to either of them one hundred pounds &c. I make my son James Feake sole executor. Reference to the lunacy of Mary Barnham.

Then follows a memorandum evidently written by James Feake, referring to things left out of his mother's will. Reference to Mrs. Blacklicke and her sister Ransom, to Barnaby Gregorye and his sister Amey, to "my cousin Sale," to "my brother Edward Boyes, my sister Bournford and cousin Bullock. Parker, 97.

[There can be but very little question that to the above family belonged Lieut. Robert Feke of Watertown, Mass., who with Serg[t] William Palmer of Yarmouth, N. E., and Judith his wife, and Tobias Feke (aged 17), son and daughter of James Feke late of London, goldsmith, deceased, made a letter of attorney (5 10[bris] 1639) to Tobias Dixon, citizen and mercer of London, to sell one tenement or house and shop in Lumbard Street, London, held of the Company of Goldsmiths in London (see Thomas Lechford's Note-Book, pp. 228–9). And I have little doubt that he was akin to the John Feke of London, goldsmith, whose pedigree is given in the Visitation of London (1633–4), published by the Harleian Society (vol. 1, p. 268). HENRY F. WATERS.]

RICHARD ATWEECKE als Weecke of Stanes, Midd., yeoman, 17 September 1592, proved 18 December 1592. To be buried in the church or churchyard of Staines. To son Richard a tenement in Thorpe (copy-hold) and land in the parish of Thorpe, with remainder to son William, next to son John the elder, then to son Poole Weeckes, then to son John the younger, next to son Josias, then to son Robert and lastly to my right heirs forever. To son William a tenement in Strowde in the parish of Egham, Surrey, late in the tenure of William Hole (and other property). To son John the elder a close of meadow in Egham &c. To son John the younger (certain tenements &c. in Staines). To his other sons. To Alice Weeckes, a daughter, ten pounds. To Joan Weeckes, a daughter, forty pounds at day of marriage or age of twenty. To Rose Weeckes, a daughter forty pounds (as above). To my brother George Weeckes twenty pounds. To either of my two brethren, William and Thomas, forty shillings apiece. To my sister Susan forty shillings. Sons Richard, William, John the elder, Poole, John the younger, evidently minors. The residue of lands to eldest son Robert and to his (Robert's) mother. The residue of goods &c. to wife Florence and son Robert, whom I make executors; and I make William Atkins, John Aldridge, Thomas Saunders and my brother George Wickes overseers. George Wickes one of the witnesses.

Harrington, 68.

GEORGE WICKES of New Windsor, Berks, gentleman, 13 December 1608, proved 10 January 1608. To be buried in the parish church of New Windsor. To my wife Judith my close of meadow in Stanes, Midd., and a close in Egham, Surrey &c. and certain grounds in Hartley Rowe in Wiltshire and my lease of a messuage in Peascod Street, New Windsor. But if she marry and take a husband then I give the said premises to my brother Thomas Wickes and his heirs and assigns forever, he to pay her a certain sum at the Bell in New Windsor &c. My brother Thomas Carter. His son William Carter, his daughter Lydia and the rest of his children. My mother Margaret Welles. Richard Springe son of my brother Francis Springe. The children of Robert Wickes of Stanes. My cousin Raphe Feilde's children which he hath by his now wife. My sister, their grand mother. Richard Wickes son of my cousin Richard Wickes. My brother Thomas Wickes his three children. Raphe Berry of New Windsor. My cousin Elizabeth Maunsell. My mother Margaret Smythe of Henley. William Jarman the younger of Eaton. William, John, Poole and Josias Wickes. My sister Florence Wickes at Stanes. Martha Steynton. Mr Barde (my book of Peter Martir) and his son William Bard. John Bartlett and Philip Bartlett sons of Mr Francis Bartlett. Sundry others. I give and bequeath unto my said brother Thomas Wickes &c. all such estate, right, title, interest &c. which I have or shall have in the goods and chattells late my brother Paule Welles by force and virtue of the last will and testament of the said Paul Welles. My wife Judith to be sole executrix; and I desire my trusty and loving brother Thomas Wickes, Mr. Hughe Evans his neighbour in London mercer, —— Turner of Cookeham Berks, gent. and —— Lawrence of Wickham Bucks to be overseers.

Dorset, 7.

HENRY WICKES of Stanes, Midd., miller, 18 August 1610, proved 23 October 1610. To daughter Johane twenty pounds, and also one peck of mault and one peck of rye to be paid unto her weekly during the time that she doth keep herself widow. To Johane Durdent, my daughter's daughter, ten pounds at marriage or age of one and twenty. To the poor of Stanes forty shillings. To wife Johane annuity of twenty pounds, with a chamber as it is furnished, to herself, and her competent diet during her natural life, to be paid out of my mills in Stanes. To son Thomas Wickes all my mills, called Hale mill houses &c. in Stanes (and other property) — and a great brass pot which was my father's. The goods unbequeathed I give unto Johane my wife and Thomas my son, whom I make executors; and I make Philip Morgan gen^t and Edward Evans gen^t overseers.   Wingfield, 83.

WILLIAM ATWICK als Wickes of Stanes, Midd. tanner, 22 September 1613, proved 11 Aug. 1620. To wife Judith the profits of all my lands, tenements &c. for eighteen years, if she live so long, for and towards the bringing up of my children till they come to the age of one and twenty or day of marriage &c. My children Obadiah, Sara. My brothers and sisters and their children. My Inn called the George. To my mother Florence Wickes forty shillings. My uncle Rubin Bicknell. My aunt Susan. My sister Feild's children. For overseers I ordain and make Mr George Bard and my brothers Robert and Richard Wickes. My wife Judith I make executrix. And it is my will that my wife shall, before her marriage to any other, give good security unto my brothers Edmond Baker and William Finche for the true payment of three hundred pounds unto my children &c.

Soame, 80.

JOSIAS WICKES of Lambeth, Surrey, brewer, 15 April 1621, proved 11 September 1621. To my brethren Robert, Richard and John Wickes and to my sister Joane Field, widow, and to my sister Judith Wickes, widow, and to Robert Field, to every of them forty shillings apiece. To my aunt Susan Worrall widow sixpence a week during her widowhood. My cousin

Elisha Knollesley, her son. I give the sum of five pounds to be spent among all my brethren to begin again their quarterly meeting, heretofore by them used, which five pounds I desire may be spent at my uncle Thomas Wickes his house in Staynes, Midd., within three months after my decease. The residue to my brother Poole Wickes, whom I make and ordain the sole and only executor of this my last will and testament; and I make my uncle Thomas Wickes and my loving friend Thomas Harris the elder, [overseers] and I give to each ten shillings. Dale, 77.

PAUL WELLS of New Windsor, Berks., gent., 11 July 1604, proved 30 July 1604. My brothers Timothy Wells and Thomas Symnell, gen^t. My lands, tenements &c. at Boveny Dorney or Burnham, Bucks. To my brother George Weekes fifty pounds which I now owe unto him. My wife Anne. The child with which she is now *grossement ensent* and great. My sisters. My mother Margaret Wells. My brother Carter. His wife my sister. William Carter, their son, and Margaret Carter, their daughter. My sister Springe. My sister Symnell. My sister Weekes. My three sisters children Margaret Symnell, Mary Carter and Elizabeth Springe. My sister Elizabeth Springe wife of Francis Springe, gen^t. Brothers Timothy Wells and Thomas Symnell to be executors and brothers George Weekes and Thomas Carter supervisors. Harte, 69.

WILLIAM FINCH the elder, of the Town of Watford in the Diocese of London and liberty of St. Albans, 17 July 1613, proved 4 September 1613. Son William. Wife Rose. Son John. William, son of Edward Finch. Son in law Thomas Tanner. Edmund Baker and his children. William Atwicke and his children. Ezekiel, son of Thomas Tanner. My sons, William, Edward, Rapho, and John Finch. My daughters Audrie Baker and Rose Tanner. My daughter Judith Atwicke. My cousin Francis Finch to be Bachelor of Arts. Brother in law John Edlin. Wife Rose Finch to be sole executor.

Book Dainty L. 41, Arch. of St. Albans.

ROSE FINCH of Waterford, Herts., widow 13 April 1630, proved 22 May 1630. The children of my daughter Judith which she had by her husband William Wickes *als* Atwicke. My son William Finch. My daughter Awdrey Baker. William son of Edward Finch and Bethia, his daughter. My son John Finch. John son of John Finch and Hannah, his daughter. John, Symon, Isaac and Raph, children of my son Raph Finch. My daughters Awdrey Baker and Rose Tanner. Others.

B. Dainty L. 204, Arch. of St. Albans.

POOLE WICKES of Lambeth, Surrey, brewer, 2 June 1632, proved 28 June 1632. To my three brothers, my sister and my uncle Wickes twenty shillings apiece. To Mr. Taylor of Clapham, my brother William Harris, my cousin Samuel Wickes the brewer, and the clerk, twenty shillings apiece. To all the brewing servants (named) ten shillings apiece. The rest of my estate, my debts being paid and funeral charges discharged, I divide between my wife and my children, she to have one-half and my children the other, the boys at twenty one and the girls at twenty one or day of marriage. The said children, to wit, John, Josias, Paul, Margaret and Elizabeth. My wife to be sole Executrix. The wife's christian name not given in Probate Act following. Awdley, 78.

ROBERT WICKES of Stanes, Midd., gen^t., 1 August 1638, proved 8 November 1638. To be buried in the churchyard of Stanes. To my son Thomas Wickes the messuage &c. in the tenure of Francis Gyles &c., he to pay to my son John Wickes, now living in New England, two hundred pounds at the Feast of the birth of our Lord God next coming &c., and if the said John happen to die before the receipt of the said sum then it shall be to the use of his children, equally, to remain in the hands of the said Thomas until they accomplish their several ages of one and twenty, and he to pay sixteen pounds a year for the use and bringing up of the said children. To my said son Thomas the parcel called Newes and those called Sharlandes and Cullverhall, he to pay to my wife Sarah twenty two pounds yearly during her natural life, and to pay her also two hundred pounds within six months next after my decease. I give to my son William three hundred pounds in manner and form following, i. e. thirty pounds in three months and the remainder in three years, and he to have ten pounds paid him every half year in the mean time. And if he should die or never come to demand the said sum then the said three hundred pounds shall be paid to my said son John Wickes and my son Robert Wickes and their children, to be equally divided. To my son Thomas the parcel called Wheatcrofts, adjoining to Culvershall he 'to pay my son John Wickes, one hundred and twenty pounds, at or on the 26th of March 1640, if the said John shall demand the same. I give to my son Robert one hundred pounds, to be paid within eight months after my deccase. To wife Sarah all the household goods that were hers before the time of our marriage. To the poor of Stanes four pounds. To all my now servants two shillings apiece. My son Thomas to be sole executor and my cousin Thomas Wickes and Daniel Enderbey overseers, giving them five shillings apiece for their love and care therein &c.	Lee, 140.

THOMAS WICKS the elder of Stanes, Midd., yeoman, 4 March 1647, proved 15 March 1647. The poor of Stanes, the poor of Egham, and the poor of Ashford, Laleham and Thorpe. Andrew Sanders. Gartred Cole my wife's daughter. Edward Holmes and Sarah Holmes. John Norwood and Sarah Rolls. Amye Whiting. My wife Mary. My mill in Staines. My cousin John Higdon the elder. My nephew Andrew Durdant the elder. My messuage and malt house in Staines. My brother Henry Wicks. Cousin Robert Durdant, son of Andrew.	Essex, 48.

HENRY WICKES of Sheere in Surrey Esq., 6 June 1657, proved 23 November 1657. To the poor of Stanes ten pounds. The poor of St. Martins in the Fields and of Sheere. The poor of Albury. My friend Mr. William Oughtred, now rector of Albury. My honored friend the Lady Baskervell. My cousin John Higdon the elder and Johane his wife, my niece. My messuages &c. in Covent Garden and Vinegar Yard in the parishes of St. Martins in the Fields and St. Pauls Covent Garden. Robert Durdant, my kinsman, eldest son of my nephew Andrew Durdant deceased. Lands and messuages &c. in Stanes and Stanwell, Midd., and in Chobham, Surrey. Grace, the wife of Robert Durdant. My godson Henry Haughton. My friend James Rice and his wife. My servant Arthur Haughton. My friend Mrs. Susanna Smith and her children, Thomas, Andrew, Mary, Susan, Margaret. — Her other daughter, Katherine Smith, my god daughter. My cousin John Harbert, William Atlee and Sarah his wife, my kinswoman. I do remit and discharge all such

moneys as are due and owing to me from Nicholas Haughton deceased. To my godson Nicholas Haughton ten pounds. My cousin John Higdon to be executor. Money due for my fee as Paymaster of His Majesty's Works.
Ruthen, 440.

[A pedigree of this family will be found in the published Visitation of Middlesex. John Wickes, a friend of Gorton's, was of Plymouth and afterwards of Rhode Island. He drew a bill of exchange, dated 24 Sept. 1639, for thirty-one pounds, on his brother Mr. Thomas Wickes' dwelling in Stanes in the County of Middlesex (England) in favor of William Withington of Aquednecke in New England, planter (see Thomas Lechford's Note-Book, pp. 188-9).
HENRY F. WATERS.]

[The following extracts from the Register of Jesus Chapel, in the parish of St. Mary Extra, co. Southampton, have been furnished me by Major F. W. T. Attree, R. E., who has before helped me. See REGISTER, vol. 46, pp. 306-7; *ante*, pp. 576-7.
H. F. WATERS.]

1738 April 23rd this is the 1st Couple for Georgia. Wm Cowel and Susannah Lester were married at J. C. (Jesus Chapel).

" May 5th John Tindall and Ann Mewle, John Gray and Mary Slade, John Hebbs and Mary Reynolds, Edward Hebbs and Elizabeth Hartoff, Joseph Salmon and Ann Smith all bound for Georgia were married at J. C.

" May 8. Zachariah Raby and Mary Taylor, Thomas Newman and Lydia West bound for Georgia were married at J. C.

" May 10th Ephraim Gordon and Sarah Coombs, Richard Bigford and Sarah Goodfellow for Georgia were married at J. C.

" May ye 18th John Fox and Elizabeth Buckle, David Marlar and Martha Heath for Georgia were married at J. C.

" May ye 21st Richard Ellit and Margaret Gardiner, Robert Collins and Lucey Tanner for Georgia were married at J. C.

" May ye 25th Charles Martin and Elizabeth Griffiths, Jnn Wakefield and Sarah Todd, Roger Usherwood and Mary Huntsman, William Owen and Mary Smith, Thomas Goss and Martha Smith all bound for Georgia were married at Jesus Chappel.

I cannot find any of these (which are, I believe, all that are contained in the Register) in Mr Moen's Marriage Licenses, Hampshire, Vol. I, men's names, A to L.

WILLIAM NICHOLLES of Witham, Essex, gentleman, 4 August 1638, proved 29 November 1638. To be buried in the parish church of Witham. An inventory to be made of my goods, &c. in my now dwelling house in Witham, there to remain during the natural life of Dorothy my wife. I give to my wife all the goods of household &c. that she had and brought to me and that were her goods at the time of our marriage. My son William Nicholles of Witham shall pay her ten pounds a year during the lease granted by the Right Worshipful Sergt Darcy of the farm called the manor of Benton's in Witham, now in the possession of the said William my son, if the said Dorothy shall so long live. And my said son William shall, the first year after my decease, give, bring in and deliver unto the said Dorothy my wife four seams of mislin, four seams of wheat and four seams of barley, good and sweet corn. Other bequests to wife and son William.

Item, I give, will and bequeath in and by this my last will and testament unto Sibrian Nicholles my son the sum of one hundred pounds at the expiration of three years after my decease, to be paid unto him by William my son. And my son William shall pay unto the said Sibrian ten pounds every year, for three years next after my decease, (to be paid half yearly) for and towards the maintenance and bringing up my said son Sibrian at Cambridge. I give Sibrian also fifty pounds, to be paid him, within a year after the decease of Dorothy my wife, by the said William my son. To my brother John Nicholles of Coggeshall, webster, five pounds. To Matthew Baxter daughter of William Baxter of Witham four pounds. To Thomas Haiword my servant twenty shillings. The residue to my son William whom I make executor and I make my wife Dorothy executrix.

Proved by William Nicholles, power reserved for Dorothy, the relict &c.
                                                                Lee, 155.

ANNE FARMER, wife of George Farmer of St. Andrew, Holborne, London, Esq,, heretofore the wife and administratrix of Thomas Gate, late one of the Barons of the Court of Exchequer, deceased, &c: her will made 24 June 1668, proved 2 November 1669. My body to be buried in the Temple Church, London, as near the body of my said late deceased husband as conveniently may be, in decent and comely manner. To my grandchild Anne Farmer, wife of Thomas Farmer of the Inner Temple, gent., my best jewell of diamonds, my silver bason and my silver salt &c. &c., and all manner of furniture in the chamber next the Dining-room, towards the street, in my house at Endfield in the Co. of Midd., as also my picture of myself &c.   Whereas I am seized in fee, according to the custom of the manor of Cheshunt, Herts., of one messuage or tenement at Lucas End and nine acres of meadow or pasture and common of pasture for cattle in Cheshunt Leyes &c — and whereas I have surrendered the said messuage and lands into the hands of Sir Clement Farnham Knight, Steward of the said manor, to the use of such person or persons and for such estate and estates as I shall by my last will and testament nominate, declare or appoint, in which Surrender my husband, Mr George Farmer, hath joined, I do declare and appoint that my said grandchild Anne Farmer shall be admitted tenant &c.; but the rents and profits shall be paid or transmitted unto Constant Morley, late wife and relict of John Morley deceased, my late brother &c., during her life, and after her decease to be and remain to the said Anne Farmer and her heirs forever. To my grandchild Edward Payne one hundred pounds at one and twenty. To my grandchildren Elizabeth and Catherine Payne ten pounds apiece (and the rest of my plate). They the daughters of my son in law Mr John Payne. Certain jewels to grandchild Anne Lane. To my son in law Sir Edward Farmer my picture of his father, drawn in little, which I used to wear. A gift to his lady. My son in law Mr Thomas Farmer. My daughter in law Mrs Elizabeth Beamond, wife of Henry Beamond Esq. My cousin Frances Norwood. Mrs. Hester Mason. Others.   Coke, 139.

[This will of Mrs. Ann Farmer is a gratifying confirmation of the suggestion advanced by me, in Gleanings of April, 1892, as to the ancestry of John Morley of Charlestown, Mass. (See REGISTER, Vol. 46, p. 156; ante, p. 568). Mrs. Farmer, by referring to her former husband Thomas Gate and also mentioning Constant Morley, the relict of her late brother John Morley, settles the matter completely.   H. F. WATERS]

RICHARD QUYNEY of Shottery, Warwick, gentleman, 25 May 1682, proved 21 November 1684. To be buried in the parish church of old Stratford, in the vault wherein my father and mother were laid. To my brother Adrian Quyney gent., all my messuages &c. in old Stratford, Shottery and Clopton (with certain exceptions) hoping the said Adrian will be as kind to my brother Thomas Quyney, gent., as I have been to him the said Adrian, if Thomas shall survive him. To Adrian the gold seal ring which was my father's, to my brother Thomas my plate hilt rapier, to my brother in law Edward Pilkington my silver plate for sweatmeats, curiously embossed, to my sister Elianor Pilkington my garter ring with a diamond therein, to my brother in law Mr. Richard Pyle my china cup curiously footed with silver, to my sister Elizabeth Pyle my curious Indian shell with a silver foot, to my brother in law Mr. Jarvis Cooper my universal ring dial, to my sister Sarah Cooper my stone jug curiously covered and footed with silver, to my nephew Mr. Robert Harvey an azimuth Equinoctial universal dial, to my niece Barbara Harvey a china bason and my china cup, to my nephew Mr. Richard Cooper my silver tobacco box, to my nephew George Lilburne a tortoise shell box with the late King's picture thereon, with scales and weights therein for gold, to my niece Elianor, daughter to my late brother Mr. John Lilburne a tortoise shell looking glass with pictures of embossed work gilded, to my niece Katherine Booth a box of Indian painted dishes and a silver spoon, to my niece Sarah Cooper my silver money box and a silver spoon gilt, to my niece Elianor Cooper a pair of " sysers," with silver tops and chain, and a silver spoon. Rings of ten shillings cost each to my cousin Richard Chandler, my cousins Richard, William, Charles and James Watts, my cousins John Sadler, William Baker and Margaret Jones, my cousin Henry Dighton and his wife, my cousin William Challoner and his wife, my cousin Reginald Forster Esq. and his wife, my cousins Francis Watts of Clifford and his wife, my cousins William and John Smith and their wives, my cousins Anne Mitchell and Elizabeth Baylye, my cousin John Frogmere, my good friends Sir William Bishop knt and Mr. Edward Harrison, Mr. Samuel Tyler and Mr. William Gibson, Mr. Robert Watkins and his wife, Capt. Richard Kinsey, William Maior, Ralph Izard and Mr. John Combes, my godson Job Watts and my god daughter Elizabeth Danvers. I commit the custody my brother William ·Quyney (whom it hath pleased God to deprive of his reason) to my said brother Adrian Quyney, earnestly desiring and strictly charging him to use his utmost care and diligence for the good and preservation of my said brother William Quyney according to the tender bowels of compassion which a good Christian and a brother ought to have to so near a relation.   The residue to my brother Adrian whom I appoint sole executor, and I make my brother Thomas Quyney overseer.   Hare, 153.

[The testator of the above will was the oldest son of Richard Quiney of London, grocer, by Ellen daughter of John Sadler of Stratford upon Avon. The wills of his father and his brother Adrian have already been given in these Gleanings, *ante*, pp. 197, 621.   His brother Thomas Quiney inherited their father's land and other property in Virginia. In the REGISTER for October, 1892, *ante*, pp. 618–621, may be found the wills of sundry relatives of this family. Their connection with Shakespeare and indirectly with John Harvard and Governor Willys of Connecticut makes them interesting.   H. F. WATERS.]

ANN QUINSIE of Wigstrapp in the parish of Lillford in the County of Northampton, widow, 29 January 1630, proved 6 April 1631. To my son in law Gabriel Munnes all my goods and household stuff now in my little parlor in Wigstrapp &c. (and other property) upon condition the said Gabriel Munnes and Christian his wife shall release unto my executor ten pounds, part of the legacy of threescore pounds bequeathed unto her the said Christian by the last will and testament of Edmond Quinsie my late husband deceased. My executor shall permit and suffer my daughter Munnes to have and enjoy free liberty in my house and to have her diet and sufficient provision until such time as it shall please God she be delivered of the child she now goeth with all and for the space of six weeks after her delivery at the only proper charges of my executor. My executor shall also at his charge board and harbor in my house at Wigstrapp my daughter Roodinge and her four children for three years after my death, she paying him ten pounds yearly. To my son William Quinsie five and forty pounds at two and twenty. To my son Thomas five and twenty pounds at one and twenty. My grandchildren Ellenor Holdich, Charity Holdich, John Holdich and John Quinsie. To my daughter in law Elizabeth Quinsie four yards of that woollen cloth which is in my house and one of my smocks. My daughter Roodinge's son and her three daughters. My daughter Binge's five sons and her daughter. My four daughters Annie Hilles, Ellen Binge, Alice Roodinge and Christian Munnes. To my son Edmund's son twelve pence in money and to his daughter one pair of hurden* sheets and twelve pence in money. Towards the reparation of the parish church of Lilford ten shillings and to the poor of Wigstrapp six pence a family. All the rest of my goods &c. to John Quinsie my son, whom I make and ordain sole executor &c.; and I appoint as supervisors John Quinsie the elder and James Holdich, and for their pains herein to be taken I give them two shillings apiece.

Among the witnesses were John Quinsie Sen[r] (by mark) and Francis Quinsy.	St. John, 44.

[* This word, written horden several times in this Will, should be harden, I suppose. These sheets probably were made of hards or coarse flax. H. F. W.]

JOHN QUINCEY of Widgthorpe, Northampthon, husbandman 18 October 1651, proved 10 December 1651. To John, my eldest son, my lease at A-church in the county aforesaid, to enter upon it at the age of one and twenty years. To Edmund, my second son, twenty pounds at one and twenty. Theophilus my third son. Gidderrill my fourth son. Joslife my fifth son. William my sixth son. Francis my seventh son. Alice my eldest daughter (under 21). Elenor my second daughter. Ann my third daughter. My sister Lewes daughter Alce Lewes. My brother Francis Quincey. My brother Thomas Quincey. Anne my now loving wife to be sole executor and my brother Francis Quincey and my cousin John Gidderrill to be supervisors. James Quincey one of the witnesses.	Grey, 246.

[These two wills are those of the mother and a brother of Edmund Quincy, born 1602, died 1635, the immigrant ancestor of the distinguished New England family of that name. An exhaustive account of this family by Prof. Edward Elbridge Salisbury, LL.D., will be found in his Family Memorials (1885), Part I. pp. 295–371, with a tabular pedigree.—EDITOR.]

JOHN PALMER of London, mercer, 1 November 1631, proved 12 February 1632. One third part of my estate, according to the laudable custom of this City of London, to my wife Elizabeth Palmer, another third to such child or children as I shall have by my wife, and to be paid them when they come to one and twenty years of age, and in case of their death, the said portion to be given to my wife; the remaining third part of my estate I give as follows. To Mr. Googe, Mr. Sibbs, Mr. Davenport and Mr. Offspring who are Feoffees, the sum of twenty pounds to be disbursed about the buying of impropriations or the like as they think fit for the church of God. To my brother Millburne Palmer ten pounds. The rest to wife Elizabeth whom I make sole executrix &c. And I desire Mr. Davenport, minister, Mr.—— French, warehouseman in Lumber and Mr. Edward Hopkins of London, merchant, that they would be pleased (after my wife's decease) to take into their custody my sons in law, Samuel and Nathaniel Browning and to educate and bring them up in the fear of the Lord and likewise to have within your own custodies their portions given them of their father for their maintenance and education, which portion of theirs is about six hundred three score and sixteen pounds or thereabouts, three hundred whereof is in the Chamberlain's hands, which I received fifteen pounds per annum for, the other three hundred threescore and sixteen pounds is in my own hand, whereof I have given a bond to Mr. Thomas Frel for a hundred of it to be paid to him for them; all which I desire may be put into their hands for their maintenance. To Matthew Barnard, porter, fifty shillings. To Ezekiell Hollyman five pounds to be bestowed upon neccessaries for the church of Wigginton. And five pounds more I desire my wife to give to two silenced ministers whom she thinks for. I also give five of my great books to my brother Francis, which he may make choice among my books. Russell, 8.

THOMAS QUINEY, citizen and brewer of London, 20 May 1701, proved 13 June 1701. As for the Harveys they shall have no reason to expect anything from me considering what they enjoy at present which of right belongs to me and what more they will at my death. I give to my loving sister Elizabeth Pyle, wife of Richard Pyle of Edmonton, Middlesex, Esq[r], for her separate maintenance all that messuage or tenement &c. in Stratford upon Avon in the Co. of Warwick, now in the occupation of William Martin &c, to hold during her natural life, and after her decease I devise the same messuage &c. to my niece Elianor Richardson, wife of Joshua Richardson, clerk, Rector of All Hallows the Wall London, for life, then to her eldest son Joshua Richardson for life, next to his heirs male &c., failing such to George Richarson second son of my said niece Elianor Richardson, then to his male issue, next to Robert Richardson, the third son &c., and lastly to the right heirs of my said niece Elianor Richardson forever.

Item, I give and bequeath all that my moyety of two plantations in Virginia, in parts beyond the Seas, lying on James River, the one called Merchants Hope, the other Martins Brandon (the other moyety whereof, equally divided, belongs to Mr. John Sadler late of London, druggist) unto my said niece Elianor Richardson until her youngest son, the said Robert Richardson, shall attain the age of one and twenty years, when I give and devise the same to him & his male issue, remainder to Joshua then to George and lastly to the right heirs of the said Elianor Richardson &c. To my niece Ellen Cooper, daughter of my sister Sarah Cooper deceased, twenty five pounds. To my said niece Elianor Richardson all my share &c. in the ship Plymouth, now out on a voyage at or returning from Virginia. To my kinswoman Elizabeth Richardson, daughter of my said niece Elianor, twenty five pounds, to be paid at her age of four and twenty years or day of marriage. The use of all the residue of my estate to my said niece Elianor Richardson and after her death I give the same outright to her children. My said niece to be sole executrix. Dyer, 83.

[This of course is the Thomas Quyney or Quiney, brother of Richard whose will I have just given and of Adrian whose will appeared *ante*, p. 621.
H. F. WATERS.]

WILLIAM SMITH of Bristol, merchant, 27 September 1704, proved 20 November 1704. To the poor of Bristol one hundred pounds. To the Work house in the Lamb Grounds, Bristol, fifty pounds for employing the poor there. To my friends Arthur Thomas, John Dyer, Thomas Dixon and Jeffry Pinnell fifty pounds to be employed by the advice and direction of the Men's Meeting of the people called Quakers within the said City of Bristol in such manner as they shall think fit. To Mary wife of John Harrode ten pounds and to my cousin Robert Wilcox ten pounds.

Item, I give unto my sister Elizabeth Wilson in Virginia thirty pounds and all my late wife's wearing apparel, both linen and woollen and silk. And my will is that my said sister shall be continued to live on my plantation in Virginia during her life and that she be supplied with necessaries from England, by my executor, as formerly it hath been done. To my cousin Abraham Wilson five hundred acres of land, to be laid out and taken from my tract of land in Virginia of eight and twenty hundred acres. And it shall be taken where it shall least incommode my said plantation, lying near Mattopony near York River in Virginia aforesaid. I give the said Abraham Wilson also fifty pounds. To my cousin John Wilson three hundred acres to be taken out (as above). The remainder of my said plantation, being two thousand acres, with all buildings, warehouses, negroes, and stock of cattle thereon, I give to my son Joseph for life, and then to his children. I give two thousand pounds to my said friends (Thomas, Dyer, Dixon and Pinnell) in trust to purchase houses and lands &c. and apply and pay the clear income thereof unto and amongst the children of my son Joseph, born of his present wife &c. during their minorities and afterwards such estates to be conveyed to them &c. To my daughter Hester, wife of the said Joseph five broad pieces of gold. Son Joseph to be sole executor. Proved by Affirmation or solemn Declaration.

Ash, 242.

WILLIAM SHAW, citizen and weaver of London 5 April 1687, proved 11 May 1693. To my brother Thomas Shaw eighty pounds. To my brother Godfrey Shaw eighty pounds and I release unto him the sum of ten pounds principal which he oweth me upon Bond and all interest due at my decease and also ten pounds more lent unto him as may appear by letters from him to me.

Item, I give and bequeath unto my brother John Shaw of Boston in New England the sum of forty pounds. To my cousin Zachariah Shaw son of my said brother Thomas sixty pounds. To my cousins Mary and Elizabeth, daughters of my said cousin Zachariah ten pounds apiece. To my cousin Tabitha Wilson daughter of my said brother Godfrey thirty pounds. To ——— Sales daughter of my said cousin Tabitha ten pounds. To my cousin Martha Blush of Boston aforesaid, daughter of my said brother John Shaw, ten pounds. To two grandchildren of my said brother John Shaw by his son John five pounds apiece. To my cousin Elizabeth Shaw daughter of my late brother Richard Shaw deceased thirty pounds. To my cousins John and Martha Barker, son and daughter of my late sister Elizabeth Barker deceased, ten pounds apiece. To my cousins Christian Smith, Mary Binks, James Hewett the younger, James Smith and William Parkin, of Attercliffe in the Co. of York, forty shillings apiece. To the poor of Attercliffe five pounds. To my cousin William Shawe, son of my brother Thomas, five hundred pounds. To Richard Shaw, son of my said cousin William, fifty pounds, to be improved by his parents until he attain the age of one and twenty years. To my said cousin William Shaw my messuage or tenement &c. wherein Mr Christmas Holloway lately dwelt, in Fetter Lane, London, to hold during the rest of the lease by which I hold the same from Sir Nicholas Bacon, knight. And if the said William shall happen to depart this life before the expiration of the said lease then I give and bequeath the said messuage &c. unto Debora Shaw, wife of the said William, and to Richard Shaw, son of the said William. To my said cousin William my two messuages &c. in Baldwin's Gardens, St. Andrew's Holborn, London, held by lease from Thomas Bedford, citizen and merchant taylor of London, he paying to my brother Thomas Shaw and his assigns out of the rent &c. three pounds per annum during the natural life of the said Thomas, if the lease shall so long continue. To my cousin David Williams, husband to my cousin Mary Williams, daughter of my said brother Thomas Shaw, three hundred pounds. To my said cousin Mary Williams one hundred pounds and to her two children, William and Mary, and to such child as she is now "ensient" with, to each of them fifty pounds. To the said Mary Williams, the mother, my messuage &c. in Gunpowder Alley, New Street, near Fetter Lane, now in the occupation of the Widow Balland &c. held by lease from the Company of Goldsmiths, next to William Williams her son. My executors not to exceed the sum of fifty pounds to be expended in my funeral. My cousins William Shaw and Mary Williams to be executors.

Coker, 87.

[John **Shaw**, butcher, of Boston, was admitted a member of the Artillery Company in 1646. He had children by wife Martha: *John*, b. 16 May, 1646, d. young; *John*, b. 1648; *Samuel*, b. 4 Nov. 1651, d. aged 10 months; *Martha*, b. 16 Sept. 1655; *Joseph*, b. 11 Nov. 1657. In 1670 he had a wife Elizabeth. He died July 29, 1687.—(*Savage*). The christian name of the husband of his daughter, Martha Blish, I presume was Abraham, as children of Abraham and Martha Blish are on record at Boston.—EDITOR.]

HANNAH WALKER of London, widow, 10 April 1675, proved 2 November 1675. I give and bequeath unto my son Thomas Walker of Sudbury in New England, in the parts beyond the seas, merchant, the sum of one hundred and fifty pounds of lawful money of England, to be paid to him or his assigns within twelve months next after my decease. In case of his death before it becomes payable I give the said sum to his wife Mary for the use of their children, if she be then living, but if dead then to the Executors of my son Thomas, for the use of the children &c. To my son in law Mr. Paul Strange five pounds to buy him mourning. A writing as to the disposition of goods &c. deposited in the hands of my dear daughter Hannah Strange, wife of the aforesaid Paul Strange. To my loving friend Mr. John Jackson of London merchant three hundred pounds, to be paid from time to time to such persons as my daughter Hannah may direct and appoint; and if she die before her husband then I give two thirds of the said three hundred pounds to the aforesaid Thomas Walker in New England, or to his executors for the use of his children, if he be dead. The other third I give to my said son in law Paul Strange. But if my daughter survive her husband then it shall be all at her dispose, living or dying. My friend Mr. John Jackson to be executor and Mr. John Smith of Lambeth, Surrey, gen^t., to be overseer.

Wit: John Ward, Hester Ward.

Commission issued 20 December 1700 to Hanna Strange widow, daughter and residuary legatee, John Jackson, the executor, having died.

Dycer, 119.

[Thomas Walker, of Sudbury, and wife Mary had eleven children, statistics of which will be found in Barry's History of Framingham, page 430. In 1664, the town of Sudbury considered if they would give Mr. Walker land for his encouragement to keep a free school in Sudbury. In 1672 he kept an ordinary there. His descendants are numerous in Sudbury and Framingham.—EDITOR.]

RICHARD WELLS Senior of the Co. of Ann Arundell in the Province of Maryland, 22 June 1667, proved in Maryland 31 August 1667 and in London 14 November 1668. To my son Richard that plantation I do now live upon, at Herring Creek, being called by the name of Wells and laid out for six hundred acres (and other tracts or parcels). To my son George my land in Baltimore County, namely three hundred acres, purchased of Capt. George Goldsmith, called the Planters Delight "being now seated." To my son John that parcel called Langford's Neck, on the N. side of Chester River in Talbot Co., being "pattented" and laid out for fifteen hundred acres, and was purchased of John Langford gen^t. To my son Robert three hundred and fifty acres called West Wells, lying on the W. side of the plantation I now live on, in Herring Creek Bay. To my son Benjamin that parcel called Benjamin's Choice, being Patented and laid out for two hundred and eighty acres, lying W. of a Dividend belonging unto Mr Francis Holland of Herring Creek. To my daughter Martha, sometime the wife of Mr. Anthony Salaway, twelve pence. To my daughter Anne, supposed wife unto Mr. John Stansby, Chirurgeon, twelve pence as a reward for her disobedience. To my daughter Mary, wife unto Mr. Thomas Stockett, three cows to be delivered, after my decease, in the Co. of Ann Arundel, and one hundred pounds of money, to be paid in the City of London within twelve months after my decease. To my five sons all my whole estate remaining, to be divided amongst them, both cattle, goods, moneys in England, tobacco, debts, servants, negroes and all things whatsoever belongeth unto me in Maryland, Virginia or in England. And they to be my executors. Wit: Francis Stockett, Bonham Turner, the mark of Wm Linckhorne.

Probate was granted (in London) to Richard Wells the eldest son, with power reserved for the others &c.   Hene, 148.

THOMAS BUSBY of Meyford, Staffordshire, gen^t., proved 19 November 1584. Wife Isabell Busby shall enjoy, during her natural life, the revenues &c. of my farms, messuages &c. in Keybulston and Meyford, lying in the Lordship of Keybulston (and other property). Agnes Haste *als* Harrison *als* Busby shall have the issues, revenues &c of those farms &c. during the residue of the term of years, during the life of the said Agnes, my daughter, and she keeping herself unmarried. My son in law Gabriel Mermyon gen^t. My brother in law John Bradshaw. My kinsman Geoffrey Busby. To my Lady Margaret Standley and Mr. Mather two gilt silver spoons, besides their "herriates" due to them. To Mr. Edward Standley, her son, my silver cup, gilt. To Isabell my wife my best silver salt, parcel gilt, and one dozen of silver spoons lately bought of her son Mr. Mermyon. My daughter in law Ellen Thacker. Oliver Thacker. Mr. Robert Thacker. Christopher Thacker. My daughter in law and her husband my cousin Calwell. My cousin John Clerke, gen^t., and his wife. Every child which my son in law Richard Holland had, before his decease, by my daughter in law Margaret, his wife, besides my godson Thomas Holland. My brother in law William Bradshaw. My cousin John Sarson and his wife. My cousin Robert Quernby of Nottingham and his wife. To my cousin William Boylston three pounds six shillings eight pence. Ann Ames, my wife's kinswoman. My kinswoman Mary Busby (her father dead). Henry Waters, if he continue with my wife until his years be expired. My executors to be Isabell Busby, my wife, Richard Winnington of London gen^t., and Geoffrey Busby, my kinsman and servant. My overseer to be M^r. Doctor Goodman, Dean of Westminister. To each of them three "Ryalls" apiece, of fifteen shillings apiece, to make them rings. Lands &c. in counties of Derby, Stafford, Leicester and Rutland.   Watson, 34.

WILLIAM MUNSEY, iremonger, 9 July 1583, proved 12 November 1584. I make my two sons William and Richard my executors and my brother James and my brother Chamberlayn and my cousin Boylson my overseers. My brother Chamberlayn may bring up William and my brother James, Richard. My brother Humprey, my daughter Margaret. The land to my son William when he comes to age. Of my goods, according to the orders of the City, one third part to my wife one third part to my children (equally) and out of my third part I give to my brother James, my brother Chamberlayn, my brother Samuel, my brother Daniel, my two sisters, my brother Humprey, my father Pipe and my cousin Boylson each a ring and a gown valued worth six pounds to each, and to my mother one also, and to her twenty pounds in money. To my wife all the plate this day in my house. The rest to my children equally. If it please God to send that the debt of Stafford's causes may be recovered then I will that there be given to the Town of Cambridge ten pounds that the Mayor of the Town and his brethern may put it to three men, five marks apiece, to have it upon good sureties for two years, and so others after to have the like from time to time. Also I give five marks to the mayor to make a dinner to the chief of the town; also ten pounds which the mayor and brethren shall cause twenty sermons to be made and to allow ten shillings for every one; and also twenty pounds to the town, which I have promised them. Also I give ten pounds for a dinner at the Iremongers Hall and to the Hospital five pounds and forty shillings to the poor of the parish. This to take effect if that the money which I have disbursed for Stafford's cause may be recovered, or if but the half thereof. Earlier in the will he says "I haue hadd greate losse."

Commission issued to Susanna Mounsey, his relict, to administer according to the tenor of the Will during the minorities of William and Richard, the sons.   Watson, 36.

JOHN BOILSTON late of London, citizen and leatherseller and free of the Worshipful Company of Merchant Adventurers, now dwelling in Newton Sowney in the Co. of Derby, 17 December 1600, proved 4 November 1601. To my wife the third part of my goods here at Newton Sowney and at Aldarley in Gloucestershire and the old rent that Master Romene payeth more than he payeth to my cousin Chamberlein; and my land at Newton Sowney during her life, and after her decease I do bequeath and give it to my daughter Elizabeth Ducye. To my daughter Elizabeth Ducye a silver chain and the great silver spoon, and the best coverlet at London. To my son Richard Ducye twenty shillings. To my son Robert

Berrye my best gown, and my best doublet at London. To his wife **six** great cushions at London. To John Boilston the son of Henry Boilston, my brother which is deceased, my lease of this house, with the years that remain after my decease, and all the land that belongeth to the same of Master Harper's, to him and his heirs conditionally that he do give unto his three youngest sisters, Joane, Jane and Katherine Boilston, ten pounds apiece, and unto his two brethren, Thomas and Edward Boilston, five pounds apiece, which is forty pounds in all. To the said John all my husbandry ware &c. To John Pratt two heifers of two years old and two of my best yearling ox calves. To my sisters eldest two daughters twenty shillings apiece. To my sister Ellin and my cousin Alman twenty shillings apiece. To my cousin Thomas Dewkesbery the rooms that he now dwelleth in for the term of years to come. To Sir William Hauline twenty shillings. To Walter Kinnersley twenty shillings. I make and ordain Walter Kinnersley, Richard Alman and Sir William Hauline my executors.

In the *sententia pro Valore* the widow's name is given as Agnes.

Woodhall, 73.

THOMAS BOYLSONN of Bewdley in the parish of Ribesfourd, in the Co. of Worcester, gen^t 14 October 1621, proved 30 November 1621. To my eldest son, William, fifty pounds. To my daughter Ann Brasier, wife of Edward Brasier, ten pounds and to their children twenty pounds. To the children of my daughter Joane deceased, late wife of Thomas Brasier, twenty shillings apiece. To Isabel Boulson, my youngest daughter, two hundred marks. To the children of Joane Paulmer my daughter, wife of Thomas Paulmer, five pounds. To the children of my daughter Jane, wife of John Milton, five pounds. To John Soley and Mary his wife, my daughter, my messuage &c. in Ludlow, Salop, in a street there called Ould Street. To Thomas Boylsonn, the son of Edmand Boylsonn, forty shillings and to Joane, the daughter of said Edmond twenty shillings, to be employed for their several uses until they shall come to age. To the daughters of Alice Cooke, my daughter, wife of William Cooke deceased, twenty shillings. To my grandchild Thomas Boylsonn, the son of Thomas Boylson deceased, my son, all my houses &c. in the City of Gloucester in a certain parish there called the Holy or Blessed Trinity, in a street called the Gorle (?) Lane and Milk Street. My will is that Edmond Boylsonn, my son, shall have and receive the profits &c. wherewith he shall maintain and keep the said Thomas at school until he shall be of ability and strength to be placed to some honest and good trade, whereunto the said Thomas shall have some liking or affection. To Joane, my wife, all my copy hold lands and tenements for life; afterwards to my son Edmond. Other bequests. Son Edmond to be executor, and Thomas Paulmer of Higgley and John Soley of Bewdley, tanner, two of my sons in law, to be my overseers.

Dale, 94.

EDWARD BOYLSON citizen and pewterer of London 18 August 1625, proved 12 November 1625. My goods, chattels &c. and other my personal estate (all just debts and duties paid and discharged) shall be praised and valued according to the custom of the City of London, one third part whereof I do leave unto Elizabeth my wife, as to her due and belonging, by the custom of the said city, another third I do leave amongst my children, as likewise belonging or due by the custom of the same city, and the other third part, being in mine power to dispose, I do reserve to pay and perform my gifts and legacies. The poor of St. Dionis Backchurch. To my loving brother Thomas Boylson, clothworker, and Mr. Talbott Fitch, merchant, whom I do intend shall be executors of this my will, to either of them five pounds apiece. Forty shillings apiece to my two apprentices and a maidservant. The rest to all my children equally. If all my children happen to die before their portions for Orphanage shall be due by the custom of the City of London all their parts to be paid unto my said brother Thomas Boylson, upon trust and confidence that he shall give and dispose a reasonable part thereof unto and between my brother John Boylson and my four sisters, according as he shall think fit. Clarke, 118.

JOHN DUDLEY of St. Dionis Backchurch, London, citizen and cloth-worker of London, 10 April 1646, proved 4 May 1646. To my wife Judith ten pounds. To my brother Robert Holmes and my sister Katherine his wife six pounds apiece. To my cousin Mary Roberts, widow, four pounds. To Giles Hubbard forty shillings. To Dorothy Yard, my present servant, three pounds. To Thomas Boylson, son of Edmond (*sic*) Boylston, late citizen and pewterer of London deceased, forty shillings. To my wife Judith Dudley a thousand and two hundred pounds &c. and the lease of my now dwelling house &c. in Fenchurch Street, parcel of the Bridgehouse Rents of the said City of London. If she should die before the expiration of the said lease then I give and bequeath it to my sister Katherine Holmes. To my said sister two hundred pounds. To my said brother Robert Holmes five pounds. To Andrew Harris, the son of my said sister Katherine Holmes, by her former husband, fifty pounds. To John Wilmot and James Wilmot the sons of Symon Wilmott, citizen and haberdasher of London, fifty pounds apiece. To my cousin Mary Roberts fifty pounds To Thomas Jeñinges son of Robert Jeñinges, clothworker, and to Gyles Hubbard fifty pounds apiece. To the said Thomas Boylston, the son of the said Edmond Boylston, and to the children of the said Thomas Boylston fifty pounds, to be equally parted, shared and divided between the said father and children, part and part alike, the part accruing unto the said Thomas to be paid unto him and the parts and shares accruing to the said children at the end of twelve months next after my death to be paid unto Thomas Boylston of the parish of Gabriel Fenchurch, London, clothworker, for the use of the said children, to be by him issued and paid to them at their several accomplishments of the age of one and twenty years, he allowing the interest for the same after the rate of six per cent per annum. To Thomas Allsopp forty shillings to buy him a ring in remembrance of me and to Elizabeth Barkham wife of William Barkham three pounds. To the poor of the parish ten pounds. Wife Judith to be executrix and brother Robert Holmes overseer. Twisse, 58.

JONAS WELLINS, citizen and stationer of London 12 January 1646, proved 26 April 1647. Wife and two daughters. To my son in law Thomas Boylestone twenty shillings and to Johane his wife, being my natural daughter, twenty shillings and to my cousin Thomas Boylestone their son, my grandchild, forty shillings at one and twenty, to buy him a ring of gold &c. To my second daughter Mary five pounds. Wife Margarett to be the residuary legatee and sole executrix. Fines, 63.

THOMAS BOYLSON citizen and clothworker of London, 1 July 1648, proved 19 August 1648. I do intend and purpose to settle a sermon or lecture within the parish church of Burton upon Trent in the County of Staff, upon the third day in every week forever, to be preached by an able, learned and Orthodox preacher of the Protestant Religion, to begin about nine of the clock in the forenoon, and for maintenance of the same have delivered into the hands of the Right Worshipful Company of Clothworkers, whereof I am a member, the sum of eight hundred pounds. They shall make a yearly payment of one and thirty pounds and four shillings for the maintaining of the said sermon &c., and to the Clerk or Sexton sixteen shillings per annum for his attendance and toleing of the bell for the said Lecture. In case the said Lecture be not continued, with an Orthodox divine minister of the Protestant Religion, according to my desire, the one half of the said yearly payment shall be yearly paid to the Treasurer of Christ's Hospital, for the better maintenance of the poor children harbored in the said Hospital, and the other half to the use of the poor of the said Company of Clothworkers &c. To my nephew John Boylson (whom in another clause he describes as Minister of Wesson) my lands, tenements &c. in Ansley in the parish of Rolleston, Staff., his mother to receive the rents during her Widowhood and have her habitation in the dwelling house there. To my nephew Henry Boylson, brother of said John, my lands and tenements &c. called Lawrence Hey, in Rollston aforesaid. To Richard Boylston my messuage wherein I now dwell, in Fanchurch Street London, out of which he shall pay to my old maid Margery, during her life, a yearly sum of ten pounds, by fifty shillings a quarter. I give to my sister in law, widow of John Boylson deceased, five pounds. To my sister Jane Cotchett, widow, at Burton, fifty pounds. To my sister Katherine Jackson twenty pounds. To my brother Jackson, her husband, five pounds. To my kinsman Samuel Brackley and his wife one hundred pounds and to their daughter thirty pounds. To the sons of my said brother John deceased I give as followeth, viz[t] to Edward Boylston, who was mine apprentice, five hundred pounds, so as he discharge his brother Thomas Boylson, pewterer, of all such money as he now oweth unto him, otherwise so much abated out of the five hundred; to the said Thomas three hundred pounds over and above that which is to be abated out of the said five hundred pounds, and the lease of the house wherein he dwelleth, in Fanchurch Street. To William Boylson lately apprentice with his brother, the said Thomas Boylson pewterer, three hundred pounds. To my kinswoman Mary, now wife of William Ball, one hundred pounds and to her husband five pounds. To Catharine Boylson one hundred pounds. To Elizabeth Boylson one hundred pounds. To Thomas Boylson, son of my brother Edward Boylson deceased, and to his wife and children (the said Thomas being a bad husband) eight hundred pounds, to remain in my executor's hands, to be paid &c. in his good discretion. To Thomas Jennings, son of Robert Jennings, who was mine apprentice and is now my partner, two hundred and fifty pounds, desiring my executor to have a care of him, that he be brought up in the fear of God. My will is that his father, Robert Jennings, shall remain partner with the said Edward and Richard Boylson and five years more &c. To the said Robert Jennings fifty pounds. To the daughter of my late brother in law Thomas Ducksberry ten pounds. To the widow of Thomas Ducksberry, son of the said Thomas deceased, twenty pounds. To her daughter Elizabeth Ducksberry, which lived with me, fifty pounds. To her other daughter, Mary Ducksberry, thirty pounds.

To the widow of William Hewes five pounds. To Margaret Gooday, for herself and her son George, thirty pounds. To the widow of Daniel Hewes five pounds. To the Parish fifty pounds. To the said John Boylson one hundred pounds and to his wife twenty pounds. To the said Richard Boylson one hundred pounds. The rest and residue of my personal estate to my said kinsman Richard Boylson and I make him sole executor. I name and entreat my loving friends Mr Thomas Burnell and Mr. Talbot Fitch to be overseers, and give to the first twenty pounds and to the other ten pounds.

A codicil was added 17 July 1648. Essex, 128.

JANE BREARE of London, widow, 29 May 1665, proved 15 June 1665. Reference to a debt of two hundred pounds due by bond from one Jonathan Newton. Testatrix indebted to cousin Thomas Blamer one hundred and sixteen pounds. To my uncle Thomas Boylstone and to Katherine his wife ten pounds apiece. To my cousins Elizabeth Smith and Anne Boylstone, daughters of the said Thomas Boylstone and Katherine his wife, ten pounds apiece. I have a bond from my father John Butten for payment of two hundred and fifty pounds. Out of it I give to my sister Mary Butten one hundred and fifty pounds and to my sister Katherine Butten one hundred pounds. I give to my father my silver tankard and six silver spoons and to my mother, Katherine Butten my diamond ring. To Jane Rycroft twenty shillings. To John Marshall and Nicholas Beebee ten shillings apiece. To John Becke five shillings. The said Jane Rycroft, John Marshall, Nicholas Beebee and John Becke being the servants of the said Thomas Boylstone. To the said Ann Boylston, my cousin, my gold ring enamelled with blue. The residue to my uncle Thomas Boylstone, whom I make sole executor &c. Hyde, 60.

THOMAS BOYLSTON, citizen and cooper of London, 11 July 1668, proved 7 December 1668. My body to be buried at the discretion of wife Katherine, whom I make sole executrix, and she shall bestow but one hundred pounds upon my funeral. My wife shall receive the rents &c. of my messuage or tenement, with the yard, garden &c. wherein I now dwell, and the rents &c. of the tenement now in the occupation of Robert Dix, in the parish of St. Gabriel Fanchurch in London, which I lately purchased of Sir John Lee, until my son Allen Boylston shall attain the full age of one and twenty years, towards the maintenance of herself and my said son; and, after he shall attain his said age, then the full moiety of the said messuage &c. wherein I now dwell unto my said wife, so long as she shall remain my widow, for her own habitation, with her family only. The other moiety I give to my son Allen Boylston. I give so much of the said messuages &c. whereof I am seized in fee simple, immediately after the determination of the estate and estates hereby given unto my said wife, unto my son Samuel and my daughter Anne Boylston forever, to be parted and divided betwixt them, and so much as I hold by lease I give to them during my lease. (Other property in the same parish bequeathed.) I give to my wife Catherine the rents &c. of my messuages, lands &c. which I purchased of my brother Henry Boylston, being in the City of Lichfield, and of a house and land at or near Fenny Stratford in Bucks which I bought of one John Somers, until my daughter Anne attain her full age of one and twenty or be married. After that I give them to Anne. In the event of the said three children dying before attaining full age &c. I give my said messuages &c. to my daughter Elizabeth Smyth and all her children, she to pay to **my** said brother Henry Boylston one thousand pounds.   The personal estate to be divided into three equal parts (according to the Custom of the City of London) of which one third to my wife another third to my said three children, Allen, Samuel and Anne (my said daughter Elizabeth Smith having already received her portion upon her marriage) and the remaining third is at my own disposing.   Then follow certain bequests, among which one to son in law John Smith and Elizabeth his wife, and to grandchildren John and Thomas Smith and Catherine Smyth, to sister Anne Serieant, to the poor in the Almshouses, belonging to the Company of Coopers of London, at Radcliffe, to the poor of Lichfield (on St Thomas' day) and to Francis Rose and John Marshall.   Reference to a gift made by an aunt Sibell Allen deceased to testator's children and a bond given to cousin Thomas Marshall that this gift shall be discharged.   Wife Catherine to be executrix.   Hene, 152.

THOMAS BOYLSTON of Bewdley in the Co. of Worcester gen^t, 29 August 1667, proved 16 July 1669.   I give &c. all my goods &c. to my dear and loving wife Alice and make her my sole executrix &c.

Among the witnesses were Margaret Boylston, Mary Boylston and Susanna Boylston.   Coke, 82.

EDWARD BOYLSTON of St. Gabriel, Fenchurch, London, citizen and clothworker of London, 11 December 1675, proved 20 December 1675. My body to be buried in the parish church of St. Dionis Backchurch London, in or near the grave of my uncle Mr. Thomas Boylston, there interred. To my sister Mrs Sarah Boylston, the widow of my brother Mr. Richard Boylston deceased, five hundred pounds.   To the eight children which she had by my said brother, her late husband, one hundred pounds apiece.   To every of the children of my brother Henry Boylston one hundred pounds apiece.   To every of the children of my sister Elizabeth Wakefield one hundred pounds apieee.   To my brother John Boylston, Doctor in Divinity, one hundred pounds.   To my loving friend John Alsop of St. Dionis, &c., scrivener, fifty pounds, and also ten pounds to buy him mourning, to be worn at my funeral.   The residue to my friend Thomas Stansall, citizen and clothworker of London, whom I appoint sole executor.   Dycer, 122.

[The following extracts are from the Register Book of St. Dionis Backchurch, London (vol. 3 of the Register Series of the Harleian Society's Publications). The wills of the persons whose names are in italics are printed in this group.

Christenings St. Dionis Backchurch.

    12 Feb. 1614 | 5, Thomas son of Edward Boylson.
    30 June 1616 Edward   "   "   "   ",
    3 May 1618 John   "   "   "   "
    12 Dec. 1619, Elizabeth dau.   "   "   "
Burials.
    11 May 1621, Anne wife of Edward Boylson buried.
    22 Aug. 1625, *Edward Boylsonne* buried.
    6 Sept. 1625, John Boylson and Edward Boylsoune, sons of Edward Boylsoune, buried.
    18 Aug. 1648, *Thomas Boylston* of Fenchurch parish, buried.
    29 Dec. 1675 *Edward Boylston*, brought from the St. Gabriell Fenchurch, buried in the North Isle, 10 feet deep.

They are evidently the New England family of Boylstons, a pedigree of which, by Thomas B. Wyman, is printed in the REGISTER, vol. 7, pp. 145-50. Thomas Boylston the ancestor of the New England family came here in the Defence in 1635, aged 20, and settled at Watertown.   In a deed dated 26th of the 5th mo. 1652, he names his kinsman "Richard Boyson," citizen and cloth-worker of London.   See Suffolk Deeds, vol. 1, p. 247.   See also Bond's Watertown and Wyman's Charlestown, under Boylston.—EDITOR.]

WILLIAM HARMAN of Moore Hall in the parish of Sutton Canfield, in the County of Warwick, gen᠎ᵗ, 1 August 1592, proved 9 October 1592. To be buried in Sutton church at the feet of my cousin Francis Atkinson late deceased. I have dwelt the most part of my time at Hampton in Arden, in the County Warwick. To Thomas Wyrley son to Thomas Wyrley, late deceased Esq., and Dorothy his wife, my sister, five pounds. Ellinor Atkinson daughter to Thomas Atkinson and Elizabeth his wife, both late deceased. Abraham Harman *alias* Cupp my reputed son.

I give and bequeath unto my " cozenn " Mr. Henry Sewell of Coventrie, alderman, four pounds and to Mr. Henry Briers of Coventry, alderman, four pounds, whom I do constitute and make my overseers of this my last will and testament. The residue to Sibell Foxall, widow, late wife to Richard Foxall of Coventry, mercer, late deceased, whom I make my sole executrix &c. Harrington, 177.

[William Harman, son of Hugh of Morehall; his elder brother John married Sibbell Fowler; on his decease she doubtless married Richard Foxall. Their sister Dorothy married Thomas Wirley of Hampsted in Staffordshire.

For the pedigree of this family, see Harleian Society's Vol. XII. Visitation of Warwickshire, p. 105.

Henry Sewall mentioned in the will, married Margaret Grazebrook, daughter of Margaret (Keene) Grazebrook, a greatniece of Hugh Harman, probably by his sister Margaret (Harman) Luson; hence the relationship mentioned of cousin. See Salisbury Memorial, Pt. 1, p. 156.—WALTER K. WATKINS.]

WILLIAM HALL of Borton in the parish of Crepredie, 6 August 1596, proved 21 October 1596. My two daughters Joane and Mary Haull. My son William Haull. If my wife marry before my son be at the age of twenty one years she shall deliver these things before mentioned (certain personal property) unto Henry Sewell my brother in law, whom I do will shall have the education and bringing up of my said son William from the time of her marriage until he shall accomplish the age of twenty one years &c. John Haull (a brother). Henry Showell a witness. Drake, 69.

[William Hall was probably of the Hall family of Oxfordshire, of which a partial pedigree of the Banbury branch of the family is given in Harleian Society publications, regular series, vol. 5.—W. K. WATKINS.]

JOHANE BROWNELL of St. Michael the Archangel, Coventry, widow, 22 July 1588, proved 22 April 1590. To be buried in the parish church of St. Michael near unto my late husband there. My son William. My son Sampson Brownell. My son in law Robert Bagnalde and Margaret his wife, my daughter. Their children Elizabeth Bagnalde and Edmond Bagnalde and the other six, Ellen, Thomas, Wynifred, Robert, Francis and Richard. Richard Butler and Elizabeth my daughter. I give to the said Elizabeth my gold ring with five stones fixed in the same and my little beer pot gilt. To Richard Butler and Elizabeth their daughter, to either of them one silver spoon with a " Lyon " on the end of them and to Rachel their daughter five shillings in money. Thomas Salter, my son in law, and Sence his wife. Johane their daughter. To my sister Alice Saunders a white silver pot with a cover and to Richard Shewell my godson a silver spoon with a maiden head upon it; and to Anne Howcott my god daughter a silver spoon with a maiden head upon it. The poor of the said city. To my " coosen " Samuel Saunders a hoop ring of gold with these letters upon it T. M. E. I do give and bequeath to my cousin Joice Shewell a hoop ring of gold. To the said Robert Bagnalde and Margaret his wife a stone pot garnished with silver, with a cover gilt without, a ring of silver and gilt about the neck thereof. My will is that my daughter Margaret should have the cover of the standing cup which my husband did give her. My cousins Richard Saunders, Thomas Saunders, Isabel Saunders and Bridget Saunders. My said two daughters Margaret and Elizabeth. My said son William Brownell to be full and sole executor.　　　Drury, 24.

WILLIAM SEWALL of the city of Coventry, vintner, 29 June 1624, proved 11 September 1624. To be buried in the parish church of St. Michael's Coventry. Elizabeth Symes, wife of Thomas Symes of Coventry brasier, and Anne Sewall both natural daughters of me the said William Sewall to be mine executors. To Elizabeth my messuage in the High Street wherein I now dwell, with the shops thereunto belonging &c. (and other property). Reference to a deed, bearing date 17 December 17 James, made between Samuel Miles of the one part and me the said William, by the name of William Sewall of the city of Coventry draper, of the other part. To my said daughter Anne the messuage &c. now or lately in the tenure of Agnes Dudly, widow, or her assigns (and other property). A messuage in Well Street in the tenure of Richard Saunders, baker. Samuel Simes my godson, one of the sons of my son in law Thomas Symes. John, Thomas, Ellen and Elizabeth Symes (other) sons and daughters of Thomas Symes my son and Elizabeth his wife. Others.

I give and bequeath to my brother Henry Sewall and Margaret his wife twenty shillings apiece. To my sister Gibbons, wife of Mr. William Gibbons, to buy her a ring in which my name shall be engraven, forty shillings. To my daughter Lucy Tadlowe, wife of Mr. Henry Tadlowe, three pounds six shillings eight pence to buy her a cup of plate on which my name shall be cut. To the band of Artillery soldiers in Coventry forty shillings to buy them powder, to be paid them upon the day of my funeral. Bequests to the poor in Bablacke &c. My two kinsmen Henry and Richard Sewall, sons of my brother Henry Sewall.　　　Byrde, 79.

ANTHONY POWER of Kenellworth, Warwick, gen[t], 21 December 1632, proved 1 May 1633. To Anne Power, my beloved wife, all my right and title that I have by virtue of any mortagege &c. to this intent that she shall be a good mother to my younger children to raise them portions and that my eldest son shall have no hand in the forenamed mortgages. My two daughters Hanna and Mary Power. Stephen Power my second son. William Power my third son. Anthony Power my fourth son. My brother Thomas Power. To Henry Power my eldest son all my inheritance lands in Kenellworth and my signet gold ring. Wife Anne to be executrix and my friends Thomas Devis and Thomas Wright, both of Kenellworth, yeomen, to be overseers.

Commission issued, 1 May 1633, to Richard Sewell, uncle (avunculo) of Stephen Power, son and executor of the will of Anne Power deceased who while living was relict and executrix of the above Anthony Power deceased &c.

Commission issued, 11 May 1640, to Stephen Power (the son) to administer *de bonis non*, Richard Sewell the former administrator being now also dead.　　　Russell, 38.

ANNE POWER of Kenellworth, Warwick, widow, 15 January 1632. William Power my third son. Anthony Power my fourth son. My two daughters Hanna and Mary Power. My brother in law William Power.

My two brothers in law Thomas Power and George Hill. Mr. Henry Wright, Richard Walton and Elizabeth Ambler. The poor of the Augmentation. Henry West my brother in law. Mr. Francis Phippes Mr. Richard Shewell Mr. Abraham Randall and William Power my brothers and dear friends.

Administration granted, 1 May 1633, to Richard Sewell uncle of Stephen Power the natural and lawful son of the deceased during his minority. The will was proved 5 February 1638 by Stephen Power the son &c.

Russell, 39.

MARGARET RANDELL of the City of Coventry, widow, 4 May 1646 proved 22 May 1646. To be buried in the Drapers' Chapel within St. Michael's Church, Coventry, near the bodies of my father and mother. My nephew Stephen Power. My two nieces, the daughters of my sister Power, namely Hannah Lee, the wife of Thomas Lee, and Mary Holbech, the wife of Amilian Holbech. My nephew Anthony Power. To my nephew Samuel Sewall, son of my brother Richard Sewall, my close or pasture called Quarry field, without Newgate on the West side of the Cawsey or pavement leading from Coventry towards Whitley on the London road. To my niece Elizabeth Seires, daughter of my brother Richard Sewall and wife of Edmond Seires, my close &c. on the back side of the said Cawsey. To my niece Anne Sewall, daughter of my brother Richard Sewall a tenement on the south side of St. Michael's Church. Another tenement to niece Prudence Sewall, daughter of my said brother Richard. To my nephew Stephen Power my parcel of land called Rowley Hill in Stoke, in the County of the city of Coventry. The residue to Stephen Power, Hannah Lee Mary Holbech and Prudence Sewall equally. The said Stephen Power to be sole executor.

John Brownell one of the witnesses. Twisse, 59.

STEPHEN POWER of Kennelworth, Warwick, gen[t], 25 July 1648 proved 15 May 1655. To my brother in law Thomas Lee of Kennelworth, gen[t], the yearly rent arising out of certain lands near Coventry called Barons Fields (in trust). My brother Henry Power. The said Thomas Lee's children. The two children of my sister Mary Holbech. My brother William Power. My uncle Thomas Power. The poor of Killingworth [sic] aforesaid. My brother Anthony Power. As for my debts owing to me by the State of England for arrears due to me for my service as a soldier, being two debentures, one of them of two hundred forty five pounds nine shillings two pence, the other of thirty seven pounds or thereabouts now in the hands or custody of my cousin Valentine Hill, I devise and bequeath the same as followeth: seven pounds thereof to the said Valentine Hill, twenty pounds to William Pynson of Coventry, gen[t], five pounds to my said uncle Power ,and the rest to my three brothers and two sisters, to be equally divided amongst them. I am engaged and stand bound, as surety with the said Valentine Hill and for the proper debt of the said Valentine, unto Major Tackington, in the sum of twenty pounds for the payment of ten pounds &c. My brother Thomas Lee to be sole executor and my brother Henry Power and my brother Amillyon Holbech to be overseers.

Aylett, 144.

[The preceding eight wills seem to refer to the Sewall family of Coventry (England) to whom the father of Judge Samuel Sewall of Boston and Major Stephen Sewall of Salem belonged. HENRY F. WATERS.

William Sewall, whose will is given, was brother of Henry Sewall the Mayor of Coventry 1589 and 1606, who was the great-grandfather of Chief Justice Samuel Sewall of Boston. Anne, wife of Anthony Power and mother of Stephen Power, was a daughter of Henry Sewall, Mayor of Coventry, as was also Margaret wife of Abraham Randall.

A pedigree of the Sewall family, compiled by Mr. William H. Whitmore, can be found on pp. xi. to xxi. of the introduction to the Sewall's Diary, published in Mass. Hist. Coll., Fifth Series, Vol. V.

Prof. E. E. Salisbury, LL.D., has also given a pedigree in Vol. I. of the Salisbury Memorial, and also referred to these wills.—WALTER K. WATKINS.]

WILLIAM BLANDE of London gentleman, 31 July 1596, proved 17 September 1596. My body to be buried at Whitechapel with my two children. Two parts of my land of my manor of Tattingston to be sold by my executrix and all my goods &c. to be sold towards the payment of my debts. My debts paid, of the overplus my wife Judith shall have the one moiety, and my son William to have the third part and the child that she now goeth withall to have the other fourth part. My wife Judith to be executrix, and I do request my brother Thomas to be my overseer.

Thomas Blande was one of the witnesses.

Confirmed by sentence diffinitive the second session of the Paschal Term A.D. 1600.   Drake, 63.

ELIZABETH BLAND, now wife of Thomas Bland of St. Martin's within Ludgate gen^t. and late executrix of the last will and testament of Margare Smithe my late mother deceased. Will made 19 July 1593 and proved 20 July 1593   One hundred pounds to be divided amongst my children had by my late husband William Yeardly, gen^t, deceased, vizt Jasper Yeardley, Margaret Yeardley, Anne Yeardly, Elizabeth Yeardley and Mary Yeardley, to be paid at days of marriage &c. To my brother Michael Harrison's children. My sister Sara Sawle. To Alice Haiwarde for her pains taken with me. My Aunt Alice Eccles. My husband Thomas Bland to be my whole executor.   Nevell, 57.

THOMAS BLAND of Sundridge, Kent, gen^t, 18 Nouember 1617, proved 15 May 1618. The poor of Sundridge and of St. Bennet's near Paul's Wharf. The children of my brother John Bland and of my brother Gregory Bland. My sister Elizabeth Burye and her children. My god daughter Judith Gilbie and the children of my sister Gilbie. My god daughter Jone Hope. My daughter in law Ellen Lewis, Margaret Ball and Emme Whitlatche. My brother Peter Blande and his children. My wife Mary. My son George Blande. My daughter Elizabeth Blande. My wife to have the occupation and use of the house and lands which I hold by lease of Mrs. Cranwell and her son. My son George to be executor and I do nominate as overseers my sons in law William Ball and John Lewis and John Blande. To son George my messuages &c. in the parishes of St. Peter's and St. Bennet's near Paul's Wharf, with remainder to the heir male of my brother John Blande, and next to my right heirs. My messuages in Shoreditch to my son George and his son Thomas Blande. John Sale referred to. The children of my son in law William Ball. My daughter in law Margaret Sale. My son in law Jasper Yardley and my daughters in law Elizabeth Cooper and Mary Yardley.

Wit. John Blande, Thomas Langhorne, Elizabeth Blande, the mark of Raphe Farrington and the mark of Sibbell Farrington, his wife.

                                                          Meade, 47.

[A pedigree of this family of Bland appears in the Visitation of London, 1633-4 (Harleian So. Pub., Vol. 1, p, 79). To it evidently belonged the Virginia family of that name, and perhaps the Maryland family. The following notes relate to these families. The printed Registers of the parish of St. Antholins, London (also published by the Harleian Society), give baptisms &c. of the family of John Bland, the father of the Virginians. HENRY F. WATERS.]

JOHN BLANDE of London, grocer, 24 September 1627, proved 20 April 1632. I will that my body be decently carried to the church between 3 and 4 clock in the afternoon with some few of my friends and neighbors and buried in the parish church of St Antholin's where I dwell. I will not have above fifty pounds bestowed at the most upon my said burial besides mourning for my children and others. Gifts to Christ Hospital and to poor prisoners. According to the city of London laws my wife is to have the thirds of my estate and the other third my children, and the other third is at my dispose. Out of my third I bequeath unto my well beloved wife Susan Blande five hundred pounds towards her widowship. If she marry then my son Thomas shall have one hundred pounds of it, John fifty and Susan Blande, my daughter, fifty pounds, if unmarried; the rest of the five hundred pounds to be divided amongst the rest of my children unmarried, by equal portions, at twenty one, the sons and the daughters at eighteen. To daughters Anne and Elizabeth Blande twenty pounds apiece over and above their parts of the children's third. My wife Susan to allow her mother fifteen pounds per annum during life, if she continues a widow, so long as her mother liveth. If she chanceth to marry and her mother living then during my mother's life. The five hundred pounds bequeathed to my children they shall enjoy till their grandmother be dead and buried. Sons Thomas and John and daughter Susan under twenty one. Son in law Emanuell Probie and my daughter Mary Probie. I give and bequeath my Ham house, after my wife's decease, among my youngest children resting from Edward Blande and so to the youngest, according to a surrender I make in the court for the use of my will. Thomas, John and Susan Blande shall allow to their grandmother Mary de Deblere, out of their legacies, three pounds per cent per annum, for every hundred pounds so long as she shall live; and if they be not of age then their legacies to be put out to use and my mother to have three per cent per annum out of it, the rest to be towards the bringing them up which are not of years. To Grace Bonde a mourning gown. Mr. Robert Edwardes' son Thomas. I give unto all my godchildren twenty shillings apiece except Lawrence Lowne's daughter and Gregory Blande's son or daughter, for Lownes played the knave with me and Gregory Blande likewise deceaved me, so they nor theirs shall have one penny of mine. To my brother Gillye forty shillings, and to each of his children by my sister forty shillings apiece, Judith Lownes not to have any thing, the wife of Lawrence Lownes. To Bedlam ten shillings. To St. Gregory's Church where I was christened, to make a stock for the poor to buy flax with, five pounds. Similar bequests to St. Antholin's church, West ham church, Aldermary church, St. Stephen's church, Coleman St., for the purchase of flax to spin or woollen yarn to knit. Johane Langhorne, my cousin Thomas Langhorne's daughter, Susan Northers and Frances Langhorne. To my son Thomas Bland my gold seal ring with my arms upon it. To John my silver mark to seal letters with. My cousin Samuel Bland. My cousin William Blande's children and my cousin Mary, his late wife. My cousin George Blande and Thomas, his son. Elizabeth my cousin Holmwood and each of her children. My sister Burie. Edward Burye. Margaret Everett, my sister's daughter. Cousin

Rosse, my sister's daughter.   Elizabeth Burye, my sister's daughter.   (All referred to as sisters of cousin Burye.)   The Lady Harbert, my niece, and each of her children.   My cousin Robert Brawler and his wife and daughter.   Thomas Northey, Mr. Isaac Jones, Mr. William Cookaine, John Duckett, Mr. Isaac Pennington, the Trinity House for old sailors.   The executors to be my loving wife Susan and Thomas my son and John my second son, and the overseers to be my son in law Emanuel Probye, my cousin Samuel Blande Robert Edwardes and Thomas Northey.

Audley, 44.

JOHN BLAND of London merchant, 3 May 1680, proved 23 June 1680. I do give and bequeath all the jewels plate and household stuff belonging to me to my dear wife Sarah Bland, feeling no greater grief under my many adversities and infirmities I now labor under than her necessary absence in Virginia about my unhappy affairs and estates there, she having "bin" the principal comfort of my past life and by her exemplary virtue, discretion, affliction (sic), prudence and patience having deserved much more from me than I am able to give, being worthy of my whole confidence and entire trust, which nevertheless by reason of the great distance she is now at and the many contingencies and accidents which may happen thereby I do think fit by a conjunction with her to commit to my choicest friend Thomas Povey Esquire, one of the Masters of Requests to the King's Majesty, who best understands all my affairs, interests and intentions, I do therefore make and constitute my said dear wife Sarah Bland and my said worthy friend Thomas Povey to be the executors &c.   Many years since I purchased a house &c. at Tangier and have laid out upon it several considerable sums of money for the improvement thereof.   It has been taken and seized upon in my absence and without my privity by the Governor there and is still possessed and applied to the service of his Majesty, for which I have not yet obtained satisfaction &c.   This entrusted to Thomas Povey.   All other lands and tenements &c. to the two executors, who are to raise money to pay the debts I shall be found to owe and a competent provision for my daughter in law Frances Bland and my grandson John Bland, her son, yet being in his infancy.

The first grant of probate was made, as above, to Thomas Povey, power reserved for Sarah Bland, the widow, to whom a grant of probate was issued 27 May 1682.   Bath, 76.

THOMAS BLAND of London, gen[t] 26 August 1674, with a codicil dated 30 October, 1674, proved 29 January 1674.   To my grand children Jane and Sarah Moyser two hundred and fifty pounds apiece, to be employed at interest or laid out in buying of several annuities for them.   To my grandson Joseph Day fifty pounds, to be employed to put him out to some decent calling when he shall attain to fifteen years of age.   To my daughter Sarah Day the wife of Joseph Day one annuity or yearly rent charge of ten pounds by the year during her natural life, issuable and payable out of my lands and tenement at Mildenhall in Suffolk.   I give to my son in law Joseph Day and Sarah his wife ten pounds apiece to buy them mourning. I appoint my son Richard Bland and my son in law Joseph Day and Sarah his wife to be executors and do appoint them to give all my linen to my grandchildren.

In the codicil he speaks of his grandson Joseph Day as "now deceased."

Dycer, 2.

THOMAS BLAND of London, merchant, 25 November 1700, proved 13 January 1700. To my sister Sarah Day ten pounds every year during her natural life, she was living with my executors. Ten pounds to Mary Keemish if she shall live to be lawfully married. Ten pounds to ——— Keenish, my sister's grandson, at one and twenty. Twenty pounds each to Sarah and Margaret Bland, my brother's two daughters if they live to be lawfully married. My cousin Lawrance Pendrill. To Ann ——— the servant in my cousin Pendrill's house forty shillings. To my said sister Sarah Day ten pounds for her mourning cloths at my funeral. To every person whose name is inserted on the back of this will one gold ring of the value about ten shillings. To my cousin Sarah Pindrell the wife of Mr. Lawrance Pindrell all my lands, plantations mortgages, houses, tobacco houses &c. in Ann Arundell County in he Province of Maryland, and also (after the payment or other accomplishment of the said contingent legacies) all my negroes, cattle, horses, mares, household stuff, debts in money and tobacco, ready money, plate, goods and chattels whatsover, either in England or Maryland or elsewhere. And I make my cousin Lawrance Pindrell and Sarah his wife my sole executors.   Dyer, 2.

July 1652. The twelvth day Adͨon issued forth to John Bland yᵉ nřall & lawful Brother of Edward Bland late in Verginia Batchelor deͨd haveing goodes etc. to Adͤter yᵉ goodes, chattles & debets of yᵉ said deͨd hee being sworne freely Adͤter etc.

Fol. 134 Admon. Act Book, 1652.

[John Bland, London, Grocer, will proved 1632, was son of Adam and Jane (Atkyns) Bland. He married Susan Deblere or Duclere of the City of Hamburg, and had twelve children; he is spoken of as of Syth Lane, London and Plaistow, Essex, Eng.

Emanuel Proby mentioned, was fourth son of Sir Peter Proby, Lord Mayor of London, afterward Lord Carysfort. His sister Elizabeth married Wm. Bury, gent.

William Blande of London, gent., an elder brother of John, married Judith Woodery, daughter of Thomas of Groby, Eng. Elizabeth, wife of Thomas Bland of St. Martin's, was the sister-in-law of the above William and John Bland. Her husband was under-sheriff of Middlesex. His will follows hers, by which we see that he had at least three wives; his first was Alice Germaine. (See p. 147, Slaughter's History of Bristol Parish, Va., 1879.)

John Bland of London, merchant, whose will was proved 1680, had with other issue Giles whose wife Frances and son John are mentioned. Frances was daughter of Thomas Probey [Povey], Master of Requests. The wife of the testator was Sarah, daughter of Giles Green, a member of Parliament for Corfe Castle, Dorset, time of Charles I.—See *Richmond Critic*, 9 July, 1888.—W. K. WATKINS.]

RICHARD BENNETT of Noansamond River in Virginia 15 March 1674, proved 3 August 1676. To the parish where I now live and have so long lived three hundred acres which Thomas Bolton holdeth by lease and on which he now lives; the rents to be received yearly by the churchwardens of the parish and disposed towards the relief of four poor aged or impotent persons whom they judge to stand in most need of help; and this to continue and be done forever as long as the land continues. To Richard, son of Thomas Buxton the rents and profits of that parcel of land on which Edmond Belson now liveth, to him and his heirs forever, the same to be paid unto him when he shall come to be twenty years of age; but if he lives not to that time or afterwards die without issue. To my daughter Anne fifty pounds sterling besides her debts which she now oweth me. To my grandchildren Elizabeth, Anne and Bennett Scarburgh, or any other of my daughter Scarburgh's children which shall be born hereafter, all that parcel of land lying on Pocomoke River on the Eastern shore in Maryland, being two thousand eight hundred acres by Patent, to them and either of them, their, or either of their, heirs forever, and also two thousand five hundred acres by Patent, lying in Wiccomoco River on the Eastern shore in Maryland. To my cousin Silvester the wife of major Nicholas Hill twelve thousand pounds of tobacco. To my cousin Mary the wife of Mr. Luke Cropley of London twenty pounds sterling. To Richard Hubard of Pigg Point one thousand pounds of tobacco. To Michael Ward and the widow of John Lewis, to each of them one thousand pounds of tobacco. To Charles Howard and Richard Higgins, to each of them one thousand pounds of tobacco, and, more to Charles Howard, the land which he lives of (sic) for eleven years. To John Chilcotes and Thomas Garratt, to each of them two thousand pounds of tobacco. To William Kitchen and John Blye, to each of them one thousand pounds of tobacco. To Patrick Edmonston and the widow Reddick, to each of them one thousand pounds of tobacco. To John Worter who married the relict of John Salsbury one thousand pounds of tobacco. To William Yearret of Pagan Creek and to the wife of Mr. Thomas Taberer, to each of them two thousand pounds of tobacco. To Elizabeth Cutland of Chuchatuke Creek and Thomas Jordan of the same place, to each of them two thousand pounds of tobacco. To James Day twelve thousand pounds of tobacco. And if Mr. Tabbarer see cause he may add three thousand more to it. I give to all my servants that now liveth with me, both Christians and Negroes, to each of them one thousand pounds of tobacco, only the two hirelings excepted, vizt Richard Higgins and John Turner.

The rest of my personal and real estate and all lands, stock, of what nature or kind soever it be, to go to my grand child Richard Bennett, to him and his heirs forever, my said grandchild now residing in Bristol, and in default of such heirs then to come to the children of Theodarick Bland and Charles Scarburgh. Lastly I do declare and ordain and appoint James Jofey, Mr Thomas Hodges and Edmond Belson, or any two of them, also Robert Peellee to be overseers.

Wit: John Speire, En^o Tarle, Charles Howard, George Davis. Proved in Nansamond court the twelvth of April 1675, by the oaths of Mr En^o Tarte (sic) Charles Howard and George Davis to be the last will and testament of Major General R: Bennett.   *Teste* Jno Lear Cler: Cur.

Bence, 99.

[Richard Bennett was a nephew of Edward Bennett, who resided for a time at Delft and was largely engaged in the Virginia trade, being a member of the Virginia company. The nephew, being his partner, came over to supervise his plantations.

Richard was a Burgess 1629 to 1631, member of the Council 1642-9, Governor 1652 to 1655 when he went to England as agent for the Colony. Returning in a few years he held various offices, and was in 1666 made Major General of the train bands.

In 1642 he had been one of those Virginia Puritans who had sent to New England for ministers, but in the last part of his life he became a Quaker.

His daughter Ann married Theoderick Bland, a son of John and Susan (Duclere) Bland, a man said to have been " in fortune and understanding inferior to no man in Virginia." See *Richmond Critic*, 9 July, 1888. See also note by R. A. Brock in these Gleanings, REGISTER, vol. 42, p. 394 (*ante*, p. 290); and Appleton's Cyclopædia of American Biography, vol. 1, p. 237.—W. K. WATKINS.]

WILLIAM SEABRIGHT of London Esq. 19 January 1618, proved 7 November 1620. To be buried in the parish church of St. Edmund the King in Lumbard street, where I do dwell, in the chancel within the vault there where the body of my most dear, virtuous and late loving wife doth rest in the Lord, as near unto her as possibly and conveniently may be placed. My said wife's grandchild Elizabeth, the elder daughter of Sir James Boucher, knight. Frances Boucher one of his daughters. My godson Thomas Boucher, eldest son of the said Sir James, James Boucher, his second son, John, his third son, Richard, his fourth son, William, his fifth son, and Henry Boucher, the youngest of the said Sir James. The good will I bear to every of them, chiefly for their good grandmother's sake. My will and desire is that after such time as the portions given to the said sons shall be paid by mine executors, then by the judgments of my loving and kind brother in law Thomas Morley their uncle, John Burnell, Richard Brigges, Edmond Page and Thomas Freeman their friends and cousins, or the more part of them for the time being, every of their said positions shall be put forth at use at the best rates they can upon as good security as they can for every hundred pounds by the year for and towards their maintenance until such time as the said friends &c. shall in their discretions think fit. My niece Sarah Astin one of the daughters of my late loving sister Eleanor Astin, widow deceased, (to whose last will and testament reference is made). My nephew Edward Seabright. Reference to will of "my good father"—"whose executor I am." My late brother in law Thomas Astin. My late brother Thomas Seabright, gen[t], deceased, made me his only executor. Have brought up all his five children. My cousin Edward Broad Esq. who married with my niece Judith. Elizabeth Blounte the late widow and administratrix of my nephew William Seabright deceased. My best and loving cousin Sir Thomas Coventrye, knight, H. M. Sollicitor General who married with my niece Sara, sithence deceased. My cousin John Burnell who married Anne my said brother's youngest daughter. Reference to "my good father Edward Seabright." The two children of my niece Sarah Coventrye, Thomas and Elizabeth. My loving sister in law Anne late the widow of my said brother and now the wife of Thomas Walsh, gentleman. The parish of Woolverley in the Co. of Worcester the place of my birth, where I was bred up a great part of my youth. I give and bequeath to my brother Thomas Morley a gown. To my sister his wife and to one of his daughters, being my god daughter, two gowns of silk "grogaron." To my brother Isaac Morley a cloak. Others. My cousin Mrs. Burnell, widow. My cousin John Huntbach and my niece his wife. My brother Walshe and my sister his wife. My cousin Page and his wife. My cousin Brigges and my cousin his wife. My cousin Simon Jenckes and his wife. My servant Edmund Nuttinge. My late servant Thomas Hale. My loving cousin Edward Broad Esq. and my loving niece his wife and their three children. My niece Anne Burnell and her children. My niece Theodicia Seabright. My nephew Edward Seabright's children and hers. My nephew William Astin's children (as I take it four in number). My loving and kind cousin Mrs Susan Colles widow. My loving sister in law Alice Boucher. Soame, 97.

[The testator of the above was Town Clerk of London and married Elizabeth, sister of Thomas Morley of London and aunt of John Morley of Charlestown, Mass. The pedigree of the family of Seabright or Sebright is given in the Visitation of Worcestershire (printed by the Harleian Society) and also in the Visitation of Essex for 1612 (Harleian So.). See also REGISTER for April, 1892 (*ante*, p. 568), in the pedigrees of Burnell and Morley, then published.
HENRY F. WATERS.

By deed dated April 2, 1624, "Edward Sebright of Prestwood, in ye Countie of Stafford Esqr ye Cozen & next heire of William Sebright Late of ye Cittie of London Esqr deceased & Theodosea ye wife of ye s^d Edward" convey to "Henry Cullicke of ye HamLett of Milton in ye Townshipp Parish or ffeilds of Prittlewell in ye Hundred of Rotchford, in ye Countie of Essex yeoman", lands in the parishes of Northshoberie, Much Wakering alias Wakering Magna and other parishes in the Hundred of Rotchford, Co. Essex, England; also lands in Strayfield (late Carters alias Friends) : land called Bangold Land; the moiety of Yokefleete and Carters Lanes.

This deed was recorded in Boston "in ye Booke of Records for deeds [IV. 325] for ye Countie of Suffolke in New England" at the request of "Richard Ely, & Elizabeth his wife, ye wife of & executrix vnto ye Late John Cullicke of Boston m^rchant."   JOHN T. HASSAM.]

HENRY WILKINSON of Nottingham town, skinner, 25 November 1642, proved 27 March 1646. To be buried in St. Peter's church within the town of Nottingham. To Mr. Robert Buckland, citizen and leatherseller of London, fifty shillings to make him a gold ring to wear for my sake. To Mrs. Anne Ball of London fifty shillings, to Mr. John Ball of London forty shillings and to Mr. Richard Ball of London forty shillings (for rings &c.). To my cousin Alice Barense of Gedlinge three pounds. To my cousin Dorothy Johnson of Ratcliffe three pounds. To my cousin Joane Skelinton of Roudington three pounds. To my cousin —— Asher of Roudington three pounds. To my cousin Anne Wilkinson at the Black Wall three pounds. To my cousin Isabel Blood in New England three pounds. To my cousin Margaret Atkinson of Nottingham four pounds. To my brother John Wilkinson forty shillings. To my cousin Robert Wilkinson three pounds. To my cousin Richard Wilkinson three pounds. To my cousin Jeffery Wilkinson three pounds. To my cousin John Wilkinson, my brother John's son, three pounds. To my cousin Mary Wilkinson four pounds. To my brother George Attenborowe twenty shillings and to my sister Mary his wife five pounds. Also to William, Jarvis, George and Richard Attenborowe, my sister's sons, to every one of them three pounds. To Anne Kirke and Elizabeth Cripel, my sister's daughters, three pounds each. To Richard Barnes of Gedlinge, my sister's son, three pounds. To my sister Jane Hardnett five pounds and my gimball gold ring and one pair spoon silver and double gilt. To my cousin Anne Beke one hoop ring of gold. My cousins Richard and Jeffery Wilkinson and their brother John. William and Henry Wilkinson and their other brother at London. Henry the son of Robert Wilkinson, my godson. My brother Hardnett and Mary his wife. My cousin Gelstrape Carpenter at Wilford. John Wilkinson, my cousin, citizen and blacksmith of London and my cousin George Wilkinson of Roudington, his brother. My loving friend Mr. Richard Hardnett citizen and skinner of London. My brother in law Richard Hardnett, skinner, to be executor.

Admon. granted (as above) to Richard Hardnett the executor of Richard Hardnett &c. to administer the goods &c.   Twisse, 37.

[Isabel Blood was the wife of Richard Blood of Groton, Mass.—EDITOR.]

JUDITH MORRIS of Dedham, Essex, widow, 25 January 1645, proved 17 March 1645. To certain preachers of the Word, vizt Mr Newcome and Mr. Smith of Dedham, Mr. Stanton of Ipswich, Mr. Edes of Lafford (Lawford?) Mr. Carr of Ardleigh, Mr. Seaborne of Langham, Mr. Cooke who was sometimes preacher at Boxted and Mr. Astey, forty shillings apiece. To Richard Jacomond's son, late of East Marsye, forty shillings. To Richard Jacomond forty shillings and to his daughter that is blind four pounds. To Martha and Elizabeth Jacomond, daughters of Richard Jacomond, all my wearing apparel. To Judith Coffeild my god daughter twenty shillings and a flockbed. To the iiij^or children of Stephen Hart, that is to say, John, Steven, Sarah and the youngest that went with her father to New England, five pounds apiece Anne Willes, my god daughter, and her brothers. To John Collens son of the widow Collins of Higham forty shillings, to be paid to his mother. My goddaughter Mary Warren and her brothers and sisters. John Morris. My brother Josuah Warren. William Morris at four and twenty. Thomas Morris, servant with Goodman Groome of Colchester. Sarah Groome my god daughter. Her father William Groome. Mary Groome. The four children of Josua Warren, vizt Josua, Sarah, Elizabeth and Hester. Mr. Strangmanes three children. The widow Woodward dwelling in St. James Parish in Colchester. Goodman Chapline of the same parish. Goodman Munson of Colchester. Thomas Roofe of Colchester, carrier, and his children. To the town of Copford five pounds towards the binding forth of two poor children apprentices. Certain poor widows in Copford. The eldest son of Parnell Cutler, sometimes my servant. Mary Harrison that dwelleth with Mr. Burrowes. To Rebecca Scolding, my god daughter now in New England, twenty shillings. The widow Pease of Colchester. To Simon Stone in New England forty shillings. The wife of Nathaniel Baker of Stratford. William Groome, my girl's father. Goodman Wood of Dedham, shoemaker, and his children. The poor of Stratford. The widow Frende and the widow Beckwaye. Mr. Nicholas Prigg. I give unto Joseph Morse in New England twenty shillings if he be living; if he be dead then my will is that William Stone in New England shall have the twenty shillings. Thomas Jacomond now servant to Mr. Barnton of Colchester. To John Bentley my bible. Robert Maken of Dedham, Sarah Warren, the wife of Thomas Beale, and her two children. Hester the wife of Mr. Strangeman above mentioned. I nominate and appoint Clement Fenne of Dedham, clothier, and John Morris of Colchester, merchant, to be my executors and Christopher Vyne of Langham supervisor.

All that my sixteenth part which I have in a ship wherein John Hayward goes master and all that I lent to the Parliament, with the profits, if any be, and all my other goods and chattels &c. not before bequeathed and given, except twenty shillings not before mentioned, which twenty shillings I now give to a kinswoman in Colchester, but all the rest of my estate unbequeathed I do give and bequeath unto my cousin Stephen Harte's children in New England, to be equally divided between them, my funeral being discharged and all other necessaries and expences being allowed to my executors. And my executors shall have power to make sale of that sixteenth part in the ship abovesaid and send the money to New England to those children to whom it is given.

Witnessed by Isaac Ham and Samuel Deacon. Probate was granted to John Morris, Clement Fenne, the other executor, being dead.

Twisse, 33.

[The above will, it will be noticed, contains a number of New England names.
H. F. W.

Stephen Hart, named in this will, came to New England (it is said in 1632,) and settled at Cambridge (then Newtown). He removed soon afterwards to Hartford and thence to Farmington. A volume was published in 1875 entitled " Genealogical History of Deacon Stephen Hart and his Descendants by Alfred Andrews." Published by Austin Hart. The compiler states that Stephen Hart was

820 GENEALOGICAL GLEANINGS IN ENGLAND.

born about 1605 at Braintree in Essex county, England. See also Paige's History of Cambridge, page 574; Memorial History of Hartford County, Conn., vol. i.. p. 242; and Savage's Genealogical Dictionary, vol. 2, p. 367-8.

Simon Stone, also named, settled at Watertown, Mass. See Bond's History of Watertown, pp. 584 to 591, for an account of him and his descendants. William Stone was, I presume, the person who settled at Guilford in Cônnecticut in 1639. See Smith's History of Guilford and Savage's Genealogical Dictionary. — EDITOR.]

FRANCIS DOUGHTIE of Hampsteed in the parish of Oldsbury and County and Diocese of Gloucester, gen‍t, 16 May 1634, proved 31 October 1634. To my son Francis my white horse or nag. To Spencer Achley, my daughter Frances' son, twenty shillings, to be paid by my executrix within six months next after my decease. To John Dauyes, the son of my daughter Margaret, ten shillings, to be paid in like manner. To the three children of my son Francis, that is to say, Mary, his daughter, and Francis and Eliah, his sons, thirty shillings, to be paid in like manner. The rest of my goods, moveable and unmoveable whatsoever, I give and bequeath to my daughter Elizabeth (excepting what I have passed by my deed bearing date 15 May 1634, made to certain uses to Humfrey Hooke, alderman of the City of Bristol, Thomas Lloyd of the same, Adam Baynham of Yate gen‍t and William Maye of Cherefield gen‍t, this excepted) and I make my daughter Elizabeth my whole and sole executrix &c.

One of the witnesses was Fr: Doughtie minist‍r. Seager, 86.

[The above will and the deed to Humfrey Hooke and others, to which it refers, gave rise to a great contention in New England, as appears from Lechford's Note-Book, pp. 133-5, 137, 171-3 and 256 (I refer to the pages of the printed book). Elizabeth Doughtie, the daughter and sole executrix of the above testator, became the wife of William Cole of Sutton in the parish of Chew Magna, in the County of Somerset, gentleman (as he calls himself in a bill of complaint to the Gov., Council and Assistants of the Jurisdiction of Massachusetts Bay) and brother of John Cole of Farrington, Somerset, yeoman, who made a deposition about Hamsteed Farm in 1639. William and Elizabeth Cole were then in New England, as was also her brother Francis Doughty, who at that time called himself a planter of Dorchester in New England. He was called a clerk in the bill of complaint by William Cole and his wife, and seems to have been a minister at Taunton (Mass.), and afterwards to have removed to Long Island. HENRY F. WATERS.]

TIMOTHY S‍t NICHOLAS of the parish of St. Marys in the Isle of Ely within the Co. of Cambridge gen‍t, 13 June 1606, proved 17 September 1606. Testator calls himself the youngest son of Vincent St. Nicholas, late of Ashe next Sandwich in the Co. of Kent, gen‍t deceased, and declares his age to be about thirty years, wishes his body to be buried within the parish church of Ahe near the grave of his father, (if it should please God to call him out of this transitory world at or near Ashe) and orders a monument to be laid upon the resting place of his body not exceeding the value of thirteen pounds six shillings eight pence. To the poor of Ospringe in Kent and of St. Marys. To every godchild. "I promised for them they shoulde constantlie professe renouncinge all poperye and Romishe Relictes and supstition." Loving brother Henry Harfleete and Thomas, his son. Brother Thomas St. Nicholas. Niece and god daughter Dorothy Bret‍t (at her age of sixteen years). Sister Brett's other daughter Deborah B rett. Niece and god daughter Deborah St. Nicholas, eldest daughter of brother Thomas. Niece Dorothy St. Nicholas (another daughter). Brother Stebbinge. Nephew Henry Harfleete. My nieces Mary, Omer (sic), Susan and Martha Harfleete. Godson John Harfleete son of William Harflete of

Sandwich gen^t. Cousin Parries children, James, Ellen, Francis and Judith, and his wife (my niece and faithful cousin). Linen &c. in their house at St. Mary Magdalens in Barmondsey near London. My cousin Christopher Lasheforde. Cousin Francis Mannocke and her children. Mary Lasheford daughter of my uncle Lasheford (if she survive her husband) and her children. "And I doe geve unto my reverend and deere frendes the zealous preachers of Gods Worde and his faithefull mynisters (vizt) to Mr. Thomas Willson my reverend teacher & instructer sixe Angells to my deere frend Mr. Anthony ffeilde of Chittenden sixe Angells To Mr. Willm̄ Syms my faithefull frend fower Angells To my deere and loving brother Stebbinge and my moste approoved faithefull frend sixe Angells To Mr Beniamyn Solley my oulde schoole fellowe and Christian frend Thirtie shillings To Mr Jacob Twentye shillinges. To Mr Snape Twentye shillinges To Mr Dampard Twentie shillinges To Mr Stoughton Twentie shillinges To Mr Egerton Twentie shillinges To Mr Brownesmithe Twentye shillings moste humblie thanckinge them for their faithefull endevor and for their earnest labour and paines for the instructyon of my conscience and the consciences of many men in the knowledge of Gods truthe and relligion. And their legacies I bestowe uppon them as a testimonie of my love and thanckfullnes towerdes them." Sundry servants &c. To Mr James Pallmer the son of Sir Thomas Pallmer, knight, my vyoll which I have often promised him. My loving friend Mr. Thomas Gellibrand of Sandwich. Cousin Rowland Engeham and cousin William Engeham.

" And whereas I haue in truste heretofore receaved of my aforesaid deere frend Mr Willm̄ Syms ffiftye powndes of lawfull money of Englande to the intente that I shoulde p^rchase therewith to the onely use of his two sonnes (vizt) Zacharye and Willm̄ Syms and of their heires landes or hereditamentes of the yearelie valewe at the tyme of the purchase thereof of Three poundes of lyke money and that untill suche purchase should be so made there shoolde be by me payd towerdes the education or mayntenñce of the said Zacharie and Willm̄ Syms the sonnes Three poundes of lawefull money of Englande yearelie at the ffeastes of the natyuitie of St^e John Baptiste and of the nativitye of oure Lord Christe by even porc̃ons: nowe therefore to thintent that I maie faithefullie pforme the said truste I doe geve" &c. (Then follows a lengthy provision for raising three pounds a year for them.) Nephew John St. Nicholas, second son of brother Thomas. Cousin Edward Upcher of Soham in Cambridgeshire. Brother Thomas and said nephew John St. Nicholas to be executors. Stafford, 66.

MARGARET FULALOVE of London, widow, 25 September 1629, proved 14 October 1629. *Imprimis* I do give and bequeath unto my cosen Zacherie Simes, whom I do make and ordain sole executor of this my last will and testament, the sum of forty shillings and to my cosen his wife my Phillip and Cheany gown and best stuff petticoat, my stuff kertle and waistcoat, all my wearing linen and twenty shillings to make her a ring. To my said cosen Simes' three children I do give and bequeath as followeth; unto William Simes three shillings of lawful money of England, unto Sarah Simes also forty shillings of like money and to Mary Simes twenty shillings of like money. I do also give and bequeath unto the said Sara Simes (a lot of bedding and household stuff, among others) two sallet dishes, one maudlin cup, a brass scummer and a brass warming pan. If any surplusage be remaining I give to my brethren Thomas and John Hickman, to each twenty shillings and twenty shillings to each of my own sisters and forty shillings to be distributed amongst my said own sisters children.   To Margaret Hayes ten shillings.   To my cousin Grantham twenty shillings and to his wife twenty shillings.   To Hulda Crooke twenty shillings.   To Sara Grantham twenty shillings.   To Caleb Grantham twenty shillings.   To my cousin Attaloone, an angel and to his wife forty shillings and a Kersey cubbord cloth.   Forty shillings to her daughter.   To my cousin Godkin's wife twenty shillings and twenty shillings to Mr. William Simes.   A silver spoon for Mary Simmes and tipt pot for my cousin Zachary.

Wit: William Symmes, Mary Symmes, her mark, Elner Godkin.

Archd. of London, B. 7 L. 62.

Against this is entered, on margin, Parish of St. Michael Bassingshawe. Married at St. Saviours Southwark, 13 August 1622, Zachery Simmes and Sara Baker.

[Zacharie Simes, named by the testator as a cousin or nephew, and as executor of her will, was evidently the Rev. Zechariah Syms or Symmes, who was the minister of Charlestown, Mass., from Dec. 22, 1634 till his death Feb. 4, 1670–1.   He was the son of Rev. William Symmes, whose father, William Symmes, was a firm protestant in the reign of Queen Mary.

Rev. Zechariah Symmes was born in Canterbury, Kent, April 5, 1599, was educated at Emmanuel College, Cambridge University, and received his A.B. in 1620.   In 1621 he was chosen lecturer at St. Antholin's in London.   About 1625 he removed to Dunstable, Beds., where he was rector for eight years.   He came to New England in the Griffin, which arrived Sept. 18, 1634.   He had a brother William who was living, probably in England, in 1664, as he names him in his will of that date.

The William Syms who had sons Zacharye and William, according to the preceding will of Timothy St. Nicholas, 1606; as well as the Mr. William Simes named by the above Margaret Fulalove, was, I presume, the father of our New England minister.   See The Symmes Memorial, by Rev. John A. Vinton, Boston, 1873.—EDITOR.]

LUDLOW (REGISTER, vol. 42, pp. 181–184; *ante*, pp. 274–277):

[On page 183 of Vol. 42 of the REGISTER (*ante*, p. 277), in the English Ludlow genealogy published by you, with special reference to Roger Ludlow of Massachusetts and Connecticut, I find the following foot-note appended to the name of *Gabriel* [Ludlow][8], of Frome, bapt. at Warminster, 27 Aug. 1634 :—
" He is said to have been the ancestor of the New York Ludlows.—G. D. SCULL."

I do not know whether the exact connection of the New York Ludlows with the English genealogy can be a matter of interest to any of your readers.   If so, here it is :—

The New York Ludlows, together with the Philadelphia branch of the family, to which belonged the Rev. John Ludlow, D.D., Provost of the University of Pennsylvania from 1834 to 1852, and his sons John Livingston Ludlow, M.D., and Judge James Ryley Ludlow, are descended from Gabriel Ludlow, who landed in New York, in his 32d year, on Nov. 24, 1694, and on April 5, 1697, was married in New York to Sarah, a daughter of the Rev. Joseph Hanmer, D.D.

In a memorandum-book belonging to Gabriel Ludlow, the entries in which are in his handwriting, which book is in the possession of Alfred Ludlow Carroll, M.D., of New York, appears the following note :—

" Gabriel Ludlow, son of Gabriel Ludlow, was born Nov[r]. the 2[d], 1663, which was on Monday night at 12 o'clock, at Castle Cary."

The next note in the memorandum-book chronicles the birth of a brother, M. Ludlow, at " ffroom " [Frome], on Dec. 2, 1666.

A letter written early in 1883 to the Vicar of Castle Cary, enquiring whether any record survived of the baptism in his parish of Gabriel Ludlow, son of Gabriel, in 1663, brought the satisfactory response that the record does survive, and the following certified copy of it:

"Copy of the baptismal certificate of Gabriel Ludlow.
'Christenings in the year 1663.
December.
The first day of this moneth Gabriell the sonne of Gabriell Ludlow of froome and of Martha his wife was Christened.'

I hereby certify that the above is a true copy of an entry in the Register of Baptisms for the Parish of Castle Cary in the County of Somerset.

REVENUE   As witness my hand this 10th day of March, 1883.
STAMP, 1D.   A. W. GRAFTON, Vicar."

THOMAS W. LUDLOW, *Cottage Lawn, Yonkers, N. Y.*
—EDITOR].

FRANCIS SCROGGES of Patmar hall in the parish of Aldebury, Herts, gentleman, 3 June 1585, proved 4 November 1585. To my wife Dionise (certain grain &c) and my whole team of horses being in number five, mostly in the keeping of John Anthony my servant and esteemed at the value of sixteen pounds (and other property). To my son Henry one hundred pounds, to my son Thomas twenty pounds, to my son William forty pounds, all within two years next after my desease. To my son Francis one hundred pounds, to be paid him at his full age of two and twenty years. To my daughter Susan twenty pounds within one quarter of a year next after my decease. To my daughters Grace and Lettece Scrogges one hundred pounds apiece at one and twenty or days of marriage. I give to my son John Scrogges all that my manor called Patmar hall and all my other lands &c to hold for three years after my decease upon condition that he shall stand bound unto Thomas Meade of Bardene, Essex, yeoman, and unto William Deane my son in law in the sum of five hundred pounds to pay the legacies I have given to his brothers and sisters, and then he shall hold the manor and lands absolutely and without condition. Provision made if he refuses &c. Henry the second son, Thomas the third son, then William, then Francis the fifth son, then the daughters, Alice, Elizabeth, Susan, Jane, Grace and Lettece. To my sister Katherine Surrye forty shillings and to Raff Surrye her son four pounds. Dionise my wife shall have her abode and dwelling in the three chambers next the kitchen in the said manor house, that is to say, over the larder there. Certain tenements &c. at Watton at Stone, Great Munden and Little Munden made over to the use of said wife, she to release to my son John all her right of dower in my manor, &c. Son John to be executor.   Brudenell, 48.

THOMAS SCROGGES of Trymley St Mary, Suffolk, 28 May 1589, proved 11 June 1589. To be buried in the church of Trimley St. Mary. My servants Jane Lambe, Elizabeth Fowles, Ann Battle and William Batle. Barnaby Gowldinge. Thomas Lambe gen^t. Lawrence Hudson of Trimley St Mary. Thomas Sagar my godchild. I am to pay to the widow Shemynge's sister in Hertfordshire and to Philip Newman and to one of Thomas Newman's children (for parcel of the purchase of Melton mill) &c. Bennett Newman my tenant. I give my lands, tenements &c. in Shotley to my brothers William and Henry and my sisters Elizabeth Anton and Susan Paye and their heirs forever. My brothers William and Henry Scrogges to be executors and William Smith *als* Randes of Walton and John Talbott overseers. If the said Bennett Newman shall think good to take my mill and lands in Melton I give him towards the purchase the seven pounds ten shillings which he shall owe me at Michaelmas next.
                                                            Leicester, 59.

JOHN SCROGGES of Patmer Hall in the parish of Alberry in the Co. of Hartford gen*, 13 August 1592, proved 14 May 1593. To be buried in the parish church of Albery. To Mary Scrogges my loving wife all my goods, debts, ready money and all such plate as she brought with her &c. To my cousin Edward Newporte one ounce of gold for a remembrance. To my three brothers, Henry, William and Francis Scrogges, to each of them one ounce of gold for a remembrance. To my three sisters, Alice Leake, Elizabeth Anton and Susan Paye, forty shillings apiece for a remembrance. To my three sisters, Jane Deane, Grace Crabbe and Lettice Scrogges, to each of them half an ounce of gold, to be paid and delivered by my executor, also for a remembrance. To my mother in law Dyonice Burton ten pounds, to buy her a mourning gown and a ring for a remembrance. To my brother in law Mr. Randolfe Symmes one ounce of gold for a remembrance and unto my sister in law Anne Symmes, the wife of the said Randolfe, forty shillings likewise for a remembrance. My servants. The parish of Albury. To my loving cousin Edward Turnor Esq. an ounce of gold for a remembrance. ˙ To my niece Dorothy Symmes, the daughter of my brother Symes, one ounce of gold. To my mother in law Dennice Scrogges forty shillings for a remembrance.

Now concerning the custody and bringing up of my son Edward Scrogges, of whose education and good nurture, both of body and mind, I have especial care and regard, and of whose inheritance, concerning the well ordering thereof, I have also great respect, I commit unto my most kind and loving mother in law Dyonice Burton, to whom I have taken order that the wardship of my son shall be assigned and made over, either mediately or immediately from Mr Sergeant Spencer who hath the grant thereof &c. &c. she to bring up my said son in good letters and nurture. My wife to be executor and my cousin Edward Turner overseer. Philip Godwynne one of the witnesses.

Proved by Mrs Mary Scrogges.   Nevell, 36.

SIR THOMAS STANLEY, knight, 26 February 1605, proved 13 May 1607. To be buried in the parish church of Albury, near my pew door, in the county of Hertford. The poor of that parish. I do give and bequeath all my lands in Sussex or elsewhere, as also my house without Temple Bar near London, to my brother Richard Stanley and his heirs forever, paying out of the said lands and house to my wife one hundred marks yearly during her life. To Dyonis Sims, my wife's kinswoman, forty pounds, within forty days after her marriage. To my wife's son Edward Scroogs, a black cloak and one to his uncle Henry Scroogs. To my cousin Joane, wife of Richard Scarlett of London, a gown of cloth. To my cousin Jone Gambell of London a gown of cloth. My servants. Six poor men that shall carry me to the church. My wife Mary to be full executrix. One little table of "currall" that standeth at Lee House in Sussex, which is my wife's mother's, Mistress Burton, my will and mind is that the same table shall be delivered to her again. To my cousin Edward Stanley in the Co. of Cumberland a gray gelding called Roger.   Hudleston, 40.

EDWARD SCROGGES of Aldbury, Herts., Esq. 2 April 1622, proved 9 October 1622. My body to be buried amongst my ancestors in Aldbury church. I do will and appoint that my loving wife Penelope (if it please God of his goodness and mercy to restore her to her health and perfect senses again and that she shall and do live and continue unmarried in my

house called Patmer Hall, of perfect sense and understanding fit and able
to govern, maintain and bring up my children in learning and virtue) for
and towards the maintenance and the bringing up of my said children shall
have the use and occupation of all my movable goods &c. within my house
of Patmer Hall and so much of my lands, tenements and rents (except
Patmer Hall woods and Shaw woods) as are now in my hands and possession by lease or otherwise till John Scrogges, mine eldest son, shall accomplish his full age of one and twenty years or be married. My two
younger sons Edward and Francis Scrogges. To my daughters Penelope
Scrogges, Smythie Scrogges, Emlyn Scrogges, Susan Scrogges and Ann
Scrogges two hundred pounds apiece. Reference to jointures settled on
mother, Dame Mary Stanley, and wife Penelope Scrogges. Provisions for
descent of property. The residue to John Smythe Esq. my father in law
and my loving mother his wife, Dame Mary Stanley, whom I do make,
ordain and constitute my executors &c.   Savile, 91.

ANNE SCROGGS of Earles Colne, Essex, maiden, 28 August 1641, proved
18 September 1641. I the daughter of Edward Scroggs late of Aldbury,
Herts., Esq. To my brother John Scroggs Esq. fifty pounds, he to pay
unto my brother William Harlakenden, executor, my whole portion of six
hundred pounds, together with all the interest thereof due unto me upon
accompt to the day of my death. My sister Goad's legacy shall be paid by my
executor and my brother Edward's legacy likewise, vizt, one hundred pounds
to my sister Goad and to my brother Edward Scroggs filty pounds. Small
bequests to Sister Scroggs, to nieces Margaret Scrogges and Susanna Goade,
to Christopher Purple my nephew and Mary Purple my niece and old Mr.
Purple their grandfather and to his wife, to Richard Harlakenden of Colne
Prior Esq. and his wife, and to Jane Clench and to my aunt Hawkesbee,
widow, and her daughter Ludgater. And to my cousin Sara Simmes (who
is now in New England) five pounds. To Mr. Daniel Rogers of Wethersfield five pounds. To Mr. Till, preacher of the Word, twenty shillings
and to my brother Sutton twenty shillings. To Mr. Josselin minister of
Earles Colne forty shillings and to my cousin Dracott five pounds. Jacob
Garret of Colne Wake, Avery Saunders of Earles Colne and John Viall
of Wethersfield. To Samuel Burton my godson forty shillings and to Mrs.
Cosen of Earles Colne twenty shillings. To my sister Smith the wife of
William Harlakenden the full sum of three hundred pounds and all such
money and other goods as are now in her custody and keeping. And if
any of those parties to whom any legacies are formerly given do depart this
life before they be due and payable then the said legacies shall remain and
be due to my sister Smith Harlakenden; and I make and ordain Mr. Stephen
Marshall, preacher of God's word at Finchingfield, and my brother in law
Mr. William Harlakenden of Earles Colne, gentleman, executors &c.
                                                        Evelyn, 115.

[The cousin Sara Simmes, described as "now in New England," was, I suppose, the "Mrs. Sarah Symmes" who had a grant of land in Cambridge, 1639,
and died there 10 June 1653 (Savage). She was undoubtedly one of the daughters
of the Randolph Symmes referred to in the preceding wills. Her relationship
with these parties must have been, I think, through the Burtons and not
through the Scrogges line. The match of Sir Thomas Stanley with the widow
Scroggs is shown in the Stanley pedigree, printed in the Visitation of Cumberland for 1615 (Harleian Society's Publications.) A very imperfect pedigree of
Scrogges may be found in the Visitation of Hertfordshire, also published by
the Harleian Society. It may prove an interesting piece of genealogical work to

attempt to enlarge and amend that pedigree with the help of the notes I have here given.

The reference to " Randall Symmes" and his wife in the following will would seem to make that worthy of preservation in connection with the foregoing wills.   HENRY F. WATERS.

Anne Scroggs, the daughter of Edward, whose will precedes hers, had a sister Smith or Smithee who married William Harlakenden, son of Thomas and Dorothy (Cheney) Harlakenden. William, who was executor of his sister in law's will, died 18 March 1674. His wife Smithee was buried 28 June 1651, as we find by the diary of Ralph Josselin, who preached her funeral sermon, published in 1652 :

" 26 June 1651. Mrs Harlakenden died; ye 28, Mrs Smitha Har. [buried, 4 Justices wch had each bur'd a wife carried her to ye grave, 2 Thess. iv. 13, 18."

This Ralph Josselin is of the same family as John, the author of Two Voyages to New England and New England's Rarities (whose pedigree is printed in the REGISTER, Vol. xl., p. 290, and in Josselyn's Voyages, ed. of 1865), and of Henry who was identified with Capt. John Mason in New England. He is the beneficiary mentioned for the sum of forty shillings. In his dairy is also to be found " Roger Har. ob. in New England 1637, or thereabts." This refers to Roger Harlakenden, who came in the *Defence*, 1635, with wife Elizabeth, who at his death married Herbert Pelham. For will of Roger Harlakenden see REGISTER, ii., p. 181. In the *Defence* also came Rev. Thomas Shepard, of Cambridge, who had been at Earles Colne; as is evidenced by the ghost story in which he is mentioned, in Richard Baxter's " Certainty of the world of Spirits fully evinced."

Richard Harlakenden, mentioned in the will, was brother of Roger of New England; he married for a second wife Mary, daughter of Sir Edward Denny.

The sister of Roger and Richard, Mabel, married Gov. John Haynes of Connecticut. As suggested by Mr. Waters, we find Sarah Simes of Cambridge died 10 June, 1653. Her will, dated 4 April, 1653, mentions "brother John Stedman" and " brother William French" (born in Halsted, Essex County, Eng.), but no relative of the name of Simes. French was one of those who came in the *Defence*, and is put down as servant to Harlakenden, probably to avoid detection. The age of Sarah Simes, who was also of the party, was given as thirty.

(See Topographer and Genealogist, Vol. i, pp. 228–258, edited by John Gough Nichols F. S. A., for a full pedigree of Harlakenden families; also REGISTER, Vol. xv., pp. 327–329).   W. K. WATKINS.]

THOMAS HEWETT, citizen and clothmaker of London, 10 October 1575, proved 19 June 1576. My body is to be buried in the parish church of St. Clement where I am a parishioner. The poor of the parish of Wales in the Co. of York where I was born. To my worshipful and loving friends and cousins Mr. Edward Osborne and Anne his wife, to either of them a ring of gold, price three pounds. To my godson Hewett Osborne five pounds. My cousin William Hewett, clothworker, and my cousin his wife. My cousin Nicholas Hewett, clothworker and my cousin his wife. To my cousin Randall Symes a ring of gold, price forty shillings, and to his wife a ring of gold, price twenty shillings. To my cousin Richard Symes of Welforde a yard and half of pewke, price twelve shillings a yard. My son in law John Hawkes, draper. Richard Foster, clothworker. My apprentices William Dawkes, Robert Bate, Henry Parker and Thomas White. My cousin George Monnox, gen^t, and his wife. Mr. Anthony Bridges of Ham and his wife and Thomas Bridges my godson. My cousin Sturdivaunt, swordbearer of London. Mr. Lewsey, gen^t. To my cousin Dummer a ring, price thirty shillings. My cousin Sandforde. Mr. Megges, draper. My son in law Richard Staper and his wife. My sons Henry and William Hewett. Henry Clyderowe. My daughter Bridget Hewett. Mr. Richard Raynolde, draper. Robert Dove, merchant taylor. Thomas Hewett, wiredrawer. Nicholas Hewett, scrivener. The house I now live in, with shop, &c. I give to my well beloved wife Elizabeth, to have and hold during her natural life, remainder to Henry Hewett my son and heir apparent. To my said wife Elizabeth my manor or grange of Sherox in the county of Nottingham or York or elsewhere, now in the tenure or occupation of John Raines and others, to hold for her life, remainder to my son Henry &c. Others mentioned, among whom, cousin John Wyghte's wife, Jasper Wraye and Mrs Wraye of Edmundton and Thomas Wraye her son, John Browne and his wife &c. My daughter Staper's four children now living. Mr. William Saye of Yesnam and my cousin Robert Saye his eldest son. Mr. Edmund Burton. My very friend Mr. Boswell of the Court of Wards. To my son William one hundred pounds over and besides his portion. I make and ordain my dear and well beloved friend and cousin Mr. Edward Osborne, alderman, and Henry Hewett my son my executors, and give to the said Mr. Edward Osborne, for his painstaking, twenty pounds. And I make and ordain my loving friends William Dummer and John Browne my overseers to see this my last will and testament in all points performed, as my special trust is in them. And I give to each of them six pounds thirteen shillings four pence.   Carew, 14.

[Tne Edward Osborne above referred to was the well-known Lord Mayor of London, and ancestor of the Duke of Leeds, about whom the romantic story is told of his leaping into the Thames from London Bridge to save from drowning the only daughter of Sir William Hewett, then Lord Mayor, to whom young Osborne was at that time apprenticed. The damsel afterwards became the wife of her preserver with the full consent of her father, who is, reported to have refused her hand to certain of the nobility and others, and to have bestowed it, together with a great dower, upon his former apprentice with the declaration that "Osborne saved her life and Osborne shall have her." Richard Staper who married the daughter of Thomas Hewett, was probably the father of the Hewyt Staper who married Elizabeth, daughter of Roger Owfellde.
                                                          HENRY F. WATERS.]

ANN BRUMPSTEAD of St. Martin in the Fields, Middlesex, widow, 5 June 1658, proved 30 September 1658. To be buried in St. Martin's near late husband John Brumpstead deceased. To my two daughters Mary Breedon, wife of John Breedon, and Rose Brumpstead five pounds apiece, to buy them mourning, and all my household goods in the Kings Head except my plate and the standards belonging to the house. To my daughter Rose a silver tankard of the value of five pounds and six silver spoons. To my daughter Mary Breedon six silver spoons. To my son in law Master John Breedon, her husband, five pounds to buy him mourning and the sum of ten pounds more. To my daughter in law Lucy Brumpstead ten pounds and also (for my grandchild Thomas Brumpstead) six silver spoons. To my cousin Thomas Pearson ten pounds. To my son Thomas Brumpstead my dwelling house known as the King's Head and all the residue of my goods and chattels &c.   Wootten, 524.

THOMAS BREEDON, 22 October 1682, proved 1 April 1689. Wife Mary to be sole executrix and to have all my outward estate &c., she to pay all my debts and to pay to my son John when he shall come to the age of twenty-four years two hundred pounds and the same to sons Zaccheus and Robert at twenty-four, and to my daughter Mary Aylemer and her three children twenty shillings apiece and to my grandson John Breedon twenty shillings.

In presence of Z. Sedgwicke, Thomas Jenings.

[The Probate Act Book shows that the testator was of Crowton in Northampton].   Ent. 48

ZACHEUS BREEDON of London, mariner, now bound to Carolina and Maryland, 21 September 1685, proved 1 September 1686. I give and bequeath unto my loving cousin Lawrence Stephenson, citizen and ironmonger of London, twenty pounds, to buy him mourning, and twenty pounds more. The residue to my honored father Thomas Breedon of Southmorton, Oxon, gen^t. And I appoint my said cousin Lawrence Stevenson full and sole executor.   Lloyd, 114.

THOMAS BRUMPSTED of Midgham, Berks Esq. 26 February 1689, proved 20 October 1690. Two leases I hold from the Dean and Chapter of Westminster settled on my wife in part of her jointure. My brother Mr Charles Brumpsted and my friend Mr Edward Noell to sell the manor of Midgham and the lands which I lately purchased from Mr. Richard Garrett and all other my estate in Berks. After payment of my debts the residue to be equally divided between my daughter Lucy Brumpsted and my son Charles (both under twenty-one). If either die the share of him or her so dieing to go to the survivor and my son John. If both die then both shares to my son John. To the said John the messuage or inn called the King's Head, in the Strand, after the death of my wife Martha. (Other property, including the Greyhound Tavern in the Strand.) Brother and sister in law Sir John Friend and the Lady Anne his wife. Brother in law and sister Timothy Dodd and Elizabeth his wife. My brother in law Robert Breedon.   Dyke, 146.

JANE BREEDON of Great Chesham, Bucks, widow, 15 September 1628, proved 15 February 1632. To my two sons Zacheus and Benaia Breedon, ten shillings apiece. To Bethsheba Grover, my daughter, twenty pounds (and certain household stuff). Priscilla Grover, her daughter. To Hanna Wigge, my daughter, other twenty pounds &c. To Obadiah Tailer, my grandchild, twenty pounds if he shall live to have children &c. The poor of Great Chesham. The residue to my daughter Abigail Gladman. I make Elkana Gladman, my son in law, full and sole executor, and my well beloved kinsmen Humphrey Greeneway of Great Chesham, Glover, and Isaac Raveninge als Carter, of West Wickcombe, overseers. Russell, 12.

[The above seemed worth saving on account of the mention of a son Zacheus Breedon, thus suggesting a relationship with our Capt. Thomas Breedon of Boston.   H. F. W.]

ROBERT DALYBER of Selliettes in the parish of Stoke Abbot, Dorset, yeoman, 20 March 1632, proved 27 May 1633. To be buried in the churchyard of Stoke Abbot before the church porch, between the Thorn and the Church porch there, near the place where my father was buried. And my will and desire is that I may have a tomb set over me, and towards that charge I give thirteen shillings four pence. The poor and the church remembered. I give to my second son Tristran Daliber fifty pounds; to be paid in two years and ten pounds more of the money due upon bond by Edward Cotherington, gen^t, at Michaelmas 1640. To son Samuel fifty pounds and also twenty pounds (as above) in May 1635. To son Joseph fifty pounds and also ten pounds (as above) 1640. To my daughter Mary Dalyber fifty pounds. To my daughter Sara Daliber fifty pounds. To my youngest daughter Rebecca Daliber fifty pounds. My two sons in law Walter Burt and John Lesty. Josias Burt eldest son of Walter. The three sons of John Lesty, John, Edward and William. My wife. The residue to my eldest son Robert Daliber whom I make sole executor.
                                        Russell, 48.

GEORGE SALTER of Dedham, Essex, grazier, 7 September 1653, proved 18 July 1654. To my son Samuel Salter my house and lands in Rattlesden, Suffolk, he paying to my loving wife four pounds a year during her natural life, she paying the fine at his admittance. And my son Samuel shall pay unto my daughter Abigail in New England, if she be yet living or if she hath any children, ten pounds within two years after my decease, and to give to my daughter Hanna in New England, if she be yet living or if she have any children, ten pounds within four years after my wife's decease. If either of them die and leave no children her portion shall be given, half of it to my son Theophilus and half of it to my daughter surviving; and if both of them depart and leave no children I give it unto my son Samuel. To my son Thomas five pounds and to Theophilus five pounds. Five shillings each to my daughters Abigail and Hannah. The remainder to my wife whom I ordain to be my sole executrix.

Proved by the oath of Mary Salter the relict and executrix.

Alchin, 65.

[A Theophilus Salter, of Ipswich 1648, was on June 30, 1653, sentenced to pay £5, the witness and fees, for endeavoring to marry Mary Smith without her friends' consent, according to Felt.—W. K. WATKINS.]

EDWARD BULLOCKE of Queen's College, Oxford, Bachelor of Arts, 10 October 19th James, proved 2 November 1621. My body to be buried in the church of the parish of St. Peter's in the East, Oxford. To my aunt Mrs. Priscilla Bullocke one hundred pounds. To aunt Mrs. Sarah Knighte, wife of Thomas Knighte, of Worlingham Suffolk, parson, forty pounds. To my uncle Rowland Wilson, citizen and vintner of London, and to Mary his wife five pounds apiece to buy them rings. To my uncle Richard Newell of London, clothworker, and Jane his wife five pounds apiece to buy them rings. To the aforesaid Thomas Knighte ten pounds. To Michael Dover of London, scrivener, forty pounds, and I forgive him twenty pounds he oweth me &c. To William Tiffin of London, mercer, his three children, vizt Benjamin, Mary and Alice, five pounds apiece. To the children of the within specified Rowland Wilson, vizt, Rowland and John, Mary Elizabeth, Jane, Sarah and Mabel, five pounds apiece. To Sarah Tiffine's four children, John, Richard, Mary and Jane, twenty pounds apiece. To the poor of St. Pancras in Soper Lane, London, ten pounds and of St. Peter's the East in Oxford five pounds. Five pounds to be bestowed in books towards the Library of Queen's College, Oxford. To my loving friend Mr. Tompson, who was my tutor, forty shillings to buy him a ring. To the minister that shall preach at my funeral twenty shillings. The residue to my loving uncles Melchesidick Bullocke and William Tiffine, whom I make my sole executors &c., and I do make Rowland Wilson and Richard Newell supervisors.

Wit: Adam Airay, Avery Thompson, Thomas Midleton.   Dale, 96.

GEORGE BENSON. Will written and subscribed with my own hand at my house at Patchinge July seventh 1629, proved 30 April 1632. My wife (whom I make my executor) shall have one fourth part of the clear temporal estate which it shall please God to grant me at my decease, and the rest to be equally divided amongst my children, whom I hope she will be careful to bring up in the nurture and admonition of the Lord. To the poor of each of the two parishes committed to my charge I do give twenty shillings. To every of them that shall be my covenant servants at my decease

I do give five shillings.   Overseers of this my will I do appoint my trusty
friends and loving brethren Mr. Henry Carleton and Mr. Thomas Vicers.
And I do desire and hope my loving nephew Mr. Rowland Wilson will be
a friend unto my children as he hath been to me at all times.

Commission issued to Henry Carlton to administer the goods &c. during
the minorities of George Michael, Edward and Alice Benson, the children,
for the reason that he named no executor.   Audley, 40.

ROBERT WILSON citizen and draper of London, 2 January 1639, proved
18 January 1639.   My body to be buried in the parish church of St. Bennett
Sherhogg in Cheap Ward in London, if I shall die in London or no further
out of the said city than Stoke Newington, Midd.   Mention of Theophilus
Biddulye and Robert Birkenad, now copartners with me.   My goods &c.
to be divided into three equal parts, according to the ancient custom of the
city of London, one part for Catharine Wilson my well beloved wife, one
to and among all my now children &c. and the third I reserve for the
performance of my will, in legacies &c.   I give to my wife my lease and
interest of and in my now dwelling house in Cheap Side London and the
lease of my house in Stoke Newington &c.   Son Thomas (under twenty-
one) to have my lease &c. of two messuages &c. in Pater Noster Row, now
or late in the tenure &c. of ———— Row and Edward Johnson, he to pay a
certain annuity to my sister Margaret Verney.   If Thomas should die before
he reaches the said age then the lease to go to my son Richard (subject to
the same condition).   To my sister in law Anne Wilson, widow, late the
wife of Samuel Wilson my brother deceased, forty pounds, and six pounds
for mourning.   To her son Samuel Wilson, whom I have placed apprentice with Mr. Roland Wilson, fifty pounds &c., and forty shillings also for
mourning.   To every other of the six children of my said late brother
Samuel, vizt Anne, Roda, Sara, Symon, Rowland and Robert Wilson, fifty
pounds apiece (with provision for education &c. during their minorities).
I give seventeen pounds to be bestowed in mourning for the said six other
children.

Item, I give and bequeath unto my brother Richard Wilson the sum of
one hundred marks, to be paid him within one year next after my decease,
or sooner if his urgent occasions require the same and he make request
therefor to my executrix.   And, if he come not over from Virginia, if he send
sufficient authority for the same his legacy shall be sent unto him in such
commodities as he shall send for.   I forgive him also and acquit and discharge him from all such sums as he doth now owe me by bond, book or
any other obligation whatsoever.   And I give him my interest in the shop
in Soper Lane which I hold by lease from him.   I give to my godson
Robert Wilson, son of my said brother Richard, fifty pounds, to be paid at
the accomplishment of his age of one and twenty years.   I give to my
brother Richard's other son, Richard Wilson, fifty pounds (as before).   I
give to the first child of my said brother Richard which was born in Virginia, begotten of the body of Katherine, now or late his wife, twenty-five
pounds, to be paid at the accomplishment of his or her age of twenty-one.
To my sister Margaret Varney one annuity of twelve pounds, payable to
the messuages &c. in Pater Noster Row aforesaid, to hold during her
natural life, &c., and I forgive and remit unto her all the debts she
oweth me, by book or otherwise.   I give to John Varney, son of my sister
Varney, fifty pounds (at one and twenty) and to Katherine Varney, her
daughter, fifty pounds.   To my sister, for mourning, six pounds and to each

of her two children forty shillings apiece. To my brother in law Edward Lycoris and to Mary his wife, my sister, fifty pounds; and twelve pounds to them also for mourning. I forgive unto my brother in law Edward Browninge twenty pounds which he did borrow of me and twenty pounds more. I also give to my said brother in law Edward Browning and his wife, my sister, twelve pounds for mourning; and to such child of my said brother Browninge and his now wife as shall be living at my decease, twenty pounds. To Sarah Watson, my said sister's daughter by a former husband deceased, fifty pounds (at one and twenty) and my executrix to allow four pounds a year toward the better education and maintenance of the same Sara &c. Provision in case she be put to service and bound apprentice. To Mary Watson, sister of the said Sarah, twenty pounds &c. To Ann Smith, daughter unto my sister Anne Smith deceased, fifty pounds (at one and twenty). To my mother in law Mrs. Rudd ten pounds and also six pounds for mourning. To my sister in law Margaret Rudd four pounds for mourning. To my sister Anne Rudd ten pounds in money and also five pounds for mourning. To my brother in law William Williams and Elizabeth his wife ten pounds for mourning and also to the said Elizabeth five pounds. I forgive to my brother Thomas Rudd, my wife's own brother, the money he oweth me by book, for goods he had of me (about three score pounds) and I give him five pounds for mourning, and five pounds more as a legacy. Sundry bequests to friends. To my cousin John Awbrey the elder forty shillings. To cousin Mr. Gilbert Harrison, alderman, and to my loving kinswoman, his wife, four pounds apiece to make them rings. To my cousin Christopher Clarke four pounds to make him a ring. To my cousin Mary Morgan three pounds. To Magdalen Burnett widow, my wife's aunt, forty shillings. To Elizabeth Burton daughter of Elizabeth Burton, my wife's kinswoman dwelling with me, ten pounds. To my aunt Ferris and her daughter forty shillings apiece. One hundred pounds to the Company of Drapers. To sundry Hospitals and parishes &c. To my cousin Ledingham and his wife twelve pounds for mourning. To his son my godson thirty pounds. The residue to my wife Catharine whom I make sole executrix. I give my lands called Gallyons, lying in Eastham and Woolwich, which I purchased of the Lord Savage, to my son Robert Wilson, with remainder to sons Richard and Thomas and next to my two eldest daughters Anne and Katharine Wilson. A messuage &c. in Swan Alley near Coleman Street to my son Richard.   Coventry, 11.

[Hotten gives in his original lists, p. 105, under date of 6 July, 1635, in the Paul of London bound for Virginia, Katherine Wilson, aged 28 years, and two children, Robert and Richard Wilson, age 6 and 5 years respectively. On p. 94, under date 20 June, 1635, in the Philip for Virginia, was Richard Wilson. The age of this Richard is given as 19 years, which, however, may be an error, and the above the Wilson family of Virginia alluded to in the will of Robert Wilson.—W. K. WATKINS.]

RAPH (RANDOLPH) INGRAM citizen and iremonger of London, 14 June 1644, proved 19 December 1644. Wife Mary. My four sons, Rowland, John, Raph and George Ingram (all under one and twenty years of age). To my mother, Mary Ingram, one hundred and fifty pounds. My brother William Ingram and his wife. My brother Robert Ingram and his wife and six children, viz' Mary, Anne, Richard, Sarah and one other whose name I do not remember. My brother in law William Harrison. My brother Thomas Ingram. My brother Arthur Ingram. The children of my brother and sister Harrison, viz' Mary and Alice. Mr. Rowland Wil-

son the elder and his wife and Mr. Rowland Wilson the younger and his
wife. My cousin Mary Crispe the wife of doctor Crispe deceased. Mr.
Henry St. John and his wife. Mr. John Wood and his wife. Others
named. Wife Mary to be executrix and Mr. Rowland Wilson the elder,
Rowland Wilson the younger, Mr. Henry St. John and my brother Robert
Ingram to be overseers. To old Mrs. Carleton at Rotterdam ten pounds
and to Mr. Edmand White of Rotterdam ten pounds. To Mary Soames
now dwelling in Duke's Place five pounds. And my desire is, in regard
of these troblesome times, to be privately buried in a decent manner, and
no mourners to be thereat but my own family.

Commission issued to Rowland Wilson Senr and Rowland Wilson jun
executors of the will of Mary Ingram who had departed this life before
taking upon herself the burden of executorship.   Rivers, 16.

MARY INGRAM widow, 10 October 1644, proved 19 December 1644.
My three sisters, Katherine, Jane and Dorothy. My mother in law Mary
Ingram. My brother Robert and his wife and their children. My brother
William Ingram and his wife. My brother Harrison and his wife and their
two daughters. Thomas and Arthur Ingram. My loving kinsman Rowland
Wilson the elder and Rowland Wilson the younger to be full and sole
executors &c. Mrs. Mary Crispe the elder. Mrs. Mary Soame. Mrs.
Boylston. All the children of Mary Crispe. Others. For mourning I
leave to my uncle and cousin Wilson to take care of and order and to see
me decently interred.   Rivers, 16.

KATHERINE HIGHLORD of London widow, 22 May 1648, proved 20 July
1648. My body to be buried in a strong wainscot coffin within the parish
church of Bennet Sherrug, London, as near unto the place there where my
first husband, Robert Wilson, lyeth buried as conveniently may be. It
shall be buried by night, within three days after my decease, without any
vain glory or pomp, and no more than friends and near acquaintance to be
invited to my burial. Bequests to the poor and to sundry prisons. The
poor where I sometimes lived in Mark Lane. To my dear mother Mrs.
Anne Rudd twenty pounds for a ring and ten pounds for mourning. To
my sister Margaret Rudd, for a ring and mourning, one hundred pounds.
To my sister Martin twenty pounds for a ring and ten pounds for mourning.
To my sister Williams twenty pounds and ten pounds for mourning. To
my sister Gower ten pounds for mourning. To my brothers in law M^r
Gower, Mr. Martin and Mr. Williams six pounds apiece for mourning cloaks.
To my brother Thomas Rudd one hundred pounds and ten pounds for
mourning and to my sister, his wife, five pounds for mourning and ten
pounds for a ring. To William and Anne Williams, my sister's children,
twenty pounds apiece to be paid at the accomplishment of their several ages
of one and twenty years, and to Katherine and Margaret Williams my
cousins (at one and twenty) fifty pounds apiece. To Robert Birkinhead,
my sister's son, fifty pounds at one and twenty. To Theophilus Birkenhead and Susan Birkenhead twenty pounds (at one and twenty). To
Thomas Rudd son of my brother Thomas one hundred pounds at twenty
one. To Anne Rudd, his daughter, twenty pounds at one and twenty. To
my aunt Mainwareing and my aunt Ferris ten pounds apiece. To my cousin
Samuel Wilson for mourning ten pounds. To my sister in law Anne Wilson ten pounds. To my cousin Sara Fowke twenty pounds. To my cousins
Robert Wilson and Rowland Wilson fifty pounds apiece at one and twenty.
To John Warney, Katherine Warney, Sarah Watson, Mary Watson, my

cousins, and to the son of my cousin Anne Wilson deceased twenty pounds apiece at one and twenty. To Robert Wilson and Richard Wilson, my cousins now in Virginia fifty pounds apiece at one and twenty. To my sister Greene and my sister Browning twenty pounds apiece to make them rings and for mourning. My cousin Sarah Parham. Mr. Taylor in Coleman St. minister. My cousin Anne Smith. My daughter Katherine Austin and her now husband. My daughter Mary Wilson (under seventeen years of age). My daughter Martha Wilson (under sixteen). My son Robert Wilson. My grandchild Thomas Awsten. My cousins Margaret, Katherine and Edith Rudd. Elizabeth, John, Robert and Richard Rudd. My cousin Thomas Rudd, son of my Uncle Thomas. Certain messuages &c., the manor of Keythorpe in the County of Leicester which I purchased of Francis Wayte Gen^t the one half I give to my son Richard Wilson and the other half to Thomas, my son Robert to have it all in his custody until both my sons accomplish the age of one and twenty years. My said son Robert to be full and sole executor and my son in law Thomas Awsten and my brother Thomas Rudd overseers. Essex, 116.

ROWLAND WILSON the younger of London Esq., one of the sheriffs of the City of London, 16 February 1649. First I do request my dear and loving wife that she accept of three thousand five hundred pounds (being the portion I had with her) and all my jewells, plate and household stuff (besides her jointure which I do hereby confirm) in lieu and satisfaction of her customary part appertaining to her by the custom of London out of my personal estate, which if she will accept of then I do will my father shall bear the funeral charges for my burial and satisfy and pay all my debts out of the residue of my estate hereafter in this will bequeathed to him. To my brother in law Samuel Wilson and his wife one hundred pounds apiece. To my brother John Carleton and his wife one hundred pounds apiece and to Bigley Carleton one hundred pounds and to Samuel Carleton my best saddle horse. To my sister Mary Crispe three hundred pounds. To William Hirdson and his wife fifty pounds apiece. To Anne Coxe and her daughter fifty pounds in lieu of what I owe them. To Joanne Hasell ten pounds. To Mrs Ingram, my cousin Raphe Ingram's mother, fifty pounds. To Mr. George Cokaine and his wife, now being with me, fifty pounds apiece. Certain bequests to the poor &c. To my brother White, for the use of his three eldest children, three hundred pounds. To my cousin George Wilson ten pounds. Others. The rest to my father Rowland Wilson Esq. My wife Mary to be sole executrix and Mr Thomas Smith the accomptant overseer.

Commission 2 April 1650 to Rowland Wilson the father to administer (with the will annexed) Mary Wilson the relict and executrix having renounced. Pembroke, 55.

JOHN CARTER of London, gentleman, 25 July 1649, proved 4 October 1650. Brother William Carter and his wife and their son William Carter. My brother in law Gabriel Miller and his son William Miller. William's mother, my sister, Anne Miller. Her two children Anne and Matthew Miller. My brother in law Richard Aspelin and my sister Aspelin, his wife and her two daughters. My brother in law Thomas Sminell and his wife, my sister, Elizabeth Sminell. My sister in law Edith Carter, late wife of my brother Nicholas Carter, and her daughter Barbara Carter. My brother in law Thomas Colpott and his sons John Colpott and Thomas Colpott. The

parish of Eaton in Bedfordshire where I was born. My cousin Francis
Wilton of that parish. My cousin Anne Wilson. Mrs. Wilkinson whose
son lives with my said cousin Wilson. My cousin Samuel Wilson's wife.
My cousin Thomas Fowke's wife. My cousin Symon Wilson. My cousins
Rowland Wilson and Robert Wilson. I make said cousins Anne Wilson,
Samuel Wilson and Thomas Fowke executors &c.

Then follows a letter ———·— For my couzin Anne Wilson at the Naggs-
head Tavern near Blackwell Hall, and for my cozen Samuel Wilson merchant in Bishopsgate Street near Gressum College and to my cozen Thomas
Fooke grocer near Lawrence Church &c. Reference made to his departure
from England. My cozen William Miller I hear is now come for Ireland.

Pembroke, 165.

ROWLAND WILSON of London, Esq. and citizen and vintner of London,
5 February 1651 proved 1 June 1654. My body to be buried in the parish
church of St. Martin Outwich, where I now dwell. My wife Mary shall
hold for life my house and site of the late Priory of Merton alias Marten &c.
in Surrey which I purchased of Sir Francis Clarke, knight, on or about 19
June 1624, and lands purchased of William Carpenter 16 August 1635 and
3 January 1628. After her decease I give said premises in trust to Samuel
Wilson merchant and Thomas Boulton cooper (my friends) to sell the same
and dispose of the proceeds according to my will. To Ellis Crispe son of
my daughter Mary Rowe my tenements in Wimbledon, Barnes, Mortlake,
and Wandsworth Surrey &c. chargeable with annuities unto his brethren
and sisters, Tobias, Samuel, Edward, Rowland and Hester Crispe. I give
my messuage or dwelling house &c. in St. Martyn Outwich unto my grandchild, Ellis Crispe, and the two tenements thereunto adjoining unto my
grandchild Tobias Crispe. I give to my two grandchildren Edmond
White and Rowland White, sons of my late daughter Elizabeth White, my
copyhold lands at Tottenham High Cross in Middlesex. My lands at Bowe
and Bromly in Middlesex I give to my daughter Mary Rowe, now wife of
Col. Owen Rowe, for life and after her decease to my grandchildren Edward
Crispe and Rowland Crispe. To my grandchild Samuel Crispe the Tavern
called the Kings Arms over against Iremonger Lane's End in St. Lawrence
in the Old Jewry, London, and the two tenements adjoining, in Basishaw
Street in the parish of St. Michael Basishaw. Other lands and houses
bequeathed. A yearly annuity to William Heardson and Anne his wife.
The Worshipful Company of Vintners whereof I am a member. My
lands, tenements and hereditaments in Greegarth in the parish of Kendall
in Westmoreland to my grandchild Ellis Crispe, subject to a trust. Refer-
ence to the sons of said daughter Mary Rowe by her late husband Doctor
Tobias Crispe. Rowland, Ellis and Mary Carleton, children of Mary
Carleton, daughter of my said daughter Mary Rowe. My brother in law
Christopher Sands, late husband of my sister Rebecka and her children.
My cousin George Wilson. My godson Rowland Ingram. My sister in
law Jane Newell. My godson Benjamin son of my brother in law William
Tiffen. All my other lands &c. to the said Samuel Wilson and Thomas
Boylston (in trust). To the wife of the said Samuel Wilson five pounds
for a ring and to my cousin Thomas Boylston's wife five pounds for a
ring.

In a codicil dated 12 April 1654 he appointed his wife Mary Wilson and
grandson Samuel Crispe executors instead of Samuel Wilson and Thomas
Boylston. Andrew Middleton and George Thimbleby to be overseers.
Another codicil was added 26 April 1654.   Alchin, 41.

The same will was also registered the next year (1655) in Book Aylett, 321, where also appears record of a sentence for confirmation of the said will in a case promoted by Mary Wilson the relict and Samuel Crispe the grandchild, executors of the said Will and Testament, against Edmund White the younger, Elizabeth Cox otherwise White, and Mary Davy, otherwise White, grandchildren also of the deceased.   Aylett, 321. Dated 25 May 1655.

JANE NEWELL of Merton Abbey, Surrey, widow, 28 December 1657, proved 26 February 1657. To be buried with decency and good order, without any pompe or vain show. To my kinsman Richard Newell the threescore pounds which I have settled in the hands of my cousin Thomas Boylston in trust, to be paid to him when he sets up his trade of vintner, as by writing dated the eight and twentieth day of November last past. If he die before this sum is due him I give twenty pounds thereof to his father Thomas Newell, ten pounds to my cousin Josias Solmes, ten pounds to Jane the daughter of Robert Newell. Gifts to Richard Newell, to cousin Solmes' children, to cousin Samuel Crispe, the writer of the will, to Mary Bodwell, to Mr. John Dawes, minister, and to Elizabeth Maior. Forty shillings to my sister Wilson to bestow on the poor. The residue to my loving cousin Henry Middleton and to Alice his wife, and I do appoint my said cousin Henry Middleton to be my sole executor, and I desire my cousin Thomas Boylston and my cousin Samuel Crispe to be overseers, and I give to each of them twenty shillings.

Wit: Tobias Crispe, Samuel Crispe.   Wootton, 80.

MARY WILSON, in the Co. of Surrey, widow, 8 September 1659, proved 3 October 1662. My body to be buried in Martin's Outwich Church, London, near my late deceased husband. To my daughter Mary Rowe one hundred and fifty pounds. To my son Col. Owen Rowe fifty pounds. To all my grandchildren living at my decease fifty pounds apiece, vizt Ellis, Tobias, Samuel, Edward and Rowland Crispe, Mary Carleton, Hester Brett, Edmond White, Elizabeth Cox and Mary Dauye. To my son Col. Rowe's three daughters, Susanna, Sarah and Hannah, two pounds apiece. To Rowland and Mary Carleton, children of my grandchild Mary Carleton, twenty pounds apiece. To Edward Brett one hundred pounds and Mary Brett ten pounds, the two children of my grandchild Hester Brett. To Samuel Wilson, my kinsman, ten pounds and to his wife five pounds. To my cousin Thomas Boylston ten pounds, and to his wife five pounds, and to his daughter Elizabeth five pounds. To Mary, Josiah and Sarah Solme, three of the children of my cousin Edward Solme. To my cousin Alice Midleton fifty pounds. To Andrew Midleton five pounds and to his wife five pounds. To Anne Hindson five pounds. Bequests to George Thimelbee, Rowland, John and Ralph Ingram. George Ingram my godson. My cousin Bishop widow. Mary Bodwell and her sister Ann Tiffin. Grace Dawson and her two daughters Jane and Beck. Mary Crisp, daughter to my grandson Ellis Crisp. Alice Clarke, daughter to my cousin Ann Cox. My old uncle of the North Countrey. My ten grandchildren. I will that Ellis Crispe shall have his grandfather's gold seal ring. My grandson Samuel Crispe to be sole executor, and for overseers I appoint my two grandchildren John Carleton and Tobias Crisp. My godson John Crispe, one of the sons of Sir Nicholas Crisp. And whereas my grandson Tobias Crisp opened and read this my will contrary to modesty and ingenuity I do for his so doing revoke my legacy to him of part of a pearl hatband and give his part to my daughter Row.

Sealed 10 September 1659. A codicil, added 16 September 1661, contains bequests to cousin Dorothy Scott, Mrs. Middleton and Mr. Scott at the Abbey gate and his wife and to others. In this she calls herself of Martine (Merton) Abbey.   Laund, 133.

EDMUND WHITE of London Esquire 4 August 1632, proved 19 February 1632. My body to be buried in the parish church of St. Laurence in the Jewry, London, as near unto the body of my late wife Elizabeth as conveniently may be. I have heretofore partly advanced my son Edmond, and have given unto him one thousand five hundred pounds and have also partly advanced my daughter Elizabeth in marriage with Gabiel Newman, citizen and goldsmith of London, and given with her one thousand pounds, and have advanced my daughter Sarah in marriage with George Hadley, citizen and grocer of London, and have given and secured to give with her one thousand pounds. I hereby devise and appoint that these several sums of money given for the advancement of my said three children shall be put into Hotch pot together with that moiety or half part of my goods and personal estate &c. which by the Custom of London shall belong unto my children at the time of my death and that then the same shall be equally divided amongst my four children, vizt Edmond, James, Elizabeth and Sara, to the end that all my children may be equally advanced out of my personal estate according to the ancient and laudable Custom of the City of London. The other half commonly called the Testator's moiety, deviseable by me, I do dispose of as followeth. Then follow certain bequests. Among others to daughter in law Elizabeth White, the wife of my said son Edmond, ten pounds to buy her a ring. To his children living at my decease one hundred pounds apiece. The children of my daughter Elizabeth Newman. The children of my daughter Sara Hadley. My sister Alice Fowlar of Mickleton, Glouc., widow. My brother John White of Patrichborne, Kent. My nephew John Fowlar of Mickleton, the son of my said sister Alice Fowlar. My kinsman Thomas Fowlar of London, cordwainer. My nephew Edmond Fowlar, another of my sister Alice Fowlar's sons. My niece Joane Fowlar her daughter. Thomas White the son of my late brother Thomas White the elder deceased. Agatha Walker the daughter of my late brother Thomas White the younger, late of Hackney, Midd^x, deceased. Her sister Ann. The poor of Mickleton in the Co. of Gloucester where I was born. My kinsman William Davies, son of Thomas Davies, citizen and merchant tailor of London. The Company of Haberdashers. Property at Powick in the Co. of Worcester. My son Edmond to be executor. My grandson Edmond White, son of my son Edmond. My son James White.   Russell, 14.

ANNE HERDSON of Merton, Surrey, widow, 30 July 1668, proved 16 March 1668. To be buried in Merton Churchyard near my late husband. Bequests to the Right Honorable the Lady Whitlocke, to Mary the wife of Col. Owen Rowe, to Lady Whitlock's son Samuel Whitlock, to Robert Wilson the son of Robert Wilson of Merton Esq., to Rowland Wilson son of Samuel Wilson of London, merchant, and to his mother, to Allan Boylston son of Thomas Boylston of London, winecooper, and to his mother, to the grandchildren of Rowland Wilson Esquire deceased, to the three children of Mr. Ellis Crispe, to my cousin Mary Bowman daughter of my brother John Besford deceased, to Elizabeth Moore daughter of my brother

Thomas Besford deceased, to Jane Randolph wife of John Randolph of Westberry in the Co. of Salop and her children John and William, to the poor of Westberry, to Mary daughter of Alice Besford late of Westberry, widow, deceased, and to her sister Martha, and to others. The two children of my late husband's brother who heretofore lived near Kendall in Yorkshire. My nieces Mary Bowman and Elizabeth Moore to be joint executrices and Samuel Wilson of Bishopsgate Street, London, merchant, and Thomas Boylston of London, winecooper, to be overseers.

Coke, 32.

EDMUND WHITE the elder, citizen and haberdasher of London, 26 November 1674, proved 5 December 1674. To my son Edmund all my estate, right, title, interest &c., granted to me by the decree of the Judicature for Determination of Differences touching Houses burnt or demolished by reason of the late dismall Fire in London, of and in those tofts and grounds in St. Laurence Jewry London and of the messuages &c. by me lately erected thereon. My said son is now indebted to me in the sum of five hundred pounds. I did heretofore send unto my son in law Humfrey Davie of Boston in New England the sum of six hundred pounds upon a mortgage of lands. Three hundred pounds of it is hereby remitted. I have two hundred and fifty pounds capital adventure in the East India Stock in the name of my son in law Mr William Coxe. The household goods in the house of my said son in law William Coxe, wherein I now dwell, I give to my daughter Elizabeth Coxe, his wife. Personal estate to be divided into two equal parts, of which one part to my three children, Edmund White, Elizabeth Coxe and Mary Davie. The other part for legacies. Ann Rogers of Hackney, my nephew John White, my cousin Baker and his wife, my cousin Ellis and his wife, my cousin Lane and his wife, my brother in law Gabriel Newman, the widow Halsted, relict of Abraham Halsted. Others.

Coke, 150.

ROBERT DAVY of Credyton als Kyrton, Devon, clothier, 30 March 1570, proved 8 June 1570. To be buried in the parish church of Crediton als Kyrton. To my two sons, Laurence and Ellis Davye my lease &c. of the Wills Parkes in Crediton &c, and to Ellis my lease of tenement in East town, Crediton. To four of the daughters of Giles Froste, named Sybbly, Katherine, Christian and Margaret, forty shillings apiece, to be paid at their several marriages. My son in law Richard Potter. My godson Robert Davie son of Gilbert Davie. The son of John Brodemeade which he had by Ware's daughter dwelling at Tyverton. My godson Robert Phillip son of John Phillip. My god daughter Annye Chease daughter of Robert Chease by his first wife. Every of John Phillippe's children. My servants John and Alice Ley. John Davye the younger, my son, dwelling in Exeter. To Laurence Davy my son my new house and garden lying over against the " bastyn " gate. John Davye son of my eldest son John Davye. Robert Davye my godson, son of John Davy my eldest son. Laurence Davye son of the aforesaid John Davye. Richard Davy of Bowe son of Thomas Davye deceased. John Kensall. Thomas Davie's daughter late the wife of one Kempe of North Bovie. To my eldest son John Davy my lease &c. of the house belonging to the Prebend of Carswell which he now dwelleth in. My executors to be Laurence and Ellis Davie.

A codicil added 17 April. Bequests to three of Johan Averie's daughters, Elizabeth, Peternell and Johan. The said Johan my daughter. Five of my son John Davie's daughters, named Elizabeth, Christian, Mary, Amye and Margaret.

Lyon, 22.

JOHN DAVIE the elder of Crediton, Devon, gen[t]., 15 October 1575, proved 30 October 1576. To be buried in the church of Crediton. The poor within the two towns of Credyton. To my wife Elizabeth my mansion house in which I now dwell, in the east town of Crediton, for forty years if she live so long and after her death to my son Lawrence Davie. To my son Lawrence ten pounds in money and ten pounds more which I owe unto him of his grandfather's "bequeathe," to be paid at his full age of one and twenty. My daughter Christian Davie. My daughter Mary Davie. My daughter Agnes Davie. My daughter Margaret Davie. Reference to bequests made to the children above named by their grandfather. My daughter Wilmott Davie. My kinsman Roger Davie. My son John to have the residue and to be my executor; and for overseers I do appoint my brothers Gilbert Davie, Lawrence Davie and John Davie of Exeter.

Carew, 28.

GILBERT DAVYE of Credyton, Devon, gen[t], 5 March 26 Eliz : proved 8 November 1585. To be buried in the church of Crediton. To the twelve governors &c. of the church twenty pounds, to be distributed amongst twenty poor persons. Robert Davye my son and heir apparent. Gilbert, Lawrence, Roger, John and Robert Trobridge, my daughter Christian's children. My son in law George Trobridge, their father. Christian his wife, my daughter. (Their daughter?) Mary at eighteen or day of marriage. My brother Ellys Davye. My brother Lawrence Davye. Anne Davye, my son's wife, and Gilbert Davye her son. Robert Alford and Thomazin his wife, my sister. My brother Lawrence Davye's children (being four of them). To my wife Mary that tenement or Barton called Bishops Leigh, in the parish of Bishops Morchard, Devon, to hold for forty years (if she so long live) in full satisfaction and recompence of her dower for all other my lands &c. The remainder to my son Robert. Other bequests to Robert. Reference to an Indenture from nephew John Davye of Crediton, gentleman. Cousin Roger Davye. Thomas, son of Ellys Davye. John Northcotte of Crediton, gen[t]. My brother John Davye of Exon gen[t]. My nephew John Davye of Credyton gen[t].   Brudenell, 49.

JOHN CORHAM the younger of Ottery S[t] Mary, Devon, 24 June 1585, proved 11 March 1586. The poor of Otery. To my brother William Corham my bow and arrows. My brother in law David Axon. My brother John Davye and my sister his wife. Raphe Baston and Katherine his wife. Edward his son and Christian their daughter. My sister Charity Corham. My sister Joane Weare. Such child as my wife shall be by God's grace delivered of. My sister Agnes Corham. Agnes, Joane and William Corham, children of my brother William. Wife Alice to be sole executrix.

William Corham, gen[t], one of the witnesses.   Spencer, 16.

LAWRENCE DAVIE of Crediton, Devon, clothier, 22 December 44th Elizabeth, proved 6 February 1601. My body to be buried in the church of Crediton. To my son Nicholas Davy and my daughter Mary Davie all my lease, title and interest in the Will Parks ground &c., the which lease was granted by Anthony Harvie Esq. To my daughter Mary Davie one hundred pounds at day of marriage. To my brother Ellis Davie twenty shillings. To the poor of the two towns of Crediton forty shillings. Towards the separation of the lower well in Kerton in the East town twenty shillings, with the five shillings that remained in my hand before. If my

daughter Mary do happen to die before she be married the hundred pounds
shall come to my son John Davy and her part of the lease &c. shall come
to my son Nicholas Davie. If Nicholas happen to die before marriage then
his portion of said lease shall go to my daughter Mary, My brother John
Davie of the city of Exon shall be my whole and sole executor and " maister "
John Trobridge and my cousin Robert Davie overseers.

Montague, 22.

MARGARET DAVEY of Exeter widow, 30 November 12th James proved
20 January 1614. To be buried in the parish church of St. Mary Arches,
Exeter. The poor of the city. The poor of Sandford in the parish of
Kyrton. The parish of Calverley. The poor of Loxbeare and of Temple.
My grandchild Johanna Haydon. Frances Haydon daughter to my son in
law Gideon Haydon and George Haydon, his son. My brother Ames
Southcott. Margaret Blackaller, daughter of Thomas Blackaller of the
parish of St. Thomas, Devon. My brother Humphrey Southcott. My
daughter Margaret Haydon. My daughter Julyan Davey. My daughter
Mary Davey. My sister Mary Blackaller. My sister Wood. My daughter
Davey's servants. My cousin Richard Southcott. My cousin Gilbert
Sweete. My brother Thomas Southcott. My son John Davey. My sister
Mary Ford. Gideon Haydon my son in law to be executor and my son
John Davey and Mr. Peter Haydon to be overseers. Rudd, 1.

THOMAS SOUTHCOTT of Calverley in the parish of Calwoodley, Devon
gent, 26 April 1618, proved 20 November 1621. The poor of said parish.
The poor of Loxbeare. The poor of Tiverton. To my daughter Mary
Colman ten pounds for to buy a piece of plate with as a token of my love
unto her. To my daughter Elizabeth Waltham (a like bequest). To my
son George Southcott (a like bequest) and to his wife. To my wife Margery
the use of all such goods as I have at Newton Petroocke, which I had
by the intermarriage with her, during her natural life, and then to my
executor. The residue to Richard, my son, whom I make sole executor;
and I ordain and make my cousin John Davie Esq. and my brother Humfry
Southcott my overseers.

John Davie, William Colman and Humfry Southcott wit:

Dale, 90.

HUMFRY SOUTHCOT of Chilton in Cheriton Fitzpaine, Devon, gent, 20
May 1643, proved 21 May 1647. To the poor of Calverly ten pounds to
be employed with those legacies and sums of money which were given to
the said parish by my brother Thomas Southcott and my sister Margaret
Davie, my cousin Mary Colman and others, entreating my overseer and
executor, with my cousin Prowse, now parson of the said parish of Calverley,
and his successors, being there resident to set down and order the disposing
and ordering of all as may continue forever. My godson Bernard
Southcott. My brother Robert Southcott if living at my decease. Ten
pounds per annum quarterly to be paid him out of my lands at Coddiford
as an addition to the annuity he is to have and now hath from my cousin
Nicholas Foord during his life. Ellen Bussell if living &c. Her husband.
The residue to my cousin and godson Thomas Southcot, willing him to
have the advice in all his proceedings, in this my last will, with my true
and ever faithful nephew Sir John Davie, Baronet, whom I make my only
overseer of this will. Fines, 209.

JOHN DAVYE of Creedy in Sandford, Devon, Esq. 20 June 15th Charles (1639), proved 7 August 1655. To be buried within the chapel of Sandford. The poor of Crediton and Sandford. To the twelve governors of the goods and hereditaments of the church of Crediton twenty pounds for and towards a workhouse &c. Have disbursed one hundred pounds towards the purchase of lands to be made over to the twelve governors for the maintenance of an English school master in Crediton &c. Provision for convenient rooms for wife in mansion house at Crediton, also garden plot and orchard. To said wife all such goods as she brought with her and such moneys as she hath put into the hands of others for employment of the same, vizt into the hands of my brother Thomas Hele one hundred pounds, in my cousin Gilbert's hands twenty pounds, in my cousin Hamon's hands two hundred pounds, in Henry Knight's hands two hundred pounds, in my sister Isack's hands twenty pounds, not doubting but she will employ the same for the best benefit of mine and her daughter Isabel Davie. Certain articles of silver to her. To my son Humfry five hundred pounds. To my daughter Margaret Davie one thousand pounds for a marriage portion. In the mean time I give her fifteen pounds per annum for her present maintenance. My son and heir shall give them their diets or twenty pounds apiece yearly until they be married. To my daughter Isabel one thousand pounds for a marriage portion, in the meantime she to be educated and maintained by her mother. Forty shillings apiece unto Sir John Younge, knight, John Willoughby of Pehembury Esq., my beloved brothers in law, and Humfrey Southcott of Chilton, gen^t, my beloved uncle, whom I make overseers, &c., the same forty shillings to be bestowed in a ring or some such other memorial as they shall like best. The residue to my son and heir John Davie whom I make sole executor.

Wit: Mary Willoughby, John Willoughby, Humfrey Southcott and John Aynell.

Proved by the oath of Sir John Davie, Baronet, the son and executor. Entered on the margin "T. dñi Johannis Davye mi^{tis}."

Aylett, 101.

[The testator, Sir John Davie, who was created a baronet Sept. 9, 1641, was the father of Humphrey Davie, a merchant of London and Boston, whose son John graduated at Harvard College in 1681. The testator was the only son of John Davie, thrice mayor of Exeter, England, who married Margaret, daughter of George Southcote of Calverly in Devon. Besides their son John, they had one daughter Margaret, wife of Gideon Haydon.

Sir John Davie, bart., was twice married; first to Juliañ, daughter of William Strode of Newnham, by whom he had four sons: 1. Sir John, his successor; 2. William, a counsellor at law, who married Margaret, daughter of Sir Francis Clark of Putney in Surrey; 3. Robert; 4. Humphrey, the New England immigrant. He had also four daughters: 1. Mary, married to John Willoughby of Payhembury in Devon; 3. Julian; 4. Margaret, married Thomas Bear of Hunsome, Devon. Sir John married 2d, Isabel Hele, by whom he had one daughter, Isabel, who married Walter Yonge of Colliton, Devon, created a baronet in 1661.

Humphrey Davie, son of the testator, married 1st, Mary, daughter of Edmund White, an abstract of whose will is given above. He emigrated in 1662 to Boston, Mass. He married for a second wife Sarah Richards, widow of James Richards and daughter of William Gibbons. He was admitted a member of the Artillery Company in 1665. He died at Hartford, Ct., Feb. 18, 1688-9. His widow married Jonathan Tyng. See REGISTER, vol. i., p. 169; Wotton's English Baronetage, 1741, vol. ii., pp. 263-9; Baronetage of England by E. Kimber and R. Johnson, 1771, vol. i., pp. 416-19; Baronetage of England by Rev. William Betham, 1801, vol. i., pp. 453-7; Whitman's History of the Ancient and Honorable Artillery Company, ed. 1842, pp. 175-6.—EDITOR.]

DAME ISABELL DAVIE, late the wife of Sir John Davie of Credie in the parish of Sandford, Devon, Baronet deceased. Her will made 20 July 1656, proved 18 November 1657. I do desire that there should be no mourning given at my funeral nor hearse set upon my grave. My executor to bestow and lay out twenty pounds for six and twenty rings with a death's head and this Poesie, to witt, " God be your guide," to be given one to each of my brothers and sisters and one apiece to each of my sons in law and daughters in law living at the time of my death. To my sons in law William Davie, Robert Davie and Humphry Davie, to each of them half a dozen silver spoons. To my cousins Richard Rowe and Joane Ford and my servant Elizabeth Wareman twenty shillings apiece. The poor of Sandford and of Crediton. My daughter Isabel Young and her children. The residue to said daughter and she to be sole executrix.

Ruthen, 433.

SIR JOHN DAVY of Creedy, Baronet, 13 April 1685, proved 9 June 1693. To be buried in the parish church of Sandford near my ancestors and relations. The manner of my funeral I leave to my executor, my dear brother William Davie, and I do hereby make him whole executor of this my last will and testament, desiring him to be dutiful to my honored mother and kind and respectful to all others our relations. And I give him all my goods, chattels and personal estate.

Proved by Sir William Davie, Baronet &c.   Coker, 94.

SIR JOHN DAVIE of Creedy in Devon, Baronet, 31 January 1677, proved 19 October 1678. To be buried in the vault or burying place which I made in the chancel of the church or chapel of the parish or hamlet of Sandford at or upon my father's death. The poor of Crediton and of Sandford and the other poor of Upton Hellions. To Dame Amy, my dear, loving and faithful wife, all the jewels, plate and books, cabinets and trunks which now are or were hers at the time of her marriage with me (and other property). My two nephews, John Davie and Nathaniel his brother, sons of my late brother Robert deceased. My nephew William Davie, second son of my late brother William Davie of Dyra Esq. deceased. The study at Creedy Widger (in Upton Hellions) which was my father Reynells. My nephew John Copplestone, son and heir of my cousin John Copplestone of Bowden Esq. My niece Mary Copplestone, eldest daughter to my brother in law Arthur Copplestone of Bowdon Esq. My sister and their children, Charles Quicke, son of John Quick jun^r of Newton St Cyers (now St. Cyres) Esq. my kinsman. Provision for a workhouse in Crediton and for an English schoolmaster in Sandford. Sir Walter Yonge of Coleton, Baronet, Thomas Reynell of Ogwells, Richard Beavis of Clisthouse, my nephew, and John Copplestone of Bowdon Esquire, my near and dear relations. Richard Beavis of Clisthouse, Devon, Esq. my well beloved brother in law.   Reeve, 109.

SIR WILLIAM DAVIE of Creedy, Devon, Baronet, 10 February 1706, proved 27 May 1707. To Dame Abigail Davie, my dear wife, all the jewels, plate, rings and cabinets which were hers at the time of my marriage with her or have been given unto her at any time since (and other property). My father John Pollixfen Esq. and my brother John Pollixfen Esq. My daughters Margaret, Frances and Trephina Davie. My brother Wollcombe Pollixfen. My daughter Mary Davie. My copyhold estates in Stratton, Somerset, &c.   Poley, 104.

SIR JOHN DAVIE late of Creedy, Devon, Baronet, 25 April 1727, proved
13 July 1728. To my son and heir John Davie all those several pictures,
with the frames thereto belonging, that is to say, the picture of my uncle
Sir John Davie, of my father and mother, of myself and my late Lady, his
brother James and his own, and my will and desire is that the same shall
be and remain to the heirs male of my family successively. Provision for
son Humphrey Davie. To my son William Davie my messuage &c. in
Holsworthy, Devon. A settlement of lands in Crediton for daughter Mary
Bishop. My son John Davie Esq. and my son in law Christopher Savery.
My daughter Mary's four daughters, Elizabeth, Jenny, Mary and Sarah
Bishop. My second daughter Sarah Savery has already received her portion. To my third daughter Elizabeth Davie two thousand five hundred
pounds, to be paid her on the day of her marriage.

Item, I further give, devise and bequeath unto my two sons Humphry
Davie and William Davie and to their heirs for ever all those my lands at
or in New England, lying and being near Boston, Groton, Milton, Rumley
als Rumney Marsh, Kennebeck River, Swan Island or elsewhere, or any
of them in New England in America or in any other town, province, Island, district or place in New England aforesaid, late or heretofore the
estate of Edmund White of London, merchant deceased, or which was formerly purchased by or in the name of Humphry Davie late of Boston, merchant deceased, for the use of or in trust for the said Edmund White. The
poor of Sandford parish. My sons Humphry and William Davie to be
executors.   Brook, 205.

[Sir John Davie, bart., the testator, was the son of Humphrey Davie referred
to above in the preceeding note on the will of Sir John Davie, the first
baronet. He was a graduate of Harvard College in 1681, and a memoir of him
will be found in the third volume of Sibley's Harvard Graduates. He married
about 1692 his step-sister, Elizabeth, daughter of James and Sarah Richards of
Hartford, Ct. He had the following children, all born in the town of Groton
(originally a part of New London), Ct., namely : 1. Mary, born June 30, 1603,
married Rev. Thomas Bishop of Barnstaple, Eng.; 2 Sarah, born October
21, 1695, married Christopher Savery of Shilson, near Modbury, Devon; 3.
Elizabeth, born March 17, 1697-8, married Ebenezer Mussell of London; 4.
John, born July 27, 1700, married Elizabeth, daughter of John Acland of Colliton,
Devon, and succeeded to the baronetcy in 1728, on the death of his father; 5.
Humphrey, born April 12, 1702, a bachelor; 6. William, born March 21, 1705-6,
married Ellen, daughter of Nicholas Jackson of Bristol, merchant. Sir John,
the testator, about 1707, on the death of his cousin William the fourth baronet,
succeeded to the baronetcy. He died in 1728. See Sibley's Harvard Graduates.
vol. iii., pp. 231-6; Caulkin's New London, pp. 415-7; Savage's Genealogical
Dictionary, vol. ii., pp, 14-15; and the other authorities cited in the preceding
note.—EDITOR.]

WILLIAM TUTTY of St. Stephens Coleman Street, London, gen^t, 10
October 1640, proved 9 January 1640. To my beloved wife Anne Tutty
all my plate and household stuff and my seal ring; only I desire her that
my children may enjoy the plate that was given them at their baptizing,
every one their own. Whereas my son William Tutty hath already had a
liberal and competent part of my estate in his maintenance in the University
of Cambridge and in a parcel of books, bought by me of Nathaniel Mickle-
thwayte, my wife's son, executor of Paul Micklethwaite late Doctor of Divinity deceased, and given to him, amounting to the sum of about forty
pounds, I therefore give unto him only the sum of ten pounds &c.

Item, because I have already given unto my eldest daughter Anne, lately
married with Alexander Knight of Ipswich in New England beyond the

seas, a competent marriage portion, I therefore give unto her, in full of her child's portion, the sum of ten pounds more to be paid her also by mine executrix within one year next after my decease. The residue of my estate to be divided into two equal parts, the one part whereof I give unto my wife Anne Tutty and the other half part to be divided équally amongst the rest of my children now living, viz' John, Joseph, Benjamin, Samuel, Elizabeth, Dorcas and Hester Tutty. My said wife to be full and sole executrix.
Commissary of London, Vol. 28 (1639-42), fol. 234.

[Alexander Knight, named in this will, resided at Ipswich, Mass., as early as 1635. He is said by P. Vincent in his History of the Pequot War, published in 1637, to have kept an inn at Chelmsford, Eng. (Coll. Mass. Hist. Society, vol. xxvi., p. 41.) The date of his marriage with Hannah or Anne, daughter of William Tutty, I have not found, though her father speaks of her as "lately married" in 1640.—EDITOR.]

JOHN TUTTIE citizen and fruiterer of London (son of William Tuttie late of London, gentleman, deceased) 3 September 1657, proved 3 October 1657 (with a codicil dated 5 September). To my sister Hannah Knight of New England for her children, or such of them living, or in case they be all deceased then for her own use if living at the time, I shall herein appoint for the payment of this and other legacies fifty pounds. To my brother William Tuttie of Totteride (sic—Totteridge?) fifty pounds. To my sister Dorcas Tuttie one hundred pounds. To my sister Hester Blissett sixty pounds. To my sister Elizabeth Tew forty pounds. To her son Nicholas Tew ten pounds. To my brother Samuel all that he owes me upon any account whatever, whether in frames or money. To each of his four children ten pounds to bind them forth to learn trades. To my brother Micklethwaight twenty pounds to buy him two pieces of plate. To my uncle John Ling forty shillings. To Richard Davies, shoemaker, five pounds. To Mary Prosser, widow, ten pounds. To Anthony Haile, trimmer, ten pounds. To Thomas Higgeson ten pounds. One hundred pounds among the poor. My wife Rachel to be sole executrix. Ruthen, 372.

WILLIAM DYRE of the Co. of Sussex in the territories of the Province of Pennsylvania Esq. I will and bequeath unto my eldest son William Dyre, now at Boston in New England, all my plantation or land in the Broad Kill, in Sussex County aforesaid, called Rumbley Place, containing two thousand acres, more or less, with ten cows, four two year old heifers, six two year old stears coming to this Spring. To my second son Edmund Dyre one plantation lying upon Loves Creek in the said County, containing six hundred acres, formerly called Sundialls (but now Beavorwick) and four hundred acres formerly in partnership with Stephen Whittman, now bounding upon the lands of Jeremiah Scott and Thomas Branscomb and to the Southward partly on John and William Roads and to the Eastward upon the marshes or Town Creek, with six cows and their increase and two two year old steers. To my youngest son James Dyre four hundred acres of land on Mispillen Creek in the County aforesaid and also three hundred acres in the fork of the Broad Kill, in the County aforesaid, part binding upon the Beaver Dam and Westward upon Prime Hook Creek, with one hundred acres of marsh adjoining, also two hundred acres in New Castle County, about seven miles from the town, butted and bounded as per "Pattent," with six cows. To my eldest daughter Sarah Dyre five hundred acres between Cold Spring and the Cypress Bridge in Sussex County, butted and bounded as by the Certificate and Plat or Draught for the same may appear, with six cows. To my youngest daughter Mary Dyre three hundred acres known by the name of the White Horse, lately bought of Charles Pickering, and two hundred and fifty five acres in Angola Neck, in the County of Sussex, some time the land of Richard Shoulster, with six cows. I give unto my dear and well beloved wife Mary Dyre twenty five hundred acres in Cedar Neck in Sussex County, as by Grant and survey for settlement of part for the whole, as also ninety six acres adjoining the town of Lewis (Lewes) in Sussex County, with two town lots in the same town, the same being begun to be built upon and improved (and other personal estate), this for her natural life and afterwards to my said children, or other ways as she shall think fit and necessary. I give her also one debt due by bond from Hendrick Vandenborgh of Newcastle for forty odd pounds silver money and a debt for six pounds, in money or corn, due from justice Andreson of Newcastle and five pounds, in wheat or pork, due from Samuel Curtis of Allawayes Creek in West Jersey, and a debt, by account or bill of Capt. William Markham for near about twenty pounds, and a debt of seventy odd pounds silver money due from William Alsberry, due by mortgage, and now in the hands of Capt. Stephanus Van Courtland of New York, with all other debts due to me from any other persons whatsoever within the said Government of New York.

I give to my wife all my land and horses in the Pequit in Narraganset Country in New England, with all my right and title of inheritance to the estate of my late father William Dyre deceased upon Rhode Island, within the Province of Providence Plantation, and also one island called Dyers Island, lying between Prudence and Rhode Island, and the balance of Mr. Thomas Lloyds bond for five hundred and ten pounds silver money payable at New York the twenty sixth of May next ensuing, being above one hundred pounds, and twenty acres of land lying at Reading in New England and two islands called Clabbord Islands in Cascoe Bay in New England, the same being all for her proper use and behoof during her natural life and afterwards to be divided amongst my said children as she shall think fit. My said dear and loving wife Mary Dyre and my said eldest son William Dyre to be my whole and sole executrix and executor for the managing my said estate; further it is my will and desire that my said wife have one hundred and fifty pounds silver money of New England, in the hands of Sir Edmund Andros. I have hereunto set my hand and seal this twentieth day of February 1687-8, and I request my friends Mr. John Hill and Mr. Samuel Gray to be assisting to my wife and children in the management of their affairs in these parts. Also I humbly request his Excellency Sir Edmund Andros, Governor General of New England, to be assistant to my said wife and children in their affairs in the parts of New England, the said Sir Edmund to be feoffee in trust to my said estate in the parts of New England.

In the presence of us, Charles Sanders and William Rodeney.

The Evidences, vizt Charles Sanders and William Rodeney attested in open Court, held for the County of Sussex the fifth day of the fourth month, called June, one thousand six hundred eighty eight, that this above written, together with the other sheet of paper hereunto annexed, is the Act and Deed of Major William Dyre deceased and that the said Major William Dyre did acknowledge the same to be his last will and testament. *Testis* Norton Claypoole, Clerk and Deputy Register.

Registered in the Public Registry of the Co. of Sussex in Book A, folio 95, 96 and 97.

Proved at London 4 September 1690 by the oath of William Dyre the son &c., power reserved for Mary Dyre the relict when she should come to ask for probate. Dyke, 136.

[William Dyre, the testator, was a son of Mary Dyer, the victim of the persecution of the Quakers, who was hanged on Boston Common, June 1, 1660. He, himself, petitioned the General Court of Massachusetts for clemency to his mother. His father, William Dyre or Dyer, a milliner from London, settled in Boston in 1635, was admitted freeman of Massachusetts March 3, 1635-6, was disarmed in 1637, and in 1638 removed to Rhode Island. See Austin's Genealogical Dictionary of Rhode Island, pp. 290-2; Record of the Dyer Family, by Cornelia C. Joy-Dyer; Savage's Genealogical Dictionary, vol. 2, p. 89; Chandler's Criminal Trials, vol. 1, pp. 31-63; and the general histories.—EDITOR.]